ECONOMICS

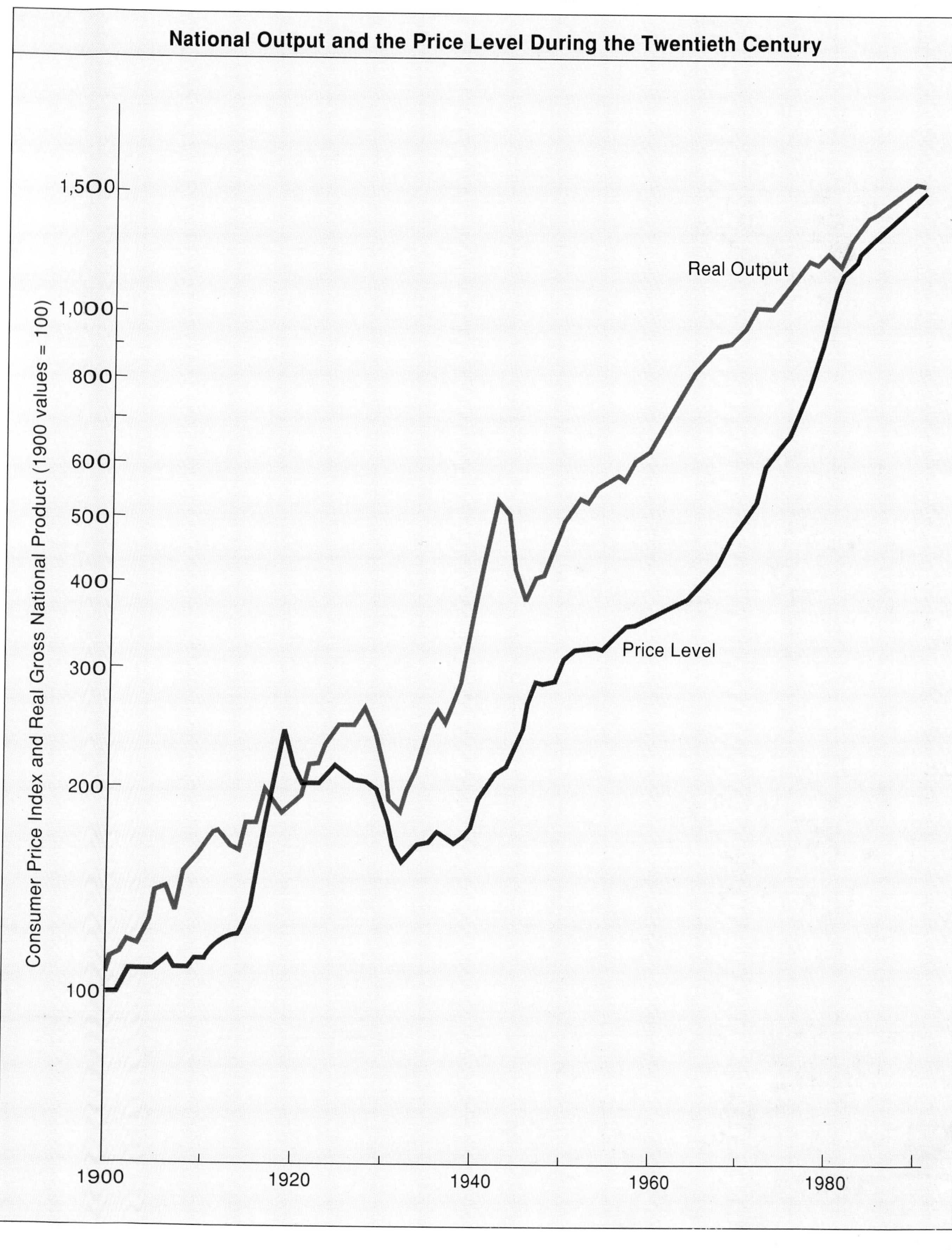
National Output and the Price Level During the Twentieth Century
Consumer Price Index and Real Gross National Product (1900 values = 100)
1,500
1,000
800
600
500
400
300
200
100
1900
1920
1940
1960
1980
Real Output
Price Level

ECONOMICS

FOURTEENTH EDITION

Paul A. Samuelson

INSTITUTE PROFESSOR EMERITUS

MASSACHUSETTS INSTITUTE

OF TECHNOLOGY

William D. Nordhaus

A. WHITNEY GRISWOLD PROFESSOR OF ECONOMICS

YALE UNIVERSITY

McGRAW-HILL, INC.

NEW YORK ST. LOUIS SAN FRANCISCO AUCKLAND BOGOTA CARACAS LISBON

LONDON MADRID MEXICO MILAN MONTREAL NEW DELHI PARIS

SAN JUAN SINGAPORE SYDNEY TOKYO TORONTO

ECONOMICS

3 4 5 6 7 8 9 0 VNH VNH 9 0 9 8 7 6 5 4 3 2

ISBN 0-07-054879-X

This book was set in Zapf Book Light by York Graphic Services, Inc.
The editors were James A. Bittker, Judith Kromm, and Ira C. Roberts;
the designer was Hermann Strohbach;
the production supervisor was Janelle S. Travers.
Drawings were done by Vantage Art Studio.
Von Hoffmann Press, Inc., was printer and binder.

Library of Congress Cataloging-in-Publication Data

Samuelson, Paul Anthony, (date).
Economics / Paul A. Samuelson, William D. Nordhaus. — 14th ed.
p. cm.
Includes index.
ISBN 0-07-054879-X
1. Economics. I. Nordhaus, William D. II. Title.
HB1715.S25 1992
330—dc20 91-37800

ABOUT THE AUTHORS

THOMAS MOON

Paul A. Samuelson, founder of the renowned MIT graduate department of economics, was trained at the University of Chicago and Harvard. His many scientific writings brought him world fame at a young age, and he was the first American to receive a Nobel Prize in economics, in 1970. One of those rare scientists who can communicate with the lay public, Professor Samuelson long wrote an economics column for *Newsweek*. He testifies often before Congress and serves as academic consultant to the Federal Reserve, the U.S. Treasury, and various private, nonprofit organizations. He was economic adviser to President John F. Kennedy. Professor Samuelson plays tennis daily, and his family's size doubled when triplets arrived.

William D. Nordhaus is one of America's eminent economists. Born in New Mexico, he was an undergraduate at Yale, received his Ph.D. in economics at MIT, and is now the A. Whitney Griswold Professor of Economics at Yale University and on the staff of the Cowles Foundation for Research in Economics. His economic research has spanned a wide variety of topics—including the environment, inflation, energy, technological change, regulation, resource economics, and trends in profits and productivity. In addition, Professor Nordhaus takes a keen interest in economic policy. He served as a member of President Carter's Council of Economic Advisers from 1977 to 1979, was Provost of Yale University from 1986 to 1988, and writes occasionally for *The New York Times* and other periodicals. He regularly teaches the Principles of Economics course at Yale. Professor Nordhaus and his family live in New Haven, Connecticut, and share an enthusiasm for music, hiking, and skiing.

TO OUR CHILDREN AND STUDENTS

ECONOMICS AND PERPETUAL YOUTH

It was never my idea to write an introductory economics textbook. My MIT department head, Ralph Freeman, came to me in 1945 and said:

> Paul, here's an offer you can't refuse. A year of economics is compulsory for our MIT students. And they find it dull.
>
> Take as much time off as you need. Write a book that people new to economics will like. It can be as short as you wish. Cover the topics *you* think important. I'm sure it will be a best seller.
>
> More importantly, you'll contribute to the education of a generation. Then you'll have two reputations. Paul Samuelson, the economic theorist who pioneers at the frontiers of high-falutin' mathematical economics. And Paul Samuelson, who has paid his dues to promoting economic literacy and rational understanding among the citizenry.

I laughed at first. I hesitated. Then I was lost. The die was cast. The rest, as they say, is history.

My publisher, McGraw-Hill, and my coauthor, Bill Nordhaus of Yale, have asked me to tell the story. So here goes.

Back to the Classroom

1945 was a crucial time. Germany and Japan were defeated, and American colleges were full to overflowing with returning service people and war workers. Economics was at a dynamic stage. The Great Depression of 1929–1935 had finally been licked by forceful programs that threw out the window the old orthodoxies of do-nothing monetary and fiscal policies. Britain and America had later mobilized their economies for a successful war in a way that Hitler, Mussolini, and the Emperor Hirohito's chieftains never dreamed of. And, though we could not know it in 1945, a successful Marshall Plan and MacArthur occupation of Japan were about to set the stage for miracle decades of postwar growth in the "Age after Keynes."

College students deserved to understand all this. But, as teachers of my generation knew to our sorrow, the best-selling economics textbooks were seriously out of date. No wonder beginners were bored—and not only at MIT. My students at Harvard often had that glassy look.

This account must not be like the fictional work the humorist Mr. Dooley attributed to Teddy Roosevelt under the mythical title "Me and Cuba." If Newton had not invented the calculus when he did, Leibniz or someone named Smith would have done so. If my 1948 *Economics* had not brought guns-and-butter choices into elementary microeconomics, someone somewhere would soon have done so. At the time of my first edition, even the word "macroeconomics"—the study of what determines a society's unemployment, its price-level inflation rate, and its rate of real GNP growth—was not yet in the dictionary! Some scholar just had to come along and revolutionize the introductory textbooks of economics.

But why me? I was back from the MIT Radiation Laboratory, where I had worked at the mathematical job of designing automatic servomechanisms to ward off enemy bombers. So to speak, I thirsted for a return to economic research and teaching. I was 30, the best age to write a text or innovate a treatise. By good chance, my advanced *Foundations of Economic Analysis,* which was to win me a Nobel Price in economics 25 years later, was already in press. Now or never to author a textbook. But first I must tell a secret. Back in those days, a promising scholar was not supposed to write textbooks—certainly not basic texts for beginning sophomores and freshmen. Only hacks were supposed to do that. But because I had already published so many research articles, it seemed that my reputation and prospects for lifetime tenure could afford me the elbow room to respond positively to MIT's request for a new textbook. Being cocky and even brash in those good old days, it was myself I had to please.

What clinched the argument for me was this: Linus Pauling, so great a scholar and humanist that he was to win two Nobel Prizes, had already written a leading chemistry text—just as the great Richard Feynman was later to publish classic physics lectures. William James had long since published his great *Principles of Psychology.* Richard Courant, top dog at Göttingen in Germany, had not been too proud to author an accurate textbook on calculus. Who was Paul Samuelson to throw stones at scholars like these? And, working the other side of the street, I thought it was high time that we got the leaders in economics back in the trenches of general education. (Running ahead of the story, one can report that by the 1990s the innovators in undergraduate economic teaching have often been those who pierced farthest out into the frontiers of economics as a scholarly discipline.)

The Long Grind of Creation

Starting a baby is easy. Bringing it to full term involves labor and travail. As soon as each chapter was written, the mimeograph machine ground it out for testing on our MIT students. I found it demanding work, but pleasant.

Rome wasn't built in a day. And what I naively thought might be a year's job turned into 3 years of writing and rewriting. For once my tennis suffered, as weekends and summer vacations had to be devoted to the task of reducing to plain and understandable prose the fundamental complexities of economic science. Even the traditional diagrams of economics, I discovered, were overdue for redesigning if the "dismal science of economics" was to become the exciting subject it really is.

Of course, the word got out that a breakthrough was in the making. And soon publishers swarmed to my office like bees around flowers. "Pick us because we're big," some said. Or, "Pick us because we're small and we'll concentrate on your needs." Or, "We have sales representatives in 48 states and 1500 colleges." I flipped a few coins and in the end decided to sign up with McGraw-Hill as publisher. Why? Because the firm was prestigious in science and business? Yes, in part. Because it had a magnificent marketing and selling staff? Yes, in part (but the other big publishers were no slouches when it came to selling college texts). What principally influenced my decision was this: (1) McGraw-Hill had published a magnificent multivolume series for the MIT Radiation Laboratory, a commercial success and a treasure house for radar and electronic sciences; and (2) McGraw-Hill had published, more for prestige than profit, the two-volume classic *Business Cycles* of Joseph Schumpeter, my famous master in the Harvard Graduate School.

The Moment of Truth

In the autumn of 1948 the first edition of *Economics* rolled off the press. No matter how hard the advance work or how optimistic the dreams, one can never be sure how the future will turn out. Fortunately, from the word "go" this novel approach to economics hit a responsive chord. Colleges big and little opted for the new. As each fresh printing was sold out, *Economics* was back again for new runs of the press.

Semester after semester our share of the market grew. In one year there was a clean sweep, with every school in the Ivy League adopting the text. As important to me were its successes at junior colleges and state universities across the map of the United States and Canada. International editions soon proliferated in English. When a Guggenheim Fellowship took me to Europe, I checked each city's main bookstore for the availability of translations into French, German, Italian, Swedish, and Portuguese.

My labor was more than rewarded. Aside from experiencing the natural vanity of an author, I was pleased as an educator to see that the citizenry, who would be deciding global policies in the last half of the century, was being exposed to the pros and cons of up-to-date mainstream economics.

Reviews of the book speeded up the bandwagon. The first one came from the pen of John Kenneth Galbraith, then an editor of the conservative business magazine *Fortune.* He predicted that the next generation would learn its economics from the Samuelson *Economics.* Praise is sweet in authors' ears, but I must confess that it was the durability of the book's dominance that surprised me. As Andy Warhol put it: We live in a time when anyone can be a celebrity for about 15 minutes. Galbraith turned out to be more prescient than I. *Economics* did set a new and lasting pattern. Most of its successful rivals are written in its general mode, and it is heartwarming that much of the competition has come from the pens of good personal friends.

One summer the U.S. Chamber of Commerce put out over the Associated Press news wires the mock charge that McGraw-Hill's Samuelson, who writes about the need for antitrust control of monopolies, ought to be indicted for controlling a lopsided share of the total textbook market! When I attended the annual meetings of the American Economic Association, instructors frequently came up to me and said, "We use your book at Siwash" or "Winnsockie" or some other far-flung place. There was always an awkward pause, as I never knew quite what to say. My problem got solved when, one day, I heard myself saying, "Mrs. Samuelson will be pleased."

When success comes into an autobiography, the going gets boring. And Joseph Schumpeter, the great Harvard expert on innovations, will remind me from the grave how important *luck* was in all this. I happened to be there, at the right time in the right place. True, luck does favor the prepared mind. But the important minds that had become prepared for the new approach to economics were those of teachers who had been debating the cons and pros of the so-called Keynesian revolution and were thirsting for a "national income" approach in *macro*economics and a "general-equilibrium" approach in *micro*economics.

The Ever-Young Child

Actually, this account is not primarily about me as author. Just as a child takes on an individual identity distinct from the parent, so it was with the brainchild *Economics*. At first I was in command of it. But then it took over in its own right and came to be in charge of me.

The years passed. My hair turned from blond to brown. Then to gray. But like the portrait of Dorian Gray, which never grew old, the textbook *Economics* remained forever 21. Its cover turned from green to blue, and then to brown and black, and to many-splendored hues. But helped by hundreds of letters and suggestions to the author from students and from professors with classroom experience, the economics inside the covers evolved and developed. A historian of mainstream-economic doctrines, like a paleontologist who studies the bones and fossils in different layers of earth, could date the ebb and flow of ideas by analyzing how Edition 1 was revised to Edition 2 and, eventually, to Edition 14.

And so it went. Hard, hard work—but ever so rewarding. Finally came the day when tennis beckoned. To McGraw-Hill I said: I've paid my dues. Let others carry on as I enjoy the good life of an emeritus professor, cultivating the researches that interest me most and letting revisions go hang.

McGraw-Hill had a ready answer: "Become a joint author. We'll make a list of congenial economists whose competence and views you admire." And so the search for the perfect William Nordhaus began. Yale is only 150 miles from MIT, and it was there that the real Nordhaus was to be found. It only helped that Bill had earned his Ph.D. at MIT. And in the days since then he has won his spurs serving on the President's Council of Economic Advisers and doing a tour of duty in Vienna with the International Institute for Applied Systems Analysis. Like Gilbert and Sullivan or Rogers and Hart, we turned out to form a congenial team.

And so, as in the classic tales, we have lived happily ever after. What matters is that the book stays young, pointing ahead to where the mainstream of economics will be flowing.

Rough Pebbles along the Way

Not always has it been fun and games. In the reactionary days of Senator Joseph McCarthy, when accusations of radicalism were being launched at the pulpit and in the classroom, my book got its share of condemnation. A conservative alumnus of MIT warned the university's president, Karl Compton, that Paul Samuelson would jeopardize his scholarly reputation if he were allowed to publish his apologetics for the "mixed economy". Dr. Compton replied that the day his faculty was subjected to censorship would be the day of his resignation from office. It all seems slightly comical four decades later, but it was no joke to be a teacher at a public university when many of the fashionable textbooks were at that time being denounced as subversive. (One excellent text, which came out a year before mine, was killed in its infancy by vicious charges of Marxism that were false on their face.) Actually, when your cheek is smacked from the Right, the pain may be assuaged in part by a slap from the Left. *Anti-Samuelson,* a two-volume critique, was authored in the 1960s when student activism was boiling over on campuses here and abroad. Apparently I was an apologist for the laissez-faire world of markets where dog eats dog.

Each cold wind imparts a useful lesson. I learned to write with special care wherever controversial matters were concerned. It was not that I was a veritable Sir Galahad in all things. Rather, it was that I could only gain by leaning over backward to state fairly the arguments against the positions popular in mainstream economics. That is why conservative schools like my Chicago alma mater were motivated to assign *Economics* at the same time that prairie progressives found it an optimal choice. Even Soviet Russia felt a translation was mandatory, and within a month the entire supply of translated copies there had been exhausted. (Experts tell me that back in Stalin's day my book was kept on the special reserve shelf in the library, along with books on sex, forbidden to all but the specially licensed readers.) With the Gorbachev thaw, new translations are planned in Hungary, Czechoslovakia, Yugoslavia, Romania, and other Eastern European countries, as well as in China, Japan, Vietnam, and other Asian lands. All in all the number of translations, published or in the pipelines, involves more than 40 languages.

Tales, Tall but True

Legends abound concerning the saga of the textbook *Economics*. Here are a few from the dregs of memory.

Some years back one of MIT's graduate students, now a college president, went to a summer program at the London School of Economics. Attending were students from all over the world, from the jungles of Africa to the rice paddies of Asia. Only one thing did they have in common, he reported. All of them had begun their study of economics with the same textbook. He said his own stock went up because he could explain what some of the American idioms meant and could pinpoint Fort Knox, Kentucky, as the place where the U.S. government stored its gold.

Japanese students are great buyers of books. *Economics* sells well there in English as well as Japanese. The erudite translator is my old Harvard classmate, Shigeto Tsuru, later to become president of Hitotsubashi University in Tokyo. With the royalties he received as translator, Dr. Tsuru purchased a luxurious condominium, and he invited various distinguished scholars to reside there during visits to Japan. As a special honor, he asked me to suggest a name for it. After some thought I came up with Royalty House, and thus it has been known ever since.

Once I received a letter from a diligent reader:

> Sir, in your textbook you say that the $24 that was paid to the Indians for the island of Manhattan—if invested at 6 percent compound interest—would have accumulated to about what all the real estate is worth today in Manhattan Island. I make that out, sir, to be several hundred billions of dollars. I don't think you can buy it for that little.

How was I to respond to her challenge? I asked my research assistant to look into the matter. The next day, Felicity Skidmore came back to say: "Tell her, boss, if 6 percent won't do it, try $6\frac{1}{2}$!"

Another time I received in the mail the following letter:

> I am a 10-year-old boy from Maine. When my Father and I were fishing last week in Lake Walden, I found a bottle floating. Inside it was the hand-printed message: If the finder of this bottle will get in touch with Professor Paul A. Samuelson of MIT, author of *Economics*, he will learn something to his advantage.
>
> Peter Quigley

Although I had not written the note (and all my department pals denied they had), I was on my mettle. But what to do? Finally, I sent this reply:

> Dear Mr. Quigley:
> Yes, I will tell you something worth knowing.
> DON'T BELIEVE EVERYTHING YOU READ IN PRINT.
> Paul A. Samuelson, Ph.D., MIT

Rumors naturally proliferate. No, the beard I don't have is not white. No, I have not been dead since 1977. No, graduate students don't ghostwrite my book—nor do clever elderly females in white sneakers. Yes, I do admit to the vice of tennis.

Samuel Butler quipped: "While others polish their style, I perfect my handwriting." That is not my way. When I try to account for the textbook's durability, I suspect that its relaxed, almost colloquial style deserves some of the credit. That ease is not easily come by. Like Macaulay the historian, I write and rewrite in the hope that each sentence and clause will, at a first reading, reveal its meaning. I don't always succeed, but I do try. For this reason I take private pleasure in the fact that the book is used to teach English to foreigners; excerpts appear in anthologies for Japanese students and also in case materials used in teaching English as a second language to immigrants. Spread the gospel of economics anyway we can, I say.

Here is not the place to describe how the various editions have changed along with the evolution of modern mainstream economics. The first edition put much stress on what might be called "Model T Keynesian macro." With each new edition, the emphasis on monetary policy grew. And with the worst wastes of the Great Depression banished, the microeconomics of efficient market pricing has come to occupy more and more of the text's pages.

Science or Art?

Economics is not an exact science. Still, it is more than an art. We cannot predict with accuracy next year's national income—just as meteorologists cannot forecast next week's weather as precisely as they can guess the day after tomorrow's. But no bank or big business would be so rash as to consult astrologers rather than trained econometricians, or try to wing it by guess and by gosh.

Firms budget their machine replacements by microeconomic principles. Several of my former students earn a million dollars per year on Wall Street. Why? Because they know rich clients or are masters of slick sales techniques? Certainly not. It is because modern theories of finance, worked out intricately in seminar rooms at the business schools of Stanford, Wharton, Chicago, MIT, and Berkeley, really do stand up to statistical testing in the real world of markets.

A beginning textbook won't teach anyone to be an expert. Still, a journey of a thousand miles begins with the first hundred yards. The great Winston Churchill, clever at writing history and heroic in leading nations, was color-blind all his life when it came to basic economic understanding. That kind of unnecessary illiteracy I and 10,000 teachers have vowed to fight.

Mine was the first generation of economists who were sought out by governments. I am the exception who never spent a full year in Washington. Still, I treasure in memory the many times I was called to testify before congressional committees or to serve as a Treasury and Federal Reserve academic consultant. Personally, most memorable were the years in which I had a chance to give economic counsel to John F. Kennedy (senator, presidential candidate, President-elect, and President in Camelot). Republican friends of mine—Fed Chairman Arthur F. Burns and Council of Economic Advisers Chairman Paul MacCracken—have similar stories to tell. Now that Eastern Europe has the need, in the "Age after Gorbachev," to move toward the market economy, Bill Nordhaus's generation is being drafted right and left.

A pseudoscience could not stand the Darwinian test of time. It was President Harry Truman who used to insist, "Give me a one-armed economist." Not for decisive Harry the adviser who says, "On the one hand this; on the other hand that." Well, I have advised legislators, candidates, and presidents. And this I have learned over a long lifetime: The prince or queen does not really want a one-armed economist. For in our profession, one-armed economists often come in two varieties: those with a Right arm only and those with only a Left arm. And then the sovereign must call in an eclectic economist like me to adjudicate between the rival zealots.

Economists are accused of not being able to make up their minds. In particular the brilliant John Maynard Keynes was accused of having volatile opinions. When a royal commission asked five economists for an opinion, it was said they would get six answers—two from Mr. Keynes. Keynes himself was quite unrepentant when pressed on the matter. He would say: "When my information changes, I change my opinion. What do you do, Sir?" He did not want to be the stopped clock that is right only twice a day.

The subject of economics is an ancient and honorable one, still growing and still having a long way to go before approaching the state of a tolerably accurate science. It began really with Adam Smith—our veritable Adam—who wrote in 1776 that great text called *The Wealth of Nations*. Then in 1848 John Stuart Mill, clocked with the highest IQ of all times, wrote *The Principles of Political Economy*, which served as the layperson's bible until 1890, when Alfred Marshall prepared his definitive *Principles of Economics*.

I would be an ingrate not to feel thrilled that, on my watch, the baton has been carried forward by this serendipitous brainchild. Science is a cooperative affair, a matter of public knowledge and never the product of one person's hand. Mostly I have been the mouthpiece of late-twentieth-century mainstream economics, but occasionally I have been able, so to speak, to get my own few licks in. Could any scholar lust for more?

Fortunately, as coauthors, William Nordhaus and I bring independent viewpoints to problems. But we are enough alike in our experiences and judgment to work the canoe forward on its steady course. The book has been lucky for the continuity plus change of its authors.

The future is longer than the present. You readers will look deep into the twenty-first century. William Nordhaus and I try to keep that ever in mind. We remember: Science progresses funeral by funeral. Science never stands still. What was great in Edition 1 is old hat by Edition 3; and maybe has ceased to be true by Edition 14. If scholars have been able to mark the evolution of economic knowledge decade by decade through study of this work's successive revisions, what never goes out of date is Respect for the Facts and for the Methods of cogent analysis and inference. If anywhere, therein resides economics' refusal to go stale and *Economics*' secret of perpetual youth.

The wood I chop warms me twice. I cannot close without remarking that the day Professor Freeman launched me on the adventure of writing a textbook for beginners in economics was the beginning of what has been sheer fun every mile of the way.

Paul A. Samuelson
Massachusetts Institute of Technology
Cambridge, Massachusetts
December 1991

PREFACE

> Books are the carriers of civilization. Without books, history is silent, literature dumb, science crippled, thought and speculation at a standstill. They are engines of change, windows on the world, lighthouses erected in a sea of time.
>
> Barbara Tuchman

Economics has developed as a science over more than 200 years. For almost half a century, this book has served as the standard-bearer for the teaching of elementary economics in classrooms in America and throughout the world. Each new edition has distilled the best thinking of economists about how markets function and about what society can do to improve people's living standards.

But economics has changed profoundly since the first edition of this text appeared in 1948. Economics is above all a living and evolving subject. In every era, it must solve emerging mysteries and grapple with current dilemmas of public policy. Over the last decade, the United States grappled with new problems of slow growth in living standards and mounting poverty; with large government budget deficits and the need to make ends meet for both private and public households; with heightened foreign competition, trade deficits, and a large foreign debt; and with growing concern about international environmental problems and the need to forge agreements to preserve our natural heritage.

But all the news was not bad during the last few years. Many middle-income countries grew quickly and slew the dragon of rapid population growth. And, in the most dramatic development of all, the nations of Eastern Europe threw off their socialist shackles and decided to cast their lot with market capitalism as a way of raising the living standards of their peoples. This was the *triumph of the market* as a way of organizing an advanced, technologically sophisticated economy.

All these and a host of other issues test the ingenuity of modern economics. The need to keep *Economics* at the forefront of modern economic analysis in the rapidly evolving world economy affords the authors an exciting opportunity to present the latest thinking of modern economists and to show how economics can contribute to a more prosperous world.

Our task in these pages is straightforward: to present a clear, accurate, and interesting introduction to the principles of modern economics and to the institutions of the American and world economy. Our primary goal is to survey economics. In doing this we emphasize the basic economic principles that will endure beyond today's headlines.

The Fourteenth Edition

Economics is a dynamic science—changing to reflect the shifting trends in economic affairs, in the environment, in the world economy, and in society at large. This book evolves along with the science it surveys. Every chapter has moved forward in time to keep pace with economic analysis and policy. What are the major changes?

1. Micro First. The major shift in this edition has been a change in the underlying organization of the text, placing microeconomics before macroeconomics. More and more today, teachers are finding that a solid background in microeconomics is indispensable for an appreciation of macroeconomic concepts and problems. Many teachers believe that the principles of macroeconomics can be more thoroughly appreciated after the rigorous reasoning of microeconomics has been mastered. This view is reinforced by the increasing emphasis on the microeconomic foundations of macroeconomics at both the introductory and the advanced levels. Understanding of almost every topic in macroeconomics is improved when the relevant microeconomic topic has been covered. In addition, surveys have found that teachers are more and more convinced that a "micro first" sequence is preferable. All these factors lead us to believe that to begin with microeconomics is to build the house of economic understanding on the firmest foundations.

2. Restructured Presentation. We have used the opportunity afforded by this fundamental change in the book's organization to restructure the coverage in both the microeconomic and the macroeconomic sections. Within the microeconomic chapters, we have deleted a great deal of institutional material that is less important for an understanding of modern economics. These pages have been replaced by a more thorough development of the basic tools of microeconomics.

Similarly, in the macroeconomic chapters, we have reoriented the chapters to focus more clearly upon the issues of short-run output determination and upon the issues of economic growth. The macroeconomic chapters begin with a complete development of the theory of aggregate demand, next develop the theory of aggregate supply, and then integrate the two parts. The chapters on macroeconomic policy are moved later in the book so that the full analytical apparatus can be deployed to analyze the difficult issues the nation faces.

3. Rediscovery of the Market. Parallel to placing microeconomics first in the sequence of topics is a leitmotif in this edition that we call "rediscovery of the market." All around the world, nations are discovering the power of the market as a tool for allocating resources. The most dramatic example of this, of course, occurred in the "velvet revolution" in Eastern Europe during 1989, and after the August 1991 putsch in the Soviet Union. Nation after nation threw out its communist leaders and rejected the command economy. In 1990, Poland undertook a grand experiment of undergoing "shock therapy" by introducing markets into much of its economy; other countries followed more gradually. These countries believed that only by allowing markets to determine prices, outputs, and incomes would people have the incentives to invest appropriately and work hard.

The rediscovery of the market was found in market economies as well. Many countries deregulated industries or "privatized" industries that had been in the public sectors. The results were generally favorable as productivity rose and prices fell. Some economists have recommended using market mechanisms to promote environmental goals, levying pollution taxes as a way of curbing harmful pollution in the most efficient manner.

4. Weight Loss. Over the last few editions, *Economics* had gained bulk as new topics were added and new economic problems were analyzed. The time had come for a fierce weight-loss campaign to reduce the weight of the material, literally and figuratively. With this objective in mind, we surveyed teachers to determine which material was least used. In addition, we questioned leading scholars to ascertain which topics could be omitted at least cost to educating an informed citizenry and a new generation of economists. We drew up a list of deletions and said sad farewell to many appendices and sections. But at every stage, the question we asked was whether the material was central to modern economics. Only when a subject failed this test was it deleted. The end result of this campaign was a book that lost more than one-quarter of its pages.

5. Incorporation of Growth Theory into Macroeconomics. One of the major recent developments in economics has been the resurgence of attention to the forces underlying long-run economic growth. Economists are increasingly examining the determinants of long-run economic growth, the sources of the slowdown in productivity growth, the generation of new technological knowledge. The fourteenth edition reflects this revival by synthesizing growth theories and findings into the section on macroeconomics. We introduce growth theory as an integral part of aggregate supply and potential output. The advantage of this approach is that the controversies about the government deficit and debt can be better understood as affecting the growth of potential output.

6. Emphasis on the Open Economy. Americans are learning that no nation is an island. Our living standards are affected by technological developments in Japan and Europe; domestic producers must contend with competitors from Korea and Mexico. Similarly, no complete understanding of modern economics is possible without a thorough grounding in the world economy. The fourteenth edition continues to increase the material devoted to international economics and the interaction between international trade and domestic economic events.

The emphasis on international affairs is contained in a revised treatment of macroeconomics. International-trade examples are woven through every chapter to highlight the importance of external events. The significance of international trade is underscored both in the overview of macroeconomics and in the chapter on output determination.

7. Microeconomic Foundations of Macroeconomics. Some may feel that an analysis of the microeconomic foundations of macroeconomics is too advanced for introductory textbooks. We disagree. Our fourteenth edition presents a straightforward survey of the economic underpinnings of modern mainstream macroeconomics. Reviewers of the last edition suggested that one area where more space was needed was in the explanation of aggregate supply and demand. We have therefore thoroughly overhauled the exposition of the analytical underpinnings of aggregate supply and demand. We have reorganized the development of macroeconomics so that the development of the material on aggregate demand is concentrated in Chapters 25 through 29, while the analysis of aggregate supply is more thoroughly developed in Chapters 26 and 30. In addition, we have streamlined the treatment of macroeconomics by shortening the analysis of rational-expectations macroeconomics and moving it from an appendix into Chapter 35.

8. Balanced Treatment of Modern Macroeconomics. The fourteenth edition features all major schools of modern macroeconomics: Keynesian, classical, and monetarist. Each is clearly presented and compared with its competitors in a balanced and even-handed way. For each, the empirical evidence is presented and evaluated.

Among the major revisions are Chapter 26's analysis of the fundamentals of aggregate supply and demand; the revised treatment of the role of money in economic activity, covered earlier in this edition in Chapters 28 and 29; integration of the rational-expectations approach into the text; and incorporation of issues of long-run economic growth into the discussion of macroeconomic policies and government deficits and debt.

9. Games and Uncertainty. The analysis of uncertainty and game theory has become an increasingly influential part of modern economics. An appreciation of how private insurance can increase consumer satisfaction relies on understanding behavior toward risk. There is much misunderstanding of the role of speculation in a market economy. In addition, game theory has gained prominence in understanding imperfect competition, the dynamics of trade negotiations, strikes, the evolution of cooperation, and even the misunderstandings that lead to war. We have highlighted the importance of game theory and uncertainty with a new chapter devoted to the subject. Even a short introduction to the economics of games and uncertainty can change the way that we look at the world around us.

10. Emphasis on History and Policy. Economics is at its core an empirical science. It first aims to explain the world around us and then helps us devise economic policies, based on sound economic principles, that can enhance the living standards of people at home and abroad.

Drawing upon history, economic chronicles, and the authors' experience, the fourteenth edition continues to emphasize the use of case studies and empirical evidence to illustrate economic theories. The rediscovery of the market is made vivid when we examine the experience of the socialist countries and their decision to become capitalist countries. The dilemmas involved in combating poverty become real when we understand the shortcomings of the present welfare system and the history of discrimination. Our comprehension of macroeconomic analysis increases when we see how government deficits in the 1980s lowered national saving and slowed capital accumulation in the United States. International economics comes to life when we study the reasons for the surging U.S. trade deficit of the 1980s or the successes of export-oriented countries.

The microeconomic chapters draw upon case studies, economic history, business decisions, and real-world experience to illustrate the fundamental principles. Examples such as Soviet economic reform, OPEC pricing, gasoline taxation, airline deregulation, antitrust policy and practice, collective bargaining by labor unions, the history of stock markets, and an analysis of tax reform help bring the theorems of microeconomics to life.

This "hands-on" approach to economics allows students to understand better the relevance of economic analysis to real-world problems.

11. Improved Exposition in Every Chapter. Although there are many new features in the fourteenth edition, the accent is upon improving the exposition of the core concepts of economics. We have labored over every page to improve this survey of introductory economics. We have received thousands of comments and suggestions from teachers, experts, and students and have incorporated their counsel in the fourteenth edition.

The attention to improved exposition will be seen in the redesign of this edition, with clearer figures and a new typeface. We have introduced scores of new end-of-chapter questions as well as new examples in the textual material. Above all, we believe that cutting out superfluous appendices, sections, and even chapters will lead to greater focus and ultimately to better understanding by the beginning student.

The Glossary, which was first introduced in the twelfth edition, has been carefully tuned to meet the needs of this edition. All major terms now have a capsule definition that students can easily turn to. As a study aid, the most important terms are printed in boldface when first defined in the text; they all then appear again in the Glossary to reinforce the indispensable vocabulary of economics in the student's mind.

One of the distinguishing features of *Economics* has been the presentation of central but somewhat advanced theories in understandable ways. For the fourteenth edition we have redrafted many chapters in both the micro and the macro parts to make these topics understandable to beginning students.

Optional Matter

Economics courses range from one-quarter surveys to year-long intensive honors courses. This textbook has been carefully designed to meet all situations. The more advanced materials have been put in separate appendices or specially designated sections. These will appeal to curious students and to demanding courses that want to survey the entire discipline thoroughly. We have included advanced problems to test the mettle of the most dedicated student.

If yours is a fast-paced course, you will appreciate the careful layering of the more advanced material. Hard-pressed courses can skip the advanced sections, covering the core of economic analysis without losing the thread of the economic reasoning. And for those who teach the bright honors students, this book will challenge the most advanced young scholar. Indeed, many of today's leading economists have written to say they've relied upon *Economics* all along their pilgrimage to the Ph.D.

Format

The fourteenth edition has changed its format to improve the readability and to emphasize the major points. Special footnotes (in displayed boxes) are reserved for important and useful illustrations of the core material in the chapter. Every figure has been redrawn with an eye to crystallizing the essential parts of the analysis.

New features in this edition include scores of fresh end-of-chapter questions, with a special accent upon short problems that reinforce the major concepts surveyed in the chapter. Terms printed in bold type mark the first occurrence and definition of the most important words that constitute the language of economics.

But these many changes have not altered one bit the central stylistic beacon that has guided *Economics* since the first edition: to use simple sentences, clear explanations, and concise tables and graphs.

For Those Who Prefer Macro First

Although this new edition has been designed to cover microeconomics first, many teachers continue to prefer beginning with macroeconomics. They may think that the first-time student finds macro more approachable and will more quickly develop a keen interest in economics when the issues of macroeconomics are encountered first. We have taught economics in both sequences and find both work well.

Whatever your philosophy, this text has been carefully designed for it. Instructors who deal with microeconomics first can move straight through the chapters. Those who wish to tackle macroeconomics first should skip from Part One directly to Part Five, knowing that the exposition and cross-references have been tailored with their needs in mind.

In addition, for those courses that do not cover the entire subject, the fourteenth edition is available in two paperback volumes, *Microeconomics* (Chapters 1 to 22 and 36 to 39 of the text) and *Macroeconomics* (Chapters 1 to 4 and 23 to 39).

Auxiliary Teaching and Study Aids

Students of this edition will benefit greatly from the *Study Guide.* This carefully designed aid has been prepared by Professor Gary Yohe of Wesleyan University, who worked in close collaboration with us in our revision. Both when used alongside classroom discussions and when employed independently for self-study, the *Study Guide* has proved to be an impressive success. There is a full-text *Study Guide* and, for the first time, micro and macro versions are also available.

In addition, instructors will find the *Instructor's Manual and Test Bank* useful for planning their courses and preparing multiple sets of test questions in both print and computerized formats. Moreover, McGraw-Hill has designed a beautiful set of two-color overhead transparencies for presenting the tabular and graphical material in the classroom. These items can all be obtained by contacting your local McGraw-Hill sales representative.

Economics in the Computer Age

This edition is accompanied by the *Interactive Economic Graphics Tutorial to accompany Samuelson/Nordhaus.* IGT III is an upgraded version of McGraw-Hill's very successful economics software program developed by H. Scott Bierman at Carlton College and Todd Proebsting at the University of Wisconsin. Thousands of students have used the *Interactive Graphics Tutorial* to learn, understand, and reinforce their study of economic graphics. This updated and technically advanced version includes microcomputer simulations, and is available for the IBM compatibles.

Acknowledgments

This book has two authors but a multitude of collaborators. We are profoundly grateful to colleagues, reviewers, students, and McGraw-Hill's staff for contributing to the timely completion of the fourteenth edition of *Economics.*

Colleagues at MIT, at Yale, and elsewhere who graciously contributed their comments and suggestions include William C. Brainard, E. Cary Brown, Robert J. Gordon, Lyle Gramley, Paul Joskow, Alfred Kahn, Richard Levin, Robert Litan, Barry Nalebuff, Merton J. Peck, Gustav Ranis, Paul Craig Roberts, Herbert Scarf, Robert M. Solow, James Tobin, Janet Yellen, and Gary Yohe.

In addition, we have benefitted from the tireless devotion of those whose experience in teaching elementary economics is embodied in this edition. We are particularly grateful to the reviewers of the Fourteenth Edition. They include:

John L. Adrian, Auburn University; **Lee J. Alston,** University of Illinois at Urbana-Champaign; **Marion S. Beaumont,** California State University, Long Beach; **Gerald Breger,** University of South Carolina; **Ernest Buchholz,** Santa Monica College; **J. S. Butler,** Vanderbilt University; **Richard Butler,** Trinity University; **Siddhartha Chib,** University of Missouri—Columbia; **Winston Chang,** S.U.N.Y. at Buffalo; **Philip Coelho,** Ball State University; **Ward Connelly,** Trinity University; **Paul Coomes,** University of Louisville; **Carl Davidson,** Michigan State University; **Edward J. Deak,** Fairfield University; **Catherine Eckel,** Virginia Polytechnic Institute and State University; **Wendy Eudy,** University of California at Berkeley; **Richard Gift,** University of Kentucky; **Jack Goddard,** Northeastern State University; **Fred Gottheil,** University of Illinois at Champaign-Urbana; **Jan M. Hansen,** University of Wisconsin-Eau Claire; **Suzanne Holt,** Cabrillo College; **James G. Ibe,** Calvin College; **Stephen Isbell,** Tennessee Technological University; **Dennis Jansen,** Texas A & M University; **Eric R. Jensen,** The College of William and Mary; **Kyoo H. Kim,** Bowling Green State University; **Felix Kwan,** Washington University; **Gary F. Langer,** Roosevelt University; **Stephen E. Lile,** Western Kentucky University; **David Loschky,** University of Missouri—Columbia; **Alfred Lubell,** State University of New York College at Oneonta; **Mark J. Machina,** University of California at San Diego; **John G. Marcis,** Illinois State University; **Thomas Mullen,** University of Wisconsin—Whitewater; **Kevin J. Murphy,** Oakland University; **Martha Paas,** Carleton College; **Andy Pienkos,** Cornell University; **James Price,** Syracuse University; **K.**

Ramagoapal, University of Vermont; **Ed Shapiro,** University of Toledo; **Ben Slay,** Bates College; **John Solow,** Stanford University; **Frank Stafford,** University of Michigan; **Michael K. Taussig,** Rutgers University; **Joseph Turek,** Lynchburg College; **John Veitch,** University of Southern California; **Darwin Wassink,** University of Wisconsin—Eau Claire; **Janice Weaver,** Drake University; **David Weinberg,** Xavier University; **William C. Wood,** James Madison University; and **Gavin Wright,** Stanford University.

Students at MIT, Yale, and other colleges and universities have served as an "invisible college." They constantly challenge and test us, helping to make this edition less imperfect than its predecessor. Although they are too numerous to enumerate, their influence is woven through every chapter. The statistical and historical material was prepared and double-checked by Tan Yong Hui. Word processing assistance was provided by Glena Ames. As a sign of the changing times, the composition for this book was set for the first time directly from floppy disks.

This project would have been impossible without the skilled team from McGraw-Hill who nurtured the book at every stage. We particularly would like to thank, in chronological order of their appearance on the scene, Senior Editor Scott Stratford, Economics Editor Jim Bittker, Development Editors Judith Kromm and Becky Ryan, Editorial Assistant Lori Ambacher, Designer Hermann Strohbach, Editing Supervisor Ira Roberts, Copy Editor Susan Gottfried, and Production Supervisor Janelle Travers. This group of skilled professionals turned a pile of floppy disks and a mountain of paper into a finely polished work of art.

A Word to the Beginning Student

Human history has witnessed waves of revolutions that shook civilizations to their roots—religious conflicts, wars for political liberation, struggles against colonialism, and nationalism. Today, the countries in Eastern Europe, in the Soviet Union, and elsewhere are wrenched by economic revolutions—people are battering down walls, overthrowing established authority, and agitating for a "market economy" because of discontent with their centralized socialist governments. Students like yourselves are marching to win the right to learn from Western textbooks like this one in hopes that they may enjoy the economic growth and living standards of market economies!

The Intellectual Marketplace

Just what is this market that Lithuanians and Poles and Russians are agitating for? In the pages that follow, you will learn about the markets for corn and wheat, stocks and bonds, French francs and Russian rubles, unskilled labor and highly trained neurosurgeons. You have probably read in the newspaper about the gross national product, the consumer price index, the stock market, and the unemployment rate. After you have completed a thorough study of the chapters in this textbook, you will know precisely what these words mean. Even more important, you will also understand the economic forces that influence and determine them.

There is also a marketplace of ideas, where contending schools of economists fashion their theories and try to persuade their scientific peers. You will find in the chapters that follow a fair and impartial review of the thinking of the intellectual giants of our profession—from the early economists like Adam Smith, David Ricardo, and Karl Marx to modern-day titans like John Maynard Keynes, Milton Friedman, and Robert Solow.

Skoal!

As you begin your journey into the land of markets and economic analysis, you may feel some apprehension. But take heart. The fact is that we envy you, the beginning student, as you set out to explore the exciting world of economics for the first time. This is a thrill that, alas, you can experience only once in a lifetime. So, as you embark, we wish you bon voyage!

Paul A. Samuelson
William D. Nordhaus

CONTENTS IN BRIEF

PART ONE

BASIC CONCEPTS

PART TWO

MICROECONOMICS: SUPPLY, DEMAND, AND PRODUCT MARKETS

PART FOUR

EFFICIENCY, EQUITY, AND GOVERNMENT

PART FIVE

FUNDAMENTAL CONCEPTS OF MACROECONOMICS

PART SIX

AGGREGATE SUPPLY AND MACROECONOMIC POLICY

CONTENTS

PART ONE

BASIC CONCEPTS

PART THREE

WAGES, RENT, AND PROFITS: THE DISTRIBUTION OF INCOME

PART FIVE

FUNDAMENTAL CONCEPTS OF MACROECONOMICS

PART SEVEN

INTERNATIONAL TRADE AND THE WORLD ECONOMY

PART ONE

BASIC CONCEPTS

The Road Ahead

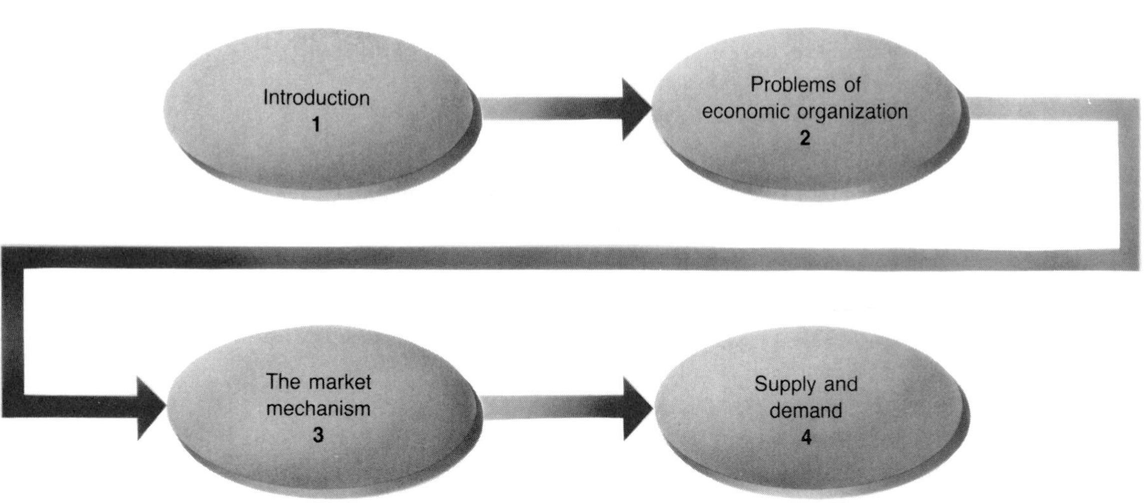

An overview of economics surveys the notions of scarcity and efficiency, the laws of supply and demand and of diminishing returns, the meaning of capital and money, the role of specialization and trade, and the functioning of the market mechanism. A complete mastery of these elementary yet profound concepts will provide a firm foundation for economic wisdom.

CHAPTER 1

INTRODUCTION

> The Age of Chivalry is gone; that of sophisters, economists, and calculators has succeeded.
>
> Edmund Burke

As you begin your reading, you are probably wondering, Why study economics? In fact, people do it for countless reasons.

Some study economics because they hope to make money.

Others worry that they will be illiterate if they cannot understand the laws of supply and demand.

People are also concerned to learn how recession or rising oil prices will affect their future.

For Whom the Bell Tolls

All these reasons, and many more, make good sense. Still, we have come to realize, there is one overriding reason to learn the basic lessons of economics.

All your life—from cradle to grave—you will run up against the brutal truths of economics. As a voter, you will make decisions on issues—on the government budget, regulating industries, taxes, and foreign trade—that cannot be understood until you have mastered the rudiments of this subject.

Choosing your life's occupation is the most important economic decision you will make. Your future depends not only on your own abilities but also upon how economic forces beyond your control affect your wages. Also, economics may help you invest the nest egg you have saved from your earnings. Of course, studying economics cannot make you a genius. But without economics the dice of life are simply loaded against you.

There is no need to belabor the point. We hope you will find that, in addition to being useful, economics is a fascinating field in its own right. Generations of students, often to their surprise, have discovered how stimulating economics can be.

What Is Economics?

Economics covers all kinds of topics. But at the core it is devoted to understanding how society allocates its scarce resources. Along the way to studying the implication of scarcity, economics tries to figure out the 1001 puzzles of everyday life.

Have You Ever Wondered . . .

You have undoubtedly asked a multitude of economic questions even before you picked up your first textbook on economics. You might come into your first class with questions like these:

Why do people worry about the government budget deficit? What are the effects of the budget deficit on inflation? For that matter, why do people worry about inflation? Why are some people rich and others poor? Why have the countries of Eastern Europe rejected socialism and why are they flocking to construct a market economy? What exactly is a market economy? What would happen if we kept foreign cars out of the United States to "protect" domestic workers and firms? Why is it sometimes hard to find a summer job? Sometimes easy? How much is it really costing me to go to college?

Rediscovery of the Market

As a scholarly discipline, economics is two centuries old. Adam Smith published his pathbreaking book *The Wealth of Nations* in 1776, a year also notable for the Declaration of Independence. It is no coincidence that both documents appeared in the same year. The movement for political freedom from the tyranny of European monarchies arose almost simultaneously with attempts to emancipate prices and wages from heavy-handed government regulation.

Adam Smith's contribution was to analyze the way that markets organized economic life and produced rapid economic growth. He showed that a system of prices and markets is able to coordinate people and businesses without any central direction. Almost a century later, as vibrant capitalist enterprises in railroads, textiles, and other sectors began to spread their influence into every region of the world, there appeared the massive critique of capitalism: Karl Marx's *Capital* (1867, 1885, 1894). Marx proclaimed that capitalism was doomed and would soon be followed by business depressions, revolutionary upheavals, and socialism.

In the decades that followed, events seemed to confirm Marx's predictions. Economic panics and deep depressions in the 1890s and 1930s led intellectuals of the twentieth century to question the viability of private-enterprise capitalism. Socialists began to apply their model in the Soviet Union in 1917 and by the 1980s almost one-third of the world was ruled by Marxian doctrines.

In 1936, in the trough of the Great Depression, however, John Maynard Keynes published *The General Theory of Employment, Interest and Money*. This landmark work described a new approach to economics, one that would help government monetary and fiscal policies tame the worst ravages of business cycles.

In the 1980s, the wheel turned full circle. The capitalist countries of the West and socialist countries of the East rediscovered the power of the market to produce rapid technological change and high living standards. In the West, governments reduced the regulatory burdens on industry and decontrolled prices. The most dramatic development occurred in Eastern Europe, where the peaceful revolution of 1989 forced the socialist countries to cast off their central-planning apparatus and allow market forces again to spring up. The fundamental insights of Adam Smith were rediscovered more than two centuries after he wrote *The Wealth of Nations*!

Definitions of Economics

What exactly is the subject that the economists from Smith to Marx to the present generation have analyzed? Here are a few definitions of economics:

- Economics asks *what* goods are produced, *how* these goods are produced, and *for whom* they are produced.
- Economics analyzes movements in the overall economy—trends in prices, output, unemployment, and foreign trade. Once such trends are understood, economics helps develop the policies by which governments can improve the performance of the economy.
- Economics is the study of commerce among nations. It helps explain why nations export some goods and import others, and analyzes the effects of putting economic barriers at national frontiers.
- Economics is the science of choice. It studies how people choose to use scarce or limited productive resources (labor, equipment, technical knowledge), to produce various commodities (such as wheat, overcoats, concerts, and missiles), and to distribute these goods for consumption.
- Economics is the study of money, banking, capital, and wealth.

The list is a good one, yet you could extend it many times over. But if we boil down all these definitions, we find a common theme:

Economics is the study of how societies use scarce resources to produce valuable commodities and distribute them among different people.

In our survey, we will distinguish between **macroeconomics,** which studies the functioning of the economy as a whole, and **microeconomics,** which analyzes the behavior of individual components like industries, firms, and households.

In our study of microeconomics, we examine the behavior of individual parts of the economy. We will study, among other things, how individual prices are set, consider what determines the price of land, labor, and capital, and inquire into the strengths and weaknesses of the market mechanism. Microeconomics is economics through a microscope.

In macroeconomics, by contrast, we examine the economy through a wide-angle lens. Macroeconomics examines how the level and growth of output are determined, analyzes inflation and unemployment, asks about the total money supply, and investigates why some nations thrive while others stagnate.

The Scientific Approach

How, you might wonder, could Smith or Keynes or today's economists hope to answer the deep and difficult questions that economics addresses? How could anyone hope to know in a precise and scientific way why Japan has grown rapidly while the Soviet Union has stagnated. Can economists really explain why some people are fabulously rich while others can hardly afford one square meal a day?

Of course, economists have no monopoly on the truth about the important issues of the day. Indeed, many phenomena are poorly understood and highly controversial. But economists and other scientists have developed techniques—sometimes called the *scientific approach*—that give them a head start in understanding the complex forces that affect economic growth, prices and wages, income distribution, and foreign trade.

Observation. One of the major sources of economic knowledge is observation of economic affairs, especially drawing upon the historical record. As an example, consider inflation, which is a term meaning a rise in the general level of prices.[1] Citizens, bankers, and political leaders often worry about inflation and take painful steps, contracting output and increasing unemployment, to prevent or slow a threatening inflation.

How can we understand the damage done by inflation? One way is to study historical inflations. For example, we will later investigate the German inflation of the 1920s, during which prices rose 1,000,000,000,000 percent in 2 years. This destroyed much of the wealth of the middle class, led to social unrest, and, many people believe, abetted Hitler's rise to power. By examining the impacts of such virulent forms of inflation, we can gain insight into the more moderate inflations of the 1970s and 1980s.

The philosopher George Santayana wrote that those who forget the past are condemned to repeat it. Economists also can learn from the study of history, and the lessons are found on virtually every page of this textbook.

Economic Analysis. History and facts are central to an empirical science like economics, but facts cannot tell their own story. To recorded history we must add economic analysis, for only by developing and testing economic theories can we simplify and organize the jumble of data and facts into a coherent view of reality.

What do we mean by *economic analysis*? This is an approach that starts with a set of assumptions and then deduces logically certain predictions about the economic behavior of people, firms, or the overall economy.

For example, consider attempts to restrict the import of foreign goods in order to "protect" domestic workers and firms from foreign competition. In recent years, the United States has bought much more from abroad than it has sold to foreigners. As a result employment in American manufacturing industries has declined. Workers in the automobile, steel, machinery, and textile industries have complained that "cheap foreign labor" is costing them their jobs. They propose limiting imports of manufactured goods to preserve the jobs of American workers. An example of such a restriction is the tight quota limiting imports of textiles.

People can argue endlessly about the impacts of such import restraints. Economists prefer to use supply-and-demand analysis to determine the impact of trade restrictions, such as on textile imports. Such an analysis shows that import restraints on textiles will tend to increase the number of jobs in the domestic textile industry, but at the same time will raise clothing prices for consumers and lower the total national income. In fact, case

[1] Developing an understanding of economic issues requires a specialized vocabulary. If you are not familiar with a particular word or phrase, you should consult the Glossary at the back of this book. The Glossary contains most of the major technical economic terms used in this book. All terms printed in boldface are also defined in the Glossary.

study piled on case study confirms the validity of these predictions.

In the pages that follow, you will find a wide variety of analytical tools: supply and demand, cost schedules, and the like. Mastery of these tools is essential for understanding the controversial economic questions of the past, present, and future.

Statistical Analyses. A complete understanding of economic activity relies upon the use of economic data and statistical analysis. Governments and businesses issue volumes of data that can help us analyze economic behavior quantitatively. While the actual application of such information requires advanced tools in probability and econometrics, understanding the results requires only careful reading and common sense.

Where might we use statistics? Let's say that you are wondering why, on average, women earn only 60 percent as much as men. With millions of workers, you can hardly hope to compile a history of every person to explain the disparity. Instead, you collect representative data on wages of men and women, along with their personal characteristics (education, years of experience, occupation, and so forth). Using these data, you then employ statistical techniques to estimate what fraction of the difference in earnings of men and women is due to differences in characteristics. For example, studies have found that a significant part of the difference in earnings is associated with the fact that men have on average spent more time in the work force and have generally entered higher-paying occupations. But after all the statistical dust has settled, a significant part of the wage differential is unexplained, and some believe this remaining differential is due to discrimination.

Experiments. The economic world is enormously complicated, with millions of households and billions of prices. In an exciting new development, economists are turning to laboratory and other controlled experiments to study economic phenomena.

What are *controlled experiments*? A scientist sets up a controlled experiment by dividing a population into two or more groups, each of which is treated in exactly the same way except for a single factor. The scientist then measures the impact of the factor under study while *holding other influences constant*.

It is more difficult to perform experiments in economics than in the laboratory sciences. To begin with, economists cannot measure economic variables with the precision that physical scientists can apply in measuring mass, velocity, or distance. Moreover, it is difficult to replicate the real economy in a laboratory.

Notwithstanding these difficulties, economists are relying more and more on experiments to explain economic behavior. For example, in one group of controlled experiments over the last two decades, economists measured people's reactions to different kinds of government programs to raise the incomes of the poor. These experiments were extremely helpful in showing how changes in government programs might affect people's work habits and saving behavior. Other experiments today examine how markets behave with small numbers of producers.

These four techniques—observation, economic analysis, statistical analyses, and experiments—form the approach by which economic science progresses. Every day a new puzzle arises. In response, economists test new ideas and reject old ones, and economics evolves and changes. Textbooks embody both the established wisdom and the hot controversies of today. But in a decade or two, new facts will have toppled old theories, and the subject will evolve anew.

Pitfalls in Economic Reasoning

In all areas of economics, old and new, certain pitfalls lie in the path of the serious economist. This section reviews a few of them.

Failing to Keep "Other Things Equal"

Most economic problems involve several forces interacting at the same time. For example, the number of cars bought in a given year is determined by the price of cars, consumer incomes, gasoline prices, and so on. How can we isolate the impact on car sales of a single variable, such as the price of gasoline?

As we noted in our discussion of controlled experiments, the key step in isolating the impact of a single variable is to hold **other things equal.** This important phrase means that the variable under consideration is changed while all other variables are held constant. If we want to measure the impact of car prices on the number of cars purchased, we must examine the effect of changing car prices while ensuring that consumer incomes, gasoline prices, interest rates, and other variables are unchanged—that these "other things are held constant."

Say that you are interested in determining the impact on car sales of the big rise in gasoline prices that followed the Persian Gulf crisis in the fall of 1990. Your analysis will be complicated because the real incomes of consumers fell at the same time that gasoline prices rose. Nevertheless, you must try to isolate the effects of the higher gasoline prices by estimating what would happen if other things were equal. Unless you exclude the effects of other changing variables, you cannot accurately gauge the impact of changing gasoline prices.

The *Post Hoc* Fallacy

A common mistake in studies of cause-and-effect relationships is the *post hoc* fallacy. A classic example of the *post hoc* fallacy is the belief held by the medicine man in a primitive society that both witchcraft and a little arsenic were necessary to kill his enemy. Then there is the observation by Dr. Optimist that, after the government has cut tax rates, the government's total tax revenues began to rise. Dr. Optimist then claims, "Aha! If we lower tax rates, we will *raise* revenues and reduce the budget deficit." In this case, too, we have the ***post hoc* fallacy.**[2]

The fact that event A takes place before event B does not prove that event A caused event B. To conclude that "after the event" implies "because of the event" is to commit the *post hoc* fallacy.

The medicine man committed the *post hoc* fallacy because he concluded that witchcraft caused death because it preceded death. Dr. Optimist's fallacy was to assume that the tax cut was responsible for the increase in government revenues; overlooked was the fact that the growing economy was raising people's incomes and might have increased tax revenues even more had taxes not been cut.

The Whole Is Not Always the Sum of the Parts

Have you ever seen people jump up at a football game to gain a better view? They usually find that, once everybody is standing up, the view has not improved at all. This example, in which what is true for an individual is not necessarily true for everyone, illustrates the "fallacy of composition," which is defined as follows:

The **fallacy of composition** is the misconception that what is true for a part is therefore true for the whole.

The following examples are true statements that might surprise people who have fallen into the fallacy of composition.

- Attempts of individuals to save more in a depression may reduce the community's total savings.
- If a single individual receives more money, that person will be better off; if everybody receives more money, no one will be better off.
- It may benefit the United States to reduce tariffs levied on imported goods, even if other countries refuse to lower their tariffs.
- If all farmers produce a big crop, total farm income will probably fall.

To see how the fallacy of composition works, take the last example. A corn farmer works from dawn to dusk to increase yields, apply the right amount of fertilizer, and so forth. If she is successful in increasing output, then her income will rise handsomely. But if *all* farmers succeed in raising their output, the price of corn may fall so sharply that the total sales of corn (price times quantity) actually fall. This shows how what holds for an individual does not necessarily hold for the group.

In the course of this book, all the apparent paradoxes listed above will be seen to be true. There are no magic formulas or hidden tricks. Rather, these are examples in which what seems to be true for individuals is not always true for society as a whole.

Subjectivity

Perhaps the greatest obstacle to mastering economics arises from the *subjectivity* we bring to

[2] In logic, this is known as the *post hoc, ergo propter hoc* fallacy (translated from the Latin as "after this, therefore necessarily because of this").

studying the world around us. We sometimes believe that the task of our studies is to uncover an objective reality—to learn the facts and laws of nature or economics.

Alas, learning is not so simple. When we are young, our minds are open to new ideas. As we grow up, we begin to organize our ideas and to learn about the world from our family, friends, and teachers. But no sooner do we begin to understand our world than we become captives of our own knowledge. Growing up on planet Earth, it was natural for early scientists to believe that the rest of the universe revolved around them. Growing up in today's America, we may find it hard to understand economic revolutions taking place in Japan or in Eastern Europe. In the end, the way we perceive the observed facts depends on the theoretical spectacles we wear.

Scientists are just like other people; they are prisoners of their theoretical preconceptions. If physicists learned Newtonian physics well, this might actually hinder their grasp of Einstein's relativity theories.

That is why science belongs to the young. The old "know" too many things that are untrue but that they cannot unlearn. A striking illustration of this is given by Nobel laureate Max Planck, the physicist renowned for his discovery of the revolutionary quantum theory. In his *Scientific Autobiography,* Planck reports what he observed in the development of physics:

> This experience gave me also an opportunity to learn a fact—a remarkable one in my opinion: A new scientific truth does not triumph by convincing its opponents and making them see the light, but rather because its opponents eventually die, and a new generation grows up that is familiar with it.

This lesson applies as well to economics, where the giants like Smith, Marx, and Keynes—indeed, all whose names appear on the family tree of economics shown on the back endpaper of this book—transformed economic understanding by converting the young and open-minded.

Is It a Bird? A simple picture illustrates the subjectivity that exists in every science. Does picture (*b*) in Figure 1-1 show a bird looking to the left? Or is it an antelope looking to the right?

There is no right answer. Either may be correct depending upon the context. In the presence of the field of birds shown in Figure 1-1(*a*), most people think the shape in (*b*) is a bird. But next to the field of antelopes in (*c*), people see it as an antelope.

So it is with scientific facts and theories. After you have studied and learned a body of economic principles, you comprehend reality in a new and different way. This insight helps us understand why people who live on the same planet can have fundamentally different economic perceptions—why some believe markets are the best way to organize the economy while others cling to socialist central

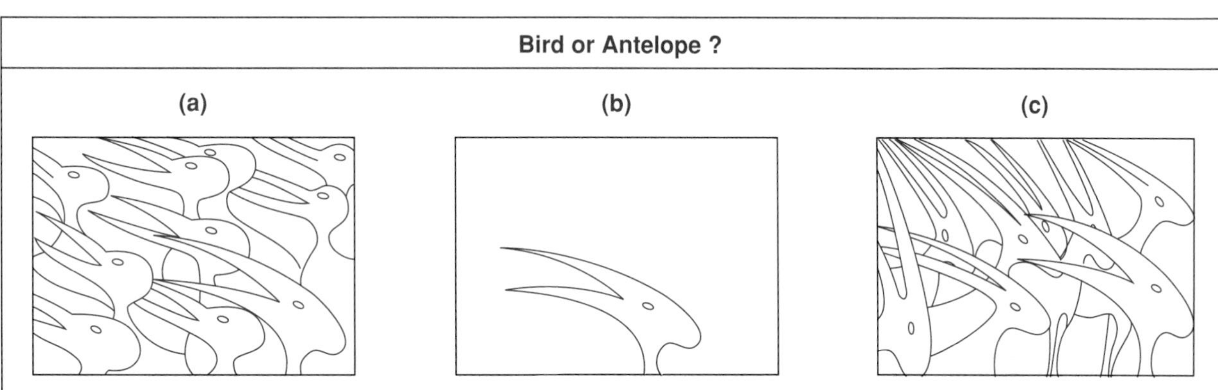

Figure 1-1. The same facts may tell different stories to scientific observers who wear different theoretical spectacles

Is **(b)** a bird or an antelope? When **(c)** is covered up, most people think it is a bird. But when **(a)** is covered, most will see it as an antelope. Thus do differences in perception affect people's views on economic policy. [Source: N.R. Hanson, *Patterns of Discovery* (Cambridge University Press, London, 1961).]

planning, or why government welfare programs are admired by some and vilified by others.

So let us be forewarned to question the inevitable subjectivity of our own beliefs and philosophies and to be open-minded about views that differ from our own.

The Law of Scarcity

Now that we have seen how economics progresses and have learned about some of the pitfalls on the road to economic understanding, let's turn to one of the fundamental concepts of economics.

At the very core of economics lies the fact of **scarcity.** Economists study the way goods are produced and consumed because people want to consume far more than an economy can produce. If infinite quantities of every good could be produced or if human desires were fully satisfied, people would not worry about the efficient use of scarce resources. Businesses would not need to fret over the efficient use of labor and materials, and governments would not need to struggle over taxes or spending. Moreover, since all of us could have as much as we pleased, no one would care about the distribution of incomes among different people or classes.

In such an Eden of affluence, there would be no **economic goods**—goods that are scarce or limited in supply. There would be no need to economize on consumption, and indeed economics would no longer be a vital science. All goods would be free, like sand in the Saudi desert or water at the beach.

But no society has reached a utopia of limitless possibilities. Goods are limited while wants seem infinite. Even in the United States, the most productive economy ever known, production is not high enough to meet everyone's desires. An investigation of consumption patterns would reveal that people want and need central heating and cooling, movies and compact disks, autos and personal computers, concerts and recreation, leisure time and privacy, clean air and pure water, safe factories and clean streets, and innumerable other goods and services. If you add up all the wants, you quickly find that there are simply not enough goods and services to satisfy even a small fraction of everyone's consumption desires. Our national output would have to be many times larger before the average American could live at the level of the average doctor or lawyer. And outside the United States, particularly in Africa and Asia, hundreds of millions of people suffer from hunger and material deprivation.

At the very core of economics is the undeniable truth that we call the **law of scarcity,** which states that goods are scarce because there are not enough resources to produce all the goods that people want to consume. All of economics flows from this central fact. Because resources are scarce, we need to study how society chooses from the menu of possible goods and services, how different commodities are produced and priced, and who gets to consume the goods that society produces.

The Uses of Economics

We suggested earlier that our economic knowledge serves us in managing our personal lives, in understanding society, and in improving the world around us. The ways that economics can help us individually will be as different as are our personal lives. Learning about the stock market may help people manage their own finances; knowledge about price theory and antitrust policy may improve the skills of a lawyer; better awareness of the determinants of cost and revenue will produce better business decisions. The doctor, the investor, and the farmer all need to know about accounting and regulation to get the most satisfaction and profit from their businesses.

Description and Policy in Economics

In addition to helping people cope with their personal concerns, economics improves knowledge of crucial national issues. People who have never made a systematic study of economics are handicapped in even thinking about national issues; they are like the illiterate trying to read.

Economics plays two distinct roles in promoting the analysis of national economic issues. It first helps to understand our society—to describe, explain, and predict economic behavior—for example, the causes of poverty. But for many people, the payoff comes when economic knowledge is applied to help design policies that will build a better society. This distinction between description and prescription is central to modern economics.

Normative vs. Positive Economics. In economics, we must be careful to distinguish between positive (or factual) statements and normative statements (or value judgments).

Positive economics describes the facts and behavior in the economy. What are the causes of poverty in the United States? What will be the effect of higher cigarette taxes on the number of smokers? How has the economic performance of socialist countries compared with that of capitalist countries? These questions can be resolved only by reference to facts—they may be easy or difficult questions, but they are all in the realm of positive economics.

Normative economics involves ethical precepts and value judgments. Should the government give money to poor people? Should the budget deficit be reduced by higher taxes or lower spending? Should the socialist countries introduce private property and stock markets? There are no right or wrong answers to these questions because they involve ethics and values rather than facts. These issues can be debated, but they can never be settled by science or by appeal to facts. There simply is no correct answer to how high inflation should be, whether society should help poor people, or how much the nation should spend on defense. These questions are resolved by political decisions, not by economic science.

Economics in Government

Economists have in recent years become the counselors of presidents and prime ministers. The political agenda is full of economic issues: Should we raise taxes to curb the budget deficit? Should the minimum wage be raised? Should the government regulate banks more closely? Political leaders need economic advisers to provide counsel on such complicated questions.

Increasingly, international aspects of economic activity concern policymakers. As the nation's trade deficit climbed in the 1980s, Congress labored to rewrite the rules of international commerce. People worry about whether the United States is losing its technological vitality and whether we will become a second-rate power behind Japan and Europe. And scientific concerns about global warming have generated support for international measures to curb energy consumption.

Heads of government must constantly make vital decisions that involve economics. Naturally, national leaders need not themselves be experts in economics. Rather, they need to be literate "consumers" of the conflicting economic advice given them. Presidents who brought major economic changes to the United States— Franklin Roosevelt, John Kennedy, and Ronald Reagan— were not professional economists. Rather, they had brain trusts of advisers who were schooled in the major economic issues and could propose solutions to the problems of the day.

Similarly, few students will become professional economists. Many will study economics for only a term or two. This book will give a thorough introductory overview of the whole subject. Your view of the world will never be the same after a single semester of economics.

Why Economists Disagree

In recent years, economists have developed a reputation for being a crotchety lot who cannot agree on anything. One writer complained, "If you laid all economists end to end, they still wouldn't reach a conclusion."

A closer look reveals that economists agree much more than is generally supposed. A broad consensus exists on many questions of positive economics, particularly on issues in microeconomics such as the importance of the market in allocating resources, the harmful effects of many government regulations (such as rent control or tariffs), and the benefits of trade and specialization.

The major disagreements among economists lie in the normative arena. Economists differ as much as the rest of the population on questions concerning the appropriate size of government, the power of unions, the relative importance of inflation and unemployment, the fair distribution of income, and whether taxes should be raised or lowered. They are as divided as their brothers and sisters on the broad political and ethical issues of today.

● At the end of our overture, let us return briefly to our opening theme, Why study economics? Perhaps the best answer to the question is a famous one given by Lord Keynes in the final lines of his 1936 classic, *The General Theory of Employment, Interest and Money*:

> The ideas of economists and political philosophers, both when they are right and when they are wrong, are more powerful than is commonly understood. Indeed the world is ruled by little else. Practical men, who believe themselves to be quite exempt from any intellectual influences, are usually the slaves of some defunct economist. Madmen in authority, who hear voices in the air, are distilling their frenzy from some academic scribbler of a few years back. I am sure that the power of vested interests is vastly exaggerated compared with the gradual encroachment of ideas. Not, indeed, immediately, but after a certain interval; for in the field of economic and political philosophy there are not many who are influenced by new theories after they are twenty-five or thirty years of age, so that the ideas which civil servants and politicians and even agitators apply to current events are not likely to be the newest. But, soon or late, it is ideas, not vested interests, which are dangerous for good or evil.

To understand the ideas of generations of economists and how they apply to the problems of personal life and national issues—ultimately, this is why we study economics. ●

SUMMARY

1. What is economics? Economics is the study of how societies choose to use scarce productive resources that have alternative uses, to produce commodities of various kinds, and to distribute them among different groups.
2. Economics is studied for a variety of reasons: to understand problems facing the citizen and family, to help governments promote growth and improve the quality of life while avoiding depression and inflation, and to analyze fascinating patterns of social behavior. Because economic questions enter into both daily life and national issues, a basic understanding of economics is vital for sound decision making by individuals and nations.
3. Economists and other scientists have a variety of weapons that can be deployed to attack economic questions. Observation of economic history provides countless episodes from which to find patterns of behavior. Economic analysis allows the facts to be arrayed into general propositions. Often statistical studies permit understanding of complex situations. And experiments allow us to test different economic hypotheses.
4. In approaching economic questions, be careful to avoid the common pitfalls. Remember to hold other things equal; keep descriptions distinct from value judgments; avoid the *post hoc* fallacy and the fallacy of composition; and recognize the necessary subjectivity in our observations and theories.
5. Economics is grounded in the law of scarcity, which holds that goods are scarce because people desire much more than the economy can produce. Economic goods are scarce, not free, and society must choose among the limited goods that can be produced with its available resources.

CONCEPTS FOR REVIEW

Economics
definitions
normative vs. positive economics
macroeconomics vs. microeconomics

Approaching economics
other things equal
controlled experiment
fallacy of composition
post hoc fallacy

The law of scarcity
free goods, economic goods

QUESTIONS FOR DISCUSSION

1. Give five definitions of economics. Which is the most comprehensive one?
2. Define each term in your own words: *post hoc* fallacy; other things equal; normative and positive economics.
3. Define economic goods and free goods. Give some examples of each. Can you think of examples of goods that used to be free goods but are now economic goods?
4. Identify which of the following are normative and which are positive statements:
   (a) The 1990 Persian Gulf crisis raised oil prices, which led to lower consumption of gasoline.
   (b) The American economy has grown more rapidly than has the Soviet economy.
   (c) The deserving poor should pay no taxes.
   (d) The oil companies are making excessive profits and should be subject to a windfall-profits tax.
   (e) Rising food prices contributed to the French Revolution.
5. Give examples of the fallacy of composition and of the *post hoc* fallacy. Is the former involved in the debate over cigarette smoking and lung cancer? (Why not?) Might the latter be involved in this debate? (Why so?) Explain carefully the paradox of farm incomes (the fourth example in the section on the fallacy of composition).
6. The following table shows data on the top federal personal-tax rate, on federal personal-tax revenues, and on total personal income.

Year	Top tax rate (%)	Tax revenues ($, billion)	Personal income ($, billion)
1980	70	244	2259
1984	50	298	3109
1988	28	401	4646

   Some might argue that lowering tax rates actually raises tax revenues. Analyze this argument. What fallacy is involved?
7. The gravestone of Karl Marx contains the following words he wrote at the age of 26:

   > Up 'til now the philosophers have only interpreted the world in various ways. The point, though, is to change it!

   Marx believed in violent revolution to overthrow the capitalist system, which he believed was exploiting workers. Are there any economic ills of society that you feel should be changed? How would you go about changing them?

A P P E N D I X 1

HOW TO READ GRAPHS

A picture is worth a thousand words.
Chinese proverb

Before you can master economics, you must have a working knowledge of graphs. They are as indispensable to the economist as a hammer is to a carpenter. So if you are not familiar with the use of diagrams, invest some time in learning how to read them—it will be time well spent.

What is a *graph*? It is a diagram showing how two or more sets of data or variables are related to one another. Graphs are useful in economics because they pack a great deal of data into a small space.

You will encounter many different kinds of graphs in this book. Some graphs show how variables change over time (see, for example, the inside of the front cover); other graphs show the relationship between different variables (such as the example we will turn to in a moment). Each graph in the book will help you to understand an important economic law or trend.

The Production-Possibility Frontier

One of the first graphs you will encounter in this text is the production-possibility frontier. At any point in time, a country can produce only a certain quantity of goods and services with its limited resources: so much gasoline, so much heating oil, so many aircraft, and so forth. Moreover, more of one good cannot be produced without giving up some of another good: for example, the more gasoline produced, the less heating oil can be produced.

In economics, we represent this limitation on a country's productive potential by the **production-possibility frontier (*PPF*).** The *PPF* represents the maximum amounts of a pair of goods or services that can both be produced with an economy's given resources assuming that all resources are fully employed.

Let's look at a basic example using food and machines. The essential data for the *PPF* are shown in Table 1A-1. Of the two sets of data, one set gives possible outputs of food; the other set gives possible outputs of machines. Each output level of food is paired with the number of machines that could be produced at the same time. You can see that as the quantity of food produced increases, the production of machines falls. Thus, if the economy produced 10 units of food, it could produce a maximum of 140 machines, but when the output of food is 20 units, only 120 machines can be manufactured.

Alternative Production Possibilities

Possibilities	Food	Machines
A	0	150
B	10	140
C	20	120
D	30	90
E	40	50
F	50	0

Table 1A-1. The pairs of possible outputs of food and machines
The table shows six potential pairs of outputs that can be produced with the given resources of a country. The country can choose one of the six possible combinations.

Production-Possibility Graph

The data shown in Table 1A-1 can also be presented as a graph. To construct the graph, we represent each of the pairs of data of Table 1A-1 by a single point on a two-dimensional plane. Figure 1A-1 displays in a graph the relationship between the food and machines outputs shown in Table

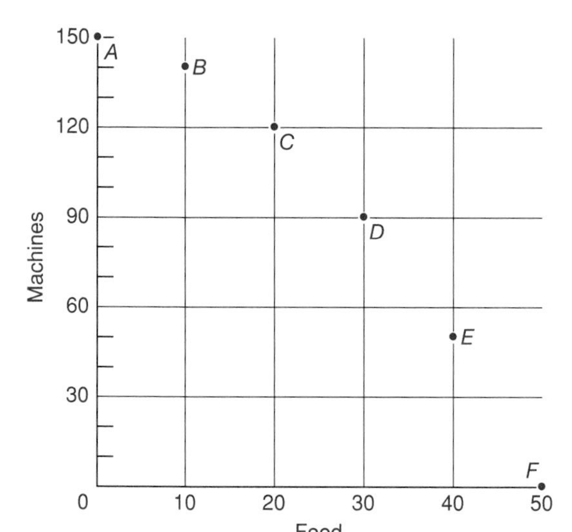

Figure 1A-1. Six possible pairs of food-machines production levels

This figure shows the data of Table 1A-1 in graphical form. The data are exactly the same, but the visual display presents the data more vividly.

1A-1. Each pair of numbers is represented by a single point in the graph. Thus the row labeled A in Table 1A-1 is graphed as point *A* in Figure 1A-1, and similarly for points *B*, *C*, and so on.

In Figure 1A-1, the vertical line at left and the horizontal line at bottom correspond to the two variables—food and machines. A *variable* is an item of interest that can be defined and measured and that takes on different values at different times or places. Important variables studied in economics are prices, quantities, hours of work, acres of land, dollars of income, and so forth.

The horizontal line on a graph is referred to as the *horizontal axis,* or sometimes the *X axis*. The horizontal axis is simply a convenient line for measuring the quantity of one of the variables. In Figure 1A-1, food output is measured on the black horizontal axis.

The vertical line at the left is known as the *vertical axis,* or *Y axis*. In Figure 1A-1, it measures the number of machines produced. Point *A* on the vertical axis stands for 150 machines.

The lower left-hand corner where the two axes meet is called the *origin*. It signifies 0 food and 0 machines in Figure 1A-1.

A Smooth Curve. In most economic relationships, variables can change by small amounts as well as by the large increments shown in Figure 1A-1. We therefore generally draw economic relationships as continuous curves. Figure 1A-2 shows the *PPF* as a smooth curve in which the points from *A* to *F* have been connected.

By comparing Table 1A-1 and Figure 1A-2 we can see why graphs are so often used in economics. The smooth *PPF* reflects the menu of choice for the economy. It is a visual device for showing what types of goods are available in what quantities. Your eye can see at a glance the relationship between machine and food production.

Slopes and Lines

In Figure 1A-2, we see a line depicting the relationship between food and machine production. One important way to describe the relationship between two variables is by the slope of the graph line.

The **slope** of a line represents the change in one variable that occurs when another variable changes. More precisely, it is the change in the variable *y* on the vertical axis per unit change in the

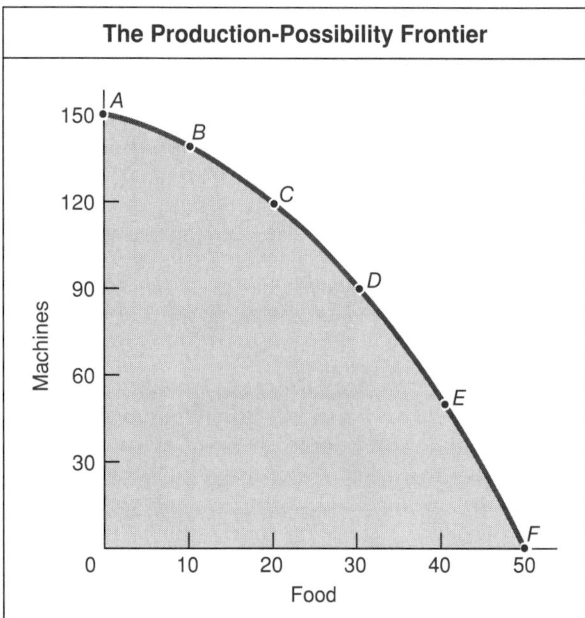

Figure 1A-2

A smooth curve fills in between the plotted pairs of points, creating the production-possibility frontier.

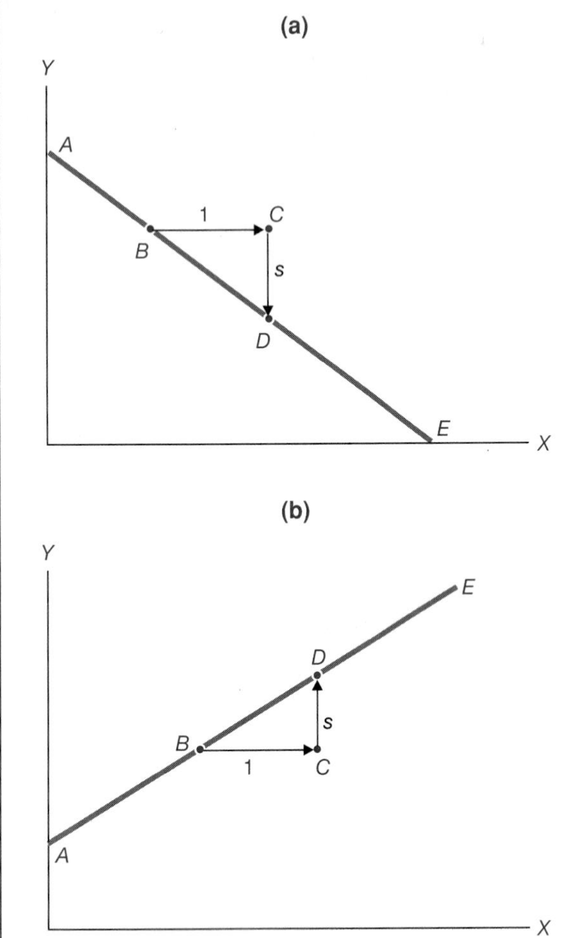

Figure 1A-3. Calculation of slope for straight lines

It is easy to calculate slopes for straight lines as "rise over run." Thus in both **(a)** and **(b)**, the numerical value of the slope is rise/run = $CD/BC = s/1 = s$. Note that in **(a)**, CD is negative, indicating a negative slope, or an inverse relationship between X and Y.

variable x on the horizontal axis. For example, in Figure 1A-2, say that food production rose from 25 to 26 units. The slope of the curve in Figure 1A-2 tells us the precise change in machinery production that would take place. *Slope is an exact numerical measure of the relationship between the change in* y *and the change in* x.

We can use Figure 1A-3 to show how to measure the slope of a straight line, say the slope of the line between points B and D. Think of the movement from B to D as occurring in two stages. First comes a horizontal movement from B to C indicating a 1-unit increase in the x value (with no change in y). Second comes a compensating vertical movement up or down, shown as s in Figure 1A-3. (The movement of 1 horizontal unit is purely for convenience. The formula holds for movements of any size.) The two-step movement brings us from one point to another on the straight line.

Because the BC movement is a 1-unit increase in x, the length of CD (shown as s in Figure 1A-3) indicates the change in y per unit change in x. On a graph, this change is called the *slope* of the line $ABDE$.

Often slope is defined as "the rise over the run." The *rise* is the vertical distance; in Figure 1A-3, the rise is the distance from C to D. The *run* is the horizontal distance; it is BC in Figure 1A-3. The rise over the run in this instance would be CD over BC. Thus the slope of BD is CD/BC.

The key points to remember are:

1. The slope can be expressed as a number. It measures the change in y per unit change in x, or "the rise over the run."
2. If the line is straight, its slope is constant everywhere.
3. The slope of the line indicates whether the relationship between x and y is *direct* or *inverse*. Direct relationships occur when variables move in the same direction (that is, they increase or decrease together); inverse relationships occur when the variables move in opposite directions (that is, one increases as the other decreases). Thus a negative slope indicates the x-y relation is inverse, as it is in Figure 1A-3(*a*). Why? Because an increase in x calls for a decrease in y.

People sometimes confuse slope with the appearance of steepness. This conclusion is often valid—but not always. The steepness depends on the scale of the graph. Panels (*a*) and (*b*) in Figure 1A-4 both portray exactly the same relationship. But in (*b*), the horizontal scale has been stretched out compared to (*a*). If you calculate carefully, you will see that the slopes are exactly the same (and are equal to $\frac{1}{2}$).

Slope of a Curved Line. A curved or nonlinear line is one whose slope changes. Sometimes we want to know the slope *at a given point*, such as point B in Figure 1A-5. We see that the slope at point B is ris-

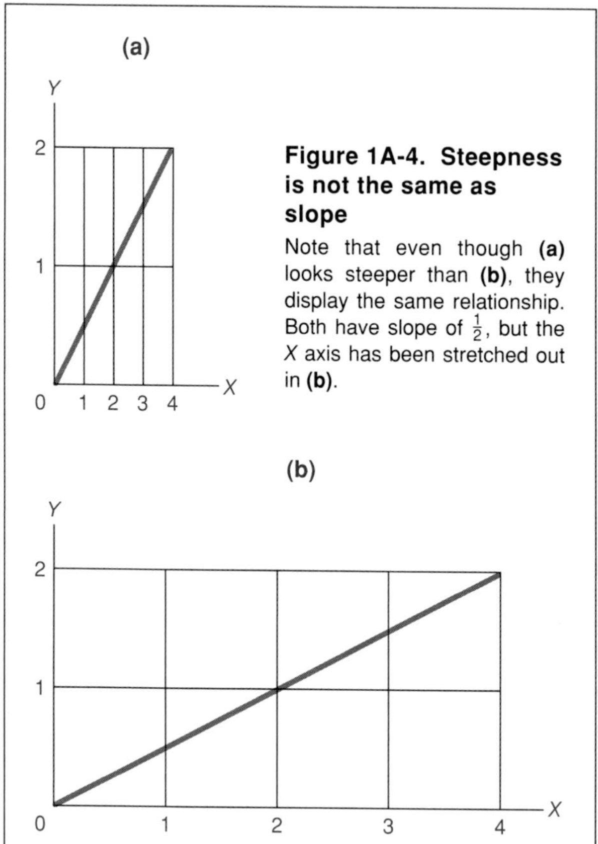

Figure 1A-4. Steepness is not the same as slope

Note that even though **(a)** looks steeper than **(b)**, they display the same relationship. Both have slope of $\frac{1}{2}$, but the X axis has been stretched out in **(b)**.

ing, but it is not obvious exactly how to calculate the slope.

To find the slope of a smooth curved line at a point, we calculate the slope of the straight line that just touches, but does not cross, the curved line at the point in question. Such a straight line is called a *tangent* to the curved line. Put differently, the slope of a curved line at a point is given by the slope of the straight line that is tangent to the curve at the given point. (Of course, we find the slope of the tangent line with the usual right-angle measuring technique discussed earlier.)

To find the slope at point *B* in Figure 1A-5, we simply construct straight line *FBJ* as a tangent to the curved line at point *B*. We then calculate the slope of the tangent as *NJ/MN*. Similarly, the tangent line *GH* gives the slope of the curved line at point *D*.

Another example of the slope of a nonlinear line is shown in Figure 1A-6. This shows a typical microeconomics curve, which is dome-shaped and has a maximum at point *C*. We can use our method

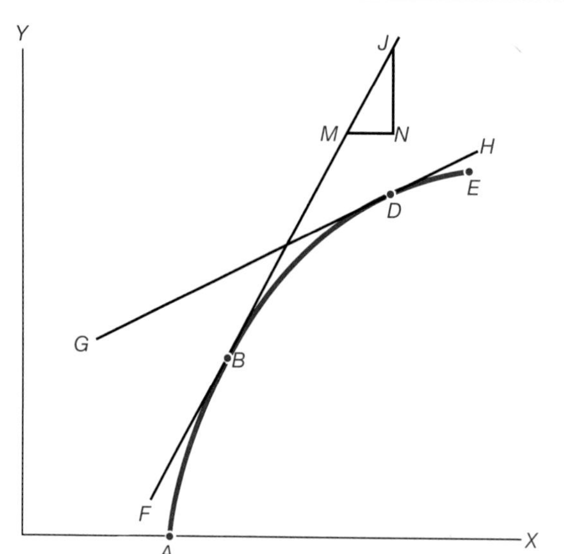

Figure 1A-5. Tangent as slope of curved line

By constructing a tangent line we can calculate the slope of a curved line at a given point. Thus the line *FBMJ* is tangent to smooth curve *ABD* at point *B*. The slope at *B* is calculated as the slope of the tangent line, i.e., as *NJ/MN*.

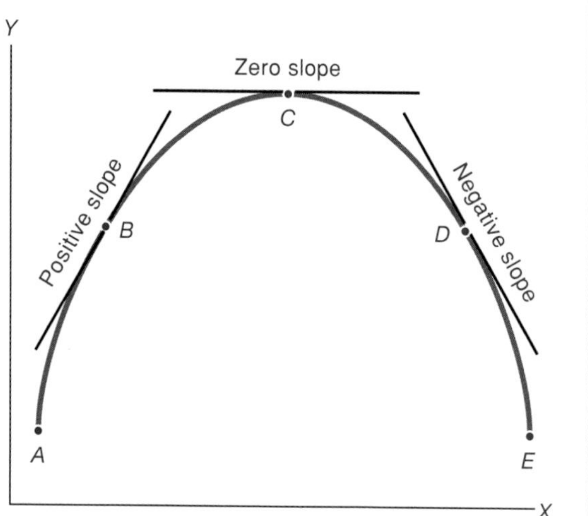

Figure 1A-6. Different slopes of nonlinear curves

Many curves in economics first rise, then reach a maximum, then fall. In the rising region from *A* to *C* the slope is positive (see point *B*). In the falling region from *C* to *E* the slope is negative (see point *D*). At the curve's maximum, point *C*, the slope is zero. (What about a U-shaped curve? What is the slope at its minimum?)

of slopes-as-tangents to see that the slope of the curve is always positive in the region where the curve is rising and negative in the falling region. At the peak or maximum of the curve, the slope is exactly zero. A zero slope signifies that a tiny movement in the x variable around the maximum has no effect on the value of the y variable.[1]

Shifts of and Movement Along Curves

An important distinction in economics is between shifts of curves and movements along curves. We can examine the distinction in Figure 1A-7. The inner production-possibility frontier reproduces the *PPF* in Figure 1A-2. At point *D* society chooses to produce 30 units of food and 90 units of machines. If society decides to consume more food *with a given PPF*, then it can *move along* the *PPF* to point *E*. This movement along the curve represents choosing more food and fewer machines.

Suppose that the inner *PPF* represents society's production possibilities for 1990. If we return to the same country in 2000, we see that the *PPF* has *shifted* from the inner 1990 curve to the outer 2000 curve. (This shift would occur because of technological change or because of an increase in labor or capital available.) In the later year, society might choose to be at point *G*, with more food and machines than at either *D* or *E*.

The point of this example is that in one case (moving from *D* to *E*) we see movement along a curve, while in the second case (from *D* to *G*) we see a shift of the curve.

[1] For those who enjoy algebra, the slope of a line can be remembered as follows. A straight line (or linear relationship) is written as $y = a + bx$. For this line, the slope of the curve is b, which measures the change in y per unit change in x.

A curved line or nonlinear relationship is one involving terms other than constants and the x term. An example of a nonlinear relationship is the quadratic equation $y = (x - 2)^2$. You can easily verify that the slope of this equation is negative for $x < 2$ and positive for $x > 2$. What is its slope for $x = 2$?

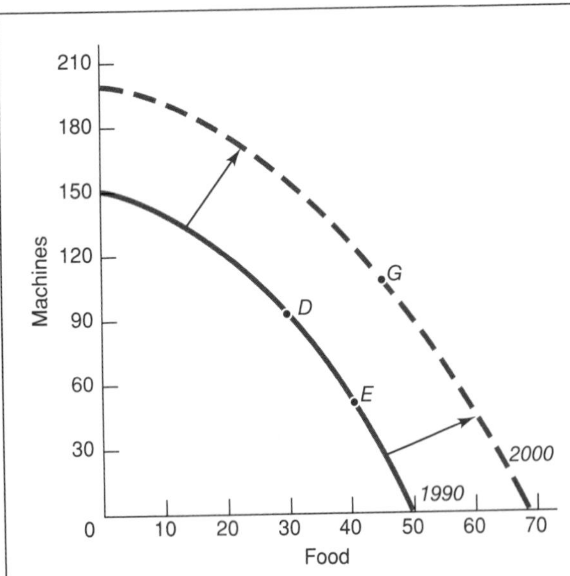

Figure 1A-7. Shift of curves versus movement along curves

In using graphs, it is essential to distinguish *movement along* a curve (such as from high-investment *D* to low-investment *E*) from a *shift of* a curve (as from *D* in an early year to *G* in a later year).

Some Special Graphs

Figure 1A-2 shows one of the most important graphs of economics, one depicting the relationship between two economic variables (such as food and machines, or guns and butter). You will encounter other types of graphs in the pages that follow.

Time Series. Some graphs show how a particular variable has changed over time. Look, for example, at the graphs on the inside front cover of this text. The left-hand graph shows a time series since the American Revolution of a significant macroeconomic variable, the ratio of the federal government debt to total gross national product or GNP—this ratio is the "debt-GNP ratio." Time-series graphs have time on the horizontal axis and variables of interest (in this case, the debt-GNP ratio) on the vertical axis. This graph shows that the debt-GNP ratio has risen sharply during every major war.

Scatter Diagrams. Sometimes individual pairs of points will be plotted, as in Figure 1A-1. Often, combinations of variables for different years will be plotted. An important example of a scatter diagram from macroeconomics is the *consumption function*, shown in Figure 1A-8. This scatter diagram shows the nation's total disposable income on the horizontal axis and total consumption (spending by households on goods like food, clothing, and hous-

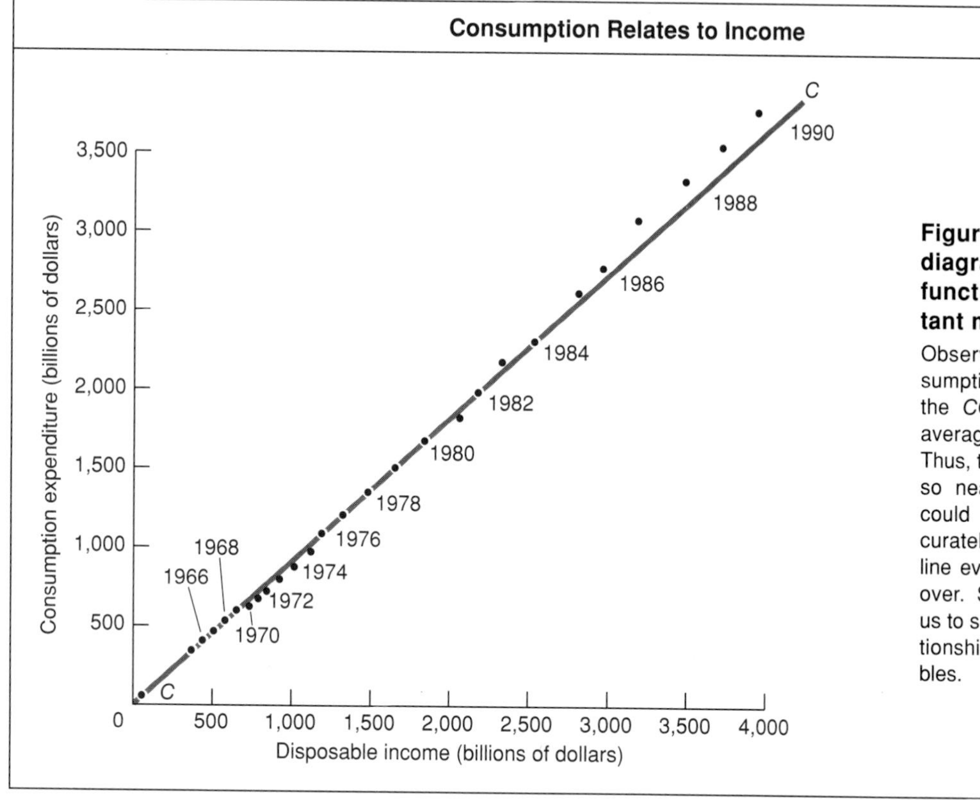

Figure 1A-8. Scatter diagram of consumption function shows important macroeconomic law

Observed points of consumption spending fall near the *CC* line, which displays average behavior over time. Thus, the blue point for 1985 is so near the *CC* line that it could have been quite accurately predicted from that line even before the year was over. Scatter diagrams allow us to see how close is the relationship between two variables.

ing) on the vertical axis. Note that consumption is very closely linked to income, a vital clue for understanding changes in national income and output.

Diagrams with More Than One Curve. Often it is useful to put two curves in the same graph, thus obtaining a "multicurve diagram." The most important example is the supply-and-demand diagram, shown in Chapter 4 (see page 55). These graphs can show two different relationships simultaneously, such as how consumer purchases respond to price (demand) and how business production responds to price (supply). By graphing the two relationships together, we can determine the price and quantity that will hold in a market.

● This concludes our brief excursion into graphs. Once you have mastered these basic principles, the graphs in this book, and in other areas, can be both fun and instructive. ●

SUMMARY TO APPENDIX

1. Graphs are an essential tool of modern economics. They provide a convenient presentation of data or of the relationship between two variables.
2. The important points to understand about a graph are: What is on each of two axes (horizontal and vertical)? What are the units on each axis? What kind of relationship is depicted in the curve or curves shown in the graph?
3. The relationship between the two variables in a curve is given by its slope. The slope is defined as "the rise over the run," or the increase in *y* per unit increase in *x*. If it is upward (or positively) sloping, the two variables are directly related; they move upward or downward together. If the graph has a downward (or negative) slope, then the two variables are inversely related.

4. In addition, we sometimes see special examples of graphs: time series, which show how a particular variable moves over time; scatter diagrams, which show the observations on a pair of variables; and multicurve diagrams, which show two or more relationships on a single figure.

CONCEPTS FOR REVIEW

Elements of graphs
horizontal, or *X*, axis
vertical, or *Y*, axis
slope as "rise over run"
slope (negative, positive, zero)
tangent as slope of curved line

Examples of graphs
time-series graphs
scatter diagrams
multicurve graphs

QUESTIONS FOR DISCUSSION

1. Consider the following problem for a student. After your 8 hours a day of sleep, you have 16 hours a day to divide between leisure and study. Let leisure be the x variable and study hours be the y variable. Plot the straight-line relationship between all combinations of x and y on a blank piece of graph paper. Be careful to label the axes and mark the origin.
2. In question 1, what is the slope of the line showing the relationship between study and leisure hours? Is it a straight line?
3. Let us say that you absolutely need 6 hours of leisure per day, no more, no less. On the graph, mark the point that corresponds to 6 hours of leisure. Now consider a *movement along the curve*: Assume that you decide that you need only 4 hours of leisure a day. Plot the new point.
4. Next show a *shift of the curve*: You find that you need less sleep, so that you have 18 hours a day to devote to leisure and study. Draw the new (shifted) curve.
5. Keep a record of your own leisure and study for a week. Plot a time-series graph of the hours of leisure and study each day. Next plot a scatter diagram of hours of leisure and hours of study. Do you see any relationship between the two variables?
6. Reread footnote 1 on page 16. Plot the straight line or linear curve $y = 10 + 0.5x$. What is its slope? Next plot the quadratic equation $y = (x - 2)^2$. What is the slope of this curve at $y = (0, 1, 2, 10)$?
7. Consider the following data. Plot the relationship on a scatter diagram. Why can't you be sure which of the variables "causes" movement in the other variable? (Remember the *post hoc* fallacy.)

Year	Money supply ($, billion)	GNP ($, billion)
1965	168	705
1970	215	1,016
1975	288	1,598
1980	409	2,732
1985	620	4,015
1990	826	5,463

Source: *Economic Report of the President,* 1991.

C H A P T E R 2

BASIC PROBLEMS OF ECONOMIC ORGANIZATION

> Every gun that is made, every warship launched, every rocket fired signifies, in the final sense, a theft from those who hunger and are not fed.
>
> President Dwight D. Eisenhower

Whenever people gather into a community, they must necessarily confront a few universal economic problems. These fundamental questions are as crucial today as they were at the dawn of human civilization. And as long as goods are scarce, these questions will surely be faced by the brave new world of the future.

In this chapter we explore the central problems of economic organization. We will see that every economy must answer a triad of questions: *what, how,* and *for whom*. This is a shorthand list that reminds us that every society must determine *what* commodities shall be produced, *how* these goods should be made, and *for whom* they will be produced.

Having described the central economic problems, we then illustrate several important choices a society must make. Because an economy's production is limited by the amount of inputs available and by its technological knowledge, society must choose between necessities and luxuries, between public and private goods, and between consumption and investment. This insight leads to the important concept of opportunity cost—which signifies that when we choose to consume a good, something else must be given up. We also discuss how the features of a modern economy—specialization and trade, money, and capital—contribute to the enormous productivity of an advanced industrial country.

A. The Three Problems of Economic Organization

Every human society—whether it is an advanced industrial nation, a centrally planned economy, or an isolated tribal society—must confront and resolve three fundamental and interdependent economic problems.

- *What* commodities are to be produced and in what quantities? How much of each of the many possible goods and services should the economy make? And when will they be produced? Should we produce pizzas or shirts today? A few high-quality shirts or many cheap shirts? Should we produce many consumption goods (like pizzas and concerts) or few consumption goods and many investment goods (like pizza factories and concert halls), allowing more consumption tomorrow?
- *How* shall goods be produced? By whom and

with what resources and in what technological manner are they to be produced? Who farms and who teaches? Is electricity to be generated from oil or from coal? With much air pollution or with little? Are goods produced by hand or with machines? In privately owned capitalist corporations or in state-owned socialist enterprises?

- *For whom* shall goods be produced? Who gets to eat the fruit of the economy's efforts? Or, to put it formally, how is the national product to be divided among different households? Are we to have a society in which a few are rich and many poor? Shall high incomes go to managers or workers or landlords? Shall the selfish inherit the earth? Shall the lazy eat well?

These three basic problems are common to all economies. But, as we will see later, different societies take different approaches in solving them.

Inputs and Outputs

In economic language, the three central economic tasks of every society are really about choices among an economy's inputs and outputs.

Inputs are commodities or services used by firms in their production processes. An economy uses its existing *technology* to combine inputs to produce outputs. **Outputs** are the various useful goods or services that are either consumed or employed in further production. Consider the "production" of an omelette. We say that the eggs, salt, heat, frying pan, and the chef's skilled labor are the inputs. The fluffy omelette is the output.

We classify inputs, also called *factors of production*, into three broad categories: land, labor, and capital.

- *Land*—or more generally natural resources—represents the gift of nature to our productive processes. It consists of the land used for farming or for underpinning houses, factories, and roads; energy resources to fuel our cars or heat our homes; and non-energy resources like copper and iron ore and sand. We should also view our physical environment—the air we breathe and the water we drink—as natural resources.
- *Labor* consists of the human time spent in production—working in automobile factories, tilling the land, teaching school, or cooking omelettes. Thousands of occupations and tasks, at all skill levels, are performed by labor. It is at once the most familiar and the most crucial input for an advanced industrial economy.
- *Capital* resources form the durable goods of an economy, produced in order to produce yet other goods. Capital goods include machines, roads, computers, hammers, trucks, steel mills, automobiles, washing machines, and buildings. As we will later see, the accumulation of specialized capital goods is essential to the task of economic development.

Restating the three economic problems in terms of inputs and outputs, a society must decide: (1) *what* outputs to produce, and in what quantity; (2) *how* to produce them—that is, by what techniques inputs should be combined to produce the desired outputs; and (3) *for whom* the outputs should be produced and distributed.

Market, Command, and Mixed Economies

In the earliest societies, custom ruled every facet of behavior. *What, how,* and *for whom* were decided by traditions passed on from elders to youths. In ancient Egypt, a son unswervingly adopted the trade of his father. In a modern economy, however, custom cannot adapt quickly enough to keep up with the rapidly evolving production and consumption patterns. Different societies face the demands for change through *alternative economic systems,* and economics studies the different mechanisms that a society can use to allocate its scarce resources.

Today, societies are generally organized in one of two fashions. In some cases, government makes most economic decisions, with those on top of the hierarchy giving economic commands to those further down the ladder. In other cases, decisions are made in markets, where individuals or enterprises voluntarily agree to trade inputs and outputs, usually through payments of money. Let's examine each of these two forms of economic organization briefly.

A **command economy** is one in which the government makes all decisions about production and distribution. In a command economy, such as has operated in the Soviet Union during most of this century, the government owns a considerable fraction of the means of production (land and capital); it also owns and directs the operations of enterprises in most industries; it is the employer of most workers and tells them how to do their jobs; and the government in a command economy decides how the output of the society is to be divided among different goods and services. In short, in a command economy, the government answers the major economic questions through its ownership of resources and its power to enforce decisions.

In the United States and most democratic countries, by contrast, most economic questions are solved by the market. Hence their economic systems are called market economies. A **market economy** is one in which individuals and private firms make the major decisions about production and consumption. A system of prices, of markets, of profits and losses, of incentives and rewards determines *what, how,* and *for whom*. Firms produce the commodities that yield the highest profits (the *what*) by the techniques of production that are least costly (the *how*). Consumption is determined by individuals' decisions about how to spend the wages and property incomes generated by their labor and property ownership (the *for whom*).

No contemporary society falls completely into either of these polar categories. Rather, all societies are **mixed economies,** with elements of market and command. There has never been a 100 percent market economy (although nineteenth-century England came close). Today most decisions in the United States are made in the marketplace. But the government plays an important role in modifying the functioning of the market; government sets laws and rules that regulate economic life, produces educational and police services, and regulates pollution and business. And the Soviet Union and the countries of Eastern Europe, unhappy with the performance of their command economies, are searching for their own particular brands of the mixed economy.

B. Society's Technological Possibilities

Why are we concerned with the fundamental questions of *what, how,* and *for whom*? Because people want to consume far more than an economy can produce. Recall the law of scarcity stated in the last chapter: goods are scarce because there are not enough resources to produce all the goods that people want to consume.

Faced with the undeniable truth that goods are scarce relative to wants, an economy must decide how to cope with limited resources. It must choose among different potential bundles of goods (the *what*), select among different techniques of production (the *how*), and decide in the end who should consume the goods (the *for whom*). In this section, we use several examples to illustrate some of the key choices that every society must make.

The Production-Possibility Frontier

Consider an economy with only so much labor, so much technical knowledge, so many factories and tools, and so much land, water power, and natural resources. In deciding *what* shall be produced and *how*, the economy is deciding in reality just how to allocate its resources among the thousands of different possible commodities. How much land should go into wheat growing? Or into housing the population? How many factories will produce computers? How many will make pizzas?

These issues are complicated even to discuss, much less resolve. Therefore, we must simplify. Let us assume that only two economic goods (or classes of economic goods) are to be produced. For dramatic purposes we can select guns and butter to illustrate the problem of choosing between military spending and civilian goods. This example applies equally to America's massive mobilization during World War II, to the issue of how to pay for operation "Desert Storm" in Saudi Arabia in 1991, and to the choices of military versus civilian spending faced by any nation.

We can begin our study of guns and butter with a numerical example. Suppose that our economy throws all its energy into producing the civilian good, butter. There is still a maximum amount of butter that can be produced per year. The maximal amount of butter depends on the quantity and quality of resources of the economy in question and the productive efficiency with which they are used. Suppose 5 million pounds of butter is the maximum amount that can be produced with the existing technology and resources.

At the other extreme, imagine that all resources are instead devoted to the production of guns. Again, because of resource limitations, the economy can produce only a limited quantity of guns. For this example, assume that the economy can produce 15 thousand guns of a certain kind if no butter is produced.

These are two extreme possibilities. In between are many others. If we are willing to give up some butter, we can have some guns. If we are willing to give up still more butter, we can have still more guns.

A schedule of possibilities is given in Table 2-1. Combination *F* shows the extreme where all butter and no guns are produced, while *A* depicts the opposite extreme where all resources go into guns. In between—at *E*, *D*, *C*, and *B*—increasing amounts of butter are given up in return for more guns.

Butter is transformed into guns, not physically, but by the alchemy of diverting the economy's resources from one use to the other.

We can represent our economy's production possibilities more vividly in the diagram shown in Figure 2-1. This diagram measures butter along the horizontal axis and guns along the vertical one.

Alternative Production Possibilities

Possibilities	Butter (millions of pounds)	Guns (thousands)
A	0	15
B	1	14
C	2	12
D	3	9
E	4	5
F	5	0

Table 2-1. Limitation of scarce resources implies the guns-butter tradeoff

As we go from *A* to *B* . . . to *F*, we are transferring labor, machines, and land from the gun industry to butter production.

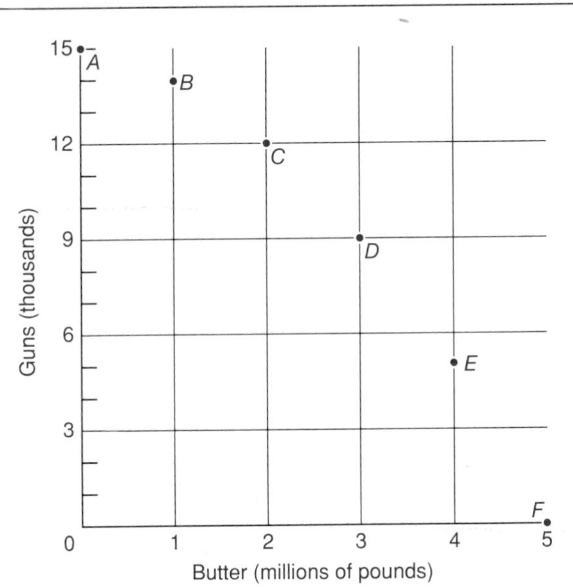

Figure 2-1. Graphical depiction of alternative production possibilities

This figure displays the alternative combinations of production pairs from Table 2-1.

Recalling the principles on using graphs outlined in Chapter 1's appendix, you should be able to go directly from the data in Table 2-1 to the figure: to *F*, by counting over 5 butter units to the right on the horizontal axis and going up 0 gun units on the vertical axis; to *E*, by going 4 butter units to the right and going up 5 gun units; and finally, to *A*, by going over 0 butter units and up 15 gun units.

If we fill in all intermediate positions with new blue points representing all the different combinations of guns and butter, we have the continuous blue curve shown as the **production-possibility frontier,** or *PPF*, in Figure 2-2.

The production-possibility frontier (or *PPF*) shows the maximum amounts of production that can be obtained by an economy, given the technological knowledge and quantity of inputs available. The *PPF* represents the menu of choices available to society.

Efficiency

Up to now, we have implicitly assumed that the economy was on, rather than inside, the production-possibility frontier. Operating on the frontier implies that the economy is producing *efficiently*.

Efficiency is one of the central concepts of economics. **Efficiency** means absence of waste, or using the economy's resources as effectively as possible to satisfy people's needs and desires. More specifically, the economy is producing efficiently when it cannot produce more of one good without producing less of another good—when it is on the production-possibility frontier.

How do we know that any point on that frontier is efficient? Let us start in the situation shown by point *D* in Figure 2-2. Decree that we want another million pounds of butter. If we ignored the constraint shown by the *PPF*, we might think it possible to produce more butter without reducing gun production, say by moving to point *I*, due east of point *D*. But point *I* is outside the frontier in the "impossible" region. Starting from *D*, we cannot get more butter without giving up some guns. Hence point *D* is efficient, and point *I* is infeasible.

The Production-Possibility Frontier

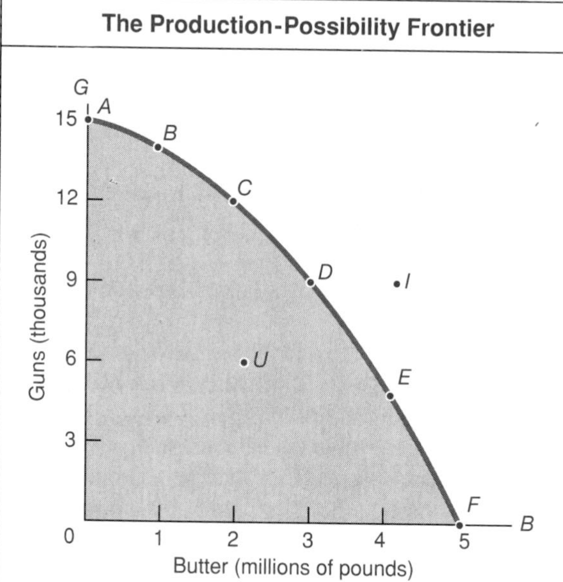

Figure 2-2. A smooth curve connects the plotted points of the numerical production possibilities

This frontier shows the schedule of choices along which society can choose to substitute guns for butter. It assumes a given state of technology and a given quantity of inputs. Points outside the frontier (such as point *I*) are infeasible or unattainable. Any point inside the curve, such as *U*, indicates that some resources are unemployed, or not used in the best possible way.

Productive efficiency occurs when society cannot increase the output of one good without cutting back on another good. An efficient economy is on its production-possibility frontier.

One further point about productive efficiency can be illustrated using the *PPF*: Being on the *PPF* means that producing more of one good inevitably requires sacrificing other goods. When we produce more guns, we are substituting guns for butter. Substitution is the law of life in a full-employment economy, and the production-possibility frontier depicts the menu of society's choices.

Unemployed Resources and Inefficiency. Even casual observers of modern life know that society has unemployed resources in the form of idle workers, idle factories, and idle land. Chapter 1 hinted that economic laws might be different when resources are less than fully employed. Being inside the *PPF* is one such instance.

When there are unemployed resources, the economy is not on its production-possibility frontier at all, but rather somewhere *inside* it. In Figure 2-2, point *U* represents a point inside the *PPF*; at *U*, society is producing only 2 units of butter and 6 units of guns. Some resources are unemployed, and by putting them to work we can have more butter and more guns. We can move from *U* to *D*, thereby producing more butter and more guns and improving the economy's efficiency.

Taking into account the possibility of unemployed resources throws light on the experience in World War II of two countries: the United States and the Soviet Union. After 1940, how was the United States able to become the "arsenal of democracy" and to enjoy civilian living standards higher than ever before? Largely by taking up the slack of unemployment from the Great Depression and moving toward the *PPF*.

The case of wartime U.S.S.R. was different. The Soviets had little unemployment before the war and were already on their rather low production-possibility frontier. To move northwest along their *PPF* the Soviets had no choice but to substitute war goods for civilian goods—with consequent privation.

Business-cycle depressions are not the only reason why an economy might be inside its *PPF*. An economy might suffer from inefficiency or dislocations because of strikes, political changes, or revolution. Such a case occurred during the early 1990s in Poland after that country substituted a free-market economy for its socialist command economy. Because of the dramatic changes in the economic system, output fell and unemployment rose as people attempted to adapt to the changed prices, laws, and incomes. A political and economic revolution pushed Poland temporarily inside its *PPF*.

Polish leaders hope that this inefficiency will be but a temporary setback. They foresee that a free market will boost incentives for efficient production. If they are right, Poland will soon move back toward its *PPF*, and indeed the *PPF* will begin to shift outward as the economy begins to grow rapidly.

Putting the *PPF* to Work

In addition to explaining efficiency, the production-possibility curve can help introduce many of the most basic concepts of economics.

1. Figure 2-2 illustrates our definition of economics as the science of choosing what goods to produce. Should we live in a fortress economy bristling with guns but with austere living habits, as at point *B* in Figure 2-2? Or should we reduce the military to a pittance and instead enjoy an economy with much bread and butter, as at point *E*?

   Such questions are debated in peacetime as well as in wartime. In the early 1980s, under the leadership of President Reagan, the United States increased real defense spending by around 50 percent. Then, following the revolutions in Eastern Europe in 1989, the Congress argued about who should receive a "peace dividend" from declining defense spending. After hostilities broke out in the Middle East in 1990, yet another debate occurred about how much to spend defending the vital oil fields of that region.
2. The production-possibility frontier provides a rigorous definition of scarcity. Economic scarcity describes the basic economic fact that—given our technical knowledge and endowment of land, labor, and capital—our economy can produce only certain maximum amounts of each economic good. The *PPF* shows the outer limit of producible goods dictated by the law of scarcity.

   Nowhere on the globe is the supply of goods so plentiful or are tastes so limited that the average family can have enough of everything it might fancy. Scarcity is a reflection of the limitation on our living standards imposed by the *PPF*.
3. The production-possibility schedule can also illustrate the three basic problems of economic life: *what, how*, and *for whom*.

   What goods are produced and consumed can be depicted by the point that ends up getting chosen on the *PPF*.

   How goods are to be produced involves an efficient choice of production techniques and a proper assignment of different quantities of different inputs to the various industries.

   For whom goods are to be produced cannot be discerned from the *PPF* alone, although you can sometimes make a guess from it. If you find a society on its *PPF* with many yachts and furs, but few houses and compact cars, you might suspect that it experiences considerable inequality of income and wealth among its people.
4. The production-possibility frontier can also illustrate the general point that we are always choosing among limited opportunities. People have limited time available to pursue different activities. For example, as a student, you might have 10 hours to study for upcoming tests in economics and history. If you study only history you will get a high grade there and do poorly in economics, and vice versa. Treating the grades on the two tests as the "output" of your studying, sketch out the *PPF* for grades, given your limited time resources.

   Alternatively, if the two student commodities are "grades" and "fun," how would you draw this *PPF*? Where are you on this frontier? Where are your lazier friends?

Pictures at an Exhibition

The same analysis that applies to choosing between the pair of goods—guns and butter—applies to any choice of goods. Thus the more resources the government uses to produce public goods (like weather forecasts), the less will be left to produce private goods (like houses); the more we choose to consume of food, the less we can consume of clothing; the more society decides to consume today, the less can be its production of capital goods (durable productive goods like equipment or factories) to turn out more consumption goods in the future.

The graphs of Figures 2-3 to 2-5 present some important applications of *PPF*s. Figure 2-3 shows the effect of economic growth on a country's production possibilities. As a result of increasing inputs of capital and labor and of improving technology, the *PPF* shifts out. A nation can have more of *all* goods as its economy grows. The figure also illustrates how poor countries must devote most of their resources to food production while rich countries can afford more luxuries as productive potential increases.

Figure 2-4 depicts how the electorate must choose between private goods (bought at a price) and public goods (paid for by taxes). Poor countries can afford little of public goods like public health and scientific research. But with economic growth, public goods as well as environmental quality take a larger share of output.

Figure 2-5 portrays how an economy chooses between (*a*) current consumption goods and (*b*) investment or capital goods (machines, factories, etc.). By sacrificing current consumption and producing more capital goods, a nation's economy can grow more rapidly, making possible more of *both* goods (consumption and capital) in the future.

These three diagrams introduce key themes of later chapters—how societies choose among different patterns of output, how they pay for their choice, how they benefit or lose in the future. A careful study of these diagrams is a good investment—just as a nation sometimes benefits from investing in capital goods for future enjoyment, so a few extra minutes spent here will bring you many rewards in your economic understanding.

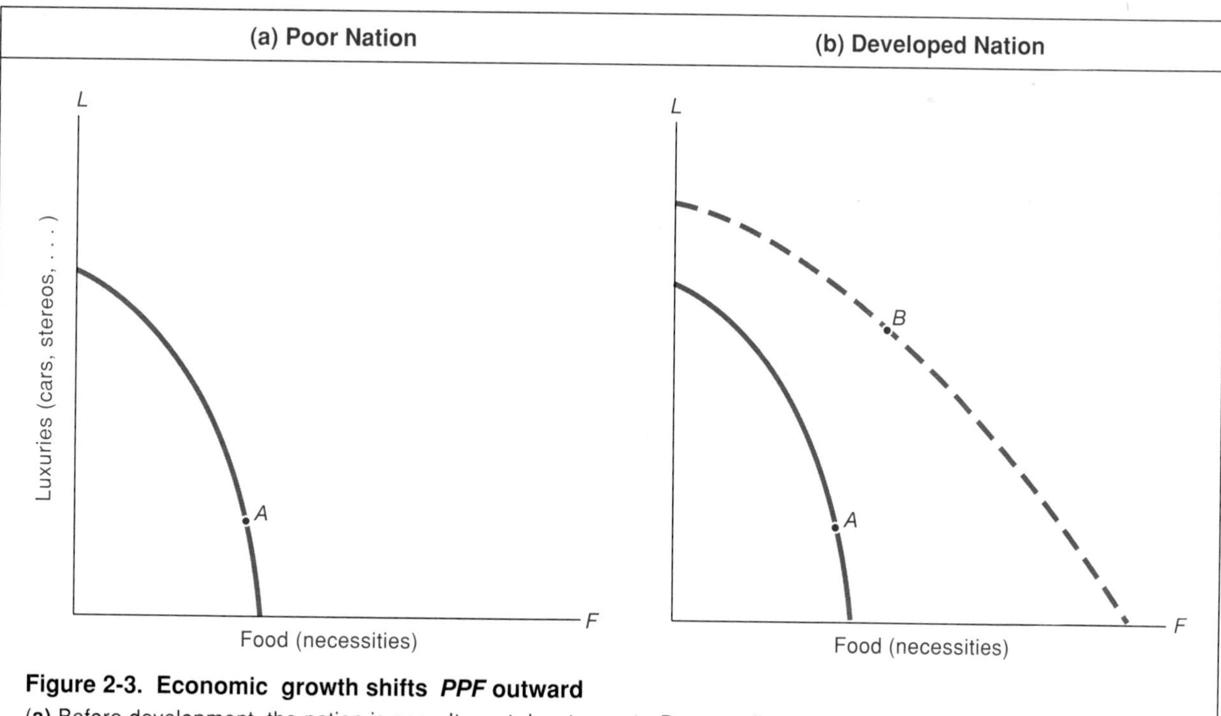

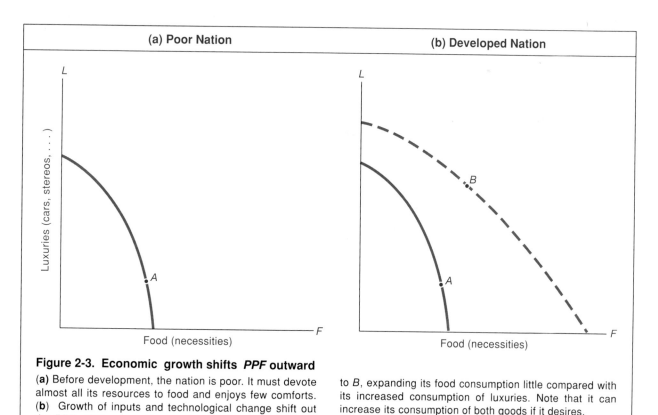

Figure 2-3. Economic growth shifts *PPF* outward

(**a**) Before development, the nation is poor. It must devote almost all its resources to food and enjoys few comforts. (**b**) Growth of inputs and technological change shift out the *PPF*. With economic growth, a nation moves from *A* to *B*, expanding its food consumption little compared with its increased consumption of luxuries. Note that it can increase its consumption of both goods if it desires.

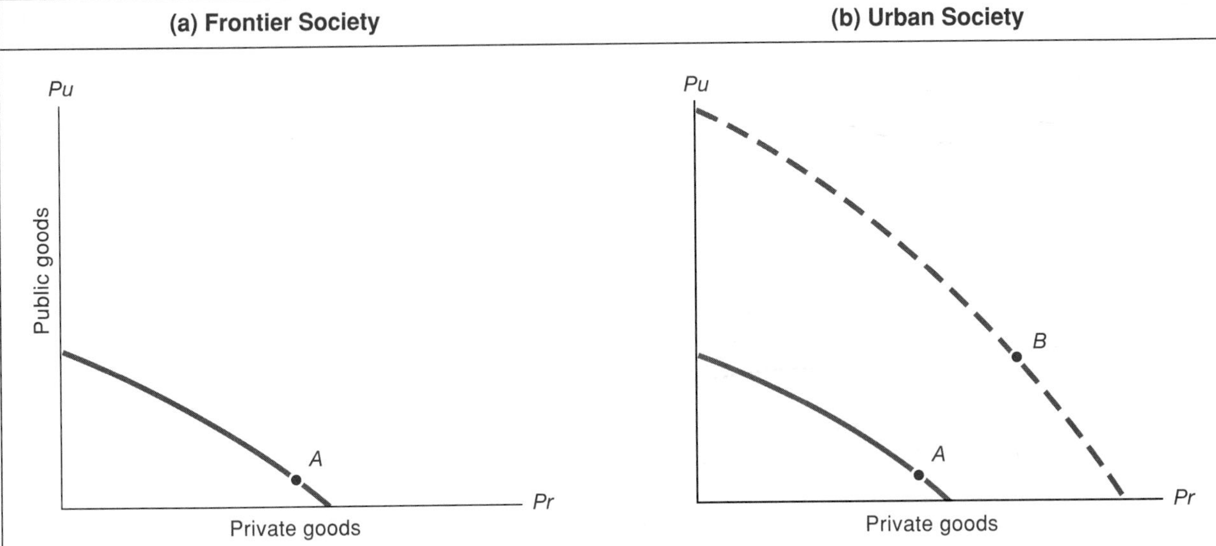

Figure 2-4. Economies must choose between public goods and private goods

(**a**) A frontier economy is poor and dispersed, as in Thomas Jefferson's days. The proportion of resources going to public goods (defense, science, public health) is low.
(**b**) A modern industrial economy is more prosperous and chooses to spend more of its higher income on public goods or governmental services (roads, defense, antipollution programs, public health, education).

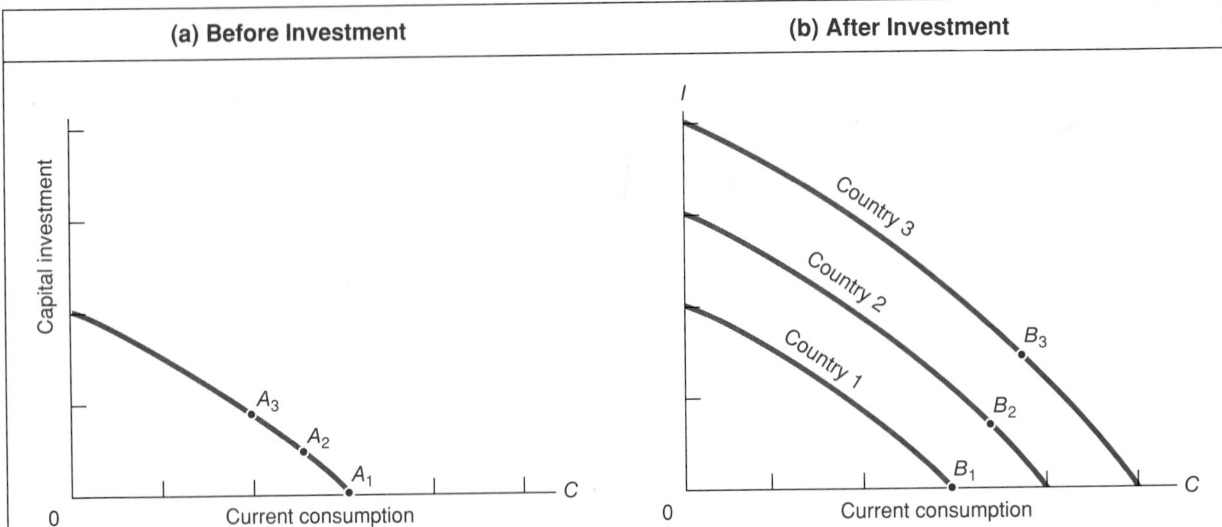

Figure 2-5. Investment for future consumption requires sacrificing current consumption

A nation can produce either current consumption goods (pizzas and concerts) or investment goods (trucks and houses).
(a) Three countries start out even. They have the same *PPF* shown in the panel on the left, but they have different investment rates. Country 1 does no investment for the future and remains at A_1 (merely replacing machines). Country 2 abstains modestly from consumption and invests at A_2. Country 3 sacrifices a great deal of current consumption and invests heavily.
(b) In the following years, countries that invest more forge ahead. Thus thrifty Country 3 has shifted its *PPF* far out, while Country 1's *PPF* has not moved at all. In the future, thrifty Country 3 continues to invest heavily but has more current consumption as well.

Opportunity Cost

Life is full of choices. Because resources are scarce, we must constantly decide what to do with our limited time and income. Should we go to a movie or read a book? Should we travel in Europe or buy a car? Should we get postgraduate or professional training or begin work right after college? In each of these cases, making a choice in a world of scarcity requires us to give up something else, in effect costing us the opportunity to do something else. The alternative forgone is called the **opportunity cost.**

To take a simple example, say that, after necessary expenses, your income is $100. With that sum you can either take a trip to Chicago or buy a radio. If you decide to go to Chicago, we would say that the opportunity cost of your trip was the pleasure of enjoying the new radio.

The concept of opportunity cost can also be illustrated using the production-possibility frontier. Look back at the frontier in Figure 2-2 on page 23. Suppose the country has decided to step up its purchases of guns from 9000 guns at *D* to 12,000 guns at *C*. What is the opportunity cost of this decision? You might calculate it in dollar terms. But on the most fundamental level, the opportunity cost is the butter that must be given up to produce the extra guns. In this example the opportunity cost of the 3000 guns is easily seen to be 1 million pounds of butter.

The **opportunity cost** of a decision arises because choosing one thing in a world of scarcity means giving up something else. The opportunity cost is the value of the good or service forgone.

The concept of opportunity cost is a useful reminder that the actual dollar outlays are not always an accurate index of true costs. For example, if the government decides to run a highway through a national park, the needed land might look cheap in out-of-pocket or budget costs. But the opportunity cost of using parkland might be quite high because people could enjoy fewer picnics or hikes or camping trips.

Another important example of opportunity cost is the cost of going to college. If you went to a public university, you might calculate the total costs of tuition, room, board, books, and travel to be about $10,000 in 1990. Does this mean that $10,000 is your opportunity cost of going to school? Definitely not! You must include as well the opportunity cost of the *time* spent studying and going to classes. A full-time job for a 19-year-old high school graduate would on average pay around $16,000 in 1990. If we add up both the actual expenses and the earnings forgone, we find the opportunity cost of college to be $26,000 (equal to $10,000 + $16,000) rather than $10,000 per year.

The Law of Diminishing Returns

We can also use the production-possibility frontier to illustrate one of the most famous economic relationships: the law of diminishing returns. This law concerns the relationship between inputs and outputs in the productive process. More specifically, *the **law of diminishing returns** holds that we will get less and less extra output when we add successive doses of an input while holding other inputs fixed.*

As an example of diminishing returns, consider the following controlled experiment: Given a fixed amount of land, say 100 acres, assume that we use no labor inputs at all. With zero labor input there is no corn output. So, in Table 2-2, we record zero product when labor is zero.

Now we make another experiment. We add 1 unit of labor to the same fixed amount of land. We observe that 2000 bushels of corn are produced. In yet another controlled experiment, we continue to

Law of Diminishing Returns

Units of labor (person-years)	Total output (bushels)	Extra output added by additional unit of labor (bushels per person-year)
0	0	
		2,000
1	2,000	
		1,000
2	3,000	
		500
3	3,500	
		____
4	3,800	
		100
5	3,900	

Table 2-2. Diminishing returns is a fundamental law of economics and technology

According to the law of diminishing returns, as additional units of labor are added, with land and other inputs held fixed, the extra output tends to decline. Fill in the extra output added by the fourth unit of labor.

hold land fixed and add exactly 1 extra unit of labor as before, going from 1 unit of labor to 2 units of labor.

What is the impact of the added labor on production? Do we have proportional returns, with an extra output of 2000 bushels added to the original output of 2000 bushels? Table 2-2 demonstrates the presence of diminishing returns. The second unit of labor adds only 1000 bushels of additional output, which is less than what the first unit of labor added. The third unit of labor adds even less output than does the second, and the fourth unit adds yet a bit less. The hypothetical experiment reported in Table 2-2 thus illustrates the law of diminishing returns.

The law of diminishing returns is an important and widely observed economic relationship. Be warned, however, that it is not universally valid for all technologies. Also, it may hold only after a few units of inputs have been added—that is, the first few units of inputs might yield increasing extra output, since a minimum amount of labor may be needed just to walk to the field and pick up a shovel. But, ultimately, diminishing returns will prevail for most technologies.

Some Examples

A little reflection suggests that the law of diminishing returns makes good sense. What happens as more and more labor cultivates the same 100-acre farm? For a while, output will increase sharply as we add labor—the fields will be more thoroughly seeded and weeded, irrigation ditches will be neater, scarecrows better oiled. At some point, however, the additional labor becomes less and less productive. The third hoeing of the day or the fourth oiling of the machinery adds little to output. Eventually, output grows very little as more people crowd onto the farm; too many tillers spoil the crop. Ultimately, output may even decline.

Diminishing returns are a key factor in explaining why many countries in Asia are so poor. Living standards in crowded China and India are low because there are so many workers per acre of land in these regions and not because land happens to be owned by the state or by absentee landlords.

We can also use the example of studying to illustrate the law of diminishing returns. You might find that the first hour of studying economics on a given day was productive—you learned new laws and facts, insights and history. The second hour might find your attention wandering a bit, with less learned. The third hour might show that diminishing returns had set in with a vengeance—so that by the next day you could remember nothing of what you had read during the third hour. Does the law of diminishing returns suggest why the hours devoted to studying should be spread out rather than crammed into the day before exams?

To summarize:

The law of diminishing returns holds that an increase in some input, with other inputs held constant, will increase total output. But after some point, the extra output resulting from additional doses of inputs will tend to become smaller and smaller.

C. Trade, Money, and Capital

No matter what system is used to organize economic activity, we will always find three distinguishing features in an advanced industrial economy: trade, money, and capital.

- An advanced economy is characterized by an elaborate network of *trade*, among individuals and countries, that depends on great specialization and an intricate division of labor.
- The economy today makes extensive use of *money*. The flow of money is the lifeblood of our system. Money provides the yardstick for measuring the economic value of things. But improper management of money by the central bank can cause inflation or depression.
- Modern industrial technologies rest on the use of vast amounts of *capital*: precision machinery,

large-scale factories, and stocks of inventories. Capital goods leverage human labor power into a much more efficient factor of production and allow productivity many times greater than in an earlier age.

Trade, Specialization, and Division of Labor

One of the major differences between a modern economy and that of frontier days is found in the extensive network of trade and specialization of individuals and firms. Western economies have enjoyed rapid economic growth over the last two centuries as increasing specialization allowed each of us to become highly productive in a particular occupation and to trade our output for the other commodities we need.

Specialization occurs when people concentrate their efforts on a particular set of tasks—it permits each person and country to use to best advantage any peculiar skills and resources. One of the facts of economic life is that, rather than have everyone do everything in a mediocre way, it is better to establish a *division of labor*—dividing production into a number of small specialized steps or tasks. A division of labor permits slow people to fish and swift people to hunt, all exchanging what they make for what they need.

To illustrate the increased productivity of specialization, Adam Smith provided the classical example of pinmaking. One worker could at best make a few dozen imperfect pins per day. But when pinmaking is broken down into a number of simple repetitive operations, a few workers can turn out hundreds of thousands of perfect pins per day.

Perhaps the epitome of specialization is the modern automobile assembly line, where cars move down a conveyor belt and workers, or even robots, perform highly specialized functions. A worker might concentrate on putting left tires on Hondas. The result of such specialization is the enormous increase in labor productivity in many manufacturing industries.

The economies of specialization allow the intricate network of trade among people and nations that we see today. Very few of us produce a single finished good; we make but the tiniest fraction of what we consume. We might teach a small part of a college curriculum, or produce buttons or zippers, or assemble part of an automobile or computer. In exchange for this specialized labor, we will receive an income adequate to buy goods from all over the world.

What determines which goods we produce? Economists emphasize the *law of comparative advantage*. This law states that individuals or nations should specialize in producing and selling those commodities which they can produce at *relatively* low cost. Similarly, an individual or nation should buy rather than produce those goods which it could produce only at a relatively high cost. The surprising feature of the law of comparative advantage is that even people or countries that are absolutely more inefficient than others will find it beneficial to specialize in the production of some goods. Thus, even the low-productivity countries of Asia or Africa can find a niche for their products in the international marketplace because they are relatively efficient at producing some goods.

The idea of *gains from trade* forms one of the central insights of economics. Different people or countries tend to specialize in certain areas and then to engage in voluntary exchange of what they produce for what they need. Many countries in the Middle East produce and export oil for food and manufactures. Japan has grown enormously productive by specializing in manufacturing goods such as automobiles and consumer electronics; it exports much of its manufacturing output to pay for imports of raw materials. Trade enriches *all* nations and increases *everyone's* living standards.

To summarize:

Advanced economies engage in specialization and division of labor, which increases the productivity of their resources. Individuals and countries then voluntarily trade goods they specialize in for others' products, vastly increasing the range and quantity of consumption and raising everyone's living standards.

Money: The Lubricant of Exchange

If specialization permits people to concentrate on particular tasks, money then allows people to trade their specialized outputs for the vast array of goods produced by others. To be sure, we could imagine a state of *barter,* where people directly trade one commodity for another. In primitive economies, food might be traded for clothing, or help in building a house might be exchanged for help in clearing a field. But exchange today in all economies—market as well as command—takes place through the medium of money.

What is money? **Money** is the means of payment or the medium of exchange; in our economy, money consists of currency and checking accounts with which households and businesses pay for things. When you buy gum with a quarter, lunch with a $10 bill, or a stereo set with a check, in each case you are employing money.

Money is a lubricant that facilitates exchange. When everyone trusts and accepts money as payment for goods and debts, trade is facilitated. Just imagine how complicated economic life would be if you had to barter goods for goods every time you wanted to buy a pizza or go to a concert. What goods could you offer Sal's Pizza or the Rolling Stones? What do you have in abundance that they want to consume? Because everyone accepts money as the medium of exchange, the need to match supplies and demands is enormously simplified.

But like other lubricants, money can get gummed up. In a barter economy, if I am hungry and you are naked, I can always sew your clothes while you bake my bread. But trade can go haywire in a monetary economy. For example, in the Great Depression of the 1930s, the banks failed, money was hoarded, some people went hungry, and other people went in rags in the world's richest country. Poverty can prevail amid plenty when money is not properly managed by the central bank.

The problems of managing money—one of the most important tasks of government today—are taken up in our chapters on macroeconomics.

Capital

We have learned that the economy depends upon three major factors of production: labor, capital, and land. Land and labor are often called *primary factors of production*. A primary factor of production is one whose quantity is determined outside the economy (by social forces in the case of labor or geological history in the case of land).

Capital is a different kind of productive factor. **Capital** *(or capital goods) is a produced factor of production, a durable input which is itself an output of the economy*. For example, we build a textile factory and use the factory to produce shirts; we assemble a computer and then employ the computer in educating students; and so forth.

Capital and Time

Capital has a special relationship to time. Why so? We will see that capital inherently involves time-consuming, indirect, roundabout methods of production. In fact, one of the paradoxes of capital is that the economy becomes enormously more productive by using indirect or roundabout methods.

If farmers had to work with their hands, without any capital in the form of tractors or shovels, farm productivity would be very low indeed. People learned long ago that direct methods of production are often less efficient than indirect or roundabout techniques. A direct method of catching fish would be to wade into the stream and catch fish with your hands, but this direct technique would yield few fish. Instead, people learned that by building nets and fishing boats (all these being capital equipment), fishing time becomes vastly more productive in terms of fish caught per day.

Other examples of efficient indirect or roundabout techniques are the following: A farmer spends time in clearing fields or digging ditches, so that the wheat yield will improve. A steelworker makes sheet steel, which will be used to manufacture a tractor, which will clear a field. A biologist injects DNA into a cell to produce a new and hardy seed. All these are roundabout ways of increasing the amount of wheat our economy can produce.

While we who toil inside the economy seldom stop to wonder about its roundaboutness, a moment's reflection will convince us that almost no one actually produces finished consumer goods. Almost everyone is doing work of a preparatory and roundabout nature, with the final consumption a distant future goal.

Growth from the Sacrifice of Current Consumption. If people are willing to *save*—to abstain from present consumption and wait for future consumption—then society can devote resources to new capital goods. A larger stock of capital helps the economy to grow faster by pushing out the *PPF*.

Look back at Figure 2-5 to see how forgoing current consumption in favor of investment adds to future production possibilities.

All this raises the question: If roundabout and indirect processes are so productive, why not replace *all* direct processes by more productive, roundabout ones, and all roundabout processes by still more roundabout processes? The advantage of using roundabout processes is offset by the initial disadvantage of having to forgo present consumption goods by diverting current consumption to investments in roundabout processes. The problem is that the roundabout processes bear fruit only after some time. We could invest time and resources in making our highways even wider and our railroad beds even flatter than they are, thereby reducing fuel and repair costs and driving time. Or students could go to school for 5 or 10 more years and acquire even greater specialized skills. We don't invest in even more roundabout investments because these would cause too great a reduction in today's consumption.

We summarize as follows:

Much of economic activity involves forgoing current consumption to increase our capital. Every time we invest—building a new factory or road, increasing the years or quality of education, or increasing the stock of useful technical knowledge—we are enhancing the future productivity of our economy.

Capital and Private Property

Physical capital goods are critical for any economy, market or command, because they help to increase productivity. But there is one significant difference between a capitalist and a socialist system: By and large, it is private firms and individuals who own the machines, buildings, and land in our market economy. What is the exception in our system—government ownership of the means of production—is the rule in a socialist state, where capital, land, and houses are collectively owned.

In a market economy, capital typically is privately owned, and the income from capital goes to individuals. Every patch of land has a deed, or title of ownership; almost every machine and building belongs to an individual or corporation. *Property rights* bestow on their owners the ability to use, exchange, paint, dig, drill, or exploit their capital goods. These capital goods also have market values, and people can buy and sell the capital goods for whatever price they will fetch. *The ability of individuals to own and profit from capital is what gives capitalism its name.*[1]

But while our society is one built on private property, property rights are limited. Society determines how much of "your" property you may bequeath to your heirs and how much must go in inheritance and estate taxes to the government. Society determines how much the owners of public utilities—such as electric and gas companies—can earn and how much pollution your car can emit. Even your home is not your castle. You must obey zoning laws and, if necessary, make way for a road.

Interestingly enough, the most valuable economic resource, labor, cannot be turned into a commodity that is bought and sold as private property. Since the abolition of slavery, it is against the law to treat human earning power like other capital assets. You are not free to sell yourself; you must rent yourself at a wage.

Property rights define the ability of individuals or firms to own, buy, sell, and use the capital goods and other property in a market economy.

● We now see how specialization, trade, money, and capital form a key to the productiveness of an advanced economy. But note as well that they are closely interrelated. Specialization creates enormous efficiencies, while increased production makes trade possible. Use of money allows trade to take place quickly and efficiently. Without the facility for trade and exchange that money provides, an elaborate division of labor would not be possible. Money and capital are related because the funds for buying capital goods are funneled through financial markets, where people's savings can be transformed into other people's capital.

Now that we have surveyed the central problems of economic organization, we can turn in the next chapter to an analysis of the way our own economy determines prices, quantities, and incomes. ●

[1] We must carefully distinguish *physical* capital from *financial* capital. Physical capital takes the form of factories, equipment, houses, and inventories; physical capital is an input or factor of production. Financial capital is "paper" assets or claims, like bonds, common stocks, checking and savings accounts, or home mortgages; financial capital is often the claim to physical capital, but it is never an input into the productive process.

SUMMARY

A. The Three Problems of Economic Organization

1. Every society must solve three fundamental problems: *what, how,* and *for whom? What* kinds and quantities shall be produced among the wide range of all possible goods and services? *How* shall resources be used in producing these goods? And *for whom* shall the goods be produced (that is, what shall be the distribution of income and consumption among different individuals and classes)?

2. Societies meet these problems in different ways. The most important forms of economic organization today are *command* and *market*. The command economy is directed by centralized control of governments; a market economy is guided by an informal system of prices and profits in which most decisions are taken by private individuals and firms. All societies have different combinations of command and market; all societies are *mixed* economies.

B. Society's Technological Possibilities

3. With given resources and technology, the production choices between two such goods as butter and guns can be summarized in the *production-possibility frontier (PPF)*. The *PPF* shows how the production of one good (such as guns) is traded off against the production of another good (such as butter).

4. Productive efficiency occurs when production of one good cannot be increased without curtailing production of another good. This is illustrated by the *PPF*. When an economy is operating efficiently—on its *PPF*—it can produce more of one good only by producing less of another good.

   Societies are sometimes inside their frontier. When unemployment is high or when government regulation hampers firms' activities, the economy is inefficient and operates inside its *PPF.*

5. Production-possibility frontiers illustrate many basic economic processes: how economic growth pushes out the frontier, how a nation chooses relatively less food and other necessities as it develops, how a country chooses between private goods and public goods, and how societies choose between consumption goods and capital goods that enhance future consumption.

6. Dollar costs are not the same as true economic costs. When we measure the total cost of making choices in a world of scarcity, we calculate the opportunity cost, which measures the value of the things given up, or opportunities forgone.

7. The law of diminishing returns holds that, after a point, as we add equal extra doses of a variable input (such as labor) to a fixed input (such as land), the amount of extra output will decline.

C. Trade, Money, and Capital

8. As economies develop, they become more specialized. Division of labor allows a task to be broken into a number of smaller chores that can be mastered and performed more quickly by a single worker. Specialization arises from the increasing tendency to use roundabout methods of production that require many specialized skills.
9. As individuals and countries become increasingly specialized, they tend to concentrate on particular commodities and trade their surplus output for goods produced by others. Voluntary trade, based on specialization and comparative advantage, benefits all.
10. Trade in specialized goods and services today relies on money to lubricate the wheels of trade. Money is the universally acceptable medium of exchange—currency and checks. It is used to pay for everything from apple tarts to zebra skins. By accepting money, people and nations can specialize in producing a few goods and trade them for others; without money, we would waste much time constantly bartering one good for another.
11. Capital goods—produced inputs such as machinery, structures, and inventories of goods in process—permit roundabout methods of production that add much to a nation's output. These roundabout methods take time and resources to get started and therefore require a temporary sacrifice of present consumption. The rules that define how capital and other assets can be bought, sold, and used are the system of property rights. In no economic system are private-property rights unlimited.

CONCEPTS FOR REVIEW

Key problems of economic organization
what, how, and *for whom*
alternative economic systems: command vs. market
inputs and outputs

Choice among production possibilities
production-possibility frontier (*PPF*)
efficiency
opportunity cost
law of diminishing returns

Features of a modern economy
specialization and division of labor
money
factors of production (land, labor, capital)
capital and private property

QUESTIONS FOR DISCUSSION

1. Define each of the following terms carefully and give examples: *PPF*, efficiency, inputs, outputs, opportunity cost.
2. Assume Econoland produces haircuts and shirts with inputs of labor. Econoland has 1000 hours of labor available. A haircut requires $\frac{1}{2}$ hour of labor, while a shirt requires 5 hours of labor. Construct Econoland's production-possibility frontier.
3. Redraw society's production-possibility frontier in Figure 2-2 after scientific inventions have doubled the productivity of its resources in butter production without any change in the productivity of gun manufacture.
4. Give three examples you know of specialization and division of labor. In what areas are you and your friends thinking of specializing? What might be the perils of *over*specialization?
5. "Lincoln freed the slaves. With one pen stroke he destroyed much of the capital the South had accumulated over the years." Comment.

6. "Compulsory military service allows the government to fool itself and the people about the true cost of a big army." Compare the budget cost and the opportunity cost of a voluntary army (where army pay is high) and compulsory service (where pay is low). What does the concept of opportunity cost contribute to analyzing the quotation?
7. Many scientists believe that we are rapidly depleting our natural resources. Assume that there are only two inputs (labor and natural resources) producing two goods (haircuts and gasoline) with no improvement in society's technology over time. Show what would happen to the *PPF* over time as natural resources are exhausted. How would invention and technological improvement modify your answer? On the basis of this example, explain why it is said that "economic growth is a race between depletion and invention."
8. Say that Diligent has 10 hours to study for upcoming tests in economics and history. Draw a *PPF* for grades, given Diligent's limited time resources. If Diligent studies inefficiently by listening to loud music and chatting with friends, where will Diligent's grade "output" be relative to the *PPF*? What would happen to the grade *PPF* if Diligent increases study inputs from 10 hours to 15 hours?
9. From 1982 to 1990, the American economy grew rapidly as unemployment fell and capital equipment was utilized more intensively. Draw *PPF*s for 1982 and 1990 and put in two points to illustrate where the economy might have been in both those years.

CHAPTER 3

MARKETS AND GOVERNMENT IN A MODERN ECONOMY

> Every individual endeavors to employ his capital so that its produce may be of greatest value. He generally neither intends to promote the public interest, nor knows how much he is promoting it. He intends only his own security, only his own gain. And he is in this led by an invisible hand to promote an end which was no part of his intention. By pursuing his own interest he frequently promotes that of society more effectually than when he really intends to promote it.
>
> Adam Smith, *The Wealth of Nations* (1776)

Both market and command economies have their roots in an earlier age. Centuries ago, government councils or town guilds directed much economic activity in regions of Europe and Asia. However, around the time of the American Revolution, governments began to exercise less and less direct control over prices and economic conditions. Feudal relationships gradually gave way to markets, or what is sometimes called "free enterprise" or "competitive capitalism."

This trend culminated in the nineteenth century, the age of **laissez-faire.** This doctrine, which translates as "leave us alone," holds that government should interfere as little as possible in economic affairs and leave economic decisions to the marketplace. Many governments followed this approach in the nineteenth century. But before full laissez-faire was achieved, the tide turned the other way. Starting at the end of the last century, in almost all countries of North America and Europe, the economic functions of government expanded steadily. The welfare state increasingly displaced the market and family in capitalist economies, while socialist governments displaced the market in many countries of Europe and Asia.

In the 1980s, the tides shifted yet again. Conservative economic policies reduced government control of the economy in the market economies. Then, in 1990, many socialist governments cast off their hierarchical central planning systems and began to grope toward "the market."

What exactly is a market economy? How does government sometimes displace the market? The time has come to understand the principles that lie behind the market economy and to review government's role in economic life.

A. How Markets Solve the Basic Economic Problems

In a country like the United States, most economic questions are resolved through the market, so we begin our systematic study there. Who solves the three basic questions—*what, how,* and *for whom*—

in a market economy? You may be surprised to learn that *no one individual or organization is responsible for solving the economic problems in a market economy*. Instead, millions of businesses and consumers engage in voluntary trade, and their actions and purposes are invisibly coordinated by a system of prices and markets.

To see how remarkable this fact is, consider the city of New York. Without a constant flow of goods into and out of the city, New Yorkers would be on the verge of starvation within a week. For New York to thrive, many kinds of goods and services must be provided. From the surrounding counties, from 50 states, and from the far corners of the world, goods travel for days and months with New York as their destination.

How is it that 10 million people can sleep easily at night, without living in mortal terror of a breakdown in the elaborate economic processes upon which the city's existence depends? The surprising answer is that these economic activities are coordinated without coercion or centralized direction by anybody through the market.

Everyone in the United States notices how much the government does to control economic activity: it places tolls on bridges, legislates police protection, controls pollution, levies taxes, sends armies to the desert, prohibits drugs, and so forth. But we seldom think about how much of our ordinary economic life proceeds without government intervention. Thousands of commodities are produced by millions of people, willingly, without central direction or master plan.

Economic Order, Not Chaos

Before people study the way the market works, they see only a jumble of different firms and products. Few of us stop to wonder how it is that food is produced in suitable amounts, gets transported to the right place, and arrives in a palatable form at the dinner table. But a close look at New York is convincing proof that a market system does not produce chaos and anarchy. A market system contains an internal logic. It works.

A market economy is an elaborate mechanism for the unconscious coordination of people, activities, and businesses through a system of prices and markets. It is a communication device for pooling the knowledge and actions of millions of diverse individuals. Without central intelligence or computation, it solves a problem that the largest supercomputer could not solve today, involving millions of unknown variables and relations. Nobody designed the market; yet it functions remarkably well.

History's most dramatic example of the effectiveness of the market economy came in West Germany after World War II. In 1947, production and consumption had dropped to a low level. Neither bombing damage nor postwar reparation payments could account for this breakdown. Paralysis of the market mechanism was clearly to blame. Price controls and overarching government regulation hobbled markets. Money was worthless; factories closed down for lack of materials; trains could not run for lack of coal; coal could not be mined because miners were hungry; miners were hungry because peasants would not sell food for money and no goods were available for them to purchase in return. Markets were not functioning properly. People could not buy what they needed or sell what they produced at free-market prices.

Then in 1948, the government freed prices from controls and introduced a new currency, quickly putting the market mechanism back into effective operation. Very quickly production and consumption soared; once again *what, how,* and *for whom* were being resolved by markets and prices. People called it "an economic miracle," but the recovery was in fact largely the result of a smoothly running market mechanism.

The point to emphasize is that markets perform similar miracles around us all the time—if only we take care to observe our economy carefully. Moreover, history records that economic and political crises often occur when the market mechanism breaks down. Indeed, the socialist economies, having seen their living standards decline relative to their Western neighbors, are in the 1990s trying to duplicate the German miracle of 1948 by turning to the market to organize economic life in their countries.

The Market Mechanism

How does a market function? Exactly how does the market mechanism go about determining prices, wages, and outputs? Originally, a market was a *place* where goods were bought and sold. Economic histories of the Middle Ages record that market stalls—filled with slabs of butter, pyramids of cheese, wet fish, and heaps of vegetables—formed the commercial centers of villages and towns. Today, important markets include the Chicago Board of Trade, where oil, wheat, and other commodities are traded, and the New York Stock Exchange, where titles to ownership of the largest American firms are bought and sold.

More generally, markets are a mechanism by which buyers and sellers meet to exchange things. The market may be centralized (as for stocks, bonds, and wheat), or decentralized (as for houses or used cars), or may even be an electronic market (as occurs for many financial assets and services). The crucial characteristic of a market is that it brings buyers and sellers together to set prices and quantities.

A market is a mechanism by which buyers and sellers of a commodity interact to determine its price and quantity.

In a market system, everything has a price, which is the value of the good in terms of money. Prices represent the terms on which people and firms voluntarily exchange different commodities. When I agree to buy a used Honda from a dealer for $3150, this indicates that the Honda is worth more than $3150 to me and that the $3150 is worth more than the Honda to the dealer. I cannot find a better value for my money than the Honda; and the dealer cannot find anyone who will pay more than I will. The used-car market has determined the price of used Hondas and, through voluntary trading, has allocated cars to the people for whom they have highest value.

In addition, prices serve as *signals* to producers and consumers. If consumers want more of any good—say, gasoline to drive their cars—the demand for gasoline will rise. As oil companies find that their inventories of gasoline are reduced, they raise the price of gasoline to ration out the limited supply. And the higher price will encourage greater oil production.

On the other hand, what if a commodity such as cars becomes overstocked at the going market price? Sellers will lower car prices in their rush to unload unwanted models. At the lower price, more consumers will want cars, and producers will want to make fewer cars. As a result, a balance, or equilibrium, between buyers and sellers will be restored.

What is true of the markets for consumer goods is also true of markets for factors of production, such as labor. If computer programmers rather than typists are needed, job opportunities will be more favorable in the computing field. The price of computer programmers (their hourly wage) will tend to rise, and that of typists will tend to fall. The shift in relative wages will cause a shift of workers into the growing occupation.

Prices coordinate the decisions of producers and consumers in a market. Higher prices tend to reduce consumer purchases and encourage production. Lower prices encourage consumption and discourage production. Prices are the balance wheel in the market mechanism.

Market Equilibrium. At every moment, innumerable factors affect economic activity. Some people are buying while others are selling; firms are inventing new products while governments are passing laws to regulate pollution; foreigners are invading our markets while American firms are moving their plants abroad. Yet in the midst of all this turmoil, markets are constantly solving the *what, how,* and *for whom*. As they balance all the forces operating on the economy, markets are finding an **equilibrium of supply and demand.**

What is a market equilibrium? It represents a *balance among all the different buyers and sellers*. Households and firms all want to buy or sell certain quantities depending upon the price. The market finds the equilibrium price that just balances the desires of buyers and sellers. Too high a price would mean a glut of goods with too much output; too low a price would produce long lines in stores and a deficiency of goods. Those prices for which buyers desire to buy exactly the quantity that sellers desire to sell yield an equilibrium of supply and demand.

How a Market Solves the Three Economic Problems

We see how prices help balance consumption and production (or supply and demand) in an individual market. What happens when we put all the different markets together—gasoline, cars, land, labor, capital, and everything else? These form a market mechanism that grinds out a *general equilibrium* of prices and production.

By matching sellers and buyers (supply and demand) in each market, a market economy simultaneously solves the three problems of *what, how,* and *for whom*. Here is the bare outline of a market equilibrium.

1. *What* things will be produced is determined by the dollar votes of consumers—not every 2 or 4 years at the polls, but in their daily purchase decisions. The money that they pay into businesses' cash registers ultimately provides the payrolls, rents, and dividends that consumers, as employees, receive as income.

   Firms in turn are driven by the desire to maximize profits—**profits** being net revenues or the difference between total sales and total costs. Firms are lured by high profits into production of goods in high demand; by the same token, firms abandon areas where they are losing money.

   Relative costs also affect the production and trade of nations. Japan produces and exports consumer electronics and imports food, while America imports consumer electronics and exports food.

   Who makes these decisions? Is it Congress? Or the Japanese government planners? In fact, neither. The price system makes the decisions. Because land is plentiful in America, land is relatively inexpensive and food costs are relatively low. Because land is scarce and expensive in Japan while engineering talent is relatively plentiful, Japanese costs are relatively high for food and low for consumer electronics. By looking at price signals on land and labor, firms, farmers, and consumers can choose the most appropriate goods to produce, trade, and consume.

2. *How* things are produced is determined by the competition among different producers. The best way for producers to meet price competition and maximize profits is to keep costs at a minimum by adopting the most efficient methods of production. Because producers are spurred on by the lure of profit, inexpensive production methods will displace more costly ones.

   History is filled with examples of how efficient technologies replaced more expensive ones. Steam engines displaced horses because steam was cheaper per unit of useful work. Diesel and electric locomotives replaced coal-driven ones because of the higher efficiency of the new technologies. In the 1990s, glass fibers and lightwave communications will displace Alexander Graham Bell's traditional copper telephone lines.

3. *For whom* things are produced is determined by supply and demand in the markets for factors of production. Factor markets determine wage rates, land rents, interest rates, and profits—such prices are called *factor prices*. By adding up all the revenues from factors we can calculate people's incomes. The distribution of income among the population is thus determined by the *amounts* of factors (person-hours, acres, etc.) owned and the *prices* of the factors (wage rates, land rents, etc.).

   Be warned, however, that the distribution of income is also affected by many influences outside the marketplace. People's incomes depend significantly upon their ownership of property (such as land or stocks), upon acquired or inherited abilities, upon luck, and upon the extent of racial and gender discrimination.

Who Governs the Market?

Who is in charge of a market economy? Do monopolistic firms call the tune? Are consumers sovereign? If we examine the structure of a market economy carefully, we see a dual monarchy shared by *consumers and technology*. Consumers direct by their innate or acquired tastes—as expressed with their dollar votes—the ultimate uses to which society's resources are channeled. They pick the point on the production-possibility frontier.

But the available resources place a fundamental constraint on consumers. The economy cannot go outside its *PPF*. You can fly to London, but there are no flights to Mars. An economy's resources, along with the available science and technology, limit the places where consumers can put their dollar votes.

In other words, consumers alone cannot dictate *what* goods should be produced. Consumer demand has to dovetail with business supply of goods. So business cost and supply decisions, along with consumer demand, help to determine what is produced. *Just as a broker helps to match buyers and sellers, so do markets act as the go-betweens who reconcile the consumer's tastes with technology's limitations.*

It is important to see the role of profits in guiding the market mechanism. Profits provide the rewards and penalties for businesses. Profits induce firms to enter areas where consumers want more goods, to leave areas where consumers want fewer goods, and to use the most efficient (or least costly) techniques of production.

Like a master using carrots and kicks to coax a donkey forward, the market system deals out profits and losses to induce firms to produce desired goods efficiently.

A Picture of Prices and Markets

We can picture the circular flow of economic life in Figure 3-1. This provides an overview of how consumers and producers interact to determine prices and quantities for both inputs and outputs. Note the two different kinds of markets in the circular flow. At the top are the product markets, or flow of outputs like tea and shoes; at the bottom are the markets for inputs or factors of production like land and labor. Further see how decisions are

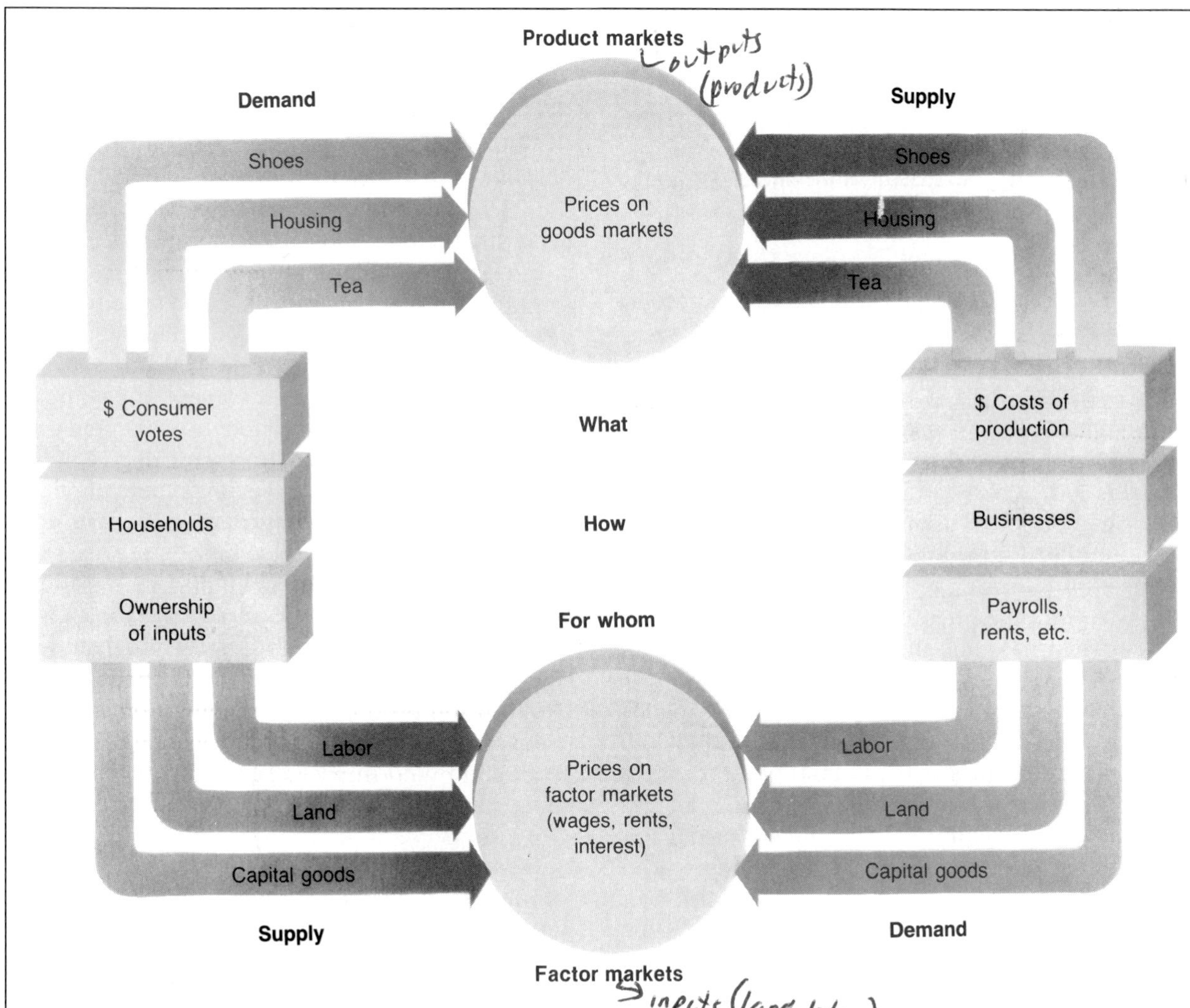

Figure 3-1. The market system relies on supply and demand to solve the trio of economic problems.

We see here the circular flow of a market economy. Dollar votes of households interact with what businesses supply in the goods markets at top, helping to determine *what* is produced. Further, business demand for inputs meets the public's supply of labor and other inputs in the factor markets below to help determine wage, rent, and interest payments. Business competition to buy factor inputs and sell goods most cheaply determines *how* goods are produced.

made by two different entities, households and businesses.

Households buy goods and sell factors of production; businesses sell goods and buy factors of production. Households use their income from sale of labor and other inputs to buy goods from businesses; businesses base their prices of goods on the costs of labor and property. Prices in goods markets are set to balance consumer demand with business supply; prices in factor markets are set to balance household supply with business demand.

All this sounds complicated. But it is simply the total picture of how the intricate web of interdependent supplies and demands interconnect through a market mechanism to solve the economic problems of *what, how,* and *for whom*. Study this figure carefully. A few minutes spent studying it will pay many dividends later in furthering your understanding of the workings of a market economy.

The Invisible Hand and "Perfect Competition"

Adam Smith, whose *The Wealth of Nations* (1776) is the germinal book of modern economics, was thrilled by his recognition of order in the economic system. Smith proclaimed the principle of the "invisible hand." This principle holds that, in selfishly pursuing only his or her personal good, every individual is led, as if by an invisible hand, to achieve the best good for all. Smith saw harmony between private interest and public interest. In his view of the economic world, any government interference with free competition is almost certain to be injurious. (Reread carefully this chapter's introductory quotation.)

Smith's *doctrine of the invisible hand* explains why the outcome of a market mechanism looks so orderly. His insight about the guiding function of the market mechanism has inspired modern economists—both the admirers and the critics of capitalism. After two more centuries of experience and thought, however, we recognize the scope and realistic limitations of this doctrine. We know that the market sometimes lets us down, that there are "market failures," and that markets do not always lead to the most efficient outcome. Important market failures, which will be extensively analyzed in this text, include imperfect competition and externalities like pollution. Let's pause to discuss the crucial role played by competition in the market system.

Perfect Competition. Smith himself recognized that the virtues of the market mechanism are fully realized only when the checks and balances of perfect competition are present. What is meant by **perfect competition?** It is a technical term that refers to a market in which no firm or consumer is large enough to affect the market price. For example, the wheat market is perfectly competitive because the largest wheat farm, producing only a minuscule fraction of the world's wheat, can have no appreciable effect upon the price of wheat.

The invisible-hand doctrine is about economies in which all the markets are perfectly competitive. In such a circumstance, markets will produce an efficient allocation of resources, so that an economy is on its production-possibility frontier. When all industries are subject to the checks and balances of perfect competition, as we will see later in this book, markets can produce the efficient bundle of outputs with the most efficient techniques and using the minimum amount of inputs.

On the other hand, when a telephone company or a labor union is large enough to influence the price of phone service or labor, some degree of "imperfect competition" has set in. When imperfect competition arises, society may move inside its *PPF*. This would occur, for example, if a single seller (a monopolist) raised the price of a good sky-high to earn extra profits. The output of that good would be reduced below the most efficient level, and the efficiency of the economy would thereby suffer. When sellers are few, inadequate checks may exist to ensure that prices are determined by the costs of production. And in such a situation, the invisible-hand property of markets may vanish.

In summary:

Adam Smith discovered a remarkable property of a competitive market economy. Under perfect competition and with no market failures, markets will squeeze as many useful goods and services out of the available resources as is possible. But where monopolies or pollution or similar market failures become pervasive, the remarkable efficiency properties of the invisible hand may be destroyed.

B. The Economic Role of Government

An ideal, perfectly competitive economy—where resource-allocation decisions are made through voluntary exchange of goods for money at market prices—squeezes the maximum quantity of useful goods and services out of a society's available resources. But the market does not always live up to its perfect ideal. Rather, market economies suffer from monopoly and pollution, along with unemployment and inflation, and the income distribution in a pure laissez-faire society is sometimes thought inequitable.

In response to the flaws in the market mechanism, nations introduce the *visible* hand of government alongside the *invisible* hand of markets. Governments displace markets by owning and operating certain enterprises (like the military); governments regulate businesses (like telephone companies); governments spend money on space exploration and scientific research; governments tax their citizens and redistribute the proceeds to poor people; and governments use fiscal and monetary powers to promote economic growth and to tame business cycles. In this section we provide a brief survey of the rationale and techniques of government intervention in a modern economy.

The Three Functions of Government

In discussing government's role, we generally take for granted that government sets the rules of the road, writing laws and enforcing contracts and property rights. But what are government's economic functions? They are to promote efficiency, to promote equity, and to foster macroeconomic growth and stability.

Governments attempt to correct market failures like monopoly and pollution to encourage *efficiency*. Government programs to promote *equity* use taxes and spending to redistribute income toward particular groups. Governments rely upon taxes, expenditures, and monetary regulation to foster *macroeconomic growth and stability*, to reduce unemployment and inflation while encouraging economic growth. We will examine briefly each function.

Efficiency

Economies sometimes suffer market failures. For example, a firm may profit as much by raising prices as by increasing production. Some firms pollute the air or dump toxic wastes into the soil. In each case, market failure leads to inefficient production or consumption, and government can play a useful role in curing the disease. But, while evaluating the role of government in curing economic ailments, we must also be alert to "government failures"—situations in which governmental attempts to cure market failures may make them worse or cause other problems.

Imperfect Competition. One serious deviation from perfect competition comes from *imperfect competition* or *monopoly* elements.

Recall how strict is the economist's definition of a "perfectly competitive market": Perfect competition in a market arises when there is a sufficient number of firms or degree of rivalry such that no one firm can affect the price of that good. An imperfect competitor is one whose actions can affect a good's price.

In reality, almost all business owners, except possibly the millions of farmers who individually produce a negligible fraction of the total crop, are imperfect competitors. At the extreme of imperfect competition is the *monopolist*—a single supplier who alone determines the price of a particular good.

What is the effect of monopoly power—the ability of a large firm to affect the price in a given market? Monopoly power leads to prices that rise above cost and consumer purchases that are reduced below efficient levels. The pattern of too high price and too low output is the hallmark of the inefficiencies associated with monopoly power.

Over the last century, governments have taken steps to curb monopoly power. Governments sometimes regulate the prices and profits of monopolies, as is now the case for local utilities. In addition, government antitrust laws prohibit actions such as price fixing or dividing up markets.

Externalities. A second type of inefficiency arises when there are spillovers or externalities. Market transactions involve voluntary exchange in which people exchange goods for money. When a firm uses a scarce resource like land, it buys the land from its owner in the land market; when a firm produces a valuable good like oil, it receives full value from the buyer in the oil market.

But many interactions take place outside markets. Firm A dumps a toxic chemical into a stream and fouls the stream for people who fish or swim downstream. Firm A has used the scarce, clean water without paying people whose water is fouled. Firm B, by contrast, provides its employees with free vaccinations against a communicable disease; once immunity is achieved, people outside the firm also benefit from the reduced danger of contracting the disease. In each case, a firm has helped or hurt people outside the market transactions; that is, there is an economic transaction without an economic payment.

Externalities (or spillover effects) occur when firms or people impose costs or benefits on others outside the marketplace.

As our society has become more densely populated and as the volume of production of energy, chemicals, and other materials increases, negative spillover effects have grown from little nuisances into major threats. This is where governments come in. Government *regulations* are designed to control externalities like air and water pollution, strip mining, hazardous wastes, unsafe drugs and foods, and radioactive materials.

Critics of regulation complain that government economic activity is unnecessarily coercive. Governments are like parents, always saying "no": Thou shalt not employ child labor. Thou shalt not pour out smoke from thy factory chimney. Thou shalt not sell dangerous drugs. Thou shalt not drive without wearing thy seat belt. And so forth.

At the same time, most people today agree that government is needed to curb some of the worst externalities created by the market mechanism.

Public Goods. It is possible to prevent firms from dumping wastes by imposing regulations; it is much more difficult for governments to encourage the production of **public goods.** These are the economic activities—conveying large or small benefits to the community—that cannot efficiently be left to private enterprise. Important examples of public goods are provision of national defense and internal law and order, the building of a highway network, and the support of basic science and public health. Adequate private production of these public goods will not occur because the benefits are so widely dispersed across the population that no single firm or consumer has an economic incentive to provide them.*

Because private provision of public goods is generally insufficient, government must step in to provide public goods. In buying public goods like national defense or lighthouses, government is behaving exactly like any other large spender. By casting sufficient dollar votes in certain directions, it causes resources to flow there. Once the dollar votes are cast, the market mechanism then takes over and channels resources to firms so that the lighthouses or roads get produced.

Taxes. Government must find the revenues to pay for its public goods and for income-redistribution programs. Such revenues come from taxes levied on personal and corporate incomes, on wages, on sales of consumer goods, and on other items. All levels of government—city, state, and federal— collect taxes to pay for their spending.

Taxes sound like another "price," in this case the price we pay for public goods. But taxes differ from prices in one crucial respect. Taxes are not voluntary. Everyone is subject to the tax laws; we are all obligated to pay for a share of the cost of public goods. Of course, through our democratic process, we as citizens impose taxes on ourselves and all of us have a right to our share of the public goods provided by government. However, the close connection between spending and consumption that

*Lighthouses are a typical example of a public good provided by government. They save lives and cargos. But lighthouse keepers cannot reach out to collect fees from ships; nor, if they could, would it serve an efficient social purpose for them to exact an economic penalty on ships who use their services. The light can be provided most efficiently free of charge, for it costs no more to warn 100 ships than to warn a single ship of the nearby rocks. We have here a positive externality, a divergence between private and social advantage. Philosophers and political leaders have always recognized the necessary role of government as provider of such public goods.

we see for private goods does not hold for taxes and public goods. I buy a hamburger or a wool sweater only if I want one, but I must pay my share of the taxes used to finance defense and public education even if I don't care a bit for these activities.

In summary, the visible hand of government is firmly grounded in economic logic. Government sets the rules of the road, levies taxes and tolls to pay for collective activities, and buys public goods such as highways. These activities facilitate the smooth driving of private enterprise, prevent abuses when firms become monopolistic road hogs, and curb firms' activities when their exhaust fumes threaten lives and property.

Equity

Our discussion of market failures like monopoly or public goods focused on defects in the allocative role of markets—imperfections that can be corrected by judicious intervention. But assume for the moment that the economy functioned with complete efficiency—always on the production-possibility frontier and never inside it, always choosing the right amount of public versus private goods, and so forth. Even if the market system worked as perfectly as just described, it might still lead to a flawed outcome. Why?

Markets do not necessarily produce a distribution of income that is regarded as socially fair or equitable. A pure laissez-faire market economy may produce unacceptably high levels of inequality of income and consumption.

Why might the market mechanism produce an unacceptable solution to the question of *for whom?* The reason is that incomes are determined by arbitrary patterns of inheritance, misfortune, hard work, and factor prices. The resulting income distribution may not correspond to a fair outcome. Moreover, recall that goods follow dollar votes and not the greatest need. A rich man's cat may drink the milk that a poor boy needs to remain healthy. Does this happen because the market is failing? Not at all, for the market mechanism is doing its job—putting goods in the hands of those who have the dollar votes. If a country spends more on pet food than on helping the poor go to college, that is a defect of income distribution, not of the market. Even the most efficient market system may generate great inequality.[1]

Often the income distribution in a market system is the result of accidents of technology or birth. Suppose the invention of robots should cause the competitive price of labor to fall greatly, thereby reducing incomes of workers and turning 95 percent of national income over to the robots' owners. Would everyone regard that as necessarily right or ideal? Probably not. Should someone be allowed to become a billionaire simply by inheriting 5000 square miles of rangeland or the family's holding of oil wells? That is the way the cookie crumbles under the market system. Would you want to tax the income of robots or levy stiff inheritance taxes on such accumulations of wealth? People are deeply divided on whether very high incomes should be heavily taxed.

Income inequalities may be politically or ethically unacceptable. A nation does not need to accept the outcome of competitive markets as predetermined and immutable; people may examine the distribution of income and decide it is unfair. If a democratic society does not like the distribution of dollar votes under a laissez-faire market system, it can take steps to change the distribution of income.

Let's say that voters decide to reduce income inequality. What tools could Congress use? First, it can engage in *progressive taxation,* taxing large incomes at a higher rate than small incomes. The federal income and inheritance taxes are examples of such redistributive progressive taxation.

Second, because low tax rates cannot help those who have no income at all, governments have in recent decades built up a system of *transfer payments,* which are money payments to people. Such transfers include aid for the elderly, blind, and disabled, and for those with dependent children, as well as unemployment insurance for the jobless. This system of transfer payments provides a "safety net" to protect the unfortunate from privation. And, finally, governments sometimes subsidize consumption of low-income groups by providing food stamps, subsidized medical care, and low-cost housing.

[1] One of the most dramatic instances of how markets can produce inequality occurred in 1848–1849, when Queen Victoria's laissez-faire government let millions of Irish children, women, and men starve in the great famine when a fungus suddenly destroyed the potato crop.

Through the process of economic growth and welfare programs that established minimum standards of living, much of the great and visible destitution of nineteenth-century capitalism has been erased in the twentieth century. But relative poverty has proven difficult to eradicate, and with changes in family structure poverty has been on the rise in recent years.

What can economics contribute to debates about equality? Economics as a science cannot answer such normative questions as how much of the competitively determined incomes—if any—should be transferred to poor families. This is a political question that must be answered at the ballot box.

Economics can analyze the costs or benefits of different redistributive systems. Economists have devoted much time to analyzing whether different income-redistribution devices (such as taxes and food stamps) lead to social waste (whereby people work less or buy drugs rather than food). They have also studied whether giving poor people cash rather than goods is likely to be a more efficient way of reducing poverty. Economics cannot answer questions of how much poverty is acceptable and fair; but it can help design more effective programs to increase the incomes of the poor.

Macroeconomic Growth and Stability

In addition to promoting efficiency and equity, governments undertake the macroeconomic functions of promoting economic growth and stabilizing the economy.

Since its origins, capitalism has been plagued by periodic bouts of inflation (rising prices) and depression (high unemployment). At times, as during the Great Depression of the 1930s, hardship persisted for a decade because governments did not yet know how to revive the economy.

Today, thanks to the intellectual contribution of John Maynard Keynes and his followers, we know how to control the worst excesses of the business cycle. We now understand that government can affect the levels of output, employment, and inflation by careful use of its fiscal and monetary powers. The *fiscal policies* of government are those just discussed—the power to tax and the power to spend. *Monetary policy* involves determining the supply of money, thereby affecting interest rates and investment and other interest-rate-sensitive spending. Through these two central tools of macroeconomic policy, governments can influence the level of total spending, the rate of growth and level of output, the levels of employment and unemployment, and the price level and rate of inflation in an economy.

Governments in advanced industrial countries successfully applied the lessons of the Keynesian revolution over the last half-century. Spurred on by expansionary monetary and fiscal policies, the market economies witnessed a period of unprecedented economic growth in the period after World War II. However, faced with economic difficulties in the 1970s—high inflation and rising unemployment, along with a slowdown in the growth of productivity—some people became skeptical about the ability of monetary and fiscal policies to stabilize the economy.

Two objectives are the focus of long-run macroeconomic policies: rapid economic growth and high productivity. *Economic growth* denotes the growth in a nation's total output, while *productivity* represents the output per unit input or the efficiency with which resources are used.

In the 1980s, governments designed macroeconomic policies to promote long-term objectives of economic growth and productivity. Fiscal policies were designed to improve incentives for production. Tax rates were lowered in most industrial countries, and the growth of expenditure programs slowed. Governments worried about the impact of their fiscal policies upon saving, investment, and innovation. In the late 1980s and early 1990s, the United States struggled to lower government budget deficits in order to raise the national investment rate and grow more rapidly. At the same time, monetary policies became more active in managing the short-run swings in output, unemployment, and inflation. The combination of growth-oriented fiscal policies and activist monetary policies produced the longest peacetime expansion in American history from 1982 to 1990.

Macroeconomic policies for stabilization and economic growth include fiscal policies (of taxing and spending) along with monetary policies (which affect interest rates and credit conditions). Since the development of macroeconomics in the 1930s, governments have succeeded in curbing the worst excesses of inflation and unemployment.

Table 3-1 summarizes the economic role played

Failure of invisible hand	Government intervention	Current examples of government policy
Inefficiency		
Monopoly	Intervene in markets	Antitrust laws
Externalities	Intervene in markets	Antipollution laws, antismoking ordinances
Public goods	Subsidize worthwhile activities	National defense, lighthouses
Inequality		
Unacceptable inequalities of income and wealth	Redistribute income	Progressive taxation of income and wealth Income-support programs (e.g., food stamps)
Macroeconomic problems		
Business cycles (high inflation and unemployment)	Stabilize through macroeconomic policies	Monetary policies (e.g., changes in money supply and interest rates) Fiscal policies (e.g., taxes and spending programs)
Slow economic growth	Stimulate growth	Invest in education Reduce budget deficit and raise national savings rate

Table 3-1. Government can remedy shortcomings of the market

by government today. It shows the important governmental functions of promoting efficiency, achieving a fairer distribution of income, and pursuing the macroeconomic objectives of economic growth and stability. In all advanced industrial economies we find a mixed economy in which the market determines most individual prices and quantities while government steers the overall economy with programs of taxation, spending, and monetary regulation. Both halves—market and government—are essential for a soundly functioning economy. Operating a modern economy without both is like trying to clap with one hand.

● We have completed our overview of the functioning of a modern mixed economy. In the next chapter we describe in detail how supply and demand interact to determine the prices and quantities of goods and see how this approach can be used to analyze a wide variety of economic problems. ●

SUMMARY

A. How Markets Solve the Basic Economic Problems

1. In an economy like the United States, most economic decisions are made in markets, which serve as mechanisms by which buyers and sellers meet to trade and determine prices and quantities for commodities. Adam Smith proclaimed that the *invisible hand* of markets would lead to the optimal economic outcome as individuals pursue their own self-interest. And while markets are far from perfect, they have proved remarkably effective at solving the problems of *how, what,* and *for whom.*
2. The market mechanism works as follows to determine the *what* and the *how:* The dollar votes of people affect prices of goods; these prices serve as guides for the amounts of the different goods to be produced. When people demand more of a good, businesses can profit by expanding production of that good. Under perfect competition, a business must find the cheapest method of production, efficiently using labor, land, and other factors; otherwise, it will incur losses and be eliminated from the market.

3. At the same time that the *what* and *how* problems are being resolved by prices, so is the problem of *for whom*. The distribution of income is determined by the ownership of factors of production (land, labor, and capital) and by factor prices. People possessing fertile land or the ability to hit home runs will earn many dollar votes to buy consumer goods. Those without property and with skills, color, or sex that the market does not value will receive low incomes.

B. The Economic Role of Government

4. Although the market mechanism is an admirable way of producing and allocating goods, sometimes market failures lead to deficiencies in the economic outcomes. Government steps in to correct these failures. Government's role in a modern economy is to ensure efficiency, to correct an unfair distribution of income, and to promote economic growth and stability.

5. Markets fail to provide an efficient allocation of resources in the presence of imperfect competition or externalities. Imperfect competition, such as monopoly, produces high prices and low levels of output. To combat these conditions, governments regulate businesses or put legal antitrust constraints on business behavior. Externalities arise when business actions impose costs or bestow benefits on others outside the marketplace without compensation. Governments may decide to step in and regulate these spillovers (as it does with air pollution) or provide for *public goods* (as in the case of national defense).

6. Markets do not necessarily produce a fair distribution of income; they may spin off unacceptably high levels of inequality of income and consumption. In response, governments generally choose to alter the pattern of incomes (the *for whom*) generated by market wages, rents, interest, and dividends. Modern governments use taxation to raise revenues for transfers or income-support programs that place a financial safety net under the poor.

7. Since the development of macroeconomics in the 1930s, government has undertaken a third role: using fiscal powers (of taxing and spending) and monetary policy (affecting interest rates and credit conditions) to promote long-run economic growth and productivity and to tame the business cycle's excesses of inflation and unemployment.

8. The prevailing mode of economic organization in modern advanced industrial economies is the *mixed economy*, in which the market determines most individual prices and quantities, while the government steers the overall economy with programs of taxation, spending, and monetary regulation.

CONCEPTS FOR REVIEW

The market mechanism
market, market mechanism
markets for goods and for factors of production
prices as signals
market equilibrium
perfect and imperfect competition

Adam Smith's invisible-hand doctrine

Government's economic role
efficiency, equity, stability
inefficiencies: monopoly and externalities
inequity of incomes under markets
macroeconomic policies: fiscal and monetary policies
stabilization and growth

QUESTIONS FOR DISCUSSION

1. Consider an economy where the only activity is farming and where land and labor produce a single output, corn. Briefly describe the solution to *what, how,* and *for whom* in this rural country. Draw a circular-flow diagram like Figure 3-1 for this economy.
2. Consider the following cases of government intervention in the economy: regulations to limit air pollution; research on an AIDS vaccine; income supplements to the elderly; price regulation of a local water monopoly; a monetary-policy step to curb inflation. What role of government is being pursued in each case?
3. In what sense does a market mechanism "ration" scarce goods and services?
4. The circular flow of goods and inputs illustrated in Figure 3-1 has a corresponding flow of dollar incomes and spending. Draw a circular-flow chart for the dollar flows in the economy, and compare it with the circular flow of goods and inputs.
5. In addition to writing the opening quotation of this chapter, Adam Smith wrote, "I have never known much good done by those who affected to trade for the public good." Explain the logic behind this statement and relate it to the invisible-hand doctrine.
6. This chapter discusses many "market failures," areas in which the invisible hand guides the economy poorly, and describes the role of government. Is it possible that there are, as well, "government failures," government attempts to curb market failures that are worse than the original market failures? Think of some examples of government failures. Can you imagine a case in which government failures are so bad that it is better to live with the market failures than to try to correct them?
7. The table below shows some of the major expenditures of the federal government. Explain how each one relates to the economic role of government.

Major Expenditure Categories for Federal Government

Budget category	Federal spending, 1992 ($, billion)
National defense	346
Social security	289
Interest on public debt	206
Unemployment insurance	27
Administration of justice	14
Pollution control	6
Basic science	4

Source: Office of Management and Budget, *Budget of the United States Government,* Fiscal Year 1992.

C H A P T E R 4

BASIC ELEMENTS OF SUPPLY AND DEMAND

You can make even a parrot into a learned economist;
all it must learn are the two words "supply" and "demand."
Anonymous

Every economy must choose the market basket of goods to be produced (the *what*), must decide *how* this market basket should be produced, and must decide who will enjoy the fruits of economic activity (the *for whom*). In the American economy, as in other advanced industrial countries, a system of markets and prices determines most economic outcomes. In a market system, consumers are like voters, using their dollar votes to buy what they want most. Your votes compete with my votes, and the people with the most dollar votes exercise the most influence over what is produced and to whom goods flow.

Our task in this chapter is to understand exactly how this system of dollar votes operates in a market economy. Why are diamonds inessential but expensive, while water is vital but cheap? Why does land in Manhattan or Tokyo command astronomical prices, while desert land in Arizona is virtually worthless? Why did few people own color televisions a few decades ago, whereas almost every American family owns one today?

The answers to these and a thousand other questions can be found in the *theory of supply and demand.* This theory shows how consumer preferences determine consumer demand for commodities, while business costs are the foundation of the supply of commodities. Finally, we will see how supply and demand are brought into balance or equilibrium by the movement of prices, by the price mechanism.

The Market Mechanism

Suppose you woke up one morning with an urge for a new stereo set. How would you get one? You wouldn't dream of saying, "I'll head down to the voting booth and vote for the president who will give me a new stereo. Of course, I mean one with twin 100-watt channels and fancy woofers."

Or to take an actual historical case, suppose that people decided to travel in automobiles rather than on horseback. How would this desire be translated into action? Would politicians tell workers and firms to move to Detroit to make cars? Would the Senate tell farmers to slow down horse production? How would government get producers to grow cotton for car seats rather than hay for horses?

Of course, the transition from horse and buggy to cars did not occur under government direction. Instead, consumers bought more cars and fewer horses. With higher profits in car production, automakers geared up, new firms like Cadillac and Ford sprang up in Detroit, and workers hungry for good jobs moved there. As horses languished in the pastures, horse prices fell and horse breeders turned to other fields. As less hay was needed for horses, the price of hay fell and other crops were planted instead. At the same time, the demand for automotive components such as steel, cotton, and rubber increased, and the prices of these goods rose, attracting manufacturers into the production of automotive-based commodities.

Through just such forces, we have witnessed a veritable revolution in American transportation during this century, with the horse population falling by 90 percent while the car population grew from nothing to 150 million vehicles. What brought about this revolution? It occurred as changes in tastes and technology operated through the forces of supply and demand.

Similar revolutions are taking place in the economic marketplace all the time. As people's tastes change and as new technologies are developed, the marketplace registers these changes in the prices and quantities of inputs and outputs.

Through changing prices and profits, the price mechanism registers changes in tastes, technologies, and trading patterns and thereby rations out the available resources among the competing uses.

Analysis of Supply and Demand

The purpose of this chapter is to show how supply and demand operate in competitive markets for *individual commodities.* We shall define first a demand curve and then a supply curve. Using these basic tools, we shall see how the market price is determined (or reaches its competitive equilibrium) where these two curves intersect—where the forces of demand and supply are just in balance.

The Demand Schedule

Both common sense and careful scientific observation have shown that the amount of a commodity people buy depends on its price. The higher the price of an article, other things being equal, the less people are willing to buy. The lower its market price, the more units of it are bought.

There exists a definite relationship between the market price of a good and the quantity demanded of that good, other things held equal. This relationship between price and quantity bought is called the **demand schedule,** or the **demand curve.**

Table 4-1 presents a hypothetical demand schedule for corn. At each price, we can determine the quantity of corn that consumers purchase. For example, at $5 per bushel, consumers will buy 9 million bushels per year.

At a lower price, more corn is bought. Thus, at a corn price of $4, the quantity bought is 10 million units. At yet a lower price (*P*) equal to $3, the quantity demanded (*Q*) is still greater at 12 million. And so forth. We can determine the quantity demanded at each listed price in Table 4-1.

Demand Schedule for Corn

	(1) Price ($ per bushel) *P*	(2) Quantity demanded (millions of bushels per year) *Q*
A	5	9
B	4	10
C	3	12
D	2	15
E	1	20

Table 4-1. The demand schedule relates quantity demanded to price

At each market price, consumers will want to buy a certain quantity of corn. As the price of corn falls, the quantity of corn demanded will rise.

The Demand Curve

The graphical representation of the demand schedule is the **demand curve.** We show the demand curve in Figure 4-1, which graphs the quantity of corn demanded on the horizontal axis and the price of corn on the vertical axis. Note that quantity and price are inversely related, *Q* going up when *P* goes down. The curve slopes downward, going from northwest to southeast. This important property is called the *law of downward-sloping demand.* It is based on common sense as well as economic theory and has been empirically tested and verified for practically all commodities—corn, gasoline, cars, and illegal drugs being a few examples.

The law of downward-sloping demand: When the price of a commodity is raised (and other things are held constant), buyers tend to buy less of the commodity. Similarly, when the price is lowered, other things being equal, quantity demanded increases.

We can illustrate the law of downward-sloping demand for the case of personal computers (PCs). In the early 1980s, the price of PCs was astronomical and only the wealthy could afford them. People used typewriters or pens to write papers and did

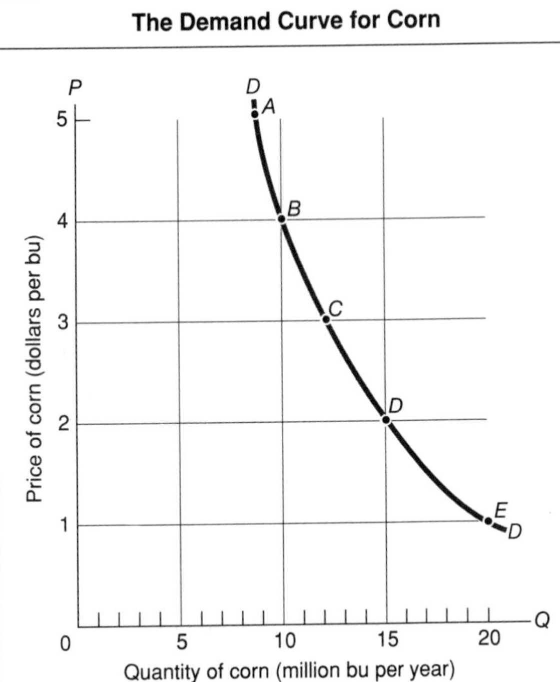

Figure 4-1. A downward-sloping demand curve relates quantity demanded to price

In the demand curve for corn, prices are measured on the vertical axis while quantity demanded is measured on the horizontal axis. Each pair of (P,Q) numbers from Table 4-1 is plotted as a point and then a smooth curve is passed through the points to give us a demand curve, DD. The negative slope of the demand curve illustrates the law of downward-sloping demand.

calculations by hand. Even today, in poor countries like India, only the richest businesses and banks own PCs.

But the prices of PCs have fallen sharply in the last decade. As more and more people could afford PCs, they came to be widely used for work, for school, and for fun. This history sheds light on one important reason for the law of downward-sloping demand: Lower prices entice new buyers.

In addition, a price reduction will induce extra purchases of goods by existing consumers. For example, when water is very expensive, we buy only enough of it to drink. Then when its price drops, we buy some to wash with. At still lower prices, we water flowers and use it lavishly for any possible purpose. Conversely, a rise in the price of a good will cause some of us to buy less.

Why does quantity demanded tend to fall as price rises? For two reasons. First is the **substitution effect.** When the price of a good rises, I will substitute other similar goods for it (as the price of beef rises, I eat more chicken). A second element is the **income effect.** This comes into play because when a price goes up, I find myself somewhat poorer than I was before. If gasoline prices double, I have in effect less income, so I will naturally curb my consumption of gasoline and other goods.

Our discussion of demand has referred to "the" demand curve. But whose demand is it? Mine? Yours? Everybody's? The fundamental building block for demand is individual tastes and needs. However, when we analyze the price and quantity for a market, we will refer to the *market demand,* which represents the sum total of all individual demands. The market demand curve is found by adding together the quantities demanded by all individuals at each price. In this chapter, we will always focus on the market demand.

Behind the Demand Curve

What determines the market demand for corn or cars or computers? Up to now, we have ignored influences other than a commodity's own price. But other influences are significant: average levels of income, the size of the population, the prices and availability of related goods, individual tastes, and special influences.

The *average income of consumers* is a key determinant of demand. As people's incomes rise, individuals tend to buy more of almost everything—apples, boats, cars, etc.

The *size of the market*—measured say by the population—clearly affects the market demand curve. California's 30 million people tend to buy 30 times more apples and cars than do Rhode Island's 1 million people.

The prices and availability of *related goods* influence the demand for a commodity. A particularly important connection exists among substitute goods—ones that tend to perform the same function, such as pens and pencils, cotton and wool, or oil and natural gas. Demand for good A tends to be low if the price of substitute product B is low. (For example, if the price of natural gas is high in Boston, will the demand for oil tend to be low or high?)

In addition to these objective elements we must add a set of subjective elements called *tastes* or *preferences.* Tastes represent a variety of social and historical influences. They may reflect genuine psychological or physiological needs (for liquids, salt, warmth, or love). And they may include artificially contrived cravings (for cigarettes, drugs, or fancy sports cars). They may contain a large element of tradition or religion (eating beef is popular in America but taboo in India, while curried jellyfish is a delicacy in Japan).

Finally, individual goods generally have *special influences* behind their demand—rainfall contributes to the demand for umbrellas, snow depth affects ski sales, and ocean temperature influences the demand for surfboards. In addition, expectations about future economic conditions, particularly prices, may have an important impact on demand.

Much of our analysis will focus on price as the variable tending to balance supply and demand. As price changes, the quantity demanded changes and we move along the demand curve. But in addition to the importance of price, we must never lose sight of these other influences that ultimately determine the strength of demand and can shift the demand curve. The different elements behind the demand for a typical good, automobiles, are sketched in Table 4-2.

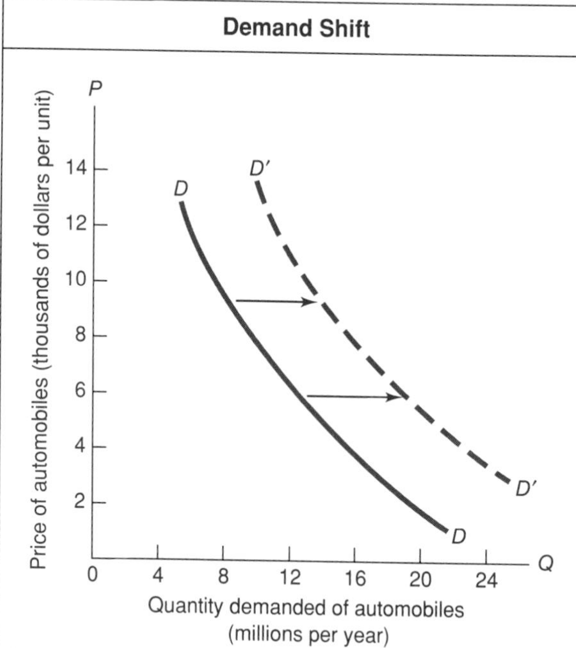

Figure 4-2. Increase in demand for automobiles

As elements underlying demand change, the demand for automobiles is affected. Here we see the effect of rising average income, increased population, and lower gasoline prices on the demand for automobiles. Why do these lead to an *increase* in demand?

Elements affecting demand	Example for automobiles
1. **The good's own price**	Higher own price reduces quantity demanded
2. **Average income**	As incomes rise, people increase car purchases
3. **Population**	Larger population increases car purchases
4. **Prices of related goods**	Lower gasoline prices raise the demand for cars
5. **Tastes**	Americans buy more cars than Europeans, other things equal
6. **Special influences**	Special influences include availability of subways, quality of road and rail network, dating patterns, expectation of future price increases, etc.

Table 4-2. Many elements, price and non-price, affect demand

A Change in Demand. As economic life evolves, demand changes incessantly. Demand curves sit still only in a textbook.

Why does the demand curve shift? Because the influences other than the good's price change. As an example, what were some possible reasons for the increase in the American demand for cars from 1950 to 1990? Many non-price influences were at work: the average real income of Americans almost doubled; the adult population rose by more than half; and there was a decline in the availability of alternative forms of transportation (bus, trolley, and rail). The result of all these changes was a rightward shift in the demand curve for cars.

The net effect of the changes in underlying influences is what we call an *increase in demand.* An increase in the demand for automobiles is illustrated in Figure 4-2 as a rightward shift in the demand curve. Note that the shift means that more cars will be bought at every price.

You can test yourself by answering the following

questions: Will a warm winter shift the demand curve for heating oil leftward or rightward? Why? What would happen to the demand for ski-lift tickets if snowfall were especially light? What will a sharp fall in the price of personal computers do to the demand for typewriters?

Supply Schedule and Supply Curve

Let us now turn from demand to supply. By "supply" we mean the quantity of a good that businesses willingly produce and sell. More precisely, we relate the quantity supplied of a good to its market price, holding equal other things such as costs of production, the prices of related goods, and the organization of the market.

The **supply schedule** (and **supply curve**) for a commodity shows the relationship between its market price and the amount of that commodity that producers are willing to produce and sell, other things held equal.

Table 4-3 shows a hypothetical supply schedule for corn, and Figure 4-3 plots the data from the table. These data show that at a corn price of $1 per bushel, no corn at all will be produced. At such a low price, farmers might devote their land to uses other than corn production. As the corn price rises (always holding constant things like the price of wheat), more land will be planted with corn. At ever-higher corn prices, farmers will find it profitable to add even more land, labor, tractors, and fertilizer. All these will increase the output of corn at the higher market prices.

The Supply Curve for Corn

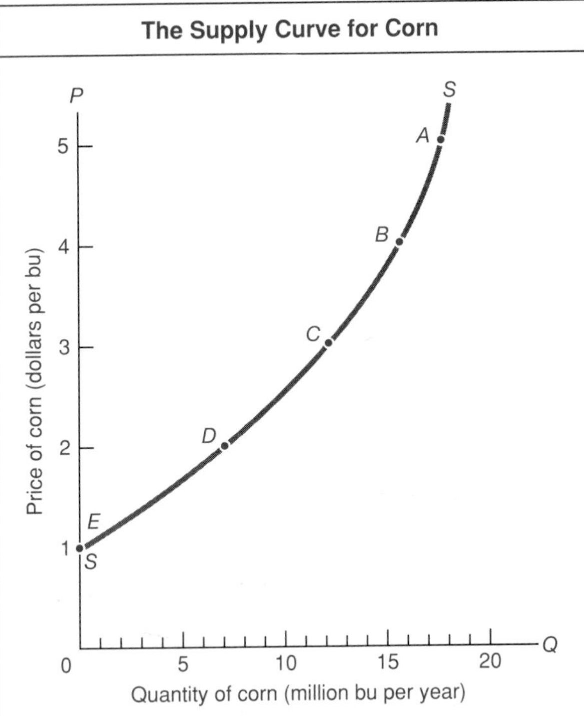

Figure 4-3. Supply curve relates quantity supplied to price

The supply curve plots the price and quantity pairs from Table 4-3. A smooth curve is passed through these points to give the upward-sloping supply curve, *SS*.

Supply Schedule for Corn

	(1) Price ($ per bushel) *P*	(2) Quantity supplied (millions of bushels per year) *Q*
A	5	18
B	4	16
C	3	12
D	2	7
E	1	0

Table 4-3. Supply schedule relates quantity supplied to price

The table shows, for each price, the quantity of corn that the country's farmers want to produce and sell. Note the direct or positive relation between price and quantity supplied.

Note that the supply curve in Figure 4-3 slopes upward and to the right. Why do supply curves for individual commodities generally slope upward? One important reason is found in the law of diminishing returns. Take the case of wine. If society wants more wine, then more and more labor will have to be added to the same limited sites suitable for producing wine grapes. Each new worker will—according to the law of diminishing returns—be adding less and less extra product; hence, the price needed to coax out additional output will have to rise. By raising the price of wine, society can persuade wine producers to produce and sell more wine; the supply curve for wine is therefore upward-sloping. Similar reasoning applies to many other goods as well.

Behind the Supply Curve

In examining the forces operating on supply, the fundamental point to grasp about businesses' supply behavior is that producers supply commodities for profit and not for fun or charity. For example, a farmer will supply more corn at higher corn prices because it is profitable to do so; conversely, when the corn price falls below the cost of production, as it did in the mid-1980s, farmers plant other crops, let the fields go to seed, or even sell their farms.

A key element underlying supply decisions, then, is the *cost of production*. When production costs for a good are low relative to the market price, it is profitable for producers to supply a great deal. When production costs are high relative to price, firms produce little or may simply go out of business.

Among the forces affecting production costs are technology and input costs. *Technological advances* certainly affect costs. A better computer program for crop rotation, genetically engineered seeds, and improved irrigation systems—all these would lower a farmer's production costs and increase supply.

Similarly, if technology did not change, but the *prices of inputs* changed, the costs of production would change and so would supply. For example, when oil prices rose in 1990, this raised production costs and lowered the supply of gasoline and diesel fuel.

Another major element influencing supply is the *prices of related goods*, particularly goods that can be readily substituted for one another in the production process. If the price of one production substitute rises, the supply of another substitute will decrease. For example, farmers can produce wheat as well as corn; an oil refinery can produce diesel fuel as well as gasoline. For each pair, as the price of one (e.g., diesel fuel) rises, this will tend to decrease the supply of the other (e.g., gasoline).

A further determinant of supply is the *market organization*. A reduction in tariffs and quotas on foreign goods will open up the market to foreign producers and will tend to increase supply. If a market becomes monopolized, the price at each level of output will increase. In general, a perfectly competitive market will produce the highest possible level of output at each price level.

Finally, *special influences* affect supply. The weather exerts an important influence on farming and on the ski industry. The computer industry has been marked by a keen spirit of innovation, which has led to a continuous flow of new products. In some industries, like railroads and telecommunications, government regulation has shunted supply decisions off the competitive track. And expectations about future prices often have an important impact upon supply decisions.

Table 4-4 highlights the important determinants of supply using automobiles as an example.

Shifts in Supply. A casual observer of markets knows that businesses are constantly changing their products and services. What lies behind changes in supply behavior?

Supply changes when any influences other than the commodity's own price changes. In terms of a supply curve, we say that supply increases (or decreases) when the amount supplied increases (or decreases) at each market price.

When automobile prices change, producers change their production and quantity supplied, but the supply and the supply curve do not shift. By contrast, when other influences affecting supply

Elements determining supply	Example for automobiles
1. **The good's own price**	Higher own price increases most profitable production level and raises quantity supplied
2. **Technology**	Computerized manufacturing lowers production cost and increases supply
3. **Input prices**	Autoworkers' wage cuts lower production costs and increase supply
4. **Prices of related goods**	If bus and truck prices fall, supply of cars increases
5. **Market organization**	Removal of quota on Japanese car imports increases supply
6. **Special influences**	If government lowers standards on pollution-control equipment, supply of cars may increase

Table 4-4. Supply is affected by price, production costs, and other influences

change, supply changes and the supply curve shifts.

We can illustrate a shift in supply for the automobile market. Supply would increase if the introduction of cost-saving computerized design and manufacturing reduced the labor required to produce cars, if autoworkers took a pay cut, if Japanese automakers were allowed to export more cars to the United States, or if the government removed some of the regulatory requirements on the industry. Any of these elements would increase the supply of automobiles in the United States at each price. Figure 4-4 illustrates an increase in supply of automobiles.

To test your understanding of supply shifts, think about the following: What happens to the supply curve for corn in Figure 4-3 after favorable weather produces a bumper crop? How does a Florida freeze affect the supply of orange juice? What would happen to the world supply of oil if political turmoil in the Soviet Union reduced its oil production?

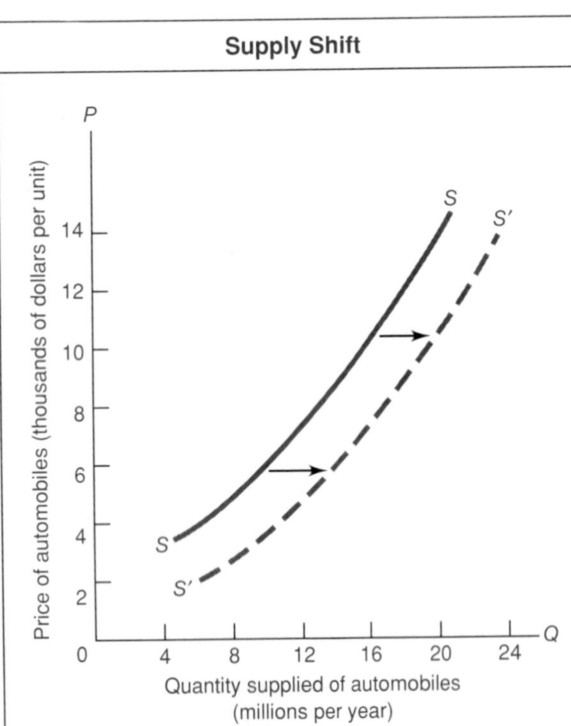

Figure 4-4. Increased supply of automobiles

As production costs fall or Japanese competition increases, the supply of automobiles increases. At each price, producers will supply more automobiles, and the supply curve therefore shifts to the right. (What would happen to the supply curve if autoworkers' wages increased sharply?)

Equilibrium of Supply and Demand

We have seen that consumers demand different amounts of corn, cars, and computers as a function of these goods' prices. Similarly, producers willingly supply different amounts of these and other goods depending on their prices. What happens when suppliers and demanders meet?

The answer is that the forces of supply and demand operate through the market to produce an equilibrium price and quantity, or a market equilibrium. The **market equilibrium** comes at that price and quantity where the supply and demand forces are in balance. At this point, the amount that buyers want to buy is just equal to the amount that sellers want to sell. At equilibrium, price and quantity tend to stay the same, as long as other things remain equal.

Let us work through the corn example in Table 4-5 to see how supply and demand determine a market equilibrium; the numbers in this table come from Tables 4-1 and 4-3. Up to this point we have been considering demand and supply in isolation. We know the amounts that are willingly bought and sold at each price. We now need to put supply and demand together to determine the actual price and quantity that the market will settle on.

To find the market price and quantity, we find a price at which the amounts desired to be bought and sold just match. If we try a price of $5 per bushel, will that prevail for long? Clearly not. As row A in Table 4-5 shows, at $5 producers would like to sell 18 million bushels per year while demanders want to buy only 9. The amount supplied at $5 exceeds the amount demanded, and stocks of corn pile up in the granary. Because too much corn is chasing too few consumers, the price of corn will tend to fall, as shown in column (5) of Table 4-5.

Say we try $2. Does that price clear the market? A quick look at row D shows that at $2 consumption exceeds production. The storehouses of corn begin to empty at that price. As people scramble around to find their desired quantity of corn, they will tend to bid up the price of corn, as is shown in column (5) of Table 4-5.

We could try other prices, but we can easily see that the equilibrium price is $3, or row C in Table

Combining Demand and Supply for Corn

	(1) Possible prices ($ per bushel)	(2) Quantity demanded (millions of bushels per year)	(3) Quantity supplied (millions of bushels per year)	(4) State of market		(5) Pressure on price
A	5	9	18	Surplus	↓	Downward
B	4	10	16	Surplus	↓	Downward
C	3	12	12	Equilibrium		Neutral
D	2	15	7	Shortage	↑	Upward
E	1	20	0	Shortage	↑	Upward

Table 4-5. Equilibrium price comes where quantity demanded equals quantity supplied

Only at the equilibrium price of $3 per bushel does amount supplied equal amount demanded. At too low a price there is a shortage and price tends to rise. Too high a price produces a surplus, which will depress price.

4-5. Only at $3 will consumers and suppliers *both* be making consistent decisions. At $3, consumers' desired demand exactly equals desired production, each of which is 12 units.

At the equilibrium price of $3, there is no tendency for price to rise or fall, and stockpiles of corn are neither growing nor declining. We also say that $3 is the market-clearing price. This denotes that all supply and demand orders are filled, the books are "cleared" of orders, and demanders and suppliers are satisfied.

Equilibrium with Supply and Demand Curves. We show a market equilibrium graphically in Figure 4-5, which combines the supply curve from Figure 4-3 with the demand curve from Figure 4-1. Combining the two graphs is possible because they are drawn with exactly the same units on each axis.

We find the market equilibrium by looking for the price at which quantity demanded equals quantity supplied. *The equilibrium price comes at the intersection of the supply and demand curves, at point* C.

How do we know that the intersection of the supply and demand curves is the market equilibrium? Let us repeat our earlier experiment. Start with the initial high price of $5 per bushel, shown at the top of the price axis in Figure 4-5. At that price, suppliers want to sell more than demanders want to buy. The result is a *surplus,* or excess of quantity supplied over quantity demanded, shown in the figure by the black line labeled "Surplus." The arrows along the curves show the direction that price tends to move when a market is in surplus.

At a low price of $2 per bushel, the market shows a *shortage,* or excess of quantity demanded over

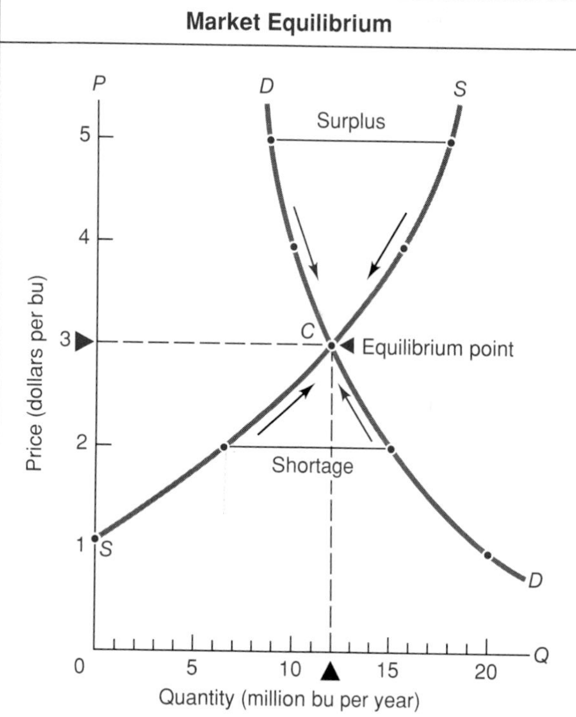

Figure 4-5. Market equilibrium comes at the intersection of supply and demand curves

The market equilibrium price and quantity come at the intersection of supply and demand curves. At a price of $3 at point *C*, firms willingly supply what consumers willingly demand. When price is too low (say at $2), quantity demanded exceeds quantity supplied, shortages occur, and prices are driven up to equilibrium. What occurs at a price of $4?

quantity supplied, here shown by the black line labeled "Shortage." Under conditions of shortage, the competition among buyers for limited goods causes the price to rise, as shown in the figure by the arrows pointing upward.

We now see that the balance or equilibrium of supply and demand comes at point *C*, *where the supply and demand curves intersect.* At point *C*, where the price is $3 per bushel and the quantity is 12 units, the quantities demanded and supplied are equal; there are no shortages or surpluses; there is no tendency for price to rise or fall. At point *C* and only at point *C*, the forces of supply and demand are in balance and the price has settled at a sustainable level.

The equilibrium price and quantity come at that level where the amount willingly supplied equals the amount willingly demanded. In a competitive market, this equilibrium is found at the intersection of the supply and demand curves. There are no shortages or surpluses at the equilibrium price.

Effect on Equilibrium of a Shift in Supply or Demand

The analysis of the supply-and-demand apparatus can do much more than tell us about the equilibrium price and quantity. It can also be used to predict the impact of changes in economic conditions on prices and quantities.

Gregory King, a seventeenth-century English writer, noticed that food prices rose when the harvest was bad. When food was plentiful, farmers got a lower price for their harvest. Let's explain this using supply and demand for corn.

A spell of bad weather reduced the amount of corn that farmers supplied at each market price; it thereby shifted the supply curve to the left. This is illustrated in Figure 4-6(*a*), where the corn supply curve has shifted from *SS* to *S′S′*. In contrast, the demand curve has not shifted; people have the same desire for food whether the harvest is good or bad.

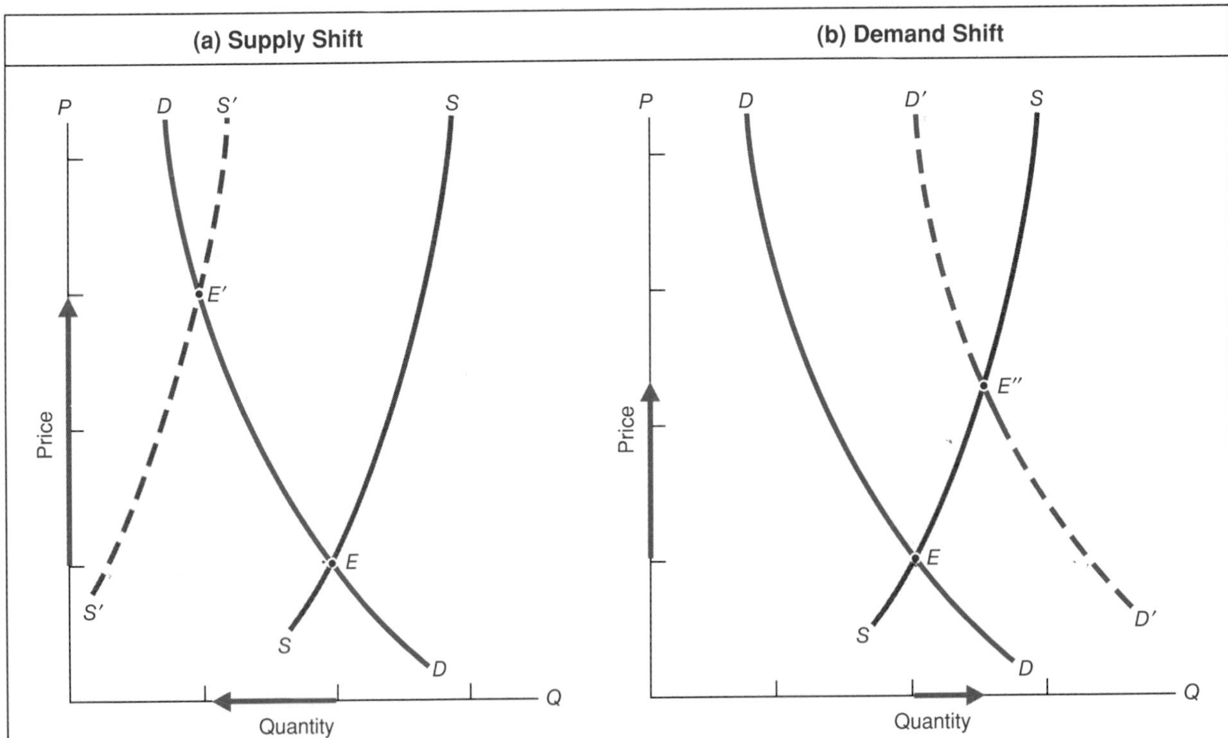

Figure 4-6. Shifts in supply or demand change equilibrium price and quantity

(a) If supply shifts leftward, a shortage will develop at the original price. Price will be bid up until quantities willingly bought and sold are equal at new equilibrium, *E′*.

(b) A shift in the demand curve leads to excess demand. Price will be bid up as equilibrium price and quantity move upward to *E″*.

What happens in the corn market? At the old price, farmers sold too little corn to satisfy consumer demand and there were shortages. Price therefore rose, encouraging production and thereby raising quantity supplied while discouraging consumption and thereby lowering quantity demanded. Price continues to rise until, at the new equilibrium price, the amounts demanded and supplied are once again equal.

As Figure 4-6(*a*) shows, the new equilibrium is found at the intersection at *E′* of the new supply curve *S′S′* and the original demand curve. Thus a bad harvest (or any leftward shift of the supply curve) raises prices and, by the law of downward-sloping demand, lowers quantity demanded.

Suppose that a decline in the price of fertilizers or a new miracle seed increased supply. Draw in a new *S″S″* curve, along with the new equilibrium *E″*. Why is the equilibrium price lower while the equilibrium quantity is higher?

We can also use our supply-and-demand apparatus to examine how changes in demand affect the market equilibrium. Suppose that there is a sharp increase in family incomes, so that everyone wants more corn. This is represented in Figure 4-6(*b*) as a "demand shift" in which, at every price, consumers demand a higher quantity of corn. The demand curve thus shifts *rightward* from *DD* to *D′D′*.

The demand shift produces a shortage of corn at the old price. A scramble for corn ensues. Prices are bid upward until supply and demand come back into balance at a higher price. Graphically, the increase in demand has changed the market equilibrium from *E* to *E″* in panel (*b*).

For both examples of shifts—a shift in supply and a shift in demand—a variable underlying the demand or supply curve has changed. In the case of supply, there might have been a change in technology or input prices or tariff policy. For the demand shift, one of the influences affecting consumer demand—incomes, population, the prices of related goods, tastes—changed and thereby shifted the demand schedule.

When elements underlying demand or supply change, this leads to shifts in demand or supply and to changes in the market equilibrium of price and quantity.

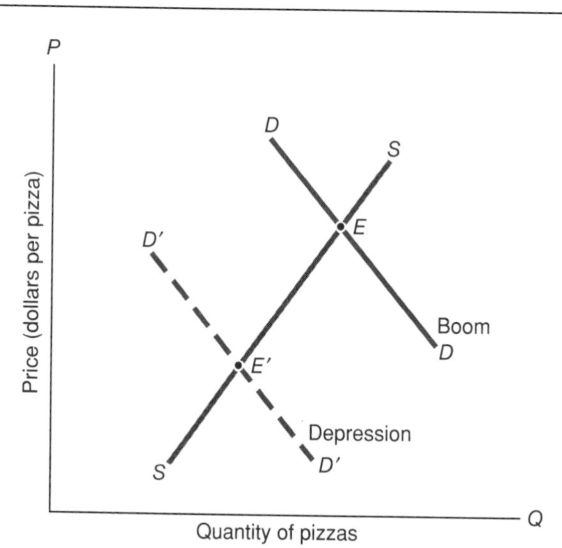

Figure 4-7. Analysis of demand must hold other things equal

Lower demand occurs when the economy is depressed, while a boom raises demand. Does the curve drawn through *E* and *E′* yield a demand curve? What is the role of "other things equal" in constructing a demand curve?

Three Hurdles

Having introduced the fundamentals of supply and demand, we pause to warn about three hurdles that must be overcome before these tools can be usefully employed. The first point is a reminder to keep other things equal. The second concerns the difference between shifts of curves and movements along curves. The third deals with the exact meaning of an equilibrium of supply and demand.

"Other Things Equal"

In analyzing supply and demand schedules, we must always be careful to analyze what would happen when *no other elements change to cloud our experiment*. Specifically, this means that, as we consider the impact of changes in the price of corn on quantity demanded, no other influence can be changed. We must hold constant family incomes, population, and the prices of other goods, along with anything else that would shift the demand schedule for corn. Like any scientist who wants to isolate the effects of one causal factor, we must vary only that one factor.

Figure 4-7 illustrates how failure to hold other

things equal can lead to erroneous reasoning. Say that Contrary is studying the market for pizzas. Contrary observes that in boom years, jobs are plentiful and people enjoy spending their high incomes in pizza parlors. When business activity is depressed and people are out of work, however, incomes are low and few pizzas are bought.

In Figure 4-7, Contrary records point E in prosperous years and E' in depression years. He takes a ruler, joins points E and E', and asserts, "I have disproved the law of downward-sloping demand. When price was lower, quantity was actually lower. My straight line joining E and E' produces an upward-sloping, not a downward-sloping, demand curve. So I have refuted a basic economic law."

Alas, poor Contrary is crestfallen to discover that he has broken one of the cardinal rules of economics: He did not hold other things equal. At the same time that price dropped, income declined. The tendency for a drop in price to raise purchases was more than masked by the countertendency of lowered income to decrease demand.

In addition, you might well be suspicious of the argument because it leads to nonsensical conclusions. Contrary would predict that corn prices will be high in years of large harvests because the demand curve is upward-sloping. Not only does such reasoning lead to absurd predictions, but it would also bankrupt the farmers or speculators who bought dear and sold cheap. Make sure, then, to hold other things equal when analyzing the impact of a change in supply or demand.

Movement along Curves vs. Shift of Curves

Great care must be taken not to confuse a *change in demand* (which denotes a shift of the demand curve) with a *change in the quantity demanded* (which means moving to a different point on the same demand curve after a price change). A similar distinction applies to supply and many other economic relationships.

A change in demand occurs when one of the elements underlying the demand curve shifts. Take the case of pizzas. If incomes increase, so will the number of pizzas that consumers want to buy at every price. In other words, higher incomes will increase demand and shift out the demand curve for pizzas.

In contrast, when the price of pizzas faced by consumers falls, and all other things remain constant, consumers will tend to purchase more pizzas. But the increased purchases result not from an increase in demand but from the price decrease. This change represents a *movement along* the demand curve, not a *shift in* the demand curve. A similar distinction applies to shifts in supply vs. changes in quantity supplied.

Figure 4-8 illustrates this crucial distinction. Figure 4-8(*a*) shows the case of an increase in demand or a shift in the demand curve. As a result of the shift, the equilibrium quantity demanded increases from 10 to 15 units.

The case of a movement along the demand curve is shown in Figure 4-8(*b*). In this case, a supply shift changes the market equilibrium from point E to point E''. As a result, the quantity demanded changes from 10 to 15 units. But demand does not change in this case; rather quantity demanded increases as consumers move along their demand curve from E to E''.

Let's put this distinction to work by analyzing the following incorrect argument: "A bad harvest need not raise price. The price might rise at first. But a higher price will diminish the demand. And a reduced demand will send the price down again. Therefore, a bad harvest might actually lower the price of corn!"

What is wrong with this statement? It errs because "demand" is used incorrectly in the third sentence; it uses the word "demand" in the sense of "quantity demanded," thus confusing a movement along a curve with a shift of the demand curve. The correct statement would run as follows:

"A bad harvest will raise price as the leftward shift in the supply curve raises the equilibrium price of corn. The higher equilibrium price will reduce the quantity demanded, as consumers move up the downward-sloping demand curve. But since no shift in the demand curve occurred, there is no reason to expect that price will fall as a result of a decrease in the quantity demanded."

Meaning of Equilibrium

The last hurdle concerns the meaning of the term "equilibrium." It is seen in the following challenge of a skeptic: "How can you say that supply and

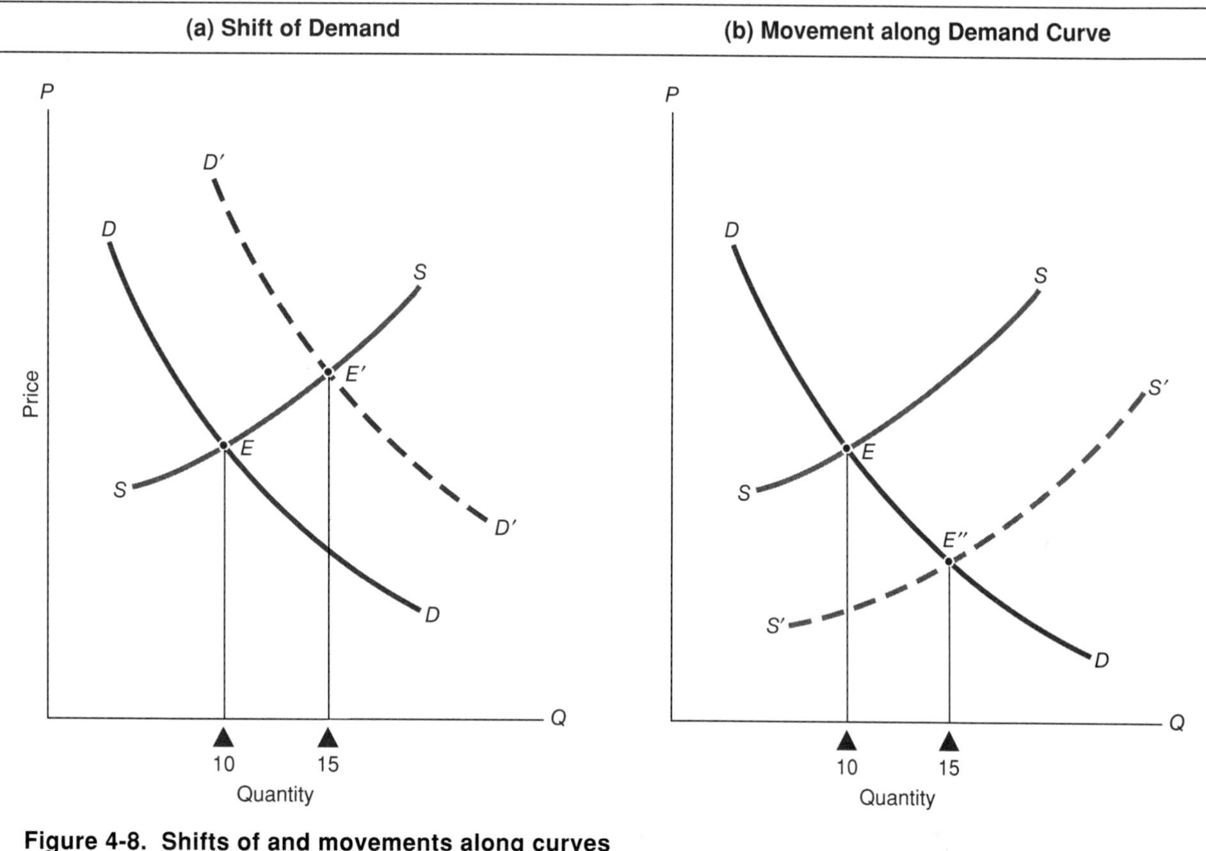

Figure 4-8. Shifts of and movements along curves

Start out with initial equilibrium at *E* and a quantity of 10 units. In **(a)**, an increase in demand (i.e., a shift of the demand curve) produces a new equilibrium of 15 units at *E*′. In **(b)**, a shift in supply results in a movement along the demand curve from *E* to *E*″.

demand determine a particular equilibrium quantity? The quantity bought must always equal the quantity sold. This is true no matter what the price and whether or not the market is in equilibrium."

This challenge emphasizes the subtlety in the term "equilibrium." We might reply as follows: You are correct that the quantity bought must be identical to the quantity sold. But we are seeking that market equilibrium for which the supply and demand are in balance. At which price is the amount that consumers willingly buy just matched by the amount that producers willingly sell? Only at such a price will buyers and sellers be satisfied with their decisions; only at the equilibrium will price tend neither to rise nor fall.

At non-equilibrium prices, the measured amounts bought and sold are obviously equal. But at too high a price there is a surplus of goods, with producers eagerly trying to sell more goods than demanders will buy. This excess of desired supply over desired demand will put downward pressure on price until price finally reaches that equilibrium level where the two curves intersect.

At the equilibrium intersection of supply and demand, and there alone, everybody will be happy: the suppliers, the demanders, and the economist who seeks the price at which there are no surpluses or shortages.

Rationing by Prices

Let us now take stock of what the market mechanism accomplishes. By determining the equilibrium prices and quantities of all inputs and out-

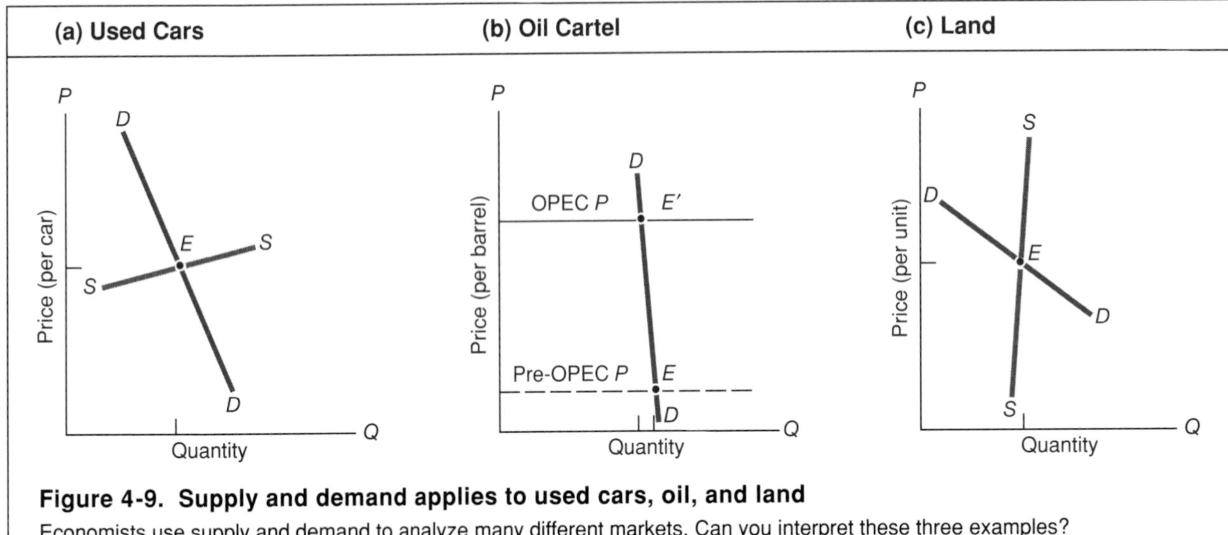

Figure 4-9. Supply and demand applies to used cars, oil, and land

Economists use supply and demand to analyze many different markets. Can you interpret these three examples?

puts, the market allocates or rations out the scarce goods of the society among the possible uses. Who does the rationing? A planning board or a legislature? No. The marketplace, through the interaction of supply and demand, does the rationing. This is rationing by the purse.

What goods are produced? This is answered by the signals of the market prices. High oil prices stimulate oil production, whereas low corn prices drive resources out of agriculture. Those who have the most dollar votes have the greatest influence on what goods are produced.

For whom are goods delivered? The power of the purse dictates the distribution of income and consumption. Those with higher incomes end up with larger houses, more clothing, and longer vacations. When backed up by cash, the most urgently felt needs get fulfilled through the demand curve.

Even the *how* question is decided by supply and demand. When corn prices are low, farmers cannot afford expensive tractors and fertilizers, and only the best land is cultivated. When oil prices are high, oil companies drill in deep offshore waters and employ novel seismic techniques to find oil.

A market economy solves the basic economic problems through the operation of supply and demand.

Three Markets

To conclude this introduction to supply and demand, let us look at three cases of markets where supply and demand can help explain how prices and quantities are determined. Figure 4-9(*a*) pictures a competitive market for used cars. What would happen to used-car prices in an economic boom when family incomes are high? Panel (*b*) shows how oil prices skyrocketed when OPEC (the Organization of Petroleum Exporting Countries) organized a price-fixing group (called a cartel). What would happen to the quantity of oil demanded if OPEC collapsed and oil prices fell sharply? The third case, in (*c*), shows the supply and demand for land in Manhattan. Note how little the supply of land responds to higher prices. Can you see why increased demand for land raises prices a great deal and hardly changes the quantity supplied of land?

These are but a small sample of the questions that supply-and-demand analysis can answer. Further study will deepen our understanding of the forces behind supply and demand and will show how this analysis can be applied to other important areas. But even this first survey will serve as an indispensable tool for interpreting the economic world in which we live.

SUMMARY

1. The analysis of supply and demand shows how a market mechanism grapples with the triad of economic problems, *what, how,* and *for whom.* It shows how dollar votes decide the prices and quantities of different goods.

2. A demand schedule represents the relationship between the quantity demanded and the price of a commodity, other things held constant. Such a demand schedule, represented graphically as a demand curve, holds equal other things like family incomes, tastes, and the prices of other goods. Almost all commodities obey the *law of downward-sloping demand,* which holds that quantity demanded falls as a good's price rises. This law is represented by a downward-sloping demand curve.

3. Many influences lie behind the demand schedule for the market as a whole: average family incomes, population, the prices of related goods, tastes, and special influences. When these influences change, the demand curve will shift.

4. The supply schedule (or supply curve) gives the relationship between the quantity of a good that producers desire to sell—other things equal—and that good's price. Quantity supplied generally responds positively to price, so that the supply curve rises upward and to the right.

5. Elements other than the good's price affect its supply. The most important influence is the commodity's production cost, determined by the state of technology and by input prices. Other elements in supply include the prices of related goods, the market organization, and special influences.

6. The equilibrium of supply and demand in a competitive market is attained at a price where the forces of supply and demand are in balance. The equilibrium price is that price at which the quantity demanded just equals the quantity supplied, which occurs graphically at the intersection of the supply and demand curves. At a price above the equilibrium, producers want to supply more than consumers want to buy, which results in a surplus of goods and exerts downward pressure on prices. Similarly, too low a price generates a shortage, and buyers will therefore tend to bid prices upward to the equilibrium.

7. Competitively determined prices ration the limited supply of goods among those with the demands and the necessary dollar votes.

8. To avoid pitfalls in the use of supply-and-demand analysis, we must observe certain strictures: (*a*) hold other things equal, which requires distinguishing the impact of a change in a commodity's price from the impact of changes in other elements; (*b*) distinguish a change in demand or supply (which produces a shift in a curve) from a change in the quantity demanded or supplied (which represents a movement along a curve); (*c*) recognize a supply-and-demand equilibrium, which is where buyers and sellers willingly engage in trades.

CONCEPTS FOR REVIEW

Supply-and-demand analysis
demand schedule or curve, *DD*
law of downward-sloping demand
supply schedule or curve, *SS*
influences affecting supply and demand curves
surplus, shortage
rationing by prices

Pitfalls in supply and demand
other things equal
shifts of curve versus movements along curve
equilibrium price and quantity

QUESTIONS FOR DISCUSSION

1. Define carefully what is meant by a demand schedule or curve. State the law of downward-sloping demand. Illustrate the law of downward-sloping demand with two cases from your own experience.
2. Define the concept of a supply schedule or curve. Show that an increase in supply means a rightward and downward shift of the supply curve. Contrast this with the rightward and upward shift in the demand curve implied by an increase in demand. Why the difference?
3. What might increase the demand for hamburgers? What would increase the supply? What would inexpensive frozen pizzas do to the market equilibrium for hamburgers? To the wages of teenagers who work at McDonald's?
4. Explain why the price in competitive markets settles down at the equilibrium intersection of supply and demand. Explain what happens if the market price started out too high or too low.
5. Explain why each of the following is false:
   (a) A freeze in Brazil's coffee-growing region will lower the price of coffee.
   (b) The high price of oil resulting from political disturbances in the Middle East will lower the demand for oil.
   (c) Concerns about the health effects of meat will lower the price of granola and raise the price of leather jackets.
   (d) The war against drugs, with increased interdiction of imported cocaine, will lower the price of domestically produced marijuana.
6. The four laws of supply and demand are the following:
   (a) An increase in demand generally raises price and raises quantity demanded.
   (b) A decrease in demand generally __________ price and __________ quantity demanded.
   (c) An increase in supply generally lowers price and raises quantity demanded.
   (d) A decrease in supply generally __________ price and __________ quantity demanded.

   Fill in the blanks. Demonstrate each law with a supply-and-demand diagram.
7. In each of the following, explain whether quantity demanded changes because of a demand shift or a price change, and draw a diagram to illustrate your answer.
   (a) As a result of increased military spending, the price of Army boots rises.
   (b) Fish prices fall after the Pope allows Catholics to eat meat on Friday.
   (c) A gasoline tax lowers the consumption of gasoline.
   (d) After a disastrous wheat blight, bread sales go down.
   (e) After a disastrous wheat blight, soybean sales go up.
   (f) After the Black Death struck Europe in the fourteenth century, wages rose.
8. "The government should protect the shoe industry from ruinous foreign competition. This will help consumers because the higher price of domestically produced shoes will lower demand and will ultimately end up lowering the price to consumers." Comment on the reasoning of this statement in terms of the discussion of "three hurdles" in the chapter. Write out a correct analysis of the impact of a restriction of foreign shoe supply on the market for shoes.
9. From the following data, plot the supply and demand curves and determine the equilibrium price and quantity.

Supply and Demand for Pizzas

Price ($ per pizza)	Quantity demanded (pizzas per semester)	Quantity supplied (pizzas per semester)
10	0	40
8	10	30
6	20	20
4	30	10
2	40	0
0	125	0

What would happen if the demand for pizzas tripled at each price? What would occur if the price were initially set at $4 per pizza?

P A R T T W O

MICROECONOMICS: SUPPLY, DEMAND, AND PRODUCT MARKETS

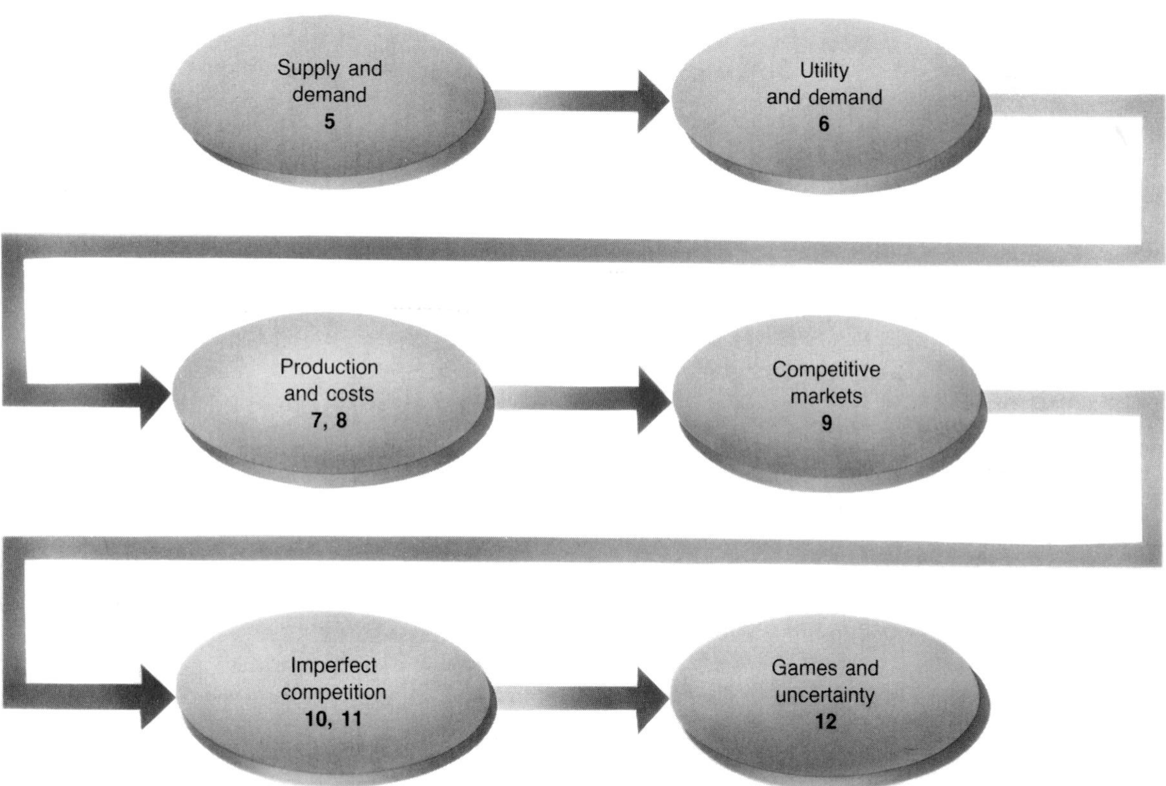

Part Two begins our detailed study of the microeconomics of product markets. After a thorough study of the supply-and-demand apparatus, we analyze how demand is grounded in individual preferences. The following chapters analyze business production and cost and then show how cost determines competitive supply. We then put the building blocks together to analyze the major market structures: perfect competition, monopoly, and oligopoly. All these tools are necessary for an understanding of the way a market economy allocates scarce resources—and how an ideal competitive economy leads to economic efficiency.

C H A P T E R 5

SUPPLY AND DEMAND IN INDIVIDUAL MARKETS

The end is easily foretold,
When every blessed thing you hold
Is made of silver, or of gold,
You long for simple pewter.

When you have nothing else to wear
But cloth of gold and satins rare,
For cloth of gold you cease to care
Up goes the price of shoddy.

Gilbert and Sullivan,
The Gondoliers

Having completed our introductory survey, we begin our study of microeconomics, which is the study of the behavior of individual parts or sectors of the economy. Our study of microeconomics will proceed in three parts.

Product markets. The next few chapters focus on the behavior of product markets. These chapters examine the principles that underlie consumer demands, the determinants of business supply, and the overall market outcomes in perfectly and imperfectly competitive markets. The major purpose of the chapters on product markets is to understand the logic of Adam Smith's *invisible hand*—to examine how prices and profits coordinate economic activity and to understand the remarkable efficiency properties of a properly functioning market mechanism.

We will also examine the market failures that arise when monopolies or other forms of imperfect competitors dominate industry. Our analysis will help answer questions like: Why is good weather bad for farmers' sales? Who ends up paying a gasoline tax—consumers or oil companies? Why do monopolies harm consumer welfare?

The last few years have shown how dependent the world is on a single commodity, oil. A thorough study of the supply and demand for oil will show why an oil embargo will drive up the price of oil; it will also reveal how a gasoline tax can reduce oil imports and make a country less vulnerable to unstable foreign sources.

Factor markets. The next set of chapters, in Part Three, analyzes the functioning of factor markets—wages of labor, interest on capital, and rent of land. We will see how prices of these factors, along with the supplies owned by households, determine people's incomes and affect the distribution of income in a market economy.

Are you concerned about the rising toll of poverty on children and minority groups? If so, you must first study carefully the economic basis of income inequality before you can hope to design lasting and efficient programs for raising the incomes of the poor.

Efficiency and fairness. The final chapters in our survey of microeconomics, in Part Four, address important policy issues in a modern market economy. These chapters examine the role of government along with the controversial issues of taxation and government spending. We will see how government plays an important role in both creating and combating market power and how it can help alleviate the poverty and hardship resulting from the market distribution of income.

Lately, scientists have warned of growing threats to our environment from toxic wastes and air pollution along with concerns about global warming. Environmental economics has begun to propose ways to halt environmental degradation without harming economic growth.

At the end of Part Four we return to the crucial issue of the appropriate role of the private and public sectors—of market and command—as alternative economic mechanisms for achieving the twin goals of economic efficiency and fairness.

A. Elasticity of Demand and Supply

In Chapter 4 we introduced the basic concepts of supply and demand. These tools, as well as the meaning of the equilibrium of supply and demand, the distinction between shifts of curves and movements along curves, and the necessity of holding other things equal, are fundamental to understanding microeconomics. If these concepts are not clear in your mind, turn back to Chapter 4 to refresh your memory about the key concepts and diagrams.

We now break fresh ground by presenting a new concept, elasticity. We then use this concept to explore further the issues in supply-and-demand analysis.

Price Elasticity of Demand

The law of downward-sloping demand tells us that quantity demanded tends to vary inversely with price. But often we want to know *how much* quantity demanded will change in response to a change in price.

The price elasticity of demand (sometimes simply called "price elasticity") measures how much the quantity demanded of a good changes when its price changes.

Elasticity denotes responsiveness. The **price elasticity of demand** (or **price elasticity**) is the responsiveness of the quantity demanded of a good to changes in the good's price, other things held equal. The precise definition of price elasticity, E_D, is the percentage change in quantity demanded divided by the percentage change in price.

We can calculate the coefficient of price elasticity numerically according to the following formula:

Price elasticity of demand = E_D

$$= \frac{\text{percentage change in quantity demanded}}{\text{percentage change in price}}$$

Let's take a close look at the meaning and economic significance of this crucial concept.

Elastic and Inelastic Demand

Demands for goods differ in their elasticities. Demand for necessities like food usually responds little to price changes, while luxuries like air travel are generally highly price-sensitive. We divide commodities into different categories depending on their demand responsiveness to price change. A good is "elastic" when its quantity demanded responds greatly to price changes and is "inelastic" when its quantity demanded responds little to price changes.

- When a 1 percent change in price calls forth more than a 1 percent change in quantity demanded, this is **price-elastic demand.**
- When a 1 percent change in price evokes less than a 1 percent change in quantity demanded, this is **price-inelastic demand.**

To illustrate the calculation of elasticities, let us examine a simple case of the response to a price

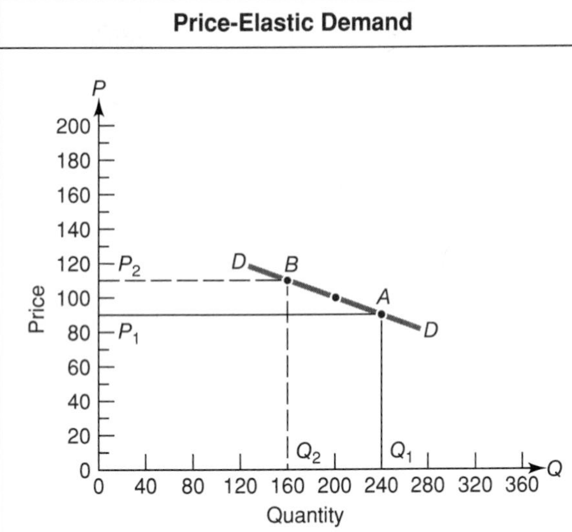

Figure 5-1. Elastic demand shows large-quantity response to price change

Market equilibrium is originally at point *A*. In response to 20 percent price increase, quantity demanded declines 40 percent to point *B*. Price elasticity is $E_D = 40/20 = 2$. Demand is therefore elastic in the region from *A* to *B*.

increase shown in Figure 5-1. In the original situation, price was 90 and quantity demanded was 240 units. A price increase to 110 led consumers to reduce their purchases to 160 units. In Figure 5-1, consumers are originally at point *A* and move along their demand schedule to point *B* when price rises.

Table 5-1 shows how we calculate price elasticity. The price increase is 20 percent with the resulting quantity decrease being 40 percent. The price elasticity of demand is evidently $E_D = 40/20 = 2$. The price elasticity is greater than 1 and this good therefore displays price-elastic demand in the region from *A* to *B*.

Case A: Price = 90 and quantity = 240
Base B: Price = 110 and quantity = 160

Percentage price change = $\Delta P/P = 20/100 = 20\%$

Percentage quantity change = $\Delta Q/Q = -80/200 = -40\%$

Price elasticity = $E_D = 40/20 = 2$

Table 5-1. Example of good with elastic demand

Consider the situation where price is raised from 90 to 110. According to the demand curve, quantity demanded falls from 240 to 160. Price elasticity is the ratio of percentage change in quantity divided by percentage change in price. We drop the minus sign from the numbers so that all elasticities are positive.

The calculation in Table 5-1 brings out three important points about elasticity measurement. First, note that prices and demands move in opposite directions because of the law of downward-sloping demand. For convenience, however, we treat all percentage changes as positive so that elasticity is always a positive number.

Second, the use of percentage changes rather than actual changes gives us the nice property that the elasticity measure is a pure number. This means that the units of measurement for quantities or for prices—bushels or tons, dollars per bushel or German marks per ton—do not affect elasticity. The percentage change in price and the percentage change in quantity are *exactly* the same in whatever units we measure quantities and prices.

A third point concerns a slight ambiguity in measuring percentage changes. The formula for a percentage change is $\Delta P/P$. The value of ΔP in Table 5-1 is clearly $20 = 110 - 90$. But what is the correct value for P in the denominator? Is it the original value of 90? The final value of 110? Or something in between?

For very small percentage changes, such as from 100 to 99, the difference in the denominator (between 99 and 100) is trivial. But for larger changes, the difference is significant. To avoid ambiguity, we always take the *average price* to be the base price for calculating price changes. In Table 5-1, we chose the average of the two prices $[P = (90 + 110)/2 = 100]$ as the base or denominator to use in the elasticity formula. Similarly, we use the *average quantity* $[Q = (160 + 240)/2 = 200]$ as the base for measuring the percentage change in quantity. The exact formula for calculating elasticity is therefore:

$$E_D = \frac{\Delta Q}{(Q_1 + Q_2)/2} \div \frac{\Delta P}{(P_1 + P_2)/2}$$

where P_1 and Q_1 represent the original price and quantity and P_2 and Q_2 stand for the new price and quantity.

Elasticity on Linear Demand Curves. Often we draw demand curves as linear or straight lines. What is the demand elasticity on a straight-line demand curve? Is demand elastic, inelastic, or what?

Numerical Calculation of Elasticity Coefficient

Q	ΔQ	P	ΔP	$\frac{Q_1 + Q_2}{2}$	$\frac{P_1 + P_2}{2}$	$E_D = \frac{\Delta Q}{(Q_1 + Q_2)/2} \div \frac{\Delta P}{(P_1 + P_2)/2}$
0		6				
	10		2	5	5	$\frac{10}{5} \div \frac{2}{5} = 5 > 1$
10		4				
	10		2	15	3	$\frac{10}{15} \div \frac{2}{3} = 1$
20		2				
	10		2	25	1	$\frac{10}{25} \div \frac{2}{1} = 0.2 < 1$
30		0				

Table 5-2. Calculation of price elasticity along a linear demand curve

ΔP denotes the change in price, i.e., $\Delta P = P_2 - P_1$, while $\Delta Q = Q_2 - Q_1$. To calculate numerical elasticity, percentage change of price equals price change ΔP divided by average price; the percentage change in output is calculated as $\Delta Q/Q$, where Q is given by the average Q. Treating all figures as positive numbers, the resulting ratio gives numerical price elasticity of demand, E_D.

The surprising answer is that the price elasticity varies from zero to infinity along a straight-line demand curve. Table 5-2 gives a detailed set of elasticity calculations using the same technique as that in Table 5-1. This table shows that linear demand curves start out with high price elasticity where price is high and quantity is low and end up with low elasticity where price is low and quantity high.

At the midpoint of the demand curve we encounter the borderline case of **unit-elastic demand,** which occurs when the percentage change in quantity is exactly the same size as the percentage change in price. We will see later that this condition implies that total sales of the commodity (which equal $P \times Q$) are constant for a unit-elastic demand curve.

Price Elasticity in Diagrams

Figure 5-2 illustrates the three cases of elasticities. In each case, price is cut in half and consumers change their quantity demanded from A to B.

In Figure 5-2(a) a halving of price has tripled quantity demanded. Like the example in Figure 5-1,

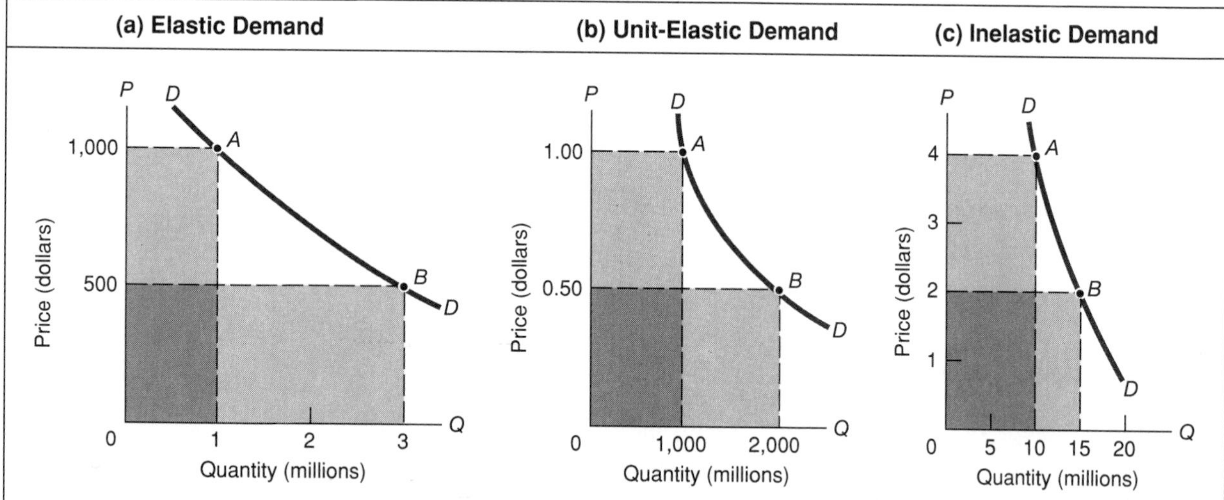

Figure 5-2. Price elasticity of demand falls into three categories: elastic, unit-elastic, and inelastic

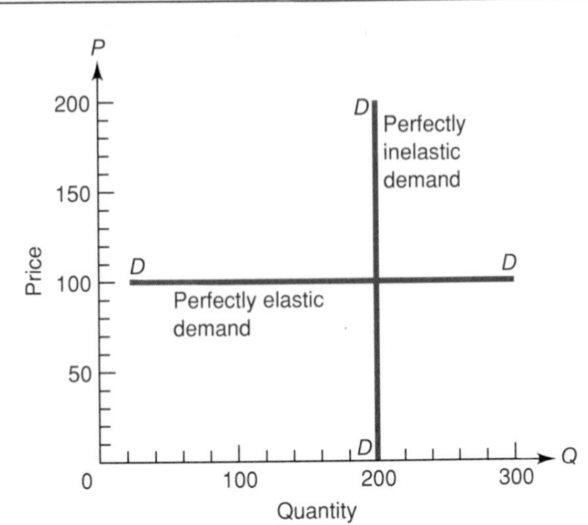

Figure 5-3. Perfectly elastic and inelastic demands

Polar extremes of demand are vertical demand curves, which represent perfectly inelastic demand ($E_D = 0$), and horizontal demand curves, which show perfectly elastic demand ($E_D = \infty$).

this case shows price-elastic demand. In Figure 5-2(*c*), cutting price in half led to only a 50 percent increase in quantity demanded, so this is the case of price-inelastic demand. The borderline case of unit-elastic demand is shown in Figure 5-2(*b*); in this example, the doubling of quantity demanded exactly matches the halving of price.

Figure 5-3 displays the important polar extremes of perfectly elastic and inelastic demands. Perfectly inelastic demands are ones where the quantity demanded responds not at all to price changes; such demand is seen to be a *vertical* demand curve. By contrast, when quantity demanded is infinitely elastic, this implies that a tiny change in price will lead to an indefinitely large change in quantity demanded, as in the *horizontal* demand curve in Figure 5-3.

Slopes vs. Elasticities

At this point, we must sound an important warning. Often the slope of a curve is confused with its elasticity. You might think a steep slope for the demand curve means inelastic demand and a flat slope signifies elastic demand.

While true for the polar cases of perfectly elastic and inelastic demands, this is not generally the case. The slope is not the same as the elasticity because the demand curve's slope depends upon the change in *P* and *Q*, whereas the elasticity depends upon their *percentage* changes.

One way to see this point is to examine Figure 5-2(*b*). This demand curve is clearly not a straight line with constant slope. Yet it has a constant demand elasticity of $E_D = 1$ because the percentage change of price is everywhere equal to the percentage change in quantity.

Figure 5-4 illustrates the pitfall of confusing slope and elasticity. This straight-line demand curve has the same slope everywhere. But the top of the line, near *A*, has a very small percentage price change and a very large percentage quantity change, and elasticity is extremely large. Therefore, price elasticity is high when we are high on the linear *DD* curve. Conversely, when price is very low, the price elasticity is close to zero.

More generally, above the midpoint *M* of any straight line, demand is elastic, with $E_D > 1$. At

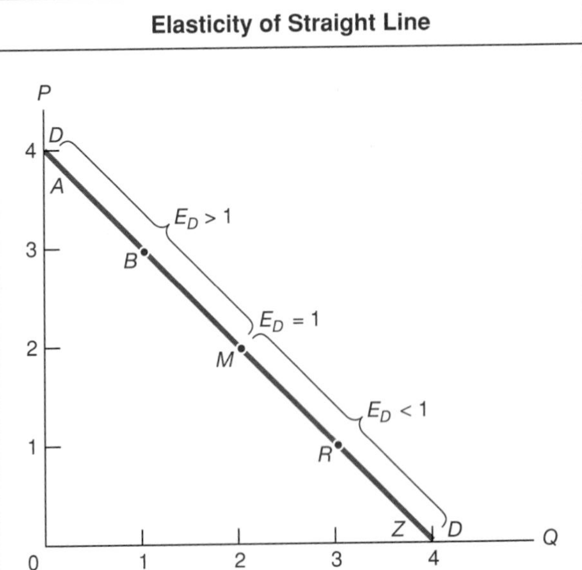

Figure 5-4. Slope and elasticity are not the same thing

All points on the straight-line demand curve have the same slope. But above the midpoint, demand is elastic; below it, demand is inelastic; at the midpoint, demand is unit-elastic. Only in the case of vertical or horizontal curves shown in Fig. 5-3 can you infer the price elasticity from slope alone.

the midpoint, demand is unit-elastic, with $E_D = 1$. Below the midpoint, demand is inelastic, with $E_D < 1$.

In summary, while the extreme cases of perfectly elastic and perfectly inelastic demand can be determined from the slopes of the demand curves alone, for the in-between cases, where reality generally lies, elasticities cannot be inferred by slope alone.*

Elasticity and Revenue

An understanding of elasticity helps clarify the impact of price changes upon total revenues of producers. Clearly, an increase in supply, arising perhaps from an abundant harvest, would tend to depress price. But the early economist Gregory King also observed a less obvious point: Farmers as a whole receive less total revenue when the harvest is good than when it is bad. Paradoxically, good weather is *bad* for farmers' incomes. The reason is that a low price elasticity of food means that large harvests (high Q) tend to be associated with low revenue (low $P \times Q$). Let's look at the relationship between price elasticity of demand and total revenue.

Total revenue is by definition equal to price times quantity (or $P \times Q$). If consumers buy 5 units at \$3 each, total revenue is \$15. The three cases of elasticity correspond to three different relationships between total revenue and price changes:

1. When demand is price inelastic, a price decrease reduces total revenue.
2. When demand is price elastic, a price decrease increases total revenue.
3. In the borderline case of unit-elastic demand, a price decrease leads to no change in total revenue.

We can easily check these three statements by referring back to Figure 5-2. We begin by showing how to measure revenue in the diagram itself. Total revenue is the product of price times quantity, $P \times Q$. Further, the area of a rectangle is always equal to the product of its base times its height. Therefore, total revenue at any point on a demand curve can be found by examining the area of the rectangle formed by the P and Q at that point.

Next, we can check the relationship between elasticity and revenue for the unit-elastic case in Figure 5-2(*b*). Note that the shaded revenue region ($P \times Q$) is \$1000 million for both points A and B. The shaded areas representing total revenue are the same because of offsetting changes in the Q base and the P height. This is what we would expect for the borderline case of unit-elastic demand.

We can also see that Figure 5-2(*a*) corresponds to elastic demand. In this figure, the revenue rectangle expands from \$1000 million to \$1500 million when price is halved. Since total revenue goes up when price is cut, demand is elastic.

In Figure 5-2(*c*) the revenue rectangle falls from \$40 million to \$30 million when price is halved, so demand is inelastic.

Which diagram illustrates Gregory King's finding that a bumper harvest means lower total revenues for farmers? Clearly it is Figure 5-2(*c*). Which represents MCI Communications' belief that a reduction in its long-distance telephone rates would induce such a large volume of calls as to increase its total sales? Surely Figure 5-2(*a*).

*A simple trick will allow you to calculate the price elasticity of a demand curve very simply. The rule is that *the elasticity of a straight line at a point is given by the ratio of the length of the line segment below the point to the length of the line segment above the point.*

To see this, first examine Fig. 5-4. Note that at the midpoint M the length of the segment above (AM) and that of the segment below (MZ) are exactly equal; hence the elasticity is $MZ/AM = 1$. At point B, this formula yields $E_D = BZ/AB = 3/1 = 3$; at R, $E_D = 1/3$.

Knowing how to calculate E_D for a straight line enables you to calculate it for any point along a curved demand curve, as shown in Fig. 5-5. (1) Draw the straight line tangent to the curve at your point (e.g., at B in Fig. 5-5) and then (2) calculate the E_D for the straight line at that point (e.g., E_D at $B = 3$). The result will be the correct elasticity for the curve at point B.

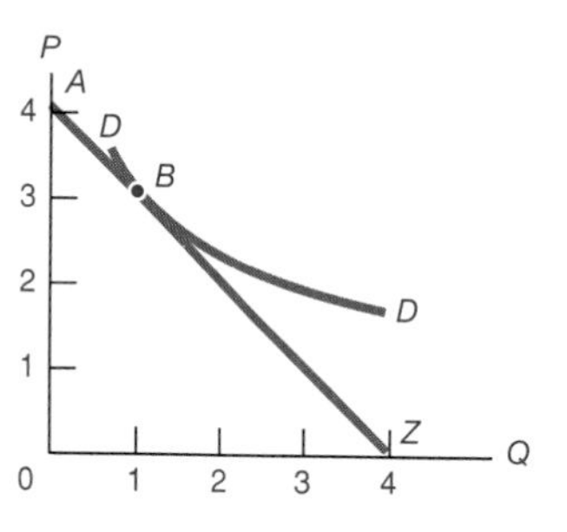

Figure 5-5

Value of demand elasticity	Description	Definition	Impact on revenues
Greater than one ($E_D > 1$)	Elastic demand	Percentage change in quantity demanded *greater* than percentage change in price	Revenues *increase* when price decreases
Equal to one ($E_D = 1$)	Unit-elastic demand	Percentage change in quantity demanded *equal* to percentage change in price	Revenues *unchanged* when price decreases
Less than one ($E_D < 1$)	Inelastic demand	Percentage change in quantity demanded *less* than percentage change in price	Revenues *decrease* when price decreases

Table 5-3. Summary of price elasticities

Make sure you understand these properties of price elasticities of demand.

Table 5-3 shows the major points to remember about price elasticities. This important table should be stored securely in your long-term memory.

A Baseball Example

An understanding of elasticity is crucial for many business decisions. Suppose you own a baseball franchise and are trying to increase your ticket revenues. Your team, the Albuquerque Dukes, usually operates with a half-empty stadium. The business manager comes in and says, "I estimate that the price elasticity for our tickets is 0.5 between $5 and $10 a ticket, 1.2 between $10 and $12 a ticket, and 2 between $12 and $15 a ticket. Our current price is $10 a ticket. What should we do?"

From the relationship between elasticity and revenue, you can see that if price is lowered below $10 a ticket, total revenues will go down because demand is price-inelastic. If price is raised above $10, total revenues will fall because demand is price-elastic in that range. Therefore, the ticket price of $10 will maximize revenues for the four ticket prices under consideration.

Determinants of Elasticities

Our analysis has concentrated solely on the measurement of elasticity. But why do some goods display elastic demands while others seem quite unresponsive to price?

For necessities like food, fuel, and shoes, demand tends to be inelastic. Such items are the staff of life and cannot easily be forgone when their prices rise. By contrast, you can substitute other goods when luxuries like ski vacations, 17-year-old Scotch whiskey, and designer clothing rise in price.

In addition, those goods that have ready substitutes tend to have higher price elasticities than those that have no substitutes. If all food or footwear prices rose 20 percent tomorrow, you would hardly expect people to stop eating or to go around barefoot, so food and footwear demands are price-inelastic. On the other hand, if hoof-and-mouth disease decimates cattle herds and drives up beef prices and the prices of leather shoes, people can turn to lamb or poultry for their meat needs and to other materials for their shoe needs. Therefore, beef and leather shoes show a high price elasticity.

The length of time that people have to respond to price changes also plays a role. A good example is that of gasoline. Suppose you are driving across the country when the price of gasoline suddenly increases. Will you consider selling your car and abandoning your vacation? Not likely. So in the short run, the elasticity of demand for gasoline may be close to zero.

In the long run, however, you can adjust your behavior to the higher price of gasoline. You can buy a smaller and more fuel-efficient car, buy a bicycle, take the train, or carpool with other people. Empirical studies confirm that in the long run the price elasticity of the demand for gasoline is around unity. For many goods, the ability to adjust consumption patterns implies that demand elasticities are higher in the long run than in the short run.

A fourth factor affecting price elasticities is the importance of a good in the consumer budget. Those goods that require a large fraction of income tend to be more responsive to price than those that are a trivial part of spending. Compare the effect of a doubling of automobile prices to a doubling of shoelace prices. People were extremely upset when gasoline prices rose in 1990, but they probably wouldn't notice if shoelace prices doubled. As a result, the demand for shoelaces is price-inelastic.

Economic factors determine the magnitude of price elasticities for individual goods: the degree to which a good is a necessity or a luxury, the extent to which substitutes are available, the time available for response, and the relative importance of a commodity in the consumer's budget.

Price Elasticity of Supply

What we did for demand, we can also do for supply. Economists define the price elasticity of supply as the responsiveness of the quantity supplied of a good to its market price.

More precisely, the **price elasticity of supply** measures the percentage change in quantity supplied in response to a 1 percent change in the good's price.

Suppose the amount supplied is perfectly fixed, as in the case of perishable fish brought to market to sell at whatever price they will fetch. This is the limiting case of perfectly inelastic supply or a vertical supply curve.

At the other extreme, say that a tiny cut in price will cause the amount supplied to fall to zero while the slightest rise in price will coax out an indefinitely large supply. Here, the ratio of the percentage change in quantity supplied to percentage change in price is extremely large and gives rise to a horizontal supply curve. This is the polar case of infinitely elastic supply.

Between these extremes, we call supply elastic or inelastic depending upon whether the percentage rise in quantity is larger or smaller than the percentage change in price. In the borderline unit-elastic case, where price elasticity of supply equals 1, the percentage increase of quantity supplied is exactly equal to the percentage increase in price.

You can readily see that the definitions of price elasticities of supply are exactly the same as those for price elasticities of demand. The only difference is that, for supply, the quantity response to price is positive, while for demand the response is negative.

The exact definition of the price elasticity of supply, E_S, is as follows:

$$E_S = \frac{\text{percentage change in quantity supplied}}{\text{percentage rise in price}}$$

Supply Elasticities

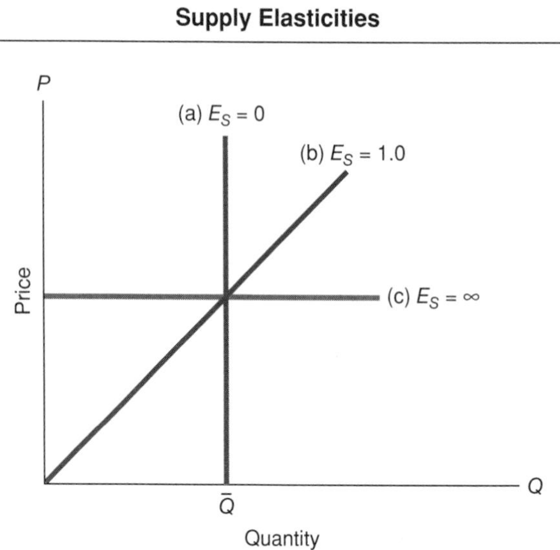

Figure 5-6. Supply elasticity depends upon producer response to price

When supply is fixed, supply elasticity is zero, as in curve **(a)**. Curve **(c)** displays an indefinitely large quantity response to price changes. Intermediate case **(b)** arises when quantity response is equal to price change.

Figure 5-6 displays three important cases of supply elasticity: the vertical supply curve showing perfectly inelastic supply, the horizontal supply curve displaying perfectly elastic supply, and an intermediate case of a straight line, going through the origin, illustrating the borderline case of unit elasticity.[1]

What factors determine supply elasticity? The major factor influencing supply elasticity is the extent to which production in the industry can be increased. If inputs can be easily found at going market prices, as is the case for the textile industry, then output can be greatly increased with little increase in price. This would indicate that supply elasticity is relatively large. On the other hand, if production capacity is severely limited, as is the case for the mining of South African gold, then even sharp increases in the price of gold will call forth

[1] You can determine the elasticity of a supply curve that is not a straight line in the fashion described for the demand curve in the footnote on page 69 by drawing the straight line that lies tangent to the curve at a point and measuring the elasticity of the tangential straight line.

but a small response in production of South African gold; this would be inelastic supply.

Another important factor in supply elasticities is the time period under consideration. A given change in price tends to have a larger effect on amount supplied as the time for suppliers to respond increases. For very brief periods after a price increase, firms may be unable to increase their inputs of labor, materials, and capital, so supply may be very price inelastic. However, as time passes and businesses can hire more labor, build new factories, and expand capacity, supply elasticities will become larger.

We have now completed our analysis of the technical aspects of elasticity and return to the mainstream of supply and demand.

B. Applications of Supply and Demand

Supply-and-demand analysis is one of the most useful tools that economics has to offer. But, as with any tool, proper application of supply and demand curves requires a great deal of practice to avoid stumbling into one of the common pitfalls of economic analysis.

We can use supply and demand to analyze a number of important microeconomic problems. One of the most interesting applications is to agriculture, where supply and demand allow us to understand the variability of farm incomes and to evaluate government measures to boost farm incomes. Another application is the effect of a tax, which is one of the ways that governments can intervene in markets.

The Economics of Agriculture

No sector provides a better laboratory to study the impact of changing supply and demand than the perfectly competitive agricultural sector. Farming is a vital part of the economy in many parts of the United States as well as in poor countries, and its products have always been one of America's major exports.

Long-Run Relative Decline of Farming

Farming was once our largest single industry. A hundred years ago, half the American population lived and worked on farms, but that number has declined to 3 percent of the work force today. What lies behind the decline of agriculture? Many people sought the higher incomes and more active social life of cities ("How can you keep them down on the farm after they've seen Paris?"); since the Civil War, black families have left the south in great numbers searching for better opportunities in northern cities.

In addition, technological progress has sharply reduced the demand for farm labor. Important advances include mechanization through tractors, combines, and cotton pickers; fertilization and irrigation; selective breeding and development of new hybrid seeds. All these innovations have vastly increased the productivity of agricultural inputs.

Finally, virtually every statistical study has shown that the demand for food tends to grow relatively slowly as incomes expand. This fact means that the demand for food tends to grow more slowly than does national income.

Decline of the Farm: Graphical Analysis

A single diagram can explain the sagging trend in farm prices better than libraries of books and editorials. Figure 5-7 shows an initial equilibrium with high prices at point *E*. Observe what happens to agriculture as the years go by. Demand for food increases with the growth of the American population and with exports to other lands. But because most foods are necessities, the demand shift is modest in comparison to growing average incomes.

What about supply? Although many people mistakenly think that farming is a backward business, statistical studies show that productivity (output per unit of input) has grown more rapidly in agri-

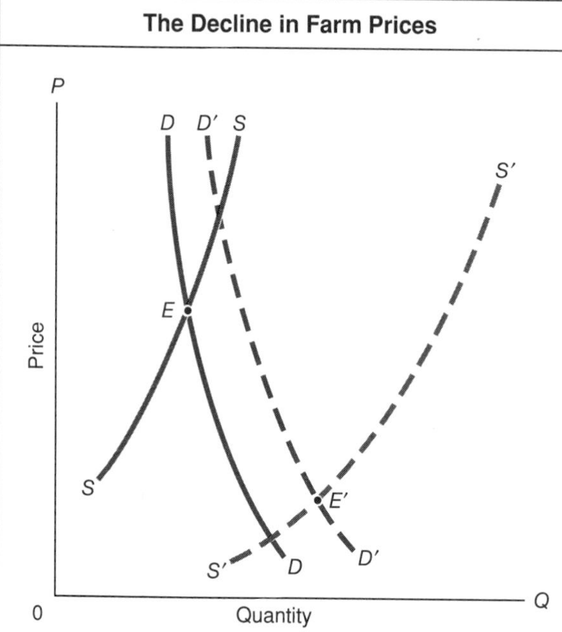

Figure 5-7. Agricultural distress results from expanding supply and price-inelastic demand

Equilibrium at *E* represents conditions in the farm sector decades ago. Demand for farm products tends to grow more slowly than the vast increase in supply generated by technological progress. Hence competitive farm prices tend to fall. Moreover, with price-inelastic demand, farm incomes decline with increases in supply.

culture than in most other industries. Rapid productivity growth has increased supply greatly as shown by the supply curve's shift from *SS* to *S′S′* in Figure 5-7.

What must happen at the new competitive equilibrium at point *E′*? Sharp increases in supply outpace modest increases in demand to produce a downward trend in farm prices. And this is precisely what has happened in recent decades: from 1951 to 1990, the prices of crops fell 67 percent relative to the overall price level! And with demand being inelastic, as prices fell, farm incomes tended to decline as well.

Crop Restrictions. In response to falling incomes, farmers often lobbied the federal government for economic assistance. Over the ages, governments here and abroad have taken many steps to help farmers. They have raised prices through price supports; they have curbed imports through tariffs and quotas; and they sometimes simply sent a subsidy check to farmers for every bushel of wheat or corn harvested.

One of the most controversial government farm programs requires farmers to restrict production. Figure 5-8 shows the economics of this policy. If the Department of Agriculture requires every farmer to "set aside" 20 percent of the corn acreage planted last year, this has the effect of shifting the supply curve of corn up and to the left. Because food demands are inelastic, crop restrictions not only raise the price of corn and other crops but also tend to raise farmers' total revenues and earnings.

Of course, consumers are hurt by the crop restrictions and higher prices—just as they would be if a flood or drought created a scarcity of foodstuffs. But this is the price society must pay when it comes to the aid of farmers by idling productive farm resources.

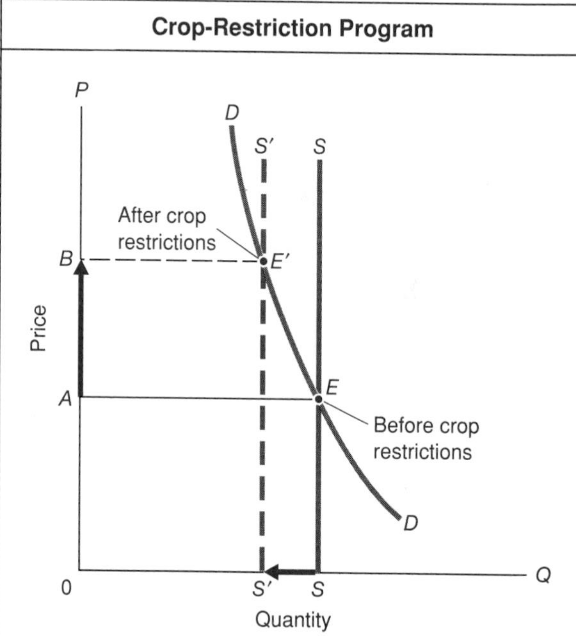

Figure 5-8. Crop-restriction programs raise both price and farm income

Before the crop restriction, the competitive market produces an equilibrium with low price at *E*. When government restricts production, the supply curve is shifted leftward to *S′S′*, moving equilibrium to *E′* and raising price to *B*. With inelastic demand, confirm that new revenue rectangle *0BE′S′* is larger than original revenue rectangle *0AES*.

Further Examples of Supply and Demand

Supply and demand apply, strictly speaking, only to perfectly competitive markets—where a homogeneous product is auctioned off in markets served by large numbers of buyers and sellers. Although perfect competition does not accurately describe most of the American economy, the supply-and-demand apparatus is a useful approximation that can be employed to analyze the impact of changing forces on prices and quantities.

Impact of a Tax on Price and Quantity

Consider the impact of a tax. Governments levy taxes on a wide variety of commodities—on cigarettes and alcohol, on payrolls and profits. Can we use supply-and-demand analysis to examine the microeconomic impact of a tax?

Yes. An important case is the gasoline tax. European countries set gasoline taxes at $2 to $4 per gallon, while in America the federal tax is but a few pennies per gallon. Advocates of higher gasoline taxes point out that the country would reap many benefits from a higher tax. The tax would bring in precious revenues to reduce our budget deficit. In addition, it would curb our growing oil consumption, reduce our dependence on insecure foreign sources of supply, and reduce pollution and other externalities of energy use.

Let us use supply and demand to analyze the incidence of a $1 tax on gasoline. By **incidence** we mean the ultimate economic impact of a tax. Is its burden shifted back completely onto the oil industry? Or will it be shifted forward to the consumers? The answer can be determined only from supply-and-demand analysis. Figure 5-9 shows the original equilibrium at *E*, the intersection of the *SS* and *DD* curves, at a gasoline price of $1 a gallon and total consumption of 100 billion gallons per year.

We portray the imposition of a $1 tax in the retail market for gasoline as an upward shift of the supply curve with the demand curve remaining unchanged. The demand curve does not shift because the quantity demanded at each price is unchanged after the gasoline tax increase. Consumers may neither know nor care whether the price at the pump goes to the government, the oil companies, or Saudi Arabia.

By contrast, the supply curve definitely does shift

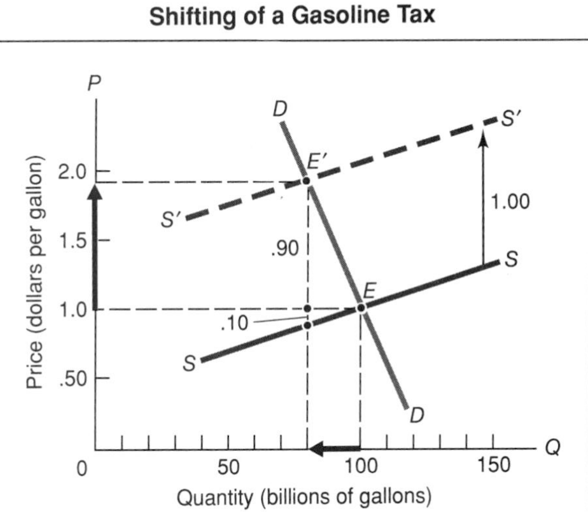

Figure 5-9. Gasoline tax falls on both consumer and producer

A $1 tax on gasoline shifts supply curve up $1 everywhere to give parallel supply curve, *S′S′*. This new supply curve intersects *DD* in new equilibrium at *E′*, where price to consumers has risen 90 cents and producers' price has fallen 10 cents. The blue arrows show changes in *P* and *Q*.

upward by $1. The reason is that producers are willing to sell a given quantity (say 100 billion gallons) only if they receive the same *net* price as before. That is, at each quantity supplied, the market price must rise by exactly the amount of the tax. If producers had originally been willing to sell 80 billion gallons at $0.90 per gallon, they would still be willing to sell the same amount at $1.90 (which, after subtracting the tax, yields the producers the same $0.90 per gallon).

What will be the new equilibrium price? The answer is found at the intersection of the new supply and demand curves, or at *E′*, where *S′S′* and *DD* meet. Because of the supply shift, the price is higher. Also, the quantity bought and sold is reduced. If we read the graph carefully, we find that the new equilibrium price has risen from $1 to about $1.90. The new equilibrium output, at which purchases and sales are in equilibrium, has fallen from 100 billion to about 80 billion gallons.

Who ultimately pays the tax? What is its incidence? Clearly the oil industry pays a small fraction, for it receives only 90 cents ($1.90 less the $1 tax) rather than $1. But the consumer bears most of the burden, with the retail price rising 90 cents, because supply is relatively price-elastic whereas demand is relatively price-inelastic.

In general, a tax will fall most heavily on consumers or on producers depending on the relative elasticities of demand and supply. A tax is shifted forward to consumers if the demand is inelastic relative to supply; a tax is shifted backward to producers if supply is relatively more inelastic than demand.

Supply-and-demand analysis can be applied to many other kinds of taxes. Using this apparatus we can understand how cigarette taxes affect both the prices and consumption of cigarettes; how taxes or tariffs on imports affect foreign trade; and how taxes on inputs like labor, capital, and land will affect wages, interest rates, and land rents.

Supply and Demand at Work

Everyday life offers countless economic issues that can be properly understood only by a careful analysis of supply and demand. Here are three:

- *Deregulation and airfares.* Until the late 1970s, the federal Civil Aeronautics Board limited competition among airlines by restricting the entry of airlines into most cities. Ticket prices were high, and many flights were virtually empty. Criticism led to deregulation by 1980 of pricing and entry on domestic routes, and the industry saw intense rivalry along with bankruptcy of poorly managed airlines.

  Figure 5-10(*a*) illustrates the effect of deregulation on airfares: increased competition increased supply, drove down the average price of air travel, and greatly increased the volume of air travel. Those who benefited most were people who bought discount fares and those flying from hub cities, such as New York and Chicago. International air service remained heavily regulated, however, and prices for regulated international travel were generally well above fares on comparable domestic routes.

- *Restriction of the supply of doctors.* The number of candidates for medical school is many times greater than is the number of students. For every medical school slot, several people take the required entrance examination. This limitation is enforced by stringent certification requirements imposed by the American Medical Association on medical schools.

  The restriction effectively decreases the supply of doctors, shifting the supply curve of physicians to the left, as shown in Figure 5-10(*b*). De-

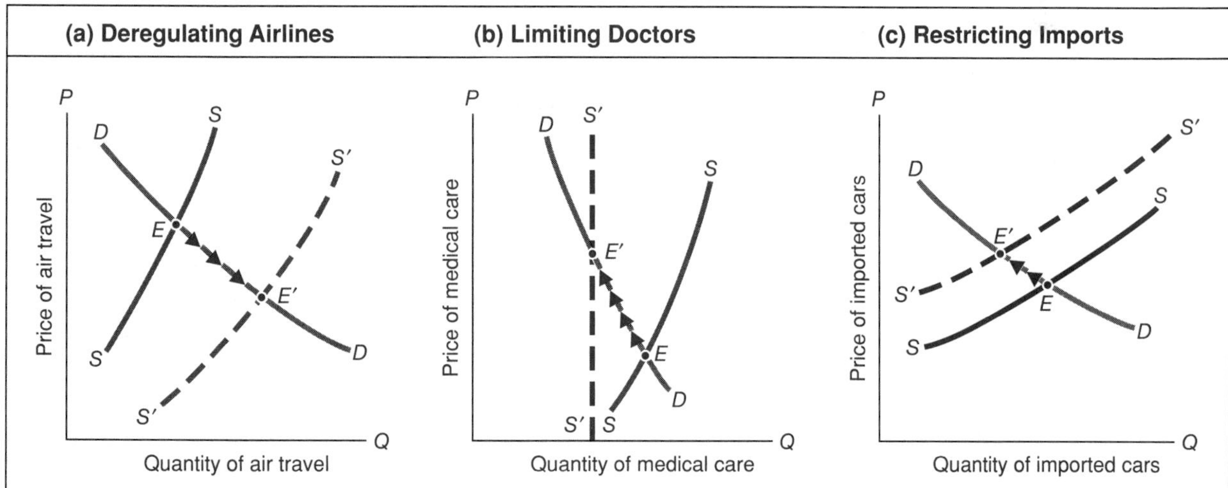

Figure 5-10. Applications of supply and demand

Supply-and-demand analysis can explain many important economic processes. Panel **(a)** shows how deregulation of the airline industry led to lower prices and more air travel; **(b)** shows how limiting the number of doctors can raise the price of medical care along with the income of doctors; **(c)** shows how an import tariff lowers the quantity and raises the price of imported cars.

fenders of this and similar certification procedures believe they are necessary to maintain the quality of medical care in the United States.

Because the demand for medical care is price-inelastic, restricting the number of medical students raises the price of medical care and increases the incomes of doctors. The higher quality comes at the expense of more costly health care for consumers.

- *A tariff on automobiles.* From the era of Henry Ford until the 1950s, the United States dominated the world automobile market. Then, with rapid technological progress in Europe and Japan came a flood of imported cars, swelling to a 25 percent market share by the 1980s. Automobile companies and unions, hit hard by excess capacity and unemployment, lobbied for restrictions on foreign-made cars.

  One proposed solution was to place a tariff on autos. (A tariff is a tax on imports.) A $2000 tariff would reduce the supply of imported autos, shifting the supply curve up and to the left. The price of imports would rise, and the quantity demanded would fall. See Figure 5-10(*c*).

  You can show in a separate diagram that a tariff increases the demand for domestic autos. Why? Because the price of a close substitute for domestic autos (imported autos) is higher after the tariff is added. Thus both the price and quantity of domestic autos rise, as the demand curve moves northeast along a given supply curve for domestic autos.

Government Intervention in Markets

Is the Law of Supply and Demand Immutable?

We now see how supply and demand work to determine prices and quantities in a competitive market economy. But we might want to ask ourselves at this point about the special role of government regulations, taxes, and spending along with the impact of foreign trade and many other factors.

We cannot deny that price depends on government actions. But they do not *add to* the forces of supply and demand; rather, they are among the numerous factors that *act through* supply and demand to determine price and quantity. If the government spends more money on boots or trucks or drug-rehabilitation research, this spending will shift out the demand for these products and raise their prices. But in the end, the competitive prices for military goods or research are still determined by supply and demand. In other words, supply and demand are not the ultimate explanations of price. They are instead useful general categories for analyzing and describing the multitude of forces impinging on price and quantity. Rather than giving final answers, supply and demand represent the beginning of economic understanding.

Once we have grasped how economic forces work through supply and demand, we can recognize the confusion of novices who declaim, "You can't repeal the law of supply and demand. King Canute knew he could not command the ocean tides to retreat from his throne on the sea. Likewise, any wise government knows it cannot evade, or interfere with, the workings of supply and demand."

It would be better not to have learned any economics than to be left with this opinion. Of course the government can affect price. Governments affect price by influencing supply or demand or both. Over the ages, governments have raised prices by restricting output. The embargo of Iraq in 1990 curbed oil production and raised oil prices sharply. Brazil has burned coffee to raise its price. We saw above how the U.S. government restricts acreage to raise food prices and farm incomes.

These governments have not violated the law of supply and demand. They have no secret economic weapons. They have simply worked through the law of supply and demand.

Prices Fixed by Law

There is one form of government interference with supply and demand that produces surprising and sometimes perverse economic effects. The government sometimes legislates maximum or minimum prices. Among the important examples are minimum wages for workers, rent controls for apartments, and interest-rate ceilings. In wartime, governments often impose wage and price controls to prevent large price changes.

This kind of interference with the laws of supply and demand is genuinely different from governments' acting through supply and demand. Let's see why.

Price Ceilings. Consider the supply and demand for gasoline. Let's say we start out in a situation where the price of gasoline is $1 a gallon. Then, because of a war or revolution, a drastic cut in oil supply occurs. Suppose that the oil prices rise sharply and the price of gasoline rises to $2 a gallon.

Populists rise to denounce the situation. They claim that consumers are being "gouged" by profiteering oil companies. Further, the rising prices threaten to ignite an inflationary spiral in the cost of living. Such are the arguments of price-control advocates everywhere.

In the face of rising prices, governments often control prices, as the American government did for oil from 1973 to 1981, a period of sharply rising energy prices. Suppose that the government passes a law setting the maximum price for gasoline at the old level of $1 a gallon. Figure 5-11 illustrates such a legal maximum price as the ceiling-price line *CJK*.

At the legal ceiling price, supply and demand do not match. Consumers want much more gasoline than producers are willing to supply at the going price. This is shown by the gap between *J* and *K*. This gap is so large that before long the pumps run dry. Somebody will have to go without the desired gasoline. If, on the other hand, the free market were allowed to operate, the market would clear with a price of $2 or more; consumers would grumble but would willingly pay the higher price rather than go without fuel.

Economic Effects of a Maximum Price Ceiling on Gasoline

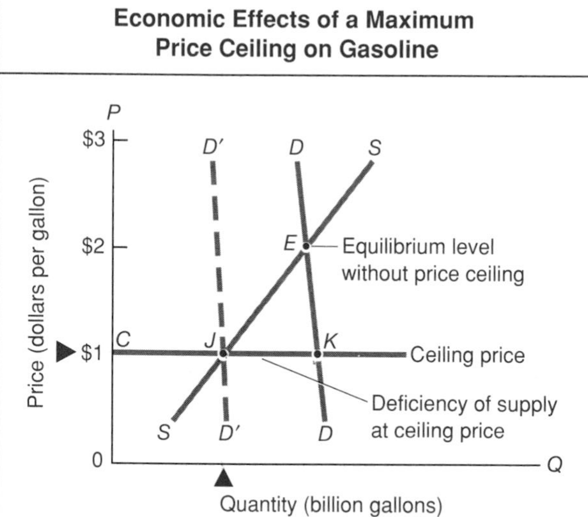

Figure 5-11. A legal maximum price, without rationing, leaves a gap between demand and supply

Without a legal price ceiling, price would rise to *E*. At the ceiling price of $1, supply and demand do not balance and some method of rationing, formal or informal, is needed to allocate the short supply and bring the actual demand down to *D′D′*.

But the market cannot clear because it is against the law for producers to charge a higher price. There follows a period of frustration and *shortage*— a game of musical cars in which somebody is left without gasoline when the pump runs dry. The inadequate supply of gasoline must somehow be rationed. At first, this may be done by "first come, first served," with or without limiting sales to each customer. Lines form, and much time has to be spent foraging for fuel.

Rationing. Eventually, some kind of *non-price rationing mechanism* evolves. For gasoline and other storable goods, the shortage is often managed by making people wait in line—rationing by the queue. Or, people who have access to the rationed good engage in *black-market sales*, which are illegal transactions above the regulated price. There is great waste as people spend valuable time trying to secure their needs. Nobody is happy, least of all the harassed seller. Eventually, governments design a more efficient way of non-price rationing through formal allocation or coupon rationing.

Under *coupon rationing*, each customer must have a coupon as well as money to buy the goods— in effect, there are two kinds of money. When rationing is adopted and coupons are meted out according to family size, occupational need, or other criteria, shortages disappear because demand is limited by the allocation of coupons.

Just how do ration coupons change the supply-and-demand picture? Clearly, the government must issue just enough of them to lower the demand curve to *D′D′* in Figure 5-11, where supply and the new demand balance at the ceiling price. If too many coupons are issued, there is excess demand and shortages and lines reappear, but to a lesser degree. If too few coupons are issued, stocks of goods will pile up and the price will fall below the ceiling. This is the signal for liberalizing the ration.

Coupon rationing has fallen out of favor in most market economies. But the lessons of rationing and price controls extend far beyond the problems of war or energy crises, for such abnormalities illuminate the function of prices in normal times.

The key point is that goods are always scarce; society can never fulfill everyone's wishes. *In normal times, price itself rations out the scarce supplies.* In periods of shortage, market prices rise to choke off excessive consumption and to encourage production; in periods of glut, prices fall to encourage consumption and discourage production. When governments step in to interfere with supply and demand, money no longer fills the role of rationer. Waste, inefficiency, and aggravation are certain companions of these interferences.

Minimum Floors and Maximum Ceilings

Although political pressures always exist to keep prices down and wages up, experience has taught that sector-by-sector price and wage controls tend to create major economic distortions. Economists therefore generally recommend that legal controls on prices be reserved for emergencies.

Nevertheless, as Adam Smith well knew when he protested against mercantilist policies of an earlier age, most economic systems are plagued by inefficiencies stemming from well-meaning but inexpert interferences with the mechanisms of supply and demand. The three examples of government intervention presented in Figure 5-12—the minimum wage, rent controls on housing, and interest-rate ceilings—illustrate the surprising side effects that can arise when governments interfere with market determination of price and quantity.

- *Minimum wage rates.* Governments sometimes legislate a minimum wage rate that sets a floor for most jobs. Although almost everyone would agree to the importance of high wages in combating poverty, studies show that a high minimum wage often hurts those it is designed to help. What does it profit an unskilled youth to know that a job will pay $4 an hour if no jobs are available? Figure 5-12(a) shows how a high minimum wage creates a pool of unemployed workers.

  We might also consider the impact of a rise in the minimum wage on the total wages of low-wage, low-skilled workers. Studies suggest that the price elasticity of demand for low-skilled workers is greater than unity, as firms substitute medium-skilled workers, capital, and low-wage

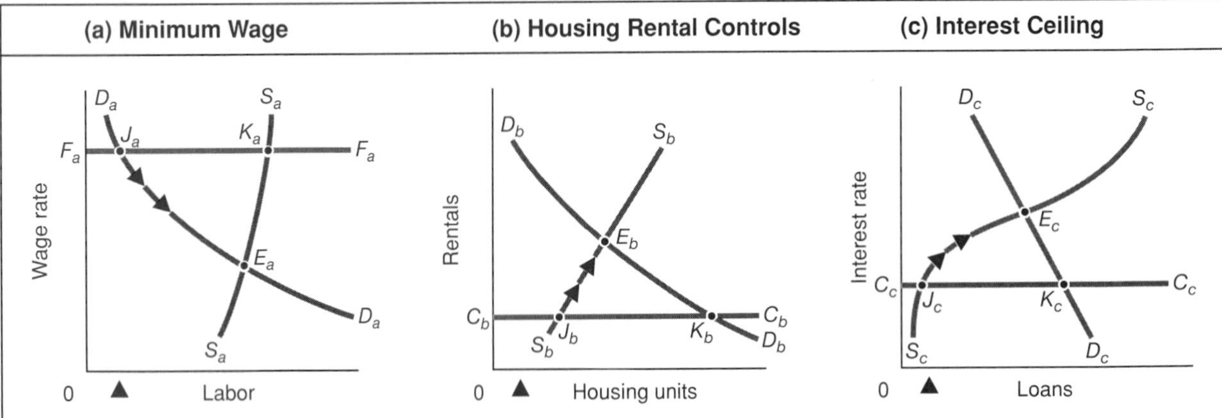

Figure 5-12. Effects of government price controls

(a) Setting minimum-wage floor at F_aF_a, high above free-market equilibrium rate E_a, results in forced equilibrium at J_a. The too-high floor freezes workers into unemployment from J_a to K_a. Lowering the minimum wage moves us down along D_aD_a, as shown by blue arrows, raising employment.

(b) Setting maximum rental ceiling at C_bC_b, far below free-market equilibrium at E_b, causes fringe of unsatisfied renters between J_b and K_b. Raising the ceiling on rentals reduces excess demand and moves industry up S_bS_b as shown by blue arrows: new construction provides more living space, and old quarters are used more efficiently.

(c) Setting maximum interest rates at C_cC_c, far below free-market equilibrium rate E_c, results in drying up of available funds. Desperate borrowers between J_c and K_c might turn to loan sharks. Raising interest ceiling can actually reduce interest rates paid by many.

foreign workers for domestic low-skilled workers. If the demand for low-wage workers is elastic, then can you see why an increase in the minimum wage will *lower* the total wages earned by this group?

- *Rent controls.* No one likes to pay rent. Yet scarcities of land and urban housing often cause rents to soar in cities. In response to rising rents and hostility toward landlords, governments sometimes impose rent controls.

  The supply-and-demand analysis shown in Figure 5-12(*b*) displays the effects of rent controls. At the controlled rental price, there is a large group of buyers who cannot find apartments. People stay too long in large apartments because rents are kept below market levels. Non-price rationing occurs, and people have to bribe landlords or pay enormous security deposits to obtain a rental apartment. New building—along with maintaining and upgrading existing rent-controlled dwellings—suffers.

  Historical experience in New York, Berkeley, Warsaw, and other cities shows perverse impacts of rent controls on new construction and maintenance. New York has seen tens of thousands of buildings abandoned because the controlled rents were too low to cover expenses and taxes. In the wry words of one European critic, "Except for bombing, nothing is as efficient at destroying a city as rent controls."

- *Interest-rate ceilings.* Interest rates are the price paid to borrow money for a period of time. For example, when you borrow $5000 to finance your education, you might have to pay 10 percent per year (i.e., $500 per year) in interest on the borrowed funds.

  Since biblical times, the charging of interest has been an object of suspicion because people object to paying lenders for the use of funds when lenders perform no visible service. In earlier times, lending at interest was a crime called *usury,* and even today some states place a legal maximum on interest rates.

  Unfortunately, the interest-rate ceiling is sometimes far below the free-market rate. While an interest rate of 12 percent per year might seem high for a credit-card or car loan, it might not cover borrowing costs, administrative costs, and the risk of default. Figure 5-12(*c*) shows the impact of too low a ceiling on interest rates. Funds dry up. Banks and other financial institutions refuse to make unprofitable loans at the legal rate. Those who are the intended beneficiaries of controls find that they cannot borrow from anyone other than a loan shark, who might charge "six for five," or $600 in payment in a week for every $500 borrowed. The inexpensive loan you cannot get does you no good.

Similar examples of interference with markets can be found in all societies. Indeed, socialist economies have attempted on a wholesale scale to circumvent supply and demand through government commands, regulations, propaganda, and penalties. The long breadlines in Moscow, Beijing, and Prague testify that the lessons of supply and demand apply everywhere and not only in countries that designate themselves as market economies.

● This concludes our survey of supply-and-demand analysis. In the next few chapters we investigate the foundations of demand and supply in consumer choice and business costs. These chapters will help to explain patterns of pricing in competitive and monopolistic markets, to analyze why vital necessities like water are cheap while luxuries like diamonds are expensive, and to show why competitive markets lead to an efficient (although possibly inequitable) allocation of resources. ●

SUMMARY

A. Elasticity of Demand and Supply

1. Price elasticity of demand measures the quantitative response of demand to a change in price. The price elasticity of demand (E_D) is defined as the percentage change in quantity demanded divided by the percentage change in price. That is:

$$\text{Price elasticity of demand} = E_D = \frac{\text{percentage change in quantity demanded}}{\text{percentage change in price}}$$

   In this calculation, the sign is taken to be positive, and P and Q are averages of old and new values.

2. We divide price elasticities into three categories. (*a*) Demand is elastic when the percentage change in quantity demanded exceeds the percentage change in price; that is, $E_D > 1$. (*b*) Demand is inelastic when the percentage change in quantity demanded is less than the percentage change in price; here $E_D < 1$. (*c*) The borderline case where percentage change in quantity demanded exactly equals percentage change in price is the unit-elastic case where $E_D = 1$.

3. Price elasticity is a pure number, involving percentages; it should not be confused with slope.

4. Demand elasticity is related to the impact of a price change on total revenue. Demand is elastic if a price reduction increases total revenue; demand is inelastic if a price reduction decreases total revenue; in the unit-elastic case, a price change has no effect on total revenue.

5. Price elasticity of demand tends to be low for necessities like food and shelter and high for luxuries like snowmobiles and air travel. Other factors affecting price elasticity are the extent to which a good has ready substitutes, the length of time that consumers have to adjust to price changes, and the fraction of the consumer budget spent on the commodity.

6. Price elasticity of supply measures the percentage change of output supplied by producers when the market price changes by a given percentage.

B. Applications of Supply and Demand

7. One of the most fruitful arenas for application of supply and demand is agriculture. Improvements in agricultural technology mean that supply increases greatly, while demand for food rises less than proportionately with income. Hence free-market prices for foodstuffs tend to fall. No wonder that governments have adopted a variety of programs, like crop restrictions, to prop up farm incomes.

8. A commodity tax shifts the supply-and-demand equilibrium. The tax's burden (or incidence) will fall more heavily on consumers than on producers to the degree that the demand is inelastic relative to supply.

9. A thousand forces affect price. But in a freely competitive market, they do so only by acting *through* supply and demand. Governments usually affect

price and quantity in individual markets by operating through supply and demand.

10. Governments occasionally interfere with the workings of competitive markets by setting maximum ceilings or minimum floors on prices. In such situations, quantity supplied need no longer equal quantity demanded; ceilings lead to excess supply while floors lead to excess demand. Distortions and inefficiencies result. Unless the discrepancies between supply and demand are removed by formal allocation or coupon rationing, disorder and black markets may result.

CONCEPTS FOR REVIEW

Elasticity concepts
price elasticity of demand, supply
elastic, inelastic, unit-elastic demand
E_D = % change in Q/% change in P
total revenue = $P \times Q$
determinants of elasticity

Applications of supply and demand
incidence of a tax:
forward-shifting onto consumers
backward shifting onto producers
rationing by price

distortions from price controls
black markets vs. coupon rationing

QUESTIONS FOR DISCUSSION

1. "A good harvest will generally lower the income of farmers." Illustrate this proposition using a supply-and-demand diagram.
2. For each pair of commodities, state which you think is the more price-elastic and give your reasons: perfume and salt; penicillin and ice cream; automobiles and automobile tires; ice cream and chocolate ice cream.
3. "The price drops by 1 percent, causing the quantity demanded to rise by 2 percent. Demand is therefore elastic, with $E_D > 1$." If you change 2 to $\frac{1}{2}$ in the first sentence, what two other changes will be required in the quotation?
4. Consider a competitive market for apartments. What would be the effect on the equilibrium output and price after the following changes (other things held equal)? In each case, explain your answer using supply and demand.
   (a) A rise in the income of consumers.
   (b) A $10-per-month tax on apartment rentals.
   (c) A government edict saying apartments could not rent for more than $200 per month.
   (d) A new construction technique allowing apartments to be built at half the cost.
   (e) A 20 percent increase in construction workers' wages.
5. A recent study concluded, "It is one of the ironies of the apartment market in New York that, although there are three times more rent-regulated apartments than free-market apartments, yet it is much easier to find a vacant, unregulated apartment." Using supply-and-demand analysis, explain this apparent paradox.
6. Explain and show graphically how the 1990–1991 embargo of Iraqi oil exports affected oil supply and demand and thereby the equilibrium oil price and quantity.
7. A conservative critic of government programs has written, "Governments know how to do one thing well. They know how to create shortages and surpluses." Explain this quotation using examples like the minimum wage or interest-rate ceilings.
8. Reread the baseball example on page 70. Create a table like Table 5-2 in which you calculate elasticities for different price changes. Assuming you sell 15,000 tickets at a ticket price of $10, add another column that shows the revenues for each price. Does this example verify the relationship between elasticities and total revenues?
9. In the third example in Figure 5-10, a tariff of $2000 is imposed on imported automobiles. Show the impact of this tariff on the supply and the demand, and on the equilibrium price and quantity, of American automobiles. Explain why American auto companies and autoworkers often support import restraints on automobiles.

10. Elasticity problems:
    (a) The demand for crude oil is estimated to have a short-run price elasticity of 0.05. If the initial price of oil were $3 per barrel, what would be the effect on oil price and quantity of an embargo that curbed world oil supply by 5 percent?
    (b) To show that elasticities are independent of units, refer back to Table 5-1. Calculate the elasticities between each demand pair. Change the price units from dollars to pennies; change the quantity units from bushels to tons, using the conversion of 30 bushels equals 1 ton. Then recalculate the elasticities in the first two rows. Explain why you get the same answer.
    (c) Demand studies find that the price elasticity of demand for crack is 0.1. Suppose that half the crack users in New York City support their habit by criminal activities. Using supply-and-demand analysis, show the impact on crime in New York City of a tough law-enforcement program that decreases the supply of crack into the New York market by 50 percent. What would be the effect on criminal activities and on drug use of legalizing crack if this lowered the price of crack by 90 percent? What would be the impact on price and addiction of a program that successfully rehabilitated half of the crack users?
11. **Advanced problem** for those who like simple geometry and algebra: Justify the E_D rule given in the footnote on page 69 for a straight line. In the triangle shown in Figure 5-13, the demand curve has the equation $Q = b - (b/a)P$, where b is the Q intercept and a the P intercept. The inverted slope of DD is $-(dQ/dP) = -(\Delta Q/\Delta P) = b/a$. Now apply the formula $E_D = -(dQ/dP)(P/Q)$ to get $E_D = (b/a)\{P/[b - (b/a)P]\} = P/(a - P)$—the ratio of the lower vertical bracket to the upper. Can you show, by the property of similar triangles, that $E_D = P/(a - P) = bC/aC$ equals "the ratio of the length of the line segment below the point to the length of the line segment above the point," as stated in the footnote on page 69?

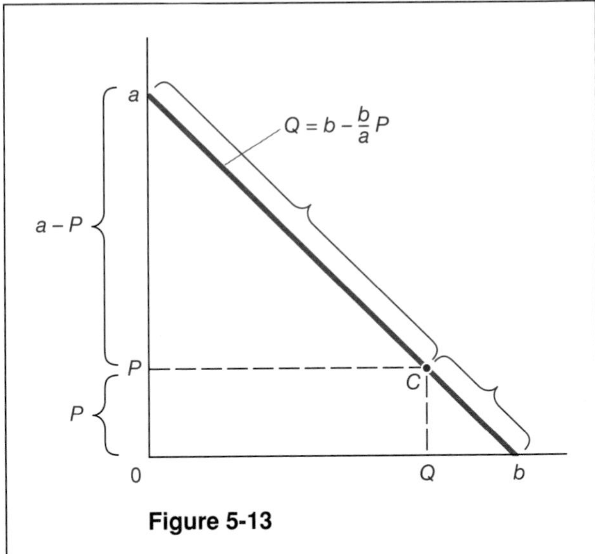

Figure 5-13

CHAPTER 6

DEMAND AND CONSUMER BEHAVIOR

What is a cynic? A man who knows the price of everything and the value of nothing.

Oscar Wilde

Each of us makes countless choices every day. Should we eat breakfast or sleep late? Drink coffee, tea, or milk at breakfast? Spend our time studying economics or enjoying a concert? Buy a new car or fix our old one? Spend our income or save for the future? These decisions, which constitute consumption choices or consumer behavior, are the stuff of our daily existence.

One of the major tasks of economics is to explain the principles of consumer behavior. We have encountered the law of demand and know that people tend to buy more of a good when its price is low than when its price is high. And in the preceding pages we learned about the price elasticities of different commodities. This chapter extends our survey of demand. We shall see how individual preferences, or utility for different bundles of consumption goods, explain consumer behavior and market demands.

The theory of utility and consumer behavior will help unravel certain mysteries. People sometimes wonder why the source of all life, water, is so cheap while useless luxuries like furs are so expensive. The concept known as consumer surplus will help explain this paradox.

Choice and Utility Theory

In explaining consumer behavior, we rely on the fundamental premise that people tend to choose those goods and services they value most highly. To describe the way consumers choose among different consumption possibilities, economists a century ago developed the notion of utility. From the notion of utility, they were able to derive the demand curve and explain its properties.

What do we mean by utility? In a word, **utility** denotes satisfaction. More precisely, it refers to the subjective pleasure or usefulness that a person derives from consuming a good or service. We should not identify utility with any precise psychological function or feeling that can be observed or measured. Rather, utility is a scientific construct that economists use to understand how rational consumers divide their limited resources among the commodities that provide them with satisfaction.

Marginal Utility and the Law of Diminishing Marginal Utility

How does utility apply to the theory of demand? Say that consuming the first unit of a good like ice cream gives you a certain level of satisfaction or utility. Now imagine consuming a second unit. Your total utility goes up because the second unit of the good gives you some additional utility. What about adding a third and fourth unit of the same good?

We now encounter a new and fundamental economic concept, that of marginal utility. When you eat a second unit of ice cream, you will get some additional satisfaction or utility. The increment to your utility is called **marginal utility.**

The expression "marginal" is a key term in economics and is always used in the sense of "extra."

A century ago economists formulated an important relationship quite analogous to the law of diminishing returns. When economists thought about utility, they enunciated the **law of diminishing marginal utility.** This law states that the amount of extra or marginal utility declines as a person consumes more and more of a good.

What is the reason for this law? Utility tends to increase as you consume more of a good. However, according to the law of diminishing marginal utility, as you consume more and more, your total utility will grow at a slower and slower rate. Growth in total utility slows because your marginal utility (the extra utility added by the last unit consumed of a good) diminishes as more of the good is consumed. The diminishing marginal utility results from the fact that your enjoyment of the good drops off as more and more of it is consumed.

The law of diminishing marginal utility states that, as the amount of a good consumed increases, the marginal utility of that good tends to diminish.

A Numerical Example

We can illustrate utility numerically in the table accompanying Figure 6-1. The table shows in column (2) that total utility (U) enjoyed increases as consumption (Q) grows, but grows at a decreasing rate. Column (3) measures marginal utility as the extra utility gained when one extra unit of the good is consumed. Thus as the individual consumes 2 units, the marginal utility is $7 - 4 = 3$ units of utility (call these units "utils").

Focus next on column (3). The fact that marginal utility declines with higher consumption illustrates the law of diminishing marginal utility.

Figure 6-1 shows both the level of total utility and the marginal utility. In part (*a*), the gray blocks add up to the total utility at each level of consumption. In addition, the smooth black curve shows the smoothed utility level for fractional units of consumption. It shows utility increasing, but at a decreasing rate. Figure 6-1(*b*) depicts marginal utilities. Each of the gray blocks of marginal utility is the same size as the corresponding block of total utility in (*a*). The straight blue line in (*b*) is the smoothed curve of marginal utility.

The law of diminishing marginal utility implies that the marginal utility (MU) curve in Figure 6-1(*b*) must slope downward. This is exactly equivalent to saying that the total utility curve in Figure 6-1(*a*) must look concave like a dome.

Relationship of Total and Marginal Utility. Using Figure 6-1, we can easily see that the total utility of consuming a certain amount is equal to the sum of the marginal utilities up to that point. For example, assume that 3 units are consumed. Column (2) of the table shows that the total utility is 9 units. In column (3) we see that the sum of the marginal utilities of the first 3 units is also $4 + 3 + 2 = 9$ units.

Examining Figure 6-1(*b*), we see that the total area under the marginal utility curve at a particular level of consumption—as measured either by blocks or by the area under the smooth MU curve—must equal the height of the total utility curve shown for the same number of units in Figure 6-1(*a*).

Whether we examine this relationship using tables or graphs, we see that total utility is the sum of all the marginal utilities that were added from the beginning.

History of Utility Theory

Modern utility theory has its source in utilitarianism, which has been one of the major currents of Western intellectual thought for the last two centuries. The notion of utility arose soon after 1700 among students of mathematical probability. Thus Daniel Bernoulli, a member of the brilliant Swiss family of mathematicians, observed in 1738 that people act as if the dollar they stand to gain in a fair bet is worth less to them than the dollar they stand to lose. This means they are averse to risk and successive new dollars of wealth bring them smaller and smaller increments of true utility.[1]

An early introduction of the utility notion into the social sciences was accomplished by the English philosopher Jeremy Bentham (1748–1831). After studying legal theory, and under the influence of Adam Smith's doctrines, Bentham turned to the study of the principles necessary for drawing up social legislation. He proposed that society should be organized on the "principle of utility," which he defined as the "property in any object . . . to pro-

[1] The economics of risk, uncertainty, and gambling are examined in Chapter 12.

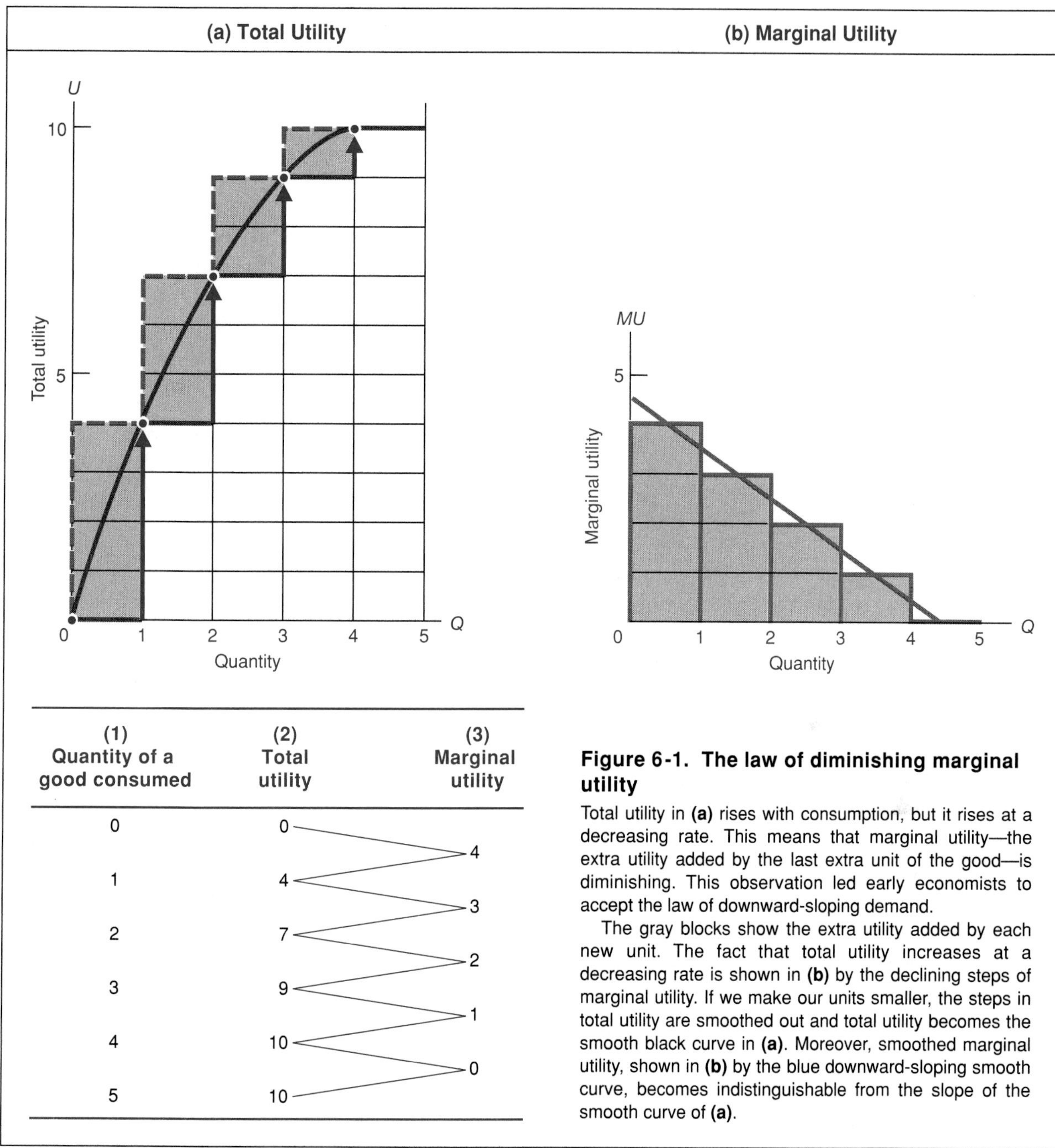

(1) Quantity of a good consumed	(2) Total utility	(3) Marginal utility
0	0	
		4
1	4	
		3
2	7	
		2
3	9	
		1
4	10	
		0
5	10	

Figure 6-1. The law of diminishing marginal utility

Total utility in **(a)** rises with consumption, but it rises at a decreasing rate. This means that marginal utility—the extra utility added by the last extra unit of the good—is diminishing. This observation led early economists to accept the law of downward-sloping demand.

The gray blocks show the extra utility added by each new unit. The fact that total utility increases at a decreasing rate is shown in **(b)** by the declining steps of marginal utility. If we make our units smaller, the steps in total utility are smoothed out and total utility becomes the smooth black curve in **(a)**. Moreover, smoothed marginal utility, shown in **(b)** by the blue downward-sloping smooth curve, becomes indistinguishable from the slope of the smooth curve of **(a)**.

duce pleasure, good or happiness or to prevent . . . pain, evil or unhappiness."[2] All legislation, according to Bentham, should be designed on *utilitarian* principles, to promote "the greatest happiness of the greatest number." Among his other legislative proposals were quite modern-sounding ideas about crime and punishment in which he suggested that raising the "pain" to the criminal by harsh punishments would deter crimes.

Bentham's views about utility seem primitive to

[2] *An Introduction to the Principles of Morals* (1789). Note that the term "utility" was used by Bentham in quite a different way from the more common usage today as something that is useful.

many people today. But 200 years ago they were revolutionary because they emphasized that social and economic policies should be designed to achieve certain practical results, whereas earlier justifications were based on tradition or on religious doctrine. Today, many political thinkers defend their legislative proposals with utilitarian notions of what will make the largest number of people best off.

The next step in the development of utility theory came when the neoclassical economists—such as William Stanley Jevons (1835–1882)—extended Bentham's utility concept to explain consumer behavior. Jevons thought economic theory was a "calculus of pleasure and pain" and showed how rational people would base their consumption decisions on the extra or marginal utility of each good. Many utilitarians of the nineteenth century believed that utility was a psychic reality—directly and cardinally measurable, like length or temperature. They looked to their own sentiments for affirmation of the law of diminishing marginal utility.

Ordinal Utility. Economists today reject the notion of a cardinal, measurable utility that is attached to consumption of ordinary goods like shoes or coffee. Indeed, we can easily derive demand curves without ever mentioning the notion of utility. What counts for modern demand theory is whether a consumer prefers certain bundles of commodities more than others, an approach represented by statements like "A is preferred to B." No more than this "ordinal utility" statement is required to establish firmly the general properties of market demand curves described in this chapter and in its appendix.[3]

[3] A statement such as "situation A is preferred to situation B"—which does not require that we know *how much* A is preferred to B—is called "ordinal," or dimensionless. Ordinal variables are ones that we can rank in order, but for which there is no measure of the quantitative difference between the situations. We might rank pictures in an exhibition in terms of the order of their beauty without having a quantitative measure of beauty.

For certain special situations the concept of "cardinal," or dimensional, utility is useful. An example of a cardinal measure comes when we say that a substance at 100 K (kelvin) is twice as hot as one at 50 K. People's behavior under conditions of uncertainty is today often analyzed using a cardinal concept of utility. This topic will be analyzed further in Chapter 12.

Equilibrium Condition: Equal Marginal Utilities per Dollar for Every Good

What is the condition under which I, as a consumer, am most satisfied with my market basket of consumption goods? We say that a consumer attempts to maximize his or her utility, or the amount of satisfaction or happiness produced by purchases of consumer goods. Can we see what a rule for such an optimal decision would be? Certainly I would not expect that the last egg I am buying brings exactly the same marginal utility as the last pair of shoes I am buying, for shoes cost much more per unit than eggs. It would seem more reasonable that I should keep buying a good which costs twice as much per unit as another good until it brings me just twice as much in marginal utility.

This leads to the conclusion that I should arrange my consumption so that every single good is bringing me the same marginal utility per dollar of expenditure. In such a situation, I am attaining maximum satisfaction or utility from my purchases.

The fundamental condition of maximum satisfaction or utility is therefore the following: A consumer with a fixed income and facing given market prices of goods will achieve maximum satisfaction or utility when the marginal utility of the last dollar spent on each good is exactly the same as the marginal utility of the last dollar spent on any other good.

Why must this condition hold? If any one good gave more marginal utility per dollar, I would increase my utility by taking money away from other goods and spending more on that good—until the law of diminishing marginal utility drove its marginal utility per dollar down to equality with that of other goods. If any good gave less marginal utility per dollar than the common level, I would buy less of it until the marginal utility of the last dollar spent on it had risen back to the common level.[4] The

[4] At a few places in economics the indivisibility of units is important and cannot be glossed over. Thus, Chevrolets cannot be divided into arbitrarily small portions the way juice can. Suppose I buy one but definitely not two Cadillacs. Then the marginal utility of the first car is enough larger than the marginal utility of the same number of dollars spent elsewhere to induce me to buy this first unit. The marginal utility that the second Cadillac would bring is enough less to ensure I do not buy it. When indivisibility matters, our equality rule for equilibrium can be restated as an inequality rule.

common marginal utility per dollar of all commodities in consumer equilibrium is called the "marginal utility of income." It measures the additional utility that would be gained if the consumer could enjoy an extra dollar's worth of consumption.

This fundamental condition of consumer equilibrium can be written in terms of the marginal utilities (*MU*) and prices (*P*) of the different goods in the following compact way:

$$\frac{MU_{\text{good 1}}}{P_1} = \frac{MU_{\text{good 2}}}{P_2} = \frac{MU_{\text{good 3}}}{P_3} = \cdots = MU \text{ per \$ of income}$$

Why Demand Curves Slope Downward

Using this fundamental rule for consumer behavior, we can easily see why demand curves slope downward. For simplicity, hold the common marginal utility per dollar of income constant. Then increase the price of good 1. With no change in quantity consumed, the first ratio (i.e., $MU_{\text{good 1}}/P_1$) will be below the *MU* per dollar of all other goods. The consumer will therefore have to readjust the consumption of good 1. How? By (*a*) lowering the consumption of good 1; (*b*) thereby raising the *MU* of good 1; until (*c*) at the new reduced level of consumption of good 1, the new marginal utility per dollar spent on good 1 is again equal to the *MU* per dollar spent on other goods.

Therefore, a higher price for a good reduces the consumer's optimal consumption of that commodity; this shows why demand curves slope downward.

Economizing on the Use of Time

The principle of stretching a budget so as to maximize satisfaction is not limited to the spending of money but applies to many other areas, such as the use of time. Our "time budget" is limited to 24 hours a day whether we are rich or poor in dollars. We can therefore apply the same concepts to time budgets that we applied earlier to dollar budgets.

Suppose that, after satisfying all your obligations, you have 3 hours a day of free time and can devote it to playing cards, listening to music, or reading. What is the best way to allocate your time? Let's ignore the possibility that time spent on some of these activities might be an investment that will enhance your earning power in the future. Rather, assume that these are all pure consumption or utility-yielding pursuits. The principles of consumer choice would suggest that you will make the best use of your time when you equalize the marginal utilities of the last minute spent on each activity.

To take another example, suppose you want to maximize your learning or your grade-point average but you have only a limited amount of time available. Should you study each subject for the same amount of time? Probably not. You may find that an equal study time for economics, history, and chemistry will not yield the same amount of learning in the last minute. If the last minute produces a greater marginal grade advantage in chemistry than in history, then you would raise your grade-point average by shifting additional minutes from history to chemistry, and so on until the last minute yields the same incremental learning in each subject.

The same rule of maximum utility per hour can be applied to many different areas of life. It is not merely a law of economics. It is a law of rational choice.

Are Consumers Wizards?

A word of caution is in order about how we view consumers. We consumers are not expected to be wizards. We may make most of our decisions unconsciously or just out of habit. What is assumed is that consumers are fairly *consistent* in their tastes and actions—that they do not flail around in unpredictable ways, making themselves miserable by persistent errors of judgment or arithmetic. If enough people act consistently, avoiding erratic changes in buying behavior, our scientific theory will provide a tolerable approximation to the facts.

An Alternative Approach: Substitution Effect and Income Effect

The concept of marginal utility has helped explain the fundamental law of downward-sloping demand. But over the last few decades, economists have developed an alternative approach to analysis of demand—one that makes no mention of marginal utility. This alternative approach uses "indifference curves," which are explained in the appendix to this chapter, to rigorously and consistently produce the major propositions about consumer behavior. This approach also helps explain the factors that tend to make the responsiveness of quantity demanded to price—the price elasticity of demand—large or small.

Indifference analysis asks about the substitution effect and the income effect of a change in price. By looking at these, we can see why the quantity demanded of a good declines as its price rises.

Substitution Effect

The first factor explaining diminishing consumption when price rises is an obvious one. If the price of coffee goes up while other prices do not, then coffee has become relatively more expensive.

When coffee becomes a more expensive source of stimulation, less coffee and more tea or cocoa will be bought. Similarly, as videocassettes decline in price relative to movie tickets, we will seek more of our amusement in the cheaper diversion. More generally, the **substitution effect** says that, when the price of a good rises, consumers will tend to substitute other goods for the more expensive good in order to achieve desired satisfaction most cheaply.

Consumers, then, behave the way businesses do when the rise in price of an input causes firms to substitute cheap inputs for the more expensive input. By this process of substitution, businesses can produce the same output at least total cost. Similarly, when consumers substitute less expensive goods, they are buying satisfaction at least cost.

Income Effect

In addition, when your money income is fixed, a price increase is just like a reduction in your real income or purchasing power. More specifically, the **income effect** signifies the impact of a price change on consumers' real incomes. When a price rises and money incomes are fixed, consumers' real incomes fall and they are likely to buy less of almost all goods (including the good whose price has risen). With a lower real income, you will now want to buy less coffee. Thus, the income effect will normally reinforce the substitution effect in making the demand curve downward sloping.

To obtain a quantitative measure of the income effect, we examine a good's **income elasticity.** This term denotes the percentage change in quantity demanded divided by the percentage change in income, holding other things, such as prices, equal. High income elasticities, such as are found for airline travel or VCRs, indicate that the demand for these goods rises rapidly as income increases. Low income elasticities, such as for food or cigarettes, denote a weak response of demand as income rises.

Income and substitution effects combine to determine the major characteristics of different commodities. Under some circumstances the resulting demand curve is very price-elastic, as where the consumer has been spending a good deal on the commodity and where ready substitutes are available. In this case both the income and substitution effects are strong and the quantity demanded responds strongly to a price increase. But if a commodity, such as salt, requires only a small fraction of the consumer's budget, is not easily replaceable by other items, and is needed in small amounts to complement more important items, then both income and substitution effects are small and demand will tend to be price-inelastic.

From Individual to Market Demand

Having analyzed the principles underlying a single individual's demand for coffee or videocassettes, next examine how the entire market demand derives from the individual demand. The demand curve for a good for the entire market is obtained by summing up the quantities demanded by all the consumers. Each consumer has a demand curve along which the quantity demanded can be plotted against the price; it generally slopes downward and to the right. If all consumers were exactly alike in their demands and if there were 1 million consumers, then we could think of the market demand curve as a millionfold enlargement of each consumer's demand curve.

But people are not all exactly alike. Some have high incomes, some low. Some greatly desire coffee; others prefer tea. To obtain the total market curve

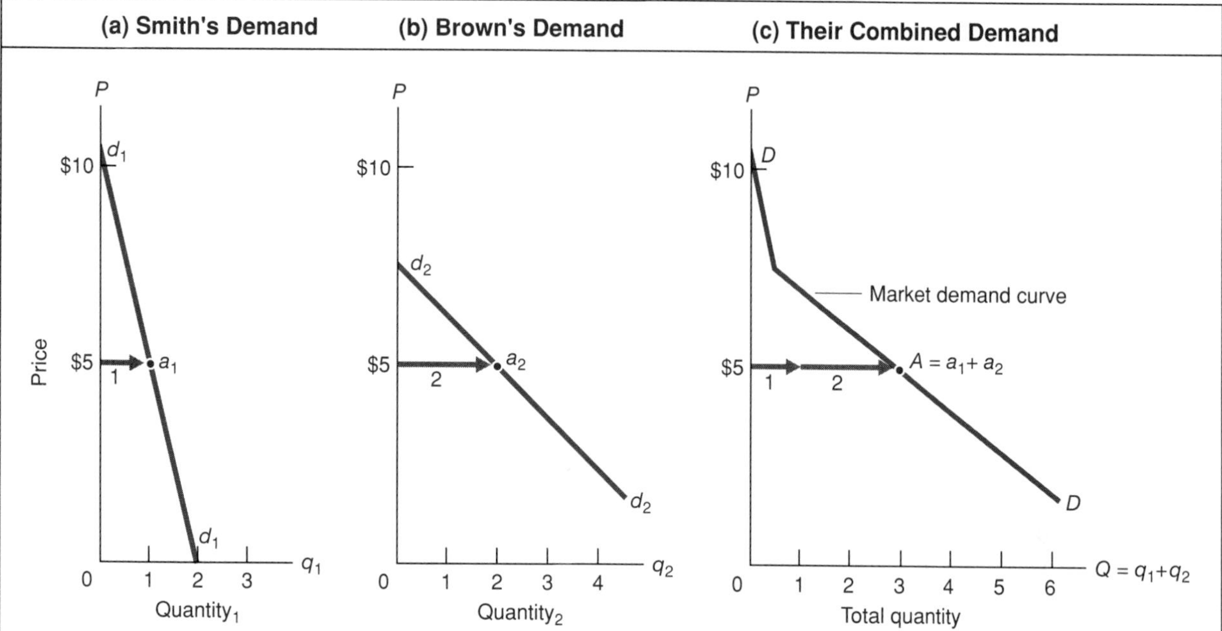

Figure 6-2. Market demand derived from individual demands

We add all individual consumers' demand curves to get the market demand curve. At each price, such as $5, we add quantities demanded by each person to get the market quantity demanded. The figure shows how, at a price of $5, we add horizontally Smith's 1 unit demanded to Brown's 2 units to get the market demand of 3 units.

all we have to do is calculate the sum total of what all the different consumers will consume at any given price. We then plot that total amount as a point on the market demand curve. Or if we like, we might construct a numerical demand table by summing the quantities demanded for all individuals at each market price.

The market demand curve is the sum of individual demands at each price. Figure 6-2 shows how to add individual *dd* demand curves horizontally to get the market *DD* demand curve.

Demand Shifts

Factors other than changes in the price of coffee can change the quantity of coffee demanded. We know this from budget studies, from historical experience, and from examining our own behavior. We discussed briefly in Chapter 5 some of the important non-price determinants of demand. We now review the earlier analysis in light of our analysis of consumer behavior.

An increase in income tends to increase the amount we are willing to buy of any good. Necessities tend to be less responsive than most goods to income changes, while luxuries tend to be more responsive to income. And there are a few abnormal goods, known as inferior goods, for which purchases may shrink as incomes increase because people can afford to replace them with other, more desirable goods. Bologna, soup bones, and shoddy merchandise are examples of inferior goods for many Americans today.

What does all this mean in terms of the demand curve? The demand curve shows how the quantity of a good demanded responds to a change in its own price. But the demand is also affected by the prices of other goods, by consumer incomes, and by special influences. The demand curve was drawn on the assumption that these other things were held constant. But what if they change? Then the whole demand curve will shift to the right or to the left.

Figure 6-3 illustrates changes in factors affecting demand. Given people's incomes and the prices for other goods, we can draw the demand curve for

Shifts in the Demand Curve

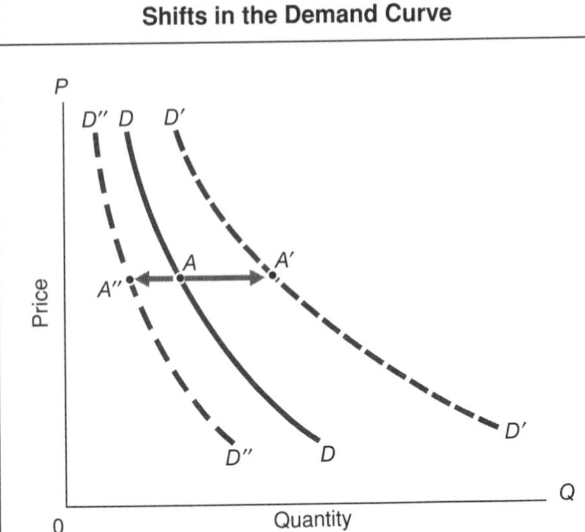

Figure 6-3. Demand curve shifts with changes in income or in other goods' prices

As incomes increase, consumers want more of a good like coffee, thus shifting *DD* to *D′D′* (explain why lower incomes shift *DD* to *D″D″*). Similarly, a rise in the price of a substitute good like cola shifts out coffee's *DD* to *D′D′*. (What would be the effect of a large increase in the price of a complementary good like sugar?)

coffee as *DD*.[5] Assume that price and quantity are at point *A*. Suppose that incomes rise while the price of coffee is unchanged. Because coffee is a normal good with a positive income elasticity, people will increase their purchases of coffee. Hence the demand curve for coffee will shift to the right, say to *D′D′*, with *A′* indicating the new quantity demanded of coffee. If incomes should fall, then we would expect a reduction in demand and in quantity bought. This downward shift we illustrate by *D″D″* and by *A″*.

Income is only one of many factors that affect the position of the demand curve. If students develop a yearning for economic knowledge and start drinking more coffee to keep them awake, the *DD* curve for coffee would shift out. Even if each individual consumed the same amount of a good, a growth in population would have the effect of increasing the total market demand for a product. If people think that a great inflation is about to get under way, they might increase their purchases now in order to beat the price rise.[6] Still other factors operate all the time to shift demand.

Cross Relations of Demand

Everyone knows that raising the price of coffee will decrease the amount of coffee demanded. We have seen that it will also affect the amounts demanded of other commodities. For example, a higher price for coffee will increase the demand for substitutes like tea. A higher coffee price may lower the demand for goods like sugar and cream that are used along with coffee. It will probably have little effect on the demand curve for pants.

We say, therefore, that coffee and tea are substitute products. Goods A and B are **substitutes** if an increase in the price of good A will increase the demand for substitute good B. Coffee and sugar, or cars and gasoline, on the other hand, are complementary products; they are called **complements** because an increase in the price of good A causes a decrease in the demand for its complementary good B. In between are **independent goods,** such as coffee and earmuffs, for which a price change for one good has no effect on the demand for the other. Try classifying the pairs turkey and cranberry sauce, oil and coal, college and textbooks, shoes and shoelaces, salt and shoelaces.

Figure 6-3 illustrates how changes in other goods' prices affect demand. A fall in the price of tea may well cause consumers to buy less coffee; the coffee demand curve shifts, say, to *D″D″*. But what if the price of coffee cups were to fall? The resulting change on *DD*, if there is one, will be in the direction of increased coffee purchases, a rightward shift of *DD*. Why this difference in response? Because tea is a rival or substitute product for coffee; coffee cups, on the other hand, are a commodity complementary to coffee.

[5] Here and in other chapters, we label *individual* demand and supply curves with lowercase letters (*dd* and *ss*), while using uppercase letters (*DD* and *SS*) for the *market* demand and supply curves.

[6] In fact, when I read in the newspaper that war fever in the Middle East will make the price of heating oil go up, I may rush out to buy more. This may seem to be an exception to the law of downward-sloping demand, but it can be reconciled with that law when we realize that I am buying more now because I want to be able to buy less of it tomorrow when its price is higher. Despite this dynamic effect of changing prices, it remains true that at a steady high price for oil I shall consume less than at a steady low price.

Empirical Estimates of Price and Income Elasticities

For many economic applications, it is essential to have numerical estimates of price elasticities. For example, an automobile manufacturer will want to know the impact on sales of the higher car prices that result from installation of costly pollution-control equipment; a college needs to know the impact of higher tuition rates on student applications; and a publisher will calculate the impact of higher textbook prices on its sales. All these applications require a numerical estimate of price elasticity.

Similar decisions depend on income elasticities. A government planning its road or rail network will estimate the impact of rising incomes on automobile travel; the federal government must calculate the effect of higher incomes on energy consumption in planning for future environmental regulations; in determining the necessary investments for generating capacity, electrical utilities require income elasticities for estimating electricity consumption.

Economists have developed important statistical techniques for estimating price and income elasticities. The quantitative estimates are derived from market data on quantities demanded, prices, incomes, and other variables. Tables 6-1 and 6-2 show selected estimates of elasticities.

Commodity	Price elasticity
Tomatoes	4.6
Green peas	2.8
Legal gambling	1.9
Marijuana	1.5
Taxi service	1.2
Furniture	1.0
Movies	0.87
Shoes	0.70
Legal services	0.61
Cigarettes	0.51
Medical insurance	0.31
Bus travel	0.20
Residential electricity	0.13

Table 6-1. Selected estimates of price elasticities of demand

Estimates of price elasticities of demand show a wide range of variation. Elasticities are generally high for goods for which ready substitutes are available, like tomatoes or peas. Low price elasticities exist for those goods like electricity which are essential to daily life and which have no close substitutes. [Source: Heinz Kohler, *Intermediate Microeconomics: Theory and Applications,* 2d ed. (Scott Foresman, New York, 1986).]

Commodity	Income elasticity
Automobiles	2.5
Housing, owner-occupied	1.5
Furniture	1.5
Books	1.4
Restaurant meals	1.4
Clothing	1.0
Physicians' services	0.75
Tobacco	0.64
Eggs	0.37
Margarine	−0.20
Pig products	−0.20
Flour	−0.36

Table 6-2. Income elasticities for selected products

Income elasticities are high for luxuries, whose consumption grows rapidly relative to income. Negative income elasticities are found for "inferior goods," whose demand falls as income rises. Demand for many staple commodities, like clothing, grows proportionally with income. [Source: Heinz Kohler, *Intermediate Microeconomics: Theory and Applications,* 2d ed. (Scott Foresman, New York, 1986).]

The Paradox of Value

The principles outlined here help answer a famous question, known as the *paradox* of value. How is it that water, which is essential to life, has little value, while diamonds, which are quite unnecessary, command an exalted price?

This paradox troubled Adam Smith 200 years ago. We now know how to resolve this paradox, as follows: "The supply and demand curves for water intersect at a very low price, while supply and demand for diamonds are such that the equilibrium price of diamonds is very high." Having said that, we would naturally go on to ask, "But *why* do supply and demand for water intersect at such a low price?" The answer is that diamonds are very scarce and the cost of getting extra ones is high, while water is relatively abundant and costs little in many areas of the world.

Yet this answer still does not reconcile the cost information with the equally valid fact that the world's water is vastly more useful than the world's supply of diamonds. To do so, we must add to the cost considerations a second truth: The utility of water as a whole does not determine its price or demand. Rather, water's price is determined by its marginal utility, by the usefulness of the *last* glass of water. Because there is so much water, the last glass sells for very little. Even though the first few drops are worth life itself, the last few are needed only for watering the lawn or washing the car. We thus find that an immensely valuable commodity like water sells for next to nothing because its last drop is worth next to nothing.

As one student put the matter: The theory of economic value is easy to understand if you just remember that in economics the tail wags the dog. It is the tail of marginal utility that wags the dog of prices and quantities.

We can resolve the paradox of value as follows: The more there is of a commodity, the less is the relative desirability of its last little unit. It is therefore clear why a large amount of water has a low price and why an absolute necessity like air could become a free good. In both cases, it is the large quantities that pull the marginal utilities so far down and thus reduce the prices of these vital commodities.

Consumer Surplus

The paradox of value emphasizes that the recorded money value of a good (measured by price × quantity) may be very misleading as an indicator of the total economic value of that good. The measured economic value of the air we breathe is zero, yet air's contribution to welfare is immeasurably large.

The gap between the total utility of a good and its total market value is called **consumer surplus.** The surplus arises because we "receive more than we pay for" as a result of the law of diminishing marginal utility.

We enjoy consumer surplus basically because we pay the same amount for each unit of a commodity that we buy, from the first to the last. We pay the same price for each egg or glass of water. Thus we pay for *each* unit what the *last* unit is worth. But by our fundamental law of diminishing marginal utility, the earlier units are worth more to us than the last. Thus, we enjoy a surplus of utility on each of these earlier units.

Figure 6-4 illustrates the concept of consumer surplus for an individual who consumes water. Say that the price of water is $1 per gallon. This is shown by the horizontal blue line at $1 in Figure 6-4. The consumer considers how many gallon jugs to buy at that price. The first gallon is highly valuable, slaking extreme thirst, and the consumer is willing to pay $9 for it. But this first gallon costs only $1—the market price—so the consumer has gained a surplus of $8.

Consider the second gallon. This is worth $8 to the consumer, but again only costs $1, so the surplus is $7. And so on down to the ninth gallon,

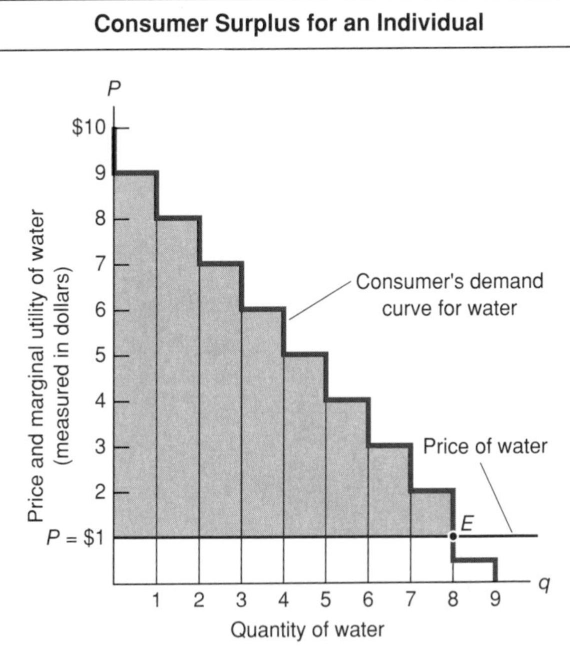

Figure 6-4. Because of diminishing marginal utility, consumer's satisfaction exceeds what is paid

The downward-stepping demand for water reflects the diminishing marginal utility of water. Note how much excess or surplus satisfaction occurs from the earlier units. Adding up all the gray surpluses ($8 of surplus on unit 1 + $7 of surplus on unit 2 + · · · + $1 of surplus on unit 8), we obtain the total consumer surplus of $36 on water purchases.

In the simplified case seen here, the area between the demand curve and the price line is the total consumer surplus.

which is worth only 50 cents to the consumer, and so it is not bought. The consumer equilibrium comes at point *E*, where 8 gallons of water are bought at a price of $1 each.

But here we make an important discovery: Even though the consumer has paid only $8, the total value of the water is $44. This is obtained by adding up each of the marginal utility columns (= $9 + $8 + ··· + $2). Thus the consumer has gained a surplus of $36 over the amount paid.

Figure 6-4 examines the case of a single consumer purchasing water. We can also apply the concept of consumer surplus to a market as a whole. The market demand curve in Figure 6-5 is the horizontal summation of the individual demand curves. The logic of the individual consumer surplus carries over to the market as a whole. The area of the market demand curve above the price line, shown as *NER* in Figure 6-5, represents the total consumer surplus.

Remember that, because consumers pay the price of the last unit for all units consumed, they enjoy a surplus of utility over cost. Consumer surplus measures the extra utility that consumers receive over what they pay for a commodity.

Consumer Surplus for a Market

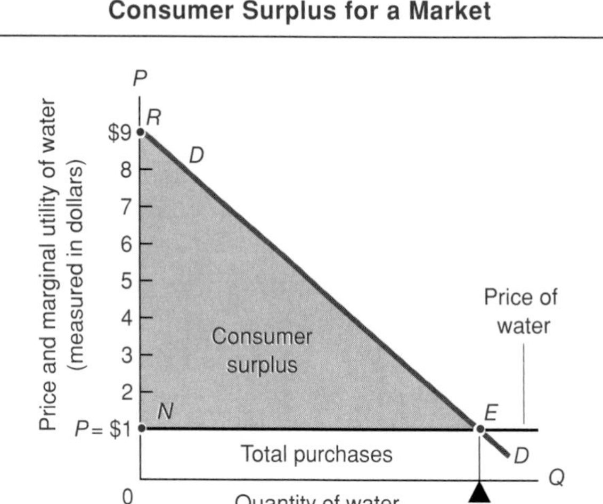

Figure 6-5. Total consumer surplus is the area under the demand curve and above the price line

The demand curve measures the amount consumers would pay for each unit consumed. Thus the total area under the demand curve (0*REM*) shows the total utility attached to the consumption of water. By subtracting the market cost of water to consumers (equal to 0*NEM*), we obtain the consumer surplus from water consumption as the triangle *NER*.

Applications of Consumer Surplus

The concept of consumer surplus is extremely useful in making decisions about public goods, notably airports, roads, dams, subways, and parks. Suppose a new highway has been proposed. Being free to all, it will bring in no revenue. The value to users will be in time saved or in safer trips and can be measured by the individual consumer surplus. To avoid difficult issues of interpersonal utility comparisons, we assume that there are 10,000 users, all identical in every respect.

By careful experimentation, we determine that each individual's consumer surplus is $350 for the highway. Consumers should vote for the road if its total cost is less than $3.5 million (10,000 × $350). And economists performing "cost-benefit analysis" generally recommend that a road should be built if its total consumer surplus exceeds its costs.

Aside from helping societies understand when it pays to build bridges or highways, consumer surplus explains why people are justifiably suspicious when price is equated with value. We have seen that water and air may have little monetary value (price times quantity) even though their total economic value far exceeds that of diamonds or furs. The consumer surplus of air and water is immense, while diamonds and furs may have little value over purchase price.

The concept of consumer surplus also points to the enormous privilege enjoyed by citizens of modern societies. Each of us enjoys a vast array of enormously valuable goods that can be bought at low prices.

This is a humbling thought. If you know people who are arrogant about their economic productivity or earnings, suggest that they pause and reflect. If they were transported to a desert island, how much would their money earnings buy? Indeed, without capital machinery, without other labor, and above all without the technological knowledge which each generation inherits from the past, how much could they produce? It is only too clear that all of us reap the consumer surplus of an economic world we never made. As L. T. Hobhouse said:

> The organizer of industry who thinks that he has "made" himself and his business has found a whole social system ready to his hand in skilled workers, machinery, a market, peace and order—a vast apparatus and a pervasive atmosphere, the joint creation of millions of men and scores of generations. Take away the whole social factor and we [are] but . . . savages living on roots, berries, and vermin.

● We have now completed our analysis of the forces that determine the demand for goods and services. The economic theory of demand emphasizes that consumers attempt to stretch their limited incomes to meet many different needs and wants; they allocate their incomes so that the utilities of the last dollars spent are equal for all goods. Such an allocation generates the vast array of demand curves for different commodities.

But what of business? What of the production and supply of the goods that consumers demand? The next two chapters turn to this other partner in supply and demand. Once our survey of business decisions is complete, we will have a fuller understanding of the forces that lie behind the two curves that dance through the pages of textbooks and indeed through economic life itself. ●

SUMMARY

1. Economists explain consumer demand by the concept of *total utility* and with the *law of diminishing marginal utility*. Utility represents the amount of usefulness or satisfaction that a consumer obtains from enjoying a commodity. The additional satisfaction obtained from consuming an additional unit of a good is given the name *marginal utility*, where "marginal" means the extra or incremental utility.

   The law of diminishing marginal utility states that as the amount of a commodity consumed increases, the marginal utility of the last unit consumed tends to decrease.

2. Economists assume that consumers allocate their limited incomes so as to obtain the greatest satisfaction or utility. To maximize utility, a consumer must equate the marginal utilities of the last dollars spent for each and every good.

   Only when the marginal utility per dollar is equal for bread and butter and everything else will the consumer attain the greatest satisfaction from a limited dollar income. But be careful to note that the marginal utility of a $50-per-ounce bottle of perfume is not equal to the marginal utility of a 50-cent glass of cola. Rather, their marginal utilities divided by price per unit—that is, their marginal utilities per last dollar, *MU/P*—are all equal in the consumer's optimal allocation.

3. Equal marginal utility per unit of resource is a fundamental rule of logic that transcends demand theory and dollars. If you want to allocate any limited resource among competing uses, you can benefit by transferring from the low marginal advantage per unit of resource to the high until a final equilibrium is reached at which all marginal advantages per unit of resource have become equal. An important application of this rule is the use of time.

4. The market demand curve for all consumers is derived by adding horizontally the separate demand curves of each consumer. A demand curve can shift for many reasons. For example, a rise in income will normally shift *DD* rightward, thus increasing demand; a rise in the price of a substitute good (e.g., tea for coffee) will also create a similar upward shift in demand; a rise

in the price of a complementary good (e.g., coffee cups for coffee) will in turn cause the *DD* curve to shift downward and leftward. Still other factors—changing tastes, population, or expectations—can increase or decrease demand.

5. We can gain added insight into the factors making for downward-sloping demand by separating the effect of a price rise into substitution and income effects. (*a*) The substitution effect occurs when a higher price leads to substitution of other goods to meet satisfactions; (*b*) the income effect means that a price increase lowers real income and thereby reduces the desired consumption of most commodities. For most goods, substitution and income effects of a price increase reinforce one another and lead to the law of downward-sloping demand. We measure the quantitative responsiveness of demand to income by the income elasticity, which measures the percentage change in quantity demanded divided by the percentage change in income.

6. Adam Smith's paradox of value—that a commodity important for welfare may sell for less in the market than other, unimportant goods—is clarified by the distinction between the concepts of marginal and total utility. The scarcity of a good, as determined by its cost and supply conditions, interacts with the market demand for the good as determined by the usefulness of its last or *marginal* unit. It is not paradoxical that total utility is high when marginal utility is low. Remember that it is the tail of marginal utility that wags the market dog of prices and quantities.

7. The fact that market price is determined by marginal rather than total utility is dramatized by the concept of *consumer surplus.* We pay the same price for each quart of milk that we buy in the market. Moreover the price is equal to the marginal utility of the last unit bought. But this means that we reap a surplus of utility over price on all earlier units, for the marginal utilities of earlier units are greater than that of the last unit by the law of diminishing marginal utility.

   The excess of total utility over market price is called consumer surplus. Consumer surplus reflects the benefit we gain from being able to buy all units at the same low price. In simplified cases, we can measure consumer surplus as the area between the demand curve and the price line. It is a concept relevant for many public decisions—such as deciding when the community should incur the heavy expenses of a road or bridge.

CONCEPTS FOR REVIEW

utility, marginal utility
utilitarianism
law of diminishing marginal utility
equating marginal utility of last dollar spent on each good: $MU_1/P_1 = MU_2/P_2 = \cdots = MU$ per \$ of income

market demand vs. individual demand
demand shifts from income and other sources
income elasticity
substitutes, complements, independent goods

substitution effect and income effect
paradox of value
consumer surplus

QUESTIONS FOR DISCUSSION

1. Explain the meaning of utility. What is the difference between total utility and marginal utility? Explain the law of diminishing marginal utility and give a numerical example.
2. Each week, Tom Wu buys two hamburgers at $2 each, eight cokes at $0.50 each, and eight slices of pizza at $1 each, but buys no hot dogs at $1.50 each. What can you deduce about Tom's marginal utility for each of the four goods?
3. Which pairs of the following goods would you classify as complementary, substitute, or independent goods: beef, ketchup, lamb, cigarettes, gum, pork, radio, television, air travel, bus travel, taxis, and paperbacks? Illustrate the resulting shift in the demand curve for one good when the price of another good goes up. How would a change in income affect the demand curve for air travel? The demand curve for bus travel?
4. Why is it wrong to say, "In equilibrium, the marginal utilities of all goods must be exactly equal"? Correct the statement and explain.
5. How much would you be willing to pay rather than give up *all* movies? How much do you spend on movies? Estimate roughly your consumer surplus.
6. Consider the following table showing the utility of different numbers of days skied each year:

Number of days skied	Total utility ($)
0	0
1	30
2	55
3	73
4	88
5	98
6	98

   Construct a table showing the marginal utility for each day of skiing. Assuming that there are 1 million people with preferences shown in the table, what would the market demand for ski-days be? If lift tickets cost $20 per day, what are the equilibrium price and quantity of days skied?
7. For each of the commodities in Table 6-1, calculate the impact of a doubling of price on quantity demanded. Similarly, for the goods in Table 6-2, what would be the impact of a 50 percent increase in consumer incomes?
8. As you add together the identical demand curves of more and more people (in a way similar to the procedure in Figure 6-2), the market demand curve becomes flatter and flatter on the same scale. Does this fact indicate that the elasticity of demand is becoming larger and larger? Explain your answer carefully.
9. What would be the features of demand for an addictive substance like cigarettes or drugs? Studies indicate that an addiction typically has a low price elasticity of demand; estimates for cigarette demand, for example, find a price elasticity of around 0.5. Assume that supply of cigarettes is perfectly elastic and that at a no-tax equilibrium of $1 per pack quantity demanded is 10 billion packs per year. If the government levies a 10-cent-per-pack tax, what would be the impact upon cigarette use and upon the price of cigarettes? What would be the tax yield? Show your answer graphically.
10. Suppose you are very rich and very fat. Your doctor has advised you to limit your food intake to 2000 calories per day. What is your consumer equilibrium for food?

APPENDIX 6

GEOMETRICAL ANALYSIS OF CONSUMER EQUILIBRIUM

A century ago, the economist Vilfredo Pareto (1848–1923) discovered that all the important elements of demand theory could be analyzed without the utility concept. Pareto developed what are today called indifference curves. This appendix presents the modern theory of indifference analysis and then derives the major conclusions of consumer behavior with that new tool.

The Indifference Curve

To depict consumer preferences or tastes graphically, we start by assuming that you are a consumer who buys different combinations of two commodities, say, food and clothing, at a given set of prices. For each combination of the two goods, we assume that you can say whether you prefer one to the other or are indifferent between the pair. For example, when asked to choose between combination A of 1 unit of food and 6 units of clothing and combination B of 2 units of food and 3 of clothing, you might (1) prefer A to B, (2) prefer B to A, or (3) be indifferent between A and B.

Suppose that A and B are equally good in your eyes—that you are indifferent as to which of them you receive. Let us consider some other combinations of goods about which you are likewise indifferent, as listed in the table for Figure 6A-1.

Figure 6A-1 shows these combinations diagrammatically. We measure units of clothing on one axis and units of food upon the other. Each of our four combinations or batches, *A, B, C, D*, is represented by its point. But these four are by no means the

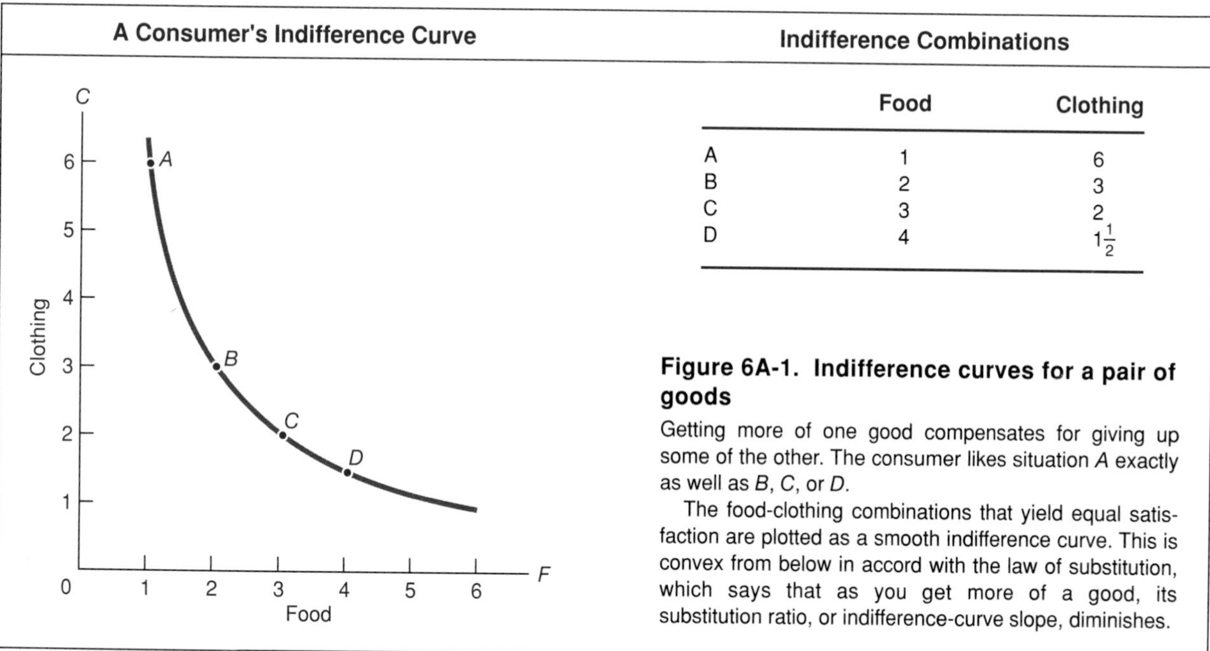

Indifference Combinations

	Food	Clothing
A	1	6
B	2	3
C	3	2
D	4	$1\frac{1}{2}$

Figure 6A-1. Indifference curves for a pair of goods

Getting more of one good compensates for giving up some of the other. The consumer likes situation *A* exactly as well as *B*, *C*, or *D*.

The food-clothing combinations that yield equal satisfaction are plotted as a smooth indifference curve. This is convex from below in accord with the law of substitution, which says that as you get more of a good, its substitution ratio, or indifference-curve slope, diminishes.

only combinations among which you are indifferent. Another batch, such as $1\frac{1}{2}$ units of food and 4 of clothing, might be ranked as equal to *A*, *B*, *C*, or *D*, and there are many others not shown.

The curved contour of Figure 6A-1, linking up the four points, is an **indifference curve.** Every point on the curve represents a different combination of the two goods, and the consumer is indifferent between any two points on the indifference curve. All combinations would be equally desirable, and the consumer would be indifferent as to which batch is received.

Law of Substitution

Indifference curves are drawn as convex to the origin, meaning that as we move you downward and to the right along the curve—a movement that implies increasing the quantity of food and reducing the units of clothing—the curve becomes more nearly horizontal. The curve is drawn in this way to illustrate a property that seems most often to hold true in real life and which we may call the *law of substitution:*

The scarcer a good, the greater its relative substitution value; its marginal utility rises relative to the marginal utility of the good that has become plentiful.

Thus, in going from *A* to *B* in Figure 6A-1, you would swap 3 of your 6 clothing units for 1 extra food unit. But from *B* to *C*, you would sacrifice only 1 unit of your remaining clothing supply to obtain a third food unit—a 1-for-1 swap. For a fourth unit of food, you would sacrifice only $\frac{1}{2}$ unit from your dwindling supply of clothing.

If we join the points *A* and *B* of Figure 6A-1, we find that the slope of the resulting line (neglecting its negative sign) has a value of 3. Join *B* and *C*, and the slope is 1; join *C* and *D*, and the slope is $\frac{1}{2}$. These figures—3, 1, $\frac{1}{2}$—are the *substitution ratios* (sometimes called the *marginal rates of substitution*) between the two goods. As the size of the movement along the curve becomes very small, the closer the substitution ratio comes to the actual slope of the indifference curve.

The slope of the indifference curve is the measure of the goods' relative marginal utilities, or of the substitution terms on which—for very small changes—the consumer would be willing to exchange a little less of one good in return for a little more of the other.

An indifference curve that is convex in the manner of Figure 6A-1 conforms to the law of substitution. As the amount of food you consume goes up—and the clothing goes down—food must become relatively cheaper and cheaper in order for you to be persuaded to take a little extra food in exchange for a little sacrifice of clothing. The precise shape and slope of an indifference curve will, of course, vary from one consumer to the next, but the typical shape will take the form shown in Figures 6A-1 and 6A-2.

The Indifference Map

The table in Figure 6A-1 is one of an infinite number of possible tables. We could start with a more preferred consumption situation and list some of the different combinations that would bring the consumer this higher level of satisfaction. One such table might have begun with 2 food and 7 clothing; another with 3 food, 8 clothing. Each table could be portrayed graphically; each has a corresponding indifference curve.

Figure 6A-2 shows four such curves; the curve from Figure 6A-1 is labeled U_3. This diagram is analogous to a geographical contour map. A person who walks along the path indicated by a particular

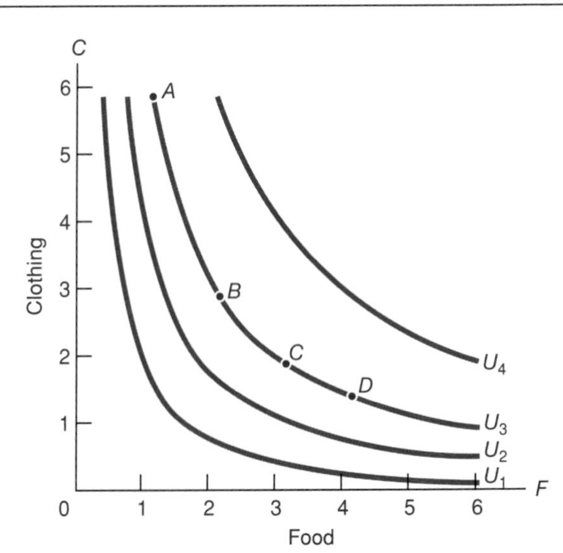

Figure 6A-2. A family of indifference curves
The curves labeled U_1, U_2, U_3, and U_4 represent indifference curves. Which of the indifference curves is preferred by the consumer?

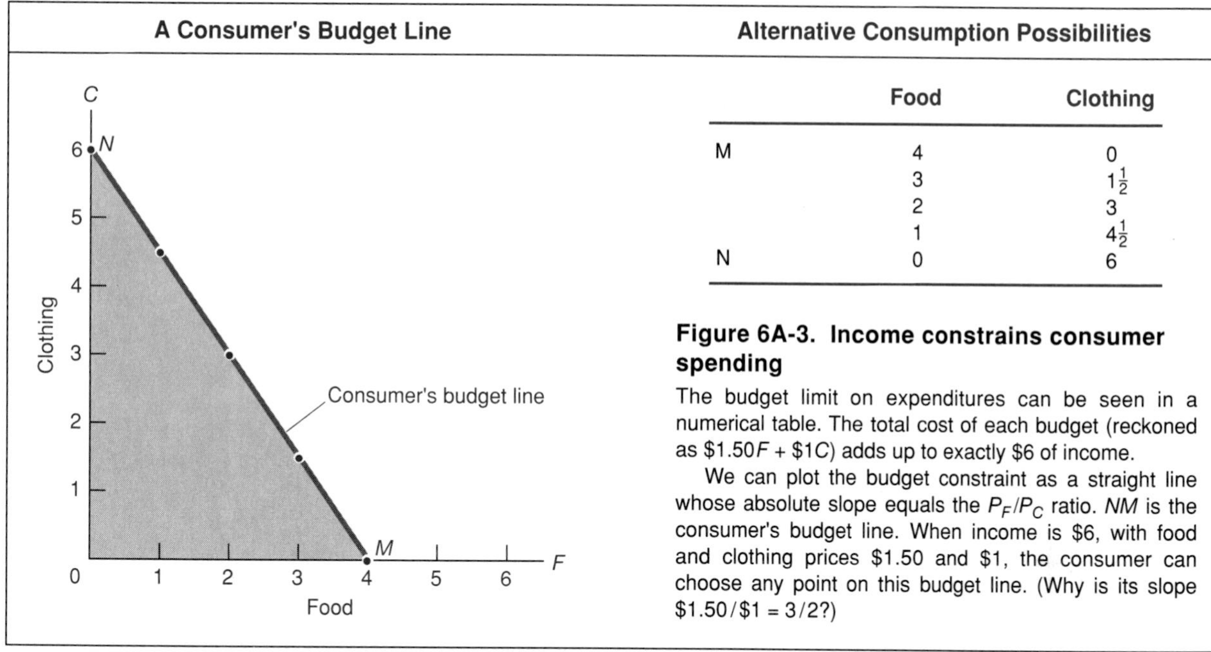

	Food	Clothing
M	4	0
	3	$1\frac{1}{2}$
	2	3
	1	$4\frac{1}{2}$
N	0	6

Figure 6A-3. Income constrains consumer spending

The budget limit on expenditures can be seen in a numerical table. The total cost of each budget (reckoned as $\$1.50F + \$1C$) adds up to exactly \$6 of income.

We can plot the budget constraint as a straight line whose absolute slope equals the P_F/P_C ratio. *NM* is the consumer's budget line. When income is \$6, with food and clothing prices \$1.50 and \$1, the consumer can choose any point on this budget line. (Why is its slope \$1.50/\$1 = 3/2?)

height contour on such a map is neither climbing nor descending; similarly, the consumer who moves from one position to another along a single indifference curve enjoys neither increasing nor decreasing satisfaction from the change in consumption. Only a few of the possible indifference curves are shown in Figure 6A-2.

Note that as we increase both goods and hence move in a northeasterly direction across this map, we are crossing successive indifference curves; we are reaching higher and higher levels of satisfaction. This assumes that the consumer gets greater satisfaction from receiving increased quantities of both goods. Hence, curve U_3 stands for a higher level of satisfaction than U_2; U_4, for a higher level of satisfaction than U_3; and so forth.

Budget Line or Budget Constraint

Now let us set a particular consumer's indifference map aside for a moment and give the consumer a fixed income. He has, say, \$6 per day to spend, and he is confronted with fixed prices for each food and clothing unit—\$1.50 for food, \$1 for clothing. It is clear that he could spend his money on any one of a variety of alternative combinations of food and clothing. At one extreme, he could buy 4 food units and no clothing; at the other, 6 clothing units and no food. The table with Figure 6A-3 illustrates some of the possible ways in which he could allocate his \$6.

Figure 6A-3 plots these five possibilities. Note that all the points lie on a straight line, labeled *NM*. Moreover, any other attainable point, such as $3\frac{1}{3}$ food units and 1 clothing unit, lies on *NM*. The straight budget line *NM* sums up all the possible combinations of the two goods that would just exhaust the consumer's income.[1]

The slope of *NM* (neglecting its sign) is $\frac{3}{2}$, which is necessarily the ratio of food price to clothing price, and the common sense of line *NM* is clear enough. Given these prices, every time our consumer gives up 3 clothing units (thereby dropping down 3 vertical units on the diagram), he can gain 2 units of food (i.e., move right 2 horizontal units).

We call *NM* the consumer's *budget line* or *budget constraint.*

[1] This is so because, if we designate quantities of food and clothing bought as *F* and *C*, respectively, total expenditure on food must be $\$1\frac{1}{2}F$ and total expenditure on clothing, $\$1C$. If daily income and expenditure is \$6, the following equation must hold: $\$6 = \$1\frac{1}{2}F + \$1C$. This is a linear equation, the equation of the budget line *NM*. Note:

$$\text{Arithmetic slope of } NM = \$1\tfrac{1}{2} \div \$1$$
$$= \text{price of food} \div \text{price of clothing}$$

The Equilibrium Position of Tangency

Now we are ready to put our two parts together. The axes of Figure 6A-3 are the same as those of Figures 6A-1 and 6A-2. We can superimpose the black budget line *NM* upon this blue consumer indifference map, as shown in Figure 6A-4. The consumer is free to move anywhere along *NM*. Positions to the right and above *NM* are not allowed because they require more than $6 of income; positions to the left and below *NM* are irrelevant because the consumer is assumed to spend the full $6.

Where will the consumer move? Obviously, to that point which yields the greatest satisfaction, or, in other words, to the highest possible indifference curve, which in this case must be at the blue point *B*. At *B*, the budget line just touches—but does not cross—the indifference curve U_3.

At this point of tangency, where the budget line just kisses but does not cross an indifference contour, is found the highest utility contour the consumer can reach.

Geometrically, the consumer is at equilibrium where the slope of the budget line is exactly equal to the slope of the indifference curve. Moreover, the slope of the budget line is the price ratio of food to clothing.

Consumer equilibrium is attained at the point where the budget line touches the highest indifference curve. At that point, the consumer's substitution ratio (or ratio of relative marginal utilities) is just equal to the ratio of food price to clothing price.

Put differently, the substitution ratio, or the slope of the indifference curve, is the ratio of the marginal utility of food to the marginal utility of clothing. So our tangency condition is just another way of stating that a good's price and its marginal utility must be proportional in equilibrium; in equilibrium, the consumer is getting the same marginal utility from the last penny spent on food as from the last penny spent on clothing. Therefore, we can derive the following equilibrium condition:

$$\frac{P_F}{P_C} = \text{substitution ratio} = \frac{MU_F}{MU_C}$$

This is exactly the same condition as we derived for utility theory in the main part of this chapter.

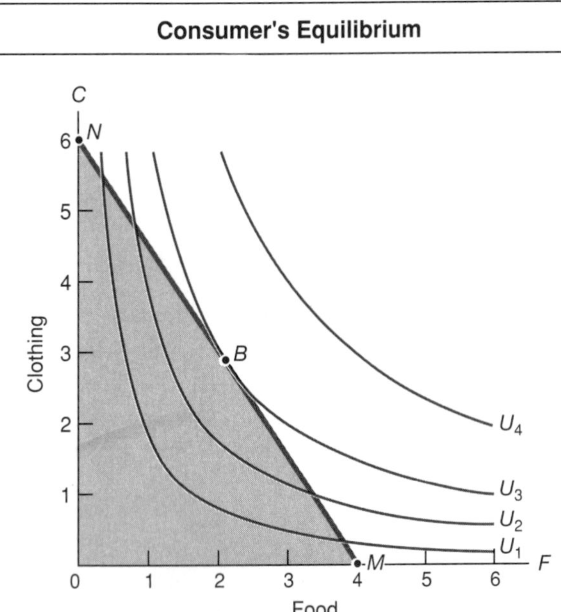

Figure 6A-4. Consumer's most preferred and feasible consumption bundle is attained at *B*

We now combine the budget line and indifference contours on one diagram. The consumer reaches highest indifference curve attainable with fixed income at point *B*; *B* represents tangency of budget line with highest indifference curve. (Why? If slopes were unequal, *NM* would intersect a *U* contour and the consumer could cross over to higher satisfaction levels.)

At tangency point *B*, substitution ratio equals price ratio P_F/P_C. This means that all goods' marginal utilities are proportional to their prices, with marginal utility of the last dollar spent on every good being equalized—as demonstrated in the chapter's main text.

Changes in Income and Price

To increase our understanding of demand we consider the effects of (*a*) a change in money income and (*b*) a change in the price of one of the two goods.

Income Change

Assume, first, that the consumer's daily income is halved while the two prices remain unchanged. We could prepare another table, similar to the table for

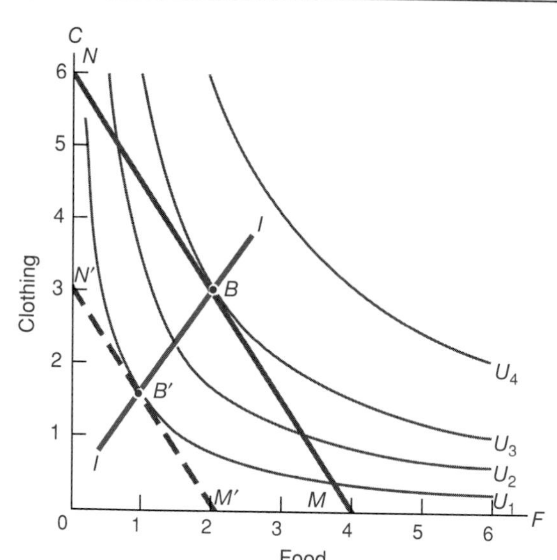

Figure 6A-5. Effect of income change on equilibrium

An income change shifts the budget line in a parallel way. Thus, halving income to \$3 shifts *NM* to *N′M′*, moving equilibrium to *B′*. (Show what raising income to \$8 would do to equilibrium. Estimate where the new tangency point would come.)

Figure 6A-3, showing the new consumption possibilities. Plotting these points on a diagram such as Figure 6A-5, we should find that the new budget line occupies the position $N'M'$ in Figure 6A-5. The line has made a parallel shift inward.[2] The consumer is now free to move only along this new (and lower) budget line; to maximize satisfaction, he will move to the highest attainable indifference curve, or to point B'. A tangency condition for consumer equilibrium applies here as before. The blue curve through $B'B$ depicts what are called *Engel curves*, showing how consumption changes when income changes.

Single Price Change

Now return our consumer to his previous daily income of \$6, but assume that the price of food rises from \$1.50 to \$3 while the price of clothing is unchanged. Again we must examine the change in the budget line. This time we find that it has pivoted on point N and is now NM'',[3] as illustrated in Figure 6A-6.

The common sense of such a shift is clear. Since the price of clothing is unchanged, point N is just as available as it was before. But since the price of food has risen, point M (which represents 4 food units) is no longer attainable. With food costing \$3 per unit, only 2 units can now be bought with a daily income of \$6. So the new budget line still passes through N, but it must pivot at N and pass through M'', which is to the left of M.

Equilibrium is now at B'', and we have a new tangency situation. Higher food price has definitely reduced food consumption, but clothing consumption may move in either direction.

To clinch understanding, you can work out the cases of an increase in income and a fall in the price of clothing or food.

2 The equation of the new $N'M'$ budget line is now $\$3 = \$1\tfrac{1}{2}F + \$1C$.

3 The budget equation of NM'' is now $\$6 = \$3F + \$1C$.

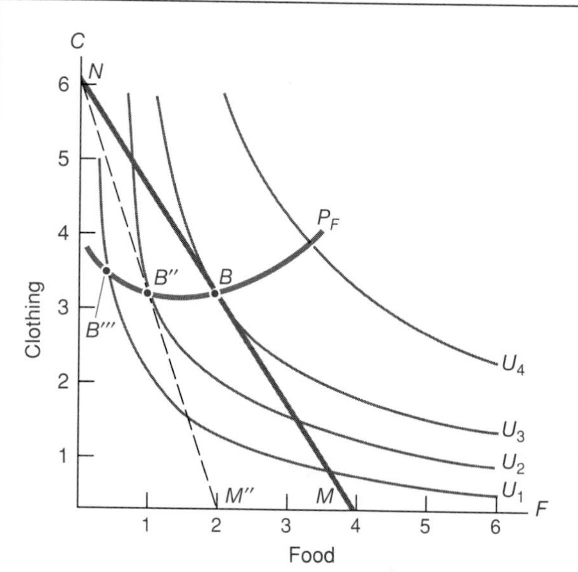

Figure 6A-6. Effect of price change on equilibrium

A rise in the price of food makes the budget line pivot on *N*, rotating from *NM* to *NM″*. New tangency equilibrium is at *B″*, with less food and either more or less clothing. (Show the change in equilibrium with a change in P_C.)

Deriving the Demand Curve

We are now in a position to derive the demand curve. Look carefully at Figure 6A-6. Note that as we increased the price of food from $1.50 per unit to $3 per unit, we kept other things constant. Tastes as represented by the indifference curves did not change, and money income and the price of clothing stayed constant. Therefore, we are in the ideal position to trace the demand curve for food. Thus at a price of $1.50, the consumer buys 2 units of food, shown as equilibrium point *B*. When price rises to $3 per unit, the food purchased is 1 unit, at equilibrium point B''. If you draw in the budget line corresponding to a price of $6 per unit of food, the equilibrium occurs at point B''', and food purchases are 0.45 unit.

Now plot the price of food against the purchases of food, again holding other things equal (this is taken up in the third question at the end of this appendix). You will have derived a neat downward-sloping demand curve from indifference curves. Note that we have done this without ever needing to mention the term "utility"—basing the derivation solely on measurable indifference curves.

SUMMARY TO APPENDIX

1. An indifference curve depicts the points of equally desirable consumption. The indifference contour is usually drawn convex (or bowl-shaped) in accordance with the empirical law of diminishing relative marginal utilities.
2. When a consumer has a fixed money income, all of which he spends, and is confronted with market prices of two goods, he is constrained to move along a straight line called the budget line or budget constraint. The line's slope will depend on the ratio of the two market prices; how far out it lies will depend on the size of his income.
3. The consumer will move along this budget line until reaching the highest attainable indifference curve. At this point, the budget line will touch, but not cross, an indifference curve. Hence, equilibrium is at the point of tangency, where the slope of the budget line (the ratio of the prices) exactly equals the slope of the indifference curve (the substitution ratio or relative-marginal-utility ratio of the two goods). This gives additional proof that, in equilibrium, marginal utilities are proportional to prices.
4. A fall in income will move the budget line inward in a parallel fashion, usually causing less of both goods to be bought. A change in the price of one good alone will, other things being equal, cause the budget line to pivot so as to change its slope. After a price or income change, the consumer will again attain a new tangency point of highest satisfaction. At every point of tangency, the marginal utility per dollar is equal in every use. By comparing the new and old equilibrium points, we trace the usual downward-sloping demand curve.

CONCEPTS FOR REVIEW

indifference curves
slope or substitution ratio
budget line or budget constraint

convexity of indifference curves and law of diminishing relative marginal utilities

optimal tangency equilibrium:
P_F/P_C = substitution ratio
$= MU_F/MU_C$

QUESTIONS FOR DISCUSSION

1. Explain why one, and only one, indifference curve will go through any point on an indifference map. Why do two indifference curves never cross?
2. If a consumer is at a point on her budget line where it crosses an indifference curve, explain why she cannot have reached equilibrium. What will she do to attain her equilibrium?
3. Use a table to list the price and quantity combinations that arise from shifting the price of food in Figure 6A-6. Then plot these on a graph. This will be the demand for food. Why does it slope downward? Show what would happen to the demand curve if the consumer's income increased?
4. In Figure 6A-4, label the indifference contours with the utility numbers 1, 2, 3, 4. Show that any other four numbers would give the same demand equilibrium, provided only that they are ordinal, or in the same more-or-less relationship. Infer from this that only dimensionless "ordinal utility" rather than numerically measurable "cardinal utility" is needed for demand economics.
5. Draw the indifference curves for a consumer who consumes each of the following pairs of goods under the listed conditions:
   (a) Pepsi and Coke are perfect substitutes and give equal enjoyment.
   (b) I like pizza but neither like nor dislike water.
   (c) I always need both a left and a right shoe.
   (d) Chocolate is tasty but celery makes me sick.

CHAPTER 7

PRODUCTION AND BUSINESS ORGANIZATION

The business of America is business.
Calvin Coolidge

Most of the economy's goods and services, from automobiles to zithers, are produced in business firms—in tiny proprietorships, in partnerships, or in giant corporations. To understand our market economy, we must first understand the organization and functioning of business enterprise in the American economy. We begin by discussing the nature of the firm and describing the major forms of business organization. We then turn to the central activity of firms: production.

A. Business Organization

The Nature of the Firm

Why do we need large organizations to produce our daily bread rather than baking our bread and producing everything ourselves? Why does production generally take place in firms rather than in our basements? Businesses exist for many reasons, but the most important are to exploit economies of mass production, to raise funds, and to organize the production process.

The most compelling factor leading to the organization of production in firms arises from *economies of mass production.* Efficient production requires specialized machinery and factories, assembly lines, and division of labor into a large number of small operations. Studies indicate that efficient production of automobiles requires production rates of at least 300,000 units per year. We could hardly expect that workers would spontaneously gather to perform each task correctly and in the right sequence; rather, firms coordinate the production process, purchasing or renting land, capital, labor, and materials. If there were no need for specialization and division of labor, we could each produce our own electricity, digital watch, and finespun shirt in our backyard. We obviously cannot perform such feats, so efficiency generally requires large-scale production in businesses.

A related function of firms is *raising resources* for large-scale production. An integrated steel mill costs $1 billion to build; the research and development expenses for a new line of aircraft might be even greater. Where are such funds to come from? In the nineteenth century, businesses could often be financed by wealthy individuals. But the days of such fabulously wealthy captains of industry are past. Today, in a private-enterprise economy, most funds for production must come from company profits or from money borrowed in financial markets. Indeed, privately financed production would be virtually unthinkable if corporations could not raise billions of dollars each year for new projects.

A third reason for firms is the provision of *management*. The manager is the person who organizes production, introduces new ideas or products or processes, makes the business decisions, and is held accountable for success or failure. Production cannot, after all, organize itself. Someone has to supervise the construction of a new factory, negotiate with labor unions, and purchase materials and supplies. Someone has to hire baseball players, find a baseball field, hire umpires, and sell tickets. Once all these factors of production are engaged, someone has to monitor their daily activities to ensure that the job is being done effectively and honestly.

Production is organized in firms because efficiency generally requires large-scale production, the raising of significant financial resources, and careful management and monitoring of ongoing activities.

Big, Small, and Infinitesimal Businesses

Production in a market economy takes place in a wide variety of business organizations—from the tiniest individual proprietorships to the giant corporations that dominate economic life in a capitalist economy. There are currently more than 18 million different businesses in America. The majority of these are tiny units owned by a single person—the individual proprietorship. Others are partnerships, owned by two or perhaps two hundred partners. The largest businesses tend to be corporations.

Tiny businesses predominate in numbers. But in sales and assets, in political and economic power, and in size of payroll and employment, the few hundred largest corporations occupy the strategically dominant position.

The Individual Proprietorship

At one end of the spectrum are the individual proprietorships, the classic small businesses often called "Mom and Pop" stores. A small store might do a few hundred dollars of business per day and barely provide a minimum wage for their owners' efforts.

These businesses are large in number but small in total sales. For most small businesses, there is a tremendous amount of personal effort required. Self-employed farmers work from 55 to 60 hours per week during the peak summer months. Still, some people will always want to start out on their own. *Theirs* may be the successful venture that gets bought out for millions of dollars.

The Partnership

Often a business requires a combination of talents—say, lawyers or doctors specializing in different areas. Any two or more people can get together and form a partnership. Each agrees to provide some fraction of the work and capital, to share some percentage of the profits, and of course to share the losses or debts.

Today, partnerships form only a small fraction of total economic activity. The reason is that partnerships pose certain disadvantages that make them impractical for large businesses. The major disadvantage is *unlimited liability*. General partners are liable without limit for all debts contracted by the partnership. If you own 1 percent of the partnership and the business fails, then you will be called upon to pay 1 percent of the bills and the other partners will be assessed their 99 percent. But if your partners cannot pay, you may be called upon to pay all the debts even if you must sell off your prize possessions.

The peril of unlimited liability and the difficulty of raising funds explain why partnerships tend to be confined to small, personal enterprises such as agriculture and retail trade. Partnerships are simply too risky for most situations.

The Corporation

The bulk of economic activity in an advanced market economy takes place in corporations. Centuries ago, corporate charters were awarded by special acts of the monarch or legislature. The British East India Company was a privileged corporation and as such it practically ruled India for more than a century. In the nineteenth century, railroads often had to spend as much money in getting a charter through the legislature as in preparing their roadbeds. Over the past century, laws have been passed that allow almost anyone the privilege of forming a corporation for almost any purpose.

Today, a **corporation** is a form of business organization, chartered in one of the 50 states or abroad and owned by a number of individual stockholders. The corporation has a separate legal identity, and indeed is a legal "person" that may on its own behalf buy, sell, borrow money, produce goods and services, and enter into contracts. In addition, the corporation enjoys the right of *limited liability*, whereby each owner's investment in the corporation is strictly limited to a specified amount.

The central features of a modern corporation are the following:

- The ownership of a corporation is determined by who holds the shares or common stock of the company. If you own 10 percent of a corporation's shares, you have 10 percent of the ownership. Publicly owned corporations are valued on stock exchanges, like the New York Stock Exchange. It is here that the titles to the largest corporations are traded and that fortunes are made and lost.
- In principle, the shareholders control the companies they own. They collect dividends in proportion to the fraction of the shares they own, and they elect directors and vote on many important issues. In practice, the millions of shareholders of our giant corporations—IBM, GM, or Exxon—exercise virtually no control because they are too dispersed to overrule the entrenched managers.
- The corporation's managers and directors have the legal power to make decisions for the corporation. They decide what to produce and how to produce it. They negotiate with labor unions and decide whether to sell the firm if another firm wishes to take it over. The shareholders own the corporation, but the managers run it.

Advantages and Disadvantages of Corporations. Why are corporations so popular in a market economy? A corporation is a legal "person" that can conduct business. Also, the corporation may have "perpetual succession" or existence, regardless of how many times the shares of stock change hands. A majority vote is needed to reach business decisions, which include making investments, setting salaries, buying or selling lines of business, and approving budgets.

In addition, corporate stockholders enjoy limited liability, which protects them from incurring the debts or losses of the corporation beyond their initial contribution. If we buy $1000 of stock, we cannot lose more than our original investment.

Corporations face one major disadvantage: There is an extra tax on corporate profits. For an unincorporated business, any income after expenses is taxed as ordinary personal income. The corporation is treated differently in that corporate income is doubly taxed—first as corporate profits and then as individual income on dividends. The double taxation of corporations has been severely criticized by some economists in recent years, although most countries continue to find corporate income a convenient tax base.

Because efficient production often requires large-scale enterprises, with billions of dollars of capital, investors need a way to pool their funds. Corporations, with limited liability and a convenient management structure, can attract large supplies of private capital, produce a variety of related products, pool risks, and utilize the economies of sizable research units and managerial know-how.

B. Theory of Production and Marginal Products

For most people, the essence of an economy is production. We visualize steamy steel mills, bustling automobile assembly lines, and amber waves of grain. Our living standards today are high primarily because the average worker can produce so much. Let's examine the major concepts concerning production.

Basic Concepts

Begin by considering the case of food production. A modern farmer uses inputs, or factors of production, such as land, labor, machinery, and fertilizer. These inputs are applied over the planting and growing season, and at harvest time the farmer will reap certain outputs, such as wheat.

Our discussion assumes that the farmer always strives to produce efficiently, or at lowest cost. That is, the farmer always attempts to produce the maximum level of output for a given dose of inputs, avoiding waste whenever possible. Later on, in deciding what crops to produce and sell, our farmer is assumed to maximize economic profits as well.

The Production Function

We have spoken of inputs like land and labor and outputs like wheat. But if you have a given quantity of land and labor, how much output can you get? In practice, the answer depends on the state of technology and engineering knowledge. At any point in time, given available technical knowledge and available labor, machinery, and fertilizer, only a certain amount of wheat can be obtained from a given plot of land. The relationship between the amount of input required and the amount of output that can be obtained is called the "production function."

The **production function** is the relationship between the maximum amount of output that can be produced and the inputs required to make that output. It is defined for a given state of technical knowledge.

For example, an agronomist has a book of agricultural production functions showing the combinations of land and labor that will produce various quantities of corn. One page has the combinations of land and labor needed to produce 100 bushels of corn; another page lists the input combinations that will produce 200 bushels of corn; and so forth.

Another production function is that for generating electricity. A book of technical specifications shows the combination of turbines, pollution-control equipment, fuel, and labor needed to produce 1 million kilowatts of power. On one page a blueprint for gas-fired plants shows low capital costs and high fuel costs. On the next page a blueprint for a coal-fired plant shows low fuel costs but high capital costs for pollution control. Yet other pages have descriptions of nuclear power plants, solar power stations, and so forth. When all the different blueprints for 1991 are put together, they form the production function for electricity generation for 1991.

A third example of a production function is the volume of crude oil that can be delivered through a pipeline. Engineers know that the amount of output depends upon the diameter of the pipe, the horsepower of the pump, and other factors such as the terrain. The list of different pipe diameters, pump sizes, and other factors, along with the associated outputs of oil, represents the production function for oil pipelines.

There are thousands of different production functions—one for each and every product—although they may not be written down in engineering handbooks. Production functions describe *how* a firm can produce its bundle of outputs, and production functions lie behind a firm's cost curves. In later chapters we will see that each factor's marginal product will determine that factor's price in competitive markets.

Total, Average, and Marginal Product

Starting with a firm's production function, we can calculate three important production concepts: total, average, and marginal product. We begin by computing the total physical product, or **total product,** which designates the total amount of output produced, in physical units such as bushels of wheat or barrels of oil pumped. Figure 7-1(*a*) and column (2) of the accompanying table illustrate the concept of total product. For this example, it shows how total product responds as the amount of labor applied is increased. The total product starts at zero for zero labor, then increases as additional units of labor are applied, reaching a maximum of 3900 units when 5 units of labor are used.

Once we know the total product, it is easy to derive the marginal product. Recall that the term "marginal" means "extra."

The **marginal product** of an input is the extra product or output added by 1 extra unit of that input while other inputs are held constant.

For example, assume that we are holding land, machinery, and all other inputs constant. Then labor's marginal product is the extra output obtained

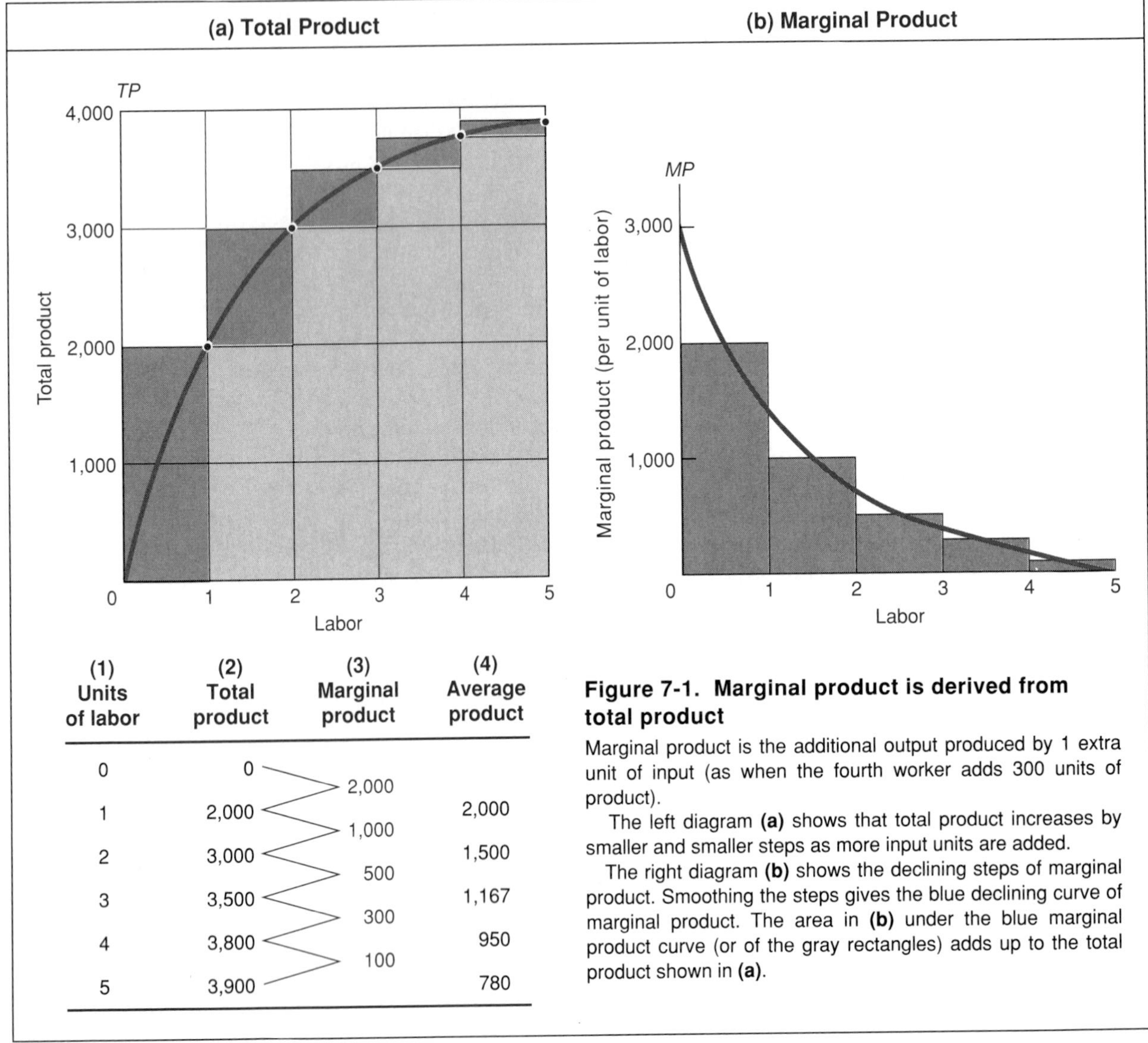

(1) Units of labor	(2) Total product	(3) Marginal product	(4) Average product
0	0		
		2,000	
1	2,000		2,000
		1,000	
2	3,000		1,500
		500	
3	3,500		1,167
		300	
4	3,800		950
		100	
5	3,900		780

Figure 7-1. Marginal product is derived from total product

Marginal product is the additional output produced by 1 extra unit of input (as when the fourth worker adds 300 units of product).

The left diagram **(a)** shows that total product increases by smaller and smaller steps as more input units are added.

The right diagram **(b)** shows the declining steps of marginal product. Smoothing the steps gives the blue declining curve of marginal product. The area in **(b)** under the blue marginal product curve (or of the gray rectangles) adds up to the total product shown in **(a)**.

by adding 1 unit of labor. The third column of the table in Figure 7-1 calculates the marginal product. The marginal product of labor starts at 2000 for the first unit of labor, then falls to only 100 units for the fifth unit. This declining marginal product in graph (*b*) will in the next section be associated with the law of diminishing returns.

The final concept is the **average product,** which measures total output divided by total units of input. The fourth column of the table in Figure 7-1 shows the average product of labor as 2000 units per worker with one worker, 1500 units per worker with two workers, and so forth. Note that the average product falls through the entire range of increasing labor input.

Marginal Products and Diminishing Returns

As noted above, each increment of labor in the marginal product column adds less and less output. The diminishing size of the added-output slabs reflects this, as does the smoothed marginal product curve, which shows a smooth downward-sloping marginal product relationship. The phenomenon of declining marginal product is just the law of diminishing returns that we first met in Chapter 2.

According to the **law of diminishing returns,** the marginal product of each unit of input will decline as the amount of that input increases, holding all other inputs constant.

Figure 7-1 illustrates the law of diminishing returns for labor, holding land and other inputs constant. What is true for labor is also true for land and any other input. We can interchange land and labor, now holding labor constant and varying land. Land's marginal product is the change in total output that results from 1 additional unit of land, with all other inputs held constant. We can calculate the marginal product of each input (labor, land, machinery, water, fertilizer, etc.); and the marginal product would apply to any output (wheat, corn, steel, soybeans, and so forth). We would find that other inputs also tend to show the law of diminishing returns.

Why do production functions generally obey the law of diminishing returns? The reason is that as more of an input such as labor is added to a fixed amount of land, machinery, and other inputs, the labor has less and less of the other factors to work with. The land gets more crowded, the machinery is overworked, and the jobs done become less important.

Diminishing returns are easily understood for inputs of water. The first units of water are vital for plant life; the next units will keep the plant healthy and growing smartly; but as more and more water gets added, the soil becomes waterlogged, and most crops will actually die.

In applying the law of diminishing returns to production, we must emphasize that it is a widely observed empirical regularity rather than a universal truth like the law of gravity. It has been found in numerous empirical studies, but exceptions have also been uncovered. Moreover, diminishing returns might not hold for all levels of production. The very first inputs of labor might actually show increasing marginal products, since a few minutes are needed just to get the machinery running and to transport the workers to the field. And the last units might actually show negative marginal products as plants suffocate from too much water. Therefore, we should always remember that the law of diminishing returns is an empirical regularity subject to exceptions and not a universal law of nature.

An Engineering Example: Oil Pipelines

An important illustration of production theory in modern business life is the economics of transporting oil by pipelines. Oil transport rests on simple physical principles yet constitutes a critical lifeline in our economic system.

We gave as an example of a production function the relationship between the quantity of crude oil transported each day through a pipeline (the output or "throughput") and the inputs, represented by the size of the pipe and the power of the pumping machinery. Engineers studying this technology have made careful measurements and have discovered a numerical relationship between the inputs and the outputs. We can use these studies to show the nature of the production function along with the total and marginal products for pipelines.

Table 7-1 lists the inputs and outputs for the oil-transport production function. The output, measured in throughput (in barrels of oil per day) is shown to be a function of two different sizes of pipes—12 inches and 24 inches—and of a variety of different horsepower settings for the pumps. Pipes come in other sizes, of course, and each would have different outputs, but two will be sufficient for this example.

Examining the table, we can determine the effect of an increase in one of the two inputs on total output. By reading down column (2) in Table 7-1, we see the effect of increasing the amount of horsepower inputs. As we move down from one row to the next, the use of horsepower increases. An estimate of the marginal product can be computed as the ratio of the increase in throughput (output) to the increase in horsepower (input). If, for example, pumping horsepower were to increase 10,000 units from 10,000 to 20,000, then throughput would climb from 43,000 barrels per day to 57,000 barrels per day for the 12-inch pipe. For this interval, the marginal product of horsepower (measured in barrels per day per horsepower) would, as a result, equal:

$$MP = \frac{57{,}000 - 43{,}000}{20{,}000 - 10{,}000} = \frac{14{,}000}{10{,}000} = 1.4$$

Moving down one row, we see that the marginal product of horsepower is 1.0 barrel per day per horsepower as power moves from 20,000 to 30,000

Total and Marginal Products for Oil Pipelines

(1)	(2)	(3)	(4)	(5)	(6)	(7)
	12-inch pipe			24-inch pipe		
Pumping horsepower	Total product (barrels per day)	Average product (barrels per day per hp)	Marginal product (barrels per day per hp)	Total product (barrels per day)	Average product (barrels per day per hp)	Marginal product (barrels per day per hp)
10,000	43,000	4.3		141,000	14.1	
			1.4			4.4
20,000	57,000	2.85		185,000	9.25	
			1.0			3.3
30,000	67,000	2.23		218,000	7.27	
			0.8			2.7
40,000	75,000	1.88		245,000	6.13	
			0.7			2.3
50,000	82,000	1.64		268,000	5.36	
			0.6			2.0
60,000	88,000	1.47		288,000	4.80	
			0.5			1.8
70,000	93,000	1.33		306,000	4.37	

Table 7-1. Engineering production function for oil pipelines

Engineering studies of oil pipelines provide the table's empirical data on the relationship between the flow of oil (in barrels per day) and the size of pipe and horsepower. The data show that diminishing returns to horsepower set in quickly, as marginal product of horsepower declines at higher levels of horsepower. [Source: L. Cookenboo, *Crude Oil Pipe Lines and Competition in the Oil Industry* (Harvard University Press, Cambridge, Mass., 1955).]

units. Our engineering study has confirmed the law of diminishing returns.

Notice that when horsepower is constant, output rises as the size of the pipe increases. For example, if 10,000 horsepower is applied, moving from a 12-inch pipe to a 24-inch pipe increases the throughput from 43,000 barrels per day to 141,000 barrels per day. In economic terms, this shows that the marginal product of pipe size is positive; employing a larger pipe increases the total output when other inputs are held constant.

Similar engineering studies have been made for many other areas of the economy, including agriculture, power plants, chemical factories, communications systems, and mines. These studies are essential for firms that wish to design their productive processes efficiently and compete effectively.

Returns to Scale

Diminishing returns and marginal products refer to the response of output to an increase of a *single* input when all other inputs are held constant. We saw that increasing labor while holding land constant would increase food output by ever-smaller increments. Similarly, Table 7-1 showed that increasing the pumping power while holding pipe size constant would increase output by smaller and smaller amounts.

But sometimes we are interested in the effect of increasing *all* inputs. For example, what would happen to wheat production if land, labor, water, and other inputs were increased by the same proportion? Or what would happen to production of automobiles if the quantities of labor, computers, robots, steel, and factory space were all doubled? These questions refer to the *returns to scale,* or the effects of scale increases of inputs on the quantity produced. Put differently, the returns to scale reflect the responsiveness of total product when all the inputs are increased proportionately. Three important cases should be distinguished:

- **Constant returns to scale** denote a case where a change in all inputs leads to an equally large increase in output. For example, if labor, land, capital, and other inputs are doubled, then under constant returns to scale output would also double. Many handicraft industries (such as handlooms operated in a developing country) show constant returns.

- **Decreasing returns to scale** occur when a balanced increase of all inputs leads to a less-than-proportional increase in total output. Say that a farmer's cornland, seed, labor, machinery, etc., were increased by 50 percent. If total output increased by only 40 percent, this situation would display decreasing returns to scale. Many productive activities involving natural resources, such as growing wine grapes or cultivating forests, show decreasing returns to scale.
- **Increasing returns to scale** arise when an increase in all inputs leads to a more-than-proportional increase in the level of output. For example, an engineer planning a small-scale chemical plant would generally find that increasing the inputs of labor, capital, and materials by 10 percent will increase the total output by more than 10 percent. Engineering studies have determined that many manufacturing processes enjoy modestly increasing returns to scale for plants up to the largest size used today.

Production shows increasing, decreasing, or constant returns to scale when a balanced increase in all inputs leads to a more-than-proportional, a less-than-proportional, or a just-proportional increase in output.

What kind of returns is most prevalent in production today? Economists often think that most production activities should be able to attain constant returns to scale. They reason that if production can be adjusted by simply replicating existing plants over and over again, then the producer would simply be multiplying both inputs and output by the same number. In such a case, you would observe constant returns to scale for any level of output.

Often, a firm can improve upon constant returns and achieve increasing returns to scale. To take our pipeline example, Table 7-1 shows that one 12-inch pipe with 10,000 horsepower of pumping can transport 43,000 barrels of oil each day. If we were to place a second 12-inch pipe alongside the first, adding an additional 10,000 horsepower, the total throughput would increase to 86,000 barrels per day. In this case, replication leads to constant returns to scale. Figure 7-2(*a*) shows this point schematically.

But the firm could do even better by building a 24-inch pipe with 20,000 horsepower of pumping capacity, shown in Figure 7-2(*b*). This new investment would double the power and double the amount of pipe. What would be its effect on total output? Table 7-1 shows that throughput increases from 43,000 barrels per day to 185,000 barrels per day, which is much more than doubled and therefore displays increasing returns to scale. This example, typical of many manufacturing processes, shows that by efficiently redesigning a process, doubling inputs may lead to a considerably larger than proportional increase in outputs.

While the pipeline example emphasizes the role of expanding the physical scale, other reasons may be equally important in contributing to increasing returns. Chapter 2 described how, as output increases, firms may break down production into

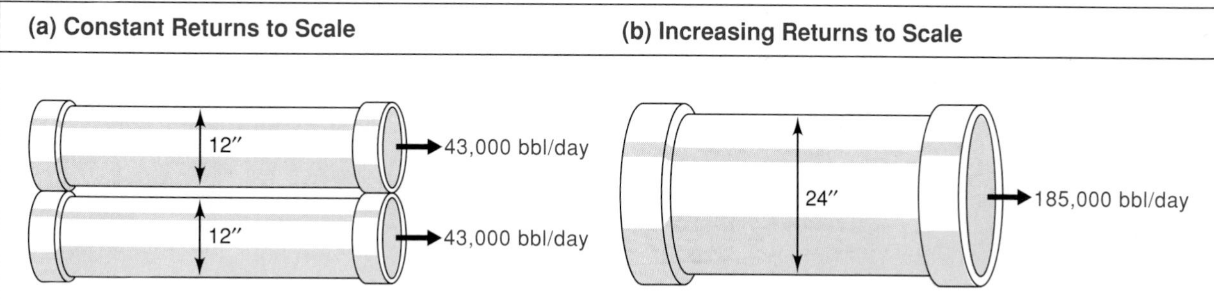

Figure 7-2. Constant and increasing returns to scale

(a) By replicating identical pipelines, a firm can double output by doubling inputs, thus enjoying constant returns to scale.

(b) Building a larger-diameter pipe along with doubling horsepower allows increasing returns to scale. (Source: Table 7-1.)

smaller steps, taking advantage of specialization and division of labor. In addition, mass production allows intensive use of specialized capital equipment, automation, and computerized design and manufacturing to perform simple and repetitive tasks quickly.

Productivity. Economies of scale and mass production have fueled much of the economic growth of nations over the last century. Most production processes are many times larger than they were during the nineteenth century. A large ship in the mid-nineteenth century could carry 2000 tons of goods, while the largest supertankers today carry over 1 million tons of oil.

What would be the effect of a general increase in the scale of economic activity? If increasing returns prevailed, then the larger scale of inputs and production would lead to greater productivity—where **productivity** is a concept measuring the ratio of total output to a weighted average of inputs. If, for example, the typical firm's inputs increased by 4 percent and output consequently increased by 10 percent, then productivity (output per unit of input) would rise by 6 percent. This example suggests that increases in a nation's per capita output and living standards may result in part from exploiting economies of scale in production.[1]

While scale economies are potentially large in many sectors, at some point decreasing returns to scale may take hold. As firms become larger and larger, the problems of management and coordination become increasingly difficult. In relentless pursuit of greater profits, a firm may find itself expanding into more geographic markets or product lines than it can effectively manage. A firm can have only one chief executive officer, one chief financial officer, one board of directors. With less time to study each market and spend on each decision, top managers may become insulated from day-to-day production and begin to make mistakes. Like empires that have been stretched too thin, such firms find themselves exposed to invasion by smaller and more agile rivals. Thus, while technology might ideally allow constant or increasing returns to scale, the need for management and supervision may eventually lead to decreasing returns to scale in giant firms.

[1] Further analysis of production, economic growth, and productivity trends is contained in Chapter 30.

Momentary Run, Short Run, and Long Run

Production requires not only labor and land but also time. Pipelines cannot be built overnight, and once built they last for decades. Farmers cannot change crops in mid-season. Large power plants take a decade to plan, construct, test, and commission. Moreover, once capital equipment has been put in the concrete form of a power plant on the Tennessee River or a petrochemical factory in Galveston, the capital cannot be economically dismantled and moved to another location or transferred to another use.

To account for the role of time in production and costs, we distinguish three different time periods. We define the **momentary run** as a period so short that production is fixed; the **short run** as a period in which firms can adjust production by changing variable factors such as materials and labor but cannot change fixed factors such as capital; and the **long run** as a period sufficiently long so that all factors including capital can be adjusted.

To understand these concepts more clearly, consider the way the production of steel might respond to changes in demand. Say that Nippon Steel is operating its furnaces at 70 percent of capacity when a sudden and unexpected increase in the demand for steel occurs because of a breakdown in a competitor's plant. In the momentary run of a day or so, the steel firm cannot adjust its production at all. It takes time to check and recheck the order books, to stoke up idle furnaces, to reschedule worker-hours, and to order the necessary materials. During the period in which such actions are taken, production will remain unchanged. Therefore, in this shortest of time periods, the momentary run, output is essentially fixed or predetermined.

As time passes, Nippon Steel can begin to adjust its production to the new level of demand. The firm can increase production by increasing worker overtime, by hiring more workers, and by operating its plants and machinery more intensively. The factors which are increased in the short run are called *variable* factors. We define the short run as the period in which production can be changed by changing variable inputs.

Suppose that the increase in steel demand persisted for an extended period of time, say 2 or 3 years or even a decade. Nippon Steel would examine its capital needs and decide that it should increase its productive capacity. More generally, it might examine all its *fixed* factors, those that cannot be changed in the short run because of physical conditions or legal contracts. The period of time over which all inputs, fixed and variable, can be adjusted is called the long run. In the long run, Nippon might add new and more efficient production processes, install a rail link or new computerized control system, or build a plant in Mexico.

Efficient production requires time as well as conventional inputs like labor. We therefore distinguish three different time periods in production and cost analysis. To summarize our definitions:

- The **momentary run** is the period of time so short that no change in production can take place.
- The **short run** is the period of time in which variable inputs, such as materials and labor, can be adjusted, but it is of insufficient length for all inputs to be changed. In the short run, fixed factors, such as plant and equipment, cannot be fully modified or adjusted.
- The **long run** is the period in which all fixed and variable factors employed by the firm can be changed, including labor, materials, and capital.

Technological Change

Economic history records that total output has grown more than tenfold since the turn of the century. But the variety and quality of goods and production processes have changed as well. Consider then how technological change operates to improve productivity and raise living standards.

We have up to now considered production with a given level of technology. The pipeline data in Table 7-1 represent the best engineering practice at a point in time, whereas the production data in Figure 7-1 might show the wheat output that was producible with the prevailing agricultural technology of 1991. A production function represents the relationship between inputs and outputs *for a given state of engineering and technical knowledge.*

But technologies change. Even the most casual historical observation finds that today's array of goods and services is far different from what prevailed a century ago. Today we use digital watches, synthetic fibers, electronic computers, space rockets, electric lights, and similar products that were unavailable in 1890. Just try to find any commodity or production process that has not changed since your grandparents were your age!

Technological change refers to changes in technology—invention of new products, improvements in old products, or changes in the processes for producing goods and services.

Technological change occurs when new engineering and technical knowledge allows more output to be produced with the same inputs, or when the same output can be produced with fewer inputs. In terms of our production terminology, technological change occurs when the production function changes. We distinguish *product innovation,* where new or improved products are introduced in the marketplace, from *process innovation,* which occurs when new or improved techniques of production are developed.

Recent technological changes include developments in microelectronics that made portable stereos and televisions possible; wide-body jets that increased the number of passenger-miles per unit of input by almost 40 percent; fiber optics that have lowered cost and improved reliability in telecommunications; and improvements in computer technologies that have increased calculation speeds by 15 percent a year for three decades. (Identify which of these are product and which are process innovations.)

Figure 7-3 illustrates how technological change would shift the total product curve. The lower line represents the feasible output, or production function, for the year 1985. If we return to the same industry or firm a decade later, we see that changes in technical and engineering knowledge have led to a 50 percent improvement in output per unit of input, or productivity.

Technological change is represented by an upward shift in the total product curve.

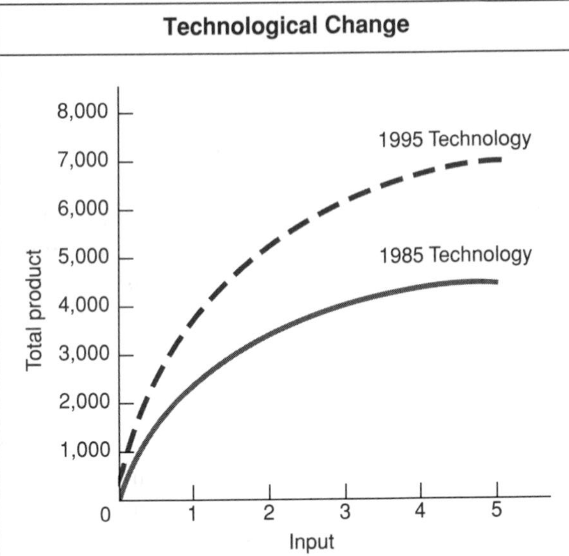

Figure 7-3. Technological advance shifts production function upward

The solid line represents maximum producible output, for each level of input, given the state of technical knowledge in 1985. As a result of computerization, new processes, better quality control, and similar factors, improved technical knowlege in 1995 allows 50 percent more output to be produced for each level of input.

Figure 7-3 shows the happy case of a technological advance. Is the opposite case—technological regress—possible? For a well-functioning market economy, the answer is no. Inferior technologies tend to be discarded in a market economy, while superior technologies—ones with higher productivity—are introduced because they will increase the profits of the innovating firms. If, for example, someone invented a new type of photocopying machine that cost twice as much as existing varieties, no sensible profit-oriented firm would build such a machine.

In perverse cases, however, technological regress might occur. An unregulated company might introduce a socially wasteful process, say one dumping toxic wastes into a stream, because the wasteful process was cheaper to operate. But the economic advantage arises only because the pollution costs are not included in the firm's calculations of costs of production. If pollution costs are included in a firm's decisions, say by taxes or regulations, no competitive firm will introduce an inferior technology.

The Aggregate Production Function for the United States

Now that we have examined the principles of production theory, we can apply these theories to measure the aggregate performance of the U.S. economy. We might investigate the behavior of total output, of different inputs (like labor, capital, and land), and total productivity. Because they involve serious problems of measurement, all such magnitudes must be calculated with great care. Yet they are useful in giving a broad description of an economy's overall behavior.

Empirical studies of the aggregate production function date back to the 1920s, when Paul Douglas (a professor at the University of Chicago and later a U.S. senator) analyzed data for manufacturing. In the 1950s and 1960s, others pursued this approach further, including Robert Solow, John Kendrick, and Edward Denison. The goal of these studies was to find how economic growth depended upon capital, labor, and productivity growth. Recall from our earlier discussion that productivity measures the total quantity of output per unit of input. **Productivity growth** denotes the rate of growth of the level of productivity. For example, if output per worker is 100 units in 1990, and it grows to 102.5 units in 1991, then we say that productivity growth was 2.5 percent per year.

In measuring productivity, we denote labor productivity as the amount of output per unit of labor; capital productivity as output per unit of capital; and total factor productivity as output per unit of total inputs of capital and labor.

Empirical Findings. What have economic studies found? Here are a few of the important results:

- Total factor productivity has been increasing throughout this century because of technological progress and higher levels of worker education and skill. The average rate of total productivity growth has been slightly under $1\frac{1}{2}$ percent per year during the twentieth century. Average real wages per worker have grown slightly faster than the rate of growth of total factor productivity.

- The capital stock has been growing faster than the number of worker-hours. As a result, labor has a growing amount of capital goods to work with; hence labor productivity and wages have tended to rise even faster than the $1\frac{1}{2}$ percent per year attributable to productivity growth alone.
- The rate of return on capital (the rate of profit) might have been expected to encounter diminishing returns because each capital unit now has less labor to cooperate with it. In fact, capital's rate of return has remained about the same.
- In the last two decades, all measures of productivity have shown a marked growth slowdown. The decades of the 1970s and 1980s experienced total factor productivity growth of only $\frac{3}{4}$ percent per year. This productivity growth slowdown has produced a markedly slower growth in real wages and in living standards in the United States.

Similar statistical measurements all over the globe help to put flesh on the bare bones of the microeconomic theory of production. They serve as factual tests of the validity of economic principles—principles that help explain the economic growth of nations.

● This analysis of trends in the aggregate production function ends our survey of the basic elements of the theory of production and marginal products. Production theory is of great importance in its own right, helping us to understand how firms manage their internal activities and to analyze underlying behavior of productivity and living standards. But production theory is also an important building block in understanding business costs, which are the central determinants of supply.

In the next chapter, then, we turn to an analysis of different cost concepts; the appendix to Chapter 8 will also provide a more complete analysis of the theory of production and cost. Mastery of these analytical tools is a prerequisite to understanding businesses' supply of goods and services and the behavior of markets, which are discussed in the remaining chapters of this part. ●

SUMMARY

A. Business Organization

1. In a market economy, production is organized in firms—some in tiny one-person proprietorships, some in partnerships, and the bulk of economic activity in corporations.

2. Each kind of enterprise has advantages and disadvantages. Small businesses are flexible, can market new products, and can disappear quickly. But they suffer from the fundamental disadvantage of being unable to accumulate large amounts of capital from a dispersed group of investors. Today's large corporation, granted limited liability by the state, is able to amass billions of dollars of capital by borrowing from banks, bondholders, and stock markets.

3. In a modern economy, firms produce most goods and services because economies of mass production necessitate that output be produced at high volumes; the technology of production requires much more capital than a single individual would willingly put at risk; and efficient production requires careful management and coordination of the tasks by a centrally directed entity.

B. Theory of Production and Marginal Products

4. To understand how business enterprises function, we begin by analyzing a firm's production behavior. The relationship between the quantity of output (such as wheat, steel, or automobiles) and the quantities of inputs (of labor, land, and capital) is called the production function.

5. Total product refers to the total output produced. Average product equals total output divided by the total quantity of inputs. We can calculate the marginal product of a factor as the extra output added for each additional unit of input while holding all other inputs constant.

6. According to the law of diminishing returns, the marginal product of each input will generally decline as the amount of that input increases, when all other inputs are held constant.

7. The returns to scale refer to the impact on output of a balanced increase in all inputs. A technology in which doubling all inputs leads to an exact doubling of outputs displays constant returns to scale. When doubling inputs leads to less than double the quantity of output, this situation is one of decreasing returns to scale. Conversely, when doubling inputs leads to greater than double the quantity of output, we have increasing returns to scale. As firms become larger and larger, difficulties of control and management may produce decreasing returns to scale.

8. Because decisions take time to implement, and because capital and other factors are often very long-lived, the reaction of production may change over different time periods. The momentary run is the brief period in which output cannot be changed. The short run is a period in which variable factors, such as labor or material inputs, can be easily changed. In the long run, the capital stock (a firm's machinery and factories) can depreciate and be replaced. In the long run, all inputs, fixed and variable, can be adjusted.

9. Technological change refers to a change in the underlying techniques of production, as when a new product or process of production is invented or an old product or process is improved. In such situations, the same output is produced with fewer inputs, or more output is produced with the same inputs. Technological change shifts the production function upward.

10. Attempts to measure an aggregate production function for the American economy tend to corroborate theories of production and marginal products. In this century, technological change has increased the productivity of both labor and capital. Total factor productivity (measuring the ratio of total output to total inputs) has averaged almost $1\frac{1}{2}$ percent per year over the twentieth century although the rate of productivity growth has slowed markedly since 1970.

CONCEPTS FOR REVIEW

Business enterprise
reasons for firms: scale economies, financial needs, management
major business forms: individual proprietorship, partnership, corporation
unlimited, limited liability

Production theory
inputs, outputs, production function
total, average, and marginal product
diminishing marginal product and the law of diminishing returns
constant, increasing, and decreasing returns to scale
momentary, short, and long run
technological change
productivity (labor, capital, total factor)
aggregate production function

QUESTIONS FOR DISCUSSION

1. Explain the concept of a production function. Describe the production function for hamburgers, concerts, haircuts, and a college education.
2. For the following table, fill in the missing values for marginal products and average products:

(1)	(2)	(3)	(4)
	18-inch pipe		
Pumping horsepower	Total product (barrels per day)	Marginal product (barrels per day per hp)	Average product (barrels per day per hp)
10,000	86,000		____
		____	
20,000	114,000		____
		____	
30,000	134,000		____
		____	
40,000	150,000		____
		____	
50,000	164,000		____

3. Using the data in question 2, plot the production function of output against horsepower. On the same graph, plot the curves for average product and marginal product.
4. Say that technological change in the form of a new pipe material allows 20 percent more output to be produced for each level of horsepower. Using the data given in question 2, plot the original production function and the new production function after the technological change.
5. Refer to Table 7-1. Calculate the marginal product of "pipe" at each level of horsepower; that is, what is the additional output obtained when the diameter of the pipe increases from 12 inches to 24 inches?
6. Refer to Table 7-1. Calculations will show that the numerical production function for throughput of oil is given by the following formula:

$$Q = 43{,}000\left(\frac{H}{10{,}000}\right)^{0.4}\left(\frac{P}{12}\right)^{1.7}$$

where Q is throughput in barrels per day, H is horsepower, and P is pipeline diameter in inches. Calculate the marginal product of additional horsepower for increments of 10,000, and calculate the marginal product of adding an additional 12 inches of pipe for the first five horsepower settings.
7. Suppose you are running the food concession at the athletic events for your college. You sell hot dogs, colas, and potato chips. What are your inputs of capital, labor, and materials? If the demand for the hot dogs declines, what steps could you take to reduce output in the short run? In the long run?
8. An important distinction in economics is between shifts in the production function and movements along the production function. For the food conces-

sion in question 7, give an example of both a shift of and a movement along the hot-dog production function. Illustrate each with a graph of the relation between hot-dog production and labor employed.

9. Consider the following changes in a firm's behavior. Which represent substitution of one factor for another with an unchanged technology, and which represent technological change? Illustrate each with a graphical production function.
   (a) When the price of oil increases, a firm replaces an oil-fired plant with a coal-fired plant.
   (b) With the introduction of laser-operated scanning machinery, a steel manufacturer improves the guarantee on the thickness of its steel plate to a tolerance of 0.01 inch from 0.05 inch in the prior year.
   (c) Over the period 1970–1985, a typesetting firm decreases its employment of typesetters by 60 percent and increases its employment of computer operators by 150 percent.
   (d) After a successful unionization drive for clerical workers, a university buys personal computers for its faculty and reduces its secretarial work force.
10. Consider a firm that produces wheat with land and labor inputs. Define and contrast diminishing returns and decreasing returns to scale. Explain why it is possible to have diminishing returns to one input and constant returns to scale for both inputs.
11. Show that if the marginal product is always decreasing, then the average product is always above the marginal product.

C H A P T E R 8

ANALYSIS OF COSTS

Costs merely register competing attractions.
Frank Knight, *Risk, Uncertainty, and Profit* (1921)

Costs lie at the heart of many business decisions. Businesses must pay careful attention to costs because every dollar of cost reduces the firm's profits. But costs are crucial for a deeper reason: firms make production and sales decisions on the basis of a good's cost and price. This chapter is devoted to a thorough analysis of different cost concepts: economic costs, including opportunity costs, and the measurement of costs in business accounts. These concepts lay the foundation for understanding the supply decisions of competitive firms and industries, taken up in the next chapter.

A. Economic Analysis of Costs

Total Cost: Fixed and Variable

Consider a firm that produces a quantity of output denoted by q using inputs of capital, labor, and materials. The firm buys these inputs in the factor markets. A profit-minded firm will keep an eagle eye on its costs to maintain profitability. The firm's accountants have the task of calculating the total dollar costs incurred at each level of q.

Table 8-1 shows the simplified total cost (TC) for each different level of output q. Looking at columns (1) and (4), we see that TC goes up as q goes up. This makes sense because it takes more labor and other inputs to produce more of a good; extra factors involve an extra money cost. It costs \$110 in all to produce 2 units, \$130 to produce 3 units, and so forth.

(1) Quantity q	(2) Fixed cost FC (\$)	(3) Variable cost VC (\$)	(4) Total cost TC (\$)
0	55	0	55
1	55	30	85
2	55	55	110
3	55	75	130
4	55	105	160
5	55	155	210
6	55	225	280

Table 8-1. Fixed, variable, and total costs
The major elements of a firm's costs are its fixed costs (which do not vary at all when output changes) and variable costs (which increase as output increases). Total costs are equal to fixed plus variable costs: $TC = FC + VC$.

Business managers know that when we write down a cost schedule like that in Table 8-1, we make the firm's job look altogether too simple. Why so? Because much hard work lies behind Table 8-1.

To attain the lowest level of costs, the firm's managers have to make sure that they are paying the least possible amount for necessary materials (such as oil or iron ore); that the latest engineering techniques are incorporated into the factory layout; and that countless other decisions are made in the most economical fashion. As a result of such managerial effort, the fixed and variable costs shown in Table 8-1 are the *minimum costs* necessary for the firm to produce that level of output.

Fixed Cost

Columns (2) and (3) break total cost into two components: total fixed cost (*FC*) and total variable cost (*VC*).

What are a firm's **fixed costs?** Sometimes called "overhead" or "sunk costs," they consist of items such as contractual payments for building and equipment rents, interest payments on debts, salaries of long-term employees, and so forth. These must be paid even if the firm produces no output, and they will not change if output changes. Because *FC* is the amount that must be paid regardless of the level of output, it remains constant at $55 in column (2).

Variable Cost

Column (3) of Table 8-1 shows variable cost (*VC*).

Variable costs are those costs that change with the level of output. Examples include materials required to produce output (such as steel to produce automobiles); production workers to staff the assembly lines; power to operate factories; and so on.

By definition, *VC* begins at zero when *q* is zero. It is the part of *TC* that grows with output; indeed, the jump in *TC* between any two outputs is the same as the jump in *VC*. Why? Because *FC* stays constant at $55 throughout and cancels out in the comparison of costs between different output levels. Let us summarize these cost concepts:

Total cost represents the lowest total dollar expense needed to produce each level of output *q*. *TC* rises as *q* rises.

Fixed cost represents the total dollar expense that is paid out even when no output is produced; fixed cost is unaffected by any variation in the quantity of output.

Variable cost represents expenses that vary with the level of output—including raw materials, wages, and fuel—and includes all costs that are not fixed.

Always, by definition,

$$TC = FC + VC$$

Definition of Marginal Cost

Marginal cost is one of the most important concepts in all economics. **Marginal cost** denotes the extra or additional cost of producing 1 extra unit of output. Say a firm is producing 1000 hard disks for a total cost of $10,000. If the total cost of producing 1001 disks is $10,015, then the marginal cost of production is $15 for the 1001st disk.

Table 8-2 uses the data from Table 8-1 to illustrate how we calculate marginal costs. The blue *MC* numbers in column (3) of Table 8-2 come from subtracting the *TC* in column (2) from the *TC* of the previous quantity. Thus the *MC* of the first unit is $30 = $85 − $55. The marginal cost of the second unit is $25 = $110 − $85. And so on.

Instead of getting *MC* from the *TC* column, we could get the *MC* figures by subtracting each *VC* number of column (3) of Table 8-1 from the *VC* in the row below it. Why? Because variable cost al-

(1) Output *q*	(2) Total cost *TC* ($)	(3) Marginal cost *MC* ($)
0	55	
		30
1	85	
		25
2	110	
		20
3	130	
		30
4	160	
		50
5	210	

Table 8-2. Calculation of marginal cost

Once we know total cost, it is easy to calculate marginal cost. To calculate the *MC* of the fifth unit, we subtract the total cost of the four units from the total cost of the five units, i.e.,

$$MC = \$210 - \$160 = \$50$$

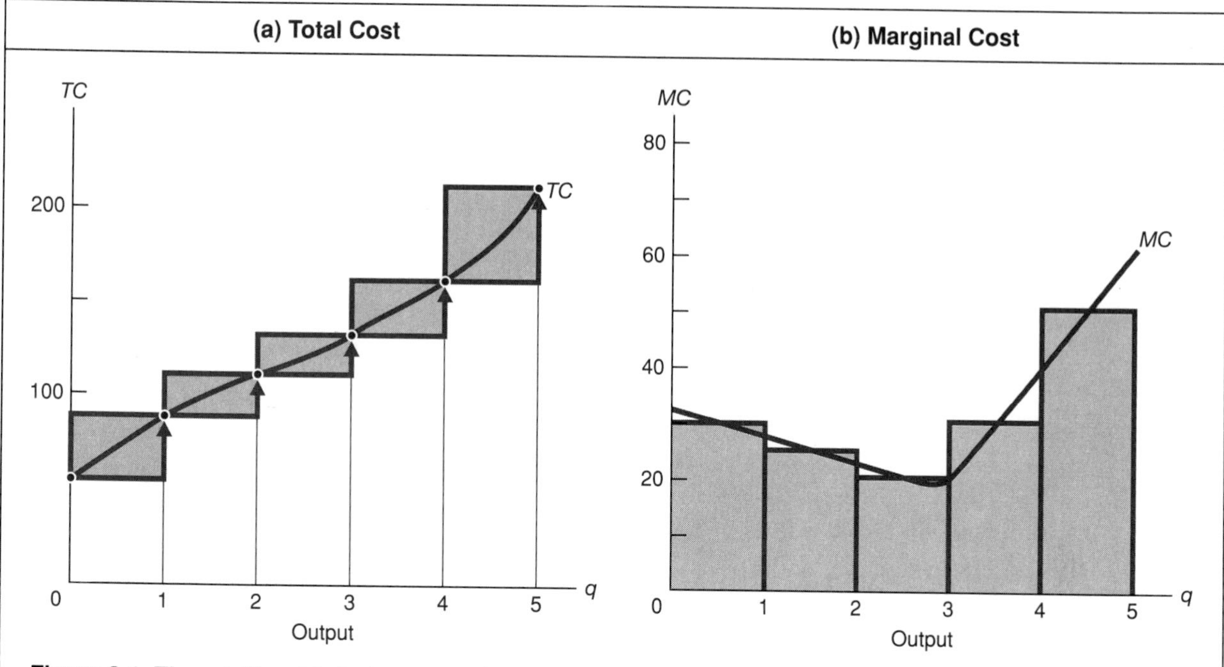

Figure 8-1. The relationship between total cost and marginal cost

This figure graphs the data from Table 8-2. Marginal cost in **(b)** is found by calculating the extra cost added in **(a)** for each unit increase in output. Thus to find the *MC* of producing the fifth unit, we subtract \$160 from \$210 to get *MC* of \$50. A smooth curve has been drawn through the points of *TC* in **(a)**, and the smooth *MC* curve in **(b)** links the discrete steps of *MC*.

ways grows exactly like total cost, the only difference being that *VC* must—by definition—start out from 0 rather than from the constant *FC* level. (Check that 30 − 0 = 85 − 55, and 55 − 30 = 110 − 85, and so on.)

The marginal cost of production is the additional cost incurred in producing 1 extra unit of output. It is calculated in Table 8-2 by comparing the total costs of producing adjacent output levels.

Marginal Cost in Diagrams. Figure 8-1 illustrates total cost and marginal cost. It shows that *TC* is related to *MC* in the same way that total product is related to marginal product or that total utility is related to marginal utility.

What kind of shape would we expect the *MC* curve to have? Empirical studies have found that for most production activities in the short run (i.e., when the capital stock is fixed), as well as for farming and many small businesses, the marginal cost curves are U-shaped like the one shown in Figure 8-1(*b*). This U-shaped curve falls in the initial phase, reaches a minimum point, and finally begins to rise.

Average Cost

We complete our catalogue of cost concepts important in economics and business with a discussion of different kinds of average or unit cost. Table 8-3 expands the data of Tables 8-1 and 8-2 to include three new measures: average cost, average fixed cost, and average variable cost.

Average or Unit Cost

One of the most important cost concepts is average cost, which, when compared with price or average revenue, will allow a business to determine whether or not it is making a profit. **Average cost** is the total cost divided by the number of units produced, as is shown in column (6) of Table 8-3. That is,

Important Cost Concepts

(1) Quantity q	(2) Fixed cost FC ($)	(3) Variable cost VC ($)	(4) Total cost $TC = FC + VC$ ($)	(5) Marginal cost per unit MC ($)	(6) Average cost per unit $AC = \frac{TC}{q}$ ($)	(7) Average fixed cost per unit $AFC = \frac{FC}{q}$ ($)	(8) Average variable cost per unit $AVC = \frac{VC}{q}$ ($)
0	55	0	55	33	Infinity	Infinity	Undefined
				30			
1	55	30	85	27	85	55	30
				25			
2	55	55	110	22	55	$27\frac{1}{2}$	$27\frac{1}{2}$
				20			
3	55	75	130	21	$43\frac{1}{3}$	$18\frac{1}{3}$	25
				30			
4*	**55**	**105**	**160**	40*	**40***	$\mathbf{13\frac{3}{4}}$	$\mathbf{26\frac{1}{4}}$
				50			
5	55	155	210	60	42	11	——
				——			
6	55	225	280	80	$46\frac{4}{6}$	$9\frac{1}{6}$	$37\frac{3}{6}$
				90			
7	55	——	370	100	$52\frac{6}{7}$	$7\frac{6}{7}$	45
				110			
8	55	——	480	120	60	$6\frac{7}{8}$	$53\frac{1}{8}$
				130			
9	55	555	610	140	$67\frac{7}{9}$	$6\frac{1}{9}$	$61\frac{6}{9}$
				150			
10	55	705	760		76	$5\frac{5}{10}$	$70\frac{5}{10}$

*Minimum level of average cost.

Table 8-3. All cost concepts derive from total cost schedule

We can derive all the different cost concepts from the *TC* in column (4). Columns (5) and (6) are the important ones to concentrate on: Incremental or marginal cost is calculated by subtraction of adjacent rows of *TC* and is shown in blue. The light blue numbers of smoothed *MC* come from Fig. 8-2(*b*). In column (6) note the point of minimum cost of $40 on the U-shaped *AC* curve in Fig. 8-2(*b*). (Can you see why the starred *MC* equals the starred *AC* at the minimum? Also, calculate and fill in all the missing numbers.)

$$\text{Average cost} = \frac{\text{total cost}}{\text{output}} = \frac{TC}{q} = AC$$

In column (6), when only 1 unit is produced, average cost has to be the same as total cost, or $85/1 = $85. But for $q = 2$, $AC = TC/2 = \$110/2 = \$55$, as shown. Note that average cost, at first, falls lower and lower. (We shall see why in a moment.) *AC* reaches a minimum of $40 at $q = 4$, and then slowly rises.

Figure 8-2 plots the cost data shown in Table 8-3. Figure 8-2(*a*) depicts the total, fixed, and variable costs at different levels of output. Figure 8-2(*b*) shows the different average cost concepts, along with a smoothed marginal cost curve. Graph (*a*) shows how total cost moves with variable cost while fixed cost remains unchanged.

Now turn to graph (*b*). This plots the U-shaped *AC* curve and aligns *AC* right below the *TC* curve from which it is derived.

Average Fixed and Variable Cost

Just as we separated total cost into fixed and variable cost, we can also break average cost into fixed and variable components. **Average fixed cost** (*AFC*) is defined as *FC*/*q*. Since total fixed cost is a constant, dividing it by an increasing output gives a steadily falling average fixed cost curve [see column (7) of Table 8-3]. The dashed black *AFC* curve in Fig-

(a) Total, Fixed, and Variable Cost

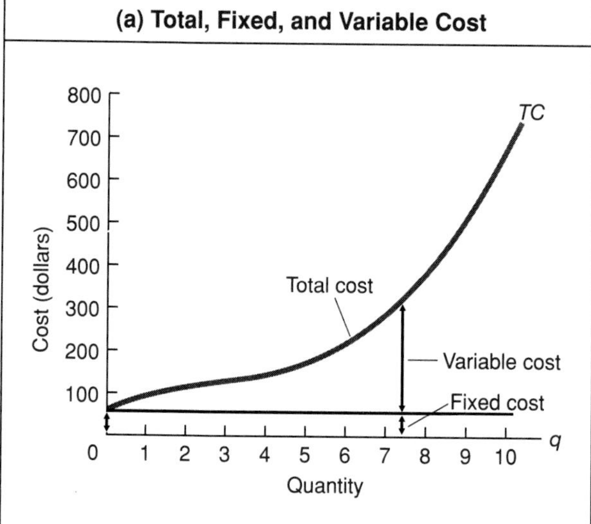

(b) Average Cost, Marginal Cost

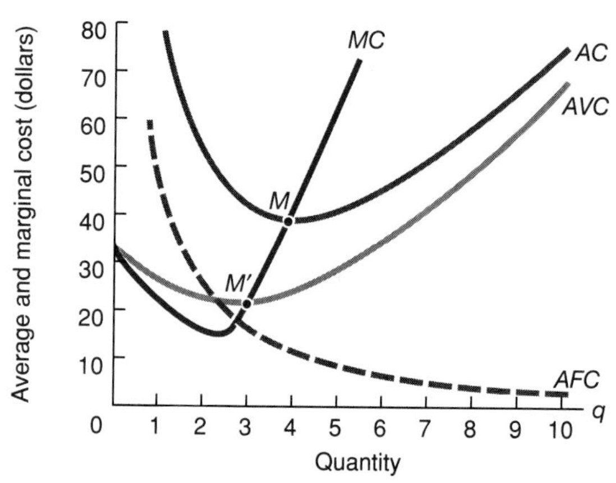

Figure 8-2. All cost curves can be derived from the total cost curve

(a) Total cost is made up of fixed cost and variable cost. **(b)** The blue curve of marginal cost falls and then rises, as indicated by the light blue *MC* figures given in column (5) of Table 8-3. The three average cost curves in **(b)** are calculated by dividing total, fixed, and variable cost by total output:

$$AC = TC/q \quad AVC = VC/q \quad \text{and} \quad AFC = FC/q.$$

Also, $AC = AVC + AFC$.

Note that *MC* intersects *AC* at its minimum.

ure 8-2(*b*) looks like a hyperbola, approaching both axes: it drops lower and lower, approaching the horizontal axis as the constant *FC* gets spread over more and more units. If we allow fractional units of *q*, *AFC* starts infinitely high as finite *FC* is spread over ever-tinier *q*.

Average variable cost (*AVC*) equals variable cost divided by output, or $AVC = VC/q$. As you can see in both Table 8-3 and Figure 8-2(*b*), for this example *AVC* first falls and then rises.

Minimum Average Cost

Figure 8-2(*b*) is a crucial diagram in economics. Fix it in your mind's eye. Note how the rising *MC* curve cuts the minimum point of the *AC* curve: *The* AC *curve is always pierced at its minimum point by the rising* MC *curve.* This means that if *MC* is below *AC* then *AC* must be falling. Why is this so? If *MC* is below *AC*, then the last unit produced costs less than the average cost of all the previous units produced. If the last unit costs less than the previous ones, then the new *AC* (i.e., the *AC* including the last unit) must be less than the old *AC*, so *AC* must be falling. In terms of our cost curves, if the *MC* curve is below the *AC* curve, then the *AC* curve must be falling.

What if *MC* is above *AC*? In this case, the last unit costs more than the average cost of the previous units. Hence the new average cost (the *AC* including the last unit) must be higher than the old *AC*. Therefore, when *MC* is above *AC*, *AC* must be rising.

Finally, when *MC* is just equal to *AC*, the last unit costs exactly the same as the average cost of all previous units. Hence the new *AC*, the one including the last unit, is equal to the old *AC*; the *AC* curve is flat when *AC* equals *MC*.

A Classroom Example. Here is an explanation of the *MC* and *AC* relationship in terms of college grade averages. Let *AG* be your average grades (or cumulative grade average up to now), and *MG* be your marginal or incremental grade average for this year. When *MG* is below *AG*, it will pull the new *AG* down. Thus if your *AG* for the first 2 years is 3, and your *MG* for your junior year is 2, then the new *AG* (at the end of your junior year) is $2\frac{2}{3}$. Similarly, if your *MG* in your third year is higher than your *AG* up to then, your new *AG* will be pulled up. Where *MG* equals *AG*, *AG* will be flat over time, or unchanged. The same relation holds for average and marginal cost.

To better understand the relationship between

MC and *AC*, study the curves in Figure 8-2(*b*) and the numbers in Table 8-3. Note that for the first 3 units, *MC* is below *AC*, and *AC* is therefore declining. At exactly 4 units *AC* equals *MC*. Over 4 units, *MC* is above *AC* and pulling *AC* up steadily.

To summarize:

When marginal cost is below average cost, it is pulling average cost down; when *MC* just equals *AC*, *AC* is neither rising nor falling and is at its minimum; when *MC* is above *AC*, it is pulling *AC* up. Hence:

At the bottom of U-shaped *AC*, $MC = AC =$ minimum *AC*.*

The Link between Production and Costs

You may be wondering, Just where do the firm's costs come from? In fact, cost curves are not the beginning of the story. Rather, they originate in the production techniques employed by the firm and in the prices the firm pays for the inputs. Now that both production and cost concepts have been presented, we describe their connection.

The link between costs and production is simple: for each level of output, firms must choose the least costly combination of inputs. A profit-oriented firm will always strive to choose the bundle of inputs that produces output at lowest cost. When the total cost of the least-cost bundle of inputs is calculated, we have the total cost shown in Tables 8-1 through 8-3.

We can see the derivation of cost from production data in a simple numerical example. Suppose Farmer Gomez rents 10 acres of land and can hire farm labor to produce wheat. Per period, land costs $5.5 per acre and labor costs $5 per worker. Using up-to-date farming methods, Gomez can produce according to the production function shown in the first three columns of Table 8-4. In this example, land is a fixed cost (because Farmer Gomez operates under a 10-year lease), while labor is a variable cost (because labor can easily be hired and fired).

Using the production data and the input-cost data, for each level of output we calculate the total cost of production shown in column (6) of Table 8-4. As an example, consider the total cost of production for 3 tons of wheat. Using the given production function, Gomez can produce this quantity with 10 acres of land and 15 farmhands. The total cost of producing 3 tons of wheat is (10 acres × $5.5 per acre) + (15 workers × $5 per worker) = $130. Similar calculations will give all the other total cost figures in column (6) of Table 8-4.

Note that these total costs are identical to the ones shown in Tables 8-1 through 8-3, so that the other cost concepts shown in the tables (i.e., *MC*, *FC*, *VC*, *AC*, *AFC*, and *AVC*) are also applicable to the production-cost example of Farmer Gomez.

Diminishing Returns and U-Shaped Cost Curves

The relationship between cost and production helps us explain why the U-shaped cost curves so prevalent in economics are grounded in the law of diminishing returns.

*One other important relation can be seen by looking at the total cost graph. In our example, we have seen large jumps in *MC* as output goes from one level to the next. Instead, focus a microscope on the total cost curve, examining the cost of going from 3.999 (thousand) *q* to 4.000 (thousand) *q*.

We saw how the slope of curved lines is measured back in the appendix to Chapter 1, and *MC* is an excellent illustration of the technique. Fig. 8-3 helps to clarify the distinction between (1) *MC* as an increment of cost for a finite step between two points of *q*, and (2) *MC* as the cost for an infinitesimal change in output measured by the tangent slope at one given *q* point. The distance from *a* to *b* represents 1 extra unit of output. The *b* to *a′* distance represents the resulting increase in total cost, which is the first and simplest definition of marginal cost.

The second definiton of marginal cost is as the slope of the total cost curve. The slope of the curve at point *a* is given by the slope of the tangent at point *a*, which is given by the distance from *b* to *c* divided by the unit distance *a* to *b*. In the limit, as the size of the extra units becomes small and we recalculate the ratios in the new smaller triangle, the discrepancy between the two definitions becomes negligible. (That is, ba'/bc approaches 1 as a' approaches a.)

Relation between Slope and Marginal Cost

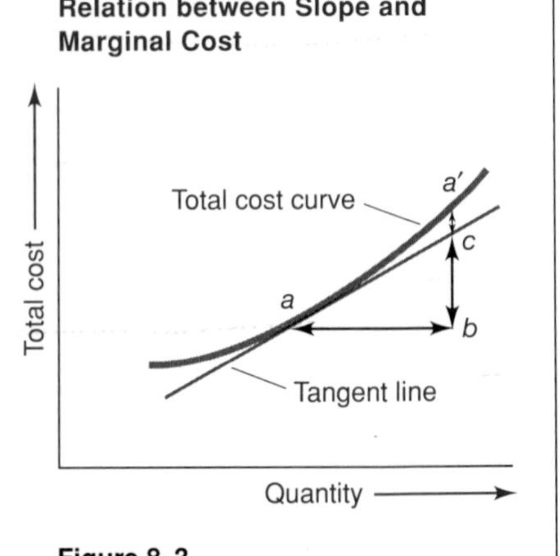

Figure 8-3

(1) Output (tons of wheat)	(2) Land inputs (acres)	(3) Labor inputs (workers)	(4) Land rent ($ per acre)	(5) Labor wage ($ per worker)	(6) Total cost ($)
0	10	0	5.5	5	55
1	10	6	5.5	5	85
2	10	11	5.5	5	110
3	10	15	5.5	5	130
4	10	21	5.5	5	160
5	10	31	5.5	5	210
6	10	45	5.5	5	280
7	10	63	5.5	5	370
8	10	85	5.5	5	480
9	10	111	5.5	5	610
10	10	141	5.5	5	760

Table 8-4. Costs are derived from production data and input costs

Farmer Gomez rents 10 acres of wheatland and employs variable labor. According to the farming production function, careful use of labor and land allows inputs and yields shown in columns (1) to (3) of the table. At input prices of $5.5 per acre and $5 per worker, we obtain Gomez' cost of production shown in column (6). All other cost concepts (such as those shown in Table 8-3) can be calculated from the total cost data.

Momentary, Short, and Long Run. The reasons for a U-shaped cost curve are best understood in terms of the time factor in production and cost. Planning and implementing decisions may take long periods of time. We therefore distinguish three different time periods in production and cost analysis. Recall our definitions of the momentary period, short run, and long run from Chapter 7 and apply those concepts to costs:

- The *momentary run* is the period of time so short that no change in production can take place; costs are fixed in this period.
- The *short run* is the period of time long enough to adjust variable inputs, such as materials and labor, but too short to allow all inputs to be changed. In the short run, overhead factors such as plant and equipment cannot be fully modified or adjusted. Therefore, in the short run, labor and materials costs are variable costs, while capital costs are fixed.
- In the *long run*, all inputs can be adjusted—including labor, materials, and capital; hence, in the long run, all costs are variable and none are fixed.[1]

In our cost analysis, consider the short run in which capital is fixed but labor is variable. Further suppose the firm operates in a competitive labor market, where each unit of labor has the same wage cost. In such a situation, the marginal cost of output will rise because the extra output produced by each extra labor unit is going down. In other words, diminishing returns to the variable factor will imply an increasing short-run marginal cost. This shows why diminishing returns leads to rising marginal costs after some point.

Figure 8-4, which contains exactly the same data as Table 8-4, illustrates the point. It shows that the region of increasing marginal product corresponds to falling marginal costs, while the region of diminishing returns implies rising marginal costs.

We can summarize the relationship between the productivity laws and the cost curves as follows:

In the short run, when factors such as capital are fixed, variable factors tend to show an initial phase of increasing returns followed by diminishing returns. The corresponding cost curves show an initial phase of declining marginal costs followed by increasing *MC* after diminishing returns have set in.

Choice of Inputs by the Firm

We can now apply the major cost concepts to the important problem of *how* a firm chooses its inputs. This section completes the link between production and cost by using the marginal product con-

[1] For a more complete discussion of momentary, short, and long runs, see Chapter 7.

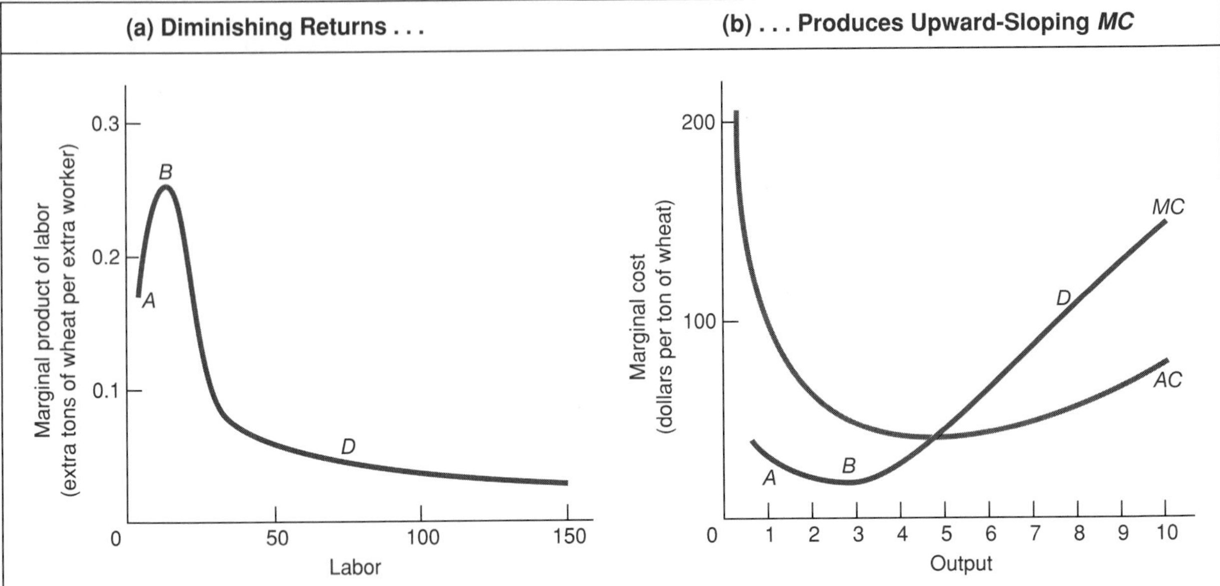

Figure 8-4. Diminishing returns and U-shaped cost curves

The U-shaped marginal cost curve in **(b)** arises from the shape of the marginal product curve in **(a)**. With fixed land and variable labor, the marginal product of labor in **(a)** first rises to the left of *B*, peaks at *B*, and then falls at *D* as diminishing returns to labor sets in.

The marginal cost curve derives from production data. In the region to the left of *B* in **(b)**—such as at point *A*—rising marginal product means that marginal cost is falling; at *B*, peak marginal product occurs at minimum marginal cost; in the region to the right of *B*, say at *D*, as marginal product of labor falls, the marginal cost of producing output increases.

Overall, increasing and then diminishing marginal product to the variable factor produces a U-shaped marginal cost curve.

cept to illustrate how firms select the least-cost combinations of inputs for a given set of input prices.

Marginal Products and the Least-Cost Rule

Every firm must decide how to produce its output. Should electricity be produced with oil or coal? Should classes be taught with faculty or graduate students? In large sections or small? In our analysis, we will rely on the fundamental assumption that *firms minimize their costs of production.* This cost-minimization assumption actually makes good sense not only for perfectly competitive firms but for monopolists or even nonprofit organizations like colleges or hospitals. It simply states that the firm should strive to produce its output at the lowest possible cost and thereby have the maximum amount of revenue left over for profits or for other objectives.

A simple example will illustrate how a firm might decide between different input combinations. Say a firm's engineers have calculated that the desired output level of 9 units could be produced with two possible options. In both cases, fuel (F) costs $2 per unit while labor ($L$) costs $5 per hour. Under option 1, the input mix is $F = 10$ and $L = 2$. Option 2 has $F = 4$ and $L = 5$. Which is the preferred option? At the market prices for inputs, total production costs for option 1 are ($2 × 10) + ($5 × 2) = $30, while total costs for option 2 are ($2 × 4) + ($5 × 5) = $33. Therefore, option 1 would be the preferred least-cost combination of inputs.

How can we generalize to cases where there are several possible input combinations? The general procedure is to begin by calculating the cost per unit of input of labor, fuel, capital, and so forth. Then calculate the marginal product of each input. The cost-minimizing combination of inputs comes when the marginal product per dollar of input is equal for all inputs. That is to say, the marginal contribution to output of each dollar's worth of labor, of land, of oil, and so forth must be just the same.

Following this reasoning, a firm will minimize its total cost of production when the marginal product per dollar of input is equalized for each factor of production. This is called the least-cost rule.

Least-cost rule: To produce a given level of output at least cost, a firm should buy inputs until it has equalized the marginal product per dollar spent on each input. This implies that

$$\frac{\text{Marginal product of } L}{\text{Price of } L} = \frac{\text{marginal product of } A}{\text{price of } A} = \cdots$$

This rule for firms is exactly analogous to what consumers do when they maximize utilities, as we saw in Chapter 6. In analyzing consumer choice, we saw that to maximize utility consumers should buy goods so that the marginal utility per dollar spent on each consumer good is equalized for all commodities.

What is the rationale for the least-cost rule? Let's say that land costs $800 an acre and labor costs $8 per hour. No one of sound mind would expect to achieve least cost if land and labor were chosen so that their marginal *physical* products were equal. If the marginal products of land and labor were both $100 worth of wheat, then equal marginal products would mean that $800 of extra land would produce $100 of wheat while $8 of extra labor would also produce $100 of wheat. Clearly this is inefficient, and the firm would want to decrease inputs of land and increase inputs of labor. Only when the marginal products per dollar of land and labor (and every other factor) were equal would the firm be minimizing its costs of production.

Another way of understanding the least-cost rule is the following: Break each factor into units worth $1 each (in our earlier fuel-labor example, $1 of labor would be one-fifth of an hour, while $1 of fuel would be $\frac{1}{2}$ unit). Then the least-cost rule states that the marginal product of each dollar-unit of input must be equalized.

Substitution Rule. A corollary of the least-cost rule is the substitution rule. If the price of one factor falls while all other factor prices remain the same, firms will profit by substituting the now-cheaper factor for all the other factors.

Let's take the case of labor (L). A fall in the price of labor will raise the ratio MP_L/P_L above the MP/P ratio for other inputs. Raising the employment of L lowers MP_L by the law of diminishing returns and therefore lowers MP_L/P_L. Lower price and MP of labor then bring the marginal product per dollar for labor back into equality with that ratio for other factors.

B. Business Accounting and Opportunity Costs

The first part of this chapter concentrated on the major concepts for measuring costs. But how do business firms actually measure costs? And what kinds of costs do economists include in their calculations?

This section explores these two questions. We first look at the rudiments of business accounting, which is the cornerstone of business decisions. We then compare the way businesses calculate costs with the broader economic concept of opportunity cost.

Principles of Accounting

Familiarity with the key concepts of accounting is a necessity for a full understanding of economics and business. Whether you run an enterprise or manage your own investments, you will depend on accounts to tell you whether you are making or losing money and which investments are thriving.

The Balance Sheet

We begin our discussion of accounting with the **balance sheet.** This is a statement that records what a firm, person, or nation is worth at a given point in time. On one side of the balance sheet are the **assets** (valuable properties or rights owned by the firm). On the other side are two items, the **liabilities** (money or obligations owed by the firm) and **net worth** (or net value, equal to total assets less total liabilities).

The fundamental identity or balancing relationship of the balance sheet is that total assets are balanced by total liabilities plus the net worth of the firm to its owners. That is,

Total assets = total liabilities + net worth

We can rearrange this relationship to find:

Net worth = assets − liabilities

Let us illustrate this by considering Table 8-5, which shows a simple balance sheet for a new international student business called Hot Dog Ventures, Inc. On the left are assets, and on the right are liabilities and net worth. A blank space (black dots) has been deliberately left next to the net worth entry because the only correct entry compatible with our fundamental balance sheet identity is $200,000. *A balance sheet must always balance* because net worth is a residual defined as assets minus liabilities.

To illustrate how net worth always balances, suppose that all the hot dogs have spoiled. Your accountant reports to you: "Total assets are down $40,000; liabilities remain unchanged. This means total net worth has decreased by $40,000, and I have no choice but to write net worth down from the previous $200,000 to only $160,000." That's how accountants keep score.

Accounting Conventions

In examining the balance sheet in Table 8-5 you might well ask, How are the values of the different items measured? How do the accountants know that the buildings are worth $100,000?

The answer is that accountants use a set of agreed-upon rules or accounting conventions to answer most questions. The most important assumption used in a balance sheet is that almost all items are measured at their transactions values or *historical costs.* This differs from the economist's concept of "value," as we will see shortly. Thus land enters the balance sheet at its purchase price; equipment and buildings enter the balance sheet at their purchase prices; and so forth. Accountants use historical cost because it reflects an objective evaluation and is easily verified.

In Table 8-5 current assets are convertible into cash within a year while fixed assets represent capital goods and land. Most of the specific items listed are more or less self-explanatory. Cash consists of coins, currency, and money on deposit in the bank. Cash is the only asset whose value is exact rather than an estimate.

Two elements of a balance sheet require mention: inventories and fixed assets. In both cases the difficulties arise because these assets are used up or consumed over time.

Inventory—consisting in the case of Hot Dog Ventures of hot dogs, buns, and storage equipment—can be valued in many different ways. Especially difficult problems arise when the costs of materials

Balance Sheet of Hot Dog Ventures, Inc. (December 31, 1992)

Assets		**Liabilities and net worth**	
		Liabilities	
Current assets:		Current liabilities:	
Cash	$ 20,000	Accounts payable	$ 20,000
Inventory	80,000	Notes payable	30,000
Fixed assets:		Long-term liabilities:	
Equipment	150,000	Bonds payable	100,000
Buildings	100,000		
		Net worth	
		Stockholders' equity:	
		Common stock	....
Total	$350,000	Total	$350,000

Table 8-5. The balance sheet records the stock of assets and liabilities, plus net worth, of a firm at a given point in time

Income Statement of Hot Dog Ventures, Inc.
(January 1, 1993, to December 31, 1993)

Net sales (after all discounts and rebates)		**$242,000**
Less cost of goods sold:		
Materials	$ 50,000	
Labor cost	90,000	
Depreciation	20,000	
Miscellaneous operating cost	10,000	
Selling and administrative costs	14,000	
Equals: Cost of goods sold	$184,000	184,000
Net operating income		$ 58,000
Less: Fixed interest charges and state and local taxes		8,500
Net income (or profit) before income taxes		$ 49,500
Less: Corporation income taxes		15,000
Net income (or profit) after taxes		**$ 34,500**
Less: Dividends paid on common stock		14,500
Addition to retained earnings		$ 20,000

Table 8-6. The income statement shows total sales and expenses for a period of time, usually a year

vary over time. Some companies value inventories at the original cost, while others value them at the price of current purchases.

The other slippery item on the balance sheet is fixed assets—buildings and equipment. A new piece of capital is valued at its purchase price (this being the historical cost convention). Older capital is "depreciated," which means that we make an allowance for using up durable capital goods.

On the liabilities side, accounts payable and notes payable are sums owed to others for goods bought or for borrowed funds. Bonds payable are long-term loans floated in the market. The last item on the balance sheet is net worth, or stockholders' equity. This is the net value of the firm's assets less liabilities, when valued at historical cost. The net worth must equal $200,000.

The Income Statement, or Statement of Profit and Loss

Let time march on. In the months following the balance sheet shown in Table 8-5, Hot Dog Ventures has earned a profit. To show its flow of income over the 12 months of the year, we must turn to its **income statement,** or—as many companies prefer to call it—the statement of profit and loss, shown in Table 8-6.

This statement reports the following: (1) Hot Dog Venture's revenues from sales in 1993, (2) the expenses to be charged against those sales, and (3) the net income, or profits remaining after expenses have been deducted. That is,

$$\text{Net income (or profit)} = \text{total revenue} - \text{total expenses}$$

which is the fundamental identity of the income statement.

Look first at the figures in the far right-hand column. Sales were $242,000; the total cost of goods sold came to $184,000. Thus $58,000 remained in net operating income. A total of $8500 plus $15,000 in interest and various taxes had to be paid out of this, leaving $34,500 in net income or profit after taxes. Dividends of $14,500 on the common stock were paid, leaving $20,000 to be plowed back as retained earnings in the business. *Note that profits are a residual of sales minus costs.*

Now turn back to the cost of goods sold. Most of these items are self-explanatory: material, labor, miscellaneous, and selling and administration. But, as with the balance sheet, there are two particularly tricky items on the income statement—inventories and depreciation. In our simple example shown in Table 8-6, Hot Dog had no change in inventories, so no problem of valuing inventories arose. If, however, there had been a change in the stock of finished goods, we would have to determine the value of the changed stock of goods.

Depreciation. The $20,000 charge for depreciation shown in Table 8-6 represents the charge for the cost of using fixed assets such as buildings and equipment. How is depreciation calculated?

Most companies own their own capital goods, but these assets do not last forever. Trucks wear out, computers become obsolete, and buildings eventually begin to deteriorate. The accountant naturally includes an appropriate charge or cost for fixed assets along with all other costs. But just how do we determine how much of an asset is "used up" in a given year?

To account for this decline in the value of fixed assets, accountants depreciate them by using a depreciation formula. There are a number of different formulas, but each follows two major principles: (*a*) The total amount of depreciation plus salvage value must equal the capital good's historical cost or purchase price; and (*b*) the depreciation is taken in annual accounting charges (even if no money ever leaves the firm) over the asset's accounting lifetime, which is usually related to the actual economic lifetime of the asset.

We can now understand how depreciation would be charged for Hot Dog Ventures. The equipment is depreciated according to a 10-year lifetime, so that the $150,000 of equipment has a depreciation charge of $15,000 per year. The $100,000 of buildings, carrying a 20-year lifetime, shows an annual depreciation charge of $5000. The total depreciation charge for 1993 is then $20,000—as is shown in Table 8-6.

We summarize our analysis of accounting concepts as follows:

- The balance sheet indicates an instantaneous financial picture or snapshot. It is like a measure of the stock of water in a lake. The major items are assets, liabilities, and net worth.
- The income statement shows the flow of sales, cost, and revenue over the year or accounting period. It measures the flow of dollars into and out of the firm—the progress of the firm over the year.

Opportunity Costs

Chapter 2 introduced the notion of opportunity cost. How do opportunity costs relate to the dollar costs measured by firms and analyzed in this chapter? In general, the economist insists on going behind the dollar transactions to measure the true *resource costs* of an activity. Economists include all costs—whether they reflect monetary transactions or not; business accounts generally exclude nonmonetary transactions.

For example, business accounts do not include a capital charge for the owner's financial contributions; nor do they count the owner's labor in a small business; nor do they include the environmental damage that occurs when a business dumps toxic wastes into a stream. But from an economic point of view, these are genuine costs to the economy and should be included.

The concept that can help us understand the distinction between money costs and true economic costs is **opportunity cost.** As was shown in Chapter 2, the opportunity cost of an action denotes the opportunities forgone, or the costs incurred, by taking that action rather than the best alternative decision.

Let's illustrate the concept of opportunity cost by considering the owner of Hot Dog Ventures. The owner puts in 60 hours a week but earns no "wages." At the end of the year, as Table 8-6 showed, the firm earns a profit of $20,000—pretty good for a neophyte firm.

Or is it? The economist would maintain that the return to a factor of production is economically important regardless of how the factor happens to be owned. We should count the owner's own labor as a cost even though the owner does not get paid directly but instead receives compensation in the form of profits. Because the owner has alternative opportunities for work, we must value the owner's labor in terms of the lost opportunities.

A careful examination might show that Hot Dog's owner could find a similar and equally interesting job working for someone else and earning $45,000. This represents the opportunity cost or earnings forgone because the owner decided to become the unpaid owner of a small business rather than the paid employee of another firm.

Therefore, the economist continues, let us calculate the true profits of the hot-dog firm. If we take the measured profits of $20,000 and subtract the $45,000 opportunity cost of the owner's labor, we find a net *loss* of $25,000. Hence, although the accountant might conclude that Hot Dog Ventures was economically viable, the economist would pronounce that the firm was an unprofitable loser.[2]

Opportunity Cost and Markets

The concept of opportunity cost applies far more broadly than simply to the unpaid factors used by a firm. It concerns the true economic cost or consequence of making decisions in a world where goods are scarce.

At this point, however, you might well say: "Now I'm totally confused. First I learned that price is a good measure of true social cost in the marketplace. Now you tell me that opportunity cost is the right concept. Isn't there an inconsistency here?"

Actually, no. You will be interested to learn that in well-functioning markets *price equals opportunity cost.* Assume that a commodity like coal is bought and sold in a competitive market. If I bring my ton of coal to market, I will receive a number of bids from prospective buyers: $25.02, $24.98, $25.01. These represent the values of my coal to, say, three electric utilities. I pick the highest—$25.02. The opportunity cost of this sale is the value of the best available alternative—that is, the second-highest bid at $25.01—which is almost identical to the price that is accepted. As the market approaches absolutely perfect competition, the bids get closer and closer until in the limit the second-highest bid (which is our definition of opportunity cost) exactly equals the highest bid (which is the price). This example shows that in competitive markets, numerous buyers compete for resources to the point where price is bid up to the best available alternative and is therefore equal to the opportunity cost.

Opportunity Costs outside Markets. The concept of opportunity cost is particularly crucial when analyzing transactions that take place outside markets. How do you measure the value of a road or a park? Of a health or safety regulation? Even the allocation of student time can be explained using opportunity cost.

- The notion of opportunity cost might explain why students watch more TV the week after exams than the week before exams. Watching TV right before an exam has a high opportunity cost, for the alternative use of time (studying) would have high value in improving grade performance. After exams, time has a lower opportunity cost.
- Say the federal government wants to drill for oil off the California coast. A storm of complaints is heard. A defender of the program states, "What's all the ruckus about? There's valuable oil out there, and there is plenty of seawater to go around. This is very low-cost oil for the nation."

  In fact, the opportunity cost might be very high. If drilling leads to oil spills that spoil the beaches, recreational activities might suffer. The opportunity cost might not be easily measured, but the recreational value of the ocean is every bit as real as the value of oil under the waters.

The Road Not Traveled. Opportunity cost, then, is a measure of what has been given up when we make a decision. Consider what Robert Frost had in mind when he wrote

> Two roads diverged in a wood, and I—
> I took the one less traveled by,
>
> And that has made all the difference.

What other road did Frost have in mind? An urban life? An avocation where he would not be able to write of roads and walls and birches? Imagine the immeasurable opportunity cost to all of us if Robert Frost had taken the road more traveled by.

But let us return from the poetic to practical concepts of cost. The crucial point to grasp is this:

Economic costs include, in addition to explicit money outlays, those opportunity costs that arise because resources can be used in alternative ways.

● Our discussion of production and cost has surveyed both economic and business definitions along with the important total, average, and marginal cost concepts. The appendix pursues those issues in greater depth. In the next chapter, we show how firms' and industries' supply decisions are directly derived from their marginal cost curves. ●

[2] If you happen to own very fertile land and persist in cultivating it by uneconomical methods, you will be paying for your folly or stubbornness by forgoing the high return such land is capable of yielding. In dollars, the land is worth more to others than to you, and if you refuse to rent or sell, you are as surely spending your sustenance to please your own tastes as you would be doing if you sold the land and spent the proceeds on wine, skiing, or song.

SUMMARY

A. Economic Analysis of Costs

1. Total cost (TC) can be broken down into fixed cost (FC) and variable cost (VC). Fixed costs are unaffected by any production decisions, while variable costs are incurred on items like labor or materials which increase as production levels rise.

2. Marginal cost (MC) is the extra total cost resulting from 1 extra unit of output. Average total cost (AC) is the sum of ever-declining average fixed cost (AFC) and average variable cost (AVC). Short-run average cost is generally represented by a U-shaped curve that is always intersected at its minimum point by the rising MC curve.

3. Useful rules to remember are:

$$TC = FC + VC \qquad AC = \frac{TC}{q} \qquad AC = AFC + AVC$$

   At the bottom of U-shaped AC, $MC = AC =$ minimum AC.

4. Costs and productivity are like mirror images. When the law of diminishing returns holds, the marginal product falls and the MC curve rises. When there is an initial stage of increasing returns, MC initially falls. If all factors of production could be bought at unchanged prices, and output were to show constant returns to scale, long-run marginal costs would be horizontal forever.

5. We can apply cost and production concepts to understand a firm's choice of the best combination of factors of production. Firms that desire to maximize profits will want to minimize the cost of producing a given level of output. In this case, the firm will follow the least-cost rule: different factors will be chosen so that the marginal product per dollar of input is equalized for all inputs. This implies that $MP_L/P_L = MP_A/P_A = \cdots$.

B. Business Accounting and Opportunity Costs

6. To understand accounting, the most important relationships are:
   (a) The fundamental balance sheet relationship between assets, liabilities, and net worth; the breakdown of each of these into financial and fixed assets; and the residual nature of net worth.
   (b) The character of the income statement (or profit-and-loss statement); the residual nature of profits; depreciation on fixed assets.

7. The economist's definition of costs is broader than the accountant's. Economic cost includes not only the obvious out-of-pocket purchases but also more subtle opportunity costs, such as the return to labor supplied by the owner of a firm. These opportunity costs are tightly constrained by the bids and offers in competitive markets, so that price is usually close to opportunity cost for marketed goods and services. The most important application of opportunity cost arises for nonmarket goods—those like clean air or

health or recreation—where the services may be highly valuable even though they are not bought and sold in markets.

CONCEPTS FOR REVIEW

Analysis of costs
total costs: fixed and variable
$TC = FC + VC$
$AC = TC/q = AFC + AVC$
marginal cost
least-cost rule:

$$\frac{MP_L}{P_L} = \frac{MP_A}{P_A} = \frac{MP_{\text{any factor}}}{P_{\text{any factor}}}$$

Concepts of accounting
fundamental balance sheet identity
assets, liabilities, and net worth
income statement
sales, cost, profits
cost concepts in economics and accounting
opportunity costs

QUESTIONS FOR DISCUSSION

1. Make a list of cost elements: wages, salaries, fuel, rentals, etc. Divide them into fixed and variable categories.
2. Explain the difference between marginal cost and average cost. Why should *AVC* always look much like *MC*? Why is *MC* the same when computed from *VC* as from *TC*?
3. To the $55 of fixed cost in Table 8-3, add $90 of additional *FC*. Now calculate a whole new table, with the same *VC* as before but new *FC* = $145. What happens to *MC, AVC*? To *TC, AC, AFC*? Can you verify that minimum *AC* is now at $q^* = 5$ with *AC* = $60 = *MC*?
4. Explain why *MC* cuts *AC* and *AVC* at the bottom of their U's.
5. Relate the rising *MC* curve to the law of diminishing returns. Contrast the falling part of the curve with that law.
6. Consider the data in the following table, which contains a situation similar to that in Table 8-4.
   (a) Calculate the *TC, VC, FC, AC, AVC*, and *MC*. On a piece of graph paper, plot the *AC* and *MC* curves.
   (b) Assume that the price of labor doubles. Calculate a new *AC* and *MC*. Plot the new curves and compare them with those in (a).
   (c) Now assume that total factor productivity doubles (i.e., that the level of output doubles for each input combination). Repeat the exercise in (b). Can you see two major factors that tend to affect a firm's cost curves?
7. Explain the fallacies in each of the following:
   (a) Average costs are minimized when marginal costs are at their lowest point.
   (b) Because fixed costs never change, average fixed cost is a constant for each level of output.
   (c) Average cost is rising whenever marginal cost is rising.
   (d) The opportunity cost of drilling for oil in Yosemite Park is zero because no firm produces anything there.
   (e) A firm minimizes costs when it spends the same amount on each input.
8. Say you are considering whether to fly or take the bus from Atlanta to New Orleans. The airfare is $100, and the flight takes 1 hour. Bus fare is $50, and the trip

(1) Output (tons of wheat)	(2) Land inputs (acres)	(3) Labor inputs (workers)	(4) Land rent ($ per acre)	(5) Labor wage ($ per worker)
0	15	0	12	5
1	15	6	12	5
2	15	11	12	5
3	15	15	12	5
4	15	21	12	5
5	15	31	12	5
6	15	45	12	5
7	15	63	12	5

takes 6 hours. Which is the most economical way to travel for: (*a*) a businessperson whose time costs $40 per hour, (*b*) a student whose time is worth $4 per hour, (*c*) you? Show how the concept of opportunity cost is crucial here.

9. In 1991 a company has $10 million of net sales and $9 million of costs of all kinds (including taxes, rentals, etc.) and rents its equipment and plant. Its inventory doesn't change in the year. It pays no dividends. Draw up its simplified 1991 income statement.

10. At the end of 1990, the company in question 9 owes no money, having been completely financed by common stock. Fill in the year-end balance sheet for 1990 using the data in the table below. Then, using the data and income statement from question 9, complete the balance sheet for 1991.

Assets (end of year)			Liabilities and net worth (end of year)		
	1990	1991		1990	1991
			Liabilities	0	0
			Net worth	....	....
Total	$50 million	....	Total	....	....

APPENDIX 8

PRODUCTION, COST THEORY, AND DECISIONS OF THE FIRM

The production theory described in Chapter 7 and the cost analysis of this chapter are among the fundamental building blocks of microeconomics. A thorough understanding of production and cost is necessary for an appreciation of how economic scarcity gets translated into prices in the marketplace. This appendix develops these concepts further and introduces the concept of an equal-product curve, or isoquant.

A Numerical Production Function

Production and cost analysis have their roots in the concept of a production function, which shows the maximum amount of output that can be produced with various combinations of inputs. Table 8A-1 starts with a numerical example of a constant-returns-to-scale production function, showing the amount of inputs along the axes and the amount of output at the grid points of the table.

Along the left-hand side are listed the varying amounts of land, going from 1 unit to 6 units. Along the bottom are listed amounts of labor, which also go from 1 to 6. Output corresponding to each land row and labor column is listed inside the table.

If we are interested in knowing exactly how much output there will be when 3 units of land and 2 units of labor are available, we count up 3 units of land and then go over 2 units of labor. The answer is seen to be 346 units of product. (Can you identify some other input combinations to produce $q =$ 346?) Similarly, we find that 3 units of land and 6 of labor produce 600 units of q. Remember that the production function shows the *maximum* output available given engineering skills and technical knowledge available at a given time.

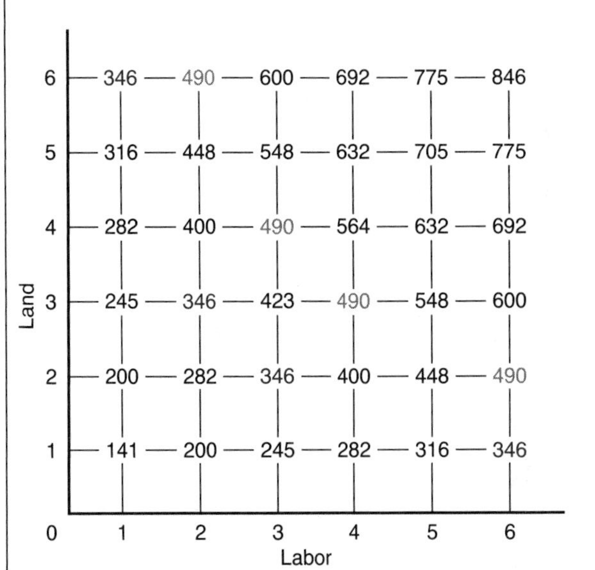

Land \ Labor	1	2	3	4	5	6
6	346	490	600	692	775	846
5	316	448	548	632	705	775
4	282	400	490	564	632	692
3	245	346	423	490	548	600
2	200	282	346	400	448	490
1	141	200	245	282	316	346
0						

Table 8A-1. A tabular picture of a production function relating amount of output to varying combinations of labor and land inputs

When you have 3 land units and 2 labor units available, the engineer tells you your maximum obtainable output is 346 units. Note the different ways to produce 346. Do the same for 490. (The production function shown in the table is a special case of the "Cobb-Douglas production function," one given by the formula $Q = 100\sqrt{2LA}$.)

The Law of Diminishing Marginal Product

Table 8A-1 can nicely illustrate the law of diminishing returns. First recall that the marginal product of labor is the extra production resulting from 1 additional unit of labor when land and other inputs are held constant. At any point in Table 8A-1, we can find the marginal product of labor by subtracting the output from the number on its right in the same row. Thus, when there are 2 units of land and 4 units of labor, the marginal product of an additional laborer would be 48, or 448 minus 400 in the second row.

By the "marginal product of land" we mean, of course, the extra product resulting from 1 additional unit of land when labor is held constant. It is calculated by comparing adjacent items in a given column. Thus, when there are 2 units of land and 4 units of labor, the marginal product of land is shown in the fourth column as 490 − 400, or 90.

We can easily find the marginal product of each of our two factors by comparing adjacent entries in vertical columns or horizontal rows of Table 8A-1.

Having defined the concept of marginal product of an input, we now can easily define the law of diminishing returns: The law of diminishing returns states that as we increase one input and hold other inputs constant, the marginal product of the varying input will, at least after some point, decline.

To illustrate this, hold land constant in Table 8A-1 by sticking to a given row—say, the row corresponding to land equal to 2 units. Now let labor increase from 1 to 2 units, from 2 to 3 units, and so forth. What happens to q at each step?

As labor goes from 1 to 2 units, the level of output increases from 200 to 282 units, or by 82 units. But the next dose of labor adds only 64 units, or 346 − 282. Diminishing returns has set in. Still further additions of a single unit of labor give us, respectively, only 54 extra units of output, 48 units, and finally 42 units. You can easily verify that the law holds for other rows, and that the law holds when land is varied and labor held constant.

We can use this example to verify our intuitive justification of the law of diminishing returns—the assertion that the law holds because the fixed factor decreases relative to the variable factor. According to this explanation, each unit of the variable factor has less and less of the fixed factor to work with. So it is natural that extra product should drop off.

If this explanation is to hold water, there should be no diminishing returns when *both* factors are increased proportionately. When labor increases from 1 to 2 and land *simultaneously* increases from 1 to 2, we should get the same increase in product as when both increase simultaneously from 2 to 3. This can be verified in Table 8A-1. In the first move we go from 141 to 282, and in the second move the product increases from 282 to 423, an equal jump of 141 units.

Least-Cost Factor Combination for a Given Output

The numerical production function shows us the different ways to produce a given level of output. But which of the many possibilities should the firm use? If the desired level of output is $q = 346$, there are no less than four different combinations of land and labor, shown as *A*, *B*, *C*, and *D* in Table 8A-2.

As far as the engineer is concerned, each of these combinations is equally good at producing an output of 346 units. But the manager interested in minimizing cost wants to find the combination that costs least.

Let us suppose that the price of labor is \$2 and the price of land \$3. The total costs when input prices are at this level are shown in the third column of the blue row of numbers in Table 8A-2. For combination *A*, the total labor and land cost will be \$20, equal to (1 × \$2) + (6 × \$3). Costs at *B*, *C*, and *D*

	(1) Input combinations	(2)	(3) Total cost when $P_L = \$2$ $P_A = \$3$	(4) Total cost when $P_L = \$2$ $P_A = \$1$
	Labor L	Land A	(\$)	(\$)
A	1	6	20	–
B	2	3	13	7
C	3	2	12	–
D	6	1	15	–

Table 8A-2. Inputs and costs of producing a given level of output

Assume that the firm has chosen 346 units of output. Then it can use any of the four choices of input combinations shown as *A*, *B*, *C*, and *D*. As the firm moves down the list, production becomes more labor-intensive and less land-intensive.

The firm's choice among the different techniques will depend on input prices. When $P_L = \$2$ and $P_A = \$3$, verify that the cost-minimizing combination is *C*. Show that lowering the price of land from \$3 to \$1 leads the firm to a more land-intensive combination at *B*.

will be, respectively, $13, $12, and $15. At the assumed input prices, *C* is the least costly way to produce the given output.

If either of the input prices changes, the equilibrium proportion of the inputs will also change so as to use less of the input that has gone up most in price. (This is just like the substitution effect of Chapter 6's discussion of consumer demand.) As soon as input prices are known, the least-cost method of production can be found by calculating the costs of different input combinations.

Equal-Product Curves

The common-sense numerical analysis of the way in which a firm will combine inputs to minimize costs can be made more vivid by the use of diagrams. We will take the diagrammatic approach by putting together two new curves, the equal-product curve and the equal-cost line.

Let's turn Table 8A-1 into a continuous curve by drawing a smooth curve through all the points that yield $q = 346$. This smooth curve, shown in Figure 8A-1, indicates all the different combinations of labor and land that yield an output of 346 units. This is called an **equal-product curve** or **isoquant** and is analogous to the consumer's indifference curve discussed in the appendix to Chapter 6. You should be able to draw on Figure 8A-1 the corresponding equal-product curve for output equal to 490 by getting the data from Table 8A-1. Indeed, an infinite number of such equal-product contour lines could be drawn in.

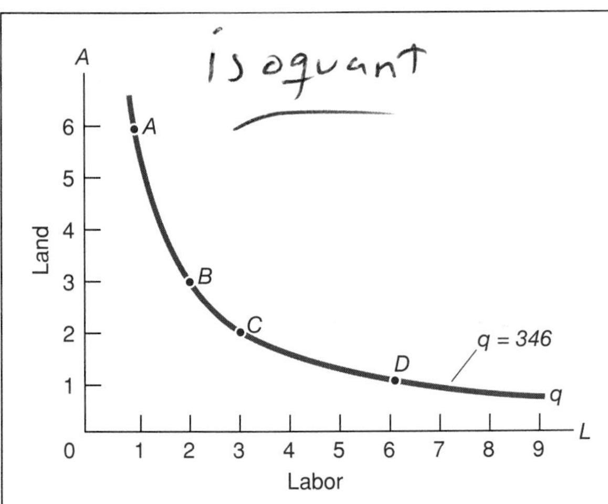

Figure 8A-1. Equal-product curve

All the points on the equal-product curve represent the different combinations of land and labor that can be used to produce the same 346 units of output.

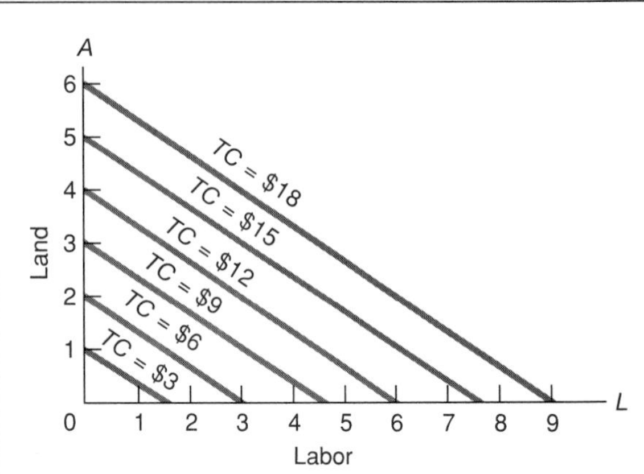

Figure 8A-2. Equal-cost lines

Every point on a given equal-cost line represents the same total cost. The lines are straight because factor prices are constant, and they all have a negative slope equal to the ratio of labor price to land price, $2/$3, and hence are parallel.

Equal-Cost Lines

Given the price of labor and land, the firm can evaluate the total cost for points *A*, *B*, *C*, and *D*, or for any other point on the equal-product curve. The firm will minimize its costs when it selects that point on its equal-product curve that has the lowest total cost.

An easy technique for finding the least-cost method of production is to construct **equal-cost lines.** This is done in Figure 8A-2, where the family of parallel straight lines represents a number of equal-cost curves when the price of labor is $2 and the price of land $3.

To find the total cost for any point, we simply read off the number appended to the equal-cost line going through that point. The lines are all straight and parallel because the firm is assumed to be able to buy all it wishes of either input at constant prices. The lines are somewhat flatter than 45° because the price of labor P_L is somewhat less than the price of land P_A. More precisely, we can always say that the arithmetic value of the slope of each equal-cost line must equal the ratio of the price of

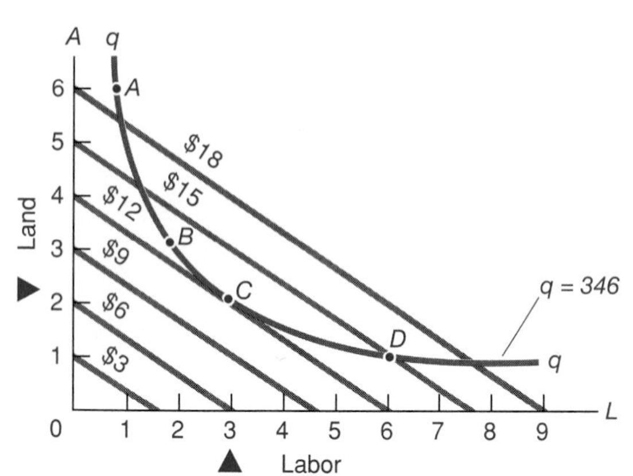

Figure 8A-3. Least-cost input combination comes at *C*

The firm desires to minimize its costs of producing a given output of 346. It thus seeks out the least expensive input combination along its blue equal-product curve. It looks for the input combination that is on the lowest of the equal-cost lines. Where the equal-product curve touches (but does not cross) the lowest equal-cost line is the least-cost position. This tangency means that factor prices and marginal products are proportional, with equalized marginal products per dollar.

labor to that of land—in this case $P_L/P_A = \frac{2}{3}$.

Equal-Product and Equal-Cost Contours: Least-Cost Tangency

Combining the equal-product and equal-cost lines, we can determine the optimal, or cost-minimizing, position of the firm. Recall that the optimal input combination comes at that point where the given output of $q = 346$ can be produced at least cost. To find such a point, simply superimpose the single blue equal-product curve upon the family of black equal-cost lines, as is shown in Figure 8A-3. The firm will always keep moving along the blue convex curve of Figure 8A-3 as long as it is able to cross over to lower cost lines. Its equilibrium will therefore be at *C*, where the equal-product curve touches (but does not cross) the lowest equal-cost line. This is a point of tangency, where the slope of the equal-product curve just matches the slope of an equal-cost line and the curves are just kissing.

We already know that the slope of the equal-cost curves is P_L/P_A. But what is the slope of the equal-product curve? Recall from Chapter 1's appendix that the slope at a point of a curved line is the slope of the straight line tangent to the curve at the point in question. For the equal-product curve, this slope is a "substitution ratio" between the two factors. It depends upon the relative marginal products of the two factors of production, namely, MP_L/MP_A—just as the rate of substitution between two goods along a consumer's indifference curve was earlier shown to equal the ratio of the marginal utilities of the two goods (see the appendix to Chapter 6).

Least-Cost Conditions

Using our graphical apparatus, we have therefore derived the conditions under which a firm will minimize its costs of production:

1. The ratio of marginal products of any two inputs must equal the ratio of their factor prices.

   Substitution ratio

$$= \frac{\text{marginal product of labor}}{\text{marginal product of land}}$$

$$= \begin{array}{c}\text{slope of}\\ \text{equal-product}\\ \text{curve}\end{array} = \frac{\text{price of labor}}{\text{price of land}}$$

2. The marginal product per dollar received from the (last) dollar of expenditure must be the same for every productive factor.

$$\frac{\text{Marginal product of } L}{\text{Price of } L} = \frac{\text{marginal product of } A}{\text{price of } A} = \cdots$$

But you should not be satisfied with abstract explanations. Always remember the common-sense economic explanation which shows how a firm will distribute its expenditure among inputs to equalize the marginal product per dollar of spending.

SUMMARY

1. A production-function table lists, for each labor column and each land row, the output that is producible. Diminishing returns to one variable factor, when other factors are held fixed or constant, can be shown by calculating the decline of marginal products in any row or column.

2. An equal-product curve depicts the alternative input combinations that produce the same level of output. The slope, or substitution ratio, along such an equal-product curve equals relative marginal products (e.g., MP_L/MP_A). Curves of equal total cost are parallel lines with slopes equal to factor-price ratios (P_L/P_A). Least-cost equilibrium comes at the tangency point, where an equal-product curve touches but does not cross the lowest TC curve. In least-cost equilibrium, marginal products are proportional to factor prices, with equalized marginal product per dollar spent on all factors (i.e., equalized MP_i/P_i).

CONCEPTS FOR REVIEW

equal-product curves
parallel lines of equal TC
substitution ratio $= MP_L/MP_A$

P_L/P_A as the slope of parallel equal-TC lines

least-cost tangency: $MP_L/MP_A = P_L/P_A$ or $MP_L/P_L = MP_A/P_A$

QUESTIONS FOR DISCUSSION

1. Show that raising labor's wage while holding land's rent constant will steepen the black equal-cost lines and move tangency point C in Figure 8A-3 northwest toward B with the now-cheaper input substituted for the input which is now more expensive. Should union leaders recognize this relationship?
2. What is the least-cost combination of inputs if the production function is given by Table 8A-1 and input prices are as shown in Figure 8A-3, where $q = 346$? What would be the least-cost ratio for the same input prices if output doubled to $q = 692$? What has happened to the "factor intensity," or land/labor ratio? Can you see why this result would hold for any output change under constant returns to scale?

CHAPTER 9

SUPPLY AND PRICING IN COMPETITIVE MARKETS

Cost of production would have
no effect on competitive price
if it could have none on supply.
John Stuart Mill

There are two sides to every market: supply and demand. If we want to understand why oil prices doubled in the fall of 1990, causing turmoil in financial markets and anxiety among consumers, we must examine carefully the complex interaction of supply and demand in the world oil market. We have to study the determinants of the demand for oil products. And, on the supply side, we must appreciate how business decisions depend upon costs of production. All these building blocks of supply and demand were explored in earlier chapters; the time has come to put the blocks together to analyze competitive markets.

First we will look at how the cost of production determines the supply behavior of competitive firms and industries. We will see that the production of a profit-maximizing firm depends upon its cost of production. The firm's marginal cost of production plays a central role in affecting its supply decisions.

The second half of the chapter shows that marginal cost is central for the industry as well as for the firm. We end by investigating the efficiency of a competitive industry. We will see that there is no reorganization of production that can improve the resource allocation generated by a competitive market, although the allocation will not necessarily be fair or equitable.

A. Supply Behavior of the Competitive Firm

Business enterprises are crucial to a market economy. This fact was captured in J. M. Keynes' remark: "If Enterprise is afoot, wealth accumulates whatever may be happening to Thrift; and if Enterprise is asleep, wealth decays whatever Thrift may be doing." But how exactly does a business enterprise behave? How much should a perfectly competitive firm produce? How much wheat should Farmer Gomez produce if wheat sells at $3 per bushel? How many tons of coal should Pittsburgh Coal and Coke produce if the market price of coal is $25 per ton?

Behavior of a Competitive Firm

In this chapter's analysis of perfectly competitive firms, we will assume that our competitive firm *maximizes profits,* which are equal to total revenues minus total costs. Profit maximization requires that the firm must manage its internal operations efficiently (prevent waste, encourage worker morale, choose efficient production processes, and so forth) and make sound decisions in the marketplace (buy the correct quantity of inputs at least cost and choose the optimal level of output).

Why would a firm want to maximize profits? Profits are like the net earnings or take-home pay of a corporation. They represent the amount a firm can reinvest in new plant and equipment, use to buy other firms, or employ to make financial investments. All these activities increase the value of the firm to its owners.

Because profits involve both costs and revenues, the firm must have a good grasp of its *cost structure.* The previous chapter analyzed the most important cost concepts. Remember the concepts of total cost and average or unit cost, as well as the crucial concept of marginal cost, which is extra cost that comes from producing an additional unit of output. Turn back to Table 8-3 on p. 122 to make sure that you are clear on these important cost concepts.

The world of perfect competition is the world of *price-takers.* A price-taker is a firm that is so small relative to its market that the firm cannot affect the market price but simply takes the price as given. When farmers are selling a homogeneous product like wheat, they can sell to a large number of buyers who are willing to pay the market price of $3 per bushel. Just as most households must accept the prices that are charged by grocery stores or movie theaters, so must competitive firms accept the market prices of the wheat or oil or coal that they produce.

We can depict a price-taking perfect competitor by examining the way the market looks to a competitive firm. Figure 9-1 shows the contrast between the industry demand curve (the *DD* curve) and the demand curve facing a single competitive firm (the *dd* curve). Because a competitive industry is populated by firms that are small relative to the market, the firm's segment of the demand curve is but a tiny segment of the industry's curve. Graphically, the competitive firm's portion of the demand curve is so small that, to the lilliputian eye of the perfect competitor, the firm's *dd* demand curve looks completely horizontal or infinitely elastic. Figure 9-1 illustrates how the elasticity of demand for a single

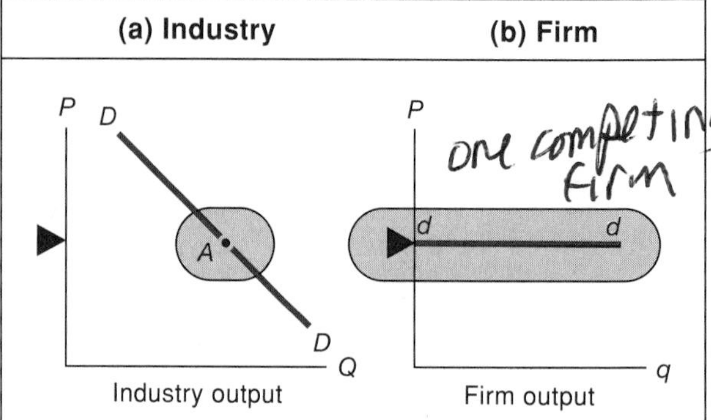

Figure 9-1. Demand curve looks horizontal to a perfect competitor

The industry demand curve is on the left, showing inelastic demand at point *A*. However, the perfect competitor has such an insignificant part of the market that demand looks completely horizontal (i.e., perfectly elastic). The perfect competitor can sell all it wants at the market price.

competitor appears very much greater than that for the entire market.

Because competitive firms cannot affect the price, for each unit sold the price is the extra revenue that the firm will earn. For example, at a market price of $40 per unit, the competitive firm can sell all it wants at $40. If it decides to sell 101 units rather than 100 units, its revenue goes up by exactly $40.

Perfect competition occurs when no producer can affect the market price. Under perfect competition, there are many small firms, each producing an identical product and each too small to affect the market price. Under such conditions, each producer faces a completely horizontal demand (or *dd*) curve; the extra revenue gained from each extra unit sold is therefore the market price.

Competitive Supply where Marginal Cost Equals Price

Given its costs, demand, and desire to maximize profits, how does a competitive firm decide on the amount that it will supply? Clearly, the amount of output supplied must depend upon the costs of production. Take the supply of bicycles as an example. No sane firm would supply bicycles at a dollar a dozen, for that price would not even cover the cost of the seats. On the other hand, if bicycles were selling at $10 million apiece, everyone would rush

Supply Decision of Competitive Firm

(1) Quantity q	(2) Total cost TC ($)	(3) Marginal cost per unit MC ($)	(4) Average cost AC ($)	(5) Price P ($)	(6) Total revenue TR ($)	(7) Profit π ($)
0	55,000					
1,000	85,000	27	85	40	40,000	−45,000
2,000	110,000	22	55	40	80,000	−30,000
3,000	130,000	21	43.33	40	120,000	−10,000
3,999	159,960.01	39.98	40.000	40	159,960	−0.01
		39.99				
4,000	**160,000**	**40**	**40**	**40**	**160,000**	**0**
		40.01				
4,001	160,040.01	40.02	40.000+	40	160,040	−0.01
5,000	210,000	60	42	40	200,000	−10,000

Table 9-1. Profit is maximized at production level where marginal cost equals price

This table uses the same cost data as that analyzed in the previous chapter (see Table 8-3). We also made a tiny adjustment in output to find the cost levels around the point of minimum average cost at 4000 units. The dark blue marginal cost figures in column (3) are the numbers that are read off the smoothed *MC* curve. The light blue *MC* numbers in column (3) between the lines are the exact *MC*.

in to open up new bicycle firms. Under normal circumstances, a firm's output decision is not so obvious and will involve the marginal cost of producing output. Let's see how.

The data in Table 9-1 can help us understand the determinants of a competitive firm's supply decision. (Note that this table contains the same cost data in thousands as Table 8-3 in the previous chapter.) For this example, we assume that the market price for the good is $40 per unit. Say the firm starts out by selling 3000 units. This yields total revenue of $40 × 3000 = $120,000 with total cost of $130,000 for a loss of $10,000.

The firm's accountant says, "Look, if we sell additional units, the revenue from each unit is $40 while the marginal cost is only $21. Additional units bring in more than they cost, so let's raise production." The firm tries a production level of 5000. At this output, the firm has revenues of $40 × 5000 = $200,000 and costs of $210,000, so it is still losing $10,000.

The accountant points out that at the output level of 5000, marginal cost is $60, which is more than price of $40, so the firm is losing $20 (equal to price less *MC*) for each unit produced. Now the firm sees the light. It sees that the maximum-profit output comes at that output where marginal cost equals price.

The reason underlying this proposition is that the firm can always make additional profit as long as the price is greater than the marginal cost of the last unit. Total profit reaches its peak—is maximized—when there is no longer any extra profit to be earned by selling extra output. At the maximum-profit point, the last unit produced brings in an amount of revenue exactly equal to that unit's cost. What is that extra revenue? It is the price per unit. What is that extra cost? It is the marginal cost.

Let's test this rule by looking at Table 9-1. Starting at the maximum-profit output of 4000 units, if the firm sold 1 more unit, that unit would bring a price of $40 while the marginal cost of that unit is $40.01. So the firm would lose money on the 4001st unit. Similarly, the firm would lose $0.01 if it produced 1 less unit. This shows that the firm's maximum-profit output comes at exactly $q = 4000$, where price equals marginal cost.

Rule for a firm's supply under perfect competition: A profit-maximizing firm will set its production at that level where marginal cost equals price:

$$\text{Marginal cost} = \text{price} \qquad \text{or} \qquad MC = P$$

Figure 9-2 illustrates a firm's supply decision diagrammatically. When the market price of output is $40, the firm consults its cost data in Table 9-1 and finds that the production level corresponding to that marginal cost is 4000 units. Hence, at a market price of $40, the firm will wish to produce and sell 4000 units, an amount that corresponds to the intersection of the price line at $40 and the *MC* curve at point *B* in Figure 9-2.

In general, then, the firm's marginal cost curve can be used to find its optimal production schedule: the profit-maximizing output will come where the price intersects the marginal cost curve.

Note as well that at a production level of 4000, Table 9-1 shows that average or unit cost is also $40, so the firm just breaks even there, with total revenues equal to total costs. Point *B* is the **break-even point,** which shows the price at which the firm makes zero profits, with revenues just covering costs.

What if the firm chooses the wrong output? If the market price were $50, the firm should choose output at intersection point *A* in Figure 9-2. We can calculate the loss of profit if the firm mistakenly produces at *B* when price was at $50 by the shaded gray triangle in Figure 9-2. This depicts the surplus of price over *MC* for production between *B* and *A*. Draw in a similar shaded triangle above *A* to show the loss from producing too much.

The general rule then is:

A profit-maximizing firm will set its output at that level where marginal cost equals price. Diagrammatically, this means that a firm's marginal cost curve is also its supply curve.

Total Cost and the Shutdown Condition

Our general rule for firm supply leaves open one possibility—that the price will be so low that the firm will want to shut down. When would this occur? Generally, a firm will want to shut down in the short run when it can no longer cover its variable costs.

For example, suppose the firm were faced with a market price of $35, shown by the horizontal *d″d″* line in Figure 9-2. At that price the firm has *MC* equal to price at point *C*, a point at which the price is actually less than the average cost of production. Would the firm want to keep producing even though it was incurring a loss? Or would it want to shut down?

The correct answer is that a firm should *mini-*

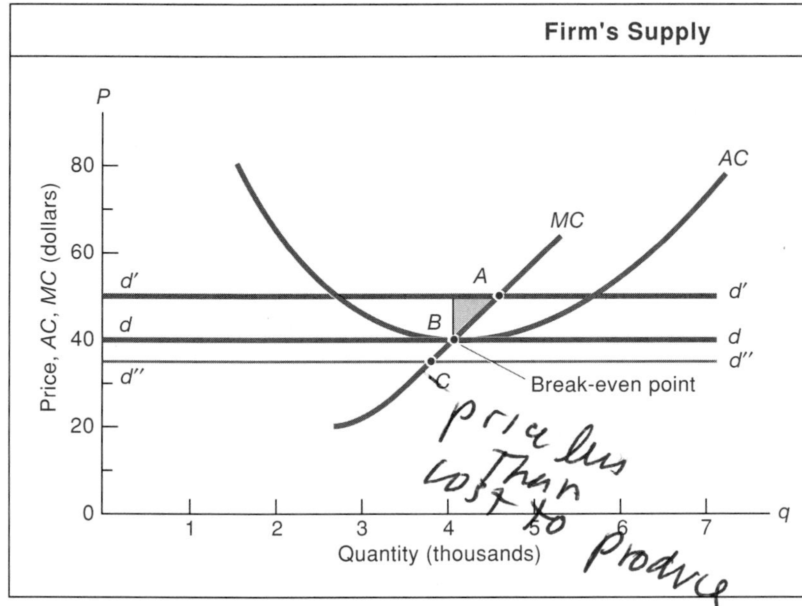

Figure 9-2. Firm's supply curve is its rising marginal cost curve

For a profit-maximizing competitive firm, the upward sloping marginal cost (*MC*) curve is the firm's supply curve. For market price at *d′d′*, firm will supply output at intersection point at *A*. Explain why intersection points at *B* and *C* represent equilibria for prices at *d* and *d″* respectively.

mize its losses. Because the firm's fixed costs are $55,000, producing at point *C* would result in a loss of only $20,000. In this situation, the firm should continue to produce where price equals marginal cost because it would lose less money than if it were to shut down completely. Continuing to operate would mean losing $20,000 whereas shutting down would involve losing $55,000.

To understand this point, remember that even when a firm produces nothing, it must still cover its contractual commitments. In the short run, the firm must pay fixed costs such as bond interest, rentals, and directors' salaries. The balance of the firm's costs are variable costs such as those for materials, production workers, and fuel. Hence, as price falls lower and lower, the firm always has the option of producing nothing at all. How much will it then lose? With its revenue zero and all its fixed costs going on anyway, its loss would exactly equal its fixed costs.

This reasoning suggests a rule governing when the firm should shut down:

When the price falls so low that total revenues are less than variable cost, and price is less than average variable cost, the firm will minimize its losses by shutting down.

The critically low market price at which revenues just equal variable cost (or equivalently at which losses exactly equal fixed costs) is called the **shutdown point.** For prices above the shutdown point, the firm will produce along its marginal cost curve because, even though the firm might be losing money, it would lose more money by shutting down. For prices below the shutdown point, the firm will produce nothing at all because by shutting down, the firm will lose only its fixed costs.

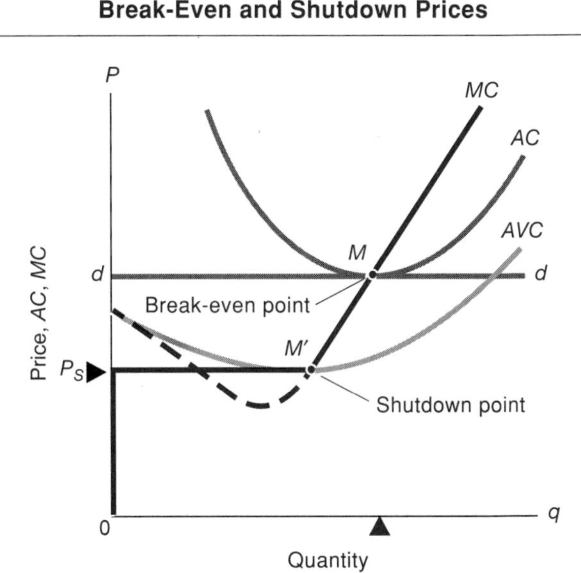

Figure 9-3. Firm's supply curve travels down the *MC* curve to the shutdown point

The firm's supply curve corresponds to its *MC* curve as long as revenues exceed variable costs. Once price falls to below P_S, the shutdown point, losses are greater than fixed costs and the firm shuts down. Hence the solid blue curve is the firm's supply curve

Figure 9-3 shows the *shutdown* and *break-even* points for a firm. The break-even point comes where price is equal to *AC*, while the shutdown level of output comes where price is equal to *AVC*. Therefore, the firm's supply curve is the solid blue line in Figure 9-3. It goes up the vertical axis to the price corresponding to the shutdown point; jumps to the shutdown point at *M′*, where *P* equals the level of *AVC*; then continues up the *MC* curve for prices above the shutdown price.

The analysis of shutdown conditions leads to the surprising conclusion that profit-maximizing firms may in the short run continue to operate even though they are losing money. This condition will hold particularly for firms that own a great deal of capital and therefore have high fixed costs; for these firms it is often less costly to continue producing at a loss than to shut down and still be forced to pay the high fixed costs.

B. Supply Behavior in Competitive Industries

We have seen that the supply decisions of competitive firms come at that output level where marginal cost is equal to price. But a competitive market is comprised of a large number of firms, and we are interested in the behavior of all firms together, not just a single firm. How can we move from the one to the many?

Summing All Firms' Supply Curves to Get Market Supply

Suppose we are dealing with a competitive market for fish. At a given price, firm A will bring so much fish to market, firm B will bring another quantity, and so on for firms C, D, etc. In each case, the quantity supplied will be determined by each firm's marginal costs. The *total* quantity brought to market at a given price will be the *sum* of the individual quantities that firms supply at that price.

This reasoning leads to the following relationship between individual and market supplies:

To get the market supply curve for a good, we must add horizontally the supply curves of all the individual producers of that good.

Figure 9-4 illustrates this for two firms. To get the industry's supply curve *SS*, add horizontally, at the same price, all firms' supply curves *ss*. At a price of $40, firm A will supply 4000 units while firm B will supply 11,000 units. Therefore the industry supply curve, shown in Figure 9-4(*c*), adds the two supplies together and finds total industry supply of 15,000 units at a price of $40. If there are two million rather than two firms, we would still derive industry output by adding all the 2 million individual-firm quantities at the going price. Horizontal addition of output at each price gives us the industry supply curve.

Momentary, Short-Run, and Long-Run Equilibrium

At the turn of the century Cambridge University's great economist Alfred Marshall helped forge the supply-and-demand tools we use today. He noticed that demand shifts produce greater price adjustments in the short run than in the long run. We can understand this observation by distinguishing three time periods for market equilibrium that correspond to different cost categories: (1) *momentary* equilibrium, when supply is fixed, (2) *short-run* equilibrium, when firms can increase their output even though plant and equipment are fixed, and (3) *long-run* equilibrium, when all factors are variable, so firms can abandon old plants or build new ones and new firms can enter or exit the industry.

Figure 9-5 shows market equilibrium for the three periods. Consider the demand for a perishable good, such as fish. Say demand increases from

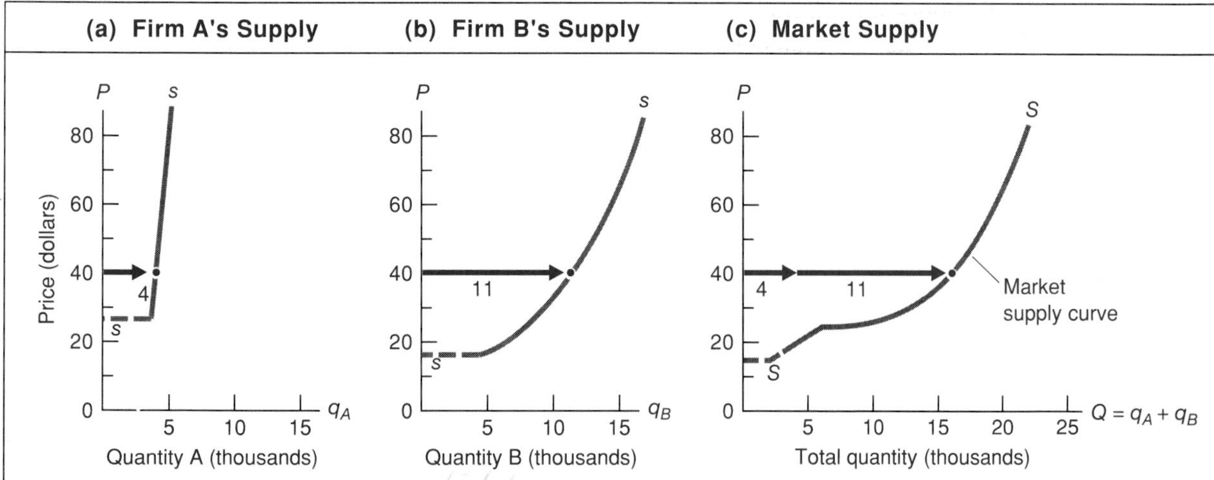

Figure 9-4. Add all firms' supply curves to derive market supply

The diagrams show how the market supply curve (*SS*) is composed of two individual supply curves (*ss*). We horizontally add quantities supplied by each firm at $40 to get total market supply at $40. This applies at each price and to any number of firms. If there were 1000 firms identical to firm A, the market supply curve would look just like firm A's supply curve with a thousandfold change of horizontal scale.

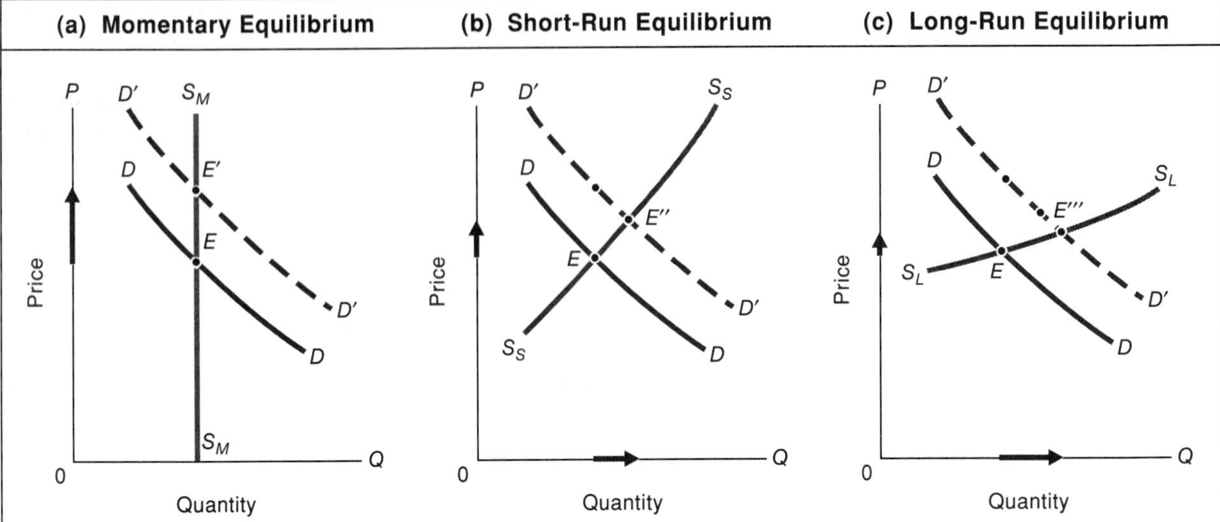

Figure 9-5. Effect of increase in demand on price varies in different time periods

We distinguish between periods in which supply elements have time to make **(a)** no adjustments (momentary equilibrium), **(b)** adjustments of labor and variable factors (short-run equilibrium), and **(c)** full adjustment of all factors, fixed as well as varying (long-run equilibrium). The longer the time for adjustment, the greater the elasticity of supply response and the less the rise in price.

DD to *D′D′*. In the momentary equilibrium, the quantity of fish supplied is fixed, so higher demand bids up sharply the price of fish. This is shown in Figure 9-5(*a*), where the increased demand runs up the vertical momentary supply curve $S_M S_M$ to determine the sharply higher price shown at *E′*. The large price rise is needed to ration the fixed supply of fish among the eager demanders.

But with so high a price, fishing captains will soon want to increase their catch. In the short run, they cannot build new boats, but they can hire larger crews and work longer hours. Increased inputs of variable factors will produce a greater quantity of fish along the *short-run supply curve* $S_S S_S$, shown in Figure 9-5(*b*). The short-run supply curve intersects the new demand curve at *E″*, the point of short-run equilibrium. Note that the short-run equilibrium price is lower than the momentary price because of the more intensive use of the fishing fleet in the short run.

In the long run, the higher prices coax out more shipbuilding, attract more sailors into the industry, and induce new firms to enter the industry. This gives us the long-run supply curve $S_L S_L$ in part (*c*). The intersection of the long-run supply curve with the new demand curve yields the long-run equilibrium attained when *all* economic conditions (including the number of ships, shipyards, and firms) have adjusted to the new level of demand.

Test your understanding of this discussion by assuming a decrease in demand. Show what happens in the new momentary equilibrium as well as in the short and long runs if people suddenly stop eating fish.

The Long Run for a Competitive Industry

Our analysis of break-even conditions showed that firms might stay in business for a time even though they are unprofitable. This situation is particularly likely for firms that have high fixed capital costs and explains why, in the steep business downturn in the early 1980s, many of America's large companies—General Motors, U.S. Steel, International Harvester—stayed in business even though they incurred losses in the billions of dollars.

But do such losses suggest a troubling conclusion? Might capitalism tend toward a "euthanasia of the capitalists," a state where chronic losses are normal? For this question, we need to analyze long-run shutdown conditions. We showed that firms shut down when they can no longer cover their variable costs. But in the long run, *all* costs are variable. The firm can pay off its bonds, release its managers, and let its leases expire. In the long run, all commitments are once again options, and firms will produce only when price is at or above the break-even point where price equals average cost.

There is, then, a critical *break-even point* below which long-run price cannot remain if firms are to stay in business. That is, long-run price must cover out-of-pocket costs such as labor, materials, equipment, taxes, and other expenses, and opportunity costs such as competitive return on the owner's invested capital.

In terms of the cost curves shown in Figure 9-3, price must be at or above point M for the firm to stay in business in the long run. If every other firm were exactly like this firm, the long-run supply would dry up completely below this critical break-even price which covers all costs of staying in business.

Now further suppose that all firms are exactly alike and that entry into the industry is absolutely free in the long run, so that any number of firms can come into the industry and produce at exactly the same costs as those firms already in the industry. In this situation, the long-run price cannot remain above the critical break-even point at which price just equals total long-run average cost.

The long-run break-even condition comes at a critical P where identical firms just cover their full competitive costs. Below this critical long-run price, firms would leave the industry until price returns to long-run average cost. Above this long-run price, new firms would enter the industry, thereby forcing market price back down to the long-run equilibrium price where all competitive costs are just covered.

When an industry is supplied by competitive firms with identical cost curves, and when firms can enter and leave the industry freely, the long-run equilibrium condition is that price equals marginal cost equals the minimum long-run average cost for each identical firm:

$$P = MC = \text{minimum long-run } AC$$
$$= \text{break-even price}$$

Long-Run Industry Supply. What is the shape of the long-run supply curve for an industry? Suppose that an industry has free entry of identical firms. If the identical firms use general inputs, such as unskilled labor, that can be attracted from the vast ocean of other uses without affecting the prices of those general inputs, we get the case of constant costs shown by the horizontal S_LS_L supply curve in Figure 9-6.

By contrast, suppose the inputs used in the industry include certain fixed factors specific to this industry alone—e.g., rare vineyard land for the wine industry or scarce beachfront properties for summer vacations. Then the supply curve for the wine or vacation industry must be upward sloping as shown by S_LS_L' in Figure 9-6.

Why must the long-run supply curve of industries with specific factors be rising? Because of the law of diminishing returns. For the case of the rare vineyard land, when firms apply increasing inputs of labor to fixed land, they receive smaller and smaller increments of wine-grape output; but each dose of labor costs the same in wages, so the MC of wine rises. This long-run rising MC means the long-run supply curve must be rising.

An interesting phenomenon occurs in industries with rising long-run MC. In such cases, owners of productive factors peculiar to this industry—fertile

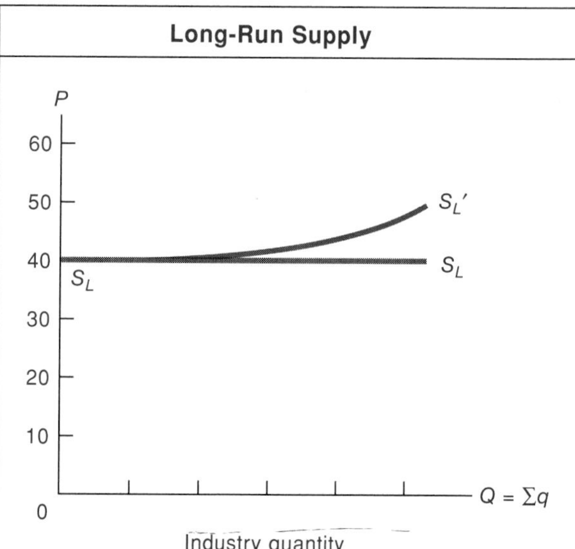

Figure 9-6. Long-run industry supply depends on cost conditions

With entry and exit free and any number of firms able to produce on identical, unchanged cost curves, the long-run S_LS_L curve will be horizontal at each firm's minimum average cost or break-even price. If the industry uses a specific factor, such as scarce beachfront property, the long-run supply curve must slope upward like S_LS_L' as higher production employs less well suited inputs.

vineyards, attractive beachfront properties, or low-cost oil fields—will earn a higher income from their properties as the industry expands.

What can we conclude about the long-run profitability of competitive capitalism? We have found that the forces of competition tend to push firms and industries toward a zero-pure-profit long-run state. Those industries that are profitable tend to attract entry of new firms, thereby driving down prices and reducing profits toward zero. By contrast, those industries which are suffering losses tend to repel firms, as firms seek industries with better profit opportunities. Prices and profits then tend to rise. *The long-run equilibrium hence is one with no pure profits.*

Decreasing Costs and the Breakdown of Perfect Competition

Earlier sections considered the cases of diminishing returns and of constant costs. What happens when marginal costs are declining and there are decreasing average costs in an industry, say because of pervasive economies of scale? We might suppose that the supply curve would slope downward, but this is definitely incorrect.

If marginal cost is declining at the point where $P = MC$, then the competitive firm can increase its profits by increasing output. This is so because if you move to the right of such a point on a falling *MC* curve, you find that the price is above marginal cost for each additional unit. Hence, in the case of decreasing marginal cost, the perfectly competitive firm can increase its profits indefinitely by expanding its output.

In other words, in a declining-cost industry, the first firm to enter will get a head start on other firms and will find its advantage increasing the larger the firm grows. If other firms contract their outputs, this will result in a competitive disadvantage as they are forced back up their declining *MC* curves.

What is the result? Under continuously decreasing costs, one or a few firms will expand their outputs to the point where they become a significant part of the industry's total output. The industry then becomes imperfectly competitive. Perhaps a single monopolist will dominate the industry; a more likely outcome is that a few large sellers will control most of the industry's output; or there might be a large number of firms, each with slightly different products. Whatever the outcome, we must inevitably find some kind of imperfect competition instead of the atomistic perfect competition of price-taking firms.

The case of decreasing costs is not an isolated phenomenon. Numerous detailed econometric and engineering studies confirm that a wide range of nonagricultural industries show declining average long-run costs. Given the prevalence of decreasing costs, we cannot be surprised at the extent of imperfect competition in the modern industrial economy.

C. Efficiency and Equity of Competitive Markets

We have now completed our basic analysis of the operation of competitive markets. How well do competitive markets perform? Do they deserve high grades for satisfying people's economic needs and using society's scarce resources efficiently? Or do they tend to waste resources?

To answer these questions, we proceed as follows: First, we review the meaning of efficiency. We then turn to see how competitive markets behave. At the end of this section, important qualifications concerning competitive markets are presented as a reminder of the shortcomings of a market economy.

The Efficiency of Competitive Markets

We have seen how competitive markets synthesize the demands of individuals for goods and services with the supply decisions of firms. The interaction of supplies and demands produces the millions of prices and quantities for goods from apples to zithers in product markets, along with the wages of labor, rents of land, and interest on capital in factor markets.

But the critical question for judging a competitive economy is, How efficient is it? Is society getting many guns and much butter for a given amount of inputs? Or does the butter melt on the way to the store, while the guns have crooked barrels?

The Concept of Efficiency

To answer this we must introduce the concept of **allocative efficiency** (or **efficiency,** for short). An economy is efficient if it is organized to provide its consumers the largest possible bundle of goods and services, given the resources and technology of the economy. That is:

Allocative efficiency occurs when no possible reorganization of production can make anyone better off without making someone else worse off. Under conditions of allocative efficiency, one person's satisfaction or utility can be increased only by lowering someone else's utility.[1]

We can think of the concept of efficiency intuitively in terms of the production-possibility frontier. An economy is clearly inefficient if it is inside the *PPF*. If we move out to the *PPF*, no one need suffer a decline in utility. An efficient economy is on its *PPF*.

Efficiency of Competitive Equilibrium

Let us examine the performance of a competitive economy in terms of the standard of allocative efficiency. We begin with a simplified example to illustrate the general principles.

Consider an idealized situation where all individuals are identical. Further simplify by assuming: (*a*) Each person works at growing food. As people increase their work and leisure hours are curtailed, each additional hour of work becomes increasingly tiresome. (*b*) Each extra unit of food consumed brings diminished marginal utility (*MU*).[2] (*c*) Because food production takes place on fixed plots of land, by the law of diminishing returns, each extra minute of work brings less and less extra food.

Figure 9-7 shows supply and demand for our simplified competitive economy. When we add the identical supply curves of our identical farmers, we get the upward-sloping *MC* curve. As we saw earlier in this chapter, the *MC* curve is also the industry's supply curve, so the figure shows *MC* = *SS*. Also, the demand curve is the horizontal summation of the identical individuals' marginal utility and demand-for-food curves; it is represented by the downward-stepping *MU* = *DD* curve for food in Figure 9-7.

The intersection of the *SS* and *DD* curves shows the competitive equilibrium for food. At point *E*, farmers supply exactly what consumers want to

Efficiency of Competitive Equilibrium

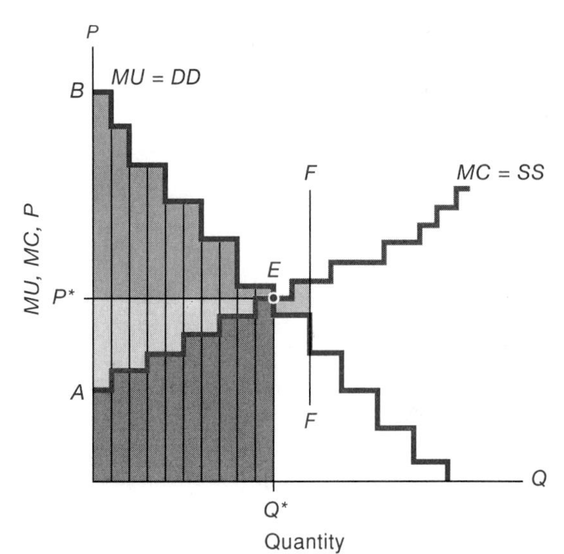

Figure 9-7. At competitive equilibrium point *E*, the marginal costs and utilities of food are exactly balanced

Many identical farmer-consumers bring their food to market. The upward-stepping *MC* = *SS* curve adds together the marginal cost curves, while the downward stepping *MU* = *DD* curve represents the consumer valuation of food. At competitive market equilibrium *E*, the marginal gain from the last unit of food is exactly equal to the marginal labor cost required to produce the last unit of food.

The cost of producing food is shown by the dark and light gray slices, showing the utility lost because of the labor needed to produce food. Vertical slices of blue under *MU* are the economic surplus that measures the excess of food utility over its cost. It is maximized at *E*: the light gray area to the right of *E* shows the economic loss from producing too much food.

[1] This concept of efficiency is also called "Pareto efficiency," after Vilfredo Pareto (1848–1923), the Italian economist who first devised the concept.

[2] To simplify the analysis, we adopt a "money metric" for utility. We adjust our utility yardstick so that the marginal utility of an additional hour of leisure is always constant and has a value of \$1. We can then express all prices in these dollar-units of leisure, so a "util" is a unit of utility in this money metric.

purchase at the equilibrium market price. Each person will be working up to the critical point where the declining marginal-utility-of-consuming-food curve intersects the rising marginal-cost-of-growing-food curve.

A careful analysis of this competitive equilibrium will show that it is efficient. At competitive equilibrium point E in Figure 9-7, the representative consumer will have higher utility than with any other feasible allocation of resources. This is so because at competitive equilibrium E, the marginal utility of the consumed good (MU) equals the price (P), which in turn equals the marginal cost of producing the good (MC). As the following three-step process shows, if $MU = P = MC$, then the allocation is efficient.

1. $P = MU$. Consumers choose food purchases up to the amount $P = MU$. As a result, every person is gaining P utils of satisfaction from the last unit of food consumed.
2. $P = MC$. As producers, each person is supplying sweaty labor up to the point where the price of food exactly equals the MC of the last unit of food supplied (the MC here being the cost in terms of the utility of leisure forgone and the disutility of sweaty labor that is needed to produce the last unit of food). The price then is the utils of satisfaction lost by working that last bit of time needed to grow that last unit of food.
3. Putting these two equations together, we see that $MU = MC$. *This means that the utils gained from the last unit of food consumed exactly equal the utils lost from the sweaty labor required to produce that last unit of food.* It is exactly this condition—that the marginal gain to society from the last unit consumed equals the marginal cost to society of that last unit produced—which guarantees that a competitive equilibrium is efficient.

Economic Surplus

The efficiency of competitive markets can also be seen using the concept of economic surplus, which is a generalization of consumer surplus. Recall from Chapter 6 that *consumer surplus* is the excess of the value or utility of a good to consumers over the price paid for a good. To this we add the excess of the revenue that producers receive over their production costs; this excess is called *producer surplus*. The total of producer and consumer surplus is called **economic surplus,** which denotes the total utility or satisfaction generated by an economy over the costs of production.

Economic surplus is the excess of utility or satisfaction over costs of production. It is equal to consumer surplus (excess of consumer utility over price paid) plus producer surplus (excess of producer revenues over cost).

How is efficiency related to economic surplus? Clearly, an economy is performing well when it generates a great deal of economic surplus, when satisfactions are high and costs are low. When an economy is squeezing the maximum amount of economic surplus out of available resources, then the economy is efficient. *Allocative efficiency requires production of the maximum amount of economic surplus out of the inputs of labor, land, and other resources.*

Figure 9-7 shows the economic surplus of our farmer-consumer economy. Each blue slab represents the surplus on that unit of food, measured by the difference between the MU of that unit and the MC (in terms of utility lost from sweaty labor) of producing that food unit. The total blue shaded area between the MU line and the MC line is the total economic surplus. At point E, the blue area is maximized, which means that the total surplus from the economy is maximized.

Moreover, if the economy operates at any point other than the competitive equilibrium point E in Figure 9-7, it will be inefficient. Assume output were by some mistake to rise from E to the level indicated by the thin line at F. Because the MC curve is above the MU curve for outputs beyond E, people would be losing utility because the extra food produced will not be worth the extra hours of sweaty labor used to produce the food. The light gray area between the MC and MU curves and between E and line FF is a measure of the loss in economic surplus that results from too high a level of output. (Show what would happen to economic surplus if output were too low.)

The competitive equilibrium of $P = MU = MC$ produces the maximum amount of economic surplus and is therefore efficient.

Equilibrium with Many Markets

Let us now turn from our simple parable about identical farmer-consumers to an economy populated by millions of different firms, hundreds of millions of people, and countless commodities. Can a perfectly competitive economy still be efficient in this more complex world?

Conditions. The answer is, "Yes," or better still, "Yes, if. . ." The most important conditions are that the economy must behave competitively and that there must be no externalities.

First, the markets must be perfectly competitive; we must rule out monopolies and oligopolies. Buyers and sellers must be well informed, and markets must exist for all commodities and even for risks that people incur. If there are monopolists or missing markets, price will not necessarily equal marginal cost for those commodities.

Second, we must rule out externalities such as pollution or invention. If some firms pour dioxin into a river without paying the social cost of that activity, we have an oversupply of river poison. In this case, the price equals the firm's private marginal costs but not social marginal costs. As we will see in Chapter 18, perfect competition is not efficient when uncorrected spillovers take place.[3]

[3] Some other technical requirements are usually given for efficiency, as is seen in Chapter 17's treatment of "general equilibrium" of competitive markets.

For those industries where there are many reasonably informed consumers, many mutually competing producers, and negligible externalities, a system of perfectly competitive markets will produce the maximum economic surplus and will earn the economist's gold star of allocational efficiency.

Market Synthesis. Figure 9-8 illustrates how a competitive system brings out a balance between utility and cost for a single commodity with nonidentical firms and consumers.

On the left, we add horizontally the demand curves for all consumers to get the market *DD* curve in the middle. On the right, we add all the separate firms' *MC* curves to get the industry *SS* curve in the middle.

At the competitive equilibrium at point *E*, consumers on the left get the quantity they are willing to purchase of the good at the price reflecting efficient social *MC*.

On the right, the equilibrium market price also allocates production efficiently among firms. The gray area under *SS* in the middle represents the minimized sum of gray cost areas on the right. Each firm is setting its output so that $MC = P$. Production efficiency is achieved because there is no

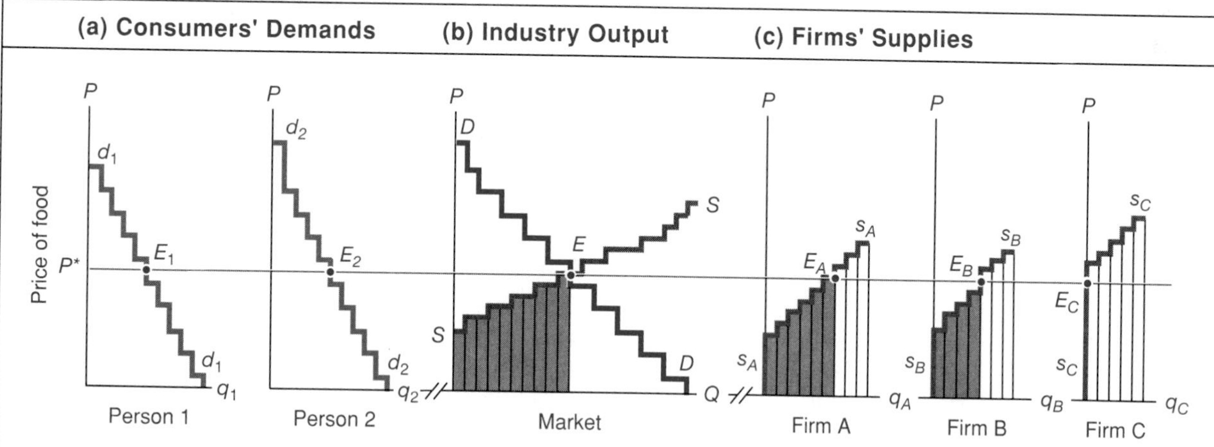

Figure 9-8. Competitive market integrates consumers' demands and producers' costs

(a) Individual demands are shown on the left. We add the consumers' *dd* curves horizontally to obtain the market demand *DD* curve in the middle.

(b) The market brings together all consumer demands and firm supplies to reach market equilibrium at *E*. The horizontal price-of-food line shows where each consumer on the left and each producer on the right reaches equilibrium. At *P**, see how each consumer's *MU* is equated to each firm's *MC*, leading to allocative efficiency.

(c) For each competitive firm, profits are maximized when the supply curve is given by the rising *MC* curve. The gray area depicts each firm's cost of producing the amount at *E*. At prices equal to marginal cost, the industry produces output at the least total cost.

reorganization of production that would allow the same level of industry output to be produced at lower cost. Note that high-cost firm C is not producing at all because the *MC* of its first unit is greater than the price.

The perfectly competitive market is a device for synthesizing (*a*) the willingness of people possessing dollar votes to pay for goods as represented by demand with (*b*) the marginal costs of those goods as represented by firms' supply. Under ideal conditions, the outcome guarantees allocative efficiency, in which no consumer's utility can be raised without lowering another consumer's utility.

Many Goods. Our economy produces not only food but also clothing, movies, vacations, and many other commodities. How does our analysis apply when consumers must choose among many products?

The principles are exactly the same, but now we recall one further condition: Utility-maximizing consumers spread their dollars among different goods until the marginal utility of the last dollar is equalized for each good consumed. In this case, as long as the qualifications discussed in the last subsection are met, a competitive economy is efficient with a multitude of goods and factors of production.

In a multiproduct and multifactor world, a perfectly competitive economy is efficient when private and social costs and demands coincide. Each industry must balance *MC* and *MU*. For example, if movies have 2 times the *MC* of hamburgers, then the *P* and the *MU* of movies must also be twice those of hamburgers. Only then will the *MU*s, which are equal to the *P*s, be equal to the *MC*s. By equating price and marginal cost, competition guarantees that an economy can attain allocative efficiency.

We must emphasize that our conclusion about the efficiency of perfect competition does not depend on any of the simplifying assumptions discussed here. It is a general conclusion subject only to the qualifications discussed above.

The Central Role of Marginal-Cost Pricing

This chapter has stressed the importance of competition and marginal cost in attaining an efficient allocation of resources. But the centrality of marginal cost extends far beyond perfect competition. Using marginal cost to achieve production efficiency holds for any society or organization trying to make the most effective use of its resources—whether that entity is a capitalist or socialist economy, a profit-maximizing or nonprofit organization, a university or a church, or even a family.

The essential role of marginal cost in a market economy is this: Only when prices are equal to marginal costs is the economy squeezing the maximum output and economic surplus from its scarce resources of land, labor, and capital. Only when each firm has its own marginal cost equal to each other firm's *MC*—as will be the case when each *MC* has been set equal to a common price—will the industry be producing its total output at minimum total cost. Only when price is equal to marginal cost for all firms will society be on its production-possibility frontier.

The use of marginal cost as a benchmark for efficient resource allocation is applicable to all economic systems and not just to market economies. If you are operating a government enterprise to generate electricity (such as the Tennessee Valley Authority), you will want to generate electricity in different power stations so as to equalize marginal costs of production. Only then can you minimize total production costs.

Or if you decide that a new form of market socialism should replace central planning in the Soviet Union or China, your socialist firms will surely want to produce wheat efficiently. Efficiency requires that the marginal cost of wheat and all other goods be set by equating some kind of price with the marginal cost of production for each and every farm and firm.[4]

Efficiency and Equity of Competitive Markets

We have seen that in certain situations competitive markets have remarkable efficiency properties. But we cannot say that laissez-faire competition produces the greatest happiness of the greatest num-

[4] The Soviet mathematician and academician L. V. Kantorovich shared the 1975 Nobel Prize in economics for his original and deep research into the use of optimal pricing mechanisms in a centrally planned economy.

ber. Nor does it necessarily result in the fairest possible use of resources.

Why not? Because people are not equally endowed with purchasing power. Some are very poor through no fault of their own, while others are very rich through no virtue of their own. So the weighting of dollar votes, which lie behind the individual demand curves, may not appear fair and equitable.

A system of prices and markets may be one in which a few people have most of the income and wealth. They may have inherited the society's scarce land or own valuable patents and oil fields. The economy might be highly efficient, squeezing a great amount of guns and butter from its resources, but the rich few are eating the butter or feeding it to their poodles while the guns are merely protecting the butter of the rich.

A perfectly competitive and efficient economy may have a high and unacceptable extent of inequality of income, consumption, and wealth.

Efficiency vs. Equity. A society does not live on efficiency alone. Philosophers and the populace ask, Efficiency *for what?* And *for whom?* A society may choose to change a laissez-faire equilibrium to improve the equity or fairness of the distribution of income and wealth. The society may decide to sacrifice efficiency to improve equity.

The conflict between efficiency and fairness is one of the most profound questions of value that a society faces. Is society satisfied with outcomes where the maximal amount of bread is produced? Or will modern democracies take loaves from the wealthy and pass them out to the poor?

There are no correct answers here. These are normative questions that are answered in the political arena by democratic voters or autocratic planners. Economics cannot say what steps governments should take to improve equity. But economics can offer some insights into the efficiency of different government policies that affect the distribution of income and consumption.

To begin with, some government policies are aimed at improving efficiency rather than redistributing income and wealth. Externalities sometimes cause harm or good that is not included in the calculations of free and unregulated markets; monopolies may take over industries and restrict output. Regulatory policies to correct deficiencies in the invisible hand may guide the economy toward a more efficient outcome.

Many direct interferences in the market are attempts to promote equity or to protect particular groups against the impersonal forces of supply and demand. Those helped are sometimes poor, sometimes affluent. For example, farm programs that restrict output and raise the price of wheat and corn boost the incomes of all farmers, rich and poor. The minimum wage raises the income of some low-wage workers at the expense of others who cannot find work or of consumers who must pay higher prices. In each case, government interferes with the market to protect a particular group.

Economists generally believe that direct government interferences with the market are an inefficient way of correcting the income distribution. The same goal can often be achieved more efficiently by using *taxes and income-tested transfers* to redistribute income. (An income-tested transfer is a government payment, say for food or housing, that depends upon the level of income of the recipient.) Rather than interfere in the labor or wheat market by raising the minimum wage or subsidizing bread, governments can equalize incomes by taxing high-income people and giving funds to low-income people.

Relying primarily upon taxes and transfers is doubly beneficial. First, this approach allows competitive markets to produce efficiently and prevents their being gummed up by price or quantity restrictions. And second, by limiting the transfer programs to those who are deserving, the costs are reduced to the bare minimum needed to help the targeted group.

● We have now completed our discussion of perfect competition. In the next chapter, we extend our analysis by examining the different market structures. ●

SUMMARY

A. Supply Behavior of the Competitive Firm

1. A perfectly competitive firm is one that can sell all the output it wants at the going market price. Competitive firms are assumed to maximize their profits. To maximize profits, the competitive firm will choose that output level at which price equals the marginal cost of production, i.e., $P = MC$. Diagrammatically, the competitive firm's equilibrium will come where the rising MC curve intersects its horizontal demand curve.

2. Variable (or avoidable) costs must be taken into consideration in determining a firm's short-run shutdown point. Below the shutdown point, the firm loses more than its fixed costs. It will therefore shut down and produce nothing when price falls below the shutdown price.

3. A competitive industry's long-run supply curve, $S_L S_L$, must take into account the entry of new firms and exodus of old ones. In the long run, all a firm's commitments expire. It will stay in business only if price is at least as high as long-run average costs. These costs include out-of-pocket payments to labor, lenders, material suppliers, or landlords and opportunity costs, such as returns on the property assets owned by the firm.

B. Supply Behavior in Competitive Industries

4. Each firm's rising MC curve is its supply curve. To obtain the supply curve of a group of competitive firms, we add horizontally their separate supply curves. The supply curve of the industry hence represents the marginal cost curve for the competitive industry as a whole.

5. Because firms can adjust production over time, we distinguish three different time periods: (*a*) momentary equilibrium of fixed supply; (*b*) short-run equilibrium with output varying within fixed plants and firms; (*c*) long-run equilibrium, when the number of firms and plants, and all other conditions, adjust completely to the new demand conditions.

6. In the long run, when firms are free to enter and leave the industry, and where no one firm has any particular advantage of skill or location, competition will eliminate any excess profits earned by existing firms in the industry. So, just as free exit means price cannot fall below the break-even point, free entry means price cannot exceed long-run average cost in long-run equilibrium.

7. When an industry can expand by replication without pushing up the prices of its factors of production, the resulting long-run supply curve will be horizontal. When an industry uses factors specific to it, its long-run supply curve will slope upward.

8. When marginal costs are declining, and firms enjoy decreasing costs as output increases, competitive firms could increase their profits by expanding output indefinitely. In this situation, one or a few firms will tend to expand and the remaining firms will tend to contract. Forever-decreasing cost curves lead to destruction of perfect competition.

C. Efficiency and Equity of Competitive Markets

9. The analysis of competitive markets sheds light on the efficient organization of a society. Allocative efficiency occurs when there is no way of reorganizing production and distribution such that everyone's satisfactions can be improved. Put differently, allocative efficiency exists when no single individual can be made better off without making another individual worse off.

10. Under ideal conditions, a competitive economy attains allocative efficiency. These conditions are: (*a*) When consumers maximize satisfaction, the marginal utility just equals the price. (*b*) When competitive producers supply goods, they choose output so that marginal cost just equals price. (*c*) Because $MU = P$ and $MC = P$, it follows that $MU = MC$. Thus the marginal social cost of producing a good under perfect competition just equals its marginal utility valuation.

11. Markets must meet three important tests before they are socially optimal. First, there must not be any imperfect competition, which means that individual producers cannot affect the price of output. Second, there must be no spillover effects or externalities where one firm imposes a social cost (or causes a benefit) without the affected party being compensated (or paying). Finally, for a competitive outcome to be optimal, the distribution of dollar votes must correspond to the society's concepts of justice.

12. Efficient competitive markets by themselves will not necessarily ensure a distribution of income and consumption that corresponds to the society's ethical ideals. Governments often modify the laissez-faire equilibrium to change the income distribution, but the most efficient redistributional method is usually through a system of taxes and income-tested transfer payments.

CONCEPTS FOR REVIEW

Competitive supply

$P = MC$ as maximum-profit condition
firm's *ss* supply curve and its *MC* curve
break-even point where $P = MC = AC$
shutdown point where $P = MC = AVC$
summing individual *ss* curves to get industry *SS*
momentary, short-run, and long-run equilibrium
long-run zero-profit condition

Efficiency and equity

allocative (Pareto) efficiency
conditions for allocative efficiency: $MU = P = MC$
efficiency of competitive markets
economic surplus = consumer surplus + producer surplus
efficiency vs. equity
government interferences:
to promote efficiency
price and quantity restrictions
income-tested transfers

QUESTIONS FOR DISCUSSION

1. Explain why each of the following statements about profit-maximizing competitive firms is incorrect. Restate each one correctly.
   (a) A competitive firm will produce output up to the point where price equals average variable cost.
   (b) A firm's shutdown point comes where price is less than minimum average cost.
   (c) A firm's supply curve depends only on its marginal

cost. Any other cost concept is irrelevant for supply decisions.

(d) The $P = MC$ rule for competitive industries holds for upward-sloping, horizontal, and downward-sloping MC curves.

(e) A competitive firm sets price equal to marginal cost.

2. Explain why a firm might supply goods at a loss.
3. One of the most important rules of economics, business, and life is the *sunk-cost principle,* "Let bygones be bygones." This means that sunk costs (which are bygone in the sense that they are unrecoverably lost) should be ignored when decisions are being made. Only future costs, involving marginal and variable costs, should count in making rational decisions.

   To see this, consider the following: We can calculate fixed costs in Table 9-1 as the cost level when output is 0. What are fixed costs? What is the profit-maximizing level of output for the firm in Table 9-1 if price is \$40 while fixed costs are \$0? \$55,000? \$100,000? \$1,000,000,000? Minus \$30,000? Explain the implication for a firm trying to decide whether to shut down.
4. Examine the cost data shown in Table 9-1. Calculate the supply decision of a profit-maximizing competitive firm when price is \$21, \$40, and \$60. What would the level of total profit be for each of the three prices? What would happen to the exit or entry of identical firms in the long run at each of the three prices?
5. Using the cost data shown in Table 9-1, calculate the price elasticity of supply between $P = 40$ and $P = 40.02$ for the individual firm. Assume that there are 2000 identical firms and construct a table showing the industry supply schedule. What is the *industry* price elasticity of supply between $P = 40$ and $P = 40.02$?
6. Examine Figure 9-8 to see that competitive firm C is not producing at all. Explain the reason why the profit-maximizing output level for firm C is at $q_C = 0$. What would happen to total industry cost of production if firm C produced 1 unit while firm B produced 1 less unit than the competitive output level?

   Say that firm C is a "Mom and Pop" grocery store. Why would chain grocery stores A and B drive C out of business? How do you feel about keeping C in business? What would be the economic impact of legislation that divided the market in three equal parts between the "Mom and Pop" store and chain stores A and B?
7. Often, consumer demand for a commodity will depend upon the use of durable goods, such as housing or transportation. In such a case, demand will show a time-varying pattern of response similar to that of supply. A good example is gasoline. In the short run, the stock of automobiles is fixed while in the long run consumers can buy new automobiles or bicycles.

   What is the relationship between the time period and the price elasticity of demand for gasoline? Sketch the short-run and long-run demand curves for gasoline. Show the impact of a decline in the supply of gasoline in both periods. Describe the impact of an oil shortage on the price of gasoline and the quantity demanded in both the long run and the short run.
8. Interpret this dialogue.

   A: "How can competitive profits be zero in the long run? Who will work for nothing?"

   B: "It is only *excess* profits that are wiped out by competition. Managers get paid for their work; owners get a normal return on capital in competitive long-run equilibrium—no more, no less."
9. **Advanced problem:** A firm can generate power from two generators; both MCs slope up, but the newer generator has lower MC at first. Show that only at peak loads, when the new generator's MC rises above the beginning MC of the older generator, should the firm use the older generator. Construct a joint MC schedule and show the generation of each at different prices.

A P P E N D I X 9

SPECIAL CASES OF COMPETITIVE MARKETS: SUPPLY AND DEMAND AT WORK

Chapters 5 through 9 have laid out the foundations of supply-and-demand analysis. This treatment put together the building blocks of utility and demand analysis for consumers, along with production, cost, and supply behavior for competitive firms. Supply-and-demand analysis is the most important item in the economist's tool kit, and it will reappear in many aspects in the chapters that follow.

Before we move on to study imperfect competition, this appendix probes more deeply into supply-and-demand analysis. We first consider certain general propositions about competitive markets and then continue with some special cases.

General Rules

We begin with two general rules about the impact of demand and supply shifts in competitive markets. These rules apply to virtually any competitive market, whether it is for codfish, brown coal, Douglas fir, Japanese yen, IBM stock, or petroleum. In the propositions that follow, we investigate the impact of shifts in supply or demand upon the price and quantity bought and sold. Recall always that by a shift in demand or supply we mean a shift in the demand or supply curve or schedule, not a movement along the curve.

Proposition 1: (*a*) As a general rule, an increase in demand for a commodity (the supply curve being constant) will raise the price of the commodity. (*b*) For most commodities, an increase in demand will also increase the quantity demanded. A decrease in demand will have the opposite effects.

Proposition 2: An increase in supply of a commodity (the demand curve being constant) will almost certainly lower the price and increase the quantity bought and sold. A decrease in supply has the opposite effect.

These two central propositions summarize the *qualitative* effects of shifts in supply and demand. But the *quantitative* effects on price and quantity depend upon the exact shapes of the supply and demand curves. In the cases that follow, we will see the response for a number of important cost and supply situations.

Case 1: Constant Cost

Imagine a manufactured item, such as pencils, whose production can be expanded by merely duplicating factories, machinery, and labor. To produce 100,000 pencils per day simply requires that we do the same thing as we did when we were manufacturing 1000 per day, but on a hundredfold scale. In addition, assume that the pencil industry uses land, labor, and other inputs in the same proportions as the rest of the economy.

In this case the long-run supply curve *SS* in Figure 9A-1 is a horizontal line at the constant level of unit costs. A rise in demand from *DD* to *D′D′* will shift the new intersection point to *E′*, raising *Q* but leaving *P* the same.

Case 2: Increasing Costs and Diminishing Returns

Suppose an industry such as wine-grape growing requires a certain kind of soil and climate. Such sites are limited in number. The annual output of wine can be increased to some extent by adding more labor and fertilizer to each acre of land. But as we saw in Chapter 7, the law of diminishing returns will eventually operate if variable factors of production, such as labor and fertilizer, are added to fixed amounts of a factor such as land.

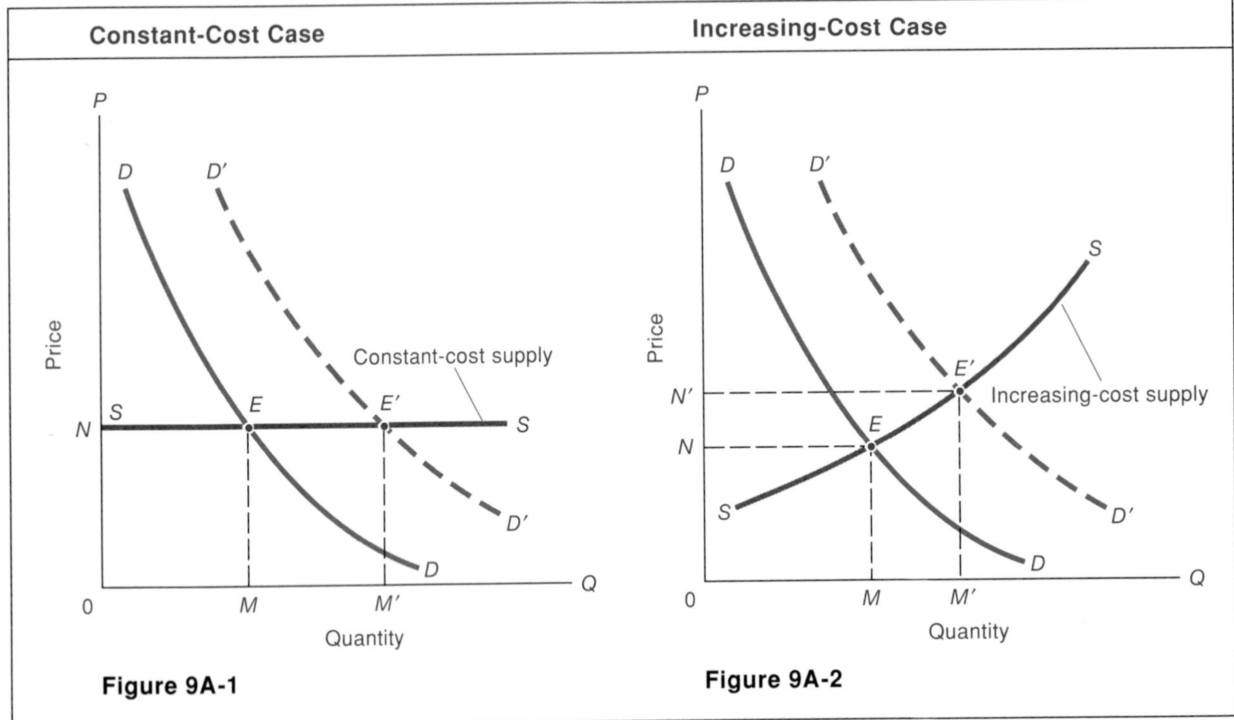

Figure 9A-1

Figure 9A-2

The result: The marginal cost of producing wine increases as wine production rises. Figure 9A-2 shows the rising supply curve *SS*. How will price be affected by an increase in demand? The figure shows that higher demand will increase the price of this good even in the long run with identical firms and free entry and exit.

Case 3: Completely Inelastic or Fixed Supply and Economic Rent

Some goods or productive factors are completely fixed in amount, regardless of price. There is only one *Mona Lisa* by da Vinci. Nature's original endowment of land can be taken as fixed in amount. Raising the price offered for land cannot create more than four corners at State and Madison in Chicago. Raising the pay of star athletes or top business executives is unlikely to change their hours of work.

In all such cases the supply curve is vertical in the relevant region. In Figure 9A-3, a higher price cannot elicit an increase in output. Land will continue to contribute to production no matter what its price. Because the same amount of land is forthcoming at every price, the price of such a factor of production is called a **pure economic rent.**

An increase in the demand for a fixed factor will affect only the price. Quantity supplied is unchanged. And the rise in price exactly equals the upward shift in demand.

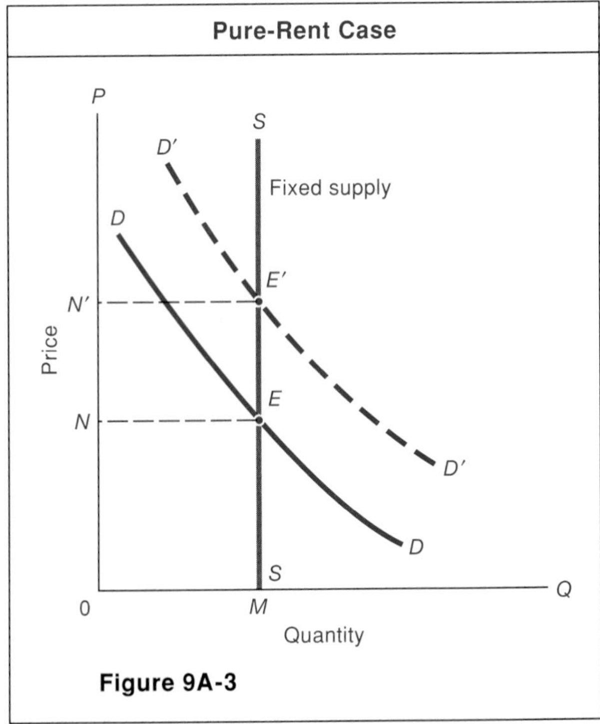

Figure 9A-3

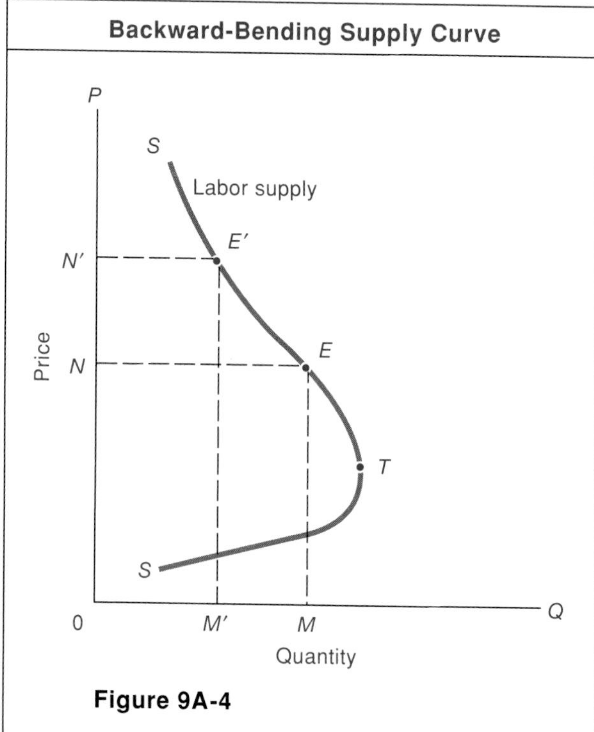

Figure 9A-4

When a tax is placed upon the fixed commodity, the effect is that the price received by the supplier is reduced by exactly the amount of the tax. The tax is completely paid by (or "shifted" to) the supplier (say, the landowner). The supplier absorbs the entire tax out of economic rent. The consumer buys exactly as much of the good or service as before and at no higher price.

Case 4: Backward-Bending Supply Curve

Firms in poor countries often noted that when they raised wages, the local workers often worked fewer hours. When the wage was doubled, instead of working 6 days a week to raise their low incomes, the workers might go fishing for 3 days. The same has been observed in high-income countries. As improved technology raises real wages, people feel that they want to take part of their higher earnings in the form of more leisure and less work. Chapter 6 described income and substitution effects, which explain why a supply curve might bend backward in this way.

Figure 9A-4 shows what a supply curve for labor might look like. At first the labor supplied rises as higher wages coax out more labor. But beyond point *T*, higher wages lead people to work fewer hours and to take more leisure. An increase in demand raises the price of labor, as was stated in Proposition 1 at the beginning of this appendix. But note why we were cautious to add "for most commodities" to Proposition 1(*b*), for now the increase in demand decreases the quantity of labor supplied.

Verification of backward-bending supply can be found in many areas. One of the most interesting examples came when oil-rich countries curbed their production of oil after the price of oil quadrupled in the early 1970s. The higher oil prices in effect induced countries like Kuwait to move from point *E* to point *E′* in Figure 9A-4.

Case 5: Shifts in Supply

All the above discussions dealt with a shift in demand and no shift in supply. To analyze Proposition 2, we must now shift supply, keeping demand constant. This is done in Figure 9A-5.

If the law of downward-sloping demand is valid, then increased supply must decrease price and

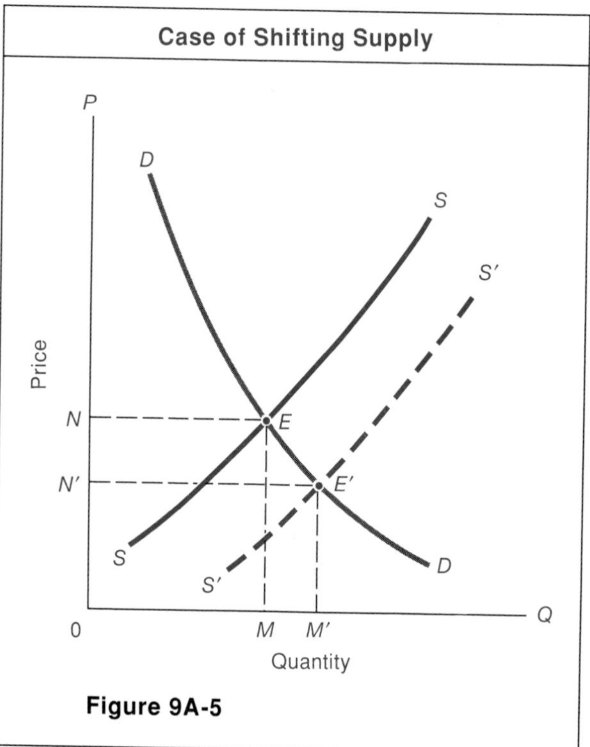

Figure 9A-5

increase quantity. You can verify the following quantitative corollaries of Proposition 2:

(*a*) An increased supply will decrease P most when demand is inelastic.
(*b*) An increased supply will increase Q least when demand is inelastic.

What are common-sense reasons for these rules? Illustrate with cases of elastic demand for autos and of inelastic demand for electricity.

Case 6: Dynamic Cobweb

A famous case shows that tools of supply and demand are not restricted to handling static and unchanging situations but can also be used to analyze economic dynamics.

Suppose that a competitive good—let us take the conventional example of hogs for pork production—is auctioned off in the market and fetches the P given by running vertically up from any given Q to the DD demand.

But now we want to introduce time into supply decisions. Suppose farmers look at today's P and use it to determine the Q they will bring to market in the *next* period. Specifically, if today's P is high, they begin breeding many new pigs, bringing them to market some months from now. The farmers have an upward-sloping supply curve, but it acts with a time lag and connects the next period's Q with this period's P. (We define a period as the time involved in producing hogs.)

If the market price were at the intersection of SS and DD in Figure 9A-6, this would represent an unchanging equilibrium in exactly the same way that it did in the nondynamic cases. Today, tomorrow, and every other period would find farmers on their SS curve producing the amount shown by E, and the amount consumers would gladly demand at that P would just match what farmers will gladly supply.

But suppose that for some reason, such as hog cholera, the crop initially drops to Q_1, which is below the equilibrium amount Q^*. We run up to E_1 on the demand curve and see that we get the higher P_1 corresponding to the reduced crop. We are not at long-run equilibrium because farmers will tomorrow move rightward on their supply curve and will in the second period produce at the

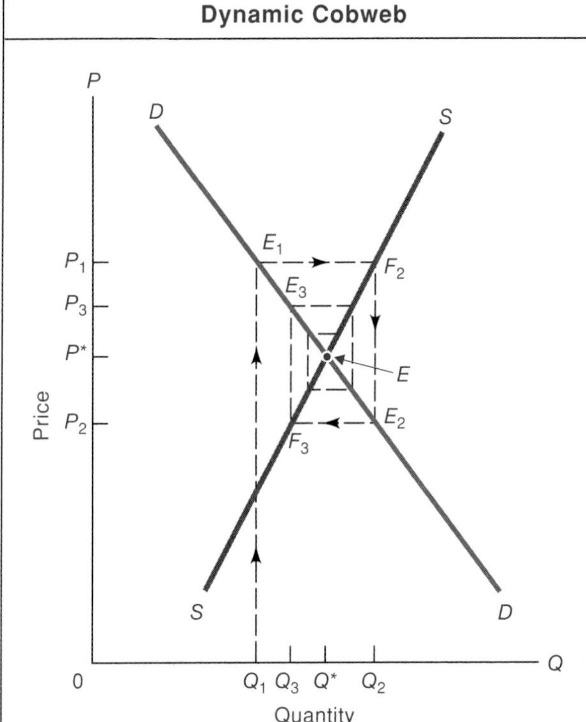

Figure 9A-6
The first period's P and Q are given by the DD curve. But now the SS curve is dynamic. It gives the amount of Q supplied in the next period for each P of the current period. So, starting at E_1, you move to F_2, down to E_2, over to F_3, up to E_3, and so forth along the converging cobweb, until reaching E.

point marked F_2. This output will now be above the equilibrium Q^*. What will it sell for in the competitive market? We run down to the demand curve and see that P_2 will have to fall to the level shown at E_2.

But we are not yet in final equilibrium. At this low price, farmers will plan to cut down production by going leftward to their SS curve and ending up at F_3. From there we move upward to the DD curve, to find the P_3 given at the E_3 point.

And thus it goes on and on. First Q is low and P is high. But high P makes next period's Q high and next period's P low. So—like an acrobat on a tightrope who goes too far on one side, then compensates by going too far on the other—market price oscillates in successive periods above and below equilibrium, tracing out a spidery cobweb.

What is the final outcome? Figure 9A-6 was

drawn with the supply curve's slope at E *steeper* than the demand curve's falling slope. The oscillations will eventually dampen and die out: the cobweb winds inward to E. We are then back at equilibrium, where we can stay until the next outside disturbance comes to set off another dying-out oscillation.

Rational Speculation

Looking at the cobweb of prices, we might wonder whether prices swing forever in this regular way without some shrewd speculators beginning to notice the pattern. Wouldn't they soon come to expect that prices were caught in some kind of regular pendular motion? Would they not then tend to buy at low P, store, and resell later at a profitable high price? Would not this speculative activity tend to wipe out the price differentials?

More advanced analysis, using the tools of *rational expectations* and dynamic analysis, shows that such effects do indeed occur under ideal speculation. Chapter 12 examines how speculators tend to even out price fluctuations over time.

SUMMARY TO APPENDIX

By way of summarizing the appendix, you should:

1. Review Propositions 1 and 2 along with their corollaries.
2. Make sure you understand important cases, such as constant and increasing costs, completely inelastic supply, backward-bending supply, and shifts in both supply and demand.

CONCEPTS FOR REVIEW

price rise from *DD* increase and probable quantity rise
constant costs, horizontal supply
increasing costs, rising *SS*
inelastic supply, vertical *SS*, rent
backward-bending supply
increased *SS* lowering *P*

QUESTIONS FOR DISCUSSION

1. For each of the following examples, decide which of the cases in this appendix applies. Use a supply-and-demand diagram to explain each of the observations.
   (a) When the federal individual income tax rate fell after 1981, a top movie star did not change her labor supplied.
   (b) As wine became more popular, wine prices rose sharply.
   (c) Even though real wages have increased considerably since 1900, hours of work have fallen.
2. What is the effect of a specific tax (i.e., $X per unit) when supply is as described in each of Cases 1 through 4?
3. Figure 9A-6 was drawn with the supply curve's slope at E *steeper* than the demand curve's falling slope. Suppose, however, that the supply curve's slope at E is *flatter* than the demand curve. Show this new case in a diagram and explain why the resulting cobweb is "dynamically unstable" and price diverges outward in explosive oscillations.

C H A P T E R 1 0

MARGINAL REVENUE AND MONOPOLY

> The monopolists, by keeping the market constantly understocked, . . . sell their commodities much above the natural price, and raise their emoluments, whether they consist in wages or profit . . .
>
> Adam Smith, *The Wealth of Nations*

Up to now we have examined the world of perfect competition in which many small firms produce and sell a standardized product. Perfect competition receives extensive attention in economics because competitive structures are relatively easy to understand; the supply-and-demand analysis of competition allows us to study the impact of taxes, demand changes, bad harvests, and a multitude of other real-world disturbances.

But the time has come to push beyond perfect competition. In all market economies, most industries have significant elements of imperfect competition. In this chapter and the next one we study the major kinds of imperfect competition—monopolistic competition, monopoly, and oligopoly. We shall see that prices are higher and outputs are lower under imperfect competition than under perfect competition. Later chapters will examine the ways that government can control imperfect competition—regulation of business and antitrust policies.

A. Patterns of Imperfect Competition

Our strict definition of a perfectly competitive market is a market in which every firm is too small to affect the market price. Think of a list of commodities: automobiles, beer, personal computers, aluminum, electricity, cigarettes, wheat, and cotton. Which fits the strict definition of perfect competition? Certainly not beer or computers. Who has heard of thousands of brewers or computer firms auctioning off their goods at the competitive Chicago Board of Trade?

Nor does the market in electricity meet the definition of perfect competition. In most towns, a single company, a monopoly, generates and markets all the electricity used by the populace.

What about aluminum or automobiles? Until World War II there was only one aluminum company, Alcoa. Even today, the four largest U.S. firms produce three-quarters of U.S. aluminum output. Aluminum would therefore be called an oligopoly, which is an industry characterized by a small number of sellers. And the automobile industry is today served by a handful of giant manufacturing firms—

General Motors, Ford, Toyota, and Honda being the most important oligopolists in this industry.

Looking at the list above, you will find that only wheat and cotton fall within our strict definition of perfect competition. All the other goods, from autos to cigarettes, fail the competitive test for a simple reason: some of the firms in the industry (General Motors for automobiles, IBM for computers, and so forth) can affect the market price by changing the quantity they sell.

Imperfect Competition Defined

If a firm can appreciably affect the market price of its output, then the firm is classified as an "imperfect competitor."

Imperfect competition prevails in an industry whenever individual sellers have some measure of control over the price of output in that industry.

Imperfect competition does not imply that a firm has absolute control over the price of its product. To call Pepsi an imperfect competitor means that it may be able to set the price of a can at 40 or 50 cents and still remain a viable firm. The firm could hardly set the price at $40 or 0.5 cent—it would go out of business. But an imperfect competitor has at least some discretion in its price decisions.

Moreover, the amount of discretion over price will differ from firm to firm. In some industries, the degree of monopoly power is very small. In the retail computer business, for example, more than a few percent difference in price will usually have a significant effect upon a firm's sales. In the monopolistic electricity distribution business, on the other hand, changes of 10 percent or more in the price of electricity will have only a small effect on a firm's sales in the short run.

Note that the existence of imperfect competition does not preclude intense rivalry in the marketplace. Imperfect competitors are often fighting to increase their market shares. Intense rivalry should be distinguished from perfect competition. Rivalry encompasses a wide variety of behavior, from advertising that attempts to shift out one's demand curve to inventing better products. Perfect competition says nothing about rivalry but simply denotes that every firm in the industry can sell all it wants at the prevailing market price.

Graphical Depiction. Figure 10-1 shows graphically the difference between perfect and imperfect competition. Figure 10-1(*a*) reminds us that a perfect competitor faces a horizontal demand curve, indicating that it can sell all it wants at the going market price. An imperfect competitor, in contrast, faces a downward-sloping demand curve. As we see in Figure 10-1(*b*), if an imperfectly competitive firm increases its sales, it will definitely depress the market price of its output.

We can also see the difference between perfect

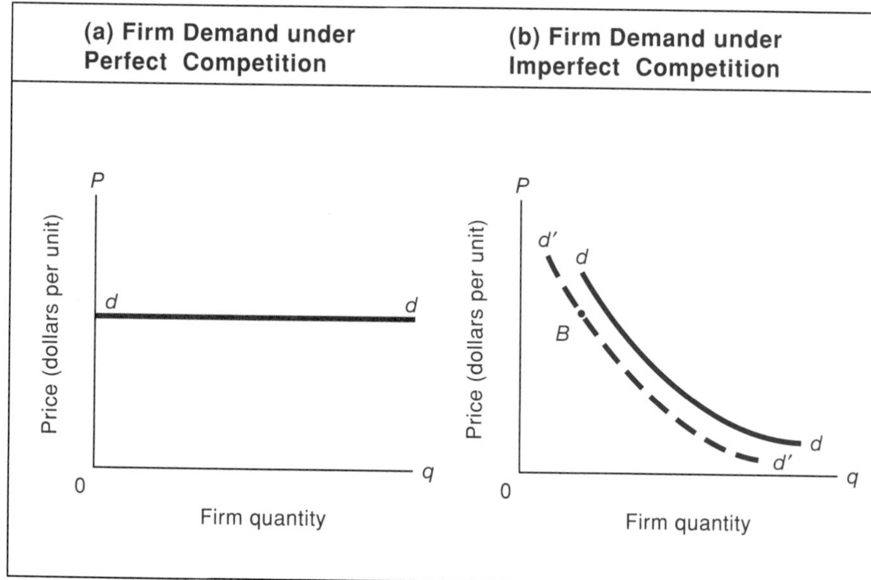

Figure 10-1. Acid test for imperfect competition is downward tilt of firm's demand curve

(a) The perfectly competitive firm can sell all it wants along its horizontal *dd* curve without depressing the market price. **(b)** But the imperfect competitor will find that its demand curve slopes downward as higher sales force its price down. And unless it is a sheltered monopolist, a cut in its rivals' prices will appreciably shift its own demand curve leftward to *d'd'*.

and imperfect competition in terms of price elasticity. For a perfect competitor, demand is perfectly elastic; for an imperfect competitor, demand has a finite elasticity. A careful measurement will show that the price elasticity is around two at point *B* in Figure 10-1(*b*).

Behavior of Imperfect Competitors

In analyzing imperfect competition, we will examine the different kinds of market imperfections, the sources of these imperfections, and the most commonly used measures of market power.

Varieties of Imperfect Competition

Let's begin by surveying the principal kinds of market structures. The *market structure* of an industry denotes the characteristics of an industry, particularly the number and size of the sellers, the extent of concentration among the firms, and the degree of homogeneity or heterogeneity of their products.

Monopoly. How imperfect can imperfect competition get? The extreme case would be monopoly: a single seller with complete control over an industry. (It is called a "monopolist," from the Greek words *mono* for "one" and *polist* for "seller.") It is the only one producing in its industry, and there is no industry producing a close substitute.

Exclusive monopolies are rare today. Only in the case of franchised local services—local telephone, gas, water, and electricity being the major examples—is there truly a single seller of a service with no close substitutes. But even these isolated monopolists must reckon with competition from other industries—cellular telephones compete with cable phones, other fuels compete with electricity or gas. In the long run, no monopolist is completely secure from attack by competitors.

Oligopoly. We have seen that oligopoly means "few sellers." Oligopolists are of two types.

First, an oligopolist may be one of a few sellers that produce an identical (or almost identical) product. If A's oil delivered in Rotterdam is much the same as B's, then the smallest price cut by B will drive consumers from A to B. Neither A nor B can be called a monopolist. Yet, if the number of sellers is few, each can have a great effect on market price.

This first type of oligopoly is common in a number of basic industries where the product is fairly homogeneous and the size of enterprise is large—as in the aluminum and oil industries. Generally, because of the high capital requirements or the high costs of obtaining the necessary technology, the costs of entering such an industry are very high.

The second type of oligopoly is typified by the industry in which there are few sellers of differentiated products. Goods are said to be *differentiated* when their important characteristics vary. The automobile industry sells differentiated products because cars have numerous distinguishing characteristics (size, power, fuel economy, and safety). Differentiation of products occurs in virtually all consumer commodities, including refrigerators and ice creams, shirts and jeans, pop singers and baseball teams, medical care and legal advice.

While the differentiated products of oligopolists are distinct, they are nonetheless close substitutes. Without being identical, Cadillacs compete with Lincolns in the luxury-car market while Canon and Minolta vie for market shares in cameras. Oligopoly is competition among the few, but the competition can be very brisk indeed.

Many Differentiated Sellers. In this last category of imperfect competition, usually called **monopolistic competition,** a large number of sellers produce differentiated products. This market structure resembles perfect competition in that there are many sellers, none of whom have a large share of the market. It differs from perfect competition in that the products are differentiated rather than identical.

The classic case of monopolistic competition is the retail gasoline market. I may go to the local Exxon station because it is convenient and provides clean water to wash my windows. But it is one of many gas stations, and I watch prices closely. If the price at Exxon rises more than a few pennies above the competition, I'll switch to the Merit station a short distance away.

We see here, then, imperfect competition among the many. The only difference between this industry and one in perfect competition is that the commodity here is slightly differentiated. What are the sources of product differentiation in monopolisti-

Types of Market Structures

Structure	Number of producers and degree of product differentiation	Part of economy where prevalent	Firm's degree of control over price	Methods of marketing
Perfect competition	Many producers; identical products	A few raw agricultural products (wheat, corn, . . .)	None	Market exchange or auction
Imperfect competition				
Monopolistic competition (many differentiated sellers)	Many producers; many real or perceived differences in product	Retail trade (food, gasoline, . . .)	Some	Advertising and quality rivalry; administered prices
Oligopoly	Few producers; little or no difference in product	Steel, chemicals	Some	Advertising and quality rivalry; administered prices
	Few producers; some differentiation of products	Autos, computers	Some	Advertising and quality rivalry; administered prices
Monopoly	Single producer; product without close substitutes	Local telephone, electricity, and gas utilities ("natural monopolies")	Considerable, but usually regulated	Advertising and service promotion

Table 10-1. Most industries are imperfectly competitive—a blend of monopoly and competition

cally competitive industries? Differentiation arises primarily from location. People want to economize on the time it takes to drive to a store, and they therefore prefer nearby locations. In addition, there are differences in quality (as in the crispness of French fries), in brands or trademarks (as in soft drinks), or in styling (as in clothing).

Table 10-1 gives a picture of the various possible categories of imperfect and perfect competition. This table is an important summary of the different kinds of market structure and warrants careful study.

In addition, imperfect competition may prevail when barriers prevent competitors from entering an industry. The barriers may arise from government laws or regulations, as when a product receives patent protection (Polaroid) or when regulations preclude competition (your local power company). In other cases, products may have well established brand images and secret formulas (Coca Cola) and competitors cannot exactly duplicate the recipe for success.

Let's examine both sources of imperfect competition.

Sources of Market Imperfections

Why do certain industries display near-perfect competition while others are dominated by a handful of large firms? Fundamentally, competition among the few tends to arise when cost conditions or entry barriers prevent a large number of firms from producing the industry's output. Cost conditions are favorable to imperfect competition when there are significant economies of large-scale production and decreasing costs; under these conditions, large firms can simply produce more cheaply and then undersell small firms, who cannot survive. Thus pervasive economies of scale generate industries with few sellers.

Cost Patterns and Structure of Market Imperfection

If every product could be made by every person at equal and constant costs, we could each produce everything ourselves and there would be no need for giant industrial firms. But the world is not made that way. Just imagine trying to produce a stereo or car or even the simplest loaf of bread starting with nothing more than seeds, iron ore, water, and so forth. It would probably take a lifetime to produce what you can buy with a week's wages. But because of specialization and economies of scale, large firms can produce our consumption needs quickly and efficiently. Our first hint about the reasons behind imperfect competition lies in the existence of economies of scale or declining average costs.

The interaction between costs and markets is illustrated in Figure 10-2. In Figure 10-2(*a*), the firm is shown to have average and marginal costs that fall forever. It displays perpetual increasing returns to scale. As output grows, the firm finds more elaborate ways of specializing its equipment; it organizes its work teams into more specialized and efficient units; it can increase capacity and net efficiency. All this without end.

No matter how big is the demand for its product—no matter how far out the industry demand curve (*DD*) happens to lie—the most efficient operating size for this one firm would be greater still. And so peaceful competitive coexistence of thousands of perfect competitors will be quite impossible because one large firm is so much more efficient than small firms. This is the case of a *natural monopoly*.

A second case, oligopoly, occurs when a firm enjoys economies of scale for some output level but after a point the scale economies are exhausted and average costs begin to increase. Figure 10-2(*b*) shows such a case. Note, however, that the *AC* curve did not turn up soon enough to avoid the breakdown of perfect competition: The industry total demand curve *DD* does not provide a big enough market to enable numerous firms to coexist at the efficient level of operation called for by the indicated cost curve.

Figure 10-2(*c*) shows a case that is favorable for perfect competition. This industry is characterized by a demand and cost structure in which the industry can support the large number of efficiently operating firms that are needed for perfect competition.

The relationship between scale economies and imperfections has been intensively studied by industrial-organization economists over the last three decades. Table 10-2 shows the results of one study of six U.S. industries. It suggests that economies of scale are an important factor in industrial concentration today.

Barriers to Competition

Although cost differences are the most important factor behind market structures, barriers to competition can also increase concentration. We can illustrate the point with reference to the data in Table

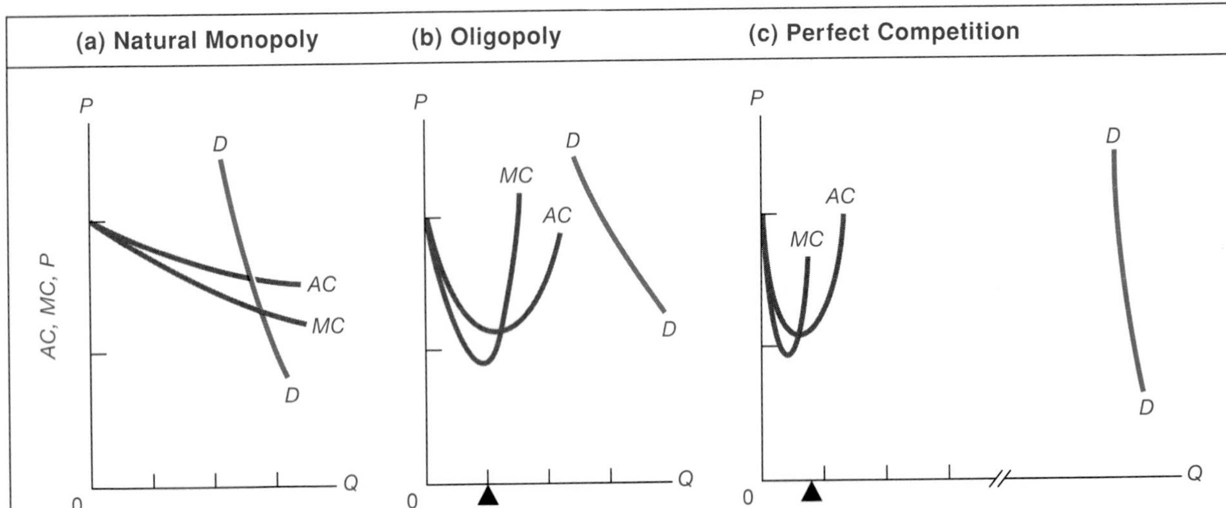

Figure 10-2. To avoid monopoly or oligopoly, average costs must turn at small fraction of industry output

Cost and demand conditions affect market structures. When costs fall indefinitely, as in the case of natural monopoly in **(a)**, one firm can expand to monopolize the industry. In **(b)**, costs eventually turn up, but not soon enough relative to total industry demand *DD*. Coexistence of numerous perfect competitors is impossible, and oligopoly will emerge. In **(c)**, total industry demand *DD* is so vast relative to efficient scale of a single seller that the market allows viable coexistence of numerous perfect competitors. Here we have perfect competition.

Industry	(1) Share of U.S. output needed by a single firm to exploit economies of scale (%)	(2) Actual average market share of top three firms (%)	(3) Main reason for economies of large-scale operations
Beer brewing	10–14	13	Need to create a national brand image and to coordinate investment
Cigarettes	6–12	23	Advertising and image differentiation
Glass bottles	4–6	22	Need for central engineering and design staff
Cement	2	7	Need to spread risk and raise capital
Refrigerators	14–20	21	Marketing requirements and length of production runs
Petroleum	4–6	8	Spread risk on crude-oil ventures and coordinate investment

Table 10-2. Economies of scale drive many industries toward concentration

Several products were studied to determine if cost conditions could lie behind existing concentration patterns. Column (1) shows the estimate of the point where the long-run average cost curve begins to turn up, as a share of output. Compare this with the average market share of each of the top three firms in column (2). [Source: F. M. Scherer, Alan Beckenstein, Erich Kaufer, and R. D. Murphy, *The Economics of Multi-Plant Operation: An International Comparisons Study* (Harvard University Press, Cambridge, Mass., 1975).]

10-2. According to those estimates, the top three cigarette firms would each need 6 to 12 percent of the national market to attain the minimum efficient scale of operation. But the actual market share of the top three firms was, on average, 23 percent of the national market. Aside from cost factors, what could account for the large actual share of the top firms?

One important answer lies in barriers to competition:

A **barrier to competition** arises when legal restrictions or product differentiation reduces the number of competitors below the number that would survive on the basis of efficiency or cost conditions alone.

Legal Restrictions. Governments sometimes restrict competition in certain industries. Important legal restrictions include patents, entry restrictions, and foreign-trade tariffs and quotas.

Patents are a very special form of legal restriction to entry. A patent is granted to an inventor to allow a temporary exclusive use (or monopoly) of the product or process that is patented. For example, Polaroid has an absolute monopoly over the market for instant cameras because of patent protection. Governments grant patent monopolies to encourage inventive activity; they are particularly beneficial to small firms and individuals. Without the prospect of monopoly protection, a sole inventor might despair of ever profiting from years devoted to the lonely search for better products or processes.

Governments also impose *entry or exit restrictions* on many industries. Governments often give *franchise monopolies* to firms; these are contracts under which the government conveys to the firm the exclusive right to provide a service (typically, water, electricity, natural gas, or telephone connections) in return for which the firm agrees to limit its profits and provide service to all customers. This arrangement is favored in industries that are natural monopolies for important goods and services. As in the case of patents, such restrictions may be beneficial to the economy, but they are undoubtedly very powerful barriers to competition and increase monopoly power. For example, until recently AT&T used government-authorized entry barriers to prevent competitors from entering the long-distance telephone industry. (We will return to this case in our discussion of antitrust policy.)

The final example of legal restrictions, *import restrictions,* has a weaker economic rationale. Suppose an industry will support perfect competition, but governments around the world impose high tariffs or quotas on foreign producers. As a result, each country's market will be much smaller, for the producers can sell only to the home markets. Each country's *DD* demand curve will lie far to the left with protectionist policies.

A protectionist pattern of world trade might change the industry structure from Figure 10-2(*c*) to 10-2(*b*) or even to 10-2(*a*). American historians know this point well when they say, "The tariff is the mother of monopolies." By contrast, when markets are broadened by abolishing tariffs in a common market, vigorous and effective competition is encouraged and prices tend to fall. One of the most dramatic examples of increased competition has come in the European Community, which has lowered tariffs among member countries steadily over the last three decades and has benefited from larger markets for firms and lower concentration of industry.

The need to reduce and keep down the barriers to competition is one of the major goals of public policy in a market economy.

Product Differentiation. In addition to legally imposed barriers to competition, there are economic barriers as well. The major hurdle for potential competitors is the pervasive presence of product differentiation that we discussed above.

Consider as an example the case of automobiles. The major industrial countries currently have among them more than a dozen large companies producing automobiles. Moreover, because transportation costs are low relative to selling prices, we might expect nearly perfect competition in this market.

In fact, because of product differentiation, the barriers to competition are relatively high. Some sources of product differentiation are natural: British cars, with steering wheels on the right side, have little attraction for American drivers. Similarly, giant American cars sell poorly in countries with narrow streets and tiny parking spaces. Some sources of product differentiation appear quite contrived. In the 1950s, cars with enormous tail fins, boosted by advertising that associated horsepower with sex appeal, were the darling of consumers. Today, German luxury cars command a premium, as do their look-alikes.

How does product differentiation, whether natural or contrived, impose a barrier to entry and increase concentration? The total demand for a product like autos or soft drinks or cigarettes will be fragmented into many smaller markets for differentiated products. The demands for each of the individual differentiated products in this market will be so small that they will not be able to support a large number of firms operating at the bottom of their U-shaped cost curves. The result is that perfect competition's *DD* curve in Figure 10-2(*c*) contracts so far to the left that it becomes like those of monopoly and oligopoly shown in Figure 10-2(*a*) and (*b*). Hence, differentiation, like tariffs, produces greater concentration and more imperfect competition.

When an industry shows pervasive economies of scale, so that the most efficient scale of a firm's production comes at a significant portion of industry demand, perfect competition is in peril. In such situations, a few firms will supply most of the industry's output. Imperfections arising from declining costs are reinforced by barriers to competition, such as legal restrictions on competition or product differentiation.

Measuring Market Power: Concentration Ratios

In terms of market organization, industries fall along a spectrum from perfect competition to pure monopoly. In many situations, particularly in assessing whether government should reduce market power, economists need a quantitative measure of the extent of market power. **Market power** signifies the degree of control that a single firm or a small number of firms have over the price and production decisions in an industry. The most common measure of market power is the *concentration ratio* for an industry, illustrated in Figure 10-3. The **four-firm concentration ratio** is defined as the percent of total industry output (or shipments) that is accounted for by the largest four firms. Similarly, the eight-firm concentration ratio is the percent of output shipped by the top eight firms. In a pure monopoly, the four- or eight-firm concentration ratio would be 100 percent, while for perfect competition, both ratios would be close to zero.

How concentrated is American manufacturing? For 1977, data show that about one-fifth of manufacturing output takes place in highly concentrated industries (those with four-firm concentration ra-

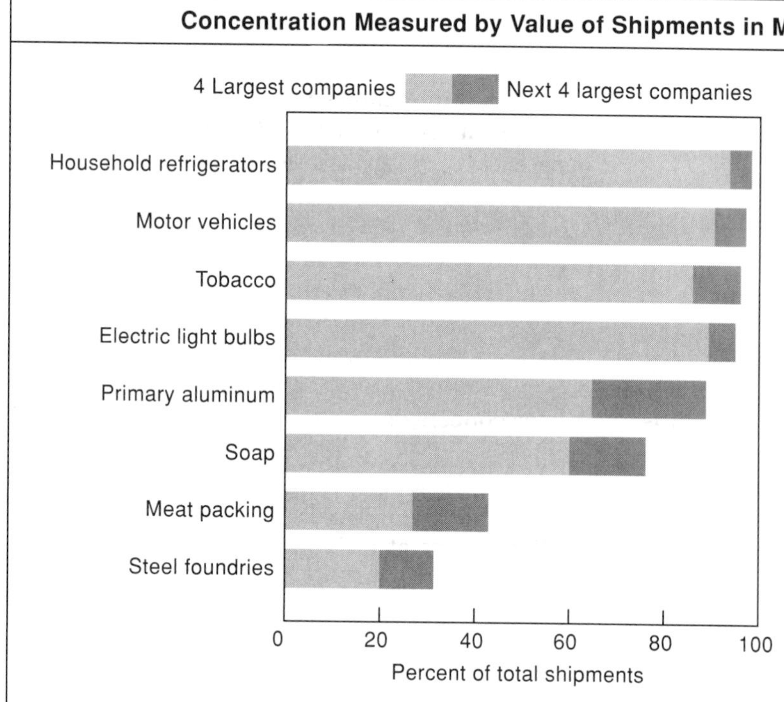

Figure 10-3. Concentration ratios measure the extent to which a few firms dominate an industry

For refrigerators, motor vehicles, and many other industries, a few firms produce most of domestic output. Compare this with the ideal of perfect competition, in which each firm is too small to affect the market price. (Source: U.S. Bureau of the Census, 1982 data.)

tios above 60 percent), while another fifth resides in unconcentrated industries (those with four-firm concentration ratios less than 20 percent).

Economists keep an eye on the historical trends in overall concentration. Data for the period since World War II indicate that the average four-firm concentration ratio in U.S. manufacturing rose slightly from 1947 to 1972 and then declined from 39.2 percent in 1972 to 37.1 percent in 1982. The actual concentration probably declined even more sharply than these data indicate because of the rise of imports, which are excluded from these estimates.

Although the measures of concentration discussed here are widely used in economic and legal analysis, they are sometimes misleading indicators of market power. In those industries that are exposed to international competition, concentration ratios will overstate the extent of market power and concentration because they include only domestic production and exclude the increasingly intense rivalry of foreign producers. Recent studies of many industries indicate that, when foreign firms are included in concentration measures, concentration ratios have been declining in recent years.

In addition, concentration measures are customarily applied to a narrow industry definition, such as mainframe computers. Sometimes, the industry definitions are too narrow, and strong competition can come from other quarters. For example, sales of personal-computer networks compete with mainframe computers even though they are in different industries. Care must always be taken to interpret quantitative indexes of market power appropriately.

B. Marginal Revenue and Monopoly

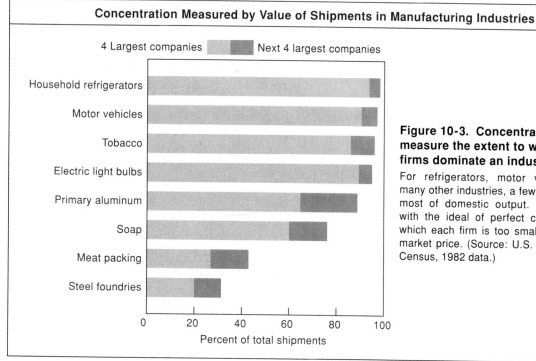

Having analyzed the major species of imperfect competitors, we will now analyze thoroughly the behavior of a monopolist. In undertaking this analysis, we will find a new concept, marginal revenue, essential for describing the equilibrium output and price. But this new concept will also apply more broadly to the analysis of oligopoly in the next chapter and indeed to the decisions of perfect competitors.

Price, Quantity, and Total Revenue

Suppose that a firm finds itself in possession of a complete monopoly in its industry. The firm might be the fortunate owner of a patent for a new anti-cancer drug, or it might have an exclusive franchise to provide cable television service. If the monopolist wishes to maximize its profits, what price should it charge? What output level should it produce?

To answer these questions, we need to compare the costs of production with the revenues from production. More precisely, we need to calculate the change in profits that occurs when production increases; we will see that this calculation is made by comparing the marginal cost of additional output with the marginal revenue of additional sales.

We developed all the relevant cost concepts in Chapter 8, where we met *TC, AC, MC,* and so forth. We will now look at the analogous revenue concepts. From the firm's demand curve, we know the relationship between price (P) and quantity sold (q): Columns (1) and (2) of Table 10-3 show the demand schedule for a hypothetical monopolist. In addition, Figure 10-4(a) depicts, in black, the demand curve (dd) for the monopolist.

We next calculate the total revenue at each sales level by multiplying price times quantity. Column (3) of Table 10-3 shows how to calculate the **total revenue** (TR), which is simply P times q. Thus 0 units bring in TR of 0; 1 unit brings in TR = \$180 × 1 = \$180; 2 units bring in \$160 × 2 = \$320; and so forth.

In this example of a straight-line or linear demand curve, total revenue at first rises with output, since the reduction in P needed to sell the extra q is moderate in this upper, elastic range of the demand curve. But when we reach the midpoint of the straight-line demand curve, TR reaches its maximum. This comes at $q = 5$, P = \$100, with TR = \$500. Increasing q beyond this point brings the firm into the inelastic demand region; for inelastic demand, a 1 percent price cut produces less than a 1 percent sales increase, so total revenue falls as price is cut. Figure 10-4(b) shows TR to be dome-shaped, rising from zero at a very high price to a maximum of \$500 and then falling to zero as price approaches zero.

Already Table 10-3 and Figure 10-4(b) illustrate the error in the following statement: "A firm out to maximize its profits will always charge the highest price that the traffic will bear." This statement is incorrect because charging the highest possible price will mean that the monopolist will sell no output and get no revenue at all! Or if we reinterpret this doctrine to mean charging the highest price at which anything at all can be sold, it is obvious that selling but 1 unit even at a high price is no way to maximize profits. Neglecting costs for the

Total and Marginal Revenue

(1) Quantity q	(2) Price $P = AR = TR/q$ (\$)	(3) Total revenue $TR = P \times q$ (\$)	(4) Marginal revenue MR (\$)
0	200	0	+200
			+180
1	180	180	+160
			+140
2	160	320	+120
			+100
3	140	420	+80
			____
4	120	480	+40
			+20
5	100	500	0
			−20
6	80	480	−40
			−60
7	60	____	−80
			−100
8	40	320	____
			−140
9	____	180	−160
			−180
10	0	0	

Table 10-3. Marginal revenue numbers can be derived from demand schedule

Total revenue in column (3) comes from multiplying P by q. To get marginal revenue, we increase q by a unit and calculate the change in total revenue. Note that MR is at first positive when demand is elastic. But after demand turns inelastic, MR becomes negative even though price never becomes negative. MR is less than P because of loss due to the necessity to lower price on previous units to sell another unit of q.

(a) Marginal Revenue

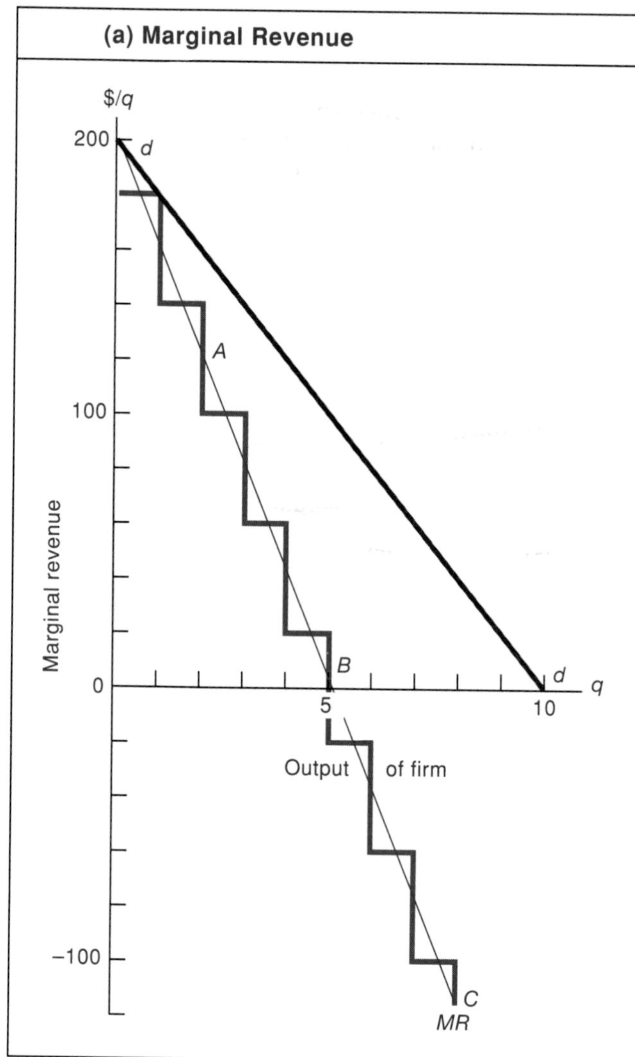

(b) Total Revenue

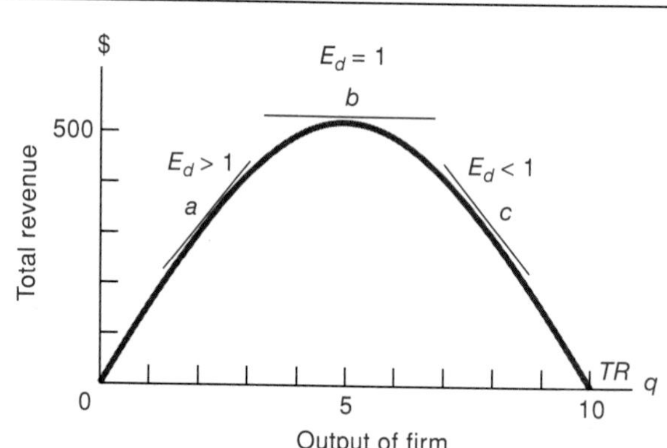

Figure 10-4. Marginal revenue curve comes from demand curve

(a) The blue steps show the increments of total revenue from each new unit of output as calculated from Table 10-3 [or from the *TR* of **(b)** in this figure]. *MR* falls below *P* from the beginning, actually dropping twice as fast as the straight-line *dd* curve. *MR* becomes negative when *dd* turns inelastic. Smoothing the incremental steps of *MR* gives the smooth, thin blue *MR* curve, which in the case of straight-line *dd* will always have twice as steep a slope as *dd*. [*Note*: These values from smoothed *MR* are the same as the light blue numbers in column (4) of Table 10-3.]

(b) Total revenue is dome-shaped—rising from zero (where $q = 0$) to a maximum (where *dd* has unitary elasticity), and then falling back to zero (where $P = 0$). *TR*'s slope gives smoothed *MR* just as jumps in *TR* give steps of incremental *MR*.

moment, the correct interpretation of charging what the traffic will bear must mean that we find the best compromise between a high *P* and a high *q*.

At what output is revenue maximized? We see in Table 10-3 that *TR* is maximized when $q = 5$ and $P = 100$. This is the point where the demand elasticity is exactly one. Thus, if a monopolist had no costs of production, it would sell, not at the maximum price, but at the price where *TR* is maximal, or where the demand elasticity is exactly unity.

Note that the price per unit can be called average revenue (*AR*) to distinguish it from total revenue. Hence, we get $P = AR$ by dividing *TR* by *q* (just as we earlier got *AC* by dividing *TC* by *q*). Verify that if column (3) had been written down *before* column (2), we could have filled in column (2) by division. To test your understanding, fill in the blanks in columns (2) to (4).

Marginal Revenue and Price

To find the highest-profit equilibrium for a monopolist, we need to measure the impact of selling an extra unit of output on total revenue; for this we need the concept of marginal revenue.

Marginal revenue (*MR*) is the increment in total revenue that comes when output increases by 1 unit. *MR* can be either positive or negative.

The blue numbers of marginal revenue are

shown in column (4) of Table 10-3. Here is how they are calculated: Subtract the TR we get by selling q units from the TR we get by selling $q + 1$ units. The difference is extra revenue or MR. Thus, from $q = 0$ to $q = 1$, we get $MR = \$180 - \$0$. From $q = 1$ to $q = 2$, MR is $\$320 - \$180 = \$140$.

MR is positive until we arrive at $q = 5$, and negative from then on. What does the strange notion of negative marginal revenue mean? That the firm is paying people to take its goods? Not at all. Negative MR means that, in order to sell additional units, the firm must decrease its price so much that its total revenues decline.

For example, when the firm sells 5 units, it gets:

$$TR \text{ (5 units)} = 5 \times \$100 = \$500$$

Now say the firm wishes to sell an additional unit of output. To do this, it must reduce the price because the demand curve slopes downward, and it can increase sales only by lowering price. So to sell 6 units, it lowers the price from \$100 to \$80. It gets \$80 of revenue from the sixth unit, but it gets only 5 × \$80 on the first 5 units, yielding:

$$TR \text{ (6 units)} = 5 \times \$80 + 1 \times \$80 = \$400 + \$80 = \$480$$

Marginal revenue between 5 and 6 units is \$480 − \$500 = minus \$20. The necessary price reduction on the first 5 units was so large that, even after adding in the sale of the sixth unit, total revenue fell. This is what happens when MR is negative.

Note that even though MR is negative, AR or price is still positive. Do not confuse marginal revenue with average revenue or price. Table 10-3 shows that they are different. In addition, Figure 10-4(*a*) plots the demand (or AR) curve and the marginal revenue (MR) curve. Scrutinize Figure 10-4(*a*) to see that the plotted blue steps of MR definitely lie below the black *dd* curve of AR. In fact, MR turns negative when AR is halfway down toward zero.

To summarize:

With demand sloping downward,

$$P > MR \; (= P - \text{loss on all previous } q)$$

Although MR is less than P for an imperfect competitor, is this also the case for a perfect competitor? Actually, no. For a perfect competitor, the sale of extra units will never depress price and the "loss on all previous q" is therefore equal to zero. Price and marginal revenue are identical for perfect competitors.

Under perfect competition, price equals average revenue equals marginal revenue. A perfect competitor's *dd* curve and its MR curve coincide as horizontal lines.

Elasticity and Marginal Revenue. What is the relationship between the price elasticity of demand and marginal revenue?

Marginal revenue is positive when demand is elastic, zero when demand is unit-elastic, and negative when demand is inelastic.

This result is really a different way of restating the definition of elasticity we used in Chapter 5. Recall that demand is elastic when a price decrease leads to a revenue increase. In such a situation, a price decrease raises output demanded so much that revenues rise, so that marginal revenue is positive. For example, in Table 10-3, as price falls in the elastic region from $P = \$180$ to $P = \$160$, output demanded rises sufficiently to raise total revenue, and marginal revenue is positive.

What happens when demand is unit-elastic? A price cut then just matches an increase in output and marginal revenue is therefore zero. Can you see why marginal revenue is always negative in the inelastic range? Why is the marginal revenue for the perfect competitor's infinitely elastic demand curve always positive?

Maximum Profit for a Monopolist

We are now ready to find the maximum-profit equilibrium of the monopolist. If a monopolist faces a given demand curve and wishes to maximize total profit (TP), what should it do? By definition, total profit = total revenue − total costs; in symbols, $TP = TR - TC = (P \times q) - TC$.

To maximize its profits, the firm must find the equilibrium price and quantity, P^* and q^*, that give the largest profit, or the largest difference between TR and TC. An important result is that *maximum profit will occur when output is at that level where the firm's marginal revenue is equal to its marginal cost.*

One way to determine this maximum-profit condition is by using a table of costs and revenues, such as Table 10-4. To find the profit-maximizing

Summary of Firm's Maximum Profit

(1) Quantity q	(2) Price P (\$)	(3) Total revenue TR (\$)	(4) Total cost TC (\$)	(5) Total profit TP (\$)	(6) Marginal revenue MR (\$)	(7) Marginal cost MC (\$)	
0	200	0	145	−145	+200	34	
					+180	30	$MR > MC$
1	180	180	175	+5	+160	27	
					+140	25	
2	160	320	200	+120	+120	22	
					+100	20	
3	140	420	220	+200	+80	21	
					+60	30	
4*	**120**	**480**	**250**	**+230**	+40	40	$MR = MC$
					+20	50	
5	100	500	300	+200	0	60	
					−20	70	
6	80	480	370	+110	−40	80	
					−60	90	
7	60	420	460	−40	−80	100	
					−100	110	
8	40	320	570	−250			$MR < MC$

* Maximum-profit equilibrium.

Table 10-4. Equating marginal cost to marginal revenue gives firm's maximum-profit q and P

Total and marginal costs of production are now brought together with total and marginal revenues. The maximum-profit condition is where $MR = MC$, with $q^* = 4$, $P^* = \$120$, and maximum $TP = \$230 = (\$120 \times 4) - \$250$. (For convenience, the light MR and MC numbers are put in to give the smoothed values at each q point.)

quantity and price, compute total profit in column (5). This column tells us that the optimal quantity, which is 4 units, requires a price of \$120 per unit. This produces a total revenue of \$480, and, after subtracting total costs of \$250, we calculate total profit to be \$230. A glance at other prices and quantities shows that no other price-output combination has as high a level of total profit.

A second way of arriving at the same answer is to compare marginal revenue, column (6), and marginal cost, column (7). (Recall that *MR* is computed from the *TR* data in Table 10-3, while *MC* is calculated from *TC* in the manner shown in Chapter 8.)

As long as each additional unit of output provides more revenue than it costs—that is to say, as long as *MR* is greater than *MC*—the firm's profit will increase. So the firm would continue to increase its output as long as *MR* is greater than *MC*. By contrast, suppose that at a given level of output *MR* is less than *MC*. This means that increasing output would lead to a *lower* level of profits, so the profit-maximizing firm should at that point cut back on output. Clearly the best-profit point then comes at the point where marginal revenue exactly equals marginal cost, as is shown by the data in Table 10-4.

The maximum-profit price and quantity of a monopolist come where its marginal revenue equals its marginal cost:

$$MR = MC, \text{ at the maximum-profit } P^* \text{ and } q^*$$

This second way of finding the optimum point, by comparing marginal cost and marginal revenue, is neither better nor worse than the first way of examining total profit. They give exactly the same answer.

These examples show the logic of the $MC = MR$ rule for maximizing profits, but what is the intuition behind this rule? Look for a moment at Table 10-4 and suppose that the monopolist is producing $q = 2$. At that point, its *MR* for producing 1 full additional unit is +\$100, while its *MC* is \$20. Thus, if it

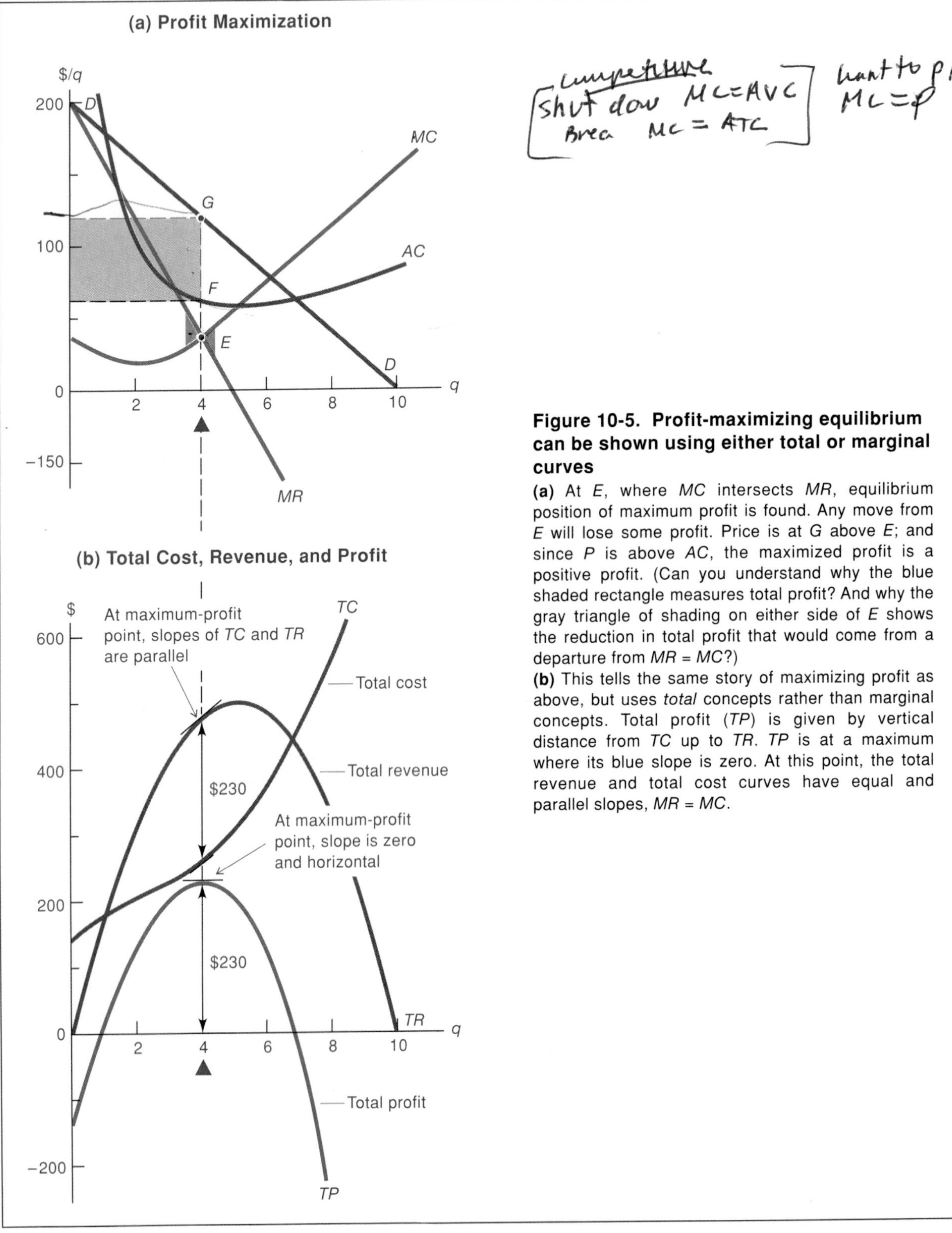

Figure 10-5. Profit-maximizing equilibrium can be shown using either total or marginal curves

(a) At *E*, where *MC* intersects *MR*, equilibrium position of maximum profit is found. Any move from *E* will lose some profit. Price is at *G* above *E*; and since *P* is above *AC*, the maximized profit is a positive profit. (Can you understand why the blue shaded rectangle measures total profit? And why the gray triangle of shading on either side of *E* shows the reduction in total profit that would come from a departure from *MR* = *MC*?)

(b) This tells the same story of maximizing profit as above, but uses *total* concepts rather than marginal concepts. Total profit (*TP*) is given by vertical distance from *TC* up to *TR*. *TP* is at a maximum where its blue slope is zero. At this point, the total revenue and total cost curves have equal and parallel slopes, *MR* = *MC*.

produced 1 additional unit, the firm would make additional profits of $MR - MC = \$100 - \$20 = \$80$. Indeed, column (5) of Table 10-4 shows that the extra profit gained by moving from 2 to 3 units is exactly \$80.

Thus when *MR* exceeds *MC*, additional profits can be made by increasing output; when *MC* exceeds *MR*, additional profits can be made by decreasing *q*. Only when $MR = MC$ can the firm maximize profits because there are no potential profits to be made by changing its output level.

Monopoly Equilibrium in Graphs

Figure 10-5 shows the monopoly equilibrium. Part (*a*) combines the firm's cost and revenue curves. The maximum-profit point comes at that output where *MC* equals *MR*, which is given at their intersection at *E*. The monopoly equilibrium, or maximum-profit point, is at an output of $q^* = 4$. To find the profit-maximizing price, we run vertically up from *E* to the *DD* curve at *G*, where $P = \$120$. The fact that average revenue at *G* lies above average cost at *F* guarantees a positive profit. The actual amount of profit is given by the gray shaded area in Figure 10-5(*a*).

The same story is told in part (*b*) with curves of total revenue, cost, and profit. Total revenue is dome-shaped. Total cost is ever rising. The vertical difference between them is total profit, which begins negative and ends negative. In between, *TP* is positive, reaching its maximum of \$230 at $q^* = 4$. At maximum-profit output, the black slopes of *TR* and *TC* (which are *MR* and *MC* at those points) are parallel and therefore equal. If the slopes were pointing outward in a nonparallel fashion (as at $q = 2$), the firm would gain extra profit by expanding *q*. At $q^* = 4$, marginal cost and marginal revenue are balanced. At that point total profit (*TP*) reaches its maximum as an additional unit adds exactly equal amounts to costs and revenues.

A monopolist will maximize its profits by setting output at the level where $MC = MR$. Because the monopolist has a downward-sloping demand curve, this means that $P > MR$. Because price is above marginal cost for a profit-maximizing monopolist, the monopolist reduces output below the level that would be found in a perfectly competitive industry.

Perfect Competition as a Polar Case of Imperfect Competition

Although we have applied the *MC* and *MR* rule to monopolists who desire to maximize profits, this rule is actually applicable far beyond the present analysis. A little thought shows that the $MC = MR$ rule applies with equal validity to a profit-maximizing perfect competitor.

Here is why: For a perfect competitor, marginal revenue turns out to be exactly the same thing as price. With no need to cut your *P* to sell an extra unit of *q*, the marginal revenue it brings you is precisely the *P* received for that last unit, with no loss on previous units being subtracted. Hence, $P = MR$ leads to the special rule for profit maximizing by a perfect competitor:

> Because a perfect competitor can sell all it wants at the market price, $P = MR$ at the maximum-profit point.

You can see this result visually by redrawing Figure 10-5(*a*). If the graph applied to a perfect competitor, the *DD* curve would be horizontal at the market price, and it would coincide with the *MR* curve. The profit-maximizing $MR = MC$ intersection would also come at $P = MC$. We see then how the general rule for profit maximization applies to perfect as well as imperfect competitors.

The Marginal Principle: Let Bygones Be Bygones

While economic theory will not necessarily make you fabulously wealthy, it does introduce you to some new ways of thinking about costs and benefits. One of the most important lessons of economics is that you should look at the *marginal* costs and benefits of decisions and ignore past or sunk costs. We might put this as follows:

> Let bygones be bygones. Don't look backward. Don't cry over spilt milk or moan about past losses. Look forward. Make a hard-headed calculation of the extra costs you'll incur by any decision and weigh these against its extra advantages. Forget about everything that will go on anyway, and make a decision based on future costs and benefits.

More formally, this is the **marginal principle,** which means that people will maximize their incomes or profits or satisfactions by counting only the marginal costs and benefits of a decision. There are countless situations in which the marginal principle applies. For instance, it clearly lies behind successful profit maximization by firms. Another example is investment decisions, in which you should forget about past gains or losses and decide whether to invest in a company or stock or house only on the basis of marginal returns and costs.*

SUMMARY

A. Patterns of Imperfect Competition

1. Most market structures today fall somewhere on a spectrum between perfect competition and pure monopoly. Under imperfect competition, a firm has some control over its price, a fact seen as a downward-sloping demand curve for the firm's output.
2. Important kinds of market structure are: (*a*) monopoly, where a single firm produces all the output in a given industry; (*b*) oligopoly, where a few sellers of a similar or differentiated product supply the industry; (*c*) monopolistic competition, where a large number of small firms supply related but somewhat differentiated products; and (*d*) perfect competition, where a large number of small firms supply an identical product. In the first three cases, firms in the industry face downward-sloping demand curves.
3. Economies of scale, or decreasing average costs, are the major source of imperfect competition. When firms can lower costs by expanding their output, this tends to destroy perfect competition because a few companies can produce the industry's output most efficiently. When the minimum efficient size of plant is large relative to the national or regional market, cost conditions produce imperfect competition.
4. In addition to declining costs, other forces leading to imperfections are barriers to competition in the form of legal restrictions (such as patents or government regulation), and natural or contrived product differentiation (such as left- versus right-hand drive in cars, or similar products made to seem different by advertising).
5. Market power is measured by concentration ratios, such as the four-firm

*An important example of the marginal principle relates to nuclear power. In the early 1990s, the U.S. had several partially completed nuclear power plants. Some had already absorbed billions of dollars of investment but were not yet ready to operate.

One particularly difficult case was the Shoreham plant on Long Island Sound, New York. By 1991 the owner had spent $6 billion on bricks, mortar, fuel rods, and interest, but the operating license had not been granted. You might ask, from a rational economic point of view, Should the plant be opened? And, more particularly, how should the $6 billion of past investments be weighed?

The *marginal principle would state that the $6 billion of past cost is irrelevant.* From an economic point of view, the only relevant issue concerns *future* costs and benefits. That is, what are the economic benefits of the electricity that Shoreham would produce? And what are the opportunity costs of producing that electricity?

The key fact to note in making this calculation is that the sunk cost of $6 billion is irrelevant to future costs and benefits. Studies indicated that, if the $6 billion were ignored, the *future* costs of the nuclear power plant would be slightly less than the next-best alternative, even though the *total* cost (with the $6 billion) would be far higher than the alternative. A pure economic analysis (ignoring safety questions) would conclude that the most efficient outcome would be to open the Shoreham nuclear power plant.

measure which calculates the percent of the market that is served by the four largest firms.

B. Marginal Revenue and Monopoly

6. We can easily derive a firm's total revenue curve from its demand curve. From the schedule or curve of total revenue, we can then derive marginal revenue, which denotes the extra revenue resulting from the sale of an extra unit of output. For the imperfect competitor, marginal revenue is less than price because of the loss on all previous units of output that will result when the firm is forced to drop its price in order to sell an extra unit of output. That is:

   With demand sloping downward,

$$P = AR > MR = P - \text{loss on all previous } q$$

7. A firm will find its maximum-profit position where $MR = MC$, that is, where the last unit it sells brings in extra revenue just equal to its extra cost. This same $MR = MC$ result can be shown graphically by the intersection of the MR and MC curves, or by the equality of the slopes of the total revenue and total cost curves. In any case, *marginal revenue* = *marginal cost* must always hold at the equilibrium position of maximum profit.
8. Economic reasoning leads to the important *marginal principle.* In making decisions, count marginal or future advantages and disadvantages and disregard sunk costs that must be paid under any circumstances.

CONCEPTS FOR REVIEW

Patterns of imperfect competition
perfect versus imperfect competition
monopoly, oligopoly, product differentiation
barriers to competition (costs, legal restrictions, product differentiation)

Marginal revenue and monopoly
marginal (or extra) revenue, MR
$MR = MC$ at maximum-profit output
$MR = P$, $P = MC$, for perfect competitor
natural monopoly
the marginal principle

QUESTIONS FOR DISCUSSION

1. List the distinguishing features of perfect and imperfect competition. What are the main varieties of imperfect competition? In which category would you place General Motors? Your local telephone company? Sears? Farmer Gomez? Your college or university?
2. "Monopolists will maximize sales. They will therefore produce more than perfect competitors and monopoly prices will be lower." Explain why the first sentence is wrong for profit-maximizing monopolists. Explain why the second sentence follows from the first sentence. What do you conclude about the validity of the second sentence?
3. What is MR's numerical value when dd has unitary elasticity?
4. Figure 10-5 shows the maximum-profit equilibrium position. Explain in detail how it really shows two different ways of describing exactly the same fact: namely, that a firm will stop expanding its production where the extra cost of further output just balances its extra revenue.

5. The market shares in the U.S. airline industry for 1986 were the following:

Firm	Market share (%)	Firm	Market share (%)
United	17	Northwest	9
American	14	TWA	8
Delta	12	Pan Am	7
Eastern	12	Eight others	2 each

Source: U.S. Department of Transportation, *Air Carrier Financial Statistics* (December 1986).

Calculate the four-firm and eight-firm concentration ratios. What would be the change in these indexes if Delta merged with United?

6. Redraw Figure 10-5(*a*) for a perfect competitor. Why is *dd* horizontal? Explain why the horizontal *dd* curve coincides with *MR*. Then proceed to find the profit-maximizing *MR* and *MC* intersection. Why does this yield the competitive condition $MR = P$?

   Now redraw Figure 10-5(*b*) for a perfect competitor. Show that the slopes of *TR* and *TC* must still match at the maximum-profit equilibrium point for a perfect competitor.

7. Pear Computer Company has fixed costs of production of \$100,000, while each unit costs \$600 of labor and \$400 of materials and fuel. At a price of \$3000, consumers would buy no Pear computers, but for each \$10 reduction in price, sales of Pear computers increase by 1000 units. Calculate marginal cost and marginal revenue for Pear Computer, and determine its monopoly price and quantity.

8. Show that a profit-maximizing monopolist will never operate in the price inelastic region of its demand curve.

9. **Advanced problem:** Firm A has *dd* demand function, $P = 15 - 0.05q$, and hence $TR = qP = 15q - 0.05q^2$. Its $TC = q + 0.02q^2$. Verify: $MR = d(TR)/dq = 15 - 0.1q$, $MC = d(TC)/dq = 1 + 0.04q$. So $d(\text{profit})/dq = 0$ at $MR = MC$ or at $15 - 0.1q = 1 + 0.04q$ or at $q^* = 100$. Then $P^* = \$15 - \$5 = \$10 > MC^* = \$5$. You can show that maximum profit $= \$1000 - (\$100 + \$200) = \$700$. Can you show that a tax of \$1 per unit will add $1q$ to *TC*, cutting q^* by 100/14 units and raising *P* by 5/14 units?

   Were A a perfect competitor, with horizontal *dd* at \$5, its maximum profit on $q^* = 100$ would have been $\$500 - \$300 = \$200$; now a \$1 per unit tax would cut competitor's q^* by more than monopolist's—namely, by $100/4 = 25$ units. Show all this.

CHAPTER 11

OLIGOPOLY AND MONOPOLISTIC COMPETITION

> We find in comparing a world of monopolized industries with a world of imperfect competition that there may be very considerable improvements in the technique of production when the unit of control in industry increases in size. But we find that an increase in the size of the unit of control will lead to an increase in the inequality of the distribution of wealth. The problem of the world of monopolists thus resolves itself into the familiar dilemma between efficiency and justice.
>
> Joan Robinson, *The Economics of Imperfect Competition* (1933)

Earlier chapters surveyed the poles of monopoly and perfect competition. But many industries in today's American economy lie between these two extremes. Many markets exhibit imperfect competition among a handful of firms. We see oligopolistic markets in manufacturing industries such as automobiles, computers, and aircraft.

Yet another important set of markets is characterized by competition among a large number of sellers of differentiated products. We see this market structure in many retail sectors, such as food stores, gasoline stations, and housing. This is the world of monopolistic competition. The different theories of imperfect competition are studied in the first section of this chapter.

The second section explores the behavior of giant corporations, moving beyond marginal revenue and cost curves to examine exactly how large companies affect our economy. We will ask, What motivates big firms? Do they really maximize profits? Who runs these giant organizations and for what purpose? Finally, we analyze the costs and benefits of imperfect competition.

A. Patterns of Imperfect Competition

A modern industrial economy like the United States contains many varieties of market structures. Glance back at Table 10-1, which shows the following major species:

- *Perfect competition* is found when a large number of firms produce an identical product—so many firms, indeed, that none of them can affect the market price. This market structure thrives mainly on farms.
- *Monopoly,* in which a single firm produces the

Characteristics of Market Structures

(1) Industrial structure (with examples)	(2) Four-firm concentration ratio, 1982 (%)	(3) Rate of profit, 1960–1979 (as % of stockholders' equity)	(4) Research and development, 1980–1982 (as % of sales)	(5) Advertising spending, 1982 (as % of sales)	(6) Degree of price flexibility, 1960–1983 (100 = flexibility for competitive industry)
High concentration (motor vehicles, tobacco, nonferrous metals)	79	13	2.7	2.3	38
Moderate concentration (paper, stone, clay, glass, chemicals)	42	12	2.1	2.2	25
Low concentration (apparel, printing, furniture)	26	11	0.6	1.3	14
Perfectly competitive (corn and wheat farming)	~ 0.01	Not available	~0	~0	100

Table 11-1. Different patterns of research, advertising, and profitability are found in different market structures

We can distinguish four major groupings: industries with high, moderate, and low levels of concentration, and perfectly competitive industries. In each category, a few important industries have been selected.

The table indicates that profit rates are only slightly elevated in concentrated industries while research and development and advertising spending are significantly higher in concentrated industries. (Sources: U.S. Bureau of the Census, *Census of Manufacturing;* National Science Foundation; Federal Trade Commission, *Quarterly Financial Report; Economic Report of the President;* Internal Revenue Service, *Corporation Income Tax*.)

entire output of an industry, was analyzed in depth in the last chapter. Such cases are rare in most market economies today.

- Between the two poles lie intermediate forms of imperfect competition. In this chapter we examine *oligopoly,* in which an industry is dominated by a few firms, as well as *monopolistic competition,* in which a large number of firms produce slightly differentiated products.

What are the salient characteristics of different market structures? Table 11-1 shows some important features for four groups of industries (those with high, moderate, and low concentration along with perfect competition).

Column (3) suggests that there is little relationship between an industry's concentration and its average rate of profit. More concentrated industries tend to have only slightly higher profits than unconcentrated ones. This finding has been a surprise to critics of capitalism, who expect supernormal monopoly profits in giant firms.

Concentrated industries tend to have much higher levels of advertising and research and development (R&D) spending per unit of sales. In perfect competition, by contrast, advertising and research are absent.

The Sources of Imperfect Competition

An economic theory of imperfect competition must account for the patterns of behavior shown in Table 11-1. In devising explanations for the origins and behavior of imperfectly competitive markets, economists stress three key factors: cost conditions, barriers to competition, and the strategic interaction among firms.

Costs

The major factors determining market structure are the technological and cost conditions of an industry. We saw above (recall page 167 and Table 10-2) that in many industries the point of minimum average cost occurs at a sizable fraction—10 or 20 or even 50 percent—of industry output. In these industries, which include petroleum refining, automobile production, and aircraft manufacturing, an efficient firm must produce a large fraction of the market output. That industry will tend to be oligopolistic, with but a few large producers.

Barriers to Competition

Chapter 10 analyzed the role of barriers to competition, which are factors that reduce the rivalry among firms in an industry. When barriers are high, an industry may have few firms and limited rivalry. Because of economies of scale and barriers to competition, oligopoly is common in manufacturing. In petroleum refining, the smallest efficient plant would cost almost $1 billion, while an automobile manufacturer would need to produce at least 300,000 units per year to attain an efficient scale of production. It is in the same manufacturing industries that we meet the highest concentration ratios in Germany, Japan, and the United States.

Strategic Interaction

When but a few firms operate in a market, they must recognize their interdependence. For example, if there are two automobile firms operating in a particular market, each firm must take into account the other firm's pricing and marketing decisions. When oligopolists recognize their mutual dependence, there will be a strategic interaction between them. **Strategic interaction** describes the condition in which each firm's business strategy depends upon its rivals' business plans. With competition among the few, firms must guess about how their rivals will react to changing tactics.

Two important kinds of strategies are *cooperative* and *noncooperative* behavior. Firms operate in a cooperative mode when they join forces to plan their business operations. Firms act noncooperatively when they act on their own without any explicit or implicit agreement with other firms. We will see that these two kinds of behavior produce major differences in market performance.

Now that we have seen the three special features of imperfect competition—high entry costs, barriers to competition, and strategic interaction—we next examine some of the most important approaches to imperfect competition.

Models of Imperfect Competition

There are many theories of imperfect competition, and advanced courses in microeconomics or business strategy describe these more fully. For an introductory taste, we will here serve up three of the most important cases of imperfect competition—collusive oligopoly, monopolistic competition, and small-number oligopoly. This appetizer will just hint at the great richness of the subject of industrial organization.

Collusive Oligopoly

An important factor influencing a market's structure is the degree of cooperation among the firms. When firms cooperate completely, they engage in **collusion.** This term denotes a situation in which two or more firms jointly set their prices or outputs, divide the market among them, or make other business decisions jointly.

Firms are tempted to collude when they recognize that their profits depend on their joint actions. To avoid ruinous rivalry, firms may collude to raise their prices. During the early years of American capitalism, oligopolists often merged or formed a trust or cartel. A **cartel** is an organization of independent firms, producing similar products, that work together to raise prices and restrict output. Meeting at celebrated dinners, such as those that Judge Gary of U.S. Steel held around 1910, the sellers' cartel would engage in *explicit collusion*.

Today, however, it is strictly illegal in the United States and most other market economies for companies to collude by jointly setting prices or dividing markets. (The antitrust laws pertaining to such behavior are discussed in Chapter 20.) Nonetheless, if there are but a few large firms in an industry, they may engage in *tacit collusion,* which occurs when they refrain from competition and set prices at inflated levels or divide up markets without explicit agreements. Firms engaged in tacit collusion refrain from using prices as a competitive tool and tend to quote rather similar prices well above the competitive level.

For example, imagine an industry of four firms with identical cost curves, each selling an identical product such as oil or industrial chemicals. Each firm—call them A, B, C, and D—currently has one-quarter of the market. Figure 11-1 illustrates oligopolist A's situation.

A's demand curve, D_AD_A, is drawn assuming that the other firms all follow firm A's price upward and downward. Thus the firm's demand curve has exactly the same elasticity as the industry's *DD* curve. Firm A will get one-fourth of the shared market as long as all firms charge the same price. In such a situation, firms may seek the **collusive oligopoly** equilibrium by colluding to maximize their joint profits.

What is the maximum-profit equilibrium for the collusive oligopolist? It is shown in Figure 11-1 at point *E*, the intersection of the firm's *MC* and *MR* curves. Here, the appropriate demand curve is D_AD_A, which recognizes that the other firms will charge the same price as A. The optimal price for the collusive oligopolist is shown at point *G* on D_AD_A, just above point *E*. This price is identical to the monopoly price; that is, the price is well above marginal cost and earns the colluding oligopolists a handsome monopoly profit.

When oligopolists can collude to maximize their joint profits, taking into account their mutual interdependence, the price and quantity will be those of a single monopolist.

Although many oligopolists would be delighted to earn such high profits, in reality many obstacles hinder effective collusion. First, collusion is illegal. Second, firms may "cheat" on the agreement by cutting their price to selected customers thereby increasing their market share. Secret price cutting is particularly likely in markets where prices are secret, where goods are differentiated, where there is more than a handful of firms, or where the technology is changing rapidly.

How prevalent, then, is collusive oligopoly? According to Adam Smith, writing in 1776:

> People of the same trade seldom meet together, even for merriment and diversion, but the conversation ends in a conspiracy against the public, or in some contrivance to raise prices.

This was undoubtedly an exaggeration, although collusion is today a real problem. A recent examination found that of 1043 major corporations, 94 have admitted to or been convicted of illegal price fixing. But most industries experience vigorous competition from both domestic and foreign firms. Moreover, the attempt to raise prices does not always succeed. The low rates of profit of concentrated industries shown in Table 11-1 suggest that few industries actually succeed in raising their profits far above competitive levels.

Two notable failures at collusion can be cited. Since 1973, the Organization of Petroleum Exporting Countries (OPEC) has attempted to set a monopoly price for oil. These attempts require that member countries curtail production to keep prices high. Sometimes OPEC succeeds, but every few years price competition breaks out. This happened in a spectacular way in 1986, when Saudi Arabia drove oil prices from $28 per barrel down to below $10.

An even more dramatic example came in the airline industry, a sector which is characterized by

Equilibrium for Collusive Oligopolist

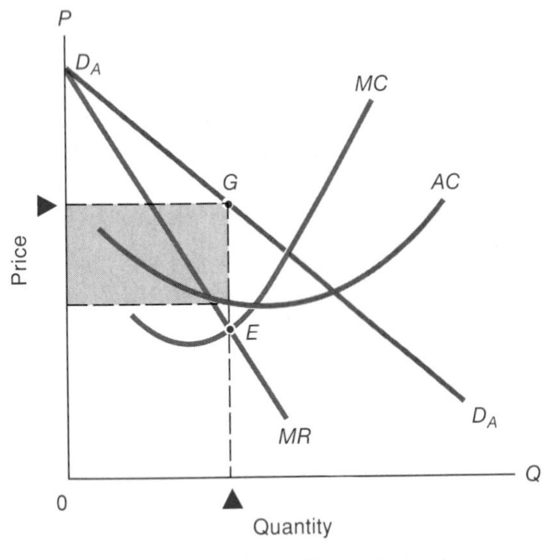

Figure 11-1. Collusive oligopoly looks much like monopoly

After experience with disastrous price wars, firms will surely recognize that each price cut is canceled by competitors' price cuts. So oligopolist A may estimate its demand curve D_AD_A by assuming others will be charging similar prices. When firms collude to set a jointly profit-maximizing price, the price will be very close to that of a single monopolist.

intense rivalry. The following conversation between the heads of Braniff and American Airlines was recorded:

Putnam (Braniff): Do you have a suggestion for me?
Crandall (American): Yes, I have a suggestion for you. Raise your . . . fares 20 percent. I'll raise mine the next morning. . . . You'll make more money and I will, too.
Putnam: We can't talk about pricing.

No one knows the frequency of such abortive attempts to rig prices.

Monopolistic Competition

A second important type of imperfect competition is **monopolistic competition,** which occurs when many firms sell similar but not identical products. Monopolistic competition resembles perfect competition in three ways: there are many buyers and sellers, entry and exit is easy, and firms take other firms' prices as given. The distinction is that products are identical under perfect competition, while products are differentiated under monopolistic competition.

To illustrate, recall that competitive firms produce standard products, like the red winter wheat sold at the Chicago Board of Trade. In contrast, monopolistic competitors sell differentiated products like different brands of gasoline, soft drinks, or prescription drugs. Within each product group, products or services are closely related but differ in some important characteristics. For our analysis, the important point is that *product differentiation leads to a downward slope in each seller's demand curve.*

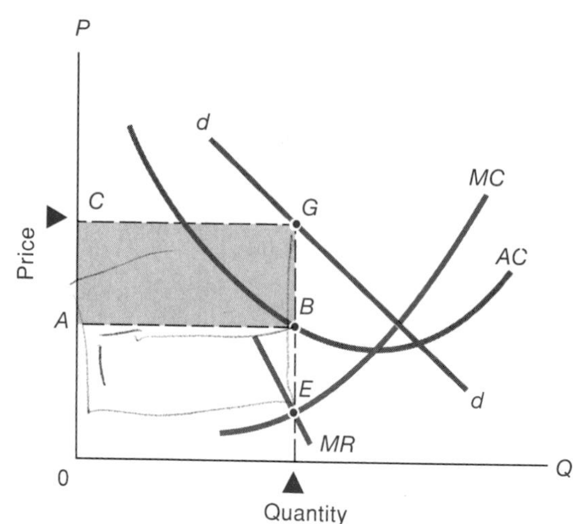

Figure 11-2. Monopolistic competitors produce many similar goods

Under monopolistic competition, numerous small firms sell differentiated products and therefore have downward-sloping demand. Each firm takes its competitors' prices as given. Equilibrium has $MR = MC$ at E, and price is at G. Because price is above AC, the firm is earning a profit, area $ABGC$.

Figure 11-2 shows a grocery store's short-run equilibrium at G. Its dd demand curve is sloped because its product is a little different from everyone else's, if only in location. The profit-maximizing price is at G, and, because price at G is above AC, the firm is making a handsome profit represented by area $ABGC$.

But our grocery store has no monopoly on land or lettuce. Firms can enter the industry by purchasing land, renting a building, entering into franchise agreements, and locating materials and supplies. For simplicity, assume that all existing and new firms have identical costs and therefore the same cost curves. Since the industry is profitable, new firms are drawn into the market. As new firms enter, the demand curve for the products of existing monopolistic competitors shifts leftward as new differentiated products nibble away at our grocery store's market.

What is the ultimate economic outcome? Grocery stores will continue to enter the market until all economic profits (including the appropriate opportunity costs for owners' time, talent, and contributed capital) have been beaten down to zero. Figure 11-3 shows the final long-run equilibrium for the typical seller. In equilibrium, the demand is reduced or shifted to the left until the new $d'd'$ demand curve just touches (but never goes above) the firm's AC curve. Point G' is a long-run equilibrium for the industry because profits are zero and no one is tempted to enter or forced to exit the industry.

In long-run equilibrium for monopolistic competition, prices are above marginal costs but economic profits have been driven down to zero.

The monopolistic competition model provides important insights into American capitalism. The surprising prediction of this model is that the rate

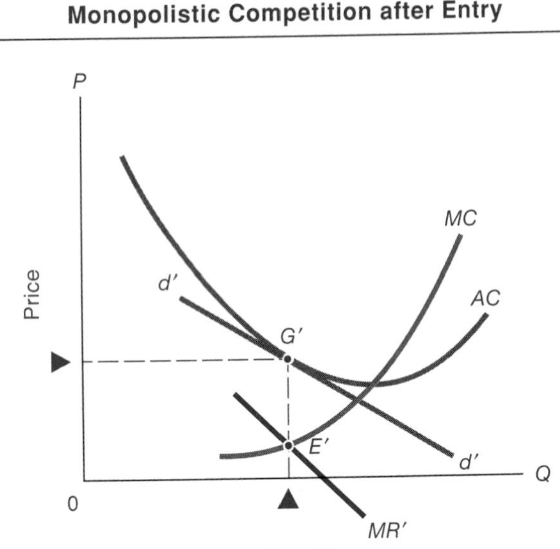

Figure 11-3. Free entry of numerous monopolistic competitors wipes out profit

The typical seller's original profitable *dd* curve in Fig.11-2 will be shifted downward and leftward by entry of new rivals. Entry ceases only when each seller has been forced into a long-run, no-profit tangency such as at *G′*. At long-run equilibrium, price remains above *MC*, and each producer is on the left-hand declining branch of its long-run *AC* curve.

of profit may be low or zero in imperfectly competitive industries. Figure 11-3 shows how monopoly profits will be competed away as firms enter with new differentiated products.

Some economists believe, in addition, that monopolistic competition is inherently inefficient. Look back at the long-run equilibrium price at *G′* in Figure 11-3. At that point, price is above marginal cost; hence, output is reduced below the ideal competitive level.

In light of its inefficiency, critics of monopolistic competition go on to a third point: "These industries are just what we don't need. We have hundreds of thousands of retail outlets, hundreds of virtually identical dog foods or cereals—all selling at prices well above marginal costs. If we could somehow get rid of a quarter or a half of these products, and standardize on just a few designs, wouldn't the economy gain enormously?"

Careful analysis finds that the answer to this question is not clear-cut. A defender of this market structure might retort: "By reducing the number of monopolistic competitors, you might well lower prices. But you might also lower ultimate consumer welfare because people would no longer have as much diversity of goods. Centrally planned socialist countries tried to standardize output on a small number of varieties, and this left their consumers highly dissatisfied. People are willing to pay a great deal to be free to choose."

Where can we look to see monopolistic competition in action? Perhaps the most familiar example is the retail gasoline market. There are 112,000 gasoline stations in the United States, each selling to an infinitesimal part of the national market. But each one has a little bit of market power, or slope to its demand curve. Its product differentiation comes from location, the type of gasoline sold, cleanliness of the station, and supplementary services.

You might think that with a bit of market power, gasoline stations would make a profit over the normal return to capital and management. In fact, they don't. Entry and exit tend to regulate the level of profits so that, over the long run, gas stations earn only a normal economic return on their invested capital.

Again and again the same story is told. In markets like retailing or wholesale trade, where barriers to entry are low and products are differentiated, numerous firms produce inefficiently small quantities and have no economic profits to show for their efforts.

Rivalry among the Few

A final situation explicitly recognizes the strategic interplay in industries with only a few firms. Often, two or three large firms will compete for market shares in a particular region or niche of an industry. In the airline industry, for example, most routes are served by one or two firms.

Take the case of *duopoly*, where a market is served by two firms. For example, Trump and Delta are duopolists that share the Washington–New York airline market. Trump cannot ignore that a cut in its prices is almost sure to be met by a price cut or some other kind of response by Delta. Where a small number of firms compete in a market, they must recognize their strategic interaction.

Strategic interactions are found in many large businesses today: in weekly magazines, in television, in automobiles, and in economics textbooks. Like a tennis player, each business must ask how its rivals will react to changes in key business decisions. If Trump cuts its fares, will its price cut be followed? Followed all the way or only partially? For how long? Will the price cuts turn into price wars or will they peter out quickly? Will Trump's adversary decide to use non-price competition, such as offering more frequent-flyer mileage or offering a two-for-one package?

The point is that there is generally no simple answer to these questions. Different situations, different industries, even different temperaments on the part of the firms' managers will lead to different responses. And businesses may respond in random ways simply to keep the opposition off balance.

Competition among the few introduces a completely new feature into economic life: It forces firms to take into account competitors' reactions to price and output deviations and brings strategic consideration into their markets.

Game Theory. To analyze strategic interplay among oligopolists, economists rely upon a fascinating area of economic theory known as **game theory,** which is the analysis of situations involving two or more decision makers who have conflicting objectives. Business life is full of strategic bargaining like that between Putnam and Crandall, or Trump and Delta. A century of theorizing by economists about what mind A thinks mind B will do if B thinks A will do such-and-such culminated in the pathbreaking work by J. von Neumann and O. Morgenstern, *The Theory of Games and Economic Behavior*.[1] While this mathematical theory cannot answer every question about how two people will interact in an interdependent world, it does offer many incisive insights for economics as well as for politics and warfare.

Some examples of game theory at work are:

- A teacher picks quiz questions at random from a book of test questions.
- A security guard makes rounds at random, not in a discernible pattern.
- Facing a shrewd rival, a military strategist will buttress the most vulnerable defense, knowing that the enemy will search for the weakest point in the defense.
- I bluff at poker, not simply to win a pot with a weak hand but also to ensure that all players do not drop out when I bet high on a good hand.

Game theory is also a key to understanding the dynamics of the arms race. It can help us understand why, when the United States developed a new weapons system (A-bomb, H-bomb, cruise missile), the military advantage was only temporary. Why? Because the Soviet Union *reacted* quickly to offset the advantage or to imitate the system itself.

In economics, game theory has been used to analyze the interaction of duopolists, labor and management (in bargaining), countries' trade policies, polluters, reputations, and a host of other situations. In the area of imperfect competition, some of the important results are the following:

- An industry made up of quantity-setting oligopolists will reach an equilibrium that lies between the high-price monopoly equilibrium and the low-price equilibrium of perfect competition. This suggests that the inefficiencies of monopoly will be reduced as more firms enter.
- As the number of noncooperative or competing oligopolists becomes large, industry price and quantity tend toward the output of the perfectly competitive market.
- If firms decide to collude rather than compete, the market price and quantity will be close to those generated by a monopoly. But experiments suggest that as the number of firms increases, collusive agreements are more difficult to police, and the frequency of cheating and noncooperative behavior increases.
- In many situations, there is no stable equilibrium for oligopoly. Strategic interplay may lead to unstable outcomes as firms threaten, bluff, start price wars, capitulate to stronger firms, punish weak opponents, signal their intentions, or simply exit from the market.

This survey concludes our analysis of different kinds of market structures. The next chapter explores the theory of games in greater depth.

[1] 3d ed. (Princeton University Press, Princeton, N.J., 1953).

B. Behavior of Large Corporations

The first part of this chapter presented the major elements of the theory of imperfect competition. We now turn to a discussion of four important controversies surrounding large firms. We begin by analyzing the structure of large firms and noting the divergence of interest between owners and managers. We then ask specifically whether firms really maximize profits. A review of the practice of markup pricing illustrates one area where firms apparently do not maximize profits. Finally, we end with a review of the Schumpeterian defense of monopoly as the major source of innovation of new products and processes.

Divorce of Ownership and Control in the Large Corporation

One of the important features of American business is that our large corporations are mostly publicly owned. Corporate shares can be bought by anyone, and ownership is spread among many pension funds, individuals, and others. Take a company like AT&T. In 1987, more than 2 million people owned its shares, but 92 percent of the stockholders had fewer than 500 shares, and no single person owned as much as 1 percent of the total. Such dispersed ownership is typical of our large publicly owned corporations.

In a classic study, Berle and Means pointed out that the wide diversification of stockholding has resulted in a separation of ownership from control.[2] Because ownership is so dispersed, owners cannot easily affect the actions of large corporations. Who then makes corporate decisions? Today, it is the salaried manager rather than the owner who is responsible for the day-to-day operation of large corporations. The managers have acquired special training and management skills and are often primarily interested in the smooth operation of the organization rather than running major risks and making revolutionary changes.

Legally, the corporation is managed by its board of directors—a group of insiders and knowledgeable outsiders. The boss usually carries the title "chief executive officer," or CEO, of the corporation. Although the board of directors is nominally responsible, most often it is the inside management that makes the major decisions about corporate strategy.

For the most part, there will be no clash of goals between the management and stockholders. Both will be interested in maximizing profits and in raising the firm's earnings growth and stock price. But in two important situations there may be a divergence of interests, often settled in favor of management.

First, insiders may vote themselves large salaries, expense accounts, bonuses, and generous retirement pensions at the stockholders' expense. A second conflict of interest may arise in connection with undistributed profits. The managers of firms have an understandable tendency to try to make firms grow and perpetuate. Some economists believe that the profits that are plowed back into a company could be more profitably invested outside the company. Indeed, a company would often be well advised to wind itself up, pay back its capital, or agree to merge with another corporation. But few are the occasions when management gladly votes itself out of jobs and the firm out of business.

Takeover! Managers are not absolute monarchs of their domain, however, for this is the age of the takeover battle. What might be the typical scenario? Let's say that Lazy-T Oil is sitting on a rich oil deposit, worth millions of dollars. But its management has become fat and happy, so Lazy-T is not drilling this rich reserve.

A group of investors, the Vulture Fund, has a large line of credit and is looking for good bargains. Vulture Fund's economists study Lazy T's income statement and balance sheet. They conclude that, although Lazy-T is currently selling for $30 per

[2] A. A. Berle, Jr., and Gardner C. Means, *The Modern Corporation and Private Property* (Commerce Clearing House, New York, 1932). R. J. Larner, in a 1966 *American Economic Review* study, suggested that the Berle-Means thesis on separation of ownership and control has been reinforced since 1929: whereas 6 of the 200 largest corporations were privately owned (80 percent or more of stock) in 1929, in 1963 there were none; 84.5 percent of the largest firms had no group of stockholders owning as much as 10 percent. The takeover movement discussed below has taken several large companies private during the 1980s.

share, Lazy-T's oil assets would bring $90 per share if the firm were broken up and sold. Vulture attempts to make a "leveraged buyout" (LBO) by offering to buy the shares of Lazy-T at $45 a share, a substantial premium over the market price. Vulture Fund raises the funds by borrowing money from banks and perhaps floating high-risk or "junk" bonds to raise the funds. After a bit of maneuvering, the directors sell out the company at $60 per share. The Vulture Fund takes control, finds a new owner who will exploit the oil field, and sells the assets for $90 a share, earning a handsome return on its investment.

The example of Lazy-T suggests that takeovers operate as a kind of market for corporate control, and as such they might provide a useful check on inefficient practices of entrenched managers. In some cases new managers do indeed shake up a firm's practices, cut costs, and improve productivity and profits. Critics of takeovers complain, however, that the threat of takeover makes managers avoid risky decisions that may bear fruit only in the long run.

Do Firms Maximize Profits?

The separation of ownership from control raises the more general question: To what degree do business firms actually try to maximize their profits? To what extent do they succeed when they try?

While we cannot give a precise answer to these questions, this much is certainly true: If a firm is reckless in making its cost, revenue, and profit decisions, then market forces will eventually eliminate that firm, or its managers, from the scene. And this is particularly true in competitive markets. Hence, to survive, a firm must pay some attention to the profitability of its actions.

But this does not necessarily mean that every oligopolist or monopolist is desperately seeking to squeeze the last dollar of profit from every transaction. As soon as a firm gains some market power, it begins to have the ability to seek objectives beyond pure profit maximization. A monopolist can set its price a bit below the profit-maximizing level without going bankrupt.

Why might a firm not maximize profits? There are two general reasons—bounded rationality and alternative goals.

Bounded rationality denotes conduct in which firms or consumers choose not to optimize their actions to the last degree. This behavior is often rational because in reality people have limited resources and information and are therefore forced to make imperfect decisions. Consumers cannot spend all day looking for the lowest-priced head of lettuce. Searching for the absolute maximum of profits would take too much time. Decision making, like all other valuable commodities, must be rationed out.

Because perfect rationality is too costly, people and firms must settle for fairly good decisions. Moreover, in some repetitive situations, the use of a "rule of thumb"—or simplified decision rule—is an economical way of making decisions.

A second reason that firms may not single-mindedly maximize profits is that managers may have *alternative goals.* We just saw that managers and shareholders may have different incentives. Shareholders are mainly interested in high dividends and stock-price increases while managers may want to earn high salaries or run a large business empire.

While some alternative goals may be innocuous, one particular conflict between management and owners raises a serious economic concern. If firms avoid worthwhile but risky investments because their managers fear the possibility of large losses, the pace of invention and innovation could be slowed. On a large scale, excessive managerial aversion to risk could retard productivity growth and thereby hurt a nation's living standard.

Markup Pricing

One of the classical instances where firms deviate from pure profit maximization is in setting prices. Observation shows that firms rarely set prices on the basis of marginal revenues and marginal costs. Most firms have only a vague idea of the shape of their demand curve. They cannot determine their optimum price and output with neat exactitude. Yet prices must be set.

Here is where average cost plays an important role. Put yourself in the seat of the president of a company producing thousands of products. You have a rough forecast of this year's sales and costs, but only a hazy idea of the demand elasticities for your various products.

You might start with your sales forecasts. Then

you turn to the cost experts to determine the average cost of producing each product in question at some standard or normal level of sales. There will be plenty of headaches in arriving at any sort of figure, but your accountants provide an estimate of the average costs.

Here is where the surprise comes: Armed with the information about sales and costs, you will probably not set your price by an *MR* and *MC* comparison. Rather, you will generally take the calculated average cost of a product and *mark it up* by adding a fixed percentage—say 20 percent of the average cost. This cost-plus-markup figure then becomes the selling price. Note that if all goes as planned, the price will cover all direct and overhead costs and allow the firm a solid profit.

Investigators of actual business pricing policies have testified that imperfectly competitive firms often follow just this practice of quoting prices on a "cost-plus-markup" basis. However realistic, this analysis is incomplete. It stops tantalizingly short of telling us *why* the average markup is 40 percent in one industry and 5 percent in another. To explain the level of the markup requires an analysis of the market structure, along with demand and costs.

Does the prevalence of markup pricing suggest that firms do not maximize profits? In some cases, yes. But a better explanation would be that markup pricing is a useful rule of thumb produced by the necessity of bounded rationality. In a large company producing thousands of products, it is simply impossible to calculate *MC* and *MR* every day for every product. Markup pricing is used as an approximation to profit maximization. Just as a baseball pitcher may not calculate the equations of motion for every pitch, so managers in search of excellence may not always have *MC* and *MR* in mind as markups are adjusted up and down in the search for higher profits.

The Schumpeterian Hypothesis

We have encountered a litany of complaints about imperfect competitors. They tend to set prices too high and quantities too low, they may earn supernormal profits, and so on. But we must now turn to one powerful point of defense of imperfect competition. Many years ago, the great Austrian-born economist Joseph Schumpeter (1883–1950) argued that the wellspring of innovation and technological change is found in giant corporations and in imperfect competitors. While it is true that imperfect competitors cause inefficiencies because their prices lie above marginal costs, Schumpeter thought that the innovation produced by large firms would more than offset the losses from too high prices.

We have already seen in Table 11-1 that research and development (R&D) is more intensively pursued in concentrated than in competitive industries. The classical case in point is the Bell Telephone Labs. This giant research organization operated with the support of the world's largest monopoly—AT&T. Over the four decades before the breakup of the Bell System, Bell Labs invented or made major contributions to transistors and semiconductors, microwave and fiber optics, bubble memory and the UNIX operating system, satellites and electronic switching. During the 1970s, fully 10 percent of all American industrial basic research was conducted by Bell Labs. Powerful R&D efforts have shown similar results in du Pont, RCA, IBM, GE, GM, and many other large companies.

What is the special economic problem concerning innovation? Why is investment in R&D different from the production of conventional goods and services? Innovation is different because it generates significant economic *externalities;* these occur, as Chapter 3 described, when costs or benefits spill over from one entity to another. When Bell Labs invented the transistor, the benefits spread around the globe in Japanese TVs, German cars, and American computers. The consumers of these goods benefited enormously from transistors and semiconductors, but the inventor, Bell Labs, received only a tiny monetary reward in the form of royalties on the inventions.

The inability of firms to capture the full monetary value of their inventions is called **inappropriability.** The rewards from inventive activity are often inappropriable because the inventions can be imitated by other firms. It is sometimes said that inventions are inherently expensive to produce but cheap to reproduce. Case studies by Edwin Mansfield and others have found that the social return to invention (that is, the value of inventions to all consumers and producers) was around 3 times the appropriable private return to the inventor (that is, the monetary value of the invention to the inventor).

To the extent that the rewards to invention are

inappropriable, we would expect private research and development to be underfunded, with the most significant underinvestment in basic research. The inappropriability and high social returns on research lead most governments to subsidize basic research in health and science and to convey patent protection on new products and processes.[3]

The inappropriability of invention also explains why large firms are much more likely to undertake R&D than are small firms. If IBM sells 65 percent of the nation's computers, then any computer invention is likely to benefit IBM in a major way, and IBM has a strong incentive to invest in R&D. By contrast, small firms have a much smaller incentive. If I were to invent a new programming language, I have such a small fraction of the nation's computer market that I would probably reap no profit at all.

It was just this view that led Joseph Schumpeter to advance his bold hypothesis.

> The modern standard of life of the masses evolved during the period of relatively unfettered "big business." If we list the items that enter the modern workman's budget and, from 1899 on, observe the course of their prices, . . . we cannot fail to be struck by the rate of the advance which, considering the spectacular improvement in qualities, seems to have been greater and not smaller than it ever was before. . . .
>
> Nor is this all. As soon as we . . . inquire into the individual items in which progress was most conspicuous, the trail leads not to the doors of those firms that work under conditions of comparatively free competition but precisely to the doors of the large concerns—which, as in the case of agricultural machinery, also account for much of the progress in the competitive sector—and a shocking suspicion dawns upon us that big business may have had more to do with creating that standard of life than keeping it down.[4]

An even greater enthusiasm was expressed by John Kenneth Galbraith:

> A benign Providence . . . has made the modern industry of a few large firms an almost perfect instrument for inducing technical change. . . . There is no more pleasant fiction than that technical change is the product of the matchless ingenuity of the small man forced by competition to employ his wits to better his neighbor. Unhappily, it is a fiction. Technical development has long since become the preserve of the scientist and the engineer.[5]

Because economists had been taught about the evils of monopoly and the wastes of imperfect competition, the bold *Schumpeterian hypothesis* came as a shock. This hypothesis has been subject to careful scrutiny for over four decades. How well have these views survived in the academic marketplace? To begin with, most economists grant the basic truth in the Schumpeterian hypothesis. We hardly see our local grocery store or tomato farmer supporting a large R&D establishment. In 1988, for example, research-performing firms with more than 25,000 employees accounted for 55 percent of privately financed R&D yet had only 7 percent of civilian employment. Of manufacturing firms with less than 1000 workers, only 4 percent had a formal R&D program, as compared to 91 percent of the large firms.

Having conceded that tiny firms do little research, many analysts draw the line. Skeptics note that many firms with low market shares have substantial and successful R&D programs. Moreover, when John Jewkes and his colleagues traced the history of the most important inventions of this century, they found that less than half came from the laboratories of large corporations. The importance of small inventors has been confirmed in recent years as major new products seem to arise from nowhere—as occurred when Apple Computer launched the microcomputer revolution in the early 1980s.

To summarize, the relationship between innovation and market power is complex. Because large firms have made a major contribution to research and innovation, we should be cautious about claims that bigness is unmitigated badness. At the same time, we must recognize that small businesses and individuals have made some of the most revolutionary technological breakthroughs. To promote rapid innovation, a nation must preserve a variety of approaches and organizations.

[3] Countries have long recognized the need for public protection for inventions. Most countries award patents to the inventor of an original product or process; in the United States a patent conveys the monopoly right to use or profit from the patented invention for a period of 17 years. By allowing monopoly in this special situation, the government increases the degree of appropriability for the invention and thus increases the incentive to invent, especially for small inventors. Examples of successful patents include those for the telephone, the Xerox machine, and the Polaroid camera.

[4] J. A. Schumpeter, *Capitalism, Socialism and Democracy* (Harper, New York, 1942), p. 81.

[5] *American Capitalism* (Houghton Mifflin, Boston, 1952), p. 91.

C. A Balance Sheet on Imperfect Competition

We have completed our survey of the basic market structures from perfect competition to pure monopoly. We have also seen that large firms may deviate from profit maximization and that large firms are often the technological leaders in a market economy.

We now turn to an assessment of the practical importance of imperfect competition in today's economy. We begin by showing how monopoly distorts resource allocation and then provide quantitative estimates of the waste due to imperfect competition. We conclude with a review of the major approaches that governments can take to control the abuses of imperfect competition.

Economic Costs of Monopoly

Deficient Output of Monopoly

Our analysis has shown how monopolists reduce output and raise price, thereby producing less than would be forthcoming in a perfectly competitive industry. To see how and why monopoly keeps output too low, imagine that all dollar votes are distributed properly and that all industries other than one are perfectly competitive, with *MC* equal to *P*. In this world, price is the correct economic standard or measure of scarcity: price measures both the marginal utility of consumption to households and the marginal cost of producing goods by firms.

Now Monopoly Inc. enters the picture. A monopolist is not a wicked firm—it doesn't rob people or force its goods down consumers' throats. Rather, Monopoly Inc. exploits the fact that it is the sole seller of a good or service. By keeping its output a little scarce, Monopoly Inc. raises its price above marginal cost. Hence society does not get as much of the monopolist's output as it wants in terms of the good's marginal cost and marginal value to consumers.

Measure of the Waste from Monopoly

We can depict the efficiency losses from monopoly by using a simplified version of our monopoly diagram, here shown in Figure 11-4. If the industry could be competitive, then the equilibrium would be reached at the point where $MC = P$ at point E. Under universal perfect competition, this industry's quantity would be 6 while the price is 100.

Now let a monopolist enter the scene, perhaps aided by tariffs, regulations, or a patent. It would set *MC* equal to *MR* (not to industry *P*), displacing the equilibrium to $Q = 3$ and $P = 150$ in Figure 11-4. The area *GBAF* is the monopolist's profit, which compares with a zero-profit competitive equilibrium.

Using our tools of consumer surplus (see Chapters 6 and 9), we can measure the deadweight loss

Losses from Monopoly

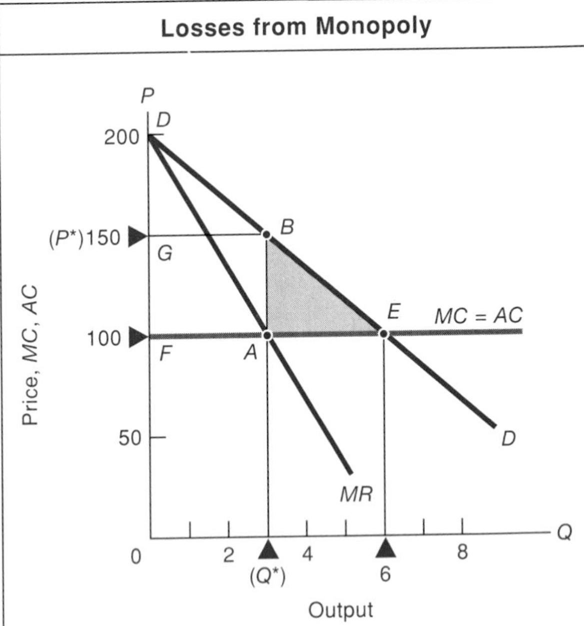

Figure 11-4. Monopolists cause economic waste by restricting output

Monopolists make their output scarce and thereby drive up price and increase profits. If industry were competitive, equilibrium would be at point *E*, where social *MC* equals social *MU* and welfare is maximized.

At monopolist's output at point *B* (with $Q^* = 3$ and $P^* = 150$), social *MU* is above social *MC*, and consumer surplus is lost. Adding together all the consumer-surplus losses between $Q = 3$ and $Q = 6$ leads to economic waste from monopoly equal to the gray shaded area *ABE*.

from monopoly. Economists measure the economic harm from inefficiency in terms of the **deadweight loss;** this term signifies the loss in real income or consumer and producer surplus that arises because of monopoly, tariffs and quotas, taxes, or other distortions. Recall that for each unit of output reduction below E, the deadweight loss or loss in consumer surplus is the vertical distance between the demand curve and the MC curve. The total deadweight loss from the monopolist's output restriction is the sum of all such losses, represented by the triangle ABE in Figure 11-4. To see this, recall that the DD curve represents consumers' marginal utility at each level of output, while the MC curve represents the opportunity cost of devoting production to this good rather than to other industries. For example, at $Q = 3$, the vertical difference between B and A represents the utility that would be gained from a small increase in the output of Q. Adding up all the lost social utility from $Q = 3$ to $Q = 6$ gives the shaded region ABE.

Empirical Studies of Costs of Monopoly. Not content with purely theoretical exercises, economists have in recent years pushed on to measure the overall costs of imperfect competition in the United States. In essence, these studies estimate the deadweight loss of consumer surplus in ABE of Figure 11-4 for all industries.

An early study by Arnold Harberger calculated the costs of monopoly in manufacturing by estimating (*a*) the difference between MC and P and (*b*) the output restriction. The deadweight loss is given by the area ABE, which is approximately $\frac{1}{2} \times (P - MC) \times$ (Q change as a result of monopoly). By summing the triangular deadweight losses across industries, Harberger obtained an estimate of the total deadweight loss from monopoly power.[6]

Harberger's finding astonished the economics community. He found that the deadweight loss from monopoly was slightly less than 0.1 percent of GNP. In today's economy, it would total about $6 billion. One economist quipped that economists might make a larger social contribution fighting fires and eradicating termites than attempting to curb monopolies.

Many studies have refined and criticized Harberger's original findings. Economists have questioned whether the parameters of the supply and demand curves were correctly estimated. In addition, critics point out that the efficiency losses may be compounded as the higher prices pile on top of each other as goods cascade from one stage of production to the other. After reviewing all these subsequent analyses, a careful recent survey concludes:

> Applying the . . . correction factors suggested in our critique of Harberger's results, it appears that the deadweight welfare loss attributable to monopolistic resource misallocation in the United States lies somewhere between 0.5 and 2 percent of gross national product.[7]

The most important reservation about this approach is that it ignores the impact of market structure upon technological advance or "dynamic efficiency." The deadweight loss measured in Figure 11-4 assumes that the cost curves are the same for perfect competitors and for imperfect competitors. But the bold Schumpeterian hypothesis presented in the last section argues that imperfect competition actually *promotes* invention and technological change. This hypothesis suggests that the gains from invention may more than offset the efficiency losses from too high prices. Economists have no consensus on this vital question, but it clearly is a major reservation to the conventional monopoly cost estimates.

Other Concerns about Market Power

Quality. We have focused on the quantity of output, but a firm's production has a *quality* dimension as well. Automobile production involves not only the number of cars but also their reliability, safety record, quality of ride, and so on. Moreover, when we examine an industry's technological progressiveness, we want to measure not only the decline in the price per unit but also quality improvement.

A common complaint about monopolists is that they pay little attention to quality of product. When AT&T had a monopoly on telephone equipment, consumers had to be satisfied with plain black phones for many years. Once competitors entered,

[6] Arnold C. Harberger, "Monopoly and Resource Allocation," *American Economic Review* (May 1954), pp. 771–787.

[7] F. M. Scherer and David Ross, *Industrial Market Structure and Economic Performance*, 3d ed. (Houghton Mifflin, Boston, 1990), p. 667.

there was a sharp increase in the variety of colors, styles, and ancillary equipment (such as answering machines). Problems of quality are endemic in socialist countries, where monopolistic state enterprises can tell consumers to take their shoddy goods or go without. No better spur to improved quality exists than a consumer's threat to take business to another establishment.

Profits. A final concern about imperfect competition arises because monopolists may be earning more than they would if forced to compete like perfect competitors. When people think of the monopoly problem, they often give most weight to the issue of monopoly profits—to the way that monopolists are supposed to enrich themselves at the expense of hapless consumers.

Intervention Strategies

We end with a review of the major approaches that governments in market economies can take to control the abuses of imperfect competition. The first three have been tried but are seldom used in modern market economies like the United States. The next three form the core of modern policies toward big business.

Over the years, governments have sometimes relied upon taxes, price controls, and government ownership to control the abuses of imperfect competition.

- *Taxes* have sometimes been used to alleviate the income-distribution effects. By taxing monopolies, a government can reduce monopoly profits, thereby softening some of the socially unacceptable effects of monopoly. But if taxation overcomes the objections to monopoly based on equity, it does little to reduce the distortion of output. A nondistorting tax drains profits but has no effect on output. If the tax increases marginal cost, it is likely to push the monopolist even further from the efficient level of output—raising price and lowering output even more.
- *Price controls* on most goods and services have been used in wartime, partly as a way of containing inflation, partly as a way of keeping down prices in concentrated industries. Studies indicate that these controls are a very blunt instrument: They lead to numerous distortions and subterfuges that undermine the economy's efficiency. During the most recent experience with price controls in the United States, in the 1970s, there were long lines for gasoline when its price was set too low, and shortages also cropped up for beef, natural gas, and even indispensables like toilet paper. Placing the entire economy under price controls to curtail a few monopolists is like poisoning the entire garden to kill a few chinch bugs.
- *Government ownership* of monopolies has been an approach widely used outside the United States. In some natural monopolies such as water, gas, and electricity distribution, it is thought that efficient production requires a single seller. In such cases, the real dilemma is whether to impose government ownership or government regulation on such firms. Most market economies have chosen the regulatory route, and in recent years many governments have "privatized" industries that were in former times public enterprises.

The first three approaches to the monopoly problem are rarely used in the United States. Instead, the United States relies on three policies to control imperfect competition: regulation, antitrust policy, and promotion of competition.

- Over the last 100 years, American government has evolved a new tool for government control of industry: *regulation.* Economic regulation allows specialized regulatory agencies to oversee the prices, outputs, entry, and exit of firms in regulated industries such as public utilities and transportation. It is, in effect, government control without government ownership. This important tool for containing monopoly is used particularly for local natural monopolies. It will be discussed in detail in Chapter 20 in our survey of government's role in curtailing market power.
- A second approach widely used to curtail anticompetitive abuses is the use of *antitrust policy.* Antitrust policies are laws that prohibit certain kinds of behavior (such as firms joining together to fix prices) or curb certain market structures (such as pure monopolies and highly concentrated oligopolies). Unlike regulation, which tells

business what to do and how to price products, antitrust policies tell businesses what *not* to do. This important policy approach will be explored in detail in Chapter 20.

- The major method of combating market power is to *encourage competition* whenever possible. There are a multitude of government policies that can promote vigorous rivalry even among large firms. Vigorous antitrust policies are an important ingredient to prevent collusion, but other policies are equally important. The most important single policy is to keep the barriers to competition at a minimum. Nothing raises prices faster or slows the pace of innovation as quickly as walling off firms and markets from actual or potential rivalry. A list of key dos and don'ts might be the following:

Remember that "the tariff is the mother of monopoly."

Promote vigorous competition from foreign firms.

Prevent states from putting up barriers to interstate trade.

Use auctions and competitive bidding for contracts whenever possible.

Remove regulatory or other constraints to competition.

Encourage small businesses to enter established arenas.

The lesson of decades of study of markets is that low barriers to entry and exit and strong prohibitions to collusion are the surest formula for preventing monopoly pricing and encouraging rapid innovation.

SUMMARY

A. Patterns of Imperfect Competition

1. Between the polar extremes of pure monopoly and perfect competition lie many species of imperfect competition. Which of these species thrives in a particular location will depend on three central factors: (*a*) the production and cost structure of the market; (*b*) the barriers to competition; and (*c*) the strategic interaction and degree of collusion among the firms.

2. If barriers to competition are high and complete collusion exists, we have the collusive oligopoly outcome: This market structure produces a price and quantity relation similar to that in a monopolistic industry.

3. Another common structure is the monopolistic competition that characterizes many retail industries. Here we see many small firms, with slight differences in the quality of products (such as different kinds of gasoline or groceries). The existence of product differentiation leads each firm to face a downward-sloping *dd* demand curve. In the long run, free entry extinguishes profits as these industries show an equilibrium in which firms' *AC* curves are tangent to their *dd* demand curves. In this tangency equilibrium, prices are above marginal costs but the industry exhibits greater diversity of quality and service than under perfect competition.

4. A final situation recognizes the strategic interplay when an industry has but a handful of firms. Where a small number of firms compete in a market, they must recognize their strategic interactions. Competition among the few introduces a completely new feature into economic life: It forces firms to take into account competitors' reactions to price and output deviations and brings strategic consideration into these markets. Game theory explores the way firms choose strategies that try to anticipate the reactions of their opponents.

B. Behavior of Large Corporations

5. As public corporations grow, and their owners become numerous and dispersed, we see the phenomenon of the separation of ownership from control. Such a trend can introduce conflicts of interest between shareholders and managers—such as when managers shun risk or pay themselves overly generous compensation. Takeovers today may help curb the most inefficient practices.

6. A careful study of the actual behavior of oligopolists shows certain kinds of behavior at variance with standard economic assumptions about profit maximization. One limit on profit maximization is bounded rationality. This principle recognizes that it is costly to make decisions, so managers may make less-than-perfect decisions, often employing rules of thumb, to economize on search and decision time. In addition, because of the divergence of interests between owners and managers, large corporations may pursue goals other than profits.

7. An important example of an action that appears not to maximize profits is the process of markup pricing. Firms seldom explicitly calculate prices by equalizing *MC* and *MR*. Rather, they use markup pricing—a rule of thumb that adds a percentage increase on top of costs of production.

8. While monopoly and oligopoly lead to price above marginal cost, and thus to short-run economic inefficiency, the Schumpeterian hypothesis holds that this traditional theory ignores the dynamics of technological change. It states that monopolies and oligopolies are the chief source of innovation and growth in living standards; to break up large firms might lower prices in the short run but would risk raising prices in the long run as the fragmentation of industry slows technological progress.

C. A Balance Sheet on Imperfect Competition

9. Exercise of monopoly power leads to economic inefficiency when price rises above marginal cost, and deterioration in quality may also occur. Empirical studies indicate that the deadweight or efficiency losses from imperfect competition are small relative to national output.

10. To curb the abuses of imperfect competition, governments in an earlier age sometimes used taxation, price controls, and nationalization. These are little used today in most market economies. The three major tools in American industrial policy are currently regulation, antitrust laws, and the encouragement of competition. Of these, the most important is to ensure vigorous rivalry by lowering the barriers to competition whenever possible.

CONCEPTS FOR REVIEW

Imperfect competition
strategic interaction
tacit and explicit collusion

imperfect competition:
- collusive oligopoly
- monopolistic competition
- small-firm oligopoly

no-profit equilibrium in monopolistic competition
inefficiency of $P > MC$

Behavior of large firms
separation of ownership from control
limits on profit maximization:
bounded rationality
alternative goals
markup pricing
takeovers as constraints on firm behavior
Schumpeterian hypothesis

Government remedies for imperfect competition
older approaches: taxation, price controls, nationalization
current approaches:
regulation, antitrust policy, pro-competitive policies

QUESTIONS FOR DISCUSSION

1. Review the first two theories of imperfect competition analyzed in the first section of this chapter. Draw up a table that compares perfect competition, monopoly, and the two theories with respect to the following characteristics: (*a*) number of firms; (*b*) extent of collusion; (*c*) price vs. marginal cost; (*d*) price vs. long-run average cost; (*e*) efficiency.
2. "The tragedy of most industries characterized by monopolistic competition is not at all excessive profits. Rather, there are no profits, and prices are excessive as resources are frittered away in low levels of production." Explain what this writer might mean in terms of the long-run equilibrium shown in Figure 11-3. Defend monopolistic competition by showing how it might lead to greater diversity of products.
3. "It is naive to try to break up monopolies into even a few effectively competing units, because the basic cause of monopoly is the law of decreasing cost with mass production. Moreover, if there are even a few firms, the price is likely to be close to marginal cost." Discuss both parts of this statement.
4. At a time when Ford had a high market share on automobiles, Henry Ford said about the Model T: "You can have any color you want, as long as it's black." Can you redraw the diagrams in this chapter using quality rather than quantity on the *X* axis? What would you predict about the quality of product under different market structures? Apply this to Ford's statement.
5. Explain the following statements:
   (a) In the retail drugstore business, each store has a little market power but fails to earn any economic profit on its activities.
   (b) According to the theory of bounded rationality, it is truly efficient for IBM not to adjust the price of its computers so that $MC = MR$ each and every day.
   (c) The government decides to tax a monopolist at a constant rate of $\$x$ per unit. Show the impact upon output and price. Is the post-tax equilibrium closer to or further from the ideal equilibrium of $P = MC$?
6. Firms often lobby for tariffs or quotas to provide relief from import competition.
   (a) Suppose that the monopolist shown in Figure 11-4 has a foreign competitor that will supply output perfectly elastically at a price slightly above the monopolist's $AC = MC$. Show the impact of the foreign competitor's entry into the market.
   (b) What would be the effect on the price and quantity if a prohibitive tariff were levied on the foreign good? (A prohibitive tariff is one that is so high as to effectively wall out all imports.) What would be the effect of a small tariff? Use your analysis to explain the statement, "The tariff is the mother of monopoly."
7. Explain in words and with the use of diagrams why a monopolistic equilibrium leads to economic inefficiency relative to a perfect competitor. Why is the condition $MC = P = MU$ of Chapter 9 critical for this analysis?
8. Often, established oligopolists or monopolists must keep an eye on *potential* as well as *actual* rivals. The following problem will show how such considerations may impose constraints on monopoly. Figure 11-5

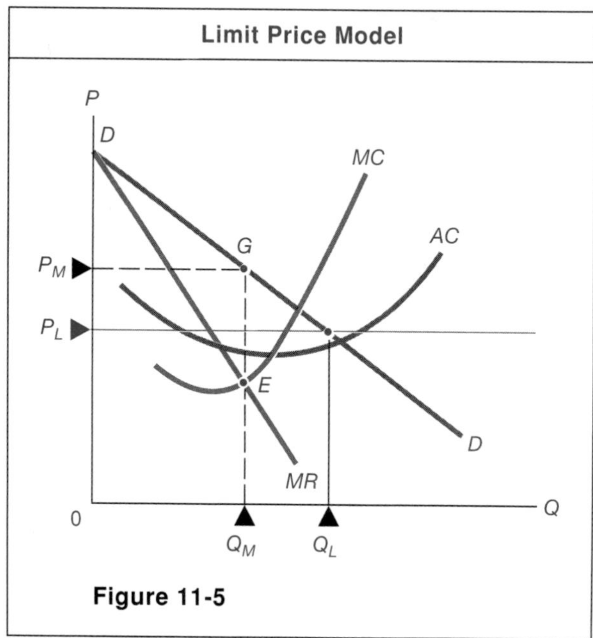

Figure 11-5

shows a conventional monopoly problem, in which the solution without rivals would be with a price of P_M and a quantity of Q_M.

Now assume that potential entrants could produce and sell with constant costs at a price P_L. Can you see how that would affect the *net* demand for the monopolist's output? What is the profit-maximizing price for the monopolist, given the threat of entry? Or, put differently, is there a *limit price* to or above which the monopolist dare not go for fear of losing every penny of profits? Why will the monopolist keep price below P_L and output above Q_L?

9. In long-run equilibrium, both perfectly competitive and monopolistically competitive markets achieve a tangency between the firm's *dd* demand curve and its *AC* average cost curve. Figure 11-3 shows the tangency for a monopolistic competitor, while Figure 11-6 displays the tangency for the perfect competitor. Discuss the similarities or differences in the two situations with respect to:

   (a) The elasticity of the demand curve for the firm's product.

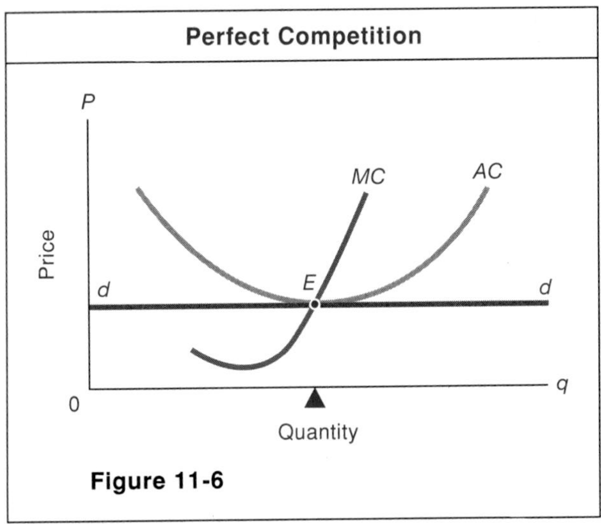

Figure 11-6

   (b) The extent of divergence between price and marginal cost.
   (c) Profits.
   (d) Economic efficiency.

C H A P T E R 1 2

UNCERTAINTY AND GAMES IN ECONOMIC BEHAVIOR

> Risk varies inversely with knowledge.
>
> Irving Fisher, *The Theory of Interest* (1930)

A textbook survey of the behavior of firms and households sometimes makes economic decisions look altogether too easy. According to elementary theory, households consult their utility functions, firms simply maximize profits, and markets work their wonders.

In reality, economic activity is much more complex than these elementary theories. One complication arises because of the uncertainties of economic life. Households must contend with uncertainty about future wages or employment and about the return on their investments in education or in financial assets. Occasionally, people suffer from misfortunes such as fires, hurricanes, or earthquakes. Firms must also contend with uncertainties about the prices of their products and inputs, political turmoil in the Middle East, the course of technological change in their industry, and the strength of rivalry from domestic and foreign competitors. The study of this first area is called the *economics of uncertainty.*

A second complication arises from the strategic interaction among economic actors. In perfectly competitive markets, all parties take prices as given and need not worry about others' reactions to their actions. In a wide variety of circumstances, however, strategic considerations are of the essence. In an oligopolistic industry, for example, each firm must worry about how other firms will react to price or output decisions. Will a price cut lead to a price war? Will the price war lead to bankruptcy? Most large firms engage in collective bargaining with a union to determine wages and conditions of work. Will too tough a position lead to a crippling strike?

We see elements of bargaining even in macroeconomics. When governments make decisions about taxes and expenditures, these often result from intricate bargaining between political parties or between the President and the Congress or among the many power brokers in the Congress. Even family life involves subtle elements of strategy and bargaining about the allocation of chores or the division of the family's income. No sphere of the economy is exempt from haggling about *what, how,* and *for whom.* The study of the economic games people, firms, and nations play is known as *game theory.*

No study of the realities of economic life is complete without a thorough study of the fascinating interplay of uncertainty and strategy.

A. Economics of Risk and Uncertainty

In our analysis of costs and demands, we have assumed that markets functioned without risk or uncertainty. We proceeded as if costs and demands were known for certain and every economic actor was able to foresee how other firms would behave.

In reality, business life is teeming with risk and uncertainty. The demand for a firm's output will fluctuate from month to month; input prices of labor, land, machines, and fuel are often highly volatile; the behavior of competitors cannot be forecast in advance. In some businesses, such as forestry or oil and gas, people make investments now in order to increase output in the future, in effect putting their investments up as hostage to future price movements. Life is a risky business.

Modern economics has recently begun to incorporate uncertainty into the analysis of business and household behavior. Here we will examine the role of markets in spreading risks over space and time, present the theory of individual behavior under uncertainty, and provide the essential theory underlying insurance markets. These topics are but a brief glimpse into the fascinating world of risk and economic life.

Speculation: Shipping Goods across Space and Time

We begin by considering the role of speculative markets, which serve society by moving goods from abundant times or places to those of scarcity. This activity is conducted by **speculators,** people who buy (or sell) a commodity with an eye to selling (or buying) it later for a profit. The commodity might be grain, eggs, or foreign currencies. Speculators are not interested in using the product or making something with it. Rather, they want to buy low and sell high. The last thing they want is to see the egg truck roll up to their door!

How do speculative activities benefit society? The economic function of speculators is to "move" goods from periods of abundance to periods of scarcity—where the "move" will be across space, time, or uncertain states of nature. Even though speculators never once see a carton of eggs or a bushel of wheat, they may help even out the price differences of these commodities among regions, or over time. They do this by buying at a time or place when goods are abundant and prices are low and selling when goods are scarce and prices are high.

Arbitrage and Geographical Price Patterns

The simplest case is one in which speculative activity reduces or eliminates regional price differences. In doing this, traders simultaneously buy in one market and sell in another market at a higher price. This activity is called **arbitrage,** which is speculation without risk.

Let's say that the price of wheat is 50 cents per bushel higher in Chicago than in Kansas City. Further, suppose that the costs of insurance and transportation are 10 cents per bushel. Then an *arbitrager* (someone engaged in arbitrage) can purchase wheat in Kansas City, ship it to Chicago, and make a profit of 40 cents per bushel. As a result of market arbitrage, the differential must disappear, so that the price differential between Chicago and Kansas City can never exceed 10 cents per bushel.

The frenzied activities of arbitragers—talking on the phone simultaneously to several brokers in several markets, searching out price differentials, trying to eke out a tiny profit every time they can buy low and sell high—tend to align the prices of identical products in different markets. Once again, we see the invisible hand at work, with the lure of profit acting to smooth out price differentials across markets and make markets function more efficiently.

Speculation and Price Behavior over Time

An ideal competitive market tends to display a definite pattern of prices over time as well as over space. But the difficulties of predicting the future make this pattern less perfect: we have an equilibrium that is constantly being disturbed but is always in the process of re-forming itself—rather like a lake's surface under the play of the winds.

Consider the simplest case of a crop like corn that is harvested once a year and can be stored for years in silos. To avoid shortages, the crop must last for the entire year. Since no one passes a law regulating the storage of corn, how does the market bring about an efficient pattern of pricing and use over the year? Through the activities of speculators trying to make a profit.

A well-informed corn speculator i ,alizes that if all the corn is thrown on the market in the autumn, it will fetch a very low price because there will be a glut on the market. Several months later, when corn is running short, the price will tend to skyrocket. Speculators can make a profit by (1) purchasing some of the autumn crop while it is cheap, (2) putting it into storage, and (3) selling it later when the price has risen.

So the speculator undertakes this set of transactions. As a result, the autumn price increases, the spring supply of corn increases, and the spring price declines. The process of speculative buying and selling tends to even out the supply and therefore the price over the year.

Moreover, if there is brisk competition among speculators, none of them will make excess profits. The returns to speculators will include the interest on invested capital, the appropriate wages for their time, plus a risk premium to compensate them for whatever risks they incur with their funds. The speculators will probably never touch a kernel of corn, nor need they know anything about the technology of storage or delivery. They merely buy and sell bits of paper.

There is one and only one monthly price pattern that will result in zero profits for competitive speculators. A little thought will show that it will not be a pattern of constant prices. Rather, the competitive speculative price pattern will produce lowest prices in the autumn glut, followed by a gradual price rise until the peak is reached just before the new corn is harvested. The price would normally rise from month to month to compensate for the storage and interest costs of carrying the crop—in exactly the same way that the price must rise over space from one mile to the next to compensate for the cost of transportation. Figure 12-1 shows the behavior of prices over an idealized yearly cycle.

We have seen how speculators even out supplies and prices. Does this process help or hurt economic efficiency? By now it is clear that effective speculation actually increases economic efficiency. By moving goods over time from periods of abundance to periods of scarcity, the speculator is buying where the price and marginal utility of the good are low and selling where the price and marginal utility of the good are high. This is a clear example of the invisible-hand principle at work: by pursuing their private interests (profits), speculators are at the same time increasing overall economic welfare (total utility).

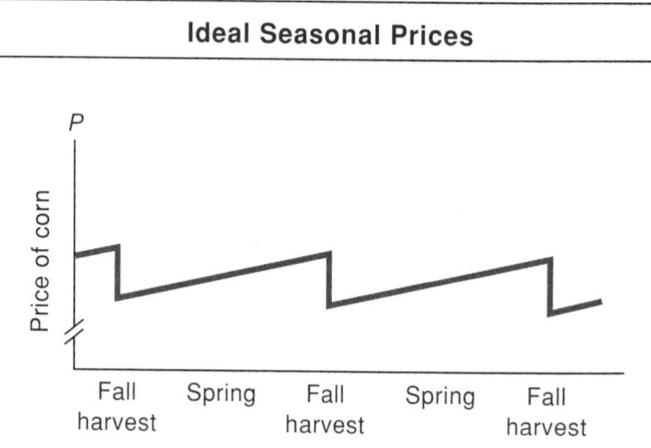

Figure 12-1. Speculators even out the price of a commodity over time

For a good to be stored, expected price rise must match holding costs. Ideally, price is lowest at harvest time, rising gently with accumulated storage, insurance, and interest costs until the next harvest. This flexible pattern tends to even out consumption over the seasons. Otherwise, a harvest glut would cause very low autumn price and sky-high spring price.

Spreading of Risks through Hedging

So far, we have seen how speculators serve to improve price and allocation patterns over space and time, but we have not really introduced any risk or uncertainty into our speculative activity. A third function of speculators is to take risk on their own shoulders, thereby absorbing risks that others do not want to bear.

As an example, consider the owner-operator of a 2-million-bushel warehouse who buys corn in Kansas in the fall, planning to sell it to the Ukrainians in the spring. She earns her living by storing corn, charging 10 cents per bushel of storage. With a full warehouse, she would earn \$200,000 before expenses, which is sufficient to cover interest, to pay her workers' wages, and to earn a competitive return on her invested capital and a fair salary for herself.

The problem she faces is that the price of corn often moves up or down by as much as $1 over the 6 months between purchase and sale. If the price of corn rises, she makes a large windfall gain. But if the price falls, she incurs a large loss which could completely wipe out her storage profits or even drive her into bankruptcy. The warehouse owner wants to earn her living by storing corn and has no interest in speculating on the price of corn. What can she do?

The answer is that by hedging her investments, she can avoid all the corn-price risk. What is **hedging?** This is the process of avoiding a risk by making a counteracting sale or investment. In our warehouse example, the owner hedges by selling the corn the moment it is bought from the farmers rather than waiting until it is sold to the Ukrainians. Upon buying 2 million bushels of corn in September, she sells the corn immediately for an agreed-upon price that will just yield the 10-cents-per-bushel storage charge and thus insulates herself from the risk of corn-price changes.

Here is where the speculator and the speculative market enter: The speculator agrees to buy the warehouse owner's corn now *for future delivery*. The current price of corn is $4 per bushel. Recalling the standard seasonal pattern of prices shown in Figure 12-1, the speculator agrees to buy 2 million bushels of corn for May delivery at a price of $4.10 per bushel. Now the owner is hedged. No matter what happens to the price of corn over the next few months, she has netted the same amount [2 million bushels × ($4.10 − $4.00) = $200,000] and bears no corn-price risk. The speculator who bought her future corn took the corn-price risk off her shoulders.

Speculative markets serve to improve the price and allocation patterns across space and time as well as to help transfer risks. These tasks are performed by speculators who, spurred on by the desire to buy low and sell high, in fact show the invisible hand at work, reallocating goods from times of feast (when prices are low) to times of famine (when prices are high).

Why Stabilization by Speculators Can Increase Utility

We can use the tools of marginal utility to show how ideal speculative markets maximize total utility over time. Say that identical consumers have utility schedules in which satisfaction in one year is independent of that in every other year. Now suppose that in the first of 2 years there is a big crop—say, 3 units per person—while the second year has a small crop of only 1 unit per person. If this crop deficiency could be foreseen perfectly, how should the consumption of the 2-year, 4-unit total be spread over the 2 years? Neglecting storage, interest, and insurance costs, *total utility for the 2 years together will be maximized only when consumption is equal in each year.*

Why is uniform consumption better than any other division of the available total? Because of the law of diminishing marginal utility. This is how we might reason: "Suppose I consume more in the first year than in the second. My marginal utility (*MU*) in the first year will be low, while it will be high in the second year. So if I carry some crop over from the first to the second year, I will be moving consumption from low *MU* times to high *MU* times. When consumption levels are equalized, *MU*s will be equal and I will be maximizing my total utility."

But this is exactly what the ideal speculative pattern accomplishes. If speculators can forecast accurately a low crop next year, they will figure it pays to carry goods over from this year's bumper crop, hoping to sell at next year's higher price. But what happens as each speculator subtracts from this year's supply and adds to next year's? Equilibrium can be reached only when the two prices have been equalized. At that point, there will be no further incentive to carry over more crops. (In reality, the speculator must augment next period's price by the cost of storage, interest, and insurance, and also add the appropriate payment for his or her effort. We here ignore all these costs just to keep the example simple.)

A graph can illuminate this argument. If utility could be measured in dollars, with each dollar always denoting the same marginal utility, the demand curves for the risky commodity would look just like the marginal utility schedule of Figure 6-1 on page 85. The two curves of Figure 12-2(*a*) show what would happen if there were no carryover—with price first determined at A_1, where S_1S_1 intersects *DD*, and second at A_2, where the lower supply S_2S_2 intersects *DD*. Total utility of the gray shaded areas would add up to only (4 + 3 + 2) + 4, or $13 per head.

But with optimal carryover of 1 unit to the sec-

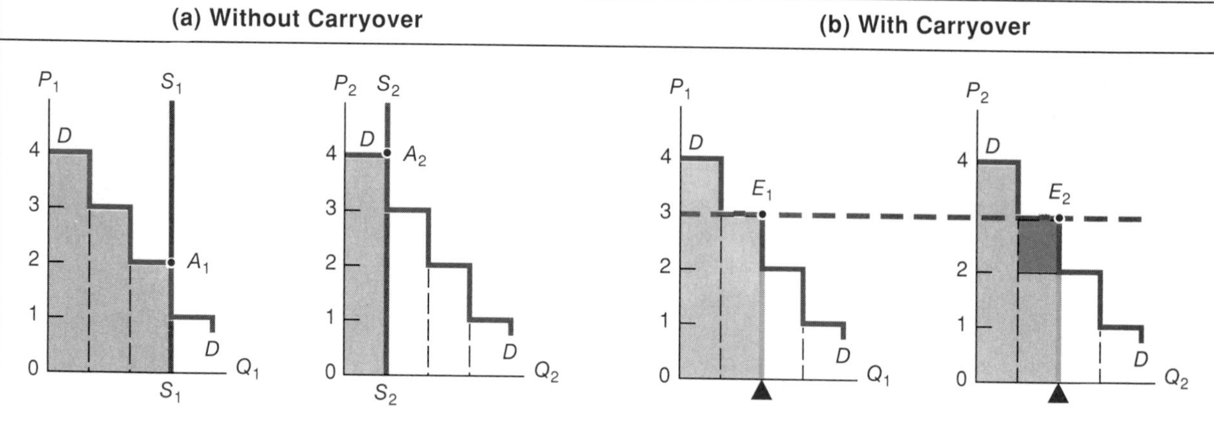

Figure 12-2. Speculative storage can improve allocation

The gray areas measure total utility enjoyed each year. Carrying 1 unit to the second year equalizes Q and also P, and increases total utility by amount of dark blue block. This diagram will apply equally well to a number of situations. It could be labeled "**(a)** without arbitrage across regional markets" and "**(b)** with arbitrage across markets." Some would even propose an extension by assuming all individuals are the same, so that it could be labeled "**(a)** without redistributive taxation" and "**(b)** with redistributive taxation."

ond year, as shown in Figure 12-2(*b*), *P*s and *Q*s will be equalized at E_1 and E_2, and the total utility of the shaded areas will add up to (4 + 3) + (4 + 3), or $14 per head. A little analysis can show that the gain in utility of $1 is measured by E_2's dark blue block, which represents the excess of the second unit's marginal utility over that of the third. Hence, one can show that equality of marginal utilities is optimal.

Ideal speculation serves the important function of reducing the variation in consumptions, and (in a world with individuals who display diminishing marginal utility) increases total utility.

Risk and Uncertainty

Having seen the way speculative markets help to transfer risks, we now consider the economics of risk and uncertainty in more detail. We begin with an analysis of uncertainty and the reason that people want to avoid risks. We then examine the institutions that a market provides to spread risks as well as some reasons why markets may fail to provide insurance in all circumstances.

Whenever you drive a car, own a house, store corn, make an investment, or even cross the street, you are risking life, limb, or fortune. How do people behave in the face of risks? We generally find that we, as drivers or owners or corn merchants or investors or consumers, want to avoid uncertainty. When we desire to avoid risk and uncertainty, we are "risk-averse."

A person is **risk-averse** when the displeasure from losing a given amount of income is greater than the pleasure from gaining the same amount of income. For example, suppose that we are offered a risky coin flip in which we will win $1000 if the coin comes up heads and lose $1000 if the coin comes up tails. This bet has *expected value* of 0 (equal to a probability of $\frac{1}{2}$ of +$1000 and a probability of $\frac{1}{2}$ of −$1000); a bet which has a zero expected value is called a *fair bet*. If we turn down all fair bets, then we are risk-averse.

In terms of the utility concept that we analyzed in Chapter 6, risk aversion is the same as *diminishing marginal utility of income*. If we are risk-averse, this implies that the gain in utility achieved by an extra amount of income is not so great as the loss in utility from losing the same amount of income. In the case of even odds, like a coin flip, the expected value is zero. But in terms of utility, the satisfaction you stand to win is less than the satisfaction you stand to lose.

For example, as a corn farmer, I clearly must contend with the natural hazards of farming. But do I also want to bear corn-price risks? Suppose that the expected value of the corn price is $4 per bushel, where this expectation arises from two equally likely outcomes with prices of $3 and $5 per bushel. Unless I can shed the price risk, I am forced into a lottery where I must sell my 10,000-bushel crop for either $30,000 or $50,000 depending upon the flip of the corn-price coin.

But by the principle of risk aversion and diminishing marginal utility, I would prefer a sure thing. That is, I would prefer to hedge my price risk by selling my corn for the expected-value price of $4, yielding a total of $40,000. Why? Because the prospect of losing $10,000 is more painful than the prospect of gaining $10,000 is pleasant. If my income is cut to $30,000, I will have to cut back on important consumption, such as meats or a new car that runs. On the other hand, the extra $10,000 might be less important, yielding only some fancy antiques or a new 100-horsepower, eight-speed, air-conditioned lawn mower.

People are generally risk-averse, preferring a sure thing to uncertain levels of consumption, other things equal. For this reason, activities that reduce the uncertainty or risk about people's consumption lead to improvements in economic welfare.

Insurance and Risk Spreading

Risk-averse individuals want to avoid risks. But risks cannot simply be buried. When a house burns down, when someone is killed in an automobile accident, or when spilled oil washes up on a beach—someone, somewhere, must bear the cost.

Markets handle risks by **risk spreading.** This process takes risks that would be large for one person and spreads them around so that they are but small risks for a large number of people. The major form of risk spreading is **insurance,** which is a kind of gambling in reverse.

For example, in buying fire insurance on a house, homeowners seem to be betting with the insurance company that the house will burn down. If it does not—and the odds are heavily in favor of it not burning—the owners forfeit the small premium charge. If it does burn down, the company must reimburse the owners for loss at an agreed-upon rate. What is true of fire insurance is equally true of life, accident, automobile, or any other kind of insurance.

The insurance company is spreading risks by pooling many different risks: it may insure millions of houses or lives or cars, thousands of factories or hotels. The advantage for the insurance company is that what is unpredictable for an individual is highly predictable for a population. Say that the Inland Fire Insurance Company insures 1 million homes, each worth $100,000. The chance that a house will burn down is 1 in 1000 per year. The *expected value* of losses to Inland is then $.001 \times \$100{,}000 = \$100$ per house per year. It charges each homeowner $100 plus another $100 for administration and for reserves.

Each homeowner is faced with the choice between the *certain* loss of $200 for each year or the *possible* 1-in-1000 catastrophic loss of $100,000. Because of risk aversion, the household will choose to buy insurance that costs more than the expected value of the loss in order to avoid the small chance of a catastrophic loss. Insurance companies can set a premium that will earn the company a profit and at the same time produce a gain in expected utility of individuals. Where does the gain come from? It arises from the law of diminishing marginal utility, which holds that the gain from winning is less valued than the pain from an equal-sized loss.

We can illustrate why risk spreading through insurance is economically advantageous with the help of Figure 12-3, which closely resembles Figure 12-2. The left-hand pair of diagrams shows what happens if the individual does not buy insurance, while the right-hand set shows what happens with insurance. There are two "states of nature" in each situation: the first and third diagrams show the case of no fire, while the second and fourth show the case of a fire.

Without insurance, people are faced with very different supplies of housing (or cars or health) depending upon chance. By purchasing insurance, people can remove the risks of fire or other catastrophic events and thereby equalize the amount of consumption in each state of nature. For example, in Figure 12-3(*a*), note that state-of-nature 1 has very high consumption while state-of-nature 2 has low consumption. In part (*b*), by paying insurance premiums, the individual lowers consumption a little but gains greatly if a fire strikes. Because of diminishing marginal utility, the situation without insurance has lower expected utility relative to a situation in which people pay a fair insurance premium to be assured of the same level of housing (or cars or health) no matter how the dice of life turn up.

We see therefore how insurance, which appears

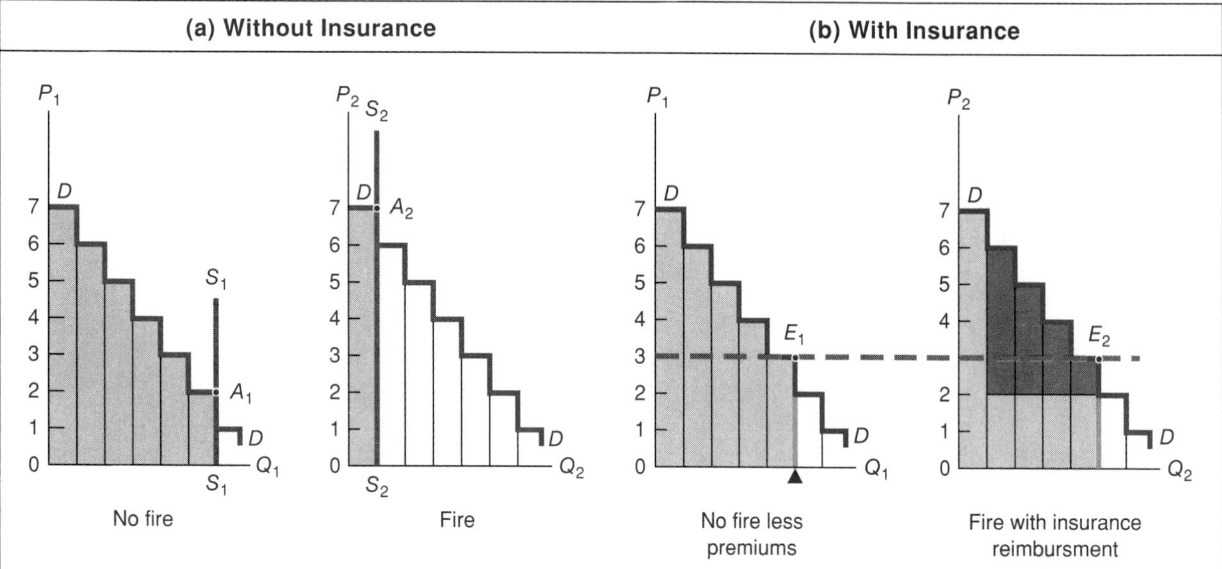

Figure 12-3. Insurance increases utility for risk-averse individuals

This diagram shows utility for different states of nature. The left-hand diagram of each pair shows a normal year while the right-hand diagram shows the impact of a disastrous fire with and without insurance. **(a)** There is much utility without insurance and with no fire, but great privation after the fire without any insurance. In **(b)**, the household sacrifices some consumption without a fire but gains greatly in case of fire. The gain in expected utility is shown by amount of dark blue block. Marginal utilities are equalized in both states, giving optimal consumption for individual with insurance.

to be just another form of gambling, actually has exactly the opposite effect. Whereas the weather creates risks, insurance helps to lessen and spread risks.

Capital Markets and Risk Sharing

We usually think of insurance as the primary way for people to shed risks, but this function is also performed by capital markets in a market economy. This occurs because the *financial* ownership of *physical* capital can be spread among many owners through the vehicle of corporate ownership.

Take the example of investment to develop a new commercial aircraft. A completely new design, including research and development, might require \$1 billion of investment spread over 10 years. Yet there is no guarantee that the plane will find a large enough commercial market to repay the invested funds. Few people have the wealth or inclination to undertake such a risky venture.

Market economies accomplish this task through publicly owned corporations. A company like Boeing is owned by millions of people and pension funds, none of whom owns a major portion of the shares. To construct a hypothetical example, divide Boeing's ownership equally among 1 million individuals. Then the \$1 billion investment becomes \$1000 per person, which is a risk that many would be willing to bear if the returns on Boeing stock appear attractive.

The principle of risk spreading extends into the international dimension as well. The risks of large-scale investment and production are shared with investors from Japan, England, Germany, and other countries when they buy shares of American corporations. And, just as an insurance company reduces its risks by insuring houses in different cities, so can we as investors reduce the riskiness of our portfolio by holding shares in companies from around the world.

By spreading the ownership of capital or of individual risky investments among a multitude of owners, capital markets can spread risks and allow much larger investments and risks than would be tolerable for individual owners.

Speculative Bubbles. Our analysis has presumed that speculators, investors, and insurers make reasonably good forecasts about uncertain events. To the extent that flesh-and-blood speculators forecast accurately, they perform a useful stabilizing function, as do government agencies that help collect and disseminate data on which these intelligent private forecasts are made. And even if a few forecasters are foolishly using astrological data for their million-dollar bets, they will be eliminated as fast as their capital is depleted.

But forecasting is hazardous, especially about the future, and we must recognize the possibility of perverse behavior. From time to time, investors lose sight of fundamentals and fall prey to rumors, hopes, and fears. Sometimes, speculation gets caught in the grip of a mass contagion, such as the inexplicable dancing crazes that swept medieval villages, the Dutch tulip mania that sent the price of a single bulb higher than that of a house, the South Sea Bubble in which companies sold stock at fabulous prices for enterprises which would "later be revealed," or, some believe, the rise and fall of the dollar in foreign exchange markets in the 1980s.

While economics may have difficulty explaining why "rational" investors would buy into such *speculative bubbles,* history documents numerous cases. From an economic point of view, such destabilizing episodes serve the economy poorly. In effect, they are activities which carry consumption from the "with insurance" to the "without insurance" phases of Figure 12-3. Destabilizing speculation leads to a deterioration in economic welfare.

Uninsurable Events and Social Insurance

While insurance is undoubtedly a useful device for spreading risks across the population, the fact is that we cannot buy insurance for all the risks of life. The reason for incompleteness of insurance markets lies in the stringent conditions that must be met for insurance to be profitably marketed.

What are these conditions? First, there must be a *large number* of events. Only then will companies be able to pool different events and spread the risks so that what is a large risk to an individual will become a small risk to many people. Moreover, the events must be relatively *independent.* No prudent insurance company would sell all its fire-insurance policies in the same building or sell only earthquake insurance in San Francisco. Rather, insurance companies strive to spread their coverage around to different and independent risks. Finally, the insurance must be relatively free of moral hazard. *Moral hazard* is at work when an insured individual can gain financially by causing the insured event to occur. When all these conditions are met—when there are many risks, all more or less independent, and where the probabilities can be accurately gauged and are not contaminated by individual gain—private-market insurance will flourish.

Social Insurance. What about cases where there are market failures because the conditions for private insurance do not hold? In these situations, there may be a role for *social insurance,* which is mandatory insurance provided by the government. Sometimes private insurance is unavailable or is priced at unfavorable terms because of moral hazard or adverse selection. *Adverse selection* arises when the people with the highest risk are the most likely ones to buy the insurance. This occurs when health insurance is bought predominantly by sick people, thus driving the cost of insurance for healthy people way above its expected value. Market failures in insurance arise in unemployment insurance, health insurance, and to some extent old-age annuities.

In these circumstances, the government may choose to step in and provide broader coverage. The huge financial reserves of government, plus the ability to avoid selection bias through universal coverage, can make government insurance a welfare-improving measure.

B. Game Theory

> Strategic thinking is the art of outdoing an adversary, knowing that the adversary is trying to do the same to you.
>
> Avinash Dixit and Barry Nalebuff, *Thinking Strategically* (1991)

Economic life is full of situations in which people or firms or countries jockey for dominance. The oligopolies that we analyzed in the last chapter sometimes break out into economic warfare. Such rivalry was seen in the last century when Vanderbilt and Drew cut and recut shipping rates on their parallel railroads. In recent years, Continental Airline tried to lure customers from its bigger rivals by offering fares far under prevailing levels. When larger airlines such as American and United were deciding how to react, they also had to take into account how Continental would react when they reacted, and so forth. These situations typify an area of economic analysis known as "game theory."

Game theory analyzes the way that two or more *players* or parties choose actions or strategies that jointly affect each participant. This theory, which may sound frivolous in its terminology borrowed from chess, bridge, and war, is in fact fraught with significance and was largely developed by John von Neumann (1903–1957), a Hungarian-born mathematical genius. We will sketch the major concepts involved in game theory and discuss some important economic applications.

Let's begin by analyzing the dynamics of price cutting, shown in Figure 12-4. The New York-based department store Macy's used to advertise, "We sell for 10 percent less." But its rival, Gimbel's, advertised, "We will not be undersold." The vertical blue arrows show Macy's price cuts; the blue horizontal arrows show Gimbel's responding strategy of matching each price cut.

By tracing through the pattern of reaction and counterreaction, you can see that this kind of rivalry will end in mutual ruin at a zero price. Why? Because the only price compatible with both strategies is a price of zero: 90 percent of zero is zero.

Macy's finally realizes that when it cuts its price, Gimbel will match the price cuts. Only if Macy's is shortsighted will it think it can undercut its rival for long. Soon Macy's will realize that the two firms are sharing a market. Indeed, if there were but two sellers and no antitrust laws to worry about, the two might even collude to raise price to the monopoly level that would maximize joint profits.

Once firms begin to worry about the effects their actions will have on other firms, we have entered the realm of game theory.

Basic Concepts

We will begin by showing the major elements of game theory in a **duopoly price war,** a situation

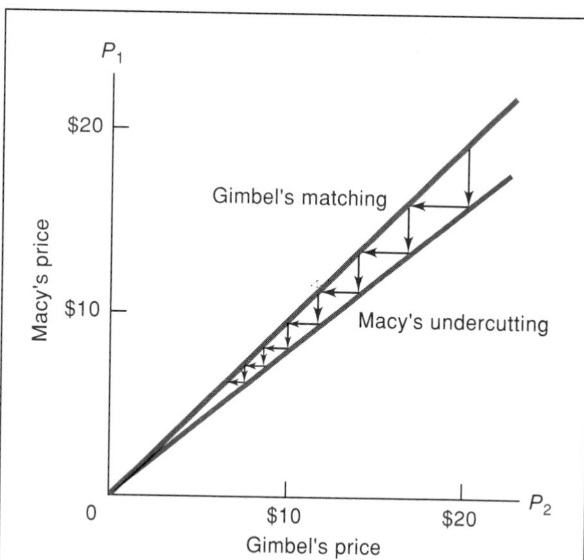

Figure 12-4. What happens when two firms insist on undercutting each other?

You can trace through the steps by which dynamic price cutting leads to ever-lower prices for two rivals.

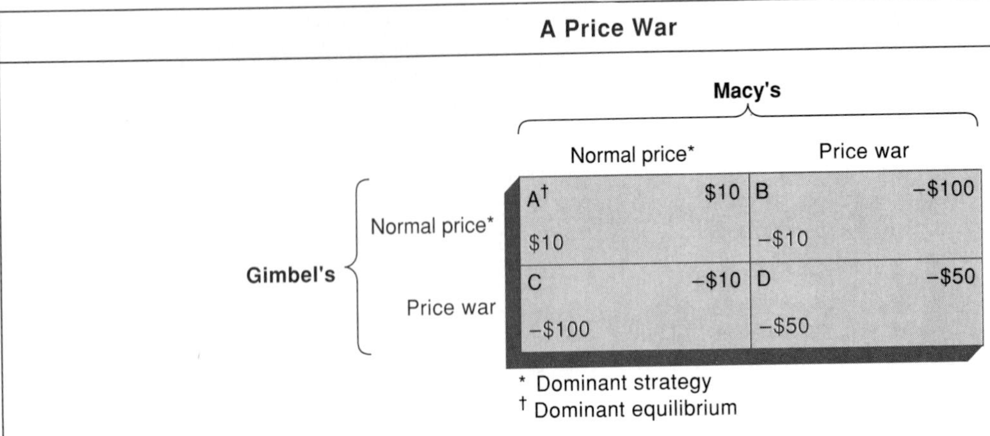

Figure 12-5. A payoff table for a price war

The payoff table shows how different strategies lead to the different payoffs or profits for the players. Gimbel's has a choice between two strategies, shown as its two rows. Macy's can choose between its two strategies, shown as two columns. The entries in the cells show the payoffs for the two players. For example, in cell C, Gimbel's plays "price war" and Macy's plays "normal price." The result is that Gimbel's has payoff of –$100 while Macy's has payoff of –$10. Thinking through the best strategies for each player leads to the dominant equilibrium in cell A.

where the market is supplied by two firms that are deciding whether to engage in economic warfare of ruinously low prices. For simplicity, we assume that each firm has the same cost and demand structure. Further, each firm can choose whether to have its normal price or to lower price below marginal costs and try to drive its rival into bankruptcy. The novel element in the duopoly game is that the firm's profits will depend on its rival's strategy as well as on its own.

A useful tool for representing the interaction between two firms or people is a two-way **payoff table.** A payoff table is a way of showing the strategies and the payoffs of a game between two players. Figure 12-5 shows the payoffs in the duopoly price game for our two stores. Suppose each firm simultaneously and independently chooses a price to charge. Each firm could either choose a normal price or decide to start a price war by choosing a price below marginal cost. In the payoff table, a firm would choose between the strategies listed in its rows or columns. For example, Macy's would choose between its two columns and Gimbel's would choose between its two rows.

Combining the two decisions of each duopolist gives four possible outcomes, which are shown in the four cells of the table. Cell A at the upper left shows the outcome when both firms choose the normal price, D is the outcome when both choose a price war, and B and C result from one having a normal price and one a war price.

The numbers inside the cells show the **payoffs** of the two firms; that is, these are the profits earned by each firm for each of the four outcomes. The blue number on the lower left shows the payoff to the player on the left (Gimbel's); the black entry on the upper right shows the payoff to the player at the top (Macy's). Because the firms are identical, the payoffs are mirror images.

Alternative Strategies

Now that we have seen the basic structure of a game, consider how you should behave as a player in the duopoly or any other game. In economics, we assume that firms maximize profits and consumers maximize utility. The new element in game theory is to think through the goals and actions of your opponent and to make *your* decision on the basis of an analysis of your opponent's goals and actions. But you must always remember that your opponent will also be analyzing your strategies. In other words, pick your strategy by asking what makes most sense for you assuming that your opponent is acting strategically and acting in his or her best interest.[1]

Let's apply this maxim to the duopoly example. First, note that our two firms have the highest *joint* profits in outcome A. Each firm earns $10 when both follow a normal-price strategy. At the other extreme is the price war where each cuts prices and runs a big loss.

In between are two interesting strategies where only one firm engages in the price war. In outcome C, for example, Macy's follows a normal-price strategy while Gimbel's engages in a price war. Gimbel's takes most of the market and loses a great deal of money because it is selling below cost. Macy's is actually better off continuing to sell at normal prices rather than responding.

Dominant Strategy. In considering possible strategies, the simplest case is that of a **dominant strategy.** This situation arises when one player has a best strategy *no matter what strategy the other player follows.*

In our price-war game, for example, consider the options open to Gimbel's. If Macy's conducts business as usual with a normal price, then Gimbel's will get $10 of profit if it plays the normal price and will have −$100 if it declares economic war. On the other hand, if Macy's starts a war, Gimbel's will lose $10 if it follows the normal price but will lose $50 if it also engages in economic warfare. You can see that the same reasoning holds for Macy's. Therefore, no matter what strategy one firm follows, the other firm's best strategy is to have the normal price. *The normal price is a dominant strategy for both firms in the price-war game.*

When both (or all) players have a dominant strategy, we say that the outcome is a **dominant equilibrium.** We can see that in Figure 12-5, outcome A is a dominant equilibrium because it arises from a situation where both firms are playing their dominant strategies.

[1] A witty and readable introduction to game theory, filled with examples from economics and daily life, is contained in Avinash Dixit and Barry Nalebuff, *Thinking Strategically* (Norton, New York, 1991).

Nash Equilibrium. Most interesting situations do not have a dominant equilibrium, and we must therefore look further. We can use our duopoly example to explore this case. In this example, which we call the **rivalry game,** each firm considers whether to have its normal price or to raise its price toward the monopoly price and try to earn monopoly profits.

The rivalry game is shown in Figure 12-6. The firms can stay at their normal-price equilibrium that we found in the price-war game. Or they can try to raise their price to earn some monopoly profits. First, note that our two firms have the highest *joint* profits in cell A, where they earn a total of $300 when each follows a high-price strategy. Situation A is one where the firms are behaving like a monopolist by having prices high. At the other extreme is the normal price, competitive-style strategy, where each has profits of $10.

In between are two interesting strategies where one firm chooses a normal-price and one a high-price strategy. In cell C, for example, Macy's follows a high-price strategy but Gimbel's undercuts. Gimbel's takes most of the market and has the highest profit of any situation, while Macy's actually loses money. In cell B, Gimbel's gambles on high price, but Macy's normal price means a loss for Gimbel's.

In this example of the rivalry game, Gimbel's has a dominant strategy; it will profit more by choosing a normal price no matter what Macy's does. On the other hand, Macy's does not have a dominant strategy, because Macy's would want to play normal if Gimbel's plays normal and would want to play high if Gimbel's plays high.

Macy's has a typical dilemma. Should it play high and hope that Gimbel's will follow suit? Or play safe by playing normal? By thinking through the structure of the payoffs, it becomes clear that Macy's should play normal price. The reason is simple. Start by putting yourself in Gimbel's shoes. You can see that Gimbel's will play "normal price" no matter what Macy's does because that is Gimbel's dominant strategy. Therefore Macy's should find its best action by assuming Gimbel's will follow Gimbel's dominant strategy, which immediately leads to Macy's playing normal. This illustrates the basic rule of basing your strategy on the assumption that your opponent will act in his or her best interest.

The Rivalry Game

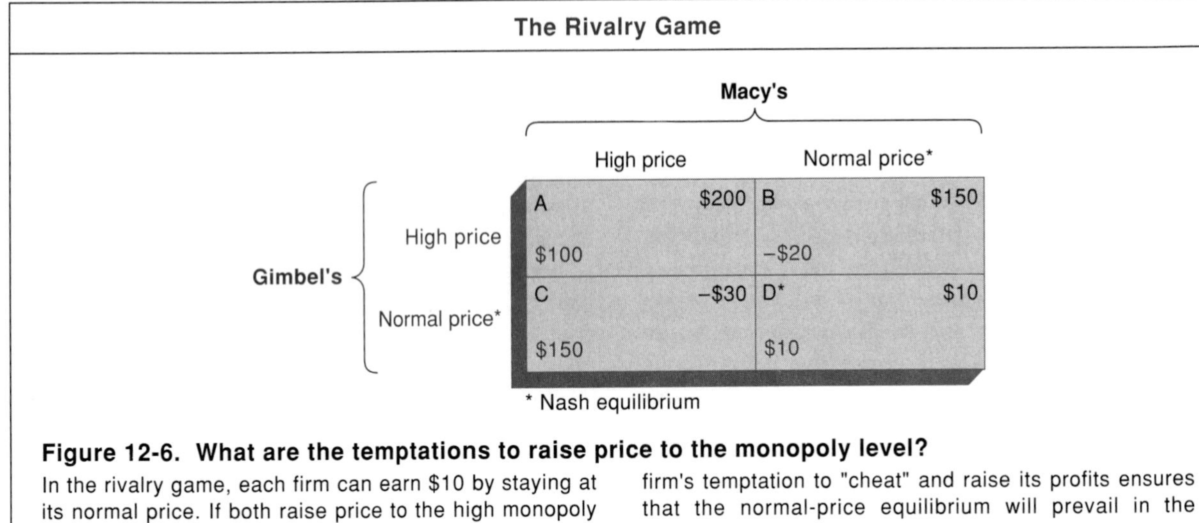

Figure 12-6. What are the temptations to raise price to the monopoly level?

In the rivalry game, each firm can earn $10 by staying at its normal price. If both raise price to the high monopoly level, their joint profits will be maximized. However, each firm's temptation to "cheat" and raise its profits ensures that the normal-price equilibrium will prevail in the absence of collusion.

The solution that we have discovered is actually a very general one which is called the **Nash equilibrium** (after mathematician John Nash). A Nash equilibrium has the characteristic that no player can improve his or her payoff given the other player's strategy. That is, given player A's strategy, player B can do no better, and given B's strategy, A can do no better. Each strategy is a best response against the other player's strategies. More precisely, let firm A pick strategy P_A while firm B picks strategy P_B. The pair of strategies (P_A^*, P_B^*) is a Nash equilibrium if no player can find a better strategy to play under the assumption that the other player sticks to his or her original strategy. That is, as long as A sticks to strategy P_A^*, B cannot do better than to stick with strategy P_B^*, and the analogous rule holds for A.

The Nash equilibrium is also sometimes called the **noncooperative equilibrium,** because each party chooses its strategy without collusion, choosing that strategy which is best for itself, without regard for the welfare of society or any other party.

We can verify that the starred strategies in Figure 12-6 are Nash equilibria. That is, neither Macy's nor Gimbel's can improve its payoffs from the (Normal, Normal) equilibrium. If Gimbel's moves to its high-price equilibrium, its profits go from $10 to −$20, while if Macy's raises its price from the normal-price Nash equilibrium, its profits go from $10 to −$30. (Verify that the dominant equilibrium shown in Figure 12-5 is also a Nash equilibrium.)

Some Important Examples of Game Theory

To Collude or Not to Collude

Figure 12-6 highlights an important fact. The starred Nash equilibrium in cell D actually brings in less total profit for the duopolists than any of the other outcomes. The best joint solution is A, with each duopolist charging the high price and earning total profits of $300. The worst is the Nash equilibrium with total profits of $20.

How can the Nash equilibrium be sensible when both oligopolists are earning less than they would with any other set of decisions? Remember Adam Smith's maxim: "People of the same trade seldom meet together . . . but the conversation ends . . . in some contrivance to raise prices." Why don't they just collude and choose the monopoly price?

The duopolists may well decide to collude, which means that they will behave in a cooperative manner. A **cooperative equilibrium** comes when the parties act in unison to find strategies that will benefit their joint payoffs. They may decide to form a cartel, setting a high price and dividing all profits equally between the firms. Clearly, this will help the duopolists at the expense of the consumers.

What are the impediments to the cooperative monopoly solution? To begin with, cartels and collusion in restraint of trade are illegal in most market economies. But there is a deeper problem for independent firms: the temptation to cheat on the cartel. Say that the price had been set (High, High) in cell A of Figure 12-6. What if Gimbel's secretly decided to sell a little output at a lower price, in effect moving to cell C? Gimbel's might be able to do this undetected for a while. During this time, Gimbel's would earn higher profits, $150 instead of $100.

Eventually, Macy's would notice that its profits had fallen. It would then reassess its strategy and, perhaps concluding that the cartel had come unglued, would also cut its price to the normal level. If the cooperative equilibrium was not enforceable, the firms would quickly gravitate to the noncooperative or Nash equilibrium in outcome D.

We can apply this reasoning to perfectly competitive markets as well. *A perfectly competitive equilibrium is a Nash or noncooperative equilibrium in which each firm and consumer makes decisions by taking the prices of everyone else as given.* In this equilibrium, each firm maximizes profits and each consumer maximizes utility, leading to a zero-profit outcome in which price equals marginal cost.

Recall Adam Smith's doctrine of the invisible hand: "By pursuing [an individual's] own interest, he frequently promotes that of society more effectually than when he really intends to promote it." The paradox of the invisible hand is that, even though each person is behaving in a noncooperative manner, the economic outcome is socially efficient. Moreover, the competitive equilibrium is a Nash equilibrium in the sense that no individual would be better off by changing strategies if all other individuals hold firm to their strategies.

In the perfectly competitive world, noncooperative behavior produces the socially desirable state of economic efficiency.

By contrast, if some parties (such as our two duopolists) were to *cooperate* and decide to move to the monopoly price in cell A, the efficiency of the economy would suffer. This suggests why governments want to enforce antitrust laws that contain harsh penalties for those who collude to fix prices or divide up the markets.

The Prisoner's Dilemma

Game theory can also shed light on the need for cooperation in economic life. In our price-cutting game in Figure 12-6, we saw that competition among firms led to the competitive outcome with low prices. Moreover, we have learned that, by an almost miraculous circumstance of economic life, Adam Smith's invisible hand produces in perfectly competitive markets an efficient allocation of resources out of individual utility or profit maximization.

But the beneficial outcome of the invisible hand is unlikely to arise in all social circumstances. The case of the "prisoner's dilemma" illustrates this basic truth in game-theoretic language. Figure 12-7

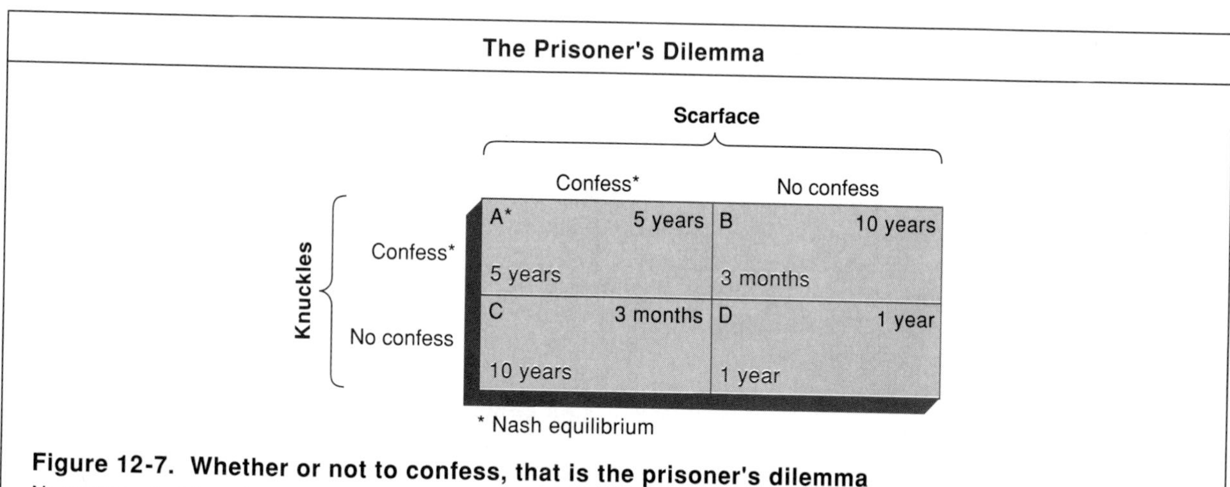

Figure 12-7. Whether or not to confess, that is the prisoner's dilemma

No matter what the other person does, it is always better for each prisoner to confess. Thus outcome A is a Nash equilibrium when both Scarface and Knuckles act selfishly and noncooperatively. Only through altruism or cooperation can the pair move to outcome D and both avoid long prison terms.

The Pollution Game

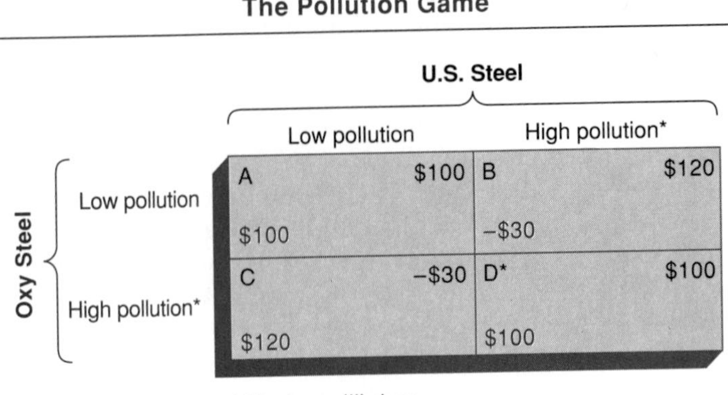

Figure 12-8. Competition and noncooperation lead to more pollution

In the deadly pollution game, each unregulated profit-maximizing steel firm emits pollution into streams and air. If a single firm tries to clean up its production, it raises prices, loses business, and suffers a decline in profits. The non-cooperative Nash equilibrium in D leads to high-pollution solution at bottom right. Governments can overcome this by enforcing the cooperative equilibrium in A, where profits are the same and the environment has been cleaned up.

is like Figure 12-5; here it refers to prisoners Scarface and Knuckles, who are partners in crime. The district attorney interviews each separately, saying, "I have enough on both of you to send you to jail for a year. But I'll make a deal with you: If you *alone* confess, you'll get off with a 3-month sentence, while your partner will serve 10 years. If you *both* confess, you'll both get 5 years."

What should Scarface do? Should she confess and hope to get a short sentence? Three months are preferable to the year she would get if she remains silent. But wait. There is an even better reason for confessing. Suppose Scarface doesn't confess and, unknown to her, Knuckles does confess. Scarface stands to get 10 years! It's clearly better in this situation for Scarface to confess and get 5 years rather than 10 years.

Knuckles is in the same dilemma: if only he knew what Scarface is thinking, or what Scarface thinks Knuckles thinks Scarface is thinking, or . . .

The significant result here is that when both prisoners act selfishly by confessing, they both end up with long prison terms. Only when they act collusively or altruistically will they end up with short prison terms.

The Pollution Game

An important economic example which uses the structure of the prisoner's dilemma is the **pollution game** shown in Figure 12-8. Consider an economy with externalities such as pollution. In this world of unregulated firms, each individual profit-maximizing firm would prefer to pollute rather than install expensive pollution-control equipment. In such a world, if a firm behaves altruistically and cleans up every particle of *its* wastes, that firm will have higher production costs, higher prices, and fewer customers. If the costs are high enough, the firm may even go bankrupt. The pressures of Darwinian competition will drive all firms to the starred Nash equilibrium in cell D in Figure 12-8; here neither firm can improve its profits by lowering pollution.

The pollution game is an example of a situation in which the invisible-hand mechanism of efficient perfect competition breaks down. In such cases, the role of government is to get firms to move to outcome A, the "Low-pollute/Low-pollute" world. In that equilibrium, the firms make the same profit as in the high-pollution world, and the earth is a greener place to live in.

Can Benevolence Survive?

The prisoner's dilemma and similar games show how self-interest may lead to a world of noncooperation, pollution, and militarism—a nasty, brutish, and short life.

But how can we account for the high degree of benevolence and cooperation within families as well as among friends, communities, and even nations? What happens when a prisoner's dilemma game like that in Figure 12-7 is played again and again? Studies indicate that people are well advised to cooperate (and often do cooperate) in *repeated* prisoner's dilemma games.

How might cooperation evolve? Let's say one player plays a *tit-for-tat* strategy, saying in effect, "An eye for an eye, and a kiss for a kiss, but start with a kiss." In the game shown in Figure 12-7, this means that Scarface will always start by cooperating—that is, by taking the decision that maximizes both prisoners' joint welfare and not confessing. If Knuckles cooperates by not confessing, Scarface will continue to play the cooperative strategy of not confessing. If Knuckles double-crosses Scarface by confessing, the next time they play, Scarface will sting Knuckles by confessing.

Recent studies show that cooperative strategies like tit for tat are the most profitable *selfish* strategies in many repeated prisoner's dilemma games. This suggests that a watchful golden rule may serve people well in many situations: "Do unto others what you would have them do unto you, but only as long as they actually are nice."

But never forget that cooperation can also be harmful to society. Tit for tat may lead to tacit collusion in otherwise-competitive markets when firms play a game that says, "Don't invade my market and I won't invade yours." Cooperation among firms may hurt consumers, as was illustrated in Figure 12-6, where collusion raised profits and hurt consumers.

Games, Games, Everywhere . . .

The insights of game theory pervade economics, the social sciences, business, and everyday life. In economics, for example, game theory can explain the dangers of trade wars as well as the risks of an arms race (some illuminating examples are provided in questions at the end of this chapter). Likewise, some believe that the phenomenon of "sticky" prices may be rooted in game theory. According to this theory, firms have reached a kind of tacit agreement about the prevailing level of price (say, in the auto or steel industry). Once this agreement has been reached, firms are reluctant to change prices lest other firms interpret this as a declaration of economic war.

Game theory can also suggest why foreign competition may lead to greater price competition. What happens when Japanese firms enter a U.S. market where firms had tacitly colluded on a price strategy that led to a high oligopolistic price? The foreign firms may "refuse to play the game." They did not agree to the rules, so they may cut prices to gain market shares. Collusion may break down.

A whole new level of complexity arises when people try to "change the game" by acting tough or changing the payoffs. A firm may change the payoffs to a potential entrant in a market by building more capacity than is needed. This is designed to "commit" the established firm to such low prices that the potential entrant will not think it profitable to enter. The most terrifying example of this kind of game is the "doomsday threat" of nuclear superpowers, in which one power threatens to launch a war of mutually assured destruction if the other power commits a lesser step of aggression.

These few examples provide a small tasting from the wide variety of fruits produced by the theory of games. This area has been enormously useful in helping economists and other social scientists think about situations where small numbers of people are well informed and interact in markets, politics, or military affairs.

SUMMARY

A. Economics of Risk and Uncertainty

1. Speculators are people who buy and sell commodities with an eye to making profits on price differentials across markets. They move goods across regions from low-price to high-price markets, across time from periods of abundance to periods of scarcity, and even across uncertain states of nature to periods when chance makes goods scarce.

2. The profit-seeking action of speculators and arbitragers tends to create certain *equilibrium patterns of price over space and time.* These market equilibria are zero-profit outcomes where the marginal costs and marginal utilities in different regions, times, or uncertain states of nature are in balance. To the extent that speculators moderate price and consumption instability, they are part of the invisible-hand mechanism that performs the socially useful function of reallocating goods from fat times (when prices are low) to lean times (when prices are high).
3. Speculative markets allow individuals to hedge against unwelcome risks. The economic principle of risk aversion, which derives from diminishing marginal utility, implies that individuals will not accept risky situations with zero expected value. Risk aversion implies that people will buy insurance to reduce the disastrous declines in utility from fire, death, or other calamities.
4. Insurance and risk spreading tend to stabilize consumption in different states of nature. Insurance takes large individual risks and spreads them so thinly that they become tolerable to a large number of individuals. Insurance is beneficial because, by helping to equalize consumption across different uncertain states, the expected level of utility rises.
5. The conditions for operation of efficient insurance markets are stringent: there must be large numbers of independent events, with little chance of moral hazard or adverse selection. When private insurance markets fail, the government may step in to provide social insurance. Even in the most laissez-faire of advanced market economies today, governments insure health and old-age pensions.

B. Game Theory

6. Economic life contains many situations of strategic interaction among firms, households, governments, or others. Game theory analyzes the way that two or more parties, who interact in a structure such as a market, choose actions or strategies that jointly affect each participant.
7. The basic structure of a game includes the players, who have different actions or strategies; and the payoffs, which describe the profits or other benefits that the players obtain in each outcome. The key new concept is the payoff table of a game, which shows the strategies and the payoffs or profits of the different players.
8. The key to choosing strategies in game theory is for players to think through both their own and their opponent's goals, never forgetting that the other side is doing the same. When playing a game in economics or any other field, assume that your opponents will choose their best options. Then pick your strategy so as to maximize your benefit, always assuming that your opponent is similarly analyzing your options.
9. Sometimes a dominant strategy is available, one that is best no matter what the opposition does. More often, we find the Nash equilibrium (or noncooperative equilibrium) most useful. A Nash equilibrium is one in which no player can improve his or her payoff given the other player's strategy. Sometimes, parties can collude or cooperate, which produces the cooperative equilibrium.

10. A Nash equilibrium produces a happy outcome in perfectly competitive markets without externalities, where the invisible-hand theorem shows how noncollusive firms produce at prices equal to marginal costs and the overall equilibrium is efficient. Sometimes, however, noncooperative behavior leads to social ruin, as when competitors pollute the planet or engage in expensive arms races. In these cases, social cooperation needs to supplant private competition.

CONCEPTS FOR REVIEW

Risk and uncertainty
spatial *P* equality
ideal seasonal price pattern
speculation, arbitrage, hedging
risk aversion and diminishing marginal utility
consumption stability vs. instability
insurance and risk spreading
insurable and uninsurable risks
social vs. private insurance
moral hazard, adverse selection

Game theory
players, strategies, payoffs
payoff table
dominant strategy and equilibrium
Nash equilibrium (or stable point)
cooperative and noncooperative equilibrium
prisoner's dilemma
competition vs. altruism
tit for tat

QUESTIONS FOR DISCUSSION

1. How does ideal speculation stabilize seasonal prices?
2. Early social reformers believed that people had essentially the same utility functions. Assuming that the parts of Figure 12-2 represent different individuals before and after income redistribution, explain how equalization of incomes would lead to the maximum total utility.
3. List some important differences between private and social insurance.
4. In the early nineteenth century, markets for agricultural crops carried little of the nation's agricultural output. Transport costs were very high. What would you expect to have been the degree of variation of prices across regions and across time?
5. Assume that a firm is making a risky investment (say, introducing a $1 million supercomputer). Can you see how the widely diversified ownership of this firm could allow near-perfect risk spreading on the computer investment?
6. In the late 1980s, "arbs" who became rich upon the illegal use of inside information gave a bad name to speculation and arbitrage. Suppose that arbitrage were made a criminal offense. Explain the economic damage that could result.
7. Superpower A wants superiority over superpower R; R wants parity with A. Hence, A in year t installs 10 percent more missiles than R had in year $t - 1$; the next year R matches A's missiles. Show how such a strategy leads to an endless arms race, using an approach like that of Figure 12-4. What is the function of an arms-control agreement that limits each side to 1000 missiles? Show graphically how an arms-control agreement changes the picture.
8. "In a world with no spillovers or externalities, collusion harms the public interest. In a world full of pollution, crime, and pestilence, cooperation is essential." Interpret in light of your understanding of game theory.
9. Show that for the prisoner's dilemma shown in Figure 12-7, the outcome in cell A is a Nash equilibrium. Also show that it is the only Nash equilibrium.
10. *Moralist:* "Speculators are no better than people who bet on the horses or enjoy cockfights. They reinforce fads and bubbles and make prices more volatile than ever. We should make speculation illegal or tax it heavily."
    Defender: "An uncertain world necessarily involves risk and someone must bear these risks. The knowledge and the venturesomeness of the speculator are chained to a socially useful purpose, thereby reducing risks and consumption fluctuation for the risk averse."
    Explain each point of view. What do *you* believe?
11. Consider the dilemma of maintaining free trade shown in the payoff table in Figure 12-9, which gives total real national incomes (in billions) of two countries as a function of foreign-trade policies. Each country can have a policy of either free trade with no

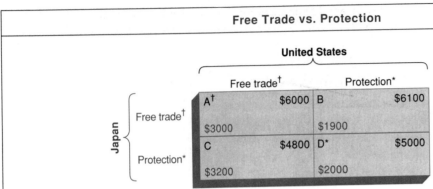

Free Trade vs. Protection

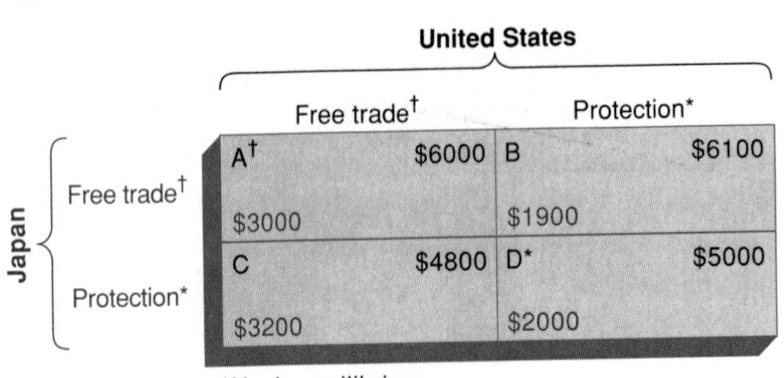

*Nash equilibrium
†Cooperative equilibrium

Figure 12-9. Countries gain from trade but lose from trade war

Japan and the U.S. can agree to the cooperative equilibrium at A in which they reduce all tariffs and quotas and enjoy the benefits of free trade. Each would, however, be tempted to "cheat" by putting trade restriction on imports, gaining income at home while hurting total world income.

tariffs or quotas or protectionism with tight quotas on imported goods and services. The payoffs are the real incomes in each country.

(a) List the four outcomes and calculate each region's national income and world income.

(b) Show how countries acting noncooperatively (without agreements and in their own selfish national interest) will be led to a trade war at the Nash equilibrium in cell D. What is the effect of the trade war on total world income?

(c) What is the impact on incomes of a trade agreement that abolishes all trade restrictions and produces free trade? Relate this result to the prisoner's dilemma.

(d) Is there an incentive for each country to "cheat" on the trade agreement? What happens if the cheating leads to retaliation and to the high-tariff outcome?

12. **Insurance problem:** Examine the problem of a consumer deciding whether to buy fire insurance illustrated in Figure 12-3. The *DD* curves drawn there, representing the marginal utility of housing services, are the same in each situation. The household consumes 6 *Q* units with no insurance and no fire, whereas a fire reduces consumption by 5 units. If the probability of a fire is one-fifth, calculate the *expected utility with no insurance,* which is the probability of each state (fire or no fire) times its utility (the area under the *DD* curve for the relevant consumption level). Explain why Figure 12-3(*a*) describes the no-insurance case.

Next, assume that the household can buy fair fire insurance with full coverage; this is a "fair bet" because the insurance premium is equal to the expected value of the loss. Explain why Figure 12-3(*b*) depicts the insurance case. Calculate the expected utility with insurance.

Finally, show that the blue shaded area in the far-right diagram measures the gain in expected utility.

13. **Advanced problem** for students of statistics: Suppose each of four cab companies faces accidents that are "normally distributed," with a standard deviation, σ_i = \$3000, around a mean loss of \$50,000. Let them now pool risks through mutual reinsurance. Show that this gives a total mean loss of \$200,000 [or still \$50,000 for each one's fair share; but now total variance is only 4 × (\$3000)^2, or $\sigma^2 = 4\sigma_i^2$ = 36,000,000 = (6000)^2]. So each ends up with a standard deviation of only \$1500 = \$6000/4—halving the risk through quadrupling the size. Can you use the same reasoning to see the following?

(a) Diversifying your wealth into four independent stocks, each with the same mean return and same (independent) variability, will halve the expected variability of your portfolio.

(b) Pooling the independent peak-load demand of two utility systems will reduce the need to have twice the stand-by capacity.

(c) A company's needed inventory tends to grow only with the square root of the number of its independent customers. Hence, a firm 4 times as big has only half the inventory cost per unit of sales.

PART THREE

WAGES, RENT, AND PROFITS: THE DISTRIBUTION OF INCOME

The Road Ahead

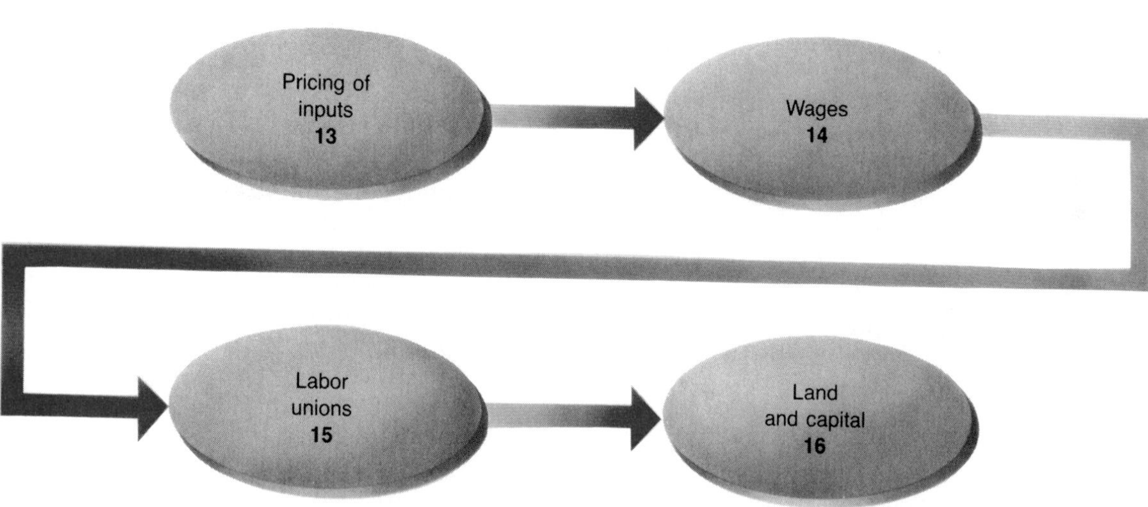

For most of this century, the fruits of economic growth were shared broadly among all groups in American society. Suddenly, in the 1980s, a new pattern emerged as upper-income groups enjoyed rising real incomes while the poor suffered from increased homelessness and deprivation. The next four chapters analyze the basic determinants of factor earnings and incomes: the wages of labor, the rents of land, and the profits earned by capital. Once the fundamentals of factor incomes are mastered, we can begin to understand the divergent fortunes of rich and poor.

CHAPTER 13

INCOMES AND THE PRICING OF FACTORS OF PRODUCTION

You know, Ernest, the rich are different from us.
F. Scott Fitzgerald

Yes, I know. They have more money than we do.
Ernest Hemingway

In the chapters on product markets we studied how markets decide on *what* is produced. Societies also are concerned with the distribution of economic activity—with the question of *who* will enjoy the goods that the economy produces. This question concerns the **theory of income distribution,** which analyzes the way that income and wealth are distributed in a society. The income distribution theory asks, Why are some people paid a million dollars a year, while others have trouble landing a job at the minimum wage? Why are the rents on real estate in Tokyo or Manhattan worth thousands of dollars a square foot, while land in the desert may sell for but a few dollars an acre? And what is the source of the billions of dollars of profits earned by giant enterprises like Exxon or Toyota?

The questions about the distribution of income are among the most controversial in all economics. Some argue that high incomes are the unfair results of past inheritance and luck while poverty stems from discrimination and lack of opportunity. Others believe that people get what they deserve and that interfering with the market distribution of income would injure an economy's efficiency and make everyone worse off. In the broad middle are those who believe that the government should exercise its power to ensure that a social safety net catches those whose incomes fall below some decent standard of living.

A. The Fruits of Industrialization

The period before the Industrial Revolution witnessed very gradual increases in the levels and distribution of incomes for the areas of the world for which we have statistical records. The advent of technological and social changes associated with the Industrial Revolution brought, starting around 1770, sharp changes in wages and the division of society along clear class lines between capitalists and workers.

This phenomenon was identified by many early critics of capitalism, particularly by Karl Marx. He and Friedrich Engels wrote in 1848:

> The modern laborer . . . , instead of rising with the progress of industry, sinks deeper and deeper below

the condition of his own class. He becomes a pauper, and pauperism develops more rapidly than population and wealth.[1]

While some of Marx's predictions about the future of industrial capitalism proved correct, his prediction about the fortunes of the working class proved to be far off the mark. His assertion that workers would become steadily poorer cannot be sustained by careful historical and statistical research.

In Europe and America, there has definitely been a steady, long-term improvement in the real wages as measured by the average worker's ability to buy food, clothing, and housing, as well as by the health and longevity of the population. This fact about industrial market economies is clear from statistics presented below. The highlights are shown graphically in Figure 13-1.

Historians sometimes dwell on the evils of the Industrial Revolution and on the poverty-ridden condition of the masses in polluted cities. In point of fact, a Dickens novel could hardly do justice to the dismal conditions of child labor, workplace dangers, and poor sanitation in early nineteenth-century factories. A workweek of 84 hours was the prevailing rule, with time out for breakfast and sometimes supper. A good deal of work could be squeezed out of a 6-year-old child, and if a woman lost two fingers in a loom, she still had eight left.

Such a lurid picture often led people to believe that the Industrial Revolution was a step backward for the working class. Weren't people better off on

[1] K. Marx and F. Engels, *The Communist Manifesto* (1848), widely reprinted.

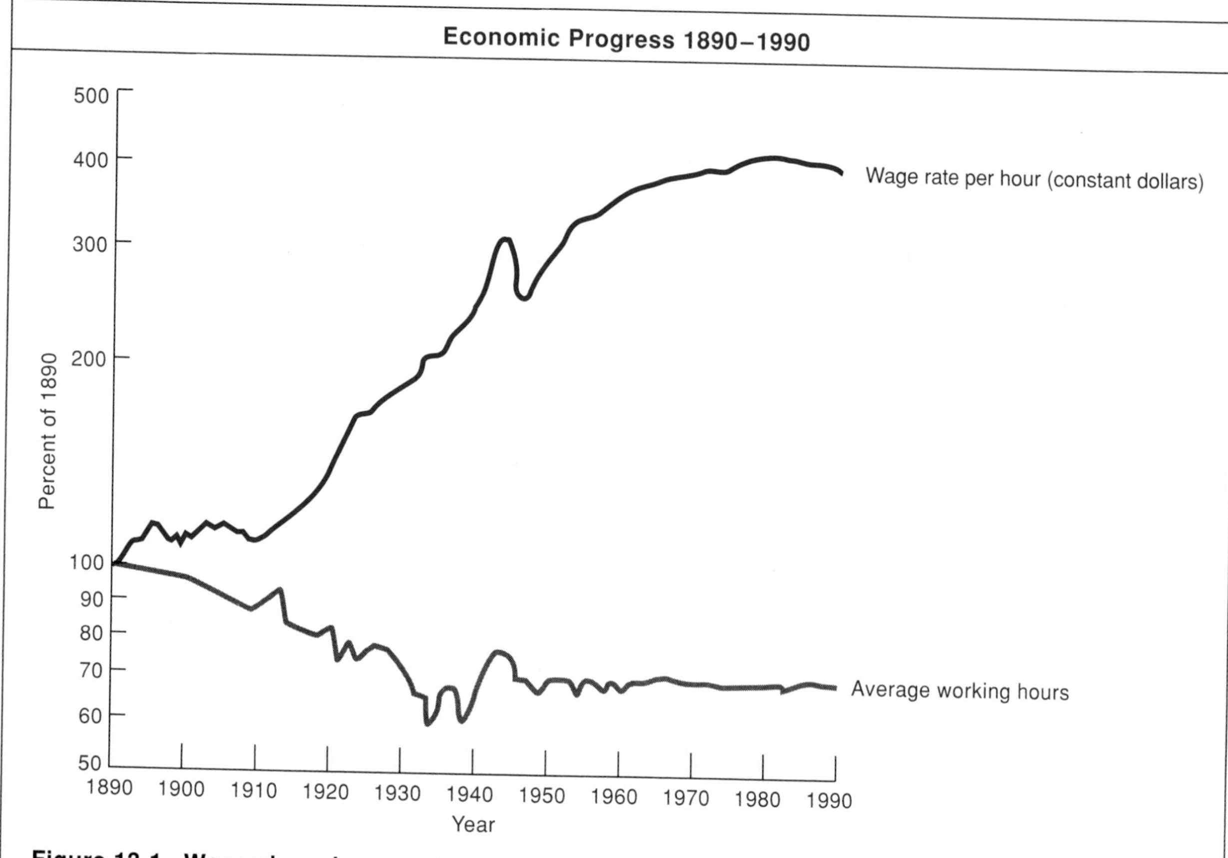

Figure 13-1. Wages have improved as hours of work declined

With advancing technology and improved capital goods, American workers enjoy higher wages while working shorter hours. Marx's prediction of impoverishment of the working class has proved far from the historical truth.

the farms than in the factories? Probably not. Poverty was simply more visible in the cities. The idyllic picture of the healthful, jolly countryside peopled by stout yeomen and happy peasantry is a historical myth unsupported by statistical research in most parts of the world.

Modern historians emphasize that the conditions of the industrial present, inadequate as they may seem, are nevertheless great improvements in living standards over earlier centuries of agrarian feudalism or unregulated laissez-faire. Real wages tended to meander up and down for the four centuries before the Industrial Revolution; since that time, wages have shown enormous gains. Today's average worker commands an income that will buy a variety of goods that would dazzle the lords of medieval times.

Income and Wealth

In measuring a person's economic condition, the two yardsticks most often used are income and wealth. We begin by defining these two key concepts and examining their major components.

Income refers to the total receipts or cash earned by a person or household during a given time period (usually a year). Income consists of wages and other labor earnings; property income such as rents, interest, and dividends; and transfer payments, or receipts from the government, such as social security or unemployment insurance.

Table 13-1 shows the average income of Americans. More precisely, it shows the total personal income of individuals in the United States divided by the number of households, for the year 1990. Labor income constitutes about two-thirds of personal income, while property income is particularly important for high-income groups. The poorer tenth of the population benefits substantially from government transfer payments such as social security and welfare payments.

Wealth consists of the net dollar value of assets owned at a point in time. Note that wealth is a stock of dollars (like the volume of a lake) while income is a flow of dollars per unit of time (like the flow of a stream). A household's wealth includes its tangible items (houses, cars and other consumer durable goods, and land) and its financial holdings (such as cash, savings accounts, bonds, and stocks). All items that are of value are called *assets*, while those that are owed are called *liabilities*. The difference between total assets and total liabilities is called wealth or *net worth*.

Table 13-2 presents a breakdown of the wealth holdings of Americans. The single most important asset of most households is the family home: 64 percent of families own houses, as compared with

Type of income	Average income per household, before taxes	Examples
Labor income:		
Wages and supplements	$29,000	Autoworker's wages; teacher's salary
Other labor income	2,800	GM's contribution to pension fund
Proprietors' income	4,300	Lawyer's share of partnership earnings
Property income:		
Rent	70	Landlord's rental from apartments
Dividend	1,300	Dividend from IBM
Interest	7,300	Interest paid on savings account
Transfer payments:		
Social security, net	1,300	Benefits less contributions
Other	3,700	Unemployment insurance, welfare, etc.
Total	**$49,800**	

Table 13-1. Major sources of personal income, 1990

American households earn most of their incomes from wages and salaries, but property incomes boost the income of the rich while government transfers are important supplements for the poor. (Source: U.S. Department of Commerce, Bureau of the Census, *Current Population Reports*. Series P-60.)

What American Households Own, 1988	
Type of asset	**Percentage of total wealth**
Tangible:	
Own home	43.0
Rental property	7.9
Motor vehicle	5.8
Other real estate	4.3
Financial:	
Checking account	0.6
Interest-earning accounts (savings accounts, time deposits, etc.)	18.3
Stocks and mutual funds	6.5
Equity in businesses	8.8
Other	4.9
Total	**100.0**
Median dollar value of assets per household, 1988	$35,800

Table 13-2. Tangible and intangible assets of households

Households hold tangible assets (such as houses and cars) as well as financial assets (such as savings accounts and stocks). Even though the average assets per household totaled almost $92,000, much of this was concentrated in a few hands, so the median value was only $35,800. (Source: U.S. Department of Commerce, Bureau of the Census, "Household Wealth and Asset Ownership: 1988," Series P-70.)

55 percent a generation ago. Most households own a modest amount of financial wealth, such as savings accounts and corporate stocks. As later chapters will show, the ownership of the nation's financial wealth is concentrated in the hands of a small fraction of the population.

B. Income Distribution and Marginal-Productivity Theory

Why do different people have such different incomes? Our starting point is to observe that the theory of income distribution in competitive markets is a special case of the theory of prices. Wages are the price of labor, rent is the price of land, and interest is the price of capital. So our first hint about income distribution comes from observing the forces lying behind supply and demand for factors of production.

But pointing to supply and demand leaves many important questions unanswered: Why are pleasant professions like law paid many times more than are unpleasant tasks like garbage collection? Why are women paid on average only 65 cents for every dollar earned by men? Is labor exploited by capital? What determines the interest and profit rates on capital? Or we might inquire about the overall distribution of income. Why are wages three-quarters of total national income?

The key to the distribution of income in a market economy is found in the marginal-productivity theory of the firm. We therefore begin by reviewing the theory of production first introduced in Chapter 7. We will see that the demand curves for the various factors of production—the demand for labor, land, and so forth—can be expressed in terms of the revenues earned on their marginal products. Putting the demand curves together with the supplies of each factor, we can calculate the incomes earned by each factor.

Marginal Productivity

Before showing how the demand for factors of production derives from their marginal productivity, we will review the essentials of Chapter 7's production theory.

The theory of production begins with the notion of the production function. If you have given quantities of land, labor, and capital, what is the maximum output of a particular good that you can produce? In technical language, the *production function* indicates the maximum amount of output that can be produced, with a given state of technical knowledge, for each combination of factor inputs. A specific production function might tell you that you can produce 1 ton of steel with 1.2 tons of iron ore, 150,000 British thermal units of energy, and 1.2 hours of labor.

The production-function concept provides a rigorous definition of *marginal product*.[2] Table 13-3 is a reminder of the way marginal products are calculated. Say we start out with 2 units of labor, plus a given dose of land and machinery, and this combination produces 30,000 bushels of corn. How much additional corn would be produced if we added 1 extra unit of labor, holding all other inputs constant? Table 13-3 provides an answer of 5000 extra bushels. We then say that the marginal product of labor at that initial input level is 5000 bushels of corn.

As a final element of review, recall the *law of diminishing returns*. Column (3) of Table 13-3 shows that each successive unit of labor has a declining marginal product. "Declining marginal product" is another name for diminishing returns. Moreover, a similar calculation of marginal product can be made for any input. We can interchange land for labor, varying the amount of land while holding constant labor and other inputs, and we would generally observe the law of diminishing returns at work for land as well as for labor.

[2] Note that the marginal product of a factor is expressed in *physical* units of product per unit of additional input. So economists sometimes use the term "marginal physical product" rather than marginal product, particularly when they want to avoid any possible confusion with a concept we will soon encounter called "marginal revenue product." For brevity, we will skip the word "physical" and abbreviate marginal product as *MP*.

Diminishing Returns Reviewed

(1) Units of labor (workers)	(2) Total product (bushels)	(3) Marginal product of labor (bushels per worker)
0	0	
		20,000
1	20,000	
		10,000
2 (initial input)	30,000	
		5,000
3	35,000	
		3,000
4	38,000	
		1,000
5	39,000	

Table 13-3. Diminishing returns is seen as diminishing marginal product

Marginal product of labor is calculated by adding 1 additional unit of labor while holding all other inputs constant. If the initial input is 2 units of labor, then adding a third produces 5000 additional bushels of corn. Diminishing returns is seen as a fall in the marginal product of labor as the number of workers increases while other inputs are unchanged.

Marginal Revenue Product

We can use the tools of production theory to devise a key concept in distribution theory, *marginal revenue product*. Suppose we are operating a giant shirt factory. We know how many shirts each additional worker produces. But as the firm's managers we want to maximize profits measured in dollars, for we pay our salaries with money, not with shirts. And workers also want to be paid in dollars rather than in clothing. We therefore need a concept that measures the additional *dollars* each additional unit of input produces. Economists give the name "marginal revenue product" to the money value of the additional output generated by an extra unit of input.

The **marginal revenue product** of input A is the additional revenue produced by an additional unit of input A.

Competitive Case. It is easy to calculate marginal revenue product when product markets are perfectly competitive. In this case, all units of the marginal product that the worker brings in (MP_L) can be sold at the competitive output price (P). Moreover, since we are considering perfect competition, the output price is unaffected by the firm's output, and price therefore equals marginal revenue (MR). If we have MP_L of 10,000 bushels and a price and MR of \$3, the dollar value of the output produced by the last worker—the marginal revenue product of labor (MRP_L)—is \$30,000 (equal to 10,000 × \$3). This is shown in column (5) of Table 13-4. Hence, under perfect competition, each worker is worth to the firm the dollar value of the last worker's marginal product; the value of each acre of land is the marginal product of land times the output price; and so forth for each factor.

Imperfect Competition. What happens in the case of imperfect competition, where the individual firm's demand curve is downward-sloping? Here, the marginal revenue received from each extra unit of output sold is less than the price because to sell an additional unit the firm must lower its price on previous units. Each unit of labor's marginal product will be worth $MR < P$ to the firm.

To continue our previous example, say that the MR was \$2 while price was \$3. Then the MRP of the second worker in Table 13-4 would be \$20,000 (equal to the MP_L of 10,000 times the MR of \$2), rather than the \$30,000 of the competitive case.

To summarize, the additional revenue gained by a firm from an additional unit of input is called the marginal revenue product. It is measured in dollar terms by the marginal revenue multiplied by the marginal product of the input.

Marginal revenue product represents the additional revenue a firm earns from employment of an additional unit of an input, with other inputs held constant. It is defined as the marginal product of the input multiplied by the marginal revenue obtained from selling an extra unit of output. This holds for labor (L), land (A), and other inputs:

$$\text{Marginal revenue product of labor } (MRP_L) = MR \times MP_L$$

$$\text{Marginal revenue product of land } (MRP_A) = MR \times MP_A$$

and so forth.

Under conditions of perfect competition, because price equals marginal revenue, these conditions simplify to marginal revenue product equals the price times the marginal product, or

$$\text{Marginal revenue product } (MRP_i) = P \times MP_i$$

for each input.

Marginal Revenue Product

(1) Units of labor (workers)	(2) Total product (bushels)	(3) Marginal product of labor (bushels per worker)	(4) Price of output ($ per bushel)	(5) Marginal revenue product of labor ($ per worker)
0	0			
		20,000	3	60,000
1	20,000			
		10,000	3	30,000
2	30,000			
		5,000	3	15,000
3	35,000			
		3,000	3	9,000
4	38,000			
		1,000	3	3,000
5	39,000			

Table 13-4. Calculation of marginal revenue product for perfectly competitive firm

Using the production data in Table 13-3 along with the price of output, we can easily calculate the marginal revenue product of labor. Marginal revenue product of labor shows how much additional revenue the firm receives when an additional unit of labor is employed. It equals the marginal product in column (3) times the competitive output price in column (4).

The Demand for Inputs

Having analyzed the underlying concepts, we now turn to the determinants of the demand for inputs. We first note two special features of factor demands—their interdependence and their derived nature. We then show how profit-maximizing firms decide upon the optimal combination of inputs, which allows us to derive the demand for inputs.

Demands for Factors Are Interdependent

A fundamental point about the demand for inputs stems from the technological fact that inputs usually do not work alone. A saw by itself is useless to me if I want to cut timber. A worker with empty hands is equally worthless. Together, the worker and the saw can cut my timber very nicely. In other words, the productivity of one factor, such as labor, depends upon the amount of other factors available to work with.

Sir William Petty put the matter in this striking way: Labor is the father of product and land the mother. We cannot say which is more essential in producing a baby—a mother or a father. So, too, it is generally impossible to say how much output has been created by any one of the different inputs taken by itself. The different inputs interact with one another.

It is this *interdependence* of productivities of land, labor, and capital goods that makes the distribution of income a complex topic. Suppose we had to distribute at one time the entire output of a nation. If land had by itself produced so much, and labor had alone produced so much, and machinery had by itself produced the rest, distribution might be easy. Under supply and demand, if each factor produced a certain amount by itself, then it would enjoy the undivided fruits of its own work.

But reread the above paragraph and underline such words as "by itself produced" and "had alone produced." They refer to a fantasy world of independent productivities which simply does not exist in reality. When an omelette is produced by chef's labor and chicken's eggs and cow's butter and land's natural gas, how can you unscramble the separate contributions of each input?

To find the answer, we must look to the interaction of supply and demand, operating in the entire set of interdependent factor markets.

Demand for Factors Is a Derived Demand

There is a second essential difference between ordinary demands and the demand by firms for inputs. Why do households demand final goods like corn muffins? They do so because of the direct enjoyment or utility these consumption goods provide. By contrast, a business does not buy inputs like cornland or ovens because they yield direct satisfaction. Rather, it buys inputs because of the production and revenue that it can gain from employment of those factors.

Satisfactions are in the picture for inputs—but at one stage removed. The satisfaction that students get from eating anchovy pizzas helps determine how many pizzas the pizzeria must make and therefore how many pizza ovens and how many anchovy boats are needed for the pizzas. An accurate analysis of the demand for inputs must, therefore, recognize that consumer demands do *ultimately* determine the pizzeria's demand for anchovies and ovens.

The firm's demand for inputs is derived indirectly from the consumer demand for its final product.

Economists therefore speak of the demand for productive factors as a **derived demand.** This means that when firms demand an input, they do so because that input permits them to produce a good which consumers are willing to buy now or in the future.

Figure 13-2 shows how the demand for a given input, such as fertile cornland, must be regarded as derived from the consumer demand curve for corn.

Factor Demands for Profit-Maximizing Firms

Where did the demand for cornland shown in Figure 13-2 come from? For that matter, what determines the demand for any factor of production? To understand these issues, we must analyze how a profit-oriented firm chooses its optimal combination of inputs.

Imagine that you are a profit-maximizing farmer. In your area, you can hire all the farmhands you want at $20,000 per year. Your accountant hands you a spreadsheet with the data in Table 13-4. How would you proceed?

You could try out different possibilities. If you hire one worker, the additional revenue (the *MRP*)

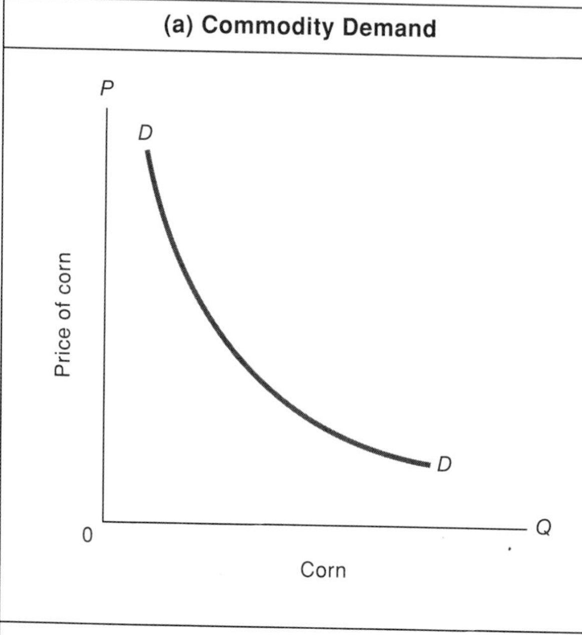

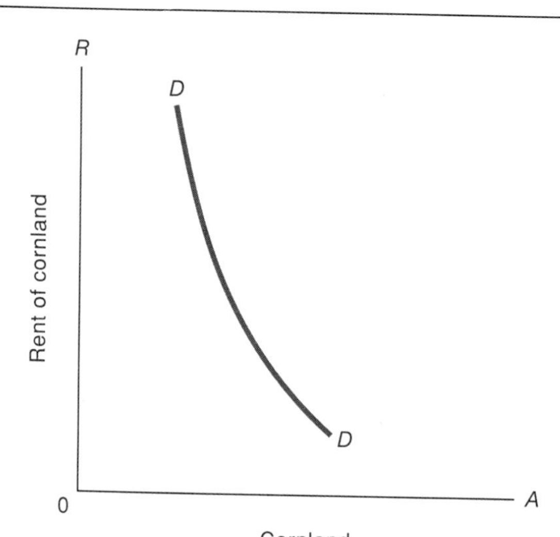

Figure 13-2. Demand for factors is derived from demand for goods they produce

The blue curve of derived demand for cornland comes from the black curve of commodity demand for corn. Shift the black curve out, and out goes the blue curve. If the black commodity curve becomes more inelastic, the same tends to happen to the blue input-demand curve.

is $60,000 while the marginal cost of the worker is $20,000, so your extra profit is $40,000. A second worker gives you an *MRP* of $30,000 for an additional profit of $10,000. The third worker produces extra output yielding revenues of only $15,000 but costs $20,000; hence, it is not profitable to hire the third worker. Table 13-4 shows that the maximum profit is earned by hiring two workers. We have by trial and error found an interesting rule:

A firm will maximize profits by hiring labor (or any factor) as long as the *MRP* of that input exceeds the extra cost of that input.

By using this reasoning, we can derive the rule for choosing the optimal combination of inputs: To maximize profits, inputs should be added as long as the marginal revenue product of the input exceeds the marginal cost or price of the input.

For perfectly competitive factor markets, the rule is even simpler. Recall that under competition the marginal revenue product equals price times marginal product ($MRP = P \times MP$).

The profit-maximizing combination of inputs for a perfectly competitive firm comes when the marginal product times the output price equals the price of the input:

$$\text{Marginal product of labor} \times \text{output price} = \text{price of labor} = \text{wage rate}$$

$$\text{Marginal product of land} \times \text{output price} = \text{price of land} = \text{rent}$$

and so forth.

We can understand this rule by the following reasoning: Say that inputs into corn production (or any competitive industry) are bundled into $1 units—$1 units of labor, $1 units of land, and so forth. The firm will want to hire that quantity of $1 units of each input which will cause the revenue earned on the last unit to also be just $1. The incremental revenue is the corn *MP* of the input times the corn price, *P*. When inputs have been added so that the $MP \times P$ just reaches $1, then the $1 of additional input cost just equals the $1 of additional revenue.

Least-Cost Rule. We can reorganize the conditions just described in a slightly different way to give the **least-cost rule for choice of inputs.** By dividing each equation by the input price, we get the following important new set of equations for perfectly competitive firms:

$$\frac{\text{Marginal product of labor}}{\text{Price of labor}} = \frac{\text{marginal product of land}}{\text{price of land}} = \cdots = \frac{1}{\text{output price}}$$

In words:

The least-cost rule states that profits are maximized when the marginal product per dollar of input is equalized for each input.

If an acre of land costs $800 while an hour of labor costs 100 times less at $8, then no rational business would decide to equalize the marginal products of the two factors. Rather, as the equation shows, costs are minimized when the marginal products *per dollar of input* are the same. Since land costs 100 times as much as labor, land's *MP* must be 100 times labor's *MP*.

This rule is identical in spirit to Chapter 6's rule for maximum consumer satisfaction; that rule states that maximum satisfaction comes when the marginal utility per dollar is equalized for each good consumed.

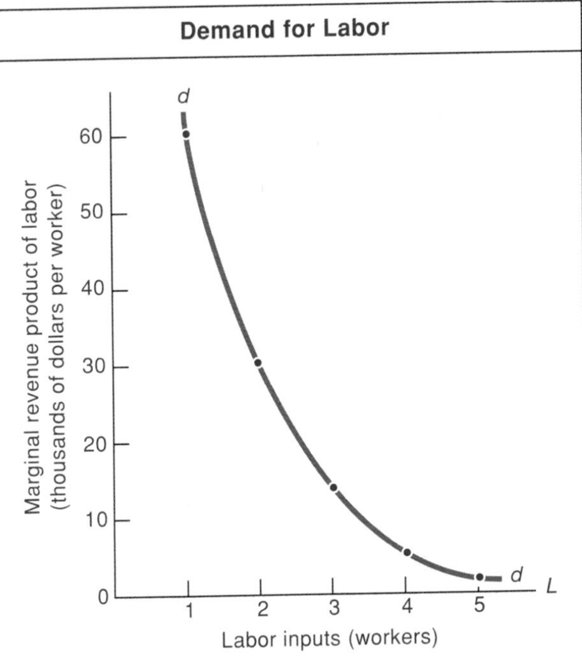

Figure 13-3. Demand for inputs derived through marginal revenue products

The demand for labor arises from the marginal revenue product of labor. This figure uses the data for the competitive firm displayed in Table 13-4.

Marginal Revenue Product and the Demand for Inputs

Having derived the *MRP* for different factors, we can now understand the demand for factors of production. We just saw that a profit-maximizing firm would choose input quantities such that the price of each input equaled the *MRP* of that input. This means that from the *MRP* schedule for an input, we can immediately determine the relationship between the price of the input and the quantity demanded of that input. This relationship is what we call the demand curve.

Glance back at Table 13-4. This table shows in the last column the *MRP* of labor for our corn farm. By the profit-maximizing condition, we know that at a wage of $60,000 the firm would choose 1 unit of labor; at a $30,000 wage, 2 units of labor would be sought; and so forth.

The *MRP* schedule for each input gives the demand schedule of the firm for that input.

We have used this result in Figure 13-3 to draw a demand curve for our corn farm using the data shown in Table 13-4. We have in addition drawn a smooth curve through the individual points to show how the demand curve would appear if fractional units of labor could be purchased.

Substitution Rule. A corollary of the least-cost rule is the following: If the price of one factor rises while other factor prices remain fixed, the firm will generally benefit from substituting more of the other inputs for the more expensive factor. A rise in labor's price, P_L, will reduce MP_L/P_L. Firms will respond by reducing employment and increasing land use until equality of marginal products per dollar of input is restored—thus lowering the amount of needed *L* and increasing the demand for land acres. A rise in land's price, P_A, alone will, by the same logic, cause labor to be substituted for more expensive land.

Supply of Factors of Production

A complete analysis of the determination of factor prices and of incomes must combine both the demand for inputs just described and the supplies of different factors. The general principles of supply vary from input to input, and this topic will be explored in depth in the next three chapters. At this point we provide a few introductory comments.

In a market economy, most factors of production are privately owned. People "own" their labor in the sense that they control its use; but this crucial "human capital" can today only be rented and cannot be sold. Capital and land are generally privately owned by households and by businesses.

Decisions about *labor* supply are determined by many economic and non-economic factors. The important determinants of labor supply are the price of labor (i.e., the wage rate) and demographic factors, such as age, gender, education, and family structure. The quantity of *land* and other natural resources is determined by geology and cannot be significantly changed, although the quality of land is affected by conservation, settlement patterns, and other improvements. The supply of *capital* depends upon past investments made by businesses, households, and governments. In the short run, the stock of capital is fixed like land, but in the long run the supply of capital is sensitive to economic factors such as incomes and interest rates.

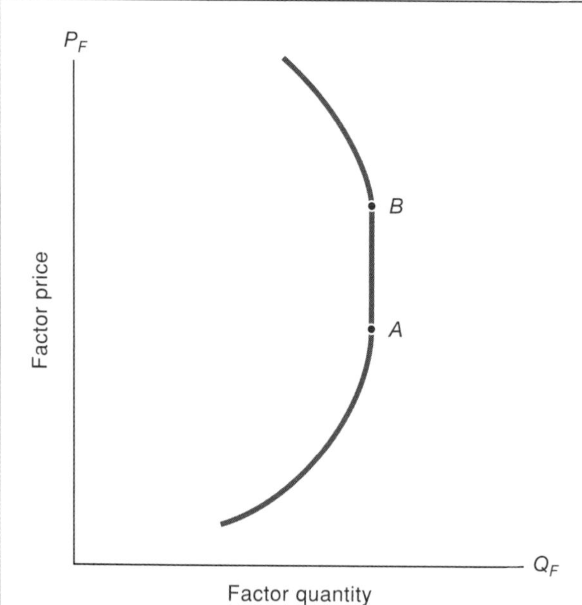

Figure 13-4. Supply curve for factors of production

Supplies of factors of production will depend upon characteristics of the factors and the preferences of their owners. Generally, supplies will respond positively to price, as in the region below *A*. For factors that are fixed in supply, like land, the supply curve will be perfectly inelastic, as from *A* to *B*. In special cases where a higher price of the factor increases the income of its owner greatly, such as for labor, the supply curve may bend backward, as in the region above *B*.

Can we say anything about the elasticity of supply of inputs? Actually, the supply curve may slope positively or negatively or even be vertical. For most goods, we would expect that the supply responds positively to its price in the long run; in this case, the supply curve would slope upward and to the right. The supply of land is usually thought to be unaffected by price, and in this case the supply of land will be perfectly inelastic, and its supply curve vertical. In some special cases, when the return to the factor increases, owners may supply less of the factor to the market. For example, if people feel they can afford to work fewer hours when wages rise, the supply curve for labor might eventually bend backward, rather than slope upward.

The different possible elasticities for the supply of factors are illustrated by the *SS* supply curve shown in Figure 13-4.

Determination of Factor Prices by Supply and Demand

A full analysis of the distribution of income must combine the supply and demand for factors of production. Earlier sections provided the underpinnings for analysis of demand and gave a brief description of supply. We showed that, for given factor prices, profit-maximizing firms would choose input combinations according to their marginal revenue products. As the price of land falls, each farmer would substitute land for other inputs such as labor, machinery, and fertilizer. Each farmer therefore would show a demand for cornland inputs like that in Figure 13-2(*b*).

How do we obtain the *market demand* for inputs (whether cornland, unskilled labor, or pizza ovens)? We add together the individual demands of each of the firms. Thus at a given price of land, we add together all the demands for land of all the firms at that price; and we do the same at every price of land. In other words, we add *horizontally* all the demand curves of the individual firms to obtain the market demand curve for an input.[3] We follow the same procedure for any input, summing up all the derived demands of all the businesses to get the market demand for each input. And in each case, the derived demand for tractors or unskilled labor or any input is based on the marginal revenue product of the input under consideration. Figure 13-5 shows a general demand curve for a factor of production as the *DD* curve.

We can perform the same operation for all the individual suppliers to the market. That is, at each level of the factor price, we add horizontally all the individual quantities supplied to obtain the market supply. The hypothetical supply curve for the factor of production is shown as *SS* in Figure 13-5.

[3] Note that this process of adding factor demand curves horizontally is exactly the same procedure that we followed in obtaining market demand curves for consumers in Chapter 6.

Competitive Pricing of Factors of Production

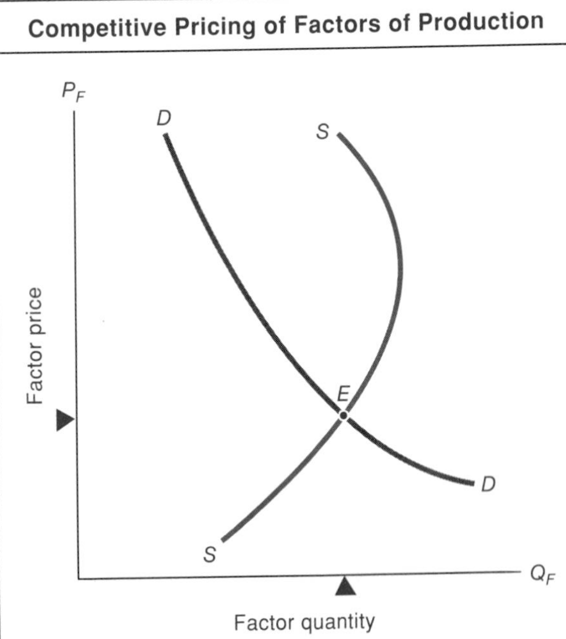

Figure 13-5. Factor supply and derived demand interact to determine factor prices and income distribution

Factor prices are determined by the interaction of factor supply and demand. If the demand for an inelastically supplied factor such as land rises, then that factor's total income will rise. Similarly, supplies and demands for trucks or computer programmers or office buildings will affect their prices and quantities sold. At what point will an increase in demand decrease both quantity supplied and total income of this factor?

The equilibrium price of the input in a competitive market comes at that level where the quantities supplied and demanded are equal—where the derived demand curve for a factor intersects its supply curve, shown at point *E* in Figure 13-5. At that price, and only at that price, will the amount that owners of the factor willingly supply just balance the amount that the buyers willingly purchase. At a lower price, eager demanders will bid up the factor's price. What happens if price is above equilibrium?

From this graph, we see the impact of shifts in the supply or demand for the factor. Pencil in an increase in demand in Figure 13-5. Show how this will tend to increase the factor's equilibrium price. In addition, show that if a factor's supply increases, shifting its supply curve down and to the right, the factor's price will definitely tend to fall.

The theory of supply and demand applied to factors of production leads to an important conclusion about incomes in a market economy: Factor prices and people's incomes are not determined at random. Rather, the forces of supply and demand operate to create high returns to factors that have either limited supply or high demand as reflected in high marginal revenue product. If a factor becomes scarcer, say because more and more farmland is converted to urban uses, then its price will rise and its lucky owner will enjoy an increase in income.

However, the income of land, labor, or capital will tend to fall if more of that factor becomes available, or if other close substitutes for it are found, or if people stop wanting the goods that the factor is best suited to make. Competition giveth, and competition taketh away.

Marginal-Productivity Theory of Distribution

We can now use marginal-productivity theory to solve the riddle of the sphinx: How do markets allocate national output among two or more factors of production?

John Bates Clark, a distinguished economist at

Columbia University, provided a simplified theory of distribution around 1900. It can be applied to competitive markets for any number of final product and factor inputs. But it is most easily grasped if we consider a simplified world with only one product in which all accounts are kept in real terms. The product could be corn or a basket of goods, but we will call it Q. Moreover, by setting the price equal to 1, we can conduct the entire discussion in real terms, with the value of output being Q and with the wage rate being the real wage in terms of goods or Q. In this situation, a production function tells how much Q is produced for each quantity of labor-hours, L, and for each quantity of acres of homogeneous land, A. Note that because $P = 1$, under perfect competition $MRP = MP \times P = MP \times 1 = MP$ and the wage $= MP_L$.

Clark reasoned as follows. A first worker has a large marginal product because there is so much land to work with. Worker 2 has a slightly smaller marginal product. But the two workers are alike: they must get exactly the same wage. Which wage? The *MP* of worker 1? The lower *MP* of worker 2? The average of these?

Under perfect competition, where landowners are free to employ as few or many workers as they like, the answer is plain: Landlords will never freely hire that second worker if the market wage they must pay exceeds the new worker's marginal product. So the demand curve for labor will ensure that *all* the workers receive a wage rate equal to the marginal product of the last worker.

But there is a surplus of total output over the wage bill because earlier workers had higher *MP*s than the last worker. What happens to the excess *MP*s produced by all the earlier workers? The excess stays with the landlords as their residual earning, which we will later call *rent*. Why do the landlords, who may be sipping their drinks thousands of miles away, earn anything on the land? Are they exploiting workers or exercising some kind of monopoly? Not really. Each landowner is a participant in the competitive market for land and rents the land for its best price. Just as worker competes with worker for jobs, landowner competes with landowner for workers. There are no conspiracies, no employer associations, and no unions in Clark's competitive world.

Figure 13-6 shows that the marginal product curve of labor gives the *DD* demand curve of all

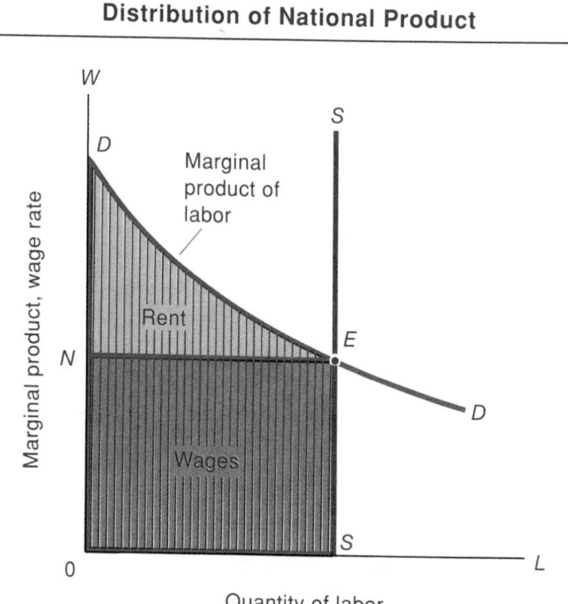

Figure 13-6. Marginal product principles determine factor distribution of income

Each vertical slice represents the marginal product of that unit of labor. Total national output is found by adding all the vertical slices up to the total supply of labor at *S*.

The distribution of output is determined by marginal product principles. Total wages are the lower rectangle (equal to the wage rate 0*N* times the quantity of labor 0*S*). Land rents get the residual upper triangle *NDE*.

employers in terms of real wages (in corn, or market baskets of goods, or Q units). The population or labor force provides us with the supply of labor (shown as *SS*), and the equilibrium wage comes at *E*. The total wage share of labor is given by $W \times L$ (for example, if $W = 5$ and $L = 1$ million, total wages = 5 million); this is shown by the dark area of the rectangle, 0*SEN*.

The surprise comes because we have found not only the wages of labor but also the distributive share of land. The light rent triangle in Figure 13-6 measures all the surplus output which was produced but was not paid out in wages. The size of the rent triangle is determined by how much the *MP* of labor declines as additional labor is added—that is, by the extent of diminishing returns. If there are a few high-quality plots, then additional units of labor will show sharp diminishing returns and rent's share will be large. If by contrast there is a great deal of homogeneous frontier land just waiting to be cleared, then there may be little tendency to diminishing returns and land's rent on the frontier may be minuscule.

Is it fair that land receive rent? Whether fair or unfair, all the workers are alike; all landlords are free competitors who can hire as much labor as they like; so it is inevitable under competition that all workers get paid the *MP* of the last worker and, because of diminishing returns, that a residual amount of rent will be left over for landowners.

We have drawn Figure 13-6 so that labor's wages are about 3 times larger than property's rents. This 3-to-1 relationship between labor income and nonlabor income reflects the fact that wages and salaries constitute about three-quarters of national income. Labor's share of national income has been remarkably stable over the twentieth century.

If mass immigration or a rise in the birth rate increase labor supply so much that society moves down the labor demand curve to a lower wage, the rectangular share of labor might or might not fall relative to the rent triangle of land.

Why is this? An increase in labor supply down the labor demand curve must always raise the absolute total of land's rent triangle. What about the absolute total of labor's rectangle? The elasticity discussion of Chapter 5 reminds us that labor's total wage rectangle will increase if *DD* has more-than-unitary price elasticity.

But can labor's rectangle grow as great in percentage as land's triangle, or even greater? Although not obvious until you experiment with drawing in labor demand curves, the answer is definitely yes. The relative share of wage's rectangle can increase and the relative share of land's triangle can decrease if the marginal product curve is sufficiently elastic.

Marginal-Productivity Theory with Many Inputs

The marginal-productivity theory discovered by J. B. Clark was a great step forward in understanding the pricing of different inputs. Clark saw that the position of land and labor could be reversed to get a complete theory of distribution.

To switch the roles of labor and land, hold labor constant and add successive units of variable land to fixed labor. Calculate each successive acre's marginal product. Then draw a demand curve showing how many acres labor-owners will demand of land at each rent rate. In the new version of Figure 13-6 that you draw, find a new E' point of equilibrium. Identify land's rectangle of rent as determined by its *MP*. Identify labor's residual wage triangle. Finally, note the complete symmetry of the factors. This new graph shows that we should think of the distributive shares of each and every factor of production as being simultaneously determined by their interdependent marginal products.

That is not all. Instead of labor and land, suppose the only two factors were labor and some versatile capital goods. Suppose a smooth production function relates Q to labor and capital with the same general properties as in Figure 13-6. In this case, you can redraw Figure 13-6 and get an identical picture of income distribution between labor and capital. Indeed, we can perform the same operation for three, four, or any number of factors.

Profit-maximizing employers in competitive factor markets will have their demand for inputs determined by the marginal products of factors. In the simplified case of a single output (with $P = 1$) we get

$$\text{Wage} = \text{marginal product of labor}$$
$$\text{Rent} = \text{marginal product of land}$$

and so forth for any factor. This distributes 100 percent of output, no more and no less, among all the factors of production.

We see then that Clark's aggregate theory of the distribution of income is compatible with the competitive pricing of any number of goods produced by any number of factors. This simple but powerful theory shows how the distribution of income is related to productivity in a competitive market economy.

Conclusions

We have now analyzed the general principles underlying the determination of the distribution of income in a competitive market economy. As in most issues, price and quantity are determined by the twin blade of supply and demand. On the demand side are the demands for factors of production. Demands are determined by both the production function and the demands for the final goods that lie behind the derived demands for factors. On the supply side is the supply of land, determined by nature's endowment; the supply of labor, determined by the size and quality of the labor force; and the supply of capital, provided by the accumulated stocks of equipment and buildings from past investments. By integrating the interdependent supplies and demands for factors, markets generate the incomes of the owners of land, labor, and capital.

Although the general principles underlying competitive determination of factor prices and incomes are the same for all the factors, each has special features. In the next two chapters, we will study the wages of labor beginning with the reasons for differences in wage rates of different groups and then examine certain imperfections in the labor market. In the final chapter of this part, we will analyze the issues of rent earned by land and interest and profit earned by capital.

SUMMARY

A. The Fruits of Industrialization

1. Distribution theory is concerned with the basic question of *for whom* economic goods are to be produced. It studies the determination of income (the flow of wages, property returns, and transfers received during a period) and wealth (the net stock of assets owned at a point in time). In examining how the different factors of production—land, labor, capital, and risk taking—get priced in the market, distribution theory examines how supplies and demands for these factors are linked and how they determine all kinds of wages, rents, interest rates, and profits.

B. Income Distribution and Marginal-Productivity Theory

2. To understand the demand for factors of production, we must analyze the theory of production and the derived demand for factors. The demand for inputs is a derived demand: we demand ovens and wheatland not for their own sake, but for the muffins and bread that they can produce for consumers. Factor demand curves are derived from commodity demand curves. An upward shift in the final demand curve causes a similar upward shift in the derived factor demand curve; greater inelasticity in commodity demand produces greater inelasticity of derived factor demand.
3. We met in earlier chapters the concepts of a production function and marginal products. The demand for a factor is drawn from the marginal revenue product (MRP), which is defined as the extra revenue earned from employing an extra unit of a factor. In any market, MRP equals the marginal revenue earned by the sale of an additional unit of the product times the marginal product of an input ($MRP = MR \times MP$). For competitive firms, because price equals marginal revenue, this simplifies to $MRP = P \times MP$.
4. A firm maximizes profits (and minimizes costs) when it sets the MRP of each factor equal to that factor's marginal cost, which is the factor's price. This can be stated equivalently as a condition in which the MRP per dollar of input is equalized for each input. This must hold in equilibrium because a profit-maximizing employer will hire any factor up to the point where the factor's marginal product will return in dollars of marginal revenue just what the factor costs.

5. To obtain the market demand for a factor, we add horizontally all firms' demand curves. This, along with the particular factor's own supply curve, determines the supply-and-demand intersection. At the equilibrium market price for the factor of production, the amount demanded and supplied will be exactly equal—only at equilibrium will the factor price have no tendency to change.
6. J. B. Clark's marginal-productivity theory of income distribution analyzes the way total national output gets distributed among the different factors. Competition of numerous landowners and laborers drives factor prices to equal their marginal products. That process will allocate exactly 100 percent of the product. Any factor, not just labor alone, can be the varying factor. Because each unit of the factor gets paid only the *MP* of the *last* unit hired, there is a residual surplus of output left over from the *MP*s of early inputs. This residual is exactly equal to the incomes of the other factors under marginal productivity pricing. Hence, Clark's theory of distribution, though simplified, is a logically complete picture of the distribution of income under perfect competition.

CONCEPTS FOR REVIEW

distribution theory
income and wealth
marginal product, marginal revenue product
derived demand
marginal revenue product of input i $= (MRP_i) = MR \times MP_i$ $= P \times MP_i$ for competitive firm
factor demands under competition:
$MP_i \times P =$ factor price$_i$
which gives least-cost rule:
$$\frac{MP_L}{P_L} = \frac{MP_A}{P_A} = \cdots = \frac{1}{\text{output price}}$$
Clark's aggregate distribution theory
MP rectangle, residual rent triangle

QUESTIONS FOR DISCUSSION

1. Define marginal product and marginal revenue product for a corn farmer. What are the units of each? Give a common-sense explanation of why maximization of profits requires that each factor's marginal revenue product must be equal to its price.
2. For each of the following factors, name the final output for which the item is a derived demand: wheatland, gasoline, barber, machine tool for skis, wine press, economics textbook.
3. In Clark's theory shown in Figure 13-6, let land rather than labor be the varying input. Draw a new figure and explain the marginal-productivity theory with this new diagram. What is the residual factor?
4. Explain the mistake in each of the following statements:
   (a) Marginal product is calculated as output per worker.
   (b) Distribution theory is simple. You simply figure out how much each factor produced, and then give it that part of output.
   (c) Under competition, workers get paid the total output produced less the costs of raw materials.
   (d) Marginal revenue product is simply the price times the marginal product.
5. Suppose GNP grows faster than total labor inputs in every decade. If, contrary to Karl Marx's predictions, wage share stays about the same fraction of GNP, show that real wage rates must rise.
6. Labor leaders used to say, "Without any labor there is no product. Hence labor deserves *all* the product." Apologists for capital would reply, "Take away all capital goods, and labor scratches a bare pittance from the earth; practically all the product belongs to capital."
   Analyze the flaws in these arguments. If you were to accept them, show that they would allocate 200 or 300 percent of output to two or three factors, whereas only 100 percent can be allocated. How does Clark's marginal-productivity theory resolve this dispute?

CHAPTER 14

WAGES AND THE LABOR MARKET

> The theory of the determination of wages in a free market is simply a special case of the general theory of value. Wages are the price of labor.
>
> J. R. Hicks, *The Theory of Wages* (1932)

Labor income is the major source of income for the vast majority of people. Wages, salaries, and other earnings today constitute 80 percent of national income in the United States. Indeed, we might say that ours is a "laboristic" rather than a capitalistic system.

Because of its importance, the labor market is a constant source of controversy, social strife, and political ferment. The pitched battles between labor and capital during the last century and the struggles today for women and minorities to gain pay equity are only two examples of clashes over labor issues.

This chapter and the next explore how wages are set in a market economy. Section A of this chapter reviews the determination of wages under competitive conditions, while the second section discusses the thorny problem of discrimination in labor markets. The next chapter then turns to an analysis of imperfect competition in labor markets, giving particular attention to the ways that unions limit the supply and raise the wages of labor.

A. Wage Determination under Perfect Competition

Wage rates differ enormously.[1] The average wage is as hard to define as the average person. An auto executive may earn $4 million a year at the same time that a clerk earns $15,000 and a farmhand $12,000. In the same factory, a skilled machinist may earn $500 a week, while an unskilled janitor gets $200. Experienced women may be paid $300 a week at the same time their younger brothers are starting at $400. Any complete theory of wages must explain these wage differentials.

But important as wage differences are, we must not overlook the general wage level. Wages of virtually every category of labor are higher than they were a century ago. As Table 14-1 demonstrates, wages are higher in North America than in Latin America; higher in Japan than in South Korea; higher in Europe than in India. By using the analytical tools of economics—particularly the supply and demand for labor—we can go far in understanding the structure of wages.

[1] In this chapter, we will generally use the term "wages" as a shorthand expression for "wages, salaries, and other forms of compensation."

Region and year	Wage rate in manufacturing ($ per hour, 1988 wage levels)
United States	
1890	2.61
1988	11.22
Great Britain	
1890	2.66
1988	8.22
West Germany (1988)	10.96
Japan (1988)	13.54
South Korea (1988)	2.066
Mexico (1988)	1.40
India (1988)	0.45

Table 14-1. General wage levels vary enormously across space and time

The United States is a high-wage country while Indian hourly wages are a tiny fraction of American levels. General wage levels are determined by supply and demand, but behind supply and demand lies the relative abundance of labor, capital, and resources, along with levels of skill and technology. (Source: International Labor Organization, Federal Reserve System.)

The General Wage Level

Why is the wage level in the United States $5\frac{1}{2}$ times that in South Korea and 25 times that in India? We can understand this phenomenon by examining the simplified case of wages paid in competitive markets to identical workers with identical jobs.

A *perfectly competitive labor market* is one in which there is a sufficiently large number of workers and employers so that no individual firm or worker has the power to affect wage rates appreciably. This definition rules out labor unions or labor markets dominated by a large firm. In reality, few labor markets are perfectly competitive, but some—such as a large city's market for inexperienced teenagers or clerical workers—approach the competitive concept tolerably well.

In a market of identical jobs and people, competition will cause the hourly wage rates to be exactly equal. No employer would pay more for the work of one person than for that person's identical twin or for a person of identical skills.

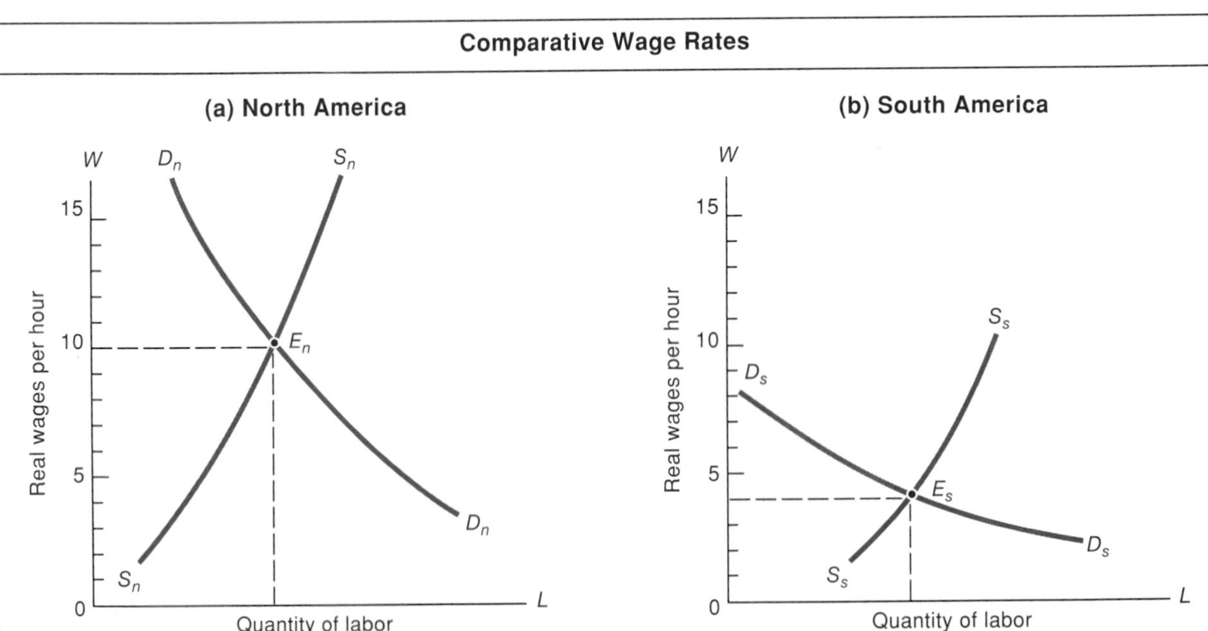

Figure 14-1. Favorable resources, skills, management, capital, and technology explain high North American wages

Supply and demand determine a higher competitive wage in North America than in South America. The major forces leading to high North American wages are a better-educated and more skilled work force, a larger stock of capital per worker, and modern technologies.

How is this single market wage determined? The answer is illustrated in Figure 14-1(*a*). Competitive supply of identical workers is shown by North America's supply curve, S_nS_n, while the demand for identical jobs is represented by D_nD_n. The equilibrium wage will settle at the level shown at E_n. If the wage were lower than E_n, shortages of labor would occur and employers would bid up wages to E_n, restoring the equilibrium.

In analyzing labor's earnings, we are interested in **real wages,** which represent the purchasing power of an hour's work or the money wages divided by the cost of living. The case shown in Figure 14-1 measures real wages in terms of how large a bundle of consumer goods the wages would buy.

Suppose that Figure 14-1(*a*) represents the state of affairs in North America while Figure 14-1(*b*) describes South America. Why are the general levels of wages so different? Is it because the minimum wage is so high in North America? Or because business monopolies are so strong in South America? Surely not. Rather, real wages differ among regions or in a given region over time through the operation of the supply and demand for labor. To understand the level of wages, therefore, we must look at the forces underlying the supply and demand for labor.

Demand for Labor

We begin our analysis of the general wage level by examining the factors that determine the demand for labor. The basic tools were provided in the last chapter, where we saw that the demand for a factor of production reflects the marginal productivity of that input.

Figure 14-2 illustrates the marginal-productivity theory. At a given time and with a given state of technology, there exists a relationship between the quantity of labor inputs and the amount of output. By the law of diminishing returns, each additional unit of labor input will add a smaller and smaller slab of output. In the example shown in Figure 14-2, at 10 units of labor, the competitively determined, general wage level will be $20 per unit.

But let's probe deeper and ask what lies behind labor's marginal productivity. Labor's marginal product depends upon the quality of labor inputs, the quantity and quality of cooperating factors of production, and the level and utilization of technical and engineering knowledge.

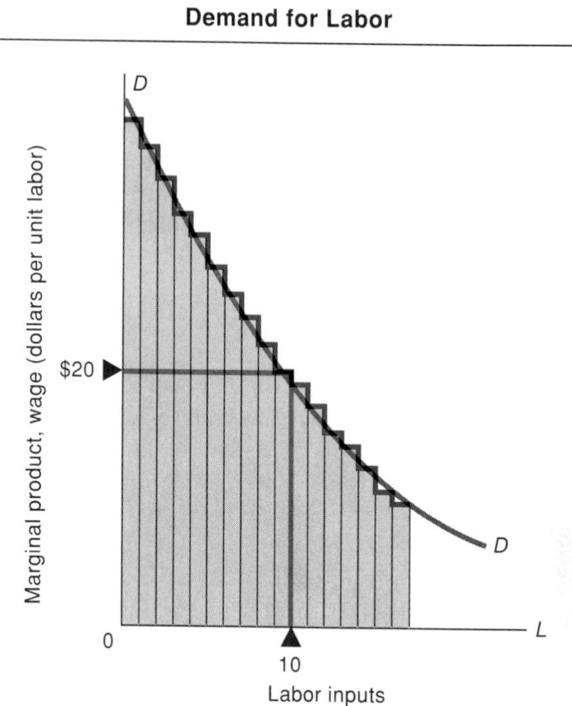

Figure 14-2. Demand for labor reflects marginal productivity

The demand for labor is determined by its marginal productivity in producing national output. The light gray vertical slices represent the extra output produced by the first, second, . . . unit of labor. The competitively determined general wage level at 10 units of labor is $20 per unit, equal to the marginal productivity of the tenth unit. The labor demand curve shifts up and out over time with capital accumulation, technological advance, and improvements in labor quality.

The quality of labor inputs refers to the literacy, education, training, and skills of the labor force. A country with an illiterate work force can hardly hope to employ modern technologies that require use of sophisticated computers and machinery. Years of education are necessary to produce an engineer capable of designing precision equipment. A decade of training must precede the ability to perform successful brain surgery. Such accumulations of human capital provide a substantial boost to the productivity of labor.

The quantity and quality of cooperating factors will also affect labor's productivity. Wages are high in the United States in part because the nation is well endowed with fertile land and other resources. Advanced countries have accumulated substantial capital stocks: dense networks of roads, rails, and telecommunications; substantial amounts of plant and equipment for each worker; and adequate inventories of spare parts. In poor countries, by contrast, roads are often unpaved and narrow, factories are generally crowded and hot, and equipment is outmoded and about to fall apart.

But the quantity and quality of inputs does not tell the whole story. Two regions may have similar resources and labor inputs, but if one uses superior managerial and technological methods, its productivity may be much higher. Britain has ample resources and a highly educated labor force, but poor management and labor strife have so hobbled Britain in the industrial race that its productivity is less than one-half that of North America. Superior technological methods arise from better basic and applied science, advanced engineering designs, and better management.

Ultimately, the combination of higher-quality labor, capital accumulation, and technological advance produces an enormous boost to labor's productivity and to the demand for labor. More than anything else, these factors lie behind the relatively high wages of advanced regions shown in Table 14-1.

Supply of Labor

Determinants of Supply

Now turn to the supply side of the labor market. Labor supply refers to the number of hours that the population desires to work in gainful activities in factories, farms, businesses, government, or not-for-profit establishments. The major determinants of labor supply are the size of the population and the way the population spends its time.

Population. Population is determined both by natural births and deaths and by immigration. Begin with the migration of labor. Before this century, the borders of most countries were open to population movement, and people left low-wage regions in search of better economic opportunities. The result was a tendency to equalize wages in different countries.

After World War I, however, laws were passed that severely limited immigration. By keeping labor supply down, a restrictive immigration policy tends to keep wages high. This interference exemplifies a basic point about the competitive determination of wages: Limiting the supply of any grade of labor relative to all other productive factors can be expected to raise its wage rate. An increase in labor supply will, other things being equal, tend to depress wage rates.

Given the downward-sloping demand for labor, it is understandable that labor unions are opposed to relaxed immigration and would like to close the borders to illegal immigration. Why might businesses be more favorable to immigration than workers are?

What about the natural increase in population? For the most part, population growth in advanced economies responds to a wide variety of religious, social, and economic factors. As a result of social trends such as the higher labor-force participation rate of women, smaller families, and later marriages, the natural growth of population in the United States and many advanced countries today is close to zero.

Labor-Force Participation and Hours Worked. What is the effect of economic conditions on the number of hours worked per year or the number of years worked per lifetime? There are many complex social and political forces at work here, in addition to the economic ones.

One of the most dramatic developments in recent decades has been the rise in women's labor-force participation. Why did the labor-force participation rate of women (i.e., the fraction of women over 15 in the labor force) jump from 40 percent in the mid-1960s to 58 percent in 1990? This explosion cannot be explained by economic analysis alone. To understand such a significant change in working patterns, one must look outside the narrow scope of economics—to changing social attitudes toward the role of women as mothers, homemakers, and workers.

"Substitution Effect" vs. "Income Effect." In analyzing labor supply, one of the most important issues is how labor responds to higher wages. What will be the effect of higher wages on the number of hours worked per lifetime? The supply curve of labor in Figure 14-3 shows one response. Note how the supply curve rises at first in a northeasterly direction; then at the critical point *C*, it begins to bend back in a northwesterly direction. How can we explain why higher wages may first increase and then decrease the quantity of labor supplied?

Put yourself in the shoes of a worker who has just been offered higher hourly rates and is free to choose the number of hours to be worked. You are tugged in two different directions. On the one hand, you are affected by the *substitution effect*, which tempts you to work longer hours because each hour of work is now better paid. Each hour of leisure has become more expensive, and you are therefore tempted to substitute extra work for leisure.

But acting against the substitution effect is the *income effect*.[2] With the higher wage, your income is higher. With a higher income, you will want to buy more goods and services and in addition you will also want more leisure time. You can afford to take a week's vacation in the winter or an extra week in the summer, or to retire earlier than you otherwise would.

Which will be more powerful, the substitution effect or the income effect? There is no single correct answer; it depends upon the individual. In the case shown in Figure 14-3, for all wage rates up to point *C*, labor supplied increases with a higher wage: the substitution effect outweighs the income effect. But from point *C* upward, the income effect outweighs the substitution effect, and labor supplied declines as wage rates climb higher.

Backward-Bending Supply Curve

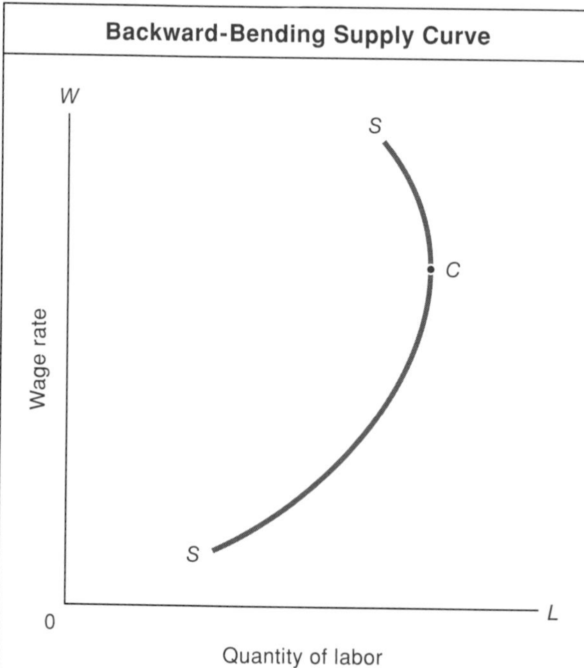

Figure 14-3. As wages rise, workers may work fewer hours

Above the critical point *C*, raising the wage rate reduces the amount of labor supplied as the income effect outweighs the substitution effect. Why? Because at higher wages workers can afford more leisure even though each extra hour of leisure costs more in wages forgone.

Empirical Findings

We often need to know the exact shape or elasticity of the labor supply curve. Will tax cuts on wages increase or decrease labor supply?[3] Will more generous welfare payments encourage or discourage work? These vital questions have interested public-policy economists attempting to propose sound policies to legislatures and presidents.

Table 14-2 presents a summary of numerous studies of the subject. This survey shows that the labor supply curve for adult males appears to be slightly backward-bending, while the response of other demographic groups looks more like a conventional upward-sloping supply curve. For the population as a whole, labor supply appears to respond very little to a change in real wages.

[2] See Chapter 6 for a discussion of substitution and income effects in connection with consumption.

[3] A group known as "supply-side economists" contend that high tax rates reduce output because they discourage the supply of labor and capital. This would occur because higher tax rates produce lower after-tax returns. Note the paradox in Fig. 14-3 that a tax cut might *decrease* labor supplied if the after-tax wage lay above point C. In that region a reduction in the tax on wages would increase the after-tax wage and decrease the amount of labor supplied.

Labor-Supply Patterns

Group of workers	Labor-force participation rate (% of population) 1960	1990	Response of labor supply to increase in real wages
Adult males	86	76	Supply curve found to be backward-bending in most studies. Thus income effect dominates substitution effect. Supply elasticity is relatively small, in the order of −0.1 to −0.2. Thus a 10 percent increase in real wage would lead to a 1 to 2 percent reduction in labor supplied.
Adult females	38	58	Most studies find positive effect of labor supplied in response to higher real wage.
Teenagers	46	54	Highly variable response. Weight of evidence is that labor supply generally responds positively to higher wages.
Entire population 16 years and over	59	67	Elasticity of total labor supply close to zero, with income effects just balancing out substitution effects. Estimated labor supply elasticity for entire population is in the range from 0 to 0.2.

Table 14-2. Empirical estimates of labor-supply responses

Economists have devoted careful study to the response of labor supply to real wages. For males, the supply curve looks firmly backward-bending, while teenagers and adult females generally respond positively to wages. For the economy as a whole, the labor supply curve is close to vertical.

Wage Differences across Groups

Having studied the general wage level, we turn now to the vital problem of wage differentials among different categories of people and jobs. Why is it that doctors earn 15 or 20 times more than lifeguards when both are saving lives? Why do workers in Alaska earn 25 percent more than those working in the same jobs in the lower 48 states?

We can start by examining patterns of wages and compensation in different industries. As is shown in Table 14-3, there is a wide range of wage rates among broad industry groups. Smaller, nonunionized sectors such as farming or retail trade tend to have low wages, while the larger firms in manufacturing and communications have wage levels 2 or 3 times higher.

To explain the wage differences across industries or individuals we must examine the influence of four factors: compensating differentials, differences in labor quality, unique elements, and labor market segmentation.

Compensating Wage Differentials

Some of the tremendous wage differentials observed in everyday life arise because of differences in the quality of jobs. Jobs differ in their attractiveness; hence wages may have to be raised to coax people into the less attractive jobs.

Compensation by Industry, 1988

Industry	Average wages per full-time employee (in $)	Average hourly earnings (in $)
Farming	12,100	—
Mining	34,900	13.27
Manufacturing	27,600	10.18
Steel mills	—	14.72
Communication	35,500	12.76
Retail trade	15,100	6.31
Variety stores	—	4.99
Services	22,300	8.91
Government	25,200	—

Table 14-3. Wages and compensation in different sectors

Average wages and salaries varied by broad industry groups from a high of $35,500 in communication to a low of $12,100 in farming. Among narrow industry groups, we see that average hourly earnings vary by a factor of 3 between the steel industry and variety stores. (Source: U.S. Department of Labor, Bureau of Labor Statistics, *Employment and Earnings;* U.S. Department of Commerce.)

Wage differentials that serve to compensate for the relative attractiveness, or nonmonetary differences, among jobs are called **compensating differentials.**

Window washers must be paid more than janitors because of the risks of climbing skyscrapers. Workers often receive 5 percent extra pay on the 4 P.M. to 12 P.M. "swing shift" and 10 percent extra pay for the 12 midnight to 8 A.M. "graveyard shift." For hours beyond 40 per week or for holiday and weekend work, $1\frac{1}{2}$ to 2 times the base hourly pay is customary. And when you read that doctors earn $150,000 a year, note that part of this is a compensating differential needed to induce people to incur many years of costs and training.

Jobs that involve hard physical labor, tedium, low social prestige, irregular employment, seasonal layoff, and physical risk all tend to be less attractive. No wonder, then, that companies must pay $50,000 or $80,000 a year to recruit people to work at dangerous and lonely jobs on offshore oil platforms. Similarly, for jobs that are especially pleasant or psychologically rewarding, such as those of park rangers and the clergy, pay levels tend to be modest.

To test whether a given difference in pay between two jobs is a compensating differential, ask people who are well qualified for both jobs: "Would you take the higher-paying job in preference to the lower?" If they are not eager to make such a choice, then it is fair to conclude that the higher-paid job is not really more attractive when due weight is given to all nonmonetary and monetary considerations.

Differences in Labor Quality

We have just seen that some wage differentials serve to compensate for the differing degrees of attractiveness of different jobs. But look around you. Clearly many high-paying jobs are more pleasant, not less pleasant, than low-paying work. We must look to factors beyond compensating differentials to explain most wage differentials.

One key to wage disparities lies in the tremendous qualitative differences among people—traceable to differences in innate mental and physical abilities, education and training, and experience. A biologist might classify all of us as members of the species *Homo sapiens*, but a personnel officer would insist that people differ enormously in their abilities to contribute to a firm's profits.

Many of the differences in labor quality are determined outside the labor force, by genetic nature or social nurture. Another important factor is *human capital*, a term that denotes the stock of useful and valuable knowledge built up in the process of education and training. Doctors, lawyers, and engineers invest many years in their formal education and on-the-job training. They spend vast sums on tuition and wages forgone—investing $100,000 to $200,000 in college and graduate training—and often work long hours. Part of the high salaries of these professions should be viewed as a return on their investment in human capital—a return on the education that makes these highly trained workers a very special kind of labor.

Rent Elements in Wages of Unique Individuals

For the lucky few, fame has lifted incomes to astronomical levels. Reported annual earnings for these stars include such enormous figures as $57 million for entertainer Bill Cosby, $5.3 million a year for baseball's Roger Clemens, $3.2 million for basketball star Michael Jordon, and $1.4 million for tennis player Martina Navratilova. Former Secretary of State Henry Kissinger is reported to bill at least $25,000 per appearance.

These extremely talented people have a particular skill that is highly valued in today's economy. Outside their specialization, they might earn only one-tenth as much. Moreover, their labor supply may be completely unaffected by their wage rate, indicating that their labor supply curve is completely inelastic or vertical for wages 20 or 80 or 120 percent of their high compensation levels. Economists term the excess of these wages above their best available incomes in other occupations a *pure economic rent*, for they are logically the same as the rent on land which is fixed in supply. Because the labor supply of these top consultants or baseball players or musicians is completely inelastic, their efforts will respond little to tax rates of 50 or 60 or 70 percent. Even when the net reward for their services is reduced by taxes or by market forces, they will continue to consult or play or sing.

Noncompeting Groups in the Labor Market

Even in a world of perfect competition, where people could move easily from one occupation to another, substantial wage differentials would appear.

These differentials would be necessary to reflect differences in the costs of education and training or in the unattractiveness of certain occupations or as rewards for unique talents.

But after accounting for all these reasons for wage differentials, we still find a large disparity in wage rates. The major reason for the difference is that labor markets are segmented into *noncompeting groups*. This fact was first pointed out by J. E. Cairnes a century ago when he wrote:

> What we find, in effect, is not a whole population competing indiscriminately for all occupations, but a series of industrial layers, superimposed on one another, . . . while those occupying the several strata are, for all purposes of effective competition, practically isolated from each other.[4]

In other words, instead of being a single factor of production, labor is many different, but closely related, factors of production. Doctors and mathematicians, for example, are noncompeting groups because it is difficult and costly for a member of one profession to enter into the other. Just as there are many different kinds of machines, each commanding a different price, so are there many different occupations and skills that compete only in a general way. Once we recognize the existence of many different submarkets of the labor market, we can see why wages may differ greatly among groups.

Why is the labor market divided into so many noncompeting groups? The major reason is that, for professions and skilled trades, it takes a large investment of time and money to become proficient. Economists can hardly hope to become cardiovascular surgeons overnight. Nor are surgeons trained to frame a house or lay a neat row of bricks. Hence, once people specialize in a particular occupation, they become part of a particular labor submarket. They are thereby subject to the supply and demand for that skill and will find that their own labor earnings rise and fall depending upon events in that occupation and industry. With this segmentation, the wages for one occupation can diverge substantially from wages in other areas.

In addition, the theory of noncompeting groups helps us understand labor market discrimination. We will see in the second section of this chapter that much discrimination arises because, by custom, law, or prejudice, workers are separated by gender, race, or ethnic background into noncompeting groups.

While the theory of noncompeting groups highlights an important aspect of labor markets, we must nonetheless recognize that some competition always exists. Just as you decide whether to rent a modern computerized tractor or hire a horse to plough your field, so you must choose between hiring a high-paid professional and a low-paid, less skilled worker. Similarly, if carpenters began to earn $200,000 per year, I might study the craft and quit being a teacher. In the long run, as people enter high-wage sectors and leave low-wage sectors, competition will beat down most of the barriers to noncompeting groups.

General Equilibrium in the Labor Market

We have seen that several forces tend to create wage differentials—those needed to compensate for different levels of unpleasantness, returns on human capital, differences in skill and talents, and segmentation of the market into noncompeting groups.

Studies of wage behavior indicate that wage differentials are surprisingly persistent. Whether we examine the relative wages of men and women, of blue-collar and white-collar workers, or of workers in different industries, we see that relative wages change very slowly from year to year.

But wage differentials are not cast in concrete. As people move into high-paying occupations and leave those that pay less, as the barriers to equal access for all groups slowly erode—as these slow-moving forces come into play, we see some tendency for wages to converge.

But for such differentials as remain, how exactly are they determined? The answer is provided by supply and demand: The market will tend toward that equilibrium pattern of wage differentials at which the total demand for each category of labor exactly matches its competitive supply. Only then will there be general equilibrium with no tendency for further widening or narrowing of wage differentials. Table 14-4 sums up our conclusions about competitive wage determination.

[4] J. E. Cairnes, *Some Leading Principles of Political Economy* (Macmillan, London, 1874), p. 72.

Summary of Competitive Wage Determination

Labor situation	Wage result
1. People all alike—jobs all alike.	No wage differentials.
2. People all alike—jobs differ in attractiveness.	Compensating wage differentials.
3. People differ, but each type of labor is in unchangeable supply ("noncompeting groups").	Wage differentials that are "pure economic rents."
4. People differ, but there is some mobility among groups ("partially competing groups").	General-equilibrium pattern of wage differentials as determined by general demand and supply (includes 1–3 as special cases).

Table 14-4. Market wage structure shows great variety of patterns under competition

Two Classical Views

The classical economists of an earlier age were fascinated by the general trend of wages and by the impacts of social legislation upon wages. Two important theories shaped views about social and economic policy during the nineteenth century and continue to have relevance today, so we review them here.

The Iron Law of Wages: Malthus and Marx

According to the Malthusian theory of population, the size of population will grow very rapidly whenever wages rise above the subsistence level (*subsistence wages* being the minimal level needed to support a person's life). In this theory, the labor supply curve should be horizontal at the subsistence wage level, which is sometimes called *the iron law of wages.*

Malthus' gloomy doctrine exerted a powerful impact upon social reformers of the nineteenth century, for this view predicted that any improvement in the living standards of the working classes would be eaten up by population increase. But a brief look at economic history shows that, in Europe and North America, people do not inevitably reproduce so rapidly that their incomes are relentlessly forced back to a bare minimum. However, perhaps there is a germ of truth in Malthus' views for the poorer countries today.

The Reserve Army of the Unemployed. Karl Marx devised quite a different version of the iron law of wages. He put great emphasis upon the "reserve army of the unemployed." In effect, employers led their workers to the factory windows and pointed to the unemployed workers outside, eager to work for less. This, Marx is interpreted to have thought, would depress wages to the subsistence level.

This view is illustrated in Figure 14-4. Suppose that the wage is pegged at $15 per hour. Employment is at the level indicated by point *A*. At this high wage, there would indeed be unemployment; the amount of unemployment would be represented by the distance *AB* between the labor sup-

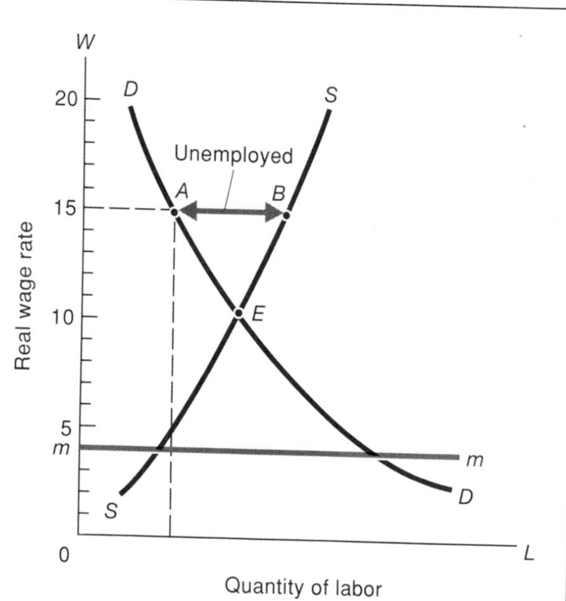

Figure 14-4. Marxists exaggerate the power of "reserve army of unemployed" to depress wages

The "reserve army of the unemployed"— as shown by *AB*—is not able to depress real wages to the minimum-subsistence level at *mm*. In a competitive labor market, the reserve army can depress wages only to equilibrium level *E*. If labor supply became so abundant that supply and demand were in equilibrium at *mm*, the wage would be at a minimum level, as in many underdeveloped countries.

plied and demanded. In our simple, idealized model of competition, such unemployment could certainly be expected to put downward pressure on wages.

But does the basic Marxian conclusion follow? Is there any tendency for real wage rates to fall to a minimum-subsistence level such as *mm* in Figure 14-4? None at all. Wage rates need never fall below the equilibrium level at *E*. In a country well endowed with technology, capital, and natural resources, this competitively determined equilibrium wage might be a very comfortable one indeed. We therefore reach an important conclusion: If competition in the labor market were really perfect, there would be no necessary tendency in an advanced country for wages to fall toward the minimum-subsistence level.

Employers might prefer to pay low wages, but that would not matter. In a competitive market, they are unable to set wage rates as they would like. As long as employers are numerous and do not act in collusion, their demands for any grade of labor will bid its wage up to the equilibrium level at which the total forthcoming labor supply is absorbed. The workers may aspire to still higher wages, but under competition they do not get what they would like; as long as they do not act collusively to limit the labor supply, their wishes will not serve to make wages rise above the competitive level.

The Lump-of-Labor Fallacy

In periods of high unemployment, people often think that a solution lies in spreading the existing amount of work more evenly. In Europe during the 1980s, for example, many labor unions proposed that the workweek be reduced to spread the declining employment among more workers. This view—that the total amount of work to be done is fixed—was sometimes espoused by classical economists and is called the "lump-of-labor fallacy."

To begin with, we must give this notion its due. To a particular group of workers, who have special skills and are stuck in one region, a reduction in the demand for labor may indeed pose a threat to their jobs. As long as wages and prices adjust slowly, these workers may face prolonged spells of unemployment. Viewed from their personal standpoint, the lump-of-labor notion may not be so fallacious. Moreover, in a major depression, when there is mass and chronic unemployment, one can understand how workers generally may yield to a lump-of-labor philosophy.

But the lump-of-labor argument implies that there is only so much useful remunerative work to be done in any economic system, and this is indeed a fallacy. A look at history in many different countries shows that there is no fixed lump of labor to be distributed—there is no need to ration out scarce work among the army of unemployed workers. It is more correct to say that an economy can adjust to create jobs for willing workers. In the longer run, as prices and wages adjust to changes in technology and tastes, jobs will come to workers or workers will move to jobs. And in the short run, this process can be lubricated by appropriate macroeconomic policies.

● We have now completed our analysis of the basic forces driving wages—both their overall levels and wage differentials among different groups. In the next section we apply these concepts to one of the most important issues of labor market policy—discrimination. ●

B. Discrimination by Race and Gender

Most of the world is nonwhite. But the white minority controls most of the economic power and enjoys a disproportionately high standard of living. Within the most advanced economic society, the United States, black citizens have long experienced a measurably lower level of income and wealth than other groups. Many other minority groups also earn markedly less than do white Americans.

Half the population is female. How is it that a woman who has the same amount of schooling as a man, the same test scores, the same social background, nonetheless ends up with a salary only two-thirds of what her brother of similar abilities gets?

Some earnings differentials arise from differences in education, work experience, and other factors; earnings disparities are inevitable in a market economy. But even after correction for such differences, a gap remains between the wages of white males and those of other groups—at least part of which is due to discrimination. In this section, we see how discrimination affects labor markets and incomes.

Earnings differentials are a universal feature of a market economy. But when a difference in earnings arises simply because of an irrelevant personal characteristic—such as race, gender, or religion—we call this **discrimination.**

Historical Roots

In the United States, discrimination has its roots in the early beliefs and institutions of society. British settlers became the dominant elite in New England 300 years ago. When other nationalities arrived, they were resented and were often kept out of the best jobs. Lodging houses and job advertisements often displayed notices such as: "No dogs or Germans need apply." Yet with time each new wave of immigrants became assimilated and accepted, working their way up from Ellis Island to corporate boardrooms and the halls of Congress.

This cheerful view of American history cannot, however, apply to all ethnic groups. American Indians resided in America long before the British; Spanish conquistadors were the first European settlers in the new world; more than 100 years have elapsed since the Emancipation Proclamation freed the slaves. Yet for these ethnic groups, discrimination in the labor market, housing, and other community activities remains a barrier to economic and social advancement.

The history of black Americans will illustrate how social processes depressed their incomes and economic status. After slavery was abolished, the black population in the south quickly fell into a caste system of peonage under "Jim Crow" legislation. Even though legally free and subject to the laws of supply and demand, black workers had average earnings far below those of whites. Why? Because, as we will see shortly, they were shunted off into menial, low-skilled occupations—into low-wage noncompeting groups. Most of the well-paid jobs were simply not open to blacks because of inferior schooling or exclusion by trade unions.

Graphical Analysis of Discrimination

Supply and demand can illustrate how exclusion lowers the incomes of groups that are targets of discrimination. Under discrimination, certain jobs are reserved for the privileged group, as is depicted in Figure 14-5(*a*). In this labor market, the supply of privileged white workers is shown by $S_w S_w$, while the demand for such labor is depicted as $D_w D_w$. Equilibrium wages occur at the high level shown at E_w.

Meanwhile, Figure 14-5(*b*) shows what is happening in the low-paid service sector or in un-

Effects of Discriminatory Exclusion

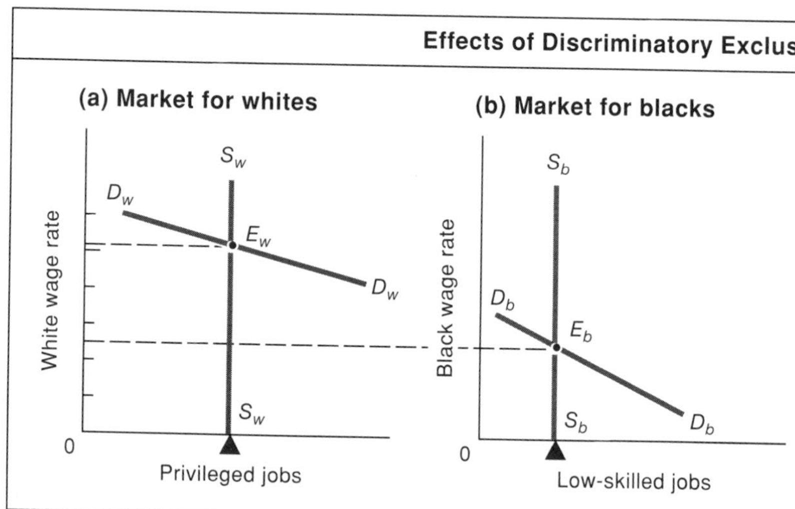

Figure 14-5. Discrimination by exclusion lowers the wage rates of blacks
Discrimination is often enforced by excluding certain groups from privileged jobs. If blacks are excluded from good jobs in market **(a)**, they must work in inferior jobs in **(b)**. Whites then end up with high wage rates at E_w while blacks earn low wage rates at E_b in market **(b)**.

skilled jobs. Black workers live in areas with poor schools and cannot afford private education, so they do not receive training for the high-paying jobs. With low levels of skills, they have low marginal revenue products in the low-skilled jobs, so their wages are depressed to the low-wage equilibrium at E_b.

Note the differential between the two markets. Exclusion has discriminated against the earning power of black workers. Because of blacks' exclusion from good jobs, market forces decreed that they would earn much lower wages than the privileged white workers. Someone might even argue that blacks "deserve" lower wages because their competitive marginal revenue products are lower. But this observation overlooks the root of the wage differentials, which is that wage differences arose because certain groups were excluded from the good jobs by their inability to obtain education and training and by the force of custom, law, or collusion.

Labor Market Segmentation, 1981

Occupation	Percentage of females
High-paid occupations:	
Sales agents, wholesale	10.7
Stock and bond salespersons	17.2
Engineering technicians	17.8
Managers and administrators	28.4
Low-paid occupations:	
Nurses' aides	84.4
Hairdressers and beauticians	84.9
Child care workers outside home	86.7
Sewers and stitchers	96.7
Practical nurses	97.7

Table 14-5. Many high-paid occupations are reserved for men

Discrimination today seldom occurs because women get lower wages for the same job. Rather, women have been limited to lower-paying occupations. Overall, the average earnings of women are only 65 percent of those of men. (Source: U.S. Department of Labor, Bureau of Labor Statistics, "Analyzing 1981 Earnings Data from the Current Population Survey," September 1982.)

Economic Discrimination against Women

The largest group to suffer from economic discrimination is women. Even year-round, full-time female workers on average earn only 65 percent as much as men of comparable education and background.

The pattern of earnings is clear. Female college graduates earn about the same amount as male high school graduates. Although white males generally receive increases in annual earnings as they grow older, income profiles show that women in their late twenties earn as much on the average as do older women.

What are the sources of income differentials between men and women? The reasons are complex, grounded in social customs and expectations as well as in economic factors such as education, training, and work experience. In general, women do not earn less than men because they are paid less for the same job. In part, the lower pay of women arose because women were excluded from certain high-paying professions, such as engineering, construction, and coal mining. In addition, women tended to interrupt their careers to have children and perform household duties. Also, economic inequality of the sexes was maintained because, until recently, few women were elected to the boards of directors of large corporations, to senior partnerships in major law firms, or to tenured professorships in top universities.

Like minority groups, then, women are often found in low-paying noncompeting groups (see Figure 14-5). The extent of labor market segmentation is detailed in Table 14-5, which shows the fraction of women in selected high-paying and low-paying occupations. To understand discrimination, we should avoid simple explanations like the picture of employers simply beating down the wage demands of women or blacks or Hispanics; rather, discrimination involves subtle exclusionary processes that prevent certain groups from participating fully in all occupations.

Empirical Evidence

Having analyzed the mechanisms by which the political process and the market economy enforce discrimination against women and minority groups, let's examine the size of earnings differentials. Table 14-6 shows the ratio of total annual earnings of males and females of different minority groups relative to those of white males. On average, earnings differentials are greatest for women and for black and Indian men as well as for men of Hispanic background. Note that women are generally penalized in the labor market only once; many minority women show earnings close to those of white women.

Discrimination vs. Personal Characteristics. It is important to understand that earnings differentials among different groups are not entirely due to discrimination. The first part of this chapter noted that there are differences in quality of labor. Black workers have historically received less education than have whites; women customarily spend more time out of the labor force than do men. Since both education and continuing work experience are linked to higher pay, it is not surprising that *some* earnings differentials exist.

Economists in recent years have conducted numerous empirical studies that attempt to separate the earnings differentials due to measurable characteristics (education, experience, etc.) from those due to discrimination and other factors. Studies indicate that from one-half to three-quarters of the male-female wage gap can be explained by differences in education and job experience. This leaves from one-quarter to one-half to be explained by discrimination and other non-measured sources.

Earnings Differentials, 1970

Group	Earnings of group (as percentage of earnings of white males)	
	Males	Females
White	100	49
Japanese-American	99	52
Chinese-American	85	46
American Indian	68	42
Mexican-American	67	36
Black	64	40
Puerto Rican	63	45

Table 14-6. Minorities and women earn substantially less than white males

Data were examined on the total annual earnings of men and women of different minority groups in the United States. These data do not correct for education, labor-force status, or previous work experience. The most disadvantaged minority-group males earn only 63 to 68 percent of white male earnings. Females earn even less, partly because of low wages, partly because of fewer hours worked.

[Source: J. D. Gwartney and J. E. Long, "The Relative Earnings of Blacks and Other Minorities," *Industrial and Labor Relations Review* (April 1978).]

Reducing Labor Market Discrimination

Over the last 25 years, governments have taken numerous steps to end discriminatory practices. But even today, the United States has been unable to eradicate discrimination based on race, sex, and other characteristics.

What approaches are available to combat discrimination? The major steps were legal landmarks, such as the Civil Rights Act of 1964 (which outlaws discrimination in hiring, firing, and employment) and the Equal Pay Act of 1963 (which requires employers to pay men and women equally for the same work).

Such laws helped to dismantle the most blatant discriminatory practices, but more subtle barriers remain. More aggressive and controversial policies include measures such as "affirmative action." This requires employers to show that they are taking extra steps to locate and hire underrepresented groups. This approach, labeled by some as "reverse discrimination," has apparently increased the representation of women and minority groups in some sectors.

Comparable Worth

In the mid-1980s, a new approach to reducing the male-female wage gap was proposed: comparable worth. This idea goes beyond the idea of "equal pay for equal work" to "equal pay for comparable worth." To understand the issue, we analyze wage structures and examine how comparable worth would attempt to equalize wages for different jobs.

Wage Structures. Most large firms administer their internal labor market by setting up a number of different job categories or grades—say, 10 grades of clerical workers, 15 grades of craft workers, 12 grades of technicians, and so forth. Each category carries a job description that varies in terms of characteristics like skill, experience, training, working conditions, etc.

Generally, firms try to set the wage levels with

Equal and Comparable Jobs

	Point scores assigned to different jobs			
	Equal jobs		Comparable jobs	
Job characteristic	Job A	Job B	Job A	Job C
Skill	80	80	80	80
Training	90	90	90	60
Responsibility	150	150	150	60
Working conditions	30	30	30	150
Total points	**350**	**350**	**350**	**350**

Table 14-7. Should comparable jobs receive equal pay?

Jobs A and B are treated as "equal jobs" and must earn equal pay. Jobs A and C have different characteristics, but by a company's point rating system are "comparable jobs." Under comparable-worth doctrine, comparable jobs should earn equal pay even though market supply and demand dictate different wages.

reference to the compensation paid for similar jobs in the relevant external labor market. For example, clerical workers will be paid more or less what other clerical workers earn in the same city, while the salaries of newly minted college professors in economics are determined relative to the national market for economists.

Where no external comparison can be easily made, firms tend to set wages for particular jobs at the level earned by similar jobs. As we will shortly see, firms sometimes assign numerical "point scores" to the skill, experience, and working conditions of jobs and then use these scores to help set wages of noncomparable jobs. Putting the external comparisons and internal evaluations together provides a firm with a wage structure for its different job categories.

Using the notion of a wage structure, we can now understand the difference between jobs of "equal worth" and those of "comparable worth." Table 14-7 shows three jobs—A, B, and C—in a particular company. Jobs A and B are assigned equal ratings on the four job characteristics (skill, training, responsibility, and working conditions). They are then designated as "equal jobs," and under the 1963 Equal Pay Act they must receive the same pay. To pay $250 per week for job A while job B pays $300 per week would represent unlawful discrimination.

Many who advocate breaking down discriminatory practices argue that comparable jobs should also receive equal pay. The last two columns of Table 14-7 show two jobs with an equal number of total points but with differing individual characteristics. Job A might be that of a technician who has major responsibilities over blood samples and who works in pleasant surroundings, while job C could be that of a forklift operator who has little skill or training but works in harsh and noisy conditions. The market wage rate in the local area, driven by ample supply of technicians and sparse supply of forklift drivers, might produce weekly wage rates of $250 for technicians and $400 for forklift operators. Under current law and practice, it would be perfectly legal for a firm to pay those differing market-based wages for comparable but dissimilar jobs.

Enter the comparable-worth doctrine. This holds that pay should be based on what a job is worth. Jobs that have comparable worth—such as A and C in Table 14-7—should be paid equally, and employers' failure to do so, according to this view, should constitute immoral and illegal discrimination. Under this approach, by equalizing wages on jobs that have comparable overall job characteristics, society can reverse decades of discrimination and eliminate the male-female wage gap.

Many analysts find fault with the concept of basing compensation on comparable worth, as exemplified in Table 14-7, rather than on the market. Critics argue that the point system is not an adequate basis for determining wages. Among potential defects in using a point system are that the factors entering the point scores are incomplete and not easily measurable in the marketplace; that a job's attributes are worth differing amounts according to the employer; and that people's disutilities of work (and therefore their required compensating differentials) may vary greatly from person to person.

Most damaging, perhaps, is that thorough investigation of the effect of these measured attributes on wages finds much left to be explained. Even when studies are confined to a single race and sex, they seldom explain more than one-third of the variations of earnings across different people. Using such point scores to predict an employee's worth is like predicting individual baseball batting averages on the basis of a player's height, weight, age, and education.

What would be the likely outcome of introducing comparable worth to determine wages in today's labor markets? The major impact would be the exclusion of market forces from wage determination. If the wages of truck drivers and telephone operators were equalized, we might find a glut of operators with too few willing to deliver the goods. Moreover, wage patterns would be frozen, locking the economy into a wage structure that is relatively unresponsive to economic shocks. If a sudden energy crisis drove up energy prices, companies would be unable to raise the relative wages of oil-drilling roustabouts and coal miners. While wage rates and pay structures tend to show considerable short-run stickiness in a modern economy, over the long run wages do adjust to major gluts and shortages in particular markets. Comparable worth would gum up an already sticky wage structure.

It should be emphasized that comparable worth is not an arcane idea confined to economics textbooks. Many unions, particularly those in which women are heavily represented, have raised the banner of comparable worth as a negotiating issue. And the courts have sometimes ruled that comparable worth is an appropriate solution to the stubborn male-female wage gap. Comparable worth is likely to persist for many years as a central public-policy issue for labor markets.

Slow Progress

Discrimination is a complex social and economic process. It is rooted in social customs and was enforced by laws that denied disadvantaged groups a decent education and good jobs. Even after equality was established by law, separation of races and sexes perpetuated social and economic stratification.

But progress is being made. In recent years, members of disadvantaged groups have entered the best educational institutions and the highest-paying professions in large numbers. For example, among those under 35 years of age, women now constitute 41 percent of mathematicians and computer scientists, 29 percent of lawyers and judges, and half of managerial and professional workers. Figure 14-6 shows the slow progress toward closing the earnings gap between black and white members of the population. But substantial differences in incomes, wealth, and jobs persist.

In sum, careful studies have convinced most analysts that objective differences explain only part of the income differentials between white men and other groups. Under such circumstances, beating down the walls of occupational protection, allowing noncompeting groups to compete, enforcing laws of equal opportunity—all these measures may help remove the stigma and economic losses of discrimination.

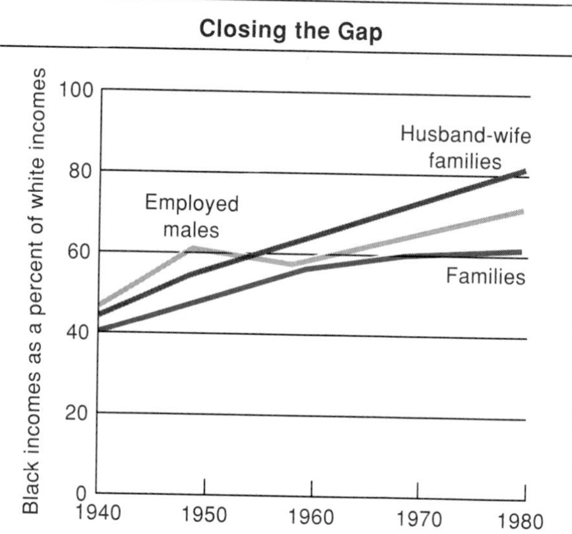

Figure 14-6. Black family income and male earnings as a percent of white earnings

The gap between whites and blacks has closed slowly in recent decades in the United States. Intact families have made the most progress, but the average family income of blacks has not succeeded in closing the gap in recent years because of the growing number of one-adult black families. (Source: RAND Corporation.)

SUMMARY

A. Wage Determination under Perfect Competition

1. In perfectly competitive equilibrium, if all people and jobs were exactly alike, there would be no wage differentials. The equilibrium wage rates determined by supply and demand would all be equal.
2. The demand for labor, as for any factor of production, is determined by labor's marginal product. A country or region will show a higher marginal product of labor and higher wages when the quality of labor inputs is higher, when the quality and quantity of cooperating inputs is greater, and when that area has access to more advanced knowledge and production techniques.
3. The supply of labor has four dimensions: population size, percentage of people gainfully employed, average number of hours worked, and quality of productive effort.
4. As wages rise, there are two opposite effects on the supply of labor. The substitution effect tempts each worker to work longer because of the higher pay for each hour of work. The income effect operates in the opposite direction because higher wages mean that workers can now afford more leisure time along with other good things of life. At some critical wage, the supply curve may bend backward. The labor supply of very gifted, unique people is quite inelastic: their wages are largely pure economic rent.
5. Once we drop unrealistic assumptions concerning the uniformity of people and jobs, we find substantial wage differentials even in a perfectly competitive labor market. Compensating wage differentials, which compensate for nonmonetary differences in the quality of jobs, explain some (but by no means all) of the differentials. But differences in the quality of various grades of labor are probably the most important cause of wage differences. Although it cannot be claimed that labor consists of wholly noncompeting groups, it is nonetheless true that there are innumerable categories of partially competing groups. The final pattern of wages would, in a perfectly competitive labor market, be determined by the general equilibrium of the interrelated schedules of supply and demand, as shown in Table 14-4.
6. Fear of unemployment often leads to acceptance of the lump-of-labor fallacy. This belief, that there is only a fixed amount of useful work to be done, may arise from experiencing technological unemployment or depression. It lies behind much of the agitation for a shorter workweek and "work-sharing" proposals. But excessively high unemployment calls for macroeconomic policies to expand employment, not for policies to decrease the supply of labor.

B. Discrimination by Race and Gender

7. By an accident of history, the minority of white males in the world has enjoyed the greatest affluence. Even a century after the abolition of slavery, inequality of opportunity and economic, racial, and sex discrimination can

be shown, by the tools of competitive supply and demand, to lead to loss of income by the underprivileged groups.

8. There are many routes to discrimination, but the most important may be the creation of noncompeting groups. By segmenting labor markets, reserving managerial positions for white men while relegating women and minorities to menial, dead-end jobs, an economy can allow inequality of earnings to persist for decades.

9. Steps to reduce labor market discrimination have been taken in many directions. Early approaches focused on outlawing discriminatory practices, while later steps mandated policies such as affirmative action. Recently, advocates of comparable worth have argued that jobs with similar value but different job characteristics should receive equal pay even if supply and demand dictate otherwise. Critics of comparable worth foresee gluts and shortages if the externally imposed comparable-worth wages differ markedly from the equilibrium of supply and demand.

CONCEPTS FOR REVIEW

Wage determination under perfect competition

elements in demand for labor: labor quality, other inputs, technology
elements in supply of labor: population, labor-force participation, hours, quality
backward-bending supply curve
income vs. substitution effect
rent element in wages
compensating differentials in wages
segmented markets and noncompeting groups
the iron law of wages of Malthus and Marx
lump-of-labor fallacy

Discrimination in labor markets

discrimination
equal jobs vs. comparable worth
earnings differentials: quality differences vs. discrimination

QUESTIONS FOR DISCUSSION

1. Make sure you understand the concepts of compensating differentials, pure economic rent, and noncompeting groups. Give examples of each from history or today's world.
2. Earnings in the United States average $450 per week, while in India workers earn but $20 per week. What forces lie behind the supply and demand for labor in the two countries that would produce such a large difference? What might India do to raise its wage level?
3. Explain what would happen to wage differentials as a result of each of the following:
   (a) Less imperfect competition among people with similar labor skills
   (b) Free migration among regions in a country
   (c) Introduction of free public education into a country where education had previously been private and expensive
   (d) A drop in popularity of television sports and entertainment programs featuring prominent stars
4. Using supply and demand, explain the impact of immigration on labor supply, quantity of labor supplied, and wage rates. Can you use this analysis to help explain why labor leaders often oppose higher levels of immigration? Also use a similar line of reasoning to explain the old labor jingle:

   Whether you work by the week or the day
   The shorter the work the better the pay.

5. Modern economic theory of discrimination states that disadvantaged groups like women or blacks have low incomes or poor jobs because they are segmented into low-wage markets. Explain how each of the following practices, which prevailed in some cases into the 1970s, helped perpetuate discriminatory labor market segmentation:
   (a) Many state schools would not allow women to

major in engineering.

(b) Many top schools would not admit women.

(c) Blacks and whites received schooling in separate school systems.

(d) Elite social clubs would not admit women, blacks, or Catholics.

(e) Many high-paid jobs (coal mining, fire fighting, construction, etc.) were thought too "tough" for women.

6. What steps could be taken to break down the segmented markets shown in Table 14-5?

7. In Europe of the 1980s, many labor groups pushed for lowering the average workweek because of the prevalence of high unemployment. What fallacy is at work here? If they succeeded, what would you expect to happen to the real wage?

8. What are the pros and cons of comparable worth? Why might it attract unions representing female workers yet find traditional male-dominated unions unsympathetic?

9. Read footnote 3 in this chapter. Define the before-tax wage as W, the post-tax wage as W_p, and the tax rate as t. Explain the relationship $W_p = (1 - t)W$. Draw up a table showing the before-tax and post-tax wages when the before-tax wage is $10 per hour for tax rates of 0, 15, 25, and 33 percent? Next sketch a supply and demand drawing upon Figure 14-3. For the regions above and below point C, show the impact of a lower tax rate upon labor supplied. In your table, show the relationship between the tax rate and the government's tax revenues.

CHAPTER 15

LABOR UNIONS AND COLLECTIVE BARGAINING

> Our empirical estimates strongly suggest that most, if not all, of the gains of union labor [in the United States] are made at the expense of nonunionized workers, and not at the expense of earning on capital.
>
> Harry G. Johnson and Peter Mieskowski (1970)

From an economic vantage point, labor is not only a central factor of production but also a unique commodity. After all, the economy is ultimately organized to enhance the well-being of people. Since the Civil War, workers cannot be bought; they can only be "rented" for wages. Moreover, workers vary enormously in their characteristics: their strength, intelligence, skill, cheerfulness, industry, and reliability.

The fact that firms rent workers has one fundamental implication: There must be some kind of understanding or *contract* between workers and employers. Sometimes the agreement is extremely casual, such as "If you work out well, the job's yours. The pay is $5 an hour." At the other extreme are tediously negotiated collective bargaining agreements between a group of firms and a union representing several thousand workers. Whether formal or casual, explicit or implicit, it is useful to think of labor "rental" in terms of contracts.

In order to study agreements between workers and firms, we concentrate on one part of the labor market where the negotiation process has been thoroughly analyzed. We focus on the formal agreements that are hammered out between labor unions and management. This discussion of the institutions of the American labor market will serve as a prelude to the analytical issues of labor market imperfections presented in section B.

A. The American Labor Movement

Some nineteen million Americans belong to unions. One-seventh of the labor force is made up of union members. If we exclude white-collar workers, supervisors, and executives, the proportion is higher still. Practically all eligible workers belong to unions in important industries such as rail, steel, autos, and mining. Few large firms avoid being organized by unions.

Growth and Decline

Figure 15-1 shows the growth of union membership since 1900 measured as a percent of the labor force. Note the slow, steady advance up to and during World War I, the explosive acquisition of new members during the New Deal of the 1930s, and the continued rapid growth during World War II. Since

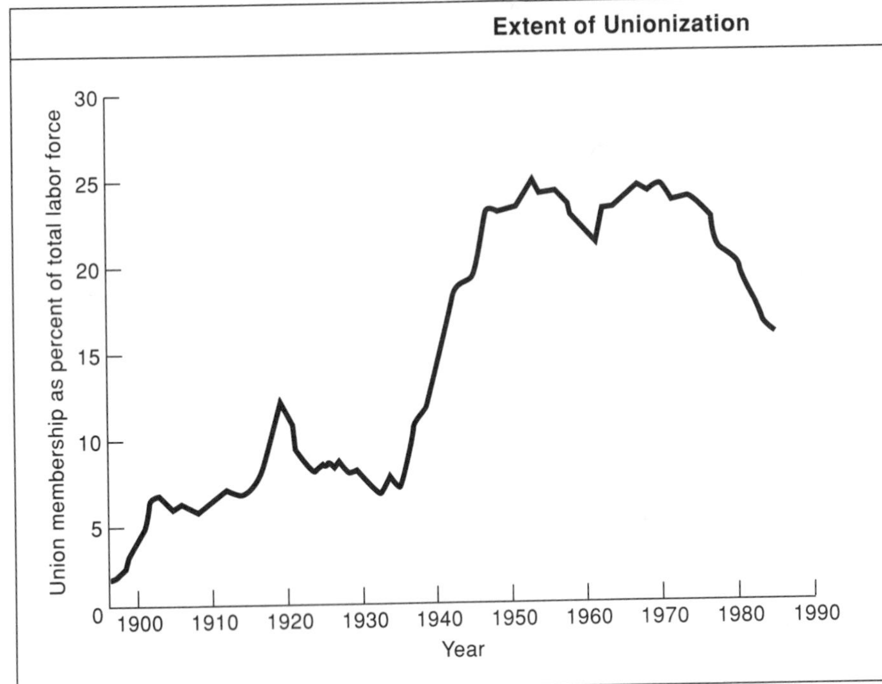

Figure 15-1. Union membership is a declining share of labor force

Of all workers, one-seventh now belong to unions—as against a fourth in 1955. Organized labor has declined sharply in the last two decades because of the declining importance of production workers in manufacturing, mining, and transport—the groups most prone to join unions. (Source: U.S. Department of Labor.)

the early 1970s, the fraction of the labor force belonging to unions in the United States has steadily declined.

Membership statistics understate the influence of unions. Many nonunion employees are covered by union agreements on wages, hours, and work conditions. In many places or industries, union wages and benefits set the standard for nonunion establishments, so that if you work for a nonunion firm you will enjoy many of the benefits of the union sector. In addition, the threat of unionization often convinces management to raise compensation levels.

Brief History of the American Labor Movement

How did labor unions first begin? What are the functions of unions? We begin with a brief history of the American labor movement.

Although the first stirrings of American labor unions predate the Civil War, it was not until the last third of the nineteenth century that labor began to revolt against big business. The first national movement was the Knights of Labor, which began as a secret society that all but "lawyers, bankers, gamblers or liquor dealers, and Pinkerton detectives" could join. Secrecy was dropped and by 1886, the high-water mark of the movement, 700,000 members had joined. The Knights represented an attempt to form one great labor union that would speak for all labor; it was more interested in political reform and social "uplift" than in bread-and-butter issues such as hours and wages. After a few unsuccessful strikes, the Knights declined in membership as rapidly as it had grown. But the lesson of the Knights was not lost on key strategists of the American labor movement: to thrive, unions must concentrate on the economic advancement of their members rather than on reforming society.

In the face of labor organizations like the Knights, employers fought back. They too learned that strength lies in cooperation; they backed up one another by keeping "blacklists" of union sympathizers and refusing to hire labor "agitators." Generally, employers were able to invoke the law on their side to "keep labor peace," and the police or the National Guard was brought in to protect company property. Some companies even hired gunmen and spies to fight unions.[1]

The American Federation of Labor

In 1881, the present-day labor movement began to take shape with the founding of the American Federation of Labor (AFL). For almost half a century until his death in 1924, Samuel Gompers dominated this organization and gave the movement its characteristic pattern. Although he was originally interested in socialist movements, he soon concluded that no movement opposed to capitalism would flourish on American soil. Gompers' main principles were simple:

- He committed the AFL to the principle of *federalism*—in which each national union had sovereignty and "exclusive jurisdiction" over its craft specialty. This meant that the AFL would not tolerate "dual unionism": two unions could not try to organize the same workers, and no group of workers could break away from a recognized national union to form its own union.
- He insisted on *voluntarism*—with labor and firms bargaining over wages, but with government staying out of collective bargaining.
- Gompers insisted on *business unionism*. Under this principle, American unions were to exist primarily to improve the economic status of workers, rather than to engage in a class struggle to alter the form of government or to promote socialism. By and large, American labor unions since Gompers' time have focused on the struggle for higher wages, shorter hours, more vacations, better working conditions, and improved fringe benefits such as pensions and health insurance. American unions were the opposite of the labor movements in many foreign countries—which, like Britain's Labour party, have dominated major political parties and waged the class struggle for major political reforms.

From its beginning, the AFL insisted on organizing *craft unions*, in which workers were grouped on the basis of a particular skill, such as carpentry or bricklaying. This strategy prevented the organization of the huge mass-production industries into a single union. Astute union advocates began to see the handwriting on the wall: *industrial unions* (those organizing an entire industry, such as steel or coal) were the wave of the future; craft unions were a relic of the past. Industrial unions were introduced in 1935 with the formation of the Congress of Industrial Organizations (CIO). Eventually, the AFL began to organize workers on an industrial basis, but its craft unions remained dominant. The AFL and CIO lived in healthy rivalry for two decades until, in 1955, they merged into the AFL-CIO, which is today the major national labor organization in the United States.

National and Local Unions and the AFL-CIO

There are three layers in the structure of American unions:

- The *local* union
- The *national* union
- The *federation* of national unions

To members, the local is the front line of unionism. Members join the local in their plant or town. They pay dues to it. Usually, the local union negotiates the collective bargaining agreement determining their wages and work conditions.

But the local is only a single chapter of the national union. Thus, an autoworker in Pontiac belongs to the local union there, which is one of hundreds of local chapters of the United Auto Workers.

Most unions belong to the AFL-CIO. Although the public thinks of the federation as the most important element of the labor movement, in reality, the AFL-CIO is the public-relations and lobbying arm for its affiliated unions and depends on its members for financial support. The AFL-CIO's power is strictly limited. Like members of the Security Council of the United Nations, each national union insists upon its "sovereignty," "right of veto," and "exclusive jurisdiction" over workers in its sphere.

[1] The chief weapons used by employers to fight unions have been (1) discriminatory discharge of union members, (2) the blacklist, (3) the "yellow-dog" contract (requiring agreement in advance not to join a union), (4) the labor spy, (5) the strikebreaker and armed guards, (6) conspiracy of town merchants, police, and judges against organizers and would-be union joiners, (7) company unions, in which the company would control the decisions of the workers' association, and (8) court injunctions.

Because national unions retain so much power, the AFL-CIO is today mainly a figurehead.

How Collective Bargaining Works

The wages and fringe benefits of unionized workers are determined by **collective bargaining.** This is the process of negotiation between representatives of firms and workers for the purpose of establishing mutually agreeable conditions of employment.

The first step in collective bargaining is union certification. Consider a production-line worker in a factory that is being organized. An AFL-CIO union has petitioned the National Labor Relations Board (NLRB) for an election to determine who will represent workers in this plant. The worker marks a secret ballot in favor of the union, and the union wins a majority. The NLRB then certifies the new union as the collective bargaining agent for the plant, prohibiting any other union from negotiating directly with management.

A day is set for the new union representatives to meet with management at the bargaining table. Seated at the table will probably be a company vice-president in charge of industrial relations; with her will be attorneys from a law firm that specializes in labor law. On the union side will be the local business agent of the union, a small committee of union officers, and an expert on negotiations from union headquarters.

What Are the Issues?

We have all heard of the last-minute, all-night sessions before a labor agreement is reached. What is actually in this agreement?

The central part, of course, is the *economic package*. This includes the basic wage rates for different job categories and the overtime rates, along with the rules for holidays and coffee breaks. In addition, the agreement will contain provisions for fringe benefits such as a pension plan, coverage for health care, and similar items. During periods of high inflation the agreement will generally contain a COLA (cost-of-living-adjustment) clause, which adjusts wages upward when consumer prices rise rapidly.

A second important and often controversial subject is *work rules*. These concern work assignments and tasks, job security, and workloads. Particularly in declining industries, the staffing requirements are a major issue because the demand for labor is falling. In the railroad industry, for example, there were decades of disputes about the number of people needed to run a train. Airlines are currently battling unions over the size of the cockpit crew.

Finally, the labor agreement has *procedural* features. These include rules of seniority—who gets laid off first or last—as well as a grievance procedure for handling discharges or disputes.

At last the contract, many pages of fine print, is signed. Everything is set down in black and white. Generally there are provisions for the arbitration of issues that arise under it. Each side agrees in advance to accept the decision of an impartial outside arbitrator in the case of disputes. The usual life of a contract is 3 years.

Collective bargaining is a complicated business—a matter of give-and-take. Much effort is spent negotiating purely economic issues, dividing the pie between wages and profits. Sometimes agreements get hung up on issues of management prerogatives, such as the ability to reassign workers or change work rules. In the end, both workers and management have a large stake in ensuring that workers are satisfied and productive on their jobs.

Government and Collective Bargaining

The history of labor unions tells the story of their gradual political acceptance and freedom from restrictive laws. Two hundred years ago, when labor first tried to organize in England and America, common-law doctrines against "conspiracy in restraint of trade" were used against union members.[2] Well into this century, unions and their members were convicted by courts, fined, jailed, and harassed by various injunctive procedures. The Supreme Court repeatedly struck down acts designed to improve working conditions for women and children and other reform legislation on hours and wages.

Gradually the pendulum swung toward support of unions and collective bargaining. A major landmark was the Clayton Act (1914), hailed as "labor's

[2] A full treatment of the economic analysis and modern legal foundations of antitrust doctrines is contained in Chapter 20.

Magna Carta" and designed to remove labor from antitrust prosecution. Other important milestones were the Railway Labor Act (1926), which accepted the basic premise of collective bargaining; the Norris-LaGuardia Act (1932), which virtually wiped out injunctive interference by the federal courts in labor disputes; and the Fair Labor Standards Act (1938), which barred child labor, called for time-and-a-half pay for weekly hours over 40, and set a federal minimum wage for most nonfarm workers.

The most important labor legislation of all was the National Labor Relations (or Wagner) Act (1935). Its section 7 stated:

> Employees shall have the right to self-organization, to form, join, or assist labor organizations, to bargain collectively through representatives of their own choosing, and to engage in concerted activities, for the purpose of collective bargaining or other mutual aid or protection.

Moreover, it set up the National Labor Relations Board (NLRB) to make sure that employers do not engage in "unfair labor practices."[3] The NLRB also holds elections in plants to see what organization will serve as the collective bargaining representative for all workers. Without doubt, this flurry of pro-union legislation helped propel unionism to its preeminent position on the eve of World War II.

After World War II, many felt that the pendulum had swung too far in labor's direction. Congress passed legislation aimed at both sides of labor disputes. The most important statute was the 1947 Taft-Hartley Act. This two-edged labor relations law prescribed standards of conduct for unions as well as employers. Among its principal features was a provision that strikes that "imperil the national health or safety" may be suspended for an 80-day "cooling off" period. This may be imposed by a court injunction requested by the attorney general.

In addition, unfair union labor practices were defined, and lawful union behavior was restricted. The "closed shop," which requires that employees join the union before they are hired, became illegal, and states were given a free hand to pass "right-to-work" or open-shop laws. Political activity and financial contributions by unions to political candidates or public officials were restricted. The free-speech rights of the employer were reaffirmed and strengthened.

With the passage of the Taft-Hartley Act, the framework for American collective bargaining was established. Although labor and business have from time to time proposed modifications of the law, no side has mustered the strength to change the status quo in a significant way since 1947.

Current Labor Issues

The issues facing labor unions in the 1990s are not unlike those of the last century. These include strikes, competition from nonunion labor, and productivity restraints.

Strikes

Unions devote their bargaining efforts to improving the wages, fringe benefits, and working conditions of their members. Only by threatening to strike can unions force concessions from management. It is not surprising, therefore, that work stoppages provide the major headlines in labor relations.

Contrary to common impressions, the power to strike is used sparingly. The time lost from strikes today is less than 0.1 percent of working time. In fact, the number of days lost from work on account of the common cold is far greater than that from all work conflicts!

Although seldom used, a union's right to strike is a crucial element in its bargaining power. Time and again concessions have been extracted by threatening employers with the heavy financial losses that result from a prolonged shutdown. Workers, too, suffer grievous financial losses and demoralization from a long strike.

In the early days of unions, governments tended to intervene on the side of business. When the Boston police struck in 1919, Massachusetts Governor Calvin Coolidge declared, "There is no right to strike against the public safety, by anybody, anywhere, any time." In railroads, steel, and coal, presidents often turned to Taft-Hartley or other injunc-

[3] The term "unfair labor practices" as used in the Wagner Act refers to employer activities that interfere with employee rights to self-organization. Examples of such employer practices are (1) firing people for joining a union, (2) refusing to hire people sympathetic to unions, (3) threatening to close an establishment if employees join a union, (4) interfering with or dominating the administration of a union, and (5) refusing to bargain with the employees' designated representatives.

tive procedures during the 1950s and 1960s. Over the last decade, however, as strikes became less prevalent and as the federal government shifted toward a less active role in economic management, direct government involvement in private labor disputes all but disappeared.

Attitudes toward strikes have changed among businesses and the public. Because of favorable interpretations of labor law by the courts and with success in breaking strikes, firms increasingly have decided to resist union strike threats. An important public demonstration was provided by President Reagan in 1981 when he refused to accept the demands of the union during an illegal strike by the air controllers. The government fired 11,400 air-traffic controllers and gradually replaced them with nonstrikers and new workers. The government's willingness to confront the controllers' union demonstrated the possible benefits to management of a tough bargaining stance.

During the 1980s, then, a new management attitude toward strikes arose. Managers began to think about the unthinkable: that they could endure a strike, perhaps by hiring nonunion workers as temporary or permanent replacements, without facing financial ruin or public censure. The increased prevalence of antilabor views both inside and outside government has led to a significant erosion in union bargaining power over the last decade.

Increasing Competitiveness

The greatest threat to unions comes from nonunion workers who supply the same product. Sometimes, the nonunion workers live in southern states that are inhospitable to unions. In the last decade, however, the greatest threat to unions arose from deregulation of domestic industries and from foreign competition.

The deregulation of many industries has opened them up to the entry of nonunionized firms. In an earlier era, a few established firms controlled most of the output in regulated industries such as trucking, airlines, telephone, and shipping. Once these firms had been unionized, the unions gained a virtual monopoly on labor sold in those sectors. After those industries were deregulated, nonunionized firms could enter and undercut established firms with lower-cost labor, thereby eroding the labor monopoly of unions.

A vivid example of competition undermining unions is the deregulation of the airlines in the early 1980s. As a result of deregulation, new carriers were allowed to enter the airline industry for the first time in decades, and low-cost airlines expanded into new markets without burdensome government constraints. A new or expanding firm could hire nonunion pilots at $40,000 a year as compared to the $80,000 a year or more paid to unionized pilots of the major airlines. As a result, the market power of unions was eroded and the average wages of union employees in the airline industry declined.

A second assault on union power came from the inroads on manufacturing industries made by foreign competitors in the early 1980s. In the first half of the 1980s, the volume of imported goods rose very rapidly. Our markets were flooded with foreign steel, chemicals, autos, and capital equipment. As a result of this import penetration, American unions no longer have a monopoly on labor supply in these industries. Foreign workers from Toyota, Mitsubishi, and Siemens now openly compete with domestic workers through foreign goods imported into American markets.

The labor embodied in imported goods posed a threat to American unions because foreign labor could undersell domestic labor in exactly the way nonunionized workers could undercut unionized workers. In response to the threat from foreign manufacturing workers, many unions reopened their labor contracts. Indeed, for the first time in modern history, steelworkers accepted a pay cut, while the Teamsters' Union froze the wages of truck drivers. The high unemployment and foreign competition of the early 1980s led to the erosion of many bastions of union strength in the American economy.

We see then how deregulation and foreign competition both undermine the strength of unions and put downward pressure on wages in unionized industries. This may be one reason why "big labor" has turned restrictionist and protectionist—to insulate its monopoly power from offshore workers and from deregulated firms.

Productivity Restraints

In an age of rapid technical change and at a time when there is increasing automation and robotization, union members are often as concerned about job security as about wage gains. What good is a pay raise for a job that no longer exists? This is not a new concern. The word "sabotage" was coined when laborers threw their wooden shoes (*sabots*) into the works of the new machines brought in by the Industrial Revolution to replace workers. *Featherbedding* refers to rules imposed on employers merely for the purpose of keeping up the demand for workers. Examples are rules that mandate the use of small shovels, limit the number of bricks laid per day, require that recording musicians be accompanied by a standby orchestra that does nothing but draw pay, and stipulate that railroad fire stokers (i.e., coal shovelers) be employed for diesel engines.

Because unions have a monopoly over the labor supplied to the affected firms or industries, entrenched unions have the power to enforce uneconomical arrangements. Railroads must bargain in good faith over work rules with their unions because they cannot legally employ nonunion workers to run the locomotives. Perhaps the most extreme example is that of the dockworkers of New York. Since 1966, senior dockworkers have received a guaranteed annual income whether or not they work. The result is that many longshoremen simply punch the clock, drive back home, and collect $35,000 a year; some of them haven't hauled a line for a decade. But the foreign competition, competition from nonunion states or firms, and deregulation of the last decade have undermined many featherbedding practices. And unions are beginning to see that in the long run featherbedding may so hamper efficiency and drive up prices that the jobs of union members become imperiled.

A study of the history of unionism will show that the controversial issues change little from decade to decade. From their infancy, unions relied upon strikes to force employers to raise wages. Once unions had gained recognition, they labored to exclude nonunion workers and to maintain their traditional work rules. But success has been gained by skillful negotiations, as the great English economist Alfred Marshall wrote at the beginning of this century:

> Trade unionism has enabled . . . workers to enter into negotiations with the same gravity, self-restraint, dignity, and forethought as are observed in the diplomacy of great nations. It has led them generally to recognize that a simply aggressive policy is a foolish policy, and that the chief use of military resources is to preserve an advantageous peace.[4]

How advantageous an economic arrangement have unions brought to their members? We turn to that issue in the next section.

B. Impact of Imperfect Competition on Wages

The last chapter analyzed the determination of wages in perfectly competitive markets. We have seen, however, that labor unions are in effect monopolists in labor markets. We now analyze the effect of labor market imperfections on wage and employment patterns.

Four Ways Unions Seek to Raise Wages

From an economic point of view, unions attempt to raise the wages of their members above competitive levels. They accomplish this goal in four ways: (1) restricting the supply of labor; (2) using their collective bargaining power to raise standard wage rates directly; (3) increasing the demand for labor; and (4) resisting employers who possess monopoly bargaining power.

Restricting the Supply of Labor

One of the primary ways that unions affect labor markets is by restricting the supply of labor. Immigration barriers, maximum-hour legislation, long apprenticeships, racial and sex barriers, and refusal

[4] *Principles of Economics*, 8th ed. (Macmillan, London, 1920), p. 703.

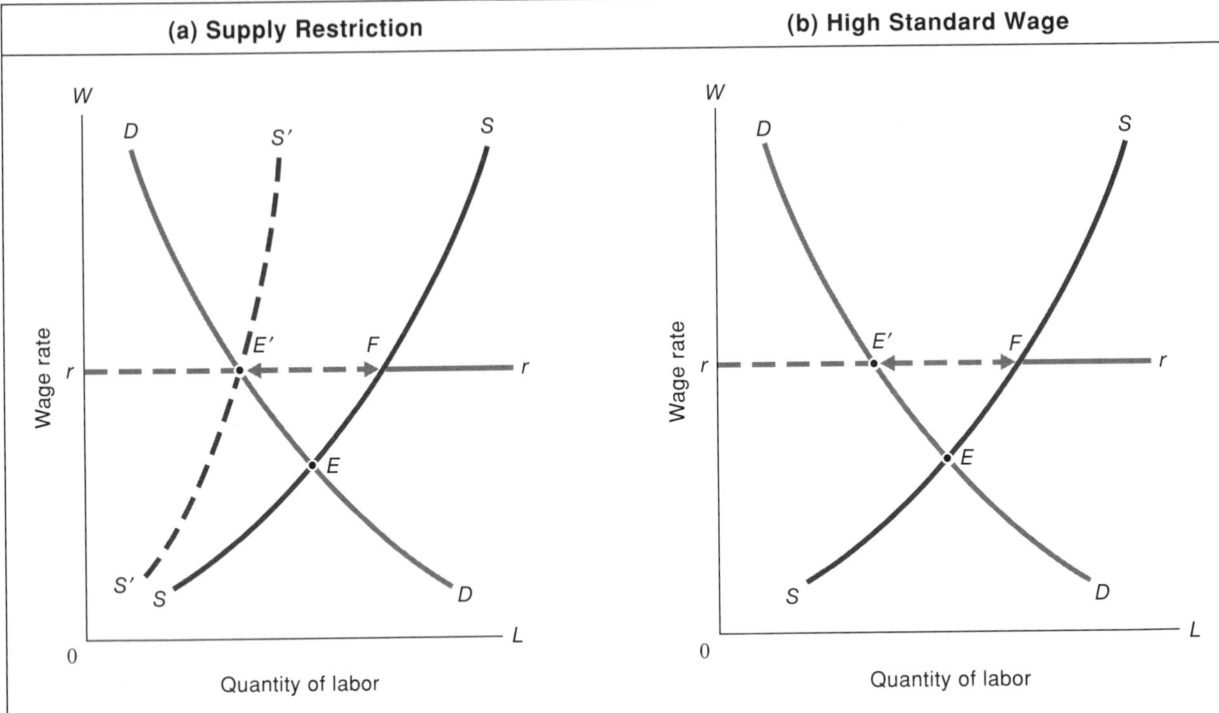

Figure 15-2. To raise pay, unions restrict supply or enforce standard wage rate

If the supply of workers is restricted from *SS* to *S′S′* in **(a)**, wages rise and employment declines. Raising the standard wage to *rr* in **(b)** has exactly the same effect on wages and employment as restricting supply. In either case, wages rise and the workers from *E′* to *F* are excluded from employment.

to admit new members into the union or to let nonunion members hold jobs—all these strategies are restrictive devices to reduce the supply of labor.

Figure 15-2(*a*) displays the effect of directly restricting labor supply. Say that unions persuade the government to pass a law (such as the Davis-Bacon Act) that effectively prohibits government contractors from hiring nonunion construction workers. The effect of this law would be to restrict the supply of construction workers from *SS* to *S′S′*. The supply restriction would lower total employment and raise wages in this labor market. What would happen if immigration restrictions limited the number of foreign agricultural workers who were allowed to harvest vegetables in California or Texas?

Raising Standard Wage Rates

Most union bargains do not directly restrict labor supply. Rather, they attempt to force employers to pay a standard wage higher than prevailing market wages. For example, if nonunion plumbers earn $15 per hour in Alabama, a union might bargain with a large construction firm to set the wage at $25 per hour for that firm's plumbers.

Such an agreement is, however, valuable to the union only if access to alternative labor supplies can be restricted. Hence, under a typical collective bargaining agreement, firms agree not to hire nonunion plumbers; nor can they contract out plumbing services; nor can they subcontract to nonunion firms. Each of these provisions helps prevent erosion of the union's monopoly lock on the supply of plumbers to the firm. In some industries, like steel and autos, unions will even try to unionize the entire industry so that firm A's unionized workers need not compete with firm B's nonunion workers. All these steps are necessary to protect high union wage rates.

Figure 15-2(*b*) shows the impact of agreed-upon high standard wages, where the union forces employers to pay wages at the standard rate shown by the horizontal line *rr*. As in panel (*a*), the equilibrium is at E', where rr intersects the employers' demand curve.

Note that the union has not directly reduced supply when it sets high standard wage rates. What then limits employment? At the above-equilibrium wage rates, employment is limited by the firms' demand for labor. The number of workers who seek employment exceeds the demand by the segment $E'F$. These excess workers might be unemployed and waiting for vacancies in the high-paying union sector, or they might become discouraged and look for jobs in other sectors. The workers from E' to F are as effectively excluded from jobs as if the union had directly limited entry.

Increasing the Demand for Labor

A third way to raise wages is to increase the demand for union labor. Figure 15-3 shows how a shift in the demand for unionized labor will shift up both wage rates and employment from E to E'.

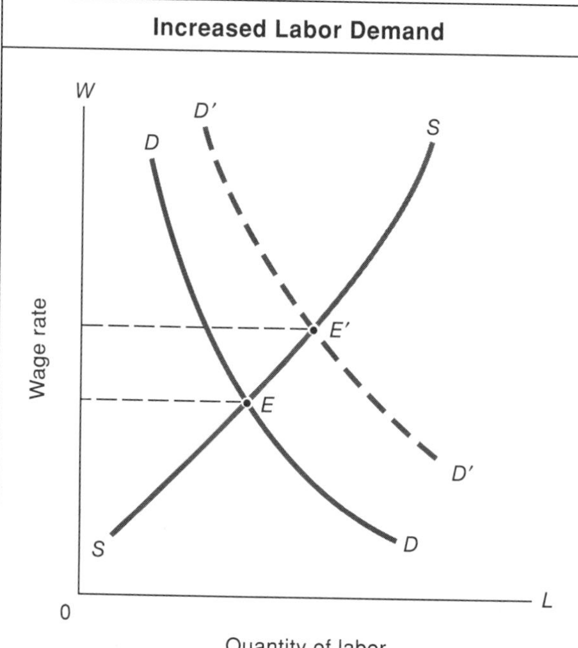

Figure 15-3. Shifting labor demand increases wage rates

Labor unions also increase wages by increasing the demand for labor. This occurs either because of increases in labor's marginal product or through means that increase the derived demand for labor by shifting the demand for the final product toward the output of union-made goods.

There are many ways to shift the labor demand curve. Labor may help industry advertise its products. Often, labor and management will lobby for an import quota on the product, thereby raising the demand for domestic workers in the industry.

Sometimes, groups that function as unions (such as professional associations of doctors) will lobby for legislation that enforces the licensing of particular professions. By limiting the practice of medicine, law, or other activities to specified groups, the supply of competing professions is reduced and the demand for the services of the preferred group is increased. (See question 7 at the end of this chapter for further analysis of the role of "quasi unions.")

In addition, unions can raise labor demand through increasing the efficiency (and therefore the marginal productivity) of labor. For example, a century ago, workers were paid so little that they were malnourished and their work was physically inefficient. Higher wages might have made them more efficient and resulted in lower production costs. Today, in the United States, few workers are still physiologically undernourished.

But psychological elements can be as important as physiological ones. Many an employer has found that low wages are bad business even from a hard-boiled, dollars-and-cents standpoint. The quality and contentment of the workers fall off so much that the company is losing from trimming the last few dollars of its wage bill. Recently, economists have begun to stress the way that wage rates can affect worker efficiency (this concept is called *efficiency wages*). Some analysts argue that farsighted employers will raise wages above competitively determined levels to attract more efficient workers, boost morale, and improve worker productivity. Recent analyses by Richard Freeman and James Medoff have thrown new light on this issue. They find evidence that unions, by serving as a collective voice of workers, may have actually increased labor productivity.[5] Some economists question the plausibility of these findings, asking why employers are so resistant to unions if they do indeed raise productivity so much.

[5] Richard B. Freeman and James L. Medoff, *What Do Unions Do?* (Basic Books, New York, 1984).

Combating Monopsony Power of Businesses

When union sympathizers first organized workers, they argued that unions were necessary as a "countervailing power" to large employers. In essence, the union's market power was necessary to offset the employers' market power. For example, suppose you live in a company town. The dominant firm is the employer of most of the people who have jobs. As an employee, you must take what this employer offers or go without work; your only alternative is to move to another region.

In this case, the employer is a **monopsonist.** Just as "monopolist" means a single seller, "monopsonist" signifies a single buyer of a commodity. How would a profit-maximizing monopsonist calculate its costs and make its hiring decisions? The monopsonist will not behave as a perfectly competitive purchaser of labor; rather, it will recognize that it can affect wages in its town. As it hires more workers, it must pay higher wages. In effect, because the firm is so large, it moves up the town's labor supply curve as it employs more workers.

Because it pays higher wages as it employs more workers, the monopsonist finds that its *marginal cost of labor is greater than the wage rate.* Why so? Because when the monopsonist hires an additional worker, it must raise the wage rate paid to all workers. Therefore the marginal cost of a new worker is equal to the wage rate of the new worker plus the higher wages paid to already-hired workers, and this sum is clearly higher than the wage rate. To maximize profits, a monopsonist should hire additional workers up to the point where its marginal revenue product is equal to the marginal cost of labor (which is greater than the wage rate). The monopsonist therefore both depresses wages and restricts employment relative to perfectly competitive labor markets.

Enter the labor union. After organizing the workers, it settles with the employer for a standard wage that is above the depressed monopsonistic wage level. At that higher standard wage, the employer can hire all the workers it needs at a given wage rate; the firm becomes a "wage taker" rather than a "wage maker." It will then become like a competitive firm that hires workers up to the point where the marginal revenue product equals the going standard wage. A union that exercises countervailing power may produce higher wages *and* higher employment.

The role of unions in combating business monopsony power proved important in their early history, particularly in isolated locations like the tin mines of Bolivia and the lumber camps of the American west. In periods when business trusts behaved like monopsonists by keeping wages low, union countervailing power may have improved wages and employment in labor markets. Countervailing power is less relevant in today's America, where labor mobility is great and where few communities are dominated by a single firm.

The Importance of Controlling Entry

For each of the four devices to raise wages, the key to success is the union's ability to control entry by potential competitors. By forming a union that comprises all the workers in a particular group, the union is able to set a monopoly price for its members. But, to succeed, it must fight off competition from nonunion labor.

This need to prevent nonunion competition is behind many of the central policies supported by labor unions. It explains why unions want to limit immigration; why unions support protectionist legislation to limit foreign goods, goods made by workers who are not members of American unions; why quasi unions like medical associations fight to restrict the practice of medicine by other groups; and why unions sometimes oppose deregulation in industries such as trucking, communications, or airlines.

Theoretical Indeterminacy of Collective Bargaining

Can economic theory accurately predict the outcome of a bargain between unions and firms? Unions sometimes realize it would not be in their interest to ask for higher wages; management sometimes takes the view that a wage increase would improve long-run corporate earnings. But both these views are exceptional. More often, at any collective bargaining negotiation, the workers will press for higher wages while management holds out for a leaner wage bill.

What will be the terms of the final agreement? Interestingly, this is one important question that no economic theory can answer with precision. This is a situation known as *bilateral monopoly*—where two parties have strong bargaining power. The result depends on psychology, politics, and countless other intangible and unpredictable factors. As far as the economist is concerned, however, the final outcome of bilateral monopoly is in principle indeterminate—as indeterminate as the haggling between two millionaires over the value of a fine painting.[6]

Effects on Wages and Employment

The advocates of labor unions claim that they have raised real wages and have benefited workers. Critics argue that the result of raising wages is high unemployment, inflation, and distorted resource allocation. What are the facts?

Has Unionization Raised Wages?

Let's start by reviewing the effects of unions on relative wages. Economists have estimated the economic impacts of unions by examining wages in unionized and nonunionized industries. On the basis of these analyses, economists have concluded that union workers receive on average a 10 to 15 percent wage differential over nonunion workers. The differential ranges from a negligible amount for hotel workers and barbers to 25 to 30 percent higher earnings for skilled construction workers or coal miners. The pattern of results suggests that where unions have the greatest difficulty monopolizing labor supply and controlling entry (as with barbers), they will be least effective in raising wages.

Another approach examines the wages of individual workers, correcting for worker characteristics and taking into account whether the worker is in a union or nonunion job. Orley Ashenfelter of Princeton examined a panel of workers over the period 1967–1975. Correcting for the influence of each worker's sex, race, education, and other personal characteristics, he found that those workers who belonged to unions in the mid-1970s had wages 17 percent above those of nonunion workers. In addition, Ashenfelter found that black males who belonged to unions obtained even higher wage differentials than other groups: 23 percent higher wages as compared to 16 percent for white males.

A final question concerns the "general-equilibrium" impact of unions. Consider an economy with different grades of labor (union and nonunion) as well as with other factors of production (such as capital). How would greater union power affect the distribution of income among *all* the different factors? This question poses great difficulties, but a tentative and surprising answer was given by economists Harry Johnson and Peter Mieskowski. Using a simplified general-equilibrium approach, they concluded that unions did not redistribute income from capital to labor but from nonunion labor to union labor. Put differently, as union wages are jacked up by union monopoly power, profits are largely maintained as prices also rise, but the real wages of nonunion workers erode.

Overall Impacts. But can unions bootstrap the entire economy to a higher real wage? Most evidence suggests not. The share of national income going to labor (including self-employment) has changed little over the last six decades. Once cyclical influences on labor's share are removed, we can see no appreciable impact of unionization on the level of real wages in the United States. The evidence from heavily unionized European countries suggests that, when unions succeed in raising money wage rates, they sometimes trigger an inflationary wage-price spiral with little or no permanent effect upon real wages. Moreover, economic history shows that when inflation heats up, governments and central banks often institute policies to slow economic activity, resulting in higher unemployment rather than higher real wages.

Effects on Employment

If unions do not affect overall wage levels, this suggests that their major impact would fall upon *relative* wages. That is, wages in unionized industries would rise relative to those in nonunionized industries. Moreover, employment would tend to be reduced in unionized and expanded in nonunionized industries.

[6] Situations like labor-management bargains are the subject of game theory, analyzed in Chapter 12. The theoretical indeterminacy of collective bargaining stems from the following result from game theory: A two-person noncooperative game does not generally have a unique outcome. Rather, as with wars or strikes, the outcome depends on many factors, such as bargaining power, prestige, bluffing ability, and even each side's perception of the strength of its opponent.

Waiting for Recall. Some economists think that the artificial wage differentials across sectors created by unions are a major cause of unemployment. They point to two mechanisms. The first is *wait unemployment*. As workers from high-paid jobs are laid off, they can collect unemployment insurance or supplemental benefits. These benefits may even exceed the take-home pay for jobs in other sectors of the economy, such as in service industries. Such workers may prefer to wait for a recall from the higher-paying manufacturing firm; they are unemployed but do not wish to work at going rates in the low-paying industries.

Classical Unemployment. A second concern is that unions and government policies have raised real wages to artificially high levels, resulting in an excess supply of labor and what is called *classical unemployment*.

This case is illustrated in Figure 15-4. Assume that unions raise wages above the market-clearing wage at *E* to a higher real wage at *r*. Then, if supply of and demand for labor in general are unchanged, the arrow between *E′* and *F* will represent the number of workers who want to work at wage *r* but cannot find work. This is called classical unemployment because it results from too high real wages. Economists often contrast classical unemployment with the unemployment that occurs in business cycles, often called Keynesian unemployment, which results from insufficient aggregate demand. The effects of too high real wages were seen after the economic unification of Germany in 1990. The economic union fixed East German wages at a level estimated to be at least two times higher than could be justified by labor's marginal revenue product. The result was a rise of classical unemployment in Eastern Germany from near zero in 1989 to over 20 percent in late 1991.[7]

This analysis suggests that when a country gets locked into real wages that are too high, high levels of unemployment may result. The unemployment will not respond to the traditional macroeconomic policies of increasing aggregate spending but rather will require remedies that lower real wages.

[7] A fascinating study of the events surrounding unification is contained in George Akerlof, Andrew Rose, Janet Yellen, and Helga Hessenius, "Germany in From the Cold," *Brookings Papers on Economic Activity*, 1991:1.

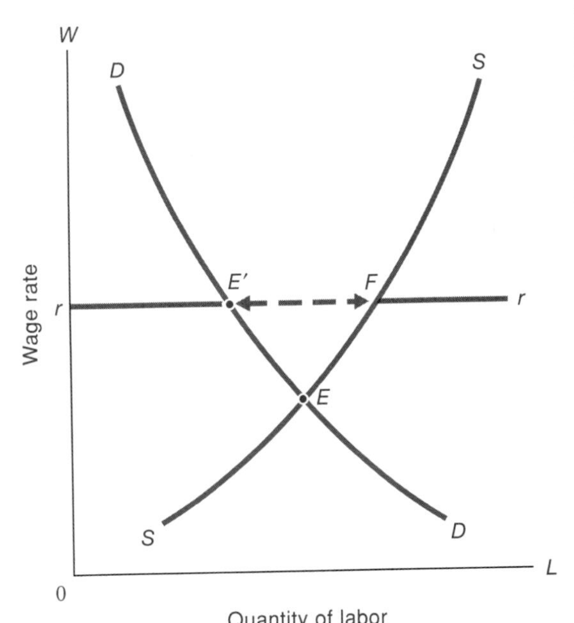

Figure 15-4. Too high real wages cause classical unemployment

If unions push real wages too high for an entire economy, firms will demand *E′*, while workers will supply *F*. Thus the black arrow from *E′* to *F* represents the amount of classical unemployment. This source of unemployment is particularly important when a country cannot affect its price level or exchange rate, and differs from the unemployment caused by insufficient aggregate demand.

The Consequences of Decline

We have traced in this chapter how labor unions became legal during this century; how they thrived during the early part of this century; and how their economic strength has eroded as blue-collar jobs became less numerous and as deregulation and foreign competition spurred businesses to fight union power.

What does this eclipse of labor unions portend for labor markets of the 1990s? Richard Freeman of Harvard offers the following reflections upon the social implications of the decline of the labor movement:

> What are the economic effects of a proportionately smaller trade union movement? From the perspective of the monopoly "face" of unionism the decline can be

expected to reduce the monopoly misallocation of resources resulting from unionism and . . . also reduce the union wage advantage. On the other hand, however, reduced unionism can be expected to affect adversely many of the positive effects of strong unionism—lower dispersion of earnings among workers; lower quit rates; and higher productivity due to pressures on management to reduce costs in organized firms. As the United Mine Workers organization and industrial relations in coal have deteriorated, productivity in union mines has fallen sharply. The broader social effects of a diminished trade union movement remain to be seen.[8]

[8] Richard B. Freeman, "The Evolution of the American Labor Market, 1948–80," in Martin Feldstein (ed.), *The American Economy in Transition* (University of Chicago Press, Chicago, 1980), p. 372.

SUMMARY

A. The American Labor Movement

1. Labor unions occupy an important but diminishing role in the American economy, in terms of both membership and influence. Their present structure is in three layers: (*a*) *local* unions, (*b*) *national* unions, and (*c*) a *federation* of unions (AFL-CIO), the first two being the most important.
2. By the 1900s, the typical American pattern of federated, nonpolitical business unionism had been established. Since 1935, the CIO and finally the AFL have modified the pattern in the direction of *industrial* unionization of whole mass-production industries rather than relying solely upon *craft* unionization of skilled workers.
3. After a union has been recognized by an NLRB election as the exclusive bargaining agent for a group of workers, management and labor representatives meet together in collective bargaining to negotiate a contract. Such agreements typically contain provisions for wages, fringe benefits, and work rules.
4. Until the mid-1930s there was bitter opposition to unions. But the pendulum of government swung to support collective bargaining, and since the Wagner Act (1935), most manufacturing industries have become unionized. The result has been less violence but still vigorous collective bargaining between unions and management.
5. Strikes have become less prevalent since World War II. Featherbedding (or work-slowing practices) is a major obstacle to productivity growth in many declining industries. The biggest threat to unions today is the competition from nonunionized firms, from imported products, and from entering firms in newly deregulated industries. These forces, together with a conservative political environment, have led to a significant decline in the economic and political power of unions.

B. Impact of Imperfect Competition on Wages

6. Unions affect wages by (*a*) restricting labor supply, (*b*) bargaining for standard rates, (*c*) following policies designed to shift productivity or the demand schedule for labor upward, and (*d*) countering monopoly bargaining power of employers (i.e., of so-called monopsonists).

   The different techniques show one important common feature: In order to raise real wages above prevailing market-determined levels, unions generally must prevent entry or competition from nonunion workers. This involves pushing for foreign-trade restrictions, regulation, and occupational licensing.

7. Economic theory states that there is no unique outcome of a collective bargaining session: bilateral monopoly or management-union bargaining (like war or two-person games) has a theoretically indeterminate solution.
8. Unions do appear to have raised the wages of union members relative to those of nonunionized workers. Studies estimate that, on average, union members have earned wages 10 to 30 percent higher than nonunion members for workers with the same characteristics. This union differential may have eroded in the last decade's period of high unemployment and competition from nonunion labor.
9. While unions may raise the wages of their members, they probably do not increase real wages or labor's share for an entire nation. They are likely to increase unemployment among union members who would prefer to wait for recall from layoff of their high-paid jobs rather than move or take low-paying jobs in other industries. And in a nation with inflexible prices, real wages that are too high may induce classical unemployment.

CONCEPTS FOR REVIEW

Labor-union history and behavior
AFL-CIO
business vs. political unionism
Wagner Act, NLRB
collective bargaining agreement

Impact of unions
standard wage rates
four ways unions raise wages
unions as monopolies
monopsony
control of entry by unions
effect of unions on real wages
wait and classical unemployment

QUESTIONS FOR DISCUSSION

1. Discuss the economic structure of unions. How are unions able to exercise monopoly power?
2. Should the police have the right to strike? Coal workers? Soldiers? Everyone? Anyone?
3. Unions favor minimum-wage laws that apply mostly to the poorer, unorganized workers. Using the concept of discrimination in segmented markets from Chapter 14, would less or more union labor be demanded with a higher minimum wage? Might the poor and unskilled be hurt—be priced out of the market—by a minimum wage that is set too high?
4. Collective bargaining contains both cooperative and antagonistic elements. List the elements of a contract that might be cooperative. Also list the antagonistic ones. Does the existence of cooperative elements in labor-management agreements suggest a reason why compulsory arbitration of labor contracts by outside arbitrators might not always be a good solution?
5. Explain, both in words and with a supply-and-demand diagram, the impact of each of the following upon the wages and employment in the affected labor market:
   (a) Upon union bricklayers: The bricklayers' union negotiated a lower standard work rule, from 26 bricks per hour to 20 bricks per hour.
   (b) Upon airline pilots: After the deregulation of the airlines, nonunion airlines like Continental increased their market share by 20 percent.
   (c) Upon M.D.s: Many states begin to allow nurses to be given more of the physicians' responsibilities.
   (d) Upon American autoworkers: Japan agreed to limit its exports of automobiles to the United States.

(e) Upon steelworkers: Through negotiations, the United Steelworkers raised its members' standard wage rates 30 percent relative to those of the average manufacturing worker.

6. If you were a union leader, would you focus your attention on (*a*) an industry that has many small firms and easy entry and exit or (*b*) a regulated monopolist that is allowed to use average cost pricing and has highly inelastic demand for its output? Justify your reasoning in terms of the ways that unions raise wages.

7. In addition to formal unions, there are many "quasi unions," which have the effect of limiting employment to their members. For example, state licensure limits the practice of medicine and law to those who pass stringent examinations; some universities limit faculty appointments to those who have a Ph.D.; social workers in some states are pressing for limitation of practice to those who have state certificates; doctors have attempted to limit the medical practice of chiropractors.

   Using supply and demand analysis, explain how such practices tend to limit supply and raise the prices of the affected professions. Under what demand conditions would these limitations increase the incomes of the affected professions?

CHAPTER 16

LAND, NATURAL RESOURCES, AND CAPITAL

In the first stone which [man] flings at the wild animal he pursues, in the first stick that he seizes to strike down the fruit which hangs above his reach, we . . . discover the origin of capital.

Robert Torrens, *An Essay on the Production of Wealth* (1821)

We have now analyzed the general theory of the demand for factors of production with an application to the labor market. This chapter turns to the major non-labor inputs: land and capital. Land and capital share many common elements. They are both durable assets that are owned by someone in a market economy. They can be bought and sold in markets, or they can be "rented" out for a period of time. The major difference between land and capital is that land is a nonproduced factor, while capital is an output of the economy, accumulated by the toil of past savers.

A complete understanding of any modern economy, whether it be capitalist or socialist, advanced or underdeveloped, requires an appreciation of the role of land and capital in economic growth.

A. Land, Natural Resources, and Rent

We begin with a survey of factors that are fixed in supply, including land and natural resources. We will pay particular attention to how markets determine *rents* on factors that are fixed in supply. We shall also see that, when rents are not charged, society may overuse common property resources, such as air or ocean fisheries.

Rent as Return to Fixed Factors

One of the peculiarities of land is that, unlike other factors, its total supply is determined by non-economic forces; land usually cannot be augmented in response to a higher price or diminished in response to a lower price. While land can sometimes be created by drainage, and the fertility of existing land can be depleted by overcropping, we can accept the complete fixity of land's supply as its characteristic feature. The classical economists referred to land as the "original and inexhaustible gift of nature" whose total supply is by definition fixed or completely inelastic. Will Rogers put this nicely when he quipped, "Land is a good investment: they ain't making it no more."

The classical economists of the last century referred to the price of such a fixed factor as **rent,** or sometimes "pure economic rent." The concept of rent applies to any factor that is fixed in supply. Da Vinci painted only one *Mona Lisa,* and if you could pay for its temporary use, you would pay rent. If you were hiring the services of performers like Whoopi Goldberg or James Taylor, you would be paying a rent for their talents.

Any payments for the use of unique factors of production are rents.

Market Equilibrium. Figure 16-1 shows the supply curve for land that is completely inelastic because its supply is fixed. The demand and supply curves intersect at the equilibrium point *E*. It is toward this factor price that the rent of land must tend. Why?

If rent rose above the equilibrium price, the amount of land demanded by all firms would be less than the existing amount that would be supplied. Some property owners would be unable to rent their land at all; they would have to offer their land for less and thus bid down its rent. By similar reasoning, the rent could not remain below the equilibrium intersection for long. If it did, the bidding of unsatisfied firms would force the factor price back up toward the equilibrium level. Only at a competitive price where the total amount of land demanded exactly equals the fixed supply will the market be in equilibrium.

A factor of production like cornland is said to earn a pure economic rent (1) when its total supply is fixed or perfectly inelastic; and (2) when the factor has no other uses, such as land being used in the production of cotton. Adam Smith's great follower in England, David Ricardo, noted in 1815 that the case of such an inelastically supplied factor could be described in the following way:

> It is not really true that the price of corn is high because the price of cornland is high. Actually the reverse is more nearly the truth. The price of cornland is high because the price of corn is high. Because the supply of land is inelastic, land will always work for whatever competition gives it. Thus the value of the land derives entirely from the value of the product, and not vice versa.

Rent Determination under Competition

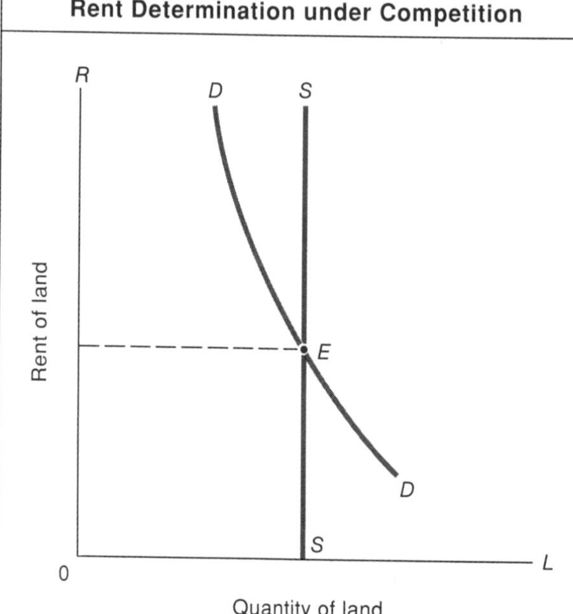

Figure 16-1. Fixed land must work for whatever it can earn

Perfectly inelastic supply characterizes the case of "rent," sometimes also called "pure economic rent." We run up the *SS* curve to the factor demand curve to determine rent. Aside from land, we can apply rent considerations to rich oil and gold properties, 7-foot basketball players, and anything else in fixed supply.

Rent and Costs

Economists sometimes go further and say, "Rent does not enter into the cost of production." There is a grain of truth in this, but still it is very dangerous reasoning. If you were a corn farmer, you would certainly have to pay your landlord just like anybody else. You would certainly include rent in your costs of production, and if you failed to pay your rent, you would end up in court.

Relativity of Viewpoint. What then are economists saying when they claim that rent does not enter into society's cost of production? They are reminding us that rent is the return to a factor that is completely inelastic in supply, so that the same quantity would be supplied whatever the price. Therefore, the prices of goods really determine land rent—rather than land rent determining the prices of goods.

In fact, the paradox of land costs involves our old enemy, the fallacy of composition. What appears as a cost of production to an individual firm using a particular kind of land may be only a price-determined rent to the whole community.

This point is most easily seen when the land is

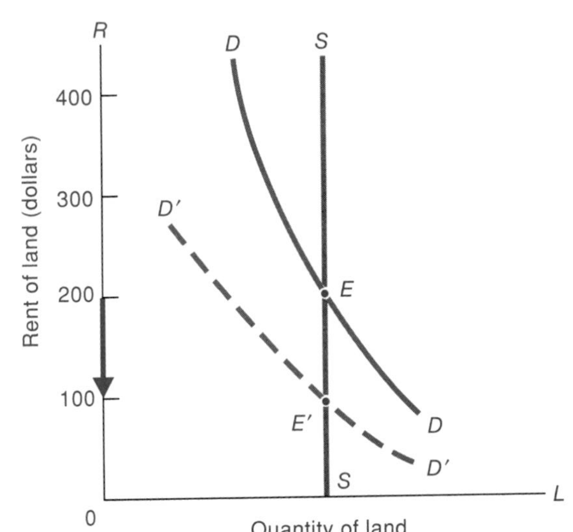

Figure 16-2. Tax on fixed land is shifted back to landowners, with government skimming off pure economic rent

A tax on fixed land leaves prices paid by users unchanged at *E* but reduces rent retained by landowners to *E*′. What can the landowners do but accept a lower return? This provides the rationale for Henry George's single-tax movement, which aimed to capture for society the increased land values that result from urbanization.

specialized and can be used for production by only one industry. If a piece of land is inelastically supplied to one industry and has no place else to go, it will always work for whatever it can earn there; its return will thus appear to every small firm as a cost like any other. But as observers of the whole industry, we still must recognize that the land return is a price-determined rent and not a price-determining cost.

In conclusion:

Whether rent is or is not a price-determining cost depends upon the viewpoint. What looks like a price-determining cost to a single firm or industry may for the entire economy be a pure economic rent paid to an inelastically supplied factor.

Henry George's Single-Tax Movement: Taxing Land's Surplus

In the late nineteenth century, America's population expanded rapidly as people migrated here from all over the world. With the growth in population, land utilization increased. Competitive land rents tended to rise. This created handsome profits for those who were lucky or farsighted enough to buy land early.

Why, some people asked, should lucky landowners be permitted to receive these "unearned land increments"? Henry George (1839–1897), a printer who thought a great deal about economics, crystallized these sentiments in the single-tax movement. This crusade agitated for heavy taxation of land rents and gained a considerable following a century ago. But it is unlikely that anyone will soon come forward and write so persuasive a bible for the single-tax movement as did Henry George in his best-selling *Poverty and Progress*.

The key economic point in George's movement concerned an important insight into the relationship between land taxation and economic efficiency. His central tenet was the following:

Pure land rent is in the nature of a "surplus" that can be taxed heavily without distorting production incentives or impairing productive efficiency.

Let us see why. Suppose that supply and demand create an equilibrium land rent, as at *E* in Figure 16-2. Now what would happen if the government introduced a 50 percent tax on all land rents? Take care to ensure that there is no tax on buildings or improvements, because that certainly would affect the volume of construction activity. All we are taxing is the income or rent on the fixed supply of agricultural and urban land sites.

After the tax, the total demand for the land's services will not have changed. At a price (*including* tax) of $200 in Figure 16-2, people will continue to demand the entire supply of land. Hence, with land fixed in supply, the market price of land services (including the tax) must be at the old intersection point *E*.

What about the rent received by the landowners? Demand and quantity supplied are unchanged, so the market price will be unaffected by the tax. Therefore, the tax must have been completely paid out of the landowner's income.

The situation can be visualized in Figure 16-2. What the farmer pays and what the landlord receives are now two quite different things. As far as the landlords are concerned, once the government steps in to take its 50 percent share, the effect is just the same as if the net demand to the owners had shifted down from *DD* to *D'D'*. Landowners' equilibrium return after taxes is now only *E'*, or only half as much as *E*. *The whole of the tax has been shifted backward onto the owners of the factor in inelastic supply.*

Landowners will surely complain. But under perfect competition there is nothing they can do about it, since they cannot alter the total supply and the land must work for whatever it can get. Half a loaf is better than none.

You might at this point wonder about the effects of such a tax on economic efficiency. The striking result is that *a tax on rent will lead to no distortions or economic inefficiencies.* Why not? Because a tax on pure economic rent does not change anyone's economic behavior. Demanders are unaffected because their price is unchanged. The behavior of suppliers is unaffected because, by supposition, the supply of land is fixed and cannot react. Hence, the economy operates after the tax exactly as it did before the tax—with no distortions or inefficiencies arising as a result of the land tax.

Ramsey Taxes

In the 1920s, the English economist Frank Ramsey asked the natural sequel to George's exploration: What are the most efficient kinds of taxes? Modern taxation theorists have developed a complete theory much along the lines first suggested by George and Ramsey.

The modern theory of *Ramsey taxes* analyzes how the government can raise the necessary taxes most efficiently—that is, with the least loss in consumer surplus. The "Ramsey tax rule" states that the government should levy the heaviest taxes on those inputs and outputs that are most price inelastic in supply or demand. Thus if land and food have very price-inelastic supply and demand curves, tax them heavily. If airline travel and cars are very price elastic, tax them lightly.

The rationale for the Ramsey tax rule is basically the same as that shown in Figure 16-2: if a commodity is very price inelastic in supply (or demand), then a tax on that commodity will have little impact upon consumption and production. In some circumstances, Ramsey taxes may constitute a way of raising revenues with a minimum of economic inefficiency.

Efficiency vs. Fairness. Both the single-tax and the Ramsey tax analyses present powerful arguments for certain kinds of taxes as the most efficient way for governments to raise their revenues. But economies and politics do not run on efficiency alone. While stiff taxation of land rents or food might be efficient, many would think them unfair.

A good example of this dilemma arose under the Thatcher government in Britain in 1990. The government proposed replacing the existing distortionary taxes with a *poll tax,* which is a fixed tax per person. The reasoning was that, like the land tax, the poll tax would induce no inefficiencies. After all, people are unlikely to emigrate or commit suicide to avoid the tax, so the economic distortions would be minimal.

Alas, the government underestimated the extent to which the populace felt this tax unfair and burdensome to low-income families. It is what is called a "regressive" tax, one that has a higher proportional burden on low-income people than on high-income people. The episode of the British poll tax illustrates clearly a central dilemma of a modern society, the need to choose between efficiency and fairness in design of economic policy.

Factor Pricing and Efficiency: Rent and Factor Prices as Devices to Ration Scarce Resources

We see that the supply and demand for factors of production help determine the distribution of income and solve the *for whom* problem. We might or might not like the wages and rents determined in the marketplace. But whether or not we like the competitive distribution of income, we must recognize that competitive pricing helps to solve the questions of *how* goods are to be produced in an efficient manner. It plays a role in the choice of the most efficient combination of factors of production.

Consider for example how different countries respond to different relative proportions of land and labor. As a result of supply and demand, in America, where land is plentiful and labor scarce, we find high land/labor ratios. In Hong Kong, where people are plentiful relative to land, we find high labor/land ratios. Do these labor/land ratios result from careful government planning and allocation?

Surely not. In a market economy, the signals transmitted by factor prices ensure that the efficient land/labor combinations are used. Land has to be auctioned off at a low price in America; labor, auctioned off at a high price. So the American farmer, seeking the least-cost combination, substitutes land for labor. In Hong Kong, by contrast, the high land price means that land is used largely for industry rather than for land-intensive agriculture. In sum:

> Prices serve as indicators of scarcity: they provide signals to producers about the relative scarcity of different inputs, thereby helping producers select the combination of inputs most appropriate for a society's factor endowments.

The Tragedy of the Commons

Charging rents on scarce resources helps an economy use its resources efficiently. This point applies with special force to vital questions about the environment. Many of our natural resources are owned by no one. Such resources are *common property resources,* like the town commons of New England villages. As has been eloquently described by the eminent biologist Garrett Hardin, a tragic outcome occurs when common land is overgrazed:

> Picture a pasture open to all. Each herdsman tries to keep as many cattle as possible on the commons. This works well for centuries because wars, poaching, and disease keep the numbers well below the carrying capacity of the land. But eventually the day of reckoning arrives. Each herdsman seeks to maximize his personal gain; he concludes that the only sensible course is for him to add another animal to his herd. And another. But this is the conclusion reached by each and every rational herdsman sharing a commons. Herds are increased without limit—in a world that is limited. Therein is the tragedy: Freedom in a commons brings ruin to all.[1]

Hardin makes an important point: When no rent is charged on a scarce good, severe misallocation or even abuse of resources can occur. In his example, no rent was charged to those who grazed their cattle on common ground. This led to overgrazing and even to destruction of the fertility of the soil. Consider these other cases:

[1] This slightly simplified paraphrase is further developed in Garrett Hardin, "The Tragedy of the Commons," *Science* (Dec. 13, 1968).

- The oceans are open to all. So everyone fishes and overfishes. Whales are threatened, and many lakes or oceans are depleted. Without an adequate fish population, breeding and maintenance of the fish schools are not possible. There would be a better use of fish resources if rents were charged to those who use fisheries—better for consumers and better for those in the fishing industry.
- During peak periods, many airports get very congested, with flights circling in the air and lined up on the runways. Economists like Alfred Kahn have proposed using peak-load "congestion fees" to ration out the scarce landing rights. These would raise ticket prices during peak periods enough to persuade some people to reschedule their flights to off-peak times.
- Factories that make chemicals or generate electricity often pump pollution into water and air. They are treating clean air and water as commons, whose disposal services they can use without paying. Why shouldn't firms pay for the use of clean air and water just as they pay for scarce capital and labor? By charging rents on the environment, we can ration out its use to those firms for whom dumping a ton of particulates or sulfur dioxide is most valuable.

Externalities in the Commons. Note that there is a shared feature in each of these three examples. The act of fishing, flying, or dumping imposes costs on other members of society. These are called *externalities,* or external diseconomies of production or consumption, such as we encountered in Chapter 3 and will discuss in greater detail in Chapter 18. Careful observation suggests that the use of common property resources often exhibits important externalities, and that these externalities can be reduced by "scarcity rents" attached to the common property resource.

Why Rents Are Absent. Why are rents generally not charged on these scarce resources? The lack of rents can be attributed to two general sources.

To begin with, for common property resources, there are no owners interested in maximizing their profits. Nobody owns the air or the oceans, so there is no one to charge and collect the appropriate rent. Sometimes, governments who own roads or waterways decide to underprice the resource, as in the case of crowded highways. Everybody's land is nobody's land, and people often feel free to pollute when they can do this at no private cost.

A second reason for abuse of common property resources is that it may be extremely costly to monitor their use and collect rents. Can you imagine a meter on every tailpipe or car or fishing rod—calculating the item's contribution to pollution, crowding, or overfishing? Because metering is so expensive, governments often choose to allow common property resources to be used free of charge.

The Commons Enclosed. But changes in the treatment of our common property resources have taken place. In the eighteenth century, the English enclosure movement turned most land over to private hands. Regulation of air and water pollution has limited the right of firms to dump wastes. The Law of the Sea Convention allows nations to regulate ocean resources as far as 200 miles from their shores. While not perfect mechanisms for charging the appropriate scarcity rents, these devices help to reduce the worst abuses of the commons.

B. Capital, Interest, and Profits

> You can have your cake and eat it too:
> Lend it out at interest.
>
> Anonymous

Basic Concepts

Economic analysis traditionally divides factors of production into three categories: land, labor, and capital. The first two of these are called primary or original factors of production, available before production takes place. To them we add a produced factor of production, capital or capital goods.

Capital consists of those durable produced goods that are in turn used as productive inputs for further production. Some capital goods might last a few years while others might last for a century or more. But the essential property of a capital good is that it is both an input and an output.

There are three major categories of capital goods: structures (such as factories and homes), equipment (consumer durable goods like automobiles and producer durable equipment like machine tools), and inventories (such as cars in dealers' lots).

Rentals on Capital Goods

Capital goods are bought and sold in capital-goods markets. For example, IBM sells computers to businesses; these computers are used by firms to help improve the efficiency of their payroll systems or production management.

Most capital goods are owned by the firm that uses them. Some capital goods, however, are rented out by their owners. Payments for the temporary use of capital goods are called *rentals.* An apartment that is owned by Ms. Landlord might be rented out for a year to a student, with the monthly payment of $300 constituting a rental.

Rate of Return on Capital Goods

One of the most important tasks of any economy, business, or household is to allocate its capital across different possible investments. Should a country invest in steel mills or in computers? Should IBM build a new plant to produce microcomputers or add to its productive capacity in mainframe processors? Should the Gomez family farm, hoping to improve its accounting records, put its funds in an IBM personal computer, an Apple, or a Leading Edge? All these questions involve costly investments—laying out money today to obtain a return in the future.

In deciding upon the best investment, we need a

measure for that yield or return on capital. One important measure is the **rate of return on capital,** which denotes the net dollar return per year for every dollar of invested capital.

Let's consider the example of a rental car company. Ugly Duckling Rental Company buys a used Ford for $10,000 and rents it out for $2500 per year. After calculating all expenses (maintenance, insurance, depreciation, etc.), and ignoring any change in car prices, Ugly Duckling earns a net rental of $1200 each year.[2] We then say that the rate of return on the Ford is 12 percent per year (= $1200 ÷ $10,000). Note also that the rate of return is a pure number per unit of time. That is, it has the dimensions of (dollars/dollars) per period of time and is usually calculated as percent per year.

You might be considering different investments: rental cars, oil wells, apartments, education, and so forth. Your financial advisers tell you that you do not have sufficient cash to invest in everything, so how can you decide which investments to make?

One useful approach is to compare the rates of return on capital of the different investments. For each one, you first calculate the dollar cost of the capital good. Then estimate the annual dollar receipts or rentals yielded by the asset. The ratio of the annual rental to the dollar cost is the rate of return on capital: it tells you the amount of money you get back for every dollar invested, measured as dollars per year per dollar of investment.

The rate of return on capital is the annual net return (rentals less expenses) per dollar of invested capital. It is a pure number—percent per year.

Of Wine, Trees, and Drills. Here are some examples of rates of return on investments:

- I buy grape juice for $10 and sell it a year later as wine for $11. If there are no other expenses, the rate of return on this investment is $1/$10, or 10 percent per year.
- I plant a pine tree with labor cost of $100. At the end of 25 years the grown tree sells for $430. The rate of return on this capital project is then 330 percent per quarter-century, which, a calculator will show, is equivalent to a return of 6 percent per year.
- I buy a $20,000 piece of oil-drilling equipment. For 10 years it earns annual rentals of $30,000, but I incur annual expenses of $26,000 for fuel, insurance, and depreciation. What is the rate of return on the drill? It is the same as the annual percentage yield of an investment of $20,000 which pays $4000 per year for 10 years. Interest tables show this drill's yield to be 15 percent per year.

Profits as Return on Capital. Where would you look to find the return on capital in the American economy? Generally, when companies own capital, the return is included in business profits. *Profits* are a residual income item equal to total revenues minus total costs. When you own shares in corporate capital, the return is your part of the overall profits of the firm. While this return has a different name (profit) and is more risky than that on many other investments, it is nonetheless a return on capital and has the dimensions of dollars of earnings per year per dollar invested. Business profits are the largest part of the return on capital in the U.S. economy today.

We will further examine the nature of profit at the end of this chapter.

Financial Assets and Interest Rates

We have spoken so far of capital goods like automobiles. But where do the resources needed to produce capital come from? Someone must be *saving,* or abstaining from current consumption, to provide funds for buying the capital goods. In a modern market economy like the United States, households and firms channel funds into capital goods by saving money in various financial assets. People buy bonds and stocks; they put money in savings accounts; they put money away for retirement in their pension funds. All these are vehicles that carry funds from savers to the investors who actually buy capital goods.

When people save, they expect a return. This is the **interest rate,** or the financial return on funds, or the annual return on borrowed funds. The yield you get when you put your money in a time deposit at a commercial bank is an example of an interest rate. At the 8 percent per year interest rate available in the early 1990s, if you deposit $1000 on January 1, 1992, you will end up with $1080 on January 1, 1993.

[2] Depreciation is an estimate of the loss in dollar value of a capital good due to obsolescence or wear and tear during a period of time.

You will usually see interest rates quoted as x percent per year. This means that the interest would be paid at that rate if the sum were borrowed for an entire year; for shorter or longer periods, the interest payment is adjusted proportionately.

There are many varieties of interest rates. There are long-term and short-term interest rates, depending on the duration of the loan or the bond; there are fixed interest-rate loans and variable interest-rate loans; there are interest rates on supersafe bonds (like U.S. government securities) and there are interest rates on highly risky "junk bonds."

To summarize:

Households and other savers provide financial resources or funds to those who want to purchase physical capital goods. The rate of interest represents the price that a bank or other financial intermediary pays a lender for the use of the money for a period of time; interest rates are quoted as a certain percent yield per year.

Present Value of Assets

Capital goods are durable assets that produce a stream of rentals or receipts over time. If you owned an apartment building, you would collect rental payments over the life of the building, much as the owner of a fruit orchard would pick fruit from the trees each season.

Suppose you became weary of tending the building and decided to sell it. To set a fair price for the building, you would need to determine the value today of the entire stream of future income. The value of that stream is called the **present value** of the capital asset.

The present value of an asset is obtained by calculating how much money invested today would be needed, at the going interest rate, to generate the asset's future stream of receipts.

Let's start with a very simple example. Let's say somebody offers to sell you a bottle of wine that matures in exactly 1 year and can then be sold for exactly $11. Assuming the market interest rate is 10 percent per year, what is the present value of the wine—that is, how much should you pay for the wine today? Pay exactly $10, because $10 invested today at the market interest rate of 10 percent will be worth $11 in 1 year. So, the present value of next year's $11 wine is today $10.

Present Value for Perpetuities

We present the first way of calculating present value by examining the case of a *perpetuity,* which is an asset like land that lasts forever and pays $\$N$ each year from now to eternity. We are seeking the present value (V) if the interest rate is i percent per year, where the present value is the amount of money invested today that would yield exactly $\$N$ each year. This is simply:

$$V = \frac{\$N}{i}$$

where V = the present value of the land

$\$N$ = permanent annual receipts

i = interest rate in decimal terms (e.g., 0.05, or $\frac{5}{100}$, or 5 percent per year)

This says that if the interest rate is always 5 percent per year, then an asset yielding a constant stream of income will sell for exactly 20 ($= 1 \div \frac{5}{100}$) times its annual income. In this case, what would be the present value of a perpetuity yielding $100 every year? At a 5 percent interest rate its present value would be $2000 ($= \$100 \div 0.05$).

General Formula for Present Value

Having seen the simple case of the perpetuity, we move to the general case of the present value of an asset with an income stream that varies over time. The main thing to remember about present value is that future payments are worth less than current payments, and they are therefore *discounted* relative to the present. Future payments are discounted because a positive interest rate means that today's dollars will grow in dollar terms in the future; hence future payments are worth less now, just as distant objects look smaller than nearby ones.

The interest rate produces a similar shrinking of time perspective. Even if I knew you would pay $1 million to my heirs 999 years from now, I would be foolish to pay you as much as a cent today. To see why, let us review the arithmetic of discounting.

The general rule for present value is the following: To figure out the value today of $1 payable t

years from now, ask yourself how much must be invested today at compound interest to grow into \$1 at the end of t years. We know that at 6 percent interest, compounded annually, any principal grows in t years proportionally to $(1 + 0.06)^t$. Hence, we need only invert this expression to find present value: the present value of \$1 payable t years from now is only $\$1/(1 + 0.06)^t$. What if the interest rate were 8 percent? Replace 0.06 by 0.08 and recalculate.

In general, there are several terms in an asset's stream of income. In present-value calculations, each dollar must stand on its own feet. Evaluate the present value of each part of the stream of future receipts, giving due allowance for the discounting required by its payment date. Then simply add together all these separate present values. This summation will give you the asset's present value.

The exact formula for present value is the following:

$$V = \frac{N_1}{1 + i} + \frac{N_2}{(1 + i)^2} + \cdots + \frac{N_t}{(1 + i)^t} + \cdots$$

In this equation, i is the one-period market interest rate (assumed constant). Further, N_1 is the net receipts (positive or negative) in period 1, N_2 the net receipts in period 2, N_t the net receipts in period t, and so forth. Then the stream of payments $(N_1, N_2, \ldots, N_t, \ldots)$ will have the present value, V, given by the formula.

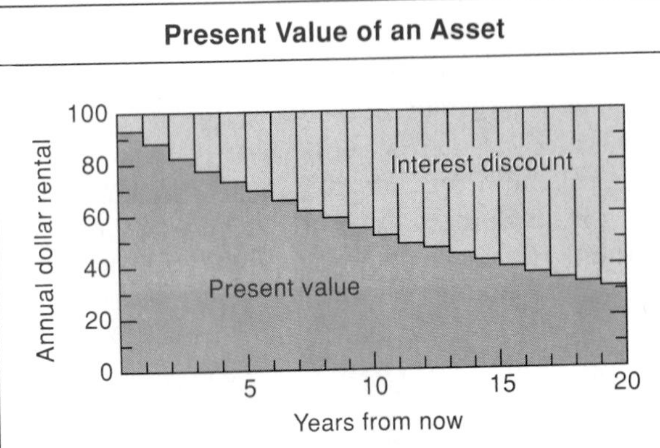

Figure 16-3. Present value of an asset
The lower blue area shows the present value of a machine giving net annual rentals of \$100 for 20 years with an interest rate of 6 percent per year. The upper gray area has been discounted away. Explain why raising the interest rate depresses the market price of an asset.

For example, assume that the interest rate is 10 percent per year, and that I am to receive \$100 next year and \$470 in 3 years. The present value of this stream is:

$$V = \frac{100}{(1.10)^1} + \frac{470}{(1.10)^3} = 444.03$$

Figure 16-3 shows the calculation of present value graphically for a machine that earns steady net annual rentals of \$100 over a 20-year period and has no scrap value at the end. Its present value is not \$2000, but only \$1147. Note how much the later dollar earnings are scaled down or discounted because of our time perspective. The total area remaining after discounting (the blue shaded area) represents the machine's total present value—the value today of the stream of all future incomes.

Acting to Maximize Present Value

The present-value formula tells us how to calculate the value of any asset once we know the earnings. But note that an asset's future receipts usually depend on business decisions: Shall we use a truck 8 or 9 years? Overhaul it once a month or once a year? Replace it with a cheap, nondurable truck or an expensive, durable one?

There is one rule that gives correct answers to all investment decisions: Calculate the present value resulting from each possible decision. Then always act so as to maximize present value. In this way you will have more wealth, to spend whenever and however you like.

Review

Let's review quickly the terms we have learned before turning to apply them:

- The economy today has accumulated large stocks of *capital*, or capital goods. These are the machines, buildings, and inventories that are so vital to an economy's productivity.
- The annual dollar receipts on capital are called *rentals*. When we divide the net receipts (rentals less costs) by the dollar value of the capital generating the rentals, we obtain the *rate of return on capital* (measured in percent per year). Note that these must be *net* receipts, after appropriate allowance for expenses such as depreciation of assets has been subtracted from *gross* rentals.

- Capital is financed by savers who lend *funds* and hold financial assets. The dollar yield on these financial assets is the *interest rate,* measured in percent per year.
- *Profits* are a residual income item, equal to total revenues minus total costs. For large corporations that own their own capital, business profits are the earnings after payment of wages, rents, and other direct factor costs.
- Capital goods and financial assets generate a stream of income over time. This stream can be converted into a *present value,* i.e., the value that the stream of income would be worth today. This conversion is made by asking what quantity of dollars today would be just sufficient to generate the asset's stream of income at going market interest rates.

Theory of Capital

Now that we have surveyed the major concepts in capital theory, we turn to an analysis of the *classical theory of capital.* This approach was developed independently by the Austrian E. V. Bohm-Bawerk, the Swede Knut Wicksell, and Yale's Irving Fisher in the United States.

Roundaboutness

In Chapter 2, we noted that investment in capital goods involves indirect or *roundabout* production. Instead of catching fish with our hands, we find it ultimately more worthwhile first to build boats and make nets—and then to use the boats and nets to catch many more fish than we could by hand.

Put differently, investment in capital goods involves forgoing present consumption to increase future consumption. Catching fewer fish today frees labor for making nets to catch many more fish tomorrow. In the most general sense, capital is productive because by forgoing consumption today we get more consumption in the future.

To see this, imagine two islands that are exactly alike. Each has the same amount of labor and natural resources. Island A uses these primary factors directly to produce consumption goods like food and clothing; it uses no produced capital goods at all. By contrast, thrifty Island B sacrifices current consumption and uses its resources and labor to produce capital goods, such as plows, shovels, and looms. After this temporary sacrifice of current consumption, B ends up with a large stock of capital goods.

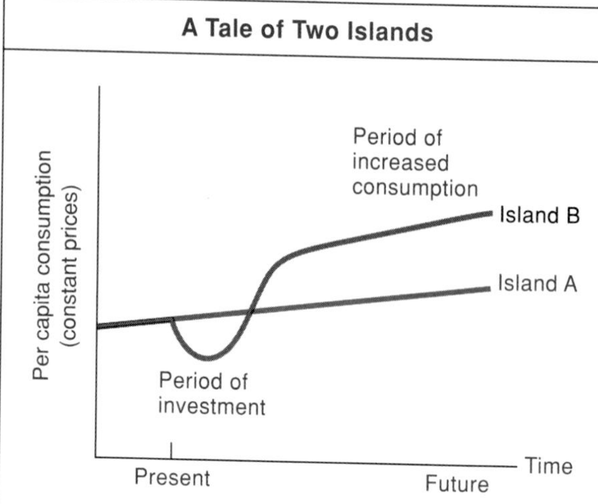

Figure 16-4. Investments today yield consumption tomorrow

Two islands begin with equal endowments of labor and natural resources. Spendthrift Island A invests nothing and shows a modest growth in per capita consumption. Thrifty Island B devotes an initial period to investment, forgoing consumption, and then enjoys the harvest of much higher consumption in the future.

Figure 16-4 shows the way that Island B forges ahead of A. For each island, measure the amount of consumption per person that can be enjoyed while maintaining the existing capital stock. Because of its thrift, Island B, using roundabout, capital-intensive methods of production, will enjoy more future consumption than Island A. B gets more than 100 units of future consumption goods for its initial sacrifice of 100 units of present consumption.

Societies invest because the sacrifices of present consumption allow increased consumption in the future.

Diminishing Returns and the Demand for Capital

What happens as a nation sacrifices more and more of its consumption for capital accumulation? As production becomes more and more roundabout or indirect? We would expect the law of diminishing returns to set in. As we add more fishing boats or power plants or computers, the extra product, or return on even more roundabout production, begins to fall. The first few fishing boats yield many fish, but too many fishing boats will simply run into each other. As capital accumulates, the rate of return on the investments falls.

Unless offset by technological change, the diminishing returns from rapid investment will drive down the rate of return on investment. Surprisingly, rates of return on capital have not fallen markedly over the course of the last 150 years, even though our capital stocks have grown manyfold. Rates of return have remained high because innovation and technological change have created profitable new opportunities as rapidly as past investment has annihilated them.

Determination of Interest and the Return on Capital

We can use the classical theory of capital to understand the determination of the rate of interest. Households *supply* funds for investment by abstaining from consumption and accumulating saving over time. At the same time, businesses *demand* capital goods—in the form of trucks, buildings, and inventories—to combine with labor, land, and other inputs. In the end, a firm's demand for capital is driven by its desire to make profits by producing goods.

Or as Irving Fisher put the matter at the beginning of this century:

> The quantity of capital and the rate of return on capital are determined by the interaction between (1) people's *impatience* to consume now rather than accumulate more capital goods for future consumption (perhaps for old-age retirement or for that proverbial rainy day); and (2) *investment opportunities* that yield higher or lower returns to such accumulated capital.

To understand how interest rates and the return on capital are determined, consider an idealized world without risk, monopoly, or inflation. In deciding whether to make an investment, a profit-maximizing firm will always compare its cost of funds with the rate of return on capital. If the rate of return is higher than the market interest rate at which the firm can borrow funds, it will undertake the investment. If the interest rate is higher than the rate of return on investment, the firm will not invest.

Where will this process end up? Eventually, firms will undertake all investments whose returns are higher than the market interest rate. In an idealized world, the equilibrium is reached when competition among firms beats down the return on investment to the level of the market interest rate.

In a world free of risk, inflation, and monopoly, the competitive rate of return on capital would be equal to the market interest rate.

Note that the market rate of interest has two functions: it rations out society's scarce supply of capital goods for the uses that have the highest rates of return; and it induces people to sacrifice current consumption in order to increase the stock of capital.

Graphical Analysis of the Return on Capital

We can illustrate classical capital theory by concentrating on a simple case in which all physical capital goods are alike. In addition, assume that the

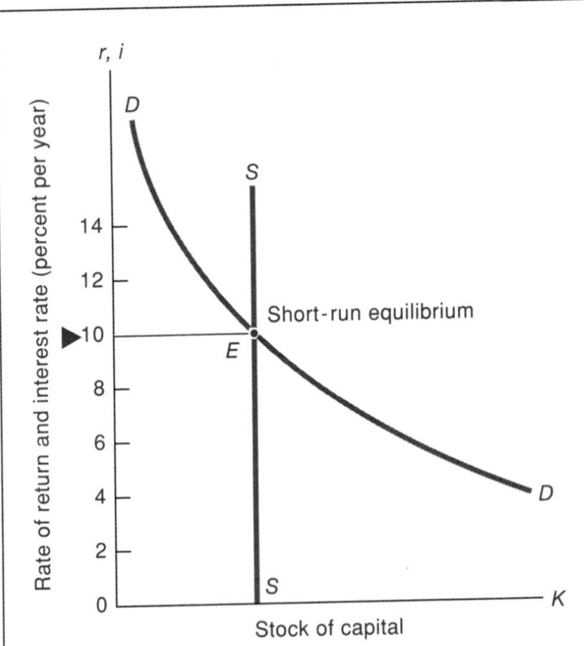

Figure 16-5. Short-run determination of interest and returns

In the short run, the economy has inherited a given stock of capital from the past, shown as the vertical *SS* supply-of-capital schedule. Intersection of the short-run supply with the demand-for-capital schedule determines the short-run return on capital, and the short-run real interest rate, at 10 percent per year.

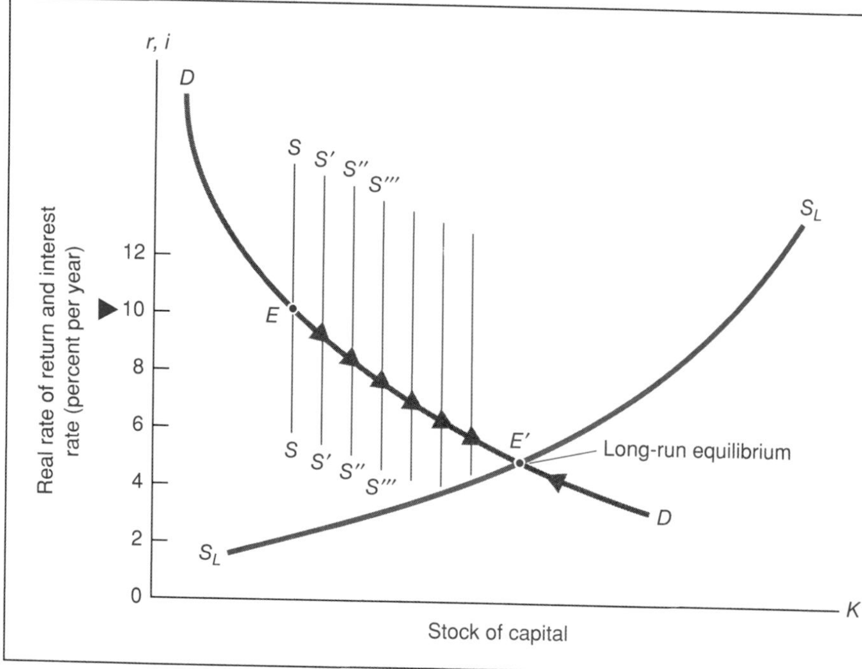

Figure 16-6. Long-run equilibration of the supply of and demand for capital

In the long run, society accumulates capital, so the supply curve is no longer vertical. As pictured here, the supply of wealth is responsive to higher interest rates. At the original short-run equilibrium at *E* there is net investment, so the economy moves down the *DD* demand curve as shown by the black arrows. Long-run equilibrium comes at *E′*, where net saving ceases.

economy is in a steady state with no population growth or technological change.

In Figure 16-5, *DD* shows the demand curve for the stock of capital; it plots the relationship between the quantity of capital demanded and the rate of return on capital. Where does the demand for capital come from? Recall from Chapter 14 that the demand for labor was derived from the marginal productivity curve for labor. Similarly, the demand for capital is a "derived demand." Ultimately, it is derived from the *marginal product of capital,* which is the extra output yielded by additions to the capital stock.

The law of diminishing returns can be seen in the fact that the demand-for-capital curve in Figure 16-5 is downward-sloping. When capital is very scarce, there are some very profitable roundabout projects that have a yield of 15 or 20 or even 40 percent per year. Gradually, as capital is accumulated and the community exploits all the high-yield projects, with total labor and land fixed, diminishing returns to capital set in. The community must then invest in lower-yield projects as it moves down the demand-for-capital curve.

Short-Run Equilibrium. We can now see how supply and demand interact. In Figure 16-5, past investments have produced a given stock of capital, shown as the vertical short-run supply curve, *SS*. Firms will demand capital goods in a manner shown by the downward-sloping demand curve, *DD*.

At the intersection of supply and demand, at point *E*, the amount of capital is just rationed out to the demanding firms. At this short-run equilibrium, firms are willing to pay 10 percent a year to borrow funds to buy capital goods. At that point, the lenders of funds are satisfied to receive exactly 10 percent a year on their supplies of capital.

Thus, in our simple riskless world, the rate of return on capital exactly equals the market interest rate. Any higher interest rate would find firms unwilling to borrow for their investments; any lower interest rate would find firms clamoring for the too scarce capital. Only at the equilibrium interest rate of 10 percent are supply and demand equilibrated.

But the equilibrium at *E* is sustained only for the short run. Why? Because, at this high interest rate, people will want to go on saving. Figure 16-6 shows how interest rates are determined in the long run. The long-run supply of capital or funds, shown as S_LS_L in Figure 16-6, slopes upward to indicate that people are willing to supply more funds at higher real interest rates. At an interest rate of 10 percent, the long-run supply of wealth or capital exceeds the demand for capital at E. People thus desire to accumulate more capital, i.e., to continue saving. This means that net capital formation is taking place at point E. So each year, the capital stock is a little higher as net investment occurs. As time passes, the community moves slowly down the DD curve as shown by the black arrows in Figure 16-6.

The March toward Equilibrium. Society moves rightward down the DD curve because positive investment means that the capital stock is increasing; the short-run supply curve is consequently being pushed further and further to the right each year. You can actually see a series of very thin short-run supply-of-capital curves in Figure 16-6—S, S', S'', S''', ... These curves show how the short-run supply of capital increases with capital accumulation.

At the same time, because of the law of diminishing returns, the rate of return and the interest rate move downward. As capital increases—while other things such as labor, land, and technical knowledge remain unchanged—the rate of return on the increased stock of capital goods falls to ever-lower levels.

Long-Term Equilibrium. Where does long-run equilibrium occur? It comes at E' in Figure 16-6; this is where the long-run supply of capital (shown as S_LS_L) intersects with the demand for capital. The long-run equilibrium is attained when the interest rate has fallen to the point where the capital stock held by firms has expanded so as to match the amount that people desire to supply.

At that point, net saving stops, net capital accumulation is zero, and the capital stock is no longer growing. The long-run equilibrium interest rate and rate of return on capital come at the point where the value of financial assets that people want to hold in the long run exactly matches the amount of capital the firms want to hold at that interest rate.

● There are two forces that drive the accumulation of capital and its return. First, the demand for capital results from the fact that indirect or roundabout production processes are productive; by abstaining from consumption today, society can raise consumption in the future. Second, people must be willing to abstain from consumption in order to accumulate financial assets, lending funds to firms that will make the productive investments in roundabout productive processes.

These two forces of technology and impatience are brought into balance by the interest rate, which ensures that society's accumulation of capital just matches the amount that people are willing to hold back from consumption in the form of saving. ●

Applications of Classical Capital Theory

We have completed our survey of the basic theory of interest and capital. But the classical theory needs some amplifications and qualifications to account for important realistic features of economic life.

Technological Disturbance

We have analyzed capital and interest in a riskless world without technological change. An accurate description would include inventions and discoveries that raise the return on capital and thereby affect equilibrium interest rates. Historical studies suggest that the tendency toward falling interest rates via diminishing returns has been just about canceled out by inventions and technological progress.

Some economists (such as Joseph Schumpeter) have likened the investment process to a plucked violin string: In a world of unchanging technology, the string gradually comes to rest as capital accumulation drives down returns on capital. But before the economy has settled into a steady state, an outside event or invention comes along to pluck the string and set the forces of investment into motion again.

Uncertainty and Expectations

Another important qualification is the extent of risk and uncertainty that exists in investment decisions. In real life no one has a crystal ball to read the future. All investments, resting as they do on estimates of future earnings, must necessarily be guesses—accurate guesses based on much thought and information in some cases, wild guesses in other cases, but in every case uncertain guesses. Each day we wake up to learn that our expectations were not quite accurate and have to be revised. Each night we go to bed realizing that the next morning will have some surprises for us.

How does the presence of uncertainty affect capital theory? Our discussion assumed that there were no risks. But in fact almost any loan or investment has an element of risk. Machines break down; an oil well may turn out to be a dry hole; your favorite computer company may go belly up. Investments differ in their degree of risk, but no investment is completely risk-free.

Investors are generally averse to holding risky assets. They would rather hold an asset that is sure to yield them 10 percent than an asset that is equally likely to yield 0 or 20 percent. Thus, you must offer an extra return, or *risk premium,* to get them to hold risky investments.

For example, raising cattle involves risks due to weather, while production of telephones does not. Suppose that investments in service industries are riskless and the normal return for such riskless investments is 10 percent per year. By contrast, owning cattle is a highly risky investment; because of bad weather, disease, and other factors you could with equal chances double your money or lose half of it. Your average return in cattle is then 25 percent per year.[3] The extra 15 percent return, over and above the riskless 10 percent return, is a risk premium required to coax cattle ranchers to endure the extra risks and sleepless nights in such an uncertain business.

In summary:

The high rates of return on risky assets or ventures include risk premiums that investors require before they will hold such risky investments.

Real vs. Nominal Interest Rates

We have up to now banished inflation from the picture. But in a world of changing prices we need to correct interest rates for the changes in the monetary yardstick caused by inflation.

The interest rates we defined above are measured in dollar or *nominal* terms and not in terms of trees or fish or wine. Interest is the yield on an investment measured in dollars per year per dollar of investment. But dollars can become distorted yardsticks. The prices of fish, trees, wine, and other goods change from year to year as the general price level rises due to inflation. We therefore need to find a *real* return on capital, one that measures the quantity of goods we get tomorrow for goods forgone today.

As an example, say that you obtain a 10 percent nominal or money yield on your investment, obtaining $110 next year for $100 invested this year. Over the course of the year, however, prices have risen 6 percent. In terms of the real amount of goods you could buy, your real yield is not 10 percent but $10 - 6 = 4$ percent. In other words, if you were to lend 100 market baskets of goods today, you could obtain only 104 market baskets of goods next year.

In a monetary economy, we must measure the return on capital by real interest rates, not money or nominal interest rates.

The real interest rate is the nominal interest rate less the rate of inflation.

The difference between real and nominal interest rates is most dramatic during periods of high inflation. During the inflationary period of 1979–1980, nominal interest rates in the United States soared to 12 percent per year. But after subtracting inflation, the real interest rates were actually near zero. This difference shows the importance of remembering the distinction between real and nominal returns when making investments.

Profits

In addition to wages, interest, and rent, economists often talk about a fourth category of income called *profits.* What are profits? How do they differ from interest and the returns on capital more generally?

Reported Profit Statistics

When accountants calculate profits, what do they usually include? **Profits** are defined as the difference between total revenues and total costs. To calculate profits, start with total revenues from sales. Subtract all expenses (wages, salaries, rents, materi-

[3] The average, or expected value, of the return is equal to the return in each state weighted by the probability of that state's occurring. Since in one state the return is 100 percent and in the other minus 50 percent, with each state having probability of one-half, the expected return is $\frac{1}{2}(100) + \frac{1}{2}(-50) = 25$ percent.

als, interest, excise taxes, and the rest). What is left over is the residual called profits.[4]

The profit figures reported in the national income accounts are limited to profits of corporations. In 1990, corporate profits before taxes were $297 billion. Companies paid $134 billion in taxes, distributed $134 billion in dividends to shareholders, and retained the balance.

How large are corporate profits? In the United States in the 1980s, corporate profits after taxes were significantly below 8 percent of total GNP. The rate of return on American corporate capital (defined as profits divided by the current dollar cost of capital goods) has averaged about 8 percent per year in the last 15 years. This return is well above the real interest rate on safe assets, which averaged around 4 percent per year over the last decade.

Determinants of Profits

What determines the rate of corporate profits in a market economy? In analyzing profits, the following list provides some of the important explanations:

1. *Profits as implicit returns.* To the economist, business profits are a hodgepodge of different elements. A large part of reported business profits is merely the return to the owners of the firm for their own labor or their own invested funds, that is, for factors of production supplied by them.

   For example, some profits are the return on the personal work provided by the owners of the firm—by the doctor or lawyer who works in a small professional corporation. Part is the rent return on self-owned natural resources. In large corporations, most profits are the opportunity costs of invested capital. These returns are called *implicit returns,* which is the name given to the opportunity costs of factors owned by firms.

   Thus some of what is ordinarily called profit is really nothing but rentals, rents, and wages under a different name. Implicit rentals, implicit rent, and implicit wages are the names economists give to the earnings on factors that the firm itself owns.

2. *Profits as reward for risk bearing and innovation.* A half-century ago, Chicago economist Frank Knight suggested that all true profit is linked with uncertainty or imperfect information. By this he meant that, once the implicit returns are subtracted, what remains is the pure profit which is the reward for undertaking investments with uncertain returns.

   In analyzing the reward for risk bearing, we would generally not count default risk or insurable risk. A provision for default risk would cover the possibility that a loan or investment could not be paid, say because the borrower went bankrupt. An insurable risk, such as those analyzed in Chapter 12, would be a risk that could be shed through purchase of insurance. These two risks are simply the normal risks of doing business and should be counted as costs.

   A kind of risk that must be considered in profit calculations is the *uninsurable risk of investments.* A company may have a high degree of sensitivity to business cycles, which means that its earnings fluctuate a great deal when aggregate output goes up or down. Because investors are averse to risky situations, they require a risk premium on this uncertain investment to compensate for their risk aversion.

   Corporate profits are the most volatile component of national income, so corporate capital must contain a significant risk premium to attract investors. Empirical studies suggest that between 3 and 6 percentage points of the annual return on corporate stocks is the risk premium necessary to attract people to hold this risky investment.

   Another way that uncertainty contributes to profits is through *reward for innovation and enterprise.* To understand this, assume that the appropriate charges for default and insurable and uninsurable risks have been subtracted from profits. In a world of perfect competition and unchanging technology, there would be no

[4] In analyzing profits, it is important to distinguish *business profits* from *economic profits.* Business profits are the residual income, equal to sales less costs, measured by accountants. Business profits include an implicit return on the capital owned by firms. Economic profits are the earnings after all costs—both money and implicit or opportunity costs—are subtracted. In large corporations, therefore, economic profits would equal business profits less an implicit return on the capital owned by the firm along with any other costs (such as unpaid management time) not fully compensated at market prices.

further profits at all. In this world, owners would be getting for their owned factors and risk incurred exactly what those services were worth in competitive markets. In other words, free entry of numerous competitors would, in a static world of unchanging technology, bring price down to cost. The only sustainable profits in a static world would be the competitive wages, rentals, rent, and return for risk bearing.

But we do not live in such a dreamworld. In reality, someone with a new idea or patent can promote a new product or lower the costs on an old one. Let's call the person who does any of these things an *innovator* or *entrepreneur.* We can identify "innovational profits" as the temporary excess return to innovators or entrepreneurs.

What do we mean by "innovators"? Such people should not be confused with managers, who are the people who run large and small companies but do not own a significant part of the equity. Innovators are different. These are people who have the vision, originality, and daring to introduce new ideas in business. History has seen great inventors like Alexander Graham Bell (the telephone), Thomas Edison (the light bulb), and Chester Carlson (xerography). Some inventors amass great fortunes from their entrepreneurship. The modern age saw Steven Jobs launch Apple Computers while Mitch Kapor became wealthy through spreadsheets he developed at Lotus Corporation. Yet for every one of these successful innovators, many others fail on the road to fame and fortune. Many try; few succeed.

Every successful innovation creates a temporary pool of monopoly. For a short time, innovational profits are earned. These profit earnings are temporary and are soon competed away by rivals and imitators. But just as one source of innovational profits is disappearing, another is being born. Innovational profits will continue to exist as long as technological change continues.

3. *Profits as monopoly returns.* Innovational profits shade off into our last category. Many people are downright suspicious of profit. The critics of profits do not see them as implicit rentals or return for risk bearing in competitive markets. Their image of the profiteer is more likely that of someone with a penchant for sly arithmetic who somehow exploits the rest of the community. What critics have in mind is a third, quite different meaning of profit: *profit as the earnings of monopoly.*

How are monopoly profits generated? Once a market departs appreciably from perfect competition, firms in the industry can earn supernormal profits by raising prices. If you are the sole owner of a valuable drug patent or if you have acquired the sole franchise to lease cable television in a city, you can raise prices above marginal cost, restrict supply, and earn monopoly profits on your investment.

What does all this add up to? It means that part of what is called profit is the return on market or monopoly power.

Awash with Profits?

This brief survey reveals many sources of profits. Given all the ways that firms can extract profits in a modern economy—implicit returns, rewards for risk bearing, and returns on monopoly power—we would expect to see the coffers of American corporations awash in cash.

Surprisingly, however, they are not. Over the last 15 years, corporations earned a modest rate of return on their investments—only about 8 percent in real terms. And for the last decade the ratio of the market value of corporations (i.e., the value of their stocks and bonds) to the value of their land, plant, and equipment (a ratio known as "Tobin's q") has been very close to one. On average, from 1980 to 1990, $100 of corporate tangible assets sold for $99 in financial markets (this being an average q of 0.99).

These data indicate that in the long run American corporations tend to earn very little supernormal returns. This finding suggests that some of the arguments about extraordinary monopoly power of large companies are exaggerated, and that competition in the markets served by corporate America is potent enough to keep the rate of return on capital close to the cost of funds.

We have now completed our survey of the incomes of the major factors of production. Armed with these tools, we are prepared to examine in Part 4 some of the major policy issues of microeconomics.

SUMMARY

A. Land, Natural Resources, and Rent

1. The unchangeable quantity of land is an interesting special case of a perfectly vertical and inelastic supply curve, whose factor return is called pure economic rent, or rent for short. Rent is more price-determined than price-determining; the return on land is more the result than the cause of the market prices for the finished commodities. Yet we must not forget that, to any small firm or industry, rent will still enter into the cost of production just like any other expense. To such a small firm or industry, rent reflects the opportunity cost of using land elsewhere and appears to be as much price-determining as any other cost element.

2. A factor like land that is inelastically supplied will continue to work the same amount even though its factor reward is reduced. For this reason, Henry George pointed out that rent is in the nature of a "surplus" rather than a reward necessary to coax out the factor's effort. This provides the basis for his single-tax proposal to tax the unearned increment of land value—without shifting the tax forward to consumers or distorting production.

3. Modern tax theory finds enduring truth in George's analysis: the theory of efficient (or Ramsey) taxes shows that the amount of economic inefficiency is minimized when taxes are levied on goods or factors that are the most inelastically supplied or demanded.

4. Many of today's environmental problems occur because rents are not charged on scarce natural resources. The "tragedy of the commons" arose when too many herds grazed common land at zero rent, thereby destroying the vegetation. Grazing, fishing, or dumping of wastes can produce externalities, or costs to society not paid for by the grazer, fisher, or dumper. In these cases, common property resources are scarce, but no rents are charged to limit their use. Creating markets for these scarce natural resources would improve resource allocation and help reduce environmental damage efficiently.

B. Capital, Interest, and Profits

5. A third factor of production is capital, a produced good that is used in further production. In the most general sense, investing in capital represents deferred consumption. By postponing consumption today and producing buildings or equipment, society increases consumption in the future. It is a technological fact that roundabout production yields a positive rate of return.

6. Recall the definitions of key terms given on pages 272–273.
   Capital goods: durable produced goods used for further production
   Rentals: net annual dollar returns on capital goods
   Rate of return on capital: net annual receipts on capital divided by dollar value of capital (measured as percent per year)
   Interest rate: yield on funds, also measured as percent per year

Present value: value today of a stream of future returns generated by an asset

Profits: a residual income item equal to revenues minus costs

7. Assets generate streams of income in future periods. By calculating the present value, we can convert the stream of returns into a single value today. This is done by asking what amount of dollars today will generate the stream of future returns, when invested at the market interest rate.
8. The exact present-value formula is as follows: Each dollar payable t years from now is worth only its present value (V) of $\$1/(1 + i)^t$. So for any net receipt stream ($N_1, N_2, \ldots, N_t, \ldots$) where N_t is the dollar value of receipts t years in the future, we have:

$$V = \frac{N_1}{1+i} + \frac{N_2}{(1+i)^2} + \cdots + \frac{N_t}{(1+i)^t} + \cdots$$

9. Interest is a device that serves two functions in the economy. It provides an incentive for people to save and accumulate wealth. But the interest rate is also a rationing device; it allows society to select only those investment projects with the highest rates of return. However, as more and more capital is accumulated, and as the law of diminishing returns sets in, the rate of return on capital and the interest rate will be beaten down by competition. Falling interest rates are a signal to society to adopt more capital-intensive projects with lower rates of return.
10. Saving and investment involve waiting for future consumption rather than consuming today. Such thrift interacts with the net productivity of capital to determine interest rates, the rate of return on capital, and the capital stock. The funds or financial assets needed to purchase capital are provided by households that are willing to sacrifice consumption today in return for larger consumption tomorrow. The demand for capital comes from firms that have a variety of roundabout investment projects. In long-run equilibrium, the interest rate is thus determined by the interaction between the net productivity of capital and the willingness of households to sacrifice consumption today for consumption tomorrow.
11. Important qualifications of classical capital theory include the following: Lack of perfect foresight means that capital's return is highly volatile as expectations, technology, and income levels change. Also, to get the real rate of interest, one must subtract the rate of inflation from the nominal rate of interest.
12. Profits are revenues less costs. Reported business profits are chiefly corporate earnings. Economically, we must distinguish three different categories. Perhaps the most important source is profits as an implicit return. Firms generally own many of their own non-labor factors of production—capital, natural resources, and patents. In these cases, the implicit return on unpaid or owned inputs is part of profits.
13. A second source of profits is uncertainty—associated with the return to cover uninsurable risks, and the profits earned by entrepreneurs who introduce new products or innovations.
14. Finally, profits may result from firms exercising monopoly power—on their patents, from special privileges, or due to regulation.

CONCEPTS FOR REVIEW

Land
rent
inelastic supply of land
efficient or Ramsey taxes
"tragedy of the commons"
scarcity rents for common property resources

Capital
capital, capital goods
rentals, rate of return on capital, interest rate, profits
indirect or roundabout production methods
present value
implicit rewards to factors in profits

real vs. nominal interest rate
twin elements in interest determination: returns to roundaboutness and impatience
uncertainty and profits: default risk, insurable and uninsurable risks, innovation

QUESTIONS FOR DISCUSSION

1. Define the "pure economic rent" case. Explain the sense in which rent of such a factor is "output-price-determined" rather than "output-price-determining." Show that, nonetheless, an increase in supply of the rent-earning factor will depress its return and lower the prices of goods that use much of it.
2. What would you expect to be the result of a tax on the earnings of top rock stars or baseball players?
3. Give some examples of efficient roundabout processes and some of durable "produced" or "intermediate" outputs that serve in their turn as inputs.
4. Contrast the following four returns on durable assets: (*a*) rent on land, (*b*) rental of a capital good, (*c*) rate of return on a capital good, and (*d*) interest rate. Give an example of each.
5. Using the supply-and-demand analysis of interest, explain how each of the following would affect interest rates in the classical analysis:
   (a) An innovation that increased the marginal product of capital at each level of capital
   (b) A decrease in the desired wealthholdings of households
   (c) A 50 percent tax on the return on capital
6. Consider each of the following sources of reported profits. Decide into which of the categories (or subcategories) of profits each falls:
   (a) The profit earned by a medical corporation in a perfectly competitive industry
   (b) The profit earned by a firm that has relatively little invested capital but is extremely cyclical
   (c) A firm, making $100,000 a year on a new video game, whose competitors are expected to invade the field and wipe out the profits
   (d) The profit of a farm that owns a prime vineyard in California
7. Looking back to Figures 16-5 and 16-6, review how the economy moved from the short-run equilibrium interest rate at 10 percent per year to the long-run equilibrium. Now explain what would occur in both the long run and the short run when innovations shifted *up* the demand-for-capital curve. What would happen if the government debt became very large and a large part of people's supply of capital was siphoned off to holdings of government debt?
8. Explain the rule for calculating present discounted value of a perpetual income stream. At 5 percent, what is the worth of a perpetuity paying $100 per year? Paying $200 per year? Paying $*N* per year? At 10 or 8 percent, what is the worth of a perpetuity paying $100 per year? What does doubling of the interest rate do to the capitalized value of a perpetuity—say, a perpetual bond?
9. Our highways have limited traffic capacity, as is illustrated by the vertical line *CS* in Figure 16-7. During peak periods, the demand curve (*DEB*) is far to the right. Explain what happens when society charges no

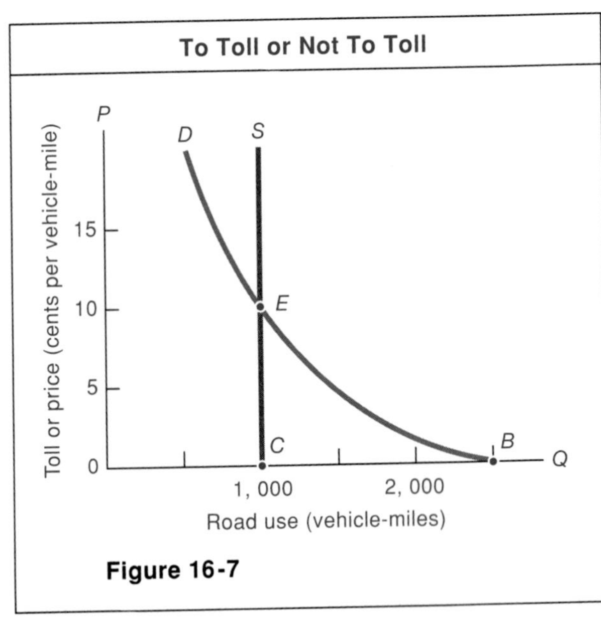

Figure 16-7

tolls for road use, so that the demand for highway use is at point B on the demand curve. Interpret segment CB.

Some have suggested using "congestion tolls" to keep demand within the available supply. What would the equilibrium congestion toll be? Explain how demand is restrained. Who would be made better off, who worse off by such a scheme?

10. Recall the algebraic formula for a convergent geometric progression:

$$1 + K + K^2 + \cdots = \frac{1}{1 - K}$$

for any fraction K less than 1. If you set $K = 1/(1 + i)$, can you verify the present-value formula for a permanent income stream, $V = \$N/i$? Provide an alternative proof using common sense. What would be the value of a lottery that paid you and your heirs $5000 per year forever at an interest rate of 6 percent per year?

PART FOUR

EFFICIENCY, EQUITY, AND GOVERNMENT

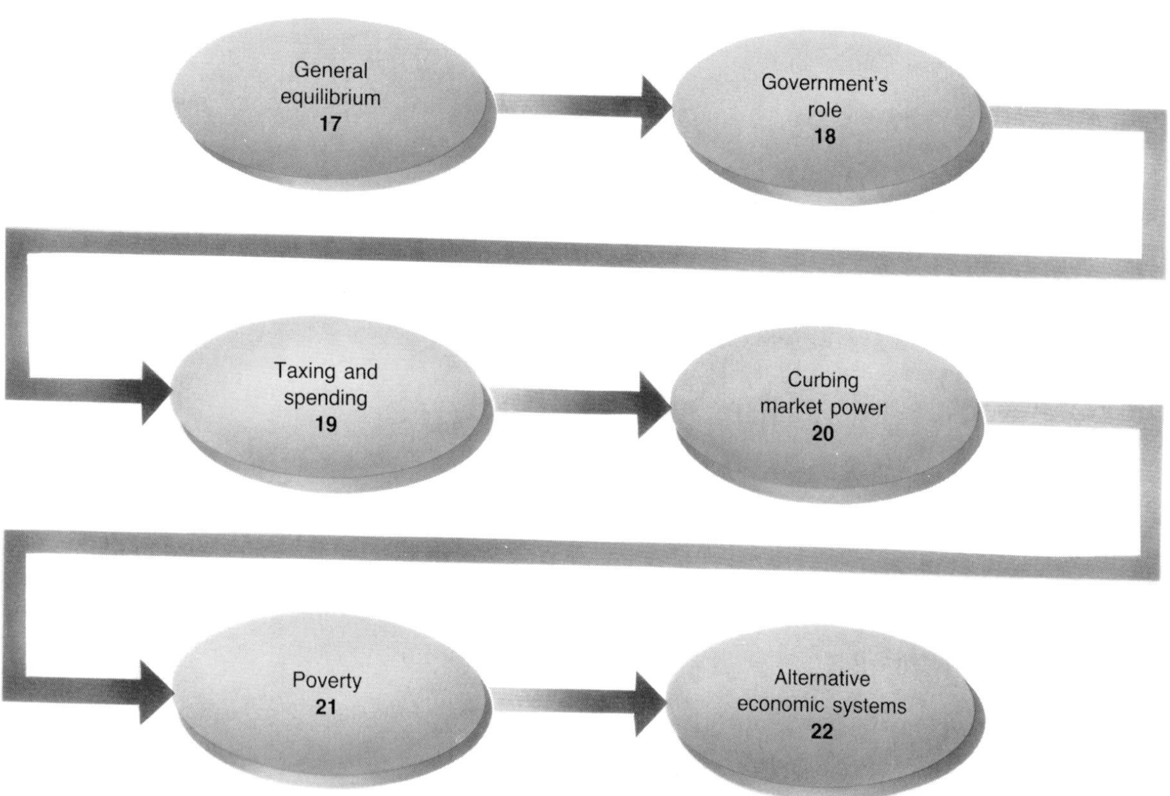

Our survey of microeconomics up to this point has examined how markets allocate resources in individual product and factor markets. In this part, we will weigh the major issues of design of an economic system: How do the prices and quantities in all the markets interact in a general equilibrium of markets? How can government intervene to change the allocation of resources? What are the possible conflicts between equity and efficiency? What are the alternative economic systems, and how do they compare with the mixed system in a modern market economy?

C H A P T E R 17

MARKETS AND ECONOMIC EFFICIENCY

The delicate, invisible web you wove . . .
T. S. Eliot

Our survey of microeconomics now turns to the vital issue of the interaction of all markets in a general equilibrium of all the products and factors together. We have seen that individual competitive markets display the invisible-hand property of efficiency, but what happens when all the markets are put together? In this chapter, we will see that the remarkable efficiency properties of competitive markets extend to the ensemble of markets under certain limited conditions. But we will also see that market failures like pollution and monopoly can mar the efficiency of a market economy.

This chapter's analysis is followed by two chapters investigating the role of government in an advanced industrialized economy. These chapters examine the nature of public choice, the patterns of government taxation and expenditure systems, and the methods government employs to cope with spillovers or externalities.

Two central economic responsibilities of government are to ensure efficiency and to promote fairness. Chapter 20 analyzes the way that governments can promote efficiency in the operation of business firms, examining how monopolies are subjected to price and service regulation, while oligopolies are constrained by antitrust laws.

Chapter 21 then studies the distribution of income in the United States. We will analyze the sources of economic inequality and survey the dilemmas that arise when societies attempt to redistribute income from the rich to the poor. How much, we will ask, must a nation sacrifice if it wishes to reduce or eradicate poverty.

Finally, Chapter 22 studies the development of economic thinking and alternative economic systems. We will review how economic analysis developed over the last two centuries and how different visions of the good society were translated into action, particularly in socialist countries. Why, we will ask, have socialist countries stagnated? Why have they rediscovered the market that they rejected decades ago?

This part, then, is devoted to the thorniest and most controversial issues of microeconomics: How well or badly does the market perform? How much should government intervene in economic activity? How much, if any, should the state tax the rich to boost the living standards of the poor? Why have socialist countries stagnated in recent years, and how can they reinvigorate their ailing economies?

General Equilibrium and the Invisible-Hand Theory

Let's review the path we have followed in understanding the behavior of individual markets:

1. Competitive supply and demand operate to determine prices and quantities in individual markets.
2. Market demand curves are derived from the marginal utilities of different goods.

3. The marginal costs of different commodities lie behind their competitive supply curves.
4. Firms calculate marginal costs of products and marginal revenue products of factors and then choose inputs and outputs so as to maximize profits.
5. These marginal revenue products, summed for all firms, provide the derived demands for the factors of production.
6. These derived demands for land, labor, or capital goods interact with their market supplies to determine factor prices such as rent, wages, and interest rates.
7. The factor prices and quantities determine incomes, which then close the circle back to steps 1 and 2 by helping to determine the demand for different commodities.

Each of these relationships is the subject of *partial-equilibrium analysis,* which analyzes the behavior of a single market, household, or firm, taking the behavior of all other markets and the rest of the economy as given. By contrast, **general-equilibrium analysis** examines how (and how successfully) the simultaneous interaction of all households, firms, and markets solves the questions of *how, what,* and *for whom.*

Interaction of All Markets in General Equilibrium

Notice how our list of steps follows a logical progression from step to step. In the textbook chapters, they follow in almost the same order. But in real life, which comes first? Is there an orderly sequence that determines prices in single markets on Monday, evaluates consumer preferences on Tuesday, and reckons business costs on Wednesday and marginal products on Thursday? Obviously not. All these processes are going on simultaneously.

That is not all. These different activities do not go on independently, each in its own little groove, careful not to get in the way of the others. All the processes of supply and demand, of cost and preference, of factor productivity and demand are really different aspects of one vast, simultaneous, interdependent process.

Thus, the supply curve for wheat depends upon the cost calculations, the production considerations, and the wage, rent, and interest determinations. Actually, you can take any one of the seven steps in the list and draw arrows connecting it causally with every other step.

Nor is the interdependence limited to the seven steps outlined above. There are also linkages across different products. For example, wheat supply and demand, and wheatland supply and demand, depend upon tastes for cornbread and oatmeal; upon how many people want to sacrifice food purchases for other products; and upon the demand for land in farming and other uses.

A Circular Flow. Like an invisible web, the many input and output markets are connected in an interdependent system we call a general equilibrium. Figure 17-1 depicts the general structure of a general equilibrium. The outer loops show the demands and supplies of all goods and factors. We speak here not of a single good or factor but of *all* different products (corn, medical care, concerts, pizzas, etc.), which are made by a vast array of factors of production (cornland, surgeons, studios, trucks, etc.).

Each good or factor is exchanged in a market, and the equilibrium of supply and demand determines the price and quantity of the item. That marriage of supply and demand is occurring millions of times every day, for all kinds of commodities from abacuses to zweiback. Note in Figure 17-1 that the upper loop carries the supplies and demands for products, while the lower loop matches it with the supplies and demands for factors of production. See how consumers demand products and supply factors; indeed, households buy their consumption goods with the incomes they earn from the factors they supply. Similarly, businesses buy factors and supply products, paying out factor incomes and profits with the revenues from the products that businesses sell.

Thus we see a logical structure behind the millions of markets determining prices and outputs: (1) Households with supplies of factors and preferences for products interact with (2) firms that, guided by the desire to maximize profits, transform factors bought from households into products sold to households. The logical structure of a general-equilibrium system is complete.

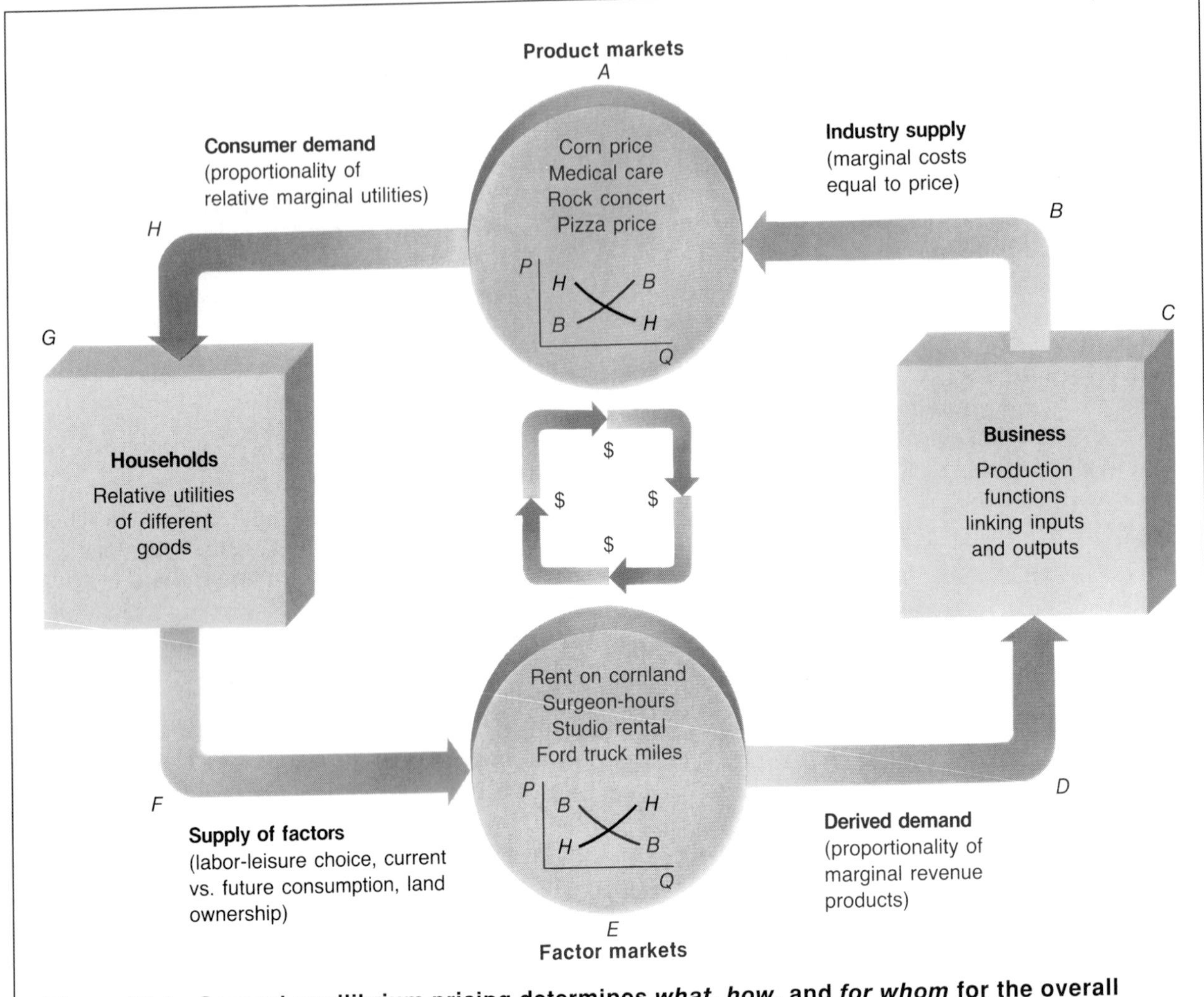

Figure 17-1. General-equilibrium pricing determines *what*, *how*, and *for whom* for the overall economy

The circular flow of economic life is described by the general economic equilibrium. Observe how profit-maximizing firms and utility-maximizing households interact in product markets at *A* and factor markets at *E*, determining the prices and quantities of each output and input. Note that the flow of money inside the figure moves in the opposite direction from the physical flow of goods and factors.

Properties of a Competitive General Equilibrium

Using partial-equilibrium analysis, earlier chapters examined the behavior of individual competitive markets for factors and products. We now consider, using general-equilibrium analysis, the properties of an ensemble of competitive markets. Such a general equilibrium contains many different kinds of labor, machines, and land, and these serve as inputs to produce dozens of different kinds of computers, hundreds of different specifications of automobiles, thousands of different items of clothing, and so on.

What are the characteristics of a general economic equilibrium? Do the efficiency properties of perfect competition in individual markets carry over to all markets together? Do prices play an important role as indicators of scarcity for the overall economy? Do the equations of supply and demand actually lead to an equilibrium, or is the overall outcome indeterminate? General-equilibrium analysis addresses these questions.

In our analysis we proceed as follows: We first describe the assumptions of our general economic equilibrium. We then describe in a summary fashion the properties of a general equilibrium. Next, in a more technical discussion, we sketch the properties of a general equilibrium in more detail. Finally, we show why a perfectly competitive general equilibrium will be efficient.

The Basic Principles. To simplify the analysis, we will consider an economy in which all markets are perfectly competitive and are subject to the relentless competition of many buyers and sellers. Firms maximize profits, while consumers choose their most preferred market baskets of goods. Further, assume that there are no natural monopolies and that each good is produced under conditions of constant or decreasing returns to scale. No pollution, entry-limiting regulations, or monopolistic labor unions mar the competitive landscape. Finally, each price, whether for an input or output, moves flexibly enough to equilibrate supply and demand at all times. Such an economy, were it to exist, would be one in which Adam Smith's invisible hand could rule without any impediment from imperfect competition.

For this economy, we can describe consumer and producer behavior and then show how they dovetail to produce an overall equilibrium. First, consumers will allocate their incomes across different goods in order to maximize their satisfactions. They choose goods such that the marginal utilities per dollar of expenditure are equal for the last unit of each commodity.

What are the conditions for the profit maximization of producers? In product markets, each firm will set its output level so that the marginal cost of production equals the price of the good. Since this is the case for every good and every firm, it follows that the competitive market price of each good reflects society's marginal cost of that good.

Putting together the conditions for perfectly competitive producers and consumers, we see that, for each consumer, the marginal utility of consumption for each good is equal to that good's marginal cost. Further, the marginal utility per last dollar of each good is equalized for every good.

In general equilibrium, marginal utilities per dollar of all consumer goods are equal to each other and are equal to the marginal social costs of production of those goods.

An example will clarify this result. Say that we have two individuals, Ms. Smith and Mr. Ricardo, and two kinds of goods, corn and clothing. In the consumer equilibrium, Ms. Smith buys corn and clothing until the *MU* per dollar of each good is 1 (Smith) util. Similarly, Mr. Ricardo distributes his income so that he gets 1 (Ricardo) util per dollar of spending. The corn and clothing producers set their output levels such that price equals marginal cost, so a dollar-bundle of corn will have a marginal cost of production of $1 for each producer, as will a dollar-bundle of clothing. If society were to produce one more dollar-bundle of corn, this would cost society exactly 1 dollar's worth of a bundle of scarce labor, land, and capital resources.

Putting these conditions together, we see that each extra dollar of consumption, by either Smith or Ricardo, yields exactly 1 extra util of satisfaction, whether that extra spending is on clothing or on food. Similarly, each extra unit of spending will have a marginal or additional cost to society of 1 extra dollar of resources, and this is so whether that extra dollar is spent by Smith or Ricardo or on food or clothing. The general equilibrium of markets therefore determines prices and outputs so that the marginal utility of each good to consumers equals the marginal cost of each good to society.

Detailed Analysis of General Equilibrium

Before we investigate why perfectly competitive markets lead to an efficient allocation of resources, we reiterate the *conditions of a competitive general equilibrium.* These conditions fall naturally into two categories; the first, relating to consumers, corresponds to the upper loop of Figure 17-1 while the second, concerning production, corresponds to the lower loop.

1. *Consumer equilibrium.* Our analysis of consumer behavior in Chapter 6 showed that, when choosing among goods, consumers would maximize their utility by equalizing the marginal utility per dollar of spending. Using this rule, we then see that the ratio of the marginal utilities of two goods, known technically as the "marginal

rate of substitution" between the two goods (or $MRS_{1,2}$ for the substitution relation between goods 1 and 2), satisfies the condition:

$$MRS_{1,2} = \frac{MU_1}{MU_2} = \frac{P_1}{P_2}$$

In words, the ratio of marginal utilities of two goods, or the relative marginal satisfactions derived from the two goods, is equal to the ratio of their prices. This condition must hold for an individual consumer who buys the two goods in question.

2. *Producer equilibrium.* The behavior of profit-maximizing firms leads to an analogous but somewhat more complex set of conditions, covered in Chapters 7 through 9. In those chapters we found that competitive firms choose input and output levels as follows:

(a) The first and most fundamental *output condition* for producers is that the level of output is set so that the price of each good equals the marginal cost of that good. By rearranging terms in this equation, we then find:

$$\frac{MC_1}{MC_2} = \frac{P_1}{P_2}$$

This equation says that, in a competitive economy, the ratio of the marginal costs of two final products is equal to their price ratio. The equality holds for all goods that are produced and for all firms that produce these goods. We can also interpret the ratio of marginal costs as the rate at which society can transform one good into another (sometimes the ratio of marginal costs is called the "marginal rate of transformation of goods" or the *MRT*). If corn's *MC* is $1 and a haircut's *MC* is $10, then, by transferring resources from barbers to farmers, society can transform one haircut into 10 units of corn.

The fundamental point to understand about a competitive economy is that the competitive prices reflect social costs or scarcities. We just noted that the ratio of marginal costs, or the *MRT* between two goods, tells us the rate at which society can transform one good into another. But because the price ratio of the two goods equals the *MRT* between the two goods, it follows that relative prices reflect social scarcities under perfect competition. It is just this essential fact, that competitive prices provide an accurate signal of the relative scarcity of different goods, that demonstrates the validity behind the invisible-hand principle that perfectly competitive markets lead to allocative efficiency.

(b) In addition to the output condition in (a), competition leads to certain relationships concerning input use. We have seen that profit-maximizing firms choose the amount of each input so that the value of its marginal product is equal to its price. Hence

Marginal product of land in good 1 × price of good 1 = rent on land

Marginal product of land in good 2 × price of good 2 = rent on land

Marginal product of labor in good 1 × price of good 1 = wage of labor

And so forth.

These relationships have several important implications. First, because each firm in a given industry faces the same prices for inputs and output, the marginal product of input A is the same for each firm in that industry.

By rearranging the terms in the above equations, we can see that the ratio of marginal products of inputs is equal to the ratio of their prices:

$$\frac{\text{Marginal product of land in good 1}}{\text{Marginal product of labor in good 1}} = \frac{\text{price of land}}{\text{price of labor}}$$

In addition, this relationship holds for all firms that use land and labor to produce good 1. Moreover, it holds for all factors of production (capital, oil, unskilled labor, etc.) and for all produced goods.

This *input condition* is important because it implies that the ratios of marginal products of factors are the same for all inputs and all firms in all uses. If labor is scarce relative to land in America, then land rents will be low relative to labor wages. This factor-price ratio will provide a signal for firms to operate with high ratios of land to labor. For inputs, as for outputs, competitive prices are reliable indexes of the economic scarcity of different factors of production.

To summarize:

In competitive general equilibrium, with utility-maximizing consumers and profit-maximizing firms:

- The ratios of marginal utilities of goods for all consumers are equal to the relative prices of those goods.
- The ratios of marginal costs of goods produced by firms are equal to the relative prices of those goods.
- The relative marginal products of all inputs are equal for all firms and all goods and are equal to those inputs' relative prices.*

Prices under Socialism. Our discussion of the relation between prices, consumers, and producers has made no mention of the organization of the economy, of whether the firms were owned by the state or by private enterprise. For an economy to be efficient, certain conditions must hold between the marginal utilities and the marginal costs of different goods. *These efficiency conditions would hold in a society organized along socialist lines as well as in a capitalist economy.*

Under most socialist systems, such as those in the Soviet Union or Eastern Europe until recently, prices were largely neglected as a means of allocating resources. The planners in these countries relied on central planning of major commodities as the means of deciding on the *what, how,* and *for whom.* Economists argued that by ignoring the role of prices, much waste would occur because some goods would be overproduced while others would be in short supply.

In recent years, economists in socialist countries have come to recognize the crucial role of prices in their systems. They recommend relying upon prices to guide firm production decisions as well as consumer choice. In the early 1990s, many socialist countries were beginning to allow prices to serve as signals of social scarcity so as to improve economic efficiency.

Allocative Efficiency in a Perfectly Competitive Economy

The first task for an economy is to solve the problems of *what, how,* and *for whom,* and just doing that is no simple task. But once an economy is actually operating, we want to know how efficiently the system performs. We have seen that a competitive market serves to allocate resources with remarkable efficiency for individual markets—that is, in partial equilibrium. Does an ensemble of markets in general equilibrium also allocate resources efficiently?

Allocative Efficiency

As we saw in Chapter 9, the concept of allocative efficiency measures the extent to which society provides consumers with the largest possible bundle of commodities, in the desired proportions. More precisely, **allocative efficiency** (sometimes called "Pareto efficiency," or "efficiency" for short) occurs when there is no way to reorganize production or consumption so that it will increase the satisfaction of one person without reducing the satisfaction of another person. Efficiency means in effect that no one can be made better off without making someone else worse off.

*A careful reader might here ask: "Are you sure that you have *exactly* the right number of equations to solve for all the unknown prices and quantities? That they will lead to a complete and consistent set of supply-and-demand equilibria for all inputs and outputs?"

Economists have pondered these profound questions for almost a century. Léon Walras, a French economist of the last century, is usually credited with discovery of the theory and equations of general equilibrium. He was, however, unable to provide a rigorous proof that there is an equilibrium of the competitive system. Only in the middle third of the twentieth century was a complete proof of the existence of a solution given, using high-powered mathematical tools such as topology and set theory, by J. von Neumann, A. Wald, and American Nobel Prize-winning economists Kenneth Arrow and Gerard Debreu. This revolutionary discovery showed that there will always exist at least one set of prices that will exactly balance the supplies and demands for all inputs and outputs—even if there are millions of inputs and outputs, in many different regions, and even if goods are produced and sold at different times.

The Utility-Possibility Frontier. We have defined efficiency as a state in which the maximum amount of goods and satisfaction is squeezed out of society's resources. This definition sounds very much as if the economy is on a frontier. And indeed it is—the *utility-possibility frontier* (or the *UPF*). This curve shows the outer limit of utilities or satisfactions that an economy can attain. Such a concept is very similar in spirit to the production-possibility frontier. The major difference is that the *UPF* places utilities or levels of satisfaction on the two axes, as is shown in Figure 17-2. The *UPF* slopes downward to indicate that, on the frontier, as one person's satisfaction increases, the other person's must decrease.

Note that the *UPF* is drawn somewhat wavy. This shape indicates that the scale of the individual utility measure is arbitrary; however, the inability to measure and compare individual utilities is unimportant for analyzing efficiency. All that matters here is that a person's level of satisfaction rises as the utility index increases. Because of this positive relation between utility and desired levels of consumption, we are guaranteed that each person will want to move out as far as possible on his or her utility axis.

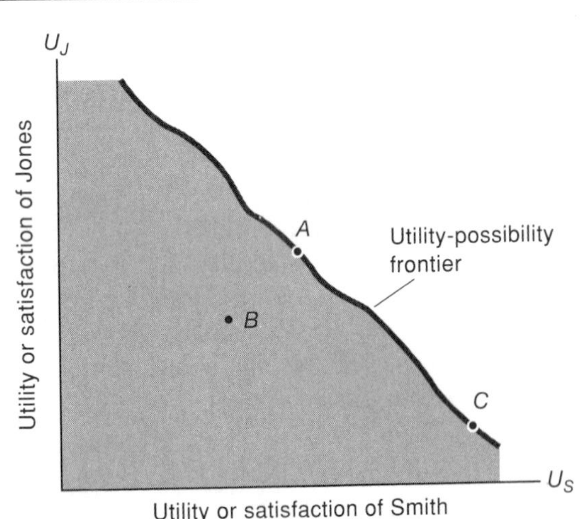

Figure 17-2. Allocations on the utility-possibility frontier are efficient

An economy is operating efficiently when no individual's satisfaction can be improved without lowering someone else's satisfaction. Efficient points are on the utility-possibility frontier (*UPF*). Moving from outcome *A* to outcome *C* can improve Smith's position only by hurting Jones; point *A* is therefore efficient. Point *B* is inside the *UPF*; it is inefficient because Jones, Smith, or both can be made better off without hurting anyone else.

The concept of allocative efficiency, so crucial to modern economics, was introduced by Vilfredo Pareto in 1906. An economic outcome is defined as possessing allocative efficiency (or Pareto efficiency) when it is on the frontier of the utility-possibility curve. One such Pareto-efficient point is shown at *A* in Figure 17-2.

Why is point *A* Pareto-efficient? Because there is no feasible economic reorganization that makes anyone better off without making someone else worse off. We can, of course, move to point *C*. Such a move would certainly delight Smith, whose consumption and satisfaction are increased. But Smith's gain comes only at Jones' expense. When all possible gains to Smith must come at Jones' expense, the economy is on its *UPF* and is operating efficiently.

Efficiency, Competition, and Welfare Economics

The study of the relationship between perfect competition and allocative efficiency lies in the realm of **welfare economics.** This is the term for the normative analysis of economic systems—the study of what is right and what is wrong, what is desirable and what is undesirable, about the economy's functioning. This subject is concerned with the best way to organize economic activity, the best distribution of income, and the best tax system.

One of the central subjects of welfare economics concerns the efficiency of a perfectly competitive economy. Two centuries ago, Adam Smith proclaimed that, through the workings of the invisible hand, those who pursue their own self-interest would most effectively promote the public welfare. But it took almost two centuries for economists to prove the kernel of truth in Smith's intuition. Today, this result is known as the *first theorem of welfare economics:*

A perfectly competitive, general-equilibrium market system will display allocative efficiency. In such a system, all goods' prices are equal to marginal costs, all factor prices are equal to the value of their marginal products, and there are no externalities. Under these conditions, when each producer maximizes profits and each consumer maximizes utility, the economy as a whole is efficient; you cannot make anyone better off without making someone else worse off.

What does all this mean? It implies that, given the resources and technology of the society, even the most skilled planner cannot come along with a computer or an ingenious reorganization scheme and find a solution superior to the competitive marketplace; no reorganization can make everyone better off. And this result is true whether the economy has one or two or two million competitive markets for goods and factors.

Rationale. What is the reason for this surprising coincidence between public and private interest? We can easily see the logic by using an example. Suppose some self-proclaimed wizard comes forth and says, "I have found a way of reorganizing the perfectly competitive economy to make everyone better off. Simply give everyone more pizzas and fewer shirts and everyone will be better off."

Unfortunately, the wizard is mistaken. Suppose the current price of shirts is $15, while the price of pizzas is $5. On the consumer's side, each individual has allocated his or her budget so that the marginal utility of the last pizza is just one-third that of the last shirt. So consumers would certainly not want to have more pizzas and fewer shirts unless they could get more than three pizzas for each shirt given up.

Can the economy squeeze out more than three pizzas for each forgone shirt? Not if it is competitively organized. Under perfect competition, the ratio of the price of shirts to the price of pizzas is the ratio of the marginal costs of the two goods. Hence if their price ratio is $15/$5 = 3, producers can squeeze out only three more pizzas for each shirt not produced. Indeed, if the production-possibility frontier is bowed out, producers will actually get somewhat less than three pizzas for every shirt forgone.

So we see why our wizard is wrong. Consumers are willing to eat more pizzas and have fewer shirts only if they can improve their satisfactions, which means that they must get more than three pizzas for every shirt forgone. But this is not possible because profit-maximizing producers cannot get more than three pizzas by producing one less shirt. Therefore the proposed reorganization will not improve everybody's economic satisfaction.

Competition and Efficiency

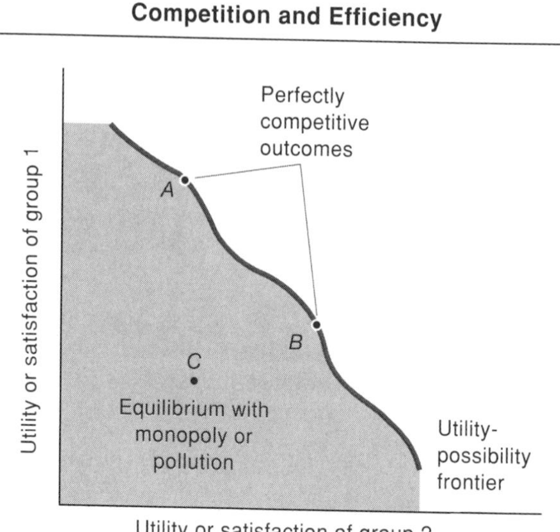

Figure 17-3. Perfectly competitive equilibria are efficient

A fundamental result of general-equilibrium theory is that perfectly competitive economies are efficient. Hence all competitive outcomes are on the production-possibility and utility-possibility frontiers. Market failures like monopoly or pollution push the economy inside both frontiers.

The reasoning, of course, extends far beyond pizzas and shirts. With a little thought you can see that it works as well for all consumer goods. With the help of an intermediate textbook, you can even see how it will extend to include reorganizations of inputs and production across firms. The basic point to see is that, because prices serve as signals of economic scarcity for producers and social utility for consumers, a competitive price mechanism allows the maximum output to be produced from a society's resources and technology.

The efficiency of perfect competition is illustrated in Figure 17-3. We have divided the population into two groups, group 1 and group 2, and have shown the satisfaction of the two groups on the two axes. Points *A* and *B* represent alternative and efficient competitive equilibria. By contrast, point *C* shows an economy laboring with much pollution or inefficient monopolies; economy C operates well inside its frontier, with groups 1 and 2 both losing consumption relative to efficiently operating economy B. We see, therefore, that all perfectly competitive economies operate efficiently and are somewhere on their utility-possibility frontiers.[1]

Qualifications

Our discussion has proceeded on the basis of some unrealistic assumptions: no monopolies, no spillovers or externalities, no government policy failures, and so forth. The perfectly competitive world of the economist is like the frictionless model of the physicist. It is not a picture of the real world we meet when we step outside the library and rub elbows with people on the street. Moreover, even if perfect competition ruled everywhere, people still might not be satisfied with the distribution of incomes generated by competition.

Let's review, then, the two qualifications of efficiency of markets—market failures and unacceptable income distribution.

Market Failures

Two different types of market failure spoil the idyllic picture of perfect competition assumed in the discussion of efficient markets: imperfect competition and externalities. We have explored issues of imperfect competition in Chapters 10 through 12; we will discuss externalities in depth in Chapter 18. The way each of these affects economic efficiency will be examined here.

The key problem in both cases is similar: the market outcome is one in which the prices do not reflect true social marginal costs and social marginal utilities.

[1] The text discussion has described what is known as the "first theorem of welfare economics." In addition, a second theorem of welfare economics is the converse of the first theorem. Consider an economy in which preferences and technology are "regular"—that is, one with diminishing marginal utilities of consumption and no increasing returns in production. Under these and a few other conditions, any efficient allocation of resources can be reached by some perfectly competitive equilibrium. Put differently, if the government wishes to reach some particular efficient outcome, such as point *A* in Fig. 17-3, in principle it can do so by redistributing initial incomes (say by ideal lump-sum taxes and transfers) and then allowing the invisible hand to guide the economy to the desired point. In such regular economies, a combination of efficient income redistribution plus competition is enough to reach any efficient allocation of resources.

Monopoly. When a firm has a monopoly over a particular market—because of a patented drug, a local electricity franchise, or an import quota on a particular brand of foreign car—the firm can raise the price of its product above its marginal cost. Consumers buy less of such goods than they would under competition, and consumer satisfaction is reduced. This kind of reduction of consumer satisfaction is typical of the inefficiencies created by imperfect competition.

Externalities. The other key market failure is externalities. Recall that externalities arise when all the side effects of production or consumption are not included in market prices. For example, a utility might pump sulfurous fumes into the air, causing damage to neighboring homes and to people's health. If the utility does not pay for these impacts, there will be inefficient levels of pollution and consumer welfare will suffer.

Not all externalities are harmful. Some are beneficial, such as the externalities that come from knowledge-generating activities. For example, when Chester Carlson invented xerography, he received only modest compensation although the world's secretaries and scribes were relieved of billions of hours of drudgery. Another positive externality arises from public-health programs, in which an inoculation protects not only the inoculated person but also others who might be infected were that person to contract a communicable disease.

Economics in a Vacuum? We have already encountered many other examples of market failure or the breakdown of competition. We have seen that prices are often rigid in contrast to the minute-to-minute flexibility of competitive auction prices seeking their equilibria. We have seen that two equally skilled people may work for different wage rates at similar jobs. We have seen how oligopolies and monopolies can restrain quantities to raise prices and profits.

We found that discrimination and segmented labor markets may lead to unequal employment opportunity, generating economic inefficiencies and social inequities. And we have seen how government interferences in markets can lead to unemployment, unavailability of credit, or apartment shortages.

After reading this list of qualifications, you might naturally wonder whether the notion of the efficient invisible hand ever applies to the world we live in. When we consider the wide range of actual market failures, should we then believe that the real-world economy bears any resemblance to the idealized general-equilibrium analysis of the textbooks?

Taken literally, there is no doubt that a perfect and absolutely efficient competitive mechanism has never existed and never will. But in a broader sense, the insights of the competitive theory retain a great deal of validity. Even though engineers know that they can never create a perfect vacuum, they still find the analysis of behavior in a vacuum extremely valuable for throwing light on many complicated problems. So it is with our competitive model. In the long run, many imperfections turn out to be transient as monopolies are eroded by competing technologies. While oversimplified, the competitive model points to many important hypotheses about economic behavior, and these hypotheses appear especially valid in the long run.

Suppose, for example, that a war cuts off the supply of oil to world markets. Competitive analysis says that the price of oil will rise and that the quantity demanded will fall. Sophisticated analysts of *n*-person game theory will fret that the world oil market is not perfectly competitive and that no hard-and-fast conclusions can be drawn. But put your money with the competitive model—betting that oil prices will rise in the short run—and you will probably end up wealthier than the sophisticated skeptics.

Initial Distribution of Income

But let us for the moment close our eyes to monopolies, pollution, labor unions, and other market failures. What do ideal competitive markets mean for the distribution of income? Is there an invisible hand in the marketplace that ensures that the most deserving people will obtain their just rewards? Or that those who toil long hours will receive a decent standard of living? No. In fact, competitive markets do not guarantee that income and consumption will necessarily go to the neediest or most deserving. Rather, the distribution of income and consumption in a market economy reflects initial endowments of inherited talents and wealth along with a variety of factors such as discrimination, effort, health, and luck.

In fact, under laissez-faire, perfect competition could lead to massive inequality, to malnourished children who grow up to produce more malnourished children, and to the perpetuation of inequality of incomes and wealth for generation after generation. Or, if the initial distribution of wealth, genetic abilities, education, and training happened to be spread quite evenly, perfect competition might lead to a society characterized by near-equality of wages, incomes, and property.

In short, Adam Smith, in the famous passage quoted on page 35, was not wholly justified in asserting that an invisible hand successfully channels individuals who selfishly seek their own interests into promoting the "public interest"—if the public interest includes a fair distribution of income and property. Smith proved nothing of this kind, nor has any economist since 1776.

A Final Word on Welfare Economics

In subsequent chapters, we will be traveling extensively in the land of welfare economics, confronting some of the major ethical and political issues of modern society. We will consider whether government should regulate industry and whether the tax system should redistribute income from rich to poor or from farm to city. We will continue to apply the results of our analysis of perfect competition, recalling the important results of the great master Adam Smith along with the refined analyses of his twentieth-century counterparts.

But economics cannot have the final word on these controversial problems. For underlying all these issues are normative assumptions and value judgments about what is good and right and just. What an economist does, therefore, is try very hard to keep positive science cleanly separated from normative judgments.

For the most part in science, scholars describe and analyze the behavior of physical or social systems. The task of positive description is kept as free as is humanly possible from the taint of wishful thinking and ethical concern about what ought to be. Why? Because scientists are cold-blooded robots? No. Rather, because experience shows that a more accurate job of positive description will be achieved if one tries to be objective.

Birds or Antelopes? Experience also shows that, try as we may, we humans never succeed in completely separating the objective and subjective aspects of a discipline. Indeed, the very choice of what economists decide to study and the perspective from which they study it both conspire against totally objective analysis and observation. Recall Chapter 1's bird-antelope paradox (page 7) and be warned that one's unconscious attitudes can color one's seemingly objective perceptions.

Moreover, a person's economic policy prescriptions will depend upon that person's political philosophy. Conservatives will legitimately interpret economic principles in terms of their version of the good society, while radicals may call for large reforms of the present structure of a mixed economy by giving their interpretation of fundamental economic laws.

Economic science cannot in the end tell us which political point of view is right or wrong. It arms us for the great debate.

SUMMARY

1. Individual markets reach a *partial equilibria* in factor markets and in final-goods markets. But the economy must reach a *general equilibrium* of all these markets. This general equilibrium of all markets is interrelated in a circular flow by a web of price connections. Households supply factors of production and demand final goods; businesses buy factors of production and transform and sell them as final goods.

2. The general-equilibrium competitive price system is logically complete. There is a sufficient number of supply-and-demand relationships to determine all relative prices and all quantities.

3. Under certain conditions, a competitive general equilibrium will display *allocative efficiency.* Allocative efficiency (sometimes called Pareto efficiency) signifies that no one person can be made better off without someone else being made worse off. In such a situation, the economy is on both its production-possibility frontier and its utility-possibility frontier. The central result of general-equilibrium analysis is this: Because prices serve as signals of economic scarcity for producers and social utility for consumers, a competitive price mechanism allows the maximum output to be produced from a society's resources and technology.

4. There are severe limits on the conditions under which an efficient competitive equilibrium can be attained: there can be no externalities, no monopolies or economies of scale, and no uninsurable risks. The presence of such imperfections leads to a breakdown of the *price ratio = marginal cost ratio = marginal utility ratio* conditions, and hence to inefficiency.

5. Even if the ideal conditions for efficient perfect competition were to hold, one major reservation about the outcome of competitive laissez-faire would remain. We have no reason to think that income under laissez-faire will be fairly distributed. The outcome might be one with enormous disparities in income and wealth that persist for generations. Or, conceivably, the outcome might be one in which there is a virtual equality of outcomes.

CONCEPTS FOR REVIEW

partial equilibrium vs. general equilibrium
allocative (or Pareto) efficiency
utility-possibility frontier (*UPF*)
invisible-hand theory: in Adam Smith's doctrine and in today's general-equilibrium theory
qualifications to the invisible-hand doctrine: market failures and arbitrary distribution of income
welfare economics
two theorems of welfare economics

QUESTIONS FOR DISCUSSION

1. Summarize how a competitive pricing system solves the three fundamental economic problems. Illustrate the price mechanism for the seven steps (pages 286–287) where the economy produces outputs of food and clothing with inputs of labor and land.
2. List the qualifications to the invisible-hand theory. Illustrate each qualification with an example from your own experience or reading.
3. List the conditions for competitive general equilibrium described in the text under "Detailed Analysis of General Equilibrium." State each condition in a sentence or two. Explain why monopoly or a pollution externality would lead to a failure of one of these conditions.
4. State carefully the two theorems of welfare economics. How would they apply to the following quotations?
   (a) "Perfect competition affords the ideal condition for the distribution of wealth." (Francis Walker, 1892)
   (b) "The invisible hand, if it is to be found anywhere, is likely to be found picking the pockets of the poor." (Edward Nell, 1982)
   (c) Adam Smith's quotation on the invisible hand (see the beginning of Chapter 3).
   (d) "Pareto . . . suggested that competition brought about a state in comparison to which no consumer's satisfaction can be made higher, within the limitations of available resources and technological know-how, without at the same time lowering at least one other consumer's satisfaction level." (Tjalling Koopmans, 1957)
   (e) "Perfect competition can achieve anything that can be obtained under socialism."
5. The analysis of efficiency of competitive economies assumes that there is no technological advance. Recall the Schumpeterian hypothesis from Chapter 11. How does this elaboration qualify the view of economic efficiency of the competitive mechanism? What kind of market failure is exemplified by invention? In a world of rapid potential technological advance, use production-possibility curves to illustrate how in the long run an innovative economy with imperfect competition might produce higher consumption than an efficient but technologically stagnant competitive economy.
6. **Advanced problem:** "The second theorem of welfare economics (page 294, footnote 1) means that all the debates about socialism vs. capitalism are vacuous. Anything that can be done by ideal, centrally planned socialism can, by the second welfare theorem, be done by competitive markets plus the proper dose of redistributive taxation." Comment on the logic behind this statement. State whether you agree or not and defend your position.

C H A P T E R 1 8

GOVERNMENT AND THE ECONOMY

Democracy is the recurrent suspicion that more than half the people are right more than half the time.

E. B. White

Markets have over the last two centuries proven to be a mighty engine for powering the economies of industrial countries. Nonetheless, starting about a century ago, governments in virtually all countries of Europe and North America began to intervene in economic activity to correct the perceived flaws in the marketplace. The increase of government involvement has brought a vast increase in the influence of the state over economic life, both in the share of national income devoted to transfers and income-support payments and in the legal and regulatory controls over economic activity.

Government encroachment on the private sector has not been continuous; rather, following the cycle of politics, capitalist economies take two steps forward, then one step backward, on the road to greater government involvement. The latest phase has seen the *reemergence of the market* in both capitalist and socialist countries. A crusade for reduced government involvement launched during the Reagan administration in the United States (1981–1989) has been joined by governments in many other countries. But even today the electorate is divided on the proper role of government. Some people want to continue expanding the scope of government; others take up the banner of the conservative revolution and strive to reduce government's role in the future.

The government has a profound effect on economic activity. In this chapter we begin by examining government's role in economic life. We then turn to the topic of public choice, which describes how democratic governments choose among the alternative programs open to their societies. The final section then examines the vital issues of externalities like pollution or knowledge and shows how governments may need to step in where markets fail.

A. Government Control of the Economy

The Instruments of Government Policy

How do governments affect the economy? There are three major instruments of government control. These are:

1. *Taxes* that serve to reduce private expenditures (such as for automobiles or restaurant food) and thereby make room for public expenditure (on goods like trucks or army rations)
2. *Expenditures* that induce firms or workers to

produce certain goods or services (such as tanks or police protection), along with *transfer payments* (like welfare payments) that provide income support

3. *Regulations* or controls that direct people to perform or desist from certain economic activities (such as rules concerning the amount that firms can pollute)

History of Taxing and Spending

For more than a century, national income and production have been rising in all industrial economies. At the same time, in most countries, government expenditure has been rising even faster. Each period of emergency—depression, war, or concern over social problems such as poverty or pollution—expands the activity of government. After the crisis has passed, government controls and spending never return to their previous levels.

Before World War I, the combined federal, state, and local government expenditure or taxation amounted to little more than one-tenth of our entire national income. The war effort during World War II compelled government to consume about half the nation's greatly expanded total output. In the 1980s, expenditure of all levels of government in the United States ran around 35 percent of GNP.

Figure 18-1 shows the trend in government taxes and expenditures for all levels of government in the United States. The rising curves indicate that the shares of taxes and spending have grown steadily upward over the course of this century.

Figure 18-2 shows how government spending as a percent of GNP varies among countries. High-income countries tend to tax and spend a larger fraction of GNP than do poor countries. Can we discern a pattern among wealthy countries? Within the high-income countries, no simple law relating tax burdens and the citizenry's well-being can do

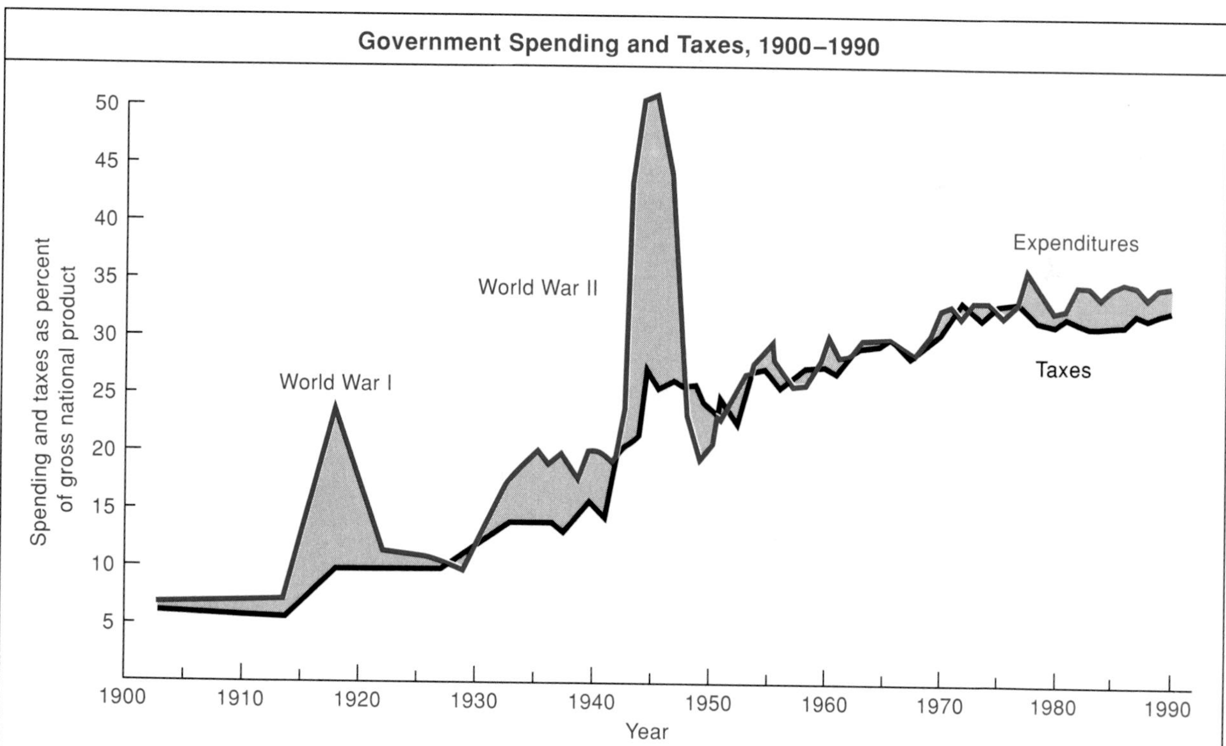

Figure 18-1. The size of government has grown sharply over the twentieth century

Government expenditures include federal, state, and local spending on goods, services, and transfers. Note that the share of spending and taxation jumped sharply during World Wars I and II and that the size of government did not return to prewar levels after these wars. The difference between the tax and spending curves represents the government deficit or surplus. (Source: U.S. Department of Commerce.)

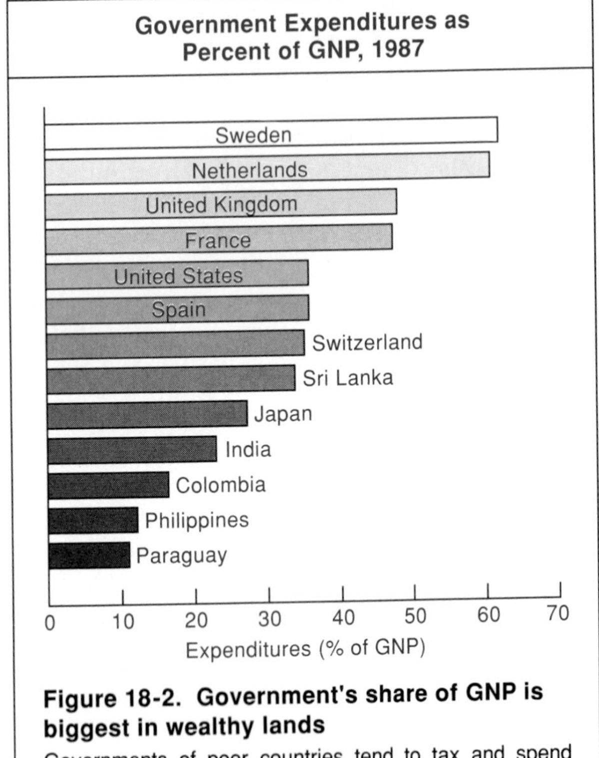

Figure 18-2. Government's share of GNP is biggest in wealthy lands

Governments of poor countries tend to tax and spend less, relative to national product, than advanced countries. With affluence come greater interdependence and the desire to meet social needs, along with less need to meet urgent private necessities. (Source: International Monetary Fund.)

justice to the true diversity of the fiscal facts of nations.[1]

The Growth of Government Controls and Regulation

The increase in collective expenditures is only part of the story. In addition to the rapid growth in spending and taxing, there has also been a vast expansion in the laws and regulations governing economic affairs.

Nineteenth-century America came as close as any economy has come to being a pure laissez-faire society—the system that the British historian Thomas Carlyle dubbed "anarchy plus the constable." This philosophy permitted people great personal freedom to pursue their economic ambitions and produced a century of rapid material progress. But critics saw many flaws in this laissez-faire idyll. Historians record periodic business crises, extremes of poverty and inequality, deep-seated racial discrimination, and poisoning of water, land, and air by pollution. Muckrakers and progressives called for a bridle on capitalism so that the people could steer this wayward beast in more humane directions.

Beginning in the 1890s, the United States gradually turned away from the belief that "that government governs best which governs least." Presidents Theodore Roosevelt, Woodrow Wilson, Franklin Roosevelt, and Lyndon Johnson—in the face of strenuous opposition—pushed out the boundaries of federal control over the economy, devising new regulatory and fiscal tools to combat the ailments of the day.

Constitutional powers of government were interpreted broadly and used to "secure the public interest" and to "police" the economic system. In 1887, the federal Interstate Commerce Commission (ICC) was established to regulate rail traffic across state boundaries. Soon afterward, the Sherman Antitrust Act and other laws were aimed against monopolistic combinations in "restraint of trade."

During the 1930s, a whole set of industries came under *economic regulation*, whereby government sets the prices, conditions of exit and entry, and safety standards. Regulated industries in recent years included the airlines, trucking, and barge and water traffic; electric, gas, and telephone utilities; financial markets; and oil and natural gas, as well as pipelines.

In addition to regulating the prices and standards of business, the nation attempted to protect health and safety through increasingly stringent *social regulation*. Following the revelations of the muckraking era of the early 1900s, pure food and drug acts were passed. Then, during the 1960s and

[1] Figures 18-1 and 18-2 show the total expenditures of governments. Such expenditures include expenditures on goods and services (like missiles and teachers) as well as transfer payments (like social security and interest on the government debt). Expenditures on goods and services make a direct claim upon the production of a country; transfer payments, by contrast, increase people's income and allow them to purchase goods and services but do not directly reduce the quantity of goods and services available for private consumption and investment.

1970s, Congress passed a series of acts that regulated mine safety and then worker safety more generally; set the framework for federal regulation of air and water pollution and of hazardous substances; authorized safety standards for automobiles and consumer products; controlled strip mining; and regulated nuclear power safety and toxic wastes.

So great was the proliferation of regulation by the late 1970s that many called the regulatory agencies a "fourth branch" of government. So powerful was the opposition to new regulatory programs that further growth of regulation was abruptly halted during the Reagan and Bush years; in addition, during this time, regulatory enforcement was relaxed.

How does it come to pass that the nation adopts such radically new doctrines? Looking back, we see that each new policy produced powerful reactions on both sides. For example, when social security was introduced by Franklin Roosevelt during the 1930s, he deemed it a public pension system essential to protecting the well-being of older citizens. But opponents denounced social security as an ominous sign of socialism. Newspapers of the day recorded similar sentiments about public subsidies for medical care, regulation of factory conditions, legal protection for unions, and antipollution laws.

With the passage of time, political attitudes evolve. The radical doctrines of one era become accepted as the gospel of the next. The much-criticized social security system of the 1930s was defended by conservative President Ronald Reagan in the 1980s as part of the "social safety net." The public has come to accept government constraints that have changed the very nature of capitalism. Private property is less and less wholly private. Free enterprise has become progressively less free. Irreversible evolution is part of history.

The Functions of Government

Philosophers since the time of Plato have debated the role of the state, and political thinkers have proposed different approaches to government. In recent years economics has developed a new field called *public choice*, which is the study of how governments make choices and direct the economy.

Our survey begins in this section with an analysis of the *normative* role of government. That is, we will explore the kind of economic functions that government ought to perform. In the next section, we present the *positive* or descriptive analysis of government behavior, describing the actual behavior of governments and legislatures. We then end with an application of these principles to the important public-policy problem of externalities.

We are beginning to get a picture of how government directs and interacts with the economy. What are the major economic functions that government performs in a modern mixed economy? In fact there are four:

1. Establishing the legal framework for the market economy
2. Affecting the allocation of resources to improve economic efficiency
3. Establishing programs to improve the distribution of income
4. Stabilizing the economy through macroeconomic policies

Let's look at each.

The Legal Framework

The government's first function, setting the legal framework, establishes the rules of the market. These rules include the definition of property, the laws of contracts and bankruptcy, the mutual obligations of labor and management, and a multitude of laws and regulations constraining the way different members of the society interact.

Although the legal framework profoundly affects economic behavior, most laws are not based on a finely honed economic cost-benefit analysis. Rather, some came from Roman times, others grew from English common law, while modern law is often driven by utilitarian reasoning or sometimes simply by what will sell in the political marketplace.

Whatever the source of our laws and customs, the legal framework strongly influences economic activity. For example, in the nineteenth century, firms were not responsible for workers who became ill while working in unsafe or unhealthful factories. Consumers had little recourse if they bought a defective product. What were the results? There were thousands of occupational illnesses, and millions of dollars were spent on snake-oil remedies that purported to cure all ailments.

During the twentieth century, the legal system evolved to make businesses legally responsible for their actions and products. Firms can now be sued if workers become ill from their work. Thousands of workers who had contracted cancer recently sued asbestos manufacturers, and one giant firm, Manville Corporation, went bankrupt under the weight of these claims. Firms are more and more often held responsible for faulty products. As a result of these legal changes, firms now pay much closer attention to the safety of their products and workplaces.

Allocation

Now that we have seen how government sets the legal framework, we turn next to a discussion of the three essential economic functions of government: allocation, income distribution, and stabilization.

A central economic purpose of government is to assist in the socially desirable allocation of resources. This is the *microeconomic* side of government policy; it concentrates on the *what* and *how* of economic life. Microeconomic policies differ among countries according to customs and political philosophies. Some countries emphasize a hands-off, laissez-faire approach, leaving most decisions to the market. Other countries lean toward heavy government regulation, or even ownership of businesses, in which production decisions are made by government planners.

Ours is fundamentally a market economy. On any microeconomic issue, most people presume that the market will be encouraged to solve the economic problem at hand. But sometimes our government chooses to override the allocational decisions of market supply and demand. Let us see why.

Hypothetical Laissez-Faire. In the first place suppose all goods can be produced efficiently by perfectly competitive firms. Also assume that all goods are like loaves of bread, the total of which can be cut up into separate consumptions for different individuals, so that the more I consume out of the total, the less you consume. And further suppose that there are no externalities like air pollution and that each person has equal initial access to human and natural resources, equal opportunity in every sense, and can carry on any activity independently of others, much as in frontier days.

If all these idealized conditions were met, the invisible hand could provide perfectly efficient and equitable production and distribution of national output, and there would be no need for government intervention in the economy.

Yet even in this case, if there were to be a division of labor among people and regions, and if a price mechanism were to work, government would have an important role. Courts and police forces would be needed to ensure fulfillment of contracts, nonfraudulent and nonviolent behavior, freedom from theft and external aggression, and the legislated rights of property.

This is the case for laissez-faire with minimal government—and indeed, it might be a good system if the idealized conditions listed above were truly present.

Realistic Interdependencies. In reality, each and every one of the idealized conditions enumerated above is violated to some extent in all human societies. Abilities, opportunities, and ownership of property do exhibit disparities, depending on inheritance and social history. Some groups are or have been systematically discriminated against. Also, many kinds of production can take place most efficiently only in units too large for truly perfect competition. And unregulated factories do tend to pollute the air, water, and land. The market is not ideal. There are market failures.

Let us review briefly how these market failures might lead to a call for government activity:

- *Discrimination in labor markets.* When some groups are discriminated against or excluded from high-paid jobs, government may decide to step in, outlaw discriminatory actions, and break down the barriers between noncompeting groups.
- *The breakdown of perfect competition.* When monopolies or oligopolies collude to reduce rivalry or drive firms out of business, government may apply antitrust policies or regulation.

- *The presence of significant externalities*—too much air pollution or too little investment in knowledge. As we will see later in this chapter, government may need to control the emissions of polluters or to support basic science.

Clearly, there is much on the agenda of possible allocational problems for government to handle.

Income Redistribution

One of the first lessons we learned is that the invisible hand might be marvelously efficient but at the same time produce a very unequal distribution of income. Under laissez-faire, people end up rich or poor depending on their inherited wealth, on their talents and efforts, on the prices of their skills, and sometimes on their luck in finding oil. To some people, the distribution of income arising from unregulated competition looks as arbitrary as the Darwinian distribution of food and plunder among animals in the jungle.

In the poorest societies, there is little excess income to take from the better off and provide to the unfortunate. But as societies become more affluent, they devote more resources to providing services for poor people; this activity—income redistribution—is the second major economic function of government. The welfare states of North America and Western Europe now devote a significant share of their incomes to maintaining minimum standards of health, nutrition, and income.

Most advanced countries now rule that children shall not go hungry because of the economic circumstances of their parents; that poor people shall not die young because of insufficient money for needed medical care; that the young shall receive free public education; and that the old shall be able to live out their years with some minimum of income. In the United States, these government activities are provided primarily by transfer programs, such as food stamps, Medicaid, and social security, which make resources available to targeted low-income groups.

Macroeconomic Stabilization

The most recent economic function assumed by the federal government is stabilization. Governments today attempt to smooth out the business cycle in order to prevent chronic unemployment, economic stagnation, and price inflation and to encourage rapid economic growth. The government's main weapons for controlling business fluctuations and promoting economic growth are monetary policy and fiscal policy. The methods that governments can use to stabilize the economy are analyzed in that part of economics devoted to macroeconomics.

This analysis of the four functions of government concludes our survey of the normative view of government's role, of how government ought to intervene to improve the functioning and fairness of a market economy.

B. Public-Choice Theory: How Governments Make Decisions

The first section of this chapter described the normative role of government in a modern economy. But do governments in fact follow the prescriptions laid down by economists and philosophers? Do governments use a "visible hand" to ensure that public-policy decisions serve to make the economy operate more smoothly and effectively? Or are there "government failures" that parallel market failures such as monopoly and pollution?

These questions are the domain of **public-choice theory,** which is the branch of economics that studies the way that governments make decisions. Here we ask how governments decide on the level of taxes and public consumption and on the size of transfer payments. Public-choice theory asks about the *how, what,* and *for whom* of the public sector, just as supply-and-demand theory examines choices for the private sector.*

How Governments Choose

In the private sector, people express their views by casting what we have metaphorically called "dollar votes" for the goods they desire. In the political sphere, they cast real votes—for representatives and for presidents. Let's review how people vote and what the consequences are.

The Political Game

The game of politics, like the market, has its rules and its players. Political decision making operates within a set of *rules:* these are the basic constitution and voting system. The most important rule of the game for our purpose is that decisions are made by elected representatives.

Who are the *players?* Voters are the consumers whose desires a democracy is ultimately supposed to serve. The other major players are the elected representatives, or politicians. This group performs a function much like that of firms in a market economy—they are the entrepreneurs who interpret the public's demand for collective goods and find ways of supplying these goods.

What motivates politicians? Most elected officials are motivated by a combination of pragmatism and ideology—joining the quest for electoral survival with their fundamental beliefs about how the nation should be governed. Some change their positions quickly as the political winds shift. Others feel so deeply about issues that they are willing to risk defeat in defense of their ideals. But the theory of public choice cuts through this thicket of complex motivations by making a simple assumption: *Politicians are assumed to behave so as to maximize their chances of election.* They are assumed to be vote maximizers—just as firms are taken to be profit maximizers.

Poised between voters and politicians stand organizations known as *interest groups,* which represent people or businesses that are organized to lobby for a specific set of interests or issues. For example, the National Rifle Association defends the right of citizens to bear arms; the Iron and Steel Institute attempts to limit steel imports; the Environmental Defense Fund presses for more stringent control of pollution. Sometimes, interest groups assume a degree of political power far beyond the numerical size of their membership. When interest groups "capture" regulatory agencies or legislative bodies, we have a case of *nonrepresentative government.*

There are other players as well. One important set of participants consists of the people who run executive agencies (such as generals in the Pentagon or farmers in the Agriculture Department). Although they exercise great power because of their expertise and long experience, these bureaucrats are ultimately subject to the decisions of political leaders.

In summary:

Public-choice theory describes how governments make decisions about taxation, expenditure, regulation, and other policies. Like the game of markets, the game of politics must match up people's de-

*Since the time of Adam Smith, economists have focused most of their energy on understanding the workings of the marketplace. But serious thinkers have also pondered the government's role in society. Joseph Schumpeter pioneered public-choice theory in *Capitalism, Socialism, and Democracy* (1942), and Kenneth Arrow's Nobel Prize-winning study on social choice (analyzed later in this chapter) brought mathematical rigor to this field. But the landmark study by Anthony Downs, *An Economic Theory of Democracy* (1957), first sketched a powerful new theory in which politicians set economic policies in order to be reelected. Downs showed how parties will tend to move toward the center of the political spectrum and suggested that it is highly irrational for people to vote given the small likelihood of any individual's affecting the outcome.

Further studies by James Buchanan and Gordon Tullock in *The Calculus of Consent* (1959) defended checks and balances and advocated the use of unanimity in political decisions—arguing that unanimous decisions do not coerce anyone and therefore impose no costs. For this and other works, Buchanan received the Nobel Prize in 1986. This brand of economics received careful study by conservative politicians during the early 1980s, and it was applied to such areas as farm policy, regulation, and the courts and formed the theoretical basis for a proposed constitutional amendment to balance the budget.

mands for collective goods with the economy's capability to supply them. The major difference lies in the fact that the central players of politics—politicians—are primarily concerned with winning elections, while the major players in markets—business firms—aim to earn profits.

Mechanisms for Public Choice

In every nation there is a political system for making collective decisions. How does this work in theory and in practice? We focus here on decision processes, particularly on voting systems, in democratic countries.

Public choice is the process by which individual preferences are combined into collective decisions. A democratic society stresses the importance of individual values and tastes in such an aggregation—"one person, one vote" expresses this individualistic underpinning of our political system.

But a crucial problem arises just because we must aggregate millions of opinions into a single decision. The United States has 250 million views about the defense budget or welfare. But in the end, there can be only one decision about whether to go to war, only one federal energy policy, and so forth. A red light means "stop" for everyone because political choices are *indivisible* for a nation. Such decisions are coercive compared to private decisions about ice cream or bread or concerts, where your choice to eat ice cream does not bind my decisions.

Unlike private decisions, collective choice contains an essential indivisibility with but one outcome on any particular issue.

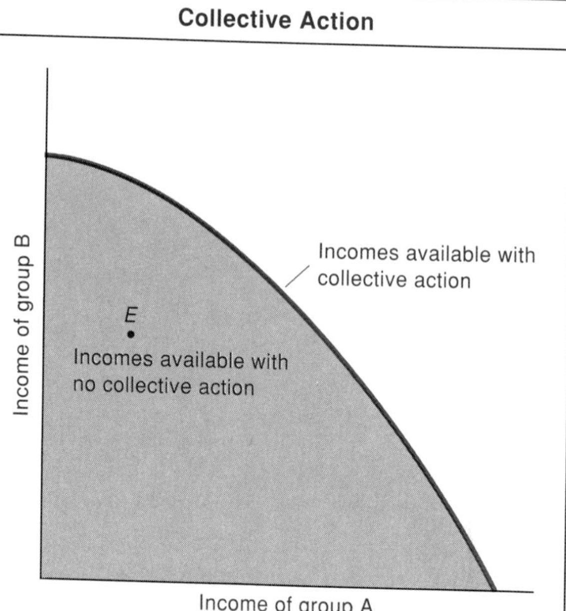

Figure 18-3. The logic of collective action
The graph shows economic performance with and without collective action. Point *E* marks the outcome of pure laissez-faire, where governments build no roads, vaccinate no children, and "leave things alone."

With collective actions such as road-building, support of science, regulation of the money supply, and so forth, incomes can be improved as society moves toward frontier from *E*.

Outcomes of Collective Choice

What is the effect of collective decisions? Figure 18-3 shows the possibilities. For this diagram we imagine a society in which there are two kinds of people, A's and B's. They may be rich and poor, Republicans and Democrats, or country and city dwellers. For the moment, think of each as a unified group with homogeneous interests and tastes.

Consider first a society that shunned any kind of government. Such a world was described by the seventeenth-century philosopher Thomas Hobbes as a state of nature where there was "no place for industry, because the fruit thereof is uncertain; no culture of the earth, no navigation, no arts; continual fear of violent death; and the life of man, solitary, poor, nasty, brutish, and short."[2] In this world with no government, society would be living in an uncivilized and dangerous jungle, with low incomes, as shown at point *E* in Figure 18-3.

Next consider the potential for a society which undertook sensible collective actions. It could build highways and encourage railroads. Public-health measures could wipe out malaria, smallpox, and plague. Government-supported education and science could produce a literate work force, probe outer space and tiny molecules, and thereby promote rapid productivity growth. Monetary policies could lead to a sound currency and viable banking system, thereby allowing people to save and businesses to invest. Police could make the streets and

[2] Thomas Hobbes, *Leviathan* (1651). This quotation has been shortened and rendered into modern English.

homes safer. Pollution-abatement programs could clean the air and water and produce a healthier populace. Income-support measures could provide food and medical care for those who are unable to care for themselves.

Successful public-sector activities push out the frontier of what the economy can produce; the frontier of society's possibilities with collective action is shown in Figure 18-3.

Is Public Choice Efficient?

When we think of the many useful activities undertaken by government, we might ask whether collective choice always enhances efficiency. Few would deny that wiping out plague was beneficial. But is there a "visible-hand" theorem by which government policies always guide the economy toward an efficient and equitable economic allocation of public goods and income?

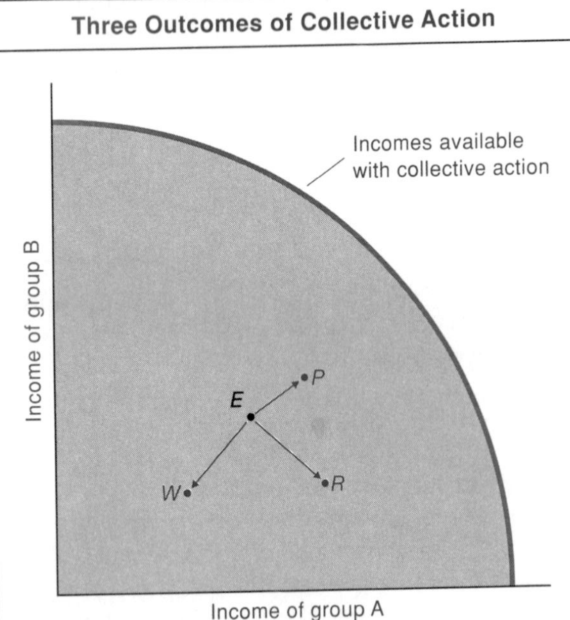

Figure 18-4. Collective actions can improve or hurt all or simply redistribute incomes
Starting at the laissez-faire point *E*, we can distinguish three kinds of outcomes of collective action. A Pareto improvement makes everyone better off by moving to point *P*. Or there might be a massive government failure (like nuclear war) which makes everyone worse off as society moves from *E* to *W*. Very often programs are redistributive, moving society from *E* to *R*.

We will later see that the answer is no. As Figure 18-4 illustrates, collective decisions can be divided into three general categories: harmful, redistributive, and efficient. A first and probably rare *harmful* case arises when governments take steps that make everyone worse off. If a particular strategy leads to nuclear war, that will surely be a total failure. Such failures are illustrated by the movement from initial point *E* to point *W* in Figure 18-4.

Second, there are simple *redistributive* outcomes, shown by the arrow from *E* to *R*. In these cases society may tax one group to benefit others, or may impose a tariff on a product that helps factors of production in that industry but hurts consumers.

Finally, collective actions may produce *Pareto improvements,* which represent actions that lead to improvements in everyone's satisfaction; they make everyone better off and no one worse off. A Pareto improvement is shown by the arrow moving northeast in Figure 18-4 from point *E* to point *P*. Examples of Pareto improvements would be government support for a new scientific advance (like communications satellites) or its help in disseminating a public-health measure (like a smallpox or polio vaccine).

We must keep this distinction among the three kinds of outcomes in mind because there are no foolproof rules that always make everyone better off.

Alternative Decision Rules

Societies have devised diverse ways of making collective decisions: some by tradition, others by monarchy, and most Western countries today by representative government. In public-choice theory, we look behind the particular forms of government to the underlying choice process. Do systems that rely on consensus or unanimity produce efficient and consistent decisions? What does "the will of the majority" really mean? Under what circumstances are the decisions of collective choice unfair or inefficient?

Unanimity

Many social and economic thinkers have stressed the advantages of making decisions by consensus

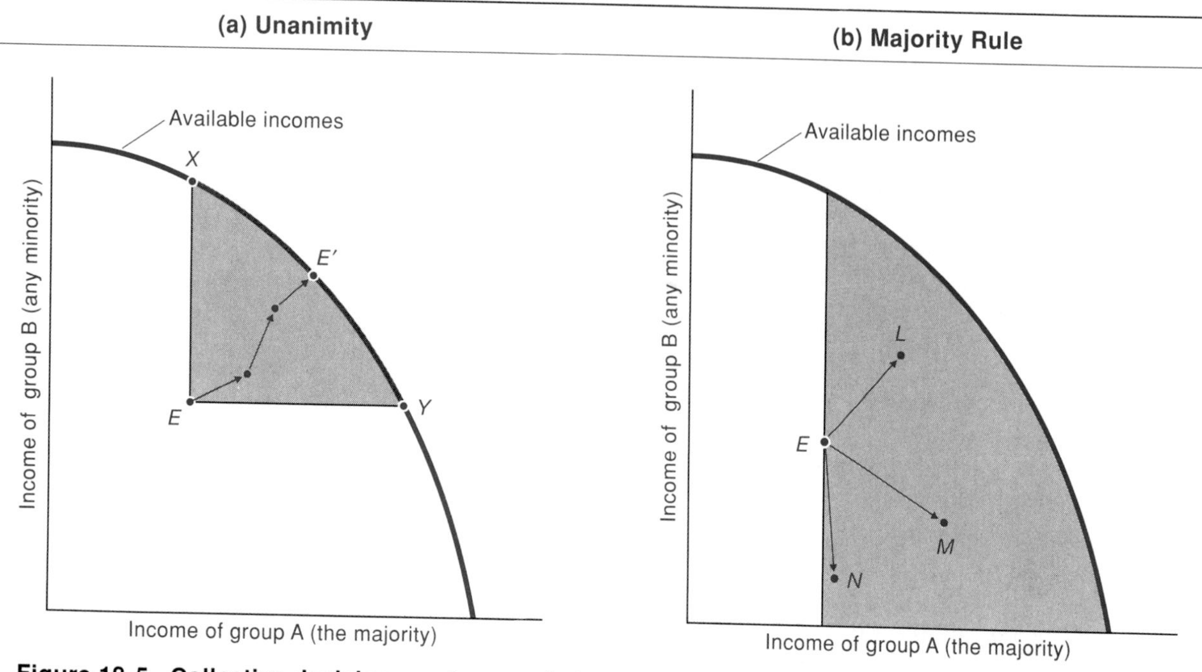

Figure 18-5. Collective decisions under unanimity and majority rule

The left panel illustrates outcomes when decisions require unanimity: if each person must agree to each decision, no one can be made worse off. Hence, starting at *E*, all outcomes must lie in the region *EXY*.

Under majority rule, shown on the right, majority group A can decide issues and would vote for any proposal improving its income (moving rightward into the shaded region). Some decisions may be efficient and fair (as in movement to *L*) or inefficient and unfair (as in movement to *N*).

or by unanimity. This approach requires that everybody agree with collective decisions. Figure 18-5(*a*) illustrates how decisions by consensus proceed. No decision can be made without the accord of each person, so each decision must improve each person's income (or, more generally, each person's level of satisfaction). It must therefore move society northeast toward the income-possibility frontier in Figure 18-5(*a*)—a process shown by the arrows. A voting system based on unanimity would guarantee that all decisions be Pareto improvements, never making anyone worse off. In addition, because each voter must agree with any decision, there can never be any coercion of minorities by larger groups.

Unfortunately, a rule of unanimity poses severe practical shortcomings. As anyone knows who has ever tried to get a group of people to agree on anything, generating a consensus takes enormous time and energy. One skeptic can hold up any measure, no matter how worthwhile that measure might be. Even worse, once the last skeptic realized how powerful he was, he could blackmail those who favored the measure. If a $100 million pollution-control or road-building program could be vetoed by a single person, this person could hold out for any number of pet projects, delaying the vote and benefiting himself or his constituents in the process.

In the end, a unanimous voting system would get so bogged down in bargaining, blackmail, and delay that virtually nothing would be accomplished. No laws would be passed. The system would be at an impasse or would have to creak along with existing arrangements. Instead of moving northeast from point *E*, the society would simply get stuck at point *E* (wherever *E* might happen to be).

Government by unanimity is likely to preserve the status quo, however bad or good it is.

Majority Rule

Virtually all voting bodies rely on majority rule for making decisions. Under this system, a law or rule is adopted when more than half the voters approve it. Majority rule is used in the U.S. Congress, the Supreme Court, and state and local governments, as well as in most corporate boards and clubs.

An idealized description of majority rule is shown on the right side of Figure 18-5. Assume that group A is in the majority. In a pure economic calculation, it will vote for any measure that increases its real income. Thus any of the three points shown—*L*, *M*, or *N*—would win over point *E* by majority vote. Of the three, *M* produces the highest income for group A and would be the ultimate winner in majority voting among the four choices.

The outcomes shown in Figure 18-5(*b*) suggest some important features of majority rule. First, majority rule does not guarantee Pareto improvements. The majority would prefer point *M* to point *E*, but point *M* makes the minority, the B's, worse off. Majority rule may lead to a "tyranny by the majority"; majorities can impose their political will on minorities, through discrimination, income redistribution, or oppressive laws. Such tyranny is not possible under unanimity.

Avoiding Tyranny by the Majority. The possibility of tyranny by the majority has haunted political philosophers for centuries. Because deep thinkers like James Madison and Alexander Hamilton feared coercive political activity, they proposed the use of *supermajorities* for many important issues (such as constitutional amendments). Supermajorities require that a measure obtain more than a simple majority, say, two-thirds of the votes, in order to pass.

In recent years, many people have proposed extending rule by supermajority to the federal budget process. Critics argue that the usual budget process allows majorities to pass extravagant spending laws, expanding the scope of government and in effect tyrannizing the minority, who are heavily taxed and coerced into participating in a society dominated by government planners.

The proposed solution is to require supermajorities for the passage of economic legislation that would lead to budget deficits or to an expansion of government expenditure programs. In the 1980s, conservatives proposed a constitutional amendment to balance the federal budget. It would require a supermajority of 60 percent to increase the share of government spending or to run a budget deficit. When the constitutional amendment failed, Congress passed the *Gramm-Rudman* bill, which mandated a gradual reduction of federal budget deficits and an eventual balanced budget. As budget deficits have climbed in the early 1990s, the pressure for legislative or constitutional supermajorities to impose a national budget constraint has continued.

Cyclical Voting and the Voting Paradox

We hear much about the "will of the majority" and "letting the majority have its way." In a deep analysis of majority rule, Nobel-laureate Kenneth Arrow of Stanford demonstrated certain fundamental flaws that could result from majority decisions. We will illustrate Arrow's results with the help of a simple example of three individuals choosing among three different options.

The situation is illustrated in Table 18-1. Each of three individuals has one vote. They must choose from three different levels of defense spending: high, medium, and low. Moreover, each person has a different idea about the way the country should be defended. Jones is a hawk, but his second choice is a small elite army rather than a poorly funded middle-sized one. Smith is a centrist: she likes both guns and butter. Brown is a pacifist, preferring the smallest possible army.

Now line this group up and try to decide the de-

	Voter's preference among different proposals on defense spending		
Voter	Low spending	Medium spending	High spending
Jones	2	3	1
Smith	3	1	2
Brown	1	2	3

Table 18-1. How cyclical voting or the voting paradox arises

Jones wants a strong army or little defense. Smith is a centrist and prefers a modest defense outlay. Brown is a pacifist.

Under majority voting, each person votes in favor of his or her preferred program. When the programs are voted upon, low spending beats medium spending 2 to 1; medium spending beats high spending 2 to 1; and high spending beats low spending 2 to 1. Like a dog chasing its tail, the majority voting rule here cycles around endlessly. Nor is there any way to resolve the paradox except by arbitrary voting procedures.

fense issue by majority vote. As Table 18-1 shows, low spending beats medium spending; medium spending beats high spending; high spending beats low spending. No program can win a majority vote against all other programs. We see here the voting paradox:

The *voting paradox* arises when no single program can command a majority against all other programs.

Setting the Agenda. There are many important implications of the voting paradox, but one particular one should be mentioned. This is the importance of the *agenda,* or the order of business. Because of the need to economize on time, legislatures must have a set of procedures. They cannot allow endless cycling around on issues where opinions are divided.

But the voting paradox shows that the agenda may be crucial to the outcome—that the order of votes may determine which program prevails. Let's return to our example of defense in Table 18-1. Say that Congress has to decide on a defense policy, but it is divided into three equal camps whose preferences are like those shown in Table 18-1. Here is where the Rules Committee becomes important. By manipulating the order of votes, the Rules Committee can actually determine the winner. Suppose that the Rules Committee is run by ultra-liberals who believe that the cold war is over and that the United States should therefore dismantle its defense establishment. It can set the agenda in a way that will guarantee its desired outcome. The group starts with a vote between high and medium spending; medium spending wins by 2 votes to 1. Then the winner is pitted against low spending, with low spending the victor. Low spending has won because of the order of the voting.

But suppose the Rules Committee is dominated by the hawkish Committee on the Present Danger. Can you see how it could engineer the high-defense outcome? By starting the low against the medium, and then letting high take on the winner.

This example suggests why chairpersons and rules committees are so important in legislatures: the power to set the agenda is often the power to determine the outcome.

Arrow's Theorem. Have political theorists devised a way of eliminating vote cycling and making good decisions? Kenneth Arrow investigated this question and found that *no majority-rule voting rule guarantees efficiency, respects individual preferences, and is independent of the agenda.* Put differently, no voting scheme has ever been devised—and Arrow proved it impossible to find one—that can guarantee majority voting will be consistent and will move the society to its most desirable position.

Applications of Public-Choice Theory

Public-choice theory also helps us understand how political forces can influence budgets and other factors affecting economic activity. While governments play a central role in modern economies, they have their own brand of imperfection. Just as real economies never attain the perfection of competitive markets, so democracies sometimes fail to respond to social needs in the most effective way. There are government failures as well as market failures:

Government failure arises when state actions fail to improve economic efficiency or when the government redistributes income unfairly.

There are two important sources of government failures: the bureaucratic imperative and short time horizons.

The Bureaucratic Imperative. Few can resist the temptation to increase their own influence or power. Governments are the same. They often do too much for too long. One reason for the tendency of government to overexpand is that there is no profit check (or what businesspeople call "the bottom line") on individual projects. If the government builds too many dams or too many bombers, there is no profit-and-loss statement by which the economic worth of these projects can be calculated. The only support such projects need is a legislative majority, and this can often be obtained by financing the campaigns of a small group of key legislators. Once they have come into existence, programs develop a strong constituency from those who work in them or those who benefit from their activities.

For many reasons, governments often have a great deal of trouble stopping a project once it has started. A classic example is the "breeder reactor."

This project involved an advanced nuclear power system that would replace the current generation of nuclear reactors when uranium runs out. The government designed the Clinch River Breeder Reactor in the late 1960s when everyone thought nuclear power would grow very rapidly. But by the mid-1970s, studies showed that the breeder reactor was going to be economically unviable. By the late 1970s, it was clear that nobody was ordering nuclear power plants anymore, and many utilities were canceling plants under construction. Yet the government continued spending hundreds of millions of dollars on the Clinch River project until 1983.

As one wit said in this regard, governments often behave like the little boy who said, "I know how to spell 'banana,' but I don't know when to stop."

Short Time Horizons. Elected political leaders in the United States must face elections frequently—every 2, 4, or 6 years—and often compete in hotly contested districts. Electoral pressures may lead to short time horizons in political decisions.

The syndrome of short time horizons was illustrated time and again during the 1980s by battles over the federal budget deficit. Almost everyone agreed that the high budget deficit was harmful to the economy. Almost everyone conceded that if the budget deficit were not reduced, productivity and prosperity would be imperiled. Yet, again and again, the federal government postponed taking the necessary steps to eliminate the deficit.

What was the source of the failure? Reducing the deficit requires painful steps *today* to improve economic performance *in the future.* In order to increase saving, investment, and productivity, taxes must be raised or spending cut in the present. But members of Congress who are running for reelection are reluctant to take measures that would lead to short-run unpopularity; they are more concerned about their reelection today than about future economic problems. And the political aspirants believe that voters would pay more attention to immediate tax increases or spending cuts than to the long-term benefits of deficit reduction.

The tendency to focus only upon the next election may lead governments to introduce and maintain programs with short payoff periods and to avoid those with immediate costs and diffuse future benefits. This focus on short time horizons tends to produce a proconsumption bias in government programs. That is, programs receive favorable treatment when they boost present consumption relative to future consumption, and long-term investments (research, conservation, and protection of the environment) may suffer in periods of particularly close political elections.

Some thoughtful analysts have remarked that public-choice theory presents a pessimistic view of government behavior. No reading of history could justify such a cynical conclusion. History is full of political leaders who have taken farsighted and wise, but unpopular, measures. But public-choice theory reminds us that collective choice in democracies does not always lead to an optimal or even efficient outcome. Democracies have elected Hitler and Mussolini and Peron, along with Lincoln and Churchill and Kennedy.

C. Public Choice and Externalities

Of all the economic problems requiring government action, some of the most serious arise when economic activity generates externalities. It is here that the need for sound decisions tests a nation's ability to avoid short time horizons and interest-group politics. In this final section we explore the nature of externalities, describe why they produce economic inefficiencies, and analyze potential remedies.

You will recall from earlier chapters that an externality or spillover effect occurs when production or consumption inflicts involuntary costs or benefits on others; that is, costs or benefits are imposed on others yet are not paid for by those who impose them or receive them. More precisely, an externality is an effect of one economic agent's behavior on another's well-being where that effect is not reflected in dollar or market transactions.

Externalities come in many guises. Some are positive (external economies), while others are negative (external diseconomies). Thus when I dump a barrel of acid into a stream, it kills fish and plants. Because I don't pay anyone for this damage, an external diseconomy occurs. When you discover a better way to clean up oil spills, the benefit will extend to many people who do not pay you for it. This is an external economy.

Some externalities are pervasive, while others have only small spillover components. When a carrier of bubonic plague entered a town during the Middle Ages, the population could be felled by the Black Death. On the other hand, when you chew an onion at a football stadium on a windy day, the external impacts are hardly noticeable.

Public vs. Private Goods

To illustrate the concept of external effects, consider the extreme example of a *public good,* which is a commodity that can be provided to everyone as easily as it can be provided to one person.

The case par excellence of a public good is national defense. Nothing is more vital to a society than its security. But national defense, as an economic good, differs completely from a private good like bread. Ten loaves of bread can be divided up in many ways among individuals, and what I eat cannot be eaten by others. But national defense, once provided, benefits everyone equally. It matters not at all whether you are hawk or dove, pacifist or militarist, old or young, ignorant or learned—you will receive the same amount of national security from the Army as does every other resident of the country.

Note therefore the stark contrast: The decision to provide a certain level of a public good like national defense will lead to a number of submarines, cruise missiles, and tanks to protect each of us. By contrast, the decision to consume a private good like bread is an individual act. You can eat four slices, or two, or a whole loaf; the decision is purely your own and does not commit anyone else to a particular amount of bread consumption.

The example of national defense is a dramatic and extreme case of a public good. But when you think of a smallpox vaccine, a park concert, a dam upstream on a river that prevents flood damage downstream—indeed, when you think of almost any government activity—you will often find elements of public goods involved. In summary:

Public goods are ones whose benefits are indivisibly spread among the entire community, whether or not individuals desire to purchase the public good. **Private goods,** by contrast, are ones that can be divided up and provided separately to different individuals, with no external benefits or costs to others. Efficient provision of public goods often requires government action, while private goods can be efficiently allocated by markets.

In addition to public goods, we often see public "bads," which are public goods that impose costs uniformly across a group. These are unintended by-products of consumption or production activities. One critical externality is the "greenhouse effect," which results from the buildup of carbon dioxide and other gases. Scientific studies indicate that in the coming decades these gases will cause the climate to become warmer, oceans to rise, and monsoons to shift. Nobody is producing carbon dioxide in order to change the climate. Rather, this externality results unintentionally from activities like the burning of fossil fuels.

Other examples include the air and water pollution that results from chemical production, energy production, and use of automobiles; "acid rain," which comes from long-distance transportation of sulfur emissions from power plants; radioactive exposure from atmospheric tests of nuclear weapons or from accidents like that at the Soviet plant in Chernobyl; depletion of the ozone layer from buildup of chlorofluorocarbons; and many other examples. Note that in all these cases, those who caused the external effect did not desire to hurt anyone. The externalities were the unintentional but harmful side effects of economic activity.

The most important favorable externalities are those associated with the generation of knowledge. When inventors at Bell Telephone Laboratories invented the transistor in 1948, this invention ushered in the electronic age, producing fast supercomputers, electronic telephone switches, stereo equipment, digital watches, and countless other useful products. Did Bell Labs profit from the value of the inventions outside the telephone industry? Very little. Rather, the transistor revolution was an externality whose benefits accrued to consumers around the world.

Nor is the transistor an isolated example. Inventions and discoveries over the ages—from the wheel and fire to the personal computer and superconductivity—inevitably spill over to benefit consumers many times more than they do their inventors.

Market Inefficiency with Externalities

Abraham Lincoln said that government is "to do for the people what needs to be done, but which they cannot, by individual effort, do at all, or do so well, for themselves." Public goods satisfy this description for these are goods that will not be efficiently provided by a pure market mechanism. No one can capture and sell the benefits of national defense; the benefits of basic science are too diffuse for profit-oriented firms to find economically attractive; firms will not voluntarily restrict emissions of noxious chemicals or abstain from dumping toxic wastes in landfills. Defense, scientific research, and pollution control are therefore generally held to be legitimate government functions.

Analysis of Inefficiency

Why do external diseconomies like pollution lead to economic inefficiency? Take a hypothetical coal-burning steel firm, American Steel, Inc., that generates an external diseconomy by spewing out tons of noxious sulfur dioxide fumes. Some of the sulfur harms the steel company, requiring more frequent repainting and raising the firm's medical bills. But most of the damage is "external" to the firm, settling throughout the region, harming vegetation and buildings, and causing various kinds of respiratory ailments in people.

Being a sound profit-maximizing enterprise, American Steel must decide how much pollution it should emit. With no pollution cleanup, its workers and plant will suffer. Cleaning up every little speck, on the other hand, will require heavy expenses for low-sulfur cleaner fuels, recycling systems, scrubbing equipment, and so forth. A complete cleanup would cost so much that American Steel could not hope to compete with other steelmakers.

The managers therefore decide to clean up just to the point where the firm's extra cost of pollution damage (marginal private damage) is equal to the extra cost of cleanup (marginal cost of abatement). The firm's engineers tell management that at the designated pollution rate of 200 tons per period, an extra ton of pollution will cost $10 in damages to the firm; these are the firm's *internal* or *private damages.* At the same time, cleaning up an additional ton of pollutant will cost $10 in capital, labor, etc. The firm has found its private optimal level of pollution: at 200 tons of pollution, the marginal private damage to the firm just equals the marginal cost of abatement. Put differently, when American Steel produces steel in a least-cost manner, it will set its pollution limit at 200 tons.

But what happens when an environmental specialist decides to undertake an audit of the steel firm? The auditor is interested in costs to society as well as private costs to American Steel. In examining social costs, the auditor finds that the marginal social costs—including health and property damage in neighboring regions—are 4 times the marginal private costs to American Steel. The damage from each extra ton costs American Steel $10, but the rest of society suffers additional damage of $30 per ton of *external costs.* Why doesn't American Steel include the $30 of additional social damages in its cost calculations? The $30 is excluded because these damages are external to the firm and cost it nothing.

We now see how pollution and other externalities lead to inefficient economic outcomes:

In an unregulated environment, firms will determine their most profitable pollution levels by equating the marginal private damage from pollution with the marginal cost of abatement. When the pollution spillovers are significant, the private equilibrium will produce inefficiently high levels of pollution and too little cleanup activity.

Socially Efficient Pollution. Let's go a step further and ask about the optimal level of pollution. *Efficiency requires that the marginal social damage from pollution equal the marginal social costs of abatement.* This equality occurs when the marginal benefits to the nation's health and property of reducing pollution by 1 unit just equal the marginal costs of that reduction.

How might an efficient level of pollution be determined? Economists recommend an approach known as *cost-benefit analysis,* in which efficient standards are set by balancing the marginal costs of abatement against the marginal benefits of pollution reduction. In the case of American Steel, suppose that experts study the cost data for abatement and environmental damage. They determine that marginal costs and marginal benefits are equalized when the amount of pollution is reduced from 200 tons to 100 tons. At the efficient pollution rate, they find that the marginal cost of abatement is $20 per ton, while the marginal damage from 1 extra ton is also $20.

Why is 100 tons the efficient level of pollution? Because at this emissions rate the net social value of production is maximized. If American Steel were to emit more than 100 tons of pollution, the marginal damage from pollution would outweigh the marginal savings from lower levels of abatement. On the other hand, if pollution were to be cut below 100 tons, the marginal costs of pollution cleanup would be greater than the marginal gains from cleaner air. Here again, as in many areas, we find the most efficient outcome by equating marginal cost and marginal benefit of an activity.[3]

Use of cost-benefit analysis will show why the extreme environmentalist position of "no risk" or "zero discharge"—to prohibit any pollution—will generally be wasteful. To reduce pollution to zero will generally impose astronomically high cleanup costs, while the marginal benefits of reducing the last few grams of pollution may be quite modest. In some cases, it may even be impossible to continue to produce with zero emissions, so a no-risk philosophy might require closing down the steel industry or banning all vehicular traffic. In most cases, economic efficiency calls for a compromise, balancing the extra value of the industry's output against the extra damage from pollution.

An unregulated market economy will generate levels of pollution (or other externalities) such that the marginal *private* damage of pollution equals the marginal private costs of abatement. Efficiency requires that marginal *social* damage equal marginal social abatement costs. In an unregulated economy, there will be too little abatement and too much pollution.

[3] A geometric approach to understanding American Steel's laissez-faire equilibrium and the optimal pollution level is given in question 9 at the end of this chapter.

Policies to Correct Externalities

What are the weapons that government can use to combat inefficiencies arising from externalities? Governments today combat externalities using either direct controls or financial incentives to induce firms to decrease harmful externalities or to increase beneficial activities. In the remainder of this section we focus primarily upon government steps to restrain pollution and other harmful activities.

Government Programs

Direct Controls. For almost all pollution, as well as health and safety externalities, governments rely on direct controls. For example, the 1970 Clean Air Act reduced allowable emissions of three major pollutants by 90 percent. In 1977, utilities were told to reduce sulfur emissions on new plants by 90 percent. In 1984, firms were required to reduce the amount of asbestos in their plants to no more than two fibers per cubic centimeter of air. And so it goes with regulation.

How does the government enforce a pollution regulation? Let us continue our example of American Steel, which might have been told that it can emit no more than 100 tons of particulate matter. The state Department of Environmental Protection would not tell American Steel *how* to meet the standard, only that it must comply. If standards are appropriately set, and if the firm duly complies, then the outcome might approach the efficient pollution level described in the previous part of this section.

Unfortunately, pollution-control programs seldom work in such an ideal fashion. Direct controls suffer from government failures of the kind discussed in section B of this chapter.

What failures arise in government pollution-abatement programs? We described above the need to compare marginal costs and marginal benefits in determining the most efficient level of pollution. In reality, cost-benefit comparisons are often not performed. Indeed, for some regulatory programs, the law prohibits cost-benefit comparison as a way of setting standards.

In addition, enforcement is often haphazard. If

the penalties for exceeding the standard are very harsh, the firm has a clear incentive to comply. But for most programs, the penalties for noncompliance are minimal (a few thousand dollars plus legal fees). As a result, the firm has a financial incentive to ignore or evade the pollution standard. Only fines in the hundreds of millions of dollars could correct this incentive problem.

Finally, standards are inherently a very blunt tool. They are generally the same for large firms and small firms, for steel mills in cities and in rural areas, and for acutely hazardous substances and mildly toxic ones. Uniform national rules prevent an efficient allocation of pollution reduction among firms; as a result, those firms whose marginal costs of pollution abatement are lowest do the most abatement. Numerous studies have shown that the bluntness of pollution standards causes the nation to pay much more than it would for the same pollution reduction efficiently engineered.

Emissions Taxes. In order to avoid some of the pitfalls of direct controls, many economists have suggested a new instrument: pollution or emissions taxes requiring that firms pay a tax on their pollution equal to the amount of external damage. If American Steel were imposing external marginal costs of $30 per ton on the surrounding community, then the appropriate emissions charge would be $30 per ton. This is in effect *internalizing* the externality by making the firm face the social costs of its activities. In calculating its private costs, American Steel would find that each additional ton of pollution would cost it $10 of internal costs to the firm plus $30 in emissions fees, for an overall marginal cost of $40 per ton of pollution. By equating the marginal cost (internal costs plus emissions fees) with the marginal abatement cost, the firm would curb its pollution back to the efficient level. If the emissions fee were correctly calculated—a big if—profit-minded firms would be led as if by a mended invisible hand to the efficient point where marginal social costs and marginal social benefits of pollution are equal.

Economists today often recommend emissions taxes (or externality taxes more generally) as a way of reducing pollution or externalities in a flexible and efficient manner. For example, if it is shown that CO_2 emissions warm the globe and cause extensive damages, nations might levy pollution taxes on CO_2 emissions as a method of slowing global warming. Some European countries have already imposed CO_2 taxes, and this proposal is being hotly debated in the United States today.

Private Approaches

Not all solutions involve direct government action. Two private approaches may provide a moderately efficient outcome: private negotiations and liability rules.

Negotiation and the Coase Theorem. Let's say that the government decides not to intervene. A startling analysis by Chicago's Ronald Coase suggested that voluntary negotiations among the affected parties would in some circumstances lead to the efficient outcome.

The conditions under which this might occur arise when there are well-defined property rights and the costs of negotiations are low. Suppose, for example, that I am spilling chemicals upstream from your fish ponds and killing many of your fish. Further, say that you can sue me for damage to your fish. In such a case, Coase argued, the two of us would have a powerful incentive to get together and agree on the efficient level of dumping. And this incentive would exist without any government antipollution program.

Some have tried to take Coase's suggestion even further, arguing that efficient bargains *will* occur. But this conclusion is surely too optimistic. To say that there is room for an efficient, cost-saving bargain does not mean that a deal will always be struck—as the history of war, labor-management disputes, and the theory of games amply demonstrate.[4]

[4] Those who have studied Chapter 12 will recognize that the theory of games can be fruitfully applied to the bargaining situations involved in this kind of an externality. What lessons emerge?

Recall that a two-person game often ends up at inefficient outcomes. The "prisoner's dilemma" game resembles a situation where polluters' private interests lead them to high levels of soot and waste. This could well be a Nash equilibrium of the pollution game. Moreover, there is no theorem from game theory proving that an invisible hand will lead two or more bargainers to the Pareto-efficient level of pollution. Coase never proved such a result, nor has anyone else.

Nevertheless, Coase's analysis does point to certain cases where private bargains may help alleviate externalities—namely, where property rights are well defined and where there are a few affected parties who can get together and negotiate an efficient solution.

Liability Rules. A second approach relies on the legal framework of liability laws or the tort system rather than upon direct government regulations. Here, the generator of externalities is legally liable for any damages caused to other persons.

In some areas, this doctrine is well established. Thus, in most states, if you are injured by a negligent driver, you can sue for damages. Or, if a company's workplace causes illness to its workers, the workers can sue the company for compensation.

Returning to our steel example, how would a perfect liability system contain the externality? If American Steel caused $30 of damages per ton of pollution, the victims would recover these damages through the courts. Thus the marginal cost faced by the firm would be $40 per ton ($10 of internal costs plus $30 of legal damages). Such costs would give firms strong incentives to reduce pollution back toward the efficient level.

Unfortunately, liability rules have shortcomings no less than other systems of attacking externalities. The major difficulty resides in the high cost of litigating damages and, for pollution, in the lack of property rights in clean air.

● Our introductory survey of government's role in the economy is a sobering reminder of the responsibilities and shortcomings of collective action. On the one hand, governments must defend their borders, stabilize their economies, protect the public health, and regulate pollution. On the other hand, many policies designed to benefit the public interest suffer from inefficiencies and inconsistencies.

Does this mean we should abandon the visible hand of government for the invisible hand of markets? Economics cannot answer such deep political questions; all it can do is examine the strengths and weaknesses of both collective and market choices, and point to mechanisms (such as pollution taxes or liability rules) by which a mended invisible hand may be more efficient than the extremes of either pure laissez-faire or unbridled bureaucratic rule making. ●

SUMMARY

A. Government Control of the Economy

1. The economic role of government has grown vastly larger over the last century. More and more activities in our complex, interdependent society have come under direct regulation and control.
2. A modern welfare state performs four economic functions: (*a*) It sets the legal framework for economic activity—constitutions, laws, and rules of the economic game. (*b*) It allocates resources to collective goods by taxing, spending, and regulating when the market mechanism falters. (*c*) It redistributes resources by social welfare transfers. (*d*) It establishes macroeconomic stabilization policy to even out the peaks and troughs of unemployment, to contain inflation, and to promote long-term economic growth.

B. Public-Choice Theory: How Governments Make Decisions

3. Public-choice theory analyzes how governments actually behave. In a complex and interdependent modern economy, government actions can serve to increase society's real income over Hobbes' brutal state of nature.

4. Public choice involves the aggregation of individual preferences into a collective choice. Under unanimity, all decisions must be made by consensus. Unanimity has the ideal property that all decisions are Pareto improvements (no one can be hurt), but the costliness of persuading everyone is so great that, in practice, no decisions are likely to be made under unanimity.

5. Most committees and legislative bodies use majority rule, which ensures that decisions will improve the welfare of at least half the voters. But majority rule can lead to "tyranny by the majority" and has the potential for cyclical voting whereby, in the face of diverse tastes, no single program commands a majority.

6. Just as the invisible hand can break down, so there are government failures. These are cases in which, because of the need for less-than-unanimous decisions, inefficient or inequitable outcomes can arise. Important examples are the capture of a legislature by well-financed minorities or lobbies, the tendency of governments to finance excessive programs for too long, and the short time horizons that plague competitive electoral arrangements.

C. Public Choice and Externalities

7. One major example of market failure that may require collective actions is external effects. These occur when the costs (or benefits) of an activity spill over to other people, without those other people being paid (or paying) for the costs (or benefits) incurred (or received).

8. The most clear-cut example of an externality is the case of public goods, like defense, where all consumers in a group share equally in the consumption and cannot be excluded. Less obvious examples like public health, inventions, parks, and dams also possess public-good properties. These contrast with private goods, like bread, which can be divided and provided to a single individual.

9. An unregulated market economy will produce too much pollution. Unregulated firms decide pollution levels (or other externalities) such that the marginal private damage of pollution equals the marginal private costs of abatement. Efficiency requires that marginal social damage equal marginal social abatement costs.

10. There are numerous steps by which governments can internalize or correct the inefficiencies arising from externalities. Alternatives include decentralized solutions (such as negotiations or legal liability rules) and government-imposed approaches (such as pollution emission standards or emissions taxes). Experience indicates that no approach is ideal in all circumstances, but many economists believe that greater use of market-like systems of regulation would improve the efficiency of regulatory systems.

CONCEPTS FOR REVIEW

Functions of government
four functions of government: framework, stabilization, allocation, distribution
market failures vs. government failures

Public choice
public choice
government failures: capture, myopia, bureaucracy
public choice by: unanimity, majority rule, supermajorities
Arrow's theorem, cyclical voting, the voting paradox

Externalities and public goods
private vs. public goods
externalities
inefficiency of externalities
internal vs. external costs, social vs. private cost
remedies for externalities: bargaining, liability, standards, taxes

QUESTIONS FOR DISCUSSION

1. Name things government does now that it once didn't do. Can you think of things government used to do that it no longer does? What does this changing pattern of government activity indicate about the changing role of government in steering the economy?
2. It is useful to think of a spectrum of goods from purely public to purely private. On a piece of paper, draw a continuum and fill it with examples that are purely private, mostly private, half-and-half, mostly public, purely public. Under what conditions would you allow the market to allocate resources and when would you have the government make the economic decisions?
3. Evaluate critically the statement regarding the proper role of government attributed to Abraham Lincoln on page 312. Could believers in big government as well as believers in small government both agree with it?
4. "Local public goods" are ones that mainly benefit the residents of a town or state—such as beaches or schools open only to town residents. Is there any reason to think that towns might act competitively to provide the correct amount of local public goods to their residents? If so, does this suggest an economic theory of "fiscal federalism" whereby local public goods should be locally supplied?
5. Decide whether each of the following externalities is serious enough to warrant collective action. If so, which of the four remedies considered in the chapter would be most efficient?
   (a) Steel mills' emitting of sulfur oxides into the Birmingham air
   (b) Smoking by people in restaurants
   (c) Smoking by students without roommates in their own rooms
   (d) Driving by persons under the influence of alcohol, involving 25,000 fatalities per year
   (e) Driving by persons under 21 under the influence of alcohol
6. Can you see why a market allocation of bread proceeds by unanimity? Why is this not possible for national defense? Does this difference suggest why the bread allocation may lead society to the utility-possibility frontier, while the national defense allocation may not?
7. In considering whether you want a pure laissez-faire economy or government regulation, discuss whether there should be government controls over prostitution, drugs, assault weapons, and alcohol. Should there be a free market for body organs and adopted babies?
8. President Ronald Reagan once stated: "A problem in one part of the country does not automatically mean that we need a new federal program in all fifty states." Consider a problem like air pollution which causes smog and health problems in California. Which of the four policies to combat externalities might cause inefficiencies because they impose a uniform national program? Which policies are more flexible and can adapt to local conditions?

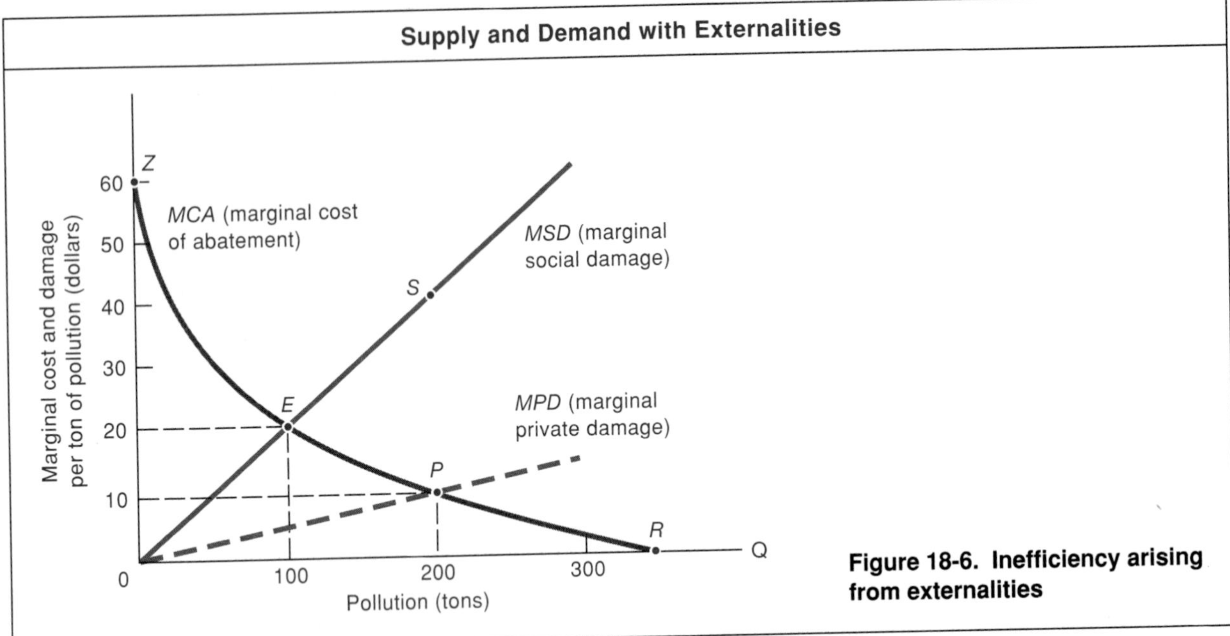

Figure 18-6. Inefficiency arising from externalities

9. **Advanced problem:** Figure 18-6 illustrates the pollution example of American Steel discussed in section C. The downward-sloping black curve shows the marginal cost of reducing pollution at each pollution level, while the solid blue line measures the marginal social damage created by American Steel's pollution. The dashed line, by contrast, shows the marginal private damage done by American Steel to itself.

   Explain why point *P* represents the inefficient laissez-faire and unregulated outcome. Further explain why point *E* is the efficient outcome.

   For extra credit, try to show how each of the four policy approaches (see pages 313–315) moves the private equilibrium from *P* to *E*.

C H A P T E R 19

GOVERNMENT TAXATION AND EXPENDITURE

> The spirit of a people, its cultural level, its social structure, the deeds its policy may prepare, all this and more is written in its fiscal history. . . . He who knows how to listen to its messenger here discerns the thunder of world history more clearly than anywhere else.
>
> Joseph Schumpeter

In all modern countries, even those which rely primarily on market forces to allocate most goods and services, governments have an important role in several key sectors. Governments today set the legal framework for the market, regulate the financial system, promote competition, and care for those unable to care for themselves.

How do governments accomplish their economic responsibilities? There is no magic secret. Governments raise resources through taxation and then use their dollar votes to purchase goods and services in the marketplace. In the first section, we survey the expenditures of government on the federal, state, and local level. Then, in the second section, we examine the principles of taxation along with the actual tax systems employed at these different levels. By understanding the nature of our fiscal institutions, we can better discern the message of fiscal history.

A. Government Expenditures

Federal, State, and Local Functions

All nations organize their governments on different levels. Americans face three levels of government: federal, state, and local. Before the twentieth century, local government was by far the most important of the three. The federal government did little more than support the military, pay interest on the national debt, finance a few public works, and pay salaries of government officials. Most of its tax collection came from liquor and tobacco excises and import tariffs. Life was simple. Local governments performed most functions and depended primarily on property taxes for their finance.

Figure 19-1 plots the trends in government spending. You can see that the share of federal spending in GNP tripled during the Great Depression and bulged temporarily during World War II. Since 1940, federal spending has surpassed state and local spending.

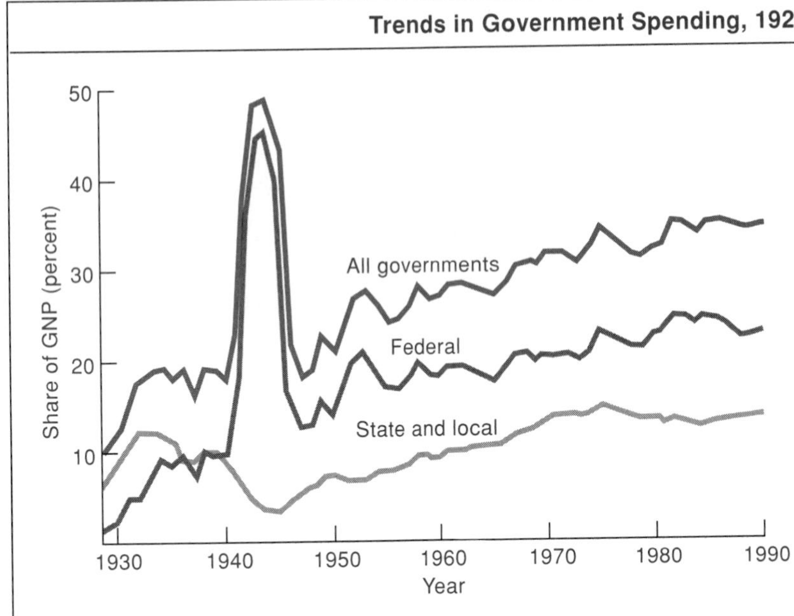

Figure 19-1. The share of government spending grew in war and peace

Federal spending rose rapidly in the Great Depression and bulged during World War II. In the 1960s and 1970s, government spending on income-support payments showed the steepest trends, while in the 1980s interest payments and defense spending grew most rapidly. Note how little the conservative policies of the last decade slowed the trend toward higher government spending. (Source: U.S. Department of Commerce.)

Federal Expenditures

The U.S. government is the world's biggest business. It buys more automobiles and steel, meets a bigger payroll, and handles more money than any organization anywhere. The numbers involved in federal finance are astronomical—in the billions and trillions of dollars. The federal budget for 1992 is projected to be $1446 billion; this enormous number amounts to $5783 for each American or approximately 2.8 months of annual GNP.

Table 19-1 lists the major categories of federal expenditure for fiscal year 1992. (The federal fiscal year 1992 covers October 1, 1991, through September 30, 1992.) The largest item is national security and international affairs, which includes primarily the cost of equipping and staffing the Department of Defense.

The most rapidly expanding item in the last two decades has been *entitlement programs*—those that provide benefits or payments to any persons who meet certain eligibility requirements set down by law. The major entitlements are social security (old-age, survivors, and disability insurance), health programs (including Medicare for those over 65 and Medicaid for indigent families), and income security programs (including payments for food, unemployment insurance, and cash payments to the poor). In fact, virtually the entire growth in federal spending can be accounted for by entitlement programs, which have grown from 20 percent of the budget in 1960 to 46 percent in 1989.

Another category includes programs for specific sectors of the economy: supporting agriculture, giving grants to local governments for sewage systems, and funding space exploration. A final category is general government. This includes traditional functions of government such as operation of Congress, the judiciary, and the presidency. It is surprising to see that the cost of these traditional functions is dwarfed by all the rest. Taken together, all programs other than entitlements have actually shrunk since 1960. The federal budget has grown during the last quarter-century because the populace has voted larger and larger transfer payments to itself.

State and Local Expenditures

Although the battles over the federal budget command the headlines, state and local units provide many of the essential functions in today's economy. Figure 19-2 illustrates the way states and localities spend their money. By far the largest item is education because most of the nation's children are educated in schools financed primarily by local governments. By attempting to equalize the educational resources available to every child, the nation

Federal Expenditure in Fiscal Year 1992

	Budget ($, billion)	Percentage of total
1. National defense, veterans, and international affairs	346	24
2. Social security	289	20
3. Interest on government debt	206	14
4. Health	195	13
5. Income security	185	13
6. Transportation, commerce, and housing	132	9
7. Education, training, and employment	46	3
8. General government	28	2
9. Energy, natural resources, and environment	23	2
10. Science, space, and technology	18	1
11. Agriculture	15	1
12. Miscellaneous and offsetting receipts	−41	−3
TOTAL	1,446	100

Table 19-1. Federal spending is dominated by defense and entitlement programs

Almost one-third of federal spending is to pay for defense and interest or pensions due to past wars. Almost half today is for rapidly growing "entitlement programs"—income security, social security, and health. Note how small is item 8's traditional cost of government. (Source: Office of Management and Budget, *Budget of the U.S. Government, Fiscal Year 1992.*)

helps to level out the otherwise great disparities in economic opportunity.

Fiscal Federalism

Students of American government are familiar with a division of political responsibilities among the different branches and levels of government. A similar division of labor occurs in economic affairs. Ours is a system of *fiscal federalism* as well as political federalism. The federal government directs activities that concern the entire nation—paying for defense, space, and foreign affairs. Local governments educate children, police streets, and remove garbage. States build highways and administer welfare programs.

As you examine Table 19-1 and Figure 19-2, you can see how the different kinds of expenditures are parceled out among the three levels of government. In analyzing the fiscal division of labor among governments, economists stress that programs have varying degrees of spillover or externalities. In general, localities are responsible for "local public goods," activities whose benefits are largely confined to local residents. Since libraries are used by townspeople and streetlights illuminate city roads, these are appropriately paid for by local residents. Many federal functions are "national public goods"

Purposes of State and Local Expenditures, Fiscal 1985

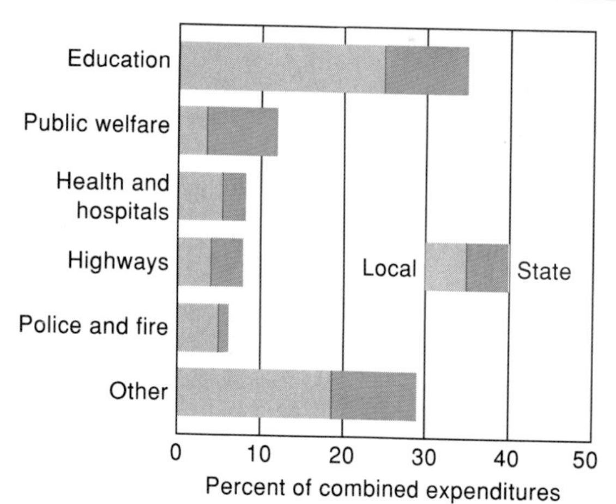

Figure 19-2. State and local governments concentrate on local public goods

State and local programs include providing education, financing hospitals, maintaining the streets, and similar tasks. In the division of labor among governments, cities pave their streets and states construct highways between cities, while the federal government pays for 90 percent of interstate highways. Do you see a pattern of fiscal federalism here? (Source: U.S. Bureau of the Census, *Government Finances in 1984–1985.*)

and provide benefits to all the nation's citizens. For example, an AIDS vaccine would benefit people from every state, not just those living near the laboratory where it is discovered; similarly, missiles sitting in Kansas silos provide a perilous deterrence for the entire country, not just for those living near the cornfields. An efficient system of fiscal federalism will take into account the nature of the spillovers of government programs.[1]

The boundaries between the fiscal functions change over time. Alexander Hamilton, Franklin Roosevelt, and Lyndon Johnson acted to broaden the federal role, while Thomas Jefferson, Calvin Coolidge, and Ronald Reagan attempted to check or reverse the accretion of fiscal powers at the federal level. One of the perennial debates of economics centers on the appropriate level for administering government programs.

B. Economic Aspects of Taxation

Taxes are what we pay for a civilized society.
Justice Oliver Wendell Holmes

Governments must pay for their programs; the funds come mainly from taxes and any shortfall is made up by borrowing from the public. But if we look behind the dollar flows, what the government needs to police the streets or fight a war in the desert is real economic resources. Government needs aluminum and teachers and microchips; it must draw upon the economy's scarce land, labor, and capital.

In taxing, governments are in reality deciding how its needed resources shall be drawn from the nation's households and businesses and put into collective consumption and investment. The money raised through taxation is the vehicle by which real resources are transferred from private goods to collective goods.

Principles of Taxation

In the distant past, taxes were levied by those in power against those out of power. A nobleman in the court of Louis XIV might go scot-free, while a peasant in Normandy was heavily burdened. Such arbitrary distribution of taxes eventually gave way to more rational fiscal principles as economists and political philosophers developed systematic approaches to tax policy.

Benefit vs. Ability-to-Pay Principles

Of the many principles underlying optimal taxation, the two most important are:

- That different individuals should be taxed in proportion to the benefit they receive from government programs. Just as people pay private dollars in proportion to their consumption of private bread, a person's taxes should be related to his or her use of collective goods like public roads or parks. This is the **benefit principle.**
- That the amount of taxes people pay should relate to their income, wealth, or ability to pay. Stated differently, taxation should be arranged to help accomplish what society regards as the proper and equitable distribution of incomes.[2] This is the **ability-to-pay principle.**

[1] What about global public goods like the global environment and climate, or the threat of extinction of species? These problems may receive insufficient government resources because of the absence of a world government.

[2] Economists following in the utilitarian tradition (see the discussion of utilitarianism in Chapter 6) used to argue that the utilities or satisfactions of different people can be added together to form a total social utility or satisfaction. If each extra dollar brings less and less extra satisfaction to each of us, and if the rich and poor are alike in their capacity to enjoy consumption, a dollar taxed away from a millionaire and given to a poor person is supposed to add more to total social utility than it subtracts. This suggests that, because those with higher income (or higher "abilities to pay") have less extra satisfaction from their last dollars than do poorer people, putting a larger tax share on higher-income people will increase total social satisfaction. Chapter 12, especially Fig. 12-2, illustrates the analysis of how redistributing income from high-income to low-income individuals can raise the average utility or satisfaction of the population.

Horizontal and Vertical Equity

In addition to these general principles, tax systems attempt to incorporate modern views about fairness or equity. One important principle is that of **horizontal equity,** which states that those who are essentially equal should be taxed equally.

The notion of equal treatment of equals has deep roots in Western culture. If you and I are alike in every way except the color of our eyes, all principles of taxation would hold that we should pay equal taxes. In the case of benefit taxation, if we receive exactly the same services from the highways or parks, the principle of horizontal equity states that we should therefore pay equal taxes. Or if a tax system followed the ability-to-pay approach, horizontal equity would dictate that people who have equal incomes should pay the same taxes.

A more controversial principle concerns **vertical equity,** which concerns the tax treatment of people with different levels of income. Abstract philosophical principles provide little guidance in resolving the issues of fairness here. Imagine that A and B are alike in every respect except that B has 10 times the property and income of A. Does that mean that B should pay the same absolute tax dollars as A for government services such as police protection? Or that B should pay the same percentage of income in taxes? Or, since the police need more time to protect the property of well-to-do B, is it perhaps fair for B to pay a larger fraction of income in taxes?

In fact, these are highly charged political issues and not narrow economic questions. General and abstract principles of taxation simply cannot decide how different groups should be taxed.

Pragmatic Compromises in Taxation

How have societies resolved these thorny philosophical questions? Governments have generally adopted pragmatic solutions that are only partially based on benefit and ability-to-pay approaches. Political representatives know that taxes are highly unpopular. After all, the cry of "taxation without representation" helped launch the American Revolution. Modern tax systems are an uneasy compromise between lofty principles and political pragmatism. As the canny French finance minister Colbert wrote three centuries ago, "Raising taxes is like plucking a goose: you want to get the maximum number of feathers with the minimum amount of hiss."

What practices have emerged? In some cases, public services at the local and national levels primarily benefit recognizable groups, and those groups have no special claim for favorable or unfavorable treatment by virtue of their average incomes or other characteristics. In such cases, modern governments generally rely on taxes of the benefit type.

Thus, local roads are usually paid for by local residents. "User fees" are charged for water and sewage treatment, which are treated like private goods. Taxes collected on gasoline may be devoted (or "earmarked") to roads.

Progressive and Regressive Taxes. Today, advanced countries rely heavily on *progressive income taxes.* A family with $50,000 of income is taxed more than one with $20,000 of income. Not only does the higher-income family pay a larger income tax, but it in fact pays a higher fraction of its income.

This progressive tax is in contrast to a strictly proportional tax, which makes all taxpayers pay exactly the same proportion of income. A regressive tax takes a larger fraction of income in taxes from poor than from rich families.

A tax is called *proportional, progressive,* or *regressive* depending upon whether it takes from high-income people the same fraction of income, a larger fraction of income, or a smaller fraction of income than it takes from low-income people.[3]

The different kinds of taxes are illustrated in Figure 19-3. What are some examples? A personal income tax that is graduated to take more and more out of each extra dollar of income is progressive. A comprehensive sales tax will be mildly regressive because the ratio of expenditure to income falls as income rises. But a tax that is strictly proportional to the size of one's estate left at death is progressive since the person with twice the income tends on the average to have and bequeath more than twice the wealth.

Direct and Indirect Taxes. Taxes are classified as direct or indirect. **Indirect taxes** are ones that are levied on goods and services and thus only "indirectly" on individuals. Examples are excise and

[3] It should be noted that the words "progressive" and "regressive" are technical economic terms relating to the proportions that taxes bear to different incomes. Do not interpret them in emotional or political terms.

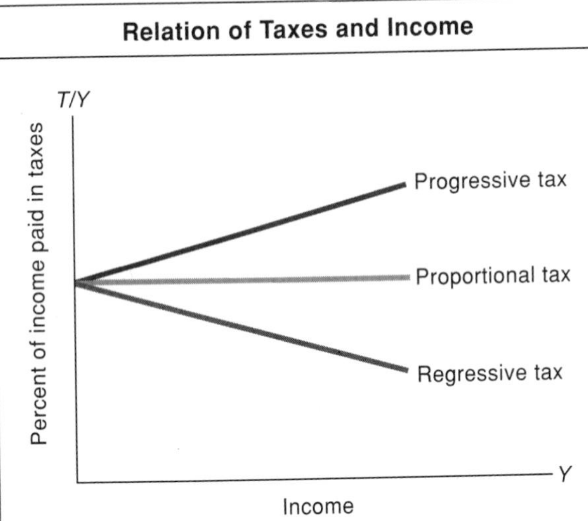

Figure 19-3. Progressive, proportional, and regressive taxes
Taxes are progressive if they take a larger fraction of income as income rises; proportional if taxes are a constant fraction of income; and regressive if they place a larger relative burden on low-income families than on high-income families.

sales taxes, cigarette and gasoline taxes, tariff duties on imports, and property taxes.

Over the last century, legislatures in all democracies have increasingly relied upon **direct taxes,** which are levied directly upon individuals or firms. Examples of direct taxes are personal income taxes, social security or other payroll taxes, and inheritance and gift taxes. Corporation income taxes are also treated as direct taxes, because people receive the income of corporations. A major reason direct taxes have become increasingly popular is that these taxes can easily be tailored to fit personal circumstances, such as size of family, income, age, and more generally the ability to pay. By contrast, adjusting indirect taxes for personal situations is relatively difficult.

Federal Taxation

Let us begin our analysis of taxation with a survey of the federal system of taxation in place in the early 1990s. Table 19-2 provides an overview of the major taxes and shows whether they are progressive, proportional, or regressive.

Sales and Excise Taxes

The United States has no national sales tax, although there are a number of federal excise taxes on specific commodities such as cigarettes, alcohol, and gasoline. Sales and excise taxes are generally regressive, because consumption in general, and purchase of these items in particular, takes a larger fraction of the income of a poor family than of a rich one.

Many economists and political leaders have argued that the United States should rely more heavily on sales or consumption taxes than it has up to now. They note that the country is currently saving and investing less than is needed for future needs; by substituting sales taxes for income taxes, they believe that the national savings rate would increase. Critics of consumption taxes respond that such a change is undesirable because sales taxes are more regressive than today's income tax.

Social Insurance Taxes

Virtually all industries now come under the Social Security Act. Workers receive retirement benefits that depend upon their earnings history and past social security taxes. The social insurance program also funds a disability program and health insurance for the poor and elderly.

Federal Tax Receipts, Fiscal Year 1992

	Receipts ($, billion)
Progressive:	
Individual income taxes	530
Death and gift taxes	13
Corporation income taxes	102
Proportional:	
Payroll taxes	429
Regressive:	
Excise taxes	67
Other taxes and receipts	24
Total	**1,165**

Table 19-2. Income and payroll taxes are the main federal revenue sources
Progressive taxes are still the leading source of federal revenues, but proportional payroll taxes are closing fast. (Source: Office of Management and Budget, *Budget of the U.S. Government, Fiscal Year 1992.*)

To pay for these benefits, employees and employers are charged a "payroll tax." In 1990, this consisted of a total of 15.3 percent of all wage income below a ceiling of about $51,300 a year per person; the tax is split between employer and employee.

Table 19-2 shows the payroll tax as a proportional tax because it taxes a fixed fraction of employment earnings. It does have some regressive features, however, because it exempts property income and does not apply to any earnings above $51,300 (for 1990).

The payroll tax has been the fastest growing source of federal revenues, rising from 0 in 1929, to 18 percent of revenues in 1960, to 37 percent in 1991.

Corporation Income Taxes

After a corporation has met all its expenses and reckoned its annual income, it must pay part of its income to the federal government. The top federal corporation tax rate in 1991 is set at 34 percent of corporate profits. Small corporations pay a slightly lower tax rate on their first $75,000 of profits.

The corporation income tax is probably the most controversial of federal taxes. Many economists oppose this tax, arguing that the corporation is but a legal fiction and should not be taxed. By taxing first corporate profits, then the dividends paid by corporations and received by individuals, the government subjects corporations to double taxation. Because of double taxation, corporate production is the most heavily taxed sector of the economy, a fact that may discourage corporate investment.

Some economists advocate abolition of the corporation income tax. They would instead credit corporate-source income to the corporation's owners and tax the income at personal tax rates. Studies indicate that this step would improve the economy's efficiency by a few billion dollars.

Value-Added Taxes

Finally, we mention a tax that has been widely used outside the United States. The **value-added tax,** or VAT for short, collects taxes at each stage of production. Thus, for a loaf of bread, VAT is collected from the farmer for wheat production, from the miller for flour production, from the baker at the dough stage, and finally from the grocer at the delivered-loaf stage.

All this sounds complicated. In fact, a VAT is essentially the same as a national sales tax; it ends up taxing the sum of labor, interest, and other values added, which sum up to total final sales.

From time to time, the idea of a VAT becomes popular in the United States as a way to raise additional revenues. Its appeal arises because the VAT is a tax on consumption, and, as noted above, many economists think that the United States should boost saving by changing its tax structure toward one based on consumption and away from one based on income. In addition, countries that are heavily involved in international trade may desire to "harmonize" their fiscal systems with European and other countries that rely on a large VAT.

Overall, is VAT a good idea? As with old age, it depends on the alternative. An objective analysis would begin by calling VAT a national sales tax and would then compare it to other tax systems.

The Individual Income Tax

The most important and complex tax is the individual income tax. All advanced industrial countries tax the incomes of their residents and citizens, but this tax is particularly important in the United States. Of all taxes, this one is most carefully tailored to an individual's ability to pay.

The individual income tax arrived late in our nation's history; the Constitution forbade any direct tax that was not apportioned among the states according to population. In 1913, the Sixteenth Amendment to the Constitution provided that "Congress shall have power to lay and collect taxes on income, from whatever source derived, without apportionment among the several States. . . ."

The individual income tax raised much controversy but little revenue until World War II. Then, to raise money for the war effort, tax rates were increased sharply with the top tax rate reaching 94 percent. After the war, the income tax continued as the most significant federal tax. However, the tax rate paid by those with the highest incomes was reduced to 70 percent in 1965, 50 percent in 1982, 28 percent in 1988, and was raised to 31 percent for 1991.

Periodically, the country rises up and, literally or figuratively, revolts against its tax system. The most recent revolt occurred in the mid-1980s when perceived inequities in the system led political figures

(1) Adjusted gross income (before exemptions and deductions) ($)	(2) Individual income tax ($)	(3) Average tax rate (%) (3) = [(2) ÷ (1)] × 100	(4) Marginal tax rate (= tax on extra dollar) (%)	(5) Disposable income after taxes ($) (5) = (1) − (2)
5,000	−702	−14	−14	5,702
10,000	−953	−10	0	10,953
20,000	956	5	15	19,044
50,000	4,744	9	15	45,256
100,000	15,886	16	33	84,114
150,000	28,756	19	33	121,244
250,000	55,156	22	28	194,844
1,000,000	224,000	22	28	776,000
10,000,000	2,240,000	22	28	7,760,000

Table 19-3. Federal income tax for a family of four, 1990

The table shows incomes, taxes, and tax rates for a representative four-person family in 1990. Because of the earned-income tax credit, low-income workers with children get a tax rebate (this being a small "negative income tax"). Marginal tax rates rise from 15 to 28 to a maximum of 33 percent of income. (This table assumes that deductions are the greater of the standard deduction or 20 percent of income.) (Source: U.S. Internal Revenue Service.)

as disparate as liberal Senator Bill Bradley and conservative President Ronald Reagan to join forces in an assault on the tax code. The result was the landmark Tax Reform Act of 1986, which represented the most sweeping change in the tax code in a generation.

How does the federal income tax work? The principle is simple, although the forms are complicated. You start by calculating your income; you then subtract certain expenses, deductions, and exemptions, to obtain taxable income. You can then calculate your taxes on the basis of your taxable income.

The calculation of individual taxes is illustrated for a simple case in Table 19-3. This table shows the taxes faced by a family of four in 1990.

Column (1) shows different levels of "adjusted gross income"—that is, wages, interest, dividends, and other income earned by the household.

Assuming that our household has four people, and takes certain deductions, column (2) shows the tax due. Note that the tax is actually negative for those with wage incomes of $5000 and of $10,000, indicating that the government is transferring income to low-income families. For people with positive taxes, the lowest "marginal tax rate," or extra tax per dollar of extra income, is 15 percent.[4] Taxes then rise rapidly in relation to income. Indeed, when income climbs to $10 million, more than 22 percent will go to the government. The current top marginal rate of 33 percent is well below the 70 percent rate of the late 1960s or the 94 percent rate of the 1940s.

Column (3) shows just how progressive the personal income-tax code really is. A $50,000-a-year family is made to bear a relatively heavier burden than a $20,000-a-year family—the former pays 9 percent of income in taxes, while the latter pays but 5 percent. Someone earning $1 million each year is made to bear a still heavier relative burden.

Column (4) records the important marginal tax rate at each level of income. This begins at minus 14 percent for poor families, rises to 15 percent for those just entering the positive tax system, and increases to 28 percent for individuals with the highest incomes.

Column (5) shows the amount of "disposable income after taxes." Note that it always pays to get more income: even when a rock star makes another million dollars, she still has $720,000 of disposable income left over (= $1,000,000 minus 28 percent of $1,000,000).

[4] Note our friend "marginal," meaning "extra." The notion of marginal tax rates is extremely important in modern economics. Remember the "marginal principle" that people should only be concerned with the extra costs or benefits that occur—"let bygones by bygones." Under this principle, the major effect of any tax on incentives to supply capital or labor comes from the marginal tax rate. This notion has formed the intellectual core of modern "supply-side economics."

Erosion of the Tax Base. The U.S. government collects a larger fraction of its revenues from individual income taxes than do most countries. Yet, the United States also has among the lowest tax rates of any major industrial country, as is shown in Table 19-4. How can the United States raise so much in taxes with such low tax rates? This paradox is easily explained: The U.S. includes more items in the definition of "taxable income" than do other countries. That is to say, the number of exclusions and deductions from taxable income are fewer here than elsewhere.

At the same time, while most people face marginal tax rates of 15 or 25 percent, individual income taxes nonetheless average less than 10 percent of GNP. The reason is that many items of income are excluded from taxation. Some call these untaxed items "loopholes," while more neutral terms are "tax preferences" and "tax expenditures."

What are some of the untaxed items? First, there are exemptions of $2050 per person for 1990. In addition, a married couple may take a "standard deduction," or subtraction from income, of $5450 in 1990. Both these amounts increase each year with inflation because of "indexation" of the tax system.

Second, some income avoids taxation by going to the "underground economy": many people fail to report all their income and fake their expense accounts. The government estimates that in recent years 10 percent of taxable income is not reported.

Third, and quantitatively more important than evasion, is legal tax avoidance. Congress legislates many tax expenditures that let certain types of income go lightly taxed or not taxed at all. Examples include interest on state and local bonds, partial exclusion of social security benefits and payments for pensions, deductibility of some state and local taxes, and special treatment of income in certain industries such as oil and gas. Table 19-5 shows the most important tax expenditures.

Top Tax Rates in Major Countries

Country	Top marginal tax rate*
Britain	40
Canada	29
France	57
Germany	53
Japan	50
Netherlands	70
Sweden	42
United States	31

*The additional amount of taxes per dollar of additional taxable income paid by taxpayers with the highest incomes.

Table 19-4. U.S. has the lowest tax rates and the broadest base

Since World War II, the U.S. has lowered the tax rate on the highest incomes from 92 percent in 1964 to 31 percent in 1991. This was accomplished by broadening the tax base and including many items of tax preference in taxable income. [Source: OECD, *The Role of Indicators in Structural Surveillance* (OECD, Paris, 1990).]

Tax Expenditures, 1992

	Amount ($, billion)
1. Exclusion of pension contributions	51
2. Deductibility of mortgage interest on owner-occupied homes	41
3. Exclusion of employer contributions for medical expenses	33
4. Capital gains carryover at death	27
5. Accelerated depreciation	26
Total:	
Top 5 items	**178**
All tax expenditures	**363**

Table 19-5. Tax expenditures erode the tax base

Analysts use the term "tax expenditures" to represent money spent by Congress through tax reductions. The table shows the major tax expenditures, which are calculated by determining the amount of income excluded from the tax base and multiplying these numbers by the applicable tax rate. (Source: Office of Management and Budget, *Budget of the U.S. Government, Fiscal Year 1992.*)

The Fiscal Revolution of the 1980s

For most of this century, the United States experienced a steady growth in the scale and scope of government. The federal government assumed many new responsibilities; it undertook the construction of dams and regulation of power plants, bolstered income-support programs, enacted social security, and printed food stamps. At the end of the 1970s, conservatives complained that the United States was becoming a planned economy.

President Ronald Reagan held an economic philosophy that marked a turning point from the earlier period. He believed that individual initiative and unfettered markets would produce the best possible economic outcome:

> My program [is] a careful combination of reducing incentive-stifling taxes, slowing the growth of federal spending and regulations, and a gradually slowing expansion of the money supply. . . . That environment will be an America in which honest work is no longer discouraged by ever-rising prices and tax rates.

This philosophy, sometimes labeled *supply-side economics*, held sway during the Reagan and early Bush presidencies.

Overall Economic Policy

During the conservative 1980s, the government held that economic policy should emphasize microeconomic measures to improve productivity and economic efficiency rather than take macroeconomic steps to stabilize the overall economy. Under the supply-side approach, macroeconomic policies, such as those involving the rate of growth of the money supply or the level of government spending, should not be "fine-tuned" in an attempt to control the business cycle but should be oriented toward the long-run goals of economic growth and efficiency.

Budget Policy

The Reagan budgetary philosophy advocated a strong military buildup, maintenance of middle-class income-support programs like social security, and sharp cutbacks in other civilian programs. But the Reagan plan was only partially successful. Defense spending grew rapidly during the 1980s, but the other goals were blunted. The attempt to cut civilian spending was thwarted by political forces that successfully protected their own spending programs. Overall, government spending as a share of GNP grew from 20 percent in the 1960s and 1970s to 23 percent in 1990. Moreover, whereas Reagan took office proclaiming the need to balance the budget, the 1980s saw the highest peacetime budget deficits in half a century.

Regulatory Relief

The years from 1965 to 1980 represented the heyday of regulatory institution-building. The United States legislated programs to deal with traffic safety, air and water pollution, hazards of the workplace, mine safety and strip mining, and the dangers from nuclear power and toxic wastes. The Reagan administration believed that this regulation was overambitious in intent and overzealous in administration—and that the United States needed "regulatory relief."

The Reagan administration's attack on regulatory programs was less visible but in many ways more effective than its budgetary and economic programs. Virtually all regulatory programs were curbed; few new regulations were issued, enforcement was relaxed, and rules were generally interpreted in ways sympathetic to free-market advocates.

Tax Policy

The 1980s hatched a string of tax changes, with radical legislation enacted in both 1981 and 1986. The 1981 Economic Recovery and Tax Act (ERTA) produced major cuts in both business and individual taxes. In keeping with the philosophy of supply-side economics, personal tax rates were cut across the board by 25 percent. Proponents promised that these cuts would not markedly reduce tax revenues.

A further step was the important Tax Reform Act (TRA) of 1986, which included a number of important new features:

- Marginal tax rates were lowered from a top rate of 50 percent to a top rate of 28 percent for individuals and from 46 percent to 34 percent for corporations.
- Numerous tax expenditures were trimmed. The most significant changes were that capital gains (income earned from sale of assets like common stocks and houses) were taxed as ordinary income rather than at preferential rates; sales taxes were no longer deductible from income; interest paid on consumer loans and student debt was no longer deductible.
- The overall impact of the TRA was "revenue neutral"—meaning that it neither raised nor lowered total revenues. However, this neutrality was attained by raising taxes on corporations and lowering taxes on individuals by the same amount.

Distributional Impact. What was the impact of the 1986 Tax Reform Act upon the distribution of income? At first blush, it might appear that high-income individuals benefit from the sharp reduction in the marginal tax rates (from 50 percent to 28 percent at the top). In fact, because the tax base was significantly broadened while the effective rate on corporations was raised significantly, the effect on taxes of the 1986 TRA was mildly progressive. Table 19-6 shows estimates of the percent change in total tax liabilities by income group. The higher tax for the top incomes results mainly from the higher corporation tax, which is assumed to fall on the owners of capital.

Recent Tax Changes. Although the 1986 tax reforms are the most significant changes in many years, Congress tinkers with the tax code almost every year to make minor adjustments. In 1990, Congress enacted a budget package that was designed to reduce the federal budget deficit, and this package included a number of significant tax changes. The 1990 act increased taxes on consumption (through raising "sin taxes" on cigarettes, alcohol, and gasoline) and increased the taxes at the highest levels of income. The basic structure of the 1986 reforms emerged largely untouched by these most recent changes.

Impact of Tax Reform on Income Distribution

Income group	Percent change in: Federal individual and corporate income taxes	Total federal taxes
Top tenth of households	+3	+2
Top 5%	+4	+3
Top 1%	+5	+5
Second tenth	−6	−4
Third tenth	−6	−3
Fourth tenth	−7	−4
Fifth tenth	−8	−4
Sixth tenth	−12	−6
Seventh tenth	−16	−7
Eighth tenth	−24	−10
Ninth tenth	−32	−11
Bottom tenth	−44	−16

Table 19-6. Change in federal taxes as a result of the 1986 Tax Reform Act

The 1986 Tax Reform Act broadened the tax base and lowered marginal tax rates. Overall, the impact was to lower the tax burden on the low-income groups and raise taxes on the highest tenth of households. In this calculation, income from corporations is imputed to households according to household ownership of corporate stocks, and the corporation tax is assumed to fall upon the owners of capital. [Source: Joseph A. Pechman, "Tax Reform: Theory and Practice," *Journal of Economic Perspectives* (Summer 1987), p. 20.]

Policy area	Economic performance: Early period (1960–1980)	Reagan years (1981–1989)
Economic policy and performance:		
Growth of money supply (% per year)	5.5	7.8
Unemployment rate (%)	5.6	7.3
Inflation rate (% per year)	5.1	4.0
Productivity growth (% per year)	1.9	1.4
Personal savings rate (% of income)	7.3	5.2
Budget policy:		
Spending/GNP (%)	20.2	23.8
Non-defense spending/GNP (%)	13.2	17.6
Taxes/GNP (%)	19.1	20.0
Deficit/GNP (%)	1.1	3.8
Tax policy:		
Income taxes/total taxes (%)	60	73
Top tax rate (%, end of period)	50	28

Table 19-7. Economic performance in the Reagan and prior years

The conservative economic policies produced little improvement in overall economic performance or in the share of GNP devoted to spending or taxation. The burden of the individual income tax grew relative to other taxes, and non-defense programs were trimmed. [Source: *Economic Report of the President* (GPO, Washington, D.C.).]

Overall Assessment

What has been the impact of the conservative fiscal revolution on the American economy? The performance of the economy during the Reagan years, as sketched briefly in Table 19-7, showed little improvement in most of the major indexes of economic policy: unemployment was higher than in the previous two decades; inflation averaged approximately the same rate (although it fell relative to the 1970s); productivity growth and the personal savings rate deteriorated from the previous two decades. In addition, the fiscal policies of the 1980s have led to major changes in the patterns of saving and investment, significantly lowering national saving in response to higher levels of public dissaving in the form of budget deficits.

Most important, perhaps, are the changing attitudes about government. In the 1980s, Presidents Reagan and Bush consistently spoke of the need for self-reliance and of the perils that exist when a free society leans too heavily on the economic intervention of government. This message had not been heard from an American President for many years.

Taxes and Efficiency

We have seen that the centerpiece of the conservative fiscal revolution was tax reform, designed to lower marginal tax rates and to improve incentives and economic efficiency. We first review the impact of taxes on efficiency and then see whether the conservative goals were fulfilled.

What is the impact of high tax rates on work, saving, and risk taking? As we have seen in Chapter 14, the impact of tax rates on hours worked is unclear because the income and substitution effects of wage changes work in opposite directions. As a result of progressive taxes, some people may choose more leisure over more work. Other people may work harder in order to make their million. Many high-income doctors, artists, celebrities, and business executives, who enjoy their jobs and the sense of power or accomplishment that they bring, will work as hard for $150,000 as for $200,000.

The effect of high taxes on property income is more clear-cut. Studies have determined that taxing a particular kind of capital or property will cause resources to move to lower-taxed sectors or even to other countries. For example, if corporate capital is double-taxed, some of people's savings will flow out of corporate stocks and into noncorporate sectors like housing. If risky investments are taxed unfavorably, investors may prefer safer investments.

The most important effect may arise not from *levels* of taxation, but from *differences* in tax rates. There are a sufficient number of respectable "tax shelters" open to wealthy people so that they may typically pay much less than the high tax rates shown in Table 19-3. For example, they may invest in tax-exempt bonds, drill for oil and gas, or put their money in vacation homes. In these sheltered sectors, investors may face low taxes or no taxes at all. Hence, high marginal tax rates may simply divert economic activity to lightly taxed sectors.

Supply-Side Economics and the Laffer Curve

An important application of the issue of the impact of taxes on incentives arose during the debate about tax reform in the 1980s. The **supply-side school** argued that the disincentive effects of high marginal tax rates were responsible for many of the nation's ills—low saving, recession, stagnant productivity, and high inflation. Led by Arthur Laffer, Norman Ture, and Paul Craig Roberts, this group emphasized the importance of low marginal tax rates for good economic performance. One of the analytical tools introduced by this group was the *Laffer curve.*

The theoretical Laffer curve is shown on the left side of Figure 19-4. The general shape can be seen in the following way: Clearly at a zero tax rate there will be no revenues. Also, when taxes reach 100 percent, no one will work, so again there would be no revenues. The Laffer curve thus shows zero revenues at 0 and 100 percent tax rates.

What lies in between? According to the supply-side school, as tax rates rise from zero, total revenues rise. Then, at some point, people begin to work less, save less, and divert their activity to the underground economy. At some point, say, point M in Figure 19-4(*a*), the total revenue received by the Treasury is maximized. The curve is sometimes drawn so that its peak comes at a 50 percent tax rate, although it is not clear that Laffer or other members of the supply-side school consistently argued that the maximum revenue point comes at a tax rate of 50 percent.

What happens when the tax rate rises above point M in Figure 19-4(*a*)? The disincentive effect outweighs the revenue effect. So government tax revenues actually begin to decline even though tax rates are raised. If you believe that the economy is to the right of maximum-revenue point M, you could recommend a policy of having your cake and eating it too: lower tax rates, increase economic efficiency, and raise revenues.

How did mainstream economists react to this radical new theory? Most economists were skeptical about the quantitative importance of significant disincentives from high tax rates in the United States. Moreover, the economic evidence does not support the supply-side theory. Figure 19-4(*b*) shows a real-world Laffer curve constructed by Vir-

The Laffer Curve in Theory and Reality

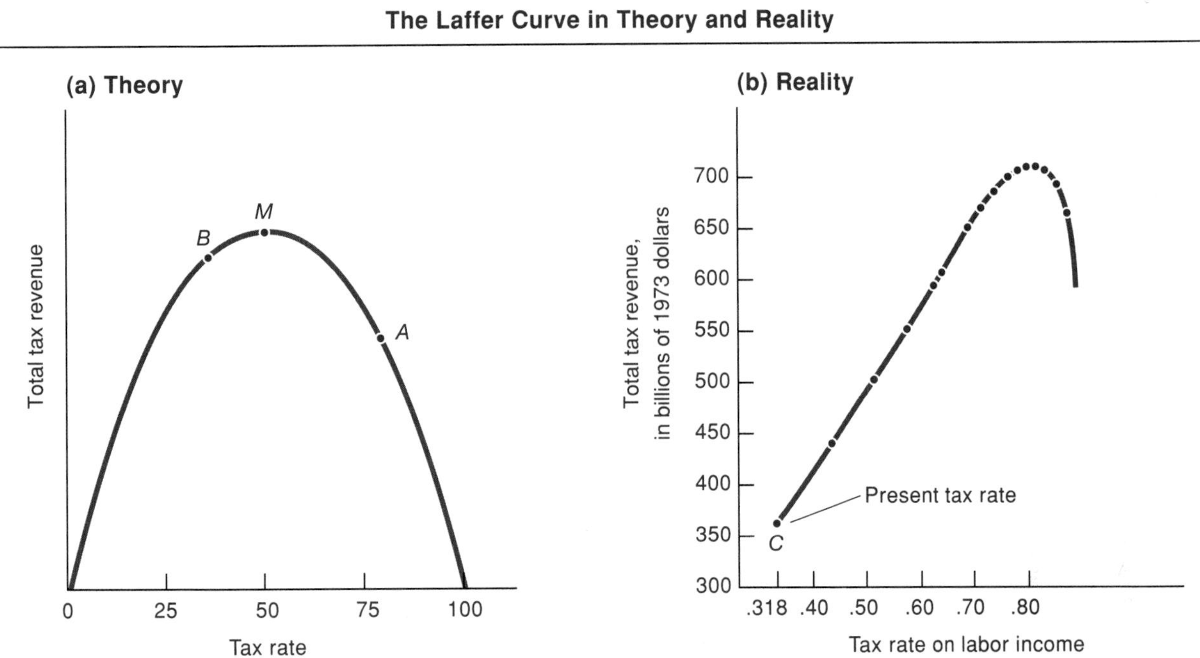

Figure 19-4. Evidence indicates that lowering tax rates would today lower revenues

The Laffer curve illustrates the relationship between tax revenues and tax rates. In the theoretical Laffer curve on the left, a tax rate of 50 percent produces maximal revenues. By reducing tax rates from *A* to *B*, revenues rise even as tax rates fall.

Careful empirical studies find a curve that tilts sharply to the right, with the U.S. tax system approximately at point *C*, as in **(b)**. In this realistic case, small movements in tax rates will have roughly proportional effects on revenues. [Source: Don Fullerton, "Relationship between Tax Rates and Government Revenue," *Journal of Public Economics* (October 1982).]

ginia's Don Fullerton after he examined several econometric studies of the response of work effort to tax rates. The maximum-revenue point comes far to the right of today's tax rates, shown as point C. Fullerton's survey predicts that a cut in taxes would produce an almost-proportional reduction in tax revenues.

The Supply-Side Experiment. Although the scientific evidence supporting the supply-side theories was weak, the Reagan administration adopted the supply-side prescription for the 1980s.* Taxes

*One of the puzzles about the supply-side revolution is how an obscure idea, which received virtually no support from empirical studies or from mainstream economists, could have achieved such legislative success in a few months. This question is addressed by David Stockman, who was an architect of supply-side policies when he served as director of the Reagan Office of Management and Budget from 1981 to 1984. This is how Stockman describes President Reagan's conversion to the Laffer curve [the following quotation is from David Stockman, *The Triumph of Politics* (Avon, New York, 1987)]:

> In January 1980, Governor Reagan's campaign managers had sent him to school for a few days to get brushed up on the national issues. There, Jack Kemp, Art Laffer, and Jude Wanniski thoroughly hosed him down with supply-side doctrine.
>
> They told him about the "Laffer curve." It set off a symphony in his ears. He knew instantly that it was true and would never doubt it a moment thereafter.
>
> He had once been on the Laffer curve himself. "I came into the Big Money making pictures during World War II," he would always say. At that time the wartime income surtax hit 90 percent.
>
> "You could only make four pictures and then you were in the top bracket," he would continue. "So we all quit working after four pictures and went off to the country."
>
> High tax rates caused less work. Low tax rates caused more. His experience proved it.

were cut sharply in the hope that increases in effort would offset reductions in tax rates. Supply siders promoted the cuts as the needed stimulants for America's sick economy and argued that the cuts would produce no unpleasant side effects.

In fact, history gives little comfort to the supply-side theories. Personal savings rates declined, rather than rose, after the tax cuts. The Laffer-curve prediction that revenues would rise following the tax cuts has proven false; indeed, federal revenues shrank relative to their trend and the federal budget consequently moved from an approximate balance in 1979 to a gaping $200 billion deficit after 1983. Subtle effects may yet appear, and, given the difficulty of performing controlled experiments in economics, no definitive appraisal of the supply-side tax cuts may be possible. But the central prediction of the supply-side economists—that working and saving would increase dramatically as marginal tax rates were cut—has up to now proven incorrect. By the usual scientific standards, the supply-side experiment suggests that the underlying theory should be rejected.

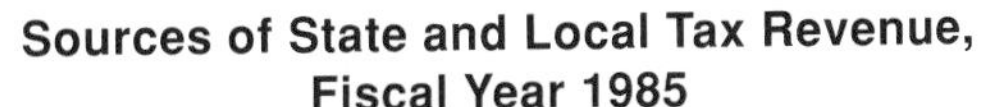

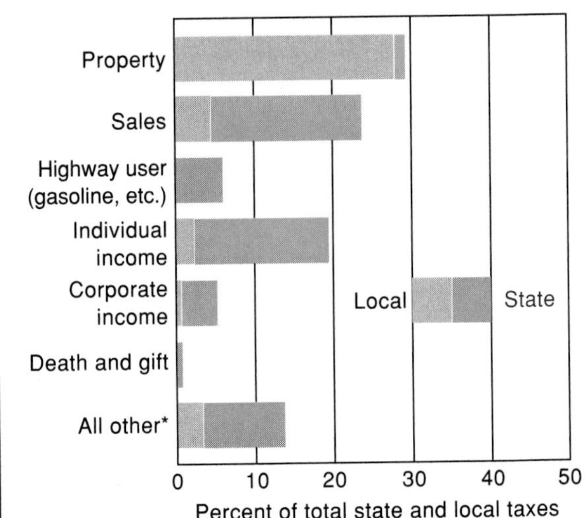

*Does not include federal revenue sharing

Figure 19-5. Property and sales taxes dominate at state and local levels

Cities rely heavily on property taxes because houses and land cannot easily flee to the next town to avoid a city's tax. (Source: U.S. Bureau of the Census, *Government Finances in 1984-85*.)

State and Local Taxes

We turn now to public finance other than federal. Although the federal government raises more taxes than other levels of government, state and local taxes have an important effect upon the economic health of these lower levels. Figure 19-5 illustrates the main sources of funds that finance state and local expenditures.

Property Tax

The property tax accounts for about 30 percent of the total revenues of state and local finance. Figure 19-5 shows that localities are the main recipient of property taxes.

The property tax is levied primarily on real estate—land and buildings. Each locality sets an annual tax rate. Chicago, for example, sets a nominal tax rate of 9.66 percent of "assessed value" (i.e., of the value as determined by the city). If my house has been assessed at $100,000, my tax is $9,660. However, in most places assessed valuations tend to be but a fraction of true market value. In Chicago, assessments are about 16 percent of market value, so the true tax rate is only 1.55 percent of market value.

The property tax became controversial in the 1970s. During the housing boom of the 1970s, housing valuations and taxes skyrocketed. Taxpayers revolted. In Massachusetts, voters passed "Proposition $2\frac{1}{2}$," limiting tax payments to $2\frac{1}{2}$ percent of market value. Today, almost half the states have limitations on property or other taxes; these will prevent state and local taxes from rising as rapidly as they did in the 1970s. During the 1990–1991 recession, these tax limits led several cities and states into severe fiscal crises as these governments ran out of tax funds and were forced to cut services.

Sales Taxes

States get most of their revenues from general sales taxes on goods and services. Each purchase at the department store, pharmacy, or restaurant incurs a percentage tax (food and other necessities are exempt in some states). Also, states usually add their own liquor and tobacco excises to the federal excises. Such taxes are often tolerated because most people—including many cigarette smokers and moderate drinkers—feel that there is something vaguely immoral about tobacco and alcohol. They think these "sin taxes" stun two birds with one stone: the state gets revenue, and vice is discouraged as higher prices reduce consumption.

Other Taxes

Most states tax the net income of a corporation and collect miscellaneous other fees from business enterprises. Forty-five states imitate the federal government, on a much smaller scale, by taxing individuals according to the size of their incomes. Even a few cities tax incomes earned by those who live or work there.

There are other miscellaneous revenues. Many states tax bequests. Some states, such as Nevada and New Jersey, tax slot machines and racetrack betting or legitimize gambling by operating lotteries. And most states levy "highway user taxes" on gasoline.

The Thorny Problem of Tax Incidence

When governments levy taxes, they generally have a clear idea of who will pay the tax. But we should not assume that the people or firms that send the tax monies to the government will end up paying that tax. This point raises the issue: Who ultimately pays a particular tax? Does its burden stay on the person or firm that actually pays the tax? Or is the tax shifted elsewhere? Businesses may be able to shift the tax "forward" onto their customers by raising their price by the amount of the tax. Or they may shift the tax "backward" onto their suppliers (owners of labor, land, and other factors), who find themselves with lower wages, rents, and other factor prices than they would have enjoyed had there been no tax.

Economists insist on examining **tax incidence**—the way the tax burden ultimately is borne and its total effects on work effort, saving, commodity prices, factor prices, resource allocations, and the composition of production and consumption.

Tax-incidence questions include: Does a 5-cent-a-gallon tax on gasoline raise the price at the pump by 5 cents so that the incidence is on the consumer? Or does the tax lower the price of crude oil so that the incidence is on the oil producers? Or is the incidence somewhere in between? Does it change coal prices? And does the tax kill off oil production, so that it has incidence effects beyond those which show up in money prices and wages and even beyond the burdens that you can allocate among the different citizens?

Microeconomics provides some important tools for analyzing tax incidence. In earlier chapters, we saw the incidence of a gasoline tax. In such simple cases, involving only supply of and demand for a single commodity, incidence analysis is straightforward. In other cases, the effects cascade through the economy, making analysis extremely complex and sometimes requiring general-equilibrium approaches.

We might want to know the *fiscal incidence* of the government tax and transfer system as a whole. Fiscal incidence examines the impact of both tax and expenditure programs on the incomes of the population. Fiscal incidence concerns the overall degree of progressivity or regressivity of government programs. It is estimated by allocating all taxes and transfer payments to different groups. Such a study can be only approximate, since no one is sure how the corporation tax or the property tax gets shifted.

The conceptual experiment we want to make is:

- To measure incomes without taxes and transfers
- Then to measure incomes with taxes and transfers
- And finally to measure *incidence* as the difference between these two situations

Of course, economists are not magicians who can make such controlled experiments, but they take careful measurements and use good judgment to estimate the effects of taxes and spending.

Incidence of Federal Taxes and Transfers

Figure 19-6 shows the results of a recent study of the incidence of all federal taxes and transfers; in this figure, transfers are measured positively while taxes are measured in the negative direction. The federal tax system is slightly regressive at the low end, and then it becomes roughly progressive at higher incomes.

However, taxes are only half the story. Transfers

Fiscal Impact of Government, 1987

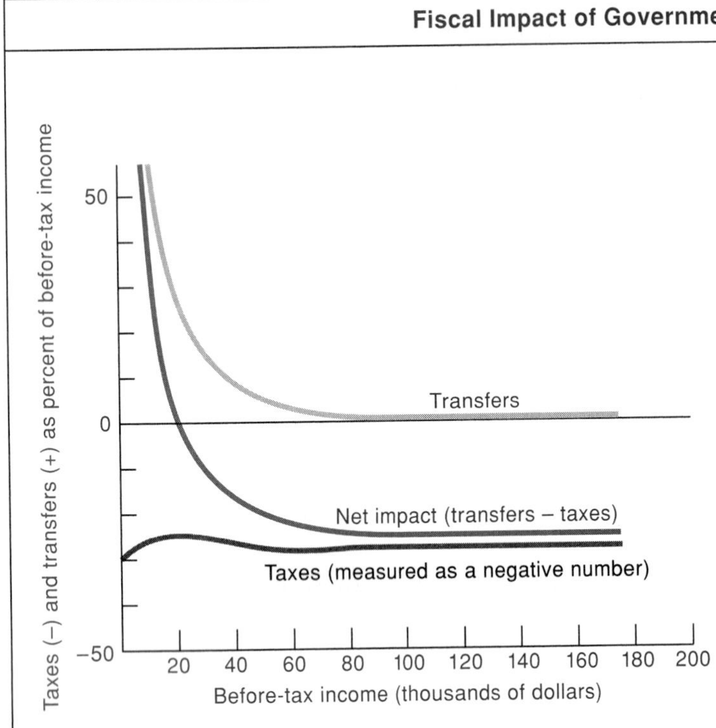

Figure 19-6. Who pays the taxes and who benefits from transfers? What is government's net fiscal impact?

How has the modern welfare state affected the real income of its citizens? The black line shows that federal taxes are regressive at low levels of income, then become progressive after that point. The light blue line of federal transfer programs—items such as welfare, social security, and unemployment insurance—is highly progressive, being concentrated in lower income groups. Therefore, the net impact, or "incidence," of federal taxes and transfers is highly progressive, as is shown by the downward-sloping blue line. Income after government tax and transfer programs is more equally distributed than is income from market sources alone.

[Source: The methodology is described in Joseph Pechman, *Who Bears the Tax Burden?* (Brookings Institution, Washington, D.C., 1974), Variant 1C. The estimates are based on unpublished data for 1985 and have been updated to incomes of 1987.]

are a substantial fraction of income for low-income households. That is, the poor receive proportionally much more in government programs than do the middle classes or the upper classes. Therefore, when the transfers and taxes are added together to get net fiscal incidence, we find that government programs as a whole are very progressive. For those with before-tax incomes under $25,000 the net impact of government taxes and transfers is positive, while for those with higher incomes the net impact is a decrease in income.

This pattern of net fiscal impact is similar to that found in most advanced market economies today. As one recent survey of the subject concluded:

> The evidence for almost all countries suggests that the tax system overall has almost no effect on income distribution. . . . This results from the progressive impact of income taxes being offset by regressive taxes, notably employers' social security contributions and indirect taxes. . . . When tax, transfer, and expenditure programmes are viewed together, it is apparent that public expenditure programmes, particularly the provision of cash transfers, have been almost totally responsible for the changes in income distribution which governments have brought about. . . .[5]

[5] Peter Saunders, "Evidence on Income Redistribution by Governments," OECD, Economics and Statistics Department, Working Papers, No. 11 (January 1984).

SUMMARY

A. Government Expenditures

1. The American system of public finance is one of fiscal federalism. The federal government concentrates its spending on issues of national concern—on national public goods like defense and space exploration. States and localities generally focus on local public goods—those whose benefits are largely confined within state or city boundaries.

2. Government spending and taxation today take approximately one-third of total GNP. Of this total, 70 percent is spent at the federal level, and the balance is divided between state and local governments. Only a tiny fraction of government outlays is devoted to traditional activities like police and the courts.

B. Economic Aspects of Taxation

3. Notions of "benefits" and "ability to pay" are two principal theories of taxation. A tax is progressive, proportional, or regressive as it takes a larger, equal, or smaller fraction of income from rich families than from poor families. Direct and progressive taxes on incomes are in contrast to indirect and regressive sales and excise taxes.
4. More than half of federal revenue comes from personal and corporation income taxes. The rest comes from taxes on payrolls or consumption goods. Local governments raise most of their revenue from property taxes, while sales taxes are most important for states.
5. The individual income tax is levied on "income from whatever source derived," less certain exemptions and deductions. The 1986 Tax Reform Act completely overhauled the federal income tax, trimming many tax expenditures and lowering marginal tax rates substantially. Even with its lower tax rates, the individual income tax is progressive, placing higher average tax burdens on rich than on poor people.
6. The fastest-growing federal tax is the payroll tax, used to finance social security. This is an "earmarked" levy, with funds going to provide public pensions and health and disability benefits. Because there are visible benefits at the end of the stream of payments, the payroll tax has elements of a benefit tax.
7. The conservative fiscal revolution of the 1980s stood on four pillars: a macroeconomic policy that emphasized economic efficiency rather than business-cycle management; a budget policy that bolstered defense, cut civilian programs, and gave little weight to fiscal deficits; a regulatory program reducing the burden of federal regulations, especially those pertaining to health, safety, and the environment; and, most important, lower tax rates and tax burdens. The major legacy of this period was the tax reforms of 1981 and 1986, which lowered marginal tax rates dramatically and completely overhauled the individual income tax.
8. Economists are divided on the extent to which taxes hurt incentives to work or save. An extreme view of this debate is provided by the supply siders. According to the theory illustrated by the Laffer curve, tax rates in the late 1970s were so high that revenues were actually reduced. This extreme view has received little empirical support.
9. The incidence of a tax refers to its ultimate economic burden and to its total effect on prices and other economic magnitudes. Those upon whom a tax is first levied may succeed in shifting part of its burden forward or backward. The progressiveness in benefits of transfer programs offsets the regressiveness of our tax structure at low incomes, so the net fiscal impact of government in today's welfare state is highly progressive.

CONCEPTS FOR REVIEW

Government expenditures and fiscal incidence
fiscal federalism and local vs. national public goods
fiscal incidence
Reagan fiscal revolution: four elements

Taxation
benefit and ability-to-pay principles
direct and indirect taxes
progressive, proportional, and regressive taxes
tax incidence and shifting
1986 Tax Reform Act
incentive effects of taxes
Laffer curve in theory and reality

QUESTIONS FOR DISCUSSION

1. Make a list of different federal taxes in order of their progressiveness. If the federal government were to trade in income taxes for consumption or sales taxes, what would be the effect in terms of overall progressiveness of the tax system?
2. "Because people don't change their smoking habits much as a result of taxation, and because the poor smoke, a tax on cigarettes is really no different from a tax on bread." What does this quotation imply about the nature of the demand for cigarettes (in terms of price and income elasticity)? Explain carefully your views on the subject of "sin taxes."
3. "I favor progressively taxing what people spend to consume, not what they earn. My consumption tax would encourage more saving and investment—since we'd then no longer double-tax both saving and the fruits of that saving." Analyze this argument in favor of taxing consumption.
4. Proponents of supply-side economics point to the experience of the 1960s as evidence that the United States was in 1960 on the wrong side of the peak of the Laffer curve in Figure 19-4(*a*). They note, "After the Kennedy-Johnson tax cuts of 1964, federal revenues actually rose from $110 billion in 1963 to $133 billion in 1966. Therefore, cutting taxes raises revenues." What fallacies are being committed here? (Recall the *post hoc* fallacy.) Give a correct analysis.
5. Is it possible that some taxes *promote* economic efficiency? Consider, for example, taxes on sulfur or carbon dioxide emissions or on leaky oil tankers. Construct a list of taxes that you think would increase efficiency and compare their effects with taxes on labor or capital income.
6. The following table gives the data for a hypothetical tax system:

(1) Adjusted gross income ($)	(2) Deductions and exemptions ($)	(3) Taxable income ($)	(4) Individual income tax ($)
5,000	5,000	0	0
10,000	9,000	1,000	150
20,000	12,000	8,000	1,200
50,000	20,000	30,000	4,500
100,000	30,000	70,000	14,500
500,000	100,000	400,000	97,000

At each income level, calculate the marginal and average tax rates on taxable income. If adjusted gross income is used as an income base, is this system one which is progressive, proportional, or regressive?

7. Consider the data on taxes, wages, and hours of work shown below. Complete the blank items in the table. Draw a Laffer curve on a sheet of graph paper. At what tax rate does the government collect maximal revenue? Explain in words what is happening in the economy as the tax rate increases.
8. Some public goods are local, spilling out to residents of small areas; others are national, benefiting an entire nation; some are global, having an effect upon all nations. A private good is one where the spillover is negligible. Give some examples of purely private goods and of local, national, and global public goods or externalities. For each, indicate the level of government that could design policies most efficiently, and suggest one or two appropriate government actions that could solve the externality.

Tax rate (%)	Pre-tax wage rate ($ per hour)	Post-tax wage rate	Hours of work	Pre-tax earnings	Tax revenues
0	10	______	2,000	______	______
10	10	______	2,000	______	______
20	10	______	1,950	______	______
30	10	______	1,900	______	______
40	10	______	1,850	______	______
50	10	______	1,800	______	______
60	10	______	1,700	______	______
70	10	______	1,600	______	______
80	10	______	1,300	______	______
90	10	______	600	______	______
100	10	______	0	______	______

C H A P T E R 2 0

CURBING MARKET POWER: REGULATION AND ANTITRUST POLICIES

Both theoretical and empirical research question the extent to which regulation can achieve the goals for which it has been promulgated.
Stephen Breyer and Paul MacAvoy, *Regulation and Deregulation*

In a modern market economy, the government has three central economic functions: to maintain efficient operation of the economy, to promote macroeconomic growth and stability, and to help ensure a fair distribution of income. As we saw in the last chapter, in pursuing efficiency, where public goods or externalities are pervasive, the government must overrule the market and direct productive activities. For the most part, however, governments in market economies rely on the force of rivalry and competition—the carrot of profits and the stick of bankruptcy—to stimulate the private sector to behave efficiently.

Yet even when the major resource-allocation decisions are made in the private sector, governments act as watchdogs to prevent the exercise of market power. When businesses have market power, they can raise prices above the competitive level where price equals marginal cost. Such high prices both reduce output below efficient levels and earn high profits for the businesses. The populace in a modern democracy demands that governments curb abuses of market power.

How can governments restrain the excesses of monopoly power while allowing private firms the freedom to compete with their rivals? To accomplish this task, governments use economic regulation and antitrust policies. Historically, governments have controlled the operations of private businesses chiefly through regulation. The first half of this chapter discusses the scope and nature of government regulation, analyzes the purpose and effect of economic regulation, and surveys the history of the deregulation movement of the last two decades. Governments also attempt to promote competition and prevent monopoly abuses; this area of government activity, antitrust policies, is the subject of the second half of this chapter.

A. Business Regulation: Theory and Practice

Review of Imperfect Competition

Chapters 10 and 11 discussed the way that imperfect competitors set their prices and quantities. Let's begin by reviewing the major elements of the economic theory that relate to government antimonopoly policies.

- Imperfect competitors are inefficient because they set prices above marginal cost. The consumers in the monopolistic or oligopolistic industry are consuming less of these goods than would be the case if they were efficiently supplied.
- Many industries have technologies that exhibit significant economies of scale. It would be unrealistic to try to produce the output of such industries with perfectly competitive firms, for that would require that the output be produced by inefficiently small firms. In the rare case where the technology in an industry can be efficiently produced only by a single firm, we call this a "natural monopoly."
- In the long run, most economic progress comes from technological change. According to the Schumpeterian hypothesis, firms with extensive market power are largely responsible for dynamic innovation. Government policies should be especially careful not to harm the incentives for innovation.
- The major abuses in markets—either in too high a price or in poor product quality—come when an industry is effectively monopolized; economists often identify an industry as monopolistic when a single firm or colluding group of firms produces more than three-quarters of the output in an industry.
- The government has taken on the responsibility to prevent monopolization from occurring and to regulate monopolies when they are inevitable. Antitrust policies attempt to prevent monopolization or anticompetitive abuses; economic regulation is used to control the exercise of monopoly power in natural monopolies.

Two Kinds of Regulation

In attempting to control or influence economic activity, governments can use market incentives or commands. *Market incentives,* such as tax or expenditure programs, coax people and firms to follow the government's will through voluntary self-interest. When the government builds a road, it harnesses the profit-oriented behavior of business firms to level the hills and pour the cement. The government is coercing no one; its dollar votes are inducing road-building just as would happen if a private party financed the road.

Another, more direct approach comes when governments issue *command-and-control orders.* In this case, governments command people to undertake or desist from certain activities through government regulation. For example, the government could command people to pave the roads in front of their houses and thereby try to improve the road network.

Regulation consists of government rules or laws issued to control the price, sale, or production decisions of firms.

It is customary to distinguish between two forms of regulation. **Economic regulation** refers to the control of prices, the variety of or standards for products, entry and exit conditions, and standards of service in a particular industry. Prominent examples are regulation of public utilities (telephone, electricity, natural gas, and water) as well as regulations in other industries (transportation, finance, radio, and TV). This is the species of regulation that will be examined in this chapter.

In addition, there is a newer form of regulation, known as **social regulation,** which is used to promote the health and safety of workers and consumers. This denotes rules aimed at correcting a wide variety of side effects or externalities that result from economic activity. Programs to clean our air and water, or to ensure the safety of nuclear power or drugs or cars, are the most prominent examples of social regulation. These programs were addressed in Chapter 18.

Economic Regulation of Imperfect Competition

Economic regulation of American industry goes back more than a century to the founding of the Interstate Commerce Commission (ICC) in 1887. The ICC was designed as much to prevent price wars and to guarantee service to small towns as it was to control monopoly. Later, federal regulation spread to banks in 1913, to electric power in 1920, and to communications, securities markets, labor, trucking, and air travel during the 1930s. There was little legislation authorizing further economic regulation after World War II.

How much of the private economy is under government economic regulation? At its peak, in 1978, industries under some kind of price or other economic regulation comprised somewhat more than 15 percent of national income. This percentage has declined dramatically since 1978 because of the deregulation movement we will discuss later in this chapter.

Why Regulate Industry?

Regulation restrains the unfettered market power of firms. Why might governments choose to regulate business even in the land of free enterprise? Governments may regulate firms, particularly natural monopolies, and limit price increases of regulated firms. In addition, many economists believe that industry regulation results from interest-group politics in which the regulatory agency has been captured by the industry and is protecting producers rather than consumers.

Containing Market Power. The traditional economic view of regulation is normative: that regulatory measures should be taken to correct major market failures. More specifically, government should regulate industries where there is too small a number of firms to stimulate vigorous rivalry. Government should regulate industry particularly in the extreme case of natural monopoly, especially where the monopoly occurs for necessities that have a low price elasticity of demand.

An important example of a natural monopoly is local telephone distribution. The cost of sending wires into every home and gathering the wires in a local telephone exchange is sufficiently great that it would not pay to have more than one firm provide such local telephone service, so this is a natural monopoly.

Another source of natural monopoly occurs when an industry has *economies of scope,* which arise when a number of different products can more efficiently be produced together than by separate firms. For example, transport-equipment firms show economies of scope—a firm producing cars and trucks has a cost advantage in producing buses and tanks. Why? Because specialized knowledge and machinery are shared across the different products. These firms have economies of scope in production of ground-based transport systems.

We know from our discussion of declining costs in Chapter 9 that pervasive economies of scale are inconsistent with perfect competition; we will see oligopoly or monopoly in such cases. But the point here is even more extreme: *When there are such powerful economies of scale or scope that only one firm can survive, we have a natural monopoly.*

Why do governments regulate natural monopolies? They do so because a natural monopolist, enjoying a large cost advantage over its competitors and facing price-inelastic demand, can jack up its price sharply, obtain enormous monopoly profits, and create major economic inefficiencies. Another reason for regulation is that consumers have inadequate information about products. For example, testing pharmaceutical drugs is expensive and scientifically complex. The government regulates drugs by allowing the sale of only those drugs which are proven "safe and efficacious." Government also prohibits false and misleading advertising. In both cases, the government is attempting to correct for a market failure to provide information efficiently. Some economists worry that such regulation will tend to inhibit innovation and introduction of new products.

In earlier times, regulation was justified on the dubious grounds that it was needed to prevent cutthroat competition. This was one argument for continued control over the railroads, trucks, airlines, and buses, as well as for regulation of the level of agricultural production. Economists have little sympathy for this argument. After all, competition with increased efficiency and low prices is exactly what will benefit consumers most.

Interest-Group Theories of Regulation. A different approach to the theory of regulation is based on positive analysis of what regulation actually does rather than a normative view of what it should do. This view, put forth by economists from the University of Chicago, holds that economic regulation results from the interplay of political forces and economic interests in regulated industries.[1] According to these economists, regulation creates an economic return for some firms or groups. This happens because regulators restrict entry into the

[1] The germinal work in this area is by George Stigler of the University of Chicago, who won a Nobel Prize for this and other contributions. James Buchanan won the 1986 Nobel Prize in economics for his studies of public-choice economics in regulation, taxation, expenditures, and other areas. The Chicago School has been highly influential in its view that government intervention in the economy often does more harm than good.

regulated industry, as when the government limited entry into the telecommunications market or prevented airlines from entering new markets. Restricting entry or otherwise restraining competition raises the profits of those firms that are established in the regulated industry. Hence, it is in the economic interest of the regulated firms to perpetuate regulation. Put differently, the economic interests of the regulated firms create a demand for regulation that will restrict competition from those outside the industry. Established firms want to maintain regulatory barriers to keep out competitors, raise prices, and keep profits high.

What about the supply of regulation? The supply is provided by legislators or administrators who operate in the political marketplace; these suppliers want to gain votes or political support to maintain themselves in office. Often the currency for supporting politicians is campaign contributions to help reelect the sympathetic legislators. In addition, those who lose from the regulation—the consumers—are too dispersed and uninformed to combat the regulated industry through offsetting political pressure or campaign contributions.

In effect, the Chicago economists argue, "You say that regulation is in the interest of consumers and is necessary to maintain low prices and curb monopoly power. Don't believe it. Rather, regulation is a political activity like paying veterans benefits or agricultural support payments. It is designed to boost the incomes of producers by limiting entry and preventing competition in the regulated industry."

This radical theory has been supported by numerous studies of economic regulation. It has been shown that regulation often held prices *up* (in trucking, in airlines, in brokerage firms, in insurance), while the economic rationale for regulation was to prevent monopoly pricing abuses by holding prices *down*. Moreover, these findings are consistent with the burgeoning public-choice literature explored in Chapter 18.

The most recent example of a regulatory program benefiting the industry it regulated is the savings and loan scandal. The federal program of deposit insurance was established in the 1930s to help restore confidence and prevent bank panics. By the early 1980s, however, it became clear that the program was poorly designed. It guaranteed deposits in banks without ensuring that banks behaved prudently with the insured deposits. Banks began to speculate with insured funds, making bad investments and paying high salaries to their executives; losses mounted to the hundreds of billions of dollars. Because of intense lobbying and generous campaign contributions, appropriate government action to stop the wasteful practices was delayed for years until President Bush acted to curb the worst abuses in 1989. Who were the major beneficiaries of the lax bank regulation? The banks. Who were the losers? The taxpayers.

Fortunately, the savings and loan scandal is not the norm. For the most part, while consumers have often been poorly served by economic regulation, legislators have generally voted to regulate industries out of a sincere belief that regulation was in the public interest and that it would prevent price discrimination among customers or ensure universal or regular service. But the road to waste is paved with good intentions, and these programs have often harmed rather than helped consumers.

Public-Utility Regulation of Natural Monopoly

A valid economic argument for regulation is to prevent monopoly pricing by natural monopolists. Let us see exactly how regulators control excessive price increases of monopolists. Recall that a natural monopoly is an industry in which the most efficient way of organizing production is through a single firm. Figure 20-1 shows the way the *AC*, *MC*, and industry demand curve might look for a natural monopoly. Note that the industry demand curve (*DD*) intersects the firm's *MC* curve where *AC* is falling. If two similar firms were to produce the industry output, the average cost for the two firms would be well above that of a single firm.

How prevalent are natural monopolies in today's American economy? Figure 20-2 shows some representative examples from regulated and unregulated industries. Note that many industries that are still regulated or were recently deregulated (airlines, trucks, banks) have a low degree of natural monopoly. This low degree of natural monopoly lends support to the interest-group theory of economic regulation—that regulation has long outlived its usefulness for consumers and lives on because of

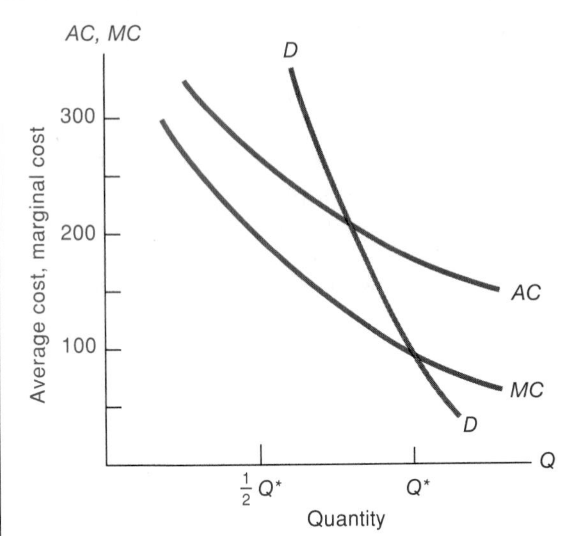

Figure 20-1. Cost curves for a natural monopolist

For a natural monopolist, the *AC* curve is still falling at the point where it cuts the industry's *DD* curve. Thus efficient production requires output to be concentrated in a single firm. (Can you estimate from the diagram how much more expensive it would be if Q^* were to be produced by two firms each producing $\frac{1}{2}Q^*$?)

political support from protected firms in regulated industries.

Suppose that the legislature decides to impose *public-utility regulation* on a particular industry. How would it proceed? It would first set up a public-utility commission to oversee prices, service, and entry into and exit from the industry. The most important decision would be to determine the pricing of the monopoly firm.

Traditionally, regulation imposes *average cost pricing* on regulated firms. For example, an electric utility would take all its costs (fixed as well as variable) and distribute them to each product sold (say, electricity and steam). Then each class of customer would be charged the *fully distributed average cost* of that type of service.

Figure 20-3 illustrates public-utility regulation. Point *M* (associated with output Q_M) is the unregulated profit-maximizing output of the monopolist we examined in Chapter 10. Here we find sky-high price, tiny quantity, and handsome profits (as shown by the difference between price and average cost).

In traditional regulation, the monopolist is allowed to charge a price only high enough to cover average cost. In this case, the firm will set its price where the demand curve *DD* intersects the *AC* curve. Hence, the equilibrium is at point *R*, with output Q_R.

How good is the solution? Economically speaking, it might represent an improvement over unregulated monopoly. First, the owners of the monopoly are presumably no more deserving than the consumers. So there is no reason to allow them to extract monopoly profits from consumers. By wiping out monopolistic profit, we may end up with what most people feel to be a more equitable distribution of income. (But remember that value judgments beyond technical economics are involved in such a conclusion.)

Second, in making the monopolist cut its price

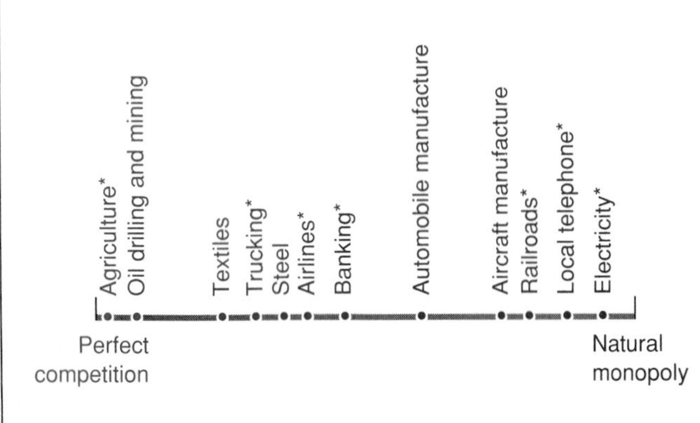

Figure 20-2. Degree of natural monopoly in different industries

This figure displays several regulated and unregulated industries by their degree of natural monopoly or of perfect competition. In perfectly competitive industries, the minimum efficient scale of firm is minuscule relative to the market, while a natural monopoly is one where *AC* is still falling sharply at the level of total industry output. Agriculture and mining are inherently quite competitive, while local telephone and electric utilities are close to polar natural monopolies. The asterisk (*) indicates industries that have historically been heavily regulated by governments.

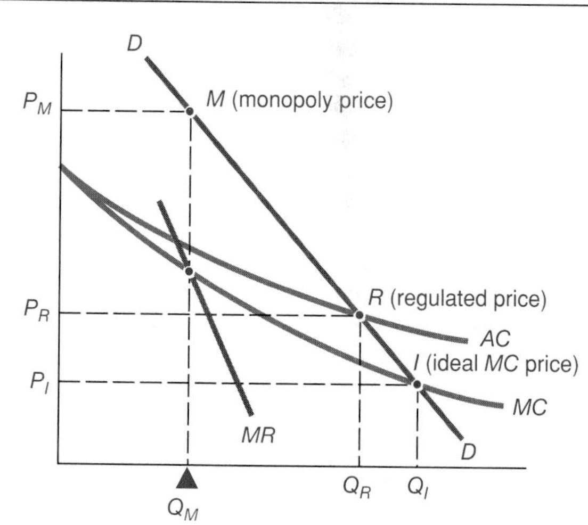

Figure 20-3. Ideal and practical regulation of monopolists

Maximum-profit equilibrium for the unregulated monopolist is at *M*, directly above the intersection of *MR* and long-run *MC*, with price above *MC*.

Public-utility commissions customarily require average cost prices at *R*—where the demand curve intersects the long-run average cost curve. This wipes out excess profit. More important, it brings price down closer to marginal cost.

Ideally, price should be forced all the way down to *I*, where price = *MC* and hence marginal social costs and benefits are appropriately balanced. At point *I*, there is no efficiency loss from price being above marginal cost.

from P_M to P_R, the regulators have lowered the discrepancy between price and marginal cost. This is deemed an improvement because the higher output is worth more to consumers in marginal utility than it costs society in terms of the marginal cost. Only when price is equal to marginal cost in all sectors is society using its resources most efficiently.

Ideally Regulated Pricing. If $P = MC$ is such a good thing, why shouldn't the regulators force the monopolist to lower price until it equals marginal cost at the intersection point of the *DD* and *MC* curves (at *I*)?

Actually, $P = MC$ or *marginal-cost pricing* is the ideal target for economic efficiency. But it presents a serious practical obstacle: if a firm with declining average cost sets price equal to marginal cost, it will incur a chronic loss. The reason is that if *AC* is falling, then $MC < AC$, so setting $P = MC$ implies having $P < AC$. When price (or average revenue) is less than average cost, the firm is losing money. To see this point visually, examine the ideal regulatory solution at point *I* in Figure 20-3. At that point, price equals marginal cost, but the *MC* is less than average cost. When average cost is greater than the price, the firm is losing money.

Firms will not operate at a loss for long. Hence the ideal regulatory solution would require that the government subsidize the decreasing-cost producer, presumably by funneling tax revenues to the firm. Raising taxes to subsidize a monopolist is not a popular idea, and this approach is rarely employed.

The Deregulation Movement

For the last two decades, many economists have argued that the regulatory process was actually creating monopoly power rather than curbing it. This idea is partially based on the interest-group view of regulation analyzed above. In addition, observers noted that economic regulation had spread far beyond the local natural monopolies. By the mid-1970s, regulators were issuing their orders to railroads and trucks, airlines and buses, radio and TV broadcasting, oil and natural gas, pecans and milk, and virtually all financial markets. Many of these regulated industries were closer to the pole of perfect competition than to natural monopoly, as Figure 20-2 suggests.

Since 1975, the federal government has deregulated many industries, including airlines, trucking, railroad, stockbroking, long-distance telephone service, and natural gas. Each of these industries has structural characteristics that are favorable to competition because their markets are large relative to the efficient size of individual firms.

The airline industry provides a dramatic example of the dilemmas of deregulation. Since its creation in the 1930s, the Civil Aeronautics Board (CAB) viewed its role as deterring competition. No major new air carriers were allowed to enter the interstate market from 1938 to 1978. When innovative, low-cost and no-frills airfares were proposed, the CAB slapped these proposals down. The CAB was (as the interest-group view of regulation predicted) devoted to keeping airfares up, not down.

In 1977, President Carter appointed Alfred Kahn chairman of the CAB. A distinguished economist and critic of regulation, Kahn set out to allow more competition by entry and fare flexibility.* In 1978, Congress passed legislation to allow free entry and exit on all domestic air routes. Airlines were freed to set whatever fares the traffic would bear.

Many non-economists worried that there would be massive layoffs and loss of service without regulation. After several years of experience, it is clear that competition has changed the entire structure of the airline industry. Studies indicate that (after correcting for inflation) average fares fell sharply over the years after deregulation; that utilization of aircraft has increased; and that airlines have become extraordinarily innovative in their pricing strategies. By most measures, the industry has operated more efficiently since deregulation. Moreover, the vision of vigorous competition has certainly been borne out, with five bankruptcies among major airlines since deregulation, the most recent being Eastern Airlines. Economists can be justly proud of their accuracy in forecasting the effects of airline deregulation.

A similar history occurred in the oil industry after its complete deregulation in February 1981. Oil companies began to introduce new forms of marketing to compete for the dwindling gasoline market. Many companies expanded self-service and introduced electronic high-speed pumps. These innovations forced the price margin between gasoline and crude oil to shrink sharply after deregulation. Instead of gouging consumers, oil companies competed with one another.

The American deregulation movement also spread to other countries, which worked to free their industries to compete for domestic and foreign markets. Although political obstacles continue to slow deregulation in many potentially competitive markets, it seems unlikely that this trend will be reversed in the years to come.

B. Antitrust Policy

As industries are increasingly controlled by the invisible hand rather than by government regulation, the major weapon in the government arsenal against market power today is antitrust policy. Antitrust policies attack anticompetitive abuses in two different ways. First, they prohibit certain kinds of *business conduct,* such as price fixing, that restrain competitive forces. Second, they restrict some *market structures,* such as monopolies, that are thought most likely to restrict commerce and abuse their economic power in other ways.

Antitrust policy has been a fruitful arena for interactions of law and economics for decades. Our survey of antitrust policy will examine one of the most critical segments of business law and at the same time show how the tools of microeconomic analysis can be usefully applied in this important area of economic policy.

*Alfred Kahn was a pioneer of regulatory economics who reshaped our world in his short term of government service. Kahn's early work involved the study of both the history of regulation and the impacts of government regulation on industries. Kahn joined the CAB and, using his powers of persuasion, began to loosen the regulatory restraints on airlines. Within 4 years, the industry became known for its vigorous and innovative competition.

Kahn is known for his wit as well as his wisdom. He once admitted to a group of airline executives that he knew nothing about the business, saying that for him an airplane was simply marginal cost with wings. In 1978, Kahn left the CAB to become President Carter's chief inflation fighter. In that post he furthered deregulation of the trucking industry. Kahn also predicted that, without an effective anti-inflation policy, the economy would soon be in a deep recession. But because White House aides fretted over his choice of words, he relabeled the recession a "banana" and spoke of the need for "bananas" to fight inflation.

Our introduction to American antitrust policy will include the following:

- The history of *legislative acts*—e.g., the Sherman Act (1890), the Clayton Act (1914), and the Federal Trade Commission Act (1914), plus later amendments.
- The evolution of *case law on structure and conduct*—the definition of different forms of illegal conduct, changing views on the role of size and structure in finding antitrust violations, and the outcomes of the major antitrust cases from Standard Oil in 1911 to AT&T in 1982.
- *The new approach to antitrust of the 1980s*—one that stresses the intrinsic rivalry of oligopolists and is skeptical of the ability of government to use antitrust policies to improve the performance of large business in a deregulated world full of intense foreign competition.

The balance of this chapter explores these three aspects of antitrust policy.

The Framework Statutes

Antitrust law is like a huge forest that has grown from a handful of seeds. The statutes on which the law is based are so concise and straightforward that they can be quoted in Table 20-1; it is astounding how much law has grown from so few words.

The Antitrust Laws

Sherman Antitrust Act (1890, as amended)

§1. Every contract, combination in the form of trust or otherwise, or conspiracy, in restraint of trade or commerce among the several States, or with foreign nations, is declared to be illegal.

§2. Every person who shall monopolize, or attempt to monopolize, or combine or conspire with any other person or persons, to monopolize any part of the trade or commerce among the several States, or with foreign nations, shall be deemed guilty of a felony. . . .

Clayton Antitrust Act (1914, as amended)

§2. It shall be unlawful . . . to discriminate in price between different purchasers of commodities of like grade and quality . . . where the effect of such discrimination may be substantially to lessen competition or tend to create a monopoly in any line of commerce. . . . *Provided,* That nothing herein contained shall prevent differentials which make only due allowance for differences in the cost. . . .

§3. That it shall be unlawful for any person . . . to lease or make a sale or contract . . . on the condition, agreement, or understanding that the lessee or purchaser thereof shall not use or deal in the . . . commodities of a competitor . . . where the effect . . . may be to substantially lessen competition or tend to create a monopoly in any line of commerce.

§7. No [corporation] . . . shall acquire . . . the whole or any part . . . of another [corporation] . . . where . . . the effect of such an acquisition may be substantially to lessen competition, or to tend to create a monopoly.

Federal Trade Commission Act (1914, as amended)

§5. Unfair methods of competition . . . and unfair or deceptive acts or practices . . . are declared unlawful.

Table 20-1. These statutes form the basis of American antitrust law

Sherman Act (1890)

Monopolies had long been illegal under the common law, based on custom and past judicial decisions. But these laws proved ineffective against the mergers and trusts[2] that began to grow in the 1880s. Populist sentiments then led to passage of the Sherman Act in 1890.

The Sherman Act made it illegal to "monopolize trade" and outlawed any "combination or conspiracy in restraint of trade." But beyond an antipathy toward "monopolizing" there is no evidence that anyone had clear notions about which actions were to be regarded as legal or illegal.

[2] A *trust* is a group of firms, usually in the same industry, that combine together by a legal agreement to regulate production, prices, or other industrial conditions.

Clayton Act (1914)

The Clayton Act was passed to clarify and strengthen the Sherman Act. It outlawed *tying contracts* (in which a customer is forced to buy product B if she wants product A); it ruled *price discrimination* and exclusive dealings illegal; it banned *interlocking directorates* (in which some people would be directors of firms in the same industry) and *mergers* formed by acquiring common stock of competitors. These practices were not illegal per se (meaning, in themselves), but only when they might substantially lessen competition. The Clayton Act emphasized prevention as well as punishment.

Another important element of the Clayton Act was that it specifically provided antitrust immunity to labor unions.

Federal Trade Commission

In 1914 the Federal Trade Commission (FTC) was established to prohibit "unfair methods of competition" and to warn against anticompetitive mergers. In 1938, the FTC was also empowered to ban false and deceptive advertising. To enforce its powers, the FTC can investigate, hold hearings, and issue cease-and-desist orders.

Basic Issues in Antitrust: Conduct, Structure, and Mergers

In the century since the Sherman Act was passed, economists and jurists have thought deeply about the proper role of large enterprises. Modern antitrust theory emphasizes the role of industrial structure and conduct in analyzing market structures.

Illegal Conduct

Some of the earliest antitrust decisions concerned illegal behavior. The courts have ruled that certain kinds of collusive behavior are illegal per se; there is simply no defense that will justify this set of actions. The offenders cannot defend themselves by pointing to some worthy objective (such as product quality) or mitigating circumstance (such as low profits).

The most important class of per se illegal conduct is agreements among competing firms to fix prices, restrict output, or divide markets. Such actions have the effect of raising prices and lowering output. Even the severest critics of antitrust policy can find no redeeming virtue in price fixing.

Other forms of conduct are also limited by antitrust laws. These include:

- *Retail price maintenance,* where retailers agree not to sell below or above a price specified by manufacturers.
- *Predatory pricing,* in which a firm sells its goods for less than production costs (usually interpreted as marginal cost or average variable cost).
- *Tying contracts* or arrangements, whereby a firm will sell product A only if the purchaser buys product B.
- *Price discrimination,* in which a firm sells the same product to different customers at different prices for reasons not related to cost or meeting competition.

As you read over this list, as well as the previous paragraph, note that these practices relate to a firm's *conduct.* Whether committed by monopolies or small firms, it is the acts that are illegal; the market power of the firm in question is not at issue.

Although conduct-related cases receive less attention than structural cases, they are an integral part of antitrust. Perhaps the most celebrated example is the great electric-equipment conspiracy.

In 1961, the electric-equipment industry was found guilty of collusive price agreements. Executives of the largest companies—such as GE and Westinghouse—conspired to raise prices and covered their tracks like characters in a spy novel by meeting in hunting lodges, using code names, and making telephone calls from phone booths. Although the top executives in these companies were apparently unaware of what the vice-presidents just below them were doing, they had put much pressure on their vice-presidents for increased sales. The companies agreed to pay extensive damages to their customers for overcharges, and some executives were jailed for their antitrust violations.

The great electrical conspiracy sent a shock through American business. While few large-scale conspiracies have been uncovered in recent years, price fixing continues to be a concern. There are on average 50 federal cases and hundreds of private cases each year attacking price fixing and other illegal behavior.

A recent case involves an investigation by the Justice Department of the setting of tuitions and scholarship aid by many colleges and universities. The government claimed that these educational institutions conspired to raise tuition levels and to reduce scholarship competition for top students. In 1991, several institutions settled with the Department of Justice in a "consent decree." The colleges and universities admitted no wrongdoing but agreed not to meet to set common policies for scholarships. This case raised novel issues about whether educational institutions lie in the scope of business activities that are regulated by antitrust law.

Structure: Is Bigness Badness?

The most visible antitrust cases concern structure rather than conduct. They consist of attempts to *break up* large firms as well as preventive *antimerger* proceedings against proposed mergers of large firms. The first surge of antitrust activity under the Sherman Act focused on dismantling existing monopolies. In 1911, the Supreme Court ordered the American Tobacco Company and Standard Oil to be broken up into many separate companies.

In condemning these flagrant monopolies, the Supreme Court enunciated the important "rule of reason": Only *unreasonable* restraints of trade (mergers, agreements, and the like) came within the scope of the Sherman Act and were considered illegal.

The rule-of-reason doctrine virtually nullified the antitrust laws' attack on monopolistic mergers, as shown by the U.S. Steel case (1920). J. P. Morgan had put this giant together by merger, and at its peak it controlled 60 percent of the market. But the court held that size alone was no offense. In that period, as today, courts focused more on anticompetitive *conduct* than on pure monopoly *structure.*

The New Deal and Alcoa. Congress passes laws. But nothing happens unless private parties or the Department of Justice brings suit to enforce them. During the roaring twenties, antitrust went into hibernation. Not until the late 1930s, when F. D. Roosevelt put Thurman Arnold in charge of antitrust, was there a real burst of federal prosecutions in this area. Arnold tackled the building industries, glass, cigarettes, cement, and many others.

The Alcoa case (1945) represents the culmination of New Deal activism, as well as the furthest boundary of trust-busting by the courts. Alcoa had gained a 90 percent market share in aluminum, but by means that were not in themselves illegal. It had installed capacity in anticipation of the growth of demand and kept prices low to prevent potential competition. It had attempted to maintain its large market share by keeping entry unprofitable rather than by engaging in anticompetitive acts. The court nonetheless found that Alcoa had violated the Sherman Act, holding that monopoly power, even if lawfully acquired, could constitute an economic ill and should be condemned. During this period, the courts came to emphasize market structure along with market conduct: *monopoly power, even without otherwise illegal conduct, was declared illegal.*

Recent Developments

Since the high-water mark in 1945, the pattern of judicial decisions and economic theory has steadily retreated from the hostility to monopoly seen in the Alcoa case. Only two major companies have been pursued in the last two decades: IBM and AT&T. Since these cases were concluded in 1982, no significant structural antitrust cases have been initiated. A review of these last two cases reveals the flavor of modern thinking about antitrust policy.

The AT&T Case. Until 1983 AT&T had a virtual monopoly on the telecommunications market. It handled more than 95 percent of all long-distance calls, provided 85 percent of all local lines, and sold most of the nation's telephone equipment. The complex of companies owned by AT&T—often called the Bell System—included Bell Telephone Labs, Western Electric Company, and 23 Bell operating companies.

Since the invention of the telephone in 1876, the company Alexander Graham Bell founded had spent many years battling with the government in numerous antitrust suits. Two earlier government antitrust suits had but a limited effect on the company.

In 1974, the Department of Justice filed yet another and more far-reaching suit. It contended that AT&T had (*a*) prevented competing long-distance carriers (like MCI) from connecting to local exchanges and (*b*) obstructed other equipment manufacturers from selling telecommunications equipment to subscribers or to Bell operating companies. The government's central legal and economic argument was that Bell had used its regulated natural monopoly in the local telephone market to create monopoly power in the long-distance and telephone-equipment markets.

Bell took two lines of defense. First, it denied many factual charges or rebutted their relevance. Second, it claimed that the U.S. telephone system was the best in the world precisely *because* Bell owned and operated most of the U.S. telephone system. In a line of argument similar to the Schumpeterian hypothesis (see Chapter 11), AT&T argued that the size and scope of the Bell System made its monopoly a reasonable and efficient way to conduct the telephone business.

The bizarre outcome surprised everyone. Fearful that the case might end unfavorably, Bell's management settled with the government in a consent decree that essentially met every point of the government's proposed remedy. Bell's local telephone operating companies were divested (or legally separated) from AT&T and, in 1984, were regrouped into seven large regional telephone holding companies. AT&T retained its long-distance operations as well as Bell Labs (the research organization) and Western Electric (the equipment manufacturer). The net effect was to reduce the size and sales of the Bell System by 80 percent.

In some respects, the AT&T settlement was a victory for competition. Local telephone companies are free to buy equipment from anyone. Consumers are free to choose among alternative long-distance providers and equipment suppliers. AT&T is no longer able to take advantage of its local franchise monopoly to block the entry of rival companies.

But many economists raised questions about the wisdom of the consent decree. They worried about the quality of telephone service in a more fragmented industry. Will Bell Labs maintain its technological virtuosity and continue to be among the most fruitful industrial research laboratories in the world? Will larger foreign companies overtake the United States in the global telecommunications industry? Questions about the long-term implications of the AT&T antitrust suit will be answered only in the years to come.

The IBM Case. The second major antitrust case in recent years was the government suit to dismember IBM. Filed in 1969, the suit charged that IBM "has attempted to monopolize and has monopolized . . . general purpose digital computers." The government charged that IBM had a dominant market share, with 76 percent of the market in 1967. Moreover, the government claimed that IBM had used many devices to prevent others from competing; the alleged anticompetitive steps included tie-in pricing, excessively low prices to discourage entry, and introduction of new products that tended to reduce the attractiveness of the products of other companies.

IBM contested the government case with tenacity and vigor. IBM's major defense was that the government was penalizing success rather than anticompetitive behavior. The fundamental dilemma in such cases was crisply stated in the Alcoa case: "The successful competitor having been urged to compete must not be turned on when he wins." IBM claimed that the government was punishing the firm that had accurately foreseen the enormous potential in the computer revolution and had dominated the industry through its "superior skill, foresight, and industry."

The case dragged along inconclusively until the Reagan administration's antitrust chief, William Baxter, undertook a careful review and, in 1982, decided to dismiss the case as "without merit." The government's reasoning was that, unlike the telecommunications industry, the computer industry was unregulated and subject to the full force of market competition. Baxter held that this industry was intrinsically competitive and that government attempts to restructure the computer market were more likely to harm than promote economic efficiency. The evolution of the microcomputer industry and the relative decline in IBM's share over the last decade bear out the government's claim that even IBM's size is no bar to intense competition.

Private Antitrust. Up to now we have considered government antitrust actions. One of the remarkable developments in recent years has been the privatization of antitrust enforcement. Under the law, private parties can bring damage suits. If the suit is successful, the private party gets *triple damages* plus reasonable costs.

Spurred by the gains from triple damages, private parties have been increasingly active in bringing antitrust suits. In the first decades of this century, the numbers of government and private antitrust suits were approximately equal. But by the late 1970s, private parties were bringing more than 1000 cases a year, compared to the government's 50 or so. Awards as high as $1.8 billion (in a preliminary judgment against AT&T) have made this a lucrative field for lawsuits.

The issues raised by the privatization of antitrust law are just beginning to be debated. On the one hand, the prospect of a billion-dollar lawsuit must surely give pause to a potential conspiracy—so in this respect the antitrust laws are probably better enforced. But to the extent that the present antitrust laws are inefficiently designed, as many economists now believe, the army of private litigators will only help enforce poorly designed laws more strictly and increase the volume of costly litigation. Some thoughtful scholars now think that damage awards are too high and should be reduced.

Mergers: Law and Practice

Companies can gain market power through growth (plowing back earnings and building new plants). But a much easier way to gain market share, or simply to get bigger, is to merge with another company. The 1980s saw a tremendous growth in merger activity.

Horizontal mergers—in which companies in the same industry combine—are forbidden under the Clayton Act when the merger is likely to reduce competition in the industry substantially. Case law and the Department of Justice's 1982 and 1984 merger guidelines clarified the meaning of the vague statutory language. Under these guidelines, industries are divided into three groups: unconcentrated, moderately concentrated, and highly concentrated. Mergers in the latter two types of industries will be challenged even in cases where the firms involved have small market shares. For example, in a highly concentrated industry, if a firm with a market share of 10 percent acquires one with a share of 2.5 percent or more, the Department of Justice is likely to challenge the merger.

Vertical mergers occur when two firms at different stages of the production process come together. In recent years, the courts have taken a hard line toward vertical mergers. They worried about the potential restriction of competition through exclusive dealings if two independent firms merged. Courts tended to pay relatively little heed to the potential efficiencies of joint operations in vertical mergers.

As part of its campaign to reduce government intervention, the Reagan administration changed the guidelines on mergers in 1982 and 1984. The new guidelines greatly relaxed enforcement with respect to both vertical and horizontal mergers. Many economists believe that these changes brought on the great wave of mergers and acquisitions of the 1980s.

A third kind of combination, called **conglomerate mergers,** joins together unrelated businesses. In a conglomerate merger, a chemical or steel company might buy an oil company, or a firm that has many lines of business (like ITT) might add yet more strings to its bow (hotels, rental cars, or whatever).

The critics of conglomerates make two points. First, they note that, in part because of merger activity, the concentration of assets in the top companies has grown steadily over this century. Figure 20-4 shows the estimated share of assets owned by the 200 largest corporations. These data suggest that the asset share of the top 200 rose from about one-third around 1910 to 61 percent in 1984. The increasing trend in asset concentration alarms many economists and policymakers, including the Federal Trade Commission, which noted a few years ago that "the giant corporations will ultimately take over the country."

The data shown in Figure 20-4 can, however, be misleading. The rise in concentration of assets does not necessarily mean that the degree of market power in individual industries is also growing. The asset share may increase because large firms are fishing in other firms' waters. When du Pont acquired the large oil firm Conoco or when the cigarette firm Philip Morris bought General Foods, the concentration of assets increased but the degree of effective competition rose in the affected industries. In addition, data on asset shares underestimate the degree of competition because they omit foreign firms, which are increasingly important in most manufacturing markets. The data in Figure 20-4 do indicate, however, that fewer people are making the crucial decisions for American industry, and this centralization of power and decision making distresses many analysts.

The second point made by the critics of conglomerates is that many of these combinations serve no economic purpose. They are, it is argued, simply a brand of boardroom poker to entertain managers bored with supervising their tiresome steel or chemical operations. And, indeed, there is a point here: What does the airplane business have in common with meat-packing? Or typewriters with birth-control pills? Or computer leasing with passenger-bus operations?

Conglomerates are not without defenders. Some economists argue that these mergers bring good modern management to backward firms and that

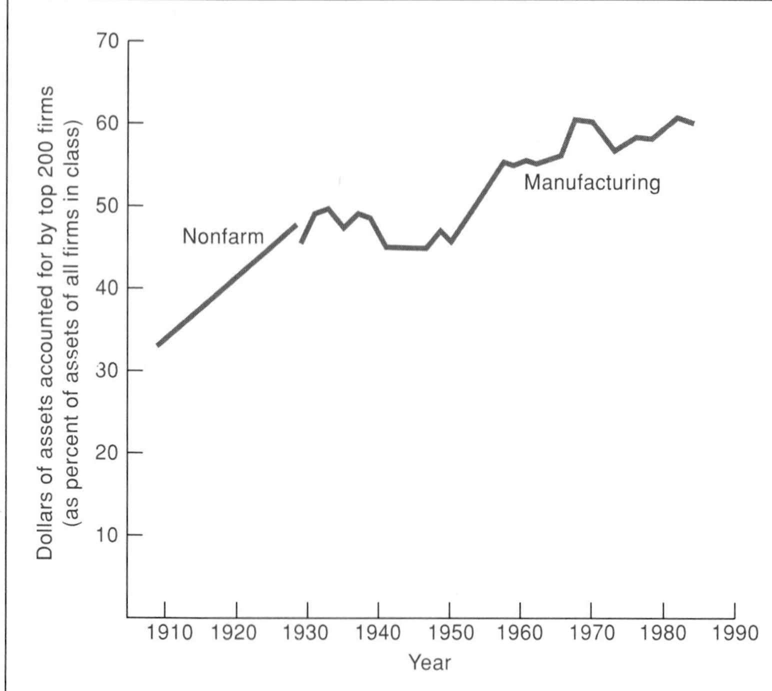

Figure 20-4. Share of assets in top 200 firms
Since the turn of the century, industrial assets have become more and more concentrated in fewer giant companies. The data are not always comparable, but they show a sharp increase during the 1920s and 1930s, as well as during the early 1950s. (The break in the series indicates a change in the method of calculating shares.) [Source: F. M. Scherer, *Industrial Market Structure and Economic Performance*, 2nd ed. (Houghton Mifflin Company, Boston, 1980); Clair Wilcox and William G. Shepherd, *Public Policies toward Business* (Irwin, Homewood, Ill., 1975); U.S. Bureau of the Census, *Concentration Ratios in Manufacturing and Statistical Abstract of the United States*.]

takeovers, like bankruptcy, represent the economy's way of eliminating deadwood in the economic struggle for survival. But there is no consensus on the merits or demerits of conglomerate mergers. No study has found major gains or costs, so perhaps the best policy is to keep a watchful eye.

Antitrust Laws and Efficiency

The dismissal of the federal antitrust case against IBM and the revision of merger guidelines of the early 1980s began a new chapter in American antitrust policy. With these steps, antitrust law has largely abandoned its mission "to put an end to great aggregations of capital because of the helplessness of the individual before them" (to quote from the 1945 Alcoa decision). During the supply-side years of the 1980s, the antitrust laws were directed solely toward the goal of improving economic efficiency. If big is efficient, big shall reign.

What prompted the changing attitude toward antitrust policy? In part, it grew out of technical developments in economic research. Economists found that performance was not always closely associated with structure. Some large firms (IBM, AT&T, and Boeing, for example) and some highly concentrated markets (computers, telecommunications, and aircraft manufacture) proved to be among the industries with the highest performance with respect to innovation and productivity growth. Whereas economic theory held that monopoly keeps prices high, historical experience indicated that highly concentrated industries often had rapidly declining prices relative to less concentrated industries. At the same time, some unconcentrated industries, such as agriculture, exhibited outstanding performance. No iron law could be found linking structure and performance.

How can we explain this paradox? Some economists invoke the Schumpeterian hypothesis. Firms in concentrated industries collect monopoly profits, to be sure. But the size of the market also means that large firms can appropriate much of the return on research and development (R&D) investments, and this explains the high levels of R&D and the rapid technological change in concentrated industries. If, as Schumpeter claimed, technological change originates in large firms, then it would be foolish to slay these giant geese who lay such golden eggs. This view has been well expressed by Lester Thurow, dean of the MIT Sloan School of

Management: "The millions spent on the IBM [antitrust] case would have been better spent if they had been plowed back into research and development on keeping America No. 1 in computers."

A second buttress of the new antitrust policy arose from revised views of the nature of competition. Considering both experimental evidence and observation, many economists have come to believe that intense rivalry will spring up even in highly concentrated markets, as long as collusion is strictly prohibited. Indeed, in the words of Richard Posner:

> The only truly unilateral acts by which firms can get or keep monopoly power are practices like committing fraud on the Patent Office or blowing up a competitor's plant, and fraud and force are in general adequately punished under other statutes.[3]

In this view, the only valid purpose of the antitrust laws should be to replace existing statutes with a simple prohibition against *agreements*—explicit or tacit—that unreasonably restrict competition.

Third, the swing of the pendulum against strict antitrust enforcement came from the movement toward laissez-faire economic views during the Reagan era. This position was inspired by proponents of the Chicago School, which held that most monopoly power is derivative of government interventions. According to this view, the major pools of monopoly power lie in areas protected by government fiat. Important examples include the exemption of labor unions from antitrust laws, monopoly protection conveyed by the patent laws, government regulation of interstate trucking rates, barriers to entry into the professions, rate setting and restrictions in medical care, and state limitations on the cable television or the taxicab industry. Advocates of the laissez-faire view, including former FTC chief James Miller, who often sported an Adam Smith necktie, argued that reducing government regulation would enhance competition.

A final reason for the more relaxed view toward antitrust has been the intensification of foreign competition. As more foreign firms gain a foothold in the American economy, they tend to compete vigorously for market share and often upset established sales patterns and pricing practices. As the sales of Japanese automakers increased, the cozy coexistence of the Big Three American auto firms dissolved. Many economists believe that the threat of foreign competition is a much more powerful tool for enforcing market discipline than are antitrust laws. Indeed, some people argue that the antitrust laws are an obstacle to American business's competing efficiently abroad because they prohibit joint ventures and operations.

Will the permissive antitrust policies of the 1980s endure? No one can predict the direction of future attitudes toward big business. There are signs of a return to a more traditional view of antitrust under the Bush administration. Nonetheless, the arguments supporting the efficiency-oriented view are shared by economists and lawyers across the political spectrum, and the intensity of foreign competition is unlikely to change, so a return to the trust-busting fervor of earlier years appears unlikely in the near future.

[3] Richard A. Posner, *Antitrust Law: An Economic Prospectus* (University of Chicago Press, Chicago, 1976), p. 212. The writing of Posner—along with that of Robert Bork, William Baxter, and William Landes—has been highly influential in determining the new climate of antitrust thinking.

SUMMARY

A. Business Regulation: Theory and Practice

1. Regulation consists of government rules commanding firms to alter their business conduct. Economic regulation refers to the control of prices, production, entry and exit conditions, and standards of service in a particular industry; social regulation consists of rules aimed at correcting externalities, particularly those that impinge on health and safety.

2. There is a spectrum of market structures between perfect competition at one pole and natural monopoly at the other. Natural monopoly occurs when average costs are falling for every level of output, so that the most

efficient organization of the industry requires production in a single firm. Few industries come close to this condition today—perhaps only local utilities like telephone, water, and electricity.

3. While control of natural monopoly is often the stated goal of economic regulation, the Chicago view holds that regulation is desired by regulated firms whose interests are furthered by exclusion of potential rivals.
4. In conditions of natural monopoly, governments regulate the price and service of private companies. Traditionally, government regulation of monopoly has required that price be set at the average cost of production. The ideal regulation would require price to be set equal to marginal cost, but this approach is impractical because it requires that government subsidize the monopolist. The deregulation movement of the 1970s reduced the extent of economic regulation markedly, with airline deregulation exemplifying the gains from deregulation.

B. Antitrust Policy

5. Antitrust policy, prohibiting anticompetitive conduct and preventing monopolistic structures, is the primary way that public policy limits abuses of market power by large firms. This policy grew out of legislation like the Sherman Act (1890) and the Clayton Act (1914). The primary purposes of antitrust are: (*a*) to prohibit anticompetitive activities (which include agreements to fix prices or divide up territories; price discrimination; and tie-in agreements) and (*b*) to break up monopoly structures. In today's legal theory, such structures are those that have excessive market power (a large share of the market) and also engage in anticompetitive acts.
6. In addition to limiting the behavior of existing firms, antitrust law prevents mergers that would lessen competition. Today, horizontal mergers (between firms in the same industry) are the main source of concern, while vertical and conglomerate mergers tend to be tolerated.
7. Antitrust policy has been significantly influenced by economic thinking during the last two decades. As a result, antitrust policy during the 1980s focused almost exclusively on improving efficiency, while it ignored earlier populist concerns with bigness itself. Moreover, in today's economy—with intense competition from foreign producers and in deregulated industries—many believe that antitrust policy should concentrate primarily on preventing collusive agreements like price fixing.

CONCEPTS FOR REVIEW

Regulation
economic vs. social regulation
natural monopoly
economic vs. interest-group theories of regulation
three price outcomes under monopoly (unregulated, regulated, ideal)
deregulation movement

Antitrust policy
Sherman, Clayton, and FTC Acts
per se prohibitions vs. the "rule of reason"
mergers: vertical, horizontal, conglomerate
efficiency-oriented antitrust policy

QUESTIONS FOR DISCUSSION

1. What are the major weapons that government has to restrain monopoly power? Describe the strengths and weaknesses of each policy.
2. Review the three pricing outcomes in Figure 20-3. Can you think of the difficulties of implementing the ideal regulated price? (*Hint:* Where does the country get the revenues? Is *MC* easy to measure?) Similarly, can you think of reasons why many economists would prefer the unregulated to the regulated outcome? (*Hint:* What if P_M is not much above P_R? What if you worried about the interest-group theory of regulation?)
3. Sketch the interest-group theory of regulation. Who are the suppliers and the demanders of regulation? What is the "price" and "quantity" in this "market"? Why is the analogy of votes and dollars imprecise?
4. "IBM is not bad just because it is big." Discuss, particularly with reference to the application of antitrust laws to large companies.
5. Examine the cost and demand curves in Figure 20-1. Using those curves, derive the monopoly price and output. Compare that with the ideal regulated output and price. Describe the difference.
6. Two important approaches to antitrust are "structure" and "conduct." The former looks only at the structure of the industry (such as the concentration of firms); the latter, at firm conduct (e.g., price fixing).
   (a) Review the various statutes and cases to see which are related to conduct and which to structure. What about the merger guidelines of the 1980s?
   (b) What are the advantages and disadvantages of each approach?
7. Make a list of the industries that you feel are candidates for the title "natural monopoly." Then review the different strategies for intervention to prevent exercise of monopoly power. What would you do about each industry on your list?
8. Show that a profit-maximizing, unregulated monopolist will never operate in the price-inelastic region of its demand curve. Show how regulation can force the monopolist onto the inelastic portion of its demand curve. What will be the impact of an increase in the regulated price of a monopolist upon revenues and profits when it is operating on (*a*) the elastic portion of the demand curve, (*b*) the inelastic portion of the demand curve, and (*c*) the unit-elastic portion of the demand curve?
9. **Advanced problem:** Some economists believe that the traditional concentration ratios do not adequately measure the impact of firm size on market power because they do not take into account the impact of dominant firms. A measure which attempts to reflect the effect of the size differences is the Herfindahl index, or *H*, which is equal to the sum of the squared market shares in percentage terms:

$$H = \sum_{i=1}^{n} S_i^2 = S_1^2 + S_2^2 + \cdots$$

where there are *n* firms and S_i is the percentage market share of the *i*th firm. When the industry is a complete monopoly, the Herfindahl index is $H = 100^2 = 10{,}000$. For a perfectly competitive industry, the Herfindahl index is $H = 0$.

According to the government's 1982 guidelines, mergers may be challenged if they significantly decrease competition in moderately concentrated or highly concentrated industries according to the Herfindahl index. The Antitrust Division is "likely to challenge" a merger if it adds more than 100 points to the Herfindahl index when the Herfindahl index is between 1000 and 1800, and it is also likely to challenge if a merger adds more than 50 points to the index for an industry whose index is more than 1800.

Consider an industry with a Herfindahl index of 1400 before a merger. Four firms are considering merger possibilities: American with a market share of 20 percent; United with a share of 10 percent; USWest with a share of 6 percent; and Piddly with a share of 4 percent. Which pairs of companies could merge without running the risk of an antitrust challenge?

C H A P T E R 2 1

INCOME DISTRIBUTION AND THE STRUGGLE AGAINST POVERTY

[The conflict] between equality and efficiency [is] our biggest socioeconomic tradeoff, and it plagues us in dozens of dimensions of social policy. We can't have our cake of market efficiency and share it equally.

Arthur Okun (1975)

We live in a double-standard economy. Our laws proclaim the rights of all women and men, the principle of one-person, one-vote, and equality of opportunity. This is the rhetoric of modern democracy. But daily life in a market economy speaks otherwise. On the streets, people are told, "Work or go hungry" and "Economic power goes to those who are white, male, and well connected."

Which face is reality? The answer is both, to some degree. Democratic countries value human rights and equality of opportunity. They have taken steps to raise living standards of the less fortunate. But in some areas, the steps are tentative, for the modern welfare state has found that there are limits to its affluence. And as nations attempt to equalize incomes among their citizens, they encounter greater and greater adverse effects on incentives and efficiency. Today, people are asking, How much of the economic pie must be sacrificed in order to divide it more equally?

The purpose of this chapter is to examine the facts concerning the distribution of income and the dilemmas that governments face when they undertake to redistribute incomes. Government policies to ensure a fair income distribution are among the most controversial and difficult issues of public policy. It is here that clear economic analysis of facts and trends in poverty, as well as of the strengths and weaknesses of different kinds of policies, will have a large payoff in promoting the smooth operation of a market society.

A. Measurement of Inequality

An analysis of the distribution of economic well-being must begin with a careful measurement of income and wealth in the past as well as today at home and in other countries. Recall that by **income** we mean the total receipts or cash earned by a person or household during a given time period (usually a year). Income consists of labor earnings, property income (such as rents, interest, and dividends), and government transfer payments. **Wealth** consists of the net dollar value of assets owned at a point in time. You can refresh your memory about the major sources of income and wealth by reviewing Tables 13-1 and 13-2 (pages 218 and 219).

The Distribution of Income and Wealth

Most of us have a general idea of what our families earn. But people are surprised to learn about the average earnings of American families. Statistics show that during the recession year of 1991, the average (or per capita) annual disposable income of Americans was approximately $16,100.

But almost no one earns the average income, and it is more revealing to know the *distribution of income,* which shows the dispersion of individual incomes. To understand the income distribution, consider the following experiment. Suppose each member of a group—or of the entire nation—writes down his or her yearly income on an index card. We can then sort these cards into *income classes.* Some of the cards will go into the lowest class, the group with under $5000 of income. Some go into the next class. A few go into the income class over $100,000.

The actual income distribution of American families in 1989 is shown in Table 21-1. Column (1) shows the different income-class intervals. Column (2) shows the percentage of families in each income class. Column (3) shows the percentage of the total national income that goes to the people in the given income class.

Columns (4) and (5) are computed from (2) and (3), respectively. Column (4) shows what percentage of the total number of families belongs to each income class or below. Column (5) shows what percentage of total income goes to the people who belong in the given income class or below.

A glance at the income distribution in Table 21-1 shows the wide spread of incomes. There's always room at the top because it is hard to get there, not because it is easy. If we made an income pyramid out of a child's blocks, with each layer portraying $500 of income, the peak would be far higher than Mount Everest, but most people would be within a few feet of the ground.

How to Measure Inequality among Income Classes

How great is the dispersion of disposable incomes, and how can we measure the degree of income inequality? A useful way to analyze inequality is to ask, What percentage of all income goes to the lowest 10 percent of the population? What percentage goes to the lowest 50 percent? The lowest 95 percent? And so forth. These questions can be answered from the data underlying Table 21-1.

(1) Income class	(2) Percentage of all families in this class	(3) Percentage of total income received by families in this class	(4) Percentage of families in this class and lower ones	(5) Percentage of income received by this class and lower ones
Under $5,000	3.6	0.2	3.6	0.2
$5,000–$9,999	6.3	1.1	9.9	1.3
$10,000–$14,999	8.1	2.4	18.0	3.7
$15,000–$24,999	16.7	8.0	34.7	11.7
$25,000–$49,999	36.3	31.8	71.0	43.5
$50,000–$74,999	17.7	25.7	88.7	69.2
$75,000–$99,999	6.5	13.3	95.2	82.5
$100,000 and over	4.8	17.5	100.0	100.0
Total	100.0	100.0		

Table 21-1. Distribution of total incomes of American households, 1989

This table shows how total incomes were distributed among households. Half of households received less than the median income of $34,200 while half received more. (Source: U.S. Bureau of the Census, *Money Income and Poverty Status in the United States, 1989,* Current Population Report, Series P-60, No. 168, September 1990.)

Income Shares, 1989

(1) Family income by rank	(2) Percent share of income	(3) Cumulative percentage of people	(4) Cumulative percentage of income: Absolute equality	(5) Absolute inequality	(6) Actual distribution
		0	0	0	0
Lowest fifth	4.6	20	20	0	4.6
Second fifth	10.6	40	40	0	15.2
Third fifth	16.5	60	60	0	31.7
Fourth fifth	23.7	80	80	0	55.4
Highest fifth*	44.6	100	100	100	100.0

* Top 5 percent receive 17.9 percent of total income.

Table 21-2. By grouping the population into fifths, we can compare actual and polar cases of inequality

We group the population into the fifth (or quintile) with the lowest income, the fifth with the second-lowest income, and so forth. Column (2) shows what fraction of total income each fifth receives. Then, by cumulating the income of each quintile, we can compare the actual distribution with polar extremes of complete inequality and equality. (Source: U.S. Bureau of the Census, *Money Income and Poverty Status in the United States, 1989,* Current Population Report, Series P-60, No. 168, September 1990.)

At one pole, if incomes were absolutely equally distributed, the lowest 20 percent of the population would receive exactly 20 percent of the total income, the highest 20 percent would also get only 20 percent of the income, and so forth.

In reality, as the first two columns of Table 21-2 show, the lowest 20 percent of the families get only 4.6 percent of the total income. The fourth 20 percent get almost 24 percent. The most affluent 20 percent of the families earn nearly 45 percent, and the upper 5 percent get almost 18 percent—more than what the bottom two-fifths of the population get all together.

We can show the degree of inequality in a diagram known as the **Lorenz curve,** a widely used device for analyzing income and wealth inequality. Figure 21-1 is a Lorenz curve showing the amount of inequality listed in the columns of Table 21-2; that is, it contrasts the patterns of (*a*) absolute equality, (*b*) absolute inequality, and (*c*) actual 1989 American inequality.

Absolute equality is depicted by the gray column of numbers in column (4) of Table 21-2. When they are plotted, these become the diagonal line of Figure 21-1's Lorenz diagram (shown as a broken line).

At the other extreme, we have the hypothetical case of absolute inequality, where one person has all the income. Absolute inequality is shown in column (5) of Table 21-2 and by the lowest curve on the Lorenz diagram—the dashed, right-angled line.

Any actual income distribution, such as that for 1989, will fall between the extremes of absolute equality and absolute inequality. The blue column in Table 21-2 presents the data derived from the first two columns in a form suitable for plotting as an actual Lorenz curve. This actual Lorenz curve appears in Figure 21-1 as the solid blue intermediate curve. The shaded area indicates the deviation from absolute equality, hence giving us a measure of the degree of inequality of income distribution.[1]

Inequality in Different Regions. Countries show quite different income distributions depending upon their economic and social structure. Lorenz curves of four countries are shown in Figure 21-2(*a*). We see that the United Kingdom and Sweden have less income inequality than does the United States. The reason for this lies partly in the high levels of redistributive taxation in the European countries. In addition, the United States has larger proportions of its population in low-income minority groups and larger numbers of one-parent families.

Because of the unreliable data in socialist countries, it is extremely difficult to compare the in-

[1] A quantitative measure of inequality is the "Gini coefficient," which is 2 times the shaded area. This measure is discussed in question 6 at the end of this chapter.

Distribution of Disposable Family Income in the United States, 1989 (Lorenz Curve)

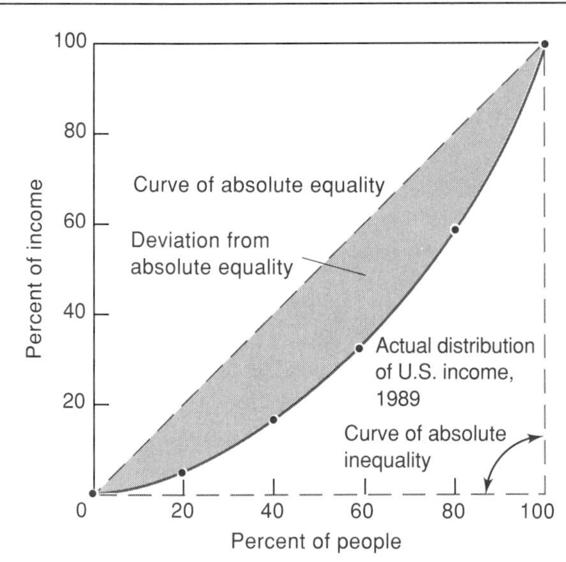

Figure 21-1. Lorenz curve shows actual income inequality as compared to polar cases

By plotting the figures from Table 21-2's column (6), we see that the blue actual distribution-of-income curve lies between the two extremes of absolute equality and absolute inequality. The shaded area of this Lorenz curve (as a percentage of the triangle's area) measures relative inequality of income. (How would the curve have looked back in the roaring 1920s when inequality was greater? In a Utopia where all have equal inheritances and opportunities?)

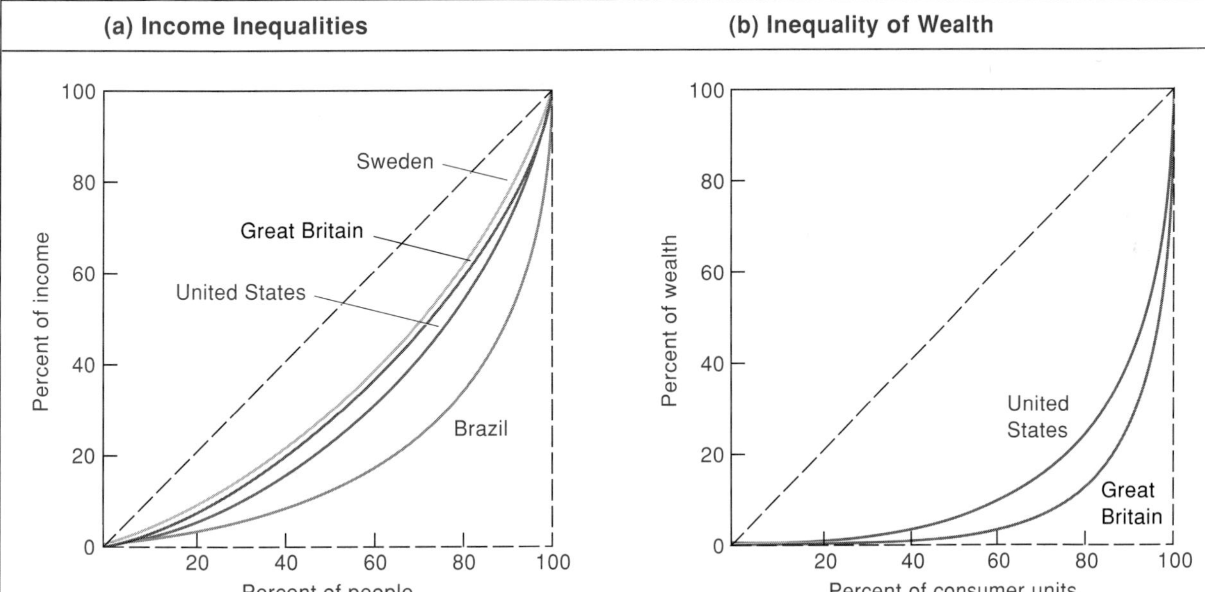

Figure 21-2. Inequality differs in different societies, and is greater for wealth than for income

(a) Advanced economies show less inequality of income distribution than do industrializing economies. Contrary to predictions of many socialists that the rich get richer and the poor get poorer under capitalism, the mixed economy shows increasing equality over time.

(b) Holdings of wealth tend to be more concentrated than do annual incomes. The U.S. and Great Britain have similar income distributions, but British wealth is much more concentrated than American. Socialist countries like China and the Soviet Union would show much less concentration of private wealth. [Source: James D. Smith and Stephen D. Franklin, "The Concentration of Personal Wealth, 1922–1969," *American Economic Review* (May 1974); A. B. Atkinson and A. J. Harrison, "Trends in the Distribution of Wealth in Britain," in A. B. Atkinson (ed.), *Wealth, Income and Inequality* (Oxford University Press, London, 1980).]

equality in the Soviet Union or China with that of advanced market economies.[2] If we confine ourselves to the advanced market economies, the greatest income equality is found in Japan and West Germany. The most unequal income distributions come in the United States, Canada, and France.

Distribution of Wealth

Another important index of economic power is *wealth,* which is the net ownership of financial claims and tangible property, or, in terms of our accounting definitions in Chapter 8, net worth (equal to assets minus liabilities).

One source of the inequality of income is inequality of ownership of wealth. Those who are fabulously wealthy—whether because of inheritance, skill, or luck—enjoy incomes far above the amount earned by the average household. Those without wealth begin with an income handicap.

By and large, wealth is much more unequally distributed in market economies than is income, as Figure 21-2(*b*) shows. In the United States, 1 percent of the people own about 19 percent of all wealth, and the richest $\frac{1}{2}$ percent own fully 14 percent of the nation's wealth. In 1988, the latest year for which extensive data are available, the net worth of American households totaled approximately $8400 billion. The top $2\frac{3}{4}$ percent owned $2280 billion of assets, representing more than one-fourth of total household net worth. The distribution of wealth is even more lopsided in Great Britain than in the United States. In part, this greater inequality exists because certain peers and tycoons in Britain own tremendous amounts of land and other property. But studies show that much of the difference comes from the fact that middle-class Americans often have considerable net worth in the houses they own, a circumstance which is much less common among the lower-income British.

The visible differences in ownership of wealth have spurred radicals over the ages to propose heavy taxation of property income, wealth, or inheritance, and revolutionaries have agitated for expropriation by the state of great accumulations of property. In recent years, however, the reemergence of the market has muted the call for redistribution of wealth, particularly in socialist countries where wealth accumulation by private individuals is now seen as a way of increasing the capital stock and economic efficiency.

Measurement and Trends in Poverty

The Bible says, "The poor, ye shall always have with you." And this was the view of the classical economists and most people until very recently; the classical economists preached the dismal science of an unalterable distribution of income.

The classical economists held that the wages of labor, the rent of land, and the profit of capital were determined by economic laws and not by political decisions. If reformers tried to use the state to modify these facts of life, they would be ineffective in the end. Such well-meaning attempts would beget a smaller national output, which would probably still be distributed in about the same way. Vexation and violence brought about by efforts to alter this social order would merely produce chaos and class warfare.

Modern societies refuse to accept all the inequalities of the distribution of income and consumption generated by laissez-faire markets. In the 1960s, the United States declared "war on poverty" and launched ambitious programs to eradicate economic privation. The results have been disappointing. But before we learn the fate of these lofty dreams, we must examine the definition of poverty, a surprisingly elusive concept.

What Is Poverty?

The word "poverty" means different things to different people. Clearly poverty is a condition in which people have inadequate incomes, but it is

[2] Studies have found that the distribution of earnings in the Soviet Union looks about as unequal as that in the United States. Top scientists and academicians in the Soviet Union probably earn relatively more than their counterparts in the United States. Soviet party chiefs, military leaders, and government ministers historically had great economic privilege, with dachas, limousines, and their own stores filled with Western goods.

Even if the structure of earnings were similar in communist and capitalist countries, one major difference remains: in capitalist countries, perhaps a tenth of national income goes to upper-income groups as property income (interest, dividends, capital gains, etc.). In the Soviet Union or China, by contrast, there are no Rockefellers or Gettys.

hard to draw an exact line between the poor and the non-poor. Economists have therefore devised certain techniques which provide the official definition of poverty.

As a starting point, economists defined poverty as a level of income below the estimated cost of living at the subsistence level. To double-check this calculation, economists have noted that poor families generally spend one-third of their income on food. Hence, from calculations on the cost of a subsistence food budget, economists can calculate a minimum-subsistence income in a second way by multiplying the minimum-food budget by a factor of 3.

These two methods agree fairly well. They indicate that the subsistence cost of living for an urban family of four was about $12,675 in 1989. This figure represents the "poverty line" or demarcation between those the government labels poor and non-poor. The poverty line also varies by family size and is adjusted over time by the consumer price index to reflect changes in the cost of living.

While an exact figure for measuring poverty is helpful, its use raises numerous conceptual issues. For one thing, only cash payments are included in measured income, and some important in-kind benefits such as food stamps or medical care are therefore omitted. Because of these omissions, the extent of poverty is overestimated. In addition, "poverty" is a relative term. The notion of a subsistence budget includes subjective questions of taste and social convention. Today's minimal food budget of $4200 per year for a family of four in the United States far surpasses the minimum required for adequate nutrition, while today's substandard housing often includes household appliances and plumbing that were unavailable to the richest citizens of an earlier era. We should keep these conceptual issues in mind as we listen to debates about poverty and income redistribution.

Poverty in Major Groups, 1989

Population group	Percent of group in poverty
Total population	12.8
By racial group:	
White	10.0
Black	30.7
Hispanic	26.2
Other	16.4
By age:	
Under 18 years	19.6
18 to 64 years	10.2
65 years and over	11.4
By type of family:	
Married couple	5.6
Female householder, no spouse present	32.2
Unrelated subfamilies	51.4
By education of householder:	
Less than 8 years	25.5
High school diploma, no college	19.0
Some college	3.6

Table 21-3. Incidence of poverty in different groups

Whites, college-educated persons, and the elderly have lower-than-average poverty rates. Blacks, Hispanics, and female-headed households have much higher poverty rates than average. (Source: U.S. Bureau of the Census, *Money Income and Poverty Status in the United States, 1989,* Current Population Report, Series P-60, No. 168, September 1990.)

Who Are the Poor?

Poverty hits some groups harder than others. Table 21-3 shows the incidence of poverty in different groups for 1989. While 12.8 percent of the total population was counted as falling below the 1989 poverty line of $12,675, the rate among black families was 3 times that of whites.

Perhaps the most ominous trend is the poverty rate among single-parent families headed by women. Between 35 and 40 percent of these families fall below the poverty line, and half of black households in this group are poor. This group represents a rapidly growing fraction of the poverty population, rising from 17 percent of the poor in 1959 to 35 percent in 1989. Social scientists worry that the children in these families will receive inadequate nutrition and education and will find it difficult to escape from poverty when they are adults.

No discussion of poverty would be accurate without an analysis of the position of minorities. Almost one-third of blacks, Hispanics, and American Indians have below-standard incomes. Table 21-4 shows some of the significant demographic characteristics of the black and white populations.

Why are so many female-headed and black fami-

Worker characteristics	White	Black
Income, 1989:		
Median income of families	$35,975	$20,209
Percent of persons in poverty	10.0	30.7
Percent of families with incomes of $25,000 or more	68.4	41.9
Education:		
Percent of persons 25–29 years old who have completed high school	86.6	80.9
Percent of persons 25–34 years old who are college graduates	24.5	13.1
Unemployment rates, 1990:		
Percent of adult men	3.9	10.8
Percent of adult women	4.1	10.0
Percent of teenagers	13.0	30.6
Occupation:		
Percent of labor force who are scientists or engineers	2.01	0.44
Percent of labor force who are doctors	0.47	0.15
Wealth, 1988:		
Median wealth of families	$43,279	$4,169
Percent of families with wealth over $500,000	3.16	0.13

Table 21-4. Discrimination and inequality of opportunity

Because of racial discrimination and less education, blacks still find fewer good jobs. The incidence of unemployment compounds the inequality. Black Americans tend to be particularly underrepresented in managerial and professional positions. (Source: U.S. Bureau of the Census; U.S. Bureau of Labor Statistics.)

lies poor? What is the role of discrimination?[3] Experienced observers insist that blatant racial or gender discrimination in which firms simply pay minorities or women less is vanishing today. Yet the relative poverty of women and blacks is increasing. How can we reconcile these two apparently contradictory trends? Two factors are probably at work. First, poorer groups often have less education and training and therefore do not qualify for high-paying jobs. A second explanation lies in the phenomenon of noncompeting groups. Discrimination today generally works not by flagrant exclusion of blacks and minorities from schools or jobs but by the more subtle means of disqualifying them, by reason of lack of suitable education and training, from the best positions in the professions or in executive and managerial areas.

Trends in Inequality and Poverty

What is happening to the degree of inequality of incomes in modern industrial economies like the United States? By calculating Lorenz and other curves, scholars find that inequality has definitely declined since the beginning of this century. But over the last decade there appears to have been a turn toward greater inequality and poverty. Between the mid-1970s and 1989, the share of income going to the upper-income groups increased, while the lowest-income group lost ground.

The trends in inequality are shown graphically in Figure 21-3. According to historical studies, the share of total income going to the poorest fifth (or quintile) of the families stood around 3.6 percent in the late 1920s. The share of the bottom quintile rose to 5 percent after World War II, as many people migrated from low-income agricultural jobs into industry. There was some increase in the income share of the bottom fifth of households until the mid-1970s, after which this share declined sharply in the 1980s, sinking to 4.6 percent of total income in 1989.

In *absolute* terms, the bottom fifth of the population has fared well over this century: the real income of the bottom fifth of the population has grown sharply since the 1920s. To a significant extent, the poor have enjoyed the fruits of economic growth along with more affluent groups. Indeed, as the light blue line shows, the share of national income drawn by the poorest fifth has increased slightly since the numbers were first collected.

[3] The economics of discrimination in the workplace is analyzed in Chapter 14.

What do official measurements of poverty tell us? The black line in Figure 21-3 shows that the percent of the population in poverty dropped sharply from the late 1950s to the early 1970s. Since 1980, however, rising unemployment, cuts in government welfare programs, and the increasing number of female-headed households have reversed the earlier trend, producing a sharp increase in the poor population.

What lies behind the changing extent of inequality? In part, inequality has been substantially reduced by government actions. Government programs like welfare and food stamps for the indigent, social security for the elderly, and unemployment insurance take the worst edge off abject poverty. Moreover, our income-tax system tends to tax high incomes more heavily than low incomes, thereby tending to reduce the degree of inequality.

The rising inequality over the last decade has several sources. Among the important ones are a rise in female-headed households, a decrease in the relative pay of low-skilled jobs, and an erosion of government transfer programs—all of which depressed the incomes of the poorest part of the population. In addition, rising interest rates, a booming stock market, and lower income-tax rates at the top raised the relative incomes of the richest groups.

Effects of Industrialization on Equality. Historians have examined the patterns of inequality as nations follow the road from isolated traditional societies through the first phases of economic development and into mature industrialization. What does the fragmentary evidence indicate?

Data on different countries show a pattern in which inequality begins to rise with economic development, after which inequality then declines. The greatest extremes of inequality—with conspicuous opulence appearing alongside the most abject poverty—occur in middle-income countries.

Those countries with the greatest inequality tend to be the middle-income countries—particularly Latin American countries like Peru, Panama, Brazil, or Venezuela. In these countries, it is not uncommon for the bottom fifth to earn only 2 percent of total income, while the top 10 percent may get 40 or even 50 percent of income.

Recent studies by the World Bank and scholars confirm that economic development itself temporarily increases income inequality. Then, as labor's share of national income rises in the mixed economy, inequality is reduced.

We have now concluded the discussion of the measurement of income and wealth inequality in the United States and other countries. We turn next to an analysis of the roots of economic inequality.

How Fared the Poor?

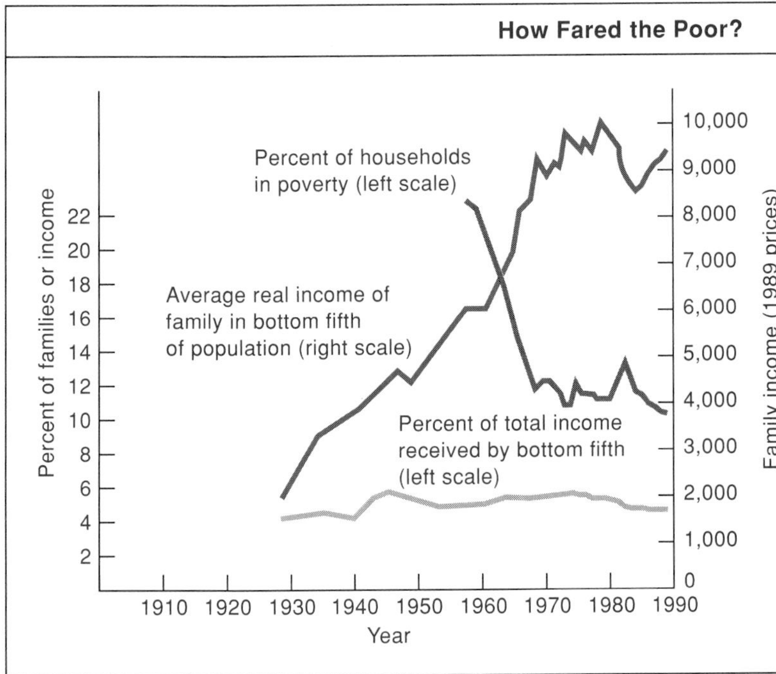

Figure 21-3. Trends in poverty and inequality

The upward-sloping heavy blue line shows the average family income (in constant 1989 prices) of a family in the bottom fifth of the population. Note how sharply it rose from 1929 to 1970, and how incomes of the poor have fallen in the 1980s.

The increase in the absolute incomes of the poor has been mainly due to a rise in average income. The light blue line shows that the share of the bottom fifth of the population has changed little since the late 1940s.

The black line shows the fraction of the population that is below the official poverty line. It shrank sharply during the 1960s, but has risen in the last few years. (Source: U.S. Bureau of the Census.)

B. The Sources of Inequality

One of the most noble aspirations of a modern democracy is to promote equality—equality of opportunity, of participation, and of political freedoms. However, direct attempts to reduce inequality of income have proven controversial because people disagree strenuously about the role of redistributive taxation and welfare programs.

Whether governments should reduce income inequality is a normative issue that economics cannot resolve. But economic analysis can help to uncover the facts so that informed choices can be made. What are the sources of poverty and wealth? How do saving and work respond to different fiscal systems? The answers to such questions will inevitably influence our attitudes toward steps to reduce inequality.

In this section we review the sources of income inequality in a market economy. We focus primarily upon labor and property incomes, the two major categories of income.

Inequality in Labor Income

Labor earnings constitute 80 percent of factor incomes. Even if property incomes were distributed equally, much inequality would remain. Let us begin then by examining the factors that produce inequalities in earnings: differences in abilities and skills of labor, in occupations and intensities of work, in levels of education, and in other factors.

Abilities and Skills

People vary enormously in their abilities—in physical, mental, and temperamental dimensions. However, these personal differences are of little help in explaining the puzzle of income dispersion. Physical traits (such as strength or height or girth) and measured mental traits (such as intelligence quotient or tone perception) explain relatively little of the differences among the earnings of people.

This is not to say that individual abilities matter little. The ability to hit a home run or charm a television audience greatly enhances a person's earning potential. But the skills valued in the marketplace are varied and often difficult to measure. Markets tend to reward willingness to take risks, ambition, luck, strokes of engineering genius, good judgment, and hard work—none of which are easily measured in standardized tests. As Mark Twain might have said, "You don't have to be smart to make money. But you *do* have to know how to make money."

Intensity of Work

The intensity of work varies enormously among individuals. The workaholic may log 70 hours a week on the job, never take a vacation, and postpone retirement indefinitely. An ascetic might work just enough to pay for life's necessities. Differences in income might be great simply because of differences in work effort, yet no one would say that economic opportunity was therefore genuinely unequal.

Differences among Occupations

One important source of income inequality lies in people's occupations. At the low end of the scale we find domestic servants, fast-food personnel, and unskilled service workers. A full-time, year-round employee at McDonald's or at a car wash might earn $8000 a year today.

At the other extreme are the high-earning professionals. What single profession seems to make the most money? In recent years it has without question been medical doctors. Physicians working in medical corporations had median earnings of $155,000 in 1990. They have moved well ahead of lawyers, who had median earnings of $52,000 in 1990.[4]

What is the source of such vast differences among occupations? Part of the disparity comes from the years of training needed to become a doctor or lawyer. Abilities also play a role, for example,

[4] Top New York law firms bill their giant corporate clients at more than $500 per hour. In 1990, top graduates of the best law schools *started out* with the big New York firms at $80,000 per year.

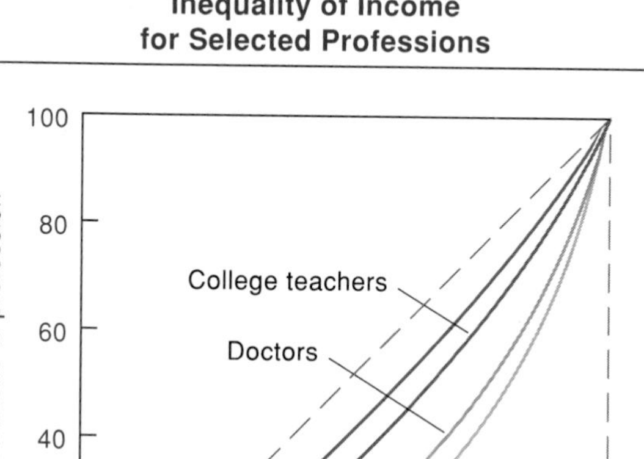

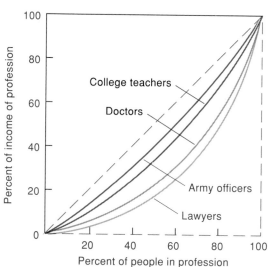

Figure 21-4. Lawyers and doctors show more inequality than salaried professors or army officers

Income inequality is highest in law. How would the curve look for clerical workers? For government janitors? Why would the curve for speculators on the stock exchange be the most unequal of all?

in limiting engineering jobs to those who have some quantitative skills. Some jobs pay more because they are dangerous or unpleasant. And in most cases (recall Chapter 5's discussion of limiting the number of doctors), restricting the supply of its members drives up the income potential of a profession.

Figure 21-4 shows how professions differ in their inequality of earnings.

Differences in Education: Is College Worthwhile?

How do education and training affect lifetime incomes? Are they worth the cost? This question is addressed by the study of **human capital,** which represents investments of time and money in improving the quality of workers through training and education. We hear often of tangible investments. But investment in improving human skills, as economists Theodore Schultz and Gary Becker have emphasized, may benefit society and individuals just as much as investment in plant and equipment.

What is an investment in human capital? When a student goes to college, each year he or she might pay $10,000 in tuition and $16,000 in opportunity costs of earnings forgone. In return for this substantial investment, the earnings of the college graduate might exceed those of a high school graduate by $10,000 per year. The higher earnings are the return on the investment in human capital.

Does college actually pay off? The evidence suggests that it does. Moreover, the returns to a college education have soared dramatically over the last 10 years. Whereas a college graduate earned 25 percent more than a high school graduate with the same background in the late 1970s, a decade later the earnings differential had widened to 75 percent. More and more, in today's service economy of computers and invoices, the skills learned in college are a prerequisite for a high-paying job. A high school dropout is generally at a severe disadvantage in the job market.

Even if you have to borrow at 10 percent interest, put off years of gainful employment, live away from home, and pay for food and books, your lifetime earnings in the occupations that are open only to college graduates will probably more than compensate you for the costs. Recent data show that an 18-year-old male who goes on to graduate from college will earn about $3,100,000 (at 1988 price and income levels) before the age of 65. Those of the same generation who graduate only from high school will earn about $2,100,000. Those who do not finish high school will earn an average of only $1,500,000.

Often, people point to the role of luck in determining economic circumstances. But, as Louis Pasteur remarked, "Chance favors only the mind that is prepared." In a world of rapidly changing technologies, education prepares people to understand and profit from new circumstances.

Other Factors

In addition to ability, occupation, and education, other factors affect the inequality of wage earnings. We saw in Chapter 14 that discrimination and exclusion from certain occupations have played an important role in keeping down the incomes of women and many minority groups.

In addition, the homelife and community experience of children have a major impact on later earnings. Children of the affluent probably don't start life ahead of the poor, but they benefit from their environment at every stage. A child of poverty often experiences crowding, poor nutrition, run-down schools, and overworked teachers. Some believe that the scales are tipped against many inner-city children before they are 10 years old.

Inequalities in Property Income

The greatest disparities in income arise from differences in inherited and acquired wealth. The history of great fortunes—associated with names like Rockefeller, Mellon, Getty, and Ford—shows that differences in wages and personal characteristics are dwarfed by differences in property income.

The Rockefellers and the Gettys are but the smallest splinter atop the pyramid of wealth. At the bottom lie people who enter this world with only a gasp for air and leave their children with no more than a few memories. The poor own few material goods and therefore earn no income on their nonexistent wealth.

It is just such disparities in wealth that have produced the most vitriolic attacks from capitalism's critics. "Property is theft!" wrote the nineteenth-century socialist Pierre Proudhon. Before deciding whether to agree, however, let's examine the sources of differences in wealth.

Inheritance

John D. Rockefeller gained a fortune by shrewd combinations of oil and steel firms. As a consequence, his heirs moved to the top of the pyramid of wealth, status, and power. The progeny of the tycoons of an earlier era are among today's top wealthholders. According to surveys, two-thirds of the top 1 percent of wealthholders in America inherited a substantial fraction of their property.

Saving and Risk Taking

Economic mythology spins tales of modern-day Horatio Algers who toil endlessly, take fantastic risks, save everything, and end up in a fabulous Park Avenue penthouse. To what extent, in fact, does America's accumulated wealth result from people's saving over their life cycle of work and retirement? A recent study by Laurence Kotlikoff and Lawrence Summers suggests that only a small fraction of personal wealth, perhaps 20 percent, can be explained by life-cycle savings. The balance, it appears, comes from other sources, such as inheritances or gifts.

America's 100 Richest People

Source of wealth	Number of persons	Amount of net worth: Billions of dollars	Amount of net worth: Percent
Inheritance	37	48.7	35
Financial acumen	7	9.6	7
Entrepreneurship	56	80.7	58
Of which:			
Oil	9	11.8	9
Real estate	12	13.0	9
Retailing	9	17.1	12
Electronics	4	8.5	6
Candy	4	4.6	3
Other	18	25.7	19
Total	100	139.0	100

Table 21-5. How did the richest Americans reach the summit?

In 1987, 100 Americans had net worth of at least $740 million, according to *Forbes* magazine. Most gained their wealth by entrepreneurship. A minority represent the beneficiaries of *earlier* entrepreneurship (like the Rockefellers). A tiny fraction gained wealth by stock market speculation or by inventing new products. [Source: *Forbes* (Oct. 26, 1987).]

A popular notion is that today's wealth is the reward for yesterday's risk taking. We cannot expect someone to incur great risk—risking millions in drilling oil wells or bringing a new technology to market—without some lure of exceptional reward.

What is the relative importance of different sources of wealth? Table 21-5 displays the experience of the top 100 wealthholders in 1987. These data suggest that entrepreneurship has been the major source of great wealth. Putting together new business organizations (such as oil-drilling companies, shopping center complexes, and even candy-bar firms) has been the surest route to great wealth in a market economy; about one-third of the 100 wealthiest got there primarily by birth.

C. Equality vs. Efficiency: How Much Redistribution?

Faced with the dilemma of poverty in the midst of plenty, all societies take steps to provide for their poorest citizens. But what is given to the poor must come from the non-poor, and that is undoubtedly the major point of resistance to redistributive taxation. In addition, philosophers and economists worry about the impact of redistribution upon the efficiency and morale of a country. In this section, we consider the costs of income redistribution and survey the current system of income maintenance.

The Cost of Equality

Political philosophers over the ages have debated the proper extent of equality. Democratic societies affirm the principle of equality of *political rights*. The United States guarantees the right to vote, trial by jury, free speech and practice of religion, and other constitutional liberties.

In the 1960s, liberal philosophers espoused the view that people should also have equal *economic opportunity*. In other words, all people should play by the same rules on a level playing field. All should have equal access to the best schools and training and jobs. Then discrimination on the basis of race or gender or religion would disappear. Many steps were taken to promote greater equality, but inequalities of opportunity have proven very stubborn, and even America of the 1990s falls far short of the goal of equal economic opportunity.

A third and most far-reaching ideal is equality of *economic outcome*. In this idealistic dream, people would have the same consumption whether they are smart or dull, eager or lazy, lucky or unfortunate. Wages would be the same for doctor and nurse, lawyer and secretary. "From each according to his abilities, to each according to his needs" was one formulation of this philosophy.

Today, even the most radical socialist recognizes that some differences in economic outcome are necessary if the economy is to function efficiently. Without some differential reward for different kinds of work, how can we ensure that people will do the unpleasant as well as the pleasant work, that they will work on dangerous offshore oil derricks as well as in pleasant parks? Insisting on equality of outcomes would severely hamper the functioning of the economy.

Equality vs. Efficiency

In taking steps to redistribute income from the rich to the poor, governments may harm economic efficiency and reduce the amount of national income available to distribute. On the other hand, if equality is an ethical good, it is one worth paying for. The question of how much we are willing to pay in reduced efficiency for greater equity was addressed by Arthur Okun in his "leaky bucket" experiment:

> If we value less inequality, we'll approve when a dollar is taken in a bucket from the very rich and given to the very poor.[5]

But suppose the bucket of redistribution has a leak in it. Suppose only a fraction—maybe one-half—of each dollar in taxes paid by the rich actu-

[5] Arthur M. Okun, *Equality and Efficiency: The Big Tradeoff* (Brookings Institution, Washington, D.C., 1975).

ally reaches the poor. Then redistribution in the name of equity has been at the expense of economic efficiency.

Okun presented a fundamental dilemma. Redistributional measures like the progressive income tax analyzed in Chapter 19 will probably reduce real output by reducing incentives to work and save. As a nation considers its income-distribution policies, it will want to weigh the benefit of greater equality against the costs resulting from a smaller national income.

Economic Costs of Redistribution. We can illustrate Okun's point by using the *income-possibility curve* of Figure 21-5. This graph shows the incomes available to different groups when government programs redistribute income.

We begin by dividing the population in half; the real income of the low-income group is measured on the vertical axis of Figure 21-5 while the income of the upper half is measured on the horizontal axis. At point *A*, which is the pre-redistribution point, no taxes are levied and no transfers are given, so people simply live with their market incomes. In a competitive economy, point *A* will be efficient and the no-redistribution policy maximizes national output.

Redistribution at Cost of Inefficiency

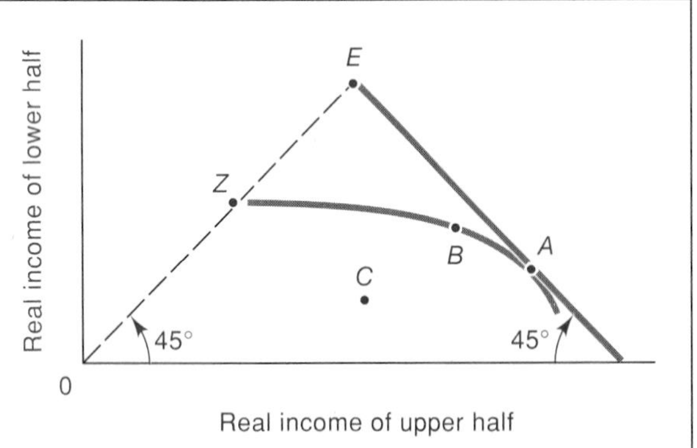

Figure 21-5. Redistributing income may harm economic efficiency

Point *A* marks the most efficient outcome, with maximal GNP. If society could redistribute with no loss of efficiency, the economy would move toward point *E*. Because redistributive programs generally create distortions and efficiency losses, the path of redistribution might move along the blue line *ABZ*. Society must decide how much efficiency to sacrifice to gain greater equality. Why would everyone want to avoid inefficient redistributional programs that take the economy to point *C*?

Unfortunately, at laissez-faire point *A*, the upper-income group receives substantially more income than the lower half. Congress might strive for greater equality by tax and transfer programs, hoping to move toward the point of equal incomes at *E*. If such steps could be taken without reducing GNP, the economy would move along the black line from *A* to *E*. The slope of the *AE* line is −45°, reflecting the assumption about efficiency that every dollar taken from the upper half increases the income of the lower half by exactly $1. Along the −45° line, total national income is constant, indicating that redistributional programs have no impact upon the total size of GNP.

If a country redistributes income by imposing high tax rates on the wealthiest people, their saving and work effort may be reduced or misdirected, with a resulting lower total national output. They may spend more money on tax lawyers, save less for retirement, or invest less in risky innovations. Also, if society puts a guaranteed floor beneath the incomes of the poor, the sting of poverty will be reduced and the poor may work less. All these reactions to redistributive programs reduce the total size of real national income.

In terms of Okun's experiment, we might find that for every $100 of taxation on the rich, the income of the poor increased by only $50, with the rest dissipated in wasted effort or administrative costs. The bucket of redistribution has developed a large leak. Costly redistribution is shown by the *ABZ* curve in Figure 21-5. Here, the hypothetical frontier of real incomes bends away from the −45° line because taxes and transfers produce inefficiencies.

Indeed, experience has shown that in some cases the distortions due to interference can become so great that the attempt to help one social class at the expense of another can end in hurting them both. Or, in the opposite case, an action that looks like it is aimed to benefit the rich ultimately profits everyone.

The experience of socialist countries exemplifies how attempts to equalize incomes by expropriating property from the rich can end up hurting everyone. By prohibiting private ownership of businesses, socialist governments reduced the inequalities that arise from large property incomes. But the reduced incentives to work, accumulate capital, and innovate crippled this radical experiment of "each according to his needs" and impoverished entire countries. By 1990, comparisons of living standards in East and West had convinced many socialist countries that private ownership of business would benefit the living standards of workers as well as capitalists.

How Big Are the Leaks?

Okun characterized our redistributive system of taxes and transfers as a leaky bucket. But just how big are the leaks in the American economy? Is the country closer to Figure 21-5's point *A*, where the leaks are negligible? Or to *B*, where they are substantial? Or to *Z*, where the redistributive bucket is in fact a sieve? To find the answer, we must examine the major inefficiencies induced by high tax rates and by generous income-support programs: administrative costs, damage to work and savings incentives, and socioeconomic costs.

- The government must hire tax collectors to raise revenues and social security accountants to disburse them. These are clear inefficiencies or regrettable necessities, but they are small: the Internal Revenue Service spends only half a penny on administrative costs for each dollar of collected revenues.
- As the tax collector's bite grows larger and larger, might I not become discouraged and end up working less? Recall from Chapter 19's Laffer curve that tax rates might conceivably be so high that total revenues are actually lower than they would be at more modest tax rates. Empirical evidence, however, suggests that the damage of taxes on work effort is limited. We saw in Chapter 14 that the labor supply curve may actually be backward-bending, indicating that a tax on wages might increase rather than decrease work effort. Few studies find the effect of taxes on work effort to be substantial. More important, perhaps, are the impacts of welfare and transfer systems on poor people, a controversial topic to which we will turn shortly.
- Perhaps the most important potential leakage from the revenue bucket is the savings component. Some believe that high tax rates discourage saving and investment. The evidence for the United States lends little support to this view. If redistributive taxation were a significant drag on saving and investment, we should detect the effect in the aggregate data. In 1929, when federal tax rates were low, the nation saved and invested 16 percent of GNP; in 1973, with all the allegedly onerous taxes, the United States still saved and invested 16 percent of GNP. And, after the major tax cuts of the early 1980s, the national savings rate fell to the lowest levels since the Great Depression. Whatever are recent trends, the potential for an adverse effect of high taxes on saving is present and will be carefully monitored in coming years.
- Some claim that the leaks cannot be found in the cost statistics of the economist; instead, the costs of equality are seen in attitudes rather than in dollars. Is the business ethic downplayed? Are young people so turned off by the prospect of high taxes that they turn on to drugs and idleness? Is the welfare system leading to a permanent underclass, a society of people who are trapped in a culture of dependency?
- Some people criticize the entire notion of costly redistribution, arguing as follows: Poverty is rooted in malnourishment in the early years, broken families, illiteracy at home, poor education, and lack of job training. Poverty begets poverty; the vicious cycle of malnutrition, poor education, drug dependency, low productivity, and low incomes leads to yet another generation of poor families. Programs providing health care and adequate food for poor families [such as the federal Women, Infants, and Children (WIC) Program] will *increase* productivity and efficiency rather than decrease output. By breaking the vicious cycle of poverty today, we will be raising the skills, human capital, and productivity of the children of poverty tomorrow. Programs to break the cycle of poverty are investments that require resources today to increase productivity tomorrow.

Adding Up the Leaks

When all the leaks are added up, how big are they? Okun argued that the leaks are small, particularly when funds for redistributive programs are drawn from the tap of a broad-based income tax. Others disagree strenuously, pointing to the dizzying array of tax loopholes and transfer programs as confusing and destructive of economic efficiency.

What is the reality? While much research has

been undertaken on the cost of redistribution, the truth has proved elusive. A cautious verdict is that there are but modest losses to economic efficiency from redistributional programs of the kind used in the United States today. The efficiency costs of redistribution appear small as compared to the economic costs of poverty in malnutrition, health, lost job skills, and human misery.

Antipoverty Policies: Programs and Criticisms

If a country decides to declare war on poverty, what weapons can it deploy? Have these programs produced counterproductive responses in the low-income population? What reforms could ameliorate the problems of today's welfare system? We address these issues in the remainder of this chapter.

The Rise of the Welfare State

We noted earlier in this chapter that the early classical economists believed the distribution of income was unalterable. They argued that attempts to alleviate poverty by government interventions in the economy were foolish endeavors that would simply end up reducing total national income.

By the end of the nineteenth century, however, political leaders in Western Europe took steps that marked a historic turning point in the economic role of government. Bismarck in Germany, Gladstone and Disraeli in Britain, followed by Franklin Roosevelt in the United States introduced a new concept of government responsibility for the welfare of the populace. This was the **welfare state,** in which the government modifies market forces to protect individuals against specified contingencies and to guarantee people a minimum standard of living.

Important provisions in the welfare state include public pensions, accident and sickness insurance, unemployment insurance, health insurance, food and housing programs, family allowances, and income supplements for certain groups of people. These policies were introduced gradually from 1880 through to the modern era, although some programs have not been universally provided (e.g., unlike many countries, the United States does not offer universal national health insurance).

Income-Security Programs

What are the major income-security programs in the welfare state today? For the United States, they are the following.

After people rediscovered hunger in this most affluent of societies in the 1960s, the United States instituted the *food-stamp program.* Under this program, low-income families receive stamps or coupons that permit them to purchase food at a small fraction of its market cost.

In every state there exists some *welfare assistance* for the destitute. These programs offer *in-kind* aid (that is, direct aid in food, clothing, or housing) as well as straight *income transfers.* The most visible and controversial form of welfare assistance is AFDC (Aid to Families with Dependent Children), which supports poor parents with small children. Governments also provide income security for the aged, blind, and disabled who demonstrate a need for aid. One of the most rapidly growing programs is *Medicaid,* which provides medical benefits for low-income families.

There are numerous other income-security programs, some of which are more or less targeted at poor families. Housing programs, social security, and disability benefits tend to bolster the incomes of the poor more than those of the population as a whole—even though they are not specifically designed for low-income families.

How much do all federal programs add up to in terms of budget expenditures? Table 21-6 shows the level of federal spending for income-security programs for both the general population and poor households. All federal poverty programs today amount to 10 percent of the total federal budget.

Even though the federal programs to assist the poor form a relatively modest part of the budget, they have dulled the sharp edge of poverty. They have provided a financial safety net that has eradicated much of the grinding poverty of earlier periods.

Two Views of Poverty

Social scientists put forth a wide variety of proposals to cure or alleviate poverty. The different approaches often reflect differing views of the roots of poverty. Proponents of strong government action see poverty as the result of social and economic conditions over which the poor have little control.

Federal Programs for the Poor, 1992		
Program	**Amount ($, billion)**	**Percent of total federal spending**
All income-security programs	**614.3**	**42.5**
General programs	**468.2**	**32.4**
Social security	288.6	
Medicare	113.8	
Other (veterans, other retirement)	38.6	
Unemployment compensation	27.2	
Programs for the poor	**146.1**	**10.1**
Medicaid	59.8	
Other income supplements	15.3	
Food and nutrition	30.2	
Housing assistance	19.9	
Aid to families with dependent children	15.1	
International development and aid	5.8	

Table 21-6. Most federal income-security dollars go for general programs like social security

Federal programs for income security are largely concentrated on the population as a whole, rather than on the poor. Only $30 billion is spent on programs that increase poor families' incomes. Note as well the high cost of health programs for both the poor and the non-poor. (Source: Office of Management and Budget, *Budget of the United States Government*, 1992.)

They stress malnutrition, poor schools, broken families, discrimination, lack of job opportunities, and a dangerous environment as central determinants of the fate of the poor. If you hold this view, you might well believe that government bears a responsibility to alleviate poverty—either by providing income to the poor or by correcting the conditions that produce poverty.

A second view holds that poverty grows out of maladaptive individual behavior—behavior that is the responsibility of individuals and is properly cured by the poor themselves. In earlier centuries, laissez-faire apologists held that the poor were shiftless, lazy, or drunk; as a charity worker wrote almost a century ago, "Want of employment . . . is, as often as not, [caused by] drink." Sometimes the government itself is blamed for breeding dependency upon a patchwork of government programs that squelch individual initiative. Critics who hold these views advocate that the government should cut back on welfare programs so that people will develop their own resources.

The poverty debate was succinctly summarized by the eminent social scientist William Wilson:

> Liberals have traditionally emphasized how the plight of disadvantaged groups can be related to the problems of the broader society, including problems of discrimination and social class subordination. . . . Conservatives, in contrast, have traditionally stressed the importance of different group values and competitive resources in accounting for the experiences of the disadvantaged.[6]

Few analysts of the problems of poverty and the welfare system fall into either of these two extreme categories. Nonetheless, much of today's debate can be better understood if these two views and their implications are factored into the political equation.

Incentive Problems of the Poor

One of the major obstacles faced by poor families is that the current welfare system severely reduces the incentives of low-income adults to seek work. If a person on welfare gets a job, the government will trim back food stamps, welfare payments, and rent subsidies. We might say that poor people face high marginal "tax rates" (or, more accurately, "benefit-reduction rates") because welfare benefits are sharply reduced as earnings rise.

The following calculation for a family of three (mother and two children) living in Pennsylvania

[6] William Julius Wilson, "Cycles of Deprivation and the Underclass Debate," *Social Service Review* (December 1985), pp. 541–559.

will illustrate the problem. We choose the example of Pennsylvania because the AFDC benefits in that state are close to the national average. In 1987, if the mother did not have a job, the family would receive AFDC benefits of $4584 and food stamps worth $1549, for a total disposable income of $6133. Suppose the parent takes a full-time job, earning $8000 a year. She would lose all the AFDC benefits, but would retain $1306 worth of food stamps. After child-care and work-related expenses of $2400, disposable income would equal $6906.

The net gain from taking this $8000 job would be a gain in disposable income of $773 a year; the increase in disposable income is only 9.7 percent of the increase in earnings. If we consider benefit reductions as a kind of "tax," the tax rates on the working poor can easily reach 90 percent—far above the rate faced by the richest Americans and surely a major disincentive to the avid pursuit of work.

One of the harshest criticisms of the current welfare system is that it provides incentives for family dissolution at a time when intact families are already an endangered species. Most states refuse to provide welfare support to a family in which both parents are present, reasoning that the second parent can be expected to support the children. In such cases, the parent (usually the father) of a family on welfare may find that his family's income rises sharply if he leaves home and disappears. Only then can his wife and children continue to get welfare support.

The Negative Income Tax

Contemplating the perverse effects of the current welfare system on economic efficiency and the social structure of the country, economists of varied political persuasions have concluded that the welfare system needs a fundamental reform. Conservatives like Milton Friedman of Chicago and liberals like James Tobin of Yale agree that it will be both cheaper and more humane to replace or supplement the incoherent set of income-support programs with a single unified program of cash assistance.

This reform, analyzed and supported by many economists, is sometimes called the **negative income tax.** Other plans with different and more appealing names have been put forth over the years, but most of them share the goal of creating a uniform, national income-support program that maintains sufficient economic incentives for poor people to work.

How It Works. The basic notion of a negative income tax is simple. When I make $25,000 a year, I pay positive income taxes (as seen in Table 19-3). When I earn an extra thousand dollars, I pay extra taxes of $150, leaving me $850 of additional disposable income. Thus the incentive to earn more is preserved.

Next consider a poor family earning, say, $8000 in 1990. The Congress might decide that such a family deserves an income above $8000, especially if it has earned its $8000 by work and if the family has small children to support. The government wants to provide further income support. Put differently, the family should not pay taxes on its income but should receive a *negative* income tax in the form of an income supplement.

The problem is how to continue to provide government income support without hurting the family's incentives to work. The way to do this is to provide a basic allowance and then permit the family to keep a significant portion of any earnings. By this reasoning, just as people with high incomes can keep most of their earnings if they earn more money, similarly a poor family could keep much of its additional earnings if a family member gets a job.

Possible Formula. How might a negative income tax work in practice? Each household would be provided with a basic allowance, say $4500 for a family of four. The family would then keep its extra earnings while the basic allowance would be reduced. If the benefit-reduction rate was 60 percent, then for every $100 of extra earnings, the government payment would be reduced by $60. The family's net income would therefore rise by $40 for each $100 of extra earnings.

Table 21-7 shows a hypothetical negative income tax with a basic allowance of $4500 and a "tax rate" or benefit-reduction rate of 50 percent. This example shows that the government can simultaneously support the poorest families and maintain an incentive for people to seek gainful employment. Compare this approach with that of the existing welfare system, examined above, to see how the

Possible Formula for Negative Income Tax

Market earnings ($)	Algebraic tax (+ if tax; – if benefits received) ($)	After-tax income ($)
0	– 4,500	4,500
4,000	– 2,500	6,500
7,000	– 1,000	8,000
8,000	– 500	8,500
9,000	0	9,000
10,000	+ 500	9,500

Table 21-7. Negative income tax sets minimum-income standards, preserving incentives and efficiency

Under a negative income tax plan, poor people receive income support from the government—in essence, getting negative taxes. The plan in the table starts with a "basic allowance" of $4500 and then reduces benefits (or "taxes income") at the rate of 50 percent of any earnings. Under this plan, incentives to work are maintained. As the last column shows, after-tax income rises significantly when the family increases its market income.

current system destroys incentives while the negative income tax would motivate people to look for work.

In the design of a negative income tax, crucial economic and social questions arise: Should the program include single persons along with families? Should supported persons be required to work (a system known as "workfare")? Should college students be eligible for benefits? And, most important, should the support levels be minimal so that welfare provides a bare pittance, thereby interfering minimally with work incentives and keeping the welfare rolls small? Or should the negative income tax be generous, greatly supplementing incomes at or above the poverty line but risking major disincentive effects and swelling the welfare rolls?

Experimental Evidence. Critics of the negative income tax argue that it would cost a great deal of money and undermine the work ethic. To assess these criticisms, economists helped design an impressive set of real-world experiments to measure the effects of a negative income tax on people's behavior.

The *negative income tax experiments* involved several thousand families in New Jersey, Indiana, Seattle, and Denver. The experiments divided a randomly selected group of families into "control" groups that would receive no special treatment and "experimental" groups that would live under a negative income tax plan for a few years. The central question was how people would react to income supplements such as those sketched in Table 21-7.

These informative experiments showed that families in the more generous plans (say, those obtaining 100 percent of the poverty line as the basic allowance) reduced their hours of work markedly—by as much as 15 percent. When extrapolated to the entire population, this work reduction—the leak in Okun's redistributive bucket—would reduce national output by 15 to 30 percent of the measured budget cost of the program. On the other hand, experiments with smaller benefit levels produced much smaller reductions in the work effort of the affected people.

What are the ultimate lessons of the negative income tax experiments? Are the efficiency losses large or small? Those who care more about the poor than about economic efficiency find much justice in a generous negative income tax program. By contrast, those primarily concerned with efficiency and who hold the poor responsible for their own economic condition argue for curbing existing welfare programs.

How has the electorate responded to the tug-of-war between efficiency and redistribution? Since about 1975, cash assistance to low-income families has been steadily reduced. A clear message about the responsibility of people to provide for themselves came in the 1988 Welfare Reform Act, which required many welfare recipients to work or to enter training programs. Faced with the alternative approaches to poverty, America has moved away from the carrots of government assistance and toward the sticks of market necessity.

SUMMARY

A. Measurement of Inequality

1. In the last century, the classical economists believed that inequality was a universal constant, unchangeable by public policy. This view does not stand up to scrutiny. Poverty has made a glacial retreat over the last few decades; absolute incomes for those in the bottom part of the income distribution have risen sharply.
2. The Lorenz curve is a convenient device for measuring the spreads or inequalities of income distribution. It shows what percentage of total income goes to the poorest 1 percent of the population, to the poorest 10 percent, to the poorest 95 percent, and so forth.
3. Poverty is essentially a relative notion. In the United States, poverty was defined in terms of the adequacy of spending on food in the early 1960s. By this standard of measured income, little progress has been made in the last decade.
4. The distribution of American income today appears to be less unequal than in the early part of this century or than in less developed countries now. But it still shows a considerable measure of inequality and even a slight increase of inequality over the last decade. Wealth is even more unequally distributed than is income, both in the United States and in other capitalist economies.

B. The Sources of Inequality

5. To explain the inequality in income distribution, we can look separately at labor income and property income. Labor earnings vary because of differences in abilities and in intensities of work (both hours and effort), and because occupational earnings differ, due to divergent amounts of human capital, among other factors.
6. Property incomes are more unevenly distributed than labor earnings, largely because of the great disparities in wealth. Inheritance helps the children of the wealthy begin ahead of the average person; only a small fraction of America's wealth can be accounted for by life-cycle savings. Entrepreneurship appears prominently as a source of the net worth of the 100 richest Americans.

C. Equality vs. Efficiency: How Much Redistribution?

7. Political philosophers write of three types of equality: (*a*) equality of political rights, such as the right to vote; (*b*) equality of opportunity, providing equal access to jobs, education, and other social systems; and (*c*) equality of outcome, whereby people are guaranteed equal incomes or consumptions. Whereas the first two types of equality are increasingly accepted in most advanced democracies like the United States, equality of outcome is extremely controversial and unacceptable to many.
8. Equality has costs as well as benefits; the costs show up as drains from

Okun's "leaky bucket." That is, attempts to reduce income inequality by progressive taxation or welfare payments may harm economic incentives to work or save and may thereby reduce the size of national output. Potential leakages are administrative costs and reduced hours of work or savings rates.

9. Major programs to alleviate poverty are welfare payments, food stamps, Medicaid, and a group of smaller or less targeted programs. As a whole, these programs are criticized because they impose high benefit-reduction rates (or marginal "tax" rates) on low-income families when families begin to earn wages or other income.

10. Prominent among proposals to reform the income-support system for the poor stands the negative income tax. This would replace the dizzying array of existing programs with a unified, cash income supplement. The supplement would be reduced (that is, income would be "taxed") at a moderate rate (say one-third or one-half), so that low-income families would have a significant incentive to seek market employment.

CONCEPTS FOR REVIEW

Measurement of inequality
trends of income distribution
Lorenz curve of income and wealth
human capital
labor and property income
relative roles of luck, life-cycle savings, risk taking, inheritance
sources of inequality

Analysis and policies to combat poverty
poverty
welfare state
equality: political, of opportunity, of outcome
Okun's "leaky bucket"
equality vs. efficiency
income-possibility curve: ideal and realistic cases
income-support programs
negative income tax: basic allowance, tax rate
benefit-reduction rate (marginal tax rate)

QUESTIONS FOR DISCUSSION

1. Let each member of the class anonymously write down on a card an estimate of his or her family's annual income. From these, draw up a frequency table showing the distribution of incomes. What is the median income? The mean income?
2. Many people believe that incomes should be more equally distributed. How unequal do *you* think incomes should be for people of different abilities? If you desired less inequality, what methods would you propose to equalize incomes? (Choose between redistributive taxation and government transfers.)
3. What effect would the following have on the Lorenz curve of after-tax incomes? (Assume that the taxes are spent by the government on a representative slice of GNP.)
   (a) A proportional income tax (i.e., one taxing all incomes at the same rate)
   (b) A progressive income tax (i.e., one taxing high incomes more heavily than low incomes)
   (c) A 5 percent national sales tax
   (d) A deep recession
   Draw five Lorenz curves to illustrate the original income distribution and the income distribution after each action, (*a*) to (*d*).
4. Discuss the three different kinds of equality. Why might equality of opportunity not lead to equality of outcome? Should persons of different abilities be given the same access to jobs and education? What might be done to ensure equality of outcome? How might such steps lead to economic inefficiencies?
5. Consider two ways of supplementing the income of the poor: (*a*) cash assistance (say, $500 per month) and (*b*) categorical benefits such as subsidized food, medical care, or housing. List the pros

and cons of using each strategy. Can you explain why the United States tends to use mainly strategy (*b*)? Do you agree?

6. Instead of using the Lorenz curve to measure inequality, calculate the area between the actual curve of inequality and the curve of equal incomes (i.e., the gray shaded region in Figure 21-1). Two times this ratio is called the "Gini coefficient."

   What is the Gini coefficient for a society with absolute equality of income? For one in which one person gets all the income? Estimate the Gini coefficients for the different Lorenz curves in Figure 21-2.

7. In a country called Econoland, there are 10 people. Their incomes (in thousands) are $3, $6, $2, $8, $4, $9, $1, $5, $7, and $5. Construct a table of income quintiles like Table 21-2. Plot a Lorenz curve. Calculate the Gini coefficient defined in question 6.

8. The following table shows the per capita incomes of the 10 most populous countries for 1990. These are converted from the national currencies into U.S. dollars by using "purchasing-power" exchange rates that measure actual buying power.

Per Capita Incomes, 1990

United States	$18,530	Nigeria	$370
Japan	15,760	Pakistan	350
Soviet Union	3,470	India	300
Brazil	2,020	China	290
Indonesia	450	Bangladesh	160

Source: World Bank, *World Development Report, 1990*, updated by authors.

   Use an encyclopedia to obtain the populations of each country. Then, assuming that each person in a given country received exactly that country's per capita GNP, construct a Lorenz curve for the 10 countries. Does this Lorenz curve show more or less inequality than the Lorenz curves for individual countries shown in Figure 21-2(*a*)?

9. Many people continue to argue about what form assistance for the poor should take. One school says, "Give people money and let them buy health services and the foods they need." The other school says, "If you give money for milk to the poor, they will spend it on beer. Your dollar goes further in alleviating malnourishment and disease if you provide the services in kind. The dollar that you earn may be yours to spend, but society's income-support dollar is a dollar that society has the right paternalistically to channel directly to its targets."

   The argument of the first school might rest on demand theory: let each household decide how to maximize its utility on a limited budget. Chapter 6 shows why this argument might be right. But what if the parents' utility includes mainly beer and lottery tickets and no milk or clothing for the children? Might you agree with the second view? From your own personal experience and reading, which of these two views do you think is more accurate? Explain your reasoning.

10. One of the central dilemmas in designing a negative income tax is the necessity to raise benefit-reduction (or tax) rates when basic allowances increase. Look again at Table 21-7, and consider different constant-tax-rate programs that have a break-even point (or zero-tax point) at $9000. What is the benefit-reduction rate when the basic allowance is $2700? $7200? $9000?

    Does the rise of the tax rate as the basic allowance increases suggest that there will be increasing inefficiency as equality is pursued more vigorously—that Okun's bucket will become leakier as antipoverty programs become more egalitarian? Does this suggest why Figure 21-5 curves inward as more income is transferred from rich to poor?

CHAPTER 22

THE WINDS OF CHANGE: THE TRIUMPH OF THE MARKET

> Come writers and critics
> Who prophesize with your pen
> And keep your eyes wide
> The chance won't come again
> And don't speak too soon
> For the wheel's still in spin . . .
> For the times they are a-changin'.
>
> Bob Dylan

Modern economics focuses primarily on the workings of a market economy like the United States, and the effectiveness of the market is today increasingly appreciated throughout the world. Nowhere is the allure of the market stronger than in socialist countries that have forcibly repressed the spontaneous decentralized exchange of private firms and households. At the end of the 1980s, the walls of the centrally planned economies of Eastern Europe were knocked down, and those countries began the swift transition to market economies. The lesson of recent history is that economic ideals can break down walls and topple governments.

These dramatic events make headlines today. But what are the historical and intellectual roots of socialist systems? We cannot ignore nonmarket economic systems and criticisms of capitalism. During this century, Marxism claimed the allegiance of nearly 2 billion people, while socialism has been championed by many of the great Western thinkers. A half-century ago, in the midst of a great depression and armies of unemployed workers, many economists and political leaders were haunted by the thought that capitalism was doomed. What were the events that led to the rejection of the Marxist model and the triumph of the market? This chapter is devoted to this question.

A. Evolution of Economic Thought

We begin with an excursion into the history of economic thought, analyzing the thinking of the great economists of the past. Once you understand how economic theories developed in the past, you will be better prepared for the modifications today's theories will surely undergo in the future.[1]

[1] Good introductions to the history of economics are Robert L. Heilbroner, *The Worldly Philosophers,* 6th ed. (Simon and Schuster, Inc., New York, 1987), or Mark Blaug, *Economic Theory in Retrospect,* 4th ed. (Cambridge University Press, London, 1985). The standard advanced reference is the posthumous classic, Joseph A. Schumpeter, *History of Economic Analysis* (Oxford University Press, New York, 1957).

The Growth of Mainstream Economics

Early Roots

Economic thinking began with Aristotle and continued through the teachings of the medieval Scholastics. These early stirrings dealt largely with normative doctrines such as the idea of a "just price," which purported to tell the genuine value of a commodity. The Scholastics rejected interest on loans as unjust "usury," and prohibitions of usury survive today as interest-rate ceilings in many states and countries.

Perhaps the first systematic thinkers were the *mercantilists* of the seventeenth and eighteenth centuries. This group of pamphleteers devised policies designed to buttress the military and economic might of emerging nation-states. Especially powerful in England and France, they espoused the accumulation of gold and silver and promoted protectionist steps like Britain's Navigation Acts, which eventually kindled the American Revolution.

Mercantilist practices spawned numerous ideas. David Hume (1711–1776) propounded his brilliant gold-flow mechanism (see Chapter 39) to demonstrate how the mercantilists' gold inflow would eventually end up raising prices rather than output. The group known as the *Physiocrats* reacted powerfully to the excesses of the French mercantilists. The Physiocrats pronounced agriculture the only source of economic surplus and attempted to remove trade restrictions from corn and other sectors. A remarkable depiction of the economy as a circular flow, still used in today's texts (see page 39), was made by Quesnay, Louis XIV's court physician. He stressed that the different elements of the economy are as integrally tied together as are the blood vessels of the body.

Classical Economics: Adam Smith, the Prophet of Laissez-Faire

The family tree of economics, shown on the back endpaper, depicts the lineage of modern economics. The early influences converge in the publication by Adam Smith (1723–1790) of *The Wealth of Nations* in 1776, which marks the birthdate of modern economics.

After beginning his career as a moral philosopher, Smith turned to the study of political economy, which culminated in his classic work. Smith's contributions were legion. He discussed the foundation of prices and the distribution of income, analyzed various theories of wages, and performed one of the earliest empirical studies of inflation.

But of all his contributions to economic analysis, the boldest was his recognition that the market mechanism is a self-regulating natural order. He saw that the price system organizes the behavior of people and does so in an automatic fashion without central direction. To mercantilists who were eager to interfere with markets, Smith in effect said:

> You think that you are improving the economy with your well-meaning laws and regulations. You are not. In a laissez-faire system, the oil of self-interest will keep the economic gears turning in a miraculous fashion. No planners are necessary; no government need issue edicts to control prices or mandate production. The market will solve all our problems.

Adam Smith was a worldly student of history, politics, and economics. He drew upon his vast storehouse of knowledge, rather than on abstract reasoning, when he wrote his famous words about the invisible hand:

> Every individual . . . neither intends to promote the general interest, nor knows how much he is promoting it. He intends only his own security, his own gain. And he is in this led by an invisible hand to promote an end which was no part of his intention. By pursuing his own interest he frequently promotes that of society more effectually than when he really intends to promote it.

Smith was unable to prove the essence of his invisible-hand doctrine. Indeed, until the 1940s no one knew how to prove, or even to state properly, the kernel of truth in this proposition about the efficiency of perfectly competitive markets (recall our analysis in Chapter 17).

Smith's approach, instead, was to prove by example. He enumerated countless cases of government follies. He mined ancient and contemporary history for illustrations of how well-meaning government interferences in economic affairs had had harmful effects upon nations. His masterpiece is a practical handbook that might be entitled *How to Make the GNP Grow*. And at the same time, it lays the foundations for modern analysis of supply and demand.

Spirit of the Bourgeois Age. But, of course, its many virtues are not enough to explain why *The Wealth of Nations* had so dramatic an impact on the century to follow. Just as important was the fact that the rising business classes needed a spokesperson for their interests. Smith provided the laissez-faire ideology that served their purposes, offering intellectual support for free enterprise with minimal government interference.

This does not imply that Smith was a flunky for the business classes. Actually, he had a healthy distrust of business owners. He wrote, for example, "People of the same trade seldom meet together, even for merriment and diversion, but the conversation ends in a conspiracy against the public, or in some contrivance to raise prices."

Smith was definitely on the side of the common people. But his advocacy of laissez-faire was derived from his conviction that government regulation would produce inefficiency and high prices and would hurt consumers. To replace monopolistic businesses with government regulation of the economy would, he thought, probably make a bad situation worse.

Smith's eclectic and pragmatic views ushered in the Industrial Revolution and the golden age of capitalism.

Classical Economics: Malthus and Ricardo

In the half-century after *The Wealth of Nations* appeared, the law of diminishing returns was discovered. Ironically, just as the Industrial Revolution in the West was offsetting the dire workings of that dismal law, the Reverend T. R. Malthus (1766–1834) enunciated the *iron law of wages,* holding that population growth will inevitably drive workers' wages down to subsistence levels.

The central figure of the age, however, was David Ricardo (1772–1823), from whose thinking both neoclassical and modern economics derive. Ricardo never went to college. Born to an affluent family, he was cut off by his father with £800 for having married outside his Jewish faith. Within 12 years, he retired from being a stockbroker with a nest egg in the millions.

Once established and affluent, he chanced to read Adam Smith. Ricardo believed that there were basic errors in Smith's microeconomic analysis and gaps in his macroeconomic writings, and was persuaded to write his *Principles of Political Economy and Taxation* (1817), which secured his fame.

One of Ricardo's contributions lay in a thorough analysis of the nature of economic rent—a theory that survives almost intact today in the form seen in Chapter 16. He presented a careful analysis of the labor theory of value (of which more is to come in our analysis of Marxian theories). His analysis of the burden of the public debt is an apt warning for the 1990s.

In addition, Ricardo analyzed the patterns of international trade. He proposed a rudimentary version of the law of comparative advantage, which holds that nations should import or export according to their relative (rather than absolute) costs. But his major accomplishment was his analysis of the laws of income distribution in a capitalist economy.

Stagnant Wage Predictions and Class Conflict. For a full half-century, from 1820 to 1870, Ricardo kept economists and statesmen hypnotized. Yet, like Malthus, he bet on the wrong horse of diminishing returns just when the technological advances of the Industrial Revolution were outpacing that law.

Ricardo's vision was that rents would rise and land would form the bottleneck to economic growth. In the century to come, in fact, landowners would wither away in importance, and capitalists would replace them as barons of the economic order.

For Ricardo, the law of distribution was the most important part of economic theory. He studied the distribution of the national product among the major classes of society: wages for workers, profits for capitalists, and rents for landowners. With a total social product limited by diminishing returns, Ricardo emphasized that what was gained by one social class had to be taken away from another one. Ricardo presented an autumnal view of capitalism—of an economy on its way to an inevitable rendezvous with stagnation—that attracted both intellectuals and the general public, both capitalists and socialists, over the next century.

No wonder the capitalists liked Ricardo. They could find quotations in his work to prove that trade unions and reforms can do little for the masses.

No wonder the socialists liked Ricardo. They found in him a proof that capitalism would have to be destroyed if workers were to win their rightful share of national output.

Decadence in Classical Economics. Historians of science observe that the progress of science is discontinuous. New schools of thought rise, spread their influence, and convince skeptics.

But schools, like people, are subject to hardening of the arteries. Students learn the embalmed truth from their teachers and sacred textbooks. The imperfections in the orthodox doctrines are ignored or glossed over as unimportant.

Decadence and senility set in. Thus, John Stuart Mill, an outstanding economist of the mid-nineteenth century, could write in his classic, *Principles of Political Economy:* "Happily, there is nothing in the laws of Value which remains for the present and any future writer to clear up. . . ."

Classical economics had grown stale. The time had come for new blood.

The Great Schism. A century ago the family tree of economics branched. One branch grew from Karl Marx's *Capital* (1867, 1885, 1894) and his earlier writings. This line, important for understanding the economic organization of socialist countries, will be analyzed in section B of this chapter. The other branch continued the tradition of Smith and Ricardo, through the neoclassical thinkers and Keynesian economics to the present-day era of modern mainstream economics.

Neoclassical Economics

Classical writers emphasized costs to the neglect of demand. They were in effect working with horizontal supply curves and ignoring the role of demand curves. Around 1870, three scholars independently laid the foundation for modern economics by devising an analysis that could synthesize both demand elements and cost elements. They were W. Stanley Jevons (1835–1882) in England, Carl Menger (1840–1921) in Austria, and Léon Walras (1834–1910) in Switzerland.

The key element in the neoclassical revolution was to understand how consumer preferences (called "utility") enter into the demand for commodities. The neoclassical economists provided the missing link in a complete theory of the market mechanism by showing that demand depends upon marginal utility. (A modern version of the neoclassical theory of utility forms the basis of the theory of demand derived in Chapter 6.)

Finally, Walras discovered how to analyze the economy as a whole—as a simultaneous general equilibrium of all the labor, land, and product markets. The late Joseph Schumpeter (1883–1950) used to say that of all great economists, surely Walras was the greatest—for it was he who discovered how all markets interact in a general equilibrium.

Welfare Economics and Policy Concerns

Ever since Adam Smith analyzed the harmful effects of government regulation of the market, economists have devised technical tools that could measure the losses that arise from misplaced government interferences with a competitive equilibrium; important innovations were the concepts of consumer surplus devised by Alfred Marshall and allocational efficiency introduced by Vilfredo Pareto. But neoclassical economists were not all devotees of laissez-faire. Most of the great economists have been critical of capitalism's inequality. Early in this century, Cambridge economist A. C. Pigou emphasized the case against laissez-faire and argued that government is necessary to mitigate inequality, offset monopoly distortions, and correct for pollution and other externalities.

Even as economics became more "scientific," it never lost its interest in policy. Most of the great economists tell us in their autobiographies that they became economists to help improve the world. But, however much the great economists wanted to bring about a more just economic order, they insisted that plans for alternative economic systems be practical.

A fascinating biography of a radical is that of the great Scandinavian economist Knut Wicksell (1851–1926). Wicksell was a counterculture bohemian who believed in birth control in the 1870s, when that was heresy. As the Czar's army stood on the Swedish borders, Wicksell disregarded the prevalent nationalism of the day and advised his fellow citizens to dismantle their army.

Though he never hesitated to speak out on behalf of unpopular causes, in economic issues Wicksell was a hard-headed realist who criticized utopian socialist ideas. His practical reform proposals anticipated the modern Swedish welfare state, with its income-redistribution programs.

Today as well, the giants of modern economics keep one eye on economic analysis and the other upon the policy implications of their theoretical studies. Economists of the late twentieth century study government deficits, the money supply, the environment, and poverty not only because they are fascinated by economic behavior. They also search endlessly for ways that the government can promote equity and economic efficiency.

The Keynesian Revolution

In the years after World War I, economics made great strides in describing and analyzing the economic world of developed and developing regions. One enormous hole, however, still remained, for neoclassical economics lacked a well-developed macroeconomics to match its microeconomics.

Finally, with the Great Depression came the breakthrough in the *General Theory of Employment, Interest, and Money* (1936) by John Maynard Keynes. Economics would never be the same. Keynes' breakthrough mortally wounded the belief in Say's Law (which held overproduction to be impossible). The neoclassical theories of money and the price level earlier developed by Alfred Marshall (1842–1924) and Yale's Irving Fisher (1867–1947) were given a more fruitful restatement in terms of the Keynesian concepts of the demand for money. And the insights and challenges of the Keynesian revolution have inspired a new generation of theorists to try to understand why wages and prices tend to be sticky, why nominal variables like money have real impacts, and how government fiscal and monetary policies can affect the macroeconomy.

Mainstream Economics

As we move on from the Keynesian revolution, we encounter the primary subject of this book, the modern mainstream economics that prevails in the mixed capitalist economies of North America, Western Europe, and Japan, and that is now taking root in formerly socialist Eastern Europe. As economic understanding improved in both microeconomics and macroeconomics, performance in the mixed economy benefited. The era since World War II has witnessed a growth in world output and living standards unmatched in recorded history.

But we should not glorify past achievements. The advanced industrial economies have not attained economic nirvana. They cannot achieve stable prices and full employment; poverty is on the rise; rapid growth threatens the ecological balance of our planet; affluence has its peril in high dependency upon oil imports from the unstable Persian Gulf region.

This sobering reminder of the ailments of a mixed economy should make us sensitive to the critiques of mainstream economics that have prevailed in the past and will undoubtedly continue to flourish in the future.

Modern Critiques

The critics of modern mainstream economics range from dissenters who question small points here or there to those who reject the entire logical structure. We concentrate here on the major non-Marxist critics, reserving Marxist thought for later in this chapter.

Chicago School

Starting at the right end of the political spectrum, we encounter first a group of *libertarians*—those who emphasize the central importance of personal freedom in economic and political affairs. These modern-day apostles of laissez-faire and the minimal state include primarily economists associated with the University of Chicago: Frank Knight, Henry Simons, and Milton Friedman, along with Austrian-born economist Friedrich Hayek.

The libertarians remind us of the accomplishments of the market mechanism and warn us of the penalties falling upon any society that ignores the market's guiding hand. In reading their works, we recall how governmental attempts to solve problems can create other difficulties. The libertarians point out that rent controls often lead to housing shortages; that labor unions raise wages and cause unemployment in unionized industries; and that putting price controls on gasoline leads to long lines at gasoline stations.

People of all political persuasions should study Friedman's *Capitalism and Freedom.*[2] It is a rigorous and persuasive elucidation of an important point of view which held sway among conservative

[2] University of Chicago Press, Chicago, 1962, hardcover and paperback. See also M. Friedman, *An Economist's Protest* (Thomas Horton & Co., Glen Ridge, N.J., 1972), a collection of his *Newsweek* columns.

thinkers in the 1980s. You might ask yourself whether you are for or against: Social security? Flood relief? Government inspection and regulation of food and drugs? Minimum wages? Mandatory installation of seat belts in cars? Compulsory and free public schooling? Prohibition of open sale of dangerous drugs like crack? Compulsory licensing of doctors? Establishment of national parks like Yellowstone or Grand Canyon?

If you read Friedman's work, you will see that he argues cogently against each one of these programs. He opposes them both because he sees them as interferences with personal freedom and because he thinks they fail to achieve their goals. Whether you ultimately agree or disagree with his views, as a thoughtful citizen you must grapple with the issues that Friedman addresses.

Rational-Expectations Macroeconomics. Related to the libertarians are a group of free-market macroeconomists, called the *rational-expectations school,* founded in the early 1970s by Robert Lucas at the University of Chicago and Stanford's Thomas Sargent. This school shares the libertarians' skepticism about government policies, arguing that systematic macroeconomic policies to combat unemployment will only end up causing inflation. Better a passive monetary and fiscal policy, they say, than one futilely trying to straighten out every twist and turning point of the business cycle.

The rational-expectations argument found little sympathy among older mainstream economists who fought to inject Keynesian thinking into national policy-making. But younger macroeconomists often take inspiration from the techniques of this new approach. And the Reagan administration adopted libertarian and rational-expectations views, arguing that limiting the role of government would expand both personal freedom and economic growth:

> Political freedom and economic freedom are closely related. Any comparison among contemporary nations or examination of the historical record demonstrates two important relationships between the nature of the political system and the nature of the economic system: [1] All nations which have broad-based representative government and civil liberties have most of their economic activity organized by the market. [2] Economic conditions in market economies are generally superior to those in nations . . . in which the government has the dominant economic role.[3]

Dissenters from the Left

The most vocal critics of the existing economic order have been radicals who argued that capitalism is fatally flawed and must be replaced by a more efficient and equitable system. The central figures were socialists like Marx and Engels, communists like Lenin, anarchists like Proudhon, and neo-Marxists of the 1950s like Baran and Sweezy. Who today takes up the revolutionary banner, calling for dismantlement of Western-style capitalism?

In fact, few today argue for radical restructuring of the mixed market economy. One economist who has voiced his criticisms over the last three decades is Harvard's John Kenneth Galbraith. Writing in *American Capitalism, The Affluent Society,* and *The New Industrial State,* Galbraith challenged prevailing views about consumers and firms. Among his major points were:

- Today's economy is directed by large bureaucracies, not by perfectly competitive markets. The technostructure (the educated elites who run firms, governments, and universities) ultimately makes the decisions that guide countries of both East and West. The idea that small firms are responsible for much of production, or that small inventors bring forth the major inventions, is a convenient myth designed to perpetuate belief in the market system of atomistic firms.
- Consumers are not masters of their own minds. Advertising shapes our preferences. The outcomes of markets are determined as much by Madison Avenue as by genuine needs.
- Ours is a society in which the public sector starves while the private sector lives high on the hog. Public goods like parks are neglected; roads crumble; bridges collapse.

The Oriental Mystique. America was the birthplace of the "factory system," mass production, the assembly line, and giant factories stretching over acres of land. While Adam Smith expounded the theoretical virtues of division of labor, American

[3] *Economic Report of the President,* 1982 (Government Printing Office, Washington, D.C.), pp. 27–28.

entrepreneurs developed its practice to the *n*th degree in large automobile plants employing thousands of workers. After Henry Ford introduced mass production of the Model T Ford, workers came to be viewed as little more than highly versatile, all-purpose machines.

As long as the United States remained king of the economic mountain, the defects of the factory system seemed a small price to pay for its marvelous contribution to productivity and living standards. Would we not rather work all day in a factory and be able to buy cars and home appliances than be self-employed on the farm and spend all day washing our clothes in a tub?

During the 1970s and 1980s, America began to fall behind Japan and other countries of the Pacific Rim in the economic growth race. One industry after another was conquered by Japan or Korea or Hong Kong. Steel, shipbuilding, radios, television, cameras, automobiles—all these industries fell under the domination of innovative firms from East Asian countries. While advanced industrial countries struggled with inflation or unemployment, while Latin American countries staggered under heavy debt burdens, while Eastern Europe tried to throw off its socialist chains, the countries of the Pacific Rim moved steadily and rapidly ahead. A striking example of success was the city-state of Singapore. So rapidly had this country of 3 million advanced that by 1990 it exported 20 percent more machinery to the West than did all the socialist countries of Eastern Europe.

As the mature capitalist countries began to falter, many economists asked whether the old factory system—giant bureaucratic corporations operating huge factories—had outlived its usefulness. Taking inspiration from Japanese-style management, these economists argued that "small is beautiful" and pointed to supposedly contented Japanese workers and to Japan's astounding productivity growth since World War II. MIT's Lester Thurow, Harvard's Robert Reich, and others argued for redesigning the workplace on cooperative rather than competitive lines.[4] These scholars argued in effect:

> People work for satisfaction as well as for money; men and women prize jobs which allow them to express their creativity and need for community. Workers must feel themselves part of the management team—sharing information and ideas, designing their jobs, helping to improve the quality of work and of the final output.

Although this group of economists has spawned numerous suggestions, one common theme has been to introduce profit sharing into compensation. Harvard's Martin Weitzman has analyzed a compensation system that shares revenues or profits with workers—a system modeled on the Japanese bonus system. He reasons that if workers are paid a share of profits or revenues rather than a straight hourly wage, the marginal cost of labor will decline relative to a straight wage system. Firms will choose to retain their workers during recessions, and the overall unemployment rate will decline.

Another strand running through this critique is that American management has lost touch with production. Trained in financial wizardry at the top business schools, today's MBAs feel more at home reading a balance sheet than managing a production line. They pay more attention to this quarter's bottom line than to the long-term viability of radical new products. They look to getting rich fast with glamorous takeovers or arbitrage rather than getting rich slowly through the dull job of constant innovation and better new products. Richard Darman, budget director under President Bush, contends that the modern company is suffering from "corpocracy"—bloated corporate bureaucracy which makes management sluggish, risk-averse, and poorly adapted to the dynamic world of international competition.

Mainstream economists may not agree with all the writings of the dissenters of the left and right, but they acknowledge that America has lost some of its earlier technological leadership. We must listen carefully to sift the sound from the shrill, for somewhere from these voices may emerge the academic scribbler who will revolutionize economics in the twenty-first century.

Radical Economics

Finally, we move to the truly radical end of the spectrum, to thinkers who would entirely reshape

[4] Among the important recent studies, see Lester Thurow, *The Zero-Sum Solution* (Simon and Schuster, New York, 1985); Robert Reich, *The New American Frontier* (New York Times Publisher, New York, 1983); and Martin Weitzman, *The Share Economy* (Harvard University Press, Cambridge, Mass., 1986).

today's mixed capitalist regime. Radical economics tends to rise and fall with the business cycle and political turmoil. During the depressed 1930s, socialist thought flourished, and again two decades ago, in the swirl of civil rights activism and revulsion against the Vietnam war, a school called the "new left" boldly attacked American economic institutions.

After an early wave of enthusiasm, the new left went underground. Its ranks dwindled as market economies survived the inflationary storms of the 1970s and as conservative governments took charge in many industrial democracies during the 1980s. But a handful of economists persisted in their vision of a better society. What were the major themes in their criticisms?[5]

- *Rejection of modern macroeconomics.* Modern mainstream macroeconomics says that there is a natural rate of unemployment—today around 6 percent—below which the economy cannot go without running the straits of inflation. Radicals reject the premise that prices and wages should be left to inflate freely. They would impose wage-and-price controls as a way of containing inflation, thereby allowing lower levels of unemployment.

  With the resources freed up by wage-and-price controls, the new radicals would pour funds into public capital—railroads, pollution control, education, and training.
- *Countering of imperialism.* A continuing theme in radical economics during this century has been the attack on economic imperialism. Harking back to the doctrines of Hobson and Lenin, radicals denounce American companies and accuse them of profiting from the racist policies of apartheid in South Africa. A rising storm of protest has forced many colleges and universities to sell their shares of companies operating in South Africa. Radicals see this movement as the first step in cleansing capitalism of its imperialist stain.
- *Reduction of inequality.* Today's radicals join forces with the old left in denouncing the great inequalities generated by markets. The radicals would hope to reimpose steeply progressive taxation, hoping to tax wealthy groups heavily and redistribute the funds to the poor. They recognize, however, that the most effective redistributional programs are provided by government spending (on welfare, food stamps, or housing programs) rather than by redistributive taxation.
- *Rejection of markets.* Modern economics views markets as reliable judges of consumer tastes and of the social costs of production. Today's radical economists dissent. Like Galbraith, they feel that our tastes are manipulated by advertising to favor trivial consumption. How can a nation spend billions of dollars playing video games or buying lethal cigarettes at a time when millions go without food, shelter, and adequate medical care? How can the nation permit firms to continue to foul our environment with sulfurous fumes and toxic wastes? Radicals argue for government planning. But while radical economists are sympathetic to participatory planning, they are suspicious of government bureaucracy and definitely reject Soviet-style socialism as repressive and destructive of individual liberty.

Appraisal. What is the verdict on the doctrines of the radical economists? One of the most thoughtful surveys comes from a Swedish economist, Assar Lindbeck.[6] This twentieth-century de Tocqueville studied radical economics while visiting the United States two decades ago, and his assessment rings true today.

Lindbeck points out that the radicals mistrust both the private market and the state bureaucracy. But that is one dislike too many, for these two systems are the only existing mechanisms by which a modern economy can allocate its resources. How can we plan without a government planning agency? How can markets allocate capital and labor without allowing private entrepreneurs to profit from their innovations and risk ruin from their blunders? This fundamental challenge has not been answered.

[5] See particularly Samuel Bowles, David Gordon, and Thomas Weisskopf, *Beyond the Waste Land* (Anchor Press, Garden City, N.Y., 1983).

[6] *The Political Economy of the New Left—An Outsider's View* (Harper & Row, New York, 1971).

B. Alternative Economic Systems

> Mankind has not managed to create anything more efficient than a market economy. . . . Its self-adjustment and self-regulation are geared to promote the best possible coordination of economic activity, rational use of labor, material, and financial resources, and balance the national economy.
>
> *The 500 Day Plan: Transition to the Market,* report of a group of Soviet economic experts to Presidents M. Gorbachev and B. Yeltsin, "The Shatalin Plan" (1990)

Since the Industrial Revolution, capitalism has been plagued by inequality and depressions. In the midst of each peril, prophets would pronounce that capitalism was on its deathbed. Others foretold a mechanical timetable of inevitable progression—savagery to feudalism, feudalism to capitalism, capitalism to socialism, socialism to communism—but these forecasts generally proved wrong. During the Great Depression of the 1930s, democracy and capitalism indeed appeared doomed. Country after country succumbed to dictatorship, and Soviet-style command economies displaced the market in Eastern Europe in the 1940s.

After World War II, the critics of capitalism were once again confounded. The mixed economies of the West and Japan formed a common pattern of rapid growth and expanding international trade. The insights of the Keynesian revolution propelled market economies to the most rapid and sustained period of expansion ever seen. Even though the market economies were hit with numerous shocks over the last two decades—three oil shocks, a debt crisis in middle-income countries, instability and insolvency in the banking system—advanced countries continued to grow rapidly, combining the ability of markets to innovate and market their products in the world market with government fiscal and monetary policies to control the business cycle and promote economic growth.

A Bouquet of Isms

Philosophers have always had visions of a more perfect society: Plato's Republic, Sir Thomas More's Utopia, and Marx's dictatorship of the proletariat were among the most influential. Visionaries often start by decrying society's present ills and then contrast them with the ideal features of a vaguely defined utopia. But beyond agreeing that the present order has faults, different schools of reform often have little in common.

At one extreme are anarchists, who believe in the elimination of all government. At the other extreme are advocates of an absolute communism, with the government operating a totalitarian, collectivized economic order in which all decisions about production, consumption, and distribution are made by the state. Between the extremes of anarchism and communism lie capitalism, Marxism, socialism, and the many combinations of these models.

1. *The market economy.* In pure form, this system is found in laissez-faire capitalism. Although pure laissez-faire never existed, it was closely approached in nineteenth-century Britain. Most of this book is devoted to describing the market economy and the mixed economy that evolved from it.
2. *Marxism.* Although Karl Marx was primarily a critic of capitalism, he believed that capitalism would be succeeded by socialism, which in turn would give way to communism. His powerful arguments have influenced economic planners in Europe, in the Soviet Union, in China, and in many developing countries.
3. *Socialism.* One offshoot from the Marxist tree was socialist thinking, which encompasses a wide variety of different approaches. In the nineteenth century, socialists were often revolutionaries who tried to topple governments through violent means; when they succeeded, they often substituted government ownership of capital and land for private ownership. Twentieth-century socialism is widespread, particularly in

Western Europe, where democratic socialist governments expanded the welfare state, nationalized industries, and planned the economy.

4. *Soviet-style command economy.* The most thoroughgoing practical alternative to the market economy has developed in the Soviet Union, with many features of the Soviet system adopted by Eastern Europe and China. Under the Soviet model, the state owns all the land and most of the capital, sets wages and most prices, and directs the microeconomic operation of the economy.

The rest of this chapter is devoted to explaining the economic ideas behind the last three of these economic systems.

The Central Dilemma: Market vs. Command

A survey of alternative economic systems may seem like a bewildering array of different economic "isms." And indeed, there is great variety in the way countries organize their economies. But one central issue pervades the entire discussion of alternative systems: Should the economy rely primarily upon the private market or upon government commands to answer the questions of *how, what,* and *for whom?*

In every economic system, a complex network of relationships determines *what* is produced, *how* it is produced, and *for whom* goods are produced. The economic system sets the laws and regulations that govern economic activity; determines property rights and ownership of factors of production; distributes the decision-making power over production and consumption; and determines the incentives motivating the different decision makers.

One important system for determining answers to the three fundamental questions is the *market economy.* In a market system, people act voluntarily and primarily for financial gain or personal satisfaction. Firms buy factors and produce outputs, selecting inputs and outputs in a way that will maximize their profits. Consumers supply factors and buy consumer goods to maximize their satisfactions. Agreements on production and consumption are made voluntarily and with the use of money, at prices determined in free markets, and on the basis of arrangements between buyers and sellers. Although individuals differ greatly in terms of economic power, the relations between individuals and firms are horizontal in nature, essentially voluntary, and non-hierarchical.

The other major system of organization is the *command economy,* where decisions are made by government bureaucracy. In this approach, people are linked by a vertical relationship, and control is exercised by a multilevel hierarchy. The planning bureaucracy determines *what* goods are produced, *how* they are produced, and *for whom* output is produced. The highest level of the pyramid makes the major decisions and develops the elements of the plan for the economy. The plan is subdivided and transmitted down the bureaucratic ladder, with the lower levels of the hierarchy executing the plan with increasing attention to detail. Individuals are motivated by coercion and legal sanctions; organizations compel individuals to accept orders from above. Transactions and commands may or may not use money; trades may or may not take place at established prices.

The tension between markets and command runs through all discussions about comparative economic systems.

Marxism

Modern socialism and communism owe much to Karl Marx (1818–1883). Marx studied law and philosophy, and his early thinking stressed technological breakthroughs and the accompanying changes in social and economic relations—particularly the accumulation of capital—as the motive forces of history. He thought that these forces, which he called economic determinism, would lead to the inevitable triumph of communism.

The center of Marx's economics was the *labor theory of value.* Marx assumed that it is labor power that gives value to a commodity—both the direct labor and the indirect labor embodied in buildings or machinery used up in the productive process. Marx realized that, under competitive capitalism, market prices would not necessarily equal labor values because capitalists receive an excess in revenues over labor costs—a surplus value.

By *surplus value* Marx meant the difference between revenues and total labor costs. A difference arises because workers are forced to sell their labor to capitalists and because capitalists pay workers for only part of the value of their output. In the simple case where no machinery is used up, the rate of surplus value (which Marx called the "rate of exploitation") is simply the ratio of profits to wages.

Someone who has mastered the concepts of modern economics might ask, What is gained by viewing a capitalist economy through Marxist lenses? A careful study shows that Marx's theory of prices differed little from the labor theory of value laid out by Ricardo a half-century earlier. Instead, Marx attempted to expose the nature of profit. In essence, he hoped to show that profits—that part of output that is produced by workers but received by capitalists—amount to "unearned income."

Prophecies. Marx attempted to deduce "scientifically" the inevitable transition from capitalism to socialism. In Marx's world, capitalists are driven to accumulate, for the pursuit of wealth becomes an end in itself and not a means for later consumption. As capital accumulates, the rate of profit falls. Under pressure to squeeze out ever more surplus value, the working class becomes increasingly "immiserized"—by which Marx meant that working conditions would deteriorate and workers would grow progressively alienated from their jobs. A growing "reserve army of the unemployed" would prevent wages from rising above the subsistence level.

As profits decline and investment opportunities at home become exhausted, the ruling capitalist classes resort to *imperialism*. Capital tends to seek higher rates of profit abroad. And, according to this theory (particularly as later expanded by Lenin), the foreign policies of imperialist nations increasingly attempt to win colonies and then mercilessly milk surplus value from them.

But the capitalist system could not continue this unbalanced growth forever. Marx predicted increasing inequality under capitalism, along with a gradual emergence of class consciousness among the downtrodden proletariat. Business cycles would become ever more violent as mass poverty resulted in macroeconomic underconsumption. Finally, a cataclysmic depression would sound the death knell of capitalism. Like an overripe fruit ready to fall off the tree, capitalism would have grown into a fat monopoly that could be plucked by the workers in a sudden and violent revolution.

These were the prophecies that inspired generations of radicals of the old and new left. As the decades passed, however, it became clear that history was not following Marx's script. Workers were enjoying ever-growing real wages and shorter hours, and labor's share of national income was slowly growing. Workers were gaining political power through ballots not bullets. The rate of profit showed no tendency to decline as innovations constantly replenished the stock of domestic investment opportunities. And when Keynes wrote his *General Theory* in 1936, it breathed new life and revived faith in mixed capitalism. History has not been kind to the Marxist prophesies over the century since *Capital*. But, as we have repeatedly seen, history rarely follows any script written by mere mortals.

The *economic interpretation of history* is one of Marx's lasting contributions to Western thought. Marx argued that economic interests lie behind and determine our values. Why do business executives vote for conservative candidates, while labor leaders support those who advocate raising the minimum wage or increasing unemployment benefits? The reason, Marx held, is that people's beliefs and ideologies reflect the material interests of their social and economic class.

In fact, Marx's approach is hardly foreign to mainstream economics. It generalized Adam Smith's analysis of self-interest from the dollar votes of the marketplace to the ballot votes of elections and the bullet votes of the barricades. When the economic theory of history is formalized in terms of utility and voting, we recognize the embryo of modern public-choice theories.

Our brief review of Marxian economics can only touch upon the sweeping analysis of this great and controversial intellect. Throughout his writings, Marx emphasized that societies are constantly evolving because of technological change. Each social system contains the elements of its own destruction. Hence, once we understand Marx's approach to history, we can no longer believe, as did the complacent Whig historians of nineteenth-century Britain, that laissez-faire British capitalism was the culmination of human civilization. Nor can we fall into the fallacy that the triumph of the proletariat will inevitably bring an end to the class struggle,[7] or even that the market economy of twentieth-century America represents the end of history.

[7] Only a supersophisticated Marxist could have coined the wry joke recently heard in Eastern Europe: "Under capitalism, it's a case of man exploiting man. Under socialism, it's the other way around."

"All these will pass away"—this is Karl Marx's ultimate thesis.

Socialism

As a doctrine, socialism developed from the ideas of Marx and other radical thinkers of the nineteenth century. Socialism is a middle ground between laissez-faire capitalism and the Soviet model to which we next turn. A few common elements characterize most socialist philosophies:

- *Government ownership of productive resources.* Socialists traditionally believed that the role of private property should be reduced. Key industries such as railroads, coal, and steel should be nationalized (that is, owned and operated by the state). In recent years, because of the poor performance of many state-owned enterprises, enthusiasm for nationalization has ebbed in most advanced democracies.
- *Planning.* Socialists are suspicious of the "chaos" of the marketplace and question the allocational efficiency of the invisible hand. They insist that a planning mechanism is needed to coordinate different sectors. In recent years, planners have emphasized subsidies to promote the rapid development of high-technology industries, such as microelectronics and biotechnology; these plans are sometimes called "industrial policies." In many European countries, capitalist management is diluted by "codetermination"—a process wherein representatives of workers and the public sit as company directors.
- *Redistribution of income.* Inherited wealth and the highest incomes are to be reduced by the militant use of government taxing powers; in some socialist countries, marginal tax rates have reached 98 percent. Social security benefits, free medical care, and cradle-to-grave welfare services collectively provided out of progressive-tax sources increase the well-being of the less privileged classes and guarantee minimum standards of living.
- *Peaceful and democratic evolution.* Socialists often advocate the peaceful and gradual extension of government ownership—evolution by ballot rather than revolution by bullet.

Soviet-Style Command Economy

We now turn to an analysis of the Soviet economy. This subject is of great importance for economics because the Soviet Union has served as a laboratory for theories about the functioning of a command economy. Some economists claimed that socialism simply could not work. The Soviet experience proves that a socialist command economy—one in which the major economic decisions are made administratively, without profits as the central motive force for production—can function and grow over long periods of time.

We will review the major issues of the Soviet economy: What are the high points of Soviet economic history? How is a command economy organized, who makes decisions, and what motivates managers? How successful was the Soviet economy in achieving its goals of rapid industrialization? And why have many socialist economies decided that they can no longer afford central planning? Why have they rediscovered the value of Adam Smith's market mechanism?

Soviet History

Czarist Russia grew rapidly from 1880 to 1914, but it was considerably less developed than industrialized countries like the United States or Britain. World War I brought great hardship to Russia and allowed Vladimir Lenin and Leon Trotsky—promising power to the workers and land to the peasants—to seize power. Upon taking power, the Soviet leaders were in a quandary for they had no economic blueprint to guide them. Marx had written extensively about the faults of capitalism, but he left communists no design for the promised land.

From 1917 to 1933, the U.S.S.R. experimented with different socialist models before settling on central planning.[8] But dissatisfaction with the pace of industrialization led Stalin to undertake a radical new venture around 1928—collectivization of agriculture and forced-draft industrialization.

Under the collectivization of Soviet agriculture

[8] A highly readable account of developments in Soviet economic history is contained in Alec Nove, *An Economic History of the U.S.S.R.*, 3d ed (Penguin, Baltimore, 1986).

between 1929 and 1935, 94 percent of Soviet peasants were forced to join collective farms. In the process, many wealthy peasants were deported, and conditions deteriorated so much that millions perished. The other part of the Soviet "great leap forward" came through the introduction of economic planning for rapid industrialization. The planners created the first 5-year plan to cover the period 1928–1933. It called for increasing investment by 150 percent over 5 years. The first plan established the priorities of Soviet planning: heavy industry was to be favored over light industry, and consumer goods were to be the residual sector after all the other priorities had been met. Through "high-pressure" or "taut" planning, the state tried to extract the maximum amount of output from workers, managers, and farmers. Although there were many reforms and changes in emphasis, the Stalinist model of the 1930s applied in the Soviet Union, and after World War II in Eastern Europe, until the "velvet revolution" of 1989.

How a Command Economy Functions

Having seen how Marxian economics sprouted in the nineteenth century and flourished in underdeveloped Russia, we now turn to examine the functioning of the Soviet-type command economy. This study of the world's largest command economy forms a valuable supplement to our understanding of economic processes.[9] But in this area we are studying a rapidly moving target. As we will explain later in this chapter, the socialist countries are today making a halting transition from a centralized to a market economy. To understand a command economy, we will examine the "Soviet-style command economy" as that system operated in the Soviet Union from the 1930s to the mid-1980s.

How does the Soviet-style command economy answer the three basic economic questions: *What* shall be produced? *How* shall it be produced? And *for whom* shall the goods be made? In broad outline, the picture is as follows.

The state owns almost all means of production—factories, equipment, and land. The major decisions about production and inputs are made by command from above, in accordance with the plan or the planners' wishes. In areas where the economy interacts with households—for consumer goods and in labor markets—prices are set by planners so that consumer demand more or less clears the markets. But the key difference from a market economy is that the direction of economic activity is set by the state, not by consumers.

What? In a command economy, the broad categories of output are determined by political decisions. Military spending in the Soviet Union has always been allocated a substantial part of output and scientific resources, while the other major priority has been investment, with a share of GNP ranging between 30 and 40 percent (as compared with 15 percent in the United States). Consumption claims the residual output after the quotas of higher-priority sectors have been filled.

By contrast with prices in a mixed capitalist system, prices in a Soviet-style command economy have little bearing on the allocation of GNP among the different sectors. Rather, planners start by dividing national output among sectors; then they use incomes and prices to help attain their planning goals.

We can illustrate how central planning works by using consumer goods as an example. Consumers' incomes are determined primarily by wages (recall that there is little property income because most property is owned by the state). But that does not mean that consumption decisions are left to the marketplace. Rather, planners first determine the levels and distribution of consumer goods (so much total consumption, so many automobiles, so many radios, and so forth). Then consumer prices are set so that demand and supply more or less balance.

More precisely, planners set prices by adjusting *turnover taxes* in order to reduce the demand for consumer goods. This process is illustrated in Figure 22-1, where the different components of the retail price are shown. The key point is that excess demand for goods can be reduced by levying a steep tax on retail purchases. For many commodities, however, prices do not clear markets because planners tend to underprice consumer goods. In addition, prices are only infrequently changed

[9] A careful study of the Soviet economic system is provided by Paul R. Gregory and Robert C. Stuart, *Soviet Economic Structure and Performance*, 4th ed. (Harper & Row, New York, 1990).

Taxes Adjust to Clear Consumer Markets

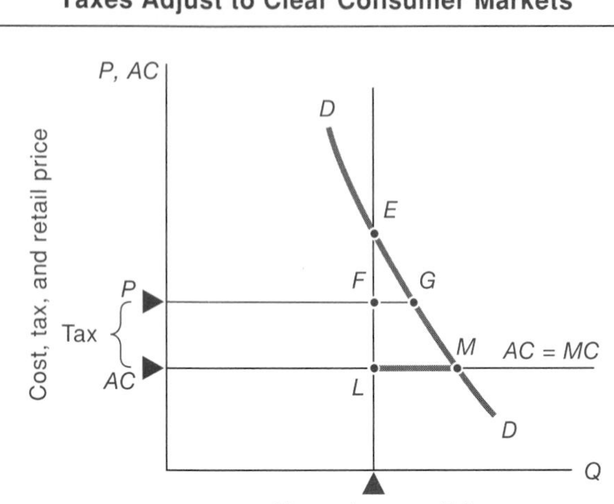

Figure 22-1. In consumer markets of a command economy, turnover taxes help to reduce consumer demand

Planners recognize that setting prices at average cost will cause drastic shortages: price at *AC* will cause shortage equal to quantity demanded *M* minus planned quantity Q^*, leading to shortage amount *LM*.

By setting turnover tax *LF* and raising retail price to *P*, planners can curb shortages or gluts. Prices are generally held fixed for several years, so wasteful mismatches of supply and demand (such as *FG*) are endemic to the Soviet-style command economy.

(most prices were fixed from 1982 to 1991 in the Soviet Union). When prices are set too low (as is the case in Figure 22-1), there is excess demand and consumers are forced to wait in long lines; in effect, lines rather than prices are rationing out goods. The long lines became a serious problem in 1990 when consumers spent on average 10 hours a week standing in line waiting to buy goods.

The role of *prices* in the Soviet-style command economy clearly differs greatly from that in a market economy. What are the principles of price determination? With few exceptions, prices are determined by planners, not by enterprises, and they bear little relationship to opportunity cost. We have already seen that retail prices (including taxes) are often set below market-clearing prices. Wholesale prices—those used by firms—are even less important and simply serve as accounting prices. Western observers stress that industrial prices (such as those on goods like steel) serve virtually no allocational role.

How? On what basis does the Soviet-style command economy determine the techniques of production? How does the command economy decide whether to use steel or aluminum, nuclear power or coal, labor or machinery? These questions can be subdivided into the question of who makes the decisions and what criteria are used.

In large part, decisions about *how* goods are to be produced are made by the planning authorities. Planners first decide on the quantities of final outputs (the *what*). Then, using a technique called *material balances,* they work backward from outputs to the required inputs and the flows among different firms. Investment decisions are specified in great detail by the planners, while firms have considerable flexibility in deciding upon their mix of labor inputs.

What motivates managers to fulfill the plans? Clearly no planning system could specify all the activities of all the firms—this would require trillions of commands every year. Many details must be left to the managers of individual factories, and *faulty managerial incentives* have been a recurrent problem for the command economy.

In contrast to the situation in a market economy, the primary goal of firms in a command economy is to fulfill the plan rather than to earn profits. Socialist managers face a number of targets by which they are judged. The major target is output; subsidiary targets include labor productivity, the product mix, and, in recent years, profits. Managers are then judged on how well their enterprise fulfills the plan: they get large bonuses if they meet the plan, while they may be dismissed (or, in an earlier era, sent to Siberia) if they fall short.

The managerial incentive system produces significant distortions in the command economy. Because such high priority is given to meeting the output or sales target, managers often hoard inputs like steel that might cause bottlenecks if they became scarce because of shortages or transport delays. Moreover, because output targets do not contain quality dimensions, there is an incentive to produce low-quality goods. Thus, if the target is 10,000 shirts, the firm might use rough cloth or sew a crooked seam. Stories are told of transportation enterprises that move carloads of water back and forth in order to fulfill their output target of logging so many physical ton-miles.

For Whom? We have already discussed the question of who is served by a Soviet-style command economy. The entire system is designed to attain the goals of the planners and of the leaders of the ruling party. In the Soviet Union, planners have emphasized military spending and rapid economic growth since the 1930s. In recent years, however, the consumer has been given greater priority. A much larger share of investment now goes to agriculture and light industry than in the time of Stalin. But consumers definitely take a backseat in the command economy.

Because of the high priority of investment and defense, consumption's share of Soviet GNP was during the 1980s about 53 percent (as opposed to 66 percent in the United States). Consumption is not equally distributed, however. Those with high positions or with labor skills much in demand have relatively high consumption levels.

Comparative Economic Performance

From World War II until the mid-1980s, the United States and the Soviet Union engaged in a superpower competition for public opinion, for military superiority, and for economic dominance. How has the economic performance of the world's largest command economy compared with that of the mixed economies? In answering this question, we examine the key indicators of economic growth, equality of income, and absence of inflation and unemployment.

Economic Growth. The central objective of Soviet leaders since the late 1920s has been rapid industrialization. It is hence appropriate to compare growth in GNP of the U.S.S.R with that of other countries. As Table 22-1 shows, Soviet economic growth was impressive from 1928 until the mid-1960s but has slowed sharply since the 1960s (be cautioned, however, that the Soviet data are questioned by many experts). While the growth experience has been impressive, some historians note that the growth has been achieved by applying brute force and by emphasizing production of intermediate goods or commodities of little value to consumers. Quantity, not quality, has been the goal.

What have been the sources of economic growth? Studies indicate that the pace of growth in the Soviet Union has been rapid because of "extensive growth" (increases in the growth of inputs of capital and labor). The rate of "intensive growth" (productivity growth, or the rate of growth of output per unit of input) in recent years has been markedly lower than that of major market economies, and in some years it has actually been negative.

During the last decade, Soviet GNP has grown at only about 2 percent per year, less than in the advanced market economies. What caused the slow-

Economic Growth in Market and Command Economies

Country and period	Average growth rate of GNP (% per year)
Soviet Union:	
1885–1913	3.3
1928–1966	5.5?*
1966–1990	1.8–2.7?*
United States:	
1834–1929	4.0
1929–1965	3.0
1965–1990	2.8
United Kingdom:	
1855–1990	2.1
Germany:	
1850–1990	2.7
Japan:	
1874–1990	4.5

*These estimates are particularly uncertain because data have often been manipulated or concealed.

Table 22-1. Long-term growth of GNP in the Soviet Union and major market economies

During its early years, the Soviet command economy grew more rapidly than the economy of Czarist Russia or than most major market economies. But since 1965, the Soviet economy stagnated, leading to the reform movement of today. Note, however, that many Soviet and American scholars question the accuracy of the Soviet national-output data. [Source: Gur Ofer, "Soviet Economic Growth: 1928–1985," *Journal of Economic Literature* (December 1987); CIA, *Impact of Gorbachev's Policies* (July 1988), SOV 88-10049; Paul R. Gregory and Robert C. Stuart, *Soviet Economic Structure and Performance*, 4th ed. (Harper & Row, New York, 1990).]

down? Factors include a deterioration of labor discipline, numerous planning errors, diversion of scientific talent and other resources to the military, depletion of low-cost oil and gas along with declining prices of oil and other exported raw materials, and the strain of using a cumbersome planning apparatus to deal with the demands of an increasingly sophisticated economy.

Where does the Soviet economy stand today? Studies today suggest that Soviet GNP was between 20 and 40 percent of American GNP in 1990. On a per capita basis, however, Soviet output was between one-sixth and one-third of that of the United States. There remains a large gap between the most advanced capitalist countries and the Soviet Union, and that gap has widened in the last few years.

Income Distribution. One of the major complaints levied by socialists has been that capitalism permits surplus value or unearned profits to flow to capitalists, making capitalism a very unequal, class-ridden society. By contrast, a socialist society would share the return to capital among the workers, thereby promoting much greater equality than a market economy.

In practice, Soviet planners allowed sizable wage differentials. And the privileges of the capitalist class have been replaced by generous benefits for the ruling-party elites. Recent estimates of income distribution indicate that, except for the absence of a super-rich class, the income distribution in the Soviet Union and Eastern Europe shows a striking similarity to that in Western countries.

Inflation and Unemployment. Finally, what of the scourges of capitalism—unemployment and inflation? Unemployment has traditionally been low in Soviet-style economies. The reason is that labor is generally in short supply because of the ambitious economic plans. Furthermore, controlled prices tend to be quite stable, so measured inflation is absent. In the late 1980s and early 1990s, however, open inflation erupted. In addition, prices were well below market-clearing levels and acute shortages arose in what is called "repressed inflation."

● How do these diverse elements of performance add up? A complete evaluation is beyond mere economic science. The Soviet model has demonstrated that a command economy is capable of mobilizing resources for rapid economic growth. But it has done so in an atmosphere of great human sacrifice, loss of life, and political repression. And it appears that in the modern world of open borders and high-quality manufactured goods, the blunt control of the command economy cannot match the finely tuned incentives and innovation of a modern mixed market economy. ●

Economic Reform: Rediscovery of the Market

In the 1970s and 1980s, socialism lost its allure as the market economies of North America, Western Europe, and the Pacific Rim left the Soviet-style economies far behind. The technological backwardness of Soviet planning is symbolized by the fact that the planning apparatus, which is supposed to allocate thousands of commodities through material balances, performs many calculations on abacuses!

It is informative to contrast East and West Germany, which had roughly equal levels of productivity and similar industrial structures at the end of World War II. After four decades of capitalism in the West and Soviet-style socialism in the East, productivity in East Germany had fallen to a level estimated between one-fourth and one-half of that in West Germany. The combination of economic stagnation and political repression led the countries of Eastern Europe to break away from the Soviet Union in 1989 and search for a more humane and efficient economic system.

Early Reform Efforts. "Economic reform" is the term given to attempts to improve the economic mechanism in Soviet-style command systems. The reform debate has most often been between those who want to improve the planned economy and those who want to decentralize decisions and give a greater role to prices, profits, and markets.

The proponents of *improved planning* stress the use of improved incentives or new tools, such as developments in mathematical economics. They would introduce input-output techniques (such as those developed by Russian-born former Harvard economist Wassily Leontief). They might use linear programming or other mathematical techniques (developed by Nobel-laureate L. V. Kantorovich and academician V. V. Novozhilov) to estimate the appropriate scarcity prices to use in executing plans.

One approach to reforms, then, would retain the key elements of the command economy, but improve the precision of its commands.

At the other pole are those who press for greater *decentralization* of decision making. This group stresses that a modern economy is too complex to be directed by a bureaucracy out of touch with production and consumers. They warn that the use of quantitative targets, such as output, leads to distortions and that distortions are worsened when consumers and producers face prices on goods that are unrelated to the social scarcity of these goods. A clear statement of the new view of the market came in the "Abalkin Report" of the Soviet deputy prime minister in late 1989:

> [T]he main features of the model of a new economic system are . . . the use of the market as the main form of coordinating the activities of the participants in production. We have become convinced on the basis of our own experience that there is no worthy alternative to the market mechanism as the method of coordinating the activities and interests of the economic subjects.

But stating the goal was not enough. To make the difficult transition from Marx to market would require both political will and the economic wisdom to take the necessary steps.

Strategies for Transition

A cruel joke heard in Eastern Europe is "Question: What is socialism? Answer: The longest road from capitalism to capitalism." Having decided to take the road back to a market economy, a command economy must remove barriers that hinder the growth of the market. Among the major obstacles on the road to reform are the following:

- *Price reform and free-market pricing.* Prices of both inputs and outputs are often far from what they would be were they market-determined. Food and housing are heavily subsidized, while automobiles and consumer durables sell for more than twice world price levels. Sooner or later, prices must be freely determined by supply and demand.
- *Hard budget constraints.* Soviet-style enterprises operate with "soft budget constraints," a term signifying that operating losses are covered by subsidies and do not lead to bankruptcy. In a market economy, firms must be fiscally responsible. Enterprises must know that unprofitability ultimately means economic bankruptcy for the firm and economic ruin for the managers.
- *Privatization.* In market economies, output is primarily produced in private firms; in the United States, for example, only 3 percent of GNP is produced by the federal government. In socialist countries, by contrast, between 80 and 90 percent of output is produced by the state. Moving to the market will require that the actual decisions about buying, selling, pricing, producing, borrowing, and lending must be made by private agents.

Other important tasks of the transition will be to set up the legal framework for a market, to establish a modern banking system, to break up the pervasive monopolies, to tighten monetary and fiscal policy in order to prevent a runaway inflation, to open up the economy to international competition, and to allow the domestic currency to be convertible into foreign currencies. Clearly, reformers in the Soviet-style economies have a big job to do.

One other critical question concerns *the sequencing of the transition.* Where should reformers begin? The reform debate is currently divided into two camps: the radical (or "big-bang" approach) and the gradual or step-by-step approach. The *big-bang approach* was tried in Poland in January 1990, when the Polish government removed controls on most prices and opened the economy to foreign trade. While it is too early to judge the success of the Polish experiment, many observers believe that it has reinvigorated the economy and introduced market forces. At the same time, rising unemployment, declining real wages, and a disruption of economic life have led to increasing disillusionment with a market economy in Poland.

A more cautious approach is *step-by-step reform,* which separates the transition into different phases. Advocates of this approach would begin by creating the legal framework for the market (law on property, law on bankruptcy, etc.). The next phase would include such steps as reducing the budget deficit, reforming prices, and closing unprofitable enterprises. The final step would be to free prices and introduce foreign competition and currency convertibility.

The step-by-step approach has been adopted by the Soviet Union and most other Eastern European countries. In the early years of *perestroika* (restructuring) under President Gorbachev, from 1985 to

1990, Soviet reforms were piecemeal and achieved very little. Under pressure from a deteriorating economy and from his political opposition, particularly Russian President Yeltsin, a group of radical economists, led by Stanislav Shatalin, proposed a "500-day plan." Under the 500-day plan, the Soviet Union would turn much of the power of the central government over to the republics and would introduce a market in a whirlwind 500 days.

The Soviet government came to the brink of this radical reform in the fall of 1990 and then retreated. The power of the entrenched management, party, and other vested interests was too strong to allow a revolution from above. The transition to the market slowed and the Soviet economy continued to deteriorate through 1991.[10] In August of 1991, an abortive coup d'état by the supporters of the old system led to an overthrow of the Communist Party and a rejection of centralized planning. Democratic and republican forces took over both the governments and the program for economic reform. By the end of 1991, the prospect for a center-designed reform appeared slight, and the several republics were charting their own course. In a sense, the 500-Day plan was precipitated by an inept coup.

Outlook for Reform. Reforms in socialist countries are in their infancy, and it will be many years before we can evaluate the results. A sober assessment of the chances for success finds many pitfalls along the road to the market. To begin with, things may get worse before they get better. A command economy is a delicately balanced web of interests and classes. A thoroughgoing reform will disrupt the normal channels of commerce and may actually slow economic growth for a time. There will be strong resistance from the entrenched bureaucracy striving to maintain its economic power. Past reform efforts have always been laid low by central planners.

Moreover, the journey from Marx to market is heading into uncharted waters. The transition from a centrally planned economy to a market economy is without precedent in economic history. We do not know whether the transition will trigger instabilities, high unemployment, rapid inflation, or political revolt.

The stakes are enormous for the Soviet Union, as is noted by one study of the Gorbachev reforms:

> Gorbachev confronts an unpleasant dilemma. Without a radical economic and political upheaval, the Soviet Union will probably be unable to sustain its economic power. . . . Essential to such an upheaval, however, is a decision to slash Soviet military expenditures and divert more resources to decentralized consumption and innovation, but this in turn will force, at the very least, a temporary reduction of military might and prestige. . . . Moreover, there is always the chance that, in the process of doing all this, Gorbachev will fail in bringing about economic reform but succeed in relegating the Soviet Union to a lesser military and political position.[11]

With this analysis of the economic reform movement, we conclude our discussion of alternative economic systems. And, indeed, the circle is closed, for we see that reform stems from the need to confront economic scarcity and to face the age-old dilemma of guns versus butter. No lesson could better illustrate the central tenet of economics—that scarcity and the limitation of economic goods is pervasive no matter what the form of economic organization.

[10] A careful survey of conditions in the Soviet Union, undertaken for the large Western democracies, is contained in a report prepared by several international organizations, *The Economoy of the USSR* (The World Bank, Washington, D.C., 1991, with three volume supplement). This group recommends the big-bang approach to economic restructuring.

[11] Marshall I. Goldman, *Gorbachev's Challenge* (Norton, New York, 1987), pp. 260–262.

SUMMARY

A. Evolution of Economic Thought

1. Growing from roots in nationalist and protectionist mercantilism, political economy as a discipline began with the classical economists: Adam Smith, whose invisible-hand doctrine proclaimed a beneficial natural order in the price system and who severely criticized government interference in the

marketplace; and Malthus and Ricardo, the gloomy prophets of diminishing returns and of the struggle over distribution of limited social income among the wage workers, landowners, and profit-seeking capitalists.

2. Flagging classicism gave way a century ago to neoclassical economics, which provided a synthesis of utility and costs, marginalism extended beyond Ricardian rent analysis to all factors of production, and modern welfare economics studying government policies for changing the income distribution or for correcting microeconomic inefficiencies.

3. The Keynesian revolution added to the microeconomics of neoclassical economics an overdue macroeconomics that eventually synthesized fiscal and monetary analysis.

4. Important counterweights to modern mainstream economics have come from both left and right. Conservative libertarian critics stress that planning and government intervention imperil personal freedoms along with economic efficiency, while rational-expectations macroeconomists argue that systematic policies cannot cure business cycles. Galbraithian iconoclasm holds that consumer tastes are shaped by advertising, while others fret over corpocracy that weakens innovativeness in large businesses. Radical economists denounce inequality, pollution, and imperialism.

B. Alternative Economic Systems

5. In reaction to the periodic crises and depressions of capitalism, critics have spawned "isms" of the Marxist, socialist, and communist varieties.

6. The Marxian offshoot from Ricardian classicism has played a pivotal role in intellectual and political history. Scientific socialism purports to predict the laws of motion of capitalism: exploitation and pauperization, class struggle and class-conditioned ideology, imperialism, cyclical crises, and ultimate proletarian victory.

7. Socialism is a middle ground between capitalism and communism, stressing government ownership of the means of production, planning by the state, income redistribution, and peaceful transition to a new world.

8. Historically, Marxism took its deepest roots in semifeudal Russia. A study of the *what, how,* and *for whom* of the Soviet-style command economy shows a much greater central planning of broad elements of resource allocation (particularly the emphasis on defense, a high rate of investment, and rapid industrialization). The Soviet economy grew rapidly in its early decades, but recent stagnation leaves a large gap between the standards of living of the U.S.S.R. and those of advanced capitalist countries.

9. Faced with slowing economic growth and the desire for economic reform, the Soviet Union and other Eastern European countries pondered the decision about whether to adopt the market mechanism. The transition faces many obstacles, such as soft budget constraints, frozen and distorted prices, and an inadequate legal framework. Two major transition strategies are the big-bang approach of multiple simultaneous measures and the more cautious step-by-step approach in which reforms would be sequenced to prevent disruption. Political opposition and worsening shortages may not allow the luxury of prudent planning of the transition.

CONCEPTS FOR REVIEW

Economic thought
mercantilism
Adam Smith:
  attack on government
  espousal of the invisible hand
Ricardian diminishing returns, class conflicts
neoclassical economics
Chicago School libertarianism
radical economics today
Marxist laws of economic evolution

Alternative economic systems
socialism, communism, Marxism
Soviet-style command economy
what, how, for whom in the command economy
two poles of socialist reform
obstacles to the market
step-by-step vs. big-bang reforms

QUESTIONS FOR DISCUSSION

1. Make a list of the key alternative economic systems, describing each and its history.
2. Analyze the way that *what, how,* and *for whom* are solved in a Soviet-style command economy, and compare your analysis with the solution of the three central questions in a market economy.
3. Which parts of a modern American economics textbook would be well—or badly—received by socialist thinkers?
4. Libertarian economists argue that the government should not regulate the quality of drugs, require seat belts, or have speed limits on highways. Devise the kind of argument a libertarian might use to support such views. Construct some opposing arguments.
5. Review the list of reservations that libertarians lodge against government interferences in the modern mixed economy (page 379). In your view, which of these interferences expand and which reduce economic freedoms? On which would you agree with Friedman's opposition?
6. Consider the Soviet-style command and the American economic models. What are the strong or weak points of each in the following tasks?
   (a) Setting a high ratio of investment to GNP
   (b) Matching shoe sizes or colors with consumer tastes
   (c) Controlling inflation and unemployment
   (d) Inventing new products or processes
7. Prices and profits play a central role in the allocation of resources in a market economy; explain briefly. Then contrast their role in a Soviet-style command economy.
8. Make a list of differences between a market economy and a Soviet-style command economy. For each of the differences, consider how an economic reformer might modify the command economy to introduce supply-and-demand determination of prices, incomes, and outputs.
9. **Advanced problem:** The basic technique of Soviet-style central planning is material balances. Under this technique, the total demand of each commodity is (in principle) adjusted to equal the total supply. More precisely, demands are set so that the sum of all demands for intermediate goods (e.g., corn for seed) plus final demands (e.g., corn for muffins) is equal to the supplies (e.g., production, imports, and decline in inventories of corn).

   Recalling the principles of efficient allocation of resources (particularly those in Chapters 9 and 17), evaluate whether a material-balances plan ensures the achievement of allocative efficiency. [*Hints:* Draw a marginal cost–based supply curve and a marginal utility–based demand diagram. Choose an arbitrary level of output, and assume this is sold at the price where output is equal to quantity demanded (i.e., the price is determined by the intersection of the planner's quantity with the demand curve). Does $MC = MU$? Can you see anything in the material-balancing technique that satisfies the fundamental conditions for allocative efficiency?] Does your analysis suggest why Soviet economists have criticized central planning and propose to introduce markets as a way of improving resource allocation?

PART FIVE

FUNDAMENTAL CONCEPTS OF MACROECONOMICS

The Road Ahead

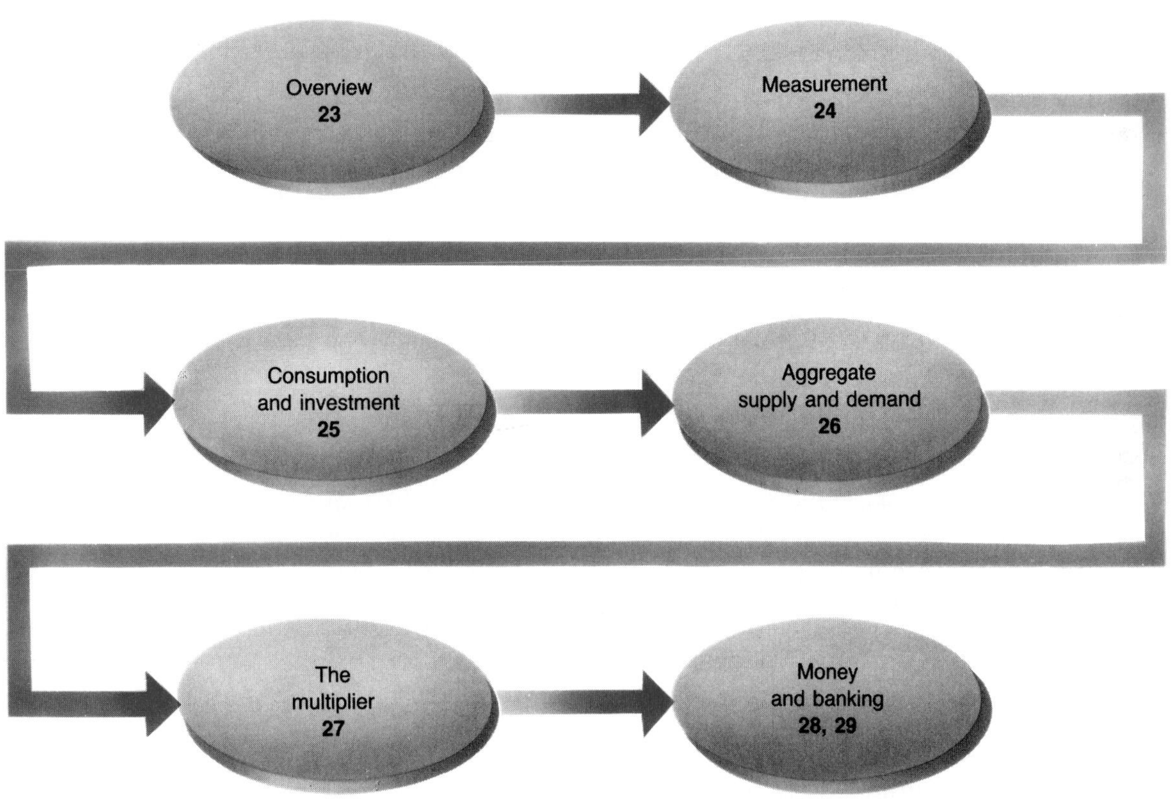

Macroeconomics is the study of the behavior of the economy as a whole. It concerns the business cycles that lead to unemployment and inflation as well as the longer-term trends in output and living standards. In Part Five, we begin with an overview of major concepts and then use aggregate supply-and-demand analysis to analyze the impact of external shocks and government policies on output, employment, and the price level.

CHAPTER 23

OVERVIEW OF MACROECONOMICS

> The whole purpose of the economy is production of goods or services for consumption now or in the future. I think the burden of proof should always be on those who would produce less rather than more, on those who would leave idle men or machines or land that could be used. It is amazing how many reasons can be found to justify such waste: fear of inflation, balance-of-payments deficits, unbalanced budgets, excessive national debt, loss of confidence in the dollar.
>
> James Tobin, *National Economic Policy*

Why did production and prices in America and much of the industrial world collapse during the Great Depression of the 1930s? Why was it during this period that millions of people were unable to find work and were living on the ragged edge of starvation? What forces propelled America into a sustained boom during World War II and then again during the Vietnam war? Why did unemployment rise to almost 11 percent of the labor force in 1982, only to decline steadily in the sustained expansion of the Reagan years? Why have prices risen a billionfold or more in some countries? And, most recently, why have sharp oil-price increases led to economic downturns three times in the last few years?

These vital questions are addressed by macroeconomics, which is introduced in this chapter. Section A examines the main macroeconomic concepts along with the central goals of macroeconomic policy. Section B then introduces the major tool of macroeconomic analysis—aggregate supply and demand—and applies this tool to analyze recent economic events in the United States.

Microeconomics vs. Macroeconomics

From Chapter 1 you will recall that **macroeconomics** is the study of the behavior of the economy as a whole. It examines the overall level of a nation's output, employment, prices, and foreign trade. By contrast, **microeconomics** studies individual prices, quantities, and markets.

A few examples will clarify this distinction. Microeconomics considers how an oil cartel might price its oil; macroeconomics asks why a sharp rise in the world price of oil causes inflation and unemployment. Microeconomics studies whether going to college is a good use of your time; macroeconomics examines the unemployment rate of young adults. Microeconomics examines the individual items of foreign trade, for example, why we import Toyotas and export heavy trucks. Macroeconomics examines overall trends in our imports and exports, asking questions such as why the exchange value of the dollar rose in the early 1980s and then fell in the late 1980s.

A. Macroeconomic Concepts and Goals

Goals and Instruments in Macroeconomics

The political, social, and military fate of nations depends greatly upon economic success, and no area of economics is today more vital to a nation's success than its macroeconomic performance. Countries like Japan, which has grown rapidly by winning export markets for its products, enjoy enhanced political power and higher living standards.

At the opposite extreme are countries that stagnate and suffer from rapid inflation, large trade deficits, and high foreign indebtedness. For example, although the Soviet Union is a vast country, well endowed with natural resources and human talent, its economic stagnation threatens to demote it to the rank of a second-rate power as its citizens scramble for bread.

A country's living standards depend crucially upon its macroeconomic policies. Before this century, countries had little understanding of how to combat periodic economic crises. But the revolutionary theory of John Maynard Keynes helped explain the forces producing economic fluctuations and devised an approach for controlling the worst excesses of business cycles. Thanks to Keynes and his modern successors, we know that in its choice of macroeconomic policies—those affecting the money supply, taxes, or government spending—a nation can speed or slow its economic growth, ignite a rapid inflation or slow price increases, produce a trade deficit or generate a trade surplus.

In analyzing macroeconomics, we always encounter a few key macroeconomic variables—the most important being gross national product (GNP), the unemployment rate, inflation, and net exports. These are the central measures by which we judge macroeconomic performance.

Table 23-1 lists the major goals and instruments of macroeconomic policy. We will now turn to a detailed discussion of each and examine some key questions that confront modern macroeconomics.

Objectives	Instruments
Output: High level Rapid growth rate	**Fiscal policy:** Government expenditure Taxation
Employment: High level of employment Low involuntary unemployment	**Monetary policy:** Control of money supply affecting interest rates
Price-level stability with free markets	**Foreign economics:** Trade policies Exchange-rate intervention
International trade: Export and import equilibrium Exchange-rate stability	**Incomes policies:** From voluntary wage-price guidelines to mandatory controls

Table 23-1. Goals and instruments of macroeconomic policy

The left-hand column displays the major goals of macroeconomic policy. These goals can be found in national laws and in the statements of political leaders. The right-hand column contains the major instruments or policy measures available to modern economies. These are the ways that policymakers can affect the pace and direction of economic activity.

Goals

To evaluate the success of an economy's overall performance, economists look at four areas: output, employment, price stability, and international trade.

Output. The ultimate objective of economic activity is to provide the goods and services that the population desires. What could be more important for an economy than to produce ample shelter, food, education, and recreation for its people?

The most comprehensive measure of the total output in an economy is the **gross national product (GNP).** GNP is the measure of the market value of all final goods and services—apples, bananas, concerts, dog races, . . . , yak coats, and zithers—produced in a country during a year. There are two ways to measure GNP. *Nominal GNP* is measured in actual market prices. *Real GNP* is calculated in constant or invariant prices (say for the year 1982).

Movements in real GNP are the best widely available measure of the level and growth of output; they serve as the carefully monitored pulse of a nation's economy. Figure 23-1 shows the history of real GNP in the United States since 1929. Note the economic decline during the Great Depression of the 1930s, the boom during World War II, the rapid and stable growth during the 1960s, the recessions in 1975 and 1982, and the steady growth in the long expansion from 1982 to 1990.

A study of the patterns of output growth in capitalist economies shows periods of expansion and contraction in real GNP. The fluctuations in overall economic activity are known as *business cycles.* During business-cycle downturns, millions of people lose their jobs, and the nation forgoes billions of dollars of goods and services because of depressed production. Business cycles have tended to be less violent since 1945 in part because progress in macroeconomics allowed policymakers to stabilize the economy after World War II.

Despite the short-term fluctuations in GNP seen in business cycles, advanced economies generally exhibit a steady long-term growth in real GNP and an improvement in living standards; this process is known as *economic growth.* The American economy has proven itself a powerful engine of progress over a period of more than a century, as shown by the growth in potential output.

Potential GNP is the long-run trend in real GNP. It represents the long-run productive capacity of the economy or the maximum amount the economy can produce while maintaining stable prices. Potential output is also sometimes called the high-

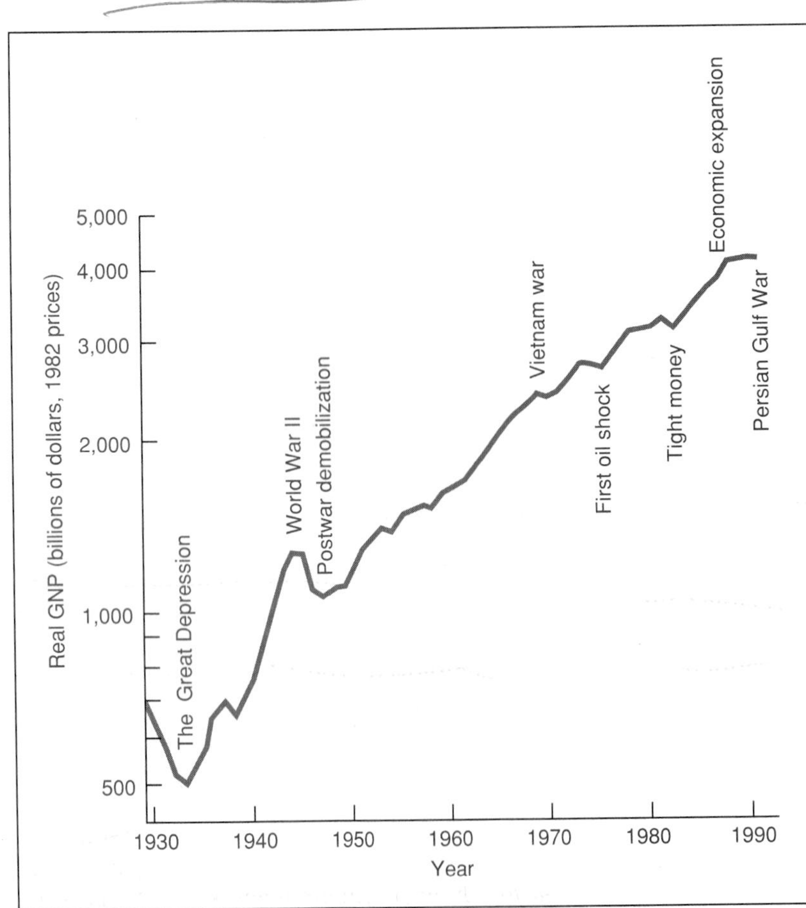

Figure 23-1. U.S. real gross national product, 1929–1991

Real GNP is the most comprehensive measure of an economy's output. Note that in the Depression output actually fell sharply. In the period since World War II, GNP growth was very steady until the economy was hit by numerous shocks in the 1970s and 1980s. (Source: U.S. Department of Commerce.)

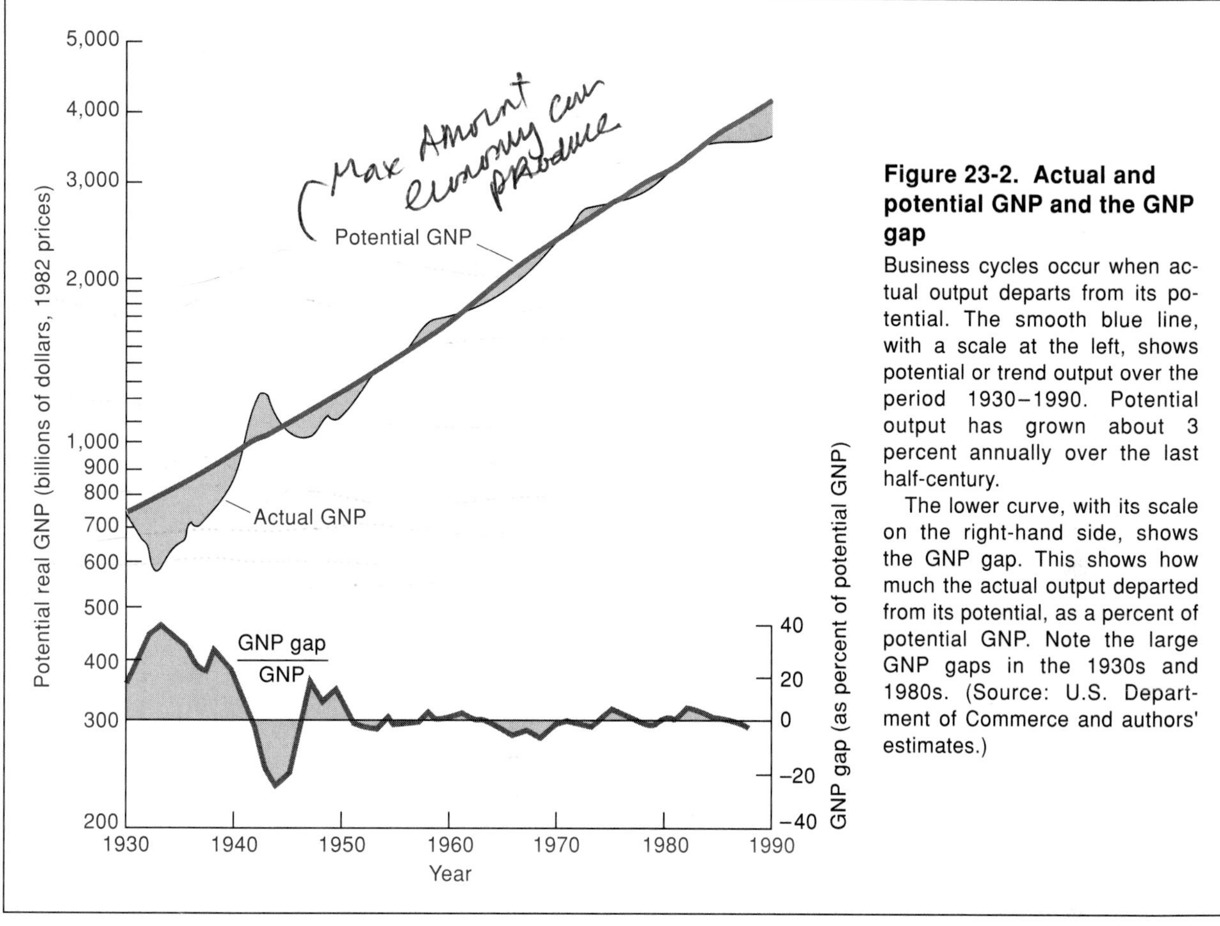

Figure 23-2. Actual and potential GNP and the GNP gap

Business cycles occur when actual output departs from its potential. The smooth blue line, with a scale at the left, shows potential or trend output over the period 1930–1990. Potential output has grown about 3 percent annually over the last half-century.

The lower curve, with its scale on the right-hand side, shows the GNP gap. This shows how much the actual output departed from its potential, as a percent of potential GNP. Note the large GNP gaps in the 1930s and 1980s. (Source: U.S. Department of Commerce and authors' estimates.)

employment level of output. When an economy is operating at its potential, unemployment is low and production is high.

During business cycles, actual GNP departs from its potential. In 1982 for example, the U.S. economy produced almost $300 billion less than potential output. This represented $5000 lost per family during a single year. The difference between potential and actual GNP is called the **GNP gap**. A large GNP gap means that the economy is in an economic downturn and is operating inside its production-possibility frontier. Economic downturns are called *recessions* when the gap is small and *depressions* when the gap is large. In years with large GNP gaps, goods are lost just as if they were dumped into the sea.

Figure 23-2 shows the estimated potential and actual output for the period 1930–1990. The gray areas between the two lines are the GNP gaps. Note the large gaps in the 1930s and the early 1980s.

High Employment, Low Unemployment. The next major goal of macroeconomic policy is *high employment,* which is the counterpart of *low unemployment.* People want to be able to find good, high-paying jobs without searching or waiting too long. Figure 23-3 shows trends in unemployment over the last six decades. The **unemployment rate** on the vertical axis is the percentage of the labor force that is unemployed. The labor force includes all employed persons and those unemployed individuals who are seeking jobs. It excludes those without work who are not looking for jobs.

The unemployment rate tends to move with the business cycle: when output is depressed, the demand for labor falls and the unemployment rate increases. Unemployment reached epidemic proportions in the Great Depression of the 1930s, when

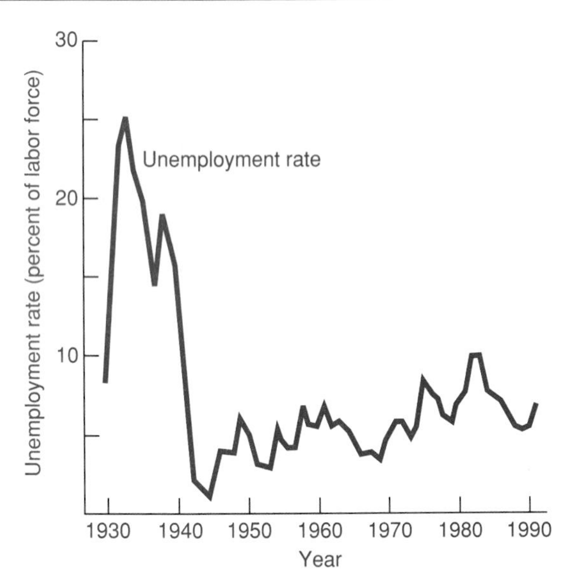

Figure 23-3. Unemployment rises in recessions, falls during expansions

The unemployment rate measures the fraction of the labor force that is looking for but cannot find work. Unemployment reached tragic proportions during the 1930s, peaking at 25 percent in 1933. Also note the upward creep of the unemployment rate since 1969, reaching a postwar high of 9.7 percent in 1982. (Source: U.S. Department of Labor.)

a quarter of the work force was idled. While the nation has avoided another Great Depression, over the last two decades there has been a marked upward drift in the fraction of the labor force that is unemployed. The goal of ensuring good jobs for all who want them has proven increasingly elusive.

Stable Prices. The third macroeconomic goal is to maintain *stable prices within free markets.* The desire to maintain free markets is a subtle concern, embodying the judgment that a smoothly functioning market economy is the most efficient way to organize most economic activity. In a free market, prices are determined by supply and demand to the maximum possible extent, and governments abstain from controlling the prices of individual goods. Only by allowing firms the ability to set prices freely can we ensure that the market will channel resources to their most effective use.

The second part of this goal is preventing the overall price level from rising or falling rapidly. Why is price stability desirable? A market economy uses prices as a yardstick to measure economic values and as a way to conduct business. When the economic yardstick changes rapidly during periods of rising prices, people become confused, make mistakes, and spend much of their time worrying about the value of their money. Rapid price changes lead to economic inefficiency.

The most common measure of the overall price level is the **consumer price index,** popularly known as the CPI. The CPI monitors the cost of a fixed basket of goods (including items such as food, shelter, clothing, and medical care) bought by the typical urban consumer. The overall price level is often denoted by the letter P.

We call changes in the level of prices the **rate of inflation,** which denotes the rate of growth or decline of the price level from one year to the next.[1] Figure 23-4 illustrates the rate of inflation for the CPI from 1929 to 1991. Over this entire period, inflation averaged 3.4 percent per year. Note that price changes fluctuated greatly over the years, varying from *minus* 10 percent in 1932 to 14 percent in 1947.

A **deflation** occurs when prices decline (i.e., the rate of inflation is negative). At the other extreme is a *hyperinflation,* a rise in the price level of a thousand or a million percent a year. In such situations, as in Weimar Germany of the 1920s and Poland in the 1980s, prices are virtually meaningless and the price system breaks down.

Most nations seek a golden mean of price flexibility, often tolerating a gentle inflation, as the best way to allow the price system to function efficiently.

International Trade. Finally, most countries strive to participate fruitfully in international trade so as to raise the living standards of their citizens. They import and export goods, services, and capital. They borrow from or lend money to foreigners. They imitate foreign technologies or sell new products abroad. Their people travel to all parts of the world for business and pleasure. And so on. For the long term, nations generally strive to keep imports

[1] More precisely the rate of inflation of the CPI is:

$$\text{Rate of inflation of consumer prices (in percent)} = \frac{\text{CPI (this year)} - \text{CPI (last year)}}{\text{CPI (last year)}} \times 100$$

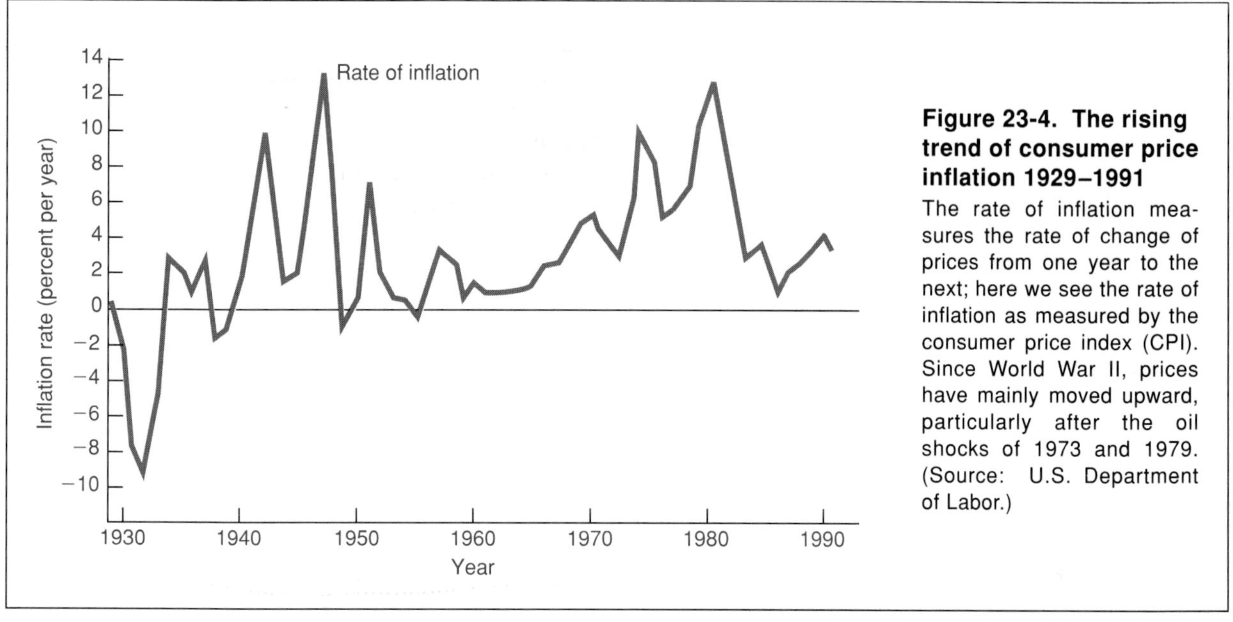

Figure 23-4. The rising trend of consumer price inflation 1929–1991
The rate of inflation measures the rate of change of prices from one year to the next; here we see the rate of inflation as measured by the consumer price index (CPI). Since World War II, prices have mainly moved upward, particularly after the oil shocks of 1973 and 1979. (Source: U.S. Department of Labor.)

and exports in balance. The numerical difference between the value of a country's exports and the value of its imports is called **net exports;** that is, net exports equal the value of exports minus the value of imports. When net exports are positive, a trade surplus exists. A trade deficit occurs when the value of imports is greater than the value of exports.

The goal of expanding international trade has become increasingly important as the nations of the globe have witnessed gains from international trade in spurring efficiency and raising economic growth. As the costs of transportation and communication links have declined, these international linkages have become tighter than they were a generation ago. International trade has replaced empire building and military conquest as the surest road to national wealth and influence. Some economies today trade over half their output.

One of the major developments of the 1980s was the change in pattern of U.S. international trade. For most of this century, the United States ran a trade surplus. That is, exports exceeded imports, yielding positive net exports. But in the 1980s, the value of imports exceeded exports and the United States incurred a trade deficit. Many Americans are concerned about the future impact of a large foreign debt.

The United States exports a variety of goods and services, including computers, grain, and aircraft, to other countries. We import oil, automobiles, electronic equipment, and a host of other commodities. Our consumption of foreign oil has been the cause of major economic disruptions in our economy over the past two decades. Most recently, when Iraq invaded the oil-rich nation of Kuwait, the sharp drop in oil supplies drove prices up, increased inflation, and contributed to an economic downturn in the United States.

Nations keep a close eye on their **foreign exchange rates,** which represent the price of their own currency in terms of the currencies of other nations. The foreign exchange rate of the U.S. dollar rose sharply against other currencies during the early 1980s and then fell sharply after 1985. For example, the U.S. dollar bought only 1.8 German marks in 1980, rose to 3.2 marks in 1985, and fell sharply to 1.8 marks in 1991.

When a nation's exchange rate rises, the prices of imported goods fall while exports become more expensive for foreigners. The result is that the nation becomes less competitive in world markets and net exports decline. Changes in exchange rates can also affect output, employment, and inflation. All these impacts make the exchange rate increasingly important for all nations.

We can summarize the goals of macroeconomic policy as follows:

1. A high and growing level of national output (i.e., real GNP)
2. High employment (with low unemployment)
3. A stable or gently rising price level, with prices and wages determined by supply and demand in free markets
4. Robust international trade in goods, services, and capital, with a stable foreign exchange rate and exports balancing imports

Policy Instruments

Put yourself in the shoes of the President or prime minister. Unemployment is rising and GNP is falling. Or, perhaps a recent rapid increase in oil prices has caused inflation to heat up, and the value of imports is rising much more rapidly than that of exports. What can your government do to improve economic performance? What policy tools can you use to reduce inflation or unemployment or to correct a trade imbalance?

Governments have certain instruments that they can use to affect macroeconomic activity. A *policy instrument* is an economic variable under the control of government that can affect one or more of the macroeconomic goals. That is, by changing monetary, fiscal, and other policies, governments can steer the economy toward a better mix of output, price stability, employment, and international trade. The four major sets of instruments of macroeconomic policy are listed on the right side of Table 23-1.

Fiscal Policy. Begin with *fiscal policy*, which denotes the use of taxes and government expenditures. The category of *government expenditure* includes government spending on goods and services—purchases of tanks and pencils, construction of dams and roads, salaries for judges and Army corporals, and so forth. Government spending determines the relative size of the public and private sectors, that is, how much of our GNP is consumed collectively rather than privately. From a macroeconomic perspective, government expenditure affects the overall level of spending in the economy and thereby influences the level of GNP.

The other part of fiscal policy, *taxation*, affects the overall economy in two ways. To begin with, taxes reduce people's incomes. By leaving households with less disposable or spendable income, taxes tend to reduce the amount people spend on goods and services. This in turn lowers the demand for goods and services, which ultimately lowers the actual GNP.

In addition, taxes affect market prices, thereby influencing incentives and behavior. For example, the more heavily business profits are taxed, the more businesses are discouraged from investing in new capital goods. In 1991 President Bush lobbied to reduce the tax on capital gains, arguing that a lower tax rate would stimulate economic growth. Many other provisions of the tax code have an important effect on economic activity.

Monetary Policy. The second major instrument of macroeconomic policy is *monetary policy*, which government conducts through the management of the nation's money, credit, and banking system. You may have read how our central bank, the Federal Reserve System, operates to regulate the money supply. But what exactly is the money supply? **Money** consists of the means of exchange or method of payment. Today, people use currency and checking accounts to pay their bills. By engaging in central-bank operations, the Federal Reserve can regulate the amount of money available to the economy.

How does such a minor thing as the money supply have such a large impact on macroeconomic activity? By changing the money supply, the Federal Reserve can influence many financial and economic variables, such as interest rates, stock prices, housing prices, and exchange rates. Restricting the money supply leads to higher interest rates and reduced investment, which, in turn, causes a decline in GNP and lower inflation. If the central bank is faced with a business downturn, it can increase the money supply and lower interest rates to stimulate economic activity.

The exact nature of monetary policy—the way in which the central bank controls the money supply and the relationships among money, output, and inflation—is one of the most fascinating, important, and controversial areas of macroeconomics. A policy of tight money in the United States—lowering the rate of growth of the money supply—raised interest rates, slowed economic growth, and raised unemployment in the period 1979–1982. Then from 1982 until 1990, careful monetary management by the Federal Reserve supported the longest economic expansion in American history. Exactly how a central bank can control economic activity will be thoroughly analyzed in the chapters on monetary policy.

International Economic Policy. As economies become more closely linked, policymakers devote increasing attention to international economic policy. The major instruments fall into two categories. The first is *trade policies,* which consist of tariffs, quotas, and other devices that restrict or encourage imports and exports. Most trade policies have little effect on macroeconomic performance, but from time to time, as was the case in the 1930s, restrictions on international trade are so severe that they cause major economic dislocations, inflations, or recessions.

A second set of policies specifically aimed at the foreign sector is *exchange-market management.* A country's international trade is influenced by its exchange rate, which represents the price of its own currency in terms of the currencies of other nations. Nations adopt different systems to regulate their foreign exchange markets. Some systems allow exchange rates to be determined purely by supply and demand; others set a fixed exchange rate against other currencies. The United States today is in the first category, generally allowing the dollar's exchange rates to be determined by market forces.

In addition, central bankers and political leaders increasingly gather to *coordinate* their macroeconomic policies, for a nation's monetary and fiscal policies can spill over to affect its neighbors. Since 1975, the leaders of the major industrial countries have met annually at economic summit meetings to discuss joint economic issues and to take appropriate measures for attaining commonly agreed-upon goals. Such meetings have dealt with a wide variety of concerns ranging from coping with oil-price increases to studying global environmental problems. They are a reminder that economies cannot manage themselves and that governments must constantly keep alert to economic instability.

Incomes Policies. When inflation threatens to get out of control, governments grope for ways to stabilize prices. The traditional route for slowing inflation has been for governments to take fiscal or monetary steps to reduce output and raise unemployment. But this traditional strategy has proven extremely costly. It takes hundreds of billions of dollars in lost GNP (or in the GNP gap) to reduce inflation by a few percentage points. Faced with the need to take such unpleasant medicine, governments have often searched for other methods of containing inflation. These alternatives range from wage and price controls (used primarily in wartime) to less drastic measures like voluntary wage and price guidelines. Policies to control wages and prices are known as **incomes policies.**

Incomes policies are the most controversial of all macroeconomic policies. A generation ago, many economists advocated wage-price policies as an inexpensive way to reduce inflation. Evidence on the impact of incomes policies along with a more conservative attitude toward government intervention has led to a general disenchantment with wage-price policies. Many economists now believe they are simply ineffective. Others think they are worse than useless—that they interfere with free markets, gum up relative price movements, and fail to reduce inflation.

A nation has a wide variety of policy instruments that can be used to pursue its macroeconomic goals. The major ones are these:

1. Fiscal policy consists of government expenditure and taxation. Government expenditure influences the relative size of collective as opposed to private consumption. Taxation subtracts from incomes and reduces private spending; in addition, it affects investment and potential output. Fiscal policy affects total spending and thereby influences real GNP and inflation.
2. Monetary policy, conducted by the central bank, determines the money supply. Changes in the money supply move interest rates up or down and affect spending in sectors such as investment, housing, and net exports. Monetary policy has an important effect on both actual GNP and potential GNP.
3. Foreign economic policies—trade policies, exchange-rate setting, and monetary and fiscal policies—attempt to keep imports in line with exports and to stabilize foreign exchange rates. Governments work together to coordinate their macroeconomic goals and policies.
4. Incomes policies are government attempts to moderate inflation by direct steps, whether by verbal persuasion or by legislated wage and price controls.

Macroeconomic Policies and Goals in Practice

Now that we have examined the major goals and instruments of macroeconomic policy, we consider the economic policies that have been pursued in the United States. Before the Great Depression of the 1930s, understanding of macroeconomics was primitive. Aside from familiar homilies like "balance the budget," there was nothing resembling a coherent theory for managing the economy.

The 1930s marked the first stirrings of the science of macroeconomics, initiated by the contribution of John Maynard Keynes.[2] After World War II, reflecting both the increasing influence of Keynesian views and the fear of a depression, the U.S. Congress formally proclaimed federal responsibility for macroeconomic performance. It enacted the landmark Employment Act of 1946, which stated:

> The Congress hereby declares that it is the continuing policy and responsibility of the federal government to use all practicable means consistent with its needs and obligations . . . to promote maximum employment, production, and purchasing power.

For the first time Congress affirmed the government's role in promoting output growth and employment and maintaining price stability. In addition to setting forth these lofty but somewhat vague goals, the Employment Act established the Council of Economic Advisers (or CEA) to be part of the presidential staff.[3]

In the 1980s, the nation's priorities shifted. During the Reagan years, the government passed large tax cuts and undertook an extensive military buildup. These policies produced a sharp increase in the federal budget deficit, which is the difference between government expenditures and tax revenues. People became alarmed about the impact of large deficits on economic growth, and in response Congress passed the Balanced Budget Act of 1985 (known as the Gramm-Rudman Act, after its chief sponsors).

Gramm-Rudman imposed a stern fiscal discipline, requiring Congress to balance the budget by 1991. If the required decline in the deficit was not met, government expenditures were to be cut automatically and across the board. The goals of the Gramm-Rudman Act proved difficult to attain as deficits climbed to record levels in early 1990; Congress repeatedly postponed the deadline for balancing the budget. In 1990, Congress modified the Gramm-Rudman Act to impose expenditure limitations on major federal budget categories.

Why has it proved so difficult to attain full employment with stable prices or a balanced budget with rapid economic growth? The answer to this question lies in the nature of the *constraints* and *tradeoffs* that face the macroeconomy. The production-possibility curve showed that we cannot have maximum guns and maximum butter, or high consumption today and high consumption tomorrow, or much private and much collective consumption. You cannot eat your cake today and have it tomorrow.

There are similar tradeoffs in macroeconomics. Macroeconomic policy requires choice among competing objectives. A nation cannot simultaneously have high consumption and rapid growth. Lowering a high inflation rate requires either a period of high unemployment and low output or interference with free markets through incomes policies. Reducing a trade deficit requires that a nation reduce domestic consumption and investment.

Of all the macroeconomic goals, the most agonizing is maintaining full employment of labor and

[2] John Maynard Keynes (1883–1946) was a many-sided genius who won eminence in the fields of mathematics, philosophy, and literature. In addition, he found time to run a large insurance company, advise the British treasury, help govern the Bank of England, edit a world-famous economics journal, collect modern art and rare books, and sponsor ballet and drama. He was also an economist who knew how to make money by shrewd speculation, both for himself and for his college, King's College, Cambridge. His 1936 book, *The General Theory of Employment, Interest and Money*, presented a profound challenge to macroeconomic thinking of the time and lay the foundation for the development of modern macroeconomics.

[3] In addition to advising the President, a major responsibility of the CEA is to prepare the *Economic Report of the President and the Council of Economic Advisers*, published annually along with the presidential budget. This document is required reading for macroeconomists. It contains a wealth of statistics and a diagnosis of current economic trends, along with analysis and defense of the administration's economic policies. Sometimes this dry document becomes controversial. A few years ago, President Reagan's Secretary of the Treasury said that the report of President Reagan's CEA was so bad that it should be "thrown in the wastebasket."

other resources. The electorate demands low unemployment and high output. But high levels of output and employment drive up prices and wages, and inflation tends to rise in periods of rapid economic growth. Policymakers are therefore forced to rein in the economy when it grows too fast, or when unemployment falls too far, in order to prevent runaway inflation.

An example of how policymakers reacted to inflation by slowing economic growth came during the oil-price shock of the late 1970s and early 1980s. After the Iranian revolution in 1978, oil production fell and oil prices jumped from $14 to $34 per barrel. Inflation in the United States rose from 6 percent in 1977 to 14 percent in 1980. Economic policymakers in the United States and abroad were frightened by the accelerating inflation. President Carter agonized: Should he slow down the economy, allow unemployment to rise, stifle economic growth, and face the wrath of the voters at the polls? Or should he introduce expansionary fiscal and monetary policies and risk igniting even greater inflation and even higher unemployment later on? Carter opted for an economic slowdown and a rise in unemployment. What would you have done?

Each country faced the same dilemma—and indeed the dilemma recurs again and again. It is impossible to escape the tradeoff between unemployment and inflation. Where prices and wages are determined in free markets, a policy to reduce inflation must pay the price in high unemployment and large GNP gaps. Conversely, if a nation wishes to grow rapidly and enjoy low unemployment, inflation will surely follow.

Other macroeconomic dilemmas confront policymakers. A country can temporarily curb inflation with wage and price controls, but the result is distorted prices and economic inefficiency. Increasing the rate of growth of potential GNP requires greater investment in knowledge and capital. This investment lowers current consumption of food, clothing, and recreation. These are the kinds of painful choices confronting macroeconomic policymakers in all market economies.

B. Aggregate Supply and Demand

We have seen that output, employment, and prices can change sharply under the influence of both economic policies and external shocks like rapid changes in oil prices. But we can go beyond description to diagnosis. What is the *economic mechanism* that transmits money or taxes or changing oil prices into output and retail prices? How can governments take steps to improve the economy's performance?

We begin our analysis of the forces determining overall economic activity by introducing a useful apparatus, aggregate supply and demand. This analysis allows us to understand how different forces affect the macroeconomy and to see how government policies can help counteract the slings and arrows of external shocks. After explaining this new tool, we conclude by using aggregate supply and demand to understand some important historical events.

Inside the Macroeconomy: Aggregate Supply and Demand

We begin with a simple picture of the forces operating on the macroeconomy, shown in Figure 23-5. This figure shows on the left the major variables affecting the macroeconomic system. First are the instruments or policy variables discussed in the last section: taxes, monetary policy, and so forth. In addition, we see a set of **external variables,** which influence economic activity but are unaffected by the economy. These variables include wars and revolutions, the weather, population growth, and many other factors.

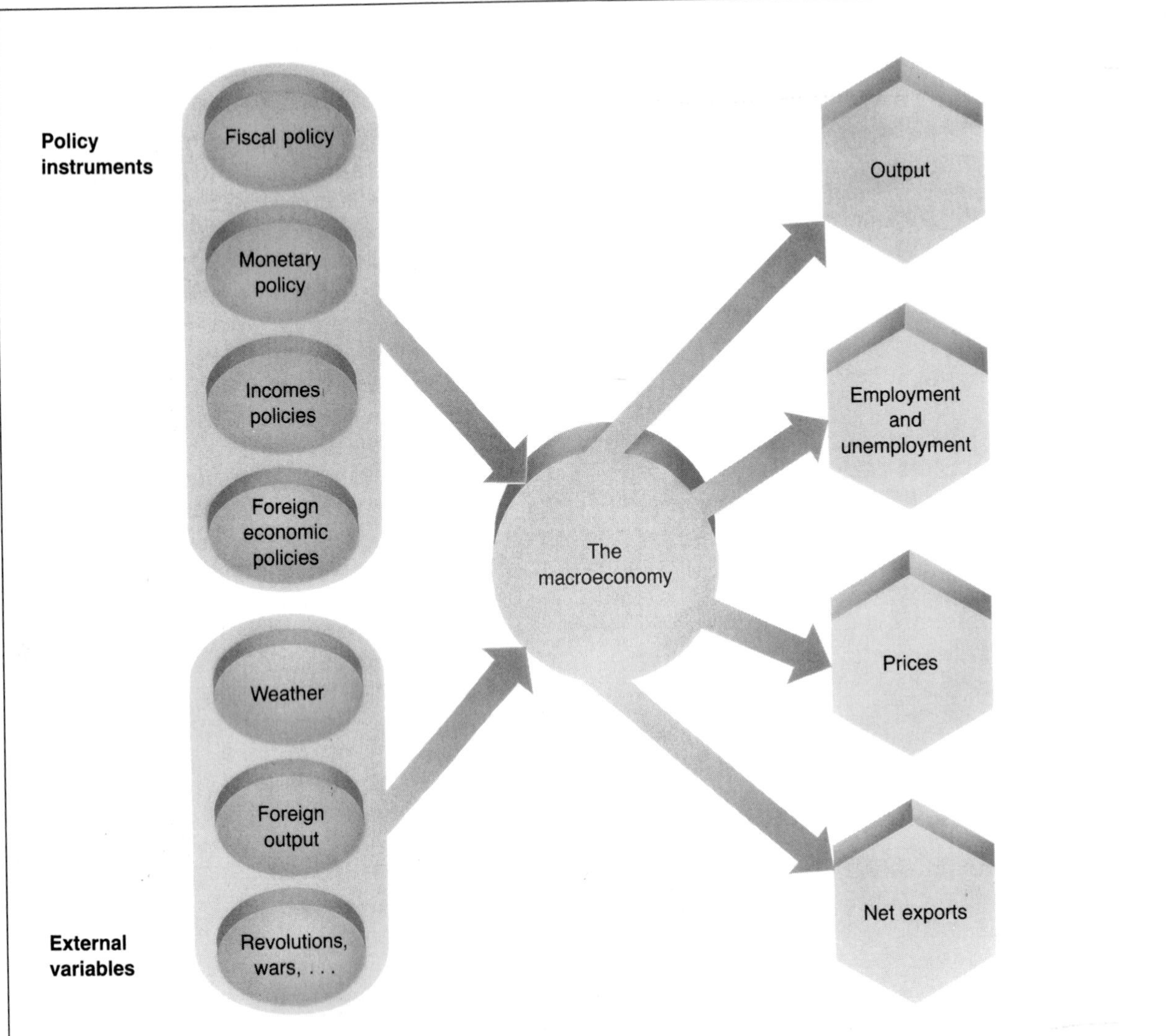

Figure 23-5. How do different factors affect the macroeconomy?
Policy variables (such as monetary or fiscal policy) along with external variables (those largely outside the control of domestic economic forces, like wars or output of foreign countries) interact to determine output, prices, employment, and net exports.

The policy and external variables interact to determine the key macroeconomic variables, shown on the right in Figure 23-5. Policy instruments and external variables determine national output, employment and unemployment, the price level, and net exports.

Definitions of Aggregate Supply and Demand

How do different forces interact to determine overall economic activity? Figure 23-6 shows the relationships among the different variables inside the macroeconomy. It separates policy and external variables into two categories: those affecting aggregate supply and those affecting aggregate demand. Dividing variables into these two categories is essential for our understanding of what determines the level of output, prices, and unemployment.

The lower part of Figure 23-6 shows the forces affecting aggregate supply. **Aggregate supply** refers to the total quantity of goods and services that the nation's businesses are willing to produce and sell in a given period. Aggregate supply (often written *AS*) depends upon the price level, the productive capacity of the economy, and the level of costs.

In general, businesses would like to produce at full capacity and sell all their output at high prices. However, in certain circumstances, prices and spending levels may be depressed, so businesses might find they have excess capacity. Under other conditions, such as during a wartime boom, factories may be operating at capacity as businesses scramble to produce to meet all their orders.

We see, then, that aggregate supply depends on the price level that businesses can charge as well as on the economy's capacity or potential output. But what determines potential output? Potential output is determined by the availability of productive inputs (labor and capital being the most important) and the efficiency with which those inputs are combined (that is, the technology of the society).

National output and the overall price level are determined by the twin blades of the scissors of aggregate supply and demand. The second blade of

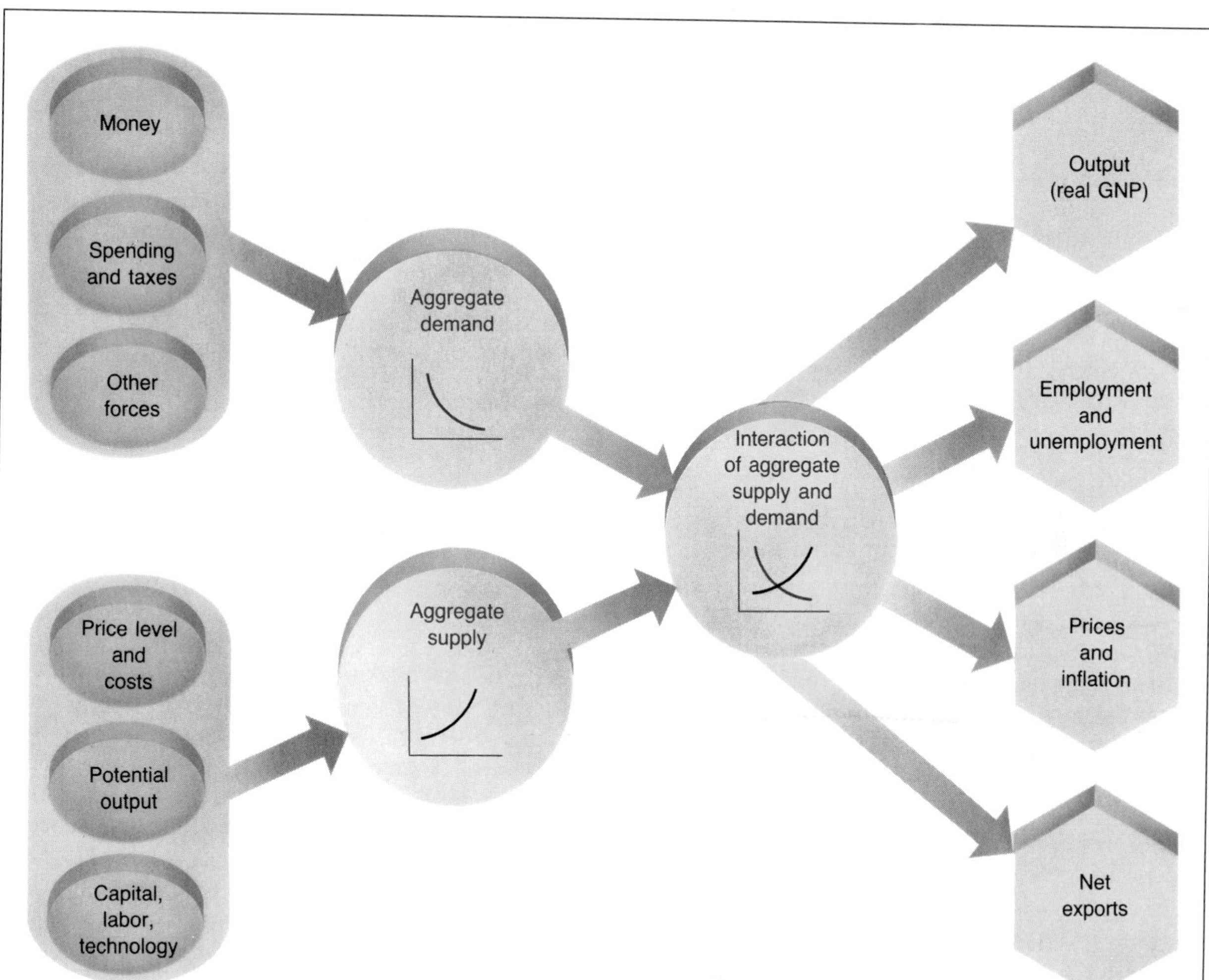

Figure 23-6. Aggregate supply and demand determine the major macroeconomic variables

This key diagram shows the major factors affecting overall economic activity. On the left are the major variables determining aggregate supply and demand: policy variables like monetary and fiscal policies along with stocks of capital and labor. In the center, aggregate supply and demand interact as the level of demand beats upon the available resources. The chief outcomes are shown on the right in hexagons: output, employment, prices, and net exports.

the scissors is **aggregate demand,** which refers to the total amount that different sectors in the economy willingly spend in a given period. Aggregate demand (often written *AD*) is the sum of spending by consumers, businesses, and other agents and depends on the level of prices, as well as on monetary policy, fiscal policy, and other factors.

In other words, aggregate demand measures total spending by all the different entities in the economy. It depends upon the cars, food, and other consumption goods bought by consumers; on plants and equipment bought by businesses; on smart bombs and computers bought by government; and on net exports. The total purchases are affected by the prices at which the goods are offered, by external forces, and by government policies.

Using both blades of the scissors of aggregate supply and demand, we can see the resulting equilibrium, as is shown in the right-hand circle of Figure 23-6. National output and the price level will move to that level where demanders willingly buy what businesses willingly sell. The resulting output and price level determine employment, unemployment, and net exports.

Aggregate Supply and Demand Curves

Supply and demand curves are often used to help analyze macroeconomic equilibrium. Recall that in Chapter 4 we used market supply and demand curves to analyze the prices and quantities of individual products. An analogous graphical apparatus can also help us understand the major macroeconomic issues of aggregate output and price determination. Using aggregate supply and demand, we can see how monetary expansion leads to rising prices and higher output. We can also see why increases in efficiency may lead to higher output and to a *lower* overall price level. Moreover, this powerful analysis will explain why a rise in world oil prices can lead to "stagflation," the unhappy circumstance where *stag*nation is combined with in*flation.*

Figure 23-7 shows the aggregate supply and demand schedules for the output of an entire economy. On the horizontal, or quantity, axis is the total output (real GNP) of the economy. On the vertical axis is the overall price level (say, as measured by the CPI).

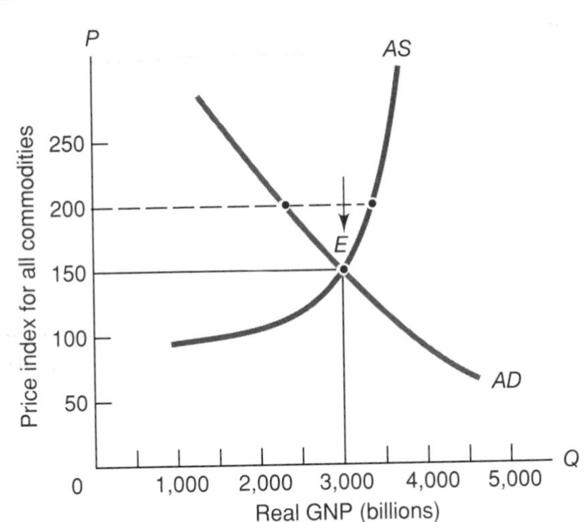

Figure 23-7. Aggregate price and output are determined by the interaction of aggregate supply and demand

National output and the overall price level are determined at the intersection of the aggregate demand and supply curves.

The *AD* curve represents the quantity of total spending at different price levels, with other factors held constant. The *AS* curve shows what firms will produce and sell at different price levels, other things equal.

The macroeconomic equilibrium lies at point *E*; this intersection occurs at an overall price level where firms willingly produce and sell an output of *Q* = 3000, and spenders willingly buy just that amount.

The downward-sloping curve is the **aggregate demand schedule,** or ***AD* curve.** It represents what all the entities in the economy—consumers, businesses, foreigners, and governments—would buy at different aggregate price levels (with other factors affecting aggregate demand held constant). From the curve, we see that at an overall price level of 150, total spending would be $3000 billion. If the price level were to rise to 200, total spending would fall to $2300 billion.

The upward-sloping curve is the **aggregate supply schedule,** or ***AS* curve.** This curve represents the quantity of goods and services that businesses are willing to produce and sell at each price level (with other determinants of aggregate supply held constant). According to the curve, businesses will want to sell $3000 billion at a price level of 150; they will want to sell a higher quantity, $3300 billion, if prices rise to 200. As the level of total output demanded rises, businesses will want to sell more goods and services at a higher price level.

It is necessary to mention one word of caution at this time: We must be careful not to confuse the macroeconomic *AD* or *AS* curves with the microeconomic *DD* or *SS* curves. The microeconomic supply and demand curves show the quantities and prices of *individual* commodities, with such things as national income and other goods' prices held as given. By contrast, the aggregate supply and demand curves show the determination of *total* output and the *overall* price level, with such things as the money supply, fiscal policy, and the capital stock held constant. The two sets of curves have a family resemblance, but they explain very different phenomena.

Macroeconomic Equilibrium. By looking at *AS* and *AD* together, we can also find the *equilibrium values of price and quantity*. That is, we can find the real GNP and the price level that would satisfy both buyers and sellers. For the *AS* and *AD* curves shown in Figure 23-7, the overall economy is in *equilibrium* at point *E*. Only at that point, where the level of output is $Q = 3000$ and $P = 150$, are spenders and sellers satisfied. Only at point *E* are demanders willing to buy exactly the amount that businesses are willing to produce and sell.

How does the economy reach its equilibrium? Indeed, what do we mean by equilibrium? A macroeconomic equilibrium is a combination of overall price and quantity at which neither buyers nor sellers wish to change their purchases, sales, or prices. Figure 23-7 illustrates the concept. If the price level were higher than equilibrium, say $P = 200$, then businesses would want to sell more than purchasers would want to buy. Goods would accumulate on the shelves as firms produce more than consumers buy. As the goods continue to pile up, firms would cut production and begin to shave their prices. As the price level declines from its original too-high level of 200, the gap between desired spending and desired sales would narrow until the equilibrium at $P = 150$ and $Q = 3000$ is reached. Once the equilibrium is reached, neither buyers nor sellers wish to change their quantities demanded or supplied, and there is no pressure on the price level to change.

Macroeconomic History: 1960–1991

We can use the aggregate supply-and-demand apparatus to analyze the recent macroeconomic history of the United States. This case study will focus on three major events: the economic expansion during the Vietnam war, the stagflation caused by the supply shocks of the 1970s, and the deep recession caused by the monetary contraction of the early 1980s.

Wartime Boom. The American economy entered the 1960s having experienced numerous recessions. John Kennedy took over the presidency hoping to resuscitate the economy. During this era the "New Economics," as the Keynesian approach was called, came to Washington. Economic advisers to Presidents Kennedy and Johnson recommended expansionary policies, and Congress enacted measures to stimulate the economy, including sharp cuts in personal and corporate taxes in 1964 and 1965. GNP grew 4 percent annually during the early 1960s, unemployment declined, and prices were stable. By 1965, the economy was at its potential output.

Unfortunately, the government underestimated the magnitude of the buildup for the Vietnam war; defense spending grew by 55 percent from 1965 to 1968. Even when it became clear that a major inflationary boom was under way, President Johnson postponed painful fiscal steps to slow the economy. Tax increases and civilian expenditure cuts came only in 1968, which was too late to prevent inflationary pressures from overheating the economy. The Federal Reserve accommodated the expansion with rapid money growth and low interest rates. As a result, for much of the period 1966–1970, the economy operated far above its potential output. Inflation gradually rose under the pressure of low unemployment and high factory utilization.

Figure 23-8 illustrates the events of this period. The tax cuts and defense expenditures increased aggregate demand, shifting the aggregate demand curve to the right from *AD* to *AD'*. Equilibrium moved from *E* to *E'*. Output and employment rose sharply, and prices began to creep upward as output exceeded capacity limits.

The lesson of this episode is that increasing aggregate demand produces higher output and employment. But if expansion takes the economy well

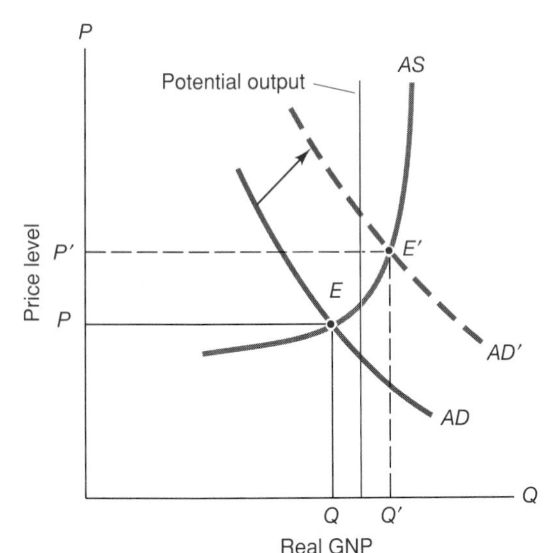

Figure 23-8. Wartime boom is propelled by increasing aggregate demand

During wartime, increased defense spending increases aggregate spending, moving aggregate demand from *AD* to *AD′*, with equilibrium output increasing from *E* to *E′*. When output rises far above potential output, the price level moves up sharply from *P* to *P′* and wartime inflation ensues.

beyond potential output, an overheated economy and price inflation will soon follow.

Supply Shocks and Stagflation. During the 1970s, the industrial world was struck by a new macroeconomic malady, supply shocks. A **supply shock** refers to a sudden change in conditions of cost or productivity that shifts aggregate supply sharply. Supply shocks occurred with particular virulence in 1973. Called the "year of the seven plagues," 1973 was marked by crop failures, shifting ocean currents, massive speculation on world commodity markets, turmoil in foreign exchange markets, and a quadrupling of the world price of crude oil.

This jolt to crude material and fuel supplies raised wholesale prices dramatically. The prices of crude materials and fuels rose more from 1972 to 1973 than they had in the entire period from the end of World War II to 1972. Shortly after the supply shock, inflation mounted sharply, and real output fell as the United States experienced a period of stagflation.

How can we understand the combination of falling output and rising prices? The sudden rise in the cost of raw materials constituted a supply shock, which we can depict as a sharp upward shift in the aggregate supply curve. An upward shift in *AS* indicates that businesses will supply the same level of output only at substantially higher prices. Figure 23-9 illustrates a supply shift.

The results of a supply shock are startling: A supply shock, seen as a sharp upward shift in the *AS* curve, results in higher prices along with a decline in output. Supply shocks thus lead to a deterioration of all the major goals of macroeconomic policy.

Tight Money, 1979–1982. By 1979 the economy had recovered from the 1973 supply shock. Output had returned to its potential. But unrest in the Mid-

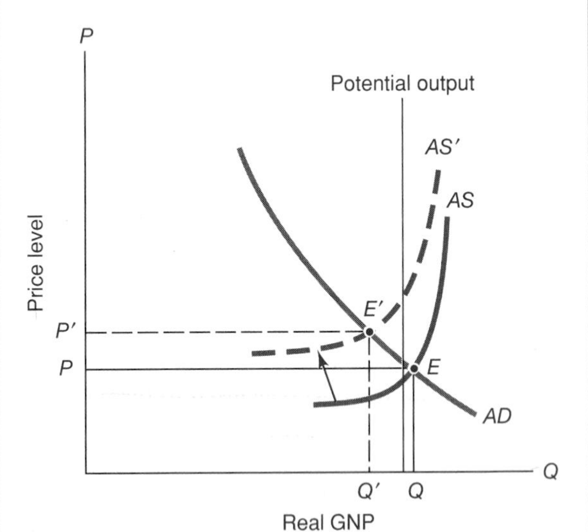

Figure 23-9. Effects of supply shocks

The effect of sharply higher oil, commodity, or labor costs is an increase in the costs of doing business. This leads to stagflation—stagnation combined with inflation.

As a result of the higher costs of oil and other inputs, businesses charge more for their products. The *AS* curve shifts up from *AS* to *AS′* and equilibrium shifts from *E* to *E′*. Output declines from *Q* to *Q′*, while prices rise. The economy thus suffers a double whammy—lower output *and* higher prices.

dle East led to another oil shock as the Iranian revolution produced a jump in oil prices from $14 per barrel in early 1978 to $34 per barrel in 1979. Inflation increased dramatically—averaging 12 percent per year from 1978 to 1980.

Double-digit inflation was unacceptable, and the Federal Reserve took steps to slow the inflation. Paul Volcker, then chairman of the Federal Reserve Board, used monetary policy to raise interest rates in 1979 (these steps constitute *tight money*). Interest rates rose sharply in 1979 and 1980, the stock market fell, and credit was hard to find. The Fed's tight-money policy slowed spending by consumers and businesses. Particularly hard-hit were interest-sensitive components of aggregate demand. After 1979, housing construction, automobile purchases, business investment, and net exports declined sharply.

Figure 23-10 shows how tight money raised interest rates and reduced aggregate demand. This result can be seen as a downward shift of the aggregate demand curve—exactly the opposite of the effect of the defense buildup during the 1960s. The decrease in aggregate demand reduced output almost 10 percent below its potential by the end of 1982, and the unemployment rate rose from below 6 percent in 1979 to more than 10 percent at the end of 1982.

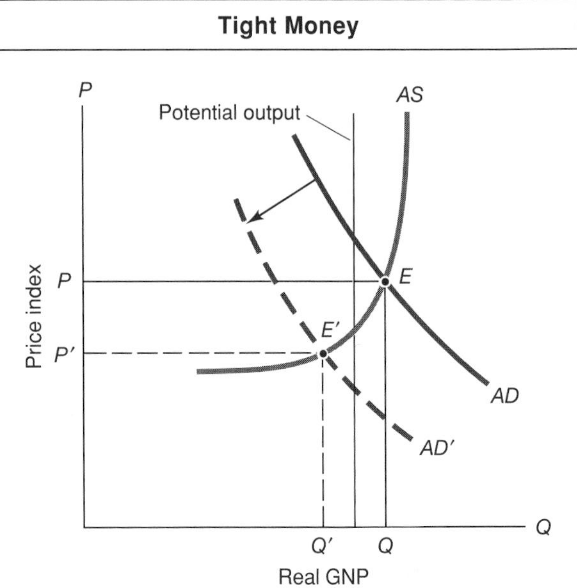

Figure 23-10. Tight money reduces output and inflation

From 1979 to 1982, the Federal Reserve slowed growth in money and credit, reducing aggregate demand, and producing a sharp downturn in economic activity. As a result, wage and price inflation slowed to a crawl for the rest of the 1980s.

The reward for these austere measures was a dramatic decline in inflation, from an average of 12 percent per year in the 1979–1980 period to 4 percent during the period from 1983 to 1988. High unemployment succeeded in wringing inflation out of the economy, but the cost was great in terms of lost output, income, and employment.

The low inflation and excess capacity of the early 1980s set the stage for the long economic expansion of the Reagan years and early part of the Bush administration. Real GNP grew steadily from 1982 to 1990, averaging $3\frac{1}{2}$ percent annually; unemployment fell from over 10 percent in 1982 to $5\frac{1}{2}$ percent in 1988–1990; and inflation remained in an acceptable region, averaging $3\frac{1}{2}$ percent from 1982 to 1990.

Economic Policy

We have seen some of the crucial forces that affect macroeconomic activity. Some factors operate on the spending side, changing aggregate demand because of shifts in consumer preferences or military expenditures. Other disturbances arise on the supply side, as when war or revolution leads to a doubling of oil prices or when bad harvests lead to major food-price increases.

The major task of macroeconomic policy today is to diagnose the different ailments affecting aggregate supply and demand and to prescribe the appropriate policies to remedy them. In some cases, policymakers face no dilemmas. For example, if the economy is heading into a recession when wartime spending begins to grow, as in early 1991, then no measures are immediately necessary to offset the higher spending. Or if the economy is operating at potential output, and the end of the cold war allows deep cuts in military spending, then the diagnosis is straightforward: the military cuts would tend to decrease aggregate demand, and most economists would agree that economic policy should offset the spending cuts by using monetary or fiscal policy to increase aggregate demand.

Other kinds of shocks pose difficult or even irreconcilable dilemmas. How should the Bush administration and the Federal Reserve respond to a major oil-price shock if one were to occur? As aggregate supply contracts (in the manner shown in Figure 23-9), should policymakers "accommodate" the price rise by increasing aggregate demand to prevent any output loss? Or should economic policy be "nonaccommodative," contracting aggregate demand to prevent any increase in the overall price level? An accommodative policy will lead to high inflation and low unemployment; a nonaccommodative approach will produce an economic downturn and high unemployment while preventing rising inflation.

Which approach is correct? Economists can provide no scientifically correct answer to such questions, for they are *normative* issues involving dilemmas of social and political values. But economics can strive to answer *positive* questions, estimating the gains and losses from inflation and unemployment associated with different policy approaches. But ultimately the painful choice between inflation and unemployment must be made by voters and their representatives.

SUMMARY

A. Macroeconomic Concepts and Goals

1. We begin the study of macroeconomics, which concerns the broad aggregates of economic life: total output, unemployment and inflation, the money supply and the budget deficit, international trade and finance. This contrasts with microeconomics, which studies the behavior of individual markets, prices, and outputs.

2. The major goals of a macroeconomy are:
   (a) High levels and rapid growth of output and consumption. Output is usually measured by the gross national product, which is the total value of all final goods and services produced in a given year. Also, GNP should be high relative to potential GNP, the maximum-sustainable or high-employment level of output.
   (b) High employment, with an ample supply of good jobs.
   (c) Price-level stability (or low inflation), through prices and wages set in free markets.
   (d) Fruitful international trade in goods, services, and capital, where exports balance imports and the nation has a stable exchange rate against foreign currencies.

3. Before the science of macroeconomics was developed, countries tended to drift around in the shifting macroeconomic currents without a rudder. Today, there are numerous instruments with which governments can steer the economy:
   (a) Fiscal policy (government spending and taxation) helps determine the allocation of resources between private and collective goods, affects people's incomes and consumption, and provides incentives for investment and other economic decisions.
   (b) Monetary policy (particularly central-bank regulation of the money supply to influence interest rates and credit conditions) affects sectors in the economy that are interest-sensitive. The most affected sectors are housing, business investment, and net exports.

(c) Foreign economic policies, affecting foreign trade and commerce and international financial flows, encourage economic gains from trade. Nations regulate international trade through trade policies and through the exchange-rate system that governs the prices of foreign goods and services.

(d) Incomes policies (government programs that directly affect wage and price decisions) attempt to control inflation without incurring the high costs of recessions and unemployment. Because they interfere with market efficiency, they are sparingly used in peacetime today.

4. The United States has developed legislative macroeconomic goals only since World War II. The Employment Act of 1946 declared a federal policy "to promote maximum employment, production, and purchasing power." The 1985 Balanced Budget (or Gramm-Rudman) Act emphasized reducing the federal budget deficit, mandating a gradual reduction of deficits toward a balanced-budget goal.

5. The United States, along with other industrial countries, was dogged by stagflation (stagnation plus inflation) during most of the 1970s and 1980s. Macroeconomic policy confronts crucial tradeoffs or choices among competing objectives. Key macroeconomic tradeoffs are those between high consumption and rapid growth and between free markets and stable prices and, most important, the cruel dilemma of choosing between unemployment and inflation.

B. Aggregate Supply and Demand

6. The central concepts for understanding the determination of national output and the price level are aggregate supply (*AS*) and aggregate demand (*AD*). Aggregate demand is composed of the total spending in an economy by households, businesses, governments, and foreigners. It represents the total real output that would be willingly bought at each price level, given the monetary and fiscal policies and other factors affecting demand. Aggregate supply describes how much output businesses would willingly produce and sell given prices, costs, and market conditions.

7. *AS* and *AD* curves have the same shapes as the familiar microeconomic supply and demand curves analyzed in Chapter 4. The *AD* curve shows the amount that consumers, firms, and other sectors would buy for each level of prices, with other factors held constant. The *AS* curve depicts the amount that businesses willingly produce and sell for each price level, other things held constant.

8. The overall macroeconomic equilibrium, determining both aggregate price and output, comes where the *AS* and *AD* curves intersect. At the equilibrium price level, purchasers willingly buy what businesses willingly sell. Equilibrium output can depart from full employment or potential output.

9. Recent American history shows an irregular cycle of aggregate demand and supply shocks and policy reactions. In the mid-1960s, Vietnam war–bloated deficits plus easy money led to a rapid increase in aggregate demand. The result was a sharp upturn in prices and inflation.

In the early 1970s, and again in 1990, adverse supply shocks led to an upward shift in aggregate supply. This led to stagflation, with a simultaneous rise in unemployment and inflation.

At the end of the 1970s, economic policymakers reacted to the rising inflation by tightening monetary policy and raising interest rates. The result was lower spending on interest-sensitive demands such as housing, investment, and net exports. The decline in aggregate demand caused a deep recession during the early 1980s, with the unemployment rate at its highest level in half a century.

CONCEPTS FOR REVIEW

Major macroeconomic concepts
macroeconomics vs. microeconomics
gross national product (GNP), actual and potential
employment, unemployment, unemployment rate
inflation, deflation
consumer price index (CPI)
incomes policy
net exports
fiscal policy (government expenditures, taxation)
money, monetary policy

Aggregate supply and demand
aggregate supply, aggregate demand
AS curve, *AD* curve
equilibrium of *AS* and *AD*
three macroeconomic shocks: wartime boom, supply shock, tight money
stagflation

QUESTIONS FOR DISCUSSION

1. What are the major goals of macroeconomics? Write a brief definition of each of the major goals. Explain why nations pursue each goal.
2. If a nation desires to have stable prices (or low inflation), why not simply pass a law that prohibits firms from changing prices?
3. If the CPI were 300 in 1993 and 315 in 1994, what would the inflation rate be for 1994?
4. What would be the effect of each of the following on aggregate demand or on aggregate supply, as indicated?
   (a) A large oil-price increase (on *AS*)
   (b) An arms-reduction agreement reducing defense spending (on *AD*)
   (c) An increase in potential output (on *AS*)
   (d) A monetary loosening that lowers interest rates (on *AD*)
5. For each of the events listed in question 4, use the *AS-AD* apparatus to show the effect on output and on the overall price level.
6. Put yourself in the shoes of an economic policymaker. The economy is in equilibrium with $P = 100$ and $Q = 3000 =$ potential GNP. You refuse to "accommodate" inflation; i.e., you want to keep prices absolutely stable at $P = 100$, no matter what happens to output. Finally, you can use monetary and fiscal policies to affect aggregate demand, but you cannot affect aggregate supply. How would you respond to:
   (a) A surprise increase in investment spending
   (b) A sharp food price increase following a major drought
   (c) A productivity decline that decreases potential output
   (d) An agreement to cut conventional military forces and associated expenditures by 20 percent
   (e) A sharp increase in net exports that followed a fall in the dollar's foreign exchange rate
7. In 1982–1983, the Reagan administration reduced taxes and increased government spending.
   (a) Explain why this policy would tend to increase aggregate demand; show the impact on output and prices assuming only an *AD* shift.
   (b) The "supply-side" school holds that tax cuts will affect aggregate supply mainly by increasing potential output. Assuming that the Reagan fiscal measures affected *AS* as well as *AD*, show the impact on output and the price level. Explain why the impact on output is unambiguous while the impact on prices is unclear.
8. After Iraq invaded Kuwait in 1990, oil prices rose sharply and the U.S. increased its defense spending. Review the impact of these two events on the econ-

omy. From what you know, write a short essay (like that under "Macroeconomic History," pages 409–411) describing the events and analyzing the period using *AS-AD* analysis.

9. Consider the data on real GNP and the price level in the table on the right.
   (a) For the years 1981 to 1985, calculate the rate of growth of real GNP and the rate of inflation. Can you guess in which year there was a steep recession?
   (b) In an *AS-AD* diagram like Figure 23-7, draw a set of *AS* and *AD* curves that would trace out the price and output equilibria shown in the table. How would you explain the recession that you have identified?

Year	Real GNP ($, billion, 1982 prices)	Price level* (1982 = 100)
1980	3,187	85.7
1981	3,249	94.0
1982	3,166	100.0
1983	3,279	103.9
1984	3,501	107.7
1985	3,619	110.9

*Note that the price index shown is the "GNP deflator," which is the price of all components of GNP.
(Source: *Economic Report of the President,* 1991.)

C H A P T E R 24

MEASURING NATIONAL OUTPUT AND INCOME

When you can measure what you are speaking about, and express it in numbers, you know something about it; when you cannot measure it, when you cannot express it in numbers, your knowledge is of a meager and unsatisfactory kind; it may be the beginning of knowledge, but you have scarcely, in your thoughts, advanced to the stage of science.

Lord Kelvin

Like other empirical sciences, economics focuses on concepts that can actually be measured—things such as prices of wheat, stock prices and interest rates, number of unemployed people, national output, or the price level. This chapter focuses on one of the most important sets of concepts in all economics, the national income and product accounts. We will learn here how to measure the gross national product (or GNP), which is the total dollar value of the national output.

Measuring national output is indispensable for macroeconomic theory and policy. It prepares us for tackling the central issues concerning economic growth, the business cycle, the relationship between economic activity and unemployment, and the measurement and determinants of inflation. Before the concept of GNP was invented, it was difficult to assess the state of the economy. Although the GNP has no patent and is not displayed in the Museum of Science and Technology, it is truly one of the great inventions of the twentieth century. Without measures of economic aggregates like GNP, macroeconomics would be adrift in a sea of unorganized data. The GNP data help policymakers steer the economy toward the nation's objectives.

In this chapter, we will also consider some of the criticisms of GNP. People do not live by bread alone, nor does society live on GNP alone. These days, we are increasingly concerned lest material growth be gained at the expense of the quality of the environment. Is it inevitable, people ask, that in driving our cars or air conditioning our houses we must also pollute the air and water and perhaps even change our climate? To answer this question, we must devise ways of converting the GNP concept into a more adequate measure of economic activity—hence the concept of *net economic welfare* or *NEW*.

Gross National Product: The Yardstick of an Economy's Performance

What is the **gross national product?** GNP is the name we give to the total dollar value of the final goods and services produced by a nation during a given year. It is the figure you arrive at when you apply the measuring rod of money to the diverse goods and services—from apples to zithers, from battleships to machine tools—that a country produces with its land, labor, and capital resources. GNP equals the sum of the money values of all consumption and investment goods, government purchases, and net exports to other lands.

GNP is used for many purposes, but the most important one is to measure the overall performance of an economy. If you ask an economic historian what happened during the Great Depression, the best short answer would be:

Between 1929 and 1933, GNP fell from $104 billion to $56 billion. This sharp decline in the money value of goods and services produced by the American economy caused hardship, bankruptcies, bank failures, riots, and political turmoil.

The gross national product (or GNP) is the most comprehensive measure of a nation's total output of goods and services. It is the sum of the dollar values of consumption, gross investment, government purchases of goods and services, and net exports.

We now discuss the elements of the national income and product accounts. We start by showing different ways of measuring GNP and distinguishing real from nominal GNP. We then analyze the major components of GNP. Finally, we reflect on the shortcomings of GNP as an index of economic welfare and suggest an alternative approach to measuring national output.

Two Measures of National Product: Goods-Flow and Earnings-Flow

How do economists actually measure GNP? One of the major surprises is that we can measure GNP in two entirely independent ways. As Figure 24-1 shows, GNP can be measured either as a flow of products or as a sum of earnings.

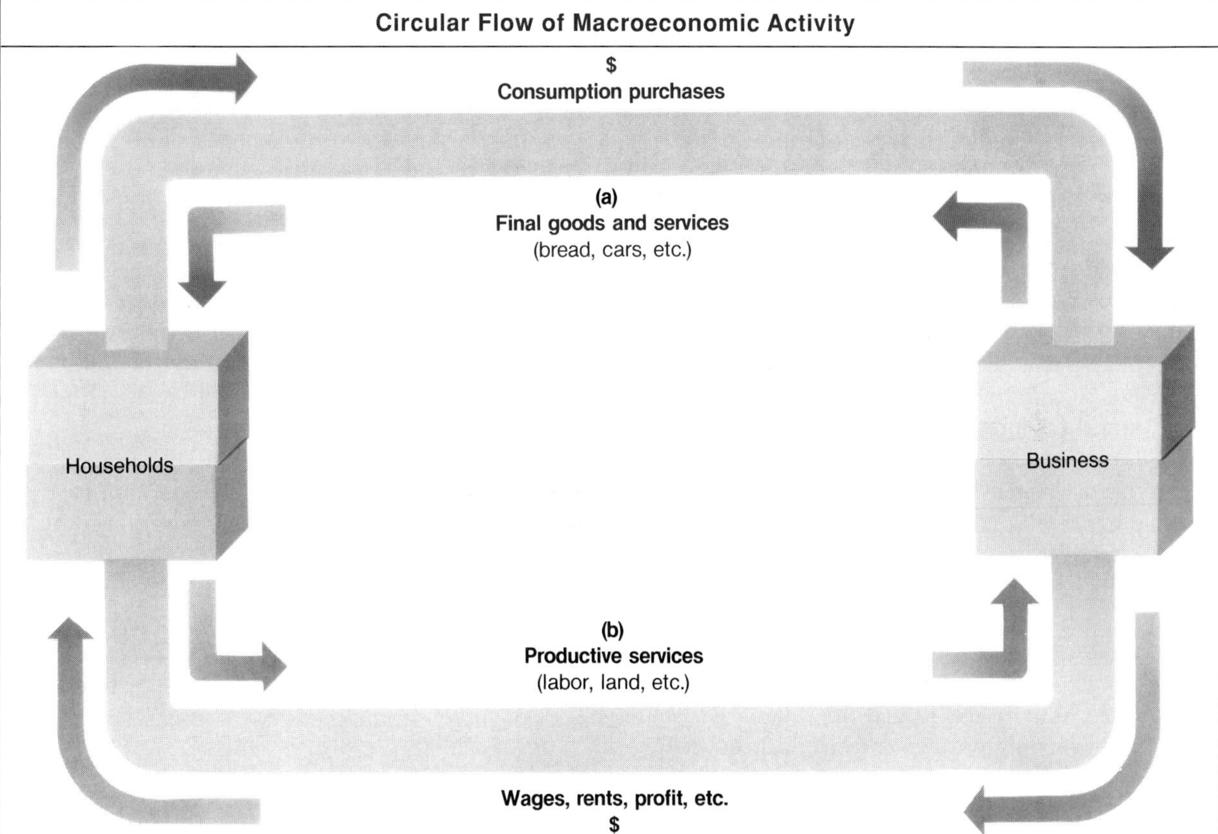

Figure 24-1. Gross national product can be measured either as (a) a flow of final products or, equally, as (b) a flow of costs

In the upper loop, people spend their money on final goods. The total dollar flow of these each year is one measure of gross national product.

The lower loop measures the annual flow of costs of output: the earnings that business pays out in wages, rent, interest, dividends, and business profits. The two measures of GNP must always be identical. Note that this figure is the *macroeconomic* counterpart of Fig. 3-1, which presented the circular flow of supply and demand.

To demonstrate the different ways of measuring GNP, we begin by considering an oversimplified world in which there is no government or foreign sector and in which no investment takes place. For the moment, our little economy produces only *consumption goods,* which are items that are purchased by households to satisfy their wants.

Flow-of-Product Approach. Each year the public consumes a wide variety of final goods and services: goods such as apples, oranges, and bread; services such as health care and haircuts. We include only *final goods*—goods ultimately bought and used by consumers. Households spend their incomes for these consumer goods, as is shown in the upper loop of Figure 24-1. Add together all the consumption dollars spent on these final goods, and you will arrive at this simplified economy's total GNP.

Thus, in our simple economy, you can easily calculate national income or product as the sum of the annual flow of *final* goods and services: (price of oranges × number of oranges) plus (price of apples × number of apples) plus. . . . The gross national product is defined as the total money value of the flow of final products produced by the nation.[1]

A crucial part of the calculation is the use of market prices as weights in valuing different commodities. Why use market prices rather than mass, volume, or labor-hours used in production? Economists use market prices because prices reflect the relative economic value of diverse goods and services. That is, the relative prices of different goods reflect how much consumers value their last (or marginal) units of consumption of these goods. Thus the choice of market prices as weights for different goods is not arbitrary; in a well-functioning market economy prices reflect the relative satisfactions that consumers receive from each good.

Earnings or Cost Approach. The second and equivalent way to calculate GNP is the earnings or cost approach. Go to the lower loop in Figure 24-1. Through it flow all the costs of doing business: these costs include the wages paid to labor, the rents paid to land, the profits paid to capital, and so forth. But these business costs are also the earnings that households receive from the firm. By measuring the annual flow of these earnings or incomes, statisticians will again arrive at the GNP.[2]

Hence, a second way to calculate GNP is as the total of factor earnings (wages, interest, rents, and profits) that are the costs of producing society's final products.

Equivalence of the Two Approaches. Now we have calculated GNP by the upper-loop flow-of-product approach and by the lower-loop earnings-flow approach. Which of these two is greater? They are *exactly* the same.

We can understand the identity of the two approaches by examining a simple barbershop economy. Say the barbers have no expenses other than labor. If they sell 10 haircuts at $6 each, GNP is $60. But the barbers' earnings (in wages and profits) are also exactly $60. Hence, the GNP here is identical whether measured as flow of products ($60 of haircuts) or as cost and income ($60 of wages and profits).

In fact, the two approaches are identical because we have included "profit" in the lower loop—along with wages and rents. What exactly is profit? Profit is what remains from the sale of a product after you have paid the other factor costs—wages, interest, and rents. It is the residual that automatically adjusts to make the lower loop's costs or earnings exactly match the upper loop's value of goods.

To sum up:

GNP, or gross national product, can be measured in two different ways: (1) as the flow of final products, or (2) as the total costs or earnings of inputs producing output. Because profit is a residual, both approaches will yield exactly the same total GNP.

Business Accounts and GNP

The national income and product accounts can be built up from businesses' income statements. An *account* for a firm or nation is a numerical record of all flows (outputs, costs, etc.) during a given period.

[1] Our oversimplified example considers only consumption expenditures. A complete definition of GNP will include *all* final goods and services; that is, GNP is consumption, private investment, government spending on goods and services, and net exports to the rest of the world.

[2] When we leave our simple world in which GNP is only consumption, we will have to introduce government transfer payments and taxes into the calculations.

(a) Income Statement of Typical Farm

Output in farming		Earnings	
Sales of goods (corn, apples, etc.)	$1,000	**Costs of production:**	
		Wages	$ 800
		Rents	100
		Interest	25
		Profit (residual)	75
Total	**$1,000**	**Total**	**$1,000**

(b) National Product Account
(Millions of Dollars)

Upper-loop flow of product		Lower-loop flow of earnings	
Final output (10 × 1,000)	$10,000	**Costs or earnings:**	
		Wages (10 × 800)	$ 8,000
		Rents (10 × 100)	1,000
		Interest (10 × 25)	250
		Profit (10 × 75)	750
GNP total	**$10,000**	**GNP total**	**$10,000**

Table 24-1. Construction of national product accounts from business accounts

Part **(a)** shows the income statement of a typical farm. The left side shows the value of production while the right side shows the firm's costs. Part **(b)** then adds up or aggregates the 10 million identical farms to obtain total GNP. Note that GNP from the product side exactly equals GNP from the earnings side.

The top half of Table 24-1 shows the results of a year's farming operations for a single, typical farm. We put sales of final products on the left-hand side and the various costs of production on the right. The bottom half of Table 24-1 shows how to construct the GNP accounts for a simple agrarian economy in which there is no government or investment and in which all final products are produced on 10 million identical farms. The national accounts simply add together the outputs and costs of the 10 million identical farms to get the two different measures of GNP.

The Problem of "Double Counting"

We defined GNP as the total production of final goods and services. A *final product* is one that is produced and sold for consumption or investment. GNP excludes *intermediate goods*—goods that are used up to produce other goods. GNP therefore includes bread but not wheat, and cars but not steel.

For the flow-of-product calculation of GNP, excluding intermediate products poses no major complications. We simply include the bread and cars in GNP but avoid including the wheat and dough that went into the bread or the steel and glass that went into the cars. If you look again at the upper loop in Figure 24-1, you will see that bread and cars appear in the flow of products, but you will not find any wheat, flour, or steel.

What has happened to products like wheat and steel? They are intermediate products and are simply cycling around inside the block marked "Business." They are never bought by consumers, and they never show up as final products in GNP.

"Value Added" in the Lower Loop. A new statistician who is being trained to make GNP measurements might be puzzled, saying:

> I can see that, if you are careful, your upper-loop product approach to GNP will avoid including intermediate products. But aren't you in some trouble when you use the lower-loop cost or earnings approach?

After all, when we gather income statements from the accounts of firms, won't we pick up what grain merchants pay to wheat farmers, what bakers pay to grain merchants, and what grocers pay to bakers? Won't this result in double counting or even triple counting of items going through several productive stages?

These are good questions, but there is an ingenious answer that will resolve the problem. In making lower-loop earnings measurements, statisticians are very careful to include in GNP only a firm's value added. **Value added** is the difference between a firm's sales and its purchases of materials and services from other firms.

In other words, in calculating the GNP earnings or value added by a firm, the statistician includes all costs that go to factors other than businesses and excludes all payments made to other businesses. Hence business costs in the form of wages, salaries, interest payments, and dividends are included in value added, but purchases of wheat or steel or electricity are excluded from value added. Why are all those purchases from other firms excluded from value added to obtain GNP? Because those purchases will get properly counted in GNP in the values added by other firms.

Table 24-2 uses the stages of bread production to illustrate how careful adherence to the value-added approach enables us to subtract the intermediate expenses that show up in the income statements of farmers, millers, bakers, and grocers. The final calculation shows the desired equality between (*a*) final sales of bread and (*b*) total earnings, calculated as the sum of all values added in all the different stages of bread production.

We can summarize as follows:

Value-added approach: To avoid double counting, we take care to include only final goods in GNP and to exclude the intermediate goods that are used up in making the final goods. By measuring the value added at each stage, taking care to subtract expenditures on the intermediate goods bought from other firms, the lower-loop earnings approach properly avoids all double counting and records wages, interest, rent, and profit exactly one time.

Details of the National Accounts

We have now studied the bare bones of the national income and product accounts. The rest of this chapter fleshes out how the various sectors fit together. Before we start on the journey to understanding the full national income and product accounts, look at Table 24-3 to get an idea of where we are going. This table shows a summary set of accounts for both the product and the income sides.

Bread Receipts, Costs, and Value Added
(Cents per Loaf)

Stage of production	(1) Sales receipts	(2) Cost of intermediate materials or goods		(3) Value added (wages, profit, etc.) (3) = (1) − (2)
Wheat	24	−0	=	24
Flour	33	−24	=	9
Baked dough	60	−33	=	27
Delivered bread	90	−60	=	30
	207	−117	=	90 (sum of value added)

Table 24-2. GNP sums up value added at each production stage

To avoid double counting of intermediate products, we carefully calculate value added at each stage, subtracting all the costs of materials and intermediate products not produced in that stage but bought from other businesses. Note that every black intermediate-product item both appears in column (1) and is subtracted, as a negative element, in the next stage of production in column (2). (How much would we overestimate GNP if we counted all receipts, not just value added? The overestimate would be 117 cents per loaf.)

National Accounts Overview	
Product approach	**Earnings approach**
Components of gross national product:	**Earnings or costs as sources of gross national product:**
Consumption (C)	Wages
+ Gross private domestic investment (I)	+ Interest, rent, and other property income
+ Government (G)	+ Indirect taxes
+ Net exports (X)	+ Depreciation
	+ Profits
Equals: Gross national product	**Equals: Gross national product**

Table 24-3. Overview of the national income and product accounts

This table shows the major components of the two sides of the national accounts. The left side shows the components of the product approach (or upper loop); the symbols C, I, G, and X are often used to represent these four items of GNP. The right side shows the components of the earnings or cost approach (or lower loop). Each approach will ultimately add up to exactly the same GNP.

If you know the structure of the table and the definitions of the terms in it, you will be well on your way to understanding GNP and its family of components.

Real vs. Nominal GNP: "Deflating" GNP by a Price Index

We define GNP as the dollar value of goods and services. In measuring the dollar value, we use the measuring rod of *market prices* for the different goods and services. But prices change over time, as inflation generally sends prices upward year after year. Who would want to measure things with a rubber yardstick—one that stretches in your hands from day to day—rather than a rigid and invariant yardstick?

The problem of changing prices is one of the problems economists have to solve when they use money as their measuring rod. Clearly, we want a measure of the nation's output and income that uses an invariant yardstick. Economists can repair most of the damage done by the elastic yardstick by using a *price index*, which is a measure of the average price of a bundle of goods.[3]

We can measure the GNP for a particular year using the actual market prices of that year; this gives us the **nominal GNP,** or GNP at current prices. Usually we are more interested in determining what has happened to the **real GNP,** which measures GNP in a set of constant or invariant prices. To obtain real GNP, we divide nominal GNP by a price index known as the **GNP deflator.**

A simple example will illustrate the general idea. Say that a country produces 1000 bushels of corn in year 1 and 1010 bushels in year 2. The price of a bushel is \$2 in year 1 and \$2.50 in year 2. We can calculate nominal GNP (PQ) as $\$2 \times 1000 = \$2000$ in year 1 and $\$2.50 \times 1010 = \$2525$ in year 2. Nominal GNP therefore grew by $26\frac{1}{4}$ percent between the two years.

But the actual amount of output did not grow anywhere near that rapidly. To find real output, we need to use the GNP deflator. We use year 1 as the *base year*, or the year in which we measure prices. We set the price index, the GNP deflator, as $P_1 = 1$ in the first year. From the data in the last paragraph, we see that the price index is $P_2 = \$2.50/\$2 = 1.25/1 = 1.25$ in year 2. Real GNP (Q) is equal to nominal GNP (PQ) divided by the GNP deflator (P). Hence real GNP was equal to $\$2000/1 = \$2000$ in year 1 and $\$2525/1.25 = \$2020$ in year 2. Thus the growth in real GNP, which corrects for the change in prices, is 1 percent and equals the growth in the output of corn, as it should.

A 1929–1933 comparison will illustrate the deflation process for an actual historical episode. Table 24-4 gives nominal GNP figures of \$104 billion for

[3] A price index is a weighted average of prices. The price index used to remove inflation (or "deflate" the GNP) is called the *GNP deflator*. It is defined as a weighted average of the prices of all commodities in the GNP, with each good's weight equal to its percentage importance in the total GNP. A full discussion will follow in Chapter 32.

1929 and \$56 billion for 1933. This represents a 46 percent drop in nominal GNP from 1929 to 1933. But the government estimates that prices on average dropped about 23 percent over this period. If we choose 1929 as our base year, with the GNP deflator of 1 in that year, this means that the 1933 price index was about 0.77. So our \$56 billion 1933 GNP was really worth much more than half the \$104 billion GNP of 1929. Table 24-4 shows that real GNP fell to only seven-tenths of the 1929 level: in terms of 1929 prices, or dollars of 1929 purchasing power, real GNP fell to \$73 billion. Hence, part of the near-halving shown by the nominal GNP was due to the optical illusion of the shrinking price yardstick.

The black line in Figure 24-2 shows the growth of nominal GNP since 1929, expressed in the actual dollars and prices that were current in each historical year. Then, for comparison, the real GNP, expressed in 1982 dollars, is shown in blue. Clearly, part of the increase in nominal GNP over the last half-century is due to inflation in the price units of our money yardstick.

To summarize:

Nominal GNP (PQ) represents the total money value of final goods and services produced in a given year, where the values are in terms of the market prices of each year. Real GNP (Q) removes price changes from nominal GNP and calculates GNP in constant prices. Because we define the GNP deflator (P) as the price of GNP, we have:

$$Q = \text{real GNP} = \frac{\text{nominal GNP}}{\text{GNP deflator}} = \frac{PQ}{P}$$

Sample Calculation of Real GNP

Date	(1) Nominal GNP (current \$, billion)	(2) Index number of prices (GNP deflator, 1929 = 1)	(3) Real GNP (\$, billion, 1929 prices) $(3) = \frac{(1)}{(2)}$
1929	104	1.00	$\frac{104}{1.00} = 104$
1933	56	0.77	$\frac{56}{0.77} = 73$

Table 24-4. Real (or inflation-corrected) GNP is obtained by dividing nominal GNP by a price index, the GNP deflator

Using price index of column (2), we deflate column (1) to get real GNP, column (3).

(Riddle: Can you show that 1929's real GNP was \$80 billion in terms of 1933 prices? *Hint:* With 1933 as a base of 1, 1929's price index is 1.30.)

Investment and Capital Formation

So far, our analysis has banished all capital goods and instead talked of an economy of consumers buying bread, apples, and other things. In real life, however, nations devote part of their output to production of investment goods. **Investment** (or purchases of capital goods) consists of the additions to the nation's capital stock of buildings, equipment, and inventories during a year. Investment involves the sacrifice of current consumption to increase future consumption. Instead of eating more bread now, people build new ovens to make it possible to produce more bread for future consumption.

A warning is in order here: To economists, investment means production of durable capital goods. In common usage, investment often denotes using money to buy General Motors stock or to open a savings account. Try not to confuse these two different uses of the word "investment."

If I take \$1000 from my safe and put it in the bank or buy a government bond, in economic terms, no investment has taken place. All that has happened is that I have exchanged one financial asset for another. Only when production of a physical capital good takes place is there what the economist calls investment.

How does investment fit into the national accounts? If people are using part of society's production possibilities for capital formation rather than for consumption, economic statisticians recognize that such outputs must be included in the upper-loop flow of GNP. Investments represent additions to the stock of durable capital goods that increase production possibilities in the future. So we must modify our original definition to read:

Gross national product is the sum of all final products. Along with consumption goods and services, we must also include gross investment.

Net vs. Gross Investment. Our revised definition included "gross investment" along with consump-

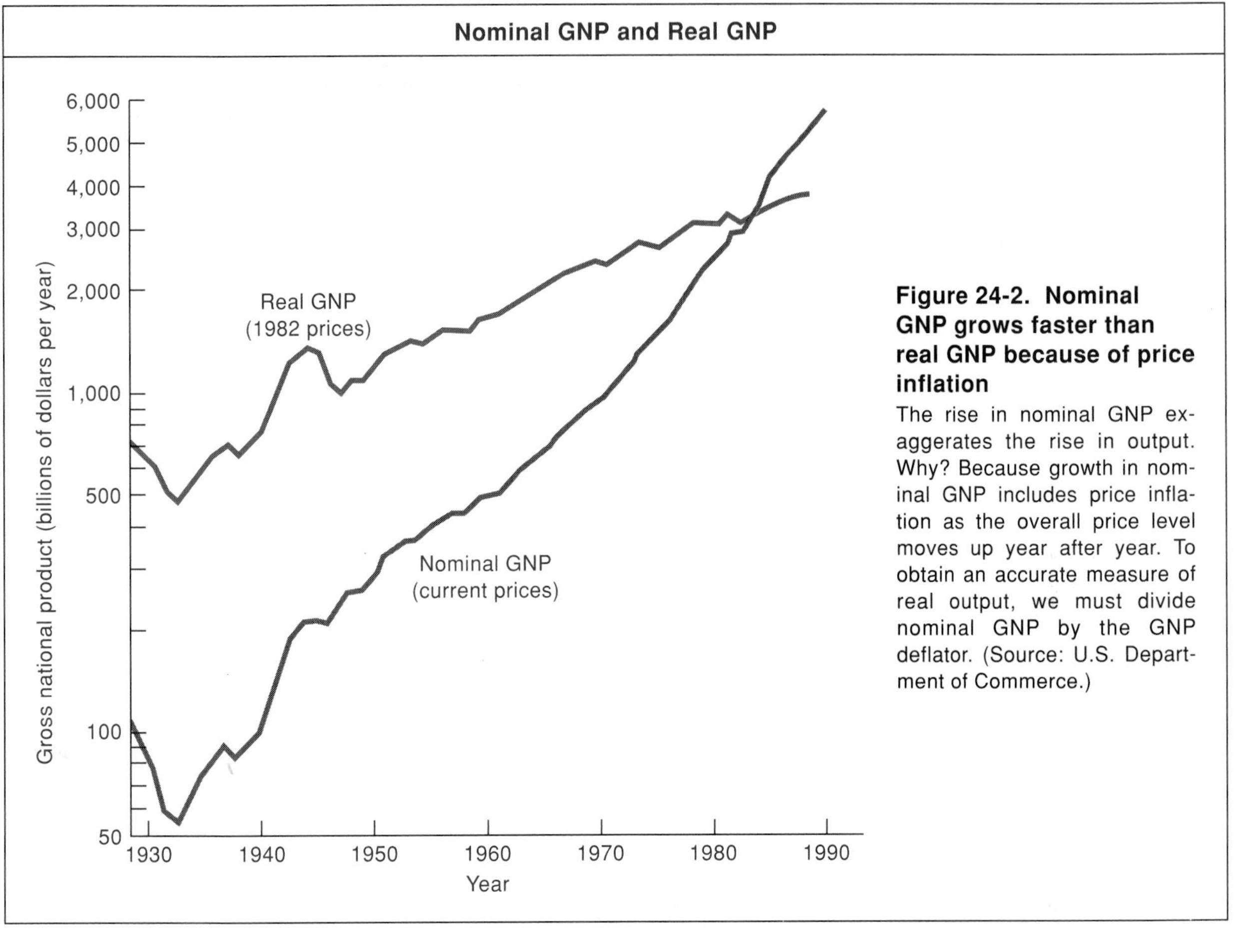

Figure 24-2. Nominal GNP grows faster than real GNP because of price inflation

The rise in nominal GNP exaggerates the rise in output. Why? Because growth in nominal GNP includes price inflation as the overall price level moves up year after year. To obtain an accurate measure of real output, we must divide nominal GNP by the GNP deflator. (Source: U.S. Department of Commerce.)

tion. What does the word "gross" mean in this context? It indicates that investment includes all investment goods produced. Gross investment is not adjusted for **depreciation,** which measures the amount of capital that has been used up in a year. Thus gross investment includes all the machines, factories, and houses built during a year—even though some were bought simply to replace some old capital goods that were thrown on the scrap heap.

If you want to get a measure of the increase in society's capital, gross investment is not a sensible measure. Because it excludes a necessary allowance for depreciation, it is too large—too gross.

An analogy to population will make clear the importance of considering depreciation. If you want to measure the increase in the size of the population, you cannot simply count the number of births, for this would clearly exaggerate the net change in population. To get population growth, you must also subtract the number of deaths.

The same point holds for capital. To find the net increase in capital, you must start with gross investment and subtract the deaths of capital in the form of depreciation, or the amount of capital used up.

Thus to estimate capital formation we measure net investment: net investment is always births of capital (gross investment) less deaths of capital (capital depreciation).

Net investment equals gross investment minus depreciation.

Table 24-5 provides data on both net investment and gross investment, which differ by the amount of depreciation. Typically net investment is substantial. In the Great Depression, however, net investment was *negative,* which indicates that the country was not investing enough to replace its capital stock.

Gross and Net Investment
(Billions of Dollars, 1982 Prices)

Investment components	1929	1933	1965	1990
Residential fixed	35.4	7.7	114.2	176.8
Business fixed	93.0	25.7	227.6	515.4
Change in business inventories	10.8	−10.7	25.2	−3.6
Gross private domestic investment	**139.2**	**22.7**	**367.0**	**688.7**
Allowances for depreciation or capital consumption (also = difference between GNP and NNP)	−86.8	−86.5	−183.6	−519.7
Net private domestic investment	**52.4**	**−63.8**	**183.4**	**169.0**

Table 24-5. To go from gross to net investment we subtract depreciation of capital

Gross births minus deaths equals any population's change. Similarly, net capital formation (or net investment) will equal gross capital formation (gross investment in all new capital goods) minus depreciation (or allowance for used-up capital goods). (Source: U.S. Department of Commerce.)

Government

Up to now we have talked about consumers but ignored the biggest consumer of all—federal, state, and local governments. Somehow GNP must take into account the billions of dollars of product a nation *collectively* consumes or invests. How do we do this?

After some debate, the income statisticians of the United States and the United Nations decided to use the simplest method of all. We simply add all government expenditures on goods and services to the flow of consumption, investment, and net exports.

These government expenditures include buying goods like roads and missiles and paying wages like those of marine colonels and weather forecasters. In short, all the government payroll expenditures on its employees plus the costs of goods (lasers, roads, and airplanes) it buys from private industry are included in this third great category of flow of products, called "government expenditure on goods and services." This category equals the contribution of federal, state, and local governments to GNP.

Exclusion of Transfer Payments. Does this mean that every dollar of government expenditure is included in GNP? Definitely not. GNP includes only government spending on goods and services; it excludes spending on transfer payments.

Government **transfer payments** are government payments to individuals that are not made in exchange for goods or services supplied. Examples of government transfers include unemployment insurance, veterans' benefits, and old-age or disability payments. They are intended to meet some form of need. Because transfers are not for purchase of a current good or service, they are omitted from GNP.

Thus if you receive a wage from the government because you are a substitute teacher, that is a factor payment and would be included in GNP. If you receive a welfare payment because you are poor, that payment is not in return for a service but is a transfer payment excluded from GNP.

One peculiar government transfer payment is the interest on the government debt. This is a return on debt incurred to pay for past wars or government programs and is not a payment for current government goods or services. Government interest payments are considered transfers and are therefore omitted from GNP.

Finally, do not confuse the way the national income accounts measure government spending on goods and services (G) with the official government budget. When the Treasury measures its expenditures, these include expenditures on goods and services (G) *plus* transfers.

Taxes. In using the flow-of-product approach to compute the GNP, we need not worry about how the government finances its spending. It does not matter whether the government pays for its goods and services by taxing, by printing money, or by borrowing. Wherever the dollars come from, the statistician computes the governmental component of GNP as the actual cost to the government of the goods and services.

It is fine to ignore taxes in the flow-of-product approach. But what about in the earnings or cost approach to GNP? Here we must account for taxes. Consider wages, for example. Part of my wages is turned over to the government through personal income taxes. These direct taxes definitely do get included in the wage component of business expenses and the same holds for direct taxes (personal or corporate) on interest, rent, and profit.

Or consider the sales tax and other indirect taxes that manufacturers and retailers have to pay on a loaf of bread (or on the wheat, flour, and dough stages). Suppose these indirect taxes total 10 cents per loaf, and suppose wages, profit, and other value-added items cost the bread industry 90 cents. What will the bread sell for in the product approach? For 90 cents? Surely not. The bread will sell for \$1, equal to 90 cents of factor costs plus 10 cents of indirect taxes.

Thus the cost approach to GNP includes both indirect and direct taxes as elements of the cost of producing final output.

Net Exports

The United States is an open economy engaged in importing and exporting goods and services. The last component of GNP—increasingly important in recent years—is **net exports,** the difference between exports and imports of goods and services.

How do we draw the line between our GNP and other countries' GNPs? The U.S. GNP represents all goods and services produced by labor, capital, and other factors owned by U.S. residents. U.S. production differs from what is purchased by all sectors in the United States in two respects. First, some of our output (Iowa wheat and Boeing aircraft) is bought by foreigners and shipped abroad. Combining these sales abroad with earnings on American capital located abroad, we obtain *exports.* Second, some of what we consume (Mexican oil and Japanese cars) is produced abroad and shipped to the United States. Adding to these purchases the earnings foreigners receive from foreign capital in the United States yields our *imports.*

For most of the last half-century, exports exceeded imports, and net exports were positive. During the 1980s, however, U.S. imports grew rapidly and net exports decreased sharply. As a result, the United States incurred a large trade deficit. We will study the sources and implications of the large trade deficit in the final four chapters of this text.

A Numerical Example. We can use a simple farming economy to understand how the national accounts work. Suppose that Agrovia produces 100 bushels of corn. Of these, 87 bushels are consumed (in *C*), 10 go for government purchases to feed the army (as *G*), and 6 go into domestic investment as increases in inventories (*I*). In addition, 4 bushels are exported while 7 bushels are imported, for net exports (*X*) of minus 3.

What then is the composition of the GNP of Agrovia? It is the following:

$$\begin{aligned} \text{GNP} &= 87 \text{ of } C + 10 \text{ of } G + 6 \text{ of } I - 3 \text{ of } X \\ &= 100 \text{ bushels} \end{aligned}$$

A Simplification. In our survey of macroeconomics, we will sometimes simplify our discussion by combining domestic investment with net exports to get *total gross national investment,* which we will call I_n. Put differently, we measure total national investment as net exports plus domestic investment in new capital goods. Let us see why. When a nation exports more than it imports, it is investing the excess (the net exports) abroad. This component is called *net foreign investment.* This foreign investment should be added to domestic capital formation to obtain the total amount that the nation is setting aside for the future—that is, the total national investment.

Gross National Product, Net National Product, and Gross Domestic Product

Although GNP is the most widely used measure of national output in the United States, two other concepts are widely cited: net national product and gross domestic product.

Recall that GNP includes *gross* investment, which is net investment plus depreciation. A little thought suggests that including depreciation is rather like including wheat as well as bread. A better measure would include only *net* investment in total output. By subtracting depreciation from GNP we obtain **net national product (NNP).**

If NNP is a sounder measure of a nation's output than GNP, why do economists and journalists work with GNP? They do so because depreciation is somewhat difficult to estimate, whereas gross investment can be estimated fairly accurately.

An alternative measure of national output, widely used outside the United States, is **gross domestic product (GDP).** This is the total output produced inside a country during a given year. For example, Fords produced with U.S.-owned capital located in Britain are included in U.S. GNP but excluded from U.S. GDP. Can you see why these Fords are in Britain's GDP but not in its GNP?

To summarize:

Net national product (NNP) equals the total final output produced by a nation during a year, where output includes net investment or gross investment less depreciation:

$$\text{NNP} = \text{GNP} - \text{depreciation}$$

Gross domestic product (GDP) is the total final output produced within a country during a year.

We can now give a final comprehensive definition of important components of GNP:

- GNP from the product side is the sum of four major components, as listed below:
  1. Personal consumption expenditure on goods and services (C)
  2. Gross private domestic investment (I)
  3. Government expenditures on goods and services (G)
  4. Net exports (X), or exports minus imports
- GNP from the cost side is the sum of the following major components:
  1. Wages, interest, rents, and profit (always with the careful exclusion, by the value-added technique, of double counting of intermediate goods bought from other firms)
  2. Indirect business taxes that show up as an expense of producing the flow of products
  3. Depreciation
- The product and cost measures of GNP yield identical amounts by definition (i.e., by adherence to the rules of value-added bookkeeping and the definition of profit as a residual).
- Net national product (NNP) equals GNP minus depreciation.

GNP and NNP: A Look at Numbers

Armed with an understanding of the concepts, we can turn to a look at the actual data in the important Table 24-6.

Flow-of-Product Approach. Look first at the left side of the table. It gives the upper-loop *flow-of-product* approach to GNP. Each of the four major components appears there, along with the production in each component for 1990. Of these, C and G and their obvious subclassifications require little discussion.

Gross private domestic investment does require one comment. Its total ($741 billion) includes all new business fixed investment in plant and equipment, residential construction, and increase in inventory of goods. This gross total excludes subtraction for depreciation of capital. After subtracting $520 billion of depreciation from gross investment, we obtain $169 billion of net investment.

Finally, note the large negative entry for *net exports,* −$31 billion. This negative entry represents the fact that in 1990 the United States imported $31 billion more in goods and services than it exported.

Adding up the four components on the left gives the total GNP of $5465 billion. This is the harvest we have been working for: the money measure of the American economy's overall performance for 1990.

Lower-Loop Flow-of-Cost Approach. Now turn to the right-hand side of the table. Here we have all *net costs of production* plus *taxes* and *depreciation.*

Wages and other employee supplements include all take-home pay, fringe benefits, and taxes on wages. *Net interest* is a similar item. Remember that interest on government debt is not included as part of G or of GNP but is treated as a transfer.

Rent income of persons includes rents received by landlords. In addition, if you own your own home, you are treated as *paying rent to yourself.* This is one of many "imputations" (or derived data) in the national accounts. It makes sense if we really want to measure the housing services the American

Gross National Product, 1990
(Billions of Current Dollars)

Product approach			Earnings or cost approach		
1. Personal consumption expenditure		$3,657	1. Wages and other employee supplements		$3,244
Durable goods	$ 480		2. Net interest		467
Nondurable goods	1,194		3. Rental income of persons		7
Services	1,983		4. Indirect business taxes, adjustments, and statistical discrepancy		526
2. Gross private domestic investment		741	5. Depreciation		520
Residential fixed	222		6. Income of unincorporated enterprises		403
Business fixed	524		7. Corporate profits before taxes		298
Change in inventories	−5		Dividends	134	
3. Government purchases of goods and services		1,098	Undistributed profits	32	
			Corporate profit taxes	132	
4. Net exports		−31			
Exports	673				
Imports	704				
Gross national product		**$5,465**	**Gross national product**		**$5,465**

Table 24-6. Here are the two ways of looking at the GNP accounts in actual numbers
The left side measures flow of products (at market prices). The right side measures flow of costs (factor earnings and depreciation plus indirect taxes). (Source: U.S. Department of Commerce.)

people are enjoying and do not want the estimate to change when people decide to own a home rather than rent one.

Indirect business taxes, as we saw earlier, must be included as a separate item in the income approach if we are to match the product approach. Any direct taxes on wages, interests, or rents were already included directly in those items, so they must not be included again. We have included with indirect business taxes some adjustments: business transfer payments and the inevitable "statistical discrepancy," which reflects the fact that the officials never have every bit of needed data.[4]

[4] Statisticians must always work with incomplete reports and fill in data gaps by estimation. Just as measurements in a chemistry lab differ from the ideal, so, in fact, do errors creep into both upper- and lower-loop GNP estimates. These are reconnected by an item called the "statistical discrepancy." Along with the civil servants who are heads of units called "Wages," "Interest," and so forth, there actually used to be someone with the title "Head of the Statistical Discrepancy." If data were perfect, that individual would have been out of a job; but because real life is never perfect, that person's task of reconciliation was one of the hardest of all.

Depreciation on capital goods that were used up must appear as an expense in GNP, just like other expenses.

Profit comes last because it is the residual—what is left over after all other costs have been subtracted from total sales. There are two kinds of profits: profit of corporations and net earnings of unincorporated enterprises.

Income of unincorporated enterprises refers to earnings of partnerships and single-ownership businesses. This includes much farm and professional income.

Finally, *corporate profits before taxes* are shown. This entry's $298 billion includes corporate profit *taxes* of $132 billion. The remainder then goes to dividends or to undistributed corporate profits; the latter amount of $32 billion is what you leave or "plow back" into the business and is called *net corporate saving.*

On the right side, the flow-of-cost approach gives us the same $5465 billion of GNP as the flow-of-product approach. The right and left sides do agree.

From GNP to Disposable Income

The basic GNP accounts are of interest not only for themselves but also because of their importance for understanding how consumers and businesses behave. Some further distinctions will help illuminate the way the nation's books are kept.

National Income. To help us understand macroeconomic activity, we sometimes want to measure the total income received by the nation. For this, we construct data on *national income* (*NI*). *NI* represents the total factor incomes received by labor, capital, and land. It is constructed principally by subtracting depreciation and indirect taxes from GNP. National income equals total wages, profits, rents, and interest.

The relationship between GNP and national income is shown in the first two bars of Figure 24-3. The left-hand bar shows GNP, while the second bar shows the subtractions required to obtain *NI.*

Disposable Income. A second important concept asks, How many dollars per year do households actually have available to spend? The concept of disposable personal income (usually called **disposable income** or *DI*) answers this question. To get disposable income, you calculate the incomes received by households and subtract personal taxes.

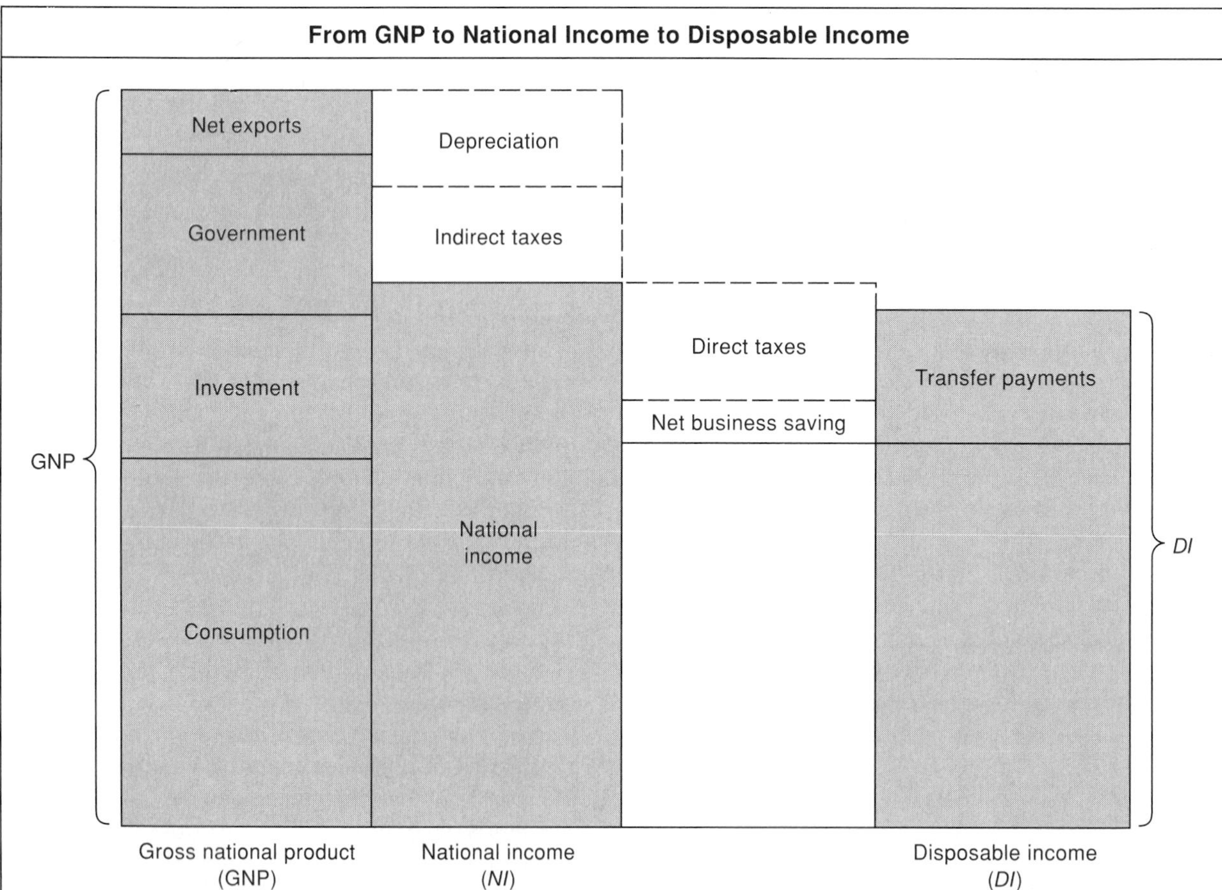

Figure 24-3. Starting with GNP, we can calculate national income (*NI*) and disposable personal income (*DI*)

Important income concepts are: (1) GNP, which is total gross income to all factors; (2) national income, which subtracts depreciation and indirect taxes and is the sum of factor incomes; (3) disposable personal income, which measures the total incomes, including transfer payments but less taxes, of the household sector.

Figure 24-3 shows the calculation of *DI*. We begin with national income in the second bar. We then subtract all direct taxes on households and corporations and further subtract business saving. Finally, we add back the transfer payments that households receive from governments. This constitutes *DI*, shown as the right-hand bar in Figure 24-3. Disposable income is what actually gets into the public's hands, to dispose of as it pleases.

As we will see in the next chapters, *DI* is what people divide between (*a*) consumption spending and (*b*) personal saving. For most of the period since World War II, personal saving represented 7 percent of disposable income, with the balance going to consumption and interest payments. Since 1985, however, the personal savings rate dropped precipitously, reaching a postwar low of 2.9 percent in 1987.

The Identity of Measured Saving and Investment

One of the most important relationships arising from national-income accounting is that between saving and investment. To pave the way for the discussion of income determination in Chapter 27, we show here that, under the accounting rules described above, *measured saving is exactly equal to measured investment.* This equality is an identity of national-income accounting and holds by definition.

What is the measure of investment? Assuming for the moment that there is no government or foreign sector, we know I is that part of the upper-loop output that is not C. What is the measure of saving, S? Again ignoring government, foreign, and corporate saving, we know that S is that part of the lower-loop disposable income, or GNP, that is not spent on C. To summarize:

$$I = \text{product-approach GNP minus } C$$

$$S = \text{earnings-approach GNP minus } C$$

But the two loops do give the same measure of GNP. Hence, we have

$I = S$: the identity between measured saving and investment

That is the simplest case. Our task will be done when we bring businesses, government, and net exports into the picture. For this discussion, total gross national investment (I_n) will include both gross domestic investment (I) and net foreign investment (X). But gross saving (S) must be divided into three different categories: (1) personal saving (PS), which comes out of disposable incomes; (2) gross business saving (GBS), which is depreciation plus any earnings retained in the firm; and (3) government surplus (GS), which represents the algebraic excess of government's tax revenues over its expenditures on goods and services and on transfers. Our identity of measured national saving and investment, S and I_n, now has to be written in terms of the three components of total S:[5]

$$I_n = PS + GBS + GS = \text{total saving}$$

Again, remember that this identity must hold whether the economy is in tranquil times, going into depression, or in a wartime boom.

Beyond GNP to Net Economic Welfare (NEW)

Advocates of the existing economic and social system often argue that free enterprise has produced a growth in real GNP never before seen in human history. But reliance on GNP has caused a backlash. Critics complain that GNP represents the excessive materialism of a society devoted to endless produc-

[5] This fundamental identity can be derived by recalling the definitions of GNP and of saving. The fundamental identity for GNP from the product side is

$$\text{GNP} = C + I + G + X$$

But gross national investment is defined as $I_n = I + X$, so the product side can be written as

$$\text{GNP} = C + I_n + G$$

Next turn to the breakdown of GNP from the earnings or cost side:

$$\text{GNP} = DI + GBS + Tx - Tr$$

where Tx = taxes and Tr = transfers. Recalling that $DI = C + PS$, we have

$$\text{GNP} = C + (PS + GBS) + (Tx - Tr - G) + G$$
$$= C + I_n + G$$

Because $GS = Tx - Tr - G$, we can cancel C and G to obtain the saving-investment identity:

$$I_n = PS + GBS + GS$$

tion of useless goods. As one dissenter said, "Don't speak to me of all your numbers and dollars, your gross national product. To me, GNP stands for gross national pollution!"

What are we to think? Isn't it true that GNP includes government purchases of bombs and missiles? Doesn't cutting our irreplaceable redwoods show up as a positive output in our national accounts? Does modern economics make a fetish of quantity of products at the expense of quality of life?

In recent years, economists have attempted to correct the defects of the official GNP numbers so that they better reflect the true satisfaction-producing products of our economy. One approach has been to construct a more meaningful measure of national output, called **net economic welfare,** or NEW. NEW is based upon GNP but makes two major changes.[6] First, NEW excludes many components of GNP that do not contribute to individual well-being; and second, some key consumption items that are omitted from GNP are included in NEW.

Net economic welfare (NEW) is an adjusted measure of total national output that includes only consumption and investment items that contribute directly to economic well-being.

We will describe the major elements of NEW.

Pluses: Value of Leisure Time. Suppose you decide, as you become more affluent, to work fewer hours, to get your psychic satisfactions from leisure as well as from goods and services. Then the measured GNP goes down even though welfare goes up. So, to correct for the psychic satisfaction of leisure, a positive correction must be added to get NEW from GNP.

Consider also do-it-yourself work done in the home—cooking meals or insulating walls. Because the values added are not bought or sold in markets, they never enter into the goods and services of the GNP—neither in the upper loop nor in the lower loop. An estimate of NEW will need to include the value of similar do-it-yourself activities.

Pluses: The Underground Economy. In recent years, many economists claim to have detected an explosive growth in the underground economy. Underground activities are of two kinds: activities that are illegal (such as the drug trade or murder for hire), and activities that are legal but unrecorded for tax purposes (such as the work of a carpenter who builds your garage in the evenings in return for your personal advice about her finances).

In general, national accountants exclude illegal activities from a measure of national output—these are by social consensus "bads" and not "goods." A swelling cocaine trade will not enter into either GNP or NEW.

What about the second source of underground activity: the array of carpenters, doctors, babysitters, and farmers who produce valuable goods and services but might escape the net of national output statisticians? Several economists, led by Edward Feige and Peter Gutmann, claim that this sector is booming. They examine financial data (particularly the use of cash, which is the major means of payment in the underground economy) and conclude that real GNP growth in the last two decades was significantly understated because of the omission of underground activity. Some point to high tax rates as an incentive to work in the underground economy.

Some evidence confirms these views. Recent studies indicate that the overall level of compliance with the federal income-tax system has been falling in recent years. The result is that a larger fraction of national income escapes the tax collector's beady eye.

Others are skeptical. While not denying that between 5 and 10 percent of economic output is unreported to the Internal Revenue Service, these skeptics doubt whether the amount is growing. They point out that the national accounts already make imputations for unreported activities.

A careful examination by Edward Denison argues that the major source of error in the national accounts would arise from understatement of employment. But the reported employment data come

[6] The discussion here is drawn from William Nordhaus and James Tobin, "Is Growth Obsolete?" in *Fiftieth Anniversary Colloquium V* (National Bureau of Economic Research, Columbia University Press, New York, 1972). We have replaced the earlier concept, a measure of economic welfare (MEW), by the more informative label "net economic welfare" (NEW). Further refinements have been undertaken by Japanese economists (who have constructed a series known as net national welfare) and by Robert Eisner, who estimates broader income and output measures in a total incomes system of accounts, or TISA [see Robert Eisner, "The Total Incomes System of Accounts," *Survey of Current Business* (January 1985), pp. 24–48].

from two completely independent sources (households and firms), and these two sources give much the same estimate of the growth of employment over the last two decades. Denison concludes that, given the consistency in the two different estimates of employment, "growth of national income and product is not being understated much as a result of growth of the underground economy."[7]

Minuses: Environmental Damage. Sometimes GNP counts the "goods" produced but ignores the "bads." For example, suppose the residents of Suburbia buy 10 million kilowatt-hours of electricity to cool their houses, paying Utility Co. 10 cents per kilowatt-hour. That $1 million covers the labor costs, plant costs, and fuel costs. But suppose the company damages the neighborhood with sulfur from fuel burned to produce electricity. It incurs no money costs for this externality. Our measure of output should not only add in the value of the electricity (which GNP does) but also subtract the environmental damage from the pollution (which GNP does not).[8]

To continue our example, suppose that in addition to paying 10 cents of direct costs, the surrounding neighborhood suffers 1 cent per kilowatt-hour of environmental damage. This is the cost of pollution (to trees, trout, streams, and people) not paid by Utility Co. Then the total "external" cost is $100,000. To correct for these hidden costs and construct NEW, we must subtract $100,000 of "pollution bads" from the $1,000,000 flow of "electricity goods."

[7] Edward F. Denison, "Is U.S. Growth Understated Because of the Underground Economy? Employment Ratios Suggest Not," *Review of Income and Wealth* (October 1982).

[8] Why do the pollution costs not enter GNP? They are omitted because no one buys or sells the damage from the sulfur emissions. Recall our discussion of externalities in Chapter 3.

Economists have just begun the difficult task of constructing measures of national output that correct the GNP for pollution, congestion, depletion of natural resources, and other shortcomings. Preliminary studies suggest that NEW grows more slowly than does GNP. This difference may be inevitable in a world in which population and congestion are increasing and in which human interventions sometimes overwhelm the capacity of nature to absorb human wastes.

Having reviewed the measurement of national output and analyzed the shortcomings of the GNP, what should we conclude about the adequacy of our national accounts as measures of economic welfare? The answer was aptly stated in a review by Arthur Okun:

> It should be no surprise that national prosperity does not guarantee a happy society, any more than personal prosperity ensures a happy family. No growth of GNP can counter the tensions arising from an unpopular and unsuccessful war, a long overdue self-confrontation with conscience on racial injustice, a volcanic eruption of sexual mores, and an unprecedented assertion of independence by the young. Still, prosperity . . . is a precondition for success in achieving many of our aspirations.[9]

[9] *The Political Economy of Prosperity* (Norton, New York, 1970), p. 124.

SUMMARY

1. The gross national product (or GNP) is the most comprehensive measure of a nation's production of goods and services. It comprises the dollar value of consumption (C), gross private domestic investment (I), government purchases of goods and services (G), and net exports (X). Recall the formula:

$$\text{GNP} = C + I + G + X$$

This will sometimes be simplified by combining domestic investment and net exports into total gross national investment (I_n):

$$\text{GNP} = C + I_n + G$$

2. Because of the way we define residual profit, we can match the upper-loop flow-of-product measurement of GNP with the lower-loop flow-of-cost mea-

surement, as shown in Figure 24-1. The flow-of-cost approach uses factor earnings and carefully computes values added to eliminate double counting of intermediate products. And after summing up all (before-tax) wage, interest, rent, depreciation, and profit income, it adds to this total all indirect tax costs of business. GNP definitely does not include transfer items such as interest on government bonds or receipt of welfare payments.

3. By use of a price index, we can "deflate" nominal GNP (GNP in current dollars) to arrive at a more accurate measure of real GNP (GNP expressed in dollars of some base year's purchasing power). Use of such a price index corrects for the rubber yardstick implied by changing levels of prices.

4. Net investment is positive when the nation is producing more capital goods than are currently being used up in the form of depreciation. Since depreciation is hard to estimate accurately, statisticians have more confidence in their measures of gross investment than in those of net investment.

5. National income and disposable income are two additional official measurements. Disposable income (*DI*) is what people actually have left—after all tax payments, corporate saving of undistributed profits, and transfer adjustments have been made—to spend on consumption or to save.

6. Using the rules of the national accounts, measured saving must exactly equal measured investment. This is easily seen in a hypothetical economy with nothing but households. In a complete economy, the identity is

$$I_n = PS + GBS + GS$$

   where total gross national investment (I_n, which equals both domestic and foreign investment) equals net personal saving (*PS*) plus gross business saving (*GBS*) plus net government saving (*GS*).

   The identity between saving and investment is just that: saving must equal investment no matter whether the economy is in boom or recession, war or peace. It is a consequence of the definitions of national-income accounting.

7. Gross national product is an imperfect measure of genuine economic welfare. An alternative approach is net economic welfare (NEW). The calculation of NEW adds to NNP certain items—such as value of leisure, the services of homemakers, and do-it-yourself activities. It also subtracts from NNP such things as unmet costs of pollution and other disamenities of modern urbanization.

CONCEPTS FOR REVIEW

GNP
GNP deflator
$GNP = C + I + G + X$
$GNP = C + I_n + G$
GNP in two equivalent views: product (upper loop) and earnings (lower loop)

intermediate goods, value added
nominal and real GNP
net investment = gross investment − depreciation
NNP = GNP − depreciation
gross domestic product (GDP)
government transfers

disposable income (*DI*)
$I_n = S$
$= PS + GBS + GS$
NEW = NNP + leisure and underground activity − pollution and disamenities

QUESTIONS FOR DISCUSSION

1. Define carefully the following and give an example of each:
   (a) Consumption
   (b) Gross private domestic investment
   (c) Government purchase of a good (in GNP)
   (d) Government transfer payment (not in GNP)
   (e) Export
2. "You can't add apples and oranges." Show that by using prices we do this in constructing GNP.
3. Consider the following data: Nominal GNP for 1990 was $5465 billion, as compared to $5201 for 1989. The GNP deflator for 1990 was 131.5, as compared to 126.3 for 1989. The GNP deflator was 100 in 1982.

   Calculate real GNP for 1989 and 1990, in 1982 prices. Calculate the rates of growth of nominal GNP and real GNP for 1990. What was the rate of inflation (as measured by the GNP deflator) for 1990?
4. Robinson Crusoe produces upper-loop product of $1000. He pays $750 in wages, $125 in interest, and $75 in rent. What *must* his profit be? If three-fourths of Crusoe's output is consumed and the rest invested, calculate Crusoeland's GNP in both the product and the income approaches and show that they must agree exactly.
5. Here are some brain teasers. Can you see why the following are *not* counted in GNP?
   (a) The home meals produced by a fine chef
   (b) Purchase of a plot of land
   (c) Purchase of an original Rembrandt painting
   (d) The value I get in 1992 from playing a 1985 Rolling Stones compact disk
   (e) Pollution damage to houses and crops from sulfur emitted by electric utilities
6. Consider the items listed in question 5. Analyze how each should be treated in NEW.
7. Consider the country of Agrovia, whose GNP is discussed in "A Numerical Example" on page 425. Construct a set of national accounts like that in Table 24-6 assuming that wheat costs $5 per bushel, there is no depreciation, wages are three-fourths of national output, indirect business taxes are used to finance government spending, and the balance of income goes as rent income to farmers.

CHAPTER 25

CONSUMPTION AND INVESTMENT

There's many a slip 'twixt the cup and the lip.
Anonymous

Patterns of consumption and investment play a crucial role in a nation's economy. Nations that consume most of their incomes, such as the United States, tend to invest relatively little and show modest rates of economic growth. By contrast, those nations that consume a small fraction of their incomes tend to invest heavily; these countries—for example, Japan or Hong Kong—have rapidly growing output and productivity.

This chapter probes the reasons lying behind trends in consumption and investment. We will attempt to understand how people choose between saving and consumption and will see that poor people tend to save less than well-to-do people. In addition, we will study the determinants of investment, including such factors as taxes, interest rates, and expectations.

We study these topics not only for their intrinsic interest but also because consumption and investment are important determinants of the overall level of output and employment in the short run. When spending on investment and consumption grows rapidly, output as a whole tends to grow as well. Why is this? We will see in the next chapters that total output in the short run is significantly affected by the interplay of consumption and investment. When favorable tax treatment or growing markets give a spur to business investment—as was the case in the 1960s and the late 1980s—aggregate demand expands and output and employment grow rapidly. When business confidence withers or when the stock market declines—as happened during the 1930s and in the early 1980s—investment declines, aggregate demand falls, and output and employment fall.

This chapter begins the thorough study of the determination of aggregate demand by focusing upon the behavior of consumption and investment. Figure 25-1 shows how this chapter's analysis fits into the overall structure of the macroeconomy. Once we have surveyed consumption and investment, we can in the next chapter put these two components together into the simplest model of income determination—the multiplier model.

The tools introduced in the next few chapters form the intellectual core of what is called *Keynesian economics.* When introduced a half-century ago by the English economist John Maynard Keynes, these concepts were as foreign to the then practicing economists as "quarks" or "charm" are to freshmen in a modern college physics course. Today, many of the elements of Keynes' thinking—such as his theories about consumption and investment—are part of the language of modern economics.

A. Consumption and Saving

We begin our discussion with an analysis of consumption and savings behavior, first examining individual spending patterns and then looking at aggregate consumption behavior. Recall from

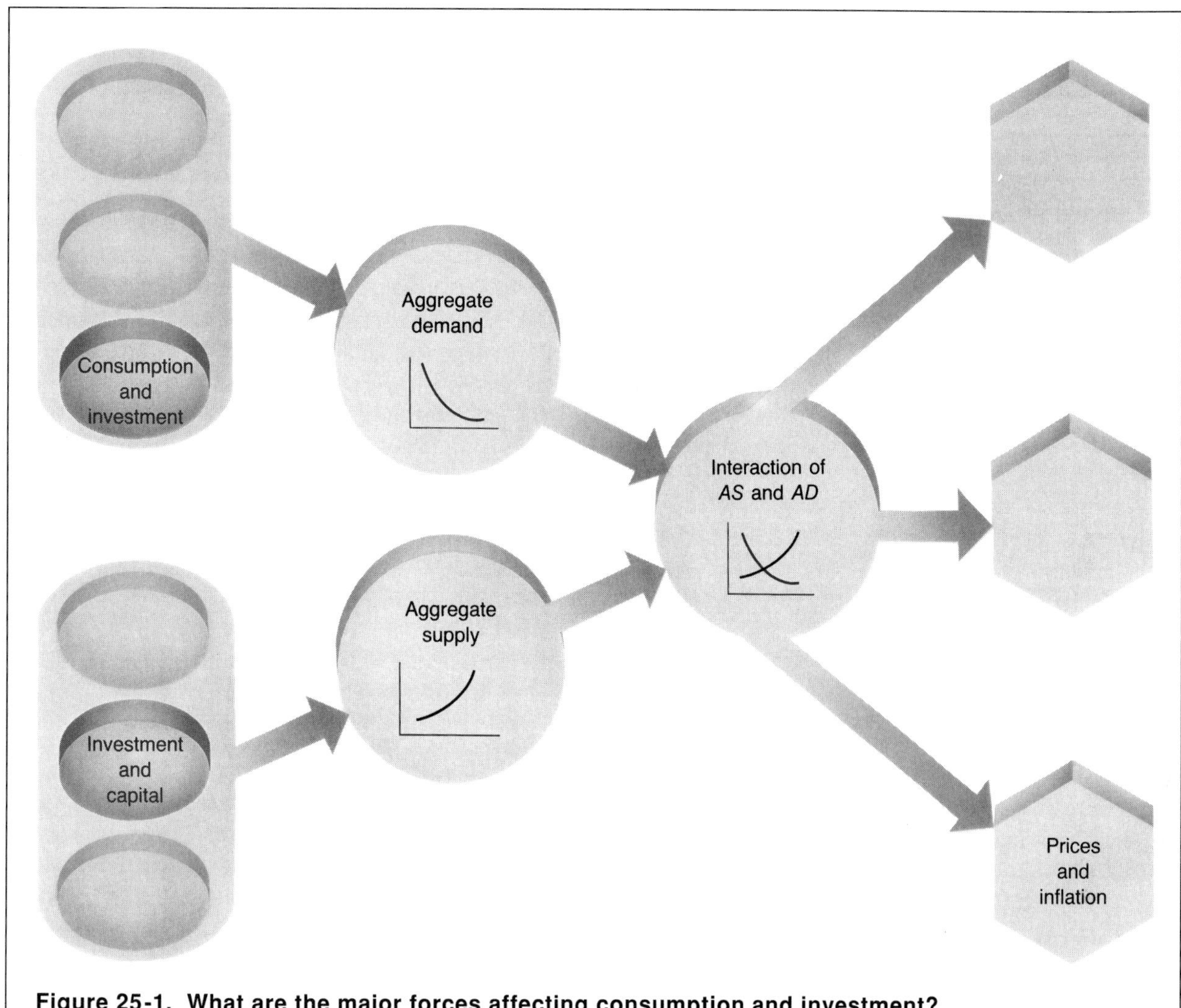

Figure 25-1. What are the major forces affecting consumption and investment?
This chapter analyzes two major components of GNP: consumption and investment. In later chapters, we will see that they affect both aggregate supply and aggregate demand.

Chapter 24 that household consumption is spending on final goods and services bought for the satisfaction gained or needs met by their use. Household saving, on the other hand, is by definition that part of income not spent on consumption.

Consumption is the largest single component of GNP, constituting 66 percent of total spending over the last decade. What are the major elements of consumption? Among the most important categories are housing, motor vehicles, food, and medical care. Table 25-1 displays the major elements, broken down into the three categories of durable goods, nondurable goods, and services. The items themselves are familiar, but their relative importance, particularly the increasing importance of services, is worth a moment's study.

Budgetary Expenditure Patterns

How do the patterns of consumption spending differ across different households in the United States?

No two families spend their disposable income in exactly the same way. Yet statistics show that there is a predictable regularity in the way people allocate their expenditures among food, clothing,

Consumption, 1990

Category of consumption	Value of category ($, billion)		Percent of total
Durable goods		480	13
Motor vehicles	213		
Household equipment	177		
Other	90		
Nondurable goods		1,194	33
Food	625		
Clothing and apparel	213		
Energy	94		
Other	262		
Services		1,983	54
Housing	570		
Medical care	483		
Personal business	159		
Education	51		
Other	720		
Total, personal consumption expenditures		3,657	100

Table 25-1. The major components of consumption

Consumption is divided into three categories: durable goods, nondurable goods, and services. The size of the service sector is becoming increasingly large as basic needs for food are met and as health, recreation, and education claim a larger part of family budgets. (Source: U.S. Department of Commerce.)

and other major items. The thousands of budgetary investigations of household spending patterns show remarkable agreement on the general, qualitative patterns of behavior.[1] Figure 25-2 tells the story. Poor families must spend their incomes largely on the necessities of life: food and shelter. As income increases, expenditure on many food items goes up. People eat more and eat better. There are, however, limits to the extra money people will spend on food when their incomes rise. Consequently, the proportion of total spending devoted to food declines as income increases.

Expenditure on clothing, recreation, and automobiles increases more than proportionately to after-tax income, until high incomes are reached. Spending on luxury items increases in greater proportion than income. Finally, as we look across families, note that saving rises very rapidly as income increases. Saving is the greatest luxury good of all.

Consumption, Income, and Saving

We suggested above that there is a close tie between income, consumption, and saving. What is the exact relationship?

Actually, the idea is simple. **Saving** is that part of income that is not consumed. That is, saving equals income minus consumption. The relationship between income, consumption, and saving for the United States in 1990 is shown in Table 25-2. Begin

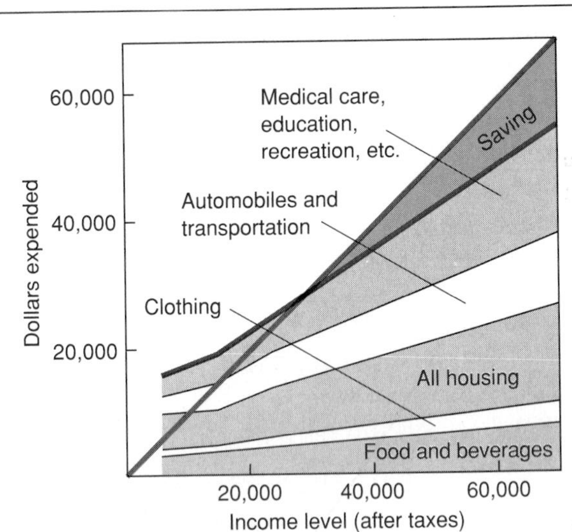

Figure 25-2. Family budget expenditures show regular patterns

Careful sampling of families and of individuals verifies the importance of disposable income as a determinant of consumption expenditure. Notice the drop in food as a percentage of higher incomes. Note also the rise in saving, from less than zero at very low incomes to substantial amounts at high incomes. [Source: U.S. Department of Labor, *Consumer Expenditure Survey: Interview Survey 1984* (August 1986), updated to 1991 prices by authors.]

[1] The spending patterns shown in Fig. 25-2 are called "Engel's Laws," after the nineteenth-century Prussian statistician Ernst Engel. The average behavior of consumption expenditure does change fairly regularly with income. But averages do not tell the whole story. Within each income class, there is a considerable spread of consumption around the average.

Item	Amount, 1990 Billions of Dollars
Personal income	**4,646**
Less: Personal tax and nontax payments	700
Equals: Personal disposable income	**3,946**
Less: Personal consumption outlays (consumption and interest)	3,767
Equals: Personal saving	**179**
Memo: Saving as percent of personal disposable income	**4.5**

Source: U.S. Department of Commerce.

Table 25-2. Saving equals disposable income less consumption

with personal income (composed, as Chapter 24 showed, of wages, interest, rents, dividends, transfer payments, and so forth). In 1990, 15 percent of personal income went to personal tax and nontax payments. This left $3946 billion of personal disposable income. Household outlays for consumption (including interest) amounted to 95.5 percent of disposable income, or $3767 billion, leaving $179 billion as personal saving. The last item in the table shows the important **personal savings rate.** This is equal to personal saving as a percent of disposable income (4.5 percent in 1990).

Economic studies have shown that income is the primary determinant of consumption and saving. Rich people save more than poor people, both absolutely and also as a percent of income. The very poor are unable to save at all. Instead, as long as they can borrow or draw down their wealth, they tend to *dissave.* That is, they tend to spend more than they earn, reducing their accumulated saving or going deeper into debt.

Table 25-3 contains illustrative data on disposable income, saving, and consumption drawn from budget studies on American households. The first column shows seven different levels of disposable income. Column (2) indicates saving at each level of income, and the third column indicates consumption spending at each level of income.

The *break-even point*—where the representative household neither saves nor dissaves but consumes all its income—comes at around $25,000. Below the break-even point, say at $24,000, the household actually consumes more than its income; it dissaves (see the −$110 item). Above $25,000 it begins to show positive saving [see the +$150 and other positive items in column (2)].

Column (3) shows the consumption spending for each income level. Since each dollar of income is divided between the part consumed and the remaining part saved, columns (3) and (2) are not independent; they must always exactly add up to column (1).

Household Saving and Consumption

	(1) Disposable income ($)	(2) Net saving (+) or dissaving (−) ($)	(3) Consumption ($)
A	24,000	−110	24,110
B	**25,000**	**0**	**25,000**
C	26,000	+150	25,850
D	27,000	+400	26,600
E	28,000	+760	27,240
F	29,000	+1,170	27,830
G	30,000	+1,640	28,360

Table 25-3. Consumption and saving are primarily determined by income

This table shows average levels of consumption and saving at different levels of disposable income. The break-even point at which people cease to dissave and begin to do positive saving is shown here at $25,000. How much of each extra dollar do people devote to extra consumption at this income level? How much to extra saving? (Answer: About 85 cents and 15 cents, respectively, when we compare row B and row C.)

To understand the way consumption affects national output, we need to introduce some new tools. We need to understand how many *extra* dollars of consumption and saving are induced by each *extra* dollar of income. This relationship is shown by:

- The consumption function, relating consumption and income; and its twin,
- The savings function, relating saving and income

The Consumption Function

One of the most important relationships in all macroeconomics is the consumption function. The **consumption function** shows the relationship between the level of consumption expenditures and the level of disposable personal income. This concept, introduced by Keynes, is based on the hypothesis that there is a stable empirical relationship between consumption and income.

We can see the consumption function most vividly in the form of a graph. Figure 25-3 plots the seven levels of income listed in Table 25-3. Disposable income [column (1) of Table 25-3] is placed on the horizontal axis, and consumption [column (3)] is on the vertical axis. Each of the income-consumption combinations is represented by a single point, and the points are then connected by a smooth curve.

The relation between consumption and income shown in Figure 25-3 is called the consumption function.

The "Break-Even" Point. To understand the figure, it is helpful to look at the 45° line drawn northeast from the origin. Because the vertical and horizontal axes have exactly the same scale, the 45° line has a very special property. At any point on the 45° line, the distance up from the horizontal axis (consumption) exactly equals the distance across from the vertical axis (disposable income). You can use your eyes or a ruler to verify this fact.

The 45° line tells us immediately whether consumption spending is equal to, greater than, or less than the level of income. The point on the consumption schedule that intersects the 45° line represents the level of disposable income at which households just break even.

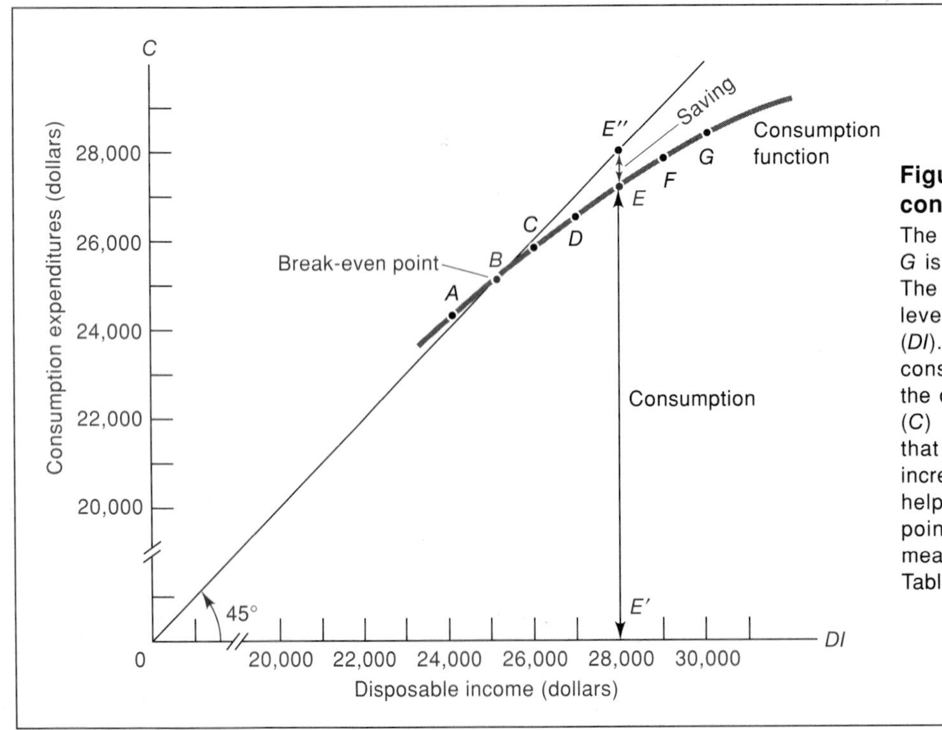

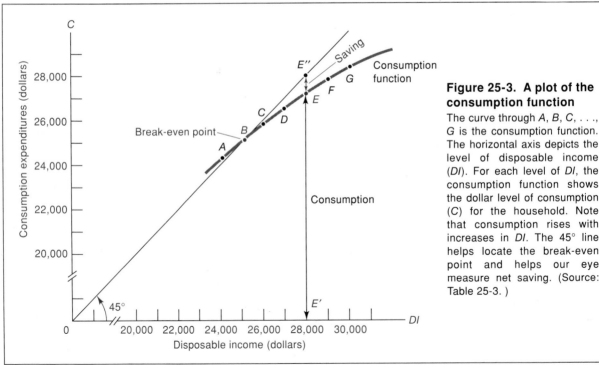

Figure 25-3. A plot of the consumption function
The curve through *A*, *B*, *C*, . . ., *G* is the consumption function. The horizontal axis depicts the level of disposable income (*DI*). For each level of *DI*, the consumption function shows the dollar level of consumption (*C*) for the household. Note that consumption rises with increases in *DI*. The 45° line helps locate the break-even point and helps our eye measure net saving. (Source: Table 25-3.)

The Savings Function

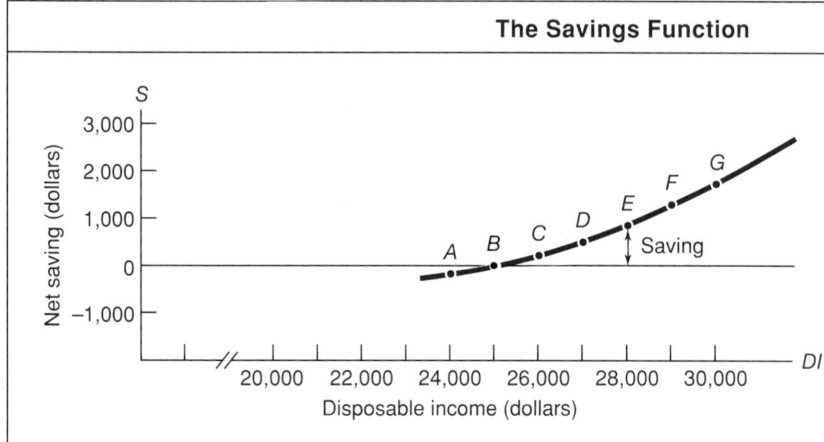

Figure 25-4. The savings function is the mirror image of the consumption function

This savings schedule is derived by subtracting consumption from income. Graphically, the savings function is obtained by subtracting vertically the consumption function from the 45° line in Fig. 25-3. Note that the break-even point *B* is at the same $25,000 income level as in Fig. 25-3.

This break-even point is at *B* in Figure 25-3. Here, consumption expenditure is exactly equal to disposable income: the household is neither a borrower nor a saver. To the right of point *B*, the consumption function lies below the 45° line. The relationship between income and consumption can be seen by examining the thin black line from *E*′ to *E* in Figure 25-3. At an income of $28,000 the level of consumption is $27,240 (see Table 25-3). We can see that consumption is less than income by the fact that the consumption function lies below the 45° line at point *E*.

What a household is not spending, it must be saving. The 45° line enables us to find how much the household is saving. Net saving is measured by the vertical distance from the consumption function up to the 45° line, as shown by the *EE*″ savings arrow in blue.

The 45° line tells us that to the left of point *B* the household is spending more than its income. The excess of consumption over income is "dissaving" and is measured by the vertical distance between the consumption function and the 45° line.

To review:

At any point on the 45° line, consumption exactly equals income and the household has zero saving. When the consumption function lies above the 45° line, the household is dissaving. When the consumption function lies below the 45° line, the household has positive saving. The amount of dissaving or saving is always measured by the vertical distance between the consumption function and the 45° line.

The Savings Function. The **savings function** shows the relationship between the level of saving and income. This is shown graphically in Figure 25-4. Again we show disposable income on the horizontal axis; but now saving, whether negative or positive in amount, is on the vertical axis.

This savings function comes directly from Figure 25-3. It is the vertical distance between the 45° line and the consumption function. For example, at point *A* in Figure 25-3, we see that the household's saving is negative because the consumption function lies above the 45° line. Figure 25-4 shows this dissaving directly—the savings function is below the zero-savings line at point *A*. Similarly, positive saving occurs to the right of point *B* because the savings function is above the zero-savings line.

The Marginal Propensity to Consume

Modern macroeconomics attaches much importance to the response of consumption to changes in income. This concept is called the marginal propensity to consume, or *MPC*.

The **marginal propensity to consume** is the extra amount that people consume when they receive an extra dollar of income.

The word "marginal" is used throughout economics to mean extra or additional. For example, "marginal cost" means the additional cost of producing an extra unit of output. "Propensity to consume" designates the desired level of consumption. *MPC*, then, is the additional or extra consumption that results from an extra dollar of income.

Table 25-4 rearranges Table 25-3's data in a more convenient form. First, verify its similarity to Table 25-3. Then, look at columns (1) and (2) to see how consumption expenditure goes up with higher levels of income.

Column (3) shows how we compute the marginal propensity to consume. From *B* to *C*, income rises by \$1000, going from \$25,000 to \$26,000. How much does consumption rise? Consumption grows from \$25,000 to \$25,850, an increase of \$850. The extra consumption is therefore 0.85 of the extra income. Out of each extra dollar of income, 85 cents goes to consumption and 15 cents goes to saving. As we move from point *B* to point *C*, we see that the marginal propensity to consume, or *MPC*, is 0.85.

You can compute *MPC* between other income levels. In Table 25-4, *MPC* begins at 0.89 for the poor and finally falls to 0.53 at higher incomes.

Marginal Propensity to Consume as Geometrical Slope. We now know how to calculate the *MPC* from data on income and consumption. We also want to understand how to calculate *MPC* graphically; we will see that the *MPC* is given by the slope of the consumption function.

Figure 25-5 shows how to calculate the *MPC* graphically. Near points *B* and *C* a little right triangle is drawn. As income increases by \$1000 from point *B* to point *C*, the amount of consumption rises by \$850. The *MPC* in this range is therefore \$850/\$1000 = 0.85. But, as the appendix to Chapter 1 showed, the slope of a line is "the rise over the

Consumption and Saving

	(1) Disposable income (after taxes) (\$)	(2) Consumption expenditure (\$)	(3) Marginal propensity to consume (*MPC*)	(4) Net saving (\$) (4) = (1) − (2)	(5) Marginal propensity to save (*MPS*)
A	24,000	24,110		−110	
			$\frac{890}{1,000} = 0.89$		$\frac{110}{1,000} = 0.11$
B	25,000	25,000		0	
			$\frac{850}{1,000} = 0.85$		$\frac{150}{1,000} = 0.15$
C	26,000	25,850		+150	
			$\frac{750}{1,000} = 0.75$		$\frac{250}{1,000} = 0.25$
D	27,000	26,600		+400	
			$\frac{640}{1,000} = 0.64$		$\frac{360}{1,000} = 0.36$
E	28,000	27,240		+760	
			$\frac{590}{1,000} = 0.59$		$\frac{410}{1,000} = 0.41$
F	29,000	27,830		+1,170	
			$\frac{530}{1,000} = 0.53$		$\frac{470}{1,000} = 0.47$
G	30,000	28,360		+1,640	

Table 25-4. The marginal propensities to consume and to save

Each dollar of income not consumed is saved. Each dollar of extra income goes either into extra consumption or into extra saving. Combining these facts allows us to calculate the marginal propensity to consume (*MPC*) and the marginal propensity to save (*MPS*).

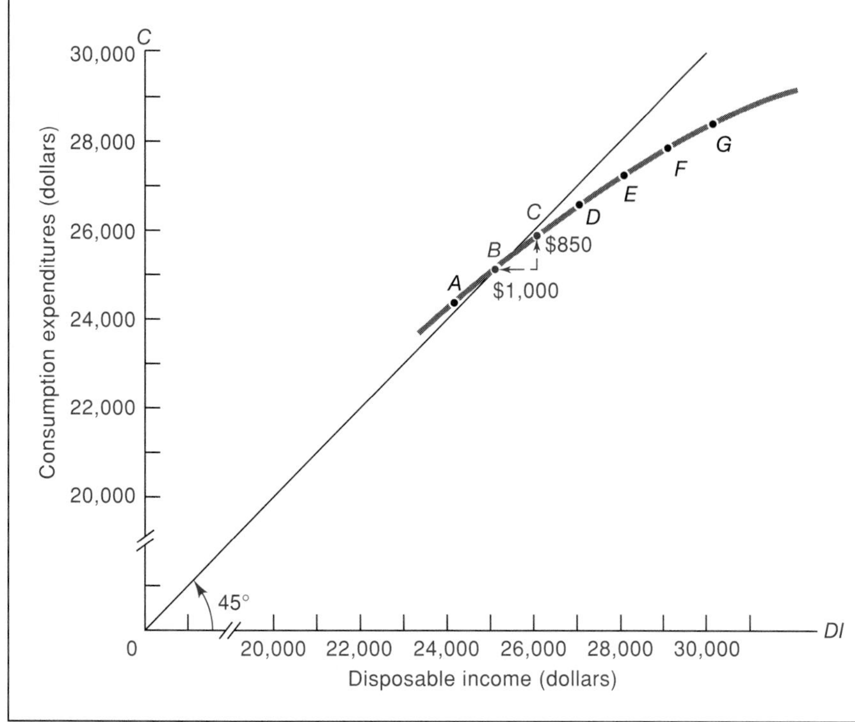

Figure 25-5. The slope of the consumption function is its *MPC*

To calculate the marginal propensity to consume (*MPC*), we measure the slope of the consumption function by forming a right triangle and relating height to base. From point *B* to point *C*, the increase in consumption is $850 while the change in disposable income is $1000. The slope, equal to the change in *C* divided by the change in *DI*, gives the *MPC*. If the consumption function is everywhere upward-sloping, what does this imply about the *MPC*?

run." We can therefore see that the slope of the consumption function between points *B* and *C* is 0.85.*

The slope of the consumption function, which measures the change in consumption per dollar change in income, is the marginal propensity to consume.

The Marginal Propensity to Save

Along with the marginal propensity to consume goes its mirror image, the marginal propensity to save, or *MPS*. The **marginal propensity to save** is defined as the fraction of an extra dollar of income that goes to extra saving.

Why are *MPC* and *MPS* related like mirror images? Recall that income equals consumption plus saving. This implies that each extra dollar of income must be divided between extra consumption and extra saving. Thus if *MPC* is 0.85, then *MPS* must be 0.15. (What would *MPS* be if *MPC* were 0.6? Or 0.99?) Comparing columns (3) and (5) of Table 25-4 confirms that at any income level, *MPC* and *MPS* must always add up to *exactly* 1, no more and

*The slope of lines was discussed in Chapter 1's appendix, but a brief review may be helpful. The numerical slope of a line can be illustrated with the help of the right triangle in Fig. 25-6. By the numerical slope of the line *XW*, we always mean the numerical ratio of the length of *ZW* to the length *XZ*. The slope is "the rise over the run."

If the line *XW* were not straight, as is the case of many curves in economics, then we would calculate the slope as the tangent. That is, if you want to find the slope at point *G* in Fig. 25-5, you (1) first place a ruler tangent to the curve at point *G*, then (2) calculate the slope as the rise over the run of the tangent line created by the ruler.

In the case of the consumption function, its slope *is* the *MPC*, or the marginal propensity to consume. Similarly, if the curve is the savings function, its slope is defined as the marginal propensity to save, or the *MPS*.

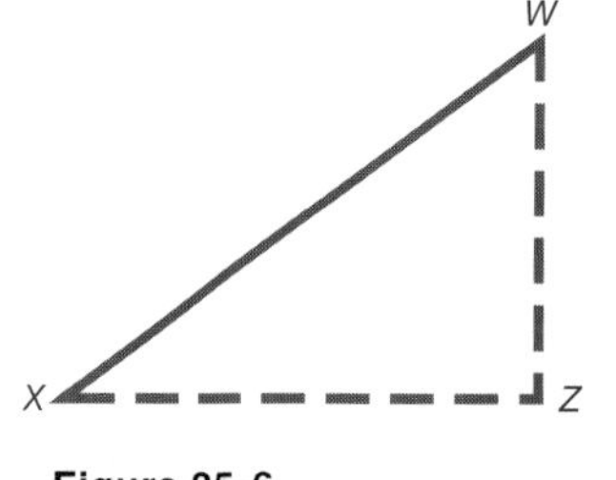

Figure 25-6

no less. Everywhere and always, $MPS \equiv 1 - MPC$.

Brief Review of Definitions

Let's review briefly the main definitions we have learned:

1. The consumption function relates the level of consumption to the level of disposable income.
2. The savings function relates saving to disposable income. Because what is saved equals what is not consumed, savings and consumption schedules are mirror images.
3. The marginal propensity to consume (MPC) is the amount of extra consumption generated by an extra dollar of income. Graphically, it is given by the slope of the consumption function.
4. The marginal propensity to save (MPS) is the extra saving generated by an extra dollar of income. Graphically, this is the slope of the savings schedule.
5. Because the part of each dollar of income that is not consumed is necessarily saved, $MPS \equiv 1 - MPC$.

National Consumption Behavior

Up to now we have examined the budget patterns and consumption behavior of typical families at different incomes. We now turn to a discussion of consumption for the nation as a whole. This transition from household behavior to national trends exemplifies the methodology of macroeconomics: we begin by examining economic activity on the individual level and then aggregate individuals to study the way the overall economy operates.

Why are we interested in national consumption trends? Consumption is important, first, because it is a major component of aggregate spending, and our task in these chapters is to understand the determination of aggregate demand. Second, what is not consumed—what is saved—is available to the nation for investment, and investment serves as a driving force behind long-term economic growth. Consumption and saving behavior are key to understanding economic growth and business cycles.

Determinants of Consumption

We begin by analyzing the major forces that affect consumer spending. What factors in a nation's life and livelihood set the pace of its consumption outlays?

Current Disposable Income. Figure 25-7 shows how closely consumption followed current disposable income over the period 1929–1991. The only period when income and consumption did not move in tandem was during World War II, when goods were scarce and rationed, and people were urged to save to help the war effort.

Informal observation and statistical studies show that the current level of disposable income is the central factor determining a nation's consumption.

Permanent Income. The simplest theory of consumption uses only the current year's income to predict consumption expenditures. Careful studies have shown that people base their consumption expenditures on long-run income trends as well as on current disposable income.

What are some examples? If bad weather destroys a crop, farmers will draw upon their previous saving. Because medical students can look forward to high professional earnings, they will borrow for consumption purposes while young. In these circumstances, consumers take the long view, asking, "Is this year's income temporarily high or low? Given my current and future income, how much can I consume today without incurring excessive debts?"

Evidence indicates that consumers generally choose their consumption levels with an eye to both current income and long-run income prospects. In order to understand how consumption depends on long-term income trends, economists have developed the *permanent-income theory* and the *life-cycle hypothesis.*

Permanent income is the level of income that households would receive when temporary or transient influences—such as the weather, a short business cycle, or a windfall gain or loss—are removed.[2] According to the permanent-income theory, consumption responds primarily to permanent income. This approach implies that

[2] The pathbreaking studies on longer-term influences were by Milton Friedman (on the permanent-income hypothesis) and Franco Modigliani (for the life-cycle model). Both received the Nobel Prize in economics for their accomplishments in these and other areas.

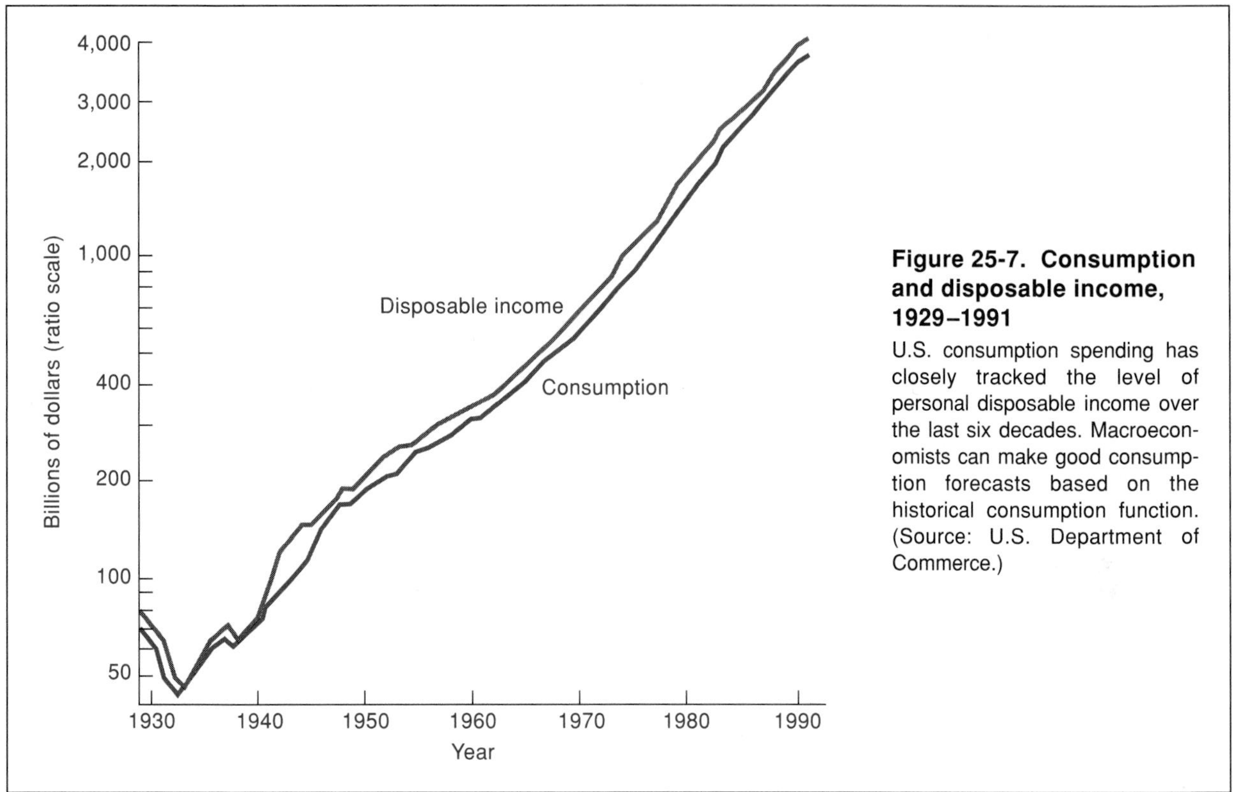

Figure 25-7. Consumption and disposable income, 1929–1991

U.S. consumption spending has closely tracked the level of personal disposable income over the last six decades. Macroeconomists can make good consumption forecasts based on the historical consumption function. (Source: U.S. Department of Commerce.)

consumers do not respond equally to all income shocks. If a change in income appears permanent (such as being promoted to a secure and high-paying job), then people are likely to consume a large fraction of the increase in income. On the other hand, if the income change is clearly transitory (for example, if it arises from a one-time bonus or a good harvest), then a significant fraction of the income change may be saved.

Wealth and Other Influences. A further important determinant of the amount of consumption is wealth. Consider two consumers, both earning $25,000 per year. One has $100,000 in the bank while the other has no saving at all. The first person may consume part of wealth, while the second has no wealth to draw down. The fact that higher wealth leads to higher consumption is called the *wealth effect.*

Normally, wealth does not change rapidly from year to year. Therefore, the wealth effect seldom causes sharp movements in consumption. From time to time, however, exceptions occur. When the stock market tumbled after 1929, fortunes collapsed and paper-rich capitalists became paupers overnight. Many wealthy people were forced to curtail their consumption. Similarly, as stock prices soared in the mid-1980s, adding more than a trillion dollars to people's wealth after 1982, consumption was probably bolstered by the flush of wealth people felt.

Other factors are identified from time to time as important determinants of saving or consumption. Some economists believe that saving has been depressed by low rates of return to savings. Martin Feldstein, Harvard professor and the chairman of the Council of Economic Advisers under President Reagan, has argued that a generous social security system reduces personal saving; because we expect to get a large government pension when we retire, we save less for retirement today.

How important are influences other than current income in determining consumption? Few doubt the importance of permanent income, wealth, social factors, and expectations in affecting savings levels. But from year to year, the major determinant of changes in consumption is actual disposable income.

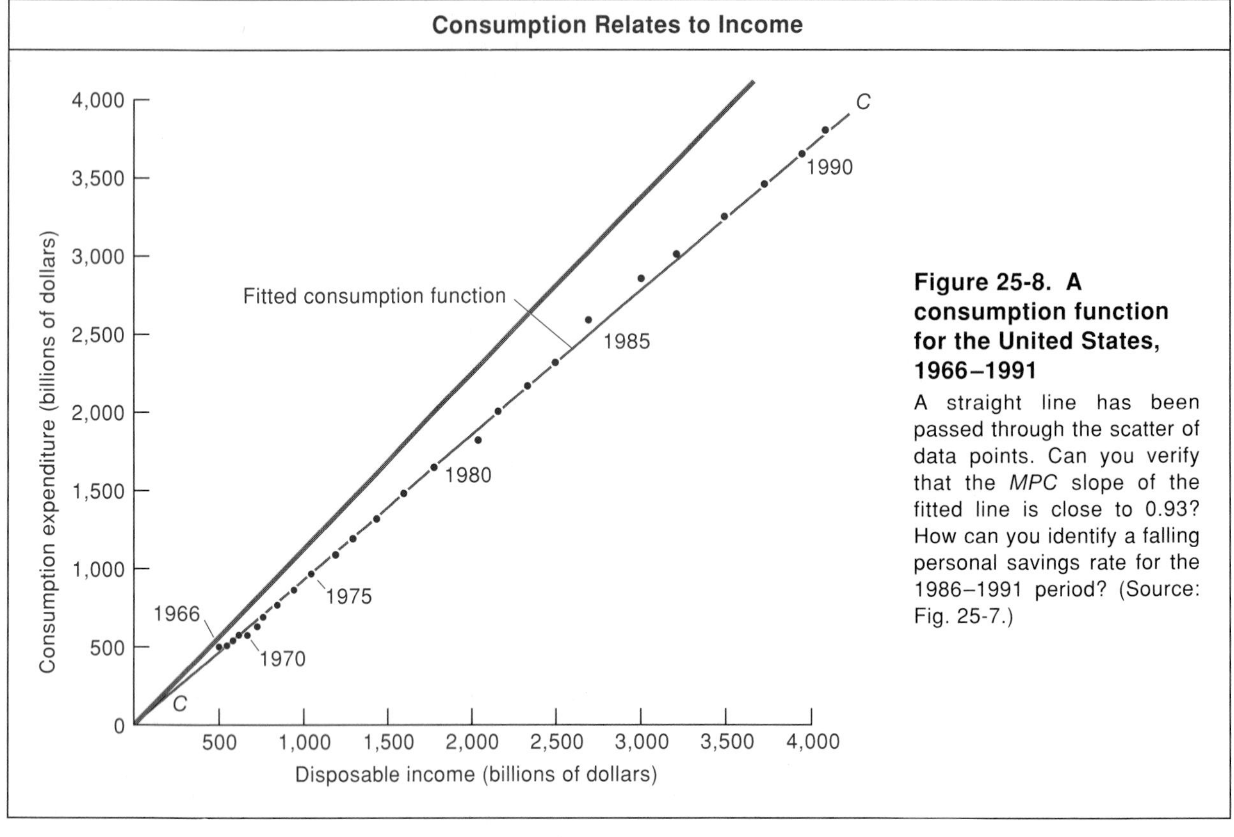

Figure 25-8. A consumption function for the United States, 1966–1991

A straight line has been passed through the scatter of data points. Can you verify that the *MPC* slope of the fitted line is close to 0.93? How can you identify a falling personal savings rate for the 1986–1991 period? (Source: Fig. 25-7.)

The National Consumption Function

Having reviewed the determinants of consumption, we may conclude that the level of disposable income is the primary determinant of the level of national consumption. Armed with this result, we can plot recent annual data on consumption and disposable income in Figure 25-8. The scatter diagram shows data for the period 1966-1991, with each point representing the level of consumption and income for a given year.

In addition, through the scatter points we have drawn a blue line—labeled *CC* and marked "Fitted consumption function." This fitted consumption function shows how closely consumption has followed disposable income over the last quarter-century. In fact, economic historians have found that a close relationship between disposable income and consumption holds back to the nineteenth century. This relationship—that consumers always save 7 percent of their disposable income—is among the most durable empirical regularities of macroeconomics. Figure 25-8 shows that the fitted line tracks the actual data very closely.

The Declining U.S. Savings Rate

Over the long run, a nation's capital formation is determined by its national savings rate. When a nation saves a great deal, its capital stock grows rapidly and it enjoys rapid growth in its potential output. When a nation's savings rate is low, its equipment and factories become obsolete and its infrastructure begins to rot away. This close relationship between saving, investment, and economic growth is the major reason why economists worry about a nation's savings rate.

Table 25-5 lists the net savings rates of major countries for the period 1960–89. It shows that Japan leads the list in saving as a percent of national income while the United States lags behind other major countries. Moreover, the already low U.S. savings rate has declined even further over the

National Savings Rates, 1960–89

Country	National savings rate (net private saving as % of GDP)
Japan	20.7
West Germany	14.0
France	13.6
Canada	9.9
United Kingdom	7.4
United States	7.2

Source: OECD, *National Accounts, 1960–89* (Paris, 1991) and U.S. Department of Commerce.

Table 25-5. U.S. savings rate trails that of other major industrial countries

The table shows net national private saving (equal to net saving of households and businesses at home and abroad) divided by GDP.

last decade. Figure 25-9 shows trends in net private saving (equal to the sum of net foreign investment and net private domestic saving) over recent decades. This measure of the national savings rate has declined from over 10 percent after World War II to around 2 percent in the late 1980s.

What are the reasons for the precipitous decline in the national savings rate? This is a highly controversial question today, but economists point to the following potential causes:

- *Federal budget deficits.* In the early 1980s, the federal government began to incur large budget deficits. The budget deficit grew from a few billion annually in the late 1970s to an average of around $150 billion annually by the late 1980s. Most economists believe that high budget deficits stimulate consumption and thereby lower national saving. Some have calculated that much of the recent decline in the national savings rate is due to the high budget deficits of the 1980s.[3]
- *Social security system.* Many economists have argued that the introduction of the social security system has removed some of the need for private saving. In earlier times, a family would

[3] One school of thought, originating in studies of Harvard's Robert Barro, holds that government deficits will not stimulate consumption. The logic of Barro's theory is that, when the government borrows to cover its deficit, people know that the government will eventually have to raise taxes to pay back the interest and principal on the debt. Rational and farsighted consumers will accordingly save just enough to offset the stimulative effect of government deficits.

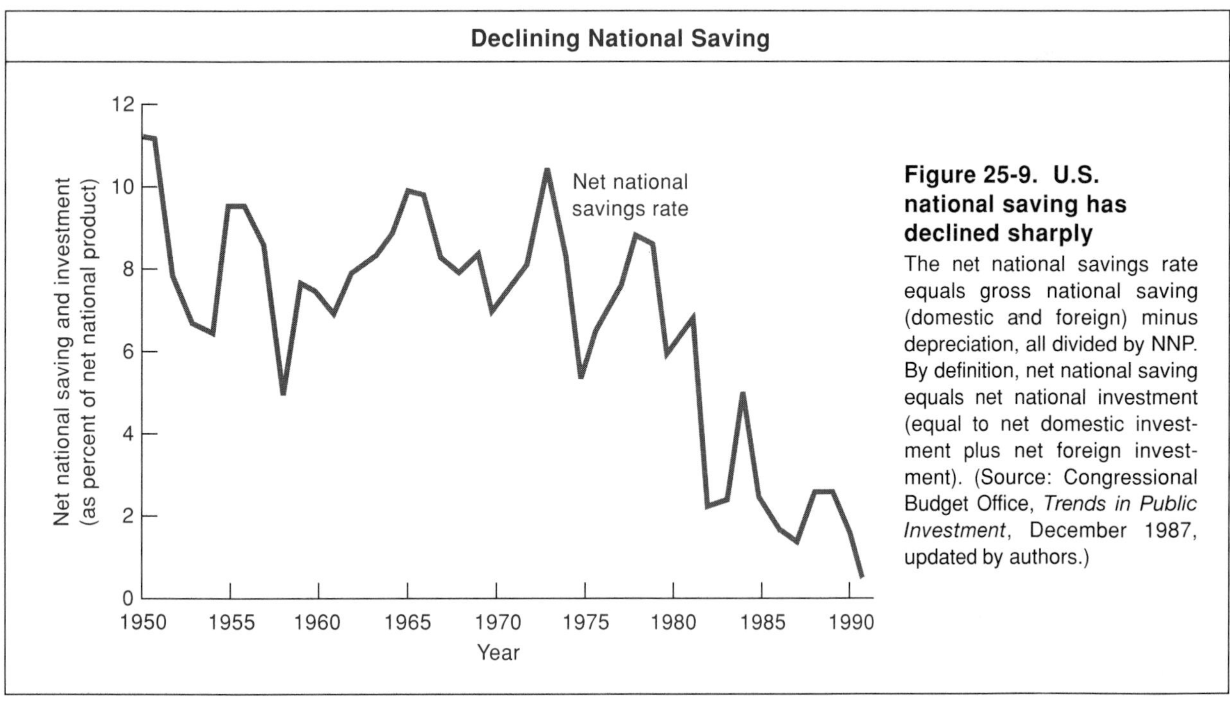

Figure 25-9. U.S. national saving has declined sharply

The net national savings rate equals gross national saving (domestic and foreign) minus depreciation, all divided by NNP. By definition, net national saving equals net national investment (equal to net domestic investment plus net foreign investment). (Source: Congressional Budget Office, *Trends in Public Investment*, December 1987, updated by authors.)

save during working years to build up a nest egg for retirement. Today, the government collects social security taxes and pays out social security benefits, displacing some of the need for private saving for retirement. Other income-support systems have a similar effect, reducing the need to save for a rainy day: crop insurance for farmers, unemployment insurance for workers, and medical care for the indigent all alleviate the precautionary motive for people to save.

- *Capital markets.* Until recently, capital markets had numerous imperfections. People found it hard to borrow funds for worthwhile purposes, whether for buying a house, financing an education, or starting a business. As capital markets developed, often with the help of government, new loan instruments allowed people to borrow more easily. One good example of this is student loans. Decades ago, college educations were financed either out of family saving or by students' working. Today, because the federal government guarantees many student loans, students can borrow to pay for their education and repay the loans from their own earnings later in life.
- *Other sources.* Many other culprits have been indicted in the case of the declining national savings rate. Some analysts pointed to high inflation in the late 1970s and early 1980s, although this cause would seem to be acquitted given the continued decline of saving as inflation disappeared in the late 1980s. Others pointed to diluted incentives to save in recent years because of high tax rates and low post-tax returns to saving; here again, the argument is unconvincing because saving did not recover even after tax rates fell and real interest rates rose in the 1980s. Further suggestions include sociological hypotheses such as a perceived decline in the Protestant ethic (an ethic that Tawney and other historians thought was a major contributor to the rise of capitalism in earlier centuries).

The declining national savings rate remains a puzzling phenomenon testing the ingenuity of macroeconomists. While no one has demonstrated conclusively why the U.S. national savings rate has dropped so sharply in recent years, virtually all believe that the savings rate is too low to guarantee a vital and healthy rate of investment in the 1990s.

B. The Determinants of Investment

The second major component of private spending is investment.[4] Investment plays two roles in macroeconomics. First, because it is a large and volatile component of spending, sharp changes in investment can have a major impact on aggregate demand. This, in turn, affects output and employment. In addition, investment leads to capital accumulation. Adding to the stock of buildings and equipment increases the nation's potential output and promotes economic growth in the long run.

Thus investment plays a dual role, affecting short-run output through its impact on aggregate demand and influencing long-run output growth through the impact of capital formation on potential output and aggregate supply.

What are the major determinants of investment? Recall from Table 24-5 that investment is broken down into three categories—purchases of residential structures, investment in business fixed plant and equipment, and additions to inventory. Of the total, about a quarter is residential housing, a twentieth normally is change in inventories, and the rest—averaging 70 percent of total investment in recent years—is investment in business plant and equipment.

Why do businesses invest? Ultimately, businesses

[4] Remember that macroeconomists use the term "investment" to mean additions to the stock of tangible capital goods—capital goods being equipment, structures, or inventories. When IBM builds a new factory or when the Smiths build a new house, these represent investments. Many people speak of "investing" when buying a piece of land, an old security, or any title to property. In economics, these purchases involve financial transactions or portfolio changes, because what one person is buying, someone else is selling. There is *investment* only when real capital is created.

buy capital goods when they expect that this action will earn them a profit—that is, will bring them revenues greater than the costs of the investment. This simple statement contains the three elements essential to understanding investment: revenues, costs, and expectations.

Revenues. An investment will bring the firm additional revenue if it helps the firm to sell more. This suggests that a very important determinant of investment is the overall level of output (or GNP). When factories are lying idle, firms have relatively little need for new factories, so investment is low. More generally, investment depends upon the revenues that will be generated by the state of overall economic activity. Some studies suggest that output fluctuations dominate the movement of investment over the business cycle. A recent example of a large output effect was seen during the business downturn of 1979–1982, when output fell sharply and investment declined by 22 percent.

Costs. A second important determinant of the level of investment is the costs of investing. Because investment goods last many years, reckoning the costs of investment is somewhat more complicated than doing so for other commodities like coal or wheat. When a purchased good lasts many years, we must calculate the cost of capital in terms of the interest rate on borrowings.

To understand this point, note that investors often raise the funds for buying capital goods by borrowing (say through a mortgage or in the bond market). What is the cost of borrowing? It is the *interest rate* on borrowed funds. Recall that the interest rate is the price paid for borrowing money for a period of time; for example, you might have to pay 13 percent to borrow $1000 for a year. In the case of a family buying a house, the interest rate is the mortgage interest rate.

The federal government sometimes uses fiscal policies to affect investment in specific sectors. In particular, *taxes* imposed by governments affect the cost of investment. The federal corporation income tax takes up to 34 cents of every dollar of corporate profits, thereby discouraging investment in the corporate sector. However, the government gives special tax breaks to oil and gas drilling, increasing activity in that sector. The tax treatment in different sectors, or even in different countries, will have a profound effect upon the investment behavior of profit-seeking companies.[5]

Expectations. The third element in the determination of investment is expectations and business confidence. Investment is above all a gamble on the future, a bet that the revenue from an investment will exceed its costs. If businesses are concerned that future economic conditions in Germany will be depressed, they will be reluctant to invest in Germany. Conversely, when businesses see the likelihood of a sharp business recovery in the near future, they begin to plan for plant expansion.

Thus investment decisions hang by a thread on expectations and forecasts about future events. But, as one wit said, predicting is hazardous, especially about the future. Businesses spend much energy analyzing investments and trying to narrow the uncertainties about their investments.

We can sum up our review of the forces lying behind investment decisions as follows:

Businesses invest to earn profits. Because capital goods last many years, investment decisions depend on (a) the demand for the output produced by the new investment, (b) the interest rates and taxes that influence the costs of the investment, and (c) business expectations about the state of the economy.

The Investment Demand Curve

To analyze how different forces affect investment, we need to understand the relationship between interest rates and investment. This relationship is especially important because it is primarily through interest rates that governments influence investment. To show the relationship between interest rates and investment, economists use a schedule called the *investment demand* curve.

[5] In assessing the impact of taxation upon investment, economists examine the "marginal tax rate" on the return on investment. The marginal tax rate is the additional tax paid on an additional dollar of income. For 1990, the marginal tax rate on income from corporate investments, including taxes levied by all levels of government (federal, state, and local), is about 38 percent (see *Economic Report of the President,* 1987, for a discussion). This means that if an investment earns $100 of profit, the corporate investor keeps $62 and governments get $38. The high tax rate on corporate profits has led some to say that government is the largest single shareholder in American capitalism.

Interest Rates and Investment

(1)	(2)	(3)	(4)	(5)	(6)	(7)
			Cost per $1,000 of project at annual interest rate of		Annual net profit per $1,000 invested at annual interest rate of	
Project	Total investment in project ($, million)	Annual revenues per $1,000 invested ($)	10% ($)	5% ($)	10% ($) (6) = (3) − 4	5% ($) (7) = (3) − (5)
A	1	1,500	100	50	1,400	1,450
B	4	220	100	50	120	170
C	10	160	100	50	60	110
D	10	130	100	50	30	80
E	5	110	100	50	10	60
F	15	90	100	50	−10	40
G	10	60	100	50	−40	10
H	20	40	100	50	−60	−10

Table 25-6. The profitability of investment depends on the interest rate

The economy has eight investment projects, ranked in order of return. Column (2) shows the investment in each project. Column (3) calculates the perpetual return each year per $1000 invested.

Columns (4) and (5) then show the cost of the project, assuming all funds are borrowed, at interest rates of 10 and 5 percent; this is shown per $1000 of the project.

The last two columns calculate the annual net profit per $1000 invested in the project. If net profit is positive, then profit-maximizing firms will undertake the investment; if negative, the investment project will be rejected.

Note how the cutoff between profitable and unprofitable investments moves as the interest rate rises. (Where would the cutoff be if the interest rate rose to 15 percent per year?)

Consider a simplified economy where firms can invest in different projects: A, B, C, and so forth up to H. These investments are so durable (like power plants or buildings) that we can ignore the need for replacement. Further, they yield a constant stream of net income each year, and there is no inflation. Table 25-6 shows the financial data on each of the investment projects.

Consider project A. This project costs $1 million. It has a very high return—$1500 per year of revenues per $1000 invested (this is a rate of return of 150 percent per year). Columns (4) and (5) show the cost of investment. For simplicity, assume that the investment is financed purely by borrowing at the market interest rate, here taken alternatively as 10 percent per year in column (4) and 5 percent in column (5).

Thus at a 10 percent annual interest rate, the cost of borrowing $1000 is $100 a year, as is shown in all entries of column (4); at a 5 percent interest rate, the borrowing cost is $50 per $1000 borrowed per year.

Finally, the last two columns show the *annual net profit* from each investment. For lucrative project A, the net annual profit is $1400 a year per $1000 invested at a 10 percent interest rate. Project H loses money.

To review our findings: In deciding among investment projects, firms compare the annual revenues from an investment with the annual cost of capital, which depends upon the interest rate. The difference between annual revenue and annual cost is the annual net profit. When annual net profit is positive, the investment makes money, while a negative net profit denotes that the investment loses money.[6]

The annual net profit on an investment is shown in the last two columns of Table 25-6. Examine the last column, corresponding to a 5 percent interest

[6] This example greatly simplifies the calculations businesses must make in actual investment analyses. Usually, investments involve an uneven stream of returns, depreciation of capital, inflation, taxes, and multiple interest rates on borrowed funds. Discussion of the economics of "discounting" and "present values" is found in analysis of capital theory and in advanced books on finance.

rate. Note that at this interest rate, investment projects A through G would be profitable. We would thus expect profit-maximizing firms to invest in all seven projects, which [from column (2)] total up to $55 million in investment. Thus at a 5 percent interest rate, investment demand would be $55 million.

However, suppose that the interest rate rises to 10 percent. Then the cost of financing these investments would double. We see from column (6) that investment projects F and G become unprofitable at an interest rate of 10 percent; investment demand would fall to $30 million.

We can show the results of this analysis in Figure 25-10. This figure shows the *demand-for-investment schedule,* which is here a downward-sloping step function of the interest rate. This schedule shows the amount of investment that would be undertaken at each interest rate; it is obtained by adding up all the investments that would be profitable at each level of the interest rate.

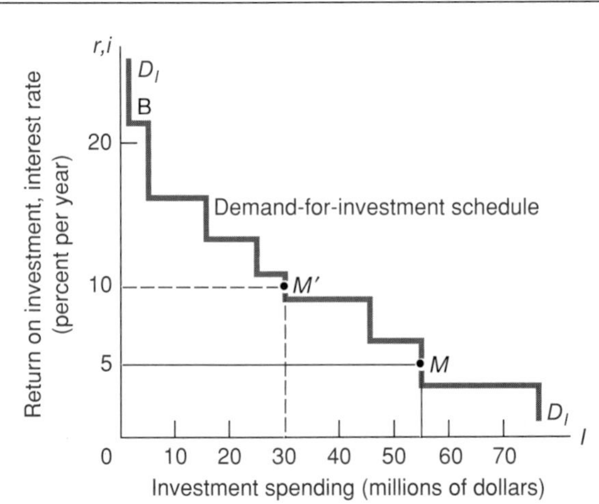

Figure 25-10. Investment depends upon the interest rate

The downward-stepping demand-for-investment schedule plots the amount that businesses would invest at each interest rate, as calculated from the data in Table 25-6. Each step represents a lump of investment: project A has such a high rate that it is off the figure; the highest visible step is project B, shown at the upper left.

At each interest rate, all investments that have positive net profit will be undertaken. Thus at an interest rate of 5 percent, $55 million of investment will take place (in projects A through G), as shown by the intersection at point *M* of the demand-for-investment curve and the solid interest-rate line. If interest rates were to rise to 10 percent, the new equilibrium would be at *M′*, with only $30 million of investment.

Hence, if the market interest rate is 5 percent, the desired level of investment will occur at point *M,* which shows investment of $55 million. At this interest rate, projects A through G are undertaken. If interest rates were to rise to 10 percent, projects F and G would be squeezed out; in this situation, investment demand would lie at point *M′* in Figure 25-10, with total investment of $30 million.

Shifts in the Investment Demand Curve

We have seen how interest rates affect the level of investment. Investment is affected by other forces as well. For example, an increase in the GNP will shift the investment demand curve out as is shown in Figure 25-11(*a*) on the following page.

An increase in business taxation would depress investment. Say that the government taxes away half the net yield in column (3) of Table 25-6, with interest costs in columns (4) and (5) not being deductible. The net profits in columns (6) and (7) would therefore decline. [Verify that at a 10 percent interest rate, a 50 percent tax on column (3) would raise the cutoff to between projects B and C, and the demand for investment would decline to $5 million.] The case of a tax increase on investment income is shown in Figure 25-11(*b*).

Finally, note the importance of expectations. What if investors become pessimistic and think that yields will soon halve? Or become optimistic and think yields will double? By working through these cases you can see how powerful an effect expectations can have on investment. Figure 25-11(*c*) displays how a bout of business pessimism would shift in the investment demand schedule, D_I.

Real vs. Nominal Interest Rates

If you look at a newspaper from the late 1970s or early 1980s, you will see *nominal* (or money) *interest rates* of 8, 15, or even 18 percent per year. These compare with rates of 3 or 4 or 5 percent in the early 1960s. Does this comparison suggest that investment should have collapsed in recent years? Or take Brazil, where interest rates have been more than 100 percent per year. Wouldn't this dampen even the most robust entrepreneurial spirits?

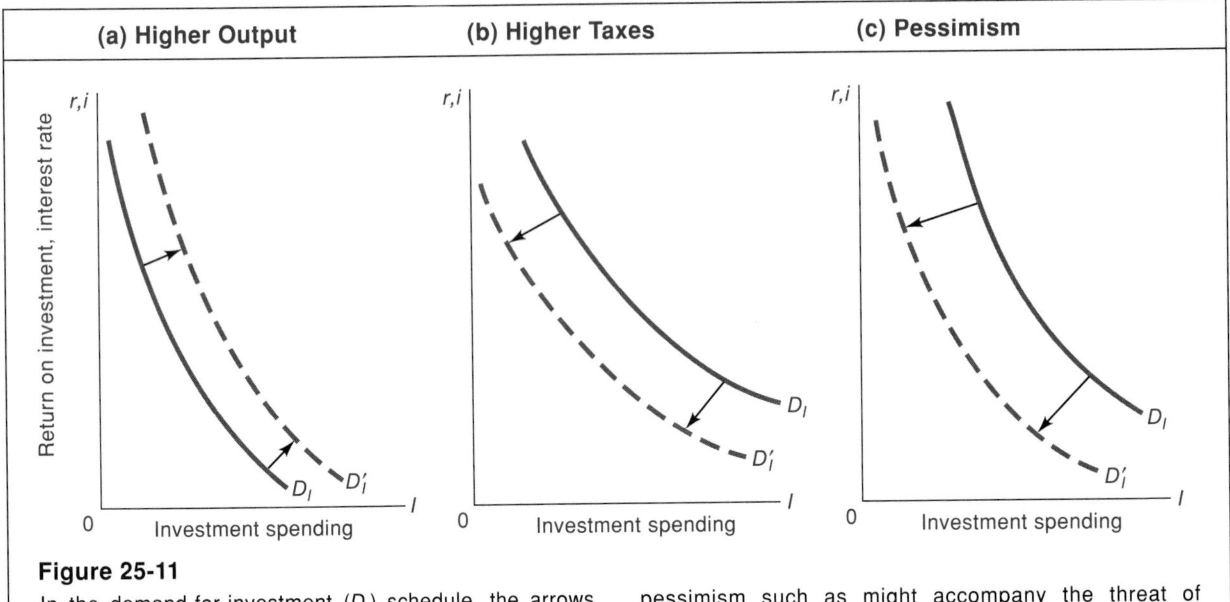

Figure 25-11

In the demand-for-investment (D_I) schedule, the arrows show the impact of **(a)** a higher level of GNP; **(b)** higher taxes on capital income; and **(c)** a burst of business pessimism such as might accompany the threat of recession, nationalization, or war in the Persian Gulf.

Surprisingly, the answer is no. Investment in the late 1970s and early 1980s in the United States was actually high by historical standards. And Brazil showed extremely high levels of real investment even though nominal interest rates were astronomical.

The key to this puzzle lies in the concept of the *real rate of interest.* In the United States and Brazil, the high money interest rates were matched by extremely high inflation rates. True, you had to pay a great deal to borrow, but when you repaid, it was in depreciated dollars or cruzados. The interest rates in terms of real goods were actually low or even negative.

An example will clarify the point. Say that the interest rate and the inflation rate are both 20 percent. If you borrow $1000 today, you have to pay back $1200 next year. But because of inflation the real value of the $1200 next year is exactly the same as the $1000 this year. So, in effect, you are repaying the exact same amount of real goods. In this case, the interest rate in terms of real goods (the *real interest rate*) is zero, not 20 percent. More generally:

The real interest rate is the interest that borrowers pay in terms of real goods and services. It is equal to the nominal (or money) interest rate less the rate of inflation.

How does this concept relate to investment? In our analysis of Table 25-6, we assumed no inflation, so the real and nominal rates of interest were equal. But if prices are rising, the income from investment is growing over time with inflation. The yield shown in column (3) is growing rather than remaining constant, and the investment would be more valuable than one with a constant yield over time.

In order to remove the distortionary effects of inflation on both revenues and on nominal interest rates, economists analyze investment in inflation-corrected terms. To do this, we examine a "real investment demand curve" that shows the effect of real output and real interest rates on real investment outlays (where "real" output and investment refer to the values of these variables in constant prices).

The concept of the real interest rate then resolves the paradox of high investment accompanying high interest rates found in Brazil and the United States in the 1970s. Although nominal interest rates were high, *real* interest rates were low. It was the low real interest rates that produced the high levels of investment.

Volatile Investment

After learning about the factors affecting investment, you will not be surprised to discover that investment is extremely volatile. Investment behaves unpredictably because it depends on such uncertain factors as the success or failure of new and untried products, changes in tax rates and interest rates, political attitudes and approaches to stabilizing the economy, and similar changeable events of economic life.

Figure 25-12 presents a picture of the instability of investment. This shows investment as a percentage of potential GNP. Note the low levels of investment during the Great Depression of the 1930s and during World War II. We can also see how the investment incentives of the 1960s increased the share of investment in GNP. Business-cycle downturns, such as in 1975 and 1982, tend to produce a sharp decline in the investment-GNP ratio.

On to the Theory of Aggregate Demand

We have now completed our introduction to the basic concepts of macroeconomics and the major components of national output. We have seen that consumption and investment can fluctuate from year to year, and in the case of investment the fluctuations can be quite sharp. This suggests that the total flow of dollar spending (aggregate demand) is not guaranteed to grow smoothly from year to year.

The next four chapters investigate how the forces of spending and production interact to give an equilibrium level of national output. We will see

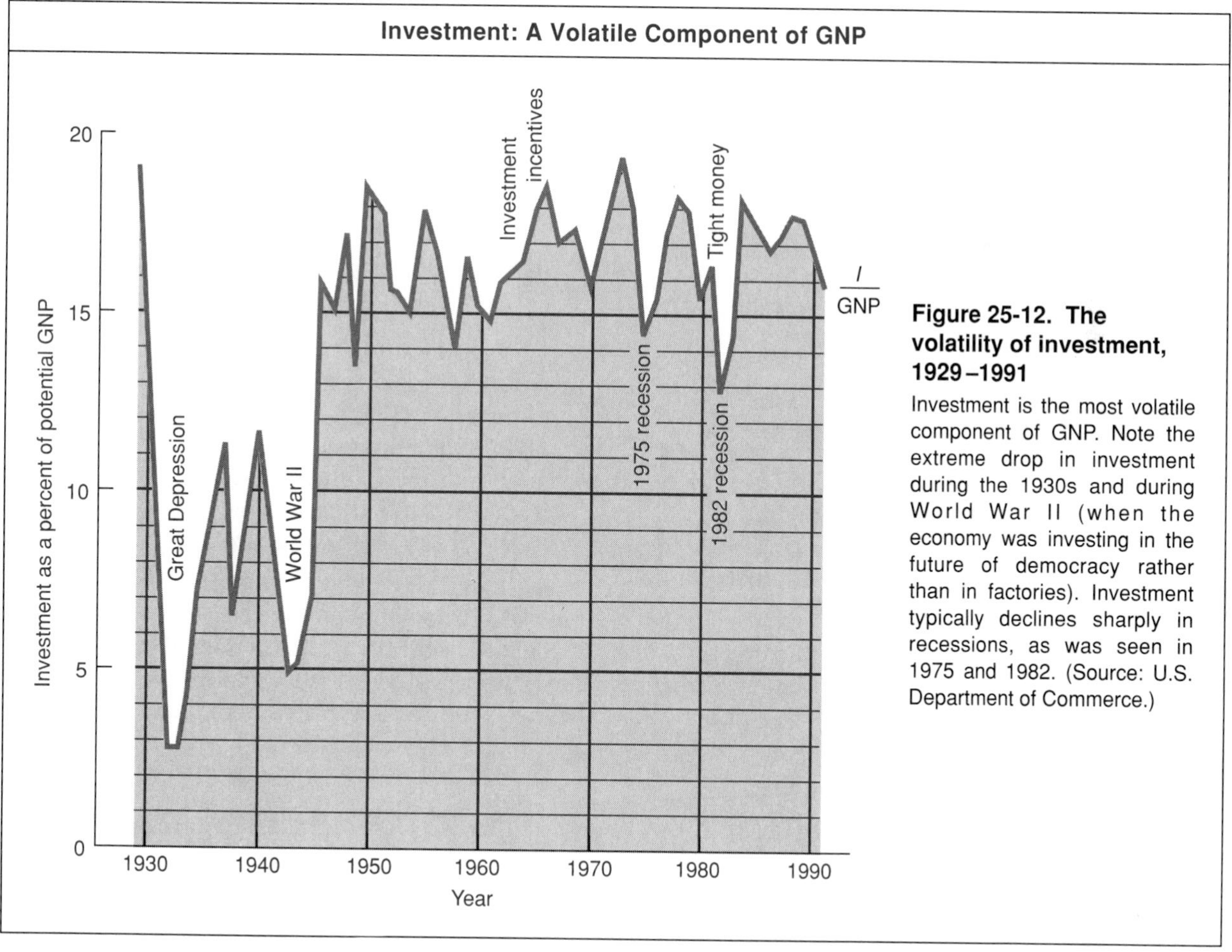

Figure 25-12. The volatility of investment, 1929–1991

Investment is the most volatile component of GNP. Note the extreme drop in investment during the 1930s and during World War II (when the economy was investing in the future of democracy rather than in factories). Investment typically declines sharply in recessions, as was seen in 1975 and 1982. (Source: U.S. Department of Commerce.)

that actual GNP can diverge from its full-employment potential. We will also see how government fiscal and monetary policies can combat recessions and booms. At the heart of the analysis is the movement of consumption and investment that we explored in this chapter.

SUMMARY

A. Consumption and Saving

1. Disposable income is an important determinant of consumption and saving. The consumption function is the schedule relating total consumption to total income. Because each dollar of income is either saved or consumed, the savings function is the other side or mirror image of the consumption function. The characteristics of the consumption and savings functions are summarized on page 442 and should be studied carefully.
2. Adding together individual consumption functions gives us the national consumption function. In simplest form, this shows total consumption expenditures as a function of disposable income. Other variables, such as wealth and expectations about future income, also have a significant impact on consumption patterns.
3. The national savings rate has declined sharply in the last decade. Studies point to the growing fiscal deficit of the federal government, to social security programs, and to changes in capital markets as possible causes. Most economists believe that a lower federal deficit is the best single way to increase the national savings rate today.

B. The Determinants of Investment

4. The second major component of spending is investment in housing, plant, and equipment. Firms invest to earn profits. The major economic forces that determine investment are therefore the revenues produced by investment (primarily influenced by the state of the business cycle), the cost of investment (determined by interest rates and tax policy), and the state of expectations about the future. Because the determinants of investment depend on highly unpredictable future events, investment is the most volatile component of aggregate spending.
5. An important relationship is the investment demand schedule, which connects the level of investment spending and the interest rate. Because the profitability of investment varies inversely with the interest rate, which is the cost of capital, we can derive a downward-sloping investment demand curve. A higher interest rate will lead firms to cancel some investment projects.
6. The real rate of interest corrects the nominal interest rate for the rate of inflation. Thus:

$$\text{Real interest rate} = \text{nominal interest rate} - \text{rate of inflation}$$

In making investment decisions, the real interest rate is particularly relevant.

CONCEPTS FOR REVIEW

Consumption and saving
budget patterns
disposable income, consumption, saving
consumption and savings functions
personal and national savings rates
marginal propensity to consume (*MPC*)
marginal propensity to save (*MPS*)
$MPC + MPS \equiv 1$
break-even point
45° line
national consumption function vs. household consumption function
determinants of consumption: current disposable income, permanent income, wealth

Investment
determinants of investment: revenues, costs, expectations
role of interest rates in *I*
investment demand function
real vs. nominal interest rate

QUESTIONS FOR DISCUSSION

1. Summarize the budget patterns for food, clothing, luxuries, saving.
2. In working with the consumption function and the investment demand schedule, we need to distinguish between shifts of and movements along these schedules.
   (a) Define carefully for both curves changes that would lead to shifts in and those that would produce movements along the schedules.
   (b) For the following, explain verbally and show in a diagram whether they are shifts of or movements along the consumption function: increase in disposable income, decrease in wealth, fall in stock prices.
   (c) For the following, explain verbally and show in a diagram whether they are shifts of or movements along the investment demand curve: expectation of a decline in output next year, rise of interest rates, decline in inflation.
3. Exactly how were the *MPC* and *MPS* in Table 25-4 computed? Illustrate by calculating *MPC* and *MPS* between points *A* and *B*. Explain why it must always be true that $MPC + MPS \equiv 1$.
4. I consume *all* my income at every level of income. Draw my consumption and savings functions. What are my *MPC* and *MPS*?
5. A noted economist has written: "The 1986 Tax Reform Act raises the tax rate on corporations by as much as 20 percentage points [e.g., from 18 percent of profits to 38 percent of profits]. In the long run, this will surely reduce the stock of plant and equipment by 10 to 15 percent." Explain the reasoning behind this statement. Illustrate using the demand-for-investment schedule.
6. Estimate your income, consumption, and saving for last year. If you dissaved (consumed more than your income) how did you finance your dissaving? Estimate the composition of your consumption in terms of each of the major categories listed in Table 25-1.
7. "Along the consumption function, income changes more than consumption." What does this imply for the *MPC* and *MPS*?
8. "Changes in disposable income lead to movements along the consumption function; changes in wealth or other factors lead to a shift of the consumption function." Explain this statement with an illustration of each case.
9. What would be the effects of the following on the investment demand function illustrated in Table 25-6 and Figure 25-10?
   (a) A doubling of the annual revenues per $1000 invested shown in column (3)
   (b) A rise in interest rates to 15 percent per year
   (c) The addition of a ninth project with data in the first three columns of: (J, 10, 70)
   (d) A 50 percent tax on *net* profits shown in columns (6) and (7)
10. Using the augmented investment demand schedule in question 9, and assuming that the interest rate is 10 percent, calculate the level of investment for cases (a) through (d) in question 9.
11. **Advanced problem:** According to the life-cycle model, people consume each year an amount that depends upon their *lifetime* income rather than

upon their current income. Assume that you expect to receive future incomes (in constant dollars) according to the following schedule:

(1) Year	(2) Income ($)	(3) Consumption	(4) Saving	(5) Cumulative saving (end of year)
1	30,000	______	______	______
2	30,000	______	______	______
3	25,000	______	______	______
4	15,000	______	______	______
5*	0	______	______	0

* Retired.

Assume that there is no interest paid on saving. You have no initial saving. Further assume that you want to "smooth" your consumption (enjoying equal consumption each year) because of diminishing extra satisfaction from extra consumption. Derive your best consumption trajectory for the 5 years, and write the figures in column (3). Then calculate your saving and enter the amounts in column (4); put your end-of-period wealth, or cumulative saving, for each year into column (5). What is your average savings rate in the first 4 years?

Next, assume that a government social security program taxes you $2000 in each of your working years and provides you with an $8000 pension in year 5. If you still desire to smooth consumption, calculate your revised savings plan. How has the social security program affected your consumption? What is the effect on your average savings rate in the first 4 years? Can you see why some economists claim that social security can lower saving?

C H A P T E R 2 6

FUNDAMENTALS OF AGGREGATE SUPPLY AND DEMAND

More generally, the classicals continue to believe that the business cycle can be understood within a model of frictionless markets, while the Keynesians believe that market failures of various sorts are necessary to explain fluctuations in the economy.

N. Gregory Mankiw (1990)

Why did the American economy sputter and enter a recession in 1990? Why was the 1990–1991 recession mild while that of the early 1980s was deep and prolonged? How did the vast expansion of military expenditure during World War II produce a major expansion of economic activity? Why did the three oil-price shocks of 1973, 1979, and 1990 lead to recessions in most industrial economies? And how can governments use monetary and fiscal policies to tame the excesses of inflation and unemployment?

The next few chapters address these central issues. This chapter begins with a detailed study of *aggregate output and the price level.* We start with an examination of the foundations of aggregate demand, building upon our analysis of consumption and investment in the last chapter. We then explain the foundations of aggregate supply, and examine the differences between the "flexible-price" and the "sticky-price" views of the economy. Finally, we will sketch the major differences between the Keynesian and the classical approaches to macroeconomics. We will see how opposing are the two views about both the functioning of the macroeconomy and the best policies for combating inflation and unemployment.

Analytical Foundations of Aggregate Demand

National output and the price level are determined by the interplay of aggregate demand and supply, as Chapter 23 showed. This means that the actual level of production is determined in part by aggregate demand (the quantity of goods and services that people, businesses, and governments want to buy) and in part by aggregate supply (the quantity of goods and services that businesses want to sell).

Aggregate demand (or *AD*) is the total or aggregate quantity of output that is willingly bought at a given level of prices, other things held constant. *AD* is the desired spending in all product sectors: consumption, private domestic investment, government purchases of goods and services, and net exports. It has four components:

1. *Consumption.* As we saw in the last chapter, consumption (*C*) is primarily determined by disposable income, which is personal income less taxes. Other factors affecting consumption are longer-term trends in income, household wealth, and the aggregate price level. Aggregate demand analysis focuses on the determinants of *real*

consumption (that is, nominal or dollar consumption divided by the price index for consumption).

2. *Investment.* Investment (*I*) spending includes purchases of structures and equipment and accumulation of inventories. Our analysis in the last chapter showed that the major determinants of investment are the level of output, the cost of capital (as determined by tax policies along with interest rates and other financial conditions), and expectations about the future. The major channel by which economic policy can affect investment is through monetary policy.
3. *Government spending.* A third component of aggregate demand is government spending (*G*) on goods and services: purchases of goods like tanks or road-building equipment as well as the services of judges and public-school teachers. Unlike consumption and investment, this component of aggregate demand is determined directly by the government's spending decisions; when the Pentagon buys a new fighter aircraft, this output immediately adds to the GNP.
4. *Net exports.* A final component of aggregate demand is net exports (*X*), which equals the value of exports minus the value of imports. Imports are determined by domestic income and output, by the ratio of domestic to foreign prices, and by the foreign exchange rate of the dollar. Exports (which are imports of other countries) are the mirror image of imports, determined by foreign incomes and outputs, by relative prices, and by foreign exchange rates. Net exports, then, will be determined by domestic and foreign incomes, relative prices, and exchange rates.

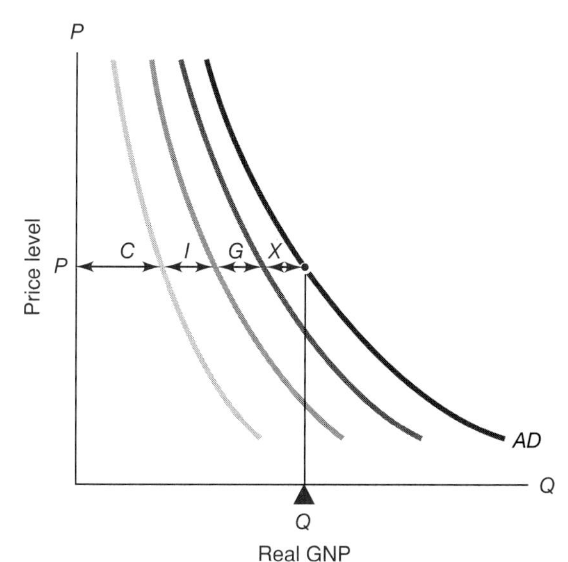

Figure 26-1. Components of aggregate demand

Aggregate demand (*AD*) consists of four streams—consumption (*C*), domestic private investment (*I*), government spending on goods and services (*G*), and net exports (*X*).

Aggregate demand shifts when there are changes in macroeconomic policies (such as monetary changes or changes in government expenditures or tax rates) or shifts in external events affecting spending (as would be the case with changes in foreign output, affecting *X*, or business confidence, affecting *I*).

Figure 26-1 shows the *AD* curve and its four major components. At price level *P*, we can read the level of consumption, investment, government spending, and net exports, which sum to *Q*. The sum of the four spending streams at the reference price level is aggregate spending, or aggregate demand, at that price level.

Behind the Aggregate Demand Curve

Figure 26-1 is a highly simplified illustration of the determinants of aggregate demand. It will aid our understanding if we explore a number of questions about aggregate demand: Why does the *AD* curve slope downward? What factors would change aggregate demand (or shift the *AD* curve)? How does this macro demand curve differ from the micro demand curves used elsewhere in economics?

The Downward-Sloping AD Curve. The *AD* curve in Figure 26-1 shows the total real (or constant-price) expenditure for each price level, other things constant. Note that the level of real spending declines as the price level rises, so the *AD* curve is downward-sloping.

Why does *AD* slope downward? Although a number of factors lead real spending to decline as the price level rises, the most important is the **money-supply effect.** The money-supply effect means that, as prices rise with a fixed nominal quantity of money, the real demand for goods and services declines.

To understand the money-supply effect, we begin by emphasizing that when we draw an *AD* curve, we hold other things like the money supply constant. More concretely, we assume that the central bank manages the nation's monetary system so that the quantity of money is unchanged for different price levels. Hence, even though the consumer price index might rise from 100 to 150, the nation's money supply would remain at $600 billion.

But if the money supply is constant while the price level rises, the real money supply must fall. We define the *real money supply* as the nominal supply of money divided by the price level. In the example in the last paragraph, the real money supply was $600 billion in the first period and fell to $400 $(= \$600 \times \frac{100}{150})$ billion in the second period.

The decline in the real money supply will affect aggregate demand through the monetary mechanism to be discussed in detail in later chapters. In brief, what happens is that, as the real money supply falls, money becomes relatively scarce and a period of tight money ensues. What are the symptoms of tight money? Interest rates and mortgage payments rise, the stock market declines, the exchange rate on the dollar rises, and credit becomes harder to obtain. Tight money leads to a decline in investment, net exports, and even consumption. In short, a rise in prices with a fixed money supply, other things equal, leads to tight money and produces a decline in total real spending. The net effect is an upward movement along a given *AD* curve.

We can continue our example of a movement along the *AD* curve in Figure 26-2(*a*). Say that the economy is in equilibrium at point *B*, with a price level of 100 (in 1990 prices), a real GNP of $3000 billion, and a money supply of $600 billion. Next assume that as a result of a bad harvest, the price level increases to 150. Because the money supply is held constant, the real money supply (in 1990 prices) declines from $600 billion to $400 billion. With money now tight, interest rates rise. The result is a decline in spending on housing, plant and equipment, automobiles, and other interest-sensitive sectors. The net effect is that total real spending declines to $2000 billion, shown as point *C*.

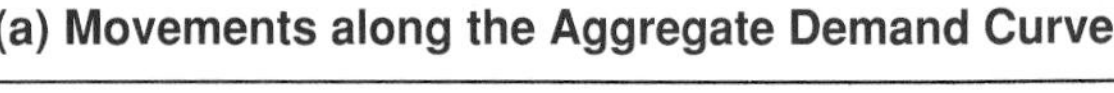

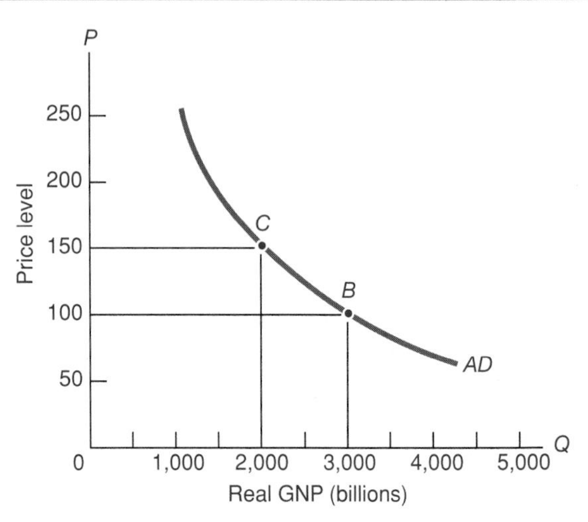

(b) Shifts of Aggregate Demand

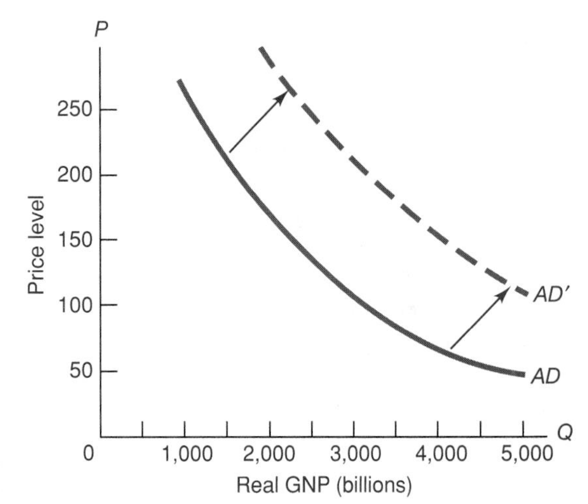

Figure 26-2. Movement along vs. shifts of aggregate demand

In **(a)**, a higher price level with a fixed money supply leads to tight money, higher interest rates, and declining spending on interest-sensitive investment and consumption. We see here a movement along the *AD* curve where other things are held constant.

In **(b)**, other things are no longer constant. Changes in variables underlying *AD*—such as money supply, tax policy, German political unification, or military spending—lead to changes in total spending at given price level.

Other factors also contribute to the relationship between real spending and the price level, although they are today quantitatively less significant than the money-supply effect.[1]

In summary:

We see that the *AD* curve slopes downward, indicating that the real output demanded declines as the price level rises. The primary reason for the downward-sloping *AD* curve is the money-supply effect, whereby higher prices operating on a fixed nominal money supply produce tight money and lower aggregate spending.

Shifts in Aggregate Demand. We have seen that total spending in the economy tends to decline as the price level rises, other things constant. But other things tend to change, and these produce changes in aggregate demand. What are the key variables that lead to shifts in aggregate demand?

We can separate the determinants of *AD* into two categories, as shown in Table 26-1. One set includes the major *policy variables* under government control. These are monetary policy—steps by which the central bank can affect the supply of money and other financial conditions—and fiscal policy—taxes and government expenditures. Table 26-1 illustrates how these government policies can affect different components of aggregate demand.

The second category is *external variables,* or variables that are determined outside the *AS-AD* framework. As Table 26-1 shows, some of these variables (such as wars or revolutions) are outside the scope of macroeconomic analysis proper, some (such as foreign economic activity) are outside the control of domestic policy, and others (such as the stock market) have significant independent movement.

What would be the effect of changes in the variables lying behind the *AD* curve? Suppose, for example, that the government increased its purchases of tanks, gas masks, and aircraft to fight in the Persian Gulf. The effect of this step would be to increase the spending on *G*. Unless some other component of spending offset the increase in *G*, the total *AD* curve would shift out and to the right as *G* increased. Similarly, an increase in the money supply, an oil-price decline, or an increase in the value of consumer wealth (say because of a stock-price increase) would lead to an increase in aggregate demand and an outward shift in the *AD* curve.

Variable	Impact on aggregate demand
Policy variables:	
Monetary policy	Increase in money supply lowers interest rates and improves credit conditions, inducing higher levels of investment and consumption of durable goods.
Fiscal policy	Increases in expenditures on goods and services directly increase spending; tax reductions or increases in transfers raise income and induce higher consumption.
External variables:	
Foreign output	Output growth abroad leads to an increase in net exports.
Asset values	Stock-price or housing-price rise produces greater household wealth and thereby increases consumption; also, this leads to lower cost of capital and increases business investment.
Oil-price decrease	Higher world oil production reduces world oil prices. Higher real incomes of consumers and higher business confidence increase consumption, automobile purchases, and investment

Table 26-1. Many factors can increase aggregate demand and shift out the *AD* curve

The simplest aggregate demand curve relates total spending to the price level. But numerous other influences affect aggregate demand—some policy variables, others external factors. The table illustrates changes that would tend to *increase* aggregate demand and shift out the *AD* curve.

Figure 26-2(*b*) shows how the changes in the variables listed in Table 26-1 would affect the *AD* curve. To test your understanding, construct a similar table showing forces that would tend to *decrease* aggregate demand (see question 2 at the chapter's end).

Microeconomic vs. Macroeconomic Demand. Having explored the *AD* curve, we pause for a warn-

[1] One famous example is the *real-balance effect* or the "Pigou effect," named after the classical economist A. C. Pigou. This effect examines the wealth effect of a lower real quantity of money on consumption spending. The rationale behind the real-balance effect is that part of people's wealth consists of money balances. As the price level rises, the real value of your money balances declines and your wealth declines. As a result of the decline of the real value of your wealth, your consumption spending will tend to decline.

ing about the difference between macroeconomic and microeconomic demand curves. Recall from our study of supply and demand that the microeconomic demand curve has the price of an individual commodity on the vertical axis and production of that commodity on the horizontal axis, with all other prices and total consumer incomes held constant.

By contrast, in the aggregate demand curve, the general price level varies along the vertical axis. Moreover, total output and incomes vary along the *AD* curve, whereas incomes and output are held constant for the microeconomic demand curve.

Finally, the negative slope of the microeconomic demand curve comes from the ability of consumers to substitute other goods for the good in question. If the meat price rises, the quantity demanded falls because consumers substitute bread and potatoes for meat, using more of the relatively inexpensive commodities and less of the relatively expensive one. The aggregate demand curve is downward-sloping for quite a different reason: Total spending falls when the overall price level rises primarily because a fixed money supply must be rationed among money demanders by raising interest rates, tightening credit, and reducing spending.

To summarize:

Macroeconomic *AD* curves differ from their microeconomic cousins because the macro curve depicts changes in prices and output for the entire economy while the micro curve analyzes the behavior of an individual commodity. In addition, the *AD* curve slopes downward primarily because of the money-supply effect, while the micro demand curve slopes downward because of the substitution effect while incomes and other goods' prices are held constant.

Alternative Views of Aggregate Demand

Understanding the determination of aggregate demand is essential for analyzing the short-run movements of output and prices as well as the distribution of GNP among different components like consumption and investment. While economists generally agree on the factors influencing demand, they differ in the emphasis they place on different forces.

In analyzing movements in aggregate demand, some economists concentrate primarily on monetary forces, especially on the role of the money supply. According to these economists, who are often called *monetarists*, the supply of money is the primary determinant of the total dollar value of spending. Monetarists hold that there is a strict relationship between the dollar value of all purchases and the amount of money available. If we identify total dollar spending with nominal GNP, then nominal GNP will be proportional to the money supply.

Other economists, on the other hand, hold that the major determinant of aggregate demand is *income and spending flows*. This approach focuses on changes in government spending and taxing, along with changes in investment and foreign economic conditions, for understanding the business cycle.

The majority of macroeconomists today adhere to an *eclectic approach*, holding that a wide variety of policy and external forces affect aggregate demand. The eclectic macroeconomists point to different forces moving the economy during different periods. For example, fiscal policy would be seen as the leading determinant of aggregate demand during World War II, when military spending was absorbing almost half of GNP. A similar analysis might have applied during the Korean and Vietnam wars. In recent years, however, as the Federal Reserve became more active in combating inflation and unemployment, monetary policy exercised the dominant influence over fluctuations in economic activity.

Often, external factors were decisive. From 1855 to 1875, investment opportunities opened up. Railroads were built all over the world, and the industrial economies enjoyed a sustained economic expansion. In the next two decades, nothing took the place of the railroads, and the United States suffered from a business depression. The early 1980s witnessed a massive decline in U.S. net exports, which deepened the economic downturn of that period.

This concludes our survey of the major elements of aggregate demand. These form one blade of the scissors that determine national output and the overall price level. We turn next to the other blade, aggregate supply, after which we will put aggregate supply and demand together and analyze today's schism between classical and Keynesian macroeconomics.

Analytical Foundations of Aggregate Supply

We turn now to the supply side of the macroeconomy. Aggregate supply (*AS*) describes the production and pricing side of the economy; it explains the behavior of businesses taken as a whole. The background factors for aggregate supply are the level of potential output and cost conditions.

Aggregate supply is central to both the long-run and the short-run evolution of the economy. In the short run, the interaction between aggregate demand and aggregate supply determines the level of output, unemployment, and capacity utilization as well as the impetus to inflation. In the long run of a decade or more, aggregate supply is the major factor behind economic growth.

This distinction between the short-run and the long-run aggregate supply is crucial to modern macroeconomics. It shows why a decline in aggregate demand, due perhaps to tight money or a decline in net exports, will lead to declining output and employment in the short run. But this same theory also explains why aggregate demand is less important than aggregate supply in explaining why North America has so much higher a living standard than does South America; it also shows why national output in the United States is so much higher in 1990 than it was in 1890.

Alternative Approaches to Aggregate Supply

Aggregate supply refers to the total national output that businesses willingly produce and sell during a given year for each level of prices, other things held constant. We can construct the **aggregate supply curve** or ***AS* curve** as the schedule showing the level of real output that will be produced at each possible price level, other things equal.

In analyzing aggregate supply, it will be crucial to distinguish *AS* curves according to the time frame. For the short run (a few months or years), we look at the **short-run aggregate supply schedule.** This relationship is depicted as an *upward-sloping AS* curve—one along which increases in prices are associated with increases in output.

For the long run (several years or a decade or more), we look at the **long-run aggregate supply schedule.** This relationship is shown as a *vertical AS* schedule, one in which increases in the price level do not generate any increase in total output supplied.

This section is devoted to explaining these central points.

Determinants of Aggregate Supply

Aggregate supply depends fundamentally upon two distinct sets of forces: potential output and wage-price behavior. Let us examine each of these influences.

Potential Output. The fundamental determinant of aggregate supply is the capacity of the economy to produce. That is, over time, aggregate supply depends primarily upon potential output.

Recall from Chapter 23 that potential GNP represents the maximum amount the economy can produce while maintaining stable prices. A more complete description of potential output would go as follows: At any time, an economy has a certain amount of labor, capital, and land available. Combining these inputs with the available technology will allow a maximum sustainable level of output to be produced. (We described this maximum sustainable level of output in Chapter 2, using the production-possibility frontier.)

If the economy attempts to produce more than its potential output, prices will begin to rise more and more rapidly as resources are utilized too intensively. If the economy produces less than its potential, high unemployment and excess capacity will prevail. Between the extremes of too-high utilization of capacity and too-high unemployment of inputs is a threshold level of output that we designate potential output.

For quantitative purposes, macroeconomists generally use the following definition of potential output:

Potential GNP is the level of real GNP that the economy would produce if the unemployment rate were at a benchmark level called the "natural rate of unemployment." Recent studies have estimated that the natural unemployment rate is around 6 percent of the labor force.

Studies of economic growth have helped economists understand the sources of the growth of potential output. Using statistical techniques, we can even estimate the quantitative contribution of inputs of labor, capital, and land, as well as the growth contributed by technological change and other improvements in efficiency.

One recent study estimated that during the period 1948–1989 real output of the private business sector grew at 3.3 percent per year. Of this, 0.7 percent per year was accounted for by growth in labor inputs, 1.2 percent per year by a larger capital stock, and 1.4 percent per year due to improved knowledge, technology, and miscellaneous sources.

What is the relation between potential output and aggregate supply? Basically, potential output represents the amount that would be supplied if aggregate demand were growing smoothly and suppliers faced no shocks. However, because of cost shocks and interruptions of aggregate demand, businesses may produce less than potential output; or, in high-pressure periods such as wartime, they may even produce more than potential output. Table 26-2 shows the key determinants of aggregate supply, broken down into factors affecting potential output and production costs.

Input Costs. Our discussion of potential output indicated that, in addition to potential output, the costs of production affect aggregate supply. As production costs rise, businesses would be willing to supply a given level of output only at a higher price. For example, if input costs rose so much that production costs exactly doubled, then the price at which businesses would supply each level of output would also double. The *AS* curve would shift upward so that each output *AS* pair (P, Q) would be replaced by $(2P, Q)$.

Table 26-2 shows some of the cost factors affecting aggregate supply. By far the most important cost is wages, which constitute about three-quarters of the overall cost of production for a country like the United States. For small open economies like the Netherlands or Hong Kong, import costs play an even greater role than wages in determining aggregate supply.

How can we graph the relationship between potential output, costs, and aggregate supply? Figure 26-3 on the following page illustrates the effect of changes in potential output and in costs on aggregate supply. The left-hand panel shows that an increase in potential output with no change in production costs would shift the aggregate supply curve outward from *AS* to *AS*′. If production costs were to increase with no change in potential output, the curve would shift straight up from *AS* to *AS*″, as shown in Figure 26-3(*b*).

Variable	Impact on aggregate supply
Potential output:	
Inputs	Available quantities of capital, labor, and land determine inputs into productive process. Potential output assumes unemployment of labor and other resources at lowest level consistent with stable prices. Growth of inputs increases potential output and aggregate supply.
Technology and efficiency	Potential output affected by level of efficiency and technologies used by businesses. Innovation and technological improvement increase level of potential output.
Wages and costs:	
Wages	Lower wages lead to lower production costs (other things equal). Lower costs for given potential output mean that quantity supplied will be higher at every price level.
Import prices	With a decline in foreign prices or an appreciation in the exchange rate, import prices fall. This leads to lower production costs and greater supply available for domestic production, raising aggregate supply.
Other input costs	Lower oil prices or less burdensome environmental regulation lowers production costs and thereby raises aggregate supply.

Table 26-2. Aggregate supply depends upon potential output and production costs

Aggregate supply relates total output supplied to the price level. Behind the *AS* curve lie fundamental factors of productivity as represented by potential output as well as the cost structure. Listed factors would increase aggregate supply, shifting the *AS* curve to the right. What would decrease aggregate supply?

The real-world shifting of *AS* is displayed in Figure 26-4. The curves are realistic empirical estimates for two different years, 1980 and 1990. The vertical lines, marked Q^P and $Q^{P\prime}$, indicate the levels of potential output in the two years. According to studies, real potential output grew about 25 percent over this period.

We see in the figure that the *AS* curve has shifted outward and upward over the 1980s. The outward

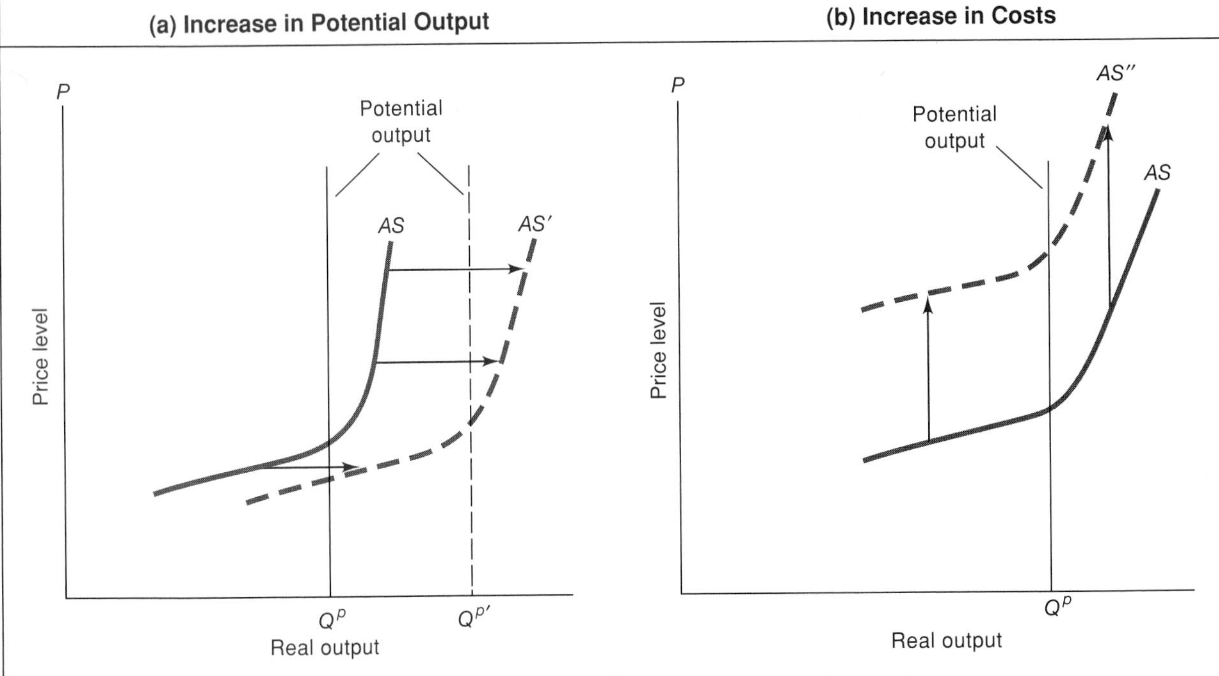

Figure 26-3. Impact of growth of potential output and costs on aggregate supply

In **(a)**, growth in potential output with no increase in production costs shifts aggregate supply curve rightward from *AS* to *AS′*. When costs increase (say because of rising wages) but potential output is unchanged, the aggregate supply curve shifts straight upward, as from *AS* to *AS″* in **(b)**.

shift was caused by the increase in potential output, say because of an increase in population and capital as well as technological change. The upward shift was caused by increases in the cost of production, as wages, energy prices, and other production costs rose. In sum, when costs increase over time along with growth in potential output, aggregate supply shifts from *AS* to *AS′* as shown in Figure 26-4.

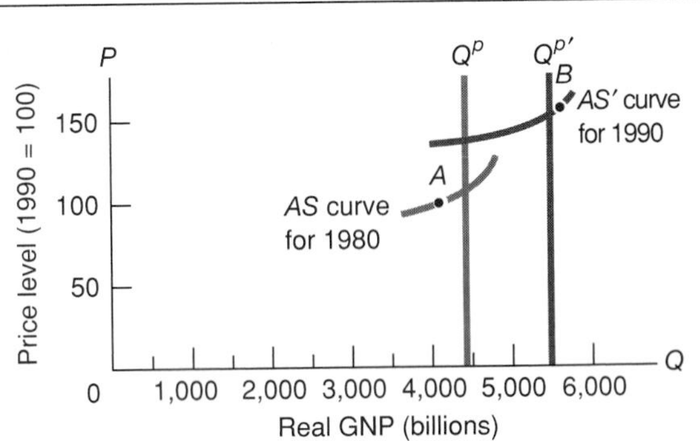

Figure 26-4. Growth in potential output increases and shifts out aggregate supply

We show potential output for 1980 and 1990 as the vertical lines marked Q^p and $Q^{p\prime}$. This increase in potential output shifted aggregate supply (*AS*) to the right.

In addition, wages, energy prices, and other input costs increased, shifting the *AS* curve upward over time. The net impact of potential-output increase and cost increases was to shift *AS* upward and to the right.

Aggregate Supply in the Short Run and Long Run

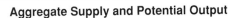

One of the major controversies about modern macroeconomics involves the determination of aggregate supply. The major bone of contention is whether the aggregate supply curve is flat, or steep, or even vertical. Many economists of the Keynesian school hold that the *AS* curve is relatively flat. This implies that changes in aggregate demand have a significant and lasting effect on output. Economists who tend toward the classical approach hold that the *AS* curve is steep or even vertical; this group believes that changes in aggregate demand have little lasting effect on output.

In fact, both views have some merit. Figure 26-5 depicts the two *AS* curves. The short-run *AS* curve on the left is upward-sloping or Keynesian. It indicates that firms are willing to increase their output levels in response to higher prices. In other words, as the level of aggregate demand rises, firms are willing to supply more output if they can also increase their prices as output rises.

Note, however, that the expansion of output cannot go on without limit in the short run. As output increases, labor shortages appear and factories operate close to capacity. In addition, firms can raise prices without losing customers to rivals. Therefore, as production rises above potential output, a larger fraction of the response to demand increases comes in the form of price increases and a smaller fraction comes in output increases. In terms of the aggregate supply curve, this implies that the short-run *AS* curve will be relatively flat to the left of the potential-output line, where output is less than potential output; but it will become steeper and steeper as output increases, that is, further and further to the right of the potential-output line.

Figure 26-5(*b*) illustrates the long-run response of aggregate supply to different price levels. We see there that the long-run *AS* curve is vertical or classical, with the output corresponding to potential output. In a classical case, the level of output supplied is independent of the price level.

Why Do Short-Run and Long-Run *AS* Differ?

Why do short-run and long-run aggregate supply behaviors differ? Why do firms raise both prices and output in the short run as aggregate demand increases? Why, by contrast, do increases in demand lead to price changes but not to output changes in the long run?

The key to these puzzles lies in the way that wages and prices are determined in a modern market economy. Some elements of business costs are *inflexible* or *sticky* in the short run. As a result of this inflexibility, businesses will respond to higher levels of aggregate demand by producing and selling higher levels of output. Put differently, because some elements of cost are constant in the short run, firms find it profitable to raise prices and sell extra output as aggregate demand increases.

Suppose that a burst of extra spending occurs. Firms know that in the short run many of their production costs are fixed in dollar terms—workers are paid \$15 per hour, rent is \$1500 per month, and so forth. If firms can successfully raise their output prices in response to the extra burst of spending, they will also find it profitable to increase their output. Hence, in the short run, before wages and

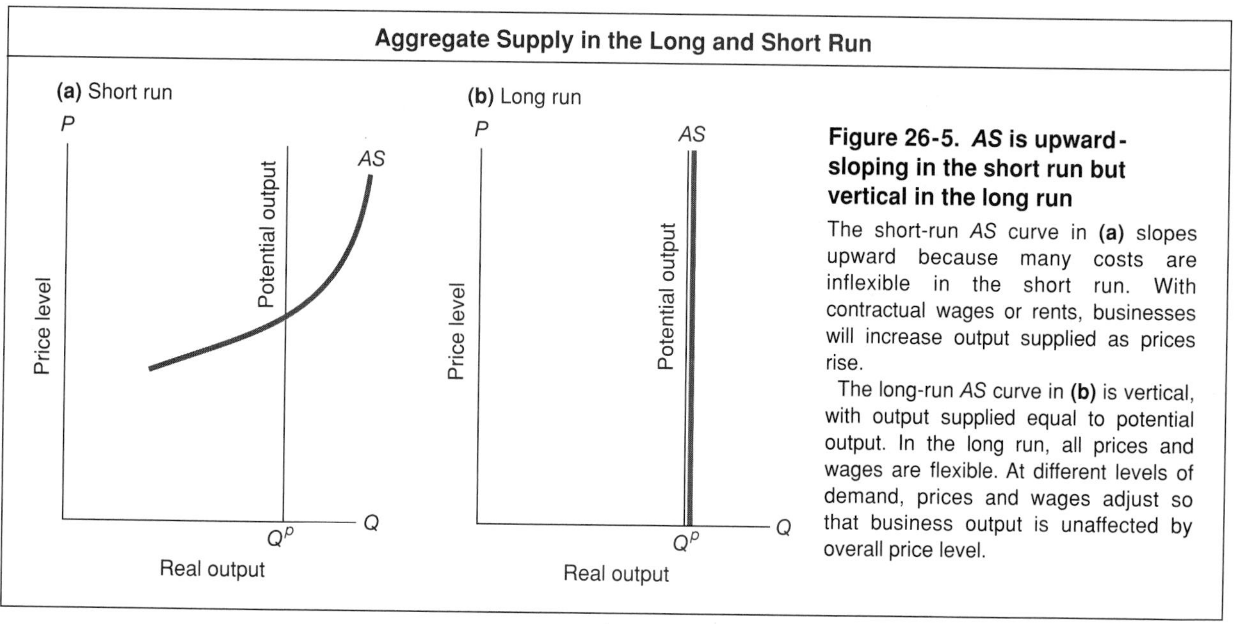

Figure 26-5. *AS* is upward-sloping in the short run but vertical in the long run

The short-run *AS* curve in **(a)** slopes upward because many costs are inflexible in the short run. With contractual wages or rents, businesses will increase output supplied as prices rise.

The long-run *AS* curve in **(b)** is vertical, with output supplied equal to potential output. In the long run, all prices and wages are flexible. At different levels of demand, prices and wages adjust so that business output is unaffected by overall price level.

rents and other dollar-fixed costs have adjusted, firms will react to aggregate demand increases by raising both prices and output. This positive association between prices and output is seen in the upward-sloping *AS* curve.

We have spoken repeatedly of "sticky" or "inflexible" costs. What are some examples? The most significant is wages. Almost half of all manufacturing workers are covered by long-term union contracts. In the United States, these contracts generally extend for 3 years and specify a dollar wage rate (with partial adjustment for price changes). Moreover, the contracts are staggered; they never expire and get renegotiated at the same time. For the life of the labor agreement, the wage rate faced by the firm will be largely fixed in dollar terms. Other prices and costs are similarly sticky in the short run. When a firm rents a building, the lease will often last for a year or more, and the rental is generally set in dollar terms. In addition, firms often sign contracts with their suppliers specifying the prices to be paid for materials or components. Some prices are fixed by government regulation, particularly those for utilities like electricity, gas, water, and local telephone service.

What happens in the long run? Eventually, the inflexible or sticky elements of cost—wage contracts, rent agreements, regulated prices, and so forth—become unstuck and negotiable. Firms cannot take advantage of fixed-money wage rates in their labor agreements forever; labor will soon recognize that prices have risen and insist on compensating increases in wages. Ultimately, all costs will adjust to the higher output prices. After the general price level has risen x percent because of the higher demand, money wages, rents, regulated prices, and other costs will in the end respond by moving up around x percent as well.

Once costs have adjusted upward as much as prices, firms will be unable to profit from the higher level of aggregate demand. The level of output will come back to its long-run equilibrium level at potential output. In the long run, after all elements of cost have fully adjusted, firms will face the same ratio of price to costs as they did before the change in demand. There will be no incentive for firms to increase their output. When we say that the *AS* curve is vertical, we mean that output supplied is independent of the level of prices and costs.

The aggregate supply for an economy will differ from potential output in the short run because of inflexible elements of cost. In the short run, firms will respond to higher demand by raising both production and prices. In the longer run, as costs respond to the higher level of prices, most or all of the response to increased demand takes the form of higher prices and little or none the form of higher output. The long-run *AS* curve is vertical because, given sufficient time, all costs adjust.

The Clash between Keynesian and Classical Views

Since the dawn of economics two centuries ago, one of the deepest controversies has concerned whether or not the economy has a tendency to move toward a long-run, full-employment equilibrium. Using modern language, we label as **classical theories** those approaches that emphasize the powerful self-correcting forces in an economy; classical macroeconomic thinking has its roots in Adam Smith, J. B. Say, and John Stuart Mill. The alternative approach, today called **Keynesian economics,** was not coherently expressed until J. M. Keynes' writings in this century.

The basic difference between classical and Keynesian approaches can be found in differing views about the behavior of aggregate supply. Keynesian economists believe that prices and wages adjust slowly, so any equilibrating forces may take many years or even decades to operate. The classical approach holds that prices and wages are flexible, so the economy moves to its long-run equilibrium very quickly. In the remainder of this chapter, we will use aggregate supply and demand analysis to explain the scientific foundations and the policy implications of these two fundamentally different approaches.[2]

The Classical Approach

Before Keynes wrote *The General Theory* in 1936, the major economic thinkers generally adhered to

[2] A brief and nontechnical survey of the debate between the new classical and Keynesian points of view can be found in N. Gregory Mankiw, "A Quick Refresher Course in Macroeconomics," *Journal of Economic Literature* (December 1990), pp. 1645–1660.

the classical view of the economy. Early economists were fascinated by the Industrial Revolution with its division of labor, accumulation of capital, and growing international trade.

Say's Law of Markets. Early economists knew about business cycles, but they viewed these as temporary and self-correcting aberrations. Their analysis revolved around *Say's Law of markets.* This theory was propounded in 1803 by the French economist J. B. Say and states that overproduction is impossible by its very nature. This is sometimes expressed today as "supply creates its own demand." What is the rationale for Say's Law? It rests on a view that there is no essential difference between a monetary economy and a barter economy—that if factories can produce more, workers will be there to buy the output.

A long line of the most distinguished economists, including D. Ricardo, J. S. Mill, and A. Marshall, subscribed to the classical macroeconomic view that overproduction is impossible. Even during the Great Depression, when a quarter of the American labor force was unemployed, the eminent economist A. C. Pigou wrote, "With perfectly free competition there will always be a strong tendency toward full employment. Such unemployment as exists at any time is due wholly to the frictional resistances [that] prevent the appropriate wage and price adjustments being made instantaneously."[3]

As the quote from Pigou suggests, the rationale behind the classical view is that wages and prices are sufficiently flexible that markets will "clear," or return to equilibrium, very quickly. If prices and wages adjust rapidly, then the short run in which prices are sticky will be so short that it can be neglected for all practical purposes. The classical macroeconomists conclude that the economy always operates at full employment or at its potential output.

The durable and valid core of Say's Law and of the classical approach is shown in Figure 26-6. This is an economy where prices and wages are determined in competitive markets, moving flexibly up and down to eliminate any excess demand or supply. In terms of our *AS-AD* analysis, it can be described by a standard, downward-sloping aggregate demand curve along with a vertical aggregate supply curve.

A Classical Macroeconomy

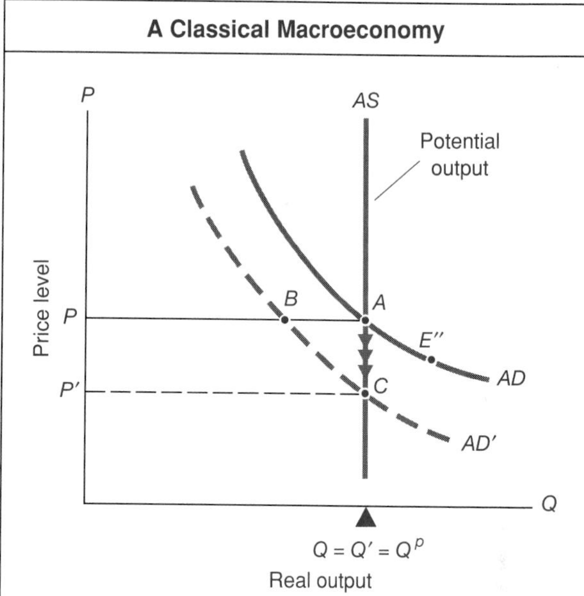

Figure 26-6. According to Say's Law, supply creates its own demand as prices move to balance demand with aggregate supply

Classical economists thought that persistent periods of glut could not occur. If *AS* or *AD* shifted, prices would react flexibly to ensure that full-employment output was sold. Here we see how flexible prices ensure that prices move down enough to increase spending to full-employment output. (What would happen if *AD* were unchanged, but potential output increased? What forces would move the economy to E″ ?)

Suppose that aggregate demand falls due to tight money or other external forces. As a result, the *AD* curve shifts leftward to *AD′* in Figure 26-6. Initially, at the original price of *P*, total spending falls to point *B*, and there might be a very brief period of falling output. But the demand shift is followed by a rapid adjustment of wages and prices, with the overall price level falling from *P* to *P′*. As the price level falls, total output returns to potential output, and full employment is reestablished at point *C*.

In the classical view, changes in aggregate demand affect the price level but have no impact upon output and employment. Price and wage flexibility ensures that the real level of spending is sufficient to maintain full employment.

[3] *The Theory of Unemployment* (1933).

Policy Consequences. The classical view has two conclusions that are vitally important for economic policy. First, the economy always enjoys full employment, and there are never any unutilized resources. The economy is always producing its potential output, and workers who want to work at the going wage rate can find jobs.

Does this proposition imply that there is no unemployment at all? Surely not, for there will always be *microeconomic* waste in any real-world economy. We would see unemployment of people who are moving between jobs or of unionized workers who have above-equilibrium wage rates. But in the classical view, an economy has no *macroeconomic* waste in the sense of underutilized resources due to insufficient aggregate demand.

The second element of the classical view is even more striking: Macroeconomic aggregate demand policies cannot influence the level of unemployment and output. Rather, monetary and fiscal policies can affect only the economy's price level, along with the composition of real GNP. This second classical proposition is easily seen in Figure 26-6. Consider an economy in equilibrium at point *C*, the intersection of the *AD*′ and the vertical *AS* curves. Say that the government decides to undertake fiscal steps to expand the economy. What happens? For a brief instant, at the initial price level *P*′, there is excess demand. However, as prices and wages quickly begin to rise under the pressure of excess demand, the economy moves to the new equilibrium at point *A*. The net effect of the expansionary economic policy has been to inflate the overall price level sufficiently to restore the initial full-employment equilibrium without changing output and employment.

At the heart of the classical view is the belief that prices and wages are flexible and that price flexibility provides a self-correcting mechanism that quickly restores full employment and always maintains potential output. And, as we will see in later chapters, the classical approach is very much alive in the writings of today's new classical school. The new classical economists base their views on modern economic developments, including imperfect information, the existence of technological shocks, and frictions from shifts of resources among industries. Although dressed in modern clothing, their policy conclusions are closely linked to the classical economists of an earlier age.

The Keynesian Revolution

While the classical economists were preaching that persistent unemployment was impossible, economists of the 1930s could hardly ignore the vast army of unemployed workers—begging for work and selling pencils on street corners. How could economics explain such massive and persistent idleness?

Keynes' *General Theory* offered an alternative macroeconomic theory, a new set of theoretical spectacles for looking at the impact of economic policies as well as external shocks. In fact, the Keynesian revolution combined two different elements. First, Keynes presented the concept of aggregate demand that we have explained in this chapter. Second, Keynes argued that prices and wages were inflexible or sticky; this meant that the vertical classical *AS* curve would have to be replaced by the upward-sloping *AS* curve.

The Surprising Consequences. By combining these two new elements, Keynes brought a veritable revolution to macroeconomics. The essence of Keynes' argument is shown in Figure 26-7. This diagram combines an aggregate demand curve along with an upward-sloping aggregate supply curve.

The first observation is that a modern market economy can get trapped in an underemployment equilibrium—a balance of aggregate supply and demand in which output is far below potential and a substantial fraction of the work force is involuntarily unemployed. For example, if the *AD* curve intersects the *AS* curve far to the left, as is illustrated at point *A*, equilibrium output may lie far below potential output. Keynes emphasized that because wages and prices are inflexible, there is no economic mechanism to restore full employment and ensure that the economy produces its potential. A nation could remain in its low-output, high-misery condition for a long time because there is no self-correcting mechanism or invisible hand to guide the economy back to full employment.

Keynes' second observation follows from the first. Through monetary or fiscal policies, the government can stimulate the economy and help maintain high levels of output and employment. For example, if the government were to increase its purchases, aggregate demand would increase, say from *AD* to *AD*′ in Figure 26-7. The impact would be

Keynesian Underemployment Equilibrium

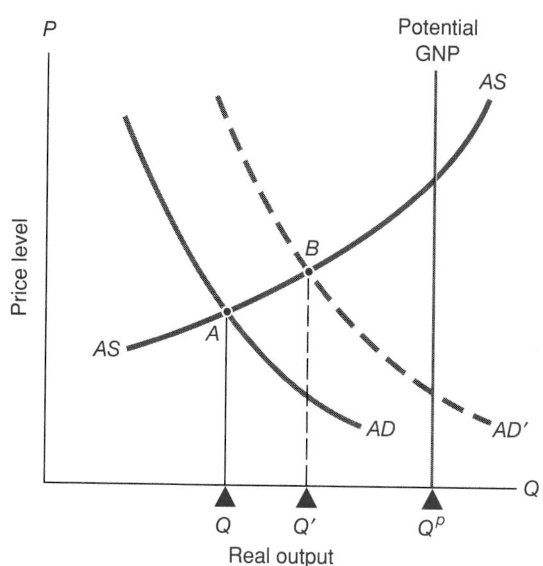

Figure 26-7. Aggregate demand determines output in the Keynesian approach

In the Keynesian model, aggregate supply slopes upward, implying that output will increase with higher aggregate demand as long as there are unused resources. When *AD* is depressed, output will be in equilibrium at point *A*, with high unemployment.

If aggregate demand increases from *AD* to *AD′*, the level of real output increases from *A* to *B*, with prices increasing as well. In this Keynesian paradigm, with *AS* upward-sloping in the short run, economic policies that increase aggregate demand succeed in increasing output and employment.

to increase output from *Q* to *Q′*, reducing the gap between actual and potential GNP. In short, with appropriate use of economic policy, government can take steps to ensure high levels of national output and employment.

Keynes' analysis created a revolution in macroeconomics, particularly among young economists who were living through the Great Depression of the 1930s and sensed something was wrong with the classical model. Of course, the Great Depression was not the first event to reveal the untenability of the classical synthesis. But for the first time, the classical approach was confronted by a competing analysis. The Keynesian approach presented a new synthesis that swept through economics and changed fundamentally the way that economists and governments think about business cycles and economic policy.

Theories and Policy

In economics, people's views on policy are often determined by the theoretical spectacles they wear. Does a President or a senator or an economist lean toward a classical or a Keynesian view? The answer to this question will often explain that person's view on many of the major economic-policy debates of the day.

Examples are legion. Economists who tend toward the classical view will often be skeptical about the need for government to stabilize business cycles. They argue that a government policy designed to increase aggregate demand will instead lead to escalating inflation. Moreover, classical economists would worry about government spending crowding out private production. By "crowding out," they mean that when the government increases its spending, production on private goods will be displaced. The higher production of guns will require resources that were previously used to produce butter.

Keynesian economists take a different tack. They think that the macroeconomy is prone to extended business cycles, with high levels of unemployed resources for long periods of time. They further hold that the government can stimulate the economy by taking monetary or fiscal steps to change aggregate demand. These policies might increase aggregate demand in periods of slow economic activity or curb spending in periods of boom with threatening inflation. The Keynesian economist might argue that government spending crowds out nothing at all because higher government spending increases output and allows private spending to continue. In essence, when the government takes a larger slice out of the pie, the pie actually becomes larger. Government spending, tax cuts, or more rapid money growth—all create more output and thus stimulate investment.

Which is the correct view—classical or Keynesian? The unalloyed truth is that both are oversimplified. In the chapters to come, we will see the strengths and weaknesses of both positions. For now, the key point to recognize is that many of the debates about economic policy arise because one participant has the classical model in mind while the other has the Keynesian view. The art of good macroeconomic judgment is to sense the strengths and weaknesses of each approach.

Toward a Better Understanding of Aggregate Demand

We have now completed our analysis of the foundations of aggregate supply and demand. The next three chapters explore the determinants of aggregate demand. We begin in the next chapter with a detailed analysis of the Keynesian multiplier model, which is the simplest example of a Keynesian approach to economic activity. We will also see how government fiscal policy and international trade feature in the multiplier framework. We then turn to an analysis of monetary economics, including the nature of money, the role of the central bank, and the way that money affects economic activity. By putting all these different elements together, we can acquire a full understanding of the forces affecting aggregate demand and of the impact of aggregate demand on the macroeconomy.

SUMMARY

1. Aggregate demand represents the total quantity of output willingly bought at a given price level, other things held constant. Components of spending include (*a*) consumption, which depends primarily upon disposable income; (*b*) investment, which depends upon present and expected future output and upon interest rates and taxes; (*c*) government spending on goods and services; and (*d*) net exports, which depend upon foreign and domestic outputs and prices and upon foreign exchange rates.
2. Aggregate demand curves differ from demand curves used in microeconomic analysis. The *AD* curves relate overall spending on all components of output to the overall price level, with policy and external variables held constant. The aggregate demand curve is downward-sloping primarily because of the money-supply effect, which occurs when a rise in the price level, with the nominal money supply constant, reduces the real money supply. A lower real money supply raises interest rates, tightens credit, and reduces total real spending. This represents a movement along an unchanged *AD* curve.
3. Factors that change aggregate demand include (*a*) macroeconomic policies, such as monetary and fiscal policies, and (*b*) external variables, such as foreign economic activity, changes in world oil prices, and shifts in asset markets. When these variables change, they shift the *AD* curve.
4. Aggregate supply describes the relationship between the output that businesses willingly produce and the overall price level, other things constant. The factors underlying aggregate supply are (*a*) potential output, determined by the inputs of labor, capital, and natural resources available to an economy along with the technology or efficiency with which these inputs are used, and (*b*) input costs, such as wages, oil and other energy prices, and import prices. Changes in these underlying factors will shift the *AS* curve.
5. In the long run, aggregate supply is closely tied to an economy's potential output. In the short run, price and wage relations will affect how production responds to different levels of aggregate demand. Accordingly, we generally treat the long-run *AS* curve as vertical or classical, indicating that

businesses will supply potential output whatever the level of prices. In the short run, because of the inflexibility of wages and prices, the *AS* curve is upward-sloping, showing that businesses will supply more output at a higher price level.

6. Two major approaches to output determination are the classical and Keynesian views:
   (*a*) The classical view is grounded in Say's Law, which states that "supply creates its own demand." In modern terms, the classical approach holds that flexible prices and wages quickly erase any excess supply or demand and reestablish full employment and full-capacity output. Moreover, macroeconomic policy can play no role in stabilizing the business cycle or reducing unemployment in a classical economy.
   (*b*) The Keynesian view holds that prices and wages are sticky in the short run due to contractual rigidities such as labor-union agreements. In this kind of economy, output responds positively to higher levels of aggregate demand because the *AS* curve is upward-sloping, particularly at low levels of output. In a Keynesian economy, the economy can experience long periods of persistent unemployment because the self-correcting mechanism of prices and wages is sluggish or absent. Monetary and fiscal policies can substitute for flexible wages and prices, stimulating the economy during depressions and helping to restore full employment or slowing the economy during booms to forestall inflationary tendencies.

7. A modern market economy combines elements of both the classical and the Keynesian models. In the short run, a period of a few months or years, the Keynesian model is most applicable. In the longer run of a decade or more, as prices and wages have time to adjust, the classical approach best describes the evolution of macroeconomic activity.

CONCEPTS FOR REVIEW

real variable
  = nominal variable/price level
aggregate demand, *AD* curve
major components of aggregate demand: *C, I, G, X*
movement along vs. shift of *AD, AS* curves
aggregate supply, *AS* curve

downward-sloping *AD* curve:
  money-supply effect
  real-balance (Pigou) effect
factors underlying and shifting *AD* curve
aggregate supply: role of potential output and production costs
short-run vs. long run *AS*

flexible vs. sticky wages and prices
Say's Law of markets
classical and Keynesian economics:
  fundamental difference on price flexibility
  impact of demand shifts
  effectiveness of policy

QUESTIONS FOR DISCUSSION

1. Define carefully what is meant by the aggregate demand curve. Distinguish between movements along the curve and shifts of the curve. What might increase output by moving along the *AD* curve? What could increase output by shifting the *AD* curve?

2. Construct a table parallel to Table 26-1, illustrating events that would lead to a *decrease* in aggregate demand. (Your response should provide different examples rather than simply change the direction of the factors mentioned in Table 26-1.)

3. What, if anything, would be the effect of each of the following on the *AS* curve in both the short run and the long run, other things constant?
   (a) Potential output increases by 25 percent.
   (b) The money supply is reduced by the Federal Reserve.
   (c) A war in the Mideast leads to a doubling of world oil prices.
   (d) A nuclear accident leads regulators to shut down all nuclear power stations.
4. In regard to the events listed in question 3, what, if anything, would be the impact on the *AD* curve?
5. Again regarding the events listed in question 3, what would be the effect on output and prices in both the short run and the long run?
6. A noted macroeconomist has written, "For a couple of years, pumping up spending and money will produce many jobs and much output, although prices are likely to rise as well. But eventually, as the economy adjusts to the new policies, output and employment will return to their 'natural' levels. It simply is not possible to keep output above its potential for long." Evaluate this quotation using the *AS-AD* apparatus of this chapter. Do you agree with the quotation?
7. Answer the following questions from both the Keynesian and the classical viewpoints using the *AS-AD* analysis of this chapter.
   (a) What will be the effect of an increase in potential output on the level of actual output if aggregate demand is unchanged?
   (b) For a given level of potential output, what is the effect of a small increase in *AD*? Of a very, very large shift in *AD*?
8. State and explain Say's Law. Starting from an equilibrium, assume that potential output increases. Show in a graphical extension of Figure 26-6 and describe in words the sense in which supply creates its own demand.
9. Restate what is meant by the "real-balance effect" (see footnote 1 of this chapter). To estimate its quantitative importance on consumption, assume the following: At an initial price level of $P = 1$, household income is 1000, non-money wealth is 4800, and money wealth is 200. The marginal propensity to consume from income is 0.80 and the marginal propensity to consume from wealth is 0.03.

   Assume that the price level rises 10 percent, with money wealth constant in nominal terms and all other variables constant in real terms. Estimate the impact of the price increase on real money wealth, on total wealth, and on consumption. Draw an *AD* curve based upon the real-balance effect only. Compare the slope with the example depicted in Figure 26-2(*a*) and the text description accompanying Figure 26-2(*a*).
10. Explain the following statement: "Higher government spending increases output and allows private spending to continue; when the government takes a larger slice out of the pie, the pie actually becomes larger." Relate this quotation to the debate between Keynesian and classical economists.

CHAPTER 27

THE MULTIPLIER MODEL

If the propensity to consume and the rate of new investment result in a deficient effective demand, the actual level of employment will fall short of the supply of labour potentially available.

J. M. Keynes, *General Theory* (1936)

All market economies experience swings in business activity when unemployment surges during depressions or when rapid increases in demand lead to inflation. Indeed, for the newborn post-socialist countries of Eastern Europe, the first taste of the market was of depression and unemployment. During the 1980s, the United States enjoyed rapid growth and falling unemployment. In 1990, under the pressure of tight money and temporarily rising oil prices, output growth slowed and unemployment began to rise.

How can we interpret these swings in economic activity? The aggregate demand-and-supply tools introduced in the last chapter can help explain the movements in output and the price level. But we also want to analyze exactly *why AS* or *AD* shifts and to predict how much output will change with changes of investment or government spending or net exports. For this task we develop the Keynesian multiplier model.

A. The Basic Multiplier Model

This chapter presents the **multiplier model,** which is a macroeconomic theory used to explain how output is determined in the short run. The name "multiplier" comes from the finding that each dollar change in certain expenditures (such as investment) leads to more than a dollar change (or a multiplied change) in GNP. The multiplier model explains how shocks to investment, foreign trade, and government tax and spending policies can affect output and employment in an economy with unemployed resources.

In this first section, we introduce the simplest multiplier model, one in which there is no government or international trade. With this background we will be able to analyze the impact of government and the foreign sector on economic activity. Figure 27-1 sketches the focus of the multiplier analysis.

As you begin your study of the multiplier, note that this approach in no way contradicts the *AS-AD* model of the last chapter. Rather, the multiplier *explains* the workings of aggregate demand by showing exactly how consumption, investment, and other variables interact to determine aggregate demand.

Chapter Overview

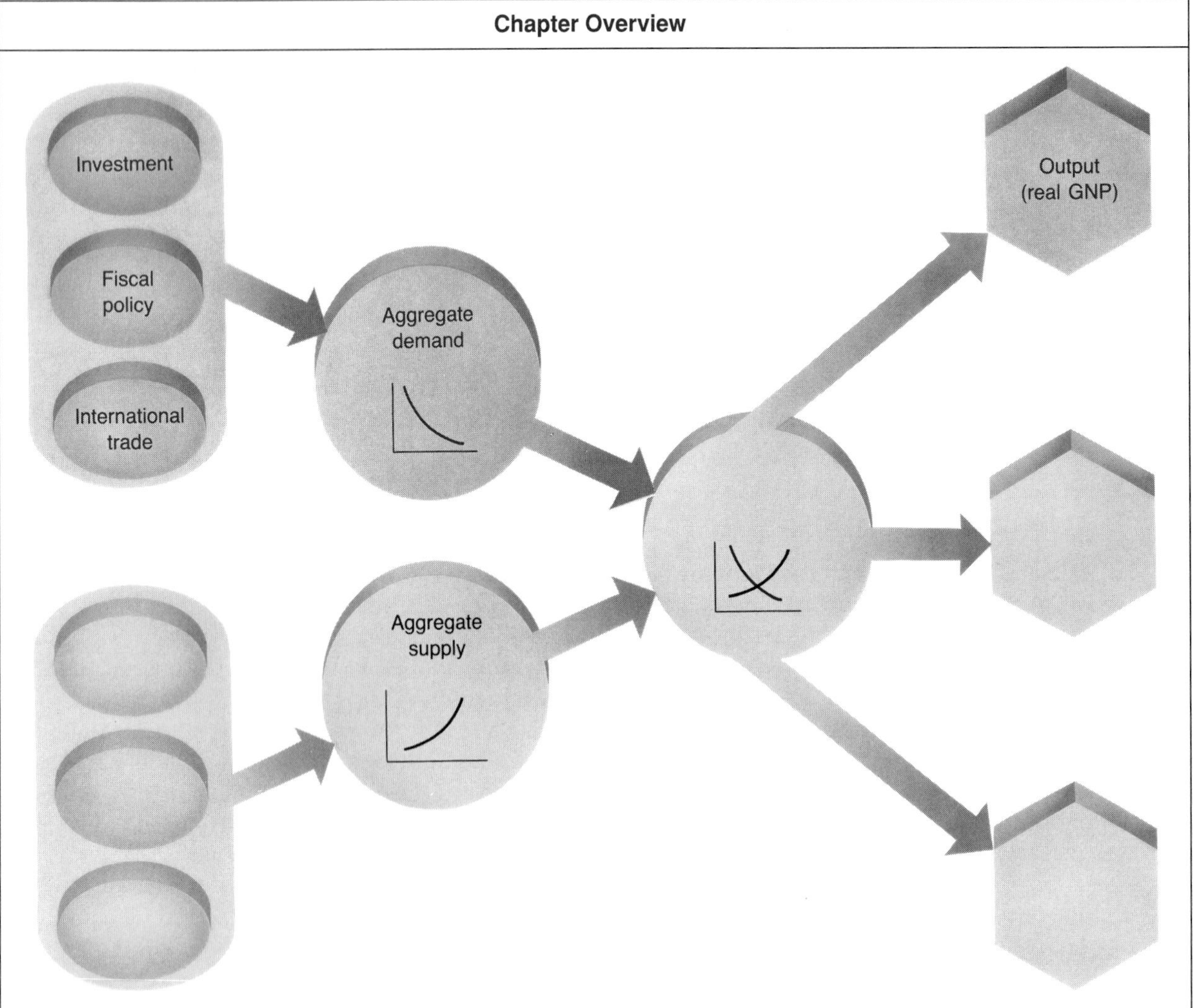

Figure 27-1. The multiplier model is a simple model of how aggregate demand determines output

This chapter develops the Keynesian multiplier model. It shows the interaction between induced consumption expenditure and autonomous variables like investment, government spending and taxation, and exports. In addition, it shows how these variables jointly determine aggregate output and employment.

Output Determination with Saving and Investment

Chapter 25 gave a simplified picture of the consumption and savings functions for the nation. These consumption and savings schedules are based on our knowledge of the budgets of different families, their wealth, and so forth. Here we shall initially simplify the picture by leaving out taxes, undistributed corporate profits, foreign trade, depreciation, and government fiscal policy. For the time being, we will assume that income is disposable income and equals GNP.

Figure 27-2 shows the national consumption and savings functions. Each point on the consumption function shows desired or planned consumption at that level of disposable income. Each point on the savings schedule shows desired or planned saving at that income level. Recall that the two schedules are closely related: since $C + S$ always equals income, the consumption and savings curves are mirror twins that will always add up to the 45° line.

We have seen that saving and investment are dependent on quite different factors: saving depends in a passive way on income, while investment depends on output and various other factors (such as expected future output, interest rates, tax policy, and business confidence).

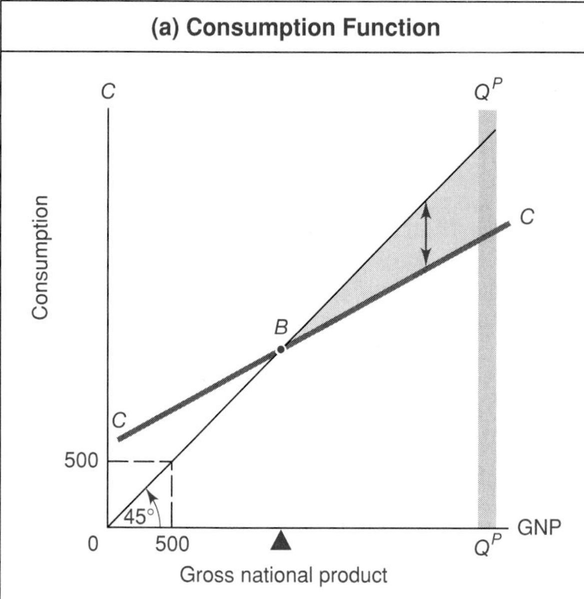

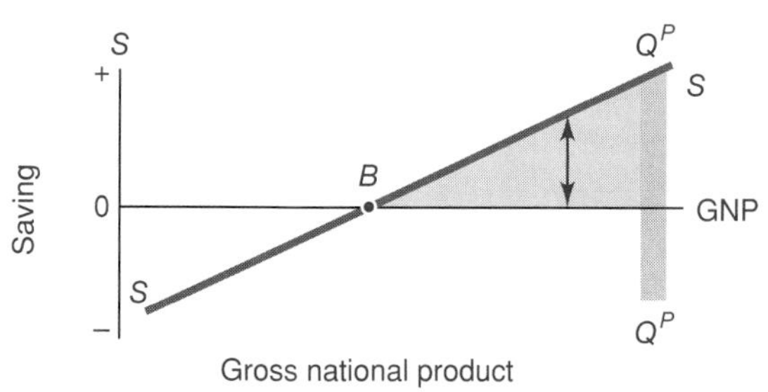

Figure 27-2. National output determines the levels of consumption and saving

CC is the consumption function for the country, while *SS* is the savings function.

Recall that these are closely related in a mirror-image fashion. The break-even point is shown at point *B*—on the upper diagram where *CC* intersects the 45° line and on the lower diagram where *SS* intersects the horizontal axis. Can you explain why the vertically aligned arrows *must* be of equal length? The two points marked "500" emphasize the important property of the 45° line: Any point on it depicts a vertical distance exactly equal to the horizontal distance. The gray band marked Q^PQ^P shows the level of potential GNP.

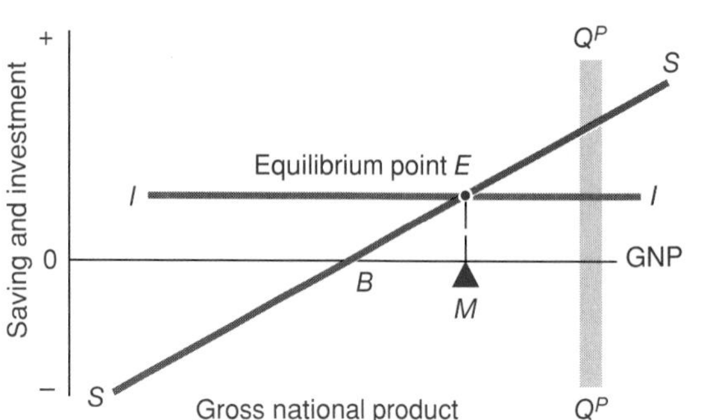

Figure 27-3. The equilibrium level of national output is determined by intersection of savings and investment schedules

The horizontal *II* line shows that investment is constant at the indicated level.

E marks the spot where investment and savings curves intersect. Equilibrium GNP comes at the intersection of the *SS* and *II* curves because this is the only level of GNP at which the desired saving of households exactly matches the desired investment of business.

For simplicity, we treat investment as an external or *autonomous* variable, one whose level is determined outside the model. Say that investment opportunities are such that investment would be exactly $200 billion per year regardless of the level of GNP. This means that, if we draw a schedule of investment against GNP, it will have to be a horizontal line—always the same distance above the horizontal axis. This case is shown in Figure 27-3, where the investment schedule is labeled *II* to distinguish it from the *SS* savings schedule. (Note that *II* does not mean Roman numeral 2.)

The savings and investment schedules intersect at point *E* in Figure 27-3. This point corresponds to a level of GNP equal to 0*M* and represents the equilibrium level of output in the multiplier model.

This intersection of the savings and investment schedules is the equilibrium level of GNP toward which national output will gravitate.

The Meaning of Equilibrium

Why is point *E* in Figure 27-3 an equilibrium? The reason is that at point *E* the desired saving of households equals the desired investment of firms. When desired saving and desired investment are not equal, output will tend to adjust up or down.

The savings and investment schedules shown in Figure 27-3 represent *desired* (or *planned*) *levels*. Thus at output level *M*, businesses will want their investment to be equal to the vertical distance *ME*. Also, households desire to save the amount *ME*. But there is no logical necessity for the actual saving (or investment) to be equal to the planned saving (or investment). People can make mistakes. Or they may forecast events incorrectly. When mistakes happen, saving or investment might deviate from planned levels.

To see how output adjusts until desired saving and desired investment are equated, we consider three cases. In the first case, the system is at *E*, where the schedule of what business firms want to invest intersects the savings schedule of what households want to save. When everyone's plans are satisfied, all will be content to go on doing just what they have been doing.

At equilibrium, firms will not find inventories piling up on their shelves; nor will their sales be so brisk as to force them to produce more goods. So production, employment, income, and spending will remain the same. In this case GNP stays at point *E*, and we can rightly call it an *equilibrium*.

The second case begins with a GNP higher than at *E*; say, GNP is to the right of *M*, at an income level where the savings schedule is higher than the investment schedule. Why can't the system stay there indefinitely? Because at this income level, families are saving more than business firms will be willing to go on investing. Firms will have too few customers and larger inventories of unsold goods than they want. What can businesses do about this situation? They can cut back production and lay off workers. This response moves GNP gradually downward, or leftward in Figure 27-3. The economy returns to equilibrium when it gets back to *E*. There the tendency to change has disappeared.

At this point, you should be able to analyze the third case. Show that if GNP were *below* its equilibrium level, strong forces would be set up to move it eastward back to *E*.

All three cases lead to the same conclusion:

The only equilibrium level of GNP occurs at *E*, where the savings and investment schedules intersect. At any other point, the desired saving of households does not coincide with the desired investment of business. This discrepancy will cause businesses to change their production and employment levels, thereby returning the system to the equilibrium GNP.

Output Determination by Consumption and Investment

In addition to the saving-investment balance, there is a second way of showing how output is determined. The equilibrium is the same, but our understanding of output determination is deepened if we work through this second approach.

This second method is called the consumption-plus-investment (or $C + I$) approach. How does the $C + I$ approach work? Figure 27-4 shows a curve of total spending graphed against total output or in-

How Consumption and Investment Determine Output

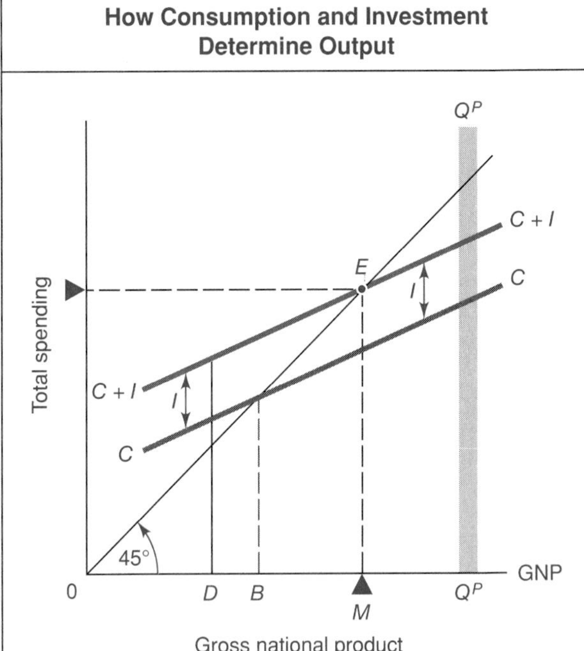

Figure 27-4. In the expenditure approach, equilibrium GNP level is found at the intersection of the $C + I$ schedule with 45° line

Adding *I* to *CC* gives the $C + I$ curve of total desired spending. At *E*, where this intersects the 45° line, we get the same equilibrium as in the savings-and-investment diagram. (Note the similarities between this figure and Fig. 27-3: the investment added to *CC* is the same as *II* of Fig. 27-3; break-even point *B* and potential-output band Q^P each come at the same GNP level on the two diagrams, and so must the *E* intersection.)

come. The black CC line is simply the consumption function, showing the level of desired consumption corresponding to each level of income. We then add desired investment (which is at fixed level I) to the consumption function. Thus the level of total desired spending is $C + I$, represented by the blue $C + I$ curve in Figure 27-4.

We next put in a 45° line to help us identify the equilibrium. At any point on the 45° line, the total level of consumption plus investment spending (measured vertically) exactly equals the total level of output (measured horizontally).

We can now calculate the equilibrium level of output in Figure 27-4. Where the desired amount of spending, represented by the $C + I$ curve, equals total output, the economy is in equilibrium. In summary:

The total spending (or $C + I$) curve shows the level of desired expenditure by consumers and businesses corresponding to each level of output. The economy is in equilibrium at the point where the $C + I$ curve crosses the 45° line—at point E in Figure 27-4. At point E the economy is in equilibrium because at that level desired spending on consumption and investment exactly equals the level of total output.

The Adjustment Mechanism. It is essential to understand why point E is an equilibrium. Equilibrium occurs when planned spending (on C and I) equals planned output. If the system were to deviate from equilibrium, say, at output level D in Figure 27-4, what would happen? At this level of output, the $C + I$ spending line is above the 45° line, so planned $C + I$ spending would be greater than planned output. This means that consumers would be buying more cars and shoes than businesses were producing. Auto dealers would find their lots emptying, and shoe stores would be running low on many sizes.

In this disequilibrium situation, auto dealers and shoe stores would respond by increasing their orders. Automakers and shoe manufacturers would recall workers from layoff and gear up their production lines. *Thus, spending disequilibrium leads to a change in output.*

By following this chain of reasoning we see that only when firms are producing what households and firms plan to spend on C and I, precisely at point E, will the economy be in equilibrium. (You should also work through what happens when output is above equilibrium.)

Planned vs. Actual Amounts. In this chapter, we repeatedly discuss "planned" or "desired" spending and output. These words call attention to the difference between (*a*) the amount of planned or desired consumption given by the consumption function or by the investment demand schedule and (*b*) the actual amount of consumption or investment measured after the fact.

This distinction emphasizes that GNP is at equilibrium only when firms and consumers are on their schedules of desired spending and investment. As measured by a national accounts statistician, saving and investment will always be exactly equal, in recession or boom. But *actual* investment will often differ from *planned* investment when actual sales are unequal to planned sales and firms consequently face an involuntary buildup or reduction of inventories. Only when the level of output is such that planned spending on $C + I$ equals planned output will there be no tendency for output, income, or spending to change.

An Arithmetic Analysis

An arithmetic example may help show why the equilibrium level of output occurs where planned spending and planned output are equal.

Table 27-1 shows a simple example of consumption and savings functions. The break-even level of income, where the nation is too poor to do any net saving on balance, is assumed to be $3000 billion ($3 trillion). Each change of income of $300 billion is assumed to lead to a $100 billion change in saving and a $200 billion change in consumption; in other words, for simplicity *MPC* is assumed to be constant and exactly equal to $\frac{2}{3}$. Therefore, $MPS = \frac{1}{3}$.

Again, we assume that investment is autonomous. Suppose that the only level of investment that will be sustained indefinitely is exactly $200 billion, as shown in column (4) of Table 27-1. That is, at each level of GNP, businesses desire to purchase $200 billion of investment goods, no more and no less.

Columns (5) and (6) are the crucial ones. Column (5) shows the total GNP—this is simply column (1) copied once again into column (5). The figures in column (6) represent what business firms would

GNP Determination Where Output Equals Planned Spending
(Billions of Dollars)

(1) Levels of GNP and *DI*	(2) Planned consumption	(3) Planned saving (3) = (1) − (2)	(4) Planned investment	(5) Level of GNP (5) = (1)		(6) Total planned spending on consumption and investment (6) = (2) + (4)	(7) Resulting tendency of output
4,200	3,800	**400**	**200**	4,200	>	4,000	Contraction
3,900	3,600	**300**	**200**	3,900	>	3,800	Contraction
3,600	**3,400**	**200**	**200**	**3,600**	=	**3,600**	**Equilibrium**
3,300	3,200	**100**	**200**	3,300	<	3,400	Expansion
3,000	3,000	**0**	**200**	3,000	<	3,200	Expansion
2,700	2,800	**−100**	**200**	2,700	<	3,000	Expansion

Table 27-1. Equilibrium output can be found arithmetically as the level where planned spending equals GNP

The blue row depicts the equilibrium GNP level, where the $3600 that is being produced is just matched by the $3600 that households plan to consume and that firms plan to invest. In upper rows, firms will be forced into unintended inventory investment and will respond by cutting back production until equilibrium GNP is reached. Interpret the lower rows' tendency toward expansion of GNP toward equilibrium.

actually be selling year in and year out; this is the planned consumption spending plus planned investment. It is the $C + I$ schedule from Figure 27-4 in numbers.

When businesses as a whole are producing too high a level of total product (higher than the sum of what consumers and businesses want to purchase), they will be involuntarily piling up inventories of unsalable goods.

Reading the top row of Table 27-1, we see that if firms are temporarily producing $4200 billion of GNP, planned or desired spending [shown in column (6)] is only $4000 billion. In this situation, excess inventories will be accumulating. Firms will respond by contracting their operations, and GNP will fall. In the opposite case, represented by the bottom row of Table 27-1, total spending is $3000 billion and output is $2700 billion. Inventories are being depleted and firms will expand operations, raising output.

We see, then, that when business firms as a whole are temporarily producing more than they can profitably sell, they will want to contract their operations, and GNP will tend to fall. When they are selling more than their current production, they increase their output and GNP rises.

Only when the level of output in column (5) exactly equals planned spending in column (6) will business firms be in equilibrium. Their sales will then be just enough to justify continuing their current level of aggregate output. GNP will neither expand nor contract.

● Let us summarize. GNP is one of the major indicators of a nation's economic health. What determines the level of GNP? In the very long run, potential output limits the amount a country can produce. But in the short run, the multiplier model suggests that aggregate demand, influenced by investment spending and the consumption function, determines GNP. Moreover, as the Keynes' quotation at the beginning of this chapter suggests, consumption and investment spending help us to understand high unemployment. While the relationships presented here have been simplified, their essence will remain valid even when extended to situations involving government fiscal policy, monetary policy, and foreign trade. ●

The Multiplier

Where is the multiplier in all this? To answer this question, we need to examine how a change in autonomous investment spending affects GNP. It is logical that an increase in investment will raise the level of output and employment. But by how much? The Keynesian multiplier model shows that an increase in investment will increase GNP by an amplified or multiplied amount—by an amount greater than itself.

The **multiplier** is the number by which the change in investment must be multiplied in order to determine the resulting change in total output.

For example, suppose investment increases by \$100 billion. If this causes an increase in output of \$300 billion, the multiplier is 3. If, instead, the resulting increase in output were \$400 billion, the multiplier would be 4.

Woodsheds and Carpenters. Why is it that the multiplier is greater than 1? Let's suppose that I hire unemployed resources to build a \$1000 woodshed. My carpenters and lumber producers will get an extra \$1000 of income. But, that is not the end of the story. If they all have a marginal propensity to consume of $\frac{2}{3}$, they will now spend \$666.67 on new consumption goods. The producers of these goods will now have extra incomes of \$666.67. If their *MPC* is also $\frac{2}{3}$, they in turn will spend \$444.44, or $\frac{2}{3}$ of \$666.67 (or $\frac{2}{3}$ of $\frac{2}{3}$ of \$1000). The process will go on, with each new round of spending being $\frac{2}{3}$ of the previous round.

Thus an endless chain of *secondary consumption respending* is set in motion by my *primary* investment of \$1000. But, although an endless chain, it is an ever-diminishing one. Eventually it adds up to a finite amount.

Using straightforward arithmetic, we can find the total increase in spending in the following manner:

$$
\begin{array}{ccc}
\$1000.00 & & 1 \times \$1000 \\
+ & & + \\
666.67 & & \frac{2}{3} \times \$1000 \\
+ & & + \\
444.44 & & (\frac{2}{3})^2 \times \$1000 \\
+ & = & + \\
296.30 & & (\frac{2}{3})^3 \times \$1000 \\
+ & & + \\
197.53 & & (\frac{2}{3})^4 \times \$1000 \\
+ & & + \\
\vdots & & \vdots \\
\hline
\$3000 & & \frac{1}{1-\frac{2}{3}} \times \$1000, \text{ or } 3 \times \$1000
\end{array}
$$

This shows that, with an *MPC* of $\frac{2}{3}$, the multiplier is 3; it consists of the 1 of primary investment plus 2 extra of secondary consumption respending.

The same arithmetic would give a multiplier of 4 for an *MPC* of $\frac{3}{4}$, because $1 + \frac{3}{4} + (\frac{3}{4})^2 + (\frac{3}{4})^3 + \cdots$ finally adds up to 4. For an *MPC* of $\frac{1}{2}$, the multiplier would be 2.

The size of the multiplier thus depends upon how large the *MPC* is. It can also be expressed in terms of the twin concept, the *MPS*. For an *MPS* of $\frac{1}{4}$, the *MPC* is $\frac{3}{4}$, and the multiplier would be 4. For an *MPS* of $\frac{1}{3}$, the multiplier is 3. If the *MPS* were $1/x$, the multiplier would be x.

By this time it should be clear that the simple multiplier is always the inverse, or "reciprocal," of the marginal propensity to save.[1] It is equal to $1/(1 - MPC)$. Our simple multiplier formula is:

$$
\begin{aligned}
\text{Change in output} &= \frac{1}{MPS} \times \text{change in investment} \\
&= \frac{1}{1 - MPC} \times \text{change in investment}
\end{aligned}
$$

In other words, the greater the extra consumption respending, the greater the multiplier.

Up to now, we have discussed the multiplier as relating to the extra consumption and saving. This is only part of the picture. Later in this chapter, we will see that the multiplier applies to changes in total spending and changes in total leakages from spending.

Graphical Picture of the Multiplier

Our discussion of the multiplier has relied up to now largely on common sense and arithmetic. Can we get the same result using our graphical analysis of saving and investment? The answer is yes.

Suppose, as back in Table 27-1, the *MPS* is $\frac{1}{3}$ and a burst of inventions gives rise to an extra \$100 billion of continuing investment opportunities. What will be the new equilibrium GNP? If the multiplier is indeed 3, the answer is \$3900 billion.

A look at Figure 27-5 can confirm this result. Our

[1] The formula for an infinite geometric progression is

$$1 + r + r^2 + r^3 + \cdots + r^n + \cdots = \frac{1}{1 - r}$$

as long as the *MPC* (r) is less than 1 in absolute value.

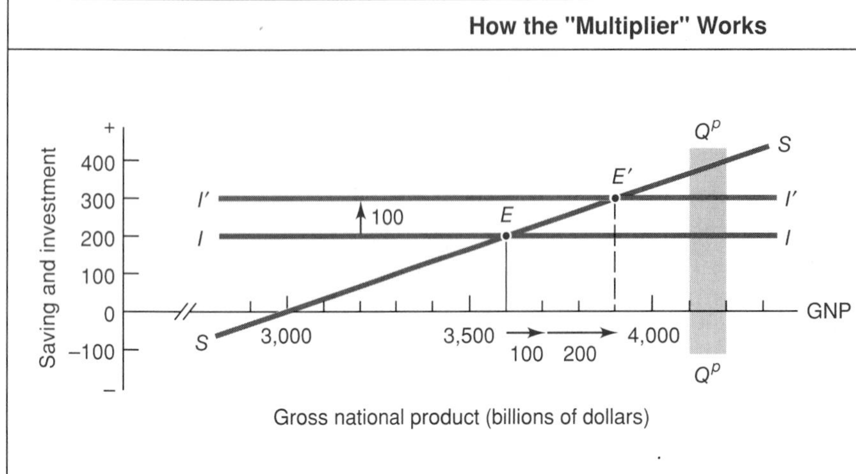

Figure 27-5. Each dollar of investment is "multiplied" into 3 dollars of output

New investment shifts *II* up to *I′I′*. *E′* gives the new equilibrium output, with output increasing by 3 for each 1 increase in investment. (*Note*: The broken horizontal blue arrow is 3 times the length of the vertical blue arrow of investment shift, and is broken to show 2 units of secondary consumption respending for each 1 unit of primary investment.)

old investment schedule *II* is shifted upward by $100 billion to the new level *I′I′*. The new intersection point is *E′*; the increase in income is exactly 3 times the increase in investment. As the blue arrows show, the horizontal output distance is 3 times as great as the upward shift in the investment schedule. We know that desired saving must rise to equal the new and higher level of investment. The only way that saving can rise is for national income to rise. With an *MPS* of $\frac{1}{3}$, and an increase in investment of $100, income must rise by $300 to bring forth $100 of additional saving to match the new investment. Hence, at equilibrium, $100 of additional investment induces $300 of additional income, verifying our multiplier arithmetic.[2]

The Multiplier in the *AS-AD* Framework

The multiplier model has been enormously influential in macroeconomic analysis over the last half-century. How does it fit into the broader macroeconomic conception of *AS* and *AD* analysis?

The relationship between the multiplier analysis and the *AS-AD* approach is shown in Figure 27-6. Part (*b*) displays an upward-sloping short-run *AS* curve that becomes relatively steep as output exceeds potential output. In the region where there are unused resources, to the left of potential output, output is determined primarily by the strength of aggregate demand. As investment increases, this increases *AD*, and equilibrium output rises.

The same economy can be described by the multiplier diagram in the top panel of Figure 27-6. The multiplier equilibrium gives the same level of output as the *AS-AD* equilibrium—both lead to a real GNP of *Q*. They simply stress different features of output determination.

These two diagrams make a key point that lies behind the multiplier diagram: The multiplier analysis applies to situations where output is less than its potential, that is, where there are unemployed resources. When there are unemployed resources, an increase in aggregate demand can raise output levels. By contrast, if an economy is producing at its maximum potential, there is simply no room for expansion when aggregate demand expands. In conditions of full employment, then, demand increases lead to higher prices rather than output increases.

Putting this in plain English, when investment or other autonomous spending increases in an economy with excess capacity and unemployed workers, most of the increments to total spending will end up in extra real output, with only small increases in the price level. However, as the economy reaches and surpasses potential output, it is not

[2] Alter Table 27-1, on p. 476, to verify this answer. In column (4), we now put $300 billion instead of $200 billion of investment. Show that the new equilibrium output now shifts one row up from the old blue equilibrium row. Can you also show that the multiplier works downward?

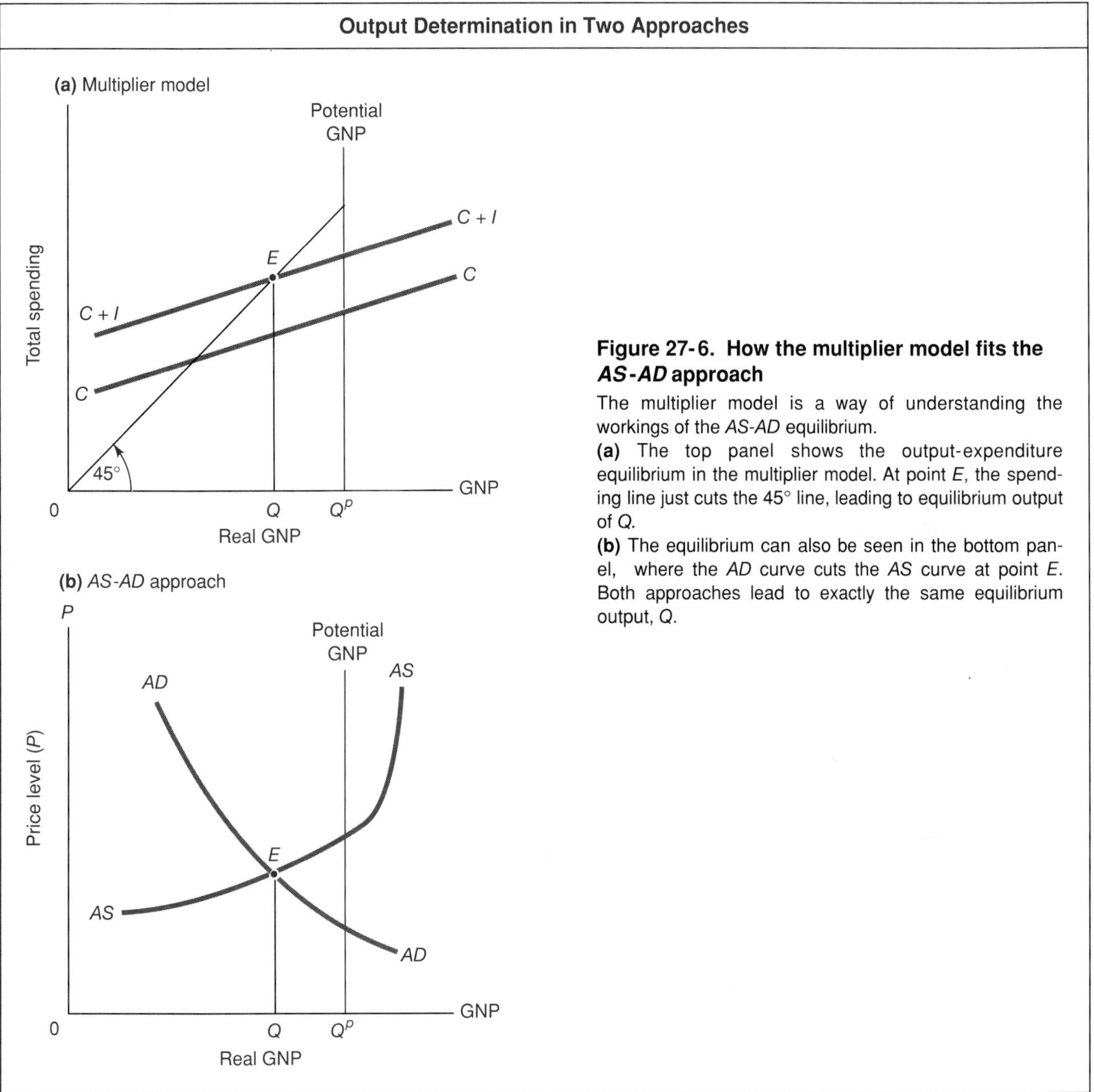

Figure 27-6. How the multiplier model fits the *AS-AD* approach

The multiplier model is a way of understanding the workings of the *AS-AD* equilibrium.

(a) The top panel shows the output-expenditure equilibrium in the multiplier model. At point *E*, the spending line just cuts the 45° line, leading to equilibrium output of *Q*.

(b) The equilibrium can also be seen in the bottom panel, where the *AD* curve cuts the *AS* curve at point *E*. Both approaches lead to exactly the same equilibrium output, *Q*.

possible to coax out more production at the going level of prices. Hence, at high levels of output, higher spending [upward shifts in the *AD* curve of Figure 27-6(*b*)] will simply result in higher price levels and little or none of the *AD* increase will end up in higher real output or employment.

This discussion points to a crucial limitation of the multiplier model. While it may be a highly useful approach to describe depressions or even recessions, it cannot apply to periods of full employment, when real GNP exceeds potential output. Once factories are operating at full capacity and when all the workers are employed, the economy simply cannot produce more output. This fact reinforces the point that the multiplier model applies only in an economy with unemployed resources.

B. Fiscal Policy in the Multiplier Model

Economies suffer from recurrent bouts of unemployment and inflation. One of the first weapons that governments deploy to moderate business cycles is *fiscal policy,* which consists of government expenditures on goods and services (G) and taxes and transfers (T). In this section, we extend our simplest multiplier model to show how, as long as there are unemployed resources, changes in G and T can influence the level of national output.

How Government Fiscal Policies Affect Output

To understand the role of government in economic activity, we need to look at government spending and taxation, along with the effects of those activities on private-sector spending. As you might guess, we now add G to get a $C + I + G$ spending schedule for charting macroeconomic equilibrium when government, with its spending and taxing, is in the picture.

It will simplify our task in the beginning if we analyze the effects of government expenditure with taxes held constant (such taxes are called "lump-sum taxes"). But even with a fixed dollar value of taxes, we can no longer ignore the distinction between disposable income and gross national product. If we rule out business saving and foreign trade, we know from Chapter 24 that GNP equals disposable income plus taxes. But with tax revenues held constant, GNP and DI will always differ by the same amount; thus, after taking account of such taxes, we can still plot the CC consumption schedule against GNP rather than against DI.

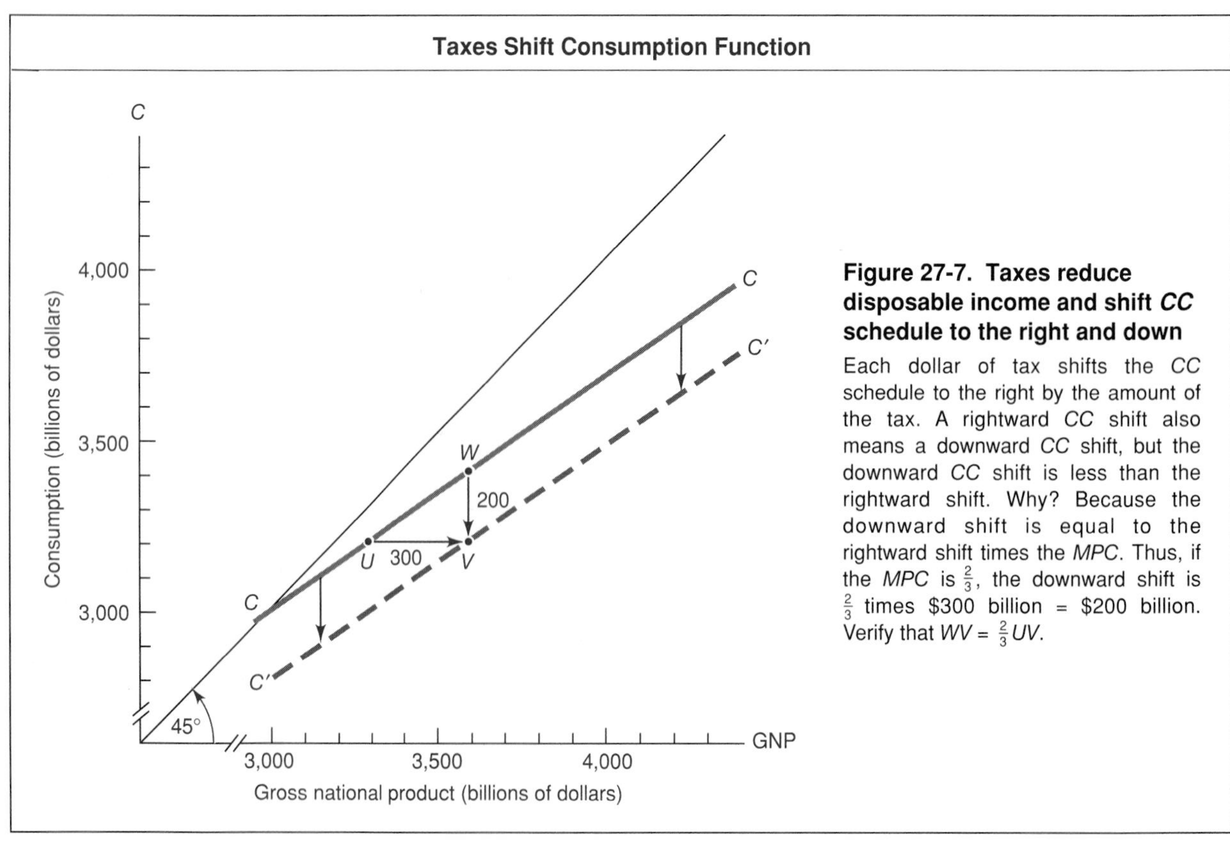

Figure 27-7. Taxes reduce disposable income and shift *CC* schedule to the right and down

Each dollar of tax shifts the CC schedule to the right by the amount of the tax. A rightward CC shift also means a downward CC shift, but the downward CC shift is less than the rightward shift. Why? Because the downward shift is equal to the rightward shift times the MPC. Thus, if the MPC is $\frac{2}{3}$, the downward shift is $\frac{2}{3}$ times \$300 billion = \$200 billion. Verify that $WV = \frac{2}{3}UV$.

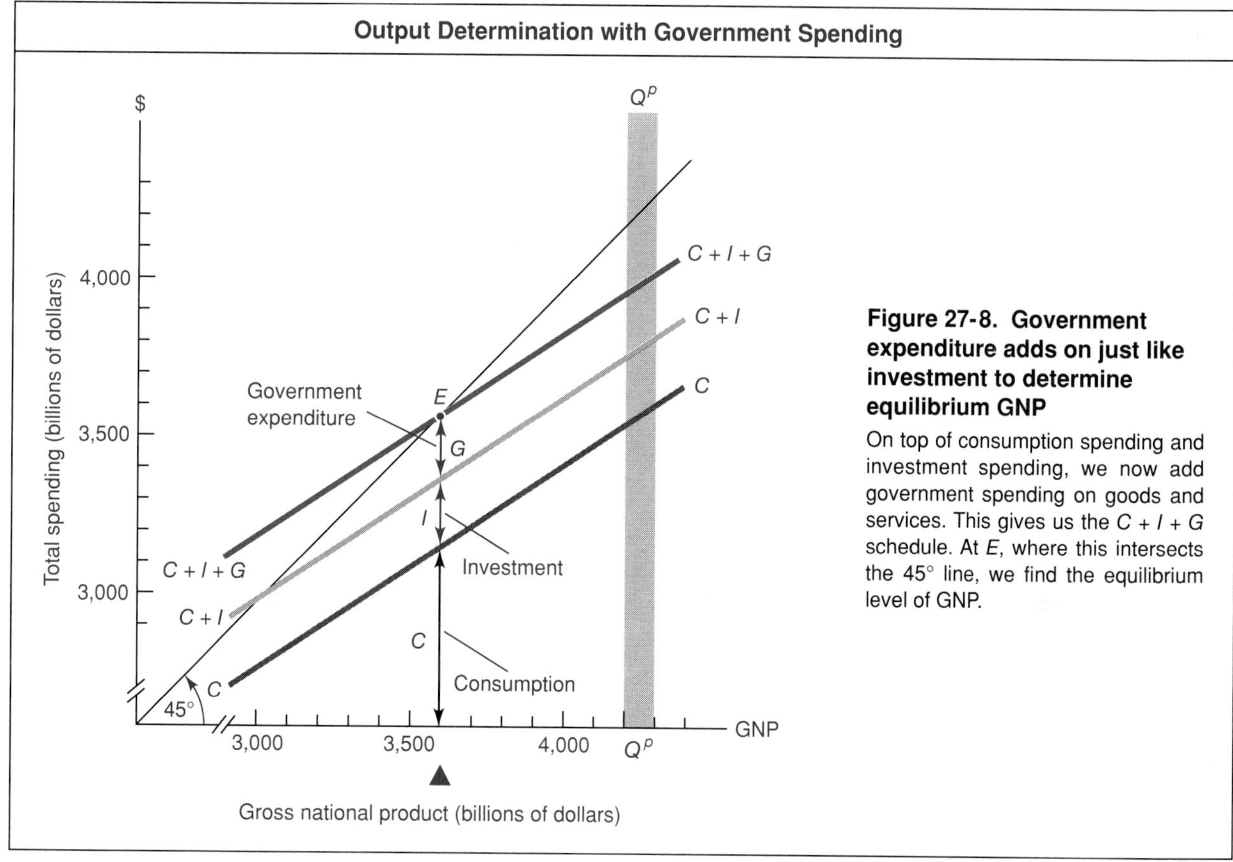

Figure 27-8. Government expenditure adds on just like investment to determine equilibrium GNP

On top of consumption spending and investment spending, we now add government spending on goods and services. This gives us the *C* + *I* + *G* schedule. At *E*, where this intersects the 45° line, we find the equilibrium level of GNP.

An example will clarify how we can depict our consumption function when taxes are present. In Figure 27-7, we have drawn our original consumption function with zero taxes as the black *CC* line. In this case, GNP = *DI*. Here, consumption is 3000 at a *DI* of 3000; consumption is also 3400 at a GNP of 3600.

Now introduce taxes of 300. At a *DI* of 3600, GNP must be equal to 3600 + 300 = 3900. Consumption is thus 3400 at a *DI* of 3600 or at a GNP of 3900. So we can write consumption as a function of GNP by shifting the consumption function to the right to the blue $C'C'$ curve; the amount of the rightward shift is exactly equal to the amount of taxes, 300.

Alternatively, we can plot the new consumption function as a parallel *downward* shift by 200. As Figure 27-7 shows, 200 is the result of multiplying a decrease in income of 300 times the *MPC* of $\frac{2}{3}$.

Turning next to the different components of aggregate demand, recall from Chapter 24 that GNP consists of four elements:

GNP = consumption expenditure
+ gross private domestic investment
+ government expenditure on goods and services
+ net exports

$$= C + I + G + X$$

For now, we assume that there is no foreign trade, so our GNP consists of the first three components, $C + I + G$. (The third section of this chapter will add the fourth component, net exports, to the multiplier model.)

Figure 27-8 shows the effect of *G*. This diagram is exactly the same as the one used in the last section. In this new diagram, we have added one new variable, *G* (government spending on goods and services), on top of the consumption function and the fixed amount of investment. That is, the vertical distance between the $C + I$ line and the $C + I + G$ line is the amount of government spending on goods and services (police, tanks, roads, etc.).

Why do we simply add G on the top? Because spending on government buildings (G) has the same macroeconomic impact as spending on private buildings (I); the collective consumption expenditure involved in maintaining a public library (G) has the same effect on jobs as private consumption expenditure for newspapers or books (C).

We end up with the three-layered cake of $C + I + G$, calculating the amount of total spending forthcoming at each level of GNP. We now must go to its point of intersection with the 45° line to find the equilibrium level of GNP. At this equilibrium GNP level, denoted by point E in Figure 27-8, total planned spending exactly equals total planned output. Point E is thus the equilibrium level of output when we add government purchases to the multiplier model.

Impact of Taxation on Aggregate Demand

How does government taxation tend to reduce aggregate demand and the level of GNP? We do not need graphs to tell us what happens when the government increases our taxes while at the same time holding its expenditures constant.

Extra taxes lower our disposable incomes, and lower disposable incomes tend to reduce our consumption spending. Clearly, if investment and government expenditure remain the same, a reduction in consumption spending will then reduce GNP and employment. Thus, in the multiplier model, higher taxes without increases in government spending will tend to reduce real GNP.

A look back at Figure 27-7 confirms this reasoning. In this figure, the upper CC curve represents the level of the consumption function with no taxes. The CC curve is unrealistic, of course, because consumers must pay taxes on their incomes. For simplicity, we assume that consumers pay \$300 billion in taxes at every level of income; thus DI is exactly \$300 billion less than GNP at every level of output. As is shown in Figure 27-7, this level of taxes can be represented by a rightward shift in the consumption function of \$300 billion. This rightward shift will also appear as a downward shift; if the MPC is $\frac{2}{3}$, then the rightward shift of \$300 billion will be seen as a downward shift of \$200 billion.

Without a doubt, taxes lower output in our multiplier model. Another glance at Figure 27-8 will show why. When taxes increase, $I + G$ do not change, but the increase in taxes will lower disposable income, thereby shifting the CC consumption schedule downward. Hence, the $C + I + G$ schedule shifts downward. You can pencil in a new, lower $C' + I + G$ schedule in Figure 27-8. Confirm that its new intersection with the 45° line must be at a lower equilibrium level of GNP.

Keep in mind that G is government outlays on goods and services. It excludes spending on transfers such as unemployment insurance or social security payments. These transfers are treated as *negative taxes*, so that the taxes (T) considered here can best be thought of as taxes less transfers. Therefore, if direct and indirect taxes total \$400 billion, while all transfer payments are \$100 billion, then net taxes, T, equal \$400 − \$100 = \$300 billion.

A Numerical Example

The points made up to now can be illustrated by Table 27-2. This table is very similar to Table 27-1, which illustrated output determination in the simplest multiplier model. The first column shows a reference level of GNP, while the second shows a fixed level of taxes, \$300 billion. Disposable income in column (3) is GNP less taxes. Consumption, taken as a function of DI, is shown in column (4). Column (5) shows the fixed level of investment, while column (6) exhibits the level of government spending. To find total aggregate demand in column (7), we add together the $C + I + G$ in columns (4) through (6).

Finally, we compare total spending in column (7) with the initial level of GNP in column (1). If spending is above GNP, output rises; if spending is below GNP, output falls. This tendency, shown in the last column, assures us that output will tend toward equilibrium at \$3600 billion.

Fiscal-Policy Multipliers

Investment, taxes, and government spending represent autonomous spending streams that interact with induced consumption spending to determine the equilibrium level of national output. We have discovered that government fiscal policy is high-powered spending much akin to investment. The parallel between investment and fiscal policy suggests that fiscal policy should also have multiplier effects upon output. And this is exactly right.

The **government expenditure multiplier** is the

Output Determination with Government
(Billions of Dollars)

(1) Initial level of GNP	(2) Taxes (*T*)	(3) Disposable income (*DI*)	(4) Planned consumption (*C*)	(5) Planned investment (*I*)	(6) Government expenditure (*G*)	(7) Total spending (*C* + *I* + *G*)	(8) Resulting tendency of economy
4,200	300	3,900	3,600	200	200	4,000 ↓	Contraction
3,900	300	3,600	3,400	200	200	3,800 ↓	Contraction
3,600	**300**	**3,300**	**3,200**	**200**	**200**	**3,600**	**Equilibrium**
3,300	300	3,000	3,000	200	200	3,400 ↑	Expansion
3,000	300	2,700	2,800	200	200	3,200 ↑	Expansion

Table 27-2. Government spending, taxes, and investment determine equilibrium GNP

This table shows how output is determined when government spending on goods and services is added to the multiplier model. In this example, taxes are "lump sum" or independent of the level of income. Disposable income is thus GNP minus \$300 billion. Total spending is $I + G +$ (the consumption determined by the consumption function).

At levels of output less than \$3600 billion, spending is greater than output, so output expands. Levels of output greater than \$3600 are unsustainable and lead to contraction. Only at output of \$3600 is output in equilibrium—that is, planned spending equals output.

The Government Expenditure Multiplier

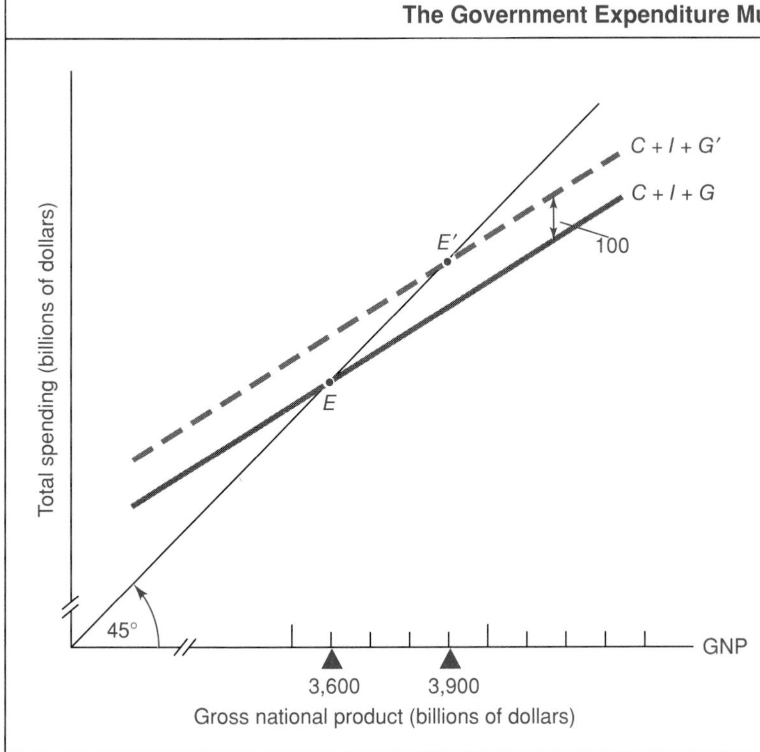

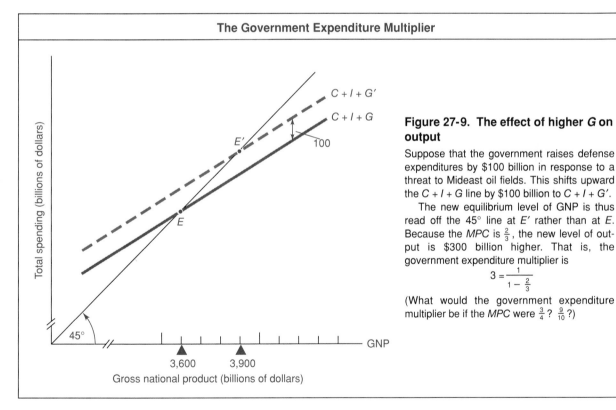

Figure 27-9. The effect of higher *G* on output

Suppose that the government raises defense expenditures by \$100 billion in response to a threat to Mideast oil fields. This shifts upward the $C + I + G$ line by \$100 billion to $C + I + G'$.

The new equilibrium level of GNP is thus read off the 45° line at E' rather than at E. Because the *MPC* is $\frac{2}{3}$, the new level of output is \$300 billion higher. That is, the government expenditure multiplier is

$$3 = \frac{1}{1 - \frac{2}{3}}$$

(What would the government expenditure multiplier be if the *MPC* were $\frac{3}{4}$? $\frac{9}{10}$?)

increase in GNP resulting from an increase of \$1 in government expenditures on goods and services. An initial government purchase of a good or service will set in motion a chain of respending: if the government builds a road, the road-builders will spend some of their incomes on consumption goods, which in turn will generate additional incomes, some of which will be respent. In the simple model examined here, the ultimate effect on GNP of an extra dollar of *G* will be the same as an extra dollar of *I*: the multipliers are equal to $1/(1 - MPC)$. Figure 27-9 shows how a change in G will result in a higher level of GNP, with the increase being a multiple of the increase in government purchases.

To show the effects of an extra $100 billion of *G*, the $C + I + G$ curve in Figure 27-9 has been shifted up by $100 billion. The ultimate increase in GNP is equal to the $100 billion of primary spending times the expenditure multiplier. In this case, because the *MPC* is $\frac{2}{3}$, the multiplier is 3, so the equilibrium level of GNP rises by $300 billion.

This example, as well as common sense, tells us that the government expenditure multiplier is exactly the same number as the investment multiplier. Because they are equal, they are both called **expenditure multipliers.**

Also, note that the multiplier horse can be ridden in both directions. If government expenditures were to fall, with taxes and other influences held constant, GNP would decline by the change in *G* times the multiplier.

The effect of *G* on output can be seen as well in the numerical example of Table 27-2. You can pencil in a different level of *G*—at $300 billion—and find the equilibrium level of GNP. It should give the same answer as Figure 27-9.

We can sum up:

Government expenditures on goods and services (*G*) are an important force in the determination of output and employment. In the multiplier model, if *G* increases, output will rise by the increase in *G* times the expenditure multiplier. Government spending therefore has the potential to stabilize or destabilize output over the business cycle.

Impact of Taxes

Taxes also have an impact upon equilibrium GNP, although the size of tax multipliers is smaller than that of expenditure multipliers. Consider the following example: Suppose the economy is at its potential GNP, and the nation raises defense spending by $200 billion. Such sudden increases have occurred at many points in the history of the United States: in the early 1940s for World War II, in 1951 for the Korean war, in the mid-1960s for the Vietnam war, and in the early 1980s during the Reagan administration's military buildup. Furthermore, say that economic planners wish to raise taxes just enough to offset the effect on GNP of the $200 billion increase in *G*. How much would taxes have to be raised?

We are in for a surprise. To offset the $200 billion increase in *G*, we need to increase tax collections by more than $200 billion. In our numerical example, we can find the exact size of the tax or *T* increase from Figure 27-7. That figure shows that a $300 billion increase in *T* reduces disposable income by just that amount and will lead to a consumption decline of just $200 billion when the *MPC* is $\frac{2}{3}$. Put differently, a tax increase of $300 billion will shift the *CC* curve down by $200 billion. Hence, while a $1 billion increase in defense spending shifts up the $C + I + G$ line by $1 billion, a $1 billion tax increase shifts down the $C + I + G$ line by only $\$\frac{2}{3}$ billion (when the *MPC* is $\frac{2}{3}$). Thus offsetting an increase in defense spending, when non-defense outlays are constant, requires a larger increase in *T* than the increase in *G*.

Dollars of tax changes are almost as powerful a weapon against unemployment or inflation as are changes in dollars of government expenditures. The tax multiplier is smaller than the expenditure multiplier by a factor equal to the *MPC*:

$$\text{Tax multiplier} = MPC \times \text{expenditure multiplier}$$

The reason the tax multiplier is smaller than the expenditure multiplier is straightforward. When government spends $1 on *G*, that $1 gets spent directly on GNP. On the other hand, when government cuts taxes by a dollar, only part of that dollar is spent on *C*, while a fraction of that $1 tax cut is saved. The difference in the response to a dollar of *G* and a dollar of *T* is enough to lower the tax multiplier below the expenditure multiplier.[3]

Fiscal Policy in Practice

Since the 1960s, fiscal policy has been one of the nation's main weapons for fighting recession or in-

[3] The different multipliers can be seen using the device of the "expenditure rounds" shown on pp. 477 ff. Let the *MPC* be *r*. Then if *G* goes up by 1 unit, the total increase in spending is the sum of secondary respending rounds:

$$1 + r + r^2 + r^3 + \cdots = \frac{1}{1 - r}$$

Now, if taxes are reduced by $1, consumers save $(1 - r)$ of the increased disposable income and spend *r* dollars on the first round. With the further rounds, the total spending is thus:

$$r + r^2 + r^3 + \cdots = \frac{r}{1 - r}$$

Thus the tax multiplier is *r* times the expenditure multiplier, where *r* is the *MPC*.

flation. The Kennedy-Johnson tax cut of 1964 lifted the economy out of a slump; but the Vietnam war buildup of 1965–1966 increased output too rapidly, and inflation began to heat up. To fight the rising inflation and offset the increased Vietnam war expenditures, Congress passed a temporary surtax on incomes in 1968. President Ford lowered taxes in 1975 to fight a deep recession; President Carter was dissatisfied with the speed of the recovery and introduced further stimulative fiscal measures in 1977 and 1978. By 1979, however, inflation became the major concern, and the Carter administration opposed further tax cuts.

The 1980s provided a dramatic demonstration of how fiscal policy works. In 1981, President Reagan proposed a tax cut along with spending reductions, but Congress passed a fiscal program that was extremely expansionary (meaning that it tends to increase real GNP). These steps propelled the American economy out of the deep recession of 1981–1982 into a rapid expansion in 1983–1985. From 1985 to 1988, however, the country became alarmed about the mounting budget deficit, and fiscal policy turned contractionary (tending to lower real GNP). The tight budget policies of the late 1980s, along with other forces, tilted the economy into recession in 1990.

With the recession alongside a large government budget deficit, Congress and the President faced a dilemma of priorities in 1990–1991. Was it more important to raise taxes and curb the deficit? Or should government spending and taxes be expansionary to soften the recession? These are typical of the difficult choices that macroeconomic policy must face today.

C. Output Determination in Open Economies

No nation is an island unto itself. Every nation is an open economy, trading goods and services with others, exporting commodities that are produced most inexpensively at home and importing products in which others have a cost advantage.

In an earlier era, foreign trade exerted only a modest influence on the macroeconomic performance of the United States. Most citizens, students, and politicians could afford to ignore the economic linkages between nations, leaving that topic to specialists who toiled in universities or in the State Department. But revolutionary developments in communications, transportation, and trade policy have increasingly linked together the economic fortunes of nations. Trading ties between Japan, Mexico, Canada, and the United States are closer today than were those between New York and California a century ago. The international business cycle exerts a powerful effect on every nation of the globe; monetary-policy actions in Washington can produce depressions, poverty, and revolution in South America; political disturbances in the Middle East can set off a spiral in oil prices that sends the world into booms or recessions. To ignore international trade is to miss half the economic ball game.

Chapters 36 through 39 analyze the theories of international trade and development in depth. In this section, we highlight some of the major trends and then show how changes in net exports affect the macroeconomy in a way similar to that of investment spending.

Foreign Trade and Economic Activity

Net Exports: Concepts and Trends

Here we turn to the fourth component of GNP: net exports. Net exports are defined as exports of goods and services minus imports of goods and services.

What are the major components of international trade? For the United States during 1990, exports totaled $673 billion while imports were $704 billion, for net exports of minus $31 billion.

The major components of exports were merchandise exports of $398 billion, of which the principal items were $35 billion of foodstuffs, $102 billion of industrial products, $154 billion of capital goods, and $36 billion of automotive goods. Other exports totaled $275 billion, including $102 billion of income on U.S. assets abroad.

Imports for 1990 totaled $704 billion. Of this, $503 billion was merchandise trade, including $27 billion of foodstuffs, $139 billion of industrial supplies, $117 billion of capital goods, $86 billion of automotive products, and $105 billion of other consumer goods. Non-merchandise imports of $201 billion included $70 billion of income from foreign assets in the United States.

Over most of the twentieth century, the United States has had a positive balance on its net exports. Net exports turned negative during the Vietnam war boom, but then improved after the depreciation of the dollar in the early 1970s and again during the deep recession of the early 1980s. A dramatic deterioration in the U.S. trade position occurred in the mid-1980s, so that by 1987 imports exceeded exports by $115 billion. The huge trade deficit has become one of the major political problems for the United States and its trading partners. Figure 27-10 displays U.S. net exports over the last three decades.

Once we acknowledge the possibility of exports and imports, we must also recognize that a nation's expenditure may differ from its production. Total *domestic expenditure* (sometimes called domestic demand) is equal to consumption plus domestic investment plus government purchases. It differs from total *national product* (or GNP) for two reasons. First, some part of domestic expenditure will be on goods produced abroad, these items being imports (denoted by m) like Mexican oil and Japanese automobiles. In addition, some part of America's production will be sold abroad as exports (denoted by e)—items like wheat and Boeing aircraft. The difference between national output and domestic expenditure is simply $e - m$ = net exports $= X$.

To calculate the *total* demand for American goods and services, we need to include not only domestic demand but also foreign demand. That is, we need to know the total spending of American residents as well as the net purchases of foreigners.

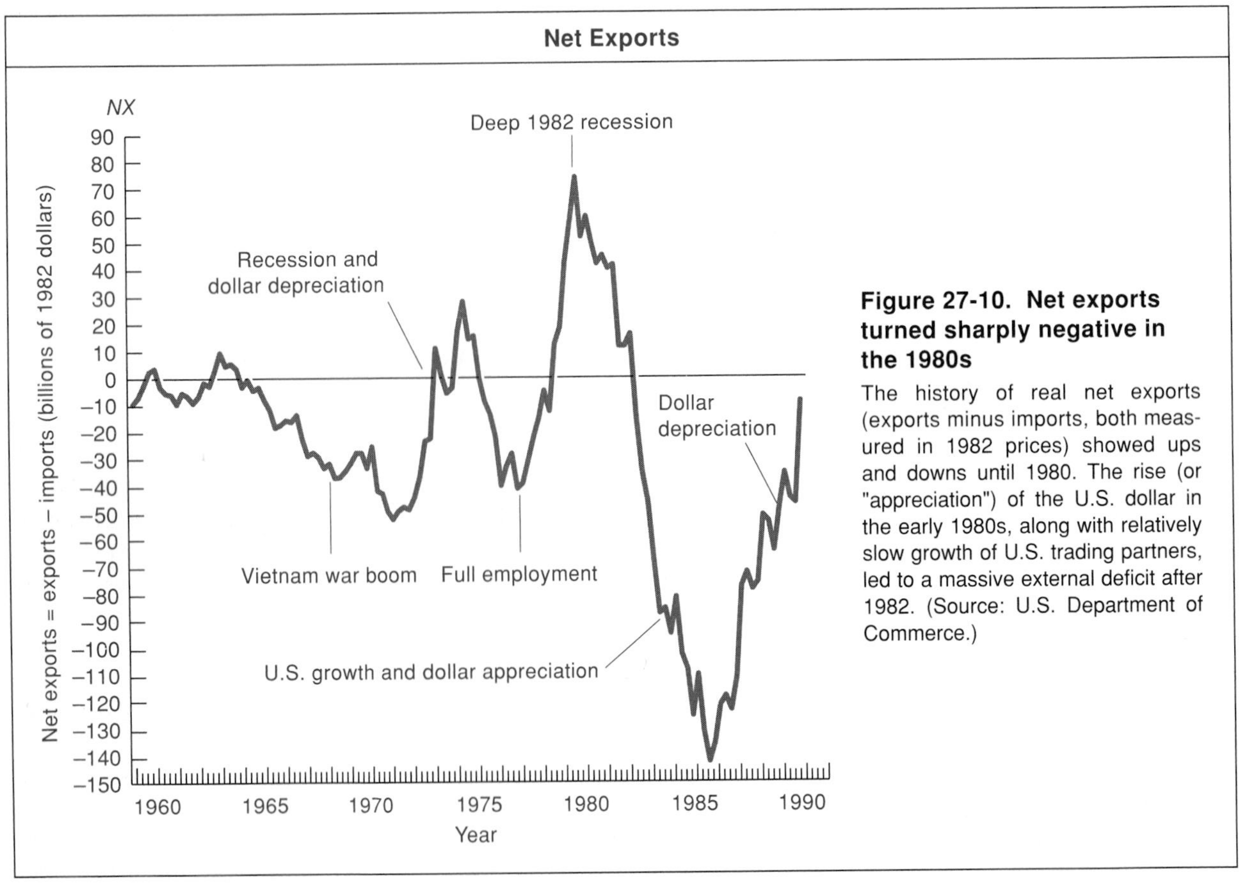

Figure 27-10. Net exports turned sharply negative in the 1980s

The history of real net exports (exports minus imports, both measured in 1982 prices) showed ups and downs until 1980. The rise (or "appreciation") of the U.S. dollar in the early 1980s, along with relatively slow growth of U.S. trading partners, led to a massive external deficit after 1982. (Source: U.S. Department of Commerce.)

This total must include domestic expenditures ($C + I + G$) plus sales to foreigners (e) less domestic purchases from foreigners (m). Expenditure on national output, or GNP, equals consumption plus domestic investment plus government purchases plus net exports:

$$\text{Total aggregate demand} = \text{GNP}$$
$$= C + I + G + X$$

Determinants of Net Exports. What determines the movements of exports and imports and therefore net exports? It is best to think of the import and export components of net exports separately. Imports into the United States are positively related to U.S. income and output. When U.S. GNP is rising rapidly, U.S. imports tend to rise even more quickly.

In addition, the choice between foreign and domestic goods responds to the relative prices of the two. If the price of domestic cars rises relative to the price of Japanese cars, say because productivity growth is more rapid in Japan or because the exchange rate on the Japanese yen falls relative to the U.S. dollar, Americans will buy more Japanese and fewer American cars. Hence the volume and value of imports will be affected by the relative prices of domestic and foreign goods, which in turn depend on both the domestic price levels and the foreign exchange rate of the dollar.[4]

Exports are the mirror image of imports: our exports are the imports of the rest of the world. Therefore, they depend primarily upon the incomes and outputs of our trading partners, as well as upon the relative prices of our exports and the goods with which they compete. As foreign output rises, or as the foreign exchange rate of the dollar falls, the volume and value of our exports tend to grow.

What caused the major changes in net exports shown in Figure 27-10? From 1960 to 1969, the American economy grew rapidly and American prices rose relative to those of its trading partners; consequently, imports tended to grow faster than exports. From 1969 to 1975, the American economy slumped. In addition, the value of the dollar fell relative to other major currencies during this period. Consequently, U.S. goods became relatively cheaper, the growth of imports slowed, exports boomed, and net exports became positive.

The early 1980s dealt a sharp blow to the U.S. trade position. The value of the dollar rose sharply from 1980 to 1985, so imports into the United States became relatively cheap while American exports became uncompetitive. Foreign economies grew less rapidly than the home economy, depressing exports, while imports grew sharply. The effect was a massive turn toward deficit in real net exports.

More recently, the trade deficit began to reverse. In the late 1980s, the exchange rate of the dollar fell, the U.S. economy grew more slowly, and as a result net exports began to climb. By 1991, the net-export deficit was down to one-quarter of its peak in 1987.

Impact of Trade on GNP

How do changes in a nation's trade flows affect its GNP and employment? Surprisingly, the answer is that this small tail can wag the entire American economy.

Table 27-3 shows how introducing net exports affects output determination. This table begins with the same components shown for a closed economy in Table 27-2. Total domestic demand in column (2) is composed of the consumption, investment, and government purchases we analyzed earlier. Column (3) then adds the exports of goods and services. As described above, these depend upon foreign incomes and outputs and upon prices and exchange rates, all of which are also taken as determined outside the model. Exports are therefore a constant level of \$360 billion of foreign spending on domestic goods and services.

The interesting new element arises from imports, shown in column (4). Like exports, imports depend upon external variables like prices and exchange rates. But in addition, imports depend upon do-

[4] Recall from Chapter 23 that the *foreign exchange rate* is the price of a nation's currency in terms of foreign currencies. Take wine as an example. The relative prices of U.S. wine and French wine will depend upon both countries' prices and upon the foreign exchange rate. Say that California chardonnay wines sell for \$6 per bottle, while the equivalent French chardonnay sells for 40 French francs. Then at the 1984 exchange rate of 10 French francs to the dollar, French wine sells at \$4 per bottle while California wine sells at \$6, giving an advantage to the imported variety.

Say that the foreign exchange rate of the dollar fell to 5 francs to the dollar. Then the French wine would sell for \$8 as compared to \$6 for the California wine. The fall in the exchange rate on the dollar would therefore turn relative prices against imports and in favor of domestic products.

Output Determination with Foreign Trade
(Billions of Dollars)

(1) Initial level of GNP	(2) Domestic demand $(C + I + G)$	(3) Exports (e)	(4) Imports (m)	(5) Net exports $(X = e - m)$	(6) Total spending $(C + I + G + X)$	(7) Resulting tendency of economy
4,200	4,000	360	420	−60	3,940 ↓	Contraction
3,900	3,800	360	390	−30	3,770 ↓	Contraction
3,600	**3,600**	**360**	**360**	**0**	**3,600**	**Equilibrium**
3,300	3,400	360	330	30	3,430 ↑	Expansion
3,000	3,200	360	300	60	3,260 ↑	Expansion

Table 27-3. Net exports add to aggregate demand of economy

To the domestic demand of $C + I + G$, we must add net exports of $X = e - m$ to obtain total aggregate demand for a country. Note that higher net exports have the same multiplier as do investment and government expenditure increases.

mestic incomes and output, which clearly change in the different rows of Table 27-3. For simplicity, we assume that the country always imports 10 percent of its total output, so imports in column (4) are 10 percent of column (1).

Subtracting column (4) from column (3) gives net exports in column (5). This is a negative number when imports exceed exports and a positive number when exports are greater than imports. Net exports in column (5) are the net addition to the spending stream contributed by foreigners. Equilibrium output in an open economy comes at the

Foreign Trade in Multiplier Model

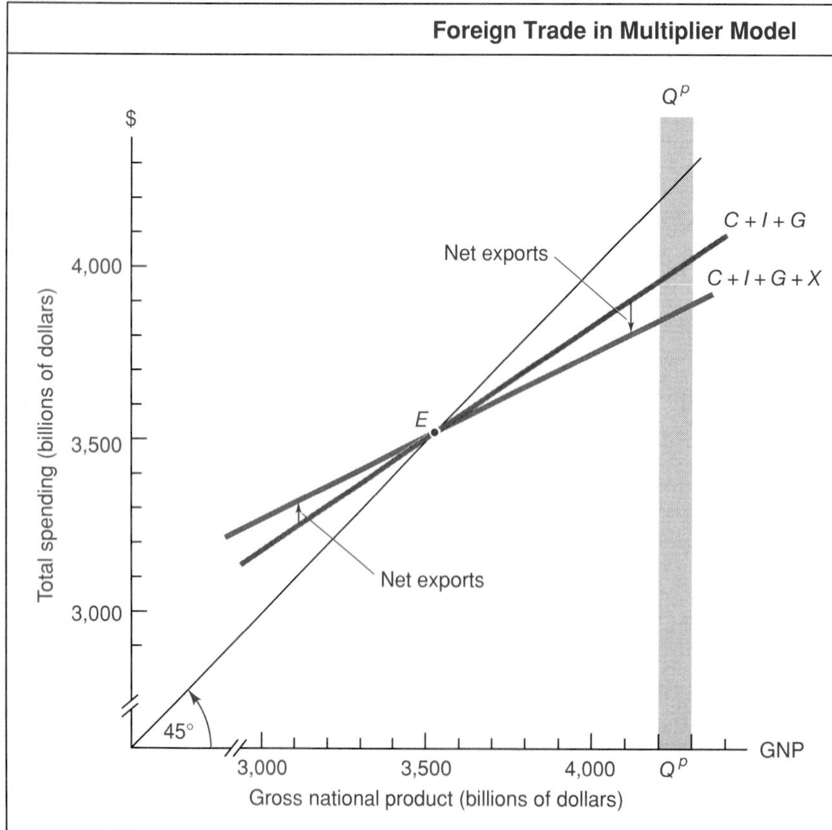

Figure 27-11. Adding net exports to domestic demand gives equilibrium GNP in open economy

The black line represents domestic demand $(C + I + G)$, purchases by domestic consumers, businesses, and governments. To this must be added net foreign spending; net exports plus domestic demand produce the blue line of total spending. Equilibrium comes at point E, where total GNP equals total spending on goods and services produced in the U.S. Note that the slope of the blue total demand curve is less than that of domestic demand to reflect the leakage from spending into imports.

point where total spending in column (6) exactly equals total output. In this case, equilibrium comes with net exports of exactly zero, although generally the net export position would differ from zero. (Make sure that you can explain why the economy is not in equilibrium when spending does not equal output.)

Figure 27-11 shows the open-economy equilibrium graphically. The upward-sloping black line marked $C + I + G$ is the same curve used in Figure 27-8 to illustrate output determination with government spending. To this line we must add the level of net exports that is forthcoming at each level of GNP. Net exports from column (5) of Table 27-3 are added to get the blue line of total aggregate demand or total spending. To the left of point E in the figure, net exports are positive so the blue line lies above the black curve; at the right, imports exceed exports and net exports are negative so the total spending line lies below the line for domestic demand.

Equilibrium GNP occurs where the blue line of total spending intersects the 45° line. This intersection comes at exactly the same point, at \$3600 billion, that is shown as equilibrium GNP in Table 27-3. Only at \$3600 billion does GNP exactly equal what consumers, businesses, governments, and foreigners want to spend on goods and services produced in the United States.[5]

The Marginal Propensity to Import and the Spending Line

Note that the aggregate demand curve, the blue $C + I + G + X$ curve in Figure 27-11, has a slightly smaller slope than the black curve of domestic demand. The explanation of this is that there is an additional leakage from spending, into imports. This new leakage arises from our assumption that 10 cents of every dollar of income is spent on imports. To handle this requires introducing a new term, the marginal propensity to import. The **marginal propensity to import,** which we will denote *MPm*, is the increase in the dollar value of imports for each \$1 increase in GNP.

Recall that we labeled the increase in consumption per unit increase of income the "marginal propensity to consume." The marginal propensity to import is closely related. It tells how much is imported for each dollar increase in total GNP. What marginal propensity to import is assumed to hold in Table 27-3? Clearly, the answer is $MPm = 0.10$, for every \$300 billion of increased income leads to \$30 billion of increased imports. (What is the marginal propensity to import in an economy with no foreign trade? Zero.)

Returning to Figure 27-11, let us examine the slope of the total spending line (that is, the line showing total spending on $C + I + G + X$). Note that the slope of the total spending line is less than the slope of the domestic demand line of $C + I + G$. As GNP and total incomes rise by \$300, spending on consumption rises by the income change times the *MPC* (assumed to be two-thirds), or by \$200. At the same time, spending on imports, or foreign goods, also rises by \$30. Hence spending on domestic goods rises by only \$170 (= \$200 − \$30), and the slope of the total spending line falls from 0.667 in our closed economy to 0.567 in our open economy.[6]

The Open-Economy Multiplier

You might suspect that the leakage of spending outside the economy into imports would change the multiplier in an open economy, especially because the import leakage changes the slope of the spending line. You would be correct. Let us see why.

One way of understanding the expenditure multiplier in an open economy is to calculate the

[5] Note that the two lines in Fig. 27-11 cross where net exports are zero, but the fact that equilibrium comes at zero net exports is purely coincidental. Change the export column to 460 in Table 27-3, recalculate the new equilibrium, and redraw the equilibrium in Fig. 27-11.

[6] Our analysis has considered only leakages from income into saving and into imports. A complete account of the economy would include two further important *leakages:* (*a*) those into taxes, because some taxes (such as income or sales taxes) rise with higher levels of income and output, and (*b*) those into business saving when businesses earn higher profits but do not pay those profits out to individuals.

In addition, a complete model would include one further item of *induced* spending: as Chapter 25 hinted, private investment tends to respond positively as output rises, for businesses tend to spend more on investment to increase capacity at higher levels of output.

These further leakages and induced-spending streams will change the slope of the aggregate spending curve and will also change the economy's multiplier.

rounds of spending and respending generated by an additional dollar of government spending, investment, or exports. For example, say that Germany needs to buy American computers to modernize antiquated facilities in what used to be East Germany. Each extra dollar of U.S. computers will generate $1 of income in the United States, of which $\$\frac{2}{3} = \$0.667$ will be spent by Americans on consumption. However, because the marginal propensity to import is 0.10, one-tenth of the extra dollar of income or $0.10 will be spent on foreign goods and services, leaving only $0.567 of spending on domestically produced goods. That $0.567 of domestic spending will generate $0.567 of U.S. income, from which $0.567 \times (\$0.567) = \$0.321$ will be spent on consumption of domestic goods and services in the next round. Hence the total increase in output, or the **open-economy multiplier,** will be

$$\begin{aligned} \text{Open-economy multiplier} &= 1 + 0.567 + (0.567)^2 + \cdots \\ &= 1 + \left(\tfrac{2}{3} - \tfrac{1}{10}\right) + \left(\tfrac{2}{3} - \tfrac{1}{10}\right)^2 + \cdots \\ &= \frac{1}{1 - \frac{2}{3} + \frac{1}{10}} = \frac{1}{\frac{13}{30}} = 2.3 \end{aligned}$$

This compares with a closed-economy multiplier of $1/(1 - 0.667) = 3$.

Another way of calculating the multiplier is as follows: Recall that the multiplier in our simplest model was $1/MPS$, where MPS = the marginal propensity to save. This result can be extended by noting that the analog to the MPS in an open economy is the *total leakage* per dollar of extra income—the dollars leaking into saving (the MPS) plus the dollars leaking into imports (the MPm). Hence, the open-economy multiplier should be $1/(MPS + MPm) = 1/(0.333 + 0.1) = 1/0.433 = 2.3$. Note that both the leakage analysis and the rounds analysis provide exactly the same answer.

To summarize:

Because a fraction of any income increase leaks into imports in an open economy, the open-economy multiplier is somewhat smaller than that of a closed economy. The exact relationship is

$$\text{Open-economy multiplier} = \frac{1}{MPS + MPm}$$

where MPS = marginal propensity to save and MPm = marginal propensity to import.

The U.S. Trade Deficit and Economic Activity

In a world where nations are increasingly linked by trade and commerce, countries must pay close attention to events abroad. If a country's policies are out of step with those of its trading partners, the roof can fall in, with recession, inflation, or major trade imbalances.

A good example of the influence of trade is shown in Figure 27-10, which depicts one of the major economic events of the last decade—the deterioration of the U.S. net export position during the early 1980s. To get a rough measure of the size of the shift, we can compare 1980 and 1986, years in which the overall utilization of resources was approximately the same. From 1980 to 1986, real net exports in 1982 prices moved from a surplus of $57 billion to a deficit of $130 billion. This decline of $187 billion in real net exports is 6 percent of the average real GNP for this period.

Unless offset by other items, this sharp decline in net exports would exert a severe contractionary effect upon the American economy. The change would be the approximate equivalent of a $187 billion decrease in government spending on goods and services. From 1980 to 1982, the decline in net exports was reinforced by monetary and fiscal policies. The result was a steep decline in U.S. aggregate demand and the deepest recession in 50 years. However, after 1982, the decrease in net exports was counteracted because the federal government budget was shifting in an *expansionary* direction. From 1982 to 1986, the federal government deficit increased by $146 billion. The fiscal expansion, along with a loosening of monetary policies, more than offset the decline in net exports; the economy pulled out of its slump.

This example serves as a warning that international conditions can have a major impact upon domestic economic activity.

How Large Are Multipliers?

In order to understand the impact of fiscal policy or of investment decisions or of changes in foreign trade, economists must be able to estimate the size of fiscal, investment, or foreign-trade multipliers. Just as a physician prescribing a pain-killer must know the effect of different dosages, so an economist must know the quantitative magnitude of expenditure and tax multipliers.

One of the recent developments in economics has been techniques for estimating econometric models of national economies. An *econometric model* is a set of equations, representing the behavior of the economy, that has been estimated using historical data. Early work in this area began with pioneers like Jan Tinbergen of the Netherlands and Lawrence Klein of the University of Pennsylvania—both winners of the Nobel Prize for constructing empirical macroeconomic models. Today, there is an entire industry of econometricians estimating macroeconomic models, determining multipliers, and forecasting the future of the economy.

Estimates of Multipliers. Textbook models give a highly simplified picture of the structure of the macroeconomy. For a more realistic picture of the response of output to changes in government expenditures, economists estimate large-scale econometric models and then perform numerical experiments by calculating the impact of a change in government expenditures on the economy. Such models serve as the basis for policy recommendations.

A recent comprehensive survey of econometric models of the United States provides a representative sample of multiplier estimates. The models surveyed include equations to predict the behavior of all major sectors of the economy (including both monetary and financial sectors, along with investment demand schedules and consumption functions) and they incorporate a full set of links with the rest of the world. In the experiments, the level of real government purchases of goods and services is permanently increased by $1 billion. The models then calculate the impact on real GNP. The change in real GNP resulting from the increase in government spending provides an estimate of the size of the government expenditure multiplier.

Figure 27-12 shows the results of this survey. The heavy blue line shows the average government expenditure multiplier estimated by eight models, while the light gray lines show the range of estimates of the individual models. The average multiplier for the first and second years is around 1.4, but after the second year the multiplier tends to decline slightly as monetary forces and international impacts come into play. (The monetary forces represent the impact of higher GNP on interest rates, which leads to a crowding out of investment, as we will explain in later chapters.)

One interesting feature of these estimates is that the different models (represented by the light gray

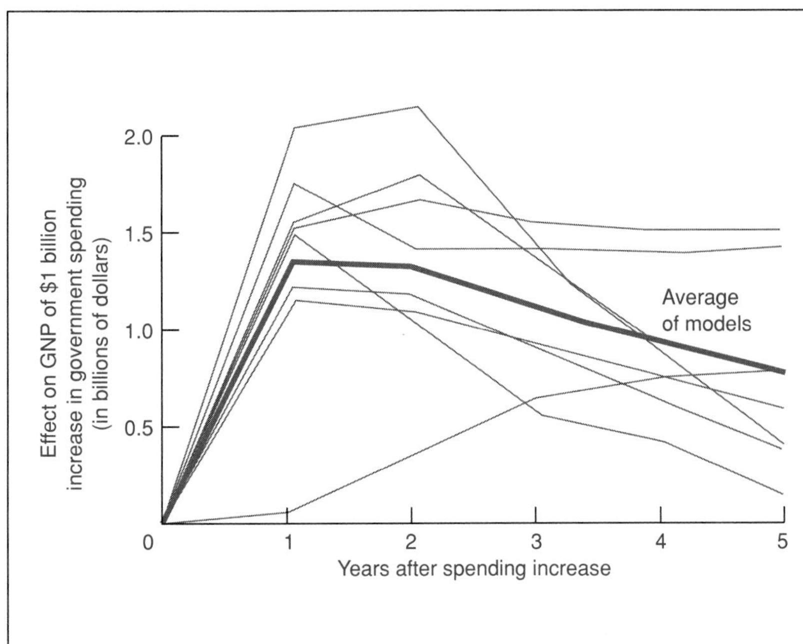

Figure 27-12. Expenditure multipliers in macroeconomic models

A recent study shows the estimated government expenditure multipliers in different macroeconomic models. These experiments show the estimated impact of a permanent $1 billion increase in the real value of government purchases of goods and services on real GNP at different intervals following the spending increase. That is, they show the impact of a $1 billion change in *G* on *Q*. The heavy blue line shows the average multiplier for the different models while the gray lines represent the multipliers for each individual model. [Source: Ralph C. Bryant, Gerald Holtham, and Peter Hooper, "Consensus and Diversity in Model Simulations," in *Empirical Macroeconomics for Interdependent Economies* (Brookings, Washington, D.C., 1988).]

lines in Figure 27-12) show considerable disagreement about the size of multipliers. Why do the estimates differ? To begin with, there is inherent uncertainty about the nature of economic relationships. Of course, uncertainty is the essence of the scientific enterprise, in both natural and social sciences. Research in economics is particularly challenging because economists cannot make controlled experiments in a laboratory. Even more perplexing is the fact that the economy itself evolves over time, so the "correct" model for 1960 is different from the "correct" model for 1990.

In addition, economists have fundamental disagreements about the underlying nature of the macroeconomy. Some economists believe that a classical approach best explains macroeconomic behavior while others are convinced that the Keynesian multiplier approach is the best starting point. Given all these hurdles, it is not surprising that there is no clear consensus about the actual multipliers for the U.S. economy.

Qualifications

We have completed our survey of the most important applications of the Keynesian multiplier model. This approach is an indispensable aid in understanding business fluctuations and the linkage between international trade and national output. It shows how government fiscal policy can be used to fight unemplovment and inflation.

But it would be a mistake to believe you can make a macroeconomist out of a parrot by simply teaching it to say "$C + I + G + X$" or "Polly has a multiplier." Behind such concepts are important assumptions and qualifications.

First, recall that the multiplier model assumes that investment is fixed and prices are inflexible. A more realistic approach takes into account that investment responds to monetary conditions and to the level of output and that prices will rise more rapidly as output and employment increase. Only after we have mastered elements of monetary theory and policy, along with the essentials of inflation analysis, can the full impact of fiscal policy and trade flows be understood. When all these elements of reality are included in the analysis, the multiplier for government purchases, taxes, or foreign trade may be attenuated; in some cases it may even approach zero.

These qualifications will concern us for the rest of the chapters on macroeconomics. We now turn to an analysis of one of the most fascinating parts of all economics, the study of money. Once we understand how the central bank determines the money supply, we will have a fuller appreciation of how governments can tame the business cycles that have run wild through much of the history of capitalism.

SUMMARY

A. The Basic Multiplier Model

1. The multiplier model provides a simple way to understand the impact of aggregate demand on the level of output. In this approach, household consumption is a function of disposable income and investment is fixed. People's desires to consume and the willingness of businesses to invest are brought into line with each other by means of changes in output. The equilibrium level of national output must be at the intersection of savings and investment schedules SS and II. Or, to put it another way, equilibrium output comes at the intersection of the consumption-plus-investment schedule $C + I$ with the 45° line.

2. If output were temporarily above its equilibrium level, businesses would find output higher than sales, with inventories piling up involuntarily and profits plummeting. Firms would therefore cut production and employ-

ment back toward the equilibrium level. The only equilibrium path of output that can be maintained is at the output level where households will voluntarily continue to save exactly as much as businesses will voluntarily continue to invest.

3. Thus for the simplified Keynesian model of this chapter, investment calls the tune, and consumption dances to the music. Investment determines output, while saving responds passively to income changes. Output rises or falls until planned saving has adjusted to the level of planned investment.

4. Investment has a *multiplier effect* on output. When investment changes, output will at first rise by an equal amount. But as the income receivers in the capital-goods industries get more income, they set into motion a whole chain of additional secondary consumption spending and employment.

   If people always spend about $\frac{2}{3}$ of each extra dollar of income on consumption, the total of the multiplier chain will be

$$1 + \tfrac{2}{3} + (\tfrac{2}{3})^2 + \cdots = \frac{1}{1 - \frac{2}{3}} = 3$$

   The multiplier works in either direction, amplifying either increases or decreases in investment. The simplest multiplier is numerically equal to the reciprocal of the *MPS* or, equivalently, to $1/(1 - MPC)$. This result occurs because it always takes more than a dollar of increased income to increase saving by a dollar.

B. Fiscal Policy in the Multiplier Model

5. Ancient societies suffered famines due to harvest failures. The modern market economy can suffer from poverty amidst plenty when business conditions deteriorate and unemployment soars. Or, excessive spending may lead to inflation. But fiscal steps, analyzed here, and monetary policies, studied later, can help smooth out the cycle of boom and bust.

6. The analysis of fiscal policy presented here elaborates the Keynesian multiplier model. For clarity, we assume a world in which prices and wages are inflexible, so that the aggregate supply curve is relatively flat for output levels below potential GNP.

7. An increase in government expenditure—taken by itself with taxes and investment unchanged—has an expansionary effect on national output much like that of investment. The schedule of $C + I + G$ shifts upward to a higher equilibrium intersection with the 45° line.

8. A decrease in taxes—taken by itself with investment and government expenditure unchanged—raises the equilibrium level of national output. The *CC* schedule of consumption plotted against GNP is shifted upward and leftward by a tax cut, but since extra dollars of disposable income go partly into saving, the dollar increase in consumption will not be quite so great as the dollars of new disposable income. Therefore, the tax multiplier is smaller than the government expenditure multiplier.

C. Output Determination in Open Economies

9. An open economy is one that engages in foreign trade, exporting goods to other countries and importing goods produced abroad. The difference between exports and imports of goods and services is called net exports. For most of the twentieth century, the United States had net exports near zero, but in the 1980s net exports moved sharply into deficit.

10. When foreign trade is introduced, domestic demand can differ from national output. Domestic demand comprises consumption, investment, and government purchases ($C + I + G$). To obtain GNP, exports (e) must be added and imports (m) subtracted, so that

$$\text{GNP} = C + I + G + X$$

where X = net exports = $e - m$. Imports are determined by domestic income and output along with the prices of domestic goods relative to those of foreign goods; exports are the mirror image, determined by foreign income and output along with relative prices. The dollar increase of imports for each dollar increase in GNP is called the marginal propensity to import (MPm).

11. Foreign trade has an effect on GNP similar to that of investment or government purchases. As net exports rise, there is an increase in aggregate demand for domestic output. Net exports hence have a multiplier effect on output. But the expenditure multiplier in an open economy will be smaller than that in a closed economy because of leakages from spending into imports. The multiplier is

$$\text{Open-economy multiplier} = \frac{1}{MPS + MPm}$$

where MPS = marginal propensity to save and MPm = marginal propensity to import. Clearly, other things equal, the open-economy multiplier is smaller than the closed-economy multiplier, where $MPm = 0$.

12. Using statistical techniques and macroeconomic models, economists have built realistic models to estimate expenditure multipliers. For mainstream models, these tend to show multipliers of between 1 and $1\frac{1}{2}$ for periods of up to 4 years.

CONCEPTS FOR REVIEW

The basic multiplier model
$C + I$ schedule
two ways of viewing GNP determination:
planned saving = planned investment
planned C + planned I = GNP
investment equals saving: planned vs. actual levels
multiplier effect of investment
multiplier
$= 1 + MPC + (MPC)^2 + \cdots$
$= \dfrac{1}{1 - MPC} = \dfrac{1}{MPS}$

Government expenditures and taxation
fiscal policy:
G effect on equilibrium GNP
T effect on CC and on GNP
multiplier effects of government spending (G) and taxes (T)
$C + I + G$ curve for closed economy

Open-economy macroeconomics
$C + I + G + X$ curve for open economy
net exports $= X = e - m$
domestic demand vs. spending on GNP
marginal propensity to import (*MPm*)
multiplier:
in closed economy $= 1/MPS$
in open economy $= 1/(MPS + MPm)$
impact of trade flows, exchange rates on GNP

QUESTIONS FOR DISCUSSION

1. In the simple multiplier model, assume that investment is always zero. Show that equilibrium output in this special case would come at the break-even point of the consumption function. Why would equilibrium output *not* occur at the break-even point when investment is not zero?
2. The savings-and-investment diagram and the 45° line $C + I$ diagram are two different ways of showing how national output is determined in the multiplier model. Describe each. Show their equivalence.
3. Reconstruct Table 27-2 assuming that net investment is equal to (*a*) \$300 billion, (*b*) \$400 billion. What is the resulting difference in GNP? Is this difference greater or smaller than the change in *I*? Why? When *I* drops from \$200 billion to \$100 billion, how much must GNP drop?
4. Give (*a*) the common sense, (*b*) the arithmetic, (*c*) the geometry of the multiplier. What are the multipliers for $MPC = 0.9$? 0.8? 0.5? For $MPS = 0.1$? 0.8?
5. Work out the explosive(!) chain of spending and respending when $MPC = 2$. Try to explain the economics of the arithmetic of the divergent infinite geometric series.
6. Explain the following concepts: government expenditure multiplier, marginal propensity to consume, marginal propensity to import, open-economy multiplier.
7. Explain in words and using the notion of expenditure rounds why the tax multiplier is smaller than the expenditure multiplier.
8. During most of the 1980s, many political leaders have argued for lowering government deficits. Analyze the impact of lower government purchases of goods and services on the government deficit and on output.
9. Explain why governments might use fiscal policy to stabilize the economy. Why would fiscal policy be effective in raising output in a Keynesian economy but not in a classical economy?
10. Explain the impact upon net exports and GNP of the following, using Table 27-3 where possible:
    (a) An increase in investment (*I*) of \$100 billion
    (b) A decrease in government purchases (*G*) of \$50 billion
    (c) An increase of foreign output which increased exports by \$10 billion
    (d) A depreciation of the exchange rate that raised exports by \$30 billion and lowered imports by \$20 billion at every level of GNP
11. What would the expenditure multiplier be in an economy without government spending or taxes where the *MPC* is 0.80 and where the *MPm* is 0? Where the *MPm* is 0.1? Where the *MPm* is 0.9? Explain why the multiplier might even be less than 1.
12. "Even if the government spends billions on wasteful military armaments, this action can create jobs in a recession and will be socially worthwhile." Discuss.

CHAPTER 28

MONEY AND COMMERCIAL BANKING

Not even love has made so many fools of men
as the pondering over the nature of money.
W. E. Gladstone (1844)

Money is so much a part of our daily lives that we pursue it relentlessly yet seldom stop to consider its vital role as the lubricant of economic activity. This chapter begins our study of monetary economics. We start by looking at the essence of money itself and then discuss the price of money, the interest rate. The second section of this chapter examines the banking system and the supply of money. This will serve as an introduction to the next chapter's analysis of central banking and of the impact of money on overall economic activity. Figure 28-1 shows, using our thematic flow diagram, the topics covered in this chapter.

The study of monetary economics is critical to an understanding of the functioning of a modern market economy and to the way that governments can control output, unemployment, and inflation. When money is well managed, output can grow smoothly with stable prices. But occasionally the monetary mechanism falters, money can grow rapidly or shrink sharply, and inflation or depression will follow on the heels of monetary disruptions. A survey of the world's economic problems today—from the hyperinflations in South America, to the economic turmoil in the Soviet Union, to the savings and loan fiasco in the United States—will usually find that a crisis in the management of money and finance is at the center of the problem.

A. The Essence of Money and Interest Rates

The Evolution of Money

Our modern financial system with currency, checks, automated teller machines, and scores of sophisticated financial instruments did not spring up overnight. It has evolved over centuries. But at the heart of the financial system is money, which is defined as follows:

Money is anything that serves as a commonly accepted medium of exchange or means of payment.

Commodities were the earliest kind of money, but over time money evolved into paper currencies and checking accounts. All these have the same essential quality: they are accepted as payment for goods and services.

Barter. In an early textbook on money, when Stanley Jevons wanted to illustrate the nature of barter, he used the following example:

Some years since, Mademoiselle Zélie, a singer of the Théâtre Lyrique at Paris, . . . gave a concert in the Soci-

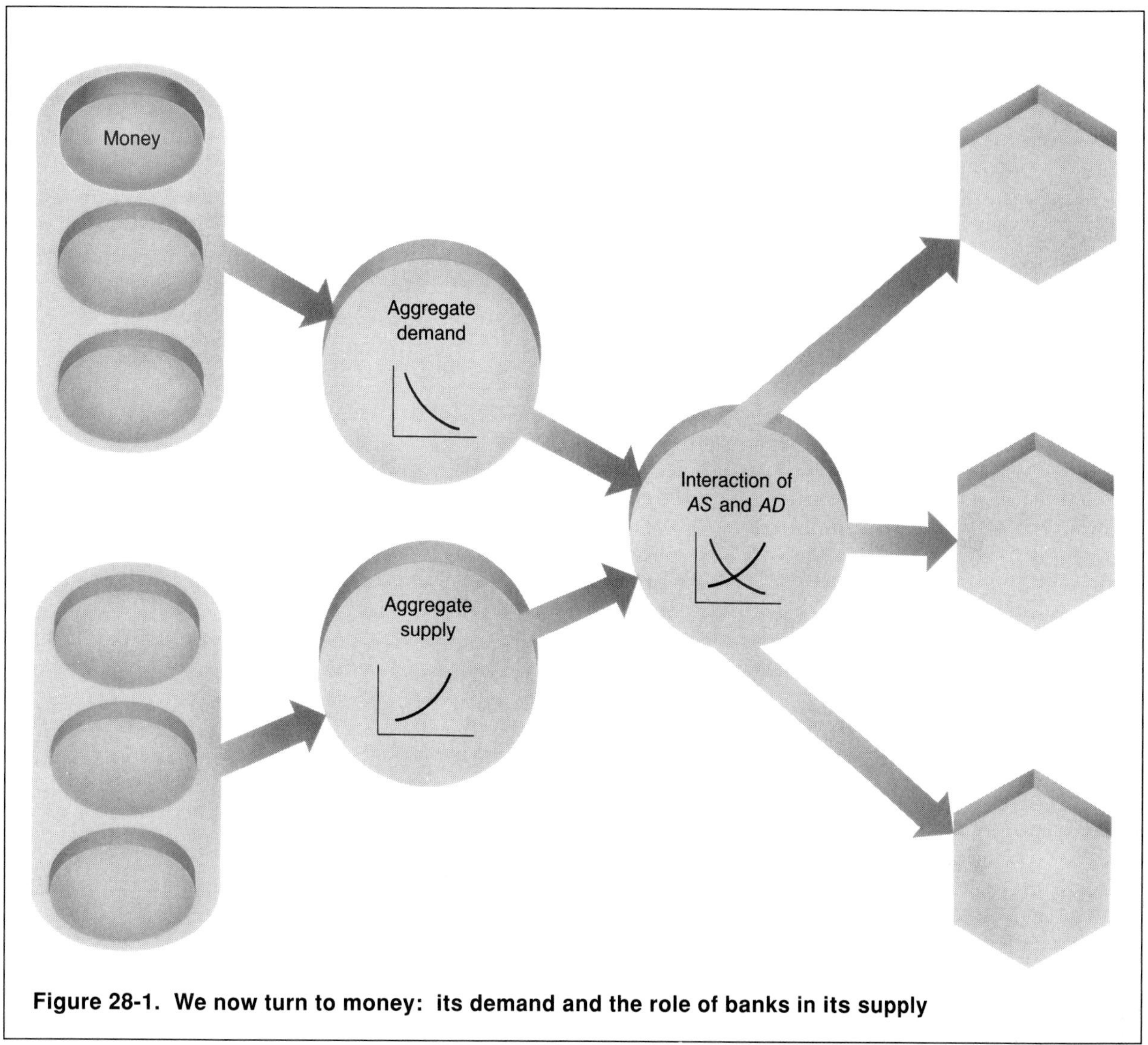

Figure 28-1. We now turn to money: its demand and the role of banks in its supply

ety Islands. In exchange for an air from *Norma* and a few other songs, she was to receive a third part of the receipts. When counted, her share was found to consist of three pigs, twenty-three turkeys, forty-four chickens, five thousand cocoa-nuts, besides considerable quantities of bananas, lemons, and oranges. . . . [I]n Paris . . . this amount of live stock and vegetables might have brought four thousand francs, which would have been good remuneration for five songs. In the Society Islands, however, pieces of money were scarce; and as Mademoiselle could not consume any considerable portion of the receipts herself, it became necessary in the mean time to feed the pigs and poultry with the fruit.

This example describes **barter,** which consists of the exchange of goods for other goods. Barter contrasts with a **monetary economy,** in which the trade takes place through a commonly accepted medium of exchange.

Inconvenient as barter obviously is, as shown by the comical example of exchanging songs for pigs, it actually represents a great step forward from the state of complete self-sufficiency. When each household must make everything it needs, everyone is a jack-of-all-trades and a master of none. Still, barter operates under grave disadvantages because an elaborate division of labor would be unthinkable without the introduction of the great social invention of money.

As economies develop, people do not directly exchange one good for another. Instead, they sell goods for money, and then use money to buy other goods they most wish to have. At first glance this seems to complicate rather than simplify matters, to replace one transaction by two. After all, you have apples and want nuts; would it not be simpler to trade one for the other rather than to sell the apples for money and then use the money to buy nuts?

Actually, the reverse is true: two monetary transactions are simpler than one barter transaction. For example, some people may want to buy apples, and some may want to sell nuts. But it would be a most unusual circumstance to find a person with trading desires that exactly complement your own—eager to sell nuts and buy apples. To use a classical economic phrase, instead of there being a "double coincidence of wants," there is likely to be a "want of coincidence." So, unless a hungry tailor happens to find an undraped farmer who has both food and a desire for a pair of pants, under barter neither can make a direct trade.

Societies that traded extensively simply could not overcome the overwhelming handicaps of barter. The use of a commonly accepted medium of exchange, money, permitted the farmer to buy pants from the tailor, who buys shoes from the cobbler, who buys leather from the farmer.

Commodity Money. Money as a medium of exchange first came into human history in the form of commodities. A great variety of items have served as money at one time or another: cattle, olive oil, beer or wine, copper, iron, gold, silver, rings, diamonds, and cigarettes.

Each of the above has advantages and disadvantages. Cattle are not divisible into small change. Beer does not improve with keeping, although wine may. Olive oil provides a nice liquid currency that is as minutely divisible as one wishes, but it is a bit messy to handle. And so forth.

By the nineteenth century, commodity money was almost exclusively limited to metals like silver and gold. These forms of money had *intrinsic value,* denoting that they had use value in themselves. Because money had intrinsic value, there was no need for the government to guarantee its value, and the quantity of money was regulated by the market through the supply and demand for gold or silver. The disadvantages of metallic money are that scarce resources are required to dig it out of the ground and that it might become scarce or abundant simply because of accidental discoveries of ore deposits.

The advent of monetary control by central banks has led to a much more stable currency system. The intrinsic value of money is now the least important thing about it.

Paper Money. The age of commodity money gave way to the age of paper money. The essence of money is now laid bare. Money is wanted not for its own sake but for the things it will buy. We do not wish to consume money directly; rather we use it by getting rid of it. Even when we choose to keep money, its value comes from the fact that we can spend it later on.

The use of paper currency has become widespread because it is a convenient medium of exchange. Currency is easily carried and stored. With careful engraving, the value of money can be protected from counterfeiting. The fact that private individuals cannot legally create money keeps it scarce.

Given this limitation in supply, currency has value. It can buy things. As long as people can pay their bills with currency, as long as it is accepted as a means of payment, it serves the function of money.

Bank Money. Today is the age of bank money—checks written on funds deposited in a bank or other financial institution. Checks are accepted in place of cash payment for many goods and services. In fact, if we calculate the total dollar amount of transactions, nine-tenths take place by bank money, the rest by currency.

Continued Evolution. Today there is extremely rapid innovation in the different forms of money. For example, some financial institutions will now link a checking account to a savings account or even to a stock portfolio, allowing customers to write checks on the value of their stock. Credit cards and traveler's checks can be used for many transactions. The fast-changing nature of money causes difficult problems for central banks, which are charged with measuring and controlling the nation's money supply.

Components of the Money Supply

Let us now look more carefully at the different kinds of money that Americans employ. The major *monetary aggregates* are the quantitative measures of the supply of money. They are known today as M_1 and M_2, and you can read about their week-to-week movements in the newspaper, along with sage commentaries on the significance of the latest wiggle. Here we will delve into the exact definitions as of 1991.

Transactions Money. One important and closely watched measure of money is *transactions money,* or M_1, which consists of items that are actually used for transactions. The following are the components of M_1:

- *Coins.* M_1 includes coins not held by banks.
- *Paper currency.* More significant is *paper currency.* Most of us know little more about a \$1 or \$5 bill than that it is inscribed with the picture of an American statesman, that it bears some official signatures, and that each has a numeral showing its face value.

  Examine a \$10 bill or some other paper bill. You will probably find it says "Federal Reserve Note." Also, it announces itself as "legal tender for all debts, public and private." But what "backs" our paper currency? Many years ago, paper money was backed by gold or silver. There is no such pretense today. Today, all U.S. coins and paper currency are *fiat money.* This term signifies that something is money because the government decrees it is money. More precisely, the government states that coins and paper currency are *legal tender,* which must be accepted for all debts, public and private.

  Coins and paper currency (the sum known as "currency") add up to about one-fourth of total transactions money, M_1.
- *Checking accounts.* There is a third component of transactions money—checking deposits or bank money. These are funds, deposited in banks and other financial institutions, that you can write checks on. These are technically known as "demand deposits and other checkable deposits."[1]

  If I have \$1000 in my checking account at the Albuquerque National Bank, that deposit can be regarded as money. Why? For the simple reason that I can pay for purchases with checks drawn on it. The deposit is like any other medium of exchange. Possessing the essential properties of money, bank checking-account deposits are counted as transactions money, as part of M_1.

Table 28-1 shows the dollar values of the different components of transactions money, M_1.

Broad Money. Although M_1 is strictly speaking the most appropriate measure of money as a means of payment, a second closely watched aggregate is *broad money,* or M_2. Sometimes called "asset money" or "near-money," M_2 includes M_1 as well as savings accounts in banks and similar assets that are very close substitutes for transactions money.

Examples of such near-monies in M_2 include deposits in a savings account in your bank; a money market mutual fund account operated by your stockbroker; a deposit in a money market deposit account run by a commercial bank. And so on.

Why are these not transactions money? Because they cannot be used as means of exchange for all purchases; they are forms of near-money, however, because you can convert them into cash very quickly with no loss of value.

Over the last decade, M_2 has been a useful indicator of trends in money-supply growth. It showed

[1] Until the late 1970s, virtually all checking accounts were "demand deposits" at commercial banks and earned no interest. Under the pressure of advancing technology and high interest rates, the sharp difference between demand deposits and other assets gradually eroded. In 1980 and 1982, Congress passed laws allowing other financial institutions to offer checking accounts (called "negotiable orders of withdrawal," or NOW accounts), and allowed payment of interest on checking accounts. By the late 1980s, interest-rate ceilings on almost all assets were removed. The result of this dismantling of regulatory restrictions between different institutions and assets is a blurring of the distinction between money and other financial assets. One of the side effects of the deregulated financial markets was the savings and loan fiasco of the late 1980s and early 1990s.

Kinds of money	Billions of dollars 1959	1971	1990
Currency (outside of financial institutions)	28.8	52.0	245.9
Demand deposits (excludes government deposits and certain foreign deposits)	110.8	175.1	277.5
NOW accounts and other checkable deposits	0.4	1.3	302.1
Total transactions money (M_1)	**140.0**	**228.4**	**825.5**
Savings accounts and small time deposits (includes money market funds)	157.8	484.3	2,497.8
Broad money (M_2)	**297.8**	**712.7**	**3,323.3**

Table 28-1. Components of the money supply of the United States

Two widely used definitions of the money supply are transactions money (M_1) and broad money (M_2). M_1 consists of currency and checking accounts. M_2 adds to these certain "near-monies" such as savings accounts and time deposits. (Source: Federal Reserve Board.)

greater stability than M_1, because when new kinds of checking accounts were introduced in the 1980s, M_1 behaved very erratically. At that time M_2 proved to be a better barometer of economic activity.

There are many other technical definitions of money that are used by specialists in monetary economics. But for our purposes, we need master only the two major definitions of money.

The major monetary concept is **transactions money,** or M_1, which is the sum of coins and paper currency in circulation outside the banks, plus checkable deposits. Less often we will also refer to **broad money** (called M_2), which includes assets such as savings accounts in addition to coins, paper currency, and checkable deposits.

The Nature of Interest Rates

In analyzing the supply and demand for money in later sections, we will need to consider the price of money, which is the interest rate:

Interest is the payment made for the use of money. The **interest rate** is the amount of interest paid per unit of time. In other words, people must pay for the opportunity to borrow money. The cost of borrowing money, measured in dollars per year per dollar borrowed, is the interest rate.

Some examples will illustrate how interest works.

- When you graduate from college you have $500 to your name. You decide to keep it in currency. If you spend none of your funds, at the end of a year you still have $500 because currency has a zero interest rate.
- You place $2000 in a savings account in your local bank, where the interest rate on savings accounts is 5 percent per year. At the end of 1 year, the bank will have paid $100 in interest into your account, so the account is now worth $2100.
- You start your first job and decide to buy a $10,000 car. You will be able to pay for it in a year. Your employer offers you a short-term loan at 12 percent per year. The loan requires you to pay interest of $100 per month (or $1200 per year) and repay the principal of $10,000 at the end of the year.
- After a few months in your new job, you find a small house to purchase and settle on a price of $100,000. You go to your local bank and find that 30-year, fixed-interest-rate mortgages have an interest rate of 10 percent per year. Each month you make a mortgage payment of $877.58. Note that this payment is a little bit more than the prorated monthly interest charge of $\frac{10}{12}$ percent per month. Why? Because it includes not only interest but also *amortization*. This is repayments of *principal*, the amount borrowed. By the time you have made your 360 monthly payments, you will have completely paid off the loan.

Fro n these examples we see that interest rates have the dimension of a pure number, in percent per year. Interest is the price paid to borrow money, which allows the borrower to obtain real resources over the time of the loan.

An Array of Interest Rates

Textbooks often speak of "*the* interest rate," but a glance at a newspaper like the *Wall Street Journal* reveals a bewildering array of interest rates in today's complex financial system. Interest rates differ mainly in terms of the characteristics of the loan or of the borrower. Let us review the major differences.

1. *Term or maturity*. Loans differ in their term or maturity—the length of time until they must be paid off. The shortest loans are overnight. For example, a bank may lend funds to a firm that is expecting payment the next day. Short-term securities are for periods up to a year. Companies often issue bonds that have maturities of 10 to 30 years, and mortgages are typically up to 30 years in maturity. Longer-term securities generally command a higher interest rate than do short-term issues because people are willing to sacrifice quick access to their funds only if they can increase their yield.
2. *Risk*. Some loans are virtually riskless while others are highly speculative. Investors require that a premium be paid when they invest in risky ventures. At the safe end of the spectrum lie the securities of the U.S. government. These bonds and bills are backed by the full faith, credit, and taxing powers of the government. These items are safe because interest on the government debt will almost certainly be paid. Intermediate in risk are borrowings of creditworthy corporations, states, and localities. Risky investments, which bear a significant chance of default or nonpayment, include those in companies close to bankruptcy, cities with shrinking tax bases, or Latin American countries with large overseas debts and little import income.

   The U.S. government pays what is called the "riskless" interest rate; over the last decade this has ranged from 5 to 15 percent per year for short-term loans. Riskier securities might pay 1, 2, or 5 percent per year more than the riskless rate; this premium reflects the amount necessary to compensate the lender for losses in case of default.
3. *Liquidity*. An asset is said to be "liquid" if it can be converted into cash quickly and with little loss in value. Most marketable securities, including common stocks and corporate and government bonds, can be turned into cash quickly for close to their current value. Illiquid assets include unique assets for which no well-established market exists. For example, if you own a house in a depressed region, you might find it difficult to sell the house quickly or at a price near its replacement cost. Similarly, it might be difficult to cash in on the full value of a small, privately owned company. The house and the small company are illiquid assets. Because of the higher risk and the difficulty of extracting the borrower's investment, illiquid assets or loans usually command considerably higher interest rates than do liquid, riskless ones.
4. *Administrative costs*. Loans differ in terms of the time and diligence needed for their oversight and administration. Some loans simply require cashing interest checks periodically. Others, such as student loans, mortgages, or credit-card advances, require ensuring timely payments. Sometimes lenders hire detectives and lawyers to track down debtors. Loans with high administrative costs may command interest rates from 5 to 10 percent per year higher than other interest rates.

When these four factors are put together, it is not surprising that we see so many different financial instruments and so many different interest rates. Figure 28-2 shows the behavior of a few important interest rates over the last three decades. In the discussion that follows, when we speak of "the interest rate" we are referring to the interest rate on short-term government securities, such as the 90-day Treasury-bill rate. As Figure 28-2 shows, most other interest rates rise and fall in step with the 3-month Treasury-bill rate.

Real vs. Nominal Interest Rates

Interest is measured in dollar terms, not in terms of fish or cars or goods in general. The *nominal interest rate* measures the yield in dollars per year per dollar invested. But dollars can become distorted yardsticks. The prices of fish, or cars, and goods in general change from year to year—these days prices generally rise due to inflation. Put differently, the interest rate on dollars does not measure what a lender really earns in terms of goods and services. Let us say that you lend $100 today at 5 percent per

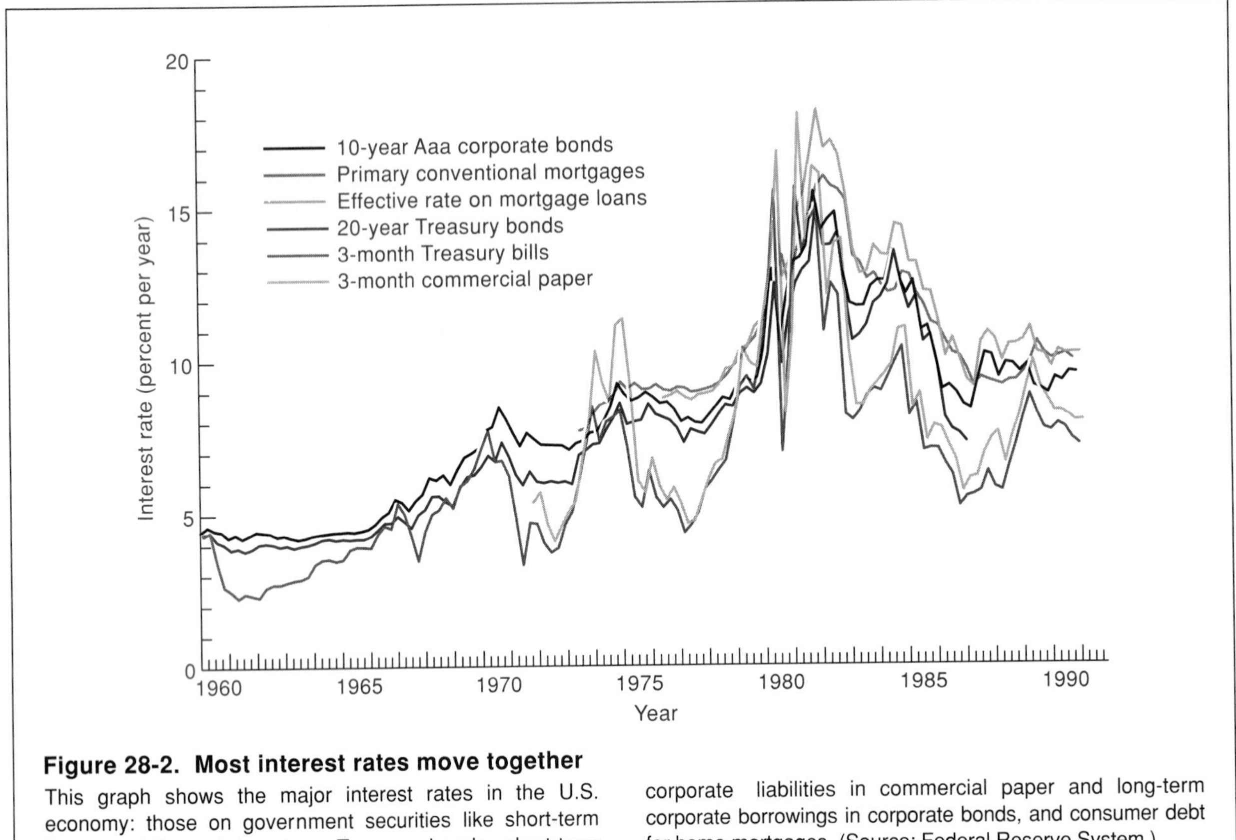

Figure 28-2. Most interest rates move together

This graph shows the major interest rates in the U.S. economy: those on government securities like short-term Treasury bills and long-term Treasury bonds, short-term corporate liabilities in commercial paper and long-term corporate borrowings in corporate bonds, and consumer debt for home mortgages. (Source: Federal Reserve System.)

year interest. You would get back $105 at the end of a year. But because prices changed over the year, you would not be able to obtain the same quantity of goods that you could have bought at the beginning of the year with the original $100.

Clearly, we need another concept of interest that measures the return on investments in terms of real goods and services rather than the return in terms of dollars. This alternative concept is the *real interest rate,* which measures the quantity of goods we get tomorrow for goods forgone today. The real interest rate is obtained by correcting nominal or dollar interest rates for the rate of inflation.

The **nominal interest rate** (sometimes also called the "money interest rate") is the interest rate on money in terms of money. When you read about interest rates in the newspaper, or examine the interest rates in Figure 28-2, you are looking at nominal interest rates; they give the dollar return per dollar of investment.

In contrast, **real interest rates** are corrected for inflation and are defined as the nominal interest rate minus the rate of inflation. As an example, suppose the nominal interest rate is 13 percent per year and the inflation rate is 7 percent per year; we can calculate the real interest rate as $13 - 7 = 6$ percent per year. In other words, if you lend out 100 market baskets of goods today, you will next year get back only 106 (and not 113) market baskets of goods as principal and real interest payments.

During inflationary periods, we must use real interest rates, not nominal or money interest rates, to calculate the yield on investments in terms of goods earned per year on goods invested. The real interest rate is the nominal interest rate less the rate of inflation.

Recent Interest-Rate Movements. The difference between nominal and real interest rates is illustrated in Figure 28-3. It shows that most of the rise in nominal interest rates from 1960 to 1980 was purely illusory, for nominal interest rates were just keeping up with inflation during those years. After 1980, however, real interest rates rose sharply.

What was the reason for the jump in real interest rates? Most macroeconomists believe that the real interest rates increased because the Federal Reserve tightened monetary policy in reaction to the high inflation of that period. (The next chapter will illustrate the mechanism by which this tightening occurs.)

The Demand for Money

The demand for money is different from the demand for ice cream or movies. Money is not desired for its own sake; you cannot eat nickels, and we seldom hang $100 bills on the wall for the artistic quality of their engraving. Rather, money is held because it serves us indirectly, as a lubricant to trade and exchange. The need to hold money to buy things is the essence of the demand for money.

Money's Functions

Before we analyze the demand for money, let's review money's functions.

1. By far the most important function of money is to serve as a *medium of exchange.* Without money we would be constantly roving around

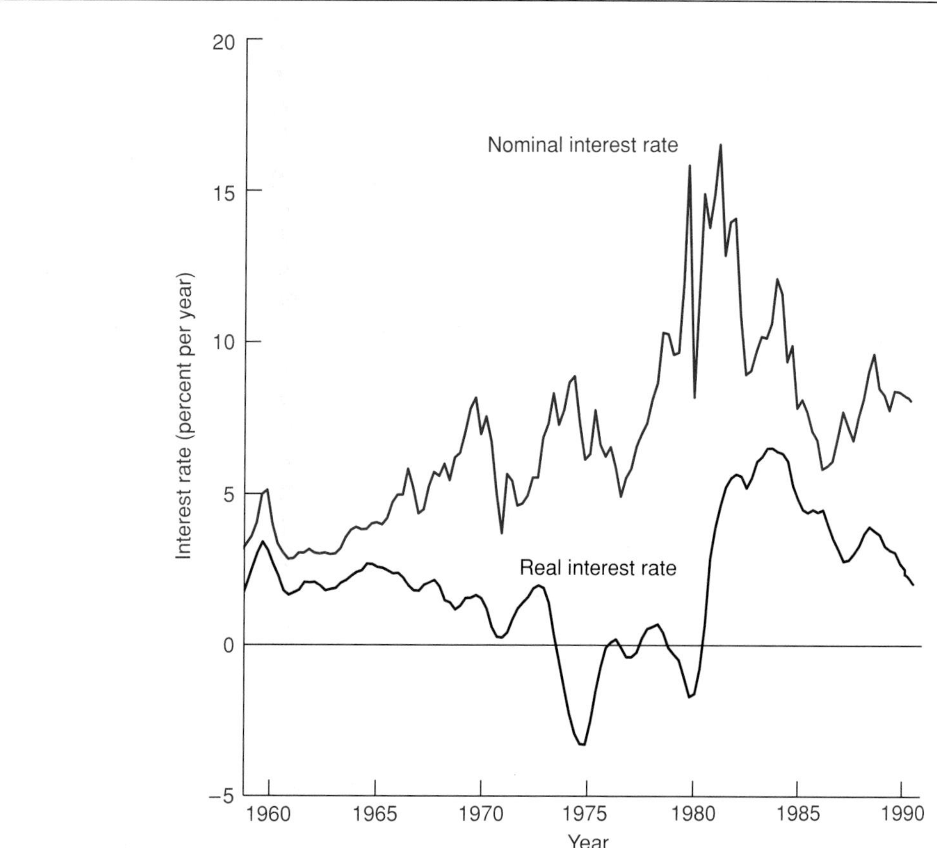

Figure 28-3. Real vs. nominal interest rates

This figure shows in blue the nominal interest rates on safe short-term securities (1-year Treasury notes). Note their upward trend over the last 25 years. Most of the upward movement can be seen as the reflection of the increase in inflation. The black curve shows the real interest rate, equal to the nominal or money rate less the realized inflation rate over the prior year. Note that real interest rates drifted downward until 1980. After 1980, however, real interest rates moved up sharply. (Source: Federal Reserve Board, U.S. Department of Labor.)

looking for someone to barter with. We are often reminded of money's utility when it does not work properly, as in the Soviet Union in the early 1990s, when people spent hours in line waiting for goods and tried to get dollars or other foreign currencies because the ruble ceased functioning as an acceptable means of exchange.

2. Money is also used as the *unit of account,* the unit by which we measure the *value* of things. Just as we measure weight in kilograms, we measure value in money. The use of a common unit of account simplifies economic life enormously.
3. Money is sometimes used as a *store of value;* it allows value to be held over time. In comparison with risky assets like stocks or real estate or gold, money is relatively riskless. In earlier days, people held currency as a safe form of wealth. Today, more and more people are holding high-yield money (such as NOW accounts) as a safe asset. But the vast preponderance of wealth is held in other assets, such as savings accounts, stocks, bonds, and real estate.

The Costs of Holding Money

These three functions of money are extremely important to people, so important that they are willing to incur a cost to hold currency or low-yielding checking accounts. What is the *cost of holding money?* It is the sacrifice in interest that you must incur by holding money rather than a riskier, less liquid asset or investment.

Say that you put \$1000 in a savings account at the beginning of 1990; you would earn about 8 percent interest and would end with \$1080 at the end of 1990. This represents an 8 percent money or nominal interest rate. By contrast, suppose that you had left your \$1000 in currency rather than in the money fund for 1990. You would end up with only \$1000, for currency pays no interest. The cost of holding money as currency in this case would be \$80.

Money allows easy and quick transactions, unambiguous determination of price, plus storage of value over time. These services are not free, however. If wealth were held in stocks, bonds, or savings accounts rather than money, it would yield a higher interest rate.

Let's consider yet another example. You have \$1000 in your checking account, or bank money (M_1). The bank pays 5 percent per year on your checking account, or \$50 per year. Alternatively, you can earn 8 percent in a savings account. Thus the net cost (or opportunity cost) of keeping your \$1000 in bank money is \$30 (= \$80 − \$50).

Why might you sacrifice the \$30? Because it is worthwhile to keep the money in your checking account to pay for food or a new bike. You are getting "money services" that are worth at least \$30 a year.

Two Sources of Money Demand

Transactions Demand. People and firms use money as a medium of exchange: households need money to buy groceries, and firms need money to pay for materials and labor. These needs constitute the *transactions demand for money.*

Figure 28-4 illustrates the mechanics of the transactions demand for money. This figure shows the average money holdings of a family that earns \$3000 per month, keeps it in money, and spends it during the month. Calculation will show that the family holds \$1500 on average in money balances.

This example can help us see how the demand for money responds to different economic influences. If all prices and incomes double, then the vertical axis in Figure 28-4 is simply relabeled by doubling all the dollar values. Clearly the nominal demand for M doubles. Thus the transactions demand for money doubles if nominal GNP doubles with no change in real GNP or other real variables.

An extremely important question is, How does the demand for money vary with interest rates? Recall that our family is paying an opportunity cost for its checking account—the interest rate on M is less than that on other assets. As interest rates rise, the family might say:

> Let's put only half of our money in the checking account at the beginning of the month, and put the other half in a savings account earning 8 percent per annum. Then on day 15, we'll take that \$1500 out of the money fund and put it in our checking account to pay the next 2 weeks' bills.

Note the net effect: As interest rates rose, and the family decided to put half its earnings in a savings account, the average money balance of our family fell from \$1500 to \$750. This shows how money holdings (or the demand for money) may be sensi-

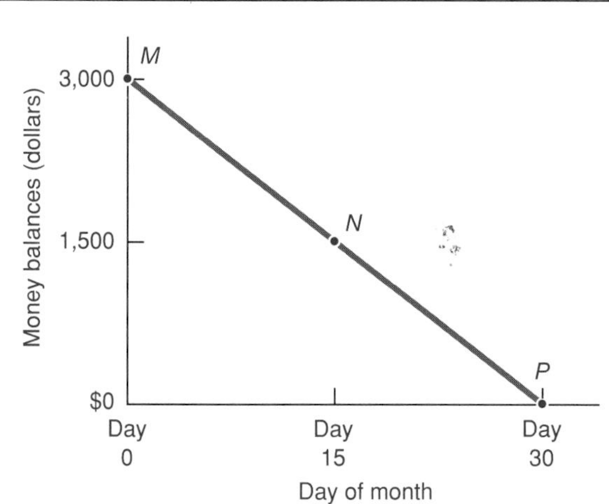

Figure 28-4. The transactions demand for money

How much money might a typical family hold? Assume that the family is paid $3000 at the beginning of the month, and spends the whole amount over the course of the month at a constant rate of $100 per day. Moreover, the family does not put any of its money in another asset during the month. Thus the family has $3000 on day 0, $1500 on day 15, and nothing at the end of the month. This is illustrated by the line *MNP*.

How much money does the family hold on average? Answer: $\frac{1}{2}$ of $3000 = $1500.

To understand the way the demand for money behaves, consider how this figure would change if all prices and incomes doubled. If real incomes doubled. If interest rates on savings accounts went to 20 percent.

tive to interest rates: *other things equal, as interest rates rise, the quantity of money demanded declines.*

You might think that the economic gain from a constant reshuffling of portfolios is so small that household money holdings are not likely to be affected by interest-rate fluctuations. Average bank balances change very little when people find they can earn 2 or 4 percent more on their money funds.

In fact, the major impact of interest rates on the demand for money comes in the business sector. Firms often find themselves with bank balances of $100 million one day, $250 million the next day, and so forth. If they do nothing, they could easily lose $20 to $50 million a year in interest payments. Since the 1970s the era of high interest rates has ushered in corporate "cash management," in which banks help their corporate customers keep their cash constantly invested in high-yield assets rather than lying fallow in zero-yield checking accounts. And with higher interest rates, corporations work a little harder to keep their cash balances at a minimum.

Asset Demand. In addition to holding money for transactions needs, people may also hold money as a store of value. As we noted in the discussion of consumption in Chapter 25, people save for retirement, for hard times, and for their children's educations. At the end of 1988, households owned about $12 trillion of financial assets of various kinds. Shouldn't money be one of these assets?

One of the most important topics of modern economics is **portfolio theory,** which describes how rational investors put their wealth into a "portfolio" (or group of securities). For example, your portfolio might consist of $10,000 worth of Treasury bonds, $5000 in a money market fund, and $14,000 in the stock market.

Portfolio theory begins with the fundamental assumption that people seek high returns on their investments but are averse to risky investments. In other words, people will generally hold risky investments only if their returns are sufficiently high. (*Returns* consist of the annual return per dollar of investment.) Given two assets with equal returns, people seek the safer investment. To draw people away from low-risk assets into risky stocks or real estate, the high-risk asset must offer a higher return.

Portfolio theory analyzes how a risk-averse investor should allocate wealth. One important rule is to diversify the portfolio among different assets. "Don't put all your eggs in one basket" is one way of expressing this rule.

In addition, advanced studies of portfolio theory show that an optimal portfolio would generally contain a mixture of low-risk and high-risk assets. The low-risk assets might well include interest-bearing checking accounts. We should not be surprised, therefore, that in today's world many households will hold money as part of their strategy for investing their wealth and not only for transactions purposes.

What of the rest of the portfolio? Calculations show (as we will see in this chapter's appendix) that by diversifying their wealth among a broad group of investments—different common stocks, different kinds of bonds, perhaps real estate—

people can attain a good return on their wealth without incurring unacceptable risks.*

We summarize as follows:

The demand for money is grounded in the need for a medium of exchange, the transactions demand. We hold currency and checking accounts to buy goods and pay our bills. As our incomes rise, the value of the goods we buy goes up, and we therefore need more money for transactions, raising our demand for money.

The transactions demand for M will be sensitive to the cost of holding money. When interest rates on alternative assets rise relative to the interest rate on money, people and businesses tend to reduce their money holdings.

In addition, people sometimes hold money as an asset. They want to protect some of their wealth against the vicissitudes of economic life, avoiding the folly of putting all their eggs in one basket. And one basket that many investors will want to use is that of an ultra-safe asset. This asset may be a high-yield checking account, part of M_1, or it may be a near-money in M_2, perhaps a savings account or a money fund.

B. Banking and the Supply of Money

Section A showed that transactions money, M_1, has two major components: currency and checking accounts. To understand the way that money affects the economy, we need to master the process by which money is created. We begin by surveying some historical and institutional aspects of commercial banking. We will then analyze the process by which banks "create" money.

Banking as a Business

Bank money and many other financial services are today provided by financial intermediaries. **Financial intermediaries** are institutions like banks, insurance companies, and a dwindling number of savings and loan associations that take deposits or funds from one group and lend these funds to another group. For example, financial intermediaries accept savings deposits from households or firms or foreigners. They then lend these funds to households and businesses for a variety of purposes.

What are the major financial intermediaries today? The largest class consists of commercial banks, which are financial institutions in which most of the nation's checkable deposits are housed; these banks have about 30 percent of the assets of financial institutions. Savings and loan associations and mutual savings banks rank second, with about 17 percent of the assets. Other important groups are life-insurance companies, pension funds, and money market mutual funds. Altogether, at the end of 1988, all such firms had a total of $9.7 trillion of assets and liabilities.

In what follows we will focus on commercial banks, or "banks" for short. We do so because these institutions are still the main source of checking accounts, or the bank-money component of M_1.

In summary:

Financial institutions transfer funds from lenders to borrowers. In doing this, they create financial instruments (like checking and savings accounts).

*The theory of portfolio choice is at the center of one of the most exciting and popular fields of intermediate economics: money and banking. This analysis uses a framework similar to that of the utility theory of Chapter 6. It assumes that people like high yields on assets but dislike risky assets. Work of Nobel-laureates Harry Markowitz and James Tobin showed that utility-maximizing consumers would spread their wealth (i.e., diversify their portfolios) among many different risky assets.

This line of research has become extremely important in modern finance theory and takes its modern form in the "capital asset pricing model," for which William Sharpe won the 1990 Nobel Prize in economics. Every good portfolio manager on Wall Street uses these techniques to bolster his or her intuition in choosing stocks and bonds.

For his contribution to portfolio theory and other aspects of monetary and macroeconomic theory, Tobin was awarded the Nobel Prize in economics in 1981.

Balance Sheet of All Commercial Banking Institutions, 1991
(Billions of Dollars)

Assets		Liabilities	
Reserves	$ 54	Checking accounts	$ 602
Loans	2,259	Savings and time deposits	1,780
Investments and securities	628	Other liabilities	998
Other assets	439		
Total	$3,380	Total	$3,380

Table 28-2. Reserves and checking deposits are major balance sheet entries of commercial banks

Reserves and checking accounts are key to bank creation of money. Checking accounts are payable on demand and thus can be drawn on quickly when customers write checks. Reserves are large primarily to meet legal requirements, not to provide against possible unexpected withdrawals. [Source: *Federal Reserve Bulletin* (June 1991).]

But from a macroeconomic vantage point the most important instrument is bank money (or checking accounts) primarily provided today by commercial banks.

A Business Venture

Banks and other financial intermediaries are much like other businesses. They are organized to earn profits for their owners. A commercial bank is a relatively simple business concern. It provides certain services for customers and in return receives payments from them.

Table 28-2 shows the consolidated balance sheet of all U.S. commercial banks. A *balance sheet* is a statement of a firm's financial position at a point in time. It lists *assets* (items that a firm owns) and *liabilities* (items the firm owes). The difference between assets and liabilities is called *net worth*. Each entry in a balance sheet is valued at its actual market value or its historical cost.[2]

Except for minor rearrangements, a bank's balance sheet looks much like the balance sheet of any business. The unique feature of the bank balance sheet is an item called "reserves," which appears on the asset side. **Reserves** are funds or assets banks hold in the form of cash on hand or of funds deposited by the bank with the central bank. A small fraction of reserves is for day-to-day business needs, but the bulk is held to meet legal reserve requirements.

[2] Balance sheets, assets, and liabilities are extensively discussed in Chapter 8.

How Banks Developed from Goldsmith Establishments

Commercial banking in England began with the goldsmiths, who developed the practice of storing people's gold and valuables for safekeeping. At first, such establishments were simply like baggage checkrooms or warehouses. Depositors left gold for safekeeping and were given a receipt. Later they presented their receipt, paid a small fee for the safekeeping, and got back their gold.

The goldsmiths soon found it more convenient not to worry about returning exactly the same piece of gold that each customer had left. Customers were quite willing to accept any gold as long as it was equivalent in value to what they had deposited. This "anonymity" was important for it freed goldsmiths to relend the gold.

What would balance sheets of a typical goldsmith establishment look like? Perhaps like Table 28-3. We assume that First Goldsmith Bank no longer hammers gold bars but is occupied solely with storing people's money for safekeeping. A total of $1 million has been deposited in its vaults, and this whole sum is held as a cash asset (this is the item "cash reserves" in the balance sheet). To balance this asset, there is a demand deposit of the same amount. Cash reserves are therefore 100 percent of deposits.

Goldsmith Balance Sheet			
Assets		**Liabilities**	
Cash reserves	$1,000,000	Demand deposits	$1,000,000
Total	$1,000,000	Total	$1,000,000

Table 28-3. First Goldsmith Bank held 100 percent cash reserves against demand deposits

In a primitive banking system, with 100 percent backing of demand deposits, no creation of money out of new reserves is possible.

The bank money would just offset the amount of ordinary money (gold or currency) placed in the bank's safe and withdrawn from active circulation. No money creation has taken place. The process would be of no more interest than if the public decided to convert nickels into dimes. We say that a 100 percent reserve banking system has a neutral effect on money, spending, and prices—not adding or subtracting from total *M*.

Modern Fractional-Reserve Banking

As profit maximizers, the goldsmith-bankers recognized that, although deposits are payable on demand, they are not all withdrawn together. Reserves equal to total deposits are necessary if all depositors suddenly had to be paid off in full at the same time, but this almost never occurred. On a given day, some people make withdrawals while others make deposits. These two kinds of transactions generally balanced out.

Funds held as reserves are sterile—sitting in a vault they do not earn interest. Early banks hit upon the idea of using the money entrusted to them to buy bonds or other earning assets. They soon found that investing their deposits was beneficial because depositors could still be paid on demand while the bank could make some extra earnings.

By putting most of the money deposited with them in earning assets and keeping only *fractional* cash reserves against deposits, banks maximize their profits. With these profits they can provide extra services or lower fees to depositors.

The decision to hold fractional rather than 100 percent reserves against deposits was revolutionary. It enabled banks to create money. That is, banks could turn 1 dollar of reserves into several dollars of deposits. In the next section we will see how this process works.

Legal Reserve Requirements

In banking, reserves are that part of a bank's assets held either as cash on hand or as deposits with the central bank. A prudent banker, concerned only with assuring customers that the bank has enough cash for daily transactions, might choose to keep 1 or 2 percent of the bank's assets in reserves. In fact, banks today set aside more than 10 percent of their checking deposits in reserves. These are held in deposits with our central bank, the Federal Reserve System, often called "the Fed."

Why are reserves in fact so high? All financial institutions are required by law and Federal Reserve regulations to keep a fraction of their deposits as reserves. Reserve requirements apply to all types of checking and savings deposits, independent of the actual need for cash on hand.

The regulatory structure that determines the legal reserve requirements is explored in the next chapter. The key point here is the following:

The main function of legal reserve requirements is to enable the Federal Reserve to control the amount of checking deposits that banks can create. By imposing high fixed legal reserve requirements, the Fed can better control the money supply.

The Process of Deposit Creation

In our simplified discussion of goldsmith banks, we suggested that banks turn reserves into bank money. There are, in fact, two steps in the process:

- The central bank (the Fed) determines the quantity of reserves of the banking system. The detailed process by which the central bank does this is discussed in the next chapter.
- Using those reserves as an input, the banking system transforms them into a much larger amount of bank money. The currency plus this bank money then is the money supply, M_1. This process is called the *multiple expansion of bank deposits.*

How Deposits Are Created: First-Generation Banks

Let us consider what happens when new reserves are injected into the banking system. Assume that the Federal Reserve buys a $1000 government bond from Ms. Bondholder, and she deposits the $1000 in her checking account at Bank 1.

The change in the balance sheet of Bank 1, as far as the new demand deposit is concerned, is shown in Table 28-4(*a*).[3] When Ms. Bondholder made the deposit, $1000 of bank money, or checking deposits, was created. Now, if the bank were to keep 100 percent of deposits in reserves, like the old goldsmiths, no extra money would be created from the new deposit of $1000. The depositor's $1000 checking deposit would just match the $1000 of reserves. But modern banks do not keep 100 percent reserves for their deposits. In our example we will assume a reserve requirement of 10 percent, for simplicity of calculations. Therefore Bank 1 must set aside as reserves $100 of the $1000 deposit.

What can Bank 1 now do? It has $900 more in reserves than it needs to meet the reserve requirement. Because reserves earn no interest, our profit-minded bank will loan or invest the excess $900. The loan might be for a car, or the investment might be a purchase of a Treasury bond.

Let's say the bank makes a loan or buys a bond. The person who borrows the money or sells the bond takes the $900 (in cash or check) and deposits it in her account in another bank. Very quickly, then, the $900 will be paid out by Bank 1.

What does the bank's balance sheet look like after all transactions and investments have been made? After it has loaned or invested $900, Bank 1's legal reserves are just enough to meet its legal reserve requirements. There is nothing more it can do until someone deposits more money. The balance sheet of Bank 1, after it has made all possible loans or investments (but still meets its reserve requirement), is shown in Table 28-4(*b*).

Note that Bank 1 has created money. How? To the original $1000 of deposits shown on the right of Table 28-4(*b*) it has added $900 of demand deposits in another account (i.e., in the checking account of the person who got the $900). Hence, the total amount of *M* is now $1900. *Bank 1's activity has created $900 of new money.*

Chain Repercussions on Other Banks

What happens after the $900 created by Bank 1 leaves the bank? It will soon be deposited in another bank, and at that point it starts up a chain of expansion whereby still more bank money is created.

[3] For simplicity, our tables will show only the *changes* in balance sheet items, and we use reserve ratios of 10 percent. Note that when bankers refer to their loans and investments, by "investments" they mean their holdings of bonds and other financial assets. They don't mean what economists mean by "investment," which is capital formation.

Bank 1 in Initial Position

Assets		Liabilities	
Reserves	+$1,000	Deposits	+$1,000
Total	+$1,000	Total	+$1,000

Table 28-4(a). Multiple-bank deposit creation is a story with many successive stages. At the start, $1000 of newly created reserves are deposited in original first-generation bank

Bank 1 in Final Position

Assets		Liabilities	
Reserves	+$ 100	Deposits	+$1,000
Loans and investments	+ 900		
Total	+$1,000	Total	+$1,000

Table 28-4(b). A profit-maximizing bank will lend or invest any excess reserves. Thus Bank 1 has kept only $100 of the original cash deposit (as required reserves) and has lent or invested the other $900

Second-Generation Banks. To see what happens to the $900, let's call all the banks that receive the $900 "second-generation banks" (or Bank 2). Their combined balance sheets now appear as shown in Table 28-4(*c*). To these banks, the dollars deposited function just like our original $1000 deposit. These banks do not know, and do not care, that they are second in a chain of deposits. Their only concern is that they are holding too much non-earning cash, or excess reserves. Only one-tenth of $900, or $90, is legally needed against the $900 deposit. They will use the other nine-tenths to acquire $810 worth of loans and investments. Hence, their balance sheets will soon reach the equilibrium shown in Table 28-4(*d*).

Second-Generation Banks in Initial Position

Assets		Liabilities	
Reserves	+$900	Deposits	+$900
Total	+$900	Total	+$900

Table 28-4(c)

At this point, the original $1000 taken out of hand-to-hand circulation has produced a total of $2710 of money. The total of M has increased, and the process continues.

Later-Generation Banks. The $810 spent by the second-generation banks in acquiring loans and investments will go to a new set of banks called "third-generation banks."

You can create the balance sheets (initial and final) for third-generation banks. Evidently, the third-generation banks will lend out their excess reserves and will thereby create $729 of new money. A fourth generation of banks will clearly end up with nine-tenths of $810 in deposits, or $729, and so on.

Final System Equilibrium

What will be the final sum: $1000 + $900 + $810 + $729 + · · · ? Table 28-5 shows that the complete effect of the chain of money creation is $10,000. We can get the answer by arithmetic, by common sense, and by elementary algebra.

Common sense tells us that the process of de-

Final Position of Second-Generation Banks

Assets		Liabilities	
Reserves	+$ 90	Deposits	+$900
Loans and investments	+ 810		
Total	+$900	Total	+$900

Table 28-4(d). Next, the money lent out by Bank 1 soon goes to new banks, which in turn lend out nine-tenths of it

Multiple Expansion of Bank Deposits Through the Banking System

Position of bank	New deposits ($)	New loans and investments ($)	New reserves ($)
Original banks	1,000.00	900.00	100.00
2d-generation banks	900.00	810.00	90.00
3d-generation banks	810.00	729.00	81.00
4th-generation banks	729.00	656.10	72.90
5th-generation banks	656.10	590.49	65.61
6th-generation banks	590.49	531.44	59.05
7th-generation banks	531.44	478.30	53.14
8th-generation banks	478.30	430.47	47.83
9th-generation banks	430.47	387.42	43.05
10th-generation banks	387.42	348.68	38.74
Sum of first 10 generations of banks	6,513.22	5,861.90	651.32
Sum of remaining generations of banks	3,486.78	3,138.10	348.68
Total for banking system as a whole	10,000.00	9,000.00	1,000.00

Table 28-5. Finally, through this long chain, all banks create new deposits of 10 times new reserves

All banks together do accomplish what no one small bank can—multiple expansion of reserves into *M*. The final equilibrium is reached when every dollar of original new reserves supports $10 of demand deposits. Note that in every generation each bank has "created" new money in the following sense: It ends up with a final bank deposit 10 times the reserve it finally retains.

posit creation must come to an end only when no bank anywhere in the system has reserves in excess of the 10 percent reserve requirement. In all our examples, no cash reserves ever leaked out of the banking system; the money simply went from one set of banks to another set of banks. The banking system will reach equilibrium when the $1000 of new reserves is all used up as required reserves on new deposits. In other words, the final equilibrium of the banking system will be the point at which 10 percent of new deposits (D) equals the new reserves of $1000. What level of D satisfies this condition? The answer is $D = \$10,000$.

We can also see the answer intuitively by looking at a consolidated balance sheet for all banks together—first, second, and hundredth generation. This is shown in Table 28-6. If total new deposits were less than $10,000, the 10 percent reserve ratio would not yet be reached, and full equilibrium would not yet be attained.[4]

[4] The algebraic solution can be shown as follows:

$$\$1000 + \$900 + \$810 + \cdots$$
$$= \$1000 \times [1 + \tfrac{9}{10} + (\tfrac{9}{10})^2 + (\tfrac{9}{10})^3 + \cdots]$$
$$= \$1000\left(\frac{1}{1-\frac{9}{10}}\right) = \$1000 \times \left(\frac{1}{0.1}\right) = \$10{,}000$$

Consolidated Balance Sheet Showing Final Position

Assets		Liabilities	
Reserves	+$ 1,000	Deposits	+$10,000
Loans and investments	+ 9,000		
Total	+$10,000	Total	+$10,000

Table 28-6. All banks together ultimately increase deposits and *M* by a multiple of the original injection of reserves

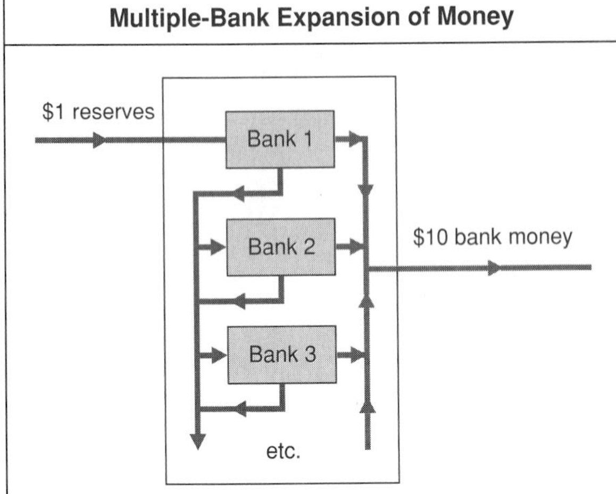

Figure 28-5. All banks can do what one can't do alone

For each dollar of new reserves deposited in a bank, the system as a whole creates about $10 of bank money. The blue arrows in the box show that Bank 1 cannot do it alone. The money supply increases as reserves spread through the banking system.

Figure 28-5 gives a schematic overview of the process. It shows how $1 of new deposits or reserves, at the upper left, is transformed into $10 of total deposits, or bank money, on the right. Inside the rectangle, which represents the banking system as a whole, Bank 1 receives the initial new deposit. The blue arrows circulating around show how reserves are redistributed while the black lines show new deposits. Though the chain has many links, each is a dwindling fraction and the whole effect does add up to the 10-to-1 total.

The Money-Supply Multiplier. We see that there is a multiplier operating on reserves. For every additional dollar in reserves provided to the banking system, banks eventually create $10 of additional deposits or bank money.

Just as the multiplier introduced in Chapter 27 made income rise threefold to generate new saving equal to the new dollar of investment, here money must increase tenfold so that 10 percent of it will match the new dollars of reserves that started the chain. Note that the arithmetic of M expansion is similar to that of the "expenditure multiplier," but don't confuse the two. The amplification here is from the stock of reserves to the stock of total M; it does not refer to the extra output induced by investment or money.

The ratio of new deposits to the increase in reserves is called the **money-supply multiplier.** In the simple case analyzed here, the money-supply multiplier is equal to

$$10 = \frac{1}{0.1} = \frac{1}{\text{required reserve ratio}}$$

The money-supply multiplier summarizes the logic of how banks create money. The entire banking system can transform an initial increase in reserves into a multiplied amount of new deposits or bank money.

Deposit Destruction

The process of deposit creation can also work in reverse when a drain in reserves reduces bank money. It is useful to reinforce your understanding of money creation by tracing in detail what happens when the Fed permanently destroys $2000 of reserves by selling a government bond to a woman who withdraws cash from her checking account to pay for it. In the end, the withdrawal of $2000 of reserves from the banking system kills off $20,000 worth of deposits throughout the whole system.

Two Qualifications to Deposit Creation

The actual financial system is somewhat more complicated than our simple banking example. We have shown that $1000 of new reserves put into a bank will ultimately result in an increase of $10,000 of bank deposits. We assumed that all the new money remained as checking accounts in the banking system, in one bank or another at every stage, and that no bank would have excess reserves. Let us see what would happen if some money leaked into circulation or if some banks had excess reserves.

Leakage into Hand-to-Hand Circulation. It is possible that, somewhere along the chain of deposit expansion, an individual who receives a check will not leave the proceeds in a bank checking account. He might put some cash in a cookie jar.

The effects of such withdrawals on our analysis are simple. When $1000 stayed in the banking system, $10,000 of new deposits was created. If $100 were to leak into circulation outside the banks and only $900 of new reserves were to remain in the banking system, then the new checking deposits created would be $9000 ($900 × 10). Therefore, the 10-to-1 amplification would occur only if no reserves leak from banks.

Possible Excess Reserves. Our analysis proceeded on the assumption that the commercial banks follow their legal reserve requirements to the letter. Might not a bank choose to keep more reserves than the legally required amount? Suppose, for example, that the original bank decided to keep $900 as additional reserves rather than lend it out. Then the whole process of multiple deposit creation would stop dead, with no expansion of deposits at all.

This decision would of course make no sense for the bank. Because the bank earns no interest on reserves, it would lose interest payments on the $900. So as long as the interest rate on investments is above zero, banks have a strong incentive to avoid holding any excess reserves.

During the Great Depression, interest rates fell to 0.12 percent per year, so banks during this period often held significant excess reserves. Another case that might lead to excess reserves would arise if the Federal Reserve paid interest on bank reserves, as some reformers have proposed. In this case, if both reserves and Treasury bills earned 4 or 6 or 10 percent per year, banks would have no incentive to invest or loan out their excess reserves.

If the interest rate on reserves were close to that on market investments, the legal reserve requirement would no longer bind banks tightly, and monetary policy would become a less useful instrument for control of the economy. For this reason, many economists strenuously oppose paying market interest rates on bank reserves.

Occasionally banks do find themselves with excess reserves. In this case they may choose to lend excess reserves to banks that are short of reserves. The amount of excess reserves is typically a very small fraction of total reserves.

With a legal reserve requirement of 10 percent, reserves will be multiplied tenfold into new deposits. However, when some of the increased deposits spill into currency or nonmonetary assets, or when banks hold excess reserves, the deposit creation will depart from the ratio of 1/(legal reserve ratio).

● We have discussed the essence of money, the return on money in the form of interest, the demand for money, and the financial system's supply of bank money. In the last section, we saw how an infusion of bank reserves leads to a multiple expansion of money. What remains for a complete understanding of monetary economics is an analysis of the Federal Reserve System. We will see in the next chapter how the Federal Reserve can manipulate bank reserves and thereby increase or decrease the total money supply. Armed with our analysis of the supply and demand for money, we can show how the money supply helps influence output, inflation, and employment. ●

SUMMARY

A. The Essence of Money and Interest Rates

1. Money is anything that serves as a commonly accepted medium of exchange or means of payment. Money also functions as a unit of value and a store of value.
2. Before money came into use, people exchanged goods for goods in a process called barter. Money arose to facilitate trade. Early money consisted of commodities, which were superseded by paper and bank money. Unlike other economic goods, money is valued because of social convention. We value money indirectly for what it buys, not for its direct utility.
3. The analysis of monetary aggregates is extremely common today among both economists and policymakers. One widely used definition of the

money supply is transactions money (M_1)—made up of currency and checking deposits. Another important concept is broad money (M_2), which includes M_1 plus highly liquid "near-monies" like savings accounts.

4. The definitions of the M's have changed over the last decade as a result of rapid innovation in financial markets. This development makes the conduct of monetary policy more difficult because monetary definitions (and thus targets for money growth) are ambiguous when new assets appear.

5. Interest rates are the price paid for borrowing money and are measured in dollars per year paid back per dollar borrowed, or in percent per year. People willingly pay interest because borrowed funds allow them to buy goods and services to satisfy consumption needs or make profitable investments.

6. Markets produce a wide array of interest rates. These rates vary because of the term or maturity of loans, because of the risk and liquidity of investments, and because of the associated administrative costs.

7. Interest rates generally rise during inflationary periods, reflecting the fact that the purchasing power of money declines as prices rise. To calculate the interest yield in terms of real goods and services, we use the real interest rate, which equals the nominal or money interest rate minus the rate of inflation.

8. The demand for money differs from that for other commodities. Money is held for its indirect rather than its direct value. But money holdings are limited because keeping assets in money rather than in other forms has an opportunity cost: we sacrifice interest earnings when we hold money.

9. The demand for money is grounded in the need to make transactions and the desire to hold assets for the future. The most important—the transactions demand—comes because people need cash or checking deposits to pay bills or buy goods. Such transactions needs are met by M_1 and are chiefly related to the value of transactions, or to nominal GNP. Other assets are held in high-yield, interest-bearing checking accounts as a supersafe part of investors' portfolios.

   Economic theory predicts, and empirical studies confirm, that the demand for money is sensitive to interest rates; higher interest rates lead to a lower demand for M.

B. Banking and the Supply of Money

10. Banks are commercial enterprises that seek to earn profits for their owners. One major function of banks is to provide checking accounts to customers. Modern banks gradually evolved from the old goldsmith establishments in which money and valuables were stored. Eventually it became general practice for goldsmiths to hold less than 100 percent reserves against deposits; this was the beginning of fractional-reserve banking.

11. If banks kept 100 percent cash reserves against all deposits, there would be no multiple creation of money when new reserves were injected by the

central bank into the system. There would be only a 1-to-1 exchange of one kind of money for another kind of money.

12. Today, banks are legally required to keep reserves on their checking deposits. These can be in the form of cash on hand or of non-interest-bearing deposits at the Federal Reserve. For illustrative purposes, we examined a required reserve ratio of 10 percent. In this case, the banking system as a whole—together with public or private borrowers and the depositing public—does create bank money 10 to 1 for each new dollar of reserves created by the Fed and deposited somewhere in the banking system.

13. Each small bank is limited in its ability to expand its loans and investments. It cannot lend or invest more than it has received from depositors; it can lend only about nine-tenths as much.

14. Although no bank alone can expand its reserves 10 to 1, the banking system as a whole can. The first individual bank receiving a new $1000 of deposits lends nine-tenths of its newly acquired cash on loans and investments. This gives a second group of banks nine-tenths of $1000 in new deposits. They, in turn, keep one-tenth in reserves and lend the other nine-tenths on new earning assets; this causes them to lose cash to a third set of banks, whose deposits have gone up by nine-tenths of nine-tenths of $1000. If we follow through the successive groups of banks in the dwindling, never-ending chain, we find for the system as a whole new deposits of

$$\begin{aligned} \$1000 + \$900 + \$810 + \$729 + \cdots &= \$1000 \times [1 + \tfrac{9}{10} + (\tfrac{9}{10})^2 + (\tfrac{9}{10})^3 + \cdots] \\ &= \$1000\left(\frac{1}{1 - \frac{9}{10}}\right) = \$1000\left(\frac{1}{0.1}\right) \\ &= \$10{,}000 \end{aligned}$$

15. Only when each $1 of the new reserves retained in the banking system ends up supporting $10 of deposits somewhere in the system will the limits to deposit expansion be reached. Then the system is loaned up; it can create no further deposits until it acquires more reserves. The 10-to-1 ratio of increased bank money to increased reserves is called the money-supply multiplier.

16. There will be some leakage of new cash reserves of the banking system into circulation outside the banks and into assets other than checking accounts. Therefore, instead of $10,000 of new checking deposits created, as in the previous examples, there may be something less than that—the difference being due to what is withdrawn from the system.

    Moreover, a bank may keep excess reserves above the legally required reserves. Excess reserves crop up when the interest rate on reserves is close to the rate on safe investments.

    When some of the new reserves leak into assets other than checking deposits, the relationship of money creation to new reserves may depart from the 10-to-1 formula given by the money-supply multiplier.

CONCEPTS FOR REVIEW

The essence of money
barter
commodity M, paper M, bank M
coins, paper currency, checking accounts
M_1, M_2

Interest rates
interest rate
riskless interest rate
interest-rate premiums due to: maturity, risk, illiquidity, administrative costs
real and nominal interest rates

Demand for money
the functions of money
motives for money demand: transactions demand, asset demand
interest as opportunity cost of holding money

Banking and money supply
banks, financial intermediaries
bank reserves (vault cash and deposits with Fed)
fractional-reserve banking
money-supply multiplier

QUESTIONS FOR DISCUSSION

1. Define M_1 and M_2. What is included in M_1? What is in M_2 but not M_1? Relate each of the components of M_2 to the factors behind the demand for money.
2. List and describe stages of money from barter to bank money. Describe how a typical transaction might occur at each stage. What institutions or laws would be necessary to pass from one stage to the next?
3. Suppose that all banks kept 100 percent reserves. Construct new versions of Tables 28-4(*a*) and 28-6 to reflect $1000 of reserves added to a banking system that keeps 100 percent reserves. What is the net effect of a reserve addition to the money supply in this case? Do banks "create" money?
4. Suppose that banks hold 20 percent of deposits as reserves and that $200 of reserves is *subtracted* from the banking system. Redo Tables 28-4(*a*) through 28-6. What is the money-supply multiplier in this case? Calculate the money-supply multiplier in a second way by using the technique shown in footnote 4.
5. What would be the effect on the demand for money (M_1) of each of the following (with other things held equal)?
   (a) An increase in real GNP
   (b) An increase in the price level
   (c) A rise in the interest rate on savings accounts and Treasury securities
   (d) Allowing banks to pay interest on checking deposits
   (e) Doubling all prices, wages, and incomes (Can you calculate exactly the effect on the demand for money?)
6. In 1937, hoping to increase M, the Federal Reserve increased bank reserves. Because interest rates were so low (around $\frac{1}{8}$ of 1 percent), excess reserves increased sharply and the money supply hardly changed at all. Explain why low interest rates encourage excess reserves, while high interest rates discourage excess reserves. Explain why changes in reserves might not be tightly linked to money-supply changes when interest rates are near zero.
7. The opportunity cost of holding money is equal to the yield on safe short-term assets (such as Treasury bills) minus the interest rate on money. What is the impact of the following on the opportunity cost of holding money in checking deposits (assume that reserve requirements are 10 percent of deposits):
   (a) Before 1980 (when checking deposits have zero yield) market interest rates increase from 8 to 9 percent.
   (b) In 1984 (when NOW accounts have a maximum yield of 5 percent) interest rates increase from 3 to 4 percent. From 8 to 9 percent.
   (c) In 1991 (when the interest rates on NOW accounts are deregulated), market interest rates increase from 3 to 4 percent. From 8 to 9 percent.

   How would you expect the demand for money to respond to the change in market interest rates in each of the above cases if the elasticity of demand for money with respect to the opportunity cost of money is 0.2?
8. Interest-rate problems (which may require a calculator):
   (a) You invest $2000 at 13.5 percent per year. What is your total balance after 6 months?
   (b) Interest is said to be "compounded" when you earn interest on whatever interest has already been paid; most interest rates quoted today are compounded. If you invest $10,000 for 3 years at a compound annual interest rate of 10 percent, what is the total investment at the end of each year?
   (c) Consider the following data: The consumer price index in 1977 was 60.6, and in 1981 it was 90.9. Interest rates on government securities in 1978

through 1981 (in percent per year) were 7.2, 10.0, 11.5, and 14.0. Calculate the average nominal and real interest rates for the 4-year period 1978–1981.

(d) Treasury bills (T-bills) are usually sold on a discounted basis; that is, a 90-day T-bill for $10,000 would sell today at a price such that collecting $10,000 at maturity would produce the market interest rate. If the market interest rate is 6.6 percent per year, what would be the price on a $10,000 90-day T-bill?

9. Explain whether you think that each of the following should be counted as part of the narrow money supply (M_1) in the United States: traveler's checks, savings accounts, subway tokens, postage stamps, credit-card balances, Canadian dollars.

10. Suppose reserve requirements were abolished. What would determine the level of reserves in the banking system? What would happen to the money-supply multiplier in this situation?

11. Suppose that one giant bank, the Humongous Bank of America, held all the checking deposits of all the people, subject to a 10 percent legal reserve requirement. If there were an injection of reserves into the economy, could the Humongous Bank lend out more than 90 percent of the deposit addition, knowing that the new deposit must come back to it? Would this change the ultimate money-supply multiplier?

12. This chapter defines money as a generally accepted and used medium of exchange. Over time, the objects used as money have evolved, and it may be difficult to identify a unique object as "the money supply." Today, assets have differing degrees of "moneyness" depending upon whether they are actually accepted as means of payment and upon the speed with which they can be converted into cash. Consider Figure 28-6's spectrum of assets from money to real capital goods. Where does the Federal Reserve draw the line between money (M_1) and other assets? Where would you draw the line? Devise some new assets, place them on the spectrum, and decide whether they should be in M_1.

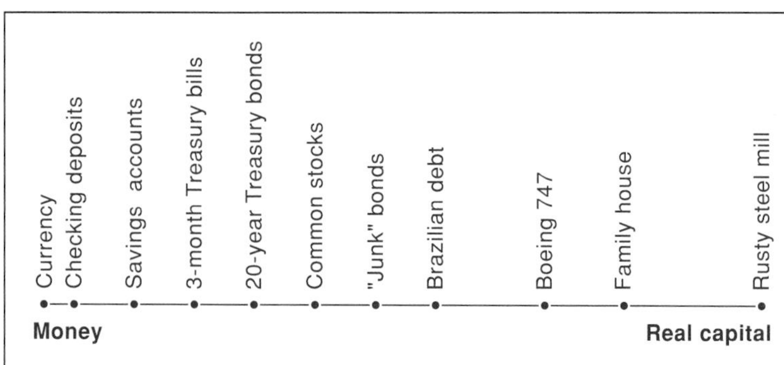

Figure 28-6. A spectrum of assets from money to capital

APPENDIX 28

STOCK MARKET FLUCTUATIONS

> The stock market is but a mirror which provides an image of the underlying or fundamental economic situation.
>
> John Kenneth Galbraith, *The Great Crash* (1955)

This chapter concentrated on monetary economics, which is crucial to an understanding of macroeconomic policy. But, as Table 28A-1 shows, households invest in many assets other than money.

Among the most fascinating assets owned by households are common stocks (or corporate equities). These are volatile securities through which people's fortunes are made and lost overnight. The 1980s illustrate the perils of "playing the market." Beginning in 1982, the stock market surged upward steadily for 5 years, gaining almost 300 percent. Those who had the luck or vision to put all their assets into stocks made a lot of money. The market peaked in the summer of 1987. On October 19, 1987—"black Monday"—the stock market lost 22 percent of its value in 6 hours. The shock to securities markets was a vivid reminder of the risks you take when you buy stocks. Nevertheless, 35 million Americans own stocks; 3 million of them are people with incomes under $10,000. Only a small fraction of shares are held by low-income households, but the fact that so many people are willing to invest their wealth this way attests to the lure of prospective gains from stock ownership.

Financial Assets of Households

Class of asset	Percent of total assets in each class: 1963	1988
Dollar-denominated:		
Currency and checking deposits (M_1)	4.6	4.2
Savings accounts	14.3	21.0
Government securities	6.4	8.5
Other	3.3	2.2
Equity in businesses:		
Corporate	31.3	18.4
Noncorporate	25.7	19.8
Pension fund and life-insurance reserves	13.4	23.9
Other	1.0	1.9
Total	100.0	100.0
Item: Total assets of households (billions)	$1,641	$12,139

Table 28A-1. Pension assets and savings accounts are largest component of household assets

This table shows how the holdings of households were divided among different assets in 1963 and 1988. Note that the share of equities fell sharply, while pension funds and savings accounts rose markedly. (Source: Federal Reserve System.)

In this appendix we explore modern theories of the behavior of the stock market. A **stock market** is a place where the shares in publicly owned companies, the titles to business firms, are bought and sold. In 1990, the value of these titles was estimated at $3 trillion in the United States. Sales in a single year might total $2 trillion. The stock market is the hub of our corporate economy.

The New York Stock Exchange is the main stock market, listing more than a thousand securities. The smaller American Stock Exchange began when brokers met on the street to buy and sell, giving hand signals to the clerks hanging out the windows to record the transactions. Only in the twentieth century did the American Stock Exchange move indoors.

Every large financial center has a stock exchange. Major ones are located in Tokyo, London, Frankfurt, Hong Kong, Toronto, Zurich, and, of course, New York. A stock exchange is the essence of a market economy. When the countries of Eastern Europe decided to scrap their centrally planned, socialist systems, one of their first acts was to introduce a stock market to buy and sell ownership rights in companies.

The Great Crash

A study of stock exchanges and financial markets relies upon both economic analysis and a careful reading of the lessons of history. One traumatic event has cast a shadow over stock markets for decades—the 1929 panic and crash. This event ushered in the long and painful Great Depression of the 1930s.

The "roaring twenties" saw a fabulous stock market boom, when everyone bought and sold stocks. Most purchases in this wild *bull* market (one with rising prices) were *on margin.* This means a buyer of $10,000 worth of stocks put up only part of the price in cash and borrowed the difference, pledging the newly bought stocks as collateral for the purchase. What did it matter that you had to pay the broker 6, 10, or 15 percent per year on the borrowings when, in one day, Auburn Motors or Bethlehem Steel might jump 10 percent in value!

A speculative mania fulfills its own promises. If people buy because they think stocks will rise, their act of buying sends up the price of stocks. This causes people to buy even more and sends the dizzy dance off on another round. But, unlike people who play cards or dice, no one apparently loses what the winners gain. Of course, the prizes are all on paper and would disappear if everyone tried to cash them in. But why should anyone want to sell such lucrative securities?

The great stock market boom of the 1920s was a classic *speculative bubble.* Prices rose because of hopes and dreams, not because the profits and dividends of companies were soaring. The crash came in "black October" of 1929. Everyone was caught, the big-league professionals as well as the piddling amateurs—Andrew Mellon, John D. Rockefeller, the engineer-turned-President in the White House, and Yale's great economics professor Irving Fisher.

When the bottom fell out of the market in 1929, investors, big and small, who bought on margin could not put up funds to cover their holdings and the market fell still further. The bull market turned into a *bear* (or declining) market. By the trough of the Depression in 1933, the market had lost 85 percent of its 1929 value.

Trends in the stock market are tracked using stock-price indexes, which are weighted averages of the prices of a basket of company stocks. Commonly followed averages include the Dow-Jones Industrial Average ("DJIA") of 30 large companies, and Standard and Poor's index of 500 companies (the "S&P 500"), which is a weighted average of the stock prices of the largest 500 American corporations.

Figure 28A-1 on the following page shows the history since 1920 of the Standard and Poor 500. The lower curve shows the "nominal" stock price average, which records the actual average during a particular year. The upper line shows the "real" price of stocks; this equals the nominal price divided by an index of consumer prices that equals 1 in 1991.

Figure 28A-1 shows that, after the banking crisis of 1933, the stock market began to recover. According to this index, real stock prices did not recover their 1929 level until 1955. Moreover, the 1991 level was just slightly shy of the all-time high of real stock prices in 1968.[1]

Where will it all end? Is there a crystal ball that will foretell the movement of stock prices? This is the subject of modern finance theory.

The Efficient-Market Theory

Economists and finance professors have long studied prices in speculative markets, like the stock market, and markets for commodities such as corn. Their findings have stirred great controversy and have even angered many financial analysts. Yet this is an area in which the facts have largely corroborated the theories.

Modern economic theories of stock prices are grouped under the heading of **efficient-market theory.**[2] One way of expressing the fundamental theory is: *You can't outguess the market.*

[1] A detailed account of the role of the stock market in the Great Depression is provided in John Kenneth Galbraith, *The Great Crash of 1929* (Avon, New York, 1988); and C. P. Kindleberger, *Manias, Panics, and Crashes* (Basic Books, New York, rev., 1989).

[2] "Efficiency" in finance theory is used differently than in other parts of economics. Here, "efficiency" means that information is quickly absorbed, not that resources produce the maximal outputs.

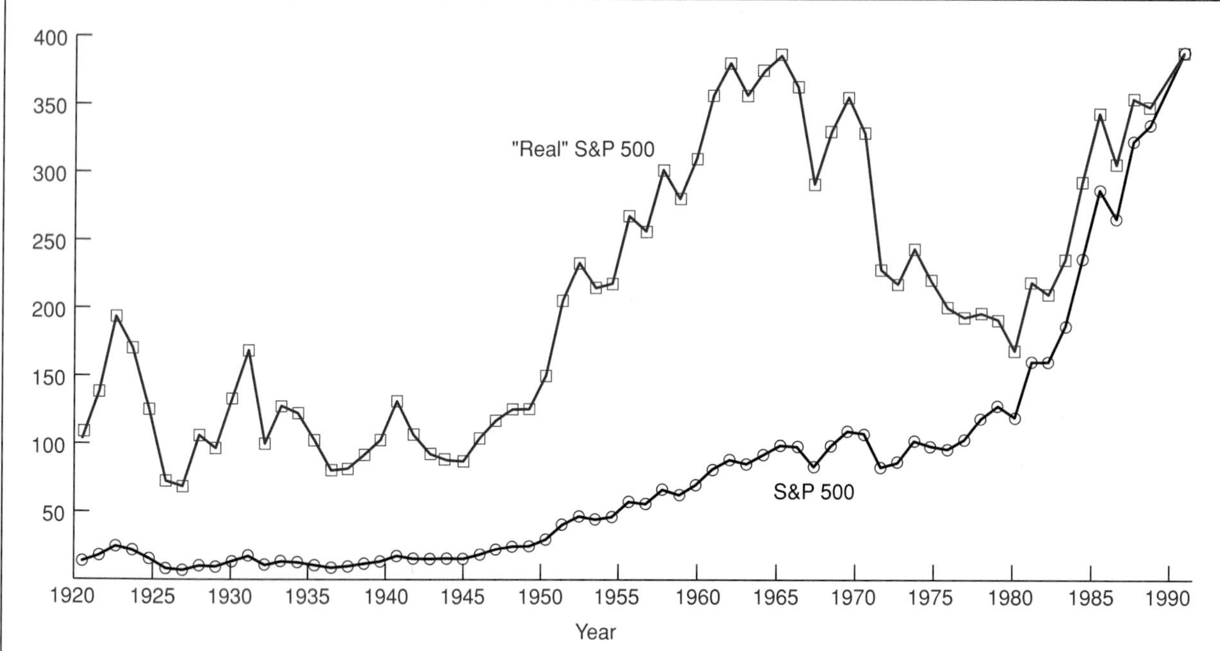

Figure 28A-1. The only guarantee about stock prices is that they will fluctuate

Stock prices in nominal terms, shown in the bottom line, tend to rise with inflation. The Standard and Poor's index (the "S&P 500") shown here tracks the value-weighted average of the stock prices of the 500 largest American companies. The top line shows the "real S&P 500" which is the S&P 500 corrected for movements in the consumer price index. The all-time high came in 1968, and by 1991 real stock prices were only two times the pre-Depression peak of 1929.

We'll see in a minute *why* this proposition is plausible. First, let's consider its factual basis. There have been numerous studies over the years about rules or formulas for making money. Typical rules are "buy after 2 days of increases" or "buy on the bad news and sell on the good news." An early study by Alfred Cowles investigated the recommendations of stockbrokers. He examined how well different brokers performed by looking at the return (in dollars of total income per year per dollar invested) on the stocks they selected. He found that, on average, a stockbroker's choices did no better than a random portfolio (or combination) of stocks. This observation led to the *dart-board theory* of stock selection:

You can throw a dart at the *Wall Street Journal* as a way of selecting stocks. Better still, buy a little of everything in the market, so that you hold a diversified "index" portfolio of the stock market. This would probably leave you better off than your cousin who follows a broker's advice. Why? Because he would have to pay more broker's commissions and his stocks, on average, would not outperform yours.

This bleak view has been generally confirmed in hundreds of studies over the last four decades. Their lesson is not that you will never become rich by following a rule or formula, but that, in general, such rules cannot outperform a randomly selected and diversified portfolio of stocks.

Rationale for the Efficient-Market View

Finance theorists have spent many years analyzing stock and bond markets in order to understand why the dart-board theory might hold. Why do well-functioning financial markets rule out persistent excess profits? The theory of efficient markets explains this.

An **efficient market** is one where all new information is quickly understood by market participants and becomes immediately incorporated into market prices. For example, say that Lazy-T Oil Company has just struck oil in the Gulf of Alaska.

This event is announced at 11:30 A.M. on Tuesday. When will the price of Lazy-T's shares rise? The efficient-market theory holds that the news will be incorporated into prices immediately. The market participants will react at once, bidding the price of Lazy-T up by the correct amount. In short, at every point in time, markets have already digested and included in stock prices or corn prices or other speculative prices all the latest available information.

This means that if you read about a heavy frost in Florida you can't enrich yourself by buying frozen orange juice futures during your lunch break: the orange juice price went up the minute the news was reported, or even earlier.[3]

The theory of efficient markets holds that market prices contain all available information. It is not possible to make profits by looking at old information or at patterns of past price changes.

A Random Walk

The efficient-market view provides an important way of analyzing price movements in organized markets. Under this approach, the price movements of stocks should look highly erratic, like a random walk, when charted over a period of time.

A price follows a *random walk* when its movements over time are completely unpredictable. For example, toss a coin for heads or tails. Call a head "plus 1" and a tail "minus 1." Then keep track of the running score of 100 coin tosses. Draw it on graph paper. This curve is a random walk. Now for comparison also graph 100 days' movement of IBM stock and of Standard and Poor's 500 index. Note how similar all three figures appear.

Why do speculative prices resemble a random walk? Economists, on reflection, have arrived at the following truths: In an efficient market all predictable things have already been built into the price. It is the arrival of *new* information—a freeze in Florida, war in the Persian Gulf, a report that the Federal Reserve has tightened the money supply—that affects stock or commodity prices. Moreover, the news must be random and unpredictable (or else it would be predictable and therefore not truly news).

To summarize: The efficient-market theory explains why movements in stock prices look so erratic. Prices respond to news, to surprises. But surprises are unpredictable events—like the flip of a coin or next month's rainstorm—that may move in any direction. Because stock prices move in response to erratic events, stock prices themselves move erratically, like a random walk.

Objections

There are four major objections to the efficient-market view of markets.

1. Suppose everybody accepts the efficient-market philosophy and stops trying to digest information quickly. If everyone assumes that stock prices are correctly valued, then will those prices *stop* being accurate?

   This is a good question, but it is unlikely that everyone will quit. Indeed, the minute too many people stopped looking ahead, the market would cease being efficient. We could then make profits by acting on old information. So the efficient market is a stable, self-monitoring equilibrium state.
2. Some people are quicker and smarter than others. Some have much money to spend on information to narrow down the odds on the uncertain future. Doesn't it stand to reason that they will make higher profits?

   There are many such people competing against each other. The Rockefellers can buy the best financial counsel there is. But so can a number of other people and institutions. Competition provides the checks and balances of efficiency and ensures minimal excess profits.

   Moreover, the efficient-market theory does suggest that a few people with special flair and skills will permanently earn high returns on their skills—just as great quarterbacks and sopranos do.
3. Economists who look at the historical record ask whether it is plausible that sharp movements in stock prices could actually reflect new information. Consider the sharp percent drop in the

[3] Scholars have attempted to measure the speed of price adjustment in such efficient markets. One study found that, if you were willing to put up $100,000, you could make a profit only if you bought stocks within 30 seconds after new information became public.

stock market from October 15 to October 19, 1987. The efficient-market view would hold that this drop was caused by economic events that depressed the value of future corporate earnings. What were those events? James Tobin, Yale's Nobel Prize–winning economist, commented, "There are no visible factors that could make a 30 percent difference in the value of stock [prices over these four days]." Efficient-market theorists fall silent before this criticism.

4. Finally, the efficient-market view applies to individual stocks but not necessarily to the entire market. Some economists have found evidence of long, self-reversing swings in stock market prices. Others believe that these swings reflect changes in the general mood of the financial community. These long-term swings may lie behind the boom psychology of the 1920s and 1980s or the depression mentality of the 1930s.

   Let us say that we believed that the whole stock market was too high in 1991 or too low in 1931. What could we do? We could not individually buy or sell enough stocks to overcome the entire national mood. So, from a macroeconomic perspective, speculative markets *can* exhibit waves of pessimism or optimism without powerful economic forces moving in to correct these swings of mood.

Financial Strategies

Only a few financial analysts are willing to accept the view that "passive" financial strategies, simply buying an indexed share of the market, are the best approach. A growing number of institutions, however, follow a passive approach, and some banks, such as Wells Fargo in San Francisco, have adopted this philosophy and now invest billions of dollars in passive accounts.

What are the lessons of the many studies of the behavior of financial markets and financial advisers?

- Be skeptical of approaches that claim to have found the quick route to success. You can't get rich by consulting the stars (although, unbelievably, some financial advisers push astrology to their clients). Hunches work out to nothing in the long run.
- The best brains on Wall Street do not, on average, beat the averages (Dow-Jones, Standard & Poor's, etc.). This is not so surprising. True, the big money managers have all the money needed for any kind of research and digging. But they are all competing with one another.
- Investors who want to achieve a good return with the least possible risk buy a broadly diversified portfolio of common stocks. They might buy an "index fund," which is a fixed portfolio of stocks with minimal management and brokerage fees. They might combine this with some diversified bonds or savings accounts. Over the longer run, such a strategy will probably earn a return of a few percentage points per year above inflation.
- Investors can also increase their expected return if they are willing to bear greater risks. Some stocks are inherently riskier than others. By investing in more cyclical stocks, in stocks that move up and down relatively more than the market as a whole, and in small companies, investors, on average, can probably beat the market. But buyer beware: When the market goes down, you will generally suffer worse-than-average losses in these riskier stocks.

If, after reading all this, you still want to try your hand in the stock market, do not be daunted. But take to heart the caution of one of America's great financiers, Bernard Baruch:

> If you are ready to give up everything else—to study the whole history and background of the market and all the principal companies whose stocks are on the board as carefully as a medical student studies anatomy—if you can do all that, and, in addition, you have the cool nerves of a great gambler, the sixth sense of a kind of clairvoyant, and the courage of a lion, you have a ghost of a chance.

SUMMARY TO APPENDIX

1. Stock markets, of which the New York Stock Exchange is the most important, are places where titles of ownership to the largest companies are bought and sold. The history of stock prices is filled with violent gyrations, such as the Great Crash of 1929. Trends are tracked by the use of stock-price indexes, such as Standard and Poor's 500 or the familiar Dow-Jones Industrial Average.
2. Modern economic theories of stock prices generally focus on the role of efficient markets. An efficient market is one in which all information is quickly absorbed by speculators and is immediately built into market prices. In efficient markets, there are no easy profits; looking at yesterday's news or past patterns of prices or elections or business cycles will not help predict future price movements.
3. Thus, in efficient markets, prices respond to surprises. Because surprises are inherently random, stock prices and other speculative prices move erratically, as in a random walk.

CONCEPTS FOR REVIEW

New York Stock Exchange
common stocks (corporate equities)
Standard and Poor's 500
efficient market
random walk of stock prices
index fund, passive strategies
new news, old information, and speculative prices

QUESTIONS FOR DISCUSSION

1. According to the efficient-market theory, what effect would the following events have on the price of GM's stock?
   (a) A surprise announcement that the government was going to undertake a new program to contract the economy by raising corporation taxes on next July 1
   (b) An increase in tax rates on July 1, six months after Congress had passed the enabling legislation
   (c) An announcement, unexpected by experts, that the United States was imposing quotas on imports of Japanese cars for the coming year
   (d) Implementation of (*c*) by issuing regulations on December 31
2. One economist commented as follows on the sharp drop in stock prices during October 1987: "There have been no events over the last few days that can rationally explain the selling frenzy during 'black October.' News about inflation, the trade balance, the budget deficit, or events in the Persian Gulf can be indicted for no more than a few dozen points of the 509 point decline in the Dow-Jones." Explain how this quotation relates to the efficient-market hypothesis. If you agree with this quotation, what would you conclude about the validity of that hypothesis?
3. Flip a coin 100 times. Count a head as "plus 1" and a tail as "minus 1." Keep a running score of the total. Plot it on a graph paper. This is a random walk. (Those with access to a computer can do this using a computer program, a random-number generator, and a plotter.)

   Next, keep track of the closing price of the stock of your favorite company for a few weeks (or get it from past issues of the newspaper). Plot the price against time. Can you see any difference in the pattern of changes? Do both look like random walks?

CHAPTER 29

CENTRAL BANKING AND MONETARY POLICY

There have been three great inventions since the beginning of time: fire, the wheel, and central banking.
Will Rogers

We learned in the last chapter about the unique properties of money. As the French economist Frederic Bastiat put it, "People are not nourished by money. They do not clothe themselves with gold; they do not warm themselves with silver." Money is held because it facilitates trade and exchange.

This chapter continues the discussion of the money supply by analyzing the tasks of central banking. The Federal Reserve System, which is the central bank of the United States, is a banker's bank. Its primary function is to control the supply of bank reserves. This activity regulates the nation's money supply and credit conditions and determines the level of interest rates. Every country has a central bank that is responsible for managing its monetary affairs.

The Federal Reserve's goals are steady growth in national output and low unemployment. Its sworn enemy is inflation. If aggregate demand is excessive and prices are being bid up, the Federal Reserve Board may reduce the growth of the money supply, thereby slowing aggregate demand and output growth. If unemployment is high and business languishing, the Fed may consider increasing the money supply, thereby raising aggregate demand and augmenting output growth. In the second half of this chapter, we will see exactly how the Federal Reserve can use its powers to pursue these goals.

A. Central Banking and the Federal Reserve System

The Federal Reserve System

Figure 29-1 shows the role of central banking in the economy and depicts its relationship to the banks and the capital markets in which interest rates and credit availability are determined. In this section we analyze how the Fed manipulates its instruments—bank reserves, the discount rate, and other tools—to determine the money supply.

Structure of the Federal Reserve

History. During the nineteenth century, the United States was plagued by banking panics. Panics occurred when people suddenly attempted to turn their bank deposits into currency. When they arrived at the banks, they found that the banks had an inadequate supply of currency because the supply of currency was fixed and smaller than the

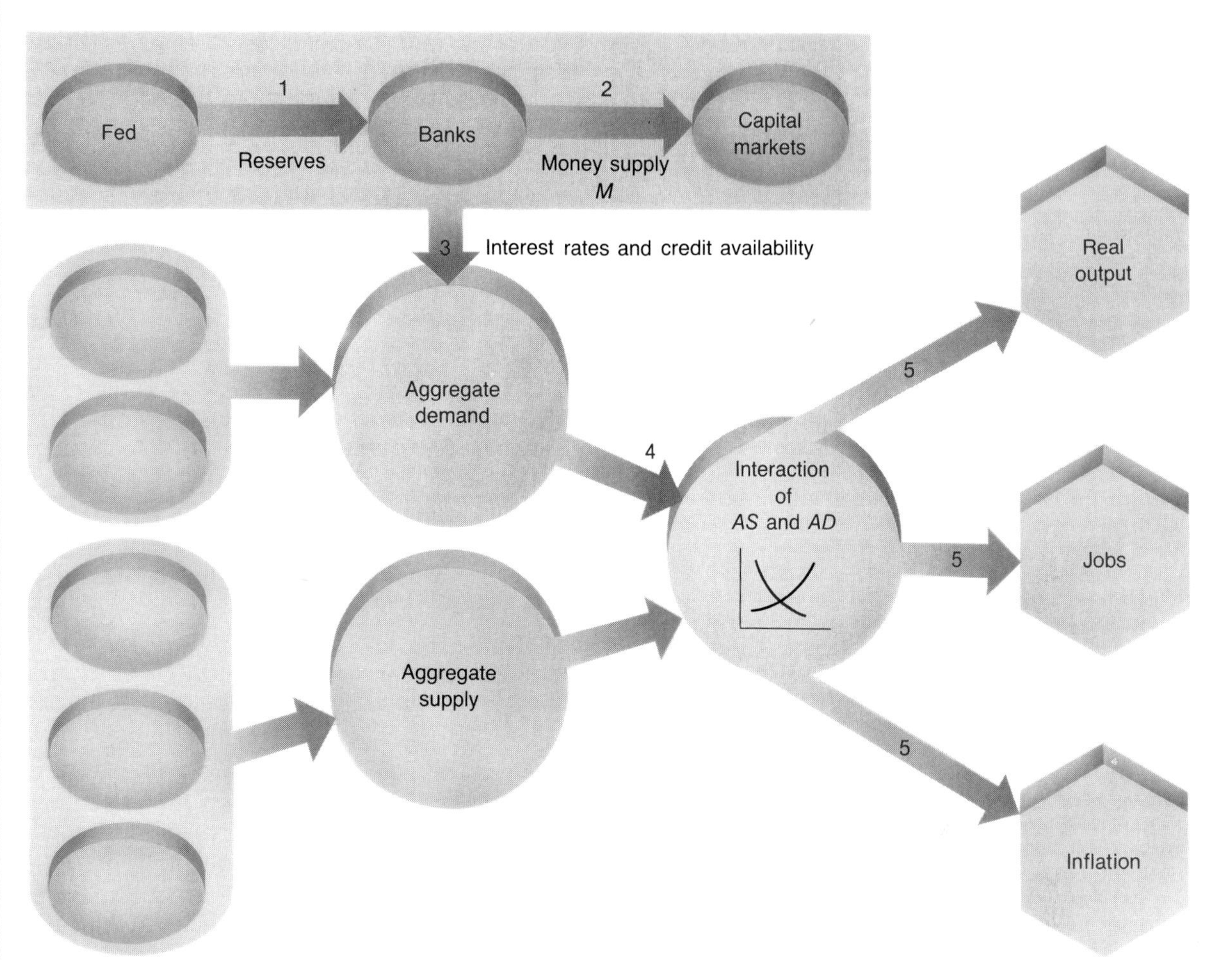

Figure 29-1. A bird's-eye view of how monetary policy affects output and inflation

This diagram shows graphically the steps by which Fed policy affects economic activity. (1) is a change in reserves; leading to (2), a change in *M*; leading to (3), changes in interest rates and credit conditions. In (4), *AD* is changed by a response of investment and other interest-sensitive spending. In (5), changes in output, employment, and inflation follow.

Remember, however, that monetary policy is not the only influence: Entering in crucial step 4, fiscal policy feeds into the aggregate demand circle.

amount of bank deposits. Bank failures and economic downturns ensued. After the severe panic of 1907, agitation and discussion led to the creation of the Federal Reserve System in 1913.

The Federal Reserve System consists of 12 regional Federal Reserve Banks, located in New York, Chicago, Richmond, Dallas, San Francisco, and other major cities. The sprawling regional structure was originally designed in a populist age to ensure that different areas would have a voice in banking matters and to avoid too great a concentration of central-banking powers in Washington or in the hands of the bankers of the eastern establishment. Each Federal Reserve Bank today manages bank operations and oversees banks in its region.

Who's in Charge? The core of the Federal Reserve is the *Board of Governors* of the Federal Reserve System, which consists of seven members nominated by the President and confirmed by the Senate to serve overlapping terms of 14 years. Members of the board are generally bankers or economists

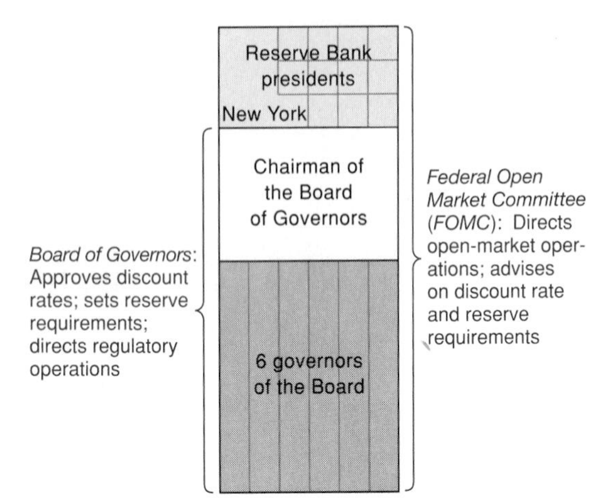

Figure 29-2. The major players in monetary policy

The powers of the Federal Reserve are lodged in two bodies. The seven-member Board of Governors approves changes in discount rates and sets reserve requirements. The 19-member FOMC directs the setting of bank reserves. The Chairman of the Board of Governors steers both committees.

The size of each box indicates that person's or group's relative power; note the size of the Chairman's box. The relative importance of different people is drawn on the basis of the study by former Fed governor Sherman Maisel, *Managing the Dollar* (Norton, New York, 1973.)

who work full-time at the job.

The key decision-making body in the Federal Reserve System is the *Federal Open Market Committee (FOMC).* The 12 voting members of the FOMC include the seven governors plus five of the presidents of the regional Federal Reserve Banks. This key group controls the single most important and frequently used tool of modern monetary policy—the supply of bank reserves.

At the pinnacle of the entire system is the *Chairman of the Board of Governors,* currently an economist, Alan Greenspan. He chairs the board and the FOMC, acts as public spokesman for the Fed, and exercises enormous power over monetary policy. He is often, and accurately, called the "second most powerful man in America," reflecting the extent to which he can influence the entire economy through his impact on monetary policy.

In spite of the formally dispersed structure of the Fed, close observers think that power is quite centralized. The Federal Reserve Board, joined at meetings by presidents of the 12 regional Federal Reserve Banks, operates under the Fed Chairman to formulate and carry out monetary policy. The informal structure of the Federal Reserve System is shown in Figure 29-2.

Independence. On examining the structure of the Fed, one might ask, "In which of the three branches of government does the Fed lie?" The answer is, "None. Legally, the 12 regional banks are private. In reality, the Fed as a whole behaves as an independent government agency."

Although nominally a corporation owned by the commercial banks that are members of the Federal Reserve System, the Federal Reserve is in fact a public agency. It is directly responsible to Congress; it listens carefully to the advice of the President; and whenever any conflict arises between its making a profit and promoting the public interest, it acts unswervingly in the public interest. The Fed is allowed to print currency, in return for which it holds interest-bearing government securities. Through this activity, it earns billions of dollars of profits each year. But, to reflect its public mission, profits above a certain return go to the U.S. government.

Above all, the Federal Reserve is an *independent* agency. While they listen carefully to Congress and the President, and even to the election returns, in the end the members of the Board of Governors and the FOMC decide monetary policy according to their views about the nation's economic interests. As a result, the Fed sometimes comes into conflict with the executive branch. The Roosevelt, Johnson, Carter, Reagan, and Bush administrations all had occasional harsh words for Fed policy. The Fed listened politely, but the President could not force the Fed to bend to his wishes.

From time to time, people argue that the Fed is too independent. "How can a democracy allow a group of private bankers to control monetary policy?" ask critics. Who, they ask, gave the Federal Reserve the authority to raise interest rates to 20 percent in 1980? Where can we read that the Fed is authorized to tighten money and create recessions? Shouldn't monetary policy be set by elected representatives in Congress or by the executive branch?

There is no right answer to these questions. On the one hand, an independent central bank is the guardian of the value of a nation's currency and the best protector against rampant inflation. Moreover, independence ensures that monetary policy is not subverted to partisan political objectives; the Fed's independence allows it the leeway to undertake policies, such as fighting inflation, that have little popular support. The elected branches will not always sacrifice their offices for long-run economic welfare.

At the same time, because they are so far removed from the political process, monetary managers at the Fed may lose touch with social and economic realities. Members of Congress are routinely forced to confront unemployed autoworkers and bankrupt farmers—groups seldom encountered in the Federal Reserve building in Washington.

The debate about the Fed's independence is neither new nor frivolous. Proposals to change the composition of the board, to put representatives of Congress or the executive branch on the FOMC or to let each new President appoint his own Chairman of the Board of Governors, are perennial topics for debate.

We can summarize the structure of the Federal Reserve System this way:

The Federal Reserve Board in Washington, together with the 12 Federal Reserve Banks, constitutes our American central bank. Every modern country has a central bank. Its primary mission is to control the nation's money supply and credit conditions.

Overview of the Fed's Operations

How does the Fed actually manage the money supply? In answering this question, it is useful to start by viewing the world as seen by the Fed. Figure 29-3 shows the various stages of Federal Reserve operations. The Federal Reserve has at its disposal a number of policy instruments that can affect certain intermediate targets (such as reserves, the money supply, and interest rates). All its operations through these instruments are intended to help achieve the ultimate objectives of a healthy economy—low inflation, rapid growth in output, and low employment. It is important to keep these three sets of variables distinct in our analysis.

The three major instruments of monetary policy are:

- *Open-market operations*—buying or selling government bonds
- *Discount-rate policy*—setting the interest rate, called the discount rate, at which member banks can borrow reserves from the Fed
- *Reserve-requirements policy*—Changing the legal reserve ratio requirements on deposits with banks and other financial institutions

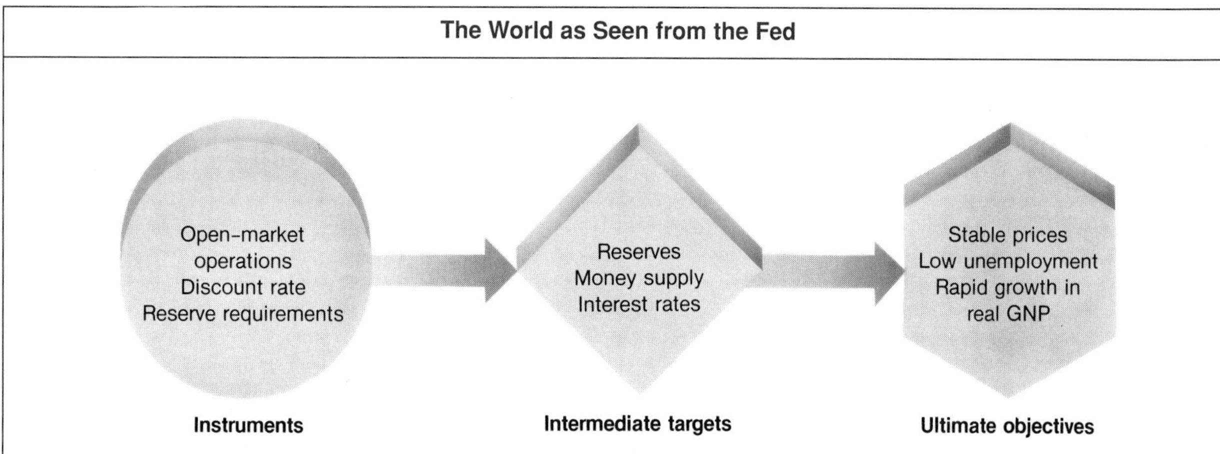

Figure 29-3. While the Fed ultimately pursues objectives like stable prices, its short-term operations focus on the intermediate targets

In determining monetary policy, the Fed directly manipulates the instruments or policy variables under its control—open-market operations, discount rate, and reserve requirements. These help determine bank reserves, the money supply, and interest rates—the intermediate targets of monetary policy. Ultimately, the Fed is a partner with fiscal policy in pursuing the major objectives of rapid growth, low unemployment, and stable prices.

In managing money, the Federal Reserve must keep its eye on a set of variables known as *intermediate targets.* These are economic variables that are neither Fed policy instruments nor true policy objectives but stand as intermediates in the transmission mechanism between Fed instruments and goals. When the Fed wants to affect its ultimate objectives, it first changes one of its instruments. This change affects an intermediate variable like interest rates, credit conditions, or the money supply. Much as a doctor interested in the health of a patient will monitor pulse and blood pressure, so will the Federal Reserve keep a careful watch on its intermediate targets.

Balance Sheet of the Federal Reserve Banks

Before analyzing the way the Fed determines the money supply, we need to describe the consolidated balance sheet of the Federal Reserve System, shown in Table 29-1. The first asset consists mostly of gold certificates, i.e., warehouse receipts from the Treasury for official gold. U.S. government securities (e.g., bonds) make up most of the rest of the assets. The small items, loans and acceptances, are primarily loans or advances to commercial banks. The interest rate the Fed charges banks for such loans, or "discounts," is called the discount rate, which is another of the Fed's tools.

Liabilities include the usual capital accounts: original capital paid in by the member banks plus retained earnings or accumulated surplus. Federal Reserve notes are the Fed's principal liabilities. This is the paper currency we use every day.

Of vital importance are the bank reserves, or balances kept on deposit by commercial banks with the Federal Reserve Banks and shown as Fed liabilities. Taken along with small amounts of the banks' vault cash, these are the reserves we have been talking about. They provide the basis for multiple deposit creation by the nation's banking system.

By altering its holding of government securities, the Fed can change bank reserves and thereby trigger the sequence of events that ultimately determines the total supply of money.

The Nuts and Bolts of Monetary Policy

Open-Market Operations

The Fed's most useful tool is "open-market operations."

By selling or buying government securities in the open market, the Fed can lower or raise bank reserves. These so-called open-market operations are a central bank's most important stabilizing instrument.

Every month the FOMC meets to decide whether to pump more reserves into the banking system by

Combined Balance Sheet of 12 Federal Reserve Banks, 1991
(Billions of Dollars)

Assets		Liabilities and net worth	
Gold certificates and other cash	$ 11.7	Capital accounts	$ 3.2
U.S. government securities	247.4	Federal Reserve notes	267.4
Loans and acceptances	0.2	Deposits:	
Miscellaneous other assets	56.0	Bank reserves	24.1
		U.S. Treasury	10.9
		Miscellaneous liabilities	9.7
Total	$315.3	Total	$315.3

Table 29-1. Federal Reserve notes and deposits underlie our money supply

By controlling its earning assets (government securities and loans), the Fed controls its liabilities (deposits and Federal Reserve notes). It determines the economy's money supply (currency and demand deposits, M_1), and thereby affects GNP, unemployment, and inflation. (Source: *Federal Reserve Bulletin.)*

Federal Reserve assets (billions)		Federal Reserve liabilities (billions)	
U.S. securities	−$1	Bank reserves	−$1
Total	−$1	Total	−$1

Commercial bank assets (billions)		Commercial bank liabilities (billions)	
Reserves	−$ 1	Checking deposits	−$10
Loans and investments	− 9		
Total	−$10	Total	−$10

Table 29-2(a). Open-market sale by Fed cuts reserves initially

Table 29-2(b). . . . and ultimately cuts deposits 10 to 1

This crucial set of tables shows how open-market operations affect the Fed's balance sheet and the balance sheet of banks.

In Table 29-2(*a*), the Fed has sold $1 billion of securities. The funds used to pay for the securities are deposited in the Fed, reducing bank reserves by $1 billion. Bank reserves thus decline by $1 billion as a result of the open-market operation.

Then in Table 29-2(*b*), we see the effect on the balance sheet of banks. With a required reserve ratio of 10 percent of deposits, the banks will be content only when they have no excess or deficit reserves. The reserve contraction cascades through the banking system. Thus deposits must fall by $10 billion for the banking system to be back in equilibrium.

In the end, an open-market operation in which the Fed sells $1 billion of securities leads to an eventual decline of $10 billion in bank money and in the money supply.

buying Treasury bills (i.e., short-term bonds) and longer-term government bonds, or whether to tighten monetary policy by selling government securities.

To see how an open-market operation changes reserves, let us suppose that the Fed thinks the economic winds are blowing up a little inflation. The FOMC holds its meeting in Washington and hears presentations and projections from its talented staff of economists. The committee decides, "Let's sell $1 billion of Treasury bills from our portfolio to contract reserves and tighten overall money and credit." The motion is unanimously approved by vote of the seven Washington governors and five regional Bank presidents.

To whom are the bonds sold? To the open market; this includes dealers in government bonds, who then resell them to commercial banks, big corporations, and other financial institutions.

The purchasers usually buy the bonds by writing checks to the Fed, drawn from an account in a commercial bank. For example, if the Fed sells $10,000 worth of bonds to Ms. Smith, she writes a check on the Farmers' Bank of Seattle. The Fed presents the check at the Farmers' Bank. When the Farmers' Bank pays the check, it will reduce its balance with the Fed by $10,000. At the end, the Farmers' Bank, and the entire commercial banking system, will lose $10,000 in reserves at the Federal Reserve System.

Table 29-2(*a*) shows the ultimate effect of a $1 billion open-market operation on the Federal Reserve balance sheet. The open-market sale changes the Federal Reserve balance sheet by reducing both assets and liabilities by $1 billion: the Fed has sold $1 billion of government bonds, and its liabilities have declined by exactly the same amount, $1 billion of bank reserves.

Effects on Money. To understand the effect of the reserve change on the money supply, we must consider the banks' response. In this chapter, we continue the algebraic convenience of assuming that banks are assumed to hold 10 percent of their deposits as reserves with the central bank; the legal reason for this practice is discussed in greater detail later in this chapter.

What happens to the money supply? Reserves go down by $1 billion, and that tends to set off a contraction of deposits. If the legal reserve requirement is 10 percent, the $1 billion sale of government bonds will result in a $10 billion cut in the community's money supply. (We saw in the last chapter how a change in bank reserves would lead to a multiplied change in total bank deposits.) Table 29-2(*b*) shows the banks' ultimate position after $1 billion of reserves have been extinguished by the open-market operation. In the end, the Fed's open-market sale has caused a $10 billion contraction in the money supply.

Operating Procedures

The FOMC meets eight times a year to give instructions to its operating arm, the Federal Reserve Bank of New York. The instructions are contained in an "FOMC policy directive." The directive has two parts: a general assessment of economic conditions and a review of the objectives of monetary policy. As an example, consider the August 1982 directive. In the midst of the deepest recession of the postwar period, the FOMC began with its review of the economy:[1]

> The information reviewed at this meeting suggests only a little further advance in real GNP in the current quarter, following a relatively small increase in the second quarter, while prices on the average are continuing to rise more slowly than in 1981.

What objectives did the Fed establish for monetary policy? It stated:

> The Federal Open Market Committee seeks to foster monetary and financial conditions that will help to reduce inflation, promote a resumption of growth in output on a sustainable basis, and contribute to a sustainable pattern of international transactions.

The most important part of the procedure is instructing the front-line troops at the New York Fed about how to manage financial markets on a day-to-day basis. The operating procedures have changed over time. Before the 1970s, the FOMC used to give such vague instructions as, "Keep credit conditions and interest rates as tight as they have been." Or, "Loosen credit a little to help expand GNP." Because the Fed acted cautiously, it was sometimes slow to react to changing business-cycle conditions.

In the late 1970s, the Federal Reserve altered its operating procedures to pay closer attention to movements in the money supply. It was accused of helping to reelect President Nixon in 1972; shortly afterward, the Fed was charged with overreacting to the sharp recession of 1974–1975 and with allowing unemployment to rise too sharply. To rein in the Fed, Congress directed it to set explicit growth-rate targets for the major monetary aggregates.

From October 1979 until late 1982, the Federal Reserve undertook a major experiment, concentrating almost exclusively on the growth of M_1, M_2, and bank reserves. It hoped that a clear and decisive strategy of targeting the monetary aggregates would help reduce an annual inflation rate that was surging beyond 10 percent. An example of the operational directive given by the FOMC dates from August 1982:

> In the short run, the Committee continues to seek behavior of reserve aggregates consistent with growth of M_1 and M_2 from June to September [1982] at annual rates of about 5 percent and about 9 percent respectively.

The shift to targeting reserves and the money supply in 1979 was highly controversial. The immediate result was a major reduction in the growth of the money supply and a consequent tightening of monetary policy. This led to an increase of market interest rates to levels not seen since the Civil War. It was followed shortly thereafter by the deepest recession since the 1930s. The policy was definitely successful in reducing inflation to 3 to 4 percent per year by the mid-1980s.

In the political hue and cry surrounding the sharp recession of 1982, the Fed concluded that its monetary policy had become overly restrictive. In addition, the definitions of the monetary aggregates became confused at this time because of the addition of a number of new assets (such as interest-bearing checking accounts) to M_1 and M_2. The Fed therefore retreated from its strict reserve and monetary targeting in the fall of 1982.

After 1982, the Fed began to downplay the use of monetary aggregates in its decisions about monetary policy. In 1987, it ceased stating explicit targets in terms of M_1, although it continued to publish monitoring ranges for other aggregates.

Choice of Policies. How does the Federal Reserve choose its money and interest-rate targets today? The process is shrouded in mystery, but firsthand accounts and memoirs of Fed governors and staff members boil down to something like the following.

The Fed staff and the FOMC have certain macroeconomic objectives, including goals for inflation, the foreign exchange rate of the dollar, real GNP, unemployment, and the trade balance. The Fed

[1] The FOMC quotations are from the *Federal Reserve Bulletin,* which contains monthly reports on Federal Reserve activities and other important financial developments.

makes regular projections on variables outside its control (such as fiscal policy, oil prices, foreign economic growth, and so forth) and then forecasts the behavior of the economy using a number of different assumptions about monetary policy.

The FOMC then debates the proper course for monetary policy. If the economy is performing satisfactorily, it might decide to leave interest rates and money-supply growth at their current levels. Or, if the FOMC thought that the current setting was encouraging inflation, it might choose to tighten monetary policy a notch. Alternatively, if the Fed thought that a recession loomed ahead, it might inject reserves into the system, increasing the money supply and consequently lowering interest rates.

It is not always easy to understand the exact chain of reasoning that led to a particular monetary-policy step. Nonetheless, historians who sift through the decisions usually find that the Fed is ultimately concerned with preserving the integrity of our financial institutions, combating inflation, defending the exchange rate of the dollar, and preventing excessive unemployment.[2]

Discount-Rate Policy: A Second Instrument

When commercial banks are short of reserves, they are allowed to borrow from the Federal Reserve Banks. Their loans were included under the asset heading "Loans and acceptances" in the Fed balance sheet in Table 29-1. We will call these loans *borrowed reserves.* When borrowed reserves are growing, the banks are borrowing from the Fed, thereby increasing total bank reserves (borrowed plus unborrowed reserves). Conversely, a drop in borrowed reserves promotes a contraction in total bank reserves.

Although borrowed reserves get multiplied into bank money just like the unborrowed reserves we discussed in the last section, they are not a precise instrument under the control of the Fed. It's like the old saying, "You can lead a horse to water, but you can't make him drink." The Fed can encourage or discourage bank borrowings, but it cannot set a precise level of borrowed reserves.

If the Fed thinks that the money supply is growing too slowly and needs to be boosted, it does not send sales agents out to drum up more borrowing. Instead, it might lower the **discount rate,** which represents the interest rate charged on bank borrowings from the 12 regional Federal Reserve Banks. But the relationship between the discount rate and bank borrowings is not very precise. In recent years, borrowed reserves have not played a major role in monetary policy.[3]

Changing the Discount Rate. For many years, the discount rate was the bellwether of monetary policy. For example, in 1965 when the Fed wanted to send a signal to markets that the Vietnam war boom threatened to become inflationary, it raised the discount rate. So powerful was this signal that Fed Chairman Martin was called to the LBJ ranch for a dressing down by President Johnson, who was afraid the higher discount rate would slow the economy. More recently, as the U.S. economy has become more integrated with other countries, the discount rate has occasionally been used to signal major changes in economic policy or to coordinate monetary policies with other countries.

Some economists would like the Federal Reserve to make the discount rate a market-based interest rate. One reform proposal would tie the discount rate directly to short-term interest rates—in principle removing any need for the Fed to ration borrowing by banks. Other economists fear that such a move would make the money supply more unpredictable. It is unlikely that such a change is in the wind today.

Changing Reserve Requirements

We noted above that, but for government rules, banks would probably keep only about 1 percent of their deposits in the form of reserves. In fact, today American banks are required to keep substantially

[2] For a careful analysis of political and economic forces operating on the Federal Reserve, see Donald Kettl, *Leadership at the Fed* (Yale University Press, New Haven, Conn., 1986).

[3] When the Federal Reserve System was started, it was thought that discount policy would be most important of all. The idea was to have banks buy their customers' promissory notes at a "discount," sending them over to the Reserve Banks in return for new cash. That way, the neighborhood banks would never run out of money to accommodate worthy farm and business borrowers. It did not work out that way. Why not? Largely because the last thing a healthy economy wants is an elastic money supply that will *automatically* expand when business is good and contract when it is bad. That way lies disastrous reinforcement of business cycles and inflation.

more reserves than are necessary for meeting customers' needs. These legal reserve requirements are a crucial part of the mechanism by which the Fed controls the supply of bank money. This section describes the nature of legal reserve requirements and shows how they affect the money supply.

Legal Reserve Requirements. We have mentioned that banks are required to hold a minimum amount as non-interest-bearing reserves. Table 29-3 shows current reserve requirements along with the Fed's discretionary power to change reserve requirements. The key concept is the level of *required reserve ratios.*[4] They range from 12 percent against checkable deposits down to zero for personal savings accounts. For convenience in our numerical examples, we use 10 percent reserve ratios, with the understanding that the actual ratio required is slightly different from 10 percent.

[4] The legislation that set out the rules for today's financial intermediaries was contained in the Depository Institutions Deregulation and Monetary Control Act of 1980 and the Garn–St Germain Depository Institutions Act of 1982. For brevity, we call these the 1980 and 1982 Banking Acts.

Type of deposit	Reserve ratio (%)	Range in which Fed can vary (%)
Checking (transaction) accounts:		
First $41 million	3	No change allowed
Above $41 million	12	8 to 14
Time and savings deposits:		
Personal	0	
Nonpersonal		
Up to 1½ years' maturity	0	0 to 9
More than 1½ years' maturity	0	0 to 9

Table 29-3. Required reserves for financial institutions

This table shows the pattern of reserve requirements for financial institutions under the 1980 Banking Act (known as the Depository Institutions Deregulation and Monetary Control Act of 1980). The reserve ratio column shows the percent of deposits in each category that must be held in non-interest-bearing deposits at the Fed or in cash on hand.

There are three classes of deposits. Checking-type accounts in large banks face required reserves of 12 percent. Checking accounts in small banks face a small reserve requirement of 3 percent. Other deposits will have no reserve requirements.

Note as well that the Fed has power to alter the reserve ratio within a given range. It does so only on the rare occasion when economic conditions warrant a sharp change in monetary policy. (Source: *Federal Reserve Bulletin,* June 1991.)

Bankers often complain that they are required to hold non-interest-bearing, barren reserve assets beyond what is needed to meet the ebb and flow of withdrawals and receipts. While this view has merit from the point of view of bankers, it misses the macroeconomic point: *Legal reserve requirements are set high in order to allow the central bank to control the money supply.* That is, by setting reserve requirements well above the level that banks themselves desire, the central bank can determine the exact level of reserves and can thereby control the money supply more precisely.

Put differently, by setting reserve requirements so high, the central bank can be confident that banks will generally want to hold no more than the legal minimum. The supply of bank money will then be determined by the supply of bank reserves (determined by the Fed through open-market operations) and by the money-supply multiplier (determined by the required reserve ratio). Because the Fed controls both bank reserves and the required reserve ratio, it has (within a small margin of error) control over the money supply.

Impacts of Changes in Required Reserves. In addition, the Fed can change reserve requirements if it wants to change the money supply quickly. For instance, if the Fed wants to tighten money overnight, it can raise the required reserve ratio for the big banks to the 14 percent statutory limit. It might even raise reserve requirements on time deposits. On the other hand, if the Fed wants to ease credit conditions, it can do the reverse and cut legal reserve ratios.

Exactly how does an increase in required ratios operate to tighten credit? Suppose the required reserve ratio is 10 percent and banks had built up their reserves to meet this requirement. Now suppose the Fed decides to tighten credit and Congress allows it to raise the required reserve ratio to 20 percent. (This fantastic figure is for algebraic simplicity. The Fed cannot and would not take such a drastic step today.)

Even if the Fed does nothing by way of open-market operations or discount policy to change bank reserves, banks now have to contract their loans and investments greatly—and their deposits as well. Why? Because (as Chapter 28 showed) bank deposits can now be only 5 times reserves, not 10 times reserves. So there must be a drop by one-half in all deposits!

This painful cut will start to take place quickly. As soon as the Federal Reserve Board signs the new rule raising the requirement to 20 percent, banks will find that they have insufficient reserves. They will have to sell some bonds and call in some loans. The bond buyers and borrowers will drain their checking accounts. The process ends only after banks have brought down their deposits to 5 rather than 10 times their reserves.

Such an enormous change in so short a time would lead to very high interest rates, credit rationing, large declines in investment, and great reductions in GNP and employment. So this extreme example warns that this powerful tool of changing reserve requirements has to be used with great caution. Changes in reserve requirements are made extremely sparingly because they present too large and abrupt a change in policy. Open-market operations can achieve the same results in a less disruptive way.

Interest-Rate Regulation

In addition to the three major instruments discussed above, the Federal Reserve (with the help of Congress and other government agencies) has historically regulated financial markets by limiting interest rates. Until the 1980s, most interest rates paid by commercial banks were controlled. Banks were not allowed to pay interest on checking accounts, and there were ceilings on interest rates on savings accounts and time deposits.

Regulated interest rates could not survive in competitive markets. Financial institutions devised new types of instruments which lured funds from low-yield deposits. The high interest rates of the late 1970s and early 1980s put further pressure on the system, because banks (which paid 5 percent per year on their savings accounts) had to compete with money market mutual funds (which paid 10 or 15 percent on their deposits). Eventually the regulatory edifice constructed during the Great Depression began to crumble. Congress reacted with the Banking Acts of 1980 and 1982, which largely deregulated interest rates.

The New Regulatory Structure. The Banking Acts of 1980 and 1982 created a new regulatory structure that has largely decontrolled interest rates in financial markets. The analytical basis of the new approach was to separate transactions accounts from non-transactions accounts. A *transactions account* is one whose primary purpose is to serve as a means of payment; these include currency and checking accounts. A *non-transactions account* is an asset whose primary purpose is to put aside funds for the future, not to pay bills (a savings account is an example of a non-transactions account).

Once this distinction had been made, the 1980 and 1982 Acts effectively deregulated non-transactions accounts. This legislation phased out interest-rate ceilings for non-transactions accounts in 1986 and set reserve requirements on these deposits at zero for personal accounts and at minimal levels for business accounts. As of the late 1980s, non-transactions accounts earn market interest rates and are effectively outside the regulatory structure of the Federal Reserve.

The remaining assets—transactions assets like checking accounts—have been largely deregulated. These accounts are subject to substantial reserve requirements (currently amounting to 12 percent of transactions deposits for large banks). However, personal transactions accounts are no longer subject to interest-rate ceilings. The result is a financial sector that has been largely removed from regulation over the last two decades.

International Reserve Movements

The dollar is today used extensively in world trade and as a safe asset by many foreign investors. Consequently, dollars are widely held abroad by those who export and import with the United States, by foreign and American investors, by those who finance trade and investments between other countries, by speculators and dealers in foreign financial markets, by foreign governments, by central banks, and by international agencies like the International Monetary Fund. Foreigners own hundreds of billions of dollars in U.S. dollar-denominated assets. Because currency itself yields no interest return, foreigners prefer to hold interest-bearing assets (bonds, stocks, etc.). However, to have a medium for buying and selling such earning assets, foreigners do hold some transactions dollars in M_1.

Why are we concerned about international money holdings at this point? The reason is that deposits by foreigners in the banking system increase the total amount of bank reserves in the same way that deposits of domestic residents do. Thus changes in foreigners' dollar money holdings can set off a chain of expansion or contraction of the U.S. money supply.

For example, say the Japanese decide to deposit $1 billion of U.S. currency in U.S. banks. What happens? There is a $1 billion increase in reserves in the domestic banking system, as illustrated in Table 28-4(*a*) in the last chapter. As a result, the banking system can expand deposits tenfold, in this case to $10 billion.

Thus the Fed's control of the nation's *M* is modified by international disturbances to bank reserves. But the Fed has the power to offset any change in reserves coming from abroad. It effects this by engaging in what is called sterilization. *Sterilization* refers to actions by a central bank that insulate the domestic money supply from international reserve flows. Sterilization usually is accomplished when the central bank implements an open-market operation that reverses the international reserve movement.

To summarize:

The central bank's control over bank reserves is subject to disturbances from abroad. These disturbances can, however, be offset if the central bank sterilizes the international flows.

In practice, the Fed routinely sterilizes international disturbances to reserves. Other countries, with less well developed financial markets and central-banking systems, sometimes have trouble fully sterilizing international reserve flows.

Other Activities

At this point, you probably have concluded that the Fed is pretty busy. But we have described only the money market functions of the Fed—those relating to control of the money supply. There are, in addition, a number of subsidiary tasks delegated to the Fed and other federal agencies:

- *Managing exchange markets.* The Fed buys and sells different currencies on foreign exchange markets on behalf of the government. While this task is generally easy, from time to time foreign exchange markets become disorderly, and the Fed, under orders from the Treasury, steps in. A full discussion of the way that central banks can intervene to affect currency values is given in Chapter 39.
- *Coordinating international finances.* The Federal Reserve took the lead during the 1980s in working with foreign countries and with international agencies to alleviate the problems of large debt burdens. The debt crisis, which surfaced in 1981, found many middle-income and poor countries, such as Mexico and Brazil, burdened with extremely high levels of interest payments relative to their export earnings. The Fed understood that the debt crisis could lead to a crisis of confidence in the financial system, because many large American banks had worthless foreign loans that were as large as their net worth. Working together with other agencies, the Fed helped manage the crisis, so that by 1991 the debt burdens of most countries, along with the risks to the international financial system, had been significantly reduced.
- *Regulating banks and insuring deposits.* Since the Great Depression, the federal government has stood behind the banks. To instill confidence in banks, the government insures bank deposits, inspects the books of banks, and takes over insolvent banks. One important function of government is the insurance of bank deposits. The government insures up to $100,000 per deposit at banks that are members of the Federal Deposit Insurance Corporation (the F.D.I.C.).

The deregulation in financial markets over the last decade, along with the structural changes in financial markets and the real economy, led to a major fiasco in the U.S. deposit insurance system. Savings and loan associations (S&Ls) were allowed to undertake risky investments with very little regulatory supervision. As a result, they paid high interest rates on insured deposits and put those funds into real estate, energy projects, and high salaries for the directors. These were "Heads I win, tails the government loses" situations. When the real estate and energy markets went sour in the late 1980s, hundreds of savings and loan associations, along with a score of commercial banks, became insolvent.

The result was that the federal government was forced to bail out banks whose insured deposits exceeded their assets by an amount estimated to be between $150 and $250 billion. Taxpayers were ultimately being forced to pay the bill. Many economists believe that the deposit insurance system must be drastically overhauled if this sad episode is not to be repeated in the future.

We have completed our analysis of the money supply. It can be summarized as follows:

The money supply is ultimately determined by the policies of the Fed. By setting reserve requirements and the discount rate, and especially by undertaking open-market operations, the Fed determines the level of reserves and the money supply.

Banks and the public are cooperating partners in this process. Banks create money by multiple expansion of reserves; the public agrees to hold money in depository institutions.

Putting these together, the Fed can determine the money supply on a medium-term basis.

B. The Effects of Money on Output and Prices

> It is only in this interval between the acquisition of money and the rise of prices that the increasing quantity of gold and silver is favorable to industry.
>
> David Hume, *Essays,* "Of Money"

Having examined the building blocks of monetary theory, we now describe the *monetary transmission mechanism,* the route by which changes in the supply of money are translated into changes in output, employment, prices, and inflation.

How Monetary Policy Works to Control Spending

We begin with an overview of the steps in the process by which the Federal Reserve affects output and prices. For concreteness, assume that the Federal Reserve is concerned about rising prices and has decided to slow down the economy. There are five steps in the process.

1. *To start the process, the Fed takes steps to reduce bank reserves.* As we saw in the first part of this chapter, the Fed reduces bank reserves primarily by selling government securities in the open market. This changes the balance sheet of the banking system by reducing total bank reserves.
2. *Each dollar reduction in bank reserves produces a multiple contraction in checking deposits, thereby reducing the money supply.* This step was described in the last chapter, where it was shown that changes in reserves lead to a multiplied change in deposits. Since the money supply equals currency plus checking deposits, the reduction in checking deposits reduces the money supply.
3. *The reduction in the money supply will tend to increase interest rates and tighten credit conditions.* With an unchanged demand for money, a reduced supply of money will raise interest rates. In addition, the amount of credit (loans and borrowing) available to people will decline. Interest rates will rise for mortgage borrowers and for businesses that want to build factories, buy new equipment, or add to inventory. Higher interest rates will also lower the values of people's assets, depressing the prices of bonds, stocks, land, and houses.
4. *With higher interest rates and lower wealth, interest-sensitive spending—especially investment—will tend to fall.* The combination of higher interest rates, tighter credit, and reduced wealth will tend to discourage investment and consumption spending. Businesses will scale down their investment plans, as will state and local governments. When a town finds it cannot float its bonds at any reasonable rate, the new road is not built and the new school is postponed. Similarly, consumers decide to buy a smaller house, or to renovate their existing one, when rising mortgage interest rates make monthly payments high relative to monthly income. And in an econ-

omy increasingly open to international trade, higher interest rates may raise the foreign exchange rate of the dollar, depressing net exports. Hence, tight money will raise interest rates and reduce spending on interest-sensitive components of aggregate demand.

5. *Finally, the pressures of tight money, by reducing aggregate demand, will reduce income, output, jobs, and inflation*. The aggregate supply-and-demand (or, equivalently, the multiplier) analysis showed how such a drop in investment and other autonomous spending may depress output and employment sharply. Furthermore, as output and employment fall below the levels that would otherwise occur, prices tend to rise less rapidly or even to fall. Inflationary forces subside. If the Fed's diagnosis of inflationary conditions was on target, the drop in output and the rise in unemployment will help relieve inflationary forces.

We can summarize the steps as follows:

$$R \text{ down} \rightarrow M \text{ down} \rightarrow i \text{ up} \rightarrow I, C, X \text{ down} \rightarrow AD \text{ down} \rightarrow \text{real GNP down and } P \text{ down}$$

This five-step sequence—from the Fed's changes in commercial bank reserves, to a multiple change in total *M*, to changes in interest rates and credit availability, to changes in investment spending that shift aggregate demand, and finally to the response of output, employment, and inflation—is vital to the determination of output and prices. If you look back at Figure 29-1, you will see how each of the five steps fits into our thematic flow chart. We have already explained the first two steps; the balance of this chapter is devoted to analyzing steps 3 through 5.

The Money Market

Step three in the transmission mechanism is the response of interest rates and credit conditions to changes in the supply of money. Recall from the last chapter that the *demand for money* depends primarily on the need to undertake transactions. Households, businesses, and governments hold money so they may buy goods, services, and other items. In addition, some part of the demand for *M* derives from the need for a supersafe and highly liquid asset.

The *supply of money* is jointly determined by the private banking system and the nation's central bank. The central bank, through open-market operations and other instruments, provides reserves to the banking system. Commercial banks then create deposits out of the central-bank reserves. By manipulating reserves, the central bank can determine the money supply within a narrow margin of error.

Supply and Demand for Money

The supply and demand for money jointly determine the market interest rates. Figure 29-4 shows the total quantity of money (*M*) on the horizontal axis and the nominal interest rate (*i*) on the vertical axis. The supply curve is drawn as a vertical line on the assumption that the Federal Reserve manipulates its instruments to keep the money supply at a given level, shown as *M** in Figure 29-4.

In addition, we show the money demand schedule as a downward-sloping curve because the holdings of money decline as the level of interest rates rises. At higher interest rates, people and busi-

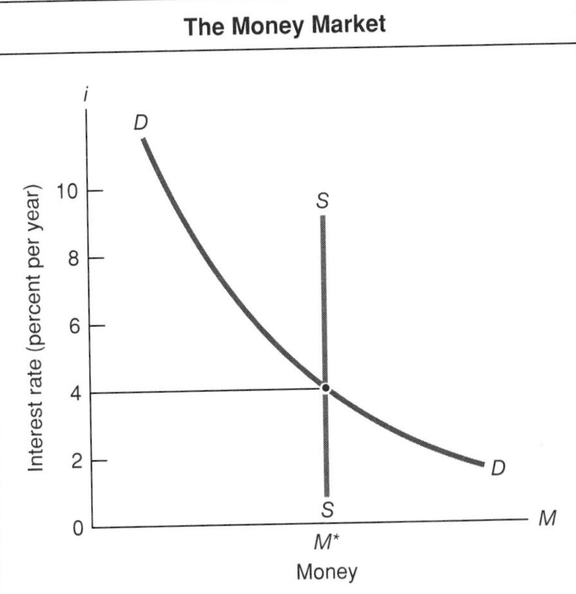

Figure 29-4. Demand and supply of money determine the interest rate

The Fed has a money target at *M**, represented by the vertical supply-of-money schedule, *SS*. The public (households and businesses) has a downward-sloping money demand schedule. In this example, the money market is in equilibrium with a nominal interest rate of 4 percent per year.

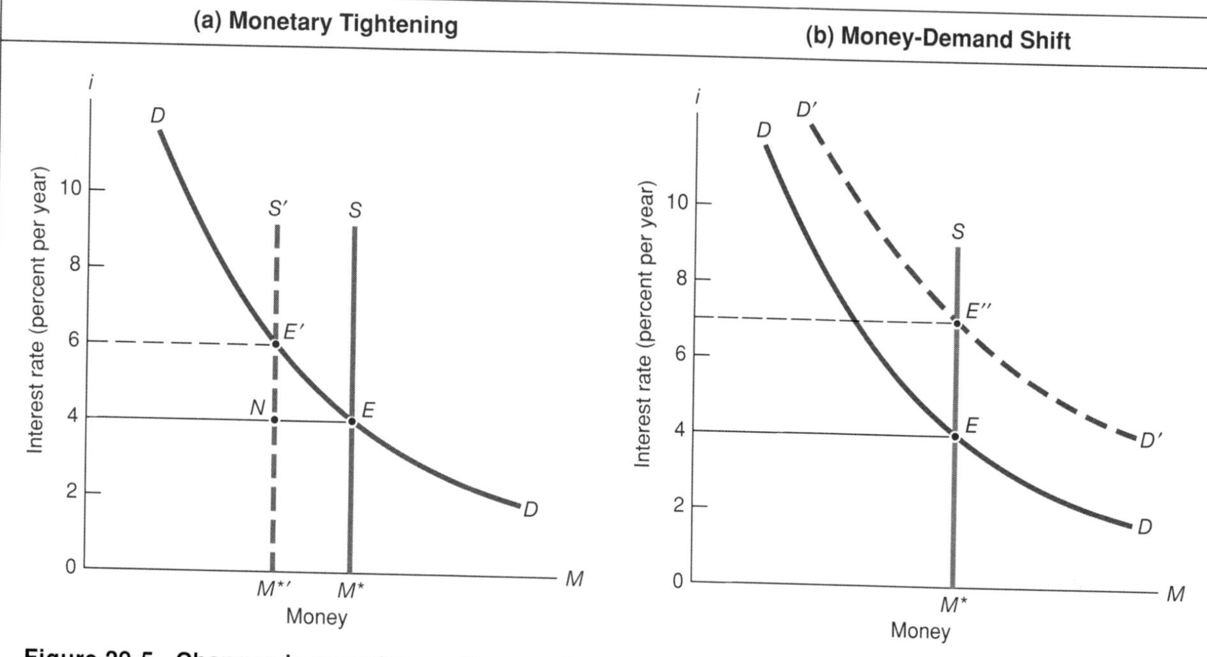

Figure 29-5. Changes in monetary policy or prices affect interest rates

In **(a)**, the Federal Reserve contracts bank reserves and the money supply in response to fears of rising prices. The lower money supply produces an excess demand for money shown by the gap *NE*. As the public attempts to attain the desired money stock, interest rates rise to the new equilibrium at *E′*.

In **(b)**, the demand for money has increased because of a run-up in the price level with real output held constant. The higher demand for money forces market interest rates upward until they in turn force the quantity of money demanded back down to M^*.

nesses shift more of their assets to higher-yield assets and away from low-yield or no-yield money. This is accomplished by shifting funds to high-interest assets more often, by holding less currency on average and replenishing cash more often, by trying to synchronize income and expenditures, and by engaging in similar cash-management schemes.

The intersection of the supply and demand schedules in Figure 29-4 determines the market interest rate. Recall that interest rates are the prices paid for the use of money. Interest rates are determined in the **money markets,** which are the markets where short-term funds are lent and borrowed. Important interest rates include short-term rates such as the rates on 3-month Treasury bills, short-term commercial paper (notes issued by large corporations), and the Federal Funds rate that banks pay each other for the overnight use of bank reserves. Longer-term interest rates include 10-year or 20-year government and corporate bonds and mortgages on real estate. (See Figure 28-2 for a graph of recent trends in interest rates.)

In Figure 29-4, the equilibrium interest rate is 4 percent per year. Only at 4 percent is the level of the money supply that the Fed has targeted consistent with the desired money holdings of the public. At a higher interest rate, there would be excessive money balances, and people would be unwilling to hold all the M^*. People would get rid of their excessive money holdings by buying bonds and other financial instruments, thereby lowering market interest rates toward the equilibrium 4 percent rate. What would happen at an interest rate of 2 percent?

We are concerned with the effects of changes in the supply or demand for money in the money market. First consider a change in monetary policy. Suppose that the Federal Reserve becomes worried about inflation and tightens monetary policy by selling securities and reducing the money supply.

The impact of a monetary tightening is shown in Figure 29-5(*a*). The leftward shift of the money supply schedule means that at the going 4 percent interest rate, money balances will not meet people's transactions and asset needs. The gap between E and N shows the extent of excess demand for money at the old interest rate. People start to sell off some of their assets and increase their money holdings. Interest rates rise until the new equilibrium is attained, shown in Figure 29-5(*a*) at point E' with a new and higher interest rate of 6 percent per year.

Another disturbance might come from higher prices. Suppose the money supply is held constant by the Fed. However, due to an increase in oil prices, the general price level rises and the money desired to finance transactions increases with no change in real GNP. In this case, shown in Figure 29-5(*b*), the demand for money would increase, shifting the money demand curve to the right from *DD* to *D'D'*, and leading to an increase in equilibrium interest rates.

The opposite cases would occur with Federal Reserve concern about a recession, a contraction in the demand for money because of a fall in prices, a decline in real output, and a shift in the public's desire to hold money.

To check your understanding, make sure you can work through the following cases using Figure 29-4: (1) The Federal Reserve has decided that unemployment is rising too sharply and wants to reverse this trend by expanding the money supply. What steps must the Fed take to expand money? What will be the impact on the money supply curve? What is the reaction in money markets? (2) As a result of a falling foreign exchange rate on the dollar, exports rise and real GNP increases. What happens to the demand for money? What is the impact upon the market interest rate? (3) As banks introduce new interest-bearing checking accounts, people decide to put more of their assets into these accounts and less into savings accounts at every level of GNP and of interest rates. The Fed is uncertain about the significance of this behavior and therefore keeps the money supply constant. What will be the impact of the asset switch on money supply and demand? On market interest rates?

To summarize our findings about the money market:

The money market is affected by a combination of (1) the public's desire to hold money (represented by the demand-for-money *DD* curve) and (2) the Fed's monetary policy (which is shown in Figure 29-4 as a fixed money supply or a vertical *SS* curve at point M^*). Their interaction determines the market interest rate, i. A tighter monetary policy shifts the *SS* curve to the left, raising market interest rates. An increase in the nation's output or price level shifts the *DD* curve to the right and raises interest rates. Monetary easing or a money-demand decline has the opposite effects.

The Monetary Mechanism

Every day, the newspapers and television feature reports on money markets and monetary policy, analyzing how monetary affairs affect interest rates, foreign exchange rates, the trade and budget deficits, output, employment, inflation, and virtually every macroeconomic variable. If you read the news recently, you might have seen the following statements:

> A big question is whether the Federal Reserve will react to the budget pact between Congress and the White House by cutting short-term interest rates. The Fed's policy-making committee faces intense pressure from White House officials to reduce short-term interest rates to help bolster the sagging economy.
>
> *(Wall Street Journal)*

> The Federal Reserve Board warned that passage of protectionist trade legislation or a higher minimum wage bill would unleash inflationary forces that the Fed would have to counter by tightening credit, perhaps severely.
>
> *(New York Times)*

> Earlier, Washington had been pressing officials to cut Japanese interest rates to enable the Federal Reserve to lower U.S. rates without risking flows of capital out of the U.S. With American's recession ending, the Fed may be less eager to trim U.S. rates. However, it is still worried that slowing growth abroad may eventually crimp American exports.
>
> *(Wall Street Journal)*

Underlying these statements are views about the way the Federal Reserve operates, the way money affects the economy, and the way political leaders and the populace want to shape monetary policy. Let us look at the impact of changing monetary conditions by using the multiplier model. We then will examine the transmission mechanism by using the aggregate demand-and-supply framework.

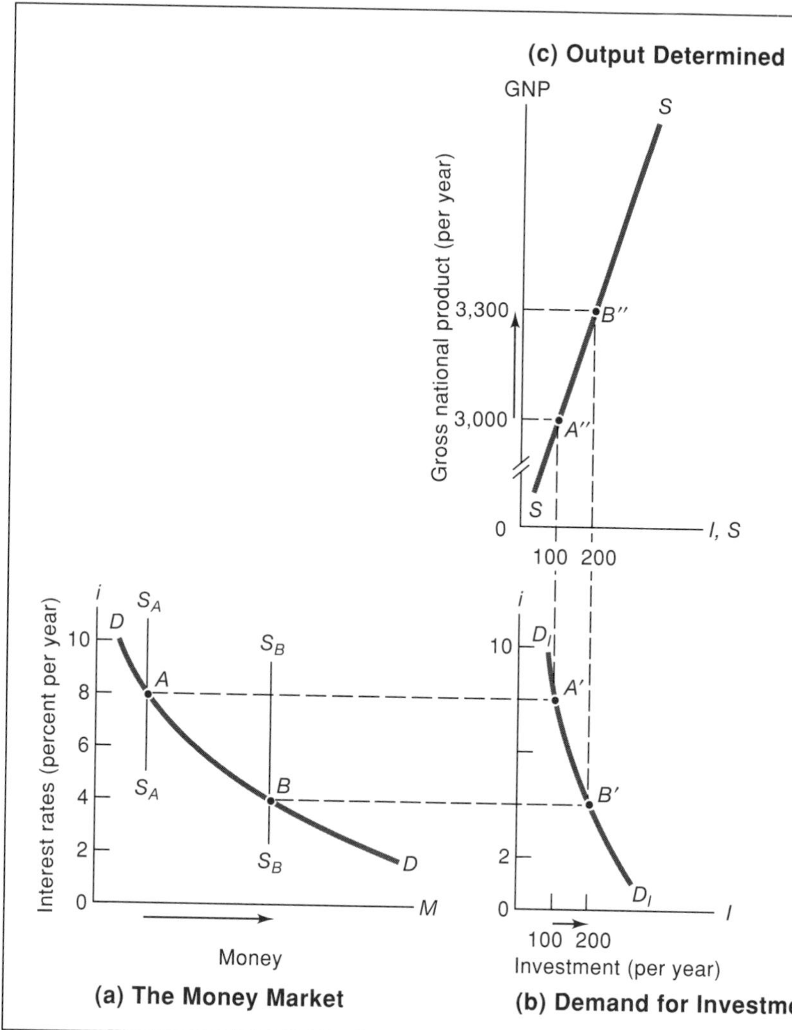

Figure 29-6. Central bank determines the money supply, changing interest rates and investment, thereby affecting GNP

When the Fed raises the money supply, from S_A to S_B, interest rates fall as people increase their money balances. That is, the economy moves down the money demand schedule in **(a)**.

Lower interest rates reduce the cost of investment, thus encouraging business purchases of plant and equipment and consumer purchases of houses. The economy moves down the demand-for-investment schedule $D_I D_I$ from A' to B' in **(b)**.

By the multiplier mechanism in **(c)**, the higher investment raises aggregate demand and GNP from A'' to B''.

Can you trace the reverse process in which open-market sales by the Fed will contract M, I, and GNP?

Graphical Analysis of Monetary Policy

Figure 29-6 shows the effects of a monetary expansion upon economic activity. Part (*a*) shows the money market in the lower left, (*b*) the determination of investment in the lower right, and (*c*) the determination of aggregate demand and GNP by the multiplier mechanism in the upper right. We can think of the causality as moving counterclockwise from the money market through investment to the determination of aggregate demand and GNP as a whole.

Starting at the lower left in Figure 29-6(*a*), we see the demand and supply for money that were depicted in Figures 29-4 and 29-5. For purposes of the present discussion, assume that in the initial state the money supply schedule was S_A and the interest rate was 8 percent per year. If the Fed was concerned about a looming recession, it might increase the money supply by making open-market purchases, shifting the curve to S_B. In the case shown in Figure 29-6(*a*), market interest rates would thereby fall to 4 percent.

Figure 29-6(*b*) picks up the story to show how lower interest rates increase spending on interest-sensitive components of aggregate demand. We saw in Chapter 25 that a decline in interest rates would induce businesses to increase their spending on plant, equipment, and inventories. The effects of eased monetary policy are rapidly seen in the housing market, where lower interest rates mean lower monthly mortgage payments on the typical house, thus encouraging households to purchase more and larger houses.

In addition, consumption spending increases, both because lower interest rates generally increase the value of wealth—as stock, bond, and housing prices tend to rise—and because consumers tend to spend more on automobiles and other big-ticket consumer durables when interest rates are low and credit is plentiful. Moreover, as we have seen in Chapter 27, lower interest rates tend to lower the foreign exchange rate on the dollar, thereby increasing the level of net exports. We see then how lower interest rates lead to increased spending in many different areas of the economy.

These consequences are evident in Figure 29-6(*b*), where the drop in interest rates (caused by the increase in the money supply) leads to a rise in investment from A' to B'. In this case, we should construe "investment" in the very broad sense sketched a moment ago: it includes not only business investment but also consumer durables and residences, as well as net foreign investment in the form of net exports.

Finally, Figure 29-6(*c*) shows the impact of changes in investment in the multiplier model. This diagram is simply Figure 27-5 turned on its side. Recall from Chapter 27 that, in the simplest multiplier model, equilibrium output is attained when desired saving equals desired investment. In Figure 29-6(*c*), we have shown this relationship by drawing the savings schedule as the *SS* schedule; this line represents the desired level of saving (measured along the horizontal axis) as a function of GNP on the vertical axis. Equilibrium GNP is attained at that level where the investment demand from panel (*b*) equals the desired saving from the *SS* schedule.

The initial level of investment was 100, as read off at A' in panel (*b*), producing a level of GNP of 3000. After easier money has lowered the interest rate from 8 to 4 percent, investment rises to 200 at point B'. This higher level of investment raises aggregate spending to the new equilibrium at B'' in panel (*c*) with a new equilibrium GNP of 3300.

What has occurred? The rise in the money supply from S_A to S_B lowered the interest rate from A to B; this caused investment to rise from A' to B'; and this in turn, acting through the multiplier, led to a rise in GNP from A'' to B''.

Such is the route by which monetary policy acts through intermediate targets like the money supply and interest rates to affect its ultimate targets.

Monetary Policy in the *AD-AS* Framework

The three-part diagram in Figure 29-6 illustrates how an increase in the money supply would lead to an increase in aggregate demand. We can now show the effect on the overall macroeconomic equilibrium by using aggregate supply and demand curves.

The increase in aggregate demand produced by an increase in the supply of money causes a rightward shift of the *AD* curve as drawn in Figure 29-7. This shift illustrates a monetary expansion in the presence of unemployed resources, with a relatively flat *AS* curve. Here, the monetary expansion

Expansionary Monetary Policy

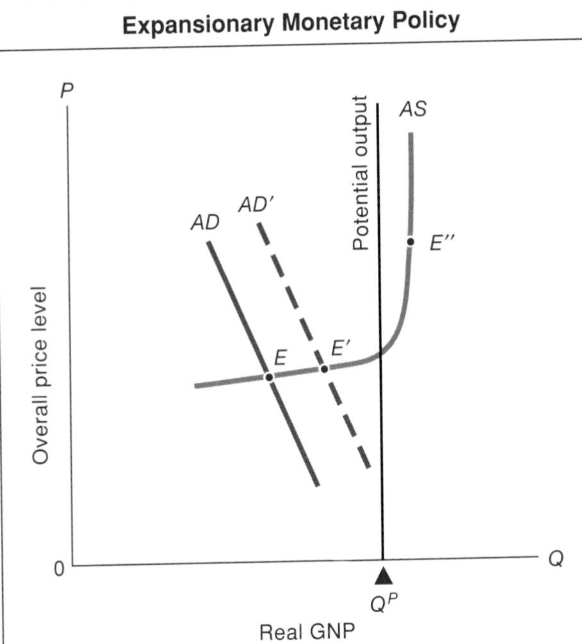

Figure 29-7. An expansionary monetary policy shifts *AD* curve to the right, raising output and prices

Earlier discussion and Figure 29-6 showed how an increase in the money supply would lead to an increase in investment and thereby to a multiplied increase in aggregate demand. This results in a rightward shift of the *AD* curve.

In the Keynesian region where the *AS* curve is relatively flat, a monetary expansion has its primary effect on real output, with only a small effect on prices. In the classical region, the *AS* curve is near-vertical (shown at point *E''*), and a monetary expansion will primarily raise prices and nominal GNP with little effect on real GNP. Can you see why in the long run money may have little impact on real output?

shifts aggregate demand from *AD* to *AD′*, and the overall equilibrium moves from *E* to *E′*. This case demonstrates how monetary expansion can increase aggregate demand and have a powerful impact on real output.

The sequence therefore runs as follows:

Monetary expansion bids down market interest rates. This stimulates interest-sensitive spending on business investment, housing, consumer durables, and the like. Via the multiplier mechanism, aggregate demand increases, raising output and prices above the levels they would otherwise attain. Therefore, the basic sequence is:

$$M \text{ up} \rightarrow i \text{ down} \rightarrow I, C, X \text{ up} \rightarrow AD \text{ up} \rightarrow \text{GNP up and } P \text{ up}$$

But what would happen if the economy were operating near its capacity? This is illustrated by point *E″* on the steeply sloping (or classical) segment of the *AS* curve in Figure 29-7. In this case, monetary changes would have little impact on real output. Rather, in the classical region of the *AS* curve, the higher money stock, chasing the same amount of output, would primarily end up raising prices.

To clinch your understanding of this vital sequence, work through the opposite case of a monetary contraction. Say that the Federal Reserve decides, as it did in 1979, to contract reserves, slow the economy, and reduce inflation. You can trace this sequence in Figure 29-6 by reversing the direction of the monetary policy, thereby seeing how money, interest rates, investment, and aggregate demand interact when monetary policy is tightened. Then see how a leftward shift of the *AD* curve in Figure 29-7 would reduce both output and prices.

Monetary Effects in the Long Run

Many economists believe that changes in the supply of money in the long run will mainly increase the price level with little or no impact upon real output. We can understand this point by analyzing the effects of monetary changes with different-shaped *AS* curves. As shown in Figure 29-7, monetary changes will affect aggregate demand and will tend to change real GNP in the short run when there are unemployed resources and the *AS* curve is relatively flat.

However, we emphasized in Chapter 26 that as prices and wages adjust over the longer run, the output effects of *AD* shifts will diminish, and the price effects will tend to dominate. Recall that the *AS* curve tends to be vertical or near-vertical in the long run as all sticky or contractual elements of wages and prices adapt to the higher expected levels of prices and wages. This means that in the long run, as prices and wages become more flexible, more and more of the effect of the money-supply change turns up in prices and less and less shows up in real output.

What is the intuition behind this difference between the short run and the long run? We can construct a highly simplified example to see the difference. Suppose we start out as in Figure 29-6 with a nominal GNP of 3000 and stable prices; then a monetary expansion that increases the money supply by 10 percent might increase nominal GNP by 10 percent to 3300. Studies by Robert J. Gordon and others indicate that, in the short run, "nominal GNP changes have been divided consistently, with two-thirds taking the form of output change and the remaining one-third the form of price change." Consequently, in the first year, the money-supply expansion might increase real GNP around 7 percent and increase prices around 3 percent.

As time passes, however, wages and prices begin to adjust more completely to the higher price and output levels. Demand inflation in both labor and product markets would raise wages and prices; wages would be adjusted to reflect the higher cost of living; cost-of-living provisions in contracts would raise wages and prices even further. After a second year, prices might rise another 1 or 2 percent, with output then being only 5 or 6 percent above its original level. In the third year, prices might rise again while output falls somewhat. Where would it end? It might continue over a period of years and decades until prices had risen by fully 10 percent and output was back to the original level. Thus, the monetary policy would have raised prices and wages by about 10 percent but would have left real output unchanged.

In this example, finally, all nominal magnitudes are increased by 10 percent, while all real magnitudes are unchanged. Nominal magnitudes like the GNP deflator, the CPI, nominal GNP, wages, the money supply, currency, checking deposits, dollar consumption, dollar imports, the dollar value of wealth, and so forth are 10 percent higher. But real GNP, real consumption, the real money supply (equal to the money supply divided by the price level), real wages, real incomes, and the real value of wealth are all unchanged by the monetary policy. In the long run, then, we say that money is *neutral.*

A word of caution is in order: The scenario that money changes lead to proportionate changes in all nominal magnitudes but no changes in real variables is intuitively plausible and supported by certain empirical evidence. But it is not a universal law. The long run may be a period of many decades; intervening events may throw the economy off the idealized long-run trajectory; and interest-rate changes along the path might have an irreversible impact upon the ultimate outcome.[5] The long-run neutrality of money is therefore only a tendency and not a universal law.

As we near the end of this chapter, we note that the discussion of the role of monetary policy has taken place without reference to fiscal policy. In reality, whatever the philosophical predilections of the government, every advanced economy simultaneously conducts both fiscal and monetary policies. Each policy has strengths and weaknesses. In the chapters that follow, we return to an integrated consideration of the roles of monetary and fiscal policies both in combating the business cycle and in promoting economic growth.

[5] An example will show how interest-rate changes might knock the economy off a neutral trajectory. When the Federal Reserve contracted the money supply and raised interest rates in 1979, the intention was to push the economy onto a low-inflation path by slowing the economy. The dramatic rise of interest rates, with short-term Treasury securities rising from 7 percent in 1978 to 14 percent in 1981, led to an appreciation of the dollar, to a massive foreign-trade deficit by the mid-1980s, and to a "debt crisis" among middle-income countries. By 1990, the United States was saddled with a foreign debt of around $400 billion, which will affect its economy for the foreseeable future.

From Aggregate Demand to Aggregate Supply

We have completed our introductory analysis of the determinants of aggregate demand. To recapitulate our findings: We examined the foundations of aggregate demand and saw that *AD* is determined by external or autonomous factors, such as investment and net exports, along with government policies, such as monetary and fiscal policies. In the short run, changes in these factors lead to an increase in spending and to increases in both output and prices.

In today's volatile world, economies are exposed to shocks from both inside and outside their borders. Wars, revolutions, debt crises, oil shocks, and government miscalculations have led to periods of high inflation or high unemployment or both in times of stagflation. Because there is no automatic self-correcting mechanism to eliminate macroeconomic fluctuations, governments today have a responsibility to moderate the swings of the business cycle. But even the wisest governments cannot eliminate unemployment and inflation in the face of all the shocks to which an economy is exposed.

Our next task is to examine more carefully issues of aggregate supply. We begin with an analysis of the process of long-run economic growth, which will deepen our understanding of the determinants of potential output and aggregate supply. We then tackle the interrelated topics of inflation and unemployment and see how modern market economies are severely constrained by the need to maintain stable prices. Finally, we return to the pressing dilemmas of macroeconomic policy today: fiscal policy and the government debt, the interrelation between fiscal policy and monetary policy, the need to promote long-term economic growth, and the new issues that arise because the United States is increasingly an open economy, exposed to the winds of international trade and finance.

SUMMARY

A. Central Banking and the Federal Reserve System

1. The Federal Reserve System is a central bank, a bank for bankers. Its function is to control the amount of bank reserves, thereby determining the nation's supply of money and affecting credit conditions and interest rates.
2. The Federal Reserve System (or "Fed" as it is often called) was created in 1913 to control the nation's money and credit. It is run by the Board of

Governors and the Federal Open Market Committee (or FOMC). The Fed acts as an independent government agency and has great discretion in determining monetary policy.

3. The Fed has three major policy instruments: (*a*) open-market operations, (*b*) the discount rate on bank borrowing, and (*c*) legal reserve requirements on depository institutions. Using these instruments, the Fed sets intermediate targets, such as the level of bank reserves, market interest rates, and the money supply. All these operations aim to improve the economy's performance with respect to the ultimate objectives of monetary policy: achieving the best combination of low inflation, low unemployment, rapid GNP growth, a sustainable trade balance, and orderly financial markets. In addition, the Fed along with other federal agencies must backstop the domestic and international financial system in times of crisis.

4. The most important instrument of monetary policy is the Fed's open-market operations. Sales by the Fed of government securities in the open market reduce the Fed's assets and liabilities and thereby reduce the reserves of banks. The effect is to decrease banks' reserve base for deposits. People end up with less *M* and more government bonds. Open-market purchases do the opposite, ultimately expanding *M* by increasing bank reserves.

5. Outflows of international reserves can reduce reserves and *M* unless offset by central-market purchases of bonds. Inflows have opposite effects unless offset. The process of offsetting international flows is sterilization. In recent years, the Fed has routinely sterilized international reserve movements.

B. The Effects of Money on Output and Prices

6. If the Fed desires to slow the growth of output, the five-step sequence goes thus:
   (a) The Fed reduces bank reserves through open-market operations.
   (b) Each dollar reduction of bank reserves produces a multiple contraction of bank money and the money supply.
   (c) In the money market, a reduction in the money supply moves along an unchanged money demand schedule, raising interest rates, restricting the amount and terms of credit, and tightening money.
   (d) Tight money reduces investment and other interest-sensitive items of spending like consumer durables or net exports.
   (e) The reduction in investment and other spending reduces aggregate demand by the familiar multiplier mechanism. The lower level of aggregate demand lowers output and the price level or inflation.
   The sequence is summarized by:

$$R \text{ down} \rightarrow M \text{ down} \rightarrow i \text{ up} \rightarrow I, C, X \text{ down} \rightarrow$$
$$AD \text{ down} \rightarrow \text{real GNP down and } P \text{ down}$$

7. Although the monetary mechanism is often explained in terms of money affecting "investment," in fact the monetary mechanism is an extremely rich and complex process whereby changes in interest rates and asset prices influence a wide variety of elements of spending. These sectors include housing, affected by changing mortgage interest rates and housing prices; business investment, affected by changing interest rates and stock prices;

spending on consumer durables, influenced by interest rates and credit availability; state and local capital spending, affected by interest rates; and net exports, determined by the effects of interest rates upon foreign exchange rates.

8. Monetary policy may have different effects in the short run and the long run. In the short run, with a relatively flat *AS* curve, most of the change in *AD* will affect output and only a small part will affect prices. In the longer run, as the *AS* curve becomes more nearly vertical, monetary shifts lead predominantly to changes in the price level and much less to output changes. In the polar case where money-supply changes affect only nominal variables and have no effects on real variables, we say money is neutral. Most real-world monetary shifts leave their footprints in the historical record.

CONCEPTS FOR REVIEW

Central banking
bank reserves
Federal Reserve balance sheet
open-market purchases and sales
discount rate, borrowings from Fed
legal reserve requirements
FOMC, Board of Governors
policy instruments, intermediate targets, ultimate objectives

The monetary transmission mechanism
demand and supply of money
five-step monetary transmission mechanism:
reserve change
reserves to money
money to interest rates
interest rates to investment
investment to GNP

interest-sensitive components of spending
monetary policy in the *AS-AD* framework
R down → M down → i up → I down → *AD* down → GNP down and P down
monetary policy in the short run and the long run
"neutrality" of money

QUESTIONS FOR DISCUSSION

1. List the policy instruments of the Fed. Explain how each changes bank reserves and the money supply. How powerful is each for controlling: (*a*) reserves, (*b*) M_1, (*c*) interest rates, (*d*) output, (*e*) prices?
2. Suppose you are the Chairperson of the Fed's Board of Governors at a time when the economy is depressed, and you are called to testify before a congressional committee. Write an explanation for an interrogating senator outlining how your expansionary acts would operate.
3. Trace the effects of a doubling of reserve requirements; a halving. Which alters bank profits more: open-market or reserve-requirements action?
4. Consider the balance sheet of the Fed in Table 29-1. Construct a corresponding balance sheet for banks (like the one in Table 28-2 in the last chapter) assuming that reserve requirements are 10 percent on checking accounts and zero on everything else.
   (a) Construct a new set of balance sheets, assuming the Fed sells $1 billion in government securities by open-market operations.
   (b) Construct another set of balance sheets to show what happens when the Fed increases reserve requirements to 20 percent.
   (c) Assume banks borrow $1 billion of reserves from the Fed. How will this action change the balance sheets?
5. Study the three quotations from newspapers on page 538. Using the theories developed in the last few chapters, explain the reasoning from each statement.
6. Discuss the following Federal Reserve statement: "The Federal Reserve System can see to it that banks have enough reserves to make money available to commerce, industry, and agriculture at low rates; but it cannot make the people borrow, and it cannot make the public spend the deposits that result when the banks do make loans and investments."
7. Using Figure 29-6, explain how the tight-money policies after 1979 lowered GNP. Also explain each of the steps in words.
8. Using a diagram like Figure 29-4, provide answers for the three examples in the paragraph on page 538.

PART SIX

AGGREGATE SUPPLY AND MACROECONOMIC POLICY

The Road Ahead

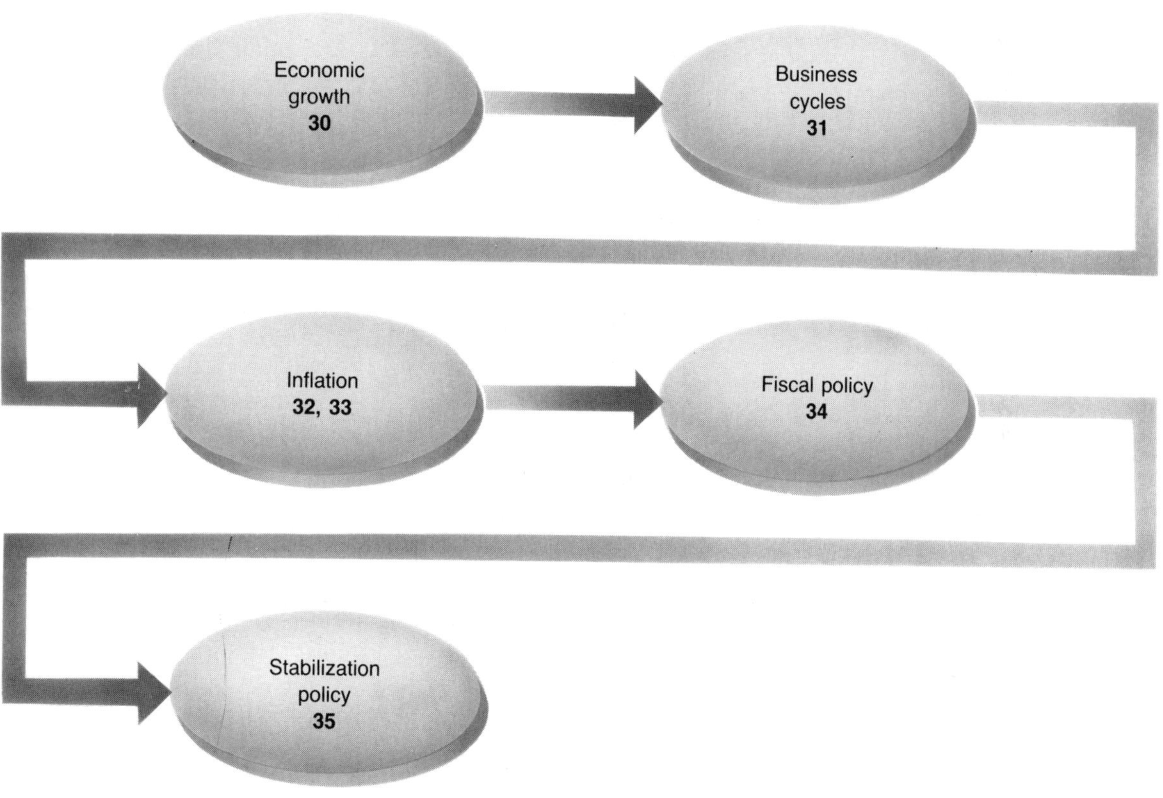

The last part derived the theory of aggregate demand, but aggregate output and prices are determined by the twin blades of aggregate supply and demand. This part begins with a description of the forces that propel long-term economic growth. It then explores the dynamics of unemployment and inflation and describes the major policy dilemmas facing a modern market economy.

C H A P T E R 30

ECONOMIC GROWTH

The Industrial Revolution was not an episode with a beginning and an end. . . . It is still going on.
E. J. Hobsbawm, *The Age of Revolution* (1962)

So far, our study of the movements in aggregate output and prices has focused primarily on the role of aggregate demand in determining the level of output. We have seen how autonomous forces like investment and exports have led to recessions, panics, and depressions. We have learned about the revolutionary analysis of J. M. Keynes, who showed how governments could tame the business cycle by applying monetary and fiscal measures that affect overall spending.

But we must now turn to the supply side of macroeconomic activity. Aggregate supply is central to both the long-run and the short-run evolution of the economy. In the short run, the interaction between aggregate demand and aggregate supply determines the level of output, unemployment, and capacity utilization and is crucial to movements in the price level and inflation. In the long run of a decade or more, aggregate supply is the major factor behind economic growth.

Our survey of aggregate supply begins in this chapter with the fundamental building block of aggregate supply: the analysis of economic growth or the growth of potential output. Figure 30-1 presents a chapter overview, using our familiar flowchart.

Long-Term Trends

Day-to-day discussion of economic issues focuses on short-run concerns like inflation, unemployment, or the latest turn in Federal Reserve policy. But these events are small ripples in the longer wave of economic growth. Year in and year out, advanced economies like the United States accumulate larger quantities of sophisticated capital equipment, push out the frontiers of technological knowledge, and increase their potential per capita GNP.

Look back to the inside frontispiece of this book, where you will see the advance of output over the twentieth century. You can see that real GNP grew *by a factor of over 15* since 1900. But this aggregate statistic hides the fortunes of individual industries experiencing evolution. Industries producing horseshoes and steam engines declined and disappeared; steel and textiles have fought for their lives against lower-cost foreign producers; aircraft and microcomputers have become the new buttress of America's industrial system—at least for a while.

Nations have long regarded economic growth as a central economic and political objective. In the United States, candidates have campaigned on platforms proclaiming the need to "get the country moving again." The recent revolutions in Eastern Europe and the Soviet Union were sparked by economic stagnation and low economic growth as compared to that of their Western neighbors. Economic growth is the single most important factor in the economic success of nations in the long run. But what exactly do we mean by economic growth?

Economic growth represents the expansion of a country's potential GNP.

Put differently, economic growth represents the

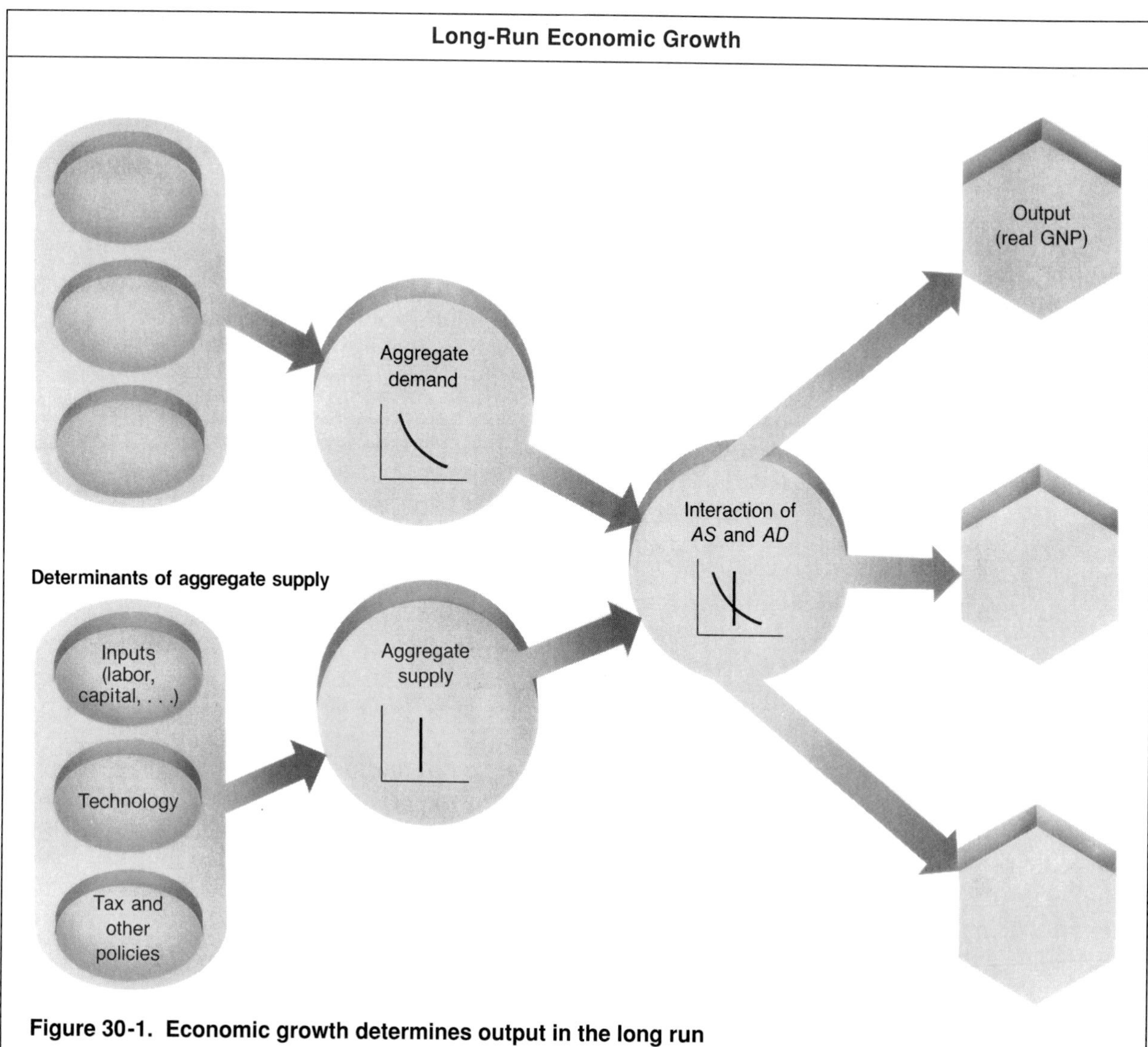

Figure 30-1. Economic growth determines output in the long run

In the long run, the growth of potential output tells the story of an economy's progress. This chapter traces the theories of economic growth and tests these theories using historical data.

expansion of a nation's production-possibility frontier (*PPF*). As economic growth occurs, a nation's *PPF* shifts outward (recall the graphs of the growing *PPF*s in Chapter 2). But economic growth is not just an abstract concept. It is vital for the citizens of a country because economic growth, in terms of growth of output per capita, means growing real wages and rising living standards. In this chapter, we will begin to understand the forces that raised consumption levels so sharply in the West over the last 200 years along with the economic policies that can be deployed to affect economic growth.

A. The Theory of Economic Growth

We begin our inquiry with a historical review of *theories of economic growth*—the factors that allow some nations to grow rapidly, some slowly, and others not at all. Our theories should help us to answer such questions as: Why have living standards risen since the Industrial Revolution? Can we discern patterns of economic growth in industrial countries? Has the period since the early 1970s witnessed a change in the patterns of economic growth?

We also want to know the sources of economic growth. Did our living standards rise because of more capital or because of technological progress? And what can a nation do to improve its economic performance?

The Magnificent Dynamics of Smith and Malthus

Even the earliest economists searched for an explanation of the evolution of output and wages. In *The Wealth of Nations* (1776), Adam Smith provided a handbook of economic development. He began with a hypothetical golden age: "that original state of things, which precedes both the appropriation of land and the accumulation of [capital] stock." This was a time when labor alone counted, when land was freely available to all, and before there was any capital to speak of.

What determines pricing and distribution in this simple and timeless dawn? Prices and outputs depend on labor alone. Every commodity trades at prices proportional to the amount of work required to produce it. If it takes twice the time to find and trap beavers than it does deer, then beavers will cost twice as much as deer. An economy in which prices are determined by the amount of labor that goes into the production of each commodity is governed by the **labor theory of value.**

In an economy such as Smith described, average labor cost would determine price no matter how many goods there were. Supply and demand are operating in this golden age, but the situation is so simple that we do not need an elaborate theory to explain it. The long-run supply curves for the different goods are simply horizontal lines at average costs, and average labor costs therefore determine prices.

Now consider the dynamics of such an economy. Population might be growing swiftly. Because land is freely available, people simply spread out onto more acres. National output exactly doubles as population doubles. The price ratio of deer to beaver remains exactly as before.

What about real wages? Wages still earn the entire national income because there is no subtraction for land rent or interest on capital. Output expands in step with population, and land is not a drag on output, so diminishing returns do not set in. The real wage per worker is therefore constant over time.

That would be the end of the story until, say, some clever hunter found a better way to catch deer or beavers. This innovation would raise the national product per capita. A balanced improvement in the productivity of labor would leave the price ratio of beaver to deer unchanged, but it would raise the real wage rate. In this world of the labor theory of value, inventions can only raise wages and speed the pace of economic growth.[1]

Scarce Land and Diminishing Returns

Eventually, as population continues to grow, all the land will be occupied, and the golden age in which only labor counts will come to an end. As we saw in Chapter 2, once the frontier of free land disappears, balanced growth of land, labor, and output is no longer possible. New laborers begin to crowd onto existing soils. Now land is scarce, and a rent is charged to ration it among different uses.

Population still grows, and so does national product. But output must grow more slowly than does population. Why? With new laborers added to fixed land, each worker now has less land to work with, and the law of diminishing returns comes

[1] Question 6 at the end of this chapter will apply the production-possibility frontier to Smith's beaver-deer economy.

into operation. The increasing labor-land ratio leads to a declining marginal product of labor and hence to declining real wage rates.[2] The classical economists believed that a clash of interests arises between classes. More people create a higher labor-land ratio, which produces lower wage rates and lower per capita incomes. At the same time, scarcer land produces higher rent rates per acre of land. Landlords gain at the expense of labor. This gloomy picture led Thomas Carlyle to criticize economics as "the dismal science."

Paradise Lost and Regained

How bad can things get? The dour Reverend T. R. Malthus thought that population pressures would drive the economy to a point where workers were at the minimum level of subsistence. Malthus reasoned that whenever wages were above the subsistence level, population would expand; below-subsistence wages would lead to high mortality and population decline. Only at subsistence wages could there be a stable equilibrium of population. He believed the working classes to be destined to a life that is brutish, nasty, and short.

But Malthus' forecast was wide of the mark, for he overlooked the future contribution of invention and technology. He failed to recognize that technological innovation could overcome the law of diminishing returns. He stood at the brink of a new era and failed to anticipate that the succeeding two centuries would show the greatest scientific and economic gains in history.

[2] The theory in this chapter relies on an important finding from microeconomics. In analysis of the determination of wages under simplified conditions, including perfect competition, it is shown that the wage rate of labor will be equal to the extra or marginal product of the last worker hired. For example, if the last worker contributes goods worth $12.50 per hour to the firm's output, then under competitive conditions the firm will be willing to pay up to $12.50 per hour in wages to that worker. Similarly, the rent on land is the marginal product of the last unit of land and the real interest rate will be determined as the marginal product of the least productive piece of capital.

Economic Growth with Capital Accumulation: The Neoclassical Model

Whereas the classical economists stressed the role of scarce land in economic growth, history records how entrepreneurs and capital—not landowners and land—have called the tune since the early nineteenth century. Land did not become increasingly scarce. Instead, the Industrial Revolution brought forth power-driven machinery that increased production, factories that gathered teams of workers into giant firms, railroads and steamships that linked together the far points of the world, and iron and steel that made possible stronger machines and faster locomotives. As market economies entered the twentieth century, important new industries grew up around the telephone, the automobile, and electric power. Capital accumulation and new technologies became the dominant force affecting economic development.

To understand how capital accumulation and technological change affect the economy, we must consider the **neoclassical model of economic growth.** This approach was pioneered by Robert Solow of MIT, who was awarded the 1987 Nobel Prize for this and other contributions to economic-growth theory.* The neoclassical growth model

*Robert M. Solow was born in Brooklyn and educated at Harvard, and then moved to MIT in 1950. In the next few years he developed the neoclassical growth model and applied it in a number of studies using the growth-accounting framework discussed in the second half of this chapter. According to the committee that awards the Nobel Prize, "The increased interest of government to expand education and research and development was inspired by these studies. Every long-term report . . . for any country has used a Solow-type analysis."

Solow is known for his enthusiasm for economics as well as for his humor. He worries that the hunger for publicity has led some economists to exaggerate their knowledge. He criticized economists for "an apparently irresistible urge to push their science further than it will go, to answer questions more delicate than our limited understanding of a complicated question will allow. Nobody likes to say 'I don't know.'"

A lively writer, Solow worries that economics is terrifically difficult to explain to the public. At his news conference after winning the Nobel Prize, Solow quipped, "The attention span of the people you write for is shorter than the length of one true sentence." Nonetheless, Solow continues to labor for his brand of economics, and the world increasingly listens to the apostle of economic growth at MIT.

serves as the basic tool for understanding the growth process in advanced countries and has been applied to empirical studies of the sources of economic growth.

Basic Assumptions

The neoclassical growth model describes an economy in which a single homogeneous output is produced by two types of inputs, capital and labor. In contrast to the Malthusian analysis, labor growth is determined by forces outside the economy and is unaffected by economic variables. In addition, we assume that the economy is competitive and always operates at full employment, so we can analyze the growth of potential output.

The major new ingredients in the neoclassical growth model are capital and technological change. For the moment, assume that technology remains constant and focus on the role of capital in the growth process. What do we mean by capital? Capital consists of durable produced goods that are used to make other goods. Capital goods include structures like factories and houses, equipment like computers and machine tools, and inventories of finished goods and goods-in-process.

For convenience, we will assume that there is a single versatile kind of capital good (call it *K*). We then measure the aggregate stock of capital as the total quantity of capital goods. In our real-world calculations, we approximate the universal capital good as the total dollar value of capital goods (i.e., the constant-dollar value of equipment, structures, and inventories). Under perfect competition and without risk or inflation, the rate of return on capital is also equal to the real interest rate on bonds and other financial assets.

Turning now to the economic-growth process, economists stress the need for **capital deepening,** which is the process by which the quantity of capital per worker increases over time. Examples of capital deepening include the multiplication of farm machinery and irrigation systems in farming, of railroads and highways in transportation, and of computers and communication systems in banking. In each of these industries, societies have invested heavily in capital goods, increasing the amount of capital per worker. As a result, the output per worker has grown enormously in farming, transportation, and banking.

What happens to the return on capital in the process of capital deepening? For a given state of technology, a rapid rate of investment in plant and equipment tends to depress the return on capital (the real interest rate). This occurs because the most worthwhile investment projects get constructed first, after which the investments become less and less valuable. Once a full railroad network or telephone system has been constructed, new investments will branch into more sparsely populated regions or duplicate existing lines. The rates of return on these late investments will be lower than the high returns on the first lines between densely populated regions.

In addition, the wage rate paid to workers will tend to rise as capital deepening takes place. Why? Each worker has more capital to work with and his or her marginal product therefore rises. As a result, the competitive wage rate rises along with the marginal product of labor. We will see the wage rate rise for farm laborers, transport workers, or bank tellers as increases in capital per worker raise marginal products in those sectors.

We can summarize the impact of capital deepening in the neoclassical growth model as follows:

Capital deepening occurs when the stock of capital grows more rapidly than the labor force. In the absence of technological change, capital deepening will produce a growth of output per worker, of the marginal product of labor, and of wages; it also will lead to diminishing returns on capital and a consequent decline in the real interest rate.

Geometrical Analysis of the Neoclassical Model

We can analyze the effects of capital accumulation using Figure 30-2. The left-hand panel shows the relationship between the capital-per-worker ratio on the horizontal axis and the rate of return on capital, or the real interest rate, on the vertical axis. This *DD* curve is downward-sloping to reflect the fact that, for given inputs of labor, capital accumulation forces the marginal product of capital to decline. This diminishing marginal productivity of capital is just the principle of diminishing returns applied to capital rather than to labor.

Figure 30-2(*b*) displays a new graph, called the *factor-price frontier*. This frontier shows the relationship between the competitively determined

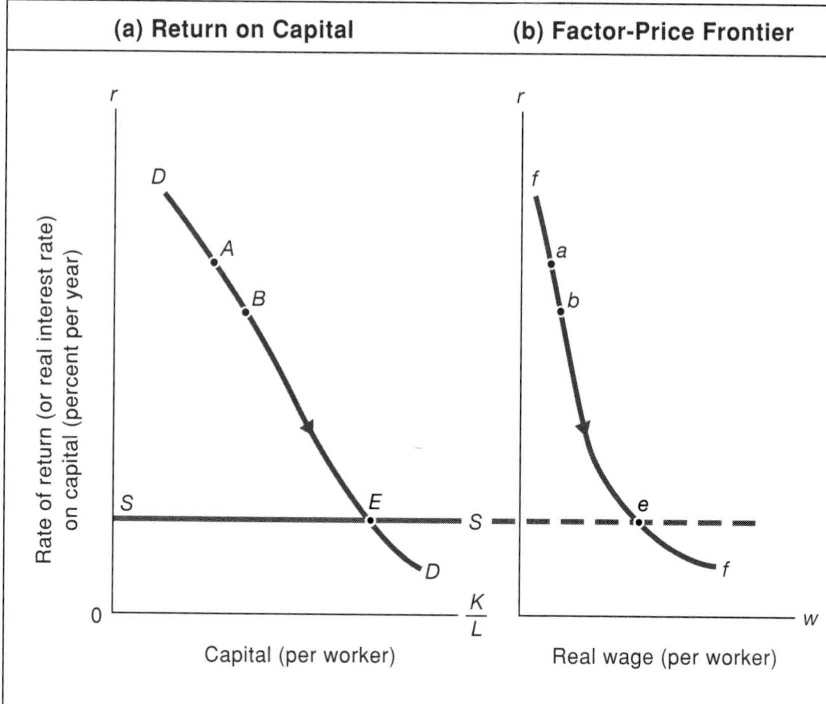

Figure 30-2. Capital accumulation raises output and wages, but depresses the return on capital

(a) Adding more capital goods to a fixed amount of labor (in the absence of technological change) will lead to diminishing returns on capital. Thus the real interest rate (which is the rate of return on capital) falls as capital increases, as is shown by the arrow on the demand curve. Capital accumulation drives the real interest rate from *A* to *B* to *E*. Eventually, the interest rate reaches a point (on the supply curve) where no further capital accumulation takes place.
(b) The factor-price frontier shows the behavior of wages in a competitive economy. Capital accumulation drives up wages at the same time that the rate of return on capital is beaten down.

wage rate and the competitive real interest rate. As capital deepens, the economy moves down and to the right on the factor-price frontier; that is, the real interest rate falls as the wage rate rises. Conversely, if a great war were to destroy much of a nation's capital, the capital-labor ratio would fall, the real interest rate would rise, and the wage rate would fall—this would represent a movement up and to the left along the factor-price frontier.

Let's use Figure 30-2 to analyze the process of economic growth with capital accumulation. Assume we have a low-income country, poorly endowed with capital per worker, shown at point *A*.

In the absence of technological change, capital accumulation takes us down the blue *DD* curve from *A* to *B*. Indeed, at some point the real interest rate might decline so far that people would feel it no longer pays them to save anything for enhanced future consumption. The *SS* line in Figure 30-2 shows the level of interest rates at which the economy's net saving is zero. At point *E*, the diminished desire for saving snuffs out further capital accumulation.

The process of capital accumulation is also shown by the factor-price frontier *ff* in Figure 30-2(*b*). In that graph, economic growth begins at an initial low-wage, high-interest equilibrium at point *a*. Then capital deepening moves the economy to point *b* with a higher wage rate and a lower real interest rate. Finally, the economy comes into equilibrium at point *e* with a still higher capital-output and capital-labor ratio.

Note that our earlier verbal summary of the impact of capital deepening is verified by the analysis in Figure 30-2.

Long-Run Steady State. What is the long-run equilibrium in the neoclassical growth model without technological change? We see a *steady state* in which capital deepening has ceased, real wages are no longer growing, and real interest rates are constant. The steady state might arrive with high wages and per capita income if a great deal of capital has been accumulated. Although there is no longer constant improvement in incomes and output, the picture of stagnation is nevertheless more optimistic than the dismal view held by Malthus.

Technological Change and Continued Growth

A glance at economic history will reveal that the pessimistic view of stagnant wages and profits was not in history's script. Rather, a never-ending stream of inventions and technological change led to a vast improvement in the production possibilities of Europe, North America, and Japan. **Technological change** denotes changes in the processes of production or introduction of new products such that more or improved output can be obtained from the same bundle of inputs. Process inventions that have greatly increased productivity were the steam engine, the Bessemer process for producing steel, the internal-combustion engine, and the wide-body jet. Fundamental technological changes include product inventions such as the telephone, the radio, the airplane, the phonograph, and television. The most dramatic technological developments of the modern era occur in electronics and computers, where today's tiny notebook computers can outperform the fastest computer of the 1960s. These inventions provide the most spectacular examples of technological change, but technological change is in fact a continuous process of small and large improvements, as witnessed by the fact that the United States has issued over 3 million patents and there are further millions of small refinements that are part of the routine progress of an economy.

For the most part, technology advances in a quiet, unnoticed fashion as small improvements increase the quality of products or the quantity of output. Occasionally, however, changes in technology create headlines and produce unforgettable visual images. During the war in the Persian Gulf in 1991, the world was stunned by the tremendous advantage that high-technology weapons—Stealth aircraft, "smart" bombs, antimissile missiles—gave to the United States and its allies against an opponent armed with a technology that was but a few years behind. Civilian technological advances are less dramatic but no less impressive in contributing to the increase in living standards of market economies.

How can we represent technological change in our neoclassical growth model? Technological change means that more output can be produced with the same inputs of capital and labor. Technological change shifts out the *PPF*.

In terms of our growth diagram, technological change shifts outward and upward the marginal product curve on the left of Figure 30-2, and it shifts out the factor-price frontier on the right side of Figure 30-2.

Figure 30-3 presents an important interpretation of economic growth. These graphs show that, instead of moving an economy to a steady state with

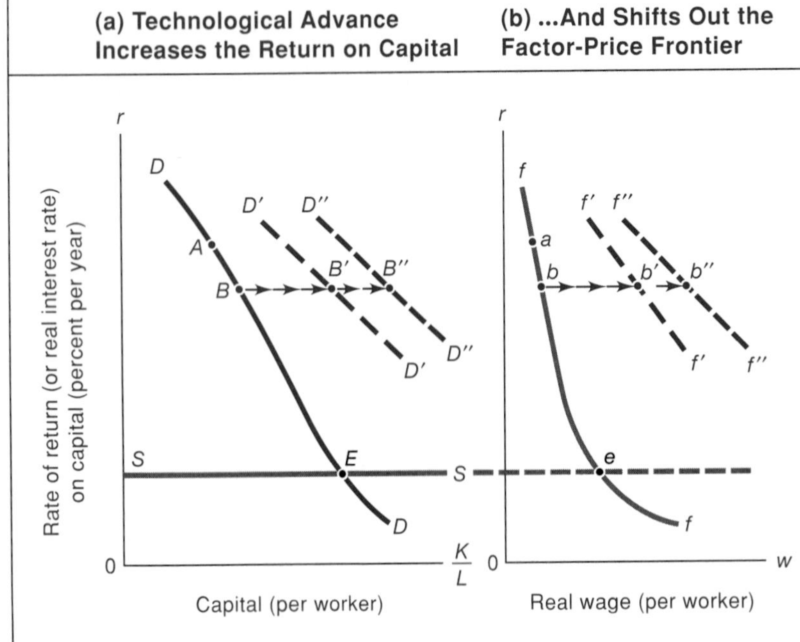

Figure 30-3. Technological advance shifts out curves, raising output and wages

Technological advance increases capital's productivity and the output that can be paid to factors of production. Hence, the productivity of capital marches out from *DD* to *D′D′* to *D″D″*, and the factor-price frontier moves from *ff* to *f′f′* to *f″f″*. These rightward shifts allow higher productivity and wages over time (as seen by shifts from *B* to *B′* to *B″* and from *b* to *b′* to *b″*).

Historically, the pace of technological change has been just fast enough to offset diminishing returns on capital—keeping interest and profit rates almost unchanged, while real wages grew steadily.

constant output, wage rates, and interest rates, inventions increase the amount of output that each unit of input can produce. As a result of technological progress, capital per worker, output per worker, and wages per worker grow over time, yet the real interest rate need not fall. Invention increases the productivity of capital and repeals the law of the falling rate of profit. In the race between diminishing returns and advancing technology, technology has won by several lengths.

Bias of Invention. Not all inventions are evenhanded. Some inventions favor capital, others labor. For example, machines and tractors reduce the need for labor and increase the demand for capital. These are thus called "labor-saving inventions," and they increase profits relative to wages. An invention that reduces the capital requirement more than the labor requirement (such as the introduction of multiple-shift workdays) is "capital-saving" and raises wages relative to profits. Between the two are "neutral inventions," which have no major effect on the relative demands of or returns to different factors. Since the Industrial Revolution, inventions appear to have been labor-saving on balance.[3]

B. The Trends and Sources of Economic Growth

We have now completed our survey of the primary theoretical approaches to economic growth. In advanced market economies, economic growth is largely determined by the growth of inputs (particularly labor and capital) and by technological change. But what are the relative contributions of labor, capital, and technology? To answer this question, we turn to an analysis of the quantitative aspects of growth and of the useful approach known as growth accounting.

The Facts of Economic Growth

Thanks to the painstaking gathering of data and construction and analysis of national accounts by Simon Kuznets, Edward Denison, Dale Jorgenson, and many others, we can discern several patterns of economic development in the United States and other advanced nations. Figure 30-4 depicts the key trends of economic development for the United States in this century. Similar patterns have been found in most of the major industrial countries.

Figure 30-4(*a*) shows the trends in real GNP, the capital stock, and population. Population and employment have more than tripled since 1900. At the same time, the stock of physical capital has risen almost tenfold. Thus the amount of capital per worker (the *K/L* ratio) has increased by a factor of almost 3. Clearly, a great deal of capital deepening has occurred.

What about the growth in output? Has output grown less rapidly than capital, as would occur in a model that ignored technological change? No. The fact that the output curve in Figure 30-4(*a*) is not in between the two factor curves, but actually lies above the capital curve, demonstrates that technological progress must have increased the productivity of capital and labor.

Indeed, the capital-output ratio—shown in Figure 30-4(*b*)—has fallen over time, rather than rising as would be expected in the capital-accumulation model without technological progress.

The average person judges an economy by the wage rate earned for working, shown in Figure 30-4(*c*) in terms of real wages (or wages corrected for inflation). Wages have shown an impressive growth

[3] The impact of invention on human society has concerned economists since the Industrial Revolution. The tools of this chapter will allow us to analyze patterns of invention and growth in a competitive economy. A vital example for humanity is the following: Some people today argue that robots and computers will make humans economically obsolete. In their view, human labor will follow the horse's role in history—from being a central economic factor to being a mere luxury.

To analyze this view, recall that robots are a different kind of capital good. The robotization of the economy suggests, then, that inventions will be highly labor-saving, and that as a result the real interest rate will rise drastically and wages will decline drastically. Hence the key variable to watch in the robotization of America is movements in the rate of return on capital.

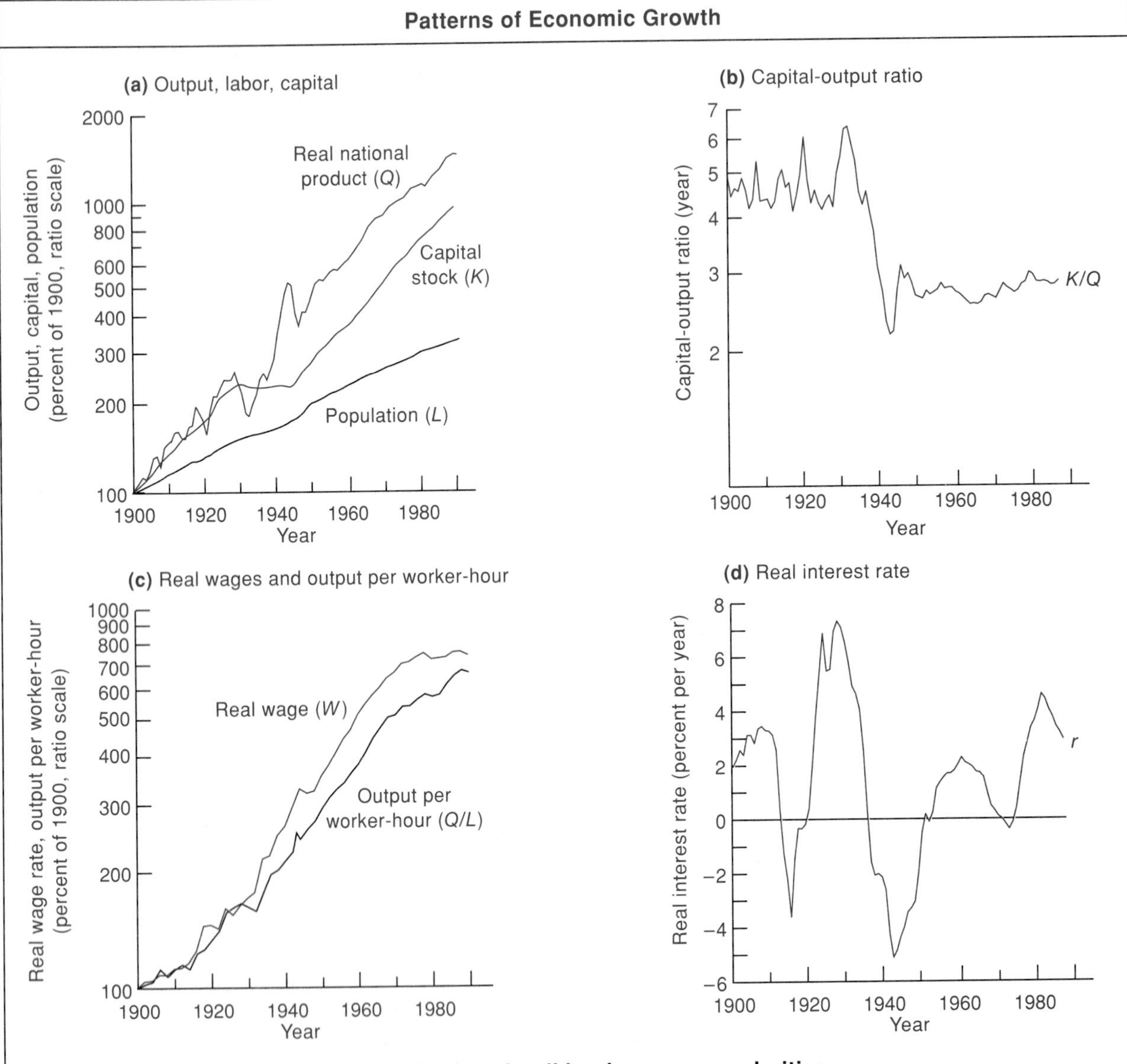

Figure 30-4. Economic growth has displayed striking long-run regularities

(a) Capital stock has grown faster than population and labor supply. Nonetheless, total output has grown even more rapidly than capital.
(b) Capital-output ratio declined sharply during the first half of the twentieth century, but has remained steady over the last four decades.
(c) Real wages have grown steadily and somewhat faster than average product per worker-hour. Note the slowdown of growth in output, real wages, and productivity since 1973. Does the productivity slowdown augur the end of the Industrial Revolution?
(d) Real interest rate has been trendless over this century, suggesting that technological change has offset diminishing returns to capital accumulation. (Source: U.S. Departments of Commerce and Labor, Federal Reserve Board, Bureau of the Census, and historical studies by John Kendrick.)

for most of this century, as we would expect from the growth in the capital-labor ratio and from steady technological advance.

The real interest rate (i.e., the money interest rate minus the rate of inflation) is shown in Figure 30-4(*d*). Interest rates and profit rates fluctuate greatly in business cycles and wars but display no strong trend upward or downward for the whole period.

Either by coincidence, or because of an economic mechanism inducing this pattern, technological change has just about offset diminishing returns.

Output per worker-hour is the solid black curve in Figure 30-4(*c*). As could be expected from the deepening of capital and from technological advance, Q/L has risen steadily.

The fact that wages rise at the same rate as output per worker does not mean that labor has captured all the fruits of productivity advance. Rather, it means that labor has kept about the same share of total product, with capital also earning about the same relative share throughout the period. Actually, a close look at Figure 30-4(*c*) shows that real wages have grown slightly faster than has output per worker-hour over the last nine decades. This trend implies a slow upward creep in the share of labor in GNP, with capital's share declining gently.

Seven Basic Trends of Economic Development

The economic history of the advanced nations can be summarized approximately by the following trends:

Trend 1. Population and the labor force have grown, but at a much more modest rate than the capital stock, resulting in capital deepening.

Trend 2. There has been a strong upward trend in real wage rates.

Trend 3. The share of wages and salaries in national income has edged up very slightly over the long run.

Trend 4. There have been major oscillations in real interest rates and the rate of profit, particularly during business cycles, but there has been no strong upward or downward trend in this century.

Trend 5. Instead of steadily rising, which would be predicted by the law of diminishing returns, the capital-output ratio has actually declined since 1900. However, it has changed little since 1950.

Trend 6. For most of the twentieth century, the ratios of national saving and of investment to GNP have been stable. Since 1980, however, the large federal budget deficit has led to a sharp decline of the national savings rate.

Trend 7. After effects of the business cycle are removed, national product has grown at an average rate of close to 3 percent per year. Output growth has been much higher than a weighted average of the growth of capital, labor, and resource inputs, suggesting that technological innovation must have played a key role in economic growth.

We must issue one warning about the trends of economic growth. The persistence of these trends might suggest that they have taken on a certain inevitability—that we can forever expect our economy to generate rapid growth in output per worker, real wages, and real output.

But this view of constant growth should be resisted, for it misreads the lessons of history and economic theory. While trends have been persistent, a closer examination shows major waves or deviations during periods of a decade or more. Moreover, there is no theoretical reason why technological innovation should remain high, forever raising living standards. Eventually, diminishing returns may become more significant, or perhaps the need to combat pollution or global environmental threats may overwhelm technological change. The period since 1973—with a marked slowdown in growth of output, real wages, and output per worker—is a reminder that there is no economic or technological reason why the future must continue the robust growth experience of the prior century.

The Economic Growth of the Mixed Economy

While the seven trends of economic history are not like the immutable laws of chemistry, they do portray fundamental facts about economic growth. How do they fit into our economic-growth theories?

Trends 2 and 1—higher wage rates when capital deepens—fit nicely together with classical and neoclassical theories of production and distribution. Trend 3—that the wage share has grown only very slowly—is an interesting coincidence that is consistent with a wide variety of production functions relating Q to L and K.

Trends 4 and 5, however, warn us that neoclassical theory cannot hold in static form. A steady profit rate and a declining, or steady, capital-output ratio cannot hold if the K/L ratio rises in a world with unchanging technology; taken together, they contradict the basic law of diminishing returns under deepening of capital. We must therefore recognize the key role of technological progress in explaining the seven trends of modern economic growth. Indeed, given the ample evidence of the contribution of science, technology, and engineering to the economy, it would be difficult to ignore advancing technology.

The trends confirm the hypothesis of technological progress shown in Figure 30-3. That figure shows an economic evolution consistent with trends 1 through 7. The tendency toward diminishing returns has been offset by technological change, with the real interest rate changing little and the wage rate rising somewhat more rapidly than output per head.

The Sources of Economic Growth

Economists have not rested contentedly with trends and theories. Under the leadership of Robert Solow, John Kendrick, and Edward Denison, economic archaeologists have begun to ferret out the sources of economic growth. Looking at theories alongside the trends shown in Figure 30-4, we now have a much better understanding of why nations grow.

The Growth-Accounting Approach[4]

Detailed studies of economic growth rely on what is called **growth accounting.** This technique is not a balance sheet or national product account of the kind we met in earlier chapters. Rather, it is a way of exhaustively accounting for the ingredients that lead to observed growth trends.

In our simple model shown in Figure 30-3, growth in output (Q) can be decomposed into three separate sources: growth in labor (L), growth in capital (K), and technological innovation itself. Momentarily ignoring technological change, an assumption of constant returns to scale means that a 1 percent growth in L together with a 1 percent growth in K will lead to a 1 percent growth in output.

But suppose L grows at 1 percent and K at 5 percent. It is tempting, but wrong, to guess that Q will then grow at 3 percent, the simple average of 1 and 5. Why wrong? Because the two factors do not necessarily contribute equally to output. Rather, the fact that three-fourths of national income goes to labor while only one-fourth goes to capital suggests that labor growth will contribute more to output than will capital growth.

If labor's growth rate gets 3 times the weight of K's, then we can calculate the answer as follows: Q will grow at 2 percent per year ($= \frac{3}{4}$ of 1% $+ \frac{1}{4}$ of 5%). To growth of inputs, we also add technological change and thereby obtain all the sources of growth.

Hence, output growth per year follows the *fundamental equation of growth accounting:*

$$\%\ Q \text{ growth} = \tfrac{3}{4}(\%\ L \text{ growth}) + \tfrac{1}{4}(\%\ K \text{ growth}) + \text{T. C.} \qquad (1)$$

where T. C. represents technological change (or total factor productivity) that raises productivity, and where $\frac{3}{4}$ and $\frac{1}{4}$ are the relative contributions of each input to economic growth, given by their relative shares of national income (of course, these fractions would be replaced by new fractions if the relative shares of the factors were to change).

To explain per capita growth, we can eliminate L as a separate growth source. Now, using the fact that capital gets one-fourth share of output, we have from equation (1):

$$\%\ \frac{Q}{L} \text{ growth} = \%\ Q \text{ growth} - \%\ L \text{ growth}$$

$$= \tfrac{1}{4}\left(\%\ \frac{K}{L} \text{ growth}\right) + \text{T. C.} \qquad (2)$$

This relation shows clearly how capital deepening would affect per capita output if technological advance were zero. Output per worker would grow only one-fourth as fast as capital per worker, reflecting diminishing returns.

One final point remains: We can measure Q growth, K growth, L growth, as well as the shares of K and L. But how can we measure T. C. (technological change)? We cannot. Rather, we must *infer* T. C. as the residual or leftover after the other components of output and inputs are calculated. Thus if we examine the equation above, T. C. is calculated by subtraction from equation (1) as:

$$\text{T. C.} = \%\ Q \text{ growth} - \tfrac{3}{4}(\%\ L \text{ growth}) - \tfrac{1}{4}(\%\ K \text{ growth}) \qquad (3)$$

[4] This discussion covers advanced materials, so short courses may skip right to the next topic, "Detailed Studies."

This equation allows us to answer critically important questions about economic growth. What part of per capita output growth is due to capital deepening and what part is due to technological advance? Does society progress chiefly by dint of thrift and the forgoing of current consumption? Or is our rising living standard the reward for the ingenuity of inventors and the daring of innovator-entrepreneurs?

Numerical Example. To determine the contributions of labor, capital, and other factors in output growth, we substitute representative numbers for the period 1900–1991 into equation (2) for the growth of Q/L above. Since 1900, L has grown 1.3 percent per year, and K has grown 2.5 percent per year, while Q has grown 3.1 percent per year. Thus, by arithmetic, we find that

$$\% \ \frac{Q}{L} \text{ growth} = \tfrac{1}{4}\left(\% \ \frac{K}{L} \text{ growth}\right) + \text{T. C.}$$

becomes

$$1.8 = \tfrac{1}{4}(1.2) + \text{T. C.} = 0.3 + 1.5$$

Thus of the 1.8 percent-per-year increase in output per worker, about 0.3 percentage point is due to capital deepening, while an astounding 1.5 percent per year stems from T. C.

Contribution of Different Elements to Growth in Real GNP, United States, 1948–1989

	In percent per year	As percent of total
Real GNP growth	**3.3**	**100**
Contribution of inputs	**1.9**	**58**
Capital	1.2	37
Labor	0.7	21
Land	0.0	0
Total factor productivity growth	**1.4**	**42**
Education	0.4	12
Advances in knowledge and other	1.0	30

Table 30-1. Education and advances in knowledge outweigh capital in contributing to economic growth

Studies using the techniques of growth accounting break down the growth of GNP in the private business sector into its contributing factors. These studies find that capital growth accounts for 37 percent of output growth. Education, technological change, and other sources make up 42 percent of total GNP growth and more than half of the growth of output per worker. [Source: Edward F. Denison, *Trends in American Economic Growth, 1929–1982* (Brookings, Washington, D.C., 1985); U.S. Department of Labor, "Multifactor Productivity Measures, 1988 and 1989," March 1991.]

Detailed Studies

More thorough studies refine the simple calculation but show quite similar conclusions. Table 30-1 presents the results of studies by Edward Denison and the Department of Labor analyzing the sources of growth over the 1948–1989 period. Over this period, output (measured as gross output of the private business sector) grew at an average rate of 3.3 percent per year. Input growth (of capital, labor, and land) contributed 1.9 percentage points per year, while **total factor productivity**—the growth of output less the growth of the weighted sum of all inputs—averaged 1.4 percent annually.

Somewhat more than one-half of the growth in output in the United States can be accounted for by the growth in labor and capital. The remaining growth is a residual factor that can be attributed to education, innovation, economies of scale, scientific advances, and other factors.

Growth accounting yields many dividends in understanding economic growth. For example, many people have wondered about the sources of growth in countries like Japan and the Soviet Union during much of this century.

Using growth accounting, scholars have uncovered some surprising answers to this puzzle. Over much of the period since World War II, Japan's GNP grew at an amazing 10 percent per year. Empirical analysis indicates that this was partly due to very rapid growth in inputs. In addition, Japan had extremely rapid technological change over this period compared to other industrial countries.

Analyses of Soviet growth show a different pattern. According to most studies, the Soviet Union grew rapidly during the period from 1930 until the mid-1960s. It appears, however, that the high growth rate came primarily from forced-draft increases in capital and labor inputs. The estimated pace of growth in total factor productivity for the Soviet Union over the last half-century has been slower than that for the United States. In the period of perestroika over the last decade, studies indicate there has been a *decline* in total factor productivity in the Soviet Union.

The Productivity Slowdown

We noted earlier that the rapid growth of output and productivity in the United States slowed abruptly around 1973. This break in the trend, which is called the **productivity slowdown,** is seen in Figure 30-4(*c*), in which labor productivity (*Q*/*L*) begins to flatten out in the early 1970s. What caused the abrupt slowdown in productivity growth?

The basic facts are shown in Table 30-2, which provides data on the growth of productivity in the U.S. economy both for the entire business sector and for different subsectors. This table shows **labor productivity,** which measures total output produced in a sector divided by the number of person-hours worked in that sector. As you can see, labor productivity slowed in all sectors in the 1970s with nonmanufacturing showing the sharpest decline. Among the areas showing the biggest deterioration in productivity were mining, construction, and services. Similar patterns, with a slowdown of productivity growth in the aggregate and in most sectors after 1973, characterize all major industrial countries.

The decline in productivity growth remains a mystery to economists. Most studies point to a number of unfavorable factors converging on the American economy at about the same time, including the following:

- In the late 1960s and early 1970s, environmental regulations required firms to spend money on plant and operations to improve health and safety, yet these improvements did not show up as measured output increases. One of the most dramatic cases was in underground mining, in which productivity declined sharply.
- The increase in energy prices in the early 1970s led firms to substitute other inputs (labor and capital) for energy. As a result, the productivity of labor and capital declined relative to earlier growth rates.
- The 1970s witnessed an infusion of inexperienced, low-wage workers into many nonmanufacturing sectors, particularly into service industries like fast-food outlets. This rapid growth increased the share of employment in the low-productivity sectors and thereby lowered overall productivity growth.

Other factors mentioned in studies of the productivity slowdown were a lower level of expenditure on civilian research and development, declining investment in plant and equipment, and higher inflation. All told, however, these factors explain only a fraction of the slowdown.

Speeding Economic Growth

In response to the lagging productivity growth, many people have called for policies to restore the earlier pace of productivity improvement. What steps can be taken to speed growth? A study by Edward Denison investigated this subject in detail, and the results appear in Table 30-3.

Labor Productivity Growth by Business Sector, 1948–1989
(Average Annual Percent Change)

			Nonfarm	
Period	Total business	Farm	Manufacturing	Nonmanufacturing
1948–1973	3.0	6.5	2.9	1.9
1973–1979	0.8	4.6	1.4	−0.1
1979–1989	1.3	3.3	3.6	0.4

Table 30-2. Labor productivity growth by sector

Labor productivity in the total business sector slowed sharply after 1973 with the most dramatic decline occurring in nonmanufacturing areas like services. Manufacturing productivity growth regained ground in the 1980s. (Source: Council of Economic Advisers, *Economic Report of the President,* 1987; U.S. Department of Agriculture; U.S. Department of Labor, Bureau of Labor Statistics.)

A Menu for Growth

Growth-encouraging steps	Estimated potential for increasing real economic growth, 1990–2000 (% per year)
1. Increase net national investment and savings rate by one-third (i.e., from 6 to 8% of GNP)	0.16
2. Increase civilian research and development by one-fifth (i.e., from 2 to 2.4% of GNP)	0.18
3. Lower the average rate of unemployment by 1% of the labor force	0.20
4. Eliminate all strikes	0.01
5. Reach an arms-control agreement that allows government to reduce strategic programs and increase government investment	0.10
Total	0.65

Table 30-3. How can the United States grow faster?

This menu of growth shows the kinds of steps that might be taken to speed the growth of potential output and labor productivity. Economists have concluded that a major increase in the growth of potential output is difficult to accomplish.

[Source: Edward Denison, *Sources of Growth in the United States* (Committee for Economic Development, New York, 1961); updated with further calculations by authors.]

These figures show that raising the growth rate of potential output or of productivity per worker is possible but difficult. The most obvious way to grow more rapidly is to increase the national savings-and-investment rate. As our discussion of fiscal and monetary policies in later chapters will show, an increase in the national savings rate could be accomplished by changing the mix of fiscal and monetary policy; for example, reducing the budget deficit and easing money would tend to increase national savings. An ambitious program might succeed in raising national net investment by 2 percent of GNP. This would lead to an increase of slightly less than two-tenths of a percentage point in the annual growth rate of potential GNP and of labor productivity over the following decade.

One cannot help but be impressed by the small magnitude of the numbers shown in Table 30-3. Increasing productivity growth is not impossible, but no easy paths have yet been found.

C. Supply-Side Economics[5]

One approach to stimulating economic growth enjoyed a meteoric rise in popularity during the 1980s. This approach, known as *supply-side economics,* motivated the fiscal policies of the Reagan administration (1981–1989). Looking back at that period, we can use our macroeconomic analysis to appraise the contribution of supply-side prescriptions for reviving the U.S. economy.

During most of the period from World War II until 1980, economic policy focused on the need to counter the evils of inflation and unemployment. Whenever unemployment rose, liberals would call for tax cuts or expenditure increases; whenever inflation threatened, conservatives would prescribe the unpleasant medicine of tight monetary or fiscal policies.

Toward the end of the 1970s, critics of the con-

[5] An excellent set of readings on the political and social debate over supply-side economics is contained in Thomas R. Swartz, Frank J. Bonello, and Andrew F. Kozak, *The Supply Side: Debating Economic Issues* (Dushkin, Guilford, Conn., 1983).

ventional approach to macroeconomics argued that economic policy had become too oriented toward the management of aggregate demand. They claimed that excessive concerns with short-run actions tended to threaten the long-run vitality of the economy. Some critics, including orthodox conservative economists, pressed for a return to more traditional policies of balancing the budget and squeezing inflation out of the economy.

At the same time, a new phalanx of theorists joined the debate. Their school of **supply-side economics** emphasized incentives for people to work and to save, downplayed the role of demand management, and proposed large tax cuts to reverse slow economic growth and slumping productivity growth. Among the proponents of this approach were economists Arthur Laffer, Paul Craig Roberts, and Norman Ture. Supply-side economics was espoused forcefully by President Reagan in the United States and by Margaret Thatcher, prime minister of Great Britain from 1979 to 1990.

Although these economists and political leaders have embraced a wide variety of positions, three central features of supply-side economics emerge: retreat from Keynesian demand-management policies, emphasis on incentives and supply effects, and advocacy of large tax cuts.

Retreat from Keynes. Keynesian economics holds that, in the short run, national output and employment are primarily determined by aggregate demand. Further, the Keynesians believe that monetary and fiscal policies should be used to combat unemployment or inflation.

Toward the end of the 1970s, disenchantment with the Keynesian approach became widespread within the economics profession. An influential article by Harvard's Martin Feldstein laid out the case against demand-oriented policies.[6] Feldstein argued for greater emphasis on factors that would increase the growth in potential output—factors such as increased saving and investment, regulatory reform, and reduced taxation of capital income. In his view, macroeconomic policies should focus primarily on increasing long-run economic growth rather than on short-run economic stabilization.

[6] See Martin Feldstein, "The Retreat from Keynesian Economics," *The Public Interest* (Summer 1981), pp. 92–105.

What was the basis of this *volte face* in economic philosophy? Although the theory was not clearly presented, it appears to be grounded in a classical view of the economy and asserts that output responds more to incentives, taxes, and post-tax factor returns than to changes in aggregate demand. In terms of the *AS-AD* framework, supply siders believe that the *AS* curve is near-vertical, so that adverse shocks to aggregate demand would have small and short-lived impacts on output and most of the effect of tight money would be on the price level.

A New Emphasis on Incentives. A second theme of supply-side economics was the key role played by *incentives,* which denote adequate returns to working, saving, and entrepreneurship. Supply siders emphasized the loss of incentives that occurs when tax rates are excessively high and argued that Keynesians, in their excessive concern with demand management, had ignored the impact of tax rates and incentives on aggregate supply. A paraphrase of the argument by a spokesman is as follows:

> Supply-side economics emphasizes the role of fiscal policy in the determination of economic growth and aggregate supply. Our analysis relies upon straight classical price theory. According to supply-side economics, tax changes affect the economy through their effect on post-tax factor rewards rather than on dollar flows of incomes and spending; tax rates affect the relative prices of goods and thereby affect supplies of labor and capital. We seek to raise the after-tax rewards to growth activities such as labor, saving, and investment relative to leisure and consumption.
>
> It is far more important to analyze the impact of a tax change on the rate of return to labor or saving or investment than to look at the dollar amount of the tax change on disposable income. By lowering tax rates on labor or interest or dividends, we can increase saving, investment, and economic growth.[7]

[7] This excerpt is a paraphrase of Stephen J. Entin, "Comments on the Critics" in a symposium, "Supply Side Economics: What Remains?" American Economic Association Annual Meeting, December 1985, *Treasury News*.

A favorable account is contained in Paul Craig Roberts, *The Supply-Side Revolution: An Insider's Account of Policymaking in Washington* (Harvard University Press, Cambridge, Mass., 1984). For a critical analysis, see the papers by Martin Feldstein, Lawrence Chimerene and Richard Young, and George von Furstenberg and F. Jeffrey Green in *American Economic Review* (May 1986).

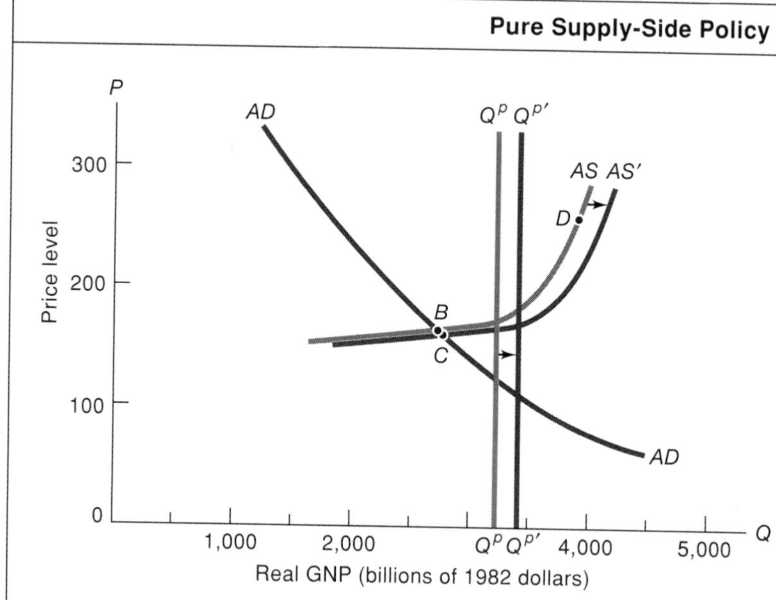

Figure 30-5. Impact of a pure supply-side policy

Before a pure supply-side policy, potential output is Q^P = 3200; an impressive increase in aggregate supply might raise potential to $Q^{P'}$ = 3400.

If the economy is on the flat portion of the *AS* curve, the impact on actual GNP will be relatively modest if *AD* does not change. In the illustrated case, actual GNP changes from *B* to *C*, with an increase of real GNP from 2700 to 2750.

On the other hand, what would happen to actual GNP if *AD* cut the *AS* curve in its near-vertical classical section, such as at point *D*? Almost all the increase in potential output would show up in actual output.

What is the hypothesized relationship between tax policy and overall economic activity? In the context of aggregate supply-and-demand analysis, lowering tax rates would raise the post-tax return to capital and labor; higher post-tax returns would induce greater labor and capital supply, along with higher rates of innovation and productivity growth; and the increase of inputs and innovation would increase the growth of potential output and thereby shift aggregate supply to the right.

Figure 30-5 illustrates the effects of a hypothetical supply-side program. Suppose that the supply-side program has the net effect of increasing the total supply of inputs like labor and capital. This increase of inputs increases potential output and shifts the *AS* curve outward as shown in the figure.

What is the impact of this supply-side measure? The answer depends upon the shape of the aggregate supply curve. If the economy is Keynesian, or in a recession, with a relatively flat *AS* curve as shown at point *B* in Figure 30-5, the impact of the supply shift on actual output will be relatively modest. In the hypothetical case, the equilibrium moves from point *B* to point *C*, with a small increase of output and a tiny decrease in the overall price level.

On the other hand, let's consider a classical economy, such as the one shown at point *D* on the *AS* curve in Figure 30-5. In this case, the increase in potential output from Q^P to $Q^{P'}$ would translate into a substantial increase in actual output, with each 1 percent increase in potential output producing almost 1 percent increase in actual output. We therefore conclude that supply-side policies are likely to be most effective when the economy behaves in a near-classical fashion.

How large an impact are supply-side policies likely to have in reality? At the beginning of the Reagan administration, supply-side enthusiasts predicted that the program would lead to rapid economic recovery, with an anticipated growth in real GNP of 4.8 percent per year over the next 4 years. In fact, the actual growth rate fell far short of the forecast, averaging only 2.5 percent per year. Given the difficulty of increasing the growth of potential output shown in the last section (see Table 30-3), we should not be surprised to learn that the supply-side policies had little impact on potential-output growth in the 1980s. The wheels of supply-side policies grind exceedingly slowly.

Tax Cuts. The final strand of supply-side thinking emerged in its advocacy of large tax cuts. We saw in our analysis of the multiplier model how taxes could affect aggregate demand and output. Supply-side economists believe that the role of taxes in affecting aggregate demand has been overemphasized. They argue that government in the 1960s and 1970s used taxes to raise revenues or stimulate demand while ignoring the impacts of the rising tax burden on incentives. The high taxes, in their view, lead people to reduce their labor and capital supply. Indeed, some supply-side economists, particularly Arthur Laffer, suggested that high tax rates might actually lower tax revenues. This "Laffer-curve" proposition held that high tax rates shrink the tax base because of a lower level of economic activity. Many mainstream economists and even some supply-side economists scoffed at the Laffer proposition.[8]

To counter earlier approaches to taxation, supply-side economists proposed a radical restructuring of the tax system, sometimes called the "supply-side tax cuts." The philosophy underlying supply-side tax cuts was that the reforms should improve incentives by lowering tax rates on the last dollar of income (or marginal tax rates); that the tax system should be less progressive (that is, it should lower the tax burden on high-income individuals); and that the system should be designed to encourage productivity or supply rather than to manipulate aggregate demand.

Figure 30-6 uses *AS-AD* analysis to illustrate the impact of a supply-side tax cut. We know from our multiplier analysis that, other things equal, tax cuts will increase consumption and increase aggregate demand. A large permanent tax cut—such as the 25 percent cut in personal taxes enacted in 1981—produces the large shift in *AD* as shown in Figure 30-6. In addition, such a tax cut might increase potential output if labor or capital supply increased. However, as the last section indicated, the size of the potential-output increase would be extremely modest in the short run. We therefore show the tax cut as shifting the *AS* curve only slightly to the right.

Just as the supply siders predict, the net effect of a massive supply-side tax cut is to increase output significantly. This change is shown by the movement from point *A* to point *B* in Figure 30-6. In the short run, the major source of the economic expansion from supply-side tax cuts is through its impact on aggregate demand rather than the effect on potential output and aggregate supply. Some

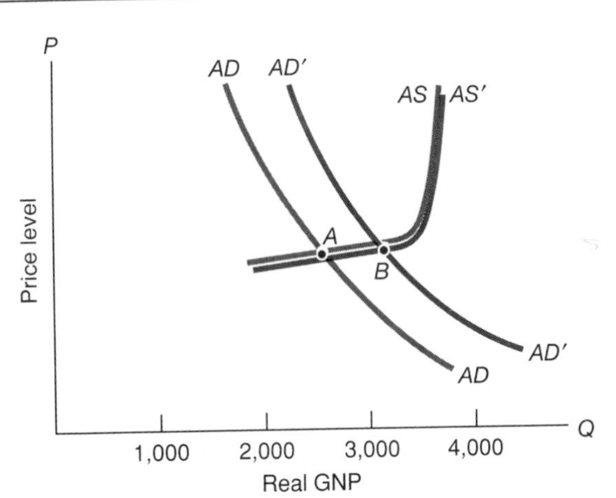

Figure 30-6. Macroeconomic impact of a supply-side tax cut

Supply-side economists recommend massive tax cuts as a measure for combating economic ailments. Tax cuts have two effects: They shift out the *AD* curve (from *AD* to *AD′*) as shown by multiplier analysis. And they may increase potential output if lower taxes induce larger quantities of labor or capital–thus shifting out the *AS* curve from *AS* to *AS′*. Such tax cuts do, as supply siders suggest, increase real GNP. But statistical studies suggest that for periods up to a decade the major impact on actual output comes through the effect upon aggregate demand.

economists have argued that the Reagan economic expansion of the mid-1980s was indeed a demand-side recovery dressed up in a supply-side cloak.

Appraisal. The radical supply-side approach to economics gradually faded after Reagan left office. What, it can be asked, is the preliminary verdict on this experiment? While many questions remain, economists generally have found that many of the supply-side propositions were not supported by economic experience in the 1980s. Among the key findings are the following:

- The supply siders predicted that the deep cuts in tax rates would stimulate economic activity and incomes so much that tax revenues would hardly fall and might even rise. In fact, tax revenues fell sharply relative to trend after the tax cuts, leading to an increase in the federal budget deficit that has persisted into the 1990s.
- Inflation was brought down sharply in the early 1980s. But the decline was, as the Keynesians had

[8] Say that R = total tax revenues, t = tax rate, and B = the tax base. For capital, R would be the total taxes on capital income, t the tax rate on capital income, and B total capital income. The Laffer proposition holds that, after a point, as t rises toward 100 percent, B shrinks so rapidly that $R = tB$ actually declines.

predicted, bought at a high price in terms of unemployment during the deep recession and high unemployment in 1981–1983.

- Supply-side economists predicted that the lower tax rates, increasing incentives for saving and investing, would increase national saving. All the supply-side encouragement of saving appears to have had no net positive effect on the national savings rate. Indeed, the national savings rate fell sharply over the 1980s and reached its lowest level since World War II in 1987.
- The fundamental goal of supply-side policies was to increase the rate of growth of potential output. The average rate of growth of potential output is estimated to have fallen from 3.6 percent per year in 1960–1970 to 3.1 percent per year in 1970–1980 to 2.3 percent per year in 1980–1990. While the fall in potential growth in the 1980s cannot be entirely attributed to macroeconomic policies, the decline does suggest that there was no sea change in economic performance in the supply-side years.

SUMMARY

A. The Theory of Economic Growth

1. Aggregate supply is derived from the economy's capability to produce—that is, from its potential output. The analysis of economic growth examines the factors that lead to the growth of potential output over the long run.
2. The classical models of Smith and Malthus describe economic development in terms of fixed land and growing population.

   In the absence of technological change, increasing population ultimately exhausts the supply of free land. The resulting increase in population density triggers the law of diminishing returns. With less and less land to work, each new worker adds less and less extra product; as a result, competitive wages fall while land rents go up. The Malthusian equilibrium is attained when the wage has fallen to the subsistence level, below which population cannot sustain itself. In reality, however, technological change has kept economic development progressing in industrial countries by continually shifting the productivity curve of labor upward.
3. Growth theories incorporating capital accumulation form the core of modern analysis. This approach examines a world in which labor grows for non-economic reasons while capital is accumulated in response to profit opportunities. In the beginning, there is a gradual increase of the amount of capital per worker, or "capital deepening." In the absence of technological change and innovation, an increase in capital per worker would not be matched by a proportional increase in output per worker because of diminishing returns. Hence, capital deepening would lower the rate of return on capital (equal to the real interest rate under risk-free competition).
4. The fundamental factor-price frontier depicts how wages must rise when the return on capital or the real interest rate falls. In a world with capital deepening, the downward trend in the real interest rate leads to a rise in real wages along the factor-price frontier.
5. Technological change, by increasing the output produced for a given bundle of inputs, pushes outward and rightward both the capital-productivity curve and the factor-price frontier, allowing output to rise even more rapidly than capital and labor inputs.

B. The Trends and Sources of Economic Growth

6. Numerous trends of economic growth are seen in data for this century. Among the key findings are that real wages and output per hour have risen steadily, although there has been some slowdown since the 1970s; the real interest rate has shown no major trend; and the capital-output ratio has declined.
7. The major trends are consistent with the simple model of capital accumulation augmented by technological advance. Thus economic theory confirms what common sense tells us—that technological advance increases the productivity of inputs and shifts out both the productivity-of-capital curve and factor-price frontiers.
8. The last trend—relatively stable growth in potential output over the last nine decades—raises the important question of the sources of economic growth. Applying quantitative techniques, economists have used growth accounting to determine that "residual" sources—such as innovation and education—outweigh capital deepening in their impact on GNP growth or labor productivity. This technique also shows the great effort required to add even a few tenths of a percentage point to the underlying potential GNP growth rate.

C. Supply-Side Economics

9. Until the 1980s, most economists focused on Keynesian remedies for stabilizing the economy; this approach emphasized changing monetary and fiscal policy to stabilize the economy. In the 1980s, supply-side economists proposed a new approach to macroeconomic policy-making: (*a*) a non-Keynesian approach to fiscal policy, focusing on the medium run, avoiding fine-tuning of the economy, and downplaying the importance of changes in aggregate demand; (*b*) a new emphasis on economic incentives—with particular attention to the impact of tax policy on post-tax returns to labor and capital as determining saving, investment, and labor supply; and (*c*) advocacy of large tax cuts, sometimes holding that these might actually pay for themselves by generating larger revenues.
10. The historical record of the 1980s suggests that supply-side policies were not successful in improving the performance of the U.S. economy. The legacy of this approach was stubborn federal budget deficits, slow growth in potential output, and a low national savings rate.

CONCEPTS FOR REVIEW

Economic-growth theory
Smith's golden age
Malthus' limited land
neoclassical growth model
K/L rise as capital deepens
capital–output ratio, *K/Q*

factor-price frontier
seven trends of economic growth
growth accounting
$\% \ Q \text{ growth} = \frac{3}{4}(\% \ L \text{ growth}) + \cdots$
$\% \ Q/L \text{ growth} = \frac{1}{4}(\% \ K/L \text{ growth}) + \text{T. C.}$

Supply-side economics
tenets of supply-side economics
impact of policies on economic performance

QUESTIONS FOR DISCUSSION

1. According to economic data, the living standards of a family in 1990 were about 7 times that of a family in 1900. What does this mean in terms of actual consumption patterns? Discuss with your parents or older relatives how your living standards today compare with those of their parents; make a comparison of the differences.
2. "If the government subsidizes science and invention and controls stagflation and cycles, we will see economic growth that would astound the classical economists." Evaluate critically.
3. "Without either population growth or technological change, persistent capital accumulation would ultimately destroy the capitalist class." Explain why such a scenario might lead to a zero interest rate and to a disappearance of profits.
4. Given that labor's share shows a slight uptrend and the capital-output ratio a slight downtrend, that the interest rate fluctuates considerably, and that the ratio of private net investment to private GNP is volatile, would you be much surprised if the basic trends on page 555 were to fluctuate sharply in the future?
5. Recall the growth-accounting equation (1) on page 556. Calculate the rate of growth of output if labor grows at 1 percent per year, capital grows at 4 percent per year, and technological change is $1\frac{1}{2}$ percent per year.

   How would your answer change if:

   (a) Labor growth slowed to 0 percent per year.
   (b) Capital growth increased to 5 percent per year.
   (c) Labor and capital had equal shares in GNP.

   Also, calculate for each of these conditions the rate of growth of output per worker.
6. Using the *PPF* discussed in Chapter 2, analyze Adam Smith's beaver-deer economy as follows.

   Assume that catching a deer takes 2 hours, while trapping a beaver requires 4 hours. For a society with 100 hours of labor, first draw the *PPF* as a straight line—going from the intercept on the vertical axis of the 50 deer producible with that much labor, to the intercept on the horizontal axis of 25 beavers. The absolute slope of this *PPF* gives the 2-to-1 price ratio prevailing at any point where both goods are being produced and consumed. (Demand curves are still needed to tell where society ends up on the *PPF*.)

   What would happen to the *PPF* if the amount of labor doubled with exactly the same technology? Also, show the effect of a doubling of labor productivity in both industries.
7. Political candidates have proposed the following policies to speed economic growth for the 1990s. For each, explain qualitatively the impact upon the growth of potential output and of per capita potential output. If possible, give a quantitative estimate of the increase in the growth of potential output and per capita potential output over the next decade:

   (a) Cut the federal budget deficit by 2 percent of GNP, increasing the ratio of investment to GNP by the same amount.
   (b) Increase the federal subsidy to research and development (R&D) by $\frac{1}{4}$ percent of GNP, assuming that this subsidy will increase private R&D by the same amount and that R&D has a social rate of return that is 3 times that of private investment.
   (c) Decrease defense spending by 1 percent of GNP, with a multiplier of 2.
   (d) Increase the labor-force participation rate of females so that total labor inputs increase by 1 percent.
   (e) Increase investments in "human capital" (or education and on-the-job training) by 1 percent of GNP.
8. A brooding pessimist might argue that 1973 marked the end of the great expansion that began with the Industrial Revolution. Assume that all the features of the earlier era were still present today *except* that technological change and innovation were to cease. What would the new seven trends look like for coming decades? What would happen to the important real wage? What steps could be taken to counteract the new trends and to put the economy back on the earlier path?
9. A supply-side economist might recommend a large tax cut to revive the economy. How might such a measure affect the *AS* curve? The *AD* curve? The resulting levels of price and real output?
10. **Advanced problem:** Many fear that robots will do to humans what tractors and cars did to horses—the horse population declined precipitously early in this century after technological change made horses obsolete. If we treat robots as a particularly productive kind of *K*, what would their introduction do to the *DD* and *ff* curves in Figure 30-2? Can total output go down with a fixed labor force? Under what conditions would the real wage decline? Can you see why the horse analogy might not apply?

CHAPTER 31

BUSINESS CYCLES AND UNEMPLOYMENT

The fault, dear Brutus, is not in our stars—but in ourselves.
William Shakespeare, *Julius Caesar*

Business conditions never stand still. Prosperity may be followed by a panic or a crash. Economic expansion gives way to recession. GNP, employment, and real incomes fall. Inflation and profits decline, and people are thrown out of work.

Eventually the bottom is reached, and recovery begins. The recovery may be slow or fast. It may be incomplete, or it may be so strong as to lead to a new boom. Prosperity may mean a long, sustained plateau of brisk demand, plentiful jobs, and rising living standards. Or it may be marked by a quick, inflationary flaring up of prices and speculation, to be followed by another slump.

Upward and downward movements in output, prices, interest rates, and employment form the business cycle that has characterized market economies for the last two centuries—ever since an elaborate, interdependent money economy began to replace the relatively self-sufficient precommercial society. In the first section of this chapter, we survey the history of business cycles and sort through the different interpretations put forth by macroeconomists over the years.

The second half of this chapter examines one of the most important features of business cycles: unemployment. We will see that changes in unemployment tend to mirror business-cycle fluctuations. The social costs of high unemployment, reflected in idle time and lost income, continue to haunt market economies and even threaten the newly emerging market economies of Eastern Europe and the Soviet Union.

Figure 31-1 shows the themes discussed in this chapter and indicates that it integrates many of the different elements of aggregate supply and demand.

A. Business Cycles

Features of the Business Cycle

Business cycles occur when economic activity speeds up or slows down. More precisely, we define a business cycle as follows:

A **business cycle** is a swing in total national output, income, and employment, usually lasting for a period of 2 to 10 years, marked by widespread expansion or contraction in many sectors of the economy.

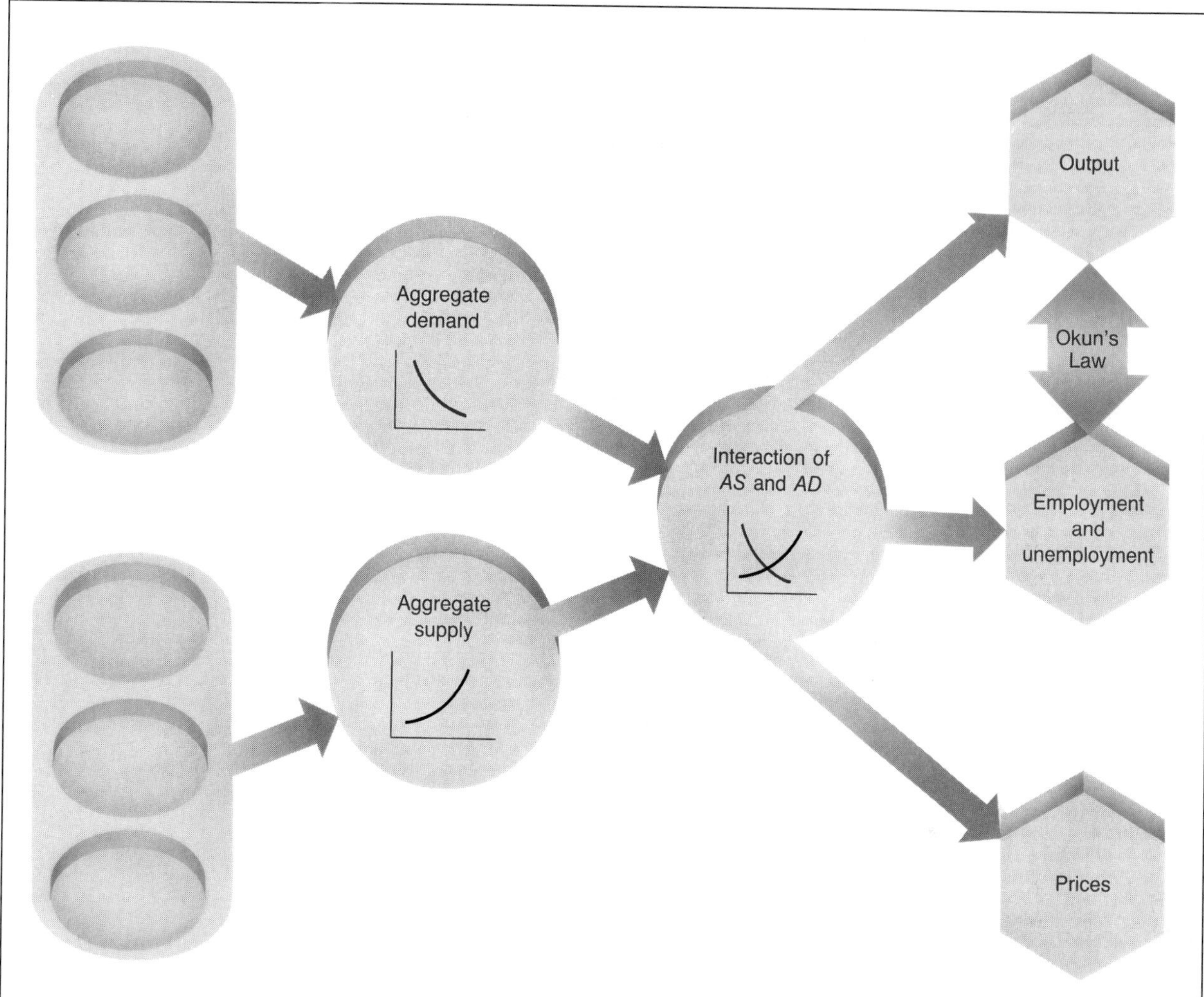

Figure 31-1. Business cycles and unemployment reflect unavoidable features of a market economy
We begin with an analysis of theories and facts of the business cycle, which combine elements of both aggregate supply and demand. Then we examine how unemployment is measured and why it fluctuates over the business cycle.

What are the common features of the business cycle? Modern analysts divide business cycles into phases. "Peaks" and "troughs" mark the turning points of the cycles, while "recession" and "expansion" are the major phases. Figure 31-2 shows the successive phases of the business cycle. The downturn of a business cycle is called a **recession,** which is defined as a period in which real GNP declines for at least 2 consecutive quarter-years. The recession begins at a peak and ends at a trough. According to the unofficial dater of business cycles, the National Bureau of Economic Research, the United States enjoyed a long expansion from late 1982 until a peak in the summer of 1990, at which time a shallow recession began.

Note that the pattern of cycles is irregular. No two business cycles are quite the same. No exact formula, such as might apply to the motions of the moon or of a pendulum, can be used to predict the duration and timing of business cycles. Rather, in their irregularities, business cycles more closely resemble the fluctuations of the weather. Figure 31-3 shows how the American economy has been battered by the business cycle throughout our re-

Four Phases of the Cycle

Recession
Peak
Peak
Peak
Business conditions
Contraction
Expansion
Trough
Recession
Trough
Recession

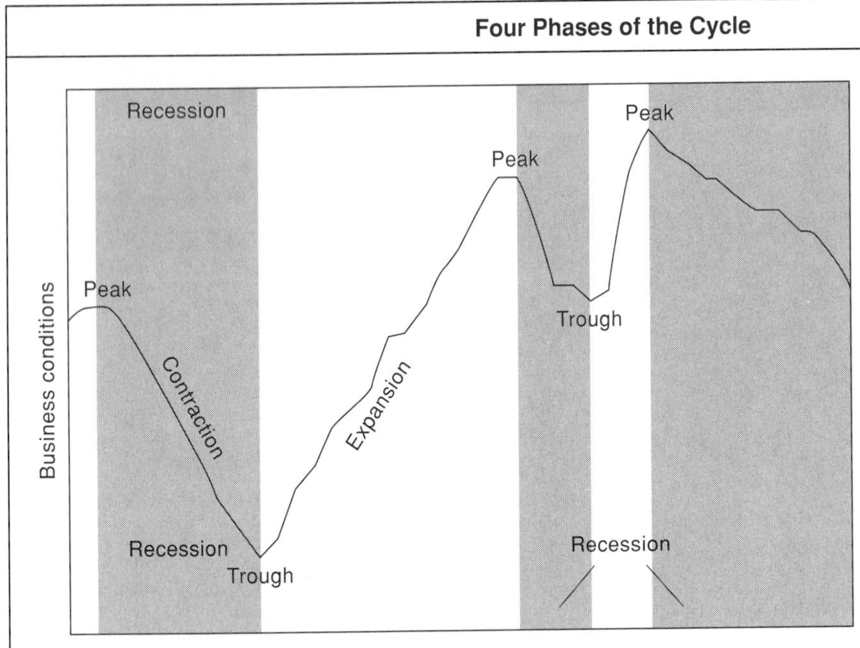

Figure 31-2. A business cycle, like the year, has its seasons

Business cycles are the irregular expansions and contractions in economic activity.

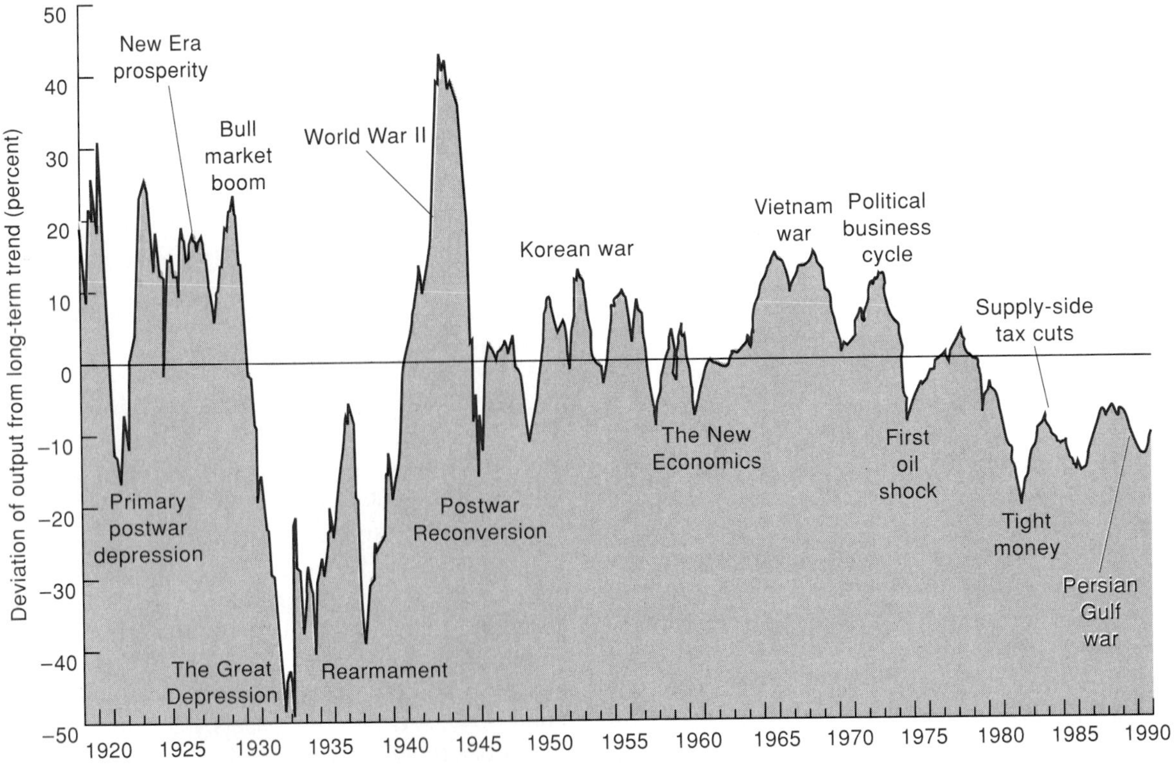

50
40
30
20
10
0
−10
−20
−30
−40
−50
Deviation of output from long-term trend (percent)
New Era prosperity
Bull market boom
World War II
Korean war
Vietnam war
Political business cycle
Supply-side tax cuts
The New Economics
First oil shock
Primary postwar depression
Postwar Reconversion
Tight money
Persian Gulf war
The Great Depression
Rearmament
1920
1925
1930
1935
1940
1945
1950
1955
1960
1965
1970
1975
1980
1985
1990

Figure 31-3. Business activity since 1919

Industrial production has fluctuated incessantly around its long-run trend. Can a more stable economy be seen over the last 30 years? (Source: Federal Reserve Board, detrended by authors.)

cent history. You can see that cycles are like mountain ranges, with different levels of heights and valleys. Some valleys are very deep and broad—as in the Great Depression; others are shallow and narrow, as was that of 1970.

While business cycles are not identical twins, they often have a familial similarity. If a reliable economic forecaster announces that a recession is about to arrive, are there any typical phenomena that you should expect to accompany the recession? The following are a few of the relationships that characterize a recession:

- Often, consumer purchases decline sharply while business inventories of automobiles and other durable goods increase unexpectedly. As businesses react by curbing production, real GNP falls. Shortly afterward, business investment in plant and equipment also falls sharply.
- The demand for labor falls—first seen in a drop in the average workweek, followed by layoffs and higher unemployment.
- As output falls, demand and supplies of crude materials decline, and the prices of many commodities tumble. Wages and manufacturing prices are less likely to decline, but they tend to rise less rapidly in economic downturns.
- Business profits fall sharply in recessions. In anticipation of this, common-stock prices usually tumble as investors sniff the scent of a business downturn. However, because the demand for credit falls, interest rates generally also fall in recessions.

We have spoken in terms of recessions. Booms are the mirror image of recessions, with each of the above factors operating in the opposite direction.

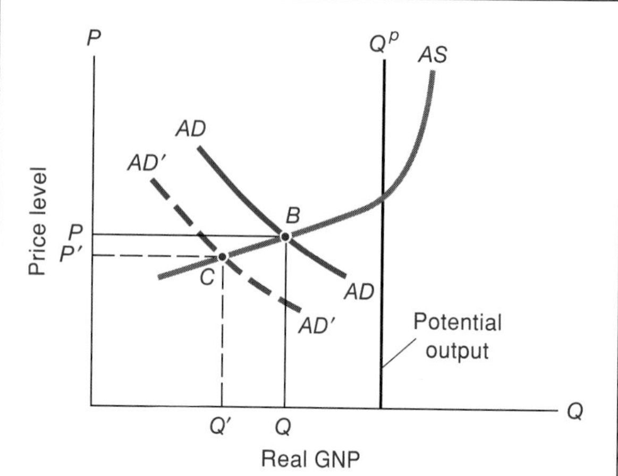

Figure 31-4. A decline in aggregate demand leads to an economic downturn

A downward shift in the *AD* curve along a relatively flat and unchanging *AS* curve leads to lower levels of output as well as lower prices or inflation. Note that as a result of the downward shift in the *AD* curve, the gap between actual and potential GNP becomes greater during a recession.

Business-Cycle Theories

Business Cycles as Shifts in Aggregate Demand

What causes business cycles? Although there is no single answer, business cycles generally occur as a result of shifts in aggregate demand. A typical cycle is illustrated in Figure 31-4, which shows how a decline in aggregate demand lowers output.

Say that the economy is originally in short-run equilibrium at point *B*. Then, as a result of a shift in consumer, government, or business spending, there is a shift to the left in the curve of aggregate spending to *AD*′. If there is no change in aggregate supply, the economy will reach a new equilibrium at point *C*. Note that output declines from *Q* to *Q*′ and that prices are lower (or in a more realistic situation, the rate of inflation falls).

The case of a boom is, naturally, just the opposite. Here, the *AD* curve shifts to the right, output approaches potential GNP or perhaps even overshoots it, and prices (and inflation) rise.

Alternative Approaches

Although the main interpretation of business cycles looks to changes in aggregate demand, we want to know more about the mechanism by which the cycle is generated. We may classify the different theories into two categories, external and primarily internal. The *external* theories find the root of the business cycle in the fluctuations of something outside the economic system—in wars, revolutions, and elections; in gold discoveries, rates of growth of population, and migrations; in discoveries of new lands and resources; in scientific breakthroughs and technological innovations; even in sunspots or the weather.

The *internal* theories look for mechanisms within the economic system itself that will give rise to self-generating business cycles. In this approach, every expansion breeds recession and contraction, and every contraction breeds revival and expansion—in a quasi-regular, repeating chain.

Here are some of the most important business-cycle theories along with their proponents:

1. *Monetary* theories attribute the business cycle to the expansion and contraction of money and credit (Hawtrey, Friedman).
2. *Innovation* theories attribute the cycle to the clustering of important inventions such as those surrounding the railroad or the automobile (Schumpeter, Hansen).
3. The *multiplier-accelerator model* proposes that external shocks are propagated by the multiplier along with an investment theory known as the accelerator, thereby generating regular, cyclical fluctuations in output (Samuelson).
4. *Political* theories of business cycles attribute fluctuations to politicians who manipulate fiscal and monetary policies in order to be reelected (Kalecki, Nordhaus, Tufte).
5. *Equilibrium-business-cycle* theories claim that misperceptions about price and wage movements lead people to supply too much or too little labor, which leads to cycles of output and employment (Lucas, Barro, Sargent).
6. *Real-business-cycle* proponents hold that productivity shocks spread through the economy and cause fluctuations (Prescott, Long, Plosser).

This list just hints at the variety of explanations of movements in output, unemployment, and prices. In looking at different business-cycle theories, however, we would want to check to see whether they correspond to the salient features described above. One important pattern, noted above, is that purchases of investment and other durable goods tend to move sharply up in expansions and down in recessions; another feature is the cyclical movement of profits. A comparison of the theories with the business-cycle facts reveals that all have elements of validity, but none is universally valid in all times and places.

Forecasting Business Cycles

Given the wide swings in economic activity, economic forecasting is one of the most important tasks of economists. Like bright headlights on a car, a good forecast illuminates the economic terrain ahead and helps decision makers adapt their actions to economic conditions.

Econometric Modeling and Forecasting

In an earlier era, economists forecasted the business cycle by looking at a wide variety of data on things like money, boxcar loadings, and steel production. Sometimes the numbers were added together to form an "index of leading indicators" which, it was hoped, would be a barometer of future economic conditions.

As economics entered the age of statistics and computers, macroeconomic forecasting has made great progress. Thanks to the pioneering work of Holland's Nobel-laureate Jan Tinbergen, today we have dozens of macroeconomic models. Lawrence Klein of the Wharton School, who won the 1980 Nobel Prize for his contribution to economic modeling, has built a number of forecasting systems over the last three decades. Commercial consulting firms, such as Data Resources Inc. (DRI), have developed models that are widely used by firms and policymakers.

How are computer models of the economy constructed? Generally modelers start with an analytical framework containing equations representing both aggregate demand and aggregate supply. Using the techniques of modern econometrics, each equation is "fitted" to the data to obtain parameter estimates (such as the *MPC*, the shape of the money-demand equation, the growth of potential GNP, etc.). Of course, at each stage modelers use their own experience and judgment to assess whether the results are reasonable.[1]

Finally, the whole "model" is put together and run as a system of equations. In small models there are one or two dozen equations. Today, large sys-

[1] The process by which forecasts are generated is somewhat mysterious to their users. The mixture of art and science has led one observer to ask: "What does an economic forecast have in common with a dog's breakfast? Simple: You never know what's in it."

tems forecast from a few hundred to 10,000 variables. Once the external and policy variables are specified (population, government spending and tax rates, monetary policy, etc.), the system of equations projects important economic variables into the future.

Often the forecasts are accurate. For example, the 1990–1991 recession was foreseen by a large number of economic forecasters. At other times, particularly when there are major policy shifts, forecasting is a hazardous profession. Table 31-1 shows the projections made by DRI, one of the nation's most influential forecasters, right after the Reagan supply-side policies were announced. With major changes in fiscal and monetary policy underway, along with dramatic movements in the dollar's exchange rate and a foreign debt crisis brewing, DRI and other forecasters missed both the deep recession and the growing federal deficit that lay over the horizon. This experience emphasizes that forecasting is as much art as science in our uncertain world. Still, the strength of economic forecasting is that, year in and year out, professional forecasters provide more accurate forecasts than do those who use unsystematic or unscientific approaches.

Is the Business Cycle Avoidable?

Just as there are waves of prosperity and recession, there also follow swings in popular views about the necessity of business cycles. From time to time, an economist or President will proclaim, "I do not believe recessions are inevitable."

Such pronouncements are overly sanguine. A more balanced view was taken by Arthur Okun:

> Recessions are now generally considered to be fundamentally preventable, like airplane crashes and unlike hurricanes. But we have not banished air crashes from the land, and it is not clear that we have the wisdom or the ability to eliminate recessions. The danger has not disappeared. The forces that produce recurrent recessions are still in the wings, merely waiting for their cue.[2]

Over the two decades since Okun wrote these words, the United States has experienced numerous cyclical ups and downs. At the same time, we have avoided *depressions*—the prolonged, cumulative slumps like those of the 1870s, 1890s, or 1930s. What has changed in the last 50 years? Pri-

[2] Arthur M. Okun, *The Political Economy of Prosperity* (Norton, New York, 1970), pp. 33 ff.

Forecasting Turbulent Times—and Results

	(1) DRI forecast of April 1981 for 4th quarter of 1982	(2) Actual data for 4th quarter of 1982	(3) Percentage error
GNP ($, billion):			
Real	1,582	1,477	7
Nominal	3,482	3,108	11
Inflation rate (% per year, GNP deflator)	10.1	3.7	63
Unemployment rate (%)	6.6	10.7	−62
Interest rates (% per year):			
3-month Treasury bills	13.8	7.9	43
Long-term bonds (AAA)	13.1	11.1	15
Federal deficit ($, billion)	24	203	−746
Stock prices (S&P 500)	146	137	6

Table 31-1. A forecast of the economy 18 months in advance

This shows the macroeconomic forecast of the performance of the U.S. economy made in spring 1981 for economic conditions 18 months later. The recession was not foreseen, nor was the accompanying reduction in inflation. Most other forecasters (including the government) did even worse. According to DRI's Otto Eckstein, "[1982] proved to be the most difficult for forecasting that has been experienced in modern memory." [Source: *The Data Resources Review of the U.S. Economy* (April 1981 and February 1983).]

marily, developments in macroeconomics now allow governments to take monetary and fiscal steps to prevent recessions from snowballing into a persistent and profound slump. If Marxists wait for capitalism to collapse in a final cataclysmic crisis, they wait in vain. The wild business cycle that ravaged mature capitalism during its early years has been tamed.

B. Unemployment

Be nice to people on your way up
because you'll meet them on your way down.
Wilson Mizner

Although the deepest depressions no longer appear to be a major threat to the American economy, the scourge of recession and unemployment still haunts us. Indeed, unemployment remains a predominant social concern of modern market economies. How can millions of people be unemployed when there is so much work to be done? What flaw in a modern mixed economy forces so many who want work to remain idle? Should nations take steps to alleviate the hardships of joblessness? Or, as some argue, do high unemployment benefits simply reduce the incentive to work and end up raising the unemployment rate? These questions, and their linkage with inflation, concern workers, policymakers, and economists more than any other economic problem.

The present section is a whirlwind tour of the meaning and measurement of unemployment. We begin with an analysis of the impact of unemployment, followed by a definition of the economic interpretation of unemployment. We then show the link between unemployment and output and discuss some of the policy questions that arise in employment policy.

Okun's Law

We have spoken about recessions as periods in which output and unemployment are high, while booms are periods in which GNP is near or above its potential, employment is high, and unemployment shrinks. But what is the exact link between unemployment and inflation? The answer to this question was provided in a striking discovery by Arthur Okun that is now known as Okun's Law.*

Okun's Law states that for every 2 percent that GNP falls relative to potential GNP, the unemployment rate rises 1 percentage point. For example, if GNP begins at 100 percent of its potential and falls to 98 percent of potential, the unemployment rate rises by 1 percentage point, say from 6 to 7 percent.[3]

[3] In early studies, Okun found that the relationship was about 3 to 1; that is, 1 point of U for every 3 points of the GNP gap. However, more recent data and more advanced econometric techniques suggest that the 2-to-1 (or perhaps a $2\frac{1}{2}$) gearing ratio between output and the unemployment rate is more representative for recent periods.

*Arthur Okun (1929–1979) was one of the most creative American economic policymakers of the postwar era. Educated at Columbia, he taught at Yale until he joined President Kennedy's Council of Economic Advisers as a staff member in 1961. He became a CEA member in 1964 and President Johnson's chairman in 1968. After he left the CEA, Okun stayed in Washington at the Brookings Institution.

One of Okun's central concerns was to find ways of containing inflation without throwing millions of people out of work. He espoused a novel approach to anti-inflation policies called "Tax-Based Incomes Policies" ("TIPs"), which we will discuss in Chapter 33.

In addition, Okun was renowned for his use of simple homilies to illustrate economic points. He compared arguments against the 1968 tax increase to his 7-year-old's arguments against taking medicine: "He is perfectly well; he is so sick that nothing can possibly help him; he will take it later in the day if his throat doesn't get better; it isn't fair unless his brothers take it too." [Arthur M. Okun, *The Political Economy of Prosperity* (Norton, New York, 1970), p. 99.] Okun proved time and again that a well-told tale is often worth more than 1000 equations.

At the beginning of this chapter, we described a typical recession as occurring when aggregate demand declines relative to aggregate supply (see Figure 31-4 on page 569). What happens to unemployment in recessions? As output falls, firms need fewer labor inputs, so workers are laid off. The result is a rise in the unemployment rate. Figure 31-5 shows the close relationship between output changes and unemployment.

You sometimes hear the expression, "You have to keep running just to stay in the same place." This is true of GNP growth and unemployment because actual GNP must grow as rapidly as potential GNP to keep the unemployment rate from rising. Say that potential GNP is growing at 3 percent per year. Then real GNP must also grow at 3 percent each year to keep the unemployment rate constant.

We can use a historical example, involving the 3 years of economic stagnation from 1979 to 1982, to illustrate Okun's Law. From 1979 to 1982, actual real GNP didn't grow at all. By contrast, potential GNP grew at 3 percent per year over this period, for a total increase of 9 percent in potential GNP from 1979 to 1982. What would Okun's Law predict about the movement of the unemployment rate from 1979 to 1982? Okun's Law holds that each 2 percent shortfall of GNP relative to potential adds 1 percentage point to the unemployment rate; therefore, a 9 percent shortfall in GNP should have led to a rise in the unemployment rate of 4.5 percentage points. Starting with an unemployment rate of 5.8 percent in 1979, then, Okun's Law would predict a 10.3 percent unemployment rate in 1982. The official statistics show that the actual unemployment rate was 9.7 percent for 1982. This is surprisingly accurate for an inexact science like economics.

Here is still another example. Let us say you are the newly elected President, planning your macroeconomic policy at the end of 1996. The unemployment rate in late 1996 is 7 percent, and you would

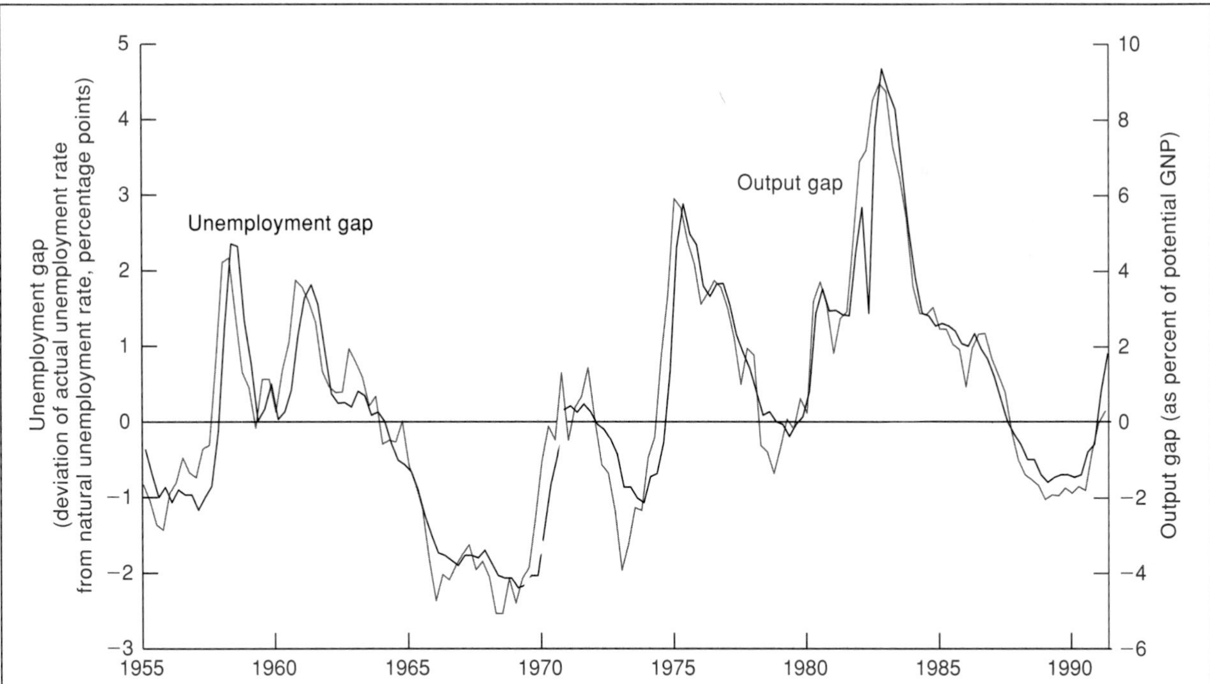

Figure 31-5. Okun's Law illustrated, 955–1990

The two lines show the output gap and the unemployment gap. The output gap is the percentage deviation of GNP from its potential. The unemployment gap is the deviation of the unemployment rate from the natural rate, in percentage points.

According to Okun's Law, whenever output moves 2 percent below potential GNP, the unemployment rate rises 1 percentage point above the natural rate. Thus in 1983, output was 7 percent below potential GNP, and the unemployment rate was $9\frac{1}{2}$ percent (= 6 percent for the natural rate plus $\frac{1}{2}$ the output gap of 7 percent).

like to get the economy back to potential GNP, with an unemployment rate of 6 percent, by the time your program is judged by the voters in November 2000.

Question: How fast must the economy grow over the 4 years from 1996 to 2000? Answer: It must grow at the growth rate of potential GNP (3 percent annually), plus enough to reduce the unemployment rate about $\frac{1}{4}$ percentage point each year. The average annual growth rate for GNP must then be $3 + \frac{1}{2} = 3\frac{1}{2}$ percent annually over the 4-year period.

Okun's Law provides the vital link between the output market and the labor market. It describes the association between short-run movements in real GNP and changes in unemployment.

Impact of Unemployment

Now that we have seen the key linkage between output and unemployment, we can understand why unemployment is a central problem in modern societies. When unemployment is high, resources are wasted and people's incomes are depressed. During such periods, economic distress spills over to affect people's emotions and family lives.

Economic Impact

Societies value high employment both because high employment means high output and incomes and because work is in many societies valued in itself. When unemployment is high, much output is lost, incomes decline, and people suffer from loss of self-esteem. During recessions, it is as if vast quantities of automobiles, housing, clothing, and other commodities were simply dumped into the ocean.

How much waste results from high unemployment? Table 31-2 provides a calculation of how far output fell short of potential GNP during the major periods of high unemployment over the last half-century. The largest economic loss occurred during the Great Depression, but the stagnant 1970s and 1980s also witnessed more than a trillion dollars of lost output.

The losses during periods of high unemployment are the greatest documented wastes in a modern economy. They are many times larger than the estimated inefficiencies from microeconomic waste due to monopoly or than the waste induced by tariffs and quotas.[4]

[4] The estimated output losses shown in Table 31-2 may overestimate the true economic cost of recessions. As Chapter 24's discussion of NEW show, some of the idle time can be usefully allocated to work around the house, such as insulating walls or tuning up the car's engine. Careful estimates by Northwestern University's Robert J. Gordon suggest, however, that this offset is only about 25 percent of the output loss due to the gap between actual and potential output. Even after these corrections, the macroeconomic losses from recessions appear very large relative to microeconomic inefficiencies.

The Cost of Stagnation

Period	Average unemployment rate (%)	Lost output: GNP loss ($, billion, 1988 prices)	Lost output: As percent of GNP during the period
Great Depression (1930–1939)	18.2	2,850	38.5
Sluggish fifties (1954–1960)	5.2	46	0.3
Stagnant seventies and eighties (1975–1984)	7.7	1,354	3.6

Table 31-2. Economic costs from periods of high unemployment

The three major periods of high unemployment since 1929 occurred during the Great Depression, the sluggish fifties, and the stagnant period from 1975 to 1984. The amount of lost output shown above is calculated as the cumulative difference between potential GNP and actual GNP. Note that during the Great Depression losses relative to GNP were more than 10 times those of recent periods of slow growth. (Source: Authors' estimates on the basis of official GNP and unemployment data.)

Social Impact

Even though the economic cost of unemployment is large, no dollar figure can adequately convey the human, social, and psychological toll from periods of persistent involuntary unemployment. The personal tragedy of unemployment is conveyed by two reminiscences. The first depicts the futility of a job search in San Francisco during the Great Depression.

> I'd get up at five in the morning and head for the waterfront. Outside the Spreckles Sugar Refinery, outside the gates, there would be a thousand men. You know dang well there's only three or four jobs. The guy would come out with two little Pinkerton cops: "I need two guys for the bull gang. Two guys to go into the hole." A thousand men would fight like a pack of Alaskan dogs to get through. Only four of us would get through.[5]

And here is the recollection of an unemployed construction worker:

> I called the roofing outfits and they didn't need me because they already had men that had been working for them five or six years. There wasn't that many openings. You had to have a college education for most of them. And I was looking for *anything*, from car wash to anything else.
>
> So what do you do all day? You go home and you sit. And you begin to get frustrated sitting home. Everybody in the household starts getting on edge. They start arguing with each other over stupid things 'cause they're all cramped in that space all the time. The whole family kind of got crushed by it.[6]

It would be surprising if such experiences did not leave scars. Public-health studies indicate that unemployment leads to a deterioration of both physical and psychological health: higher levels of heart disease, alcoholism, and suicide. The leading expert on the subject, Dr. M. Harvey Brenner, estimates that a 1-percentage-point rise in the unemployment rate sustained over a period of 6 years would lead to 37,000 early deaths in the United States. Psychological studies indicate that being fired from a job is generally as traumatic as the death of a close friend or failing school.

[5] Studs Terkel, *Hard Times: An Oral History of the Great Depression in America* (Pantheon, New York, 1970).

[6] Harry Maurer, *Not Working: An Oral History of the Unemployed* (Holt, New York, 1979).

Measuring Unemployment

Changes in the unemployment rate make monthly headlines. What lies behind the numbers? Data on work and unemployment are among the most carefully designed and comprehensive economic data the nation collects. The data are collected monthly in a procedure known as *random sampling* of the population.[7] Each month about 60,000 households are interviewed about their recent work patterns.

The survey divides the population 16 years and older into three groups:

- **Employed.** These are people who perform any paid work, as well as those who have jobs but are absent from work because of illness, strikes, or vacations.
- **Unemployed.** This group includes people who are not employed but are actively looking for work or waiting to return to work. More precisely, a person is unemployed if he or she is not working and (*a*) has made specific efforts to find a job during the last 4 weeks, (*b*) is laid off from a job and is waiting to be recalled, or (*c*) is waiting to report to a job in the next month. To be counted as unemployed a person must do more than simply think about work or, for example, contemplate the possibility of making a movie or being a rock star. A person must report specific efforts (like visiting local firms or answering want ads) to find a job. Those who are either employed or unemployed are in the **labor force.**
- **Not in the labor force.** This includes the 34 percent of the adult population that is going to school, keeping house, retired, too ill to work, or simply not looking for work.

The government's definitions are the following:

People with jobs are employed; people without jobs but looking for work are unemployed; people without jobs who are not looking for work are outside the labor force. The **unemployment rate** is the number of unemployed divided by the total labor force.

[7] Random sampling is an essential technique for estimating the behavior or characteristics of an entire population. It consists of choosing a subgroup of the population at random (say, by selecting telephone digits through a computer-generated series of random numbers) and then surveying the selected group. Random sampling is used in many social sciences, as well as in market research.

Deployment of the Population

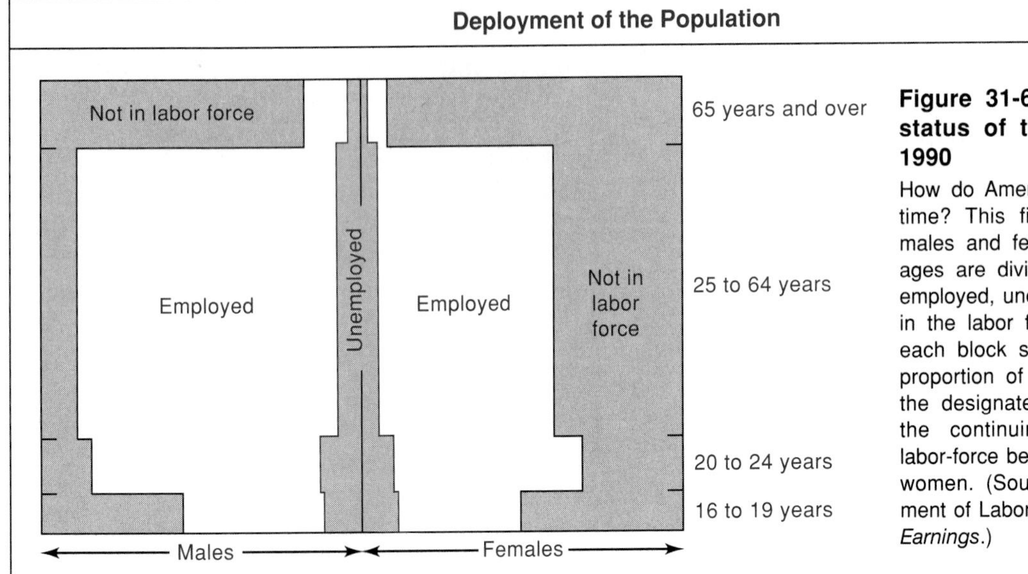

Figure 31-6. Labor-force status of the population, 1990

How do Americans spend their time? This figure shows how males and females of different ages are divided among being employed, unemployed, and not in the labor force. The size of each block shows the relative proportion of the population in the designated category. Note the continuing difference in labor-force behavior of men and women. (Source: U.S. Department of Labor, *Employment and Earnings*.)

Figure 31-6 shows how the male and female populations in the United States are divided among the three categories.

Economic Interpretation of Unemployment

We turn now from the way the government counts the unemployed to the economic analysis of unemployment. Some of the important questions we address are: What are the reasons for being unemployed? What is the distinction between "voluntary" and "involuntary" unemployment? What is the relationship between different kinds of unemployment and the business cycle?

Three Kinds of Unemployment

In sorting out the structure of today's labor markets, economists identify three different kinds of unemployment: frictional, structural, and cyclical.

Frictional unemployment arises because of the incessant movement of people between regions and jobs or through different stages of the life cycle. Even if an economy were at full employment, there would always be some turnover as people search for jobs when they graduate from school or move to a new city. Women may reenter the labor force after having children. Because frictionally unemployed workers are often moving between jobs, or looking for better jobs, it is often thought that they are "voluntarily" unemployed.

Structural unemployment signifies a mismatch between the supply and the demand for workers. Mismatches can occur because the demand for one kind of labor is rising while the demand for another kind is falling, and supplies do not quickly adjust. We often see structural imbalances across occupations or regions as certain sectors grow while others decline. For example, an acute shortage of nurses arose in the mid-1980s as the number of nurses grew slowly while the demand for nursing care grew rapidly because of an aging population and other forces. Not until nurses' salaries rose rapidly and the supply adjusted did the structural shortage of nurses decline. By contrast, the demand for coal miners has been depressed for decades because of the lack of geographical mobility of labor and capital; unemployment rates in coal-mining communities remain high today.

Cyclical unemployment exists when the overall demand for labor is low. As total spending and output fall, unemployment rises virtually everywhere. In the recession year 1982, the unemployment rate rose in 48 of the 50 states. This rise in unemployment signaled that the increased unemployment was largely cyclical.

The distinction between cyclical and other kinds of joblessness helps economists diagnose the general health of the labor market. High levels of frictional or structural unemployment can occur even though the overall labor market is in balance, for example, when turnover is high or when geographical imbalances are large. Cyclical unemployment occurs when employment falls as a result of an imbalance between aggregate supply and demand.

Microeconomic Foundations[8]

No topic has generated more controversy among economists than the causes of unemployment in a market economy. Economics teaches that prices rise or fall to clear competitive markets. At the market-clearing price, buyers willingly buy what sellers willingly sell. But something is gumming up the workings of the labor market; many hospitals are searching for nurses but cannot find them, while thousands of coal miners want to work at the going wage but cannot find a job. Similar symptoms of labor market failures are found in all market economies.

Economists look to microeconomics to help understand the existence of unemployment. Although no universally accepted theory has emerged, many analyses share the common observation that unemployment arises because wages are not flexible enough to clear markets. We explore below why wages are inflexible and why inflexible wages lead to involuntary unemployment.

We begin our analysis of the microeconomic foundations of unemployment theory by considering a typical labor market. A group of workers has a labor supply schedule shown as *SS* in Figure 31-7. The supply curve becomes completely inelastic at

[8] This topic may be omitted in short courses.

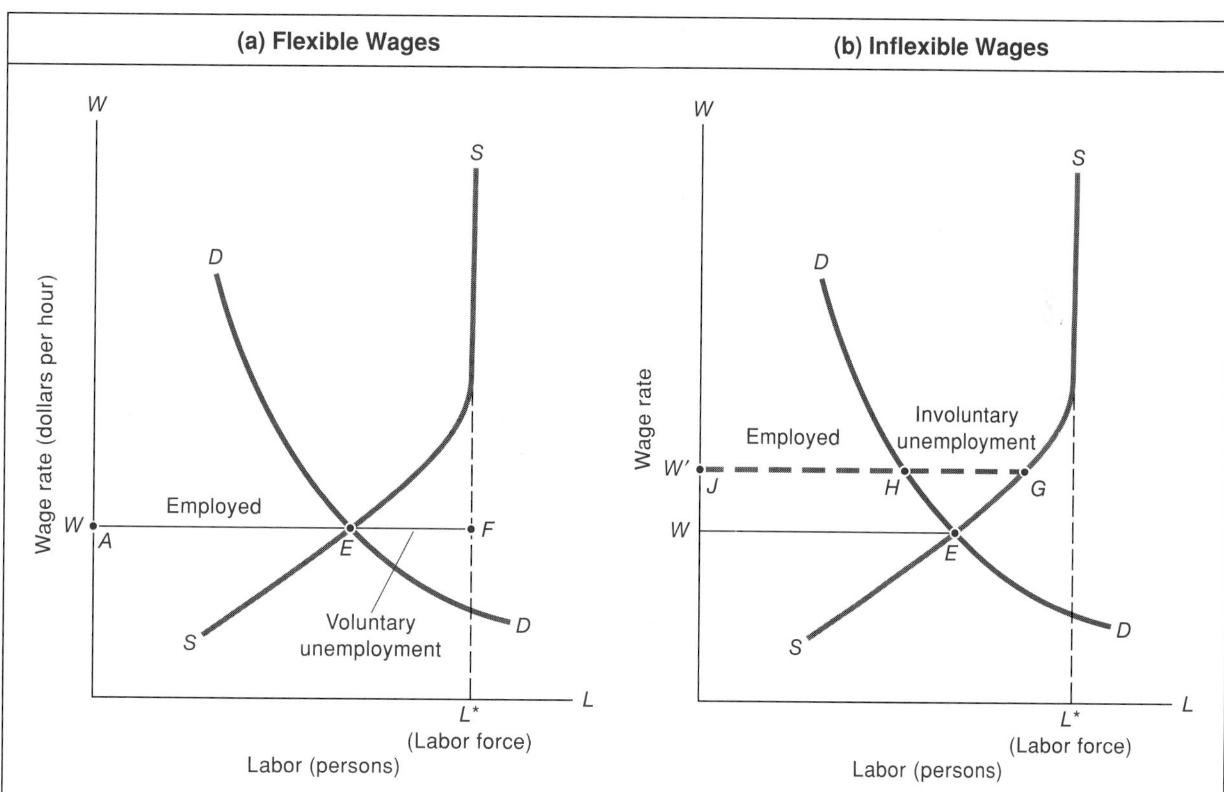

Figure 31-7. Inflexible wages can lead to involuntary unemployment

We can depict different kinds of unemployment using the microeconomic supply-and-demand framework. In **(a)**, wages move up or down to clear the labor market. There is never any involuntary unemployment.

Part **(b)** shows what happens if wages do not adjust to clear the labor market. At the too high wage at *W′*, *JH* workers are employed, but *HG* workers are involuntarily unemployed.

labor quantity L^* when wage levels are high. We will call L^* the labor force.

Voluntary Unemployment. The left-hand panel of Figure 31-7 shows the usual picture of competitive supply and demand, with a market equilibrium at point E and a wage of W. At the competitive, market-clearing equilibrium, firms willingly hire all qualified workers who want to work at the market wage. The number of employed is represented by the line from A to E. Some members of the labor force, shown by the segment EF, would like to work, but only at a higher wage rate. *The unemployed workers, represented by the segment from* E *to* F, *are* ***voluntarily unemployed*** *in the sense that they do not want to work at the going market wage rate.*

The existence of voluntary unemployment points to an important misconception about unemployment. An economy may well be performing at the peak of efficiency even though it generates a certain amount of unemployment. The voluntarily unemployed workers might prefer leisure or other activities to jobs at the going wage rate. Or they may be frictionally unemployed, perhaps moving from college to their first job. Or they might be low-productivity workers who prefer leisure to low-paid work. There are countless reasons why people might voluntarily choose not to work at the going wage rate, yet some of these people would be officially counted as unemployed.

It is important to note that voluntary unemployment might well be economically efficient even though a philosopher or politician might bemoan the fact that everybody cannot obtain a high-paying job. Just as a factory needs spare parts in case a critical piece of machinery breaks down, maybe an economy needs spare, unemployed workers, willing to go to work immediately when a critical job vacancy arises. This example shows why a complex modern economy, operating at the peak of its productivity, may generate unemployment.

In summary, a labor market characterized by perfectly flexible wages will not contain involuntary unemployment. Prices and wages simply float up or down until the markets are cleared. In any economy with perfectly flexible wages, widespread unemployment such as that in the 1930s or 1980s would simply not exist.

Involuntary Unemployment. Reread the quotations from unemployed workers on page 575. Who would seriously argue that these workers are voluntarily unemployed? They surely do not sound like consumers carefully balancing the value of work against the value of leisure. Nor do they resemble people choosing unemployment as they search for a better job. To understand cyclical unemployment we need to construct a theory of involuntary unemployment. Keynes' great breakthrough was to let the facts oust a beautiful but irrelevant theory. He explained why we see occasional bouts of *involuntary unemployment,* periods in which qualified workers are unable to get jobs at the going wage rates.

The key to his approach was to note that wages do not adjust to clear labor markets. Rather, wages tend to respond sluggishly to economic shocks. If wages do not move to clear markets, a mismatch between job seekers and job vacancies can arise. This mismatch may lead to the patterns of unemployment that we see today.

We can understand how inflexible wages lead to involuntary unemployment with an analysis of *a non-clearing labor market,* shown in Figure 31-7(*b*). This example assumes that in the wake of an economic disturbance the labor market finds itself with too high a wage rate. Labor's price is at W' rather than at the equilibrium or market-clearing wage of W.

At the too-high wage rate, there are more qualified workers looking for work than there are jobs looking for workers. The number of workers willing to work at wage W' is at point G on the supply curve, but firms only want to hire H workers, as shown by the demand curve. Because the wage exceeds the market-clearing level, there is a surplus of workers. The unemployed workers represented by the dashed line segment HG are said to be **involuntarily unemployed,** signifying that they are qualified workers who want to work at the prevailing wage but cannot find jobs. When there is a surplus of workers, firms will ration out the jobs by setting more stringent skill requirements, adding to the workload, and hiring the most qualified or most experienced workers.

The opposite case occurs when the wage is too low. Here, in a labor-shortage economy, employers cannot find enough workers to fill the existing vacancies. Firms put "Help Wanted" signs in their windows, advertise in the newspaper, and even recruit people from other towns.

Sources of Inflexibility. The theory of involuntary unemployment assumes that wages are inflexible. But this raises a further question: Why do wages not move up or down to clear markets? Why are labor markets not like the auction markets for grain, corn, and common stocks?

These questions are among the deepest unresolved mysteries of modern economics. Few economists today would argue that wages move quickly to erase labor shortages and surpluses. Yet no one completely understands the reasons for the sluggish behavior of wages and salaries. We can therefore provide no more than a tentative assessment of the sources of wage inflexibility.

A helpful distinction is that between auction markets and administered markets. An *auction market* is a highly organized and competitive market where the price floats up or down to balance supply and demand. At the Chicago Board of Trade, for example, the prices of "number 2 stiff red wheat delivered in St. Louis" or "dressed 'A' broiler chickens delivered in New York" change every minute to reflect market conditions—market conditions that are seen in frantic buy and sell orders of farmers, millers, packers, merchants, and speculators.

But 90 percent of all goods, as well as 100 percent of all labor, is sold in administered markets and not in competitive auction markets. Nobody grades labor into "number 2 subcompact-automobile tire assembler" or "class 'AAA' assistant professor of economics." No specialist burns the midnight oil trying to make sure that steelworkers' wages or professors' salaries are set at just the level where all qualified workers are placed into jobs.

Rather, most firms *administer* their wages and salaries, setting fixed pay scales and hiring people at an entry-level wage or salary. These wage scales are generally fixed for a year or so, and when they are adjusted, the pay for almost all categories goes up by the same percentage. For example, a bank might have 15 different categories of staff: three grades of secretaries, two grades of tellers, and so forth. Each year, the bank managers will decide how much to increase wages and salaries—say 5.5 percent in 1993—and the compensation in each category will then move up by that percentage. On infrequent occasions the bank might decide to move one category up or down more than the average. Given the procedure by which wages and salaries are determined, there is little room for major adjustments when the firm finds shortages or gluts in a particular area. Except in extreme cases, the firm will tend to adjust the minimum qualifications required for a job rather than its wages when it finds labor market disequilibrium.[9]

For unionized labor markets, the wage patterns are even more rigid. Wage scales are typically set for a 3-year contract period; during that period, wages are not adjusted for excess supply or demand in particular areas. Moreover, unionized workers seldom accept wage cuts even when many of their workers are unemployed.

To summarize, a careful look at wage setting in America and other market economies today reveals a highly administered process. Wages and salaries are generally set infrequently (usually no more than once a year), and relative wages tend to change very slowly.

Wages and salaries adjust to reflect shortages or surpluses in a particular market only over an extended period of time.

Let's go a step further and ask, What is the economic reason for the sluggishness of wages and salaries? Most economists believe that the inflexibility arises because of the costs of administering compensation. To take the example of union wages, negotiating a contract is a long process that requires much worker and management time and produces no output. It is because collective bargaining is so costly that such agreements are generally negotiated only once every 3 years.

Setting compensation for nonunion workers is less costly, but it nevertheless requires considerable scarce management time and has important effects on worker morale. Every time wages or sala-

[9] The example of college admissions illustrates the kind of adjustment that takes place when shortages or gluts occur. Many colleges found that applications for places soared in the 1980s. How did they react? Did they raise their tuition enough to choke off the excess demand? No. Instead, they raised their admission standards, requiring better grades in high schools and higher average SAT scores. Upgrading the requirements rather than changing wages and prices is exactly what happens in the short run when firms experience excess supply of labor.

ries are set, every time fringe benefits are changed, earlier compensation agreements are changed as well. Some workers will feel the changes are unfair, others will complain about unjust procedures, and grievances may be triggered.

Personnel managers therefore prefer a system in which wages are adjusted infrequently and most workers in a firm get the same pay increase, regardless of the market conditions for different skills or categories. This system may appear inefficient to economists, because it does not allow for a perfect adjustment of wages to reflect market supply and demand. But this approach does economize on scarce managerial time and helps promote a sense of fair play and equity in the firm. In the end, it may be cheaper to recruit workers more actively or to change the required qualifications than to upset the entire wage structure of a firm simply to hire a few new workers.

To summarize:

The theory of sticky wages and involuntary unemployment holds that the slow adjustment of wages produces surpluses and shortages in individual labor markets. But labor markets do eventually respond to market conditions; wages of high-demand occupations move up relative to low-demand occupations. Therefore, labor markets look very much like the non-clearing labor market example of Figure 31-7(*b*) in the short run. In the long run, wages tend to move to balance supply and demand, so major pockets of unemployment or of job vacancies tend to disappear as wages and quantities adjust to market conditions. But the long run may be many years, and periods of unemployment can therefore persist for many years.

Labor Market Issues

Having analyzed the causes of unemployment, we turn next to major labor market issues for today. Which groups are most likely to be unemployed? How long are they unemployed? Why is teenage unemployment so high?

Who Are the Unemployed?

In attempting to understand who the unemployed workers are, it is useful to track labor market conditions in periods of low unemployment (as in 1973) as well as in recession years (such as 1982).

Table 31-3 shows unemployment statistics for boom and recession years. The first two columns of numbers are the unemployment rates by age, race, and sex. These data show that the unemployment rate of every group tends to rise during recession.

Labor market group	Unemployment rate of different groups (% of labor force)		Distribution of total unemployment across different groups (% of total unemployed)	
	Boom (1973)	Recession (1982)	Boom (1973)	Recession (1982)
By age:				
16–19 years	14.5	23.2	28.5	18.5
20 years and older	3.8	8.6	71.5	81.5
By race:				
White	4.3	8.6	79.2	77.2
Black and other	8.9	17.3	20.8	22.8
By sex (adults only):				
Male	3.3	8.8	51.8	58.5
Female	4.8	8.3	48.2	41.5
All workers	**4.9**	**9.7**	**100.0**	**100.0**

Table 31-3. Unemployment by demographic group

This table shows how unemployment varies across different demographic groups in boom and recession years. The first set of figures shows the unemployment rate for each group in 1973 and 1982. The last two columns show the percent of the total pool of unemployed that lies in each group. (Source: U.S. Department of Labor, *Employment and Earnings*.)

The last two columns show how the total pool of unemployment is distributed among different groups; observe that the distribution of unemployment across groups changes relatively little throughout the business cycle.

Note also that nonwhites tend to experience unemployment rates twice those of whites. The relative unemployment rates of males and females, on the other hand, have reversed over the last decade. Women have generally faced higher unemployment rates than men, but this was not the case in 1982. Note as well that teenagers are a larger fraction of the unemployed in boom than in recession.

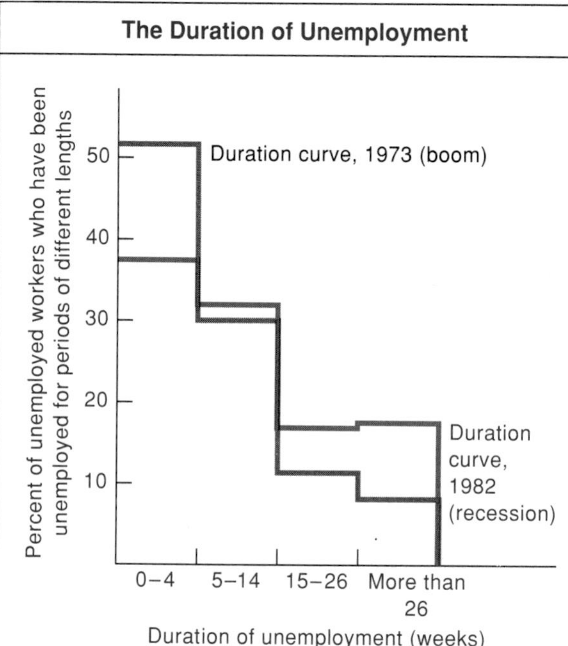

Figure 31-8. Most unemployment in the United States is short-term, but long-term unemployment increases in recessions

How long does it take workers to find jobs? The "duration curves" in the figure show what percent of the unemployed have been unemployed for different periods. Thus in the boom year 1973, only 8 percent of the unemployed were unemployed for more than 26 weeks. In the deep-recession year of 1982, the incidence of very long term unemployment (over 26 weeks) had increased to 17 percent of the unemployed. Thus the duration curve in recession tends to flatten, with more people having to wait longer to find jobs and therefore with fewer people daring to quit jobs they don't like. (Source: U.S. Department of Labor, *Employment and Earnings*.)

Duration of Unemployment

Another key question concerns duration. How much of the unemployment experience is long-term and of major social concern, and how much is short-term as people move quickly between jobs?

Figure 31-8 shows the duration of unemployment in boom and recession, again using 1973 and 1982 data. A surprising feature of American labor markets is that a very large fraction of unemployment is of very short duration. Thus in the boom year of 1973, less than one-fifth of unemployment lasted more than 14 weeks. In recessions, however, it takes considerably longer to find a job. The number of workers out of a job for more than 6 months rose from 340,000 in 1973 to 2,600,000 at the end of 1982. And in Europe, with lower mobility and greater legal obstacles to social change, long-term unemployment in the mid-1980s reached 50 percent of unemployed. Long-term unemployment poses a serious social problem because the resources that families have available—their savings, unemployment insurance, and goodwill toward one another—begin to run out after a few months.

Source of Joblessness

Why are people unemployed? Figure 31-9 shows how people responded when asked the source of their unemployment, again for 1973 and 1982.

There is always some unemployment that results from changes in people's residence or from the life cycle—moving, entering the labor force for the first time, and so forth. The major changes in the unemployment rate over time arise from the increase in job losers. This source swells enormously in recession for two reasons: First the number of people who lose their jobs increases, and then (as shown in Figure 31-8) it takes longer to find a new job.

Sources of Teenage Unemployment

Teenagers generally have the highest unemployment rate of any demographic group, and black teenagers in recent years have experienced unemployment rates between 30 and 50 percent. Is this unemployment frictional, structural, or cyclical?

Recent evidence indicates that, particularly for whites, teenage unemployment has a large frictional component. Teenagers move in and out of

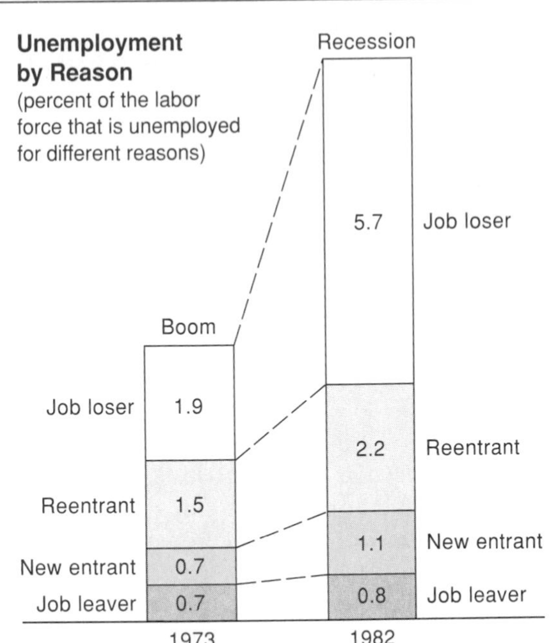

Figure 31-9. Distribution of unemployment by reason

Why did people become unemployed? Less than 1 percent of those in the labor force are unemployed because they left their jobs, and another 2 to 3 percent are new entrants into the labor force (say, because they just graduated from college) or reentrants (people who earlier left the labor force and are back looking for a job). The major change from boom to recession, however, is found in the number of job losers. From 1973 to 1982 the fraction of those in the labor force unemployed because they lost their jobs rose by a factor of 3. (Source: U.S. Department of Labor, *Employment and Earnings*.)

the labor force very frequently. They get jobs quickly and change jobs often. The average duration of teenage unemployment is only half that of adults; by contrast, the average length of a typical job is 12 times greater for adults than teenagers. In most years, half the unemployed teenagers are "new entrants" who have never had a paying job before. All these factors suggest that teenage unemployment is largely frictional; that is, it represents the job search and turnover necessary for young people to discover their personal skills and to learn what working is all about.

But teenagers do eventually learn the skills and work habits of experienced workers. Table 31-4 shows the unemployment rate at different ages for blacks and whites in 1990. The acquisition of experience and training, along with a greater desire and need for full-time work, is the reason middle-aged workers have much lower unemployment rates than teenagers.

Age	Unemployment rate (% of labor force) White	Black
16–17	15.7	36.7
18–19	12.0	28.0
20–24	7.2	19.9
25–34	4.6	11.7
35–44	3.6	7.8
45–54	3.3	5.3
55–64	3.2	4.6
65 and over	2.8	5.3

Table 31-4. Unemployment rate at different ages, 1990

As workers search for jobs and gain training, they settle on a particular occupation; they tend to stay in the labor force; and they find a preferred employer. As a result, the unemployment rates of older people fall to a fraction of that of teenagers. (Source: U.S. Department of Labor, *Employment and Earnings*, January 1991.)

Black Teenage Unemployment. While most evidence suggests that unemployment is largely frictional for white teenagers, the labor market for young black workers has behaved quite differently. After World War II, the labor market data for black teenagers was virtually identical to that for white teenagers. The labor-force participation rates and unemployment rates of black and white teenagers were virtually identical until 1955. Since that time, however, unemployment rates for black teenagers have risen relative to those of other groups while their labor-force participation rates fell. By 1990, 31 percent of black teenagers (16 to 19 years of age) were unemployed, compared to 13 percent of white teenagers. The employment rate (equal to the ratio of total employment to total population) was only 27 percent for black teenagers as opposed to 50 percent for white teenagers.

What accounts for this extraordinary divergence in the experience of the two groups? One explanation might be that labor market forces (such as the composition or location of jobs) have worked against black workers in general. This explanation does not tell the whole story. While adult black workers have always suffered higher unemployment rates than adult white workers—because of lower education levels, fewer contacts with people who can provide jobs, less on-the-job training, and racial discrimination—the ratio of black to white adult unemployment rates has not increased since World War II.

Numerous studies of the sources of the rising black teenage unemployment rate have turned up no clear explanations for the trend. One possible source is discrimination, but a rise in the black-white unemployment differential would require an increase in racial discrimination—for which there is no evidence.

Another theory holds that a high minimum wage tends to drive low-productivity black teenagers into unemployment. The change in the relation of the minimum wage to average wages allows a test of this hypothesis. From 1981 to 1989, the ratio of the minimum wage to average wages in nonfarm establishments fell from 46 percent to 34 percent, yet no improvement in the relative unemployment situation of black teenagers occurred. That no improvement took place casts doubt on the minimum wage as the prime suspect. Some conservative critics of the modern welfare state blame high unemployment of blacks on the culture of dependency that is nurtured by government aid to the poor, although there is little firm data to support these propositions.

Does high teenage unemployment lead to long-lasting labor market damage, with permanently lower levels of skills and wage rates? This question is a topic of intensive ongoing research, and the tentative answer is, Yes, particularly for minority teenagers. It appears that when youths are unable to develop on-the-job skills and work attitudes, they earn lower wages and experience higher unemployment when they are older. To the extent that this research is validated, it suggests that public policy has an important stake in devising programs to reduce teenage unemployment among minority groups.

SUMMARY

A. Business Cycles

1. Business cycles are swings in total national output, income, and employment, marked by widespread expansion or contraction in many sectors of the economy. They occur in all advanced market economies. We distinguish the phases of expansion, peak, recession, and trough.

2. Most modern business-cycle theories stress the role of shifts in aggregate demand in causing business fluctuations. In recent years, supply shocks (such as oil-price changes) have added to the list of factors affecting cycles.

3. Economists have suggested a wide variety of reasons for business cycles. Theories differ in their emphasis on external and internal factors. Importance is often attached to fluctuations in such external factors as population growth, gold discoveries, and political events or wars leading to oil-price shocks. Most theories emphasize that these external shocks interact with internal mechanisms, such as the multiplier and investment-demand shifts, to produce cyclical behavior.

4. Economic forecasting is still inexact. The most successful forecasters use computer models, based on statistical estimates, to forecast changes in the economy.

B. Unemployment

5. There is a clear connection between movements in output and the unemployment rate over the business cycle. According to Okun's Law, for every 1 percent that actual GNP declines relative to potential GNP, the unemployment rate rises $\frac{1}{2}$ percentage point. This rule is useful in translating cyclical movements of GNP into their effects on unemployment.
6. Although unemployment has plagued capitalism since the Industrial Revolution, understanding its causes and costs has been possible only with the rise of modern macroeconomic theory. It is now apparent that recessions and the associated high unemployment are extremely costly to the economy. Major periods of slack like the 1970s and 1980s cost the nation hundreds of billions of dollars and have great social costs as well.
7. The government gathers monthly statistics on unemployment, employment, and the labor force in a sample survey of the population. People with jobs are categorized as employed; people without jobs who are looking for work are said to be unemployed; people without jobs who are not looking for work are considered outside the labor force. Over the last decade, 65 percent of the population over 16 was in the labor force, while 7 percent of the labor force was unemployed.
8. Economists classify unemployment into three groups: (*a*) frictional unemployment, workers who are between jobs; (*b*) structural unemployment, workers who are in regions or industries that are in a persistent slump; and (*c*) cyclical unemployment, workers laid off when the overall economy suffers a downturn.
9. A careful look at the unemployment statistics reveals several regularities:
   (a) Recessions hit all groups in roughly proportional fashion—that is, all groups see their unemployment rates go up and down in proportion to the overall unemployment rate.
   (b) A very substantial part of unemployment is short-term. In low-unemployment years (such as 1973) more than 90 percent of unemployed workers are unemployed less than 26 weeks. The average duration of unemployment rises sharply in deep and prolonged recessions.
   (c) In most years, a substantial amount of unemployment is due to simple turnover, or frictional causes as people enter the labor force for the first time or reenter. Only during recessions is the pool of unemployed composed primarily of job losers.
10. Understanding the causes of unemployment has proved one of the major challenges of modern macroeconomics. Some unemployment (often called voluntary) would occur in a flexible-wage, perfectly competitive economy when qualified people chose not to work at the going wage rate. Voluntary unemployment might be the efficient outcome of competitive markets.
11. Most economists believe that some unemployment, particularly the high cyclical unemployment that occurs during recessions, does not reflect voluntary decisions of qualified workers not to work at going wages. Rather, cyclical unemployment occurs because wages are inflexible, failing to adjust quickly to labor surpluses or shortages. If a wage is above the market-

clearing level, some workers are employed, but other qualified workers cannot find jobs. Such unemployment is involuntary and also inefficient in that both workers and firms could benefit from an appropriate use of monetary and fiscal policies.

12. The key element to understanding involuntary unemployment is the inflexibility of wages in the face of economic shocks. Inflexibility arises because of costs involved in administering the compensation system. These costs are seen in the long duration of union contracts—which typically last 3 years. In nonunion settings, wages and salaries are generally set no more than once a year. Frequent adjustment of compensation would command too large a share of management time, would upset workers' perceptions of fairness, and would undermine worker morale and productivity.

CONCEPTS FOR REVIEW

Business cycles
business cycle
business-cycle phases: peak, trough expansion, contraction
recession
external and internal cycle theories
macroeconomic models

Unemployment
Okun's Law
unemployed, employed, labor force, not in labor force, unemployment rate
frictional, structural, and cyclical unemployment
flexible-wage (market-clearing) unemployment vs. rigid-wage (non-market-clearing) unemployment
voluntary vs. involuntary unemployment

QUESTIONS FOR DISCUSSION

1. Describe the different phases of the business cycle. In which phase is the economy now?
2. Assume that the unemployment rate is 8 percent and GNP is $4000. What is a rough estimate of potential GNP if the natural rate of unemployment is 6 percent? Assume that potential GNP is growing at 3 percent annually. What will potential GNP be in 2 years? How fast will GNP have to grow to reach potential GNP in 2 years?
3. Some business cycles originate from the demand side, while others arise from supply shocks.
   (a) Give examples of each. Explain the observable differences between the two kinds of shocks for output, prices, and unemployment.
   (b) State whether each of the following would lead to a supply-side business cycle or a demand-side cycle and illustrate the impact using the *AS-AD* diagram: a wartime increase in defense spending; devastation from wartime bombing of factories and power plants; a decrease in net exports from a debt-induced recession in Latin America; an oil-price increase following a Mideast revolution; a sharp slowdown in the rate of productivity growth.
4. What is the labor-force status of each of the following?
   (a) A teenager who is searching for a first job
   (b) An autoworker who has been dismissed and has given up hope of finding work but would like to work
   (c) A retired person who moved to Florida but reads the want ads to find a part-time job
   (d) A parent who works part-time, wants a full-time job, but doesn't have time to look
   (e) A teacher who has a job but is too ill to work
5. Think about your work status during the last 2 or 3 years. For each month, decide what your labor-force status was (employed, unemployed, not in labor force). Then for the periods you were unemployed, classify your unemployment as frictional, structural, or cyclical. What has been your personal unemployment rate? What does your experience tell you about the sources of teenage unemployment? Compare notes with your classmates.
6. Assume that Congress is considering a minimum-wage law that sets the minimum wage above the market-clearing wages for teenagers but below that for adult workers. Using supply-and-demand diagrams, show the impact of the minimum wage on the

employment, unemployment, and incomes of both sets of workers. Is the unemployment voluntary or involuntary? What would you recommend if you were called to testify about the wisdom of this measure?

7. Do you think that the economic costs or stress of a teenager unemployed for 1 month of the summer might be less or more than a head-of-household unemployed for a year? Do you think that this suggests that public policy should have a different stance with respect to these two groups?
8. **Advanced problem:** In recent years, a new theory of "equilibrium business cycles" has been proposed. This suggests that workers work harder or firms produce more as a result of misperceptions about relative prices. Thus firms are thought to move up their supply curves because they think their prices have risen in booms, when in fact the economywide price level P has risen. Such a view also holds that people have "rational" expectations—being excellent forecasters of future events.

   Could such a theory explain: (*a*) why output may rise above potential output (and unemployment may fall below its natural rate) when prices rise unexpectedly, and (*b*) how business downturns may persist for many years, as in the 1930s?
9. **Advanced problem:** Find two dice and use the following technique to see if you can generate something that looks like a business cycle. Record the numbers from 20 or more rolls of the dice. Take five-period moving averages of the successive numbers. Then plot these. They will look very much like movements in GNP, unemployment, or inflation.

   One sequence thus obtained was 7, 4, 10, 3, 7, 11, 7, 2, 9, 10 . . . . The averages were $(7 + 4 + 10 + 3 + 7)/5 = 6.2$, $(4 + 10 + 3 + 7 + 11)/5 = 7$, . . . and so forth.

   Why does this look like a business cycle? [*Hint:* The random numbers generated by the dice are like exogenous shocks of investment or wars. The moving average is like the economic system's (or a rocking chair's) internal multiplier or smoothing mechanism. Taken together, they produce what looks like a cycle.]
10. **Advanced problem:** An eminent macroeconomist, George Perry of Brookings, wrote the following after the Persian Gulf war of 1990–1991:

    > Wars have usually been good for the U.S. economy. Traditionally they bring with them rising output, low unemployment, and full use of industrial capacity as military demands add to normal economic activity. This time, for the first time, war and recession occurred together. What does this anomaly tell us about the recession? (*Brookings Review*, Spring 1991)

    Go to the library and find data on the major determinants of aggregate demand during the 1990–1991 period as well as during earlier wars (World War II, Korean war, Vietnam war). Examine particularly government spending on goods and services (especially defense spending), taxes, and interest rates. Can you explain the anomaly that Perry describes?

CHAPTER 32

THE COST OF INFLATION

> Lenin is said to have declared that the best way to destroy the capitalist system was to debauch the currency. By a continuing process of inflation, governments can confiscate, secretly and unobserved, an important part of the wealth of their citizens.
>
> J. M. Keynes

In the last chapter, we reviewed the characteristics of business cycles, with particular attention to the cyclical nature of unemployment. But to understand why society tolerates high unemployment, we need also to grasp the tradeoff between unemployment and inflation. This dilemma was aptly described by Arthur Okun:

> The task of combining prosperity with price stability now stands as the major unsolved problem of aggregative economic performance. [W]e must find a satisfactory compromise that yields growth and unemployment rates that we can be proud of, on the one hand, and a price performance that we can be comfortable with, on the other.[1]

Inflation is a major problem in many developing countries and has been the hallmark of socialist countries making the transition to the market, such as Poland and Yugoslavia. Many observers fear that the Soviet Union is on the verge of a major inflation in 1991.

It is time to analyze questions of aggregate price behavior and inflation. Why are nations so concerned about galloping inflation? What steps can be taken to keep inflation in the barn rather than running wild? Answers to these questions must be found if we are to understand why nations take stern measures and tolerate high unemployment to beat down high inflation rates.

[1] Arthur M. Okun, *The Political Economy of Prosperity* (Norton, New York, 1970), p. 130.

Figure 32-1 provides an overview of this chapter, which is concerned with the definition, measurement, and history of the price level and inflation.

What Is Inflation?

Inflation is widespread but widely misunderstood. Let us begin with a careful definition:

Inflation denotes a rise in the general level of prices. The **rate of inflation** is the rate of change of the general price level and is measured as follows:

Rate of inflation (year t)

$$= \frac{\text{price level (year } t) - \text{price level (year } t-1)}{\text{price level (year } t-1)} \times 100$$

But how do we measure the "price level" that is involved in the definition of inflation? Conceptually, the *price level* is measured as the weighted average of the goods and services in an economy. In practice, we measure the overall price level by constructing *price indexes*, which are averages of consumer or producer prices.

As an example, take the year 1990, when consumer prices rose 5.4 percent. In that year, the prices of all major product groups rose: food, beverages, shelter, apparel, transportation, medical care, and so forth. It is this general upward trend in prices that we call inflation.

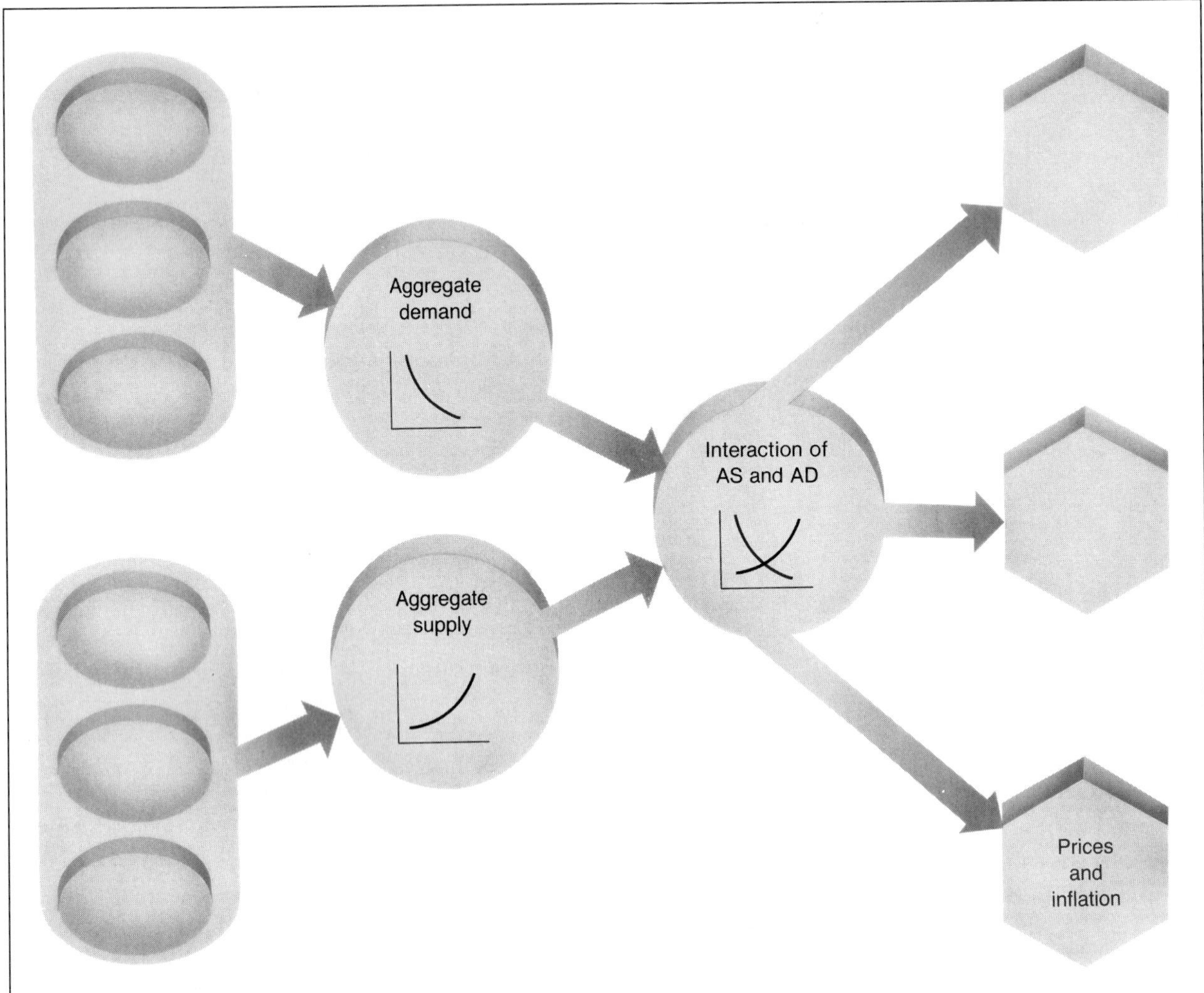

Figure 32-1. We now study the measurement and costs of inflation

Having analyzed the fundamentals of aggregate demand and unemployment, we now examine the determination of changes in the overall price level. How do we measure the overall price level and the rate of inflation? What are the major kinds of inflations? And do people react so adversely to high and variable inflation rates? These questions will be addressed in this chapter.

Not all prices rise by the same amount during inflationary periods, however. During 1990, for example, energy prices rose more than 5.4 percent while food prices rose less; but the increase in the *average price level* was 5.4 percent.

Deflation. The opposite of inflation is **deflation,** which occurs when the general level of prices is falling. Deflations have been rare in the late twentieth century. In the United States, the last time consumer prices actually fell from one year to the next was 1955. Sustained deflations, where prices fall steadily over a period of several years, are associated with depressions, such as the 1930s or the 1890s. The advent of active government stabilization policies, which have eradicated deep depressions in most advanced industrial market countries, has also eliminated deflations from the economic scene.

A related term is **disinflation,** which denotes a decline in the rate of inflation. The most recent period of disinflation occurred in the early 1980s, when the high inflation rate, reaching double-digit levels, was reduced through a policy of tight money.

Price Indexes

When newspapers tell us "Inflation is rising" or "The Federal Reserve reacted to increased inflationary tendencies," they are really reporting the movement of a price index. A **price index** is a weighted average of the prices of a number of goods and services; in constructing price indexes, economists weight individual prices by the economic importance of each good. The most important price indexes are the consumer price index, the GNP deflator, and the producer price index.

The Consumer Price Index (CPI). The most widely used measure of inflation is the consumer price index, also known as the CPI. The CPI measures the cost of a market basket of consumer goods and services, including prices of food, clothing, shelter, fuels, transportation, medical care, college tuition, and other commodities purchased for day-to-day living. Prices on 364 separate classes of commodities are collected from over 21,000 establishments in 91 areas of the country.

How are the different prices weighted in constructing price indexes? It would clearly be silly merely to add up the different prices or to weight them by their mass or volume. Rather, a price index is constructed by *weighting each price according to the economic importance of the commodity in question.*

In the case of the CPI, each item is assigned a *fixed* weight proportional to its relative importance in consumer expenditure budgets; the most recent weights for each item are proportional to the total spending by consumers on that item as determined by a survey of consumer expenditures in the 1982–1984 period.

Numerical Example. We can use a numerical example to help clarify the idea of how inflation is measured. Assume that consumers buy three commodities: food, shelter, and medical care. A hypothetical budget survey finds that consumers spend 20 percent of their budgets on food, 50 percent on shelter, and 30 percent on medical care.

Using 1995 as the *base year*, we reset the price of each commodity at 100 so that differences in the units of commodities will not affect the price index. This implies that the CPI is also 100 in the base year $[= (0.20 \times 100) + (0.50 \times 100) + (0.30 \times 100)]$. Next, we calculate the consumer price index and the rate of inflation for 1996. In 1996, food prices rise 2 percent to 102, shelter prices rise 6 percent to 106, and medical care prices are up 10 percent to 110. We recalculate the CPI for 1996 as follows:

$$\text{CPI (1996)} = (0.20 \times 102) + (0.50 \times 106) + (0.30 \times 110) = 106.4$$

In other words, if 1995 is the base year in which the CPI is 100, then in 1996 the CPI is 106.4. The rate of inflation in 1996 is then $[(106.4 - 100)/100] \times 100 =$ 6.4 percent per year. Note that in a fixed-weight index like the CPI, the *prices* change from year to year but the *weights* remain the same.

This example captures the essence of how inflation is measured. The only difference between this simplified calculation and the real one is that the CPI in fact contains many more commodities. Otherwise, the concepts are exactly the same.

GNP Deflator. We met the GNP deflator in the discussion of national income and output accounting in Chapter 24. Recall that the GNP deflator is the ratio of nominal GNP to real GNP and can thus be interpreted as the price of *all* components of GNP (consumption, investment, government purchases, and net exports) rather than of a single sector. This index differs from the CPI also because it is a variable-weight index, weighting prices by the current-period quantities. In addition, there are deflators for components of GNP, such as for investment goods, personal consumption, and so forth, and these are sometimes used to supplement the CPI.

The Producer Price Index (PPI). This index, dating from 1890, is the oldest continuous statistical series published by the Labor Department. It measures the level of prices at the wholesale or producer stage. It is based on approximately 3400 commodity prices, including prices of foods, manufactured products, and mining products. The fixed weights used to calculate the PPI are the net sales of the commodity. Because of its great detail, this index is widely used by businesses.

Index-Number Problems. While price indexes like the CPI are enormously useful, they are not without their faults. Some problems are intrinsic to price indexes. One issue is the *index-number problem,* which concerns the choice of an appropriate period for the base year. Recall that the CPI uses a fixed weight for each good. As a result, the cost of living is overestimated compared to the situation where consumers substitute relatively inexpensive for relatively expensive goods. For example, the weighting in the CPI neglects the fact that the amount of gasoline bought by consumers declined after gasoline prices rose sharply in the early 1970s. One could change the base year, or devise more elaborate weighting methods, but there is no way of solving the index-number problem perfectly.

Another difficulty arises because the CPI does not accurately capture changes in the quality of goods. For example, the CPI is not corrected for quality improvements such as better sound reproduction in phonographic equipment, safer air travel, or more accurate watches. Studies indicate

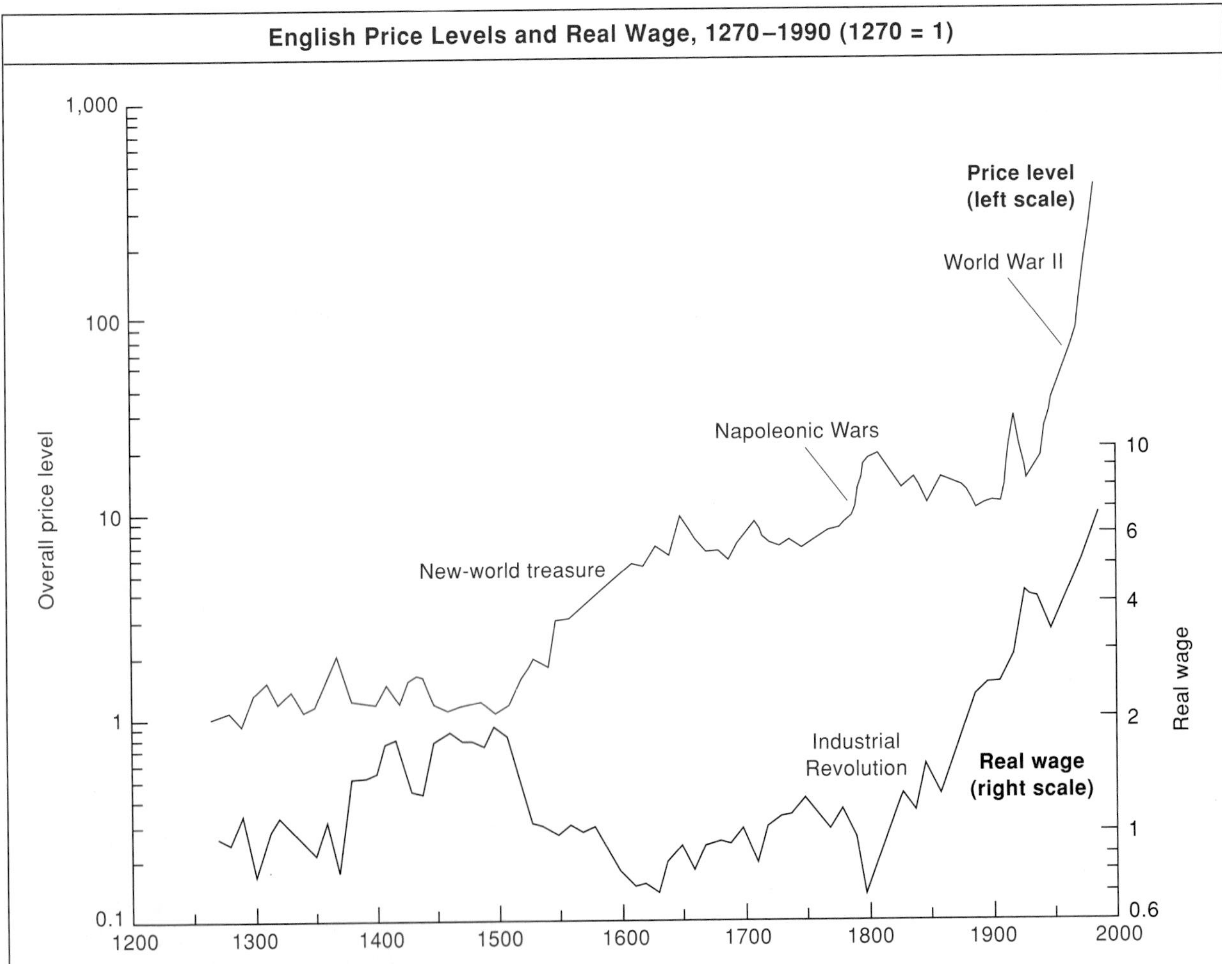

Figure 32-2. Price inflation has dogged markets since the earliest times

The graph shows England's history of prices and real wages since the Middle Ages. Note that the price of a market basket of goods has risen almost 400-fold since 1270. In early years, price increases were associated with increases in the money supply, such as from discoveries of new-world treasure and the printing of money during the Napoleonic Wars.

Note the meandering of the real wage (money wage divided by the price level) prior to the Industrial Revolution. Since then real wages have risen sharply and steadily. (Source: E. H. Phelps Brown and S. V. Hopkins, *Economica*, 1956, updated by authors.)

U.S. Prices since the Civil War (1860 = 100)

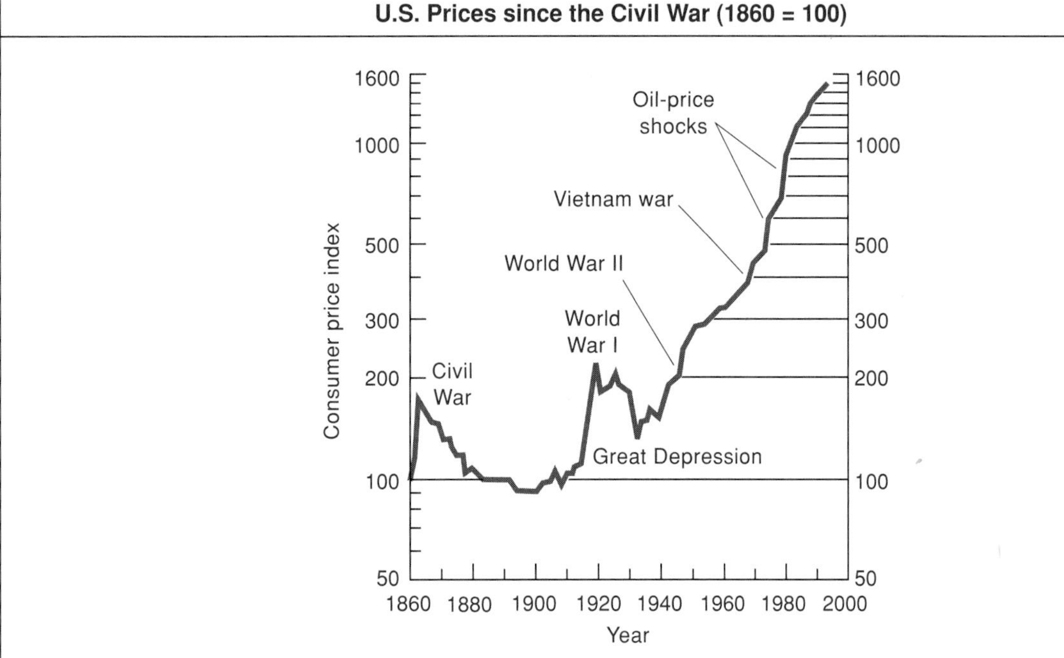

Figure 32-3. Inflations came with wars, but now they don't go away afterward

This figure shows the history of American consumer prices since 1860. Prices went up with each war, then drifted down afterward. But since 1940, the trend has been upward, both here and abroad. The only changes today are in the *rate* of inflation, not in the *fact* of inflation. (Source: U.S. Department of Labor, Bureau of Labor Statistics.)

that if quality change were properly incorporated into price indexes, the CPI would have risen less rapidly in recent years.

Misconceptions. People often get confused about inflation. Here are some questions that reflect common misconceptions along with the correct answers.

Does inflation mean that goods are expensive? No, inflation means that the average price level is rising.

Does inflation mean that we are getting poorer? Not necessarily. Our nominal incomes tend to rise rapidly during inflationary periods, so our real incomes (incomes corrected for the cost of living) may go up or down during inflationary times.

Do companies get rich at workers' expense during inflationary times? Not necessarily. The effect of inflation on the distribution of income depends on the cause of the inflation.

You will hear many more misconceptions about inflation, but you can avoid adopting them if you remember the definition of inflation given above.

The Long History of Inflation

Inflation is as old as market economies. Figure 32-2 depicts the history of English inflation since the thirteenth century. Over the long haul, prices have generally risen, as the blue line reveals. But examine also the black line, which plots the path of *real wages* (the wage rate divided by consumer prices). Real wages meandered along until the Industrial Revolution. Comparing the two lines shows that inflation is not necessarily accompanied by a decline in real income. You can see, too, that real wages have climbed steadily since around 1800, rising more than tenfold.

Figure 32-3 focuses on the behavior of consumer prices in the United States since the Civil War. Until

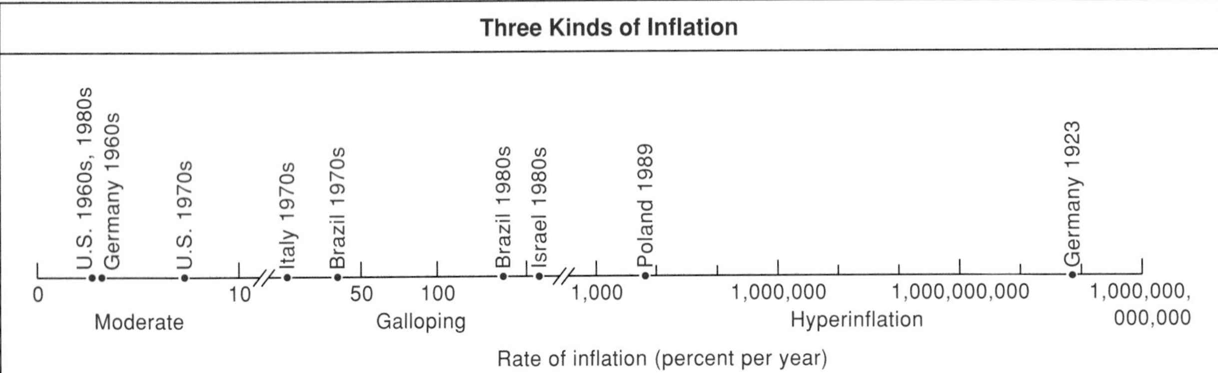

Figure 32-4. Inflations come in many varieties, sometimes mere annoyances, at other times highly destructive

The figure shows the three kinds of inflation that occur. Moderate inflation is typical today in most industrialized countries. In galloping inflation, such as that seen in Brazil and Israel during recent years, inflation jumps around from year to year, but does not explode. Hyperinflation occurs when prices rise at a thousand, million, or trillion percent annually.

1945, the pattern was regular: prices would soar during wartime, then fall back during the postwar slump. But the pattern changed ominously after World War II. Prices and wages now travel on a one-way street upward. They rise rapidly in periods of economic expansion; in recessions they do not fall but merely rise less rapidly. In other words, price and wage behavior has undergone a major structural change since 1940: it is now inflexible downward.

Three Strains of Inflation

Like diseases, inflations exhibit different levels of severity. It is useful to classify them into three categories: moderate inflation, galloping inflation, and hyperinflation. A pictorial description is shown in Figure 32-4.

Moderate Inflation. Moderate inflation is characterized by slowly rising prices. We might arbitrarily classify this as single-digit annual inflation rates. When prices are relatively stable, *people trust money.* They are willing to hold on to money because it will be almost as valuable in a month or a year as it is today. People are willing to write long-term contracts in money terms because they are confident that the price level will not get too far out of line for the good they are selling or buying. People do not waste time or resources trying to put their wealth into "real" assets rather than "money" or "paper" assets because they believe their money assets will retain their real value.

Galloping Inflation. Inflation in the double- or triple-digit range of 20, 100, or 200 percent a year is labeled "galloping inflation." At the low end of this spectrum we sometimes find advanced industrial countries like Italy. Many Latin American countries, such as Argentina and Brazil, had inflation rates of 50 to 700 percent per year in the 1970s and 1980s.

Once galloping inflation becomes entrenched, serious economic distortions arise. Generally, most contracts get indexed to a price index or to a foreign currency, like the dollar. In these conditions, money loses its value very quickly; real interest rates can be minus 50 or 100 percent per year. Consequently, people hold only the bare minimum amount of money needed for daily transactions. Financial markets wither away, and funds are generally allocated by rationing rather than by interest rates. People hoard goods, buy houses, and never, never lend money at low nominal interest rates.

The surprise is that economies with 200 percent annual inflation manage to survive even though the price system is behaving so badly. These economies tend to develop major economic distortions, however, as people send their investment funds abroad and domestic investment withers away.

Hyperinflation. While economies seem to survive under galloping inflation, a third and deadly strain takes hold when the cancer of hyperinflation strikes. Nothing good can be said about a market economy in which prices are rising a million or even a trillion percent per year.

Hyperinflations are particularly interesting to students of inflation because they highlight its effects. Consider this description of hyperinflation in the Confederacy during the Civil War:

> We used to go to the stores with money in our pockets and come back with food in our baskets. Now we go with money in baskets and return with food in our pockets. Everything is scarce except money! Prices are chaotic and production disorganized. A meal that used to cost the same amount as an opera ticket now costs twenty times as much. Everybody tends to hoard "things" and to try to get rid of the "bad" paper money, which drives the "good" metal money out of circulation. A partial return to barter inconvenience is the result.

The most thoroughly documented case of hyperinflation took place in the Weimar Republic of Germany in the 1920s. Figure 32-5 shows how the government unleashed the monetary printing presses, driving both money and prices to astronomical levels. From January 1922 to November 1923, the price index rose from 1 to 10,000,000,000. If a person had owned $300 million worth of bonds in early 1922, this amount would not have bought a piece of candy 2 years later.

Studies have found several common features in hyperinflations. First, the real demand for money (measured by the money stock divided by the price level) falls drastically. By the end of the German hyperinflation, real money demand was only one-thirtieth of its level 2 years earlier. People are in effect rushing around, dumping their money like hot potatoes before they get burned by money's loss of value. Second, relative prices become highly unstable. Under normal conditions, the real wages of a person move only a percent or less from month to month. During 1923, German real wages changed on average one-third (up or down) each month. This enormous variation in relative prices and real wages—and the inequities and distortions caused by these fluctuations—illustrates the major cost of inflation.

Perhaps the most profound effect of a hyperinflation is on wealth distribution. The British economist Lionel Robbins summarized the impact:

> The depreciation of the mark . . . destroyed the wealth of the more solid elements in German society; and it left behind a moral and economic disequilibrium, apt breeding ground for the disasters which have followed. Hitler is the foster-child of the inflation.[2]

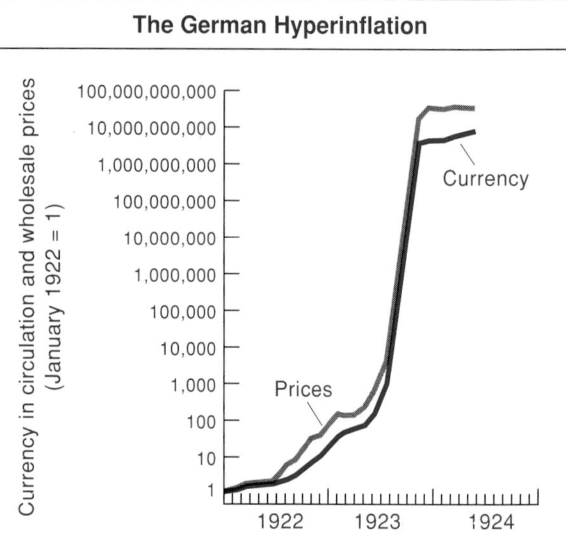

Figure 32-5. Money and inflation in Germany, 1922–1924

In the early 1920s, the young Weimar Republic of Germany was struggling to meet harsh reparations payments and satisfy creditors. It could not borrow or raise enough taxes to pay for government spending, so it turned to the printing press. The stock of currency rose astronomically from early 1922 to December 1923, and prices spiraled upward as people frantically tried to dump their money before it lost all value. If you held a billion marks in January 1922, what would be left of your riches at the end of this hyperinflation?

Do Inflations Accelerate?

Many people fear inflation, even moderate inflation rates of 6 or 9 percent, because they worry that prices will begin to gallop upward, or perhaps that the moderate inflation will degenerate into a hyper-

[2] The history of the German hyperinflation is told in detail in C. Bresciani-Turroni, *The Economics of Inflation: A Study of Currency Depreciation in Post-War Germany,* 3d ed. (Augustus M. Kelley, London, 1968). The quotation from Professor Robbins is from the introduction to the book.

inflation. Does creeping inflation inevitably become a trot? A trot become a canter? A canter become a gallop?

The history of inflations suggests that there is no such inevitable sequence. Hyperinflations are extremely rare. They occur mainly during wartime or in the backwash of war and revolution. The most recent hyperinflations occurred in countries making the revolutionary transition from socialism to market economy; in Poland, prices rose over 1000 percent a year in 1989–1990.

Galloping inflation, on the other hand, is not rare. Like periods of prolonged unemployment, galloping inflation breaks out occasionally even in advanced economies. Since the oil shock of 1973, France, Italy, and Britain have experienced bouts of galloping inflation. In general, however, nations are able to use macroeconomic policies to keep inflation at a moderate creep and hold its costs down to tolerable levels.

The Impact of Inflation

Politicians and central bankers pronounce daily on the dangers of inflationary expectations. Public-opinion polls often find that inflation is economic enemy number one. What is so dangerous and costly about inflation?

Identifying the costs of inflation has proven a difficult task. We noted above that during periods of inflation all prices and wages do not move at the same rate; that is, changes in *relative prices* occur. As a result of the diverging relative prices, two definite effects of inflation are:

- A *redistribution* of income and wealth among different classes
- *Distortions* in the relative prices and outputs of different goods, or sometimes in output and employment for the economy as a whole

Impacts on Income and Wealth Distribution

The major distributional impact of inflation arises from differences in the kinds of assets and liabilities that people hold.[3] When people owe money, a sharp rise in prices is a windfall gain for them. Suppose you borrow $100,000 to buy a house and your annual mortgage payments are $10,000. Suddenly, a great inflation doubles all wages and prices. Your dollar income doubles although the amount of goods that your income can buy is unchanged. But what has happened to the real cost of your mortgage? Your mortgage payment is still $10,000 per year, but you will need to work only half as long as before to make your mortgage payment. The great inflation has increased your wealth $50,000 by halving the real value of your mortgage debt.

This kind of thinking may encourage people to borrow heavily to buy houses or farmland. Then, when inflation slows and recession hits, the mortgage payments are so burdensome that thousands of people end up in bankruptcy court.

If you are a lender and have assets in mortgages or long-term bonds, the shoe is on the other foot. A sudden rise in prices will leave you the poorer because the dollars repaid to you are worth less than you originally expected.

Real-Interest-Rate Adjustment. If an inflation persists for a long time, people come to anticipate it and markets begin to adapt. An allowance for inflation will gradually be built into the market interest rate. Say the economy starts out with interest rates of 3 percent and stable prices. Once people expect prices to rise at 9 percent per year, bonds and mortgages will tend to pay 12 percent rather than 3 percent. The 12 percent nominal interest rate reflects a 3 percent real interest rate plus a 9 percent inflation premium. There are no further major redistributions of income and wealth once interest rates have so adjusted.

Adjustment of interest rates to chronic inflation has been observed in Brazil, Chile, and other countries with a long history of rising prices. In the 1980s, we saw a similar inflation premium built into American and European interest rates.[4]

The major redistributive impact of inflation occurs through its effect on the real value of people's wealth. In general, unanticipated inflation redistributes wealth from creditors to debtors (that is, unanticipated or unforeseen inflation helps those who have borrowed money and hurts those who

[3] The important elements of balance sheets were described in Chapters 8 and 28.

[4] Figure 28-3 shows movements in nominal and real interest rates for the United States in recent years.

have lent money). An unanticipated decline in inflation has the opposite effect.

Special Cases. Governments find that the burden of their debt shrinks during inflation. Someone who invests money in real estate or gold will make a large profit during unforeseen inflation. It used to be thought that common stocks were also a good inflation hedge, but their performance was disappointing in recent years. When inflation jumped in 1990, stock prices fell sharply all around the world as investors anticipated that central banks would tighten money.

Because of institutional changes, some old myths are no longer applicable. It used to be said that widows and orphans were hurt by inflation; today, they receive social security pensions that are "indexed" to the CPI so they are insulated from inflation because benefits automatically increase as the CPI increases. Also, many kinds of debt (like "floating-rate" mortgages) have interest rates that move up and down with market interest rates, so unanticipated inflation benefits debtors and hurts lenders less than before.

There have been volumes of research on the redistributional impacts of inflation. The summary wisdom of these studies indicates that the overall impact is highly unpredictable. Those who live on capital income tend to lose from inflation, while wage earners tend to gain. Contrary to stereotypes, statistics indicate that poor families often gain from inflation at the expense of the affluent.

But the main conclusion is that inflation mainly churns income and assets, randomly redistributing wealth around the population with little significant impact on any single group.

Effects on Output and Economic Efficiency

In addition to redistributing incomes, inflation affects the real economy in two specific areas: it affects total output and it influences economic efficiency.

Macroeconomic Impacts. The first impact is on the level of *output as a whole.* Until the 1970s, high inflation usually went hand in hand with high employment and output. Rising inflation occurred when investment was brisk and jobs were plentiful. Periods of unanticipated declines in inflation—the 1930s, 1954, 1958, and 1982—were times of high unemployment of labor and capital. Indeed, periods where declining inflation supposedly left banks and other creditors "better off" actually left them with uncollectible debts—whether owed by farmers in the 1930s or by Latin Americans in the mid-1980s.

In analyzing this experience, we must be cautious in interpreting the causality. In the observed association between inflation and output, which was cause and which effect? Was the rising output caused by the rising prices? Or were the rising prices the result of rising output? Or were both the result of a third factor that moved prices and output?

Today, macroeconomists believe that there is no necessary relationship between prices and output. An increase in aggregate demand will increase both prices and output; but a supply shock, shifting up the aggregate supply curve, will raise prices and *lower* output.[5]

We conclude with the surprising result that inflation may be associated with either a higher or a lower level of output and employment.

Microeconomic Impacts. Another, more subtle effect of inflation is the microeconomic impact on *economic efficiency.* Generally the higher the inflation rate, the greater are the distortions of relative prices.

What do we mean by price distortions? These occur when prices get out of line relative to costs and demands. A humorous example of a distortion is found in many Eastern European countries where bread prices are held far below costs. Often, bread prices are lower than fodder, and farmers have been seen feeding bread to pigs. Little wonder that there are bread lines when the price distortion is so severe.

A less humorous example concerns the distortions in the use of money, whose return is severely distorted by inflation. Currency does not receive interest. But recall that the real interest rate (the interest rate in terms of real goods) is defined as the nominal interest rate minus the rate of inflation. Thus, the real interest rate on currency is equal to

[5] These two cases were shown in our overview of macroeconomics, in Figures 23-8 and 23-9 respectively.

minus the inflation rate. For example, those who held currency in 1980 earned a real return equal to minus 13 percent (since 13 percent was the inflation rate). The upshot here is that the real interest rate on currency is dramatically affected by inflation; people will tend to unload their currency and acquire other assets when prices begin to rise rapidly. People expend real resources trying to economize on their paper money holdings.

Also, the prices of inputs or goods that are priced under long-term arrangements (labor contracts and prices in regulated or state-owned industries) tend to become more out of line with the general price level during inflationary periods. We will analyze these and other inefficiencies below.

Analysis of Inflation's Costs

As we have seen, inflation distorts relative prices and reduces economic efficiency. In addition, the severity of inflation's effects depends on whether or not the inflation is anticipated. The impact of inflation will be analyzed first by considering what happens in an idealized inflation that is both anticipated and balanced. By a "balanced" inflation, we mean one in which relative prices do not change.

Balanced, Anticipated Inflation

Suppose that all prices are rising at 10 percent each year. Nobody is surprised by the price changes. Food and clothing, wages and rents are all rising at 10 percent each year, and all real interest rates (that is, interest rates corrected for inflation) are just the same as they would be if all prices were stable.

Would anyone be concerned about such an inflation? Would the efficiency of resource use or real GNP be any smaller or larger? The answer to both questions is, No. *There is no effect on real output, efficiency, or income distribution of an inflation that is both balanced and anticipated.* My income is rising 10 percent faster than it would be with stable prices but the cost of living is also rising 10 percent faster. There is no gain or loss to different kinds of assets. Prices are, in this case, simply a changing yardstick to which people completely adjust their behavior.

This idealized case raises an unsettling thought: Is the social cost of inflation an illusion? Do people overestimate the economic costs of inflation. Do people dislike inflation because they see their living costs rise but forget that their incomes are rising in step with costs?

There is no correct answer to these questions. Economists believe that people often misunderstand the nature of inflation, confusing high *inflation* with high *prices.* In fact, the low cost of balanced and anticipated inflation suggests that popular perceptions about the ills of inflation may sometimes be inaccurate.

Unbalanced Inflation: Inflation-Induced Distortions

Let us take a step toward realism by recognizing that inflation affects relative prices, costs, and tax burdens. For the moment, let us stay with the case of anticipated inflation.

One inefficiency resulting from unbalanced inflation occurs because some prices do not adjust to reflect inflationary trends; money and taxes are two important examples. Currency is money that bears a zero nominal interest rate. If the inflation rate rises from 0 to 10 percent annually, then the real interest rate on currency falls from 0 to −10 percent per year. There is no easy way for a central bank or government to correct this distortion.

How does the negative real interest rate on currency or other kinds of money lead to inefficiency? Studies show that when inflation rises, people devote real resources to reducing their money holdings. They go to the bank more often—using up "shoe leather" and valuable time. Corporations set up elaborate "cash management" schemes. Real resources are thereby consumed to cope with the changing monetary yardstick. Empirical studies indicate, however, that this cost is modest.

The impact of inflation on taxes is potentially more significant. Under a tax system in which people pay higher taxes as their nominal incomes rise, inflation automatically raises people's average tax rates. It thus allows the government to raise taxes without passing laws. Such "taxation without legislation" has led many countries to index their tax laws to prevent inflation-induced tax increases. Parts of the U.S. tax code were indexed during the 1980s.

Indexing alone will not purge the tax system of the impacts of inflation because inflation distorts the measurement of income. For example, if you earned an interest rate of 10 percent on your funds in 1990, half of this simply replaced your loss in the purchasing power of your funds from a 5 percent inflation rate. Yet the tax code does not distinguish between real return and the interest that just compensates for inflation. Many similar distortions of income and taxes are present in the tax code today.

Some economists point to "menu costs" of inflation. The idea is that when prices are changed, restaurants will have to reprint their menus, and that task uses real resources. Other examples of menu costs are the cost of reprinting catalogues, of remetering taxis, or of changing the price tags of goods in stores.

Inflation causes many similar distortions in the economy. Often governments let the real value of their programs erode as prices rise. A recent study shows that government payments for medical care for poor people have declined in real terms as governments failed to increase their budgets in line with the rising cost of medical care. Regulated industries sometimes find that their requests for price increases are trimmed or rejected during inflationary periods. Many company pension plans provide benefits that are fixed in nominal terms so that the real benefits decline if inflation strikes. These are among the many examples of how inflation can affect people's incomes in unexpected ways.

Inflation Destroys Information. A final point to stress is that prices contain information that is valuable to consumers. We may remember that Elm City sells gas for $1.20 a gallon; with this in mind, it is easy to compare Elm City's prices with those of Exxon or Arco.

Inflation can destroy information. In rapid inflations, price tags are changed frequently and consumers have difficulty comparing prices. Consequently, consumers may mistakenly pay more than necessary for goods.

An analogy shows how a rapid change in prices destroys valuable information. Imagine that every year telephone numbers were increased a bit as we experience "telephone-number inflation." Think of how much trouble it would cause you if telephone-number inflation were rapid, and you had to find out the number for your home every day. What if the number for the operator and directory assistance also changed daily?

Unanticipated Inflation

We turn next to unanticipated inflations. Changes in inflation are usually a big surprise, even to professional forecasters. Generally, unanticipated moderate inflation has a more significant effect on the distribution of income and wealth than on the efficiency of the system. An unexpected jump in prices will impoverish some and enrich others, but will have little impact on how effectively farms and factories are run.

How costly is this redistribution? Perhaps "cost" does not describe the problem. The effects may be more social than economic. An epidemic of burglaries may not lower GNP, but it causes great distress. Similarly, randomly redistributing wealth by inflation is like forcing people to play a lottery they would prefer to avoid.

Moreover, the effect of a redistribution due to inflation depends on how big the inflation is. There is no doubt that galloping inflation or hyperinflation saps the morale and vitality of an economy. On the other hand, an inflation rate of 3 to 5 percent, such as that in the United States in the early 1990s, probably has but a minor impact on the distribution of income and wealth.

Unbalanced and Unanticipated Inflation

In reality, most inflations are both unbalanced and unanticipated. The most recent surge of inflation came in the fall of 1990, when a surprise attack on Kuwait led to an unanticipated temporary doubling of oil-prices. Like the earlier oil-price increases of 1973 and 1979, a certain amount of redistribution occurred. Fortune smiled on those lucky enough to own oil wells, oil-bearing land, or oil companies. By contrast, people who owned gas-guzzling cars, airplanes, or airline companies suffered economic losses.

The history of these oil-price shocks and the accompanying inflation is an instructive lesson on the impact of inflation. Much of the perceived cost of inflation did not stem from the inflation per se. Rather, social frictions arose from the changes in relative prices. Real incomes fell because people had to pay more for oil products, not because the general price level rose. Even if the inflation rate had been zero, the rising relative price of oil would still have hurt oil-consuming households and nations.

Recapitulation

Table 32-1 summarizes this discussion. In addition to the size of the inflation, two facets of inflation will determine its severity: whether it is balanced and whether it is anticipated. The mildest effects will be found when inflations are at a low rate. Such inflations are shown in the upper left corner of this table—small, anticipated, and balanced. Galloping inflations and hyperinflations lead to major economic and social dislocations; in these cases, high inflation rates are unanticipated and unbalanced.

Two Dimensions of Inflation's Costs

	Balanced inflation	Unbalanced inflation
Anticipated inflation	Inflation has no cost	Efficiency losses
Unanticipated inflation	Income and wealth redistribution	Efficiency losses and redistribution

Table 32-1. The impacts of inflation are governed by two main factors: whether it is balanced and whether it is anticipated

The costs of inflation depend on two different factors. First, is it a balanced inflation, where no relative prices are being changed and there are no inflation-induced distortions? Second, is it anticipated?

The Macroeconomic Reaction

Whatever the real or perceived costs of inflation, most nations today will not tolerate high inflation rates for long. Sooner or later, they take steps to reduce inflation—by restraining the growth of real output and raising unemployment, or sometimes by putting controls on prices and wages. The result is almost always a painful period of stagnation, as workers are pinched by layoffs, short hours, and poor job prospects. Indeed, the decision by governments to contain inflation was the prime cause of the long period of stagnation in Europe and North America that followed the 1979 oil-price increase and lasted until the end of the 1980s in Europe.

Thus, whatever economists may conclude about the "menu costs" or other microeconomic costs of inflation, the reaction of monetary and fiscal policy must be counted as one of the costs of inflation. And that reaction has generally been to contain inflation by high unemployment and low GNP growth; as the next chapter shows, the amount of output and jobs that must be lost to curb inflation is very large.

Final Appraisal

Inflation is a complex phenomenon, with many different kinds of costs. Can we make a final estimate of inflation's burdens? Does inflation markedly lower a nation's real output? Are the measurable costs to GNP or the unmeasured costs to morale and social stability great or small?

A careful sifting of the evidence suggests that moderate inflation like that seen recently in the United States has only a modest impact on productivity and real output. It is difficult to find studies that can point to yearly effects of more than a few billion dollars in a $6 trillion economy. Even during the German hyperinflation, output and employment fell less than in the Great Depression. On the other hand, the consequences of sudden inflation-induced distortions or changes in income and wealth undoubtedly are severe and unpleasant for many individuals, not unlike the experience of being robbed.

And, finally, even though the costs of inflation appear modest, the electorate responds forcefully to an upsurge in prices. People vote for leaders who promise to take measures to reduce inflation, and the leaders in turn take measures to curb inflation by slowing output growth and raising unemployment. This reaction is the most visible and dramatic effect of inflation in a modern economy.

SUMMARY

1. Changes in aggregate demand lead to changes in prices as well as output. Indeed, because of the inflexibility of wages, prices may be rising even though the economy still has high unemployment and unutilized capacity.

2. Inflation occurs when the general level of prices is rising (and deflation occurs when they are generally falling). Today, we calculate inflation by using price indexes—weighted averages of the prices of thousands of individual products. The consumer price index (CPI) measures the cost of a market basket of consumer goods and services relative to the cost of that bundle during a particular base year. The GNP deflator is the price of GNP.

3. Until World War II, prices rose during wartime and fell afterward. These days, we see that inflation rises during booms and subsides during recessions. But the overall price level almost never declines.

4. Like diseases, inflations come in different strains. We generally see moderate inflation in the United States (a few percentage points annually). Sometimes, galloping inflation produces price rises of 50 or 100 or 200 percent each year. Hyperinflation takes over when the printing presses spew out currency and prices start rising many times each month. Historically, hyperinflations have almost always been associated with war and revolution.

5. Inflation affects the economy by redistributing income and wealth and by changing the level and efficiency of production. When inflations and deflations are balanced and anticipated, all prices and wages are expected to move by the same percentage, with no one helped and no one hurt by the process. This type of inflation is rare. Unforeseen inflation usually favors debtors, profit seekers, and risk-taking speculators. It hurts creditors, fixed-income classes, and timid investors.

6. Because of the costs of inflation, containing inflation is one of the prime targets of macroeconomic policy. Unbalanced inflations distort relative prices, tax rates, and real interest rates. People take more trips to the bank, taxes may creep up, and measured income may become distorted. Also, unanticipated inflations lead to mistaken investments and to demoralizing and random income redistributions. And when society determines to take steps to lower inflation, the real costs of such steps in terms of lower output and employment can be painful.

CONCEPTS FOR REVIEW

inflation, deflation, disinflation
price index (CPI, GNP deflator, PPI)
strains of inflation (moderate, galloping, hyperinflation)
balanced and unbalanced inflation
impacts of inflation (redistributional, on output and employment)
costs of inflation: "shoe leather," "menu costs," income and tax distortions, loss of information
anticipated and unanticipated inflation
macroeconomic reaction to inflation

QUESTIONS FOR DISCUSSION

1. Define a price index. Define carefully the CPI and the GNP deflator. Explain the similarities and differences between these two indexes.
2. The following statements have been made about inflation. Which ones correctly describe a cost of inflation and which are misdiagnoses? Explain.
   (a) Inflation is just big oil companies ripping off the little people.
   (b) Inflation is theft. Governments can increase their taxes without passing a tax bill.
   (c) Inflation lowers our living standards by raising the cost of living.
   (d) The main cost of inflation is the unemployment that follows as governments attempt to lower inflation.
   (e) When oil prices rose after Iraq's invasion of Kuwait, the inflation hurt airlines and the automobile industry.
3. Consider the following impacts of inflation: tax distortions, income and wealth redistribution, shoe leather costs. For each, define the cost and provide an example.
4. Imagine that you were in an economy in which prices were rising 10 percent each month. What kinds of changes in the economy would you expect? Which of these changes impose serious economic costs and which are simply minor nuisances?
5. "During periods of inflation, people use real resources to reduce their holdings of fiat money. Such activities produce a private benefit with no corresponding social gain, which illustrates the social cost of inflation." Explain this quotation and give an example.
6. Consider an economy that starts out with money wages rising 2 percent each year while prices are stable. Describe whether each of the following would be balanced or unbalanced, and anticipated or unanticipated inflation:
   (a) There is a sharp upturn in wage settlements so that wages are rising at 4 percent annually, while prices remain stable.
   (b) Prices soon catch up, so that workers are surprised to find that prices are now rising at 2 percent per annum.
   (c) A decade later, wages are still rising at 4 percent each year, and prices are climbing at 2 percent annually.
7. Unanticipated deflation also produces serious social costs. For each of the following, describe the deflation and analyze the associated costs:
   (a) During the Great Depression, prices of major crops fell along with the prices of other commodities. What would happen to farmers who had large mortgages?
   (b) Many students have borrowed more than $20,000 to pay for their college education, hoping that inflation would allow them to pay off their loans in depreciated dollars. What would happen to these students if wages and prices began to *fall* at 5 percent per year?
8. The following are data on the CPI and nominal interest rates:

Year	Consumer price index (1982–1984 = 100)	Nominal interest rate (% per annum)
1979	72.6	10.0
1980	82.4	11.4
1981	90.9	13.8
1982	96.5	11.1
1983	99.6	8.8
1984	103.9	9.8
1985	107.6	7.7
1986	109.6	6.0
1987	113.6	6.1

Calculate the rate of inflation for each year from 1980 to 1987. Then calculate the real rate of interest. Do you see any major shift in the level of the real interest rate over this period?

CHAPTER 33

INFLATION AND UNEMPLOYMENT

> In no period during the past forty years has the American economy been free of excessive unemployment and inflationary tendencies simultaneously. Nor has any other industrial nation found the happy combination. Hitting the dual target of high utilization and essential price stability remains the most serious unsolved problem of stabilization policy throughout the Western world.
>
> Arthur Okun, *The Political Economy of Prosperity*

Can market economies simultaneously enjoy the blessings of full employment and price stability? Is there no way to control inflation other than by economic slowdowns that keep unemployment undesirably high? If recessions are too high a price to pay for the control of inflation, do we need "incomes policies" that can lower inflation without raising unemployment?

Questions, questions, questions. Yet answers to these are critical to the economic health of modern mixed economies. To some of these questions—such as how economists today view the inflation-unemployment tradeoff—we will be able to provide clear answers. But the fundamental dilemma remains. No jury of economic experts would agree on the formula for full employment and stable prices in a market economy. All the proposed solutions are controversial, and many have side effects that are worse than the disease. Figure 33-1 shows the road map for the present chapter.

A. Sources of Inflation

There is no single source of inflation. Like illnesses, inflations occur for many reasons. Some inflations come from the demand side, others from the supply side. But one key fact about modern inflations is that they develop an internal momentum and are hard to stop once under way.

Inertial Inflation

In modern industrial economies, inflation is highly *inertial.* That is, it will persist at the same rate until economic events cause it to change. We can compare inertial inflation to a sleepy old dog. If the dog is not "shocked" by the push of a foot or the pull of a stray cat, it will stay where it is. Once disturbed, the dog may move around, but then it eventually lies down in a new spot where it stays until the next shock.

During the mid-1980s, prices in the United States rose steadily at around 4 percent annually, and most people came to expect that inflation rate. This expected rate of inflation was built into the economy's institutions. Wage agreements between labor and management were designed around a 4

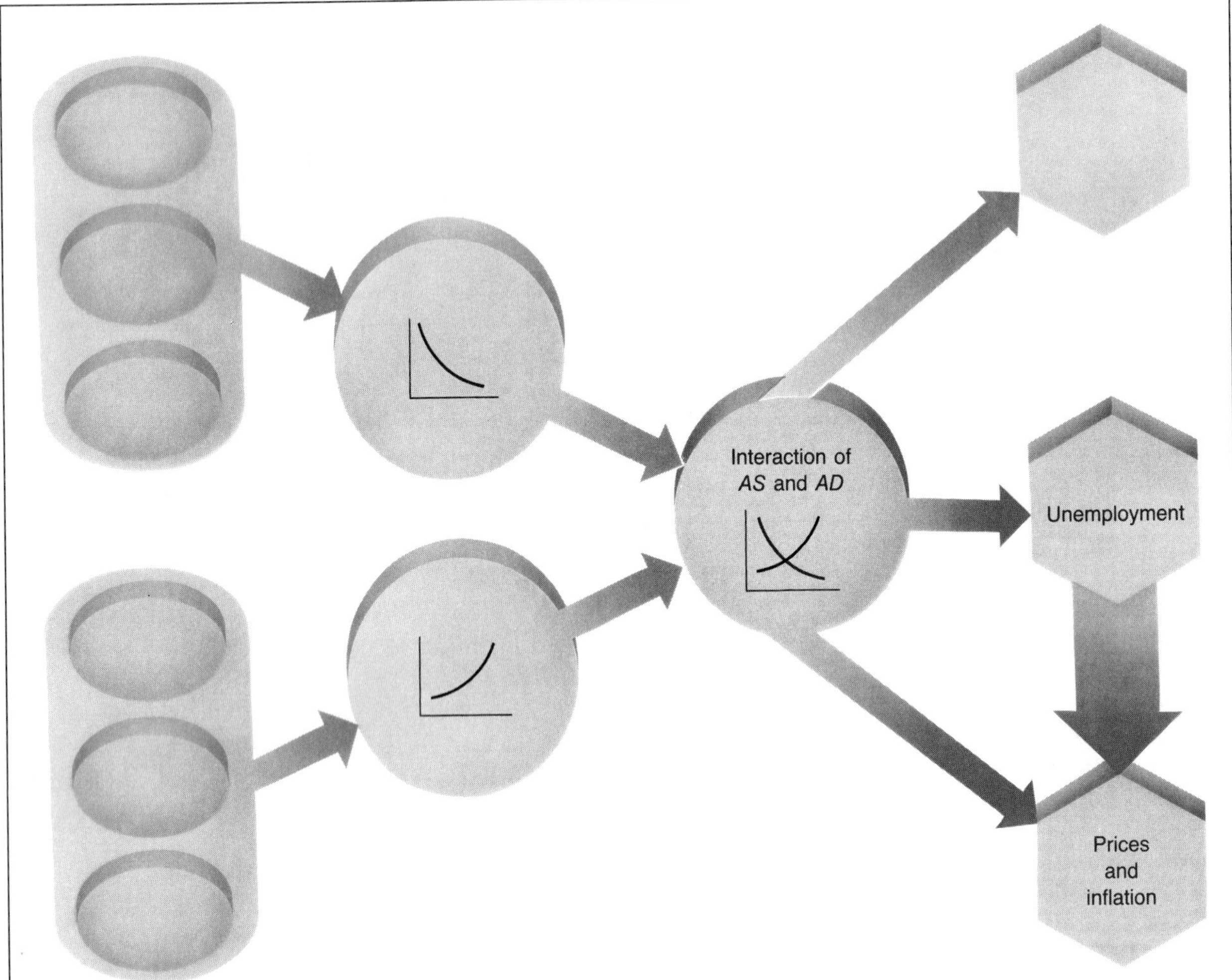

Figure 33-1. Aggregate supply and demand interact to determine prices and inflation
In this chapter, we study how *AS* and *AD* interact to determine the rate of inflation. We will analyze the connection between unemployment and inflation.

percent inflation rate; government monetary and fiscal plans assumed a 4 percent rate. Nominal GNP could grow at 7 percent (3 percent growth of output and 4 percent inflation) without any major surprises. During this period, the *inertial rate of inflation* was 4 percent per year. Other names sometimes heard for this concept are the core, underlying, or expected inflation rate.

The rate of inflation that is expected and built into contracts and informal arrangements is the inertial or core rate of inflation.

Inertial inflation can persist for a long time—as long as most people expect the inflation rate to remain the same. Under this condition, inflation is built into the system. A fully built-in inflation represents a *neutral* equilibrium, one which is able to sustain itself at a particular rate for an indefinite period of time.

But history shows that inflation does not remain undisturbed for long. Frequent shocks from changes in aggregate demand, sharp oil-price changes, poor harvests, movements in the foreign exchange rate, productivity changes, and countless other economic events move inflation above or below its inertial rate. The major kinds of shocks are demand-pull and cost-push. In summary:

At a given time, the economy has an ongoing rate of inflation to which people's expectations have adapted. This built-in inertial inflation rate tends to persist until a shock causes it to move up or down.

Demand-Pull Inflation

One of the major shocks to inflation is a change in aggregate demand. In earlier chapters we saw that changes in investment, government spending, or net exports can change aggregate demand and propel output beyond its potential. We also saw how a nation's central bank can affect economic activity. Whatever the reason, **demand-pull inflation** occurs when aggregate demand rises more rapidly than the economy's productive potential, pulling prices up to equilibrate aggregate supply and demand. In effect, demand dollars are competing for the limited supply of commodities and bid up their prices. As unemployment falls and workers become scarce, wages are bid up and the inflationary process accelerates.

One influential demand-pull theory holds the supply of money to be a prime determinant of inflation. The reasoning behind this approach is that money-supply growth increases aggregate demand which in turn increases the price level. In this example, the direction of causation is clear-cut. It proceeds from the money supply through aggregate demand to inflation. Thus, when the German central bank printed billions and billions of paper marks in 1922–1923 and these came into the marketplace in search of bread or housing, it was no wonder that the German price level rose a billionfold, making the currency worthless. This was demand-pull inflation with a vengeance. This scene was replayed when the Soviet government financed its budget deficit by printing rubles in the early 1990s.

Demand-pull inflation can arise from other sources as well; for example, during the Vietnam war, excessive fiscal deficits raised the demand for output well above its potential and ignited a rapid inflation.

Figure 33-2 illustrates the process of demand-pull inflation in terms of aggregate supply and demand. Starting from an initial equilibrium at point *E*, suppose there is an expansion of spending that pushes the *AD* curve up and to the right. The economy's equilibrium moves from *E* to *E'*. At this higher level of demand, prices have risen from *P* to *P'*. Demand-pull inflation has taken place.

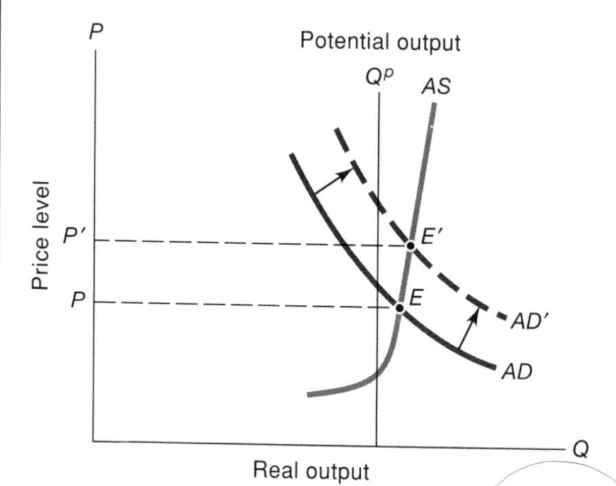

Figure 33-2. Demand-pull inflation occurs when too much spending chases too few goods

At high output levels, when aggregate demand increases, the rising spending is competing for limited goods. With a steep *AS* curve, much of the higher aggregate spending ends up in higher prices. Prices rise from *P* to *P'*. Hence, it is higher demand that pulls up the prices—demand-pull inflation. How would cost-push inflation be analyzed in this framework?

Cost-Push Inflation

The rudiments of demand-pull inflation were understood by the classical economists and used by them to explain historical price movements. But during the last half-century, the inflation process changed, as a glance back at the history of prices on page 591 reminds us. Prices today travel a one-way street—up in recession, up faster in boom. And this is true for all the market economies of the world. What differentiates modern inflation from the simple demand-pull variety is that prices and wages begin to rise before full employment is reached. They rise even when 30 percent of factory capacity lies idle and 10 percent of the labor force is unemployed. This phenomenon is known as "cost-push" or "supply-shock" inflation.

Inflation resulting from rising costs during periods of high unemployment and slack resource utilization is called **cost-push** or supply-shock **inflation.**

Cost-push inflation does not appear to have been present in the early stages of market economies. It first appeared during the 1930s and 1940s, leading to a dramatic change in the pattern of price behavior after World War II, as shown in Figure 32-3.

In looking for explanations of cost-push inflation, economists often start with wages, which are clearly an important part of business costs. In 1982, for example, when the unemployment rate was almost 10 percent, wages rose 5 percent. Some economists point to unions as the responsible parties because they force money wages to rise even though many of their members are out of work.

This view of unions as the clear-cut villains of cost-push inflation does not fit the complex historical facts. In 1982, when unemployment averaged 9.7 percent of the labor force, labor costs for union workers rose 7.2 percent, but the cost of nonunion labor also rose, by 6 percent. Both union and nonunion wages increased in spite of high unemployment.

Since the 1970s, cost-push shocks have often come from sharp changes in the prices of oil and food and from exchange-rate movements. In 1973, in 1978, and again briefly in 1990, countries were minding their own macroeconomic business when severe shortages in oil markets occurred. Oil prices rose sharply, and business costs of production increased. The outcomes were not identical for the three cases, but in each period a sharp burst of cost-push inflation followed the oil-price increase.

As an exercise, make sure you understand how a cost-push inflation works. Say that the torching of the Kuwaiti oil fields leads to an increase in oil prices and business production costs that shifts the aggregate supply curve upward by 10 percent. In Figure 33-2, draw in the effect on prices, assuming that the aggregate demand curve is unchanged. What is the impact on prices and output? You have depicted cost-push or supply-shock inflation.

Expectations and Inertial Inflation

Why, you might ask, does inflation have such strong inertia or momentum? The answer is that most prices and wages are set with an eye to future economic conditions. When prices and wages are rising rapidly and are expected to continue doing so, businesses and workers tend to build the rapid rate of inflation into their price and wage decisions. High or low inflation expectations tend to be self-fulfilling prophesies.

We can use a hypothetical example to illustrate the role of expectations in inertial inflation. Say that in 1991, Brass Mills Inc., a nonunionized light-manufacturing firm, was contemplating its annual wage and salary decisions for 1992. Its sales were growing well, and it was experiencing no major supply or demand shocks. Brass Mill's chief economist reported that prices and wages were currently rising in the range of 3 to 5 percent per year, and the major forecasting services were expecting national wage growth of 4 percent in 1992. Brass Mills had conducted a survey of local companies and found that most employers were planning on increases in compensation of $3\frac{1}{2}$ to $4\frac{1}{2}$ percent during the next year. All the signals, then, pointed to wage increases of around 4 percent for 1992 over 1991.

In examining its own "internal labor market," Brass Mills determined that its wages were in line with the local labor market. Because the managers did not want to fall behind local wages, Brass Mills decided that it would try to match local wage increases. It therefore set wage increases at the expected market increase, an average 4 percent wage increase for 1992.

The process of setting wages and salaries with an eye to expected future economic conditions can be extended to virtually all employers. This kind of reasoning also applies as well to many product prices—such as college tuitions, automobile model prices, and long-distance telephone rates—that cannot be easily changed after they have been set. Because of the length of time involved in modifying inflation expectations and in adjusting most wages and prices, inertial inflation will yield only to major shocks or changes in economic policy.

Figure 33-3 illustrates the process of inertial inflation. Suppose that potential output is constant and that there are no supply or demand shocks. When everyone expects wages and prices to rise at 4 percent each year, average costs will rise at that rate, and the *AS* curve will shift upward at 4 percent per year. If there are no demand shocks, the *AD* curve

Changing Prices, Unchanging Inflation

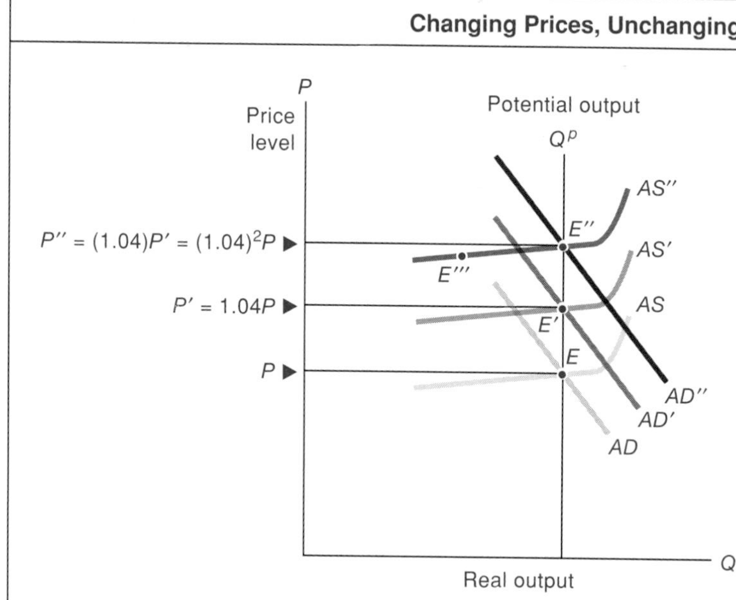

Figure 33-3. An upward spiral of prices and wages occurs when aggregate supply and demand shift up together

In this example, production costs are rising by 4 percent each year. Thus, for every level of output, the *AS* curve will be 4 percent higher next year; another 4 percent higher the year after; and so on.

If *AD* moves up at the same pace, output will stay close to potential, and prices will also rise by 4 percent. As the macroequilibrium moves from *E* to *E′* to *E″*, prices march up steadily because of inertial inflation.

Using this framework, can you depict an inertial rate of inflation of 2 or 8 percent per year?

will also shift up at that rate. The intersection of the *AD* and *AS* curves will be 4 percent higher each year. Hence, the macroeconomic equilibrium moves from *E* to *E′* to *E″*. Prices are rising 4 percent from one year to the next: inertial inflation has set in at 4 percent.

Inertial inflation occurs when the *AS* and *AD* curves are moving steadily upward at the same rate.

Price Levels vs. Inflation

Using Figure 33-3, we can make the useful distinction between movements in the price level and movements in inflation. In general, an increase in aggregate demand, a rightward shift of the *AD* curve, will raise prices, other things equal. Similarly, an upward shift in the *AS* curve resulting from an increase in aggregate supply will raise prices, other things equal.

In general, however, we must recognize that other things change. In particular, the *AD* and *AS* curves are almost always shifting over time. Figure 33-3 shows, for example, the *AS* and *AD* curves marching up together.

What if there was an unexpected shift in the *AS* or *AD* curve during the third period? How would prices and inflation be affected? Suppose for example that the third period's *AD″* curve shifted to the left because of a monetary contraction. This might cause a recession, with a new equilibrium at *E‴* on the *AS″* curve. At this point, output would have fallen below potential; prices and the inflation rate would be lower than at *E″*, but the economy would still be experiencing inflation because the price level at *E‴* is still above the previous period's equilibrium *E′* with price *P′*.

Economic forces may reduce the price level below the level it would otherwise have attained. Nonetheless, because of the momentum of costs and prices, the economy may continue to experience inflation even in the face of these contractionary shocks.

This point is central for understanding the phenomenon of *stagflation,* or high inflation in periods of high unemployment. As long as the inertial elements driving up costs are powerful, a recession may occur simultaneously with high inflation (although with inflation below the previous inertial rate). This point is shown in Figure 33-3, where output is well below its potential at recessionary point *E‴*. But prices are still rising since the price level corresponding to *E‴* is perhaps 3 percent above the previous period's price level at *P′*.

B. Modern Inflation Theory

The Phillips Curve

A useful way of representing the process of inflation was developed by the economist A. W. Phillips, who quantified the determinants of wage inflation. After careful study of more than a century's worth of data on unemployment and money wages in the United Kingdom, Phillips found an inverse relationship between unemployment and the changes in money wages. He found that wages tended to rise when unemployment was low and vice versa. Why might high unemployment lower the growth in money wages? The reason is that workers would press less strongly for wage increases when fewer alternative jobs were available, and in addition firms would resist wage demands more firmly when profits were low.

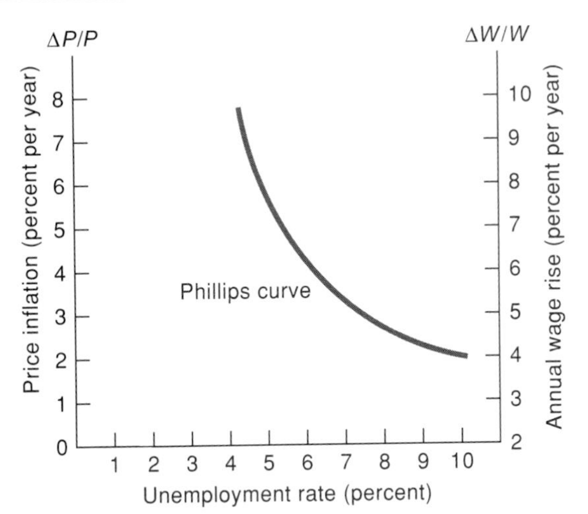

Figure 33-4. The Phillips curve depicts the tradeoff between inflation and unemployment

The Phillips curve shows the inverse relationship between inflation and unemployment. The blue wage-change scale on the right-hand vertical axis is higher than the black left-hand inflation scale by the assumed 2 percent rate of growth of average labor productivity.

The Phillips curve is useful for analyzing short-run movements of unemployment and inflation. The simplest version is shown in Figure 33-4. On the diagram's horizontal axis is the unemployment rate. On the black left-hand vertical scale is the annual rate of price inflation. The blue right-hand vertical scale shows the rate of money-wage inflation. As you move leftward on the Phillips curve by reducing unemployment, the rate of price and wage increase indicated by the curve becomes higher.

An important piece of inflation arithmetic underlies this curve. Say that labor productivity (output per worker) rises at a steady rate of 2 percent each year. Further, assume that firms set prices on the basis of average labor costs, so prices always change just as much as average labor costs per unit of output. If wages are rising at 6 percent, and productivity is rising at 2 percent, then average labor costs will rise at 4 percent. Consequently, prices will also rise at 4 percent.*

Using this inflation arithmetic, we can see the relation between wage and price increases in Figure 33-4. On the right-hand side, the blue scale shows the percentage change in money wage rates while the left-hand side shows the rate of price inflation. These two scales differ only by the assumed rate of productivity growth (so that the price change of 6 percent per year would correspond to a wage change of 8 percent per year if productivity grew by 2 percent per year and if prices always rose as fast as average labor costs). Hence:

The Phillips curve illustrates the "tradeoff" theory of inflation. According to this view, a nation can buy a lower level of unemployment if it is willing to

*This calculation can be formalized as follows: Because prices are based on average labor costs per unit of output, this implies that P is always proportional to WL/X, where P is the price level, W is the wage rate, L is labor-hours, and X is output. Further, average labor productivity (X/L) is growing smoothly at 2 percent per year. Hence, if wages are growing at 6 percent annually, prices will grow at 4 percent annually (= 6 growth in wages minus 2 growth in productivity). More generally,

$$\begin{pmatrix}\text{Rate}\\ \text{of}\\ \text{inflation}\end{pmatrix} = \begin{pmatrix}\text{rate}\\ \text{of wage}\\ \text{growth}\end{pmatrix} - \begin{pmatrix}\text{rate of}\\ \text{productivity}\\ \text{growth}\end{pmatrix}$$

pay the price of a higher rate of inflation. The terms of the tradeoff are given by the slope of the Phillips curve.

According to the Phillips curve shown in Figure 33-4, inflation will be 4 percent per year if the unemployment rate is 6 percent. How much would inflation rise if the unemployment rate were to fall by 1 percentage point?

Interpretation

How does the Phillips curve fit into our model of aggregate supply and demand? The best way to think of the Phillips curve shown in Figure 33-4 is as a *short-run relationship between inflation and unemployment when aggregate demand shifts but aggregate supply continues to change at its inertial rate.* This can be understood by comparing Figures 33-3 and 33-4.

Assume that the 6 percent unemployment rate corresponds to potential output. Then, as long as output stays at its potential, unemployment stays at 6 percent, and inflation continues to rise at 4 percent per year. Suppose, however, that a shift in aggregate demand occurs in the third period, so the equilibrium is at point E''' rather than E'' in Figure 33-3. Then output will be below potential, unemployment will rise above 6 percent, and inflation will fall. To cement your understanding of this point, pencil into Figure 33-4 the unemployment and inflation rates that correspond to points E'' and E''' in Figure 33-3.

This explanation indicates why the Phillips curve drawn in Figure 33-4 is only a short-run curve and may shift in the long run. A shock to inflation will alter people's expectations, and eventually wages and other costs will change. Aggregate supply will reflect these changes, so that a new rate of inertial inflation will emerge. This process will lead to a *shift* in the Phillips curve.

The Changing Menu. The Phillips curve has been described as a "menu for choice between inflation and unemployment." But sometimes the diners found that the prices were changing even as they ate their meal. That is, because of changes in the inertial rate of inflation, the Phillips curve shifted over time. Figure 33-5 shows the plot of inflation and unemployment over the period 1961–1990. There surely is no stable curve here; rather, the points appear to circle clockwise, with some drift outward and inward.

The observation of the clockwise rotation in the Phillips curve led economists to revise the simple Phillips curve. The fruitful result of this collision between theory and historical evidence was the natural-rate inflation theories of today.

The Natural Rate of Unemployment

To explain the strange looking "Phillips curl" in Figure 33-5, economists have constructed a modification known as the "natural-rate Phillips curve." Growing out of theoretical work of Edmund Phelps and Milton Friedman, and tested by scores of econometricians, the natural-rate theory distinguishes between the long-run Phillips curve and the short-run Phillips curve. It asserts that the downward-sloping Phillips curve of Figure 33-4 holds only in the short run. In the long run, there is only one unemployment rate that is consistent with steady inflation; that unemployment rate is called *the natural rate of unemployment.* This theory implies that the long-run Phillips curve is vertical.

To understand the new theories, we need a careful definition of the natural rate of unemployment.

The **natural rate of unemployment** is that rate at which upward and downward forces on price and wage *inflation* are in balance. At the natural rate, inflation is stable, with no tendency to show either accelerating or declining inflation. In an economy concerned with preventing high inflation rates, the natural rate of unemployment is the lowest level that can be sustained; it thus represents the highest sustainable level of employment and corresponds to a nation's potential output.

We can understand this theory in the following way: At any point in time, the economy has inherited a given inertial or expected rate of inflation. If (*a*) there is no excess demand and if (*b*) there are no supply shocks, then actual inflation will continue at the inertial rate. What do these conditions signify? Condition (*a*) means that unemployment is at that level—the natural rate of unemployment—at which the upward pressure on wages from vacancies just matches the downward wage pressure from unemployment. Condition (*b*) denotes the absence of unusual changes in the costs of materials like oil and imports, so that the aggregate sup-

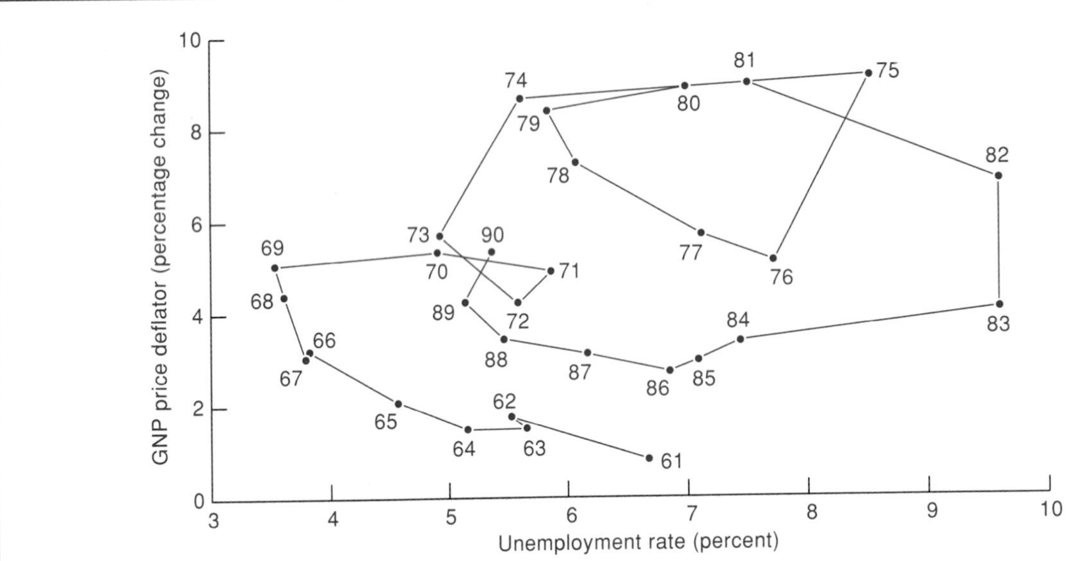

Figure 33-5. The Phillips curve or the Phillips curl?
Data on unemployment and inflation over the last three decades show a more complicated relationship than the simple short-run Phillips curve. Modern natural-rate theories explain the Phillips curl and the inward and outward drift. (Source: *Economic Report of the President,* 1982, updated by the authors; the price index here is the GNP deflator.)

ply curve is rising at the inertial rate of inflation. Putting conditions (*a*) and (*b*) together leads to a state in which inflation can continue to rise at its inertial or expected rate.

What would happen if there were either demand or cost shocks? At very low unemployment, such as that during the Vietnam war, inflation will be pushed above its inertial rate as we move along the

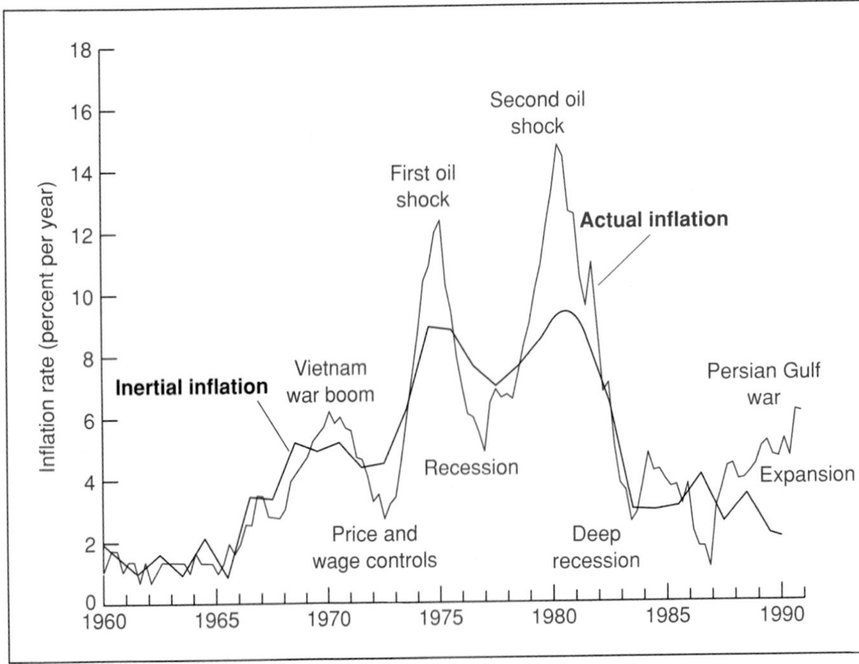

Figure 33-6. How inflation shocks affect the inertial inflation rate
Inertial inflation adjusts gradually when inflationary shocks occur. See how the Vietnam war, the first oil shock, and the second oil shock all propelled the inertial inflation rate upward. Then the period of tight money after 1979 reduced inflation, and the inertial rate declined. What is happening now to change the inertial rate of inflation? (The price index shown here is the CPI.)

short-run Phillips curve. By contrast, if unemployment rises to levels far in excess of the natural rate, as occurred in the early 1980s, inflation will decline below its inertial rate as we move down the short-run Phillips curve.

But the story does not end here. Once actual inflation rises above its inertial or expected level, people begin to adjust to the new level of inflation and to expect higher inflation. The inertial rate of inflation then adjusts to the new reality. And the short-run Phillips curve shifts.

The historical process of shock and adjustment is illustrated in Figure 33-6. Rapid growth and low unemployment during the Vietnam war led to the bidding up of prices and wages—a demand shock occurred. Actual inflation rose, and inertial inflation quickly followed suit.

Oil-price shocks in 1973 and 1979 raised actual inflation, and again inertial inflation followed. In 1980–1982, however, policymakers decided to pay almost any price in a crusade against inflation. The subsequent recession drove down actual inflation, and inertial inflation declined sharply in the late 1980s.

This brief narrative makes a crucial point about inflation: The tradeoff between inflation and unemployment remains stable only as long as the inertial or expected inflation rate remains unchanged. But when the inertial inflation rate changes, the short-run Phillips curve will shift.

A Boom Cycle

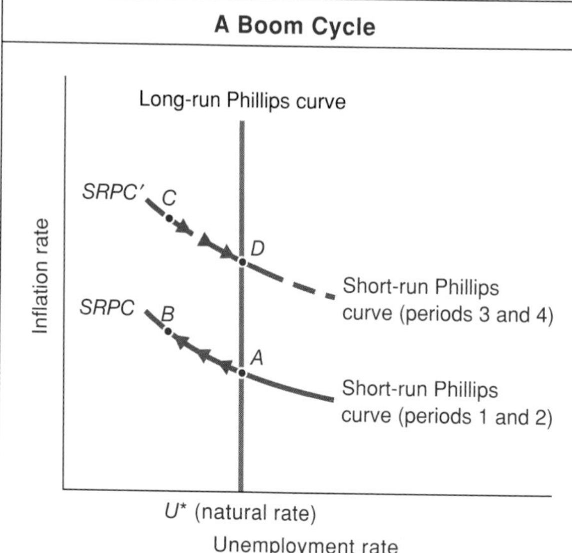

Figure 33-7. How shocks move the Phillips curve

This figure shows how a period of low unemployment shifts the short-run Phillips curve. The economy starts at point *A*. The economy then expands, with unemployment falling below the natural rate at point *B* in period 2. As a result, inflation rises above the inertial rate.

As time passes, however, the higher inflation becomes anticipated and gets built into the new short-run Phillips curve, *SRPC′*. When the economy comes back to the natural rate at point *D* in period 4, it is now saddled with higher inertial and actual inflation rates.

Note that if points *A*, *B*, *C*, and *D* represent different years, you can connect the dots. The shifting curve has produced a clockwise loop like that seen in Fig. 33-5.

The Shifting Phillips Curve

This important idea—that shocks shift the Phillips curve—can be understood as a sequence of steps, illustrated by a "boom cycle" described here and in Figure 33-7.

Period 1. In the first period, unemployment is at the natural rate. There are no demand or supply surprises, and the economy is at point *A* on the lower short-run Phillips curve (*SRPC*) in Figure 33-7.

Period 2. A rapid increase in output during an economic expansion lowers the unemployment rate. As unemployment declines, firms tend to recruit workers more vigorously, and some firms decide to increase their compensation more rapidly than they did in the previous period. As output exceeds its potential, capacity utilization rises and price markups increase. Wages and prices begin to accelerate. In terms of our Phillips curve, the economy moves up and to the left to point *B* on its short-run Phillips curve (along *SRPC* in Figure 33-7). Inflation expectations have not yet changed, but the lower unemployment rate raises inflation during the second period.

Period 3. With the higher rate of wage and price inflation, firms and workers begin to *expect* higher inflation. The higher expected rate of inflation is incorporated into wage and price decisions. The inertial or expected rate of inflation thus increases.

How does higher expected inflation show up in the Phillips-curve framework? The short-run Phillips curve shifts upward. The new Phillips curve (labeled *SRPC′* in Figure 33-7) lies above the original Phillips curve. The new short-run Phillips curve reflects the higher expected rate of inflation.

Period 4. In the final period, as the economy slows, the contraction in economic activity brings output back to its potential, and the unemployment rate returns to the natural rate. Inflation declines because of the higher unemployment.

Note the surprising outcome. Because the expected or inertial inflation rate has increased, the rate of inflation at the natural rate is higher in period 4 than during period 1. Even though aggregate supply and demand are in balance, firms and workers have come to expect a higher inflation rate. The economy will experience the same *real* GNP and unemployment levels as it did in period 1, even though the *nominal* magnitudes (prices and nominal GNP) are now growing more rapidly than they did before the expansion raised the expected rate of inflation.

We sometimes see an "austerity cycle" that occurs when unemployment rises and the actual inflation rate falls below the inertial rate. In this case, the inertial rate of inflation declines, and the economy enjoys a lower inflation rate when it returns to the natural unemployment rate. Something like this painful cycle of austerity occurred during the Carter and Reagan wars against inflation during 1979–1982.

The Vertical Long-Run Phillips Curve

We have seen that when the unemployment rate diverges from the natural rate of unemployment, the inflation rate will tend to change. What happens if the gap between the actual unemployment rate and the natural rate persists? For example, say that the natural rate is 6 percent, while the actual unemployment rate is 4 percent. Because of the gap, inflation will tend to rise from year to year. Inflation might be 6 percent in the first year, 7 percent in the second year, 8 percent in the third year, and might continue to move upward thereafter.

When would this upward spiral stop? According to the natural-rate theory, it will stop only when unemployment moves back to its natural rate. Put differently, as long as unemployment is below the natural rate, inflation will tend to increase.

The opposite behavior will be seen at high unemployment. In that case, inflation will tend to fall (or perhaps decline toward zero) as long as unemployment is above the natural rate.

Only when unemployment is *at* the natural rate will inflation stabilize; only then will the shifts of supply and demand in different labor markets be in balance; only then will inflation—at whatever is its inertial rate—tend neither to increase nor to decrease.

According to the natural-rate theory, the only level of unemployment consistent with a stable inflation rate is the natural rate of unemployment. The long-run Phillips curve must, in this theory, be drawn as a vertical line, rising straight up at the natural unemployment rate, as shown by the vertical *DA* line in Figure 33-7.

The natural-rate theory of inflation has two important implications for economic policy. First, it implies that there is a minimum level of unemployment that an economy can sustain in the long run. According to this view, a nation cannot push unemployment below the natural rate for long without igniting an upward spiral of wage and price inflation.

Second, a nation may be able to ride the short-run Phillips curve. An expansionist President can drive the unemployment rate below the natural rate and the nation can temporarily enjoy low unemployment, but at the expense of rising inflation. Conversely, when a nation thinks that its inertial inflation rate is too high, as was the case in 1979–1982, it can steel itself for a period of austerity, induce a recession, and thereby reduce inflation.

Quantitative Estimates

Although the natural unemployment rate is an important macroeconomic concept, precise numerical estimates of the natural rate have proven elusive. One of the leading experts on the subject, Robert J. Gordon, estimates that the natural rate was around 6 percent of the labor force in the 1980s. His estimates, along with the actual unemployment rate, are shown in Figure 33-8. Other economists have produced different numbers for the late 1980s, with the range of informed opinion putting the natural rate between 5 and 6 percent.

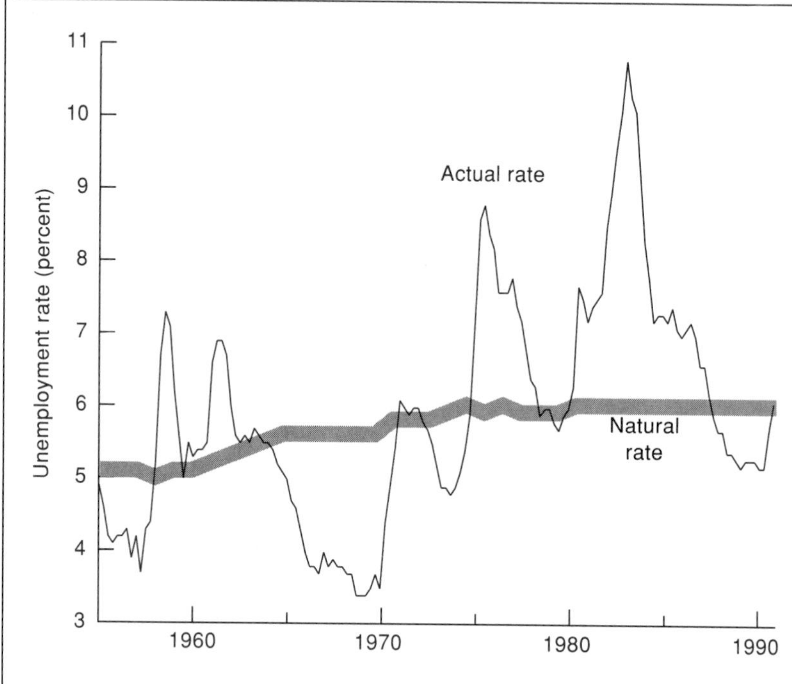

Figure 33-8. Actual and natural rates of unemployment, 1955–1990

The natural rate of unemployment is that level at which forces acting on wages and prices are in balance. Below that rate, inflation generally tends to rise; above it, inflation tends to subside.

Note that the natural rate has risen substantially over the last quarter-century. Today, it appears to be around 6 percent. Also note that the natural rate is given as a wide band to reflect the fact that it is difficult to estimate the natural rate precisely. (Source: Actual unemployment rate from U.S. Department of Labor, *Employment and Earnings;* natural unemployment rate from Robert J. Gordon, "Understanding Inflation in the 1980s," *Brookings Papers on Economic Activity,* 1985, pp. 263–302, for 1954–1984, and updates.)

Most economists hold that, given today's price-and-wage-setting institutions, the United States could not maintain an unemployment rate well below 6 percent without experiencing rising inflation.

Many people are discouraged that the natural rate is so high. Why can the nation not guarantee good jobs to all without accelerating inflation? One reason is simply that in America the amount of turnover, or frictional unemployment, is high when job opportunities are plentiful. Thus in the last year in which the economy was near its natural rate, 1990, over one-third of the unemployed workers were young (less than 25 years old). Only $2\frac{1}{2}$ percent of those in the labor force were unemployed job losers. Of 174 million adults, only 560 thousand were counted as unemployed over 26 weeks.

In addition to the frictional component of unemployment, there is normally a great deal of structural and involuntary unemployment. Even when the unemployment rate is low, a substantial fraction of the unemployed consists of job losers and long-term unemployed. Labor markets do not quickly match up job vacancies and the unemployed.

In sum, the natural rate is high in the United States in part because mobility of workers is so great, and in part because the labor market is unable to match up quickly job vacancies with unemployed workers.

The Rising Natural Rate. The best data suggest the natural rate in the United States has drifted upward substantially in recent decades. In the early 1960s, President Kennedy's economists concluded that at full employment of the labor force, the unemployment rate would be below 4 percent; the number was estimated to be 5 percent in the early 1970s. By the 1980s, as we have just seen, the natural rate was thought to be between $5\frac{1}{2}$ and 6 percent of the labor force. What is the reason for this trend? Economists point to three factors: demographic changes, government policy, and structural change.

A first factor originates in the changing demographic structure of the labor force, particularly in the rising participation of teenagers, minorities, and women. As more teenagers and women entered the labor force, the average unemployment rate rose because these groups tend to experience higher unemployment rates than adult males. This change in composition of the labor force raised the overall natural unemployment rate even though the natural unemployment rate for each group stayed the same.

In addition, some analysts believe that government social policies have also led to an upward shift in the natural rate. One often-cited example is unemployment insurance (UI). In most states, a worker who is fired or laid off qualifies for UI and, for up to 26 weeks, the unemployed person can collect around 50 percent of prior wages. As a result, workers search somewhat less assiduously for a new job when they are collecting UI. They are also understandably more likely to refuse a low-paying job. Consequently, the unemployment rate is higher. Some economists have estimated that the expansion of unemployment insurance might have added as much as 1 percentage point to the natural rate, but other economists dispute this finding.

A final contribution to the rising natural rate comes from the possibility of increasing structural unemployment. Economists note that the 1970s and 1980s produced severe shocks to industries and regions dependent on energy or exposed to international trade—auto and steel were depressed, oil drilling grew and then collapsed. The Northeast prospered and then slumped, and electronics boomed. These factors might raise the natural unemployment rate because they increase the amount of structural unemployment. It would take longer for workers and firms to match up just as it would take longer for men and women to find the right mate if men lived in one town and women in another. Studies by David Lilien and James Medoff suggest that the natural rate in the 1970s and 1980s may have increased by as much as 1 percentage point because of increasing structural unemployment, although the amount of structural unemployment appears to have declined in the last few years.

Doubts about the Natural Rate

The concept of the natural rate of unemployment, along with its output twin, potential GNP, is crucial for understanding inflation and the connection between the short run and the long run in macroeconomics. Some economists raise concerns about the validity of the natural-rate concept. One issue is whether the natural rate is a stable magnitude. Some believe that an extended period of high unemployment will lead to a deterioration of job skills, loss of on-the-job training and experience, and thereby to a higher natural rate of unemployment. Might not slow growth of real GNP reduce investment and leave the country with a diminished capital stock? Might that capacity shortage produce rising inflation even with unemployment rates above the natural rate?

Experience in Europe over the last two decades confirms some of these worries. In the early 1960s, labor markets in Germany, France, and Britain appeared to be in equilibrium with unemployment rates between 1 and 2 percent. By the late-1980s, after a decade of stagnation and slow job growth, labor market equilibrium seemed to be in balance with unemployment rates in the 7 to 12 percent range. On the basis of recent European experience, many macroeconomists are looking for ways to explain the instability of the natural rate and its dependence upon actual unemployment as well as labor market institutions.

Review

Let us review the highlights of this section:

- Inflation has great momentum and is highly inertial. It tends to persist until shocked either by demand or by costs.
- In the short run, an increase in aggregate demand which lowers the unemployment rate below the natural rate will tend to increase the inflation rate; similarly, a demand decrease will tend to lower inflation. In the short run, while the Phillips curve is stable, there is a tradeoff between inflation and unemployment.
- In the long run, Phillips curves tend to be unstable. A period of low unemployment and increasing inflation will lead people to expect higher inflation and will tend to shift up the short-run Phillips curve.
- According to the natural-rate theory, the long-run Phillips curve is completely vertical at the natural unemployment rate; as long as the unemployment rate is below the natural rate, inflation will tend to rise continually.

C. Dilemmas of Anti-inflation Policy

The economy evolves in response to political forces and technological change. Our economic theories, designed to explain issues like inflation and unemployment, must also adapt. In this final section on inflation theory, we discuss the pressing issues that arise in combating inflation.

How Long Is the Long Run?

The natural-rate theory holds that the Phillips curve is vertical in the long run. Just how long *is* the long run for this purpose? The length of time that it takes the economy to adjust fully to a shock is not precisely known. Recent studies suggest that full adjustment takes at least 5 years, and some studies conclude that the Phillips curve would not become vertical until more than a decade. These analyses indicate that it takes a long time for expectations to adjust, for labor and other long-term contracts to be renegotiated, and for all these effects to percolate through the economy. In addition, the length of time it takes for the economy to adjust probably depends on the type and novelty of the shock.

How Much Does It Cost to Reduce Inflation?

Our analysis suggests that a nation can reduce the inertial rate of inflation by reducing output and raising unemployment for a time. But in weighing anti-inflation policies, policymakers may want to know just how much it costs to squeeze inflation out of the economy. How costly is *disinflation,* the policy of lowering the rate of inflation? This is equivalent to asking about the shape of the short-run Phillips curve. If the Phillips curve is relatively flat, reducing inflation will require a big increase in unemployment; if the Phillips curve is steep, a small rise in unemployment will bring down inflation quickly and relatively painlessly.

Macroeconomists have studied this issue in great depth, and the cost assessment varies depending upon the country, the initial inflation rate, and the policy used. Studies of the cost of disinflation for the United States give a reasonably consistent answer. These studies indicate that raising unemployment to reduce the underlying inflation rate by 1 percentage point will cost the nation about 4 percent of 1 year's GNP. In terms of the current level of GNP, this amounts to a cost of about $220 billion (in 1990 prices) to reduce the inflation rate by 1 percentage point.

We can explain this estimate using the Phillips curve. According to recent studies, when the unemployment rate rises 1 percentage point above the natural rate of unemployment for 1 year, and then returns to the natural rate, the inflation rate will decline about $\frac{1}{2}$ percentage point. Therefore, to reduce inflation by 1 full percentage point, unemployment must be held 2 percentage points above the natural unemployment rate for 1 year.

Recall that Okun's Law (discussed in Chapter 31) states that when the unemployment rate is 2 percentage points above the natural rate, actual GNP is 4 percent below potential GNP. In 1990 terms, with a potential GNP (in 1990 prices) of $5500 billion, reducing inflation by 1 percentage point would require about 2 percentage points increase in the unemployment rate (U) for 1 year. In dollars, then, a disinflation of 1 percentage point would cost 2 U points × 2 percent of GNP per U point × $5500 billion of GNP = $220 billion. Other estimates of the cost range from $100 to $300 billion per point of inflation reduction.

This statistical estimate of the cost of reducing inflation can be compared to the American experience during the deep recession in the early 1980s. Table 33-1 shows a calculation of the estimated output loss from the recession (compared to producing at potential output), along with the estimated decline in the inertial inflation rate. This calculation indicates that the disinflation of the 1980–1984 period cost the nation approximately $215 billion of lost output (in 1990 prices) per percentage-point reduction in inflation. This episode corroborates statistical estimates of the cost of disinflation.

Credibility and Inflation. Recent experience in the United States can help address another impor-

The Costs of Disinflation, 1980–1984

Inertial rate of inflation:

1979	9%
1984	4%
Change:	−5 percentage points

Difference between potential and actual GNP (1990 prices):

1980	$ 128 billion
1981	144
1982	356
1983	311
1984	136
Total:	$1075 billion

Cost of disinflation = $1075 billion/5 percentage points
= $215 billion per percentage point

Table 33-1. Illustration of the cost of disinflation

This table illustrates the cost of reducing the inertial rate of inflation from around 9 percent in 1979 to around 4 percent in 1984. Over that period the inertial rate declined 5 percentage points, while the economy produced $1075 billion less than its potential GNP. Dividing these two figures provides an estimate of $215 billion of output lost per percentage-point reduction in inflation. This figure has been confirmed by numerous statistical studies of the American economy. (Source: Authors' estimates.)

tant issue. In the last decade, many economists argued that the Phillips-curve approach was too pessimistic. The dissenters held that *credible* and publicly announced policies—for example, adopting fixed monetary rules or the gold standard—would lead to a rapid and inexpensive reduction in inflation. These economists backed up their recommendations by citing "regime changes," such as monetary and fiscal reforms, that ended Austrian and Bolivian hyperinflations at relatively low cost in terms of unemployment or lost GNP. Other economists argued that, while such policies might work in countries torn by hyperinflation, war, or revolution, no realistic policy could hope to work miracles in the United States.

The bold experiment of 1980–1984 provided a good laboratory to test the credibility view against the mainstream approach. During this period, monetary policy was tightened in a clear and forceful manner. Yet the price tag was extremely high, as Table 33-1 shows. Using tough, preannounced policies to enhance credibility did not appear effective in lowering the cost.

The finding that it costs the nation $100 to $300 billion per point of inflation reduction provokes different responses from people. Some people ask whether the costs are worth the benefits of lower inflation. Others ask if there are not cheaper ways to lower inflation. These are questions that arise in the design of anti-inflation policies, to which we turn next.

Can We Lower the Natural Rate of Unemployment?

When considering the predicament raised by the conflict between high employment and stable prices, we should first analyze potential labor market policies. This raises the important question: Is the natural rate the optimal level of unemployment? If not, what can we do to lower it toward a more desirable level?

To begin with, we observe that, although it has become common parlance among macroeconomists, the term "natural rate" is misleading. The natural rate is in no way natural; it is influenced by the pattern of demographic change, by the kinds of shocks the economy experiences, by government's labor market policies, and perhaps even by the past history of unemployment itself. Some economists prefer more neutral terms such as the "inflation-safe unemployment rate" or the "non-accelerating-inflation rate of unemployment" or "NAIRU."

Moreover, the natural rate is not necessarily the optimal unemployment rate. The optimal level of unemployment for an economy would come where net economic welfare was maximized. Those who have studied the relationship of unemployment to economic welfare believe that the optimal unemployment rate is lower than the natural rate. They note that there are many spillovers or externalities in the labor market. For example, workers who have been laid off suffer from a variety of social and economic hardships. Yet employers do not pay the costs of unemployment; most of the costs (unemployment insurance, health costs, family distress, etc.) spill over as external costs and are absorbed by the worker or by the government. To the extent that unemployment has external costs, the natural unemployment rate is likely to be higher than the optimal rate.

The natural rate of unemployment is likely to be above the optimal unemployment rate, that is, above that level of unemployment where net economic welfare is maximized.

If the natural rate is neither natural nor optimal, why not simply aim for a lower level of unemployment? The reason is, as we have stressed above, that such a step would lead to rising, and unacceptable, inflation. An enormous social dividend, therefore, would reward the society that discovers how to reduce the natural unemployment rate significantly.

What measures might lower the natural rate? Some important suggestions include the following:

- *Improve labor market services.* Some unemployment occurs because job vacancies are not matched up with unemployed workers. Through better information, such as computerized job lists, the amount of frictional and structural unemployment can be reduced.
- *Bolster government training programs.* If you read the "help wanted" section of your Sunday newspaper, you will find that most of the job vacancies call for skills held by few people. Conversely, most of the unemployed are unskilled or semiskilled workers, or find themselves in the wrong job or in a depressed industry. Many believe that government training programs can help unemployed workers retool for better jobs in growing sectors. If successful, such programs provide the double bonus of allowing people to lead productive lives and of reducing the burden on government transfer programs.
- *Remove government obstacles.* We noted above that, in protecting people from the hardships of unemployment and poverty, the government has at the same time removed the sting of unemployment and reduced incentives to seek work. Some economists call for reforming the unemployment-insurance system; reducing the disincentives for work in welfare, disability, and social security programs; and strengthening work requirements in welfare programs.

Having reviewed the options for reducing the natural unemployment rate, we must add a cautionary note. Three decades of research and labor market experiments on this subject have led objective analysts to be extremely modest in their claims. Short of solutions that force the unemployed to go hungry in the cold, most proposals would probably have minimal effect on the natural rate.

Elimination or Adaptation?

Given the costs of eliminating inflation, and the difficulty of reducing the natural unemployment rate, people often ask whether it is really desirable to eliminate inflation through recession and high unemployment. Wouldn't it be better to learn to live with inflation as the lesser evil as has been done by many countries in Latin America and elsewhere?

One technique for adaptation is to "index" the economy. **Indexing** is a mechanism by which wages, prices, and contracts are partially or wholly compensated for changes in the general price level. Examples of partial indexation are found in many labor contracts which guarantee workers cost-of-living adjustments (or *COLAs*). A typical example would run as follows: Next year a firm will give a worker a 2 percent wage increase if there is no inflation. However, if prices rise 10 percent over the next 12 months, the firm will add another 4 percent as a cost-of-living adjustment. Other sectors that are sometimes indexed include the tax system, rents, and long-term industrial contracts.

Why not index the entire economy? In such a world, inflation would not matter for anything "real," and we could ignore inflation and concentrate on reducing unemployment. This sounds like a good idea, but in practice it has serious drawbacks. Full indexation is impossible because it guarantees a certain level of *real* incomes that may simply not be producible. Moreover, the greater the indexation, the more an inflationary shock will rage through the economy like an epidemic.

A high rate of indexation is like a big multiplier—it amplifies outside price shocks. Full indexation is an invitation to galloping inflation. Adaptation to inflation thus contains a paradox: the more a society insulates its members from inflation, the more unstable inflation is likely to become. Countries that have thoroughly indexed their economies (such as Brazil) have found it virtually impossible to eradicate inflation even through draconian measures.

Wanted: A Low-Cost Anti-inflation Policy

How can nations resolve the dilemma of inflation versus unemployment? Policies that attempt to lower inflation without raising unemployment are sometimes called "incomes policies." **Incomes**

policies are government actions that attempt to moderate inflation by direct steps, whether by verbal persuasion, legal controls, or other incentives. In terms of our economic analysis, they are attempts to shift the Phillips curve inward.

What are some approaches to anti-inflation policies? How successful have they been? Here are some examples:

- *Peacetime wage-price controls* have been used in Scandinavia, the Netherlands, and elsewhere. Although they have sometimes been effective for a short time, in the longer run controls have either blown up or become ineffective because people evaded them. In some cases, such as the United States during 1971–1974, price and wage controls appear to have been totally ineffective in the struggle to slow the wage-price spiral.
- *Voluntary wage-price guidelines* showed some modest success in the Netherlands, and also in the United States during the Kennedy, Johnson, and Carter years. But with time they tended to become ineffective and inequitable—particularly when accompanied by excessively stimulative fiscal and monetary policies that ignited demand-pull price pressures.
- A *market strategy* has been urged by many economists. This approach would rely on the natural discipline of markets to restrain price and wage increases. Advocates emphasize strengthening market forces by deregulation of regulated industries; removing market impediments to competition in perverse antitrust laws and in retail-price maintenance; repealing government laws that inhibit competition such as foreign-trade quotas and minimum-wage laws; banning labor-union monopolies; and above all encouraging international competition. Policies that strengthen market forces may increase the resistance to price and wage increases, particularly in imperfectly competitive labor and product markets.
- *Tax-based incomes policies* (sometimes dubbed "TIP") have been proposed as a way of using the market mechanism to attain macroeconomic objectives. TIP would use fiscal carrots and sticks to encourage anti-inflationary actions by taxing those whose wages and prices are rising rapidly and subsidizing those whose wages and prices are rising slowly. TIP has been used in socialist countries such as Hungary and Poland with some success, and has sometimes been proposed for the United States. Even the enthusiasts of TIP stress, however, that it is a complement and not a substitute for the discipline of the market mechanism and tight fiscal and monetary policies to contain inflation.

The search for an effective and durable incomes policy has not found the Holy Grail. As a thorough study of the subject by Lloyd Ulman and Robert Flanagan summarized:

> Incomes policy, to generalize from the experience of the [seven] countries studied in this account, has not been very successful. [Experience] suggests that in none of the variations so far turned up has incomes policy succeeded in its fundamental objective, as stated, of making full employment consistent with a reasonable degree of price stability.

The Cruel Dilemma

Many economists today think that there is a natural rate of unemployment below which our economies can go only at the risk of spiraling inflation. Moreover, the natural rate of unemployment is often thought to be excessively high. Critics of capitalism find the high unemployment that prevails in North America and Europe to be the central flaw in modern capitalism. The search for a way to resolve the cruel dilemma of needing high unemployment to contain inflation continues to be one of the most pressing concerns of modern macroeconomics.

SUMMARY

A. Sources of Inflation

1. At any time, an economy has a given *inertial* or expected inflation rate. This is the rate that people have come to anticipate and that is built into labor contracts and other agreements. The inertial rate of inflation can chug along at the same rate each year without a strong tendency to rise or fall.

The inertial rate of inflation is a short-run equilibrium, and persists until the economy is shocked.

2. In reality, the economy receives incessant price shocks. The major kinds of shocks that propel inflation away from its inertial rate are demand-pull and cost-push.

   Demand-pull inflation results from too much spending chasing too few goods, causing the aggregate demand curve to shift up and to the right. Wages and prices then are bid up in markets. *Cost-push* inflation is a new phenomenon of modern industrial economies. It arises when the costs of production rise even in periods of high unemployment and idle capacity. Cost-push pressures dominate when labor unions or businesses exercise market power by raising wages or prices despite high unemployment or excess capacity, or when external factors drive up commodity prices unexpectedly.

B. Modern Inflation Theory

3. The Phillips curve shows the inverse relationship between inflation and unemployment. In the short run, lowering one rate means raising the other. Suppose in a given year the inertial inflation rate is 4 percent and the natural rate of unemployment is 6 percent. If output growth drives unemployment below the natural rate, inflation will rise above the inertial rate, perhaps to an inflation rate of 5 or 6 percent or more. Similarly, if unemployment rises above the natural rate, inflation tends to fall below the inertial rate.

4. But the short-run Phillips curve tends to shift over time as expected inflation and other factors change. If inflation persists above the expected or inertial inflation rate, the expected inflation rate itself rises. If policymakers attempt to hold unemployment below the natural rate for long periods, inflation will tend to spiral upward.

5. Modern inflation theory relies on the concept of the natural rate of unemployment. The natural unemployment rate is the lowest sustainable rate that the nation can enjoy without risking an upward spiral of inflation. It represents the level of unemployment of resources at which labor and product markets are in inflationary balance.

6. Under the natural-rate theory, there is no permanent tradeoff between unemployment and inflation, and the long-run Phillips curve is vertical.

7. While many macroeconomists accept the natural-rate theory, it leaves many questions unanswered, such as the reasons for the upward drift in unemployment rates in Europe over the last two decades. The natural rate of unemployment is estimated to be between $5\frac{1}{2}$ and 6 percent in the United States today. The upward creep in the natural rate came from a mixture of demographic trends, changes in social policies, and increases in structural unemployment.

C. Dilemmas of Anti-inflation Policy

8. A central concern for policymakers is the cost of reducing inertial inflation—i.e., what are the costs of disinflation? Current estimates indicate that a substantial recession—reducing GNP by \$100 to \$300 billion below

its potential for 1 year—is necessary to slow inertial inflation by 1 percentage point.

9. Economists have put forth many proposals for lowering the natural unemployment rate; notable proposals include improving labor market information, improving education and training programs, and refashioning government programs so that workers have greater incentives to work. Sober analysis of politically viable proposals leads most economists to expect only small improvements from such labor market reforms.

10. Because of the high costs of reducing inflation through recessions, nations have often looked for other approaches. These are incomes policies such as wage-price controls and voluntary guidelines, tax-based approaches, and market-strengthening strategies. In the end, no economy has succeeded in maintaining full employment, stable prices, and free markets. The dilemma of anti-inflation policy remains.

CONCEPTS FOR REVIEW

Causes and theories of inflation
inertial inflation
sources of shock to inflation (demand-pull and cost-push)
short-run and long-run Phillips curves
natural rate of unemployment and the long-run Phillips curve
boom cycle, austerity cycle, Phillips-curve loops
natural vs. optimal rate of unemployment

Anti-inflation policy
costs of disinflation
indexing, COLA adjustments
measures to lower the natural rate of unemployment
incomes policies: wage-price controls and guidelines, competition, TIP

QUESTIONS FOR DISCUSSION

1. "Unemployment in the steel industry is 9 percent in 1991, yet wage rates in the steel industry are rising at 6 percent per year." Show that this is cost-push and not demand-pull inflation in the labor market. What reasons might exist for this phenomenon?
2. What is a short-run Phillips curve? What is on its horizontal axis? On its vertical axis? What can cause the short-run Phillips curve to shift up or down?
3. The data on the right describe inflation and unemployment in the United States in the 1980s.

   Note that the economy started out near the natural rate of unemployment in 1979 and ended near the natural rate in 1990. Can you explain the decline of inflation over these years? Do so by drawing the short-run and long-run Phillips curves for each of the years from 1979 to 1990.

Year	Unemployment rate (%)	Inflation rate, CPI (% per year)
1979	5.8	11.3
1980	7.1	13.5
1981	7.6	10.3
1982	9.7	6.2
1983	9.6	3.2
1984	7.5	4.3
1985	7.2	3.6
1986	7.0	1.9
1987	6.2	3.6
1988	5.5	4.1
1989	5.3	4.8
1990	5.5	5.4

Source: *Economic Report of the President,* 1991.

4. Many economists argue as follows: "Because there is no long-run tradeoff between unemployment and inflation, there is no point in trying to shave the peaks and troughs from the business cycle." Does this view suggest that we should not care whether the economy is stable or fluctuating widely as long as the average level of unemployment is the same? Would you agree?
5. Is unemployment above or below the natural rate

today? What are the arguments for leaving the unemployment rate where it is? For moving it toward the natural rate? How do you resolve these two views?

6. A leading economist has written: "If you think back to our discussion of the social costs of inflation, at least of moderate inflation, it is hard to avoid coming away with the impression that they are minor compared with the costs of unemployment and depressed production." Write a short essay describing your views on this issue.
7. What is the natural rate of unemployment? Why is it not zero? Why is it so high in the United States? What would you expect the natural rate to be in a country like Japan, which has a "lifetime employment system," a kind of job tenure for most of its workers?
8. Can the government set policies that will put the actual unemployment rate below the natural rate for a year or two? For several decades?
9. The following policies and phenomena affected labor markets during the 1980s. Explain the likely effect of each on the natural rate of unemployment:
   (a) The minimum wage fell 40 percent relative to the average wage rate.
   (b) Unemployment insurance became subject to taxation.
   (c) Funds for training programs for unemployed workers were cut sharply by the federal government.
   (d) Because of high cyclical unemployment, many minority-group teenagers received little on-the-job training.
   (e) Because of the decline of labor unions, a smaller fraction of the work force operated under 3-year collective bargaining agreements.
10. Examine the data on inflation and unemployment in question 3. Plot a series of short-run Phillips curves along with a long-run Phillips curve that might be consistent with that data.
11. Incomes policies are attempts to shift the Phillips curve in a favorable direction. Choose two examples of incomes policies given in the text. For each, describe the policy and show how it might affect the short-run and the long-run Phillips curves.
12. Consider the following anti-inflation policies: high unemployment, wage and price controls, and tax-based incomes policies. For each, list the advantages and disadvantages in terms of inflation control and other economic objectives. Which would you choose if the President asked for your recommendation?

C H A P T E R 3 4

FISCAL POLICY, DEFICITS, AND THE GOVERNMENT DEBT

> The only good budget is a balanced budget.
>
> Adam Smith of Glasgow (1776)

> The only good rule is that the budget should never be balanced—except for an instant when a surplus to curb inflation is being altered to a deficit to fight recession.
>
> Warren Smith of Ann Arbor (1965)

Since the American Revolution, the federal government of the United States has generally balanced its fiscal budget. Heavy military spending during wartime has customarily been financed by borrowing, so the government debt tended to soar in wartime. In peacetime, the government would pay off some of the debt, and the debt burden would shrink.

This pattern changed during the 1980s. The Reagan administration pursued a new economic philosophy that emphasized reducing taxes while sharply increasing America's military spending. Balancing the budget was sacrificed for other objectives, and the federal budget deficit soared to over $200 billion a year in the mid-1980s. The government debt grew from $660 billion when President Reagan was inaugurated to nearly $2000 billion when he left office in 1989. The policies of the Reagan period marked a turning point in America's fiscal history, leading to a struggle to contain the deficit that has lasted well into the 1990s.

What were the causes of the surging deficits in the 1980s? How did the large deficits affect the economy's pattern of investing and saving? Did government deficits "crowd out" investment? And what will be the long-lasting impact of the government debt upon economic growth? We will consider these crucial questions in this chapter.

Figure 34-1 shows the topics to be analyzed in this chapter. We begin with an analysis of the major institutional features of government budgeting and then survey the economic effects of deficits and the government debt.

A. Budgets and Fiscal Policy

Basic Definitions

Governments use budgets to control and record their fiscal affairs. A **budget** shows, for a given year, the planned expenditures of government programs and the expected revenues from tax systems. The budget typically contains a list of specific programs (education, welfare, defense, etc.), as well as tax sources (individual income tax, social-insurance taxes, etc.).

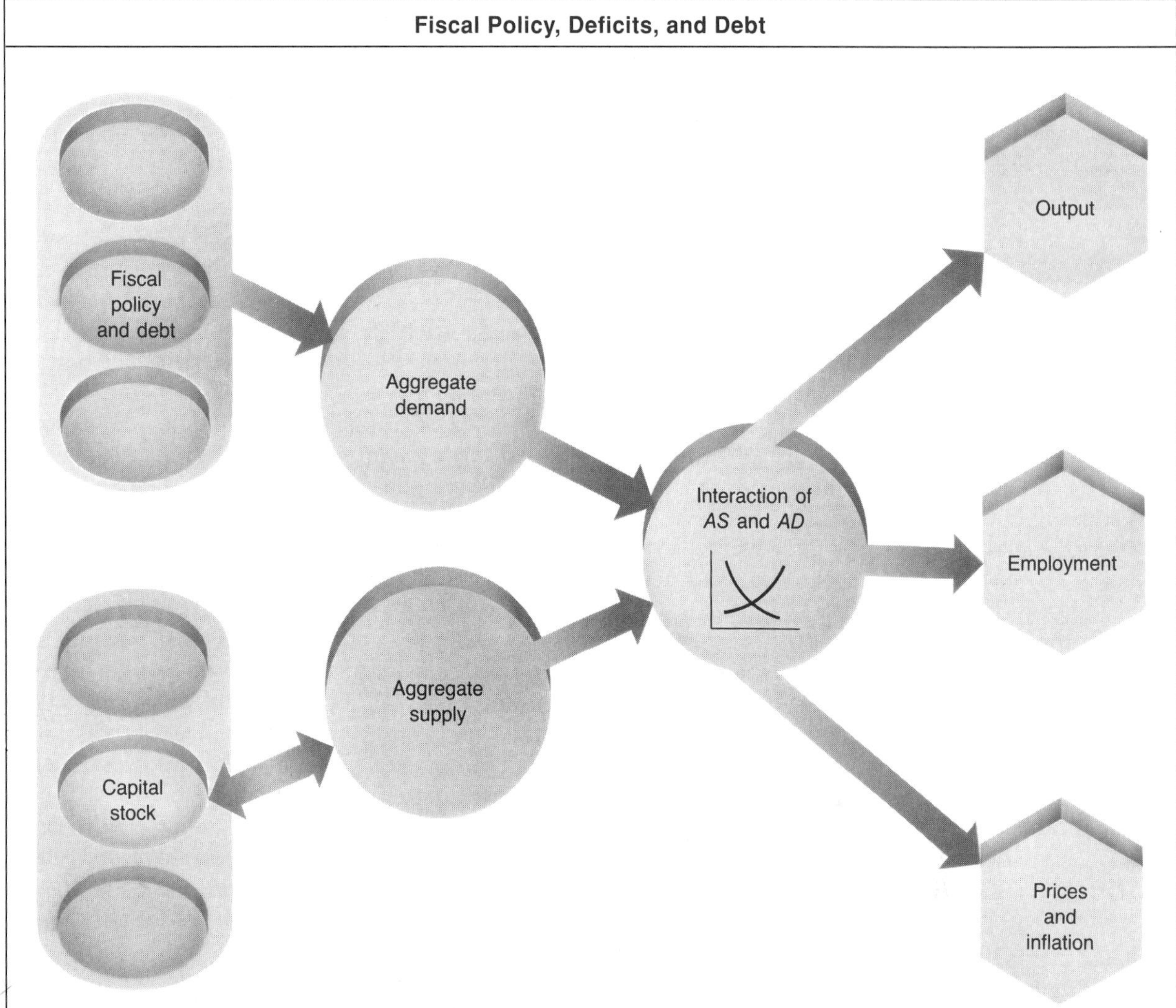

Figure 34-1. What is fiscal policy? What are the impacts of deficits? What is the burden of government debt?

This chapter explores the economic impact of fiscal policy, deficits, and government debt. Note how the causal arrows point both toward and away from the capital stock, reminding us that fiscal policies leave a significant mark on investment, capital, and economic growth.

In a given year, budgets are generally out of balance. A **budget surplus** occurs when all taxes and other revenues exceed government expenditures. A **budget deficit** is incurred when expenditures exceed taxes. When revenues and expenditures are equal during a given period, the government has a **balanced budget.**

As an example, consider President Bush's budget for fiscal year 1992. Submitted to Congress in February 1991, the proposal outlines taxes and expenditures for the 1992 fiscal year (October 1, 1991, to September 30, 1992). Bush's budget called for receipts of $1165 billion and expenditures of $1446 billion. The planned deficit was $281 billion.

When the government incurs a budget deficit, it must borrow from the public to pay its bills. To borrow, the government issues bonds, which are IOUs that promise to pay money at some time in the future. The **government debt** (sometimes called the public debt) consists of the total or accumulated borrowings by the government; it is the total dollar value of government bonds owned by the public (households, banks, businesses, foreigners, and other non-federal entities). In the pages that follow, we will study the impact of government deficits and debt upon the economy.

The Making of Fiscal Policy

Many early enthusiasts of the simple Keynesian multiplier analysis believed that fiscal policy was the philosopher's stone, the answer to prayers for curbing business cycles. If unemployment strikes, simply raise spending or cut taxes; if inflation threatens, do the opposite. Today, no one holds such naively optimistic views about banishing the business cycle to the history books. Business cycles are still with us, and fiscal policy works better in theory than in practice.

By *fiscal policy,* we mean the process of shaping taxation and public expenditure in order (*a*) to help dampen the swings of the business cycle, and (*b*) to contribute to the maintenance of a growing, high-employment economy, free from high or volatile inflation.

Suppose the economic system in a particular year is threatened with a deep and prolonged recession. What action might people call for? The Federal Reserve might use monetary policy to try to stimulate investment. Additionally, Congress and the President might alter fiscal policy, changing tax and public expenditure programs to help reach their output and inflation targets. Alternatively, if inflation is unacceptably high, Congress might raise tax rates and trim expenditure programs, or the Federal Reserve might reduce the growth of the money supply and raise interest rates.

In summary:

Fiscal policies dealing with taxes and public expenditure, in cooperation with monetary policies, have as their goals rapid economic growth with high employment and stable prices.

Automatic Stabilizers

You might get the impression that fiscal policy requires round-the-clock vigilance by the government. In fact, the modern fiscal system has inherent *automatic stabilizing properties.* All through the day and night, whether or not Congress is in session, taxes and spending are stabilizing the economy. If a recession gets under way, powerful automatic forces will instantly begin to counter the economic slowdown.

What are these automatic stabilizers? They are primarily the following:

- *Automatic changes in tax receipts.* Our federal tax system depends on progressive personal and corporate income taxes. (Progressive taxes are those for which the average tax rate rises as income rises.) How does progressive taxation ensure stability? As soon as income begins to fall off, even if Congress makes no change in tax rates, the government tax receipts decline. Today, for each $10 billion drop in GNP, total federal tax receipts drop by about $3½ billion.

  Why are such tax changes useful? They may be the right medicine for an unexpected change in the economy. If output drops, tax receipts will automatically fall so that personal incomes and spending will be cushioned; output will not fall as much as it otherwise would have. In inflationary times, an increase in tax revenues will lower personal income, dampen consumption spending, reduce aggregate demand, and slow the upward spiral of prices and wages.

  A century ago, economists thought that stability of tax revenue was a good thing; they felt that taxes should be invariant to business conditions. From a macroeconomic point of view, exactly the opposite is true. We are fortunate, therefore, that our present tax system possesses a high degree of automatic flexibility, with receipts tending to rise in inflationary times and to fall in times of recession. This is a powerful factor stabilizing the economy and moderating the business cycle.
- *Unemployment insurance, welfare, and other transfers.* The modern welfare state has an elaborate system of transfer payments that are designed to supplement incomes and relieve economic hardship. An important example is unemployment insurance (UI). Soon after employees are laid off, they begin to receive UI; when they go back to work, the payments cease. Thus UI pumps funds into or out of the economy in a countercyclical, stabilizing way. Similar features are seen in other income-support programs such as food stamps, aid to families with dependent children, and Medicaid.

Limitations of Automatic Stabilizers

Automatic stabilizers are a first line of defense but are not by themselves sufficient to maintain full stability. To see why, consider the example of taxes.

Recall that in the multiplier model, a shock to spending (in, say, investment, net exports, or government spending) will have a multiplied impact on output. However, the automatic tendency for taxes to take away a fraction of each extra dollar of income reduces the size of the multiplier. But the impact of the shock will be *reduced,* not completely eliminated. Say the *MPC* in the economy without taxes is 0.9; here the multiplier would be 10. If taxes took one-third of all income, then the multiplier would be reduced to $2\frac{1}{2}$. Instead of disturbances having their effects on GNP multiplied 10 times, because of the automatic stabilizing effect of taxes, the impact would be much smaller.[1]

Automatic stabilizers act to reduce business-cycle fluctuations in part, but they cannot wipe out 100 percent of the disturbance. Whether to reduce the balance of a disturbance, and how, remains the task of discretionary monetary and fiscal policy.

Discretionary Stabilization Policy

Even after automatic stabilizers have done their job, fluctuations in economic activity remain. In the United States today, short-run economic stabilization is handled primarily through monetary policy. (Recall our discussion in Chapter 29 of how money affects economic activity.)

In addition, at certain times, governments use discretionary fiscal policy to combat business cycles. A *discretionary fiscal policy* is one in which the government changes tax rates or spending programs. In contrast to automatic stabilizers, discretionary policies generally involve passing legislation to change the structure of the fiscal system. The principal weapons of discretionary fiscal policy are public works, other capital programs, public-employment projects, and changes in tax rates.

[1] The partial stabilizing effect can be illustrated as follows: Assume that without any taxes, government, foreign sector, etc., the *MPC* is $\frac{9}{10}$; this implies that the multiplier is 10. Now assume that $33\frac{1}{3}$ percent of any additional income is taxed away, so for every dollar of increase in GNP, $\$\frac{1}{3}$ goes to taxes and $\$\frac{2}{3}$ goes to disposable income (*DI*). And of the $\$\frac{2}{3}$ going to *DI,* 90 percent (or 60 cents of the original dollar) is spent. The multiplier is now only 2.5.

Public Works. When governments first searched for ways to counteract depressions, they often relied on public investment projects to create jobs for the unemployed. Some public-works investments, such as rural electrification, proved enormously beneficial to underdeveloped areas. Others, such as raking leaves, were no more than inefficient "make-work" projects that produced little of value.

Planners realize that it takes a long time to start a post office or implement a road-building or pollution-abatement program. Plans must be made; blueprints drawn; land acquired by purchase or court condemnation; buildings razed; new structures built.

It may be years before a significant part of the funds is spent and people are employed. Given the difficulty of forecasting more than a year or two into the future, we might find that the antirecession public-works project is just coming on stream as the economy is recovering from the recession and inflation is heating up. Today, the economic impacts of countercyclical programs are well understood and seldom relied upon to combat recessions.

Public-Employment Projects. At the other extreme from highly capital-intensive, long-duration public-works projects are public-employment projects. These programs are designed to hire unemployed workers for periods of a year or so, after which people can move to regular jobs in the private sector. Public jobs avoid one of the major shortcomings of public-works projects; they can be started up and phased out very quickly. Critics find them wasteful, citing that the projects are often of secondary importance. In addition, the transition from special public jobs to regular jobs has been a rocky one; most studies indicate that getting a public-employment job does not markedly improve one's chances of holding a regular private-sector job later.

Variation of Tax Rates. A third approach to discretionary fiscal policy is to cut income-tax rates temporarily in order to keep disposable incomes from falling and to prevent a decline from snowballing into a deep recession. Varying tax rates can be used to either stimulate or restrain an economy.

Many advocates of discretionary stabilization policy see varying tax rates as the ideal weapon. Once taxes have been changed, consumers react quickly; a tax cut is spread widely over the population, stimulating spending on consumption goods and inducing an economic upturn.

Unfortunately, experience has revealed serious shortcomings in varying taxes countercyclically. It usually takes Congress a long time to debate and enact tax proposals. Moreover, taxes are very controversial; politicians who favor raising taxes are often defeated at the polls. In addition, economists point to a technical defect in temporary countercyclical taxes: If people know tax changes are temporary, they may alter their consumption very little, thus making the countercyclical impact small.

The Advantage of Monetary Policy

These shortcomings of fiscal policy stand in sharp contrast to the potential of discretionary monetary policy. Monetary policy can be changed quickly; the Federal Reserve is an independent agency and does not need an act of Congress to change interest rates and credit conditions. Moreover, monetary policy has been shown to be extremely effective in expanding or contracting the economy. For these reasons, most economists prefer monetary policy as the primary tool for short-run stabilization. Fiscal policy would, in this view, be used to correct the nation's investment-saving balance and perhaps to counter any deep recessions or great inflations that cannot be handled by monetary policy alone.

Fiscal Deficits: Concepts and Trends

Old-Fashioned Public Finance

Sixty years ago, economic tracts dealing with public finance differed little from those in Adam Smith's time. From 1776 to 1929 there was little discernible change in public-finance theory. Democratic Presidents Grover Cleveland and Woodrow Wilson differed not a bit in their ideology of public finance from Republicans William McKinley and Herbert Hoover. What were the classical precepts of public finance?

- Public finance is simply an application of family finances. If each month a couple spends more than their monthly income, they go bankrupt and misery follows. The same is true of Uncle Sam.
- The budget should be balanced in every year; in addition, the budget should be small, with expenditure prudent and purposes strictly limited.
- The government debt is a burden on the backs of our children and grandchildren; every dollar of debt is like a heavy rock that we must carry on our shoulders.

Although economic thinking about public finance has advanced a great deal, these simple homilies resurface periodically. During the 1980s, with escalating deficits and a rapid buildup of government debt, people harked back to these early views about the virtues of a balanced budget. But few experienced public-finance specialists today agree completely with the three precepts of our forebears. Our task is to understand the logic and experience behind modern views about budgets.

Modern Public Finance[2]

Our earlier analysis of appropriate fiscal policy focused on the need to stabilize the economy: higher deficits combat recession while lower deficits or even surpluses curb inflation. (See the quotation from Keynesian economist Warren Smith at the beginning of this chapter.) But what if the needs of stabilization policy drive deficits and government debt ever upward? Or down to zero? Should we be as concerned about the deficits and debt as our grandparents were?

There are no simple answers to these questions. To find answers, we must consider the impacts of the deficits and debts upon the economy:

- Are the deficits recession-induced or policy-induced?
- Do deficits "crowd out" investment or do they "encourage" it?
- What is the true economic burden of the government debt, and how does the debt affect economic growth?

The balance of this chapter focuses on these crucial questions.

[2] In 1974, Congress established the nonpartisan Congressional Budget Office (CBO), whose first chief was economist Alice Rivlin, to analyze the economy and appraise different options for fiscal policy. The CBO has provided valuable independent economic commentary and serves as a particularly important source of information on the federal budget.

Structural vs. Cyclical Deficits

One of the most important distinctions in modern public finance is that between structural and cyclical deficits.[3] The idea is simple. The *structural* part of the budget is active—determined by discretionary policies such as setting tax rates, social security benefits, or the size of defense spending. In contrast, the *cyclical* part of the budget is determined passively by the state of the business cycle, that is, by the extent to which national income and output are high or low.

Economists define structural and cyclical budgets quantitatively as follows:

The **actual budget** records the actual dollar expenditures, revenues, and deficits in a given period.

The **structural budget** calculates what government revenues, expenditures, and deficits would be if the economy were operating at potential output.

The **cyclical budget** calculates the effect of the business cycle on the budget—measuring the changes in revenues, expenditures, and deficits that arise because the economy is not operating at potential output but is in boom or recession. The cyclical budget is the difference between the actual budget and the structural budget.

In fact, the distinction between structural and cyclical budgets parallels the difference between discretionary and automatic stabilizers. Structural spending and revenues consist of the discretionary programs enacted by the legislature; cyclical spending and deficits consist of the taxes and spending that adjust automatically to the state of the economy. For example, during a recession, every percentage-point increase in the unemployment rate today increases the deficit by about $40 billion. This increase in the cyclical deficit comes as tax revenues fall and unemployment insurance and welfare payments rise.

By contrast, say that Congress undertakes a deficit-reduction plan like that enacted in 1990. This plan raised tax rates and cut expenditures by $100 billion annually over the 1991–1996 period. These steps reduced the structural deficit—the budget deficit at full employment or potential output—by $100 billion. Or suppose that Congress decides to enact a $10 billion program for subsidizing child care. This would add $10 billion to structural expenditures and would therefore increase the structural deficit by that amount.

Generally, fiscal-policy actions change both the structural and the cyclical deficits (at least for the short run). If the government were to sign an arms-control agreement that cut $30 billion from defense spending, the result would be a reduction in the structural deficit by $30 billion. If this spending reduction were not offset by increases in other areas, it would also tend to contract the economy, thereby also increasing the cyclical deficit. Statistical studies indicate that the net effect of a measure that changes the structural budget deficit is to change the actual budget deficit in the same direction.

[3] The following discussion analyzes government deficits in light of the prevalent budgetary imbalance of the 1990s; the principles apply equally to a budget surplus with the appropriate change in sign.

Applications of Cyclical and Structural Budgets

By distinguishing cyclical deficits from structural deficits, we get a better reading of the true impact of fiscal policy. To gauge the impact of fiscal policy, it is necessary to watch the structural budget. If the actual deficit increases in a given year, one might be tempted to say, "The deficit is up, therefore the government is stimulating the economy." But this assessment could be dead wrong. Indeed, a higher deficit stemming from lower tax rates or higher defense spending (i.e., because the structural deficit rose) would tend to increase aggregate demand. On the other hand, a higher budget deficit arising from an economic downturn (a higher cyclical deficit coming from the operation of the automatic stabilizers) would not be a sign of fiscal expansion; it would mark an economic downturn.

Figure 34-2 illustrates this lesson. Note how the structural budget moved sharply toward deficit during the Vietnam war, again before the 1972 election, and once again after 1982. These were periods of strong fiscal expansion.

But the figure also indicates that movements in the actual deficit can be misleading indicators of the direction of fiscal policy. From 1979 to 1982, the cyclical budget moved sharply into deficit while the structural budget changed little. Why? As the economy went into recession, tax receipts fell off. Fiscal policy did not become more expansionary until

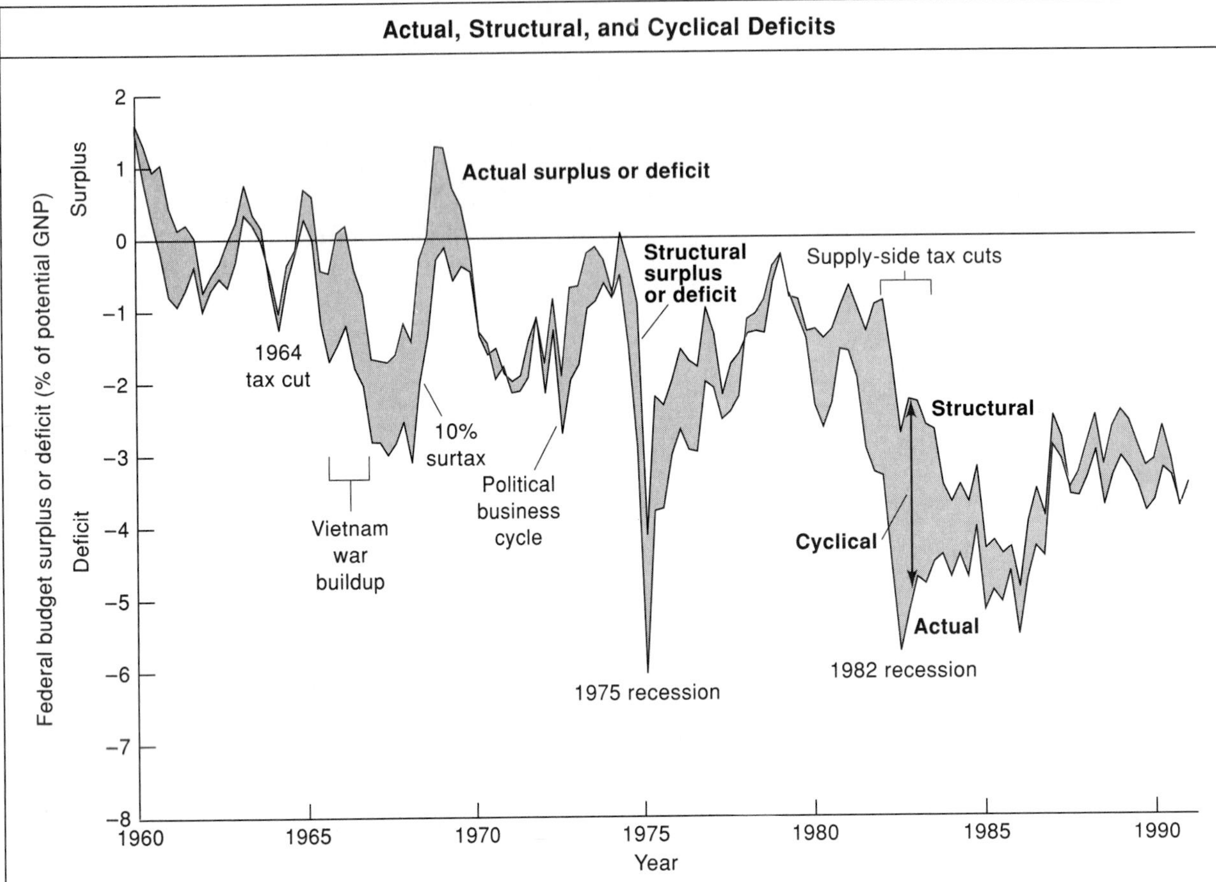

Figure 34-2. Structural, actual, and cyclical budget deficits

The blue line shows the actual budget deficit or surplus over the last three decades (as a percentage of potential GNP). The black curve depicts the structural component, i.e., what the budget deficit or surplus would have been if the economy had been at potential output.

The difference between the actual and structural deficits or surpluses is the cyclical deficit or surplus. Where the shaded area is blue, the economy had high unemployment and the cyclical budget was in deficit. Where the gap is shaded gray, output was above potential and the cyclical budget showed surplus. (Source: U.S. Department of Commerce, modified by authors to reflect the definition of potential output used in this text.)

after 1982, so the deficit increase was largely cyclical, not structural.

The structural budget is one of the most important analytical tools of macroeconomics. It allows us to separate changes in policy from the effects of the business cycle, enabling us to make a better diagnosis of where fiscal policy is leading the economy.

The Soaring Fiscal Deficits after 1979

Since the early 1980s, the most perplexing macroeconomic issue revolved around the mounting federal budget deficit. Deficits are not new to the American economy; indeed, the federal government incurred deficits throughout the 1970s. But after 1979, the size of the federal deficit jumped sharply both in absolute terms and as a fraction of GNP.

Congress passed laws attempting to stop the rising tide of red ink, but deficits climbed throughout this period. Republicans blamed the deficits on 50 years of poorly designed Democratic welfare programs and on the Democratic philosophy of "tax and spend." Democrats counterattacked that Republican presidents were responsible for the deficits and pointed to the supply-side policies as the culprit in the mounting government debt.

Deficit or contributing factor	Amount ($, billion) 1979	1982	1986
A. Budget deficit:			
Actual	16	146	207
Cyclical	−4	88	34
Structural	20	58	173
B. Increase in budget deficit from 1979:			
Actual	0	130	191
Cyclical	0	92	38
Structural	0	38	153
C. Major contributing factor:			
Increased defense spending	0	40	72
Increased interest payments	0	31	64
Increased transfer payments	0	57	39
Decreased taxes	0	2	24
Total, major contributing factors	0	130	199

Table 34-1. Sources of the rising deficit

From 1979 to 1986, the federal budget deficit rose sharply. In the early period, from 1979 to 1982, most of the increase was due to the rising cyclical deficit. In the second part of the period, structural factors were at work.

Part C of the table shows the most important contributing factors. For each, we have shown the increase in the deficit relative to a situation where it remained a constant fraction of GNP (using 1979 as a base). By this test, the most important factors were the increase in defense spending and the rise of interest payments. Tax cuts and larger transfer payments contributed as well. Note that the sum is not equal to the change in the deficit because other parts of the budget are omitted. (Source: U.S. Department of Commerce.)

What are the facts? No simple analysis can resolve this complex question, but Table 34-1 helps illustrate the fiscal trends of the 1980s. This table shows the actual, structural, and cyclical deficits in 1979 (a high-employment year), 1982 (at the trough of a deep recession), and 1986 (a year of stable macroeconomic conditions). In addition, part C of the table shows how much each of four contributing factors changed from 1979 to the reference year. These benchmark comparisons exhibit the change in each factor as a share of GNP.

What conclusions can we draw from this table and other studies? First, during the early 1980s, most of the increase in the deficit was due to the deep recession, with only a modest increase in the structural deficit. After 1982, the structural deficit rose sharply as the cyclical deficit shrank.

Looking at components, the deficit rose because all four contributing factors moved toward deficit: taxes were cut, while defense spending, interest payments, and transfer payments increased. The two largest increases came in defense spending and in interest payments. The former was due largely to the military buildup and was a conscious policy step; the latter was the inadvertent result of the tight money and higher government debt. In the end, no single source can be identified. Rather, it was the combination of policies and events, all interacting and moving in the same direction, that led to the soaring deficits.

B. The Economic Consequences of the Deficit

No macroeconomic issue has generated more controversy than the impact of government deficits and debt upon the economy. In this section, we sort through the debates to uncover the basic principles.

What are the various economic problems created

by large deficits? What is the relationship between private saving and public saving? Answering these questions is an important task for macroeconomics. At one extreme, we must avoid the customary practice of assuming that public deficits are bad because private debtors are punished. On the other hand, we must recognize the genuine problems associated with excessive government deficits.

Meaning and History of Government Debt

Definitions

The accumulated amount of what government has borrowed to finance past deficits is called the *government* or *public debt.* Most government debt is in short-term interest-bearing securities, such as Treasury bills or notes.

The government debt has a simple relationship to the government deficit: *the increase in the government debt over a given year is equal to the budget deficit.* For example, at the beginning of fiscal year 1992, $2484 billion of federal debt was held by the public. The total budget deficit for 1992 (including so-called off-budget items) was estimated to be $281 billion. Ignoring any changes in the government's bank balances or in the Federal Reserve's holdings, borrowing requirements for 1992 would be $281 billion. So at the end of 1992, federal debt would be $2484 + $281 = $2765 billion.

Most government debt is owned by financial institutions, such as banks and insurance companies. These groups receive interest on the government debt (at an average rate of 8 percent per year in 1990).

Historical Trends

To assess the importance of the present public debt, it is always useful to start by placing the problem in historical perspective.[4] Do interest payments on the debt swallow up much of the GNP? How does the total of all public interest payments compare with the figures for past years and with the experience of other countries?

To see how America's present debt compares with that of the past and with Britain's debt, look at Table 34-2. This shows each nation's government debt in relation to size of gross national product and interest payments. In 1991 our national debt of about $2484 billion represented 44 percent of our annual $5620 billion GNP. The debt's interest payments represented 3.7 percent of that GNP.

How "large" are these numbers? Note that Britain in 1818 had an internal debt estimated at double its GNP, and interest on its debt as a percentage of GNP far exceeded anything that we can look forward to; yet the century from 1818 to World War I was Britain's greatest century in terms of power and material progress. By contrast, Britain's modest-sized debt of the 1970s was accompanied by stagnation. With an eye to history, we can see that there are no magic ratios linking a nation's debt to its glory or decline.

Long-run data for the United States appear in the figure on the front endpaper of this text, which shows the ratio of federal debt to GNP since 1789. Notice how wars drove up the ratio of debt to GNP, but rapid growth with roughly balanced budgets in peacetime normally reduced the ratio of debt to GNP. After 1980, the historical patterns changed. With the implementation of supply-side policies, government deficits climbed well above those seen in earlier periods of peace and prosperity. The debt-GNP ratio rose sharply, and the United States entered a period when high deficits would constrain the growth of government programs. This unprecedented increase in the peacetime federal debt gives added importance to a careful analysis of the impact of deficits and debt.

Short Run vs. Long Run. To understand how government debt and deficits affect the economy, it is useful to analyze the short-run and the long-run outcomes separately.

- In the short run, the stock of government debt is given, and we must allow for variations of output around its potential. The short-run impact of budget deficits upon the economy is known as the question of "crowding out," which is addressed first.

[4] In measuring the federal government debt, we exclude debt held by government agencies (which the government owes itself) and debt held by the Federal Reserve System (which is part of bank reserves and costs the government no interest since the Federal Reserve does not pay interest on bank reserves). Debt held by government agencies and the Fed at the beginning of fiscal year 1992 adds another $1140 billion to the federal debt, the total known as the "gross federal debt" as opposed to the "debt held by the public" analyzed here.

Government Debt and Interest Charges Relative to Gross National Product

(1) Year	(2) Federal government debt (billions)	(3) Interest charges on government debt (billions)	(4) GNP (billions)	(5) Debt as percentage of GNP (5) = 100 × (2)/(4)	(6) Interest charges as a percentage of GNP (6) = 100 × (3)/(4)
United States:					
1990	$2,176	$184	$5,463	40	3.4
1980	588	52.5	2,732	22	1.9
1945	213	3.1	213	100	1.5
1940	40.3	0.86	100.4	40	0.9
1930	16.0	0.61	90.8	18	0.7
1920	24.1	1.02	91.9	26	1.1
1915	0.97	0.02	40.2	2	0.05
1868	2.60	0.13	6.8	38	1.9
Britain:					
1985	£158	£14	£355	45	3.9
1975	46.4	2.8	106	44	2.6
1945	21.4	0.4	9.9	216	4.3
1925	7.6	0.3	4.9	155	6.3
1915	1.1	0.02	3.3	33	0.6
1818	0.8	0.03	0.4	200	7.5

Table 34-2. Alternative measures of the size of the debt

The absolute size of the government debt is always frighteningly large. From an economic perspective, it is important to compare the size of the debt to GNP [in column (5)], or to measure the amount of GNP that must go to cover interest payments [in column (6)].

Note how Britain's debt burden in the past was many times larger than it is today. Also, see how American fiscal policies of the 1980s led to a dramatic increase in U.S. debt burdens. (For the United States, government debt is defined to be all federal interest-bearing debt held outside the federal government and outside the Federal Reserve System.)

(Source: U.S. Departments of Commerce and Treasury; Great Britain, Central Statistical Office, *Annual Abstract of Statistics;* authors' updating.)

- In the long run, the government debt varies with different fiscal and monetary paths, and output tends toward its potential. The long-run issues concerning fiscal policies, which are addressed in turn, involve the impact of government debt on capital formation and consumption of future generations and are known as the "burden of the debt."

The Crowding-Out Controversy

Politicians and business leaders often argue that government spending undermines the economy, saying in effect, "Government spending saps our nation's vitality. When the government spends people's money on public-works projects or pours money into health programs for the poor or elderly, these funds simply crowd out private investment. Public spending crowds out private projects with higher yields and greater social utility."

This argument that government spending reduces private investment invokes the **crowding-out hypothesis.** In its extreme form, this hypothesis suggests that when government spends $100 more on goods and services, private investment falls by $100.

Crowding Out and the Money Market

What is the crowding-out mechanism? Suppose that the government starts a road-building project, which increases government spending on goods and services. Our multiplier model says that in the short run, with no change in financial conditions, GNP will rise by 2 or 3 times the increase in G. The same argument applies to reductions in taxes.

But we must also take into account the reaction of financial markets. Because GNP is higher, the transactions demand for money rises. A higher level of GNP is likely to provoke a monetary tightening by the Federal Reserve. The rising interest rates and tightening of credit will tend to choke off or "crowd out" investment and other interest-sensitive spending.[5]

How does this chain of events relate to deficits? Our example assumes that there is a discretionary increase in G or cut in T, implying that the structural deficit is increased. This analysis shows that budget deficits may crowd out investment through the workings of monetary policy and financial markets.

Crowding out occurs in the short run when the effectiveness of fiscal policy is reduced by money market reactions. An increase in the structural deficit, through tax cuts or higher government spending, will tend to raise interest rates and therefore lower investment. Thus some of the induced increase in GNP may be offset as the higher structural deficit crowds out investment.

Crowding Out from Structural Deficits. Crowding out is primarily concerned with the effects of structural rather than cyclical deficits. If the deficit rises because of a recession (a cyclical deficit), the logic of crowding out simply does not apply. Why not? Because a recession causes a *decline* in the demand for money and leads to *lower* interest rates. The relationship between deficits, interest rates, and investment during recessions shows why there is no automatic crowding out of investment by higher deficits.

Impact of Structural Deficits

What is the impact of higher structural deficits on investment? Most macroeconomists agree that at least some investment is crowded out by government deficits. However, they debate about *how much* investment is reduced. Is investment reduced by only a small fraction of the government deficit? Or by virtually the whole amount?

Complete Crowding Out. At one extreme is a case of complete crowding out of investment by government spending when the monetary reaction is powerful. Suppose that the Federal Reserve determines that any rise in output would be inflationary. The Fed therefore boosts interest rates to curb investment. If the Fed has an output target, then the effect will be to crowd out investment 100 percent.[6]

This case is illustrated in Figure 34-3, which employs a Keynesian-cross diagram. The solid $C + I + G + X$ line shows the situation before any government spending increase, with an equilibrium at E. Next the government enacts a spending program, increasing government spending on goods and services from G to G'. As a result, we have the new $C + I + G' + X$ line. If there were no monetary reaction, GNP would rise from Q to Q'.

However, because of the monetary reaction, in-

[5] Recall that tight money will lead to a reduction in spending in a wide variety of interest-sensitive sectors, including business investment, housing, consumption spending on consumer durables, net exports, and capital items of state and local governments. In the discussion that follows, we will examine the impact on "investment," but keep in mind that these other components of spending are just as important.

[6] The next chapter will show that this case also holds for the strict "monetarist" world where the demand for money is completely inelastic with respect to interest rates.

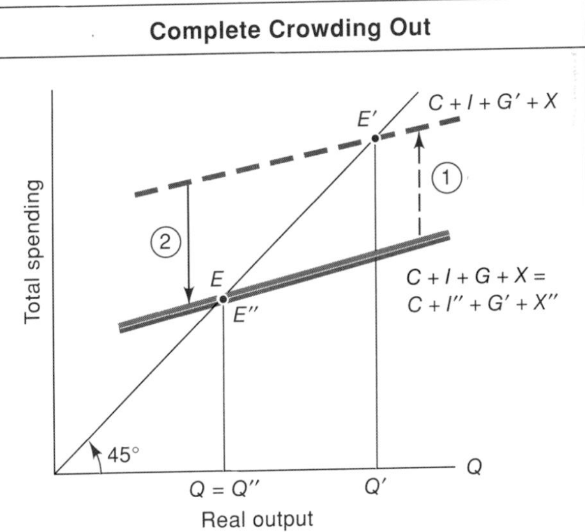

Figure 34-3. Strong monetary reaction can lead to complete crowding out

Crowding out can occur when the Federal Reserve moves to offset the impact of fiscal expansions through monetary tightening. In step **1**, an increase in government spending on goods and services shifts upward the $C + I + G + X$ line to $C + I + G' + X$. The monetary reaction in step **2** raises interest rates and lowers interest-sensitive components, leading to $C + I'' + G' + X''$ and a new equilibrium at E'', which is identical to the initial equilibrium at E. In this case, investment and net exports have been 100 percent crowded out by government spending.

terest rates rise and reduce investment and net exports. Indeed, the reaction is so powerful that the new spending line is $C + I'' + G' + X''$, with a new equilibrium (E''), which is exactly at the old equilibrium (E).

What has happened? As the fiscal policy stimulated the economy, monetary policy tightened and interest rates rose; business cut back on capital projects, and the rising exchange rate on the dollar reduced exports and increased imports. In the end interest rates had to rise by enough to reduce investment and net exports by just the amount of the G increase. *Hence, in the polar case of a strong monetary response, investment is 100 percent crowded out by an increase in government spending.*

Investment Encouragement. At the other extreme is a situation where, in the short run, investment is actually *encouraged* (or "crowded in") by larger deficits. This point of view runs as follows: We have seen that high interest rates discourage investment. On the other hand, investment is boosted by higher GNP because businesses need to buy more plant and equipment as their current plant and equipment are more intensively used. This reasoning suggests that investment might actually increase if output is stimulated by fiscal policy when productive capacity is underutilized.

This case is illustrated in Figure 34-4. This diagram differs from our earlier analyses because the investment curve is drawn as *upward-sloping* rather than horizontal. The positive slope signifies that investment rises with higher GNP because of the capacity effect. In addition, we assume that there is no monetary effect, so there is no interest-rate impact of the kind shown in Figure 34-3. In this example, equilibrium occurs where the total spending line (the $C + I + G + X$ line) intersects the 45° line.

What is the effect of higher G in this case? As fiscal policy raises spending from G to G', the spending line shifts upward to the new aggregate spending line, and the equilibrium level of output increases from Q to Q'. But the higher level of output induces higher investment, and investment increases from I to I' in Figure 34-4, so the final equilibrium is shown by $C + I' + G' + X$. *Investment is encouraged and ends up higher than it was before the fiscal expansion.* We conclude that in an underemployed economy a fiscal expansion with accommodating monetary policy may actually raise investment.

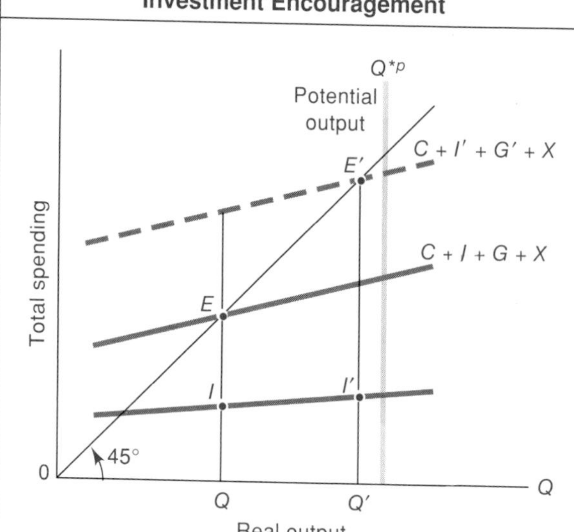

Figure 34-4. Investment may be encouraged if there are unemployed resources

Investment may be encouraged by higher deficits when there are unutilized resources and when investment responds to higher output. An increase in G shifts up the $C + I + G + X$ curve. Equilibrium output rises from Q to Q'. But because investment responds positively to the higher level of output, I increases as a result of the higher government spending.

Empirical Evidence

Such are the theories. Which of these extremes is closer to actual experience? History provides no clear-cut answer. During the 1960s, fiscal expansions appear to have encouraged investment, partly because there were ample unutilized resources and partly because the Federal Reserve allowed the economy to expand without raising interest rates.

The earlier pattern reversed during the 1980s as higher government deficits brought about a sharp monetary response, which led to a decline in net exports and private investment. The actual pattern of saving and investment for the 1980s is given in Table 34-3. The historical record shows two major conclusions. First, personal saving did not rise to offset the lower public saving; personal saving fell despite lower tax rates and higher post-tax real returns on saving.

Impact of Deficits on Saving and Investment, 1979–1986

Sector	1979	1986	Change
Gross saving (as % of GNP):			
Personal	4.7	2.9	−1.8
Business	13.1	13.9	0.8
Government			
Federal	−0.6	−4.9	−4.3
State and local	1.1	1.3	0.2
Gross investment (as % of GNP):			
Private investment			
Residential housing	5.5	5.1	−0.4
Business	12.6	10.6	−2.0
Net foreign investment (net exports)	0.1	−2.5	−2.6

Table 34-3. Increase in fiscal deficit produced surprising results

The increase in deficits of the 1980s provided a laboratory for different macroeconomic theories. From 1979 to 1986, the federal government deficits (or dissaving) increased from 0.6 percent to 4.9 percent of GNP. What was the impact upon private saving and investment? The public dissaving was, surprisingly, reinforced rather than offset by lower personal saving.

In terms of investment, a small part of the decline in total saving was reflected in residential housing; the share of business investment declined modestly. The largest part of the investment decline came in net foreign investment. (Source: U.S. Department of Commerce.)

The second and surprising result came when there was a sharp decline in net exports (or net foreign investment). The higher interest rates after 1979 led to an appreciation of the dollar, which in turn led to higher imports and lower exports and depressed real net exports from a surplus of $4 billion in 1979 to a deficit of $130 billion in 1986.[7]

What can we conclude about the extent of crowding out? The events of the last decade confirm the views of those who argue that monetary policy and financial-market reactions tend largely to offset or crowd out the impact of government spending. It is important to note, however, that the extent of the crowding out depends on the stance of the Federal Reserve; an aggressive anti-inflation Fed will produce more crowding out than a complacent and accommodative central bank. Because the link between deficits and investment is so complex—involving savings behavior, the foreign sector, financial markets, and monetary policy—it is difficult to predict which route crowding out will follow in the next fiscal expansion.

[7] We cannot say, however, that the increase in the federal deficit *caused* the changes in personal saving, business investment, and net foreign investment. To make that claim without showing the causal linkage would be to commit the *post hoc, ergo propter hoc* fallacy. While many analysts believe that the change in the federal deficit was the major force causing the changes shown in Table 34-3, other forces—such as the tight monetary policies of 1979–1982 and the debt crisis after 1982—also exerted important influences on saving and investment during this period.

Government Debt and Economic Growth

We turn now from the short-run impact of government deficits to the longer-run issue of how government debt affects economic growth. Will the high public debt lower future living standards for the average American? This question raises three specific issues: the difficulties of servicing a large external debt, the inefficiencies of levying taxes to pay interest on the debt, and the diminished economic growth that occurs when a large debt displaces capital accumulation.

External vs. Internal Debt

The first distinction to be made is between an internal and an external debt. An *internal debt* is owed by a nation to its own citizens. Many argue that an internal debt poses no burden because "we owe it all to ourselves." While this statement is oversimplified, it does represent a genuine insight. If every citizen owned $10,000 of government bonds and all were equally liable for the taxes to service that debt, it would not make sense to think of a heavy load of debt that each citizen must carry; the citizens simply owe the debt to themselves.

An *external debt* is owed by a nation to foreigners. This debt does involve a net subtraction from the resources available to people in the debtor nation. In the 1980s, many nations experienced severe economic hardships after they incurred large external debts. They were forced to export more than they imported—to run trade surpluses—in order to "service their external debts," that is, to pay the interest and principal on their past borrowings. In the late 1980s, countries like Brazil and Mexico needed to set aside one-fourth to one-third of export earnings to service their external debts. The debt-service burden on an external debt represents a reduction in the consumption possibilities of a nation.

In the late 1980s, the United States joined the list of debtor countries. Its large external deficit (large negative net exports) turned the United States from a creditor nation to a debtor nation. By 1990, the United States owed over $400 billion to foreigners. How will this affect the U.S. economy? The United States must eventually generate positive net exports, or run a trade surplus, to pay the interest on its foreign loans; it will need to export many billions of dollars more in aircraft, food, and other goods than it imports. The difficulties of making this adjustment will be studied in the final chapters of this text.

Efficiency Losses from Taxation

An internal debt requires payments of interest to bondholders, and taxes must be levied for this purpose. But even if the same people were taxed to pay the same amounts they receive in interest, there would still be the *distorting effects on incentives* that are inescapably present in the case of any taxes. Taxing Paula's interest income or wages to pay Paula interest would introduce microeconomic distortions. Paula might work less and save less; either of these outcomes must be reckoned a distortion of efficiency and well-being.

Displacement of Capital

Perhaps the most serious consequence of a large public debt is that it displaces capital from the nation's stock of wealth. As a result, the pace of economic growth slows and future living standards will decline.

What is the mechanism by which debt affects capital? Recall from our earlier discussion that people accumulate wealth for a variety of purposes such as retirement, education, and housing. People save by purchasing different assets, such as houses, stocks and bonds of corporations, savings accounts, and government bonds. We can separate the assets into two piles: (*a*) government debt and (*b*) assets that ultimately represent ownership of the stock of private capital and other durable goods. The effect of government debt is this:

As the government debt grows, people will accumulate government debt instead of private capital, and the nation's private capital stock will be displaced by public debt.

To illustrate this point, suppose that people desire to hold exactly 1000 units of wealth for retirement and other purposes. As the government debt increases, people's holdings of other assets will be reduced dollar for dollar. This occurs because as the government sells its bonds, other assets must be reduced since total desired wealth holdings are fixed. But these other assets ultimately represent the stock of private capital; stocks, bonds, and mortgages are the counterpart of factories, equipment, and houses. In this example, if the government debt goes up 100 units, we would see that people's holdings of capital and other private assets fall by 100 units. This is the case of 100 percent displacement (which is the long-run analog of 100 percent crowding out).

Full displacement is unlikely to hold in practice. In the discussion below, we will use supply-and-demand analysis to demonstrate that a higher government debt will produce higher interest rates and may stimulate higher levels of accumulation to accommodate part of the higher debt. In an open economy, the country may borrow abroad rather than reduce its domestic capital stock. The exact amount of displacement will depend on the conditions of production and on the savings behavior of domestic households and foreigners.

A Geometric Analysis.[8] The process by which the stock of capital is displaced in the long run is illustrated in Figure 34-5. In the left panel we show the supply and demand for capital as a function of the real interest rate or return on capital. As interest rates rise, firms demand less capital, while individuals may want to supply more. The equilibrium shown is for a capital stock of 4000 units with a real interest rate of 4 percent.

Now say that the government debt rises from 0 to 1000—because of war, recession, supply-side fiscal policies, or some other reason. We can analyze the impact of the increase in debt in the right-hand

[8] The balance of the discussion of displacement is somewhat more technical and can be omitted in short courses.

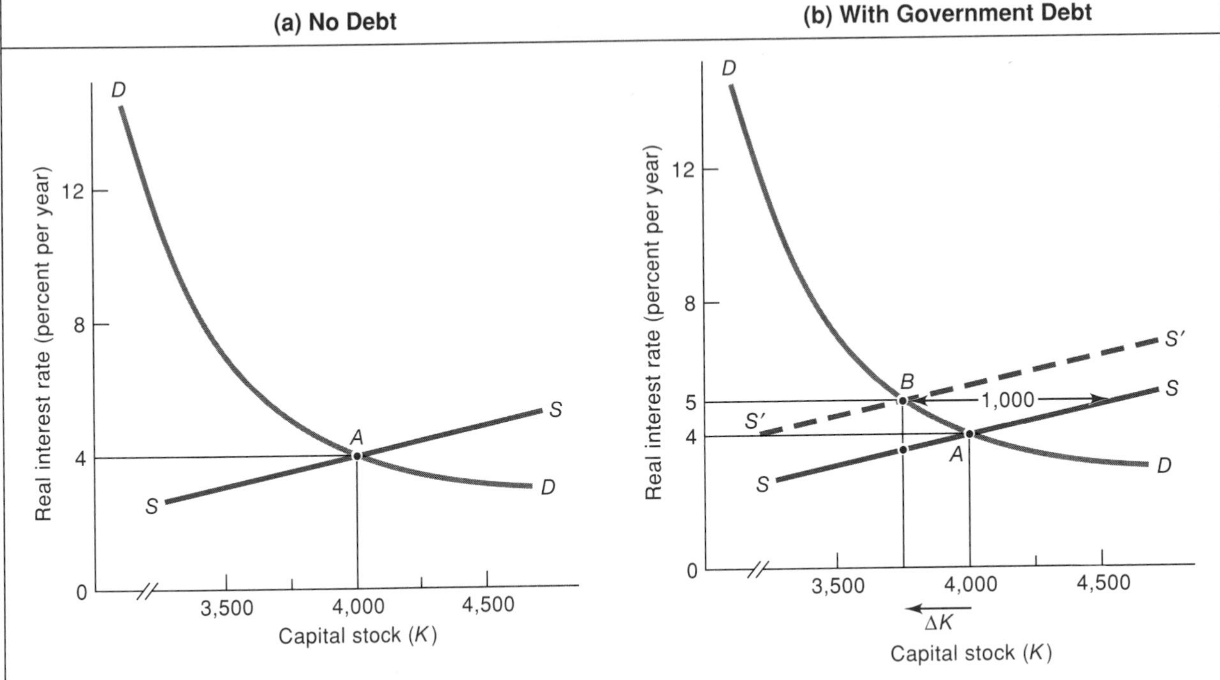

Figure 34-5. Government debt displaces private capital

Firms demand capital, while households supply capital by saving in private and public assets. The demand curve is the downward-sloping business demand for K, while the supply curve is the upward-sloping household supply of K.

Panel **(a)** shows the equilibrium without government debt. K is 4000 and the real interest rate is 4 percent.

Panel **(b)** shows the impact of 1000 units of government debt. The government debt will be sold off for what it will yield, so government securities are the bedrock of households' portfolios. Thus the curve showing the *net* supply of K shifts to the left by the 1000 units of the government debt. The new equilibrium arises northwest along the demand-for-K curve, moving from point A to point B. The interest rate is higher, firms are discouraged from holding K, and the capital stock falls.

In the long run, the 1000 units of government debt displace 250 units of society's capital stock, and output is therefore smaller. (These numbers are hypothetical for we do not know the extent to which public debt displaces private capital.)

diagram of Figure 34-5. This figure shows the 1000-unit increase in debt as a shift in the supply-of-capital (or *SS*) curve. As depicted, the households' supply-of-capital schedule shifts 1000 units to the left, to *S′S′*.

We represent an increase in government debt as a leftward shift in the households' supply-of-capital schedule. To see why, note that, because the *SS* curve represents the amount of capital that people willingly hold at each interest rate, the capital holdings are equal to the total wealth holdings minus the holdings of government debt. Since the amount of government debt (or assets other than capital) rises by 1000 and the government debt must be sold, the amount of private capital that people can buy after they own the 1000 units of government debt is 1000 less than total wealth at each interest rate. Therefore, if *SS* represents the total wealth held by people, *S′S′* (equal to *SS* less 1000) represents the total amount of capital held by people. In short, after 1000 units of government debt are sold, the new supply-of-capital schedule is *S′S′*.[9]

What is the net impact of a 1000-unit increase in government debt? As the supply of capital dries up—with national saving going into government

[9] An argument by Robert Barro of Harvard suggests that because of future taxes, government bonds may not be net wealth for the nation. For every dollar of government bonds there is an equal present value of taxes for which taxpayers are liable now or in the future. If people are very farsighted and take their heirs' well-being into account, then they may reduce their consumption by just the present value of taxes—completely offsetting the wealth effect of the bonds. In such a case, there will be no shift in the supply curve of Fig. 34-5(b).

bonds rather than into housing or into companies' stocks and bonds—the market equilibrium moves northwest along the demand-for-*K* curve. Interest rates rise. Firms slow their purchases of new factories, trucks, and computers.

In the new long-run equilibrium, the capital stock falls from 4000 to 3750. Thus, in this example, 1000 units of government debt have displaced 250 units of private capital. Such a reduction has significant economic effects, of course. With less capital, potential output, wages, and the nation's income are lower than they would otherwise be.

The diagram shown in Figure 34-5 is purely hypothetical. How large is the displacement effect in reality? Does the $2484 billion of government debt at the beginning of fiscal 1992 displace $2484 billion of capital? Or $1000 billion? Or none? And what fraction of the additional government debt will be held by foreigners?

In fact, there are no accurate estimates of the displacement effect. Looking at historical trends, particularly in the United States since World War II, the best evidence suggests that capital is partially displaced by government debt. It is clear, however, that the possibility of capital displacement is extraordinarily important for the United States as the debt continues to climb in the next few years.

Debt and Growth

If we consider all the effects of government debt on the economy, we see that a large public debt can be detrimental to long-run economic growth. Figure 34-6 illustrates this connection. Say that an economy were to operate over time with no debt. According to the principles of economic growth outlined in Chapter 30, the capital stock and potential output would follow the hypothetical path indicated by the solid lines in Figure 34-6.

Next consider policies that incur a large government deficit and debt. As the debt accumulates over time, more and more capital is displaced, as shown by the dashed capital line in the bottom of Figure 34-6. As taxes are raised to pay interest on the debt, inefficiencies further lower output. Also, an increase in external debt lowers national income and raises the fraction of national output that has to be set aside for servicing the external debt. Taking all the effects together, output and consumption will grow more slowly than they would had there been no large government debt and deficit, as is shown by comparing the top lines in Figure 34-6.

This is the major point about the long-run impact of a large government debt on economic growth:

A large government debt tends to reduce a nation's growth in potential output because it displaces private capital, increases the inefficiency from taxation, and forces a nation to service the external portion of the debt.

A New Discipline?

We have seen that modern macroeconomics has destroyed the shibboleth of the balanced budget. But this does not mean that government can go wild and let legislators' pet projects gobble up an ever-increasing portion of the national pie. Resources are limited, so some new discipline must replace the budget-balancing maxim.

Many people, particularly conservatives, believe that Congress lacks the self-control to prevent the continued growth of transfer programs and public

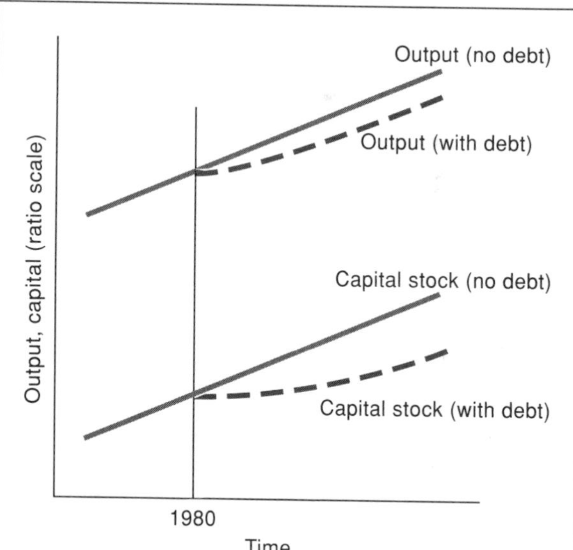

Figure 34-6. Impact of government debt on economic growth

Solid lines show the path of capital and output if the government balances its books and has no debt.

A more realistic case occurs when the government incurs a large debt. As private capital is displaced by public debt, the nation's capital stock stagnates, and the nation must pay interest on foreign holdings of its external debt. The dashed lines illustrate the impact on capital and output of the higher government debt.

works. Fiscal conservatives called for a constitutional amendment to balance the budget and contain the growth in federal spending. A dramatic turn came when Congress passed the *Gramm-Rudman Act,* which mandated a decline in the budget deficit. This bill required Congress to reduce the deficit to no more than a specified dollar amount each year and targeted a balanced budget by 1991. If Congress was unable to meet the quantitative Gramm-Rudman target, expenditures would be automatically cut across the board.

The Gramm-Rudman bill went into effect in late 1985 but the ambitious targets were not met. Congress responded by amending the bill in 1987, and in 1990 replaced the deficit targets with spending limitations in different parts of the budget. Under the 1990 amendments, Congress must find the revenues to pay for new spending programs or tax cuts; otherwise, automatic spending cuts will be imposed to offset the increased deficit.[10]

What has been the impact of the Gramm-Rudman approach? It does provide a kind of "budget constraint" on the federal government. Moreover, the process has imposed a new budgetary discipline, albeit a somewhat imperfect one, on the federal budget. While the budget is not balanced, the ratio of the federal deficit to GNP has declined. Moreover, new programs cannot be introduced without budgeting new taxes or spending cuts. But any rule legislated by Congress can be changed by Congress, so the future of this self-imposed discipline is uncertain.

Valediction

As we end our discussion of the government debt and its impact on economic growth, we should pause to reflect upon the fiscal difficulties faced by the United States. Those who study economics or make economic policies in the 1990s will confront the need to service a large external debt and the possibility of sluggish economic growth. But in the midst of today's tempest, keep in mind the observations on growth and debt of the English historian Lord Macaulay, written more than a century ago:

> At every stage in the growth of that debt, the nation has set up the same cry of anguish and despair. At every stage in the growth of that debt, it has been seriously asserted by wise men that bankruptcy and ruin were at hand. Yet still the debt went on growing; and still bankruptcy and ruin were as remote as ever. . . .
>
> The prophets of evil were under a double delusion. They erroneously imagined that there was an exact analogy between the case of an individual who is in debt to another individual and the case of a society which is in debt to a part of itself. . . . They made no allowance for the effect produced by the incessant progress of every experimental science, and by the incessant efforts of every man to get on in life. They saw that the debt grew; and they forgot that other things grew as well.

What can Macaulay teach us for the 1990s? We can hardly doubt that high fiscal deficits are producing an unprecedented growth in peacetime debt in the United States. Because much of the debt is flowing abroad to finance a large trade deficit, the nation will face rising interest payments, debt burdens, and taxes to service the debt. At some point, the trade deficit will have to turn to a surplus as we export our future production to pay for current consumption. It is possible that the transition from today's low-saving economy to a high-saving economy may be accompanied by reductions in living standards for consumers.

But it would be unwise to forecast economic collapse. The specter of national bankruptcy or financial ruin is remote for the United States in the 1990s.

[10] The budget procedures appear in the 1990 Omnibus Budget Reconciliation Act. A description of new procedures along with an analysis in terms of modern public finance theory is contained in the *Economic Report of the President,* 1991.

SUMMARY

A. Budgets and Fiscal Policy

1. Budgets are systems used by governments and organizations to indicate planned expenditures and revenues for a given year. Budgets are in surplus or deficit depending on whether the government has revenues greater or less than its expenditures.

2. Fiscal policy refers to taxation and expenditure policies. In this connection, the modern economy is blessed with important "built-in stabilizers." Requiring no discretionary action, tax receipts change automatically when income changes, reducing the multiplier and offsetting part of any disturbance. The same stabilizing effect is produced by unemployment compensation and other welfare transfers that grow automatically as income falls.
3. Automatic stabilizers never fully offset the instabilities of an economy. They reduce the multiplier, but do not make it zero. Scope is left for discretionary programs. Discretionary policies include public works, jobs programs, and various tax programs. Public works involve such long time lags in getting under way as to make their use for combating short recessions impractical. Discretionary variations in tax rates offer greater short-run flexibility but suffer from severe political complications in the United States. Most macroeconomists believe that monetary policy is more useful than fiscal policy for combating the short-term fluctuations of the business cycle.
4. When people began to drop the notion that the government's budget had to be balanced in every year or month, they first thought it would be in balance over the business cycle—with boom-time surpluses matching depression deficits. Today, we realize that only by coincidence would the surpluses in prosperous years just balance deficits in recession years.
5. To get a better measure of changes in discretionary fiscal policy, economists supplement knowledge of the budget by separating the actual budget into its structural and cyclical components. The structural budget calculates how much the government would collect and spend if the economy were operating at potential output. The cyclical budget accounts for the impact of the business cycle on tax revenues, expenditures, and the deficit. To assess the impact of fiscal policy on the economy, we should pay close attention to the structural deficit; changes in the cyclical deficit are a result of changes in the economy rather than a cause of changes in the economy.

B. The Economic Consequences of the Deficit

6. The government debt represents the accumulated borrowings from the public. It is the sum of past deficits. A useful measure of the size of the debt is the debt-GNP ratio, which for the United States has tended to rise during wartime and fall during peacetime. The decade of the 1980s was an exception, for the debt-GNP ratio rose sharply during this period.
7. In analyzing fiscal impacts, it is useful to separate the short-run and long-run effects of deficits and debts. For the short run, a pervasive concern has been that government deficits crowd out investment. This statement makes sense only for policies that raise the structural deficit.
8. The extent to which active fiscal policy will crowd out investment also depends upon financial markets, the determinants of investment, and how deficits are financed. Investment is likely to be largely crowded out when the central bank and financial markets react to higher output with tight money. In this case, investment and other interest-sensitive sectors may decline by the entire increase in government spending.

9. Active fiscal policy, if introduced during deep recessions with accommodative monetary policies, may instead encourage investment. An increase in investment occurs when output rises and businesses are induced to spend on plant and equipment because capacity utilization increases. This encouragement effect can outweigh interest-rate, crowding-out effects until the system begins to approach high employment.
10. There is mixed evidence on the extent of crowding out. Evidence from the high-deficit era of the 1980s points to a complex set of reactions to deficits, including lower domestic and foreign investment. In other periods, crowding out appears to have been minimal. The best bet today is that, outside of deep recessions, investment will be significantly crowded out by government spending.
11. The public debt need not burden the shoulders of a nation as if its citizens were forced to carry rocks on their backs. To the degree that we borrow from abroad for consumption and pledge posterity to pay back the interest and principal on such external debt, our descendants will indeed find themselves sacrificing consumption to service this debt.
12. To the degree that we leave future generations an internal debt but no change in capital stock, there are various internal effects. The process of taxing Peter to pay Paula, or taxing Paula to pay Paula, can involve various distortions of production and efficiency but should not be confused with owing money to another country.
13. In addition, economic growth may slow if the public debt displaces capital in people's portfolios. This syndrome occurs because firms' bonds and common stocks are good substitutes for government bonds. Hence, an increase in government debt may reduce the economy's capital stock.
14. In the long run, a larger government debt may slow the growth of potential output and consumption because of the costs of servicing an external debt, the inefficiencies that arise from taxing to pay the interest on the debt, and the diminished capital accumulation that comes from capital displacement.

CONCEPTS FOR REVIEW

Budgets and fiscal policy
government budget
budget deficit, surplus, and balance
discretionary policies vs. automatic stabilizers
automatic stabilization and the reduced multiplier
tools of discretionary policy
budget: actual, structural, cyclical

Economics of debt and deficits
relation of debt to past deficits
ratios of debt to GNP over space and time
short-run impact: crowding out vs. investment encouragement
long-run impacts on economic:
growth
internal vs. external debt
distortions from taxation
displacement of capital
Gramm-Rudman Act

QUESTIONS FOR DISCUSSION

1. Define automatic and discretionary stabilizers. What would be your preferred discretionary stabilizer for fighting inflation? For fighting recessions? Which discretionary stabilizers seem least useful? Why?
2. Recall the definitions of structural and cyclical deficits. For each of the following, analyze the effects on

the actual, structural, and cyclical deficits:
(a) A permanent tax cut
(b) A sharp decrease in private investment
(c) A tightening of monetary policy
(d) An increase in exports
(e) An increase in welfare benefit levels

3. In year 0, GNP is 1000, taxes are 200, and government spending is 250. Output is equal to potential output. In year 1, the government increases G to 270. If revenues are "lump-sum" taxes that are unaffected by changes in income, and if the expenditure multiplier is 2, what is the impact of the fiscal expansion upon the structural and cyclical budgets? How would your answer change if tax revenues rise 20 cents for every dollar increase in GNP?
4. J. M. Keynes wrote, "If the Treasury were to fill old bottles with banknotes, bury them in disused coal mines, and leave it to private enterprise to dig the notes up again, there need be no more unemployment and the real income of the community would probably become a good deal greater than it actually is." (*The General Theory*, p. 129, edited from the original). Explain why Keynes' analysis of the utility of a discretionary public-works program might be correct during a depression. How could well-designed fiscal or monetary policies have the same macroeconomic impacts while producing a larger quantity of useful goods and services?
5. Is it possible that government *promises* might have a displacement effect along with government debt? Thus, if the government were to promise large future social security benefits to workers, would workers feel richer? Might they reduce saving as a result? Could the capital stock end up smaller? Illustrate using Figure 34-5.
6. Trace the impact upon the government debt, the nation's capital stock, and real output of a government program that borrows abroad and spends the money on the following:
   (a) Capital to drill for oil, which is exported (as did Mexico in the 1970s)
   (b) Grain to feed its population (as did the Soviet Union in the early 1990s)
7. Professor Robert Eisner of Northwestern University wrote: "Significant cuts in our budget deficits, whether by slashing expenditures or raising taxes, pose a serious danger. They will hold down consumption, but in the process they are likely to drag down investments and along with them GNP, employment, and profits." Analyze the reasoning behind this statement in terms of the crowding-out debate. What do the lessons of history suggest about Eisner's contention?
8. Construct a graph like that in Figure 34-6 showing the path of consumption and net exports with and without a large government debt.
9. **Advanced problem:** Figure 34-7 shows a recent estimate of the accumulation of assets by the social security trust fund (which is, in effect, the opposite of government debt) over the next seven decades, as a percent of GNP. Assuming that the rest of the budget is balanced after 1995, what would be the impact of the buildup of the trust fund on the capital stock and national output:
   (a) Assuming that the trust fund retires government debt
   (b) Assuming that the Barro hypothesis (in footnote 9, page 634) is correct
   (c) Assuming that people change their private pension contributions to offset payments to social security on a dollar-for-dollar basis

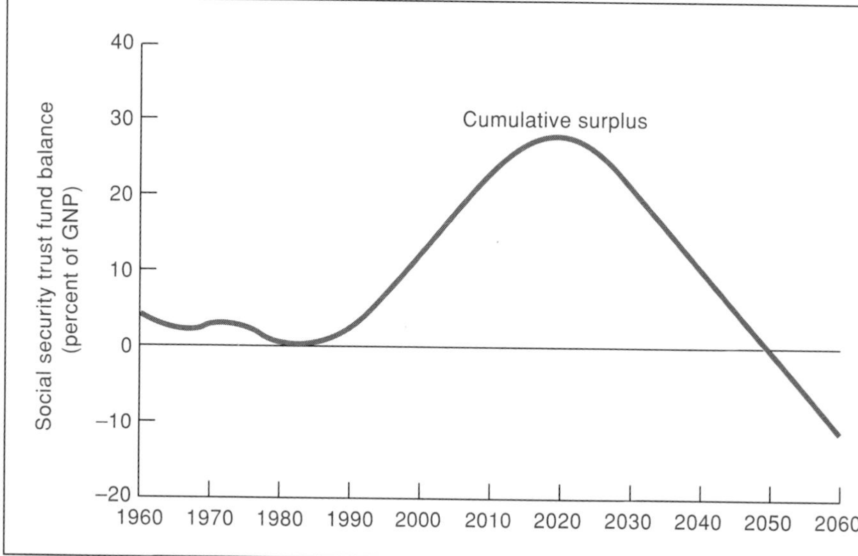

Figure 34-7. Estimated accumulation of assets in social security trust fund
Estimates show the extent to which cumulative social security taxes plus interest on balances exceed cumulative benefits. What will be the effect on the capital stock and national output? [Source: Henry Aaron, Barry Bosworth, and Gary Burtless, *OASDI Trust Fund Policy, National Saving, and the Economy* (Brookings, Washington, D.C., 1988).]

C H A P T E R 35

ISSUES IN ECONOMIC STABILIZATION

> Money is the centre around which economic science clusters; that is so, not because money or material wealth is regarded as the main aim of human effort, but because in this world of ours it is the one convenient means of measuring human motive on a large scale.
>
> Alfred Marshall, *Principles of Economics,* 8th edition (1912)

We have seen how governments must constantly battle against unemployment and inflation in their attempts to foster economic growth and provide good jobs and a decent living standard for their citizens. But economists are divided on the best way to stabilize the economy. Some believe that governments should take an active role, while others hold that a government operating with fixed rules rather than discretion will produce superior economic performance. In this final chapter, we deploy all our tools to explore today's macroeconomic controversies.

A. Velocity and Monetarism

> Inflation is always and everywhere a monetary phenomenon in the sense that it is and can be produced only by a more rapid increase in the quantity of money than in output.
>
> Milton Friedman, *The New Palgrave Dictionary of Economics* (1987)

Money cannot manage itself. Central bankers must decide on the supply of money and the degree of tightness of money and credit. Today, there are many different philosophies about the best way to manage monetary affairs. Some believe in an active policy that "leans against the wind" by slowing money growth when inflation threatens, and vice versa. Others are skeptical about the ability of policymakers to use monetary policy to "fine-tune" the economy. At the far end of the spectrum are the monetarists, who believe that discretionary monetary policy should be replaced by a fixed rule.

The Roots of Monetarism

Monetarism holds that the money supply is the major determinant of short-run movements in nominal GNP and of long-run movements in prices. Of course, Keynesian macroeconomics also emphasizes the role of money in determining aggregate demand. The main difference between monetarists and others lies in their approaches to the determination of aggregate demand. While Keynesian theories hold that many different forces affect aggregate demand, monetarists argue that changes in the money supply are the primary factor that determines output and price movements.

In order to understand monetarism, we need to introduce a new concept—the *velocity of money*—and describe a new relationship—the *quantity theory of prices.*

The Velocity of Money

Sometimes money turns over very slowly; it sits in cookie jars or in bank accounts for long periods between transactions. At other times, particularly during rapid inflation, people get rid of money quickly and money circulates rapidly from hand to hand. The speed of turnover of money is described by the concept of the velocity of money, introduced at the turn of this century by Cambridge University's Alfred Marshall and Yale's Irving Fisher. It measures the speed at which money is changing hands or circulating through the economy. When the quantity of money is large relative to the flow of expenditures, the velocity of circulation is low; when money turns over rapidly, money's velocity is high.

More precisely, we define the **income velocity of money** as the ratio of total nominal GNP to the stock of money. Velocity measures the rate at which the stock of money turns over relative to the total income or output of a nation. Formally:[1]

$$V \equiv \frac{\text{GNP}}{M} \equiv \frac{p_1q_1 + p_2q_2 + \cdots}{M} \equiv \frac{PQ}{M}$$

Here P stands for the average price level and Q stands for real GNP. Velocity (V) is defined as the amount of nominal GNP each year divided by the money stock.

We can think of the income velocity of money intuitively as the speed at which money changes hands in the economy. As a simple example, assume that the economy produces only bread, and GNP consists of 48 million loaves of bread each selling at a price of \$1, so GNP $= PQ =$ \$48 million per year. If the money supply is \$4 million, then by definition $V =$ \$48/\$4 $= 12$. This means that money turns over once a month as earnings are used to buy monthly bread.[2]

Figure 35-1 shows the recent history of the income velocity of transactions money (M_1). Note that nominal GNP has been rising faster than the money supply over the last four decades. We can thus conclude that the income velocity of money has been rising over time. The question of the stability and predictability of the velocity of money is central to macroeconomic policy.

The Quantity Theory of Prices

Having defined an interesting new variable called velocity, we now describe how some economists use the concept of velocity to explain movements in the overall price level. The key assumption here is that *the velocity of money is relatively stable and predictable.* The reason for stability, according to monetary economists, is that velocity mainly reflects underlying patterns in the timing of income and spending. If people get paid once a month and tend to spend all their incomes evenly over the course of the month, income velocity will be 12 per year. Incomes could double, prices might rise 20 percent, and total GNP may be up many times—yet with unchanged spending patterns the income velocity of money would remain unchanged. Only as people or businesses modify their asset holdings or the way they pay their bills does the velocity of income change.

On the basis of this insight about the relative stability of velocity, some early writers, particularly the classical economists, used velocity to explain changes in the price level. This approach, called the **quantity theory of prices,** rewrites the definition of velocity as follows:

[1] The definitional equations have been written with the three-bar identity symbol rather than with the more common two-bar equality symbol. This usage emphasizes that they are "identities"—statements which tell us nothing about reality but which hold true by definition even if the United States experienced a hyperinflation or were in a deep depression.

[2] The velocity of money is closely related to the demand for money. If we rewrite the velocity equation, we have $M/PQ \equiv 1/V$. The left-hand side is the demand for money per unit of GNP. Our earlier discussion of money demand applies equally well to an analysis of velocity.

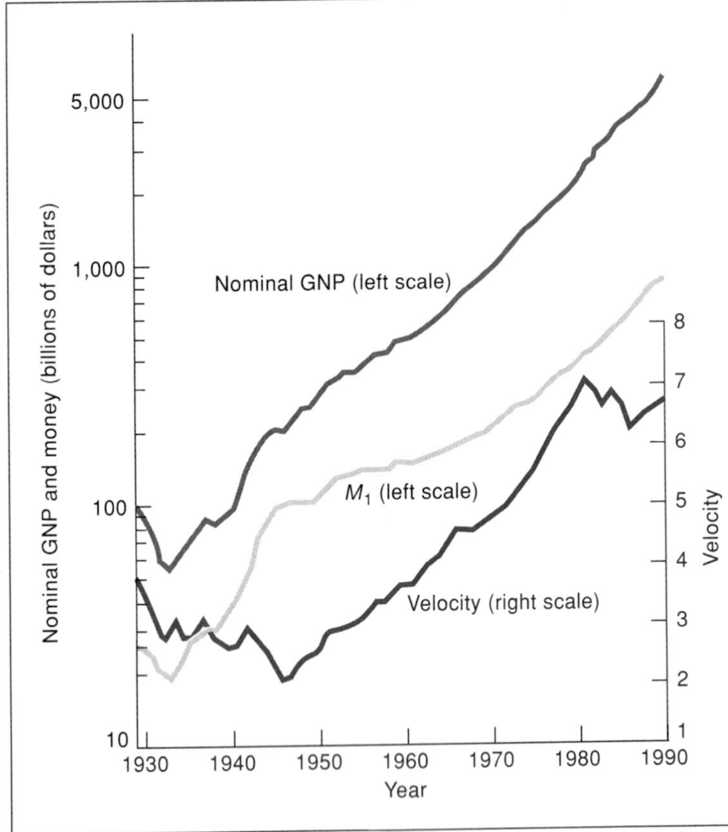

Figure 35-1. Velocity and its components, 1929–1990

Income velocity for transactions money is the ratio of nominal GNP to M_1. Over the period since 1929, money has grown 32-fold while nominal GNP has grown 53-fold.

One of the tenets of monetarism is that V is relatively stable and predictable. How stable does V appear? Can you think of some reasons why V has grown over time? *Hint*: Think of the determinants of the demand for money. (Source: V constructed by the authors from data of the Federal Reserve Board and the Department of Commerce.)

$$P \equiv \frac{MV}{Q} \equiv \left(\frac{V}{Q}\right)M \equiv kM$$

This equation is obtained from the earlier definition of velocity by substituting the variable k as a shorthand for V/Q. We write the equation this way because many classical economists believed that, if transactions patterns were stable, k would be constant. In addition, they generally assumed full employment, which meant real output would grow smoothly and would equal potential GNP. Putting these two assumptions together, k $(= V/Q)$ would be near-constant in the short run and a smoothly growing trend in the long run.

What are the implications of the quantity theory? As we can see from the equation, if k were constant, the price level would then move proportionally with the supply of money. A stable money supply would produce stable prices; if the money supply grew rapidly, so would prices. Similarly, if the money supply was multiplied by 10 or 100, the economy would experience galloping inflation or hyperinflation. Indeed, the most vivid demonstrations of the quantity theory of prices can be seen in hyperinflations. Turning back to Figure 32-5, page 593, note how prices rose a billionfold in Weimar Germany after the central bank unleashed the monetary printing presses.

This is the quantity theory with a vengeance. It can also usefully be applied to countries like Poland and the Soviet Union which are moving toward a market system. By applying the quantity theory, we can make a rough estimate of the impact of price decontrols on the price level.

To understand the quantity theory of prices, it is essential to recall that money differs fundamentally from ordinary goods like bread or cars. We want bread to eat and cars to drive. But we want money only for the work it does in buying us bread or cars. If prices in Brazil today are 50 times what they were a decade ago, then it is natural that people will need about 50 times as much money to buy things as they did 10 years ago. Here lies the core of the quantity theory of money: the demand for money rises proportionally with the price level.

The quantity theory of prices holds that prices move proportionally with the supply of money. Although the quantity theory of prices is only a rough approximation, it does help explain why countries with low money growth have moderate inflation while others with rapid money growth find their prices galloping along.

Modern Monetarism

Modern monetary economics was developed after World War II by Chicago's Milton Friedman and his numerous colleagues and followers. Under Friedman's leadership, monetarists challenged the Keynesian approach to macroeconomics and emphasized the importance of monetary policy in macroeconomic stabilization. About two decades ago, the monetarist approach branched. One fork continued the older tradition that we will now describe. The younger offshoot became the influential rational-expectations school that is analyzed later in this chapter.

The monetarist approach postulates that the growth of money determines nominal GNP in the short run and prices in the long run. This analysis operates in the framework of the quantity theory of prices and relies on the analysis of trends in velocity. Monetarists argue that the velocity of money is relatively stable (or in extreme cases constant). If correct, this is an important insight, for the quantity equation shows that, if V is constant, then movements in M will affect PQ (or nominal GNP) proportionally.

The Essence of Monetarism

Like all serious schools of thought, monetarism has differing emphases and degrees. The following points are central to monetarist thinking:

1. *Money-supply growth is the prime systematic determinant of nominal GNP growth.* Monetarism, like Keynesian multiplier theory, is basically a theory of the determinants of aggregate demand. It holds that nominal aggregate demand is affected primarily by changes in the money supply. Fiscal policy is important for some things (like the fraction of GNP devoted to defense or private consumption), but the major macroeconomic variables (aggregate output, employment, and prices) are affected mainly by money. This was put neatly in the following oversimplified way: "Only money matters."

   What is the basis for monetarist belief in the primacy of money? It is based on two central propositions. First, as Friedman has stated, "There is an extraordinary empirical stability and regularity to such magnitudes as income velocity that cannot but impress anyone who works extensively with monetary data." Second, many monetarists used to argue that the demand for money is completely insensitive to interest rates.[3]

   Why do these two assumptions lead to the monetarist view? From the quantity equation of exchange, if velocity V is stable, then M will determine $PQ \equiv$ nominal GNP. Similarly, fiscal policy is irrelevant according to the monetarists because, if V is stable, the only force that can affect PQ is M. With constant V, there is simply no door by which taxes or government expenditures can enter the stage.
2. *Prices and wages are relatively flexible.* Recall that one of the precepts of Keynesian economics is that prices and wages are "sticky." While generally accepting the view that there is *some* inertia in wage-price setting, monetarists argue that the Phillips curve is relatively steep even in the short run and insist that the long-run Phillips curve is vertical. In the *AS-AD* framework, monetarists hold that the short-run *AS* curve is quite steep.

The monetarists put points 1 and 2 together. Because (1) money is the prime determinant of nominal GNP and (2) prices and wages are fairly flexible around potential output, this implies that money moves real output only modestly and for a short time. M mainly affects P.

Accordingly, money can affect both output and prices in the short run. But in the long run, because the economy tends to operate near full employment, money's main impact is on the price level. Fiscal policy affects output and prices negligibly in both the short run and the long run. This is the essence of monetarist doctrine.

[3] The proposition that the demand for money is insensitive to the interest rate has been discredited and has generally fallen out of favor in recent years.

3. *The private sector is stable.* Finally, monetarists believe that the private economy is relatively stable. Since V is stable, most fluctuations in nominal GNP result from changes in the money supply—and the money supply, in turn, depends on actions of the central bank.

Comparison with Modern Keynesian Macroeconomics

How do monetarist views compare with modern Keynesian approaches? In fact, there has been considerable convergence in views between the two schools over the last two decades, and the disputes today are ones of emphasis rather than of fundamental beliefs.

We depict the major differences between monetarists and modern Keynesians in Figure 35-2. This figure shows both views in terms of the behavior of aggregate supply and demand. Two major differences stand out.

First, the two schools disagree about the forces that operate on aggregate demand. Monetarists believe that aggregate demand is affected only (or primarily) by the money supply and that the impact of money on aggregate demand is stable and reliable. They also believe that fiscal policy or autonomous changes in spending, unless accompanied by monetary changes, will have negligible effects upon output and prices.[4]

Keynesian economists, by contrast, hold that the world is more complex. While agreeing that money

[4] Note as well that the *AD* curve is drawn as a "rectangular hyperbola" for the monetarist assumptions. Recall that an equation $xy = constant$ describes a rectangular hyperbola in a graph of x and y. For given M and V, the aggregate demand curve is described by $PQ = constant$, so the *AD* curve is a rectangular hyerbola.

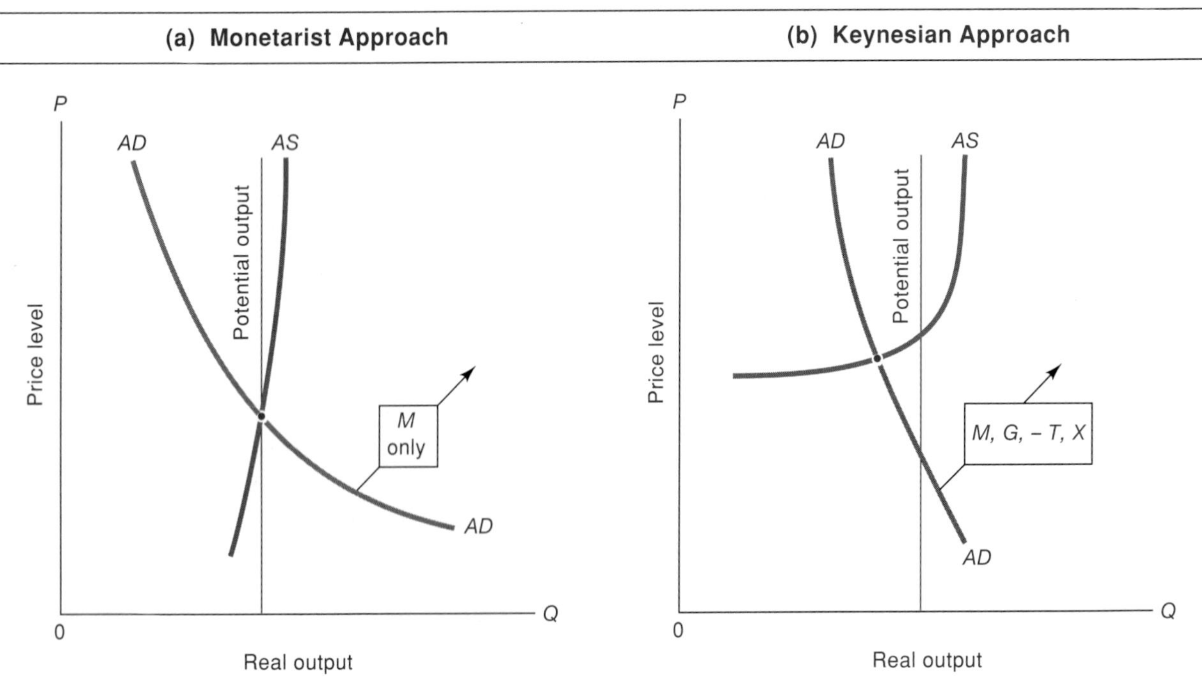

Figure 35-2. Comparison of monetarist and Keynesian views

What are the differences between monetarist and Keynesian macroeconomics? Monetarists emphasize the primacy of the money supply in determining aggregate demand. This is seen by the box, next to the *AD* curve, that contains only *M*. Eclectic Keynesians believe a wide variety of variables, including money, affect the economy. To simplify, monetarists say, "Only money matters." Mainstream macroeconomists say, "Money matters, but so does fiscal policy."

The second difference revolves around aggregate supply, where Keynesian economists stress that the *AS* curve is relatively horizontal in the short run for low GNP, while monetarists hold that prices and wages are relatively flexible, so that the short-run *AS* curve is near-vertical. For monetarists, *AD* changes mainly affect prices; for mainstream economists, *AD* changes affect both prices and output, at least in the short run.

has an important effect upon aggregate demand, output, and prices, they argue that other factors also matter. In other words, Keynesian economists hold that money enters into output determination *along with* spending variables like fiscal policy and net exports.

The second major difference between monetarists and Keynesian economists concerns the behavior of aggregate supply. Keynesian economists emphasize the inertia in prices and wages. Monetarists think that Keynesian economists exaggerate the economy's wage-price stickiness and believe that the short-run *AS* curve is quite steep—not vertical, perhaps, but much steeper than a Keynesian economist would allow.

Because they hold differing views about the slope of the *AS* curve, Keynesian economists and monetarists disagree on the short-run impact of changes in aggregate demand. Keynesian economists believe that a change in (nominal) demand will significantly change output with little effect on prices in the short run. Monetarists hold that a shift in demand will primarily end up changing prices rather than quantities.

In sum, the essence of monetarism in macroeconomic thinking centers on the importance of money in determining aggregate demand and on the relative flexibility of wages and prices.

The Monetarist Platform: Constant Money Growth

Over the last two decades, monetarism has played a significant role in shaping economic policy. Monetarist economists often espouse free markets and laissez-faire microeconomic policies. But the foremost contribution to macroeconomic policy has been their advocacy of fixed monetary rules in preference to discretionary fiscal and monetary policies.

In principle, a monetarist might recommend using monetary policy to fine-tune the economy. But monetarists have taken a different tack, arguing that the private economy is stable and that the government tends to destabilize the economy. Moreover, monetarists believe that money affects output only after long and variable lags, so the design of effective stabilization policies is a formidable task.

Thus a cardinal part of the monetarist economic philosophy is a **monetary rule:** Optimal monetary policy sets the growth of the money supply at a fixed rate and holds to that rate through all economic conditions.

What is the rationale for this view? Monetarists believe that a fixed growth rate of money (at 3 to 5 percent annually) would eliminate the source of instability in a modern economy—the capricious and unreliable shifts of monetary policy. If we replaced the Federal Reserve with a computer program that always produces a fixed *M* growth rate, there would be no bursts in *M* growth. With stable velocity, money GNP would grow at a stable rate. And if *M* grew at about the growth rate of potential GNP, the economy would soon attain price stability.

The Monetarist Experiment

Monetarist views gained widespread influence in the late 1970s. In the United States, many thought that Keynesian stabilization policies had failed to contain inflation. When inflation moved up into the double-digit range in 1979, many economists and policymakers believed that monetary policy was the only hope for an effective anti-inflation policy.

In October 1979, the new Chairman of the Federal Reserve, Paul Volcker, launched a fierce counterattack against inflation in what has been called a *monetarist experiment.* In a dramatic change of its operating procedures, the Fed decided to stop smoothing interest rates and instead focused on keeping bank reserves and the money supply on predetermined growth paths.

The Fed hoped that a strict quantitative approach to monetary management would accomplish two things. First, it would allow interest rates to rise sharply enough to brake the rapidly growing economy, raising unemployment and slowing wage and price growth through the Phillips-curve mechanism. In addition, some believed that a tough and credible monetary policy would deflate inflationary expectations, particularly in labor contracts, and demonstrate that the high-inflation period was over. Once people's expectations were deflated, the economy could experience a relatively painless reduction in the underlying rate of inflation.

The monetarist experiment was largely successful in reducing inflation. As a result of the high interest rates induced by slow money growth, interest-sensitive spending slowed. Consequently, real GNP stagnated from 1979 to 1982, and the unemployment rate rose from under 6 percent to a peak of $10\frac{1}{2}$ percent in late 1982. Inflation fell sharply. Any lingering doubts about the effectiveness of monetary policy were stilled. Money works.

But what of the monetarist claim that a tough and credible monetary policy was a low-cost anti-inflation strategy? Numerous economic studies of this question over the last decade suggest that the tough monetarist policy did not change the tradeoff between inflation and unemployment (recall the analysis of the "credibility view" in Chapter 33). In terms of unemployment and output losses, the economic sacrifices of the monetarist disinflation policy were about as large, per point of disinflation, as those of anti-inflation policies in earlier periods. Money works, but it does not work miracles.

One of the paradoxes of this period lay in the behavior of velocity. Recall that monetarists hold that velocity is relatively stable and predictable. Given stable velocity, changes in the money supply would get smoothly translated into changes in nominal GNP. But just as the monetarist doctrine was adopted, velocity became extremely unstable. Indeed, M_1 velocity changed more in 1982 than it had in several decades (see Figure 35-1). Some believe that the instability in velocity was actually produced by the heavy reliance placed upon monetary policy during this period.

B. Rational Expectations in Macroeconomics

Although most macroeconomists believe that systematic economic policy can affect unemployment and output, at least in the short run, a radical new approach departs from the standard approach. This theory, called "rational-expectations" (RE) macroeconomics, or the new classical economics, was developed by Robert Lucas (Chicago), Thomas Sargent (Stanford), Neil Wallace (Minnesota), and Robert Barro (Harvard). These researchers emphasize the role of expectations and flexible wages and prices in macroeconomics.

The Rational-Expectations Postulates

Rational-expectations macroeconomics closely resembles the classical approach to macroeconomics. It holds that (1) people use all available information and (2) prices and wages are flexible. These two postulates are the essence of the rational-expectations revolution.

The first hypothesis holds that people form their expectations on the basis of the best available information. Under this assumption, the government cannot "fool" the people, for people are well informed and have access to the same information as the government.

The second hypothesis states that prices and wages are flexible; this familiar assumption simply means that prices and wages adjust rapidly to balance supply and demand.

Together, these two postulates lead to striking results, but first we will explore the significance of each assumption.

Rational Expectations

Expectations are important in economic life. They influence how much investors will spend on investment goods and whether consumers spend or save for the future. But what is a sensible way to treat expectations in economics? The rational-expectations theorists answer this question with the **rational-expectations hypothesis.** According to rational expectations, forecasts are unbiased and are based on all available information.

To begin with, the rational-expectations hypothesis holds that people make unbiased forecasts.[5] It goes further by assuming that people use all available information and economic theory. This implies that people understand how the economy works and what the government is doing. Thus, say that the Fed always cuts its M targets when infla-

[5] A forecast is "unbiased" if it contains no systematic forecasting errors. Clearly a forecast cannot always be perfectly accurate—you cannot foresee how a coin flip will come up on a single toss. But you should not commit the statistical sin of *bias* by predicting that a fair coin would come up tails 90 percent of the time. By contrast, predicting that 50 percent of tosses come up tails would be an *unbiased* forecast.

tion reaches 10 percent, or that Congress always cuts taxes in election years. RE theory assumes that people will anticipate this kind of behavior and act accordingly.

The first important point about rational expectations is that the government cannot fool the people about systematic economic policies.

Flexible Prices and Wages

The second central assumption is that prices and wages are flexible. This assumption is familiar and holds that every price and wage moves quickly to balance supply and demand. In other words, prices are flexible, and all markets clear at all times.

By combining the assumptions of rational expectations and flexible prices, the RE macroeconomists can show certain surprising implications for macroeconomic theory and policy.

Rational Expectations and Macroeconomics

The concepts of rational expectations can be fruitfully applied in many areas of economics. Here we concentrate on two implications for macroeconomics: the nature of the labor market and the Phillips curve.

Unemployment

Is unemployment voluntary or involuntary? In our discussion in Chapter 31, we defined involuntary unemployment as a situation where qualified workers are unable to find jobs at the going wage. Refresh your memory with a glance back at Figure 31-7, which illustrates both voluntary and involuntary unemployment. Also recall that Keynesian economists think that a sizable fraction of unemployment, particularly in recessions, is involuntary.

By contrast, the rational-expectations school thinks that most unemployment is voluntary. In their view, labor markets adjust quickly after shocks as wages change to rebalance supply and demand. Unemployment, in this view, increases because more people are hunting for better jobs during recessions, not because they cannot find jobs. People are unemployed because they think that their real wages are too low, not because wages are too high as in the case of sticky-wage unemployment.

To summarize:

Rational-expectations macroeconomics holds that prices and wages are sufficiently flexible so as to ensure continuous clearing of all markets, including the labor market. This assumption implies that unemployment is voluntary. People are unemployed because they think that real wages are too low to induce them to work.

The Rational-Expectations Phillips Curve

If all unemployment is voluntary, why is unemployment so high during recessions? Why did the unemployment rate reach 25 percent in 1933 or 10 percent in 1982? Was there an epidemic of idleness in the 1930s? Did the American people take a \$300 billion vacation in 1982? Few economic historians could swallow such notions.

RE macroeconomists look to people's *misperceptions* as the key to business cycles. They believe that high unemployment arises because workers are confused about economic conditions; workers voluntarily quit their jobs in the hope of getting better ones but are surprised to find themselves in the unemployment office. High output and low unemployment, by contrast, occur when people are fooled into working harder because they overestimate real wages.

This line of reasoning leads to the *rational-expectations Phillips curve*, shown in Figure 35-3. Denote the expected rate of change of money wages as W^e, and assume prices rise as fast as wages. If the actual rate of increase of wages (W) is equal to the expected rate (so $W = W^e$), nobody is surprised or fooled, and unemployment is equal to the natural rate. Thus point A represents the no-surprise, natural-rate outcome.

How do we get points B and C? Each case arises from some kind of economic shock. To generate point B, assume that the Federal Reserve has unexpectedly increased the money supply. As a result, wages and prices also increase unexpectedly, and workers misperceive economic events, not knowing that prices are rising as rapidly as wages. They supply more labor, unemployment falls, and the economy goes to point B. You should trace through how we can generate point C by an unexpected cut in wages and prices.

Surprisingly, if we connect points B and C, they trace out a downward-sloping line that resembles the Phillips curve. Thus the downward-sloping *ap-*

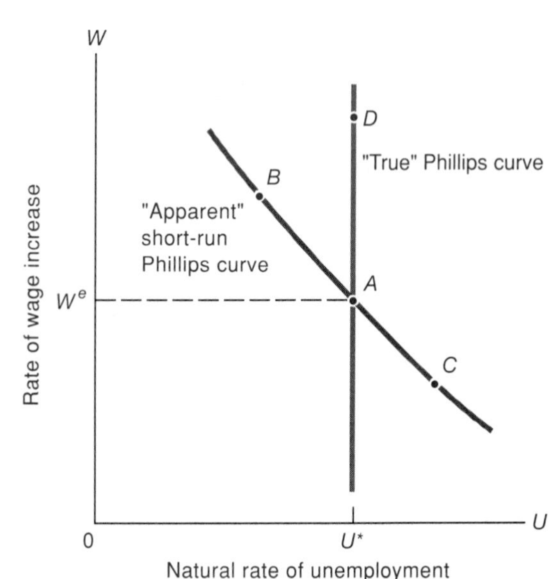

Figure 35-3. The rational-expectations Phillips curve

According to rational-expectations macroeconomics, the true Phillips curve is vertical. But we may observe an "apparent" short-run Phillips curve, drawn through points *B*, *A*, and *C*.

Point *B* arises when an inflationary shock raises money wages above their expected levels. Workers are confused, thinking that their real wages have increased, they decide to work more, and unemployment falls. Thus the economy moves from point *A* to point *B*. (Trace through the opposite pathway to *C*.)

As a result, economic historians see a scatter of points that look like *A*, *B*, and *C* and erroneously conclude that a stable short-run Phillips curve exists.

parent short-run Phillips curve arises from misperceptions of real wages or relative prices.

Policy Implications

Policy Ineffectiveness

Rational-expectations theory has important implications for the conduct of macroeconomics. The first concerns the effect of economic policy. Given the RE view of labor markets, you might say to yourself: "Okay, so RE economists believe that the Phillips curve is downward-sloping because people are fooled about what is happening to their real wages. But it's no tragedy if the people are fooled off the vertical Phillips curve. It's all for their own benefit anyway, because unemployment will be lower."

Not so, say the rational-expectations theorists. They demonstrate that, under their assumptions, government attempts to affect output and employment through monetary and fiscal policies would be fruitless. To understand the argument, imagine the government saying, "Election time is coming. Let's pump up the money supply a little." But people would say to themselves, "Yes, elections are coming. From past experience, I know that the government always pumps up the money supply before elections. They can't fool *me* and get me to work any harder." In terms of the Phillips curve of Figure 35-3, the government tries to stimulate the economy and move it from point *A* to point *B*. But as people anticipate the government's economic stimulation, the economy ends up at point *D*, with unemployment equal to the natural rate, but with higher inflation.

This is the *policy ineffectiveness theorem:*

With rational expectations and flexible prices and wages, anticipated government policy cannot affect real output or unemployment.

The policy ineffectiveness theorem depends on both rational expectations and flexible prices. The assumption of flexible prices implies that the only way that economic policy can affect output and unemployment is by surprising people and causing misperceptions. But you can hardly surprise people if your policies are predictable. Hence predictable policies cannot affect output and unemployment.

Fixed Rules Optimal

Earlier, we described the monetarist case for fixed rules. The RE approach put this argument on a much firmer footing. An economic policy can be divided into two parts, a predictable part (the "rule") and an unpredictable part ("discretion"). RE macroeconomists argue that discretion should be avoided like the plague.

Why so? They reason that policymakers cannot forecast the economy any better than the private sector can. Therefore, by the time policymakers act on the news—a war in the desert sands, a declining dollar, a corn blight—flexibly moving prices in markets populated by well-informed buyers and sellers have already incorporated the news. Markets have attained their efficient supply-and-demand equilibria. Unemployment has gravitated to its natural rate. There are simply no discretionary steps the government can take to improve the outcome or prevent the brief spells of involuntary unemployment that are caused by transient misperceptions.

Government policy can make things worse, however, with unpredictable discretionary policies that give misleading economic signals, confuse people, distort their economic behavior, and cause waste. Rather than risk such confusing "noise," say the RE economists, governments should completely avoid any discretionary macroeconomic policies.

Monetarist Rules and the Lucas Critique

The rational-expectations revolution has provided support for the monetarist advocacy of fixed rules. But at the same time it levied a devastating argument against a key monetarist assumption. Monetarists note that the velocity of money has shown a remarkable stability. Thus, they conclude, we can stabilize $MV \equiv PQ \equiv$ nominal GNP by imposing a fixed-money rule.

But the *Lucas critique,* named after RE economist Robert Lucas, argues that people may change their behavior when policy changes. Just as the apparent short-run Phillips curve might shift when Keynesian governments attempt to manipulate it, so might the apparently constant velocity change if the central bank adopts a fixed-money-growth rule.

This insight was borne out in the period from 1979 to 1982, when the United States conducted the monetarist experiment described in the last section. Velocity became extremely unstable, and 1982 showed the biggest decrease in velocity since the Federal Reserve began collecting the data.

The Lucas critique is a stern warning that economic behavior can change when policymakers rely too heavily upon past regularities.

State of the Debate

The RE theory has not been favorably received by mainstream macroeconomists. Criticisms have centered principally on the issue of flexible prices and wages. Much evidence suggests that prices often move slowly in response to shocks, and few economists believe that labor markets are in constant supply-demand equilibrium. What happens to the rational-expectations theory when the assumption of perfectly flexible wages and prices is abandoned? In general, policy will regain its power to affect the real economy in the short run.[6]

A second set of criticisms aims at the rational-expectations assumption, taking issue with the assertion that humans incorporate the latest forecast or data into their behavior like supercomputers. Empirical studies of behavior have uncovered significant elements of non-rational expectations, even among the most sophisticated professional economic forecasters.

Finally, critics argue that the predictions of the RE theory are inaccurate. The theory forecasts that misperceptions lie behind business-cycle fluctuations. But can misperceptions about wages and prices really explain deep depressions and persistent bouts of unemployment? Did it really take people a full decade to learn how hard times were in the Great Depression? Most mainstream economists believe that these implications tend to discredit the theory.

A New Synthesis?

After two decades of analysis and econometric testing of the RE approach to macroeconomics, elements of a synthesis of old and new theories are beginning to appear. What are some of the lessons? To begin with, economists now must pay careful attention to expectations in economic activity. Approaches that assume that expectations react mechanically will no longer survive careful scrutiny, particularly in auction markets like those in the financial sector.

Some macroeconomists have begun to fuse the

[6] Perhaps the best example is work that maintains the rational-expectations framework except for one modest change. Studies of "overlapping wage contracts," particularly by John Taylor (Stanford), a member of the Council of Economic Advisers under President Bush, recognize that a substantial part of the labor force works under long-term contracts that are written in *nominal* (rather than real) terms. A typical labor contract will specify a fixed money wage rate. During the period of the contract, anticipated macroeconomic policy can affect unemployment. Put in terms of the expectational view, the macroeconomic policymakers can use information that comes available *after* the contract is written but was unavailable when workers agreed to a particular money-wage path.

new view of expectations with the modern mainstream (or neo-Keynesian) view of product and labor markets. This synthesis is embodied in macroeconomic models that assume (*a*) labor and goods markets display inflexible wages and prices, (*b*) the prices and quantities in financial auction markets adjust rapidly to economic shocks and expectations, and (*c*) the expectations in auction markets are formed in a forward-looking way.

A recent survey compares the behavior of macroeconomic models that incorporate the adaptive ("backward-looking") approach to expectations with models that incorporate the rational ("forward-looking") approach. The adaptive assumption holds that people form their expectations simply and mechanically on the basis of past information. The forward-looking or rational approach is as described above.

A model comparison finds a number of important differences. One salient feature is that forward-looking models tend to have large "jumps" or discontinuous changes in interest rates, stock prices, or exchange rates when major changes in policy or external events occur. For example, an election of an expansionist President or prime minister might lead people to think that inflation was on the horizon. This perception could result in a sharp jump in interest rates along with a fall in the stock market and exchange rates. The prediction of "jumpy" prices replicates one realistic feature of auction markets and thus suggests where forward-looking expectations might be important in the real world.

Figure 35-4 compares the predictions of different models. It shows the expenditure multipliers of four forward-looking models and of seven adaptive-expectations models. Note that the multipliers of the forward-looking models are significantly smaller than those of the adaptive models.

The smaller multipliers in the forward-looking models occur for two reasons: First, after a fiscal expansion, interest rates generally rise more rapidly in forward-looking than in adaptive models. This occurs because forward-looking market participants predict a future expansion of output after an increase in government spending. A higher expected future output tends to increase interest rates *today*, and crowding out therefore occurs rapidly in forward-looking models.

Second, as interest rates rise quickly in response to a fiscal stimulus in forward-looking models, the flexible exchange rate on the dollar tends to jump upward. A rise in the exchange rate of the dollar leads to a reduction in net exports and tends to reduce the size of the fiscal stimulus.

Although this discussion touches on only two of many differences between the rational-expectations approach and more traditional macroeconomics, it does point to an important set of results that every serious macroeconomist must study carefully. Economic relationships with rational expectations may differ from those with adaptive expectations. The reaction of markets to external events, and even to policies and policymakers themselves, cannot be ignored.

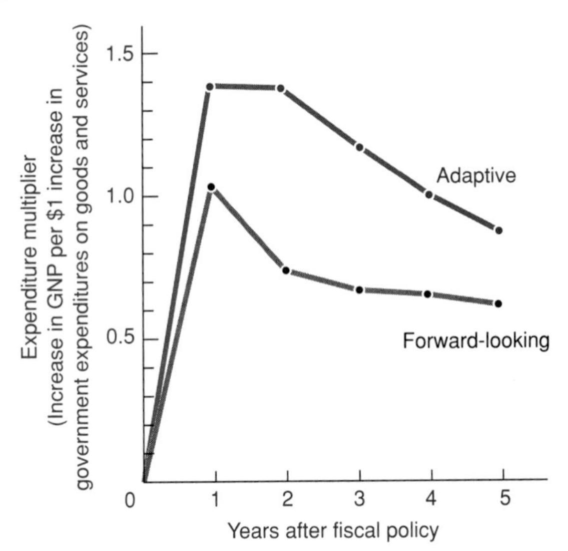

Figure 35-4. Comparison of multipliers in forward-looking and adaptive models

This graph shows the difference in expenditure multipliers of models that are adaptive (or backward-looking) and forward-looking (or rational).

Because interest rates crowd out domestic investment and exchange rates affect net exports, adjustment takes place more rapidly in forward-looking models. Forward-looking expenditure multipliers are considerably smaller than those in adaptive models. [Source: Ralph C. Bryant, Gerald Holtham, and Peter Hooper, "Consensus and Diversity in the Model Simulations," in Ralph C. Bryant et al. (eds.), *Empirical Macroeconomics for Interdependent Economies* (Brookings, Washington, D.C., 1988), Fig. 3-33.]

C. Current Issues in Stabilization Policy

Although academic scribblers will wrangle endlessly about the best macroeconomic model, policymakers cannot wait for the final scientific verdict. They must cope with this year's inflation or recession and confront the big macroeconomic tradeoffs. In this section, we evaluate the principles that lie behind monetary and fiscal policies today.

The Interaction of Monetary and Fiscal Policies

A government can use either monetary or fiscal policy to stabilize the economy. But what should be the division of labor between monetary and fiscal policies? There is no simple answer to this question. Rather, the best setting for monetary and fiscal policy will depend upon two factors: the need for demand management and the desired fiscal-monetary mix.

Demand Management

The first consideration in determining the appropriate combination of monetary and fiscal policies is the overall state of the economy and the need for adjusting aggregate demand. When the economy is stagnating, fiscal and monetary policies can be used to stimulate the economy and promote economic recovery. When inflation threatens, monetary and fiscal policies can help to slow the economy and dampen inflationary fires. These are examples of *demand management*, which refers to the use of monetary and fiscal policies to set aggregate demand at the desired level.

Suppose, for example, that the economy is entering a severe recession. Aggregate demand is depressed relative to potential output. What can the government do to revive the lagging economy? It can manage aggregate demand by raising money growth, or increasing the structural budget deficit, or both. After the economy has responded to the monetary and fiscal stimulus, output growth and employment would increase and unemployment would fall. (What steps could the government take during inflationary periods?)

The first consideration in setting monetary and fiscal policies is the state of the business cycle and the requirements of demand management.

The Policy Mix

The second factor affecting fiscal and monetary policy is the desired **fiscal-monetary mix,** which refers to the relative strength of fiscal and monetary policies and their effect on different components of output. In other words, monetary and fiscal policies can be used to affect not only the *level* of GNP but also the *composition* of GNP. By varying the mix of taxes, government spending, and monetary policy, the government can change the fraction of GNP devoted to business investment, consumption, net exports, and government purchases of goods and services.

Example 1. Let's say that the people empower a President to start a big defense buildup, leaving overall output unchanged, by having housing and other investment contract to provide the necessary resources. What could be done? The President could increase defense spending, leave taxes alone, and tighten money, thereby raising interest rates enough to squeeze investment and net exports to make room for the added government purchases. This policy would also lead to an increase in the structural budget deficit and higher real interest rates. Such a fiscal course was followed in the United States from 1981 to 1988.

Example 2. Suppose that a country became concerned about a low national savings rate and desires to raise investment so as to increase the capital stock and boost the growth rate of potential output. Moreover, this step should not change the overall level of GNP; rather, higher investment should come at the expense of private consumption. What policy mix should be pursued?

Undertake an expansionary monetary policy to lower interest rates and raise investment; keep government spending on goods and services unchanged; raise taxes and squeeze transfer payments so as to reduce disposable income and thereby lower consumption. This change in the policy mix would encourage private investment by increasing public saving (taxes less spending). Such a change was the purpose of the deficit-reduction package of 1990 in the United States and has been repeatedly proposed by economists.

What has been the actual practice in the United States? Federal fiscal policies generally bear little resemblance to rational responses to the need for an appropriate monetary-fiscal mix. Fiscal deliberations are subject to accusations that one group wants to "tax and spend" while the other supports "tax cuts for the rich." The deadlock over the appropriate balance of spending and taxing has resulted in rising fiscal deficits and increasingly tight money. Given the stance of the monetary-fiscal mix, who can be surprised that the United States has settled into a syndrome of low domestic saving and investment coupled with a large foreign deficit and debt? These are the inevitable consequences of the monetary-fiscal mix of the last few years.

Current Issues

The last three decades have witnessed a steady evolution in economic views about stabilization policy. In the early stages of the Keynesian revolution, macroeconomists emphasized fiscal policy as the most powerful and balanced remedy for demand management. Later, emphasis shifted toward monetary policy, culminating in the 1979–1982 monetarist experiment. In the 1980s, fiscal policy became increasingly paralyzed because of the large budget deficit, and the Federal Reserve gained a virtual monopoly on short-run stabilization policy. During the late 1980s and early 1990s, monetary policymakers adopted an eclectic philosophy, tightening or easing money depending upon trends in inflation, unemployment, and the exchange rate on the dollar.

Policymakers the world over have wrestled with the same dilemmas: How effective is monetary policy? What are the relative merits of rules and discretion? How should macroeconomic policy take into account the growing importance of foreign trade? To conclude our discussion of macroeconomics, we will sketch current thinking on these crucial issues.

Effectiveness of Monetary Policy

In our analysis of monetary policy, we examined the qualitative impacts of money on output. In implementing policy, the central bank must go beyond qualitative discussion to quantitative estimates. For example, say that in November 1993 the Federal Reserve forecasts that current monetary

Money, Output, and Prices

Affected variable	Response of affected variable to 4 percent change in money supply (% change in affected variable from baseline path) Year 1	Year 2	Year 3	Year 4	Year 5
Real GNP	0.9	1.1	1.2	1.1	0.8
Consumer prices	0.2	0.7	1.1	1.5	1.8
Nominal GNP	1.1	1.8	2.3	2.5	2.7

Table 35-1. Estimated effect of monetary policy on output and prices

A survey studied the impact of a change in monetary policy in eight different econometric models. In each case, a baseline run of the model was "shocked" by adding 4 percent to the money supply in year 1 and holding the money supply 4 percent above the baseline in all years thereafter. Estimates in the table show the average calculated response of the models.

Note the rapid response of real output to a monetary-policy shift, with the peak response coming in year 3. The impact upon the price level builds up gradually because of the inertial response of price and wage behavior. Note that the impact on nominal GNP is less than proportional to the money growth even after 5 years.

[Source: Ralph C. Bryant, Peter Hooper, and Gerald Holtham, "Consensus and Diversity in the Model Simulations," in Ralph Bryant et al. (eds.), *Empirical Macroeconomics for Interdependent Economies* (Brookings, Washington, D.C., 1988).]

and fiscal policy will produce an expansion with real GNP growth of 5 percent in the coming year; further, the Fed believes that a growth rate of 4 percent is the most that the economy can sustain for 1994 without the risk of an unacceptable inflation. The Fed wishes to know how much money growth must be slowed to bring real GNP growth down to the target level.

Economists use statistical techniques to estimate the quantitative impacts of monetary policy on the economy. The results of a recent study of a number of macroeconomic models are shown in Table 35-1. This study estimates the impact on the U.S. economy of increasing the money supply by 4 percent above the money supply of a "baseline" projection, with the money supply remaining 4 percent higher than the baseline for the indefinite future.

The results show a rapid response of real GNP to an increase in the money supply. By contrast, the increase in the price level builds up slowly over time, with less than one-fifth of the increase in nominal GNP in year 1 coming in prices. At the end of 5 years, according to the model simulations, most of the increase in nominal GNP shows up in prices rather than in real output. The models confirm the Keynesian prediction of a sluggish reaction of wages and prices to changes in the money supply.

What then might the staff of the Federal Reserve say when asked what change in the money supply would be needed to slow the rate of growth of real GNP by 1 percentage point? They might respond that the money supply would have to be slowed by somewhat more than 4 percent to produce a 1-percentage-point decrease in real GNP.

Fixed Rules vs. Discretion

In our discussions of monetarism, we laid out the case for fixed policy rules. Advocates of fixed rules argue that, because the private economy is relatively stable, active policy-making is likely to destabilize rather than stabilize the economy. In addition, stable rules help reinforce expectations.

Other economists counter that discretionary policies, within a realistic framework, can improve upon a fixed rule. The major economic argument against a constant-money-growth rule is that velocity is unpredictable and that erratic changes may throw the economy into recession or inflation. It would be better to allow the central bank to adjust monetary policies to changes in velocity or to other structural changes. Critics point to the sobering experience with constant-money-growth rules during the 1979–1982 period as evidence of the realistic disadvantages of following such an approach.

In a broader perspective, critics question whether rigid rules are feasible in a democratic society. A rule is set up by discretion, followed by discretion, interfered with by discretion, and abandoned by discretion. Any policy, whether a fixed rule or a discretionary one, will inevitably become unpopular at some point. The Federal Reserve is a creature of Congress, and even the Fed watches the election returns. What Federal Reserve is so self-confident as to believe that a fixed rule can be followed in the face of great inflations or deep recessions that threaten political unrest?

The debate over rules versus discretion is one of the oldest debates of political economy. There is no single best approach for all times and places. Indeed, the dilemma may reflect a deeper problem in democratic societies: the tradeoff between short-run policies intended to attract political support and long-run policies designed to enhance the general welfare. What is needed is not rigid adherence to rules, but farsighted dedication to the public good. Ironically, one of the most acclaimed economic policymakers of the postwar period has been Federal Reserve Chairman Paul Volcker whose tenure (1979–1987) was marked by sharp, discretionary policy changes aimed at reducing inflation and protecting the nation's financial system. His success in both areas testifies to the power of wise and disinterested discretionary policies.

Monetary Policy in an Open Economy

In recent years, the interaction between the domestic economy and foreign economies has come to dominate economic policy. The relationship between monetary policy and foreign trade has always been a major concern for smaller and more open economies like Canada and Britain. However, after the introduction of flexible exchange rates in 1973, with a growing share of imports and exports, and in the presence of increasingly closely linked financial markets, international trade and finance have come to play a central role in U.S. macroeconomic policy during the 1980s and early 1990s.

The imprint of economic openness on policy is clearest for monetary policy. Let's review briefly the route by which monetary policy affects trade and then output. Suppose the Federal Reserve decides to slow money growth to fight inflation, as occurred in the 1979–1982 period. This process drives up interest rates on assets denominated in U.S. dollars. Attracted by higher dollar interest rates, investors will buy dollar securities, driving up the foreign exchange rate on the dollar. The high exchange rate on the dollar encourages the United States to import and hurts U.S. exports. Net exports fall, decreasing aggregate demand. This has the impact of both lowering real GNP and lowering prices or the rate of inflation.

Note that the direction of the effect of monetary policy is the same for the trade impact as for the impact on domestic investment: tight money lowers output and prices. *The trade impact reinforces the domestic-economy impact.* But the open-economy issues pose additional complications for policymakers.

The first complication arises because the quantitative relationships between monetary policy, the exchange rate, foreign trade, and output and prices are intricate and imperfectly understood. The weak point in our understanding comes at the very first link. Current economic models cannot accurately predict the impact of monetary-policy changes on exchange rates. Further, even if we knew the money–exchange-rate relationship, the impact of exchange rates on net exports is complicated and difficult to predict. On balance, confidence in our ability to determine the best timing and likely effects of monetary policies has eroded in recent years.

Foreign economic relations add another dimension to economic policy. Domestic policymakers must concern themselves with foreign repercussions of domestic policies. Rising interest rates at home change interest rates, exchange rates, and trade balances abroad, and these changes may be unwelcome. In heavily indebted countries, such as Brazil and Mexico, higher interest rates increase debt-service burdens. In the 1980s, skyrocketing interest rates caused severe hardships for these countries. To complicate matters, these countries owe billions of dollars to American banks, and loan defaults could cause untold damage to the U.S. financial system. Finally, the nation cares not only about the total of its GNP; the composition of output matters as well. Because of shifting patterns of foreign trade, the United States has witnessed stagnation in its "tradable" sectors (manufactures, mining, and agriculture) since the early 1980s.

Open-economy macroeconomics is one of the most exciting areas of modern economics. Economists clearly have much to learn about the interactions between monetary policy and economic performance in a world increasingly open to foreign trade and financial flows.

SUMMARY

A. Velocity and Monetarism

1. Monetarism relies upon the analysis of trends in the velocity of money to understand the impact of money on the economy. The income velocity of circulation of money (V) is defined as the ratio of the dollar GNP flow to the stock of M:

$$V \equiv \frac{\text{GNP}}{M} \equiv \frac{PQ}{M}$$

   While V is definitely not a constant—if only because it rises with interest rates—its movements are somewhat regular and predictable.

2. From velocity's definition comes the quantity theory of prices:

$$P \equiv kM \qquad \text{where } k \equiv \frac{V}{Q}$$

The quantity theory of prices regards P as almost strictly proportional to M. This view is useful for understanding hyperinflations and certain long-term trends, but it should not be taken literally.

3. Monetarism has grown into a major economic school. It rests on three propositions:
   (a) The growth of the money supply is the major systematic determinant of nominal GNP growth.
   (b) Prices and wages are relatively flexible.
   (c) The private economy is stable.

   These propositions suggest that macroeconomic fluctuations arise primarily from erratic money-supply growth.
4. Monetarism is generally associated with a laissez-faire and anti-big-government political philosophy. Because of a desire to avoid active government and a belief in the inherent stability of the private sector, monetarists often propose that the money supply grow at a fixed rate of 3 or 5 percent annually. Some monetarists believe that this will produce steady growth with stable prices in the long run.
5. The Federal Reserve conducted a full-scale monetarist experiment from 1979 to 1982. The experience from this period convinced most observers that:
   (a) Money is a powerful determinant of aggregate demand.
   (b) Most of the short-run effects of money changes are on output rather than on prices.
   (c) A firm and credible monetary policy does not appear to reduce inflation at lower cost than other anti-inflation policies.
   (d) Velocity may become quite unstable when a monetarist approach is followed.

B. Rational Expectations in Macroeconomics

6. Rational-expectations (RE) macroeconomics rests on two fundamental hypotheses: People's expectations are formed efficiently and rationally, and prices and wages are flexible. In the RE economy, all unemployment is voluntary, and the Phillips curve is vertical in the short run, even though it may appear otherwise.
7. The policy ineffectiveness theorem holds that predictable government policies cannot affect real output and unemployment. The RE theory states that, while we may *observe* a downward-sloping short-run Phillips curve, we cannot *exploit* the slope for the purposes of lowering unemployment. If economic policymakers systematically attempt to increase output and decrease unemployment, people will soon come to understand and to anticipate the policy. When such a policy is anticipated, prices and wages will adjust in advance. People will remain on their supply and demand

curves, and unemployment will stay at the natural rate. Fixed policy rules will produce better economic outcomes.

8. Critics argue that there are several weaknesses in the RE theory. The assumptions of flexible prices and rational expectations are not borne out by empirical studies, especially for labor markets. And the predictions—particularly that business cycles are caused by misperceptions—seem farfetched as an explanation of serious downturns, like those of the 1930s and the early 1980s.

C. Current Issues in Stabilization Policy

9. Nations face two considerations in setting monetary and fiscal policies: the appropriate level of aggregate demand and the best monetary-fiscal mix. The mix of fiscal and monetary policies helps determine the composition of GNP. A high-investment strategy would call for a budget surplus along with an expansionary monetary policy. The mix in practice has evolved toward a very loose fiscal and tight monetary policy—a sure recipe for a low ratio of investment to GNP and for slow growth of potential output.
10. In attempting to stabilize the economy, the United States today relies almost completely upon monetary policy. Econometric models, which use statistical techniques to estimate the impact of monetary-policy changes on the macroeconomy, generally find that money-supply changes have their primary impact upon output in the short run, with a larger and larger share of the impact on nominal GNP coming in inertial prices and wages as time proceeds.
11. Should governments follow fixed rules or discretion? The answer involves both economics and political values. Conservatives often espouse rules while liberals advocate active fine-tuning of monetary policy to attain economic goals. More basic is the question of whether active and discretionary policies stabilize or destabilize the economy. Increasingly, economists stress the need for *credible* policies, whether credibility is generated by rigid rules or by wise leadership.
12. One of the major challenges for macroeconomic policy has been the increasing globalization of trade and finance. In a regime of flexible exchange rates, changes in monetary policy can affect the exchange rate and net exports, adding yet another complication to the monetary mechanism. This influence led to a major shift in the composition of GNP away from tradable goods to non-tradable goods in the early 1980s. Open-economy considerations complicate the life of central banks both because the links between money and net exports are imprecise and because additional political and economic concerns are raised by the impact of domestic policies on foreign economies, on the composition of GNP, and on third-world debt.

CONCEPTS FOR REVIEW

Velocity and monetarism
velocity of circulation of money:
$MV \equiv PQ$
quantity theory of prices:
$P \equiv kM$
modern monetarism
1979–1982 monetarist experiment

Rational expectations in macroeconomics
rational (forward-looking) expectations
adaptive (backward-looking) expectations
key assumptions: rational expectations and flexible prices and wages
policy ineffectiveness theorem

Lucas critique

Current issues of stabilization policy
demand management
fiscal-monetary mix
effectiveness of monetary policy
fixed rules vs. discretion

QUESTIONS FOR DISCUSSION

1. Define income velocity (V). For the following data, calculate the annual growth rate of the money supply and the level and rate of change of velocity:

Year	Nominal GNP	Money supply, M_1
	Billions of dollars	Billions of dollars, lagged 12 months
1981	3,053	408.9
1982	3,166	436.5
1983	3,406	474.5
1984	3,772	521.2
1985	4,015	552.1
1986	4,232	620.1
1987	4,516	724.7
1988	4,874	750.4
1989	5,201	787.5
1990	5,463	794.8

2. In the discussion of the demand for money, and in the demand-for-money schedule in Figure 29-4, it was shown that the demand for money would be sensitive to interest rates. What would be the impact of higher interest rates on velocity for a given level of nominal GNP? What are the implications of interest-sensitive demand for money on monetarist arguments that rely upon constant velocity of money?
3. Marxists used to argue, "War is necessary for full employment." How would an increase in military expenditures help cure a depression? Are there any other fiscal or monetary steps that might serve equally well to reduce unemployment and raise output?
4. Monetarists say, "Only money matters." Eclectic Keynesians answer, "Money matters, but other things, like fiscal policy, matter too." Explain and evaluate each position. Could you disagree with monetarists and still believe that monetary policy should be used to counter recessions? Explain.
5. Explain how a change in the mix of monetary and fiscal policies could reduce the budget deficit, increase domestic investment, and maintain the same level of real GNP and inflation.
6. What phase of the business cycle is the country now in? What is the current fiscal-monetary mix? What tax and expenditure policies seem appropriate? How would you vary the relative mix of policy (expenditures, taxes, and the money supply) to fight unemployment or inflation?
7. Examine the econometric estimates shown in Table 35-1. Compare them with the predictions of the quantity theory of prices. Can you think of any way to reconcile the two?
8. If, in boom times, we printed and spent $100 trillion in new greenbacks, what would happen to prices? Is there some truth, then, to the quantity theory? What might happen to prices if M were increased 1 percent in a depression?
9. The *Economic Report of the President*, 1991, contains the following analysis of monetary policy after an oil-price shock:

> Given the stability of the relationship between GNP and money, keeping money supply growth from falling in the face of a downturn in GNP caused by an oil price shock is essential to preventing an unnecessarily large and prolonged decline in economic growth. Depending on the size of the shock, a temporary increase in the money supply growth might be necessary to stabilize economy-wide spending and to help offset the decline in GNP that occurs when an oil price shock reduces real income and raises the general price level. (p. 94)

Explain the reasoning behind this statement in terms of the *AS-AD* analysis. Analyze whether this passage tends to reflect monetarist reasoning.

10. What are the various arguments for and against a fixed-money-growth rule? Consider specifically factors such as the inherent stability of the private economy, the ability to forecast the economy, the stability of the demand-for-money schedule, and expectations about macroeconomic policy.
11. Consider what monetarists and Keynesian economists would predict to be the impacts of each of the following on the course of prices, output, and employment (in each case, hold taxes and the money supply constant unless specifically mentioned):
    (a) A large tax cut
    (b) A large cut in the money supply
    (c) An increase in oil prices
    (d) A wave of innovations that increase potential output by 10 percent
    (e) A burst of exports
12. **Advanced problem** (on rational expectations): Consider the effect of rational expectations on consumption behavior. Say the government proposes a temporary tax cut of \$20 billion, lasting for a year. Consumers with adaptive expectations might assume that their disposable incomes would be \$20 billion higher every year. What would be the impact on consumption spending and GNP in the simple multiplier model of Chapter 27?

    Next suppose that consumers have rational expectations. They rationally forecast that the tax cut is for only 1 year. Being "life-cycle" consumers, they recognize that their average lifetime incomes will increase (say) only \$2 billion per year, not \$20 billion per year. What would be the reaction of such consumers? Analyze, then, the impact of rational expectations on the effectiveness of temporary tax cuts.

PART SEVEN

INTERNATIONAL TRADE AND THE WORLD ECONOMY

The Road Ahead

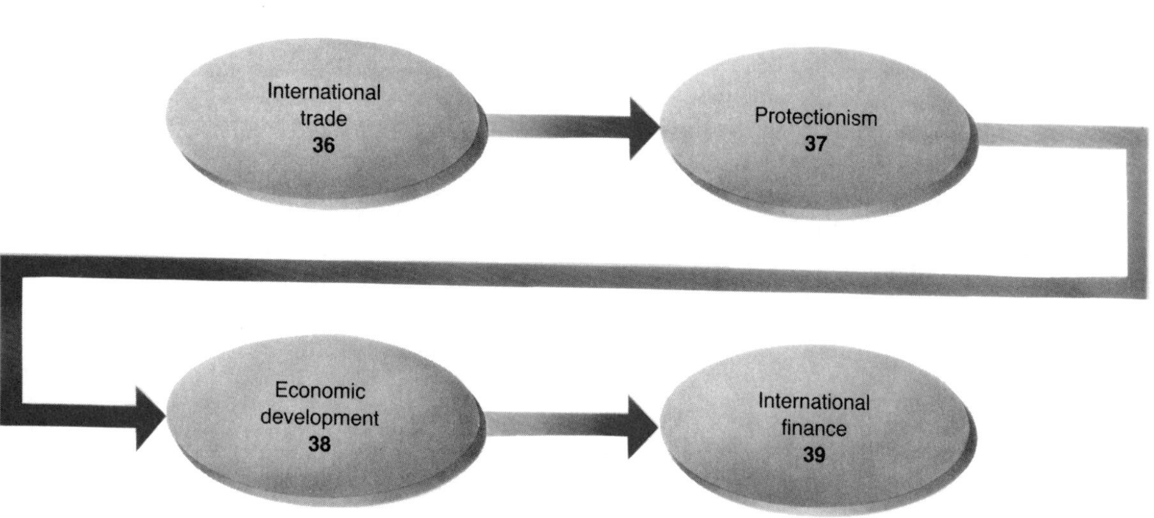

International trade is vital to economic growth because it expands a nation's consumption possibilities. Japan sells America cameras; America sells computers to Australia; Australia closes the circle by selling coal to Japan. By specializing in its areas of greatest relative productivity, each nation can consume more than it could produce alone. This is the simple yet elusive essence of foreign trade.

C H A P T E R 36

INTERNATIONAL TRADE AND THE THEORY OF COMPARATIVE ADVANTAGE

The benefit of international trade—a more efficient employment of the productive forces of the world.
John Stuart Mill

Economics shows that specialization increases productivity and living standards. We will apply this principle to the field of *international trade and finance*, the process by which nations export and import goods, services, and financial capital. International trade and finance involve many of the most controversial questions of today: Why does the United States import shoes and textiles and export food and computers? Why does Japan usually have a large trade surplus while the Philippines usually runs trade deficits? And how did it come to pass that the United States, which a few years ago was the world's largest creditor nation, has now become the largest debtor nation of all?

International vs. Domestic Trade

Analysis of international trade differs from analysis of self-sufficient economies in two ways. First, international trade involves exchange among different nations. Sometimes, political barriers to trade are erected when some groups object to foreign trade and nations impose tariffs or quotas. This practice, called protectionism, will occupy us in Chapter 37.

The other new feature raised by international trade is exchange rates. Most nations have their own currencies. I want to pay for a Japanese car in dollars, while Toyota wants to be paid in Japanese yen. As we will see in Chapter 39, the international financial system must ensure a smooth flow of dollars, yen, and other currencies—or else risk a breakdown in trade.

Economic protectionism and a diversity of national currencies are at the heart of international economic issues today.

A. Economic Basis for International Trade

Trends in Foreign Trade

We begin by examining the patterns of international trade. Figure 36-1 is a "trade map," showing how the world would look if each country's geographical size were proportional to its share of world trade. Notice how large the United States, Western Europe, and Japan loom, while the U.S.S.R. and China appear as but tiny principalities.

An economy that engages in international trade is called an *open economy*. A useful measure of

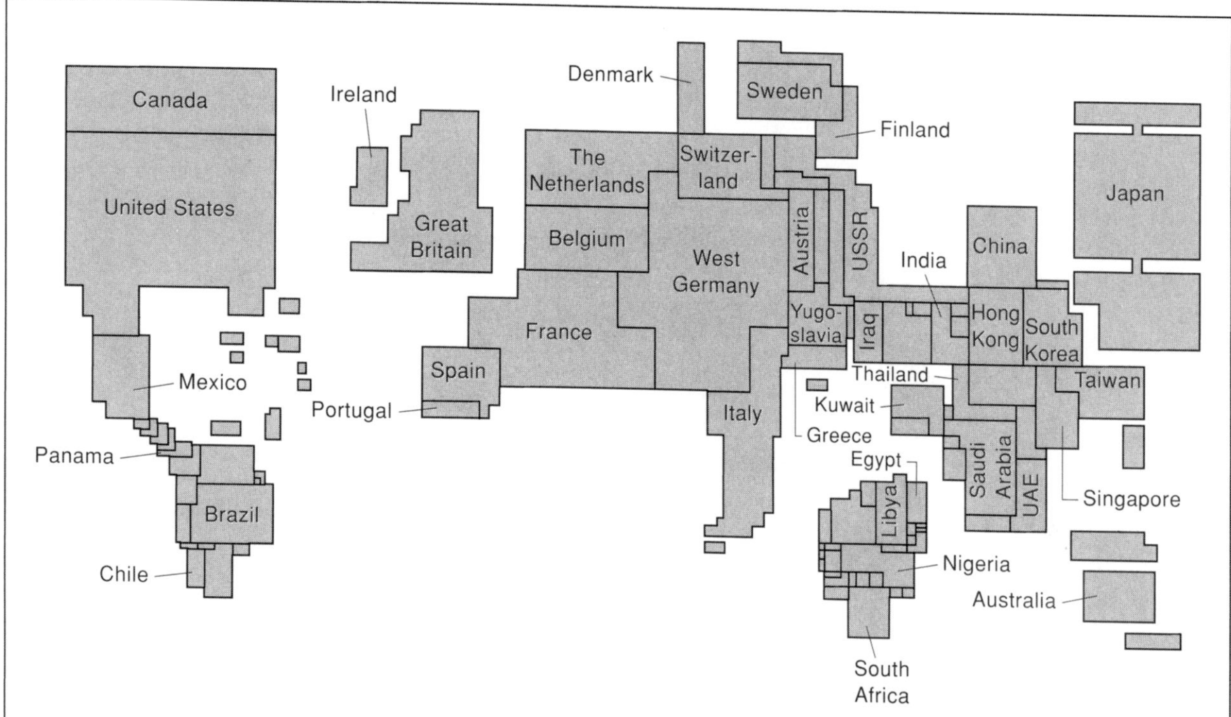

Figure 36-1. Countries of the world scaled to their international trade

In this map, the area of each country is drawn proportional to its share of total world trade in 1985. Compare the size of the advanced industrial countries with that of Africa and Asia. [Adapted from Michael Kidron and Ronald Segal, *The New State of the World Atlas* (Simon and Schuster, New York, 1987).]

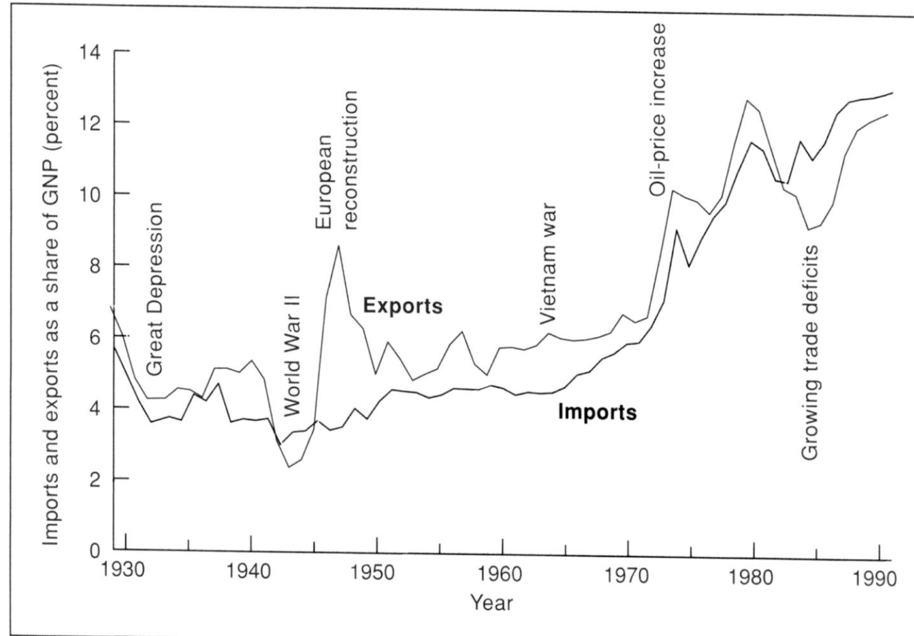

Figure 36-2. Growing U.S. openness

The United States is becoming more and more exposed to the winds of international competition. Like all major market countries, the United States has opened its borders to greater amounts of foreign trade over the last half-century. The greatest growth of the dollar value of imports came with higher oil prices and with the rise in the dollar's foreign exchange rate. In the late 1980s, imports far outdistanced exports, causing the United States to become the world's largest debtor nation. (Source: U.S. Department of Commerce.)

openness is the ratio of a country's exports or imports to its GNP. Figure 36-2 reveals that the United States is quite a self-sufficient economy. Many nations, particularly in Western Europe and East Asia, are very open economies and export and import more than 50 percent of their GNP.

The degree of openness is much higher in many U.S. industries—such as steel, textiles, and shoes—than it is for the U.S. economy as a whole. Table 36-1 shows the commodity composition of U.S. foreign trade for 1989. These data reveal that the United States exports surprisingly large amounts of primary commodities (such as food) and imports large quantities of sophisticated, capital-intensive manufactured goods (like automobiles or telecommunications equipment). Moreover, we find a great deal of two-way, or intra-industry, trade. That is, even within a particular industry (like textiles or steel), the United States both exports and imports at the same time.

What economic principles lie behind the patterns of international trade? We next turn to this issue.

U.S. Trade, 1989

Commodity classification	Share of each commodity as percent of total: Exports	Share of each commodity as percent of total: Imports
Industrial supplies:		
Oil, coal, and other fuels	4	13
Food	9	6
Other	23	16
Manufactures:		
Motor vehicles	9	17
Computers and machinery	31	21
Other	24	27
Total	100	100

Table 36-1. The United States exports surprising amounts of primary goods, imports many manufactures

The composition of U.S. total merchandise exports and imports for recent years shows a number of surprises. The United States exports a large volume of primary commodities, especially food and coal, mainly because of its ample resource base. At the same time, the United States imports many manufactures, like cars and cameras, even though manufacturing is highly capital-intensive. (Source: U.S. Bureau of the Census.)

The Sources of International Trade

Nations find it beneficial to participate in international trade for many reasons: because of diversity in the conditions of production among regions, because of decreasing costs of production, and because of differences in tastes.

Diversity in Conditions of Production

Trade may take place because of the diversity in productive possibilities among countries. As examples, look at foods and recreational activities. Countries with tropical climates will naturally specialize in bananas, coffee, and citrus fruits; these goods and services will be traded for other commodities. Countries with frostier climates are more likely to produce goods and services like maple syrup, salmon, reindeer meat, and skiing.

Decreasing Costs

A second reason for trade arises when there are increasing returns to scale, or decreasing costs of large-scale production. Many manufacturing processes enjoy economies of scale; that is, they tend to have lower average costs of production as the volume of output expands. And what better way to expand production than to sell output in the vast global marketplace?

How might the scenario run? Suppose that a particular country gets a head start in a given sector. It might be Britain with textiles in the early 1800s, the United States with automobiles in the 1920s, or Japan with consumer electronics in the 1980s. Once the country begins to produce and export the product, the economies of scale give it a significant cost and technological advantage over other countries.

The example of decreasing cost helps explain the important phenomenon of extensive intra-industry trade shown in Table 36-1. Why is it that the United States both imports and exports automobiles? The reason is that the United States has exploited the economies of scale in large-car production and is specialized there, while Japan enjoys a cost advantage in small cars and tends to specialize and export in that part of the market. Similar patterns of intra-industry specialization are seen with computers, steel, textiles, and many other manufactured products.

Differences in Tastes

Yet a third cause of trade lies in preferences. Even if the conditions of production were identical in all regions, countries might engage in trade if their tastes for goods were different.

For example, suppose that Norway and Sweden produce fish from the sea and meat from the land in about the same amounts, but the Swedes have a great fondness for meat while the Norwegians are partial to fish. In this case, a mutually beneficial export of meat from Norway and fish from Sweden would take place. Both countries would gain from this trade; the sum of human happiness is increased, just as when Jack Sprat trades fat meat for his wife's lean.

The Principle of Comparative Advantage

Uncommon Sense

The three reasons for trade listed above provide the common-sense reasons for international trade. But there is a deeper principle underlying *all* trade—in a family, within a nation, and among nations—that goes beyond common sense. The *principle of comparative advantage* holds that a country can trade even if it is absolutely more efficient (or more inefficient) than other countries in the production of every good.

Say that the United States has higher output per worker (or per unit of input) than the rest of the world in making computers and steel. But suppose the United States is relatively more efficient in computers than it is in steel. For example, U.S. productivity might be 50 percent higher than that of other countries in computers and 10 percent higher in steel. In this case, it would benefit the United States to export that good in which it is relatively more efficient (computers) and import that good in which it is relatively less efficient (steel).

Or consider a poor country like India. How could impoverished India, whose productivity per worker is only a fraction of that of industrialized countries, hope to export any of its textiles or wheat? Surprisingly, according to the doctrine of comparative advantage, India can and will trade by exporting the goods in which it is *relatively* more efficient (like wheat and textiles) and importing the goods in which it is *relatively* less efficient (like turbines and supercomputers).

The **principle of comparative advantage** holds that each country will specialize in the production and export of those goods that it can produce at relatively low cost (in which it is relatively more efficient than other countries); conversely, each country will import those goods which it produces at relatively high cost (in which it is relatively less efficient than other countries).

This simple principle provides the unshakable basis for international trade.

The Logic of Comparative Advantage

The principle of comparative advantage explains why countries specialize in the production of particular commodities. We begin with a simple example of specialization among people and then move to the more general case of specialization and comparative advantage among nations.

Consider the case of the best lawyer in town who is also the best typist in town. How should the lawyer spend her time? Should she write and type her own legal briefs? Or should she leave the typing to her secretary? Clearly, the lawyer should concentrate on legal activities, where her *relative* or *comparative* skills are most effectively used, even though she has *absolutely* greater skills in both typing and legal work.

Or look at it from the secretary's point of view. He is a fine typist, but to undertake legal research would be laborious at best and impossible at worst. He is *absolutely* less efficient than the lawyer in both legal research and in typing, but he is *relatively* or *comparatively* more efficient in typing.

The upshot of this analysis is that the most efficient outcome is for the lawyer to specialize in legal work and the secretary to concentrate on typing. The most efficient and productive pattern of specialization is that people or nations should concentrate on activities in which they are relatively or comparatively more efficient than others; this efficient pattern of specialization may imply that people or nations specialize in areas in which they are absolutely less efficient than others. And even though individual people or countries may be absolutely less or more efficient than all other people and countries, each and every person or country will have a definite comparative advantage in some goods and a definite comparative disadvantage in other goods.

Ricardo's Analysis of Comparative Advantage

Let us illustrate the fundamental principles of international trade by considering America and Europe of a century ago. If labor (or resources more generally) is absolutely more productive in America than in Europe, does this mean that America will import nothing? And is it economically wise for Europe to "protect" its markets with tariffs or quotas?

These questions were first answered by the English economist David Ricardo in 1817. Ricardo supplied a beautiful proof that international specialization benefits a nation, calling the result the law of comparative advantage.

For simplicity, Ricardo worked with only two countries and only two goods, and he chose to measure all production costs in terms of labor-hours. We shall follow his lead here, analyzing food and clothing for Europe and America.[1]

Table 36-2 portrays the principle of comparative advantage. In America, it takes 1 hour of labor to produce a unit of food, while a unit of clothing costs 2 hours of labor. In Europe the cost is 3 hours of labor for food and 4 hours of labor for clothing. We see that America has *absolute advantage* in both goods, for it can produce them with greater absolute efficiency than can Europe. However, America has *comparative advantage* in food, while Europe has comparative advantage in clothing, because food is relatively inexpensive in America while clothing is relatively less expensive in Europe.

From these facts, Ricardo proved that both countries will benefit if they specialize in their areas of comparative advantage—that is, if America specializes in the production of food while Europe specializes in the production of clothing. In this situation, America will export food to pay for European clothing while Europe exports clothing to pay for American food.

To analyze the effects of trade and the benefits of specializing in areas of comparative advantage, we must measure the amounts of food and clothing that can be produced and consumed in each country (*a*) if there is no international trade and (*b*) if there is free trade with each country specializing in its area of comparative advantage.

Before Trade. Start by examining what occurs in the absence of any international trade, say because all trade is illegal or because of a prohibitive tariff. Table 36-2 shows the real wage of the American worker for an hour's work as 1 unit of food or $\frac{1}{2}$ unit of clothing. The European worker is less well off in a no-trade position, getting only $\frac{1}{3}$ unit of food or $\frac{1}{4}$ unit of clothing per hour of work.

Clearly, if perfect competition prevails in each isolated region, the prices of food and clothing will be different in the two places because of the difference in production costs. In America, clothing will be 2 times as expensive as food because it takes twice as much labor to produce a unit of clothing as it does to produce a unit of food. In Europe, clothing will be only $\frac{4}{3}$ as expensive as food.

After Trade. Now suppose that all tariffs are repealed and free trade is allowed. For simplicity, further assume that there are no transportation costs. In this case, goods will flow from their low-price region to their high-price region. Indeed, with no transportation costs, all prices in the two regions must be equalized, just as the water in two connecting pipes must come to a common level once you remove the barrier between them. Hence food sells for the same price everywhere, as will clothing.

What is the flow of goods when trade is opened up? Clothing is relatively more expensive in Amer-

[1] The analysis of comparative advantage with many countries and many commodities is presented later in this chapter.

American and European Labor Requirements for Production

	Necessary labor (labor-hours)	
Product	**In America**	**In Europe**
1 unit of food	1	3
1 unit of clothing	2	4

Table 36-2. Comparative advantage depends only on relative costs

In a hypothetical example, America has lower labor costs in both food and clothing. American labor productivity is between 2 and 3 times Europe's (twice in clothing, thrice in food). Yet it benefits both regions to trade with each other.

ica, and food is relatively more expensive in Europe. Given these relative prices, and with no tariffs or transportation costs, this means that food will soon be shipped from America to Europe and clothing from Europe to America.

As European clothing penetrates the American market, American clothiers will find prices falling and profits shrinking, and they will begin to shut down their factories. The opposite will occur in Europe. European farmers will find that the prices of foodstuffs begin to fall when American products hit the European markets; they will suffer losses, some will go bankrupt, and resources will be withdrawn from farming.

After all the adjustments to international trade have taken place, we will see that the prices of clothing and food are equalized in Europe and America. Without further information, we cannot know the exact level to which prices will move. But we do know that the relative prices of food and clothing must lie somewhere between the European price ratio (which is $\frac{3}{4}$ for the ratio of food to clothing prices) and the American price ratio (which is $\frac{1}{2}$). Let us say that the final price ratio is $\frac{2}{3}$, so that 2 units of clothing trade for 3 units of food. For simplicity, we measure prices in American dollars and assume that the free-trade price of food is $2 per unit, which means that the free-trade price of clothing is $3 per unit.

Moreover, the regions have shifted their productive activities; America has withdrawn resources from clothing and invested in food while Europe has contracted its farm sector and expanded its clothing manufacture. Under free trade, countries shift production toward their areas of comparative advantage.

The Economic Gains from Trade

What are the economic effects of opening up the two regions to international trade? America as a whole benefits from the fact that imported clothing costs less than clothing produced at home. Likewise, Europe benefits from specializing in clothing and getting food more cheaply by importing than it can by domestic production.

We can most easily reckon the gains from trade by calculating the effect of trade upon the real wages of workers. Real wages are measured by the amount of goods and services that a worker can buy with an hour's pay. From Table 36-2, we can see that the real wages after trade will be greater than the real wages before trade for workers in both Europe *and* America. For simplicity, assume that each worker buys 1 unit of clothing and 1 unit of food. Before trade, this bundle of consumer goods costs an American worker 3 hours of work and a European worker 7 hours of work.

After trade has opened up, recall that the price of clothing is $3 per unit while the price of food is $2 per unit. An American worker must still work 1 hour to buy a unit of food; but at the price ratio of 2 to 3, the American worker need work only $1\frac{1}{2}$ hours to produce enough to buy 1 unit of European clothing. Therefore the bundle of goods costs the American worker $2\frac{1}{2}$ hours of work when trade is allowed—this represents an increase of $16\frac{2}{3}$ percent in the real wage of the American worker.

For European workers, a unit of clothing will still cost 4 hours of labor in a free-trade situation, for clothing is domestically produced. To obtain a unit of food, however, the European worker need produce only $\frac{2}{3}$ of a unit of clothing (which requires $\frac{2}{3} \times 4$ hours of labor) and then trade that $\frac{2}{3}$ unit for 1 unit of American food. The total European labor needed to obtain the bundle of consumption is then $4 + 2\frac{2}{3} = 6\frac{2}{3}$, which represents an increase in real wages of about 5 percent over the no-trade situation.

When trade opens and each country concentrates on its area of comparative advantage, everyone is better off. Workers in each region can obtain a larger quantity of consumer goods for the same amount of work when people specialize in the areas of comparative advantage and trade their own production for goods in which they have a relative disadvantage. When borders are opened to international trade, the national income of each and every trading country rises.

Effects of Tariffs and Quotas

We have analyzed the cases of free trade and no trade. What are the impacts of **tariffs** (taxes levied on imports) and **quotas** (quantitative restrictions on imports)?

One effect of restrictions on foreign trade is easily seen from our discussion up to this point. We know that a nation benefits from foreign trade, as opposed to a no-trade situation. It follows therefore that a prohibitive tariff or quota (one stringent enough to shut off all foreign trade) will unambiguously hurt a country:

A prohibitive tariff or quota, far from helping consumers in a country, reduces their real incomes by making imports too expensive and by making the whole world less productive. Countries lose from protectionism because reduced international trade eliminates the efficiency inherent in specialization and division of labor.

Extensions to Many Commodities and Countries

The world of international trade consists of more than two countries and two commodities. However the principles we explained in the example above are essentially unchanged in more realistic situations.

Many Commodities

When two countries produce many commodities at constant costs, they can be arranged in order according to the comparative advantage or cost of each. For example, the commodities might be wheat, aircraft, computers, automobiles, wine, and shoes—all arranged in the comparative-advantage sequence shown in Figure 36-3. As you can see from the figure, of all the commodities, wheat is least expensive in America relative to the costs in Europe. Europe has its greatest comparative advantage in shoes, while its advantage in wine is somewhat less than that in shoes.

We can be virtually sure that the introduction of trade will cause America to produce and export wheat, and Europe will produce and export shoes. But where will the dividing line fall? Between automobiles and computers? Or wine and shoes? Or will the dividing line fall on one of the commodities rather than between them—so that, say, automobiles might be produced in both places?

You will not be surprised to find that the answer depends upon the comparative strength of international demands for the different goods. We can think of the commodities as beads arranged on a string according to their comparative advantage; the strength of supply and demand will determine where the dividing line between American and European production will fall. An increased demand for aircraft and wheat, for example, would tend to shift prices in the direction of American goods. The shift might lead America to specialize so much more in areas of its comparative advantage that it would no longer be profitable to produce in areas of comparative disadvantage, like wine.

Many Countries

What about the case of many countries? Introducing many countries need not change our analysis. As far as a single country is concerned, all the other nations with which it trades can be lumped together into one group as "the rest of the world." The advantages of trade have no special relationship to national boundaries. The principles already developed apply between groups of countries and, indeed, between regions within the same country. In fact, they are just as applicable to trade between our northern and southern states as to trade between the United States and Canada.

Triangular and Multilateral Trade

With many countries brought into the picture, all will find it beneficial to engage in *triangular* or *multilateral trade* with a multitude of other countries. Generally *bilateral* trade between two countries is unbalanced.

A simple example of triangular trade flows is illustrated in Figure 36-4, where the arrows show the

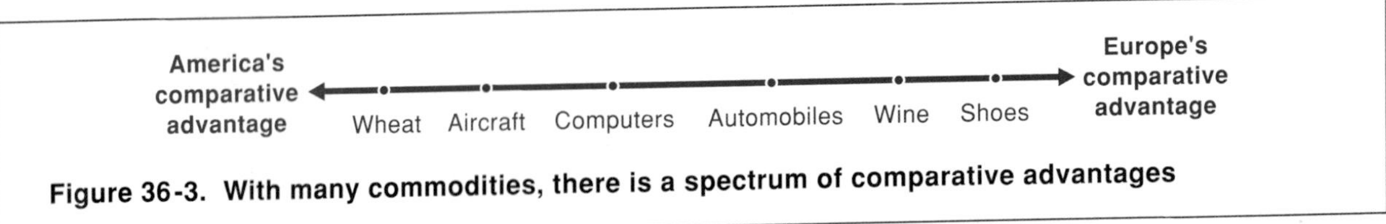

Figure 36-3. With many commodities, there is a spectrum of comparative advantages

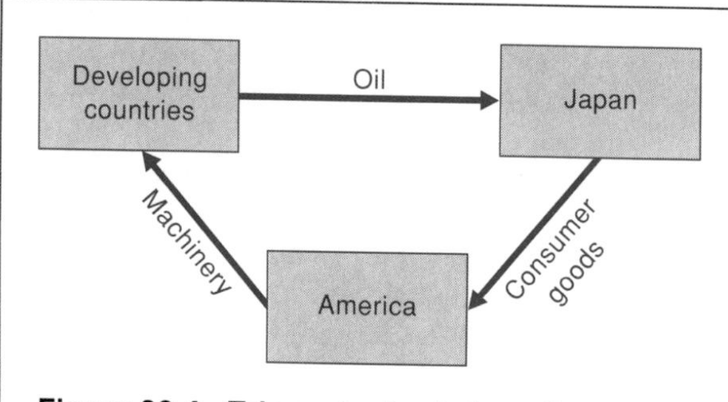

Figure 36-4. Triangular trade benefits all

Advantages of multilateral trade would be much reduced if bilateral balancing were required.

direction of exports. America buys consumer goods from Japan, Japan buys oil and primary commodities from developing countries, and developing countries buy machinery and computers from America. In reality, trade patterns are even more complex than this triangular example.

The multilateral nature of trade should give caution to those who argue for bilateral balance between particular countries, as was the case in recent proposals in the United States. What would happen if all nations signed bilateral trade agreements that balanced trade between each pair of countries? Trade would be sharply curbed; imports would balance exports, but at the level of whichever was the smaller. The gains from trade would be severely reduced.

Graphical Analysis of Comparative Advantage

We can use the production-possibility frontier (*PPF*) to expand our analysis of comparative advantage. We will continue the numerical example based upon labor costs, but the theory is equally valid in a competitive world with many different inputs.

America without Trade

Chapter 2 introduced the *PPF*, which shows the combinations of commodities that can be produced with a society's given resources and technology. Using the simple production data shown in Table 36-2, and assuming that both Europe and America have 600 units of labor, we can easily derive each region's *PPF*. The table that accompanies Figure 36-5 shows the possible levels of food and clothing that America can produce with its inputs and technology. Figure 36-5 plots the production possibilities; the blue line *DA* shows America's *PPF*. The *PPF* has a slope of $-\frac{1}{2}$, for this represents the terms on which food and clothing can be substituted in production; in competitive markets with no international trade, the price ratio of food to clothing will also be one-half.

So far we have concentrated on production and ignored consumption. However, if America is isolated from all international trade, then what it can produce is also what it can consume. Say that, for the incomes and demands in the marketplace, point *B* in Figure 36-5 marks America's production

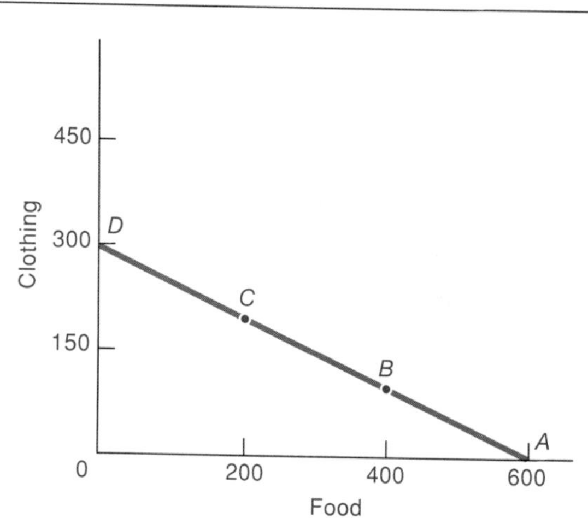

America's Production-Possibility Schedule
(1-to-2 Constant-Cost Ratio)

Possibilities	Food (units)	Clothing (units)
A	600	0
B	400	100
C	200	200
D	0	300

Figure 36-5. American production data

The constant-cost line *DA* represents America's domestic production-possibility frontier. America will produce and consume at *B* in the absence of trade.

and consumption in the absence of trade. Without trade, America produces and consumes 400 units of food and 100 units of clothing.

We can do exactly the same thing for Europe. But Europe's *PPF* will look different from America's because Europe has different efficiencies in producing food and clothing. Europe's price ratio is $\frac{3}{4}$, reflecting Europe's relative productivity in food and clothing.

Opening Up to Trade

Now admit the possibility of trade between the two regions. Food can be exchanged for clothing at some price ratio, or **terms of trade,** which denote the ratio of export prices to import prices. To indicate the trading possibilities, we put the two *PPF*s together in Figure 36-6. America's blue *PPF* shows its domestic production possibilities, while Europe's black *PPF* shows the terms on which it can domestically substitute food and clothing. Note that Europe's *PPF* is drawn closer to the origin than America's. Why? Because Europe has lower productivities in both industries; it has an absolute disadvantage in the production of both food and clothing.

However, Europe need not be discouraged by its absolute disadvantage, for it is the difference in *relative* productivities or *comparative* advantage that makes trade beneficial. The gains from trade are illustrated by the outer lines in Figure 36-6. If America could trade at Europe's relative prices, it could produce 600 units of food and move northwest along the outer black line in Figure 36-6(*a*)—where the black line represents the price ratio or terms of trade that are generated by Europe's *PPF*. Similarly, if Europe could trade with America and not affect America's relative prices, then Europe could specialize in clothing and move southeast along the blue line in Figure 36-6(*b*)—where the blue line is

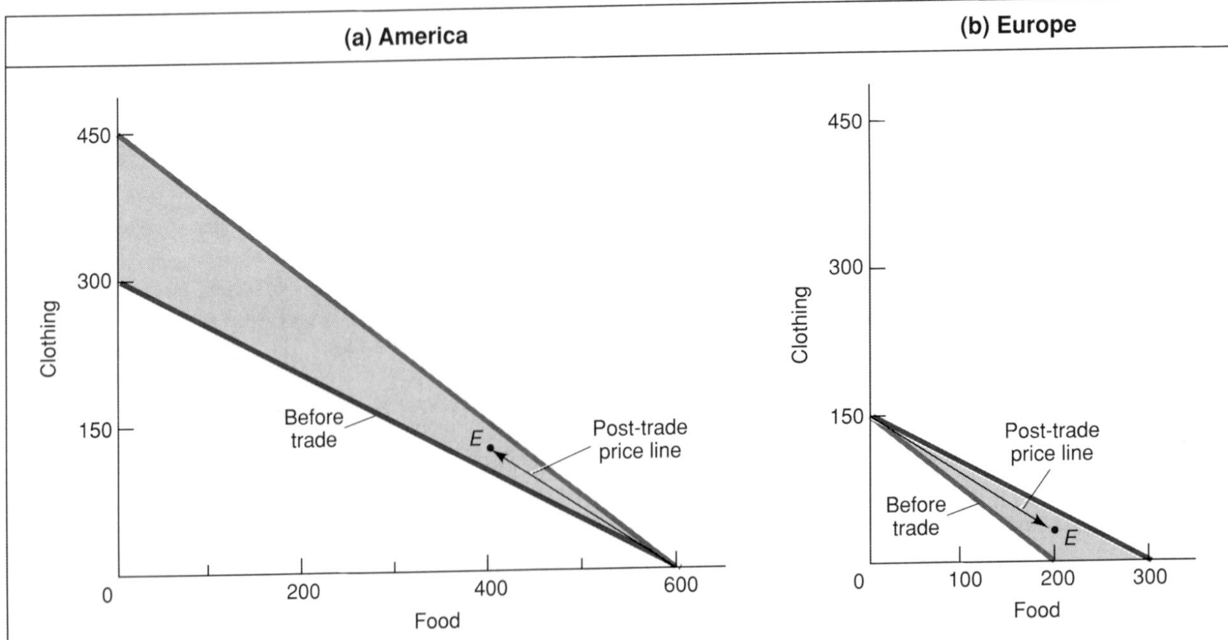

Figure 36-6. Comparative advantage illustrated

Through trade, both Europe and America improve their available consumption. If no trade is allowed, each region must be satisfied with its own production. It is therefore limited to its production-possibility curve, shown for each region as the line marked "Before trade." After borders are opened and competition equalizes relative prices of the two goods, the relative-price line will be as shown by the arrow. It lies somewhere between the blue price line (America's prices before trade) and the black price line (Europe's prices before trade).

If each region is faced with prices given by the arrows, can you see why its consumption possibilities must improve?

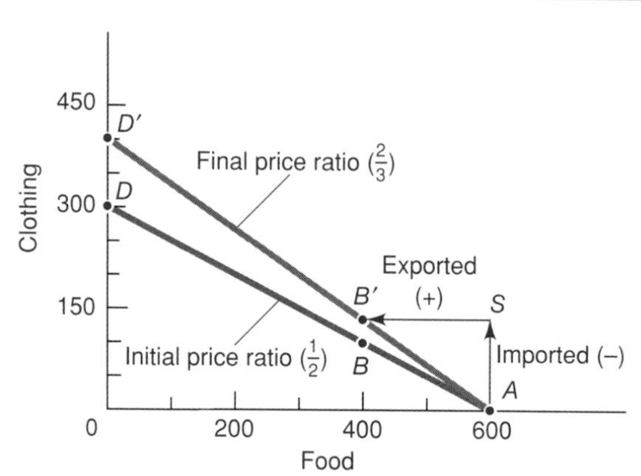

Figure 36-7. America before and after trade

Free trade expands the consumption options of America. The blue line *DA* represents America's domestic production-possibility curve; the black line *D′A*, its new consumption-possibility curve when it is able to trade freely at the price ratio $\frac{2}{3}$ and in consequence to specialize completely in the production of food (at *A*). The blue arrows from *S* to *B′* and *A* to *S* show the amounts exported (+) and imported (–) by America. As a result of free trade, America ends up at *B′* with more of both goods available than before trade at *B*.

America's pre-trade price ratio.[2]

Equilibrium Price Ratio. Once trade opens up, some set of prices must hold in the world marketplace. What prices? To dramatize this question, let us suppose that an auctioneer stands in mid-ocean and attempts to find the prices that balance supply and demand. That is, she wants to find the food and clothing prices at which the offers of food and clothing are exactly equal. She does this by calling out prices and adjusting them when imbalances occur. When she arrives at the equilibrium price level, she raps her gavel and shouts, "Going, going, gone!"

What will be the final prices? Without further information we cannot specify the exact price ratio, but we can determine what the price range will be. The prices must lie somewhere between the prices of the two regions. That is, we know that the relative price of food and clothing must lie somewhere in the range [$\frac{1}{2}$, $\frac{3}{4}$].

The final price ratio will depend upon the relative demands for food and clothing. If food is very much in demand, then the food price would be relatively high. If food demand were so high that Europe produced food, then the price ratio would be at Europe's relative prices, or $\frac{3}{4}$. On the other hand, if clothing demand were relatively high, then the relative price of clothing would rise; if clothing demand were so strong that America produced clothing, then the terms of trade would equal America's price ratio of $\frac{1}{2}$. If each region specializes completely in the area of its comparative advantage, with Europe producing only clothing and America producing only food, then the price ratio will lie somewhere between $\frac{1}{2}$ and $\frac{3}{4}$. The exact ratio will depend on the strength of demand.

For our example, we assume that the levels of demand are such that the final price ratio is $\frac{2}{3}$, with 3 units of food selling for 2 units of clothing. With this price ratio, each region can then specialize—America in food and Europe in clothing—and export some of its production to pay for imports at the world price ratio of $\frac{2}{3}$.

Figure 36-6 illustrates how trade will take place. Each region will face a *consumption-possibility curve* according to which it can produce, trade, and consume. This consumption-possibility curve begins at the region's best point of specialization and then runs out at the world price ratio of $\frac{2}{3}$. Figure 36-6(*a*) shows America's consumption possibilities as a thin black arrow with slope of $-\frac{2}{3}$ coming out of its best production point at 600 units of food and no clothing. Similarly, Europe's post-trade consumption possibilities are shown in Figure 36-6(*b*) by the black arrow running southeast from its point of best specialization with a slope of $-\frac{2}{3}$.

The final outcome is shown by the points *E* in Figure 36-6. At this free-trade equilibrium, Europe specializes in producing clothing and America specializes in producing food. Europe exports $133\frac{1}{3}$ units of clothing for 200 units of America's food. Both regions are able to consume more than they would produce alone; both regions have benefited from international trade.

Figure 36-7 illustrates the benefits of trade for America. The blue inner line shows the *PPF*, while the black outer line shows the consumption possi-

[2] This discussion demonstrates a paradox: Little countries have the most to gain from international trade. They affect world prices the least and therefore can trade at world prices that are very different from domestic prices. Why might large countries gain least from international trade?

bilities at the world price ratio of $\frac{2}{3}$. The blue arrows show the amounts exported and imported. America ends up at the point B'. Through trade it moves onto the black line $D'A$ just as if a fruitful new invention had pushed out its *PPF*.

The lessons of this analysis are summarized in Figure 36-8. This figure shows the *world* production-possibility frontier. How is the world *PPF* obtained? It represents the maximum output that can be obtained from the world's resources when goods are produced in the most efficient manner, that is, with the most efficient division of labor and regional specialization.

The world *PPF* is built up from the two regional *PPF*s (see Figure 36-6) by determining the maximum level of world output that can be obtained from the individual region *PPF*s. For example, the maximum quantity of food that can be produced (with no clothing production) is seen in Figure 36-6 to be 600 units in America and 200 units in Europe, for a world maximum of 800 units. This same point (800 food, 0 clothing) is then plotted in the world *PPF* in Figure 36-8. Additionally, we can plot the point (0 food, 450 clothing) in the world *PPF* by inspection of the regional *PPF*s. All the individual points in between can be constructed by a careful calculation of the maximum world outputs that can be produced if the two regions are efficiently specializing in the two goods.

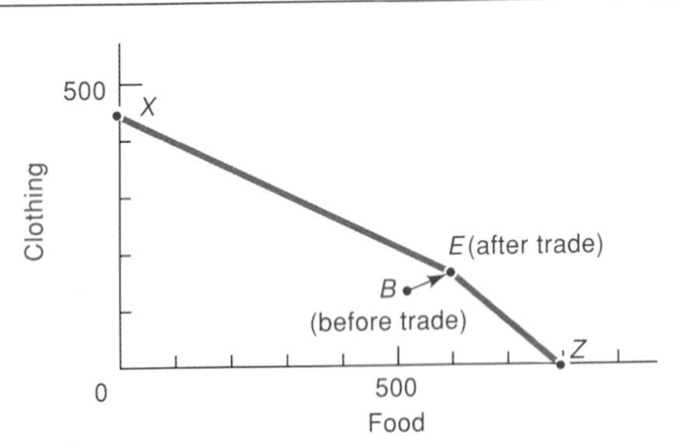

Figure 36-8. Free trade allows world to move to its production-possibility frontier

We here show the effect of free trade from the viewpoint of the world as a whole.

Before trade is allowed, each region is on its own national *PPF*. Without trade, regions are producing goods in which they are relatively inefficient, so the world is *inside* the *world PPF*, shown as the blue line *XEZ*.

Free trade allows each region to specialize in the goods in which it has comparative advantage. As a result of the specialization, the world as a whole moves out to point *E*, which is on the world *PPF*.

Before opening up borders to trade, the world is at point *B*. This is an inefficient point—inside the world *PPF*—because regions have different levels of *relative* efficiency in different goods.

After opening the borders to trade, the world moves out to point *E*, the free-trade equilibrium. At *E*, countries are specializing in areas of comparative advantage. With free trade in competitive markets, the world is on its production-possibility frontier.

Qualifications and Conclusions

We have now completed our look at the elegant theory of comparative advantage. Its conclusions apply for any number of countries and commodities. Moreover, it can be generalized to handle many inputs, changing factor proportions, and diminishing returns.

But comparative advantage has its limitations. The major defect lies in its classical assumptions, for it assumes a smoothly working economy with flexible prices and wages and no involuntary unemployment. Would the theory still hold if autoworkers, laid off when the share of Japanese cars sold in the American market rises rapidly, cannot easily find new jobs? What if an overvalued foreign exchange rate reduces the demand for manufacturing workers and these workers cannot find comparable jobs in other sectors? In such cases, trade might well push a nation *inside* its *PPF* as unemployment rose and GNP fell, and the gains from trade along with the theory of comparative advantage would fail.

Given this reservation, there can be little wonder that the theory of comparative advantage sells at a big discount during periods of major macroeconomic dislocations. During the Great Depression of the 1930s, as unemployment soared and real outputs fell, nations built high tariff walls at their borders and the volume of foreign trade shrank sharply. Comparative advantage gained prestige in the period after World War II as economic integration among the world's industrial nations led to a period of unprecedented economic growth. But, in every recession, underutilized labor and capital lobby to protect their markets from foreign competition. These epochs of history remind us that the classical theory of comparative advantage is strictly valid only when exchange rates, prices, and wages are at appropriate levels and when macroeconomic policies banish major business cycles or trade dislocations from the economic scene.

Notwithstanding its limitations, the theory of comparative advantage provides a most important glimpse of truth. A nation that neglects comparative advantage may pay a heavy price in terms of living standards and economic growth.

B. The Balance of International Payments

Balance-of-Payments Accounts

The affairs of nations today are heavily involved in their trade deficits and foreign debts or credits. The press is full of stories about the trade deficit or growing indebtedness of the United States, or the need for balance-of-payments adjustments in Latin American countries. In order to master the elements of international trade, a general understanding of the nature of balance-of-payments accounting is essential.

Up to now we have treated international trade as if nations simply barter goods—oil for aircraft or bananas for computers. In fact, international exchange, like domestic exchange, takes place through the medium of money, and the monetary flows into and out of a country are measured in a nation's balance of payments.

A country's **balance of international payments** is a systematic statement of all economic transactions between that country and the rest of the world; it forms an overall measure of the flows of goods, services, and capital between a country and the rest of the world. The U.S. Department of Commerce keeps records of U.S. transactions, makes official estimates of all international transactions, and publishes the U.S. balance-of-payments statistics. These include data on merchandise exports and imports, money lent or borrowed abroad, tourist expenditures, interest and dividends paid or received, and so forth.

The balance of international payments is listed in four sections:

I. Current account
  - Private:
    - Merchandise (or "trade balance")
    - Invisibles (services and net investment income)
    - Governmental exports or imports and grants

II. Capital account
  - Private
  - Government

III. Statistical discrepancy

IV. Official settlements

We will now explain each of these major components of the balance of payments.

Debits and Credits

Like other accounts, balance-of-payments accounts record pluses and minuses. A plus item is called a *credit,* while a minus item is called a *debit.*

In general, exports are **credits** and imports are **debits.** A good rule to use in deciding how any item should be treated is to ask whether it earns foreign currencies for the country. *Foreign currencies* are other countries' monies.

Remember the following rule:

If an item provides us with more foreign currency, as exports do, it is called a "credit." If the item is like imports and draws down our stock of foreign currencies, it is called a "debit."

How is the U.S. import of a Japanese camera recorded? It is clearly a debit, for it depletes our stock of Japanese yen. How shall we treat interest and dividend income on investments received by Americans from abroad? Clearly, they are credit items like exports because they provide us with foreign currencies.

Details of the Balance of Payments

Balance on Current Account. The totality of items under section I is usually referred to as the **balance on current account.** This summarizes the difference between our total exports and imports of goods and services. It is almost identical to net exports in the national output accounts.

In the past, many writers concentrated on the **trade balance,** which consists of merchandise imports or exports. The composition of merchandise imports and exports was shown in Table 36-1; it consists mainly of primary commodities (like food and fuels) and manufactured goods. In an earlier era, the mercantilists strove for a trade surplus (an excess of exports over imports), calling this a "favorable balance of trade." They hoped to avoid an "unfavorable trade balance," by which they meant a trade deficit (an excess of imports over exports). This choice of terms has carried over to today as many nations seek trade surpluses; economics teaches, however, that trade deficits are sometimes economically advantageous for countries that need an infusion of foreign capital.

In addition to the trade balance, we must not forget the increasing role played by *invisibles,* which include services and investment income. Services consist of such items as shipping, financial services, and foreign travel. Investment income includes the net earnings on investment abroad (that is, earnings on U.S. assets abroad less payments on foreign assets in the U.S.). The invisibles component was an important positive or credit item for the United States from World War II until the 1980s, although the U.S. international debt position has reduced this surplus item in the early 1990s.

Table 36-3 presents a summary of the U.S. balance of international payments for 1990. Note its four main divisions: current account, capital account, statistical discrepancy, and official settlements. (Each row is numbered to make reference easy.) Each item is listed by name in column (a). Credits are listed in column (b) while column (c) shows the debits. Column (d) then lists the net

U.S. Balance of Payments, 1990
(Billions of Dollars)

Section	(a) Items	(b) Credits (+)	(c) Debits (−)	(d) Net credits (+) or debits (−)
I.	**Current account**			
	1. Merchandise trade balance	390	−498	−108
	2. Invisibles (services, investment income, other)			9
	3. Balance on current account			−99
II.	**Capital account** [lending (−) or borrowing (+)]			
	4. Capital flows	88	−59	
	5. Balance on capital account			29
III.	**Statistical discrepancy**			73
	6. Total needing to be offset (line 3 + line 5 + statistical discrepancy)			2
IV.	**Official settlements**			
	7. Official settlements balance (net change in U.S. official assets)			−2
	8. Formal overall net total			0

Table 36-3. By definition, current account plus capital account plus statistical discrepancy must be offset by official government settlements
(Source: Adapted from U.S. Department of Commerce.)

credits or debits; it shows a credit if the item added to our stock of foreign currencies or a debit if, on balance, it subtracted from our foreign currency supply.

In 1990 our merchandise exports gave us credits of $390 billion. But our merchandise imports gave us debits of $498 billion. The *net* difference between credits and debits was a debit of $108 billion. This "trade deficit" is listed in column (d), on the first row. (Be sure you know why the algebraic sign is shown as − rather than as +.) From the table we see that services or invisible items plus transfers were slightly in surplus. Our current account deficit was thus $99 billion for 1990.

Capital Account. We have now completed analysis of the current account. But how did the United States "finance" its $99 billion current account deficit in 1990? The United States must have either borrowed or reduced its foreign assets. For it is definitional that what you buy you must either pay for or owe for. This means that the balance of international payments as a whole must by definition show a final zero balance.

Capital movements are loans private citizens or governments make to or receive from foreign private citizens or governments. Capital movements occur, for example, when a Japanese pension fund buys U.S. government securities or when an American buys stock in a British firm.

It is easy to decide which are credit and which are debit items in the capital account if you use the following rule: Always think of the United States as exporting and importing stocks, bonds, or other securities—or, for short, exporting and importing IOUs in return for foreign currencies. Then you can treat these exports and imports like any other exports and imports. When we borrow abroad to finance a current account deficit, we are sending IOUs (like Treasury bills) abroad and gaining foreign currencies. Is this a credit or a debit? Clearly this transaction gives rise to a credit.

Similarly, if our banks lend abroad to finance a steel mill in Brazil, this means the U.S. banks are importing IOUs from Brazilians and losing foreign currencies; this is clearly a debit item.

Line 5 shows that in 1990 the United States was a net *borrower:* we borrowed abroad more than we lent to foreigners. The United States was a net exporter of IOUs (a net borrower) in the amount of $29 billion.

Part III shows that there was a huge statistical discrepancy (the net sum of all unrecorded transactions) accounting for $73 billion. This indicates that $73 billion of unrecorded funds entered the United States.

Adding all current and capital account items to the statistical discrepancy, we find a net surplus of $2 billion.

Official Settlements. When the United States was on the gold standard and the government followed a strict laissez-faire policy, any amount remaining on line 6 had to be settled by exporting or importing gold. Now that countries are no longer on the gold standard, they balance their books with government payments or receipts of foreign currencies. These balancing flows provided by governments are called "official settlements." The most common way of providing official settlements today is for countries to buy or sell U.S. government securities. Note that in line 7 there was a small addition ($2 billion) to U.S. official assets in 1990.

Stages of the Balance of Payments

A review of the economic history of advanced industrial countries reveals that they go through four stages in their balance of payments as they grow from young debtor to mature creditor. This sequence is found, with variations related to their particular histories, in the advanced economies of North America, Europe, and Southeast Asia. We can illustrate the stages by recounting briefly the history of the balance of payments of the United States.

- *Young and growing debtor nation.* From the Revolutionary War until after the Civil War, the United States imported on current account more than it exported. Europe lent the difference, which allowed the country to build up its capital stock. The United States was a typical young and growing debtor nation.
- *Mature debtor nation.* From about 1873 to 1914, the U.S. balance of trade moved into surplus. But growth of the dividends and interest that were owed abroad on past borrowing kept the current account more or less in balance. Capital movements were also nearly in balance as lending just offset borrowing.
- *New creditor nation.* During World War I, the

United States expanded its exports tremendously. American citizens and the government lent money to allies England and France for war equipment and postwar relief needs. The United States emerged from the war a creditor nation.

- *Mature creditor nation.* In the fourth stage, earnings on foreign capital and investments provided a large surplus on invisibles that was matched by a deficit on merchandise trade. This pattern was followed by the United States until the early 1980s. Countries like Japan and West Germany today play the role of mature creditor nation as they enjoy large current account surpluses which they in turn invest abroad.

The United States, surprisingly, has moved out of the mature creditor nation stage, as the balance-of-payments data in Table 36-3 shows. The United States is once again a debtor nation, borrowing large amounts from stage-4 countries. The difference between this new situation and stage 1 is that the borrowings are now for consumption rather than for investment.

Some economists wonder whether the United States has entered a fifth stage, that of *senile debtor nation.* They note that the macroeconomic policy mix of tight money and high government deficits of the 1980s has lowered national saving. The United States is now unable to generate a volume of saving sufficient to provide its capital requirements, and we must turn to thriftier nations to do our saving for us. The counterpart of American dissaving is that foreigners, particularly Japanese investors, are purchasing substantial American assets for their portfolios.

Is this new stage of the U.S. balance of payments a transient period? Or does it mark the beginning of a long period of "structural" trade deficits that will last for decades to come? No one can answer this question with certainty. Corrective forces in the early 1990s appear to be returning the U.S. current account back toward balance, but with a heavy foreign debt to service. When that occurs, the United States will once again be a mature debtor nation, going back to stage 2 above.

SUMMARY

A. Economic Basis for International Trade

1. As soon as differences in productivities arise within a country, specialization and exchange become beneficial. The same holds across nations. International exchange allows an efficient degree of specialization and division of labor—one that is more efficient than relying only on domestic production.

2. Diversity is the fundamental reason that nations engage in international trade. Within this general principle, we see that trade occurs: (a) because of differences in the conditions of production; (b) because of decreasing costs (or economies of scale); and (c) because of diversity in tastes.

3. The most profound reason for international trade is the Ricardian principle of comparative advantage. This principle holds that trade between two regions is advantageous even if one region is absolutely more or less productive than the other in all commodities. As long as there are differences in *relative* or *comparative* efficiencies among countries, every country must enjoy a comparative advantage or a comparative disadvantage in some goods. Powerful benefits arise when countries specialize in the production of goods in their areas of comparative advantage, exporting those goods and trading them for goods in which other nations have a comparative advantage.

4. The law of comparative advantage predicts more than just the geographical pattern of specialization and direction of trade. It also demonstrates that countries are made better off and that the real wages (or, more generally,

returns to the factors of production taken as a whole) are improved by trade and the resulting enlarged totals of world production. Prohibitive quotas and tariffs, designed to "protect" workers or industries, will lower a nation's total income and consumption possibilities.

5. When there are many goods or many countries, the same principles of comparative advantage apply. With many commodities, we can arrange products along a continuum of comparative advantage, from relatively more efficient to relatively less efficient. With many countries, trade may be "triangular" or multilateral, with countries having large bilateral (or two-sided) surpluses or deficits with other individual countries. Triangular trade allows imbalances in bilateral trade, but this reflects the fact that a nation's accounts must balance only multilaterally—between a nation and the rest of the world. Imposing bilateral balance would hamper economic efficiency.

B. The Balance of International Payments

6. The balance of international payments is the set of accounts that measures all the economic transactions between a nation and the rest of the world. It includes exports and imports of goods, services, and financial capital. Exports are credit items, while imports are debits. More generally, a country's credit items are transactions that make foreign currencies available to it; debit items are ones that reduce its holdings of foreign currencies.

7. The major components of the balance of payments are:
   I. Current account (including the merchandise or trade balance along with invisibles like services and investment income)
   II. Capital account (private and government purchases and sales of assets like stocks, bonds, and real estate)
   III. Statistical discrepancy
   IV. Official settlements

   The rule of balance-of-payments accounting is that the sum of all items must equal zero: I + II + III + IV = 0.

8. Historically, countries tend to go through stages of the balance of payments: from the young debtor borrowing for economic development, through mature debtor and young creditor, to mature creditor nation living off earnings from past investments. In the 1980s, the United States moved to yet a different stage where low domestic saving again led it to borrow heavily abroad and become a debtor nation.

CONCEPTS FOR REVIEW

Principles of international trade
open economy
sources of trade: cost differences, decreasing costs, differences in tastes, comparative advantage
absolute and comparative advantage (or disadvantage)
principle of comparative advantage

economic gains from trade
effects of tariffs and quotas
spectrum of comparative advantage
triangular and multilateral trade
terms of trade
consumption vs. production possibilities with trade
world vs. national *PPF*s

Balance of payments
balance of payments (current account, capital account, official settlements)
balance of payments must total zero: I + II + III + IV = 0
debits and credits
stages of balance of payments

QUESTIONS FOR DISCUSSION

1. "Buying a good abroad cheaper than we can produce it at home is to our advantage." Is this consistent with comparative advantage?
2. State whether or not each of the following is correct and explain your reasoning. If the quotation is incorrect, provide a corrected statement.
   (a) "We Mexicans can never compete profitably with the Northern colossus. Her factories are too efficient, she has too many computers and machine tools, and her engineering skills are too advanced. We need tariffs, or we can export nothing!"
   (b) "Because of international trade, a nation can consume outside its production-possibility curve."
   (c) "If American workers are subjected to the unbridled competition of cheap foreign labor, our real wages must necessarily fall drastically."
   (d) "The current account for a country need not balance bilaterally (i.e., with each country), but it must balance multilaterally (i.e., with all countries)."
   (e) "The principle of comparative advantage applies equally well to families, cities, and states as it does to nations and continents."
3. Reconstruct Figure 36-5 and its accompanying table to show the production data for Europe; assume that Europe has 600 units of labor and that labor productivities are those given in Table 36-2.
4. What if the data in Table 36-2 changed from (1, 2; 3, 4) to (1, 2; 2, 4)? Show that all trade is killed off. Use this to explain the adage, *"Vive la différence!"* (freely translated as, "Let diversity thrive!").
5. *Follow-up to question 4:* Suppose that the data in Table 36-2 pertain to Korea and America. What are the gains from trade between the two countries? Now suppose that Korea adopts American technology, grows rapidly, and has a technology identical to that in the American column of Table 36-2. What will happen to international trade? What will happen to Korean living standards and real wages? What will happen to American living standards? Is there a lesson here for the impact of converging economies on trade and welfare?
6. Why do the largest gains in trade flow to small countries whose pre-trade prices are very different from prevailing world prices?
7. Why might a newly discovered continent have a comparative advantage in the production of food and raw materials?
8. Draw up a list of items that belong on the credit side of the balance of international payments and another list of items that belong on the debit side. What is meant by a trade surplus? By the balance on current account?
9. Construct hypothetical balance-of-payments accounts for a young debtor country, a mature debtor country, a new creditor country, and a mature creditor country.
10. A Middle East nation suddenly discovers huge oil resources. Show how its balance of trade and current account suddenly turn to surplus. Show how it can acquire assets in New York as a capital account offset. Later, when it uses the assets for internal development, show how its current and capital items reverse their roles.
11. A nation records the following data for 1994: Exports of automobiles ($100) and corn ($150); imports of oil ($150) and steel ($75); tourist expenditures abroad ($25); lending to foreign countries ($50); borrowing from foreign countries ($40); official settlements ($30 accumulation by domestic central bank). Calculate the statistical discrepancy and create a balance-of-payments table like Table 36-3.
12. A U.S. senator recently wrote the following:

    > Trade is supposed to raise the incomes of all nations involved—or at least that is what Adam Smith and David Ricardo taught us. If our economic decline has been caused by the economic growth of our competitors, then these philosophers—and the entire discipline of economics they founded—have been taking us on a 200-year ride.

    Explain why the first sentence is correct. Also explain why the second sentence does not follow from the first. Can you give an example of how economic growth of Country J could lower the standard of living in Country A? (*Hint:* The answer to question 5 will help uncover the fallacy in the quotation.)

CHAPTER 37

PROTECTIONISM AND FREE TRADE

To the Chamber of Deputies: We are subjected to the intolerable competition of a foreign rival, who enjoys such superior facilities for the production of light that he can inundate our national market at reduced price. This rival is no other than the sun. Our petition is to pass a law shutting up all windows, openings and fissures through which the light of the sun is used to penetrate our dwellings, to the prejudice of the profitable manufacture we have been enabled to bestow on the country.

Signed: Candle Makers.
F. Bastiat

The theory of comparative advantage shows how countries can benefit from specialization and international division of labor. Notwithstanding these established economic findings, legislatures are continuously besieged by groups lobbying for "protective" measures—import barriers in the form of tariffs or quotas. In the United States, Congress and the President struggle every year over whether to enact measures to protect domestic industries from inexpensive imports.

Is protectionism sound economic policy? Economists generally agree that it is not. They believe that trade promotes a mutually beneficial division of labor among nations and that free and open trade allows *each* nation to expand its production and consumption possibilities, raising the world's living standard.

But many people disagree with this assessment. Just as Alexander Hamilton wanted to build tariff walls around our manufacturing industries in 1789, so today people argue that we need to protect our industries against foreign competition.

In this chapter we begin by showing how tariffs affect prices and outputs in an industry. We then evaluate the arguments for and against economic protectionism.

Supply-and-Demand Analysis of Trade and Tariffs

In the last chapter, we analyzed the theory of comparative advantage, which shows that countries can engage in trade even though they are absolutely more efficient (or less efficient) than every other country. This doctrine can be illuminated through the use of supply and demand for goods in foreign trade.

Supply-and-Demand Analysis of a Single Traded Good

Consider only the clothing market in America. Assume for simplicity that America is a small part of the market and therefore cannot affect the world price of clothing. (This assumption will allow us to analyze supply and demand very easily; the more realistic case in which a country can affect world prices will be considered later in this chapter.)

Figure 37-1 shows the supply and demand curves for clothing in America. The demand curve of American consumers is drawn as *DD* and the domestic supply curve of American firms as *SS*. We assume that the price of clothing is determined in

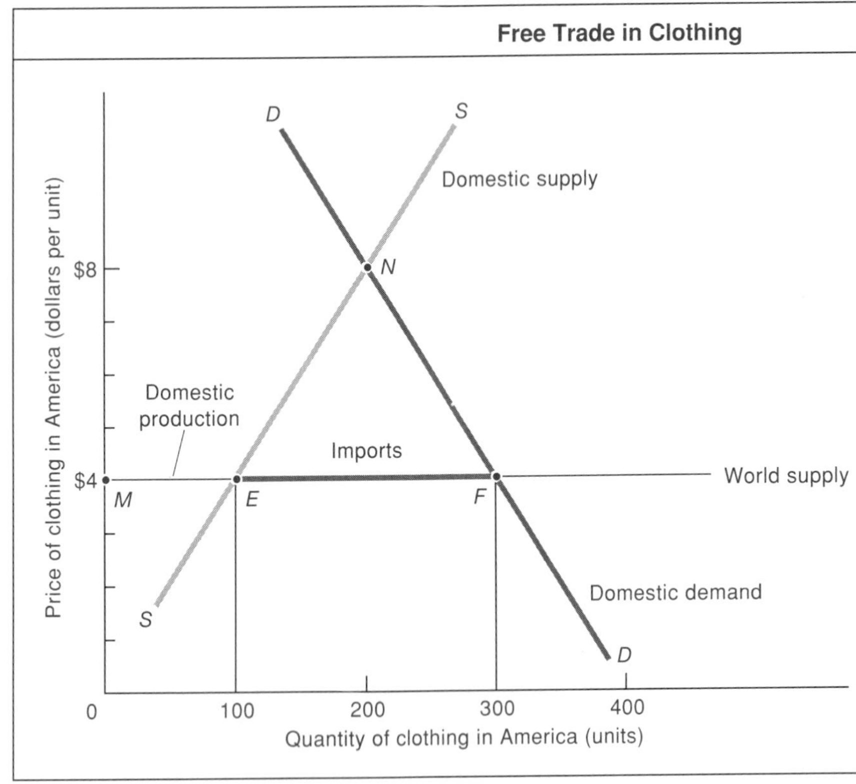

Figure 37-1. American production, imports, and consumption with free trade

We see here the free-trade equilibrium in the market for clothing. America has a comparative disadvantage in clothing. Therefore, at the no-trade equilibrium at *N*, America's price would be $8, while the world price is $4.

Assuming that American demand does not affect the world price of $4 per unit, the free-trade equilibrium comes when America produces *ME* (100 units) and imports the difference between demand and domestic supply shown as *EF* (or 200 units).

the world market (assumed to be much larger than the American market) and is equal to $4 per unit.

Later, we will take into account that transactions in international trade are carried out in different currencies. But for now we can simplify by translating each of those foreign currencies into dollars. For example, although French suppliers want to be paid in francs, we can convert the French supply schedule into a dollar supply curve by using the current exchange rate.

No-Trade Equilibrium. Suppose that transportation costs or tariffs for clothing were prohibitive (say, $100 per unit of clothing). Where would the no-trade equilibrium lie? In this case, the American market for clothing would be at the intersection of domestic supply and demand, shown at point *N* in Figure 37-1. At this no-trade point, prices would be relatively high at $8 per unit, and domestic producers would be meeting all the demand.

Free Trade. Next open up trade in clothing. In the absence of transport costs, tariffs, and quotas, the price in America must be equal to the world price. Why? Because if the American price were above the European price, sharp-eyed entrepreneurs would buy where clothing was cheap (Europe) and sell where clothing was expensive (America)—Europe would export clothing to America. Once trade flows fully adapted to supplies and demands, the price in America would equal the world price level. (In a world *with* transportation and tariff costs, the price in America would equal the world price adjusted for these costs.)

Figure 37-1 illustrates how prices, quantities, and trade flows will be determined under free trade in our clothing example. The horizontal line at $4 represents the supply curve for imports; it is horizontal, or perfectly price elastic, because American demand is assumed to be too small to affect the world price of clothing.

Once trade opens up, imports flow into America, lowering the price of clothing to the world price of $4 per unit. At that level, domestic producers will supply the amount *ME*, or 100 units while at that price consumers will want to buy 300 units. The difference, shown by the heavy line *EF*, is the amount of imports.

Who decided that we would import just this amount of clothing and that domestic producers would supply only 100 units? A European planning agency? A cartel of clothing firms? No, the amount of trade was determined by supply and demand.

Moreover, we can say that the level of prices in the no-trade equilibrium determined the direction of the trade flows. America's no-trade prices were higher than Europe's, so goods flowed into America. Remember this paradoxical rule: *Under free trade, goods flow uphill from low-price regions to high-price regions.* Clothing flows uphill from the low-price European market to the higher-price American market when markets are opened to free trade.

The supply and demand curves are highly useful in understanding the forces operating on a single industry, but they are incomplete. What determines the world price of clothing? Why is the no-trade equilibrium clothing price higher in America than in Europe? To answer these questions we have to analyze the supplies and demands for all industries. In the last chapter, we used general-equilibrium analysis to look at an economy's comparative advantage. The same principles of comparative advantage explain why Europe would export clothing and import food.[1]

Tariffs and Quotas

For centuries, governments have used tariffs and quotas to raise revenues and influence the development of individual industries. Since the eighteenth century—when the British Parliament attempted to impose tariffs on tea, sugar, and other commodities on its American colonies—tariff policy has proved fertile soil for revolution and political struggle.

We can use supply-and-demand analysis to understand the economic effects of tariffs and quotas. To begin with, note that a **tariff** is a tax levied on imports. Table 37-1 shows some representative tariff rates for the United States and Japan in the 1980s. To take an example, the United States today has a 2.5 percent tariff on automobiles. If a foreign car costs $10,000, then the domestic price including the tariff would be $10,250. A **quota** is a limit on the quantity of imports. The United States has quotas on many products, including peanuts, textiles, and beef.

	Average tariff rate, 1987 (%)	
Commodity class	United States	Japan
Agricultural products	1.8	18.4
Food products	4.7	25.4
Wearing apparel	22.7	13.8
Printing and publishing	0.7	0.1
Iron and steel	3.6	2.8
Transport equipment	2.5	1.5
Average, industrial products	4.4	2.8

Table 37-1. Average tariff rates for United States and Japan

Tariff rates for industrial countries like the United States and Japan are generally low today. High tariffs or import quotas are found in politically sensitive sectors like agriculture in Japan and clothing in the United States. [Source: Congressional Budget Office, *The GATT Negotiations and U.S. Trade Policy* (U.S. Government Printing Office, Washington, June 1987).]

Prohibitive Tariff. The easiest case to analyze is a *prohibitive tariff*—one that is so high as to completely discourage any imports. Looking back at Figure 37-1, what would happen if the tariff on clothing is more than $4 per unit (that is, more than the difference between America's no-trade price of $8 and the world price of $4)? This would be a prohibitive tariff, shutting off all clothing trade. Any importer who buys clothing at the world price of $4 can sell it in America for at most the no-trade price of $8. But the tariff the importer has to pay would come to more than the difference between the U.S. price and the world price. Prohibitive tariffs thus kill off all trade.

Nonprohibitive Tariff. More moderate tariffs (less than $4 per unit of clothing) would injure but not kill off trade. Figure 37-2 shows the equilibrium in the clothing market with a $2 tariff. Again assuming no transportation costs, a $2 tariff means that foreign clothing will sell in America for $6 per unit (equal to the $4 world price plus the $2 tariff).

The equilibrium result of a $2 tariff is to lower

[1] Economists explain that these supply and demand curves depict only "partial equilibrium." They must be anchored in general-equilibrium analysis, of which the Ricardian theory of comparative advantage described in Chapter 36 is a special case.

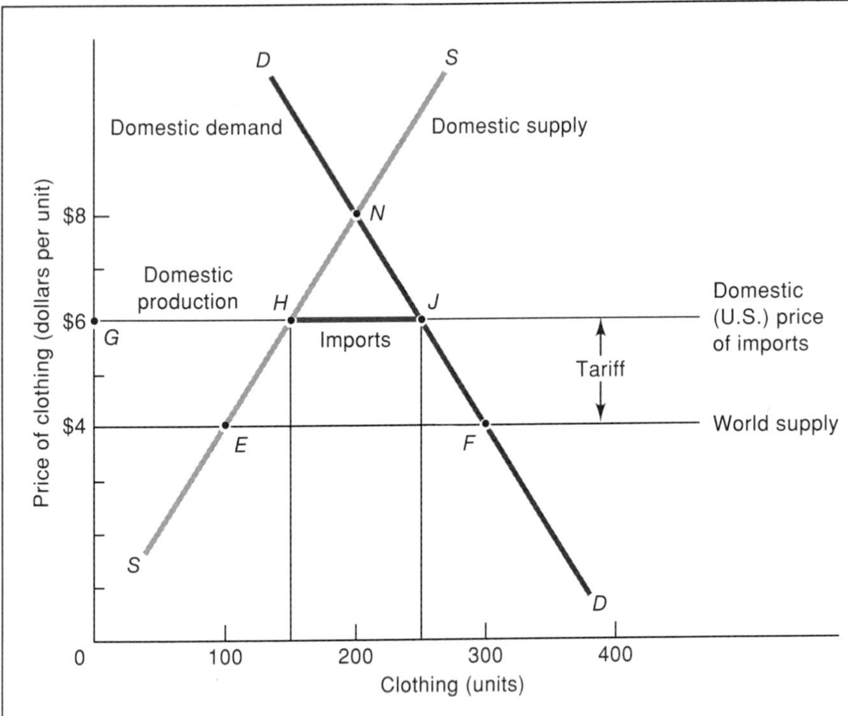

Figure 37-2. Effect of tariff

A tariff lowers imports and consumption, raises domestic production and price. Starting from the free-trade equilibrium in Fig. 37-1, America now puts a $2 tariff on clothing imports. The price of European clothing imports rises to $6 (including the tariff).

The market price rises from $4 to $6, so the total amount demanded falls. Imports shrink from 200 units to 100 units, while domestic production rises from 100 to 150 units.

domestic consumption (or quantity demanded) from 300 units in the free-trade equilibrium to 250 units after the tariff is imposed, to raise the amount of domestic production by 50 units, and to lower the quantity of imports by 100 units. This example summarizes the economic impact of tariffs:

A tariff will tend to raise price, lower the amounts consumed and imported, and raise domestic production.

Quotas. Quotas have the same qualitative effect as tariffs. A prohibitive quota (one that prevents all imports) would achieve the same result as a prohibitive tariff. The price and quantity would move back to the no-trade equilibrium at *N* in Figure 37-2. A less stringent quota might limit imports to 100 clothing units; this quota would equal the heavy line *HJ* in Figure 37-2. A quota of 100 units would lead to the same equilibrium price and output as did the $2 tariff.

Although there is no essential difference between tariffs and quotas, some subtle differences do exist. A quota makes an industry more prone to supply shocks. Moreover, a tariff gives revenue to the government, perhaps allowing other taxes to be reduced and thereby offsetting some of the harm done to customers in the importing country. A quota, on the other hand, puts the profit from the resulting price difference into the pocket of the importers lucky enough to get a permit or license to import. They can afford to wine and dine, or even bribe, the officials who give out import licenses.

Because of these differences, economists generally regard tariffs as the lesser evil. They advise that, if a government is determined to impose quotas, it should auction off the scarce import-quota licenses. An auction will ensure that the government rather than the importer or the exporter gets the revenue from the scarce right to import; and in addition, the bureaucracy will not be tempted to allocate quota rights by bribery, friendship, or nepotism.

Transportation Costs. What of transportation costs? The cost of moving bulky and perishable goods has the same effect as tariffs, reducing the extent of beneficial regional specialization. For example, if it costs $2 per unit to transport clothing from Europe to the United States, the supply-and-demand equilibrium would look just like Figure 37-2, with the American price $2 above the European price.

But there is one difference between protection and transportation costs: transport costs are imposed by nature—by distances, mountains, and rivers. Restrictive tariffs are squarely the responsibility of nations. Indeed, one economist called tariffs "negative railroads." Imposing a tariff has the same economic impact as throwing sand in the engines of vessels that transport goods to our shores from other lands.

The Economic Costs of Tariffs

In the last chapter, we saw that all countries would benefit by opening up their borders to international trade. We can also use our supply-and-demand apparatus to analyze the economic costs of tariffs.

What happens when America puts a tariff on clothing, such as the $2 tariff shown in Figure 37-2? We have seen that there are three effects: (*a*) The domestic producers, operating under a price umbrella provided by the tariff, can now expand production; (*b*) consumers are faced with higher prices and therefore reduce their consumption; and (*c*) the government gains tariff revenue. What is the net economic impact of the tariff?

Tariffs create economic inefficiency. More precisely, when tariffs are imposed, the economic loss to consumers exceeds the revenue gained by the government plus the extra profits earned by producers.

Diagrammatic Analysis

Figure 37-3 shows the economic cost of a tariff. The supply and demand curves are identical to those in Figure 37-2, but three areas are highlighted.

A. A tariff raises the price in domestic markets from $4 to $6. Businesses are thereby induced to increase their domestic production using relatively costly capacity. They produce output up to the point where marginal cost is $6 per unit (instead of up to $4 per unit under free trade). Firms reopen inefficient old factories or work existing factories extra shifts. From an economic point of view, using these high-cost plants is inefficient, for the new clothing produced by these factories

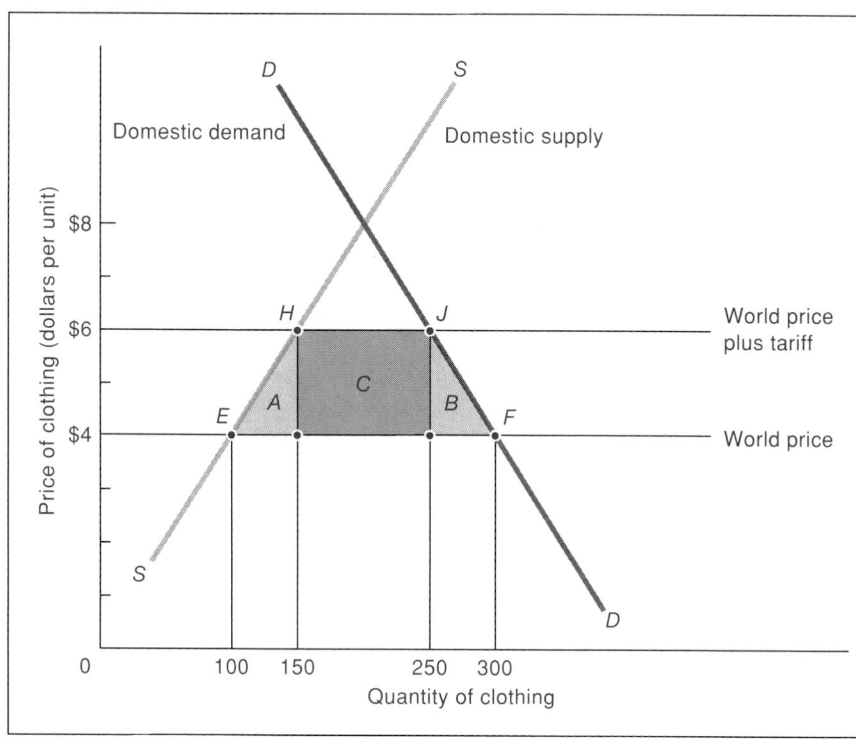

Figure 37-3. Economic cost of tariff

Imposing a tariff raises revenues and leads to inefficiency. We see the impact of the tariff as three effects. Triangle *A* is the cost of the inefficiency in production induced by a higher domestic price. Triangle *B* is the loss in consumer surplus from the inefficiently high price. Rectangle *C* is the tariff revenue gained by the government —a transfer from consumers to the government but not necessarily an efficiency loss.

at costs between $4 and $6 could be bought from abroad at $4.

We can easily depict the amount of this waste as area *A* in Figure 37-3. This area is the sum of the marginal costs of domestic producers (represented by the domestic supply curve) minus the marginal costs of foreign producers ($4). The total loss in *A* is $50 (which, by geometry, is equal to $\frac{1}{2}$ times the tariff times the induced domestic production).

B. In addition, there is a loss of consumer surplus from the too high price. Recall that the demand curve represents the marginal utilities of consumers, or the value of the different units of clothing. The resource cost of each unit of clothing is the world price, $4. Hence, triangle *B* measures the loss in consumer satisfaction from having to cut back on consumption. It is also equal to $50 (which is calculated as equal to one-half the price difference times the consumption reduction).

C. Area *C* is simply the tariff revenue, equal to the amount of the tariff times the units of imports. Revenues in Figure 37-3 are $200. Note that, unlike triangles *A* and *B*, revenue rectangle *C* need not be an efficiency cost or a deadweight loss. The government revenues raised by tariffs can be employed to finance useful government programs or can be returned to consumers.

Figure 37-3 illustrates one feature that is important in understanding the politics and history of tariffs. When a tariff is imposed, part of the impact is upon economic efficiency but the largest effect is often redistributive. In the example shown in Figure 37-3, areas *A* and *B* represent efficiency losses from inefficiently high domestic production and inefficiently low consumption, respectively. Under the simplifying assumptions used above, the efficiency losses are equal to the two little triangles and sum up to $100. The redistribution involved and shown as area *C* is much larger, however, equaling $200 raised in tariff revenues levied upon consumers of the commodity. Consumers will be unhappy about the higher product cost, and producers may attempt to capture the potential revenues by shifting from tariffs to quotas. We can see why battles over import restrictions generally center more on the redistributive gains and losses than on the issues of economic efficiency.

Imposing a tariff has three effects. It encourages inefficient domestic production; it induces consumers to reduce their purchases of the tariffed good below efficient levels; and it raises revenues for the government. Only the first two of these necessarily impose efficiency costs on the economy.

An Example of Tariffs on Textiles

Let's put some flesh on this analysis with the example of a particular tariff, such as a tariff on clothing. Today, tariffs on imported textiles and apparel are among the highest levied by the United States (see Table 37-1). How do these high tariffs affect consumers and producers?

To begin with, the tariff raises domestic clothing prices; it costs more to buy a suit or dress than it would under free trade. Because of the higher prices, many factories, which would otherwise be bankrupt in the face of a declining comparative advantage in textiles, remain open. They are just barely profitable, but they somehow manage to eke out enough sales to continue domestic production. A few more workers are employed in textiles than would otherwise be the case although, because of pressure from foreign competition, textile wages remain among the lowest of any manufacturing industry.

From a national point of view, we are wasting resources in textiles. These workers, materials, and capital would be more productively used in other sectors—perhaps in producing computers or corn or aircraft. The nation's productive potential is lower because it keeps factors of production in an industry in which it has lost its comparative advantage.

Consumers, of course, pay for this protection of the textile industry with higher prices. They get less satisfaction from their incomes than they would if they could buy textiles from Hong Kong, Korea, or China at prices that exclude the high tariffs. Consumers are induced to cut back on their clothing purchases, channeling funds into food, transportation, or recreation, whose relative prices are lowered by the tariff.

In addition, the government gets a few million dollars of revenues from tariffs on textiles. These revenues can be used to buy public goods or to reduce other taxes, so (unlike the consumer loss or the productive inefficiency) this effect is not a real social burden.

Now that we have completed our examination of the way that tariffs affect the price and quantity of a good, we turn to an analysis of the arguments for and against protecting a nation's industries from foreign trade.

The Economics of Protectionism

The arguments for tariff or quota protection against the competition of foreign imports take many different forms. Here are the main categories:

- Non-economic arguments that suggest it is desirable to sacrifice economic welfare in order to subsidize other national objectives
- Arguments that are economically false: some that are clearly defective and some whose falsity can be detected only by subtle and sophisticated economic reasoning
- A few analyses that are invalid in a perfectly competitive full-employment world, but that contain kernels of truth for a nation large enough to affect its import or export prices or for a nation suffering from unemployment

Many of these arguments are a century old; others have been devised by a school known as the "new international economics."[2]

Non-Economic Goals

The first category is most easily considered. If you ever are on a debating team given the assignment of defending free trade, you will strengthen your case at the beginning by conceding that economic welfare is not the only goal in life. A nation surely should not sacrifice its liberty and national security for a few dollars of extra real income gained in trade.

Consider the example of oil. If foreign supplies of oil are insecure, subject to sabotage and monopolization, then it would surely be reasonable for a nation to attempt to reduce its dependence on imported oils.

In some cases, a nation might not produce enough of a product for its essential military needs. This might be true for cobalt or copper. The domestic copper industry might come before Congress and lobby for a high tariff on copper, arguing that only by this means can the nation guarantee an adequate supply in wartime. A careful analysis of this contention reveals that there are often more efficient ways of ensuring the needed amount of strategic materials than by raising tariffs—a particularly useful policy being the storage of such materials in a strategic stockpile.

Yet another argument is that the nation's scientific resources (in aircraft, microelectronics, or computers) will wither away if they are not kept hard at work, protected from foreign competition. Tariffs are sometimes seen as part of a social strategy—to preserve the family farm or the centuries-old tradition of Swiss watchmaking.

A thoughtful analyst cannot dismiss such objectives out of hand. But most economists prefer the use of subsidies rather than quotas or tariffs as a way of attaining non-economic goals. A *subsidy* is a direct payment to a person or a firm that performs a desired service. For example, if the United States wants to maintain its peanut-farming tradition, subsidizing peanut farms would be more efficient than imposing a prohibitive quota on peanuts. Subsidies are preferable because they are more visible and can be debated openly; they prevent sky-high prices that are sometimes produced when supply shocks occur; they do not raise all prices, but affect only the returns of the subsidized firms or workers; and they are subject to periodic review by legislatures.

There are many non-economic goals in a humane society. But attaining them by economic protectionism is usually inefficient and costly.

Grounds for Tariffs Not Based on Sound Economics

Mercantilism. To Abraham Lincoln has been attributed the remark, "I don't know much about the tariff. I do know that when I buy a coat from England, I have the coat and England has the money. But when I buy a coat in America, I have the coat and America has the money."

This reasoning represents an age-old fallacy typi-

[2] An official statement on trade policy is contained in the *Economic Report of the President,* 1991 (Governent Printing Office, Washington, 1991). For a nontechnical account of the sources of the trade deficit and an account of the "new international economics" as told by one of its leading practitioners, see Paul Krugman, *The Age of Diminished Expectations: U.S. Economic Policy in the 1990s* (MIT Press, Cambridge, Mass., 1990).

cal of the so-called mercantilistic writers of the seventeenth and eighteenth centuries. They considered a country fortunate which sold more goods than it bought because such a "favorable" balance of trade meant that gold would flow into the country to pay for its export surplus.

The mercantilist argument confuses the means and the ends of economic activity. Accumulating gold or other monies will not improve a country's living standard. Money is worthwhile not for its own sake, but for what it will buy from other countries. Most economists today therefore reject the idea that raising tariffs to run a trade surplus will improve a country's economic welfare.

Tariffs for Special-Interest Groups. The single most important source of pressure for protective tariffs comes from powerful special-interest groups. Both business and labor know very well that a tariff on their products will help *them*, whatever its effect on total production and consumption. Adam Smith understood this point well when he wrote:

> To expect . . . freedom of trade . . . is as absurd as to expect . . . Utopia. Not only the prejudices of the public, but what is much more unconquerable, the private interests of many individuals, irresistibly oppose it.

A century ago, outright bribery was used to get the votes necessary to pass tariff legislation. Today, powerful political action committees (PACs), financed by labor or business, drum up support for tariffs or quotas on textiles, autos, steel, sugar, and other goods.

If free trade is so beneficial to the nation as a whole, why do the proponents of protectionism continue to wield such a disproportionate influence in Congress? The answer lies in the structure of public choice: free trade helps most people only a little, while protection helps a few people a great deal. If political votes were cast in proportion to total economic benefit, every nation would legislate most tariffs out of existence.

But all dollars of economic interests do not always get proportional representation. It is much harder to organize the masses of consumers and producers to agitate for the benefits of free trade than it is to organize a few companies or labor unions to beat the drums against "cheap foreign labor" or "unfair Japanese competition." In every country, the tireless enemies of free trade are the special interests of protected firms and workers.

The most dramatic case is the U.S. quota on sugar, which benefits a few producers while costing American consumers over $1 billion a year. The average consumer is probably unaware that the sugar quota costs $1\frac{1}{2}$ cents a day, and there is little incentive to lobby for free trade.

Competition from Cheap Foreign Labor. Another argument for protection, gauged to appeal to workers, has been the most popular of all in American history. This argument holds that it is impossible for American workers to compete with foreign workers who cost but a small fraction of American wages.

The flaw in the argument is that it ignores the basic principle of comparative advantage. The reason American workers have higher wages is that they are on average more productive. If our equilibrium wage is 10 times that in East Asia, it is because we are on average roughly 10 times more productive in the manufacture of tradable goods. To put this differently, the principle of comparative advantage shows that it will be beneficial for Country A to trade with Country B even if Country B can produce every good more efficiently than can Country A. Trade flows according to comparative advantage, not absolute advantage.

Having shown that the nation gains from importing the goods produced by "cheap foreign labor" in which a nation has a comparative disadvantage, we should not ignore the costs that this strategy may temporarily impose on the affected workers and firms. If plants in a particular locality are unexpectedly shut down because production moves overseas, the local labor market may be inundated with job seekers. Older workers with outdated job skills may have trouble finding attractive jobs and will suffer a decline in their real incomes. The difficulties of displaced workers will be greater when the overall economy is depressed or when the local labor markets have high unemployment. Over the long run, labor markets will reallocate workers from declining to advancing industries, but the transition may be painful for many people.

In summary, the economic answer to the "cheap foreign labor" argument rests on the comparative-advantage analysis. This shows that a country will benefit from trade even though its wages are far above those of its trading partners. High wages come from high efficiency, not from tariff protection.

Retaliatory Tariffs. While many people would agree that a world of free trade would be the best of all possible worlds, they note that this is not the world we live in. They reason, "As long as other countries impose import restrictions or otherwise discriminate against our products, we have no choice but to play the same game in self-defense. We'll go along with free trade only as long as it is fair trade. But we must play on a level playing field."

While this argument seems sensible, it is not well grounded in economic analysis or history. As we have seen, when another country increases its tariffs, this is akin to increasing its transportation costs. But if France decided to let its roads go to ruin, should we therefore chop holes in ours? Few would think so. Similarly, if another country chose to injure its economic vitality by imposing tariffs on its imports, it would not be sensible to add damage to injury by adding tariffs on ours.

The only possible sense in the argument that we should retaliate when a foreign country raises tariffs is that our threat of retaliation may deter the country from raising tariffs in the first place. This rationale was endorsed by the U.S. government in a 1982 analysis of protection (in the *Economic Report of the President*):

> Intervention in international trade . . . , even though costly to the U.S. economy in the short run, may, however, be justified if it serves the strategic purpose of increasing the cost of interventionist policies by foreign governments. Thus, there is a potential role for carefully targeted measures . . . aimed at convincing other countries to reduce their trade distortions.

But this argument should be used with great caution. Just as building missiles leads to an arms race as often as to arms control, protectionist bluffs may end up hurting the bluffer as well as the opponent. Historical studies show that retaliatory tariffs usually lead other nations to raise their tariffs still higher and are rarely an effective bargaining chip for multilateral tariff reduction.

Import Relief. Today, relatively little direct tariff business is conducted on the floor of Congress. Congress realized that tariff politics was too hot to handle and delegated most authority to the President. Trade barriers are generally imposed in response to a complaint filed by an industry that feels itself to be adversely affected by foreign competition. The complaint is analyzed by the U.S. International Trade Commission, which makes recommendations for final action by the President. Relief measures include the following actions:

- *The escape clause* allows temporary import relief (tariffs, quotas, or export quotas negotiated with other countries) when an industry has been "injured" by imports. Injury occurs when the output, employment, and profits in a domestic industry have fallen while imports have risen. "Escape clause" relief has been provided for television sets, shoes, steel, CB radios, and even nuts and bolts.
- *Antidumping tariffs* are levied when foreign countries sell in the United States at prices below their average costs or at prices lower than those in the home market. Such duties have been levied on steel imports and semiconductor chips.
- *Retaliation for unfair trade practices* is imposed when other countries discriminate against, or unjustifiably restrict, U.S. commerce. Since 1985, for example, the United States has initiated actions against Japan for restricting sales of American cigarettes, against Korea for restrictions on insurance, against Taiwan for restrictions on alcoholic beverages, and against Brazil for restrictions in the computer industry. The United States has also threatened to levy general tariff increases against countries that systematically engage in "unfair" trading practices.

What is the justification for enacting such retaliatory measures or for protecting an industry threatened by imports? Import relief may sound reasonable, but it actually runs completely counter to the economic theory of comparative advantage. The theory of comparative advantage says that an industry that cannot compete with foreign firms *ought* to be injured by imports. In one sense, the less productive industries are actually being killed off by the competition of more productive *domestic* industries.

This sounds ruthless indeed. No industry willingly dies. No region gladly undergoes conversion to new industries. Often the shift from old to new industries involves considerable unemployment and hardship. The weak industry and region feel they are being singled out to carry the burden of progress.

One compromise that recognizes the costs of adjusting to economic dislocations is to reduce tariffs gradually, so that unemployed workers will have time to retrain or move to regions with growing job opportunities. Also, Congress has decided to provide "trade adjustment assistance," or federal aid to displaced factors of production. Such assistance may lower the transitional burdens of moving resources from declining to growing industries and lessen opposition to a free-trade policy.

Potentially Valid Arguments for Protection

Finally, we can consider three arguments for protection that may have true economic merit:

- Tariffs may move the terms of trade in favor of a country.
- Temporary tariff protection for an "infant industry" with growth potential may be efficient in the long run.
- A tariff may under certain conditions help reduce unemployment.

The Terms-of-Trade or "Optimal-Tariff" Argument. One valid argument for imposing tariffs is that doing so will shift the terms of trade in a country's favor and against foreign countries. (Recall that the *terms of trade* represent the ratio of export prices to import prices.) The idea is that when a large country levies tariffs on its imports, this will reduce the world price of its imports while increasing the prices of its exports. By shifting the terms of trade in its favor, the United States can export less wheat and fewer aircraft in order to pay for imports of oil and cars. The set of tariffs that maximizes our domestic real incomes is called the *optimal tariff.*

The terms-of-trade argument goes back 150 years to the free-trade proponent John Stuart Mill and has been recently dusted off for modern approaches. It is the only argument for tariffs that would be valid under conditions of full employment and perfect competition. We can understand it by considering the simple case of an optimal tariff on oil. The optimal tariff on oil will raise the price here above the foreign price. But because our demand is curtailed as a result of the tariff, and because we are a significant part of the world demand for oil, the world market price of oil will be bid down. So part of the tariff really falls on the oil producer. (We can see that a very small country could not use this argument since it cannot affect world prices.)

Have we not therefore found a theoretically secure argument for tariffs? The answer would be yes if we could forget that this is a "beggar-thy-neighbor" policy and could ignore the reactions of other countries. But other countries are likely to react. After all, if the United States were to impose an optimal tariff of 30 percent on its imports, why should the European Community and Japan and Brazil not put 30 or 40 percent tariffs on their imports? In the end, as every country calculated and imposed its own domestic optimal tariff, the overall level of tariffs might climb to 30 or 50 percent.

Ultimately, such a situation would surely not represent an improvement of either world or individual economic welfare. When *all* countries impose optimal tariffs, it is likely that *everyone's* economic welfare will decline as the impediments to free trade become great. All countries are likely to benefit if they abolish trade barriers.

Tariffs for "Infant Industries." In his famous *Report on Manufactures* (1791), Alexander Hamilton proposed to encourage the growth of manufacturing by protecting youthful industries from foreign competition. According to this doctrine, which received the cautious support of free-trade economists like John Stuart Mill and Alfred Marshall, there are lines of production in which a country could have a comparative advantage if only they could get started.

Such "infant industries" would not be able to weather the initial period of start-up and experimentation if they had to face unprotected the gales of international competition. With some temporary shelter, however, they might develop economies of mass production, a pool of skilled labor, inventions well adapted to the local economy, and the technological efficiency typical of many mature industries. Although protection will raise prices to the consumer at first, the industry will be so efficient once it has grown up that cost and price will actually fall. A tariff is justified if the benefit to consumers at that later date would be more than enough to make up for the higher prices during the period of protection.

This argument must be weighed cautiously. Historical studies have turned up some genuine cases of infant industries that grew up to stand on their own feet. And studies of successful newly industrialized countries (such as Singapore and Korea) show that they have often protected their manufacturing industries from imports during the early stages of industrialization. But the history of tariffs reveals even more contrary cases in which perpetually protected infants have not shed their diapers after lo these many years.

Tariffs and Unemployment. Historically, a powerful motive for protection has been the desire to increase employment during a period of recession or stagnation. Protection creates jobs by raising the price of imports and diverting demand toward domestic production; Figure 37-2 demonstrates this effect. As domestic demand increases, firms will hire more workers, and unemployment will fall.[3] This too is a "beggar-thy-neighbor" policy, for it raises domestic demand at the expense of output and employment in other countries.

However, while economic protection may raise employment, it does not constitute an effective program to pursue high employment, efficiency, and stable prices. Macroeconomic analysis shows that there are better ways of reducing unemployment than by imposing import protection. By the appropriate use of monetary and fiscal policy, a country can increase output and lower unemployment. Moreover, the use of general macroeconomic policies will allow workers displaced from low-productivity jobs in industries losing their comparative advantage to move to high-productivity jobs in industries enjoying a comparative advantage.

This lesson was amply demonstrated during the 1980s. From 1982 to 1987, the United States created 15 million net new jobs while maintaining open markets and low tariffs and sharply increasing its trade deficit; by contrast, the European Community created virtually no new jobs while moving toward a position of trade surpluses.

Another way of analyzing the impact of trade barriers upon employment is to measure the "cost of a job created by import restraints." Numerous economic studies have analyzed the economic cost imposed when tariffs or quotas are put on an industry. As an example, consider the voluntary import quotas on Japanese cars during the 1980s. According to government studies, these quotas increased employment in the automobile industry by around 30,000 workers during 1983 and 1984. For the 7 million cars bought annually during that period, it is estimated that consumers paid an average of $500 per car more than they would have without the quotas. The consumer cost then averaged about $3.5 billion/30,000 = slightly over $100,000 per job.[4] Calculations such as these show that protection is a highly inefficient way to increase employment.

In summary:

Tariffs and import protection are an inefficient way to create jobs or to lower unemployment. A more effective way to increase productive employment is through domestic monetary and fiscal policy.

Other Barriers to Trade

While this chapter has mainly spoken of tariffs, most points apply equally well to any other impediments to trade. Quotas have much the same effects as tariffs, for they prevent the comparative advantages of different countries from being determined in the marketplace. In recent years, countries have negotiated quotas with other countries. The United States, for example, forced Japan to put "voluntary" export quotas on automobiles and negotiated similar export quotas on televisions, shoes, and steel.

Finally, we should mention the so-called nontariff barriers (or NTBs). These consist of informal restrictions or regulations that make it difficult for

[3] Those who have studied the chapters on macroeconomics can understand the mechanism by which tariffs increase employment as follows: Recall that higher investment or government spending increases aggregate demand, output, and employment. By similar reasoning, greater protection or higher tariffs lower imports, increase net exports, and thereby increase aggregate demand. The higher net exports will have a multiplier effect much like that of investment or government spending on goods and services.

[4] These figures are drawn from the Congressional Budget Office, *Has Trade Protection Revitalized Domestic Industries?* (U.S. Government Printing Office, Washington, 1986), Chap. V.

countries to sell their goods in foreign markets. The growth of NTBs was one of the major problems trade negotiators faced in the 1980s.

Multilateral Trade Negotiations

Given the tug-of-war between the economic benefits of free trade and the political appeal of protection, which force has prevailed? The history of U.S. tariffs, shown in Figure 37-4, has been bumpy. For most of American history, we have been a high-tariff nation. The pinnacle came after the infamous Smoot-Hawley tariff of 1930, which was opposed by virtually every American economist yet sailed through Congress.

The trade barriers erected during the Depression helped raise prices and exacerbated economic distress. The 1930s witnessed trade wars in which countries attempted to raise employment and output by raising trade barriers at the expense of their neighbors. Nations soon learned that at the end of the tariff-retaliation game, all were losers.

Negotiating Free Trade

At the end of World War II, nations designed a number of institutions to promote peace and economic

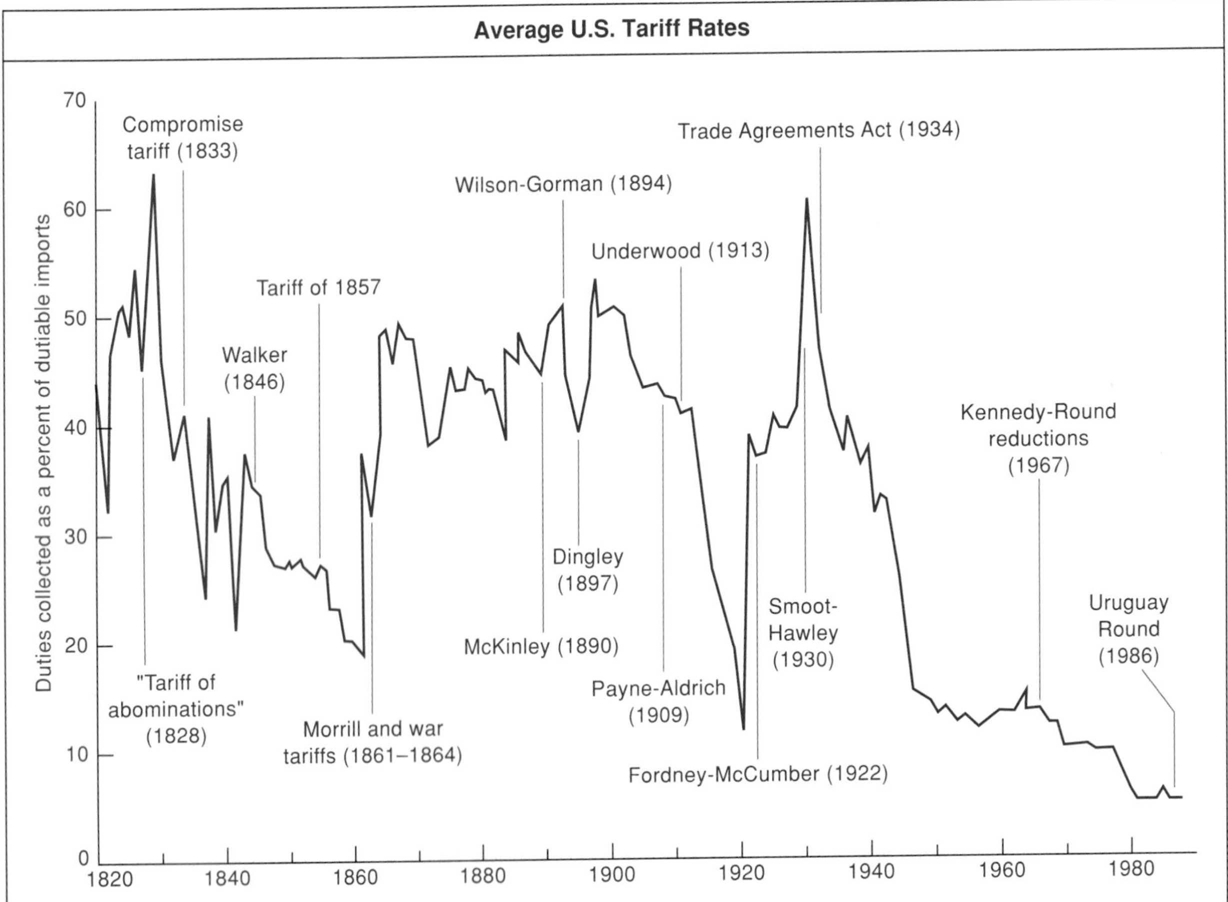

Figure 37-4. America was historically a high-tariff nation

Duties were high for most of our nation's history, but have come down in a series of trade negotiations since the 1930s. The newest threat comes from non-tariff barriers, particularly negotiated quotas. Workers and firms in industries such as textiles, shoes, steel, and autos want competing imports kept out in order to maintain their wages and profits. High tariffs depress a nation's real wages as it loses the efficiencies of specialization and regional division of labor.

prosperity through cooperative policies. One of the most successful of these was the General Agreement on Tariffs and Trade (GATT), whose charter speaks of raising living standards through "substantial reduction of tariffs and other barriers to trade and the elimination of discriminatory treatment in international commerce." The GATT currently has almost 100 member countries, accounting for 85 percent of international trade.

Among the principles underlying the GATT are: (1) countries should work to lower trade barriers; (2) all trade barriers should be applied on a nondiscriminatory basis (i.e., all nations should enjoy "most-favored-nation" status); (3) when a country increases its tariffs above agreed-upon levels, it must compensate its trading partners for their economic injury; and (4) trade conflicts should be settled by consultations and arbitration.

The history of trade negotiations has proved one of the major successes in international economic cooperation. Every few years, major industrial countries gather under the auspices of the GATT to identify major trade barriers and negotiate their removal. The current negotiations are called the "Uruguay Round." In addition to the traditional goal of reducing tariff and quota barriers, the new round has undertaken the ambitious goals of lowering trade barriers and subsidies in agriculture and removing quotas on textiles. In addition, these negotiations hope to extend free trade to services and intellectual property.

Recent Steps. Over the last few years, governments took a number of steps to promote free trade or to broaden markets. Among the most important were the following:

- In 1987, the United States and Canada negotiated a set of principles for free trade between the two countries. This agreement was particularly significant because Canada is the largest trading partner of the United States, with total trade flows between the two of $176 billion in 1990. Canada's tariff rates are among the highest of the major industrial countries, and Canada curtails foreign investment on nationalist grounds. Economists have estimated that a free-trade agreement would raise real incomes in Canada by 5 percent and those in the United States by 1 percent.
- The Bush administration has proposed extending the North American free trade region to include Mexico. Mexico is the third-largest trading partner of the United States, and most U.S.-Mexico trade is in manufactured goods. Proponents of the plan argue that it would allow a more efficient division of labor and would enable U.S. firms to compete more effectively against firms in other countries. The proposal has been severely criticized by labor groups, who believe that it will increase the supply of goods produced by low-skilled labor and thereby depress the wages of workers in the affected industries.
- "Europe 1992" is another movement toward a regional free-trade zone. This plan for the 12 nations of the European Community is scheduled to be completed in 1992. It will reduce all internal tariff and regulatory barriers to trade, harmonize taxes and subsidies, and allow companies operating in Europe to manage their production and trade with much the same freedom as do companies in the United States. Some economists believe that with a huge free-trade area, Europe may soon challenge the United States as the world's leading economic superpower.

Appraisal. How successful have nations and the GATT been in achieving the goal of reducing trade barriers? Figure 37-4 shows dramatically how, as a result of the many rounds of successful tariff negotiations, the United States has ceased to be a high-tariff nation. Indeed, the average tariff rate in the United States has fallen to less than one-tenth of the level reached under the Smoot-Hawley tariff, and similar reductions have been achieved in other nations. But the political proponents of protection remain powerful. Many fear that the industrial world is perilously near the point where a spark of protection and retaliation like that of the 1930s might ignite a major trade war between nations. Up to now, however, the forces of conciliation have prevailed.

SUMMARY

1. Completely free trade equalizes prices at home with those in world markets. Under trade, goods flow uphill from low-price to high-price markets.
2. A tariff raises the domestic prices of imported goods, leading to a decline in consumption and imports along with an increase in domestic production. Quotas have very similar effects and may, in addition, lower government revenues.
3. A tariff causes economic waste. The economy suffers losses from decreased home consumption and from wasting resources on goods lacking comparative advantage. The losses generally exceed government revenues from the tariff.
4. Most arguments for tariffs simply rationalize special benefits to particular pressure groups and cannot withstand economic analysis. Three arguments that can stand up to careful scrutiny are:
   (a) The terms of trade or "optimal tariff" can in principle raise the real income of a large country at the expense of its trading partners.
   (b) In a situation of less than full employment, tariffs might push an economy toward fuller employment, but monetary or fiscal policies could attain the same employment goal with fewer inefficiencies than this "beggar-thy-neighbor" policy.
   (c) Sometimes, infant industries may need temporary protection in order to realize their true long-run comparative advantages.

CONCEPTS FOR REVIEW

price equilibrium with and without trade
tariff, quota
effects of tariffs on price, imports, and domestic production
mercantilist, cheap foreign labor, and retaliatory arguments
terms-of-trade shifts and the optimal tariff
unemployment and tariffs
infant-industry tariff
GATT and trade negotiations

QUESTIONS FOR DISCUSSION

1. What do you think are the most favorable arguments for and against protection?
2. What arguments have been made for import protection of the computer or automobile industry? Weigh the pros and cons. Present your point of view carefully.
3. Analyze the infant-industry argument for tariffs. What is its relation to comparative advantage? What are today's infant industries?
4. The 1988 Trade Act allows for tariff protection for industries "injured" by imports. Construct the best possible defense for this provision; attack it with the most weighty opposing arguments.
5. Since the 1930s, industrial nations have negotiated a series of agreements in which they lowered their tariff barriers. Explain how a mutual reduction of tariffs helps countries in *four* ways. (*Hint:* Each side's tariff reductions help both itself and its trading partners.)
6. The "new international economics" developed theories that might support the following arguments for protecting domestic industries against foreign competition:
   (a) "In some situations, a country could improve its standard of living by imposing protection if no one else retaliated."
   (b) "If the marketplace is not working well, and there

is excessive unemployment, tariffs might lower the unemployment rate."

(c) "A country might be willing to accept a small drop in its living standard to preserve certain industries that it deems necessary for national security, such as supercomputers or oil, by protecting them from foreign competition."

(d) "Wages in Korea are but one-tenth of those in the United States. Unless we limit the imports of Korean manufactures, we face a future in which our trade deficit continues to deteriorate under the onslaught of competition from low-wage East Asian workers."

In each case, relate the argument to one of the traditional defenses of protectionism. State the conditions under which it is valid and decide whether you agree with it.

7. The United States has quotas on steel, shipping, automobiles, textiles, and many other products. Economists estimate that by auctioning off the quota rights, the Treasury would gain at least $10 billion annually. Use Figure 37-3 to analyze the economics of quotas as follows: Assume that the government imposes a quota of 100 on imports, allocating the quota rights to importing countries on the basis of last year's imports. What would be the equilibrium price and quantity of clothing? What would be the efficiency losses from quotas? Who would get revenue rectangle C? What would be the effect of auctioning off the quota rights?

8. Consider a situation in which the industrial countries import all their oil from oil-exporting OPEC countries and in which OPEC countries are competitive suppliers with a completely inelastic supply curve. What would be the effect on oil imports, OPEC oil prices, and industrial-country oil prices if all oil-consuming countries placed a $10-per-barrel import tariff on oil? Which tariff argument might be used to support such a tariff on oil imports?

C H A P T E R 38

THE ECONOMICS OF DEVELOPING COUNTRIES

I believe in materialism. I believe in all the proceeds of a healthy materialism—good cooking, dry houses, dry feet, sewers, drain pipes, hot water, baths, electric lights, automobiles, good roads, bright streets, long vacations away from the village pump, new ideas, fast horses, swift conversation, theatres, operas, orchestras, bands—I believe in them all for everybody. The man who dies without knowing these things may be as exquisite as a saint, and as rich as a poet; but it is in spite of, not because of, his deprivation.

Francis Hackett

Of the 5 billion people on this planet, perhaps 1 billion live in absolute poverty—barely able to survive from day to day. At the same time that poor countries are struggling to rise out of abject poverty, their rapid population growth has reduced the benefits of improved agricultural technologies.

What causes the great differences in the wealth of nations? Can the world peacefully survive with poverty in the midst of plenty, with agricultural surpluses in America alongside starvation in Africa? What steps can poorer nations take to improve their living standards?

This chapter explores some of the obstacles facing less developed countries. The first part of the chapter describes the characteristics of developing countries and explores the issue of population growth. The chapter then turns to the sources of global poverty and examines strategies countries can follow to raise the incomes of their people.

A. Developing Countries and the Population Problem

Aspects of a Developing Country

What is meant by a developing country, or a less developed country (LDC). A **developing country** is one with real per capita income that is low relative to that in advanced countries like the United States, Japan, and those in Western Europe. In human terms, developing countries have populations with poor health, low levels of literacy, inadequate dwellings, and meager diets.

Table 38-1 is a key source of data for understanding the major players in the world economy, as well as indicators of underdevelopment. Countries are grouped into the categories of low-income, lower-middle income, upper-middle income, and high-income economies.

Country group	Population 1989 (millions)	Gross National Product: Level 1989 ($, billions)	per capita: 1989 ($)	per capita: Growth 1965–1989 (% per year)	Adult illiteracy 1980 (%)	Life expectancy at birth (years)	Rural population 1989 (% of total)
Low-income economies (e.g., China, India)	2,948	956	330	2.9	44	62	64
Lower–middle-income economies (e.g., Egypt, Philippines, Mexico)	682	911	1,360	2.0	26	65	47
Upper–middle-income economies (e.g., Brazil, Korea, Iran)	423	1,207	3,150	2.6	24	67	34
High-income economies (e.g., United States, Japan, France)	830	14,764	18,330	2.4	5	76	23

Table 38-1. Important indicators for different country groups

Countries are grouped by the World Bank into four major categories depending upon their per capita incomes. In each, a number of important indicators of economic development are shown. Note that low-income countries tend to have high illiteracy, low life expectancy, and a large fraction of their labor force in agriculture. [Source: World Bank, *World Development Report, 1991* (World Bank, Washington, 1991).]

A number of interesting features emerge from the table. Clearly, low-income countries are much poorer than advanced countries like the United States. Their calculated per capita incomes are about one-fiftieth of those in high-income countries. Be warned, however, that standard comparisons are distorted by the use of official exchange rates to compare living standards. A newer technique, looking at "purchasing-power parity," or what incomes will buy, suggests that incomes in poorer countries are probably considerably understated—but a large gap still remains.

In addition, many social and health indicators show the effects of poverty in low-income nations. Life expectancy is low, and educational attainment and literacy are modest, reflecting low levels of investment in human capital. In these countries, most people live and work on farms, whereas few do in wealthier countries.

Table 38-1 also shows that there is a great diversity among developing countries. Some remain at the ragged edge of starvation—these are the very poorest countries like Chad, Bangladesh, or Ethiopia. Other countries that were in that category two or three decades ago have graduated to the rank of middle-income countries. The more successful—Hong Kong, South Korea, and Taiwan—are called the "newly industrializing countries," or "NICs." Yesterday's successful developing countries, which are today's NICs, will probably be tomorrow's advanced countries.

Life in Low-Income Countries

To bring out the contrasts between advanced and developing economies, imagine that you are a typical 21-year-old in one of the low-income countries Haiti, India, or Bangladesh. You are poor. Even after making generous allowance for the goods that you produce and consume, your annual income averages barely $300. Your counterpart in North America might have more than $20,000 in average earnings. Perhaps you can find cold comfort in the thought that only 1 person in 4 in the world averages more than $3000 in annual income.

For each of your fellow citizens who can read, there is one like you who is illiterate. Your life expectancy is four-fifths that of the average person in an advanced country; already two of your brothers and sisters have died before reaching adulthood.

Most people in your country work on farms. Few can be spared from food production to work in factories. You work with but one-sixtieth the horsepower of a prosperous North American worker. You know little about science, but much about your village traditions.

You and your fellow citizens in the 40 poorest countries constitute 55 percent of the world population, but must divide among each other only 5 percent of world income. You are often hungry, and the food you eat is mainly roughage or rice. While you were among those who got some primary schooling, like most of your friends you did not go on to high school, and only the wealthiest go to a university. You work long hours in the fields without the benefit of machinery. At night you sleep on a mat. You have little household furniture, perhaps a table and a radio. Your only mode of transportation is an old pair of boots.

Such is the way of life in the poorest countries of the world.

Population: The Legacy of Malthus

Some nations are endowed with few people, enjoying a vast continent teeming with minerals and fertile land; others see their people crowded into small plots, leaving no tillable corner untouched. The theory of population can help to explain such disparities among countries.

One of the earliest writers to analyze the relation between population and the economy was T. R. Malthus. He first developed his views while arguing at breakfast against his father's perfectionist view that the human race was always improving. Finally the son became so agitated that he wrote *An Essay on the Principle of Population* (1798). This was an instantaneous best-seller and since then has influenced the thinking of people all over the world about population and economic growth.

Malthus began with the observation of Benjamin Franklin that, in the American colonies where resources were abundant, population tended to double every 25 years or so. He then postulated a universal tendency for population—unless checked by limited food supply—to grow exponentially, or by a geometric progression.[1] Eventually, a population which doubles every generation—1, 2, 4, 8, 16, 32, 64, 128, 256, 512, 1024, . . . —becomes so large that there is not enough space in the world for all the people to stand.

But Malthus had one further card to play. At this point he unleashed the devil of diminishing returns.He argued that because land is fixed while labor inputs keep growing, food would tend to grow by an arithmetic progression and not by a geometric progression. (Compare 1, 2, 3, 4, . . . , with 1, 2, 4, 8, ...) Malthus concluded:

> As population doubles and redoubles, it is as if the globe were halving and halving again in size—until finally it has shrunk so much that the supply of food falls below the level necessary for life.
>
> When the law of diminishing returns is applied to a fixed supply of land, food production tends not to keep up with a population's geometric-progression rate of growth.

Now, Malthus did not say that population necessarily would increase at a geometric rate. This was only its tendency if unchecked. He described the checks that operate, in all times and places, to hold population down. And in his later, little-read editions, Malthus retreated from his gloomy doctrine, holding out hope that population growth could be slowed by birth prevention, rather than by pestilence, famine, and war.

This important application of diminishing returns illustrates the profound effects a simple theory can have. Malthus' ideas had wide repercussions. His book was used to support a stern revision of the English poor laws. Under the influence of Malthus' writings, people argued that poverty should be made as uncomfortable as possible. His opinions also bolstered the argument that trade unions could not improve the welfare of workers—since any increase in their wages would allegedly

[1] Exponential (or geometric) growth occurs when a variable increases at a constant proportional rate from period to period. Thus, if a population of 200 is growing at 3 percent per year, it would equal 200 in year 0, 200×1.03 in year 1, $200 \times 1.03 \times 1.03$ in year 2, $200 \times (1.03)^3$ in year 3, . . . , $200 \times (1.03)^{10}$ in year 10, and so on. Money earning compound interest grows geometrically. For example, at 6 percent compound interest, money doubles in value every 12 years. It has been estimated that the $24 received by the Indians for Manhattan Island would, if deposited at compound interest, be worth as much today as all property on the island.

only cause workers to reproduce until all were reduced to a bare subsistence.

Flawed Prophecies of Malthus. Despite his careful statistical studies, demographers today think that Malthus' views were oversimplified. In his discussion of diminishing returns, Malthus never fully anticipated the technological miracle of the Industrial Revolution. Nor did he foresee that after 1870 population growth in most Western nations would begin to decline just as living standards and real wages grew most rapidly.

In the century following Malthus, technological advance shifted out the production-possibility frontiers of countries in Europe and North America. This rapid technological change allowed output to far outstrip population, resulting in a rapid rise in real wages.

Nevertheless, the germs of truth in Malthus' doctrines are still important for understanding the population behavior of India, Ethiopia, China, and other parts of the globe where the balance of numbers and food supply is a vital consideration.

Sources of Population Growth, 1988
(Rates per 1,000 of Population per Year)

	Birth rate	Death rate	Natural growth rate
Low-income countries:			
Zambia	49	13	36
Malawi	54	19	35
India	31	11	20
Middle-income countries:			
Venezuela	29	5	24
Brazil	27	8	19
Thailand	22	7	15
High-income countries:			
United States	15	9	6
France	14	10	4
Germany	10	11	−1

Table 38-2. Birth, death, and population growth rates

Data for three groups of countries illustrate how patterns of population growth change with levels of development. Poor countries have high birth and death rates. When health conditions improve in the course of economic development, countries experience a fall in death rates. In the richest countries, birth rates fall, population growth declines, and population stabilizes. (Source: World Bank, *World Development Report, 1991.*)

Modern Views on Population

The history of population in developed countries did not follow Malthus' script. In fact, populations stabilized in most advanced countries as these countries made the transition from high birth and death rates in preindustrial times to low birth and death rates today. Before we can fully understand this important shift, we must master some of the concepts of modern **demography,** the study of the behavior of population.[2]

Birth and Death Rates

Basic to understanding population are the concepts of *crude birth and death rates.* These are simply the number of births or deaths per year per 1000 people. If we subtract the death rate from the birth rate, we get the rate of population growth.[3] Birth, death, and population growth rates for representative countries are shown in Table 38-2.

The Demographic Transition

We are now in a position to understand the demographic transition that occurs during the course of economic development. An idealized picture of the stages is shown in Figure 38-1. Here, population growth proceeds through four stages:

1. Traditional, preindustrial societies, in which high birth and death rates lead to low population growth. These societies are today found only in remote and isolated populations.

[2] An informative summary of the relationship between population and the overall economy is contained in Gary Becker's presidential address to the American Economic Association, "Family Economics and Macro Behavior," *American Economic Review* (March 1988), pp. 1–13.

[3] When applied to a specific country, this calculation assumes no migration. If there is net immigration (or emigration), then this figure would have to be added to (or subtracted from) births minus deaths to get net increase in population.

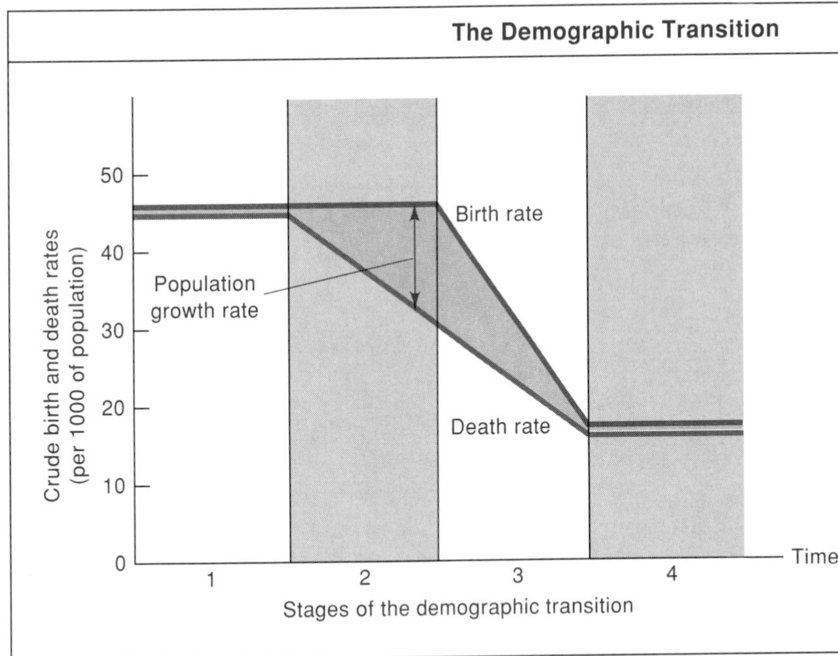

Figure 38-1. The stages of the demographic transition

This figure shows how countries have often made the transition from slow population growth with high birth and death rates to slow population growth with low birth and death rates.

Stage 1: Traditional society with little growth.

Stage 2: With the introduction of modern medical practices, deaths fall but births stay high and population growth rises.

Stage 3: The birth rate begins to recede and population growth diminishes.

Stage 4: In a mature society, couples have 2 children on average and population stabilizes.

2. Early economic development, in which advances of better nutrition and improved public health produce a decline in death rate with little effect on the birth rate. Population spurts upward.
3. Later development, in which lower infant mortality, urbanization, and education lead many couples to desire smaller families, cutting back the birth rate. Population growth may be rapid, but it is slowing.
4. Maturity, in which couples practice birth control successfully and both spouses tend to work outside the home. The desired (and actual) number of children per family drops to around 2, and after a time net population growth is close to zero.

We see, then, that the pessimistic population forecasts of Malthus appear correct in stages 1 and 2. But affluence in stages 3 and 4 leads to declining population growth.

Population Explosion

The demographic transition to low population growth holds out hope that many poor countries will not get forever caught in a Malthusian trap. Evidently, the transition has not yet been completed, as is shown by Table 38-2. Faced with the prospect of continued rapid population growth, many observers fear the globe will have to display signs saying, "Standing Room Only."

Controlling Population Growth. In the face of the Malthusian specter, countries have begun to take an active role in curbing growth of population, even when such actions run against prevailing religious norms. Many countries have introduced educational campaigns, subsidized birth control, or, in extreme cases, implemented mandatory sterilization. China has been particularly forceful in curbing population growth among its more than 1 billion inhabitants.

Slowly, we begin to see the results of economic development and birth control. The birth rate in poor countries has declined from 43 per 1000 in 1965 to 31 per 1000 in 1989. Although these countries are probably still in stage 2 of the demographic transition (see Figure 38-1), their population growth rates have declined over the last two decades. The struggle against poverty induced by excessive population growth is still under way on two-thirds of the globe.

B. The Process of Economic Development

The Four Elements in Development

Having seen what it means to be a developing country, we now turn to an analysis of the nature of the development process.

In our study of economic growth in Chapter 30, we explored how a nation expands its productive potential over time. Economic growth in developing countries is no different; the engine of economic progress must ride on the same four wheels, no matter how rich or poor the country. These four factors are:

- Human resources (labor supply, education, discipline, motivation)
- Natural resources (land, minerals, fuels, climate)
- Capital formation (machines, factories, roads)
- Technology (science, engineering, management, entrepreneurship)

Let's see how each of the four wheels contributes to growth, as well as how public policy can steer the growth process in desirable directions.

Human Resources

In addition to excessive population growth, developing countries must also be concerned with the quality of their human resources. Economic planners in developing countries emphasize the following specific programs:

- Control disease and improve health and nutrition—both to make people happier and to make them more productive workers. Health-care clinics and sewerage projects are vitally useful social capital.
- Improve education, reduce illiteracy, and train workers. Educated people become more productive workers, who can use capital more effectively, adopt new technologies, and learn from their mistakes. For advanced learning in science, engineering, medicine, and management, countries will benefit by sending their best minds abroad to bring back the newest advances. (But countries must beware of the *brain drain*, in which the most able people get drawn off to high-wage countries.)

Many economists believe that the quality of labor inputs, human capital, is the single most important catalyst to economic development. Virtually every other ingredient in production—capital goods, raw materials, and technology—can be bought or borrowed from advanced countries. But applying high-productivity techniques to local conditions almost always requires management, production workers, and engineering know-how found only in a literate and highly skilled work force. Modern technologies are often embodied in capital goods, as can be seen in telecommunications devices, computers, electricity-generating equipment, and fighter aircraft. However, these capital goods require complementary trained labor for effective use and maintenance. The crucial role of skilled labor has been shown again and again when sophisticated mining, defense, or manufacturing machinery fell into disrepair and disuse because the labor force of developing countries had not acquired the necessary maintenance skills.

Natural Resources

Some poor countries of Africa and Asia have meager endowments of natural resources, and such land and minerals as they do possess must be divided among dense populations. Perhaps the most valuable natural resource of developing countries is arable land. As Table 38-1 shows, much of the labor force in developing countries is employed in farming. Hence the productive use of land—with appropriate conservation, fertilizers, and tillage—will go far in increasing a poor nation's output. Moreover, landownership patterns are a key to providing farmers with strong incentives to invest in capital and technologies that will increase their land's yield. If farmers own their own land, they will be willing to make improvements, such as in irrigation systems, and undertake appropriate conservation practices.

Capital Formation

While the hands of people are much the same the world around, workers in advanced countries have their hands on a great deal more capital—and are therefore much more productive.

Accumulating capital, as we have seen, requires a sacrifice of current consumption over many decades. But there's the rub, for the poorest countries are near a subsistence standard of living. When you are poor to begin with, reducing current consumption to provide for future consumption seems impossible.

In advanced economies, 10 to 20 percent of income may go into capital formation. By contrast, the poorest agrarian countries are often able to save only 5 percent of national income. Moreover, much of the low level of saving goes to provide the growing population with housing and simple tools. Little is left over for development.

But let's say a country has succeeded in hiking up its rate of saving. Even so, it takes many decades to accumulate the railroads, electricity-generating plants, equipment, factories, and other capital goods that underpin a productive economic structure.

In many developing countries, the single most pressing problem is too little saving. Particularly in the poorest regions, urgent current consumption competes with investment for scarce resources. The result is too little investment in the productive capital so indispensable for rapid economic progress.

Social Overhead Capital. When we think of capital, we must not concentrate only on trucks and steel mills. Many large social investments must precede industrialization, or even the efficient marketing of farm products.

To develop, a private economy must have **social overhead capital.** This consists of the large-scale projects that precede trade and commerce—roads, railroads, irrigation projects, public-health measures, etc. All these involve large investments that tend to be "indivisible," or lumpy, and sometimes have increasing returns to scale. No small farm or family can profitably undertake to build a railroad system; no pioneering private enterprise can hope to make a profit from a telephone or irrigation system before the markets have been developed. These large-scale investment projects spread their benefits widely across the economy.

Often these projects involve external economies, or spillovers that private firms cannot capture. For example, a regional agricultural adviser can help all farmers in an area; or a public-health program inoculating people against typhoid or diphtheria protects the population beyond those inoculated. In each of these cases it would be impossible for an enterprising firm to capture the social benefits because the firm cannot collect fees from the thousands or even millions of beneficiaries. Because of the large indivisibilities and external effects, the government must step in, provide the necessary funds and initiative, and ensure that these social overhead investments are undertaken.

Foreign Borrowing and the Debt Crisis

If there are so many obstacles to finding domestic saving for capital formation, why not rely more heavily on foreign sources? Does not economic theory tell us that a rich country, which has tapped its own high-yield investment projects, can benefit both itself and the recipient by investing in high-yield projects abroad?

Actually, prior to 1914, economic development did proceed in this fashion. Britain in the last century saved about 15 percent of its GNP and invested fully half this amount abroad. And during most of the period after World War II, the United States and other advanced countries lent large sums to developing countries. The figures on foreign investment in low- and middle-income countries show an impressive record of capital transfer: foreign loans averaged $112 billion annually in the period 1980–1982. Investors in wealthy countries sent their funds abroad in search of higher returns than were available at home; poor countries, hungry for funds to finance investment projects or even consumption, welcomed this flow of foreign capital.

By the end of the 1970s, however, the extent of foreign borrowing by developing countries had become unsustainably large. Total outstanding debt grew almost 20 percent per year and increased by almost $500 billion from 1973 to 1982. Some of these loans were put to good use in investments in oil drilling, textile factories, and coal-mining equipment, but others simply raised consumption levels.

As long as the exports of these countries grew at the same rate as borrowings, all was well. But with the rise in world interest rates and the slowdown in the world economy after 1980, many countries found that their borrow-and-invest strategy had led them to the brink of financial crisis. Some countries (such as Bolivia and Peru) needed all their export earnings simply to pay the interest on their foreign debt. Others found themselves unable to meet debt-repayment schedules. Almost all indebted developing countries were staggering under heavy debt-service burdens (i.e., the need to repay the interest and principal on their loans). As a result, country after country, particularly in Latin America, failed to make interest payments and had their debts "rescheduled," or postponed.

By the early 1990s, the debt crisis continued to pose serious problems for heavily indebted countries. What does economic history suggest will be the future course of events in the area of foreign debt? If no severe shocks hit the world economy, indebted countries can probably move back toward lower levels of foreign debt. However, a severe shock to output, interest rates, or confidence might weaken the international financial system so much that loans to poor countries would once again be severely restricted.

Technological Change and Innovations

In addition to the fundamental factors of population, natural resources, and capital formation, development depends on the vital fourth factor, technology. Here developing countries have one potential advantage: they can hope to benefit by relying on the technological progress of more advanced nations.

Imitating Technology. Poor countries do not need to find modern Newtons to discover the law of gravity; they can read about it in any physics book. They don't have to repeat the slow, meandering climb of the Industrial Revolution; they can buy tractors, computers, and power looms undreamed of by the great merchants of the past.

Japan and the United States clearly illustrate this in their historical developments. Japan joined the industrial race late and only at the end of the nineteenth century sent students abroad to learn Western technology. The Japanese government took an active role in stimulating the pace of development and in building railroads and utilities. Relying on the adaptation of foreign technologies, Japan moved into its position today as the world's second-largest industrial economy.

The case of the United States itself provides a hopeful example to the rest of the world. Only in the 1930s did America reach the front rank in the field of pure science. Yet for a century its applied technology was outstanding. The key inventions involved in the automobile originated almost exclusively abroad. Nevertheless, Henry Ford and General Motors applied foreign inventions and outproduced the rest of the world. The examples of the United States and Japan show how countries can thrive by adapting foreign science and technology to local market conditions.

Entrepreneurship and Innovation. From the histories of Japan and the United States, it might appear that adaptation of foreign technology is an easy recipe for development. You might say: "Just go abroad; copy more efficient methods; put them into effect at home; then sit back and wait for the extra output to roll in."

In fact, technological change is not that simple. You can send a textbook on chemical engineering to Poorovia, but without skilled scientists, engineers, and entrepreneurs and without adequate capital, Poorovia couldn't even think about building a working petrochemical plant. Remember, the advanced technology was itself developed to meet the special conditions of the advanced countries—including high wages, plentiful capital relative to labor, and ample skilled engineers. These conditions do not prevail in poorer countries.

One of the key tasks of economic development is the fostering of an entrepreneurial spirit. A country cannot thrive without a group of owners or managers willing to undertake risks, open new plants, adopt new technologies, confront strife, and import new ways of doing business. Government can help entrepreneurship by setting up extension services for farmers, educating and training the work force, establishing management schools, and making sure that government itself maintains a healthy respect for the role of private initiative.

Vicious Cycle

We have emphasized that poor countries face great obstacles in combining the four elements of progress—labor, capital, resources, and entrepreneurship. In addition, countries find that the difficulties reinforce each other in a *vicious cycle of poverty*.

Figure 38-2 illustrates how one hurdle raises yet other hurdles. Low incomes lead to low saving; low saving retards the growth of capital; inadequate capital prevents introduction of machinery and rapid growth in productivity; low productivity leads to low incomes. Other elements in poverty are also self-reinforcing. Poverty is accompanied by low levels of skill and literacy; these in turn prevent the adaptation of new and improved technologies.

Overcoming the barriers of poverty often requires a concerted effort on many fronts, and some development economists recommend a "big push" forward to break the vicious cycle. If a country is fortunate, simultaneous steps to invest more, develop skills, and curb population growth can break the vicious cycle of poverty and stimulate a virtuous cycle of rapid economic development.

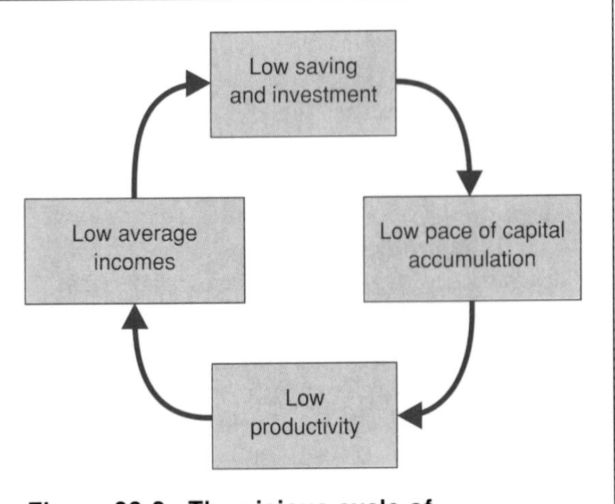

Figure 38-2. The vicious cycle of underdevelopment

Many obstacles to development are reinforcing. Low levels of income prevent saving, retard capital growth, hinder productivity growth, and keep income low. Successful development may require taking steps to break the chain at many points.

Strategies of Economic Development

We see how countries must combine labor, resources, capital, and technology in order to grow rapidly. But this is no real formula; it is the equivalent of saying that an Olympic sprinter must run like the wind. Why do some countries succeed in running faster than others? How do poor countries ever get started down the road of economic development?

Comprehensive Theories

Historians and social scientists have long been fascinated by the differences in the pace of economic growth among nations. Some early theories stressed climate, noting that all advanced countries lie in the earth's temperate zone. Others have pointed to the importance of custom, culture, or religion as a key factor. Max Weber emphasized the "Protestant ethic" as a driving force behind capitalism. More recently, Mancur Olson has argued that nations begin to decline when their decision structure becomes brittle and when interest groups or oligarchies prevent social and economic change.

No doubt each of these theories has some validity for a particular time and place. But they do not hold up as universal explanations of economic development. Weber's theory leaves unexplained why the cradle of civilization appeared in the Near East and Greece while the later-dominant Europeans lived in caves, worshiped trolls, and wore bearskins. Where is the Protestant ethic in a sleek Japanese factory in which workers gather to pay homage to Buddha? How can we explain that a country like Japan, with a rigid social structure and powerful lobbies, has become the world's most productive economy?

To understand the diversity of economic experience, we must turn to broader explanations.

Recent Approaches to Development

For decades economists have been intensely interested in economic development. The following account represents a montage of important ideas developed in recent years. Each theory attempts to describe how countries break out of the vicious cycle of poverty and begin to mobilize the four wheels of economic development.

The Takeoff. Human history is long, and the era of economic development has come only recently. During most of history, life was nasty, brutish, and short. But, in a few places over a brief period, superior production techniques were introduced. Great inequality of income allowed a few to funnel saving into capital formation. Economic development could take place.

So dramatic was the discontinuity between earlier periods and the Industrial Revolution that scholars like W. W. Rostow developed a theory stressing stages of economic growth. One of Rostow's stages is called the *takeoff,* the analogy being with an airplane, which can fly only after attaining a critical speed.

Different countries had their takeoffs in different periods: England at the beginning of the eighteenth century, the United States around 1850, Japan in 1910, and Mexico after 1940.

The takeoff is impelled by "leading sectors," such as a rapidly growing export market or an industry displaying large economies of scale. Once these leading sectors begin to flourish, a process of *self-sustaining growth* (the takeoff) occurs. Growth leads to profits; profits are reinvested; capital, productivity, and per capita incomes spurt ahead. The virtuous cycle of economic development is under way.

The Backwardness Hypothesis. A second view emphasizes the international context of development. We saw above that poorer countries have important advantages that the first pioneers along the path of industrialization did not. Developing nations can now draw upon the capital, skills, and technology of more advanced countries. This hypothesis, advanced by Alexander Gerschenkron of Harvard, suggests that *relative backwardness* itself may aid development. Countries can buy modern textile machinery, efficient pumps, miracle seeds, chemical fertilizers, and medical supplies. Because they can lean on the technologies of advanced countries, today's developing countries can grow more rapidly than did Britain or Western Europe in the period 1780–1850.

Balanced Growth. The takeoff and backwardness hypotheses have caught the attention of scholars and experts. But we must step back and assess history to see whether they fit the facts. Some writers suggest that growth is a *balanced* process with countries progressing steadily ahead. In their view, economic development resembles the tortoise, making continual progress, rather than the hare, who runs in spurts and then rests when exhausted.

The three alternatives can be seen graphically in Figure 38-3. Here we see how the takeoff, the backwardness hypothesis, and the balanced-growth views would appear over time for three countries—advanced A, middle-income B, and low-income C.

Which of these three views appears most closely to explain history? In one outstanding study, Nobel-laureate Simon Kuznets examined the history of 13 advanced countries, going back as far as 1800.[4] He concluded that the balanced-growth model is most consistent with the countries he studied. He saw no significant rise or fall in economic growth as development progressed.

Note one further important difference between the three theories. The takeoff theory suggests that there will be increasing *divergence* among countries (some flying rapidly, while others are unable to leave the ground). The backwardness hypothesis suggests *convergence,* while the Kuznets view suggests roughly constant differentials. Empirical evidence shown in Table 38-3 indicates that there has

[4] Simon Kuznets, *Economic Growth of Nations* (Harvard University Press, Cambridge, Mass., 1971).

Recent Growth Trends

Country group	Rate of growth of real GNP (% per year) 1965–1980	1980–1989
Low-income:		
China and India	5.0	7.6
Other	4.6	3.4
Middle-income:		
Lower-middle	5.5	2.5
Upper-middle	6.8	3.2
Industrial market economies	3.8	3.0

Table 38-3. Poorer countries are slowly closing the income gap

Data on the growth in total output show that poor countries were unable to close the gap between themselves and the industrial market economies during the 1960s, but middle-income or newly industrializing countries grew rapidly. Stagnation in high-income market economies during the 1970s allowed the relative output gaps to close by 10 to 25 percent. (Source: World Bank, *World Development Report, 1991.*)

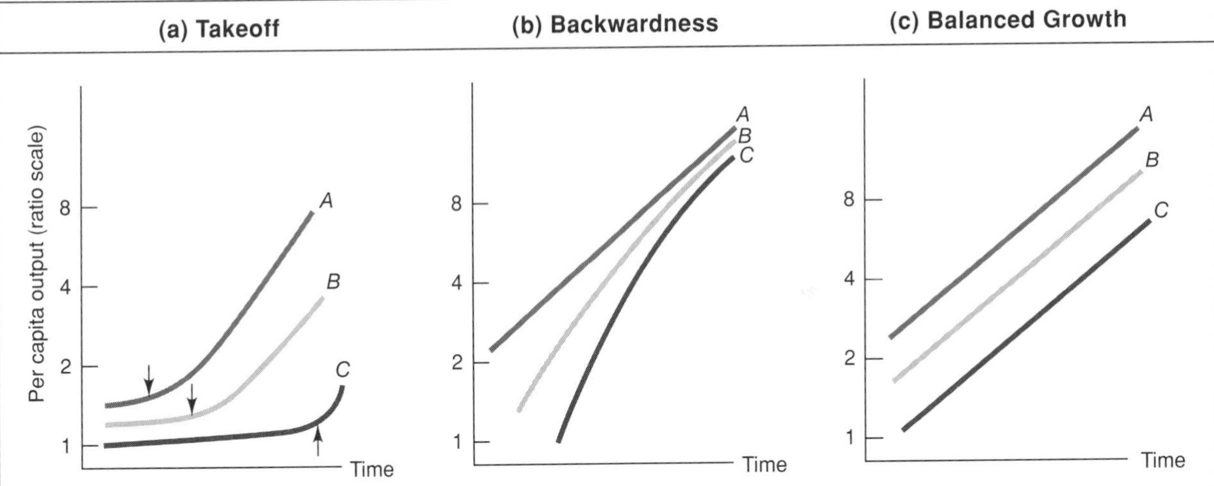

Figure 38-3. Three views of the development process

Consider advanced Country A, middle-income Country B, and low-income Country C. In part **(a)**, leading sectors such as exports promote a takeoff (shown by arrows) into rapid self-sustaining growth. In part **(b)**, backward countries rely on and adopt technologies invented by richer countries. They thus grow rapidly and gradually catch up with advanced countries. In the final scheme, **(c)**, countries grow at the same rate, and the relative gap between countries is roughly constant.

Note that output is shown on a ratio scale, meaning that the *slope* of each line represents the *growth* rate of output. Thus a constant slope, as in part **(c)**, indicates a constant annual growth rate of output; while an increasing slope, as in part **(a)**, indicates an increasing growth rate of output. What is occurring in part **(b)**? [Adapted from Bruce Herrick and Charles P. Kindleberger, *Economic Development* (McGraw-Hill, New York, 1983)].

been little convergence between advanced and developing countries in the last quarter-century (although the performance of individual countries has varied greatly from the average)—a pattern of growth rates most consistent with the balanced-growth view.

Issues in Economic Development

To say that countries must encourage rapid growth in capital and technology does not answer *how* these key ingredients are to be deployed. Among the vast array of issues that arise in development planning, we focus here on four recurrent themes: the balance between industry and agriculture, the role of outward orientation, the risks of overspecialization, and the role of the market.

Industrialization vs. Agriculture. In most countries, incomes in urban areas are almost double those in rural agriculture. And in affluent nations, much of the economy is in industry, particularly manufacturing. Hence, many nations jump to the conclusion that industrialization is the cause rather than the effect of affluence.

We must be wary of such inferences, which often fall into the *post hoc* fallacy. You sometimes hear, "Rich men smoke cigars, but smoking a cigar will not make you a rich man." Similarly, there is no economic justification for a poor country to insist upon having its own national airline and large steel mill. These are not the fundamental necessities of economic growth.

The lesson of decades of attempts to accelerate industrialization at the expense of agriculture has led many analysts to rethink the role of farming. Industrialization tends to be capital-intensive, attracts workers into crowded cities, and often produces high levels of unemployment. Raising productivity on farms may require less capital, while providing productive employment for surplus labor.

Indeed, if Bangladesh could increase the productivity of its farming by 20 percent, that would do more to release resources for the production of comforts than would trying to construct a domestic steel industry that would displace imported metals.

Inward vs. Outward Orientation. A fundamental issue of economic development concerns a country's stance toward international trade. Should developing countries attempt to be self-sufficient, replacing most imports with domestic production? (This is known as a strategy of *import substitution.*) Or should a country strive to pay for the imports it needs by improving efficiency and competitiveness, developing foreign markets, and giving incentives for exports? (This is called a strategy of *outward orientation.*)

Policies of import substitution have often been popular in Latin America. The policy most frequently used toward this end has been to build high tariff walls around manufacturing industries so that local firms can produce and sell goods that would otherwise be imported. For example, Brazil has placed high tariffs on automobiles to encourage firms to assemble autos at home rather than import much less expensive cars from North America or Japan.

Critics observe that such subsidized import substitution generally limits competition, dampens innovation and productivity growth, and keeps the country's real income low. This approach ignores the benefits of specialization and comparative advantage. The consumers and the entire economy might be better off if the emphasis on import substitution were replaced by an emphasis on outward orientation. Outward expansion sets up a system of incentives that stimulates exports. Key features of this approach are maintaining a competitive foreign exchange rate, choosing foreign-trade policies that encourage firms to produce for export, and minimizing unnecessary government regulation of businesses, especially of small firms.

The success of outward-expansion policies is best illustrated by the East Asian NICs. A generation ago, countries like Taiwan, South Korea, and Singapore had per capita incomes one-quarter to one-third of those in the wealthiest Latin American countries. Yet, by saving large fractions of their national incomes and channeling these to high-return export industries, the East Asian NICs overtook every Latin American country by the late 1980s. The secret to success was not a complete laissez-faire policy, for the governments in fact engaged in some planning and intervention. Rather, the outward orientation allowed the countries to reap economies of scale and the benefits of international specialization and thus to increase employment, effectively use domestic resources, enjoy rapid productivity growth, and provide enormous gains in living standards.

A recent study of the economic prospects of Latin America concludes with the following assessment of the effects of outward expansion:

> Outward orientation is the keystone of the strategies of virtually all the "success stories" [of economic development]—in East and southeast Asia, in Latin America in certain periods, in Turkey, and elsewhere. Even where success has been limited, as in Africa, relatively outward-oriented countries have done much better than inward-oriented.[5]

The Dangers of Overspecialization. We have repeatedly emphasized the economic gains from specialization, whether within a nation or among nations, because division of labor allows a vast increase in the quantity and variety of producible goods and services. But can a nation become dangerously overspecialized? Imagine the fate of a nation with big cost advantages that specialized completely in horseshoe manufacture in 1900, in production of vacuum tubes in 1945, or in construction of nuclear reactors in 1975?

Some degree of diversification is essential. If Venezuela exports mainly oil and Zambia mainly copper, price fluctuations in these markets will have a large effect on their foreign-trade balances and real incomes. Table 38-4 shows the degree to which some economies engage in "monoculture"—that is, have most of their exports concentrated in a single product. The oil-exporting countries are the most vulnerable to the dangers of overspecialization, followed by producers of other primary commodities.

[5] Bela Belassa et al., *Toward Renewed Economic Growth in Latin America* (Institute for International Economics, Washington, D.C., 1986), p. 24. This study points out that microeconomic government regulations may be as important as macroeconomic policies, with the following example: "The state as regulator has stifled much entrepreneurial initiative throughout [Latin America]. In several countries, numerous licenses are needed even to begin exporting—hardly an auspicious framework within which to promote outward expansion. In Peru, it recently took 289 days to register a new corporation—compared with four hours in Miami" (p. 30).

Exports of the Most Important Product, 1984			
	As percent of total exports	As percent of GNP	Commodity
Iran	98.0	34.6	Oil
Nigeria	97.3	16.0	Oil
Saudia Arabia	93.0	34.6	Oil
Zambia	83.8	21.7	Copper
Venezuela	82.6	21.7	Oil
Colombia	53.2	6.4	Coffee
South Africa	42.1	13.6	Gold
Tanzania	38.5	2.9	Coffee
Jamaica	38.0	11.4	Alumina
Sweden	9.7	3.0	Paper
United States	2.5	0.1	Corn

Table 38-4. Degree of specialization in exports

Many countries, particularly oil exporters, are dangerously specialized in a single commodity. These countries court disaster when primary commodity prices fall. Advanced countries like the United States tend to be much more diversified and therefore suffer little from price swings in individual sectors. (Source: International Monetary Fund and U.S. Department of Commerce.)

When a country is overspecialized, prudent planning suggests that special efforts should be taken to diversify into different areas (particularly areas where the price swings are independent of, or even inverse to, those in the current area of specialization). If coffee demand and supply are volatile, and if sound investment opportunities can be found in coal mining or cut flowers, a country like Colombia may be well advised to limit the market's tendency to specialize in coffee production.

"Don't put all your beans in one bag" is a good rule for countries as well as people.

State vs. Market. The cultures of many developing countries are hostile to the operation of markets. Often, competition among firms or profit-seeking behavior is contrary to traditional practices, religious beliefs, or vested interest. Yet decades of experience suggest that markets provide the most effective way of managing an economy and promoting rapid economic growth.

Some of the elements of a market-oriented policy have been described above. The important elements include an outward orientation in trade policy, low tariffs and few quantitative restrictions, easy entry and exit, the promotion of small business, and the fostering of competition. Moreover, markets work best in a stable macroeconomic environment—one in which taxes are predictable, prices are stable, and the government budget is balanced.

At the same time, the government has a vital role in establishing and maintaining a healthy economic environment. Government must keep law and order, enforce contracts, and orient its regulations toward competition and innovation. Government often plays a leading role in investment in human capital through education, health, and transportation, but government should minimize its intervention or control in sectors where it has no comparative advantage. Government should focus its efforts in areas where there are clear signs of market failures and should dismantle regulatory impediments to the private sector in areas where government has comparative disadvantage.

Responsibilities of the Affluent

This chapter has addressed the problems of poor countries. These regions are, however, part of a larger network of markets and policies. What are the responsibilities of the developed world? An eminent development scholar, T. N. Srinivasan, writes this:

> [W]ithout a liberal global trading and financing environment, the efforts of developing countries . . . would be frustrated. A protectionist surge in the industrialized world . . . would be extremely harmful. A successful completion of the Uruguay Round that eliminates most tariff and nontariff barriers to exports from developing countries and the acceptance by developing countries of full rights and obligations of the GATT system . . . is a must. Above all, the multilateral lending agencies, with augmented resources, should return to their primary role of providing development finance at suitable terms for countries with a credible commitment to pursuing a viable development strategy and capable of implementing it, and move away from acting as "debt collection" agents for imprudent lenders from improvident borrowers.[6]

[6] T. N. Srinivasan, "Development Thought, Strategy and Policy: Then and Now," background paper for *World Development Report 1991*, October 1990. The *World Development Report 1991* contains a detailed, nontechnical survey of theory and experience of economic development.

SUMMARY

A. Developing Countries and the Population Problem

1. Most of the world consists of developing countries, which have relatively low per capita incomes. Such countries often exhibit rapid population growth and low literacy and have a high proportion of their population living and working on farms. Within the group of developing countries, some are middle-income newly industrializing countries, or NICs. This group has been successful in breaking the vicious cycle of underdevelopment.

2. Malthus' theory of population rests on the law of diminishing returns. He contended that population, if unchecked, would tend to grow at a geometric (or exponential) rate, doubling every generation or so. But each member of the growing population would have less land and natural resources to work with. Because of diminishing returns, income could grow at an arithmetic rate at best; output per person would tend to fall so low as to stabilize population at a subsistence level of near-starvation.

3. Over the last century and a half, Malthus and his followers have been criticized on several grounds: for ignoring the possibility of technological advance and for overlooking the significance of birth control as a force in lowering population growth.

4. The concept of the demographic transition helps explain historical trends in population. This is the four-stage process by which a traditional society moves from stable population with high birth and death rates to stable population with low birth and death rates. In the interval, countries generally find that their death rates fall before their birth rates, so that a population explosion may occur. Many poorer and middle-income countries are still in the middle of their demographic transition.

B. The Process of Economic Development

5. The key to development lies in four fundamental factors: human resources, natural resources, capital formation (domestic or imported), and technology. Population causes problems of explosive growth as death rates fall before birth rates; the Malthusian prediction of diminishing returns stalks less developed countries. On the constructive agenda, improving the population's health, education, and technical training has high priority.

6. Rates of productive capital formation in poor countries are low because incomes are so depressed that little can be saved for the future. The financing of growth in poorer countries has always been an unstable link in the productive mechanism. The most recent crisis arose when many middle-income countries borrowed heavily in the 1970s to finance ambitious development programs. The economic slowdown of the early 1980s led to swollen debts, which left these countries unable to export enough to cover their debt service and customary import levels.

7. Technological change is often associated with investment and new machin-

ery. It offers much hope to the developing nations inasmuch as they can adapt the more productive technologies of advanced nations. This requires entrepreneurship. One task of development is to spur internal growth of the scarce entrepreneurial spirit.

8. Numerous theories of economic development help explain why the four fundamental factors are present or absent at a particular time. Geography and climate, custom, religious and business attitudes, class conflicts and colonialism—each affects economic development. But none does so in a simple and invariable way.

   More convincing are the takeoff theory (whereby increasing returns and social overhead capital combine to allow rapid growth in a short period); the backwardness hypothesis (in which less advanced countries can converge quickly toward the more advanced by borrowing their technology and technologists); and the balanced-growth view (in which countries tend to grow at pretty much the same rate whether advanced or backward).

CONCEPTS FOR REVIEW

Basic concepts
developing country, LDC
indicators of development
Malthusian population theory
demographic transition
(stages 1, 2, 3, 4)
social overhead capital, externalities

Development strategies
four elements in development:
human resources, natural resources, capital, technology and innovation
takeoff, backwardness, and balanced-growth hypotheses
inward vs. outward orientation
overspecialization in exports

QUESTIONS FOR DISCUSSION

1. Examine each of the countries in Table 38-2. Can you say where each is in its demographic transition?
2. Many economists believe that the state should not interfere in a market where there are no important externalities—this being the "liberal" or laissez-faire tradition. Are there externalities in population growth that would lead to positive or negative spillovers? Consider such items as education, national defense, roads, pollution, and the creation of geniuses like Mozart or Einstein.
3. A *geometric progression* is a sequence of terms ($g_1, g_2, \ldots, g_t, g_{t+1}, \ldots$) in which each term is the same multiple of its predecessor, $g_2/g_1 = g_3/g_2 = \cdots = g_{t+1}/g_t = \beta$. If $\beta = 1 + i > 1$ the terms grow exponentially like compound interest. An *arithmetic progression* is a sequence ($a_1, a_2, a_3, \ldots, a_t, a_{t+1}, \ldots$) in which the difference between each term and its predecessor is the same constant: $a_2 - a_1 = a_3 - a_2 = \cdots = a_{t+1} - a_t = \alpha$. Give examples of each. Satisfy yourself that any geometric progression with $\beta > 1$ must eventually surpass any arithmetic progression. Relate this to Malthus' theory.
4. Recall that Malthus asserted that unchecked population would grow geometrically, while food supply—constrained by diminishing returns—would grow only arithmetically. Use a numerical example to show why per capita food production must decline if population is unchecked while diminishing returns lead food production to grow more slowly than labor inputs.
5. Would you expect everyone to agree with the praise of material well-being expressed in the chapter's opening quotation?
6. Delineate each of the four important factors driving economic development. With respect to these, how was it that the high-income oil-exporting countries became rich? What hope is there for a country like Bangladesh, which has very low per capita resources of capital, land, and technology?
7. Some fear the "vicious cycle of underdevelopment."

Rapid population growth eats into whatever improvements in technology occur and lowers living standards. With a low per capita income, the country cannot save and invest and mainly engages in subsistence farming. With most of the population on the farm, there is little hope for education, decline in fertility, or industrialization. If you were to advise such a country, how would you break through the vicious cycle?

8. Compare the situation a developing country faces today with that it might have faced (at an equivalent level of per capita income) 200 years ago. Considering the four wheels of economic development, explain the advantages and disadvantages that today's developing country might experience.

9. **Advanced problem** (for those who have also studied economic-growth theory in Chapter 30): We can extend our growth-accounting equation to include three factors and write the following equation:

$$g_Q = s_L g_L + s_K g_K + s_R g_R + \text{T. C.}$$

where g_Q = the growth rate of output, g_i = the growth rate of inputs (i = inputs to production = L for labor, K for capital, and R for land and other natural resources), and s_i = the contribution of each input to output growth as measured by its share of national income ($0 \le s_i \le 1$ and $s_L + s_K + s_R = 1$). T. C. measures technological change.

(a) In the poorest developing countries, the share of capital is close to zero, the main resource is agricultural land (which is constant), and there is little technological change. Can you see why per capita output is likely to be stagnant or even to decline (i.e., $g_Q < g_L$)? Explain the Malthusian hypothesis in terms of this model.

(b) In advanced industrial economies, the share of land resources drops to virtually zero. Why does the generalized growth-account equation then become identical to that given in Chapter 30? Can you explain the failure of the Malthusian hypothesis in terms of this equation?

(c) According to economists who are pessimistic about future prospects (including a group known as "neo-Malthusians"), T. C. is close to zero, the available supply of natural resources is declining, and the share of resources is large and rising. Does this explain why the future of industrial societies might be bleak? What assumptions of the neo-Malthusians might you question?

C H A P T E R 39

EXCHANGE RATES AND THE INTERNATIONAL FINANCIAL SYSTEM

Before I built a wall I'd ask to know
What I was walling in or walling out . . .
Robert Frost

Like other industrial economies, the United States is part of a vast global marketplace. Events in distant lands sometimes have a profound effect upon economic conditions at home. Bad harvests in the Soviet Union can drive up food prices in American grocery stores. Technological advances in the Japanese automobile industry have thrown people out of work in Detroit. A dispute between two oil-rich countries led to military conflict and plunged world oil markets into turmoil, hurt consumer confidence, and contributed to a sharp recession in the industrial world. Economically, no nation is an island unto itself. When the bell tolls for one nation, it tolls for all.

What are the economic mechanisms that increasingly link nations together? We saw in the last three chapters the way international trade allows nations to specialize in areas of comparative advantage, exporting goods in which they have relative efficiency and importing those in which they are relatively inefficient. But how does international exchange take place? Not by bartering American computers for Japanese cars, but through the medium of money—by buying or selling commodities for dollars or yen or pounds or francs or other currencies. To understand the mechanism of international trade, we must apply the principles of international finance.

This concluding chapter examines the essentials of exchange rates and the international financial system. The first section examines exchange rates between different currencies and explains different exchange-rate systems. The second part analyzes the evolution of the international financial system and examines some of the key issues in international economics.

The history of international finance has been marked by alternating periods of calm, breakdown, and reconstruction. During the 1980s, many economists and policymakers felt a strong dissatisfaction with the current international financial system, and they searched actively for a more stable system. But, whatever are the shortcomings of the international financial system, we might say that it resembles democracy—an imperfect system, but the best that we know.

A. The Determination of Foreign Exchange Rates

Foreign Exchange Rates

We are all familiar with domestic trade. When I buy Florida oranges or California shirts, I naturally want to pay in dollars. Luckily, the orange grower and the shirt manufacturer want payment in U.S. dollars, so all trade can be carried on in dollars. Economic transactions within a country are simple.

If I want to buy a British bicycle, however, the transaction becomes more complicated. The bicycle manufacturer needs to be paid in British money rather than in dollars. Similarly, if the British want to buy U.S. merchandise, they must obtain U.S. dollars. International trade therefore introduces a new element: the **foreign exchange rate,** which denotes the price of a foreign country's currency in terms of our own.

For example, the U.S. dollar price of a British pound was recently \$1.80; for a British resident wanting to buy U.S. goods, the price of a dollar was £1/\$1.80 = £0.56. There is a foreign exchange rate between U.S. dollars and the currency of each and every country. In mid-1991, the foreign exchange rate was 54 cents for a German mark, 16 cents for a French franc, 87 cents for a Canadian dollar, and 0.72 cent for a Japanese yen. For foreigners desiring to buy dollars, the reciprocal prices were 1.84 German marks, 6.06 French francs, 1.14 Canadian dollars, or 138 Japanese yen for each U.S. dollar.

With the foreign exchange rate, it is now possible for me to buy an English bicycle. Suppose its quoted price is £100. All I have to do is look in the newspaper for the foreign exchange rate for pounds. If this is \$1.80 per pound, I simply go to a bank with \$180 and ask that the money be used to pay the English bicycle exporter. Pay with what? The bank pays with pounds—the kind of money the exporter needs.

You should be able to show what British importers of American trucks have to do if they want to buy, say, a \$36,000 shipment from an American exporter. Here pounds must be converted into dollars. You will see that, when the foreign exchange rate is \$1.80 per pound, the truck shipment costs them £20,000.

Businesses and tourists do not have to know anything more than this for their import or export transactions. But the economics of foreign exchange rates cannot be grasped until we analyze the forces underlying the supply and demand for foreign currencies and the functioning of the foreign exchange market.

The Foreign Exchange Market

To understand how foreign exchange rates are determined, we need to analyze the workings of the foreign exchange market. The **foreign exchange market** is the market in which currencies of different countries are traded; it is here that foreign exchange rates are determined. Foreign exchange is traded at the retail level in many banks and firms specializing in that business. Organized markets in New York, Tokyo, London, and Zurich trade hundreds of billions of dollars' worth of currencies each day.

We can use our familiar supply and demand curves to illustrate how markets determine the price of foreign currencies. Figure 39-1 shows the supply and demand for British pounds in a simplified example in which we consider only the bilateral trade between Britain and the United States. The demand for British pounds comes from people who need pounds to purchase British goods, services, or financial instruments; the supply of pounds comes from people who are supplying goods, services, or investments to the British and who accordingly have been paid for these items in pounds. The price of foreign exchange—the foreign exchange rate—settles at that price where supply and demand are in balance.

Let us first consider the demand side. The demand for British pounds originates when Americans need pounds to buy British bicycles and other commodities, to vacation in London, to hire British insurance services, and to pay for similar items in the British current account (recall the discussion of the balance of payments in Chapter 36). In addition, foreign exchange is required if Americans

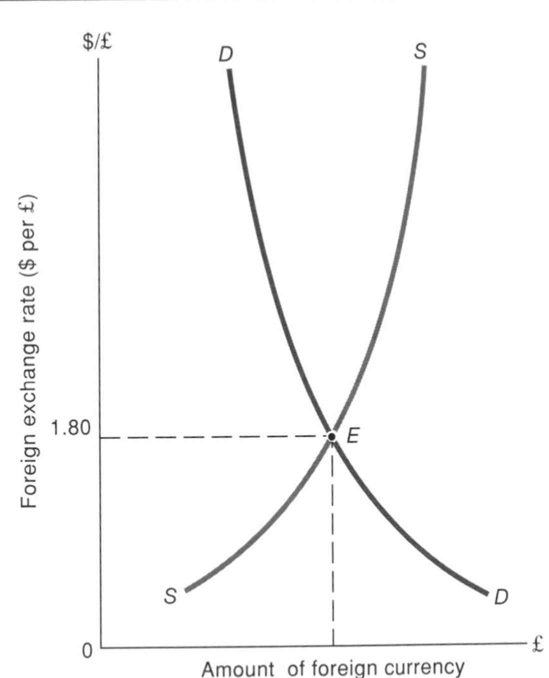

Figure 39-1. Exchange-rate equilibrium

The market exchange rate comes when supply and demand for goods, services, and capital flows are in balance. Behind demand is the desire to import British goods, buy British securities, visit the Bard's grave, and so forth. Behind the supply of pounds to be traded for dollars is British desire for U.S. goods, services, and capital. If the rate were above *E*, there would be an excess supply of foreign currency; market forces would push the exchange rate back down to *E*, where the supply and demand for foreign currency are just in balance.

want to buy land in Britain or to purchase shares in British companies. In short, we demand foreign currencies when we purchase foreign goods, services, and assets. The demand curve shown in Figure 39-1 is represented by the downward-sloping *DD* curve, with the vertical axis representing the price of the British pound. The demand curve generally slopes downward to indicate that as the price of the British pound falls, foreigners tend to want to buy more British goods. For example, if the pound were to fall from $1.80/£ to $1.20/£, other things being equal, Americans would want to buy more British bicycles and spend more time visiting Britain.

What lies behind the supply of foreign currency (represented in Figure 39-1 by the *SS* supply curve of British pounds)? The British supply their currency when they import goods, services, and assets. For example, when a British student buys an American book or takes a trip to the United States, she supplies the British pounds necessary for the expense. Or when the British government purchases an American supercomputer for weather forecasting, this increases the supply of British pounds. In short, the British supply pounds to pay for their purchases of foreign goods, services, and financial assets. The supply curve in Figure 39-1 slopes upward to indicate that as the pound's value rises (and the dollar therefore becomes less expensive) British residents will want to buy more foreign goods, services, and investments and will therefore generally supply more of their currency to the foreign exchange market.

The supply and demand for British pounds interact in the foreign exchange market. Market forces move the foreign exchange rate up or down to balance the inflows and outflows of pounds; the price will settle at the equilibrium foreign exchange rate at which the pounds willingly bought just equal the pounds willingly sold.

The balance of supply and demand for foreign exchange determines the foreign exchange rate of a currency. At the market exchange rate of $1.80 per £1, shown at point *E* in Figure 39-1, the exchange rate is in equilibrium and has no tendency to rise or fall.

We saw above that the exchange rate is a reciprocal relationship. Just as we sell a British pound for $1.80, we buy a dollar for £0.56. We could also have drawn the reciprocal demand-and-supply relationship by analyzing the demand and supply of U.S. dollars. In our simplified bilateral trading world, the British supply of pounds would translate into a demand for dollars, while the American demand for pounds would represent a supply of dollars. We could then draw the supply and demand for the dollar foreign exchange, and the equilibrium would come at £0.56/$ rather than $1.80/£.

Moreover, this supply and demand for foreign exchange exists for every currency. And in a world of many nations, it is the many-sided exchange and trade, with demands and supplies coming from all quarters, that determines the entire array of foreign exchange rates.

Effects of Changes in Trade. What would happen if there were changes in the volume of international trade? For example, what would happen if the United States withdrew its troops from Europe or decided to curb imports from Britain, or if we traveled less abroad?

In each of these cases, America's demand for foreign currencies would decrease. The result is shown in Figure 39-2 for the case where the shift affects Britain. The decline in purchases of goods, services, and investments decreases the demand for foreign currencies. This change is represented by a leftward shift in the demand curve. The result will be a lower price of foreign currencies, that is, a lower exchange rate on the pound and a higher exchange rate on the dollar. How much will exchange rates change? Just enough so that British exports and capital flows to America are increased, and imports and capital flows from America to Britain are decreased, until supply and demand are again in balance. In the example shown in Figure 39-2, the pound has declined from \$1.80 to \$1.25 per £1.

A Shift in Demand

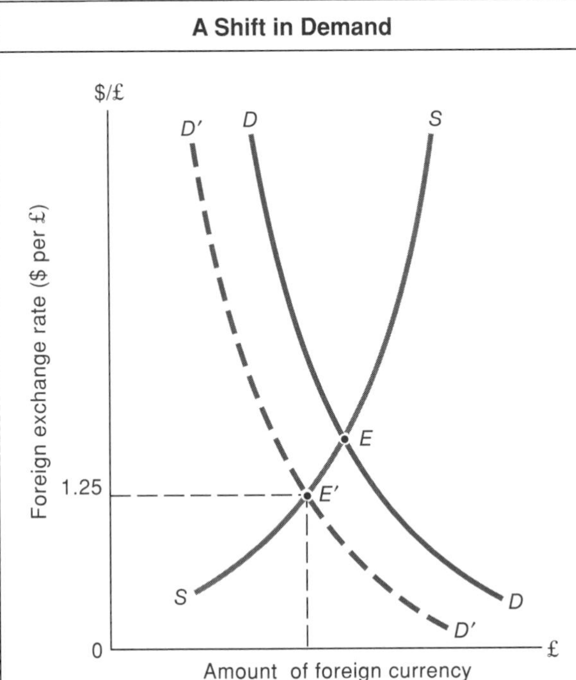

Figure 39-2. A decrease in American imports leads to a dollar appreciation

Suppose Americans travel less to Britain or decide to withdraw troops from Europe. This will lower the imports from Britain and decrease the demand for British pounds, shifting the *DD* curve to the left to *D′D′*. As a result, the exchange rate of the pound falls to \$1.25 per £1 (similarly, the exchange rate of the dollar rises to £0.80/\$). At the new exchange rate at *E′*, British exports are stimulated and American imports decline until the supply and demand for British pounds are once more in balance. (What would be the impact of a decision by the British government to stop buying American military equipment?)

Terminology for Exchange-Rate Changes

Foreign exchange markets have a special vocabulary. By definition, a fall in the price of one currency in terms of one or all others is called a "depreciation." A rise in the price of a currency in terms of another currency is called an "appreciation." In our example above, when the price of the pound went from \$1.80 to \$1.25, the pound depreciated and the dollar underwent an appreciation.

The term "devaluation" is often confused with the term "depreciation." Devaluation is confined to situations in which a country has officially pegged its exchange rate to another currency or to gold and in which the pegged rate or "parity" is changed by raising the price of the other currency or gold.

For example, in 1971 the United States changed the official price of gold from \$35 to \$38 per ounce, so we say the dollar was devalued. But when the dollar fell from 150 yen/\$ to 120 yen/\$ in the marketplace, the dollar depreciated.

When a country's foreign exchange rate declines relative to that of another country, we say that the domestic currency **depreciates** while the foreign currency **appreciates.**

When a country's official foreign exchange rate (relative to gold or other currencies) is lowered, we say that the currency has undergone a **devaluation,** while an increase in the official foreign exchange rate is called a **revaluation.**

Three Major Exchange-Rate Systems

Having reviewed the principles underlying the market determination of exchange rates, we can now turn to an analysis of the **exchange-rate system,** which denotes the set of rules, arrangements, and institutions under which payments are made and received for transactions reaching across national boundaries.

At the outset, we must ask why there is an exchange-rate system to regulate exchange rates, when there is no "lettuce system" to regulate lettuce prices or even a "machinery system" to affect the machinery market. The reason is that foreign exchange rates affect output, inflation, foreign trade, and many other central economic goals, so it is natural that governments will regulate exchange markets in an attempt to improve international economic performance.

The importance of the international monetary system was well described by economist Robert Solomon:

> Like the traffic lights in a city, the international monetary system is taken for granted until it begins to malfunction and to disrupt people's lives. . . . A well-functioning monetary system will facilitate international trade and investment and smooth adaptation to change. A monetary system that functions poorly may not only discourage the development of trade and investment among nations but subject their economies to disruptive shocks when necessary adjustments to change are prevented or delayed.[1]

There are three major exchange-rate systems:

- The gold standard
- A system of "pure" floating exchange rates, in which exchange rates fluctuate with private supply and demand so as to balance the exchange market
- A hybrid system of "managed" floating exchange rates, which involves some currencies whose values float freely, some currencies whose values are determined by a combination of government intervention and the market, and some that are pegged or fixed to one currency or a group of currencies

The Classical Gold Standard

Historically, one of the most important exchange-rate systems was the gold standard. This system held sway in its purest form during the period 1880–1913. In this system, countries defined their currencies in terms of a fixed amount of gold, thereby establishing fixed exchange rates among the countries on the gold standard.

The functioning of the gold standard can be seen easily by a simplified example. Suppose people everywhere insisted on being paid in bits of pure gold metal. Then buying a bicycle in Britain would merely require payment in gold at a price expressed in ounces of gold. By definition there would be no foreign-exchange-rate problem. Gold would be the common world currency.

This example captures the essence of the gold standard. It became customary for each country to issue gold coins carrying the seal of the state to guarantee purity and weight. Once gold coins became the medium of exchange—money—foreign trade was no different from domestic trade; everything could be paid for in gold. Differences arose only if countries chose different *units* for their coins. Thus, Queen Victoria chose to make British coins about $\frac{1}{4}$ ounce of gold (the pound) and President McKinley chose to make the U.S. unit $\frac{1}{20}$ ounce of gold (the dollar). In that case, the British pound, being 5 times as heavy as the dollar, had an exchange rate of $5 to £1.

In the years before 1914, this was basically how the gold standard worked. Of course, countries tended to use their own coins. But anyone was free to melt down coins and sell them at the going price of gold. So, exchange rates were fixed for all countries on the gold standard; the rates of exchange (also called "par values" or "parities") for different currencies were determined by the gold content of their monetary units.

Only minor qualifications need be brought to the gold-standard example analyzed above. Because gold is quite inconvenient to carry around, governments inevitably issued paper certificates that were pledged to be redeemable in gold metal. People had the right to exchange gold for certificates and certificates for gold, and they often exercised that right. Also, in those days ocean transport was slow and costly, and there were in reality costs of melting and recoining. Therefore, exchange rates were not exactly fixed but fluctuated in a narrow band.

Hume's Gold-Flow Equilibrating Mechanism

Under the gold standard, what kept America from buying more British goods and services and lend-

[1] Robert Solomon, *The International Monetary System, 1945–1976: An Insider's View* (Harper & Row, New York, 1977), pp. 1, 7.

ing more capital to Britain than Britain bought from or lent to America? Put differently, what kept us from demanding more British pounds than Britain wanted to supply? We would have had to ship gold to Britain to pay for our trade deficit. Wouldn't we eventually lose all our gold?

Mercantilists fretted that there would be a drain of a country's gold and argued that the government should halt this drain by placing tariffs and quotas on imports, subsidizing exports, and invoking numerous other interferences.

Mercantilism came under attack from Adam Smith. But the clearest refutation of mercantile reasoning flowed from the pen of the British philosopher David Hume in 1752. His argument is as valid today as it was then for understanding how trade flows get balanced.

First of all, Hume pointed out, all countries could not be simultaneously losing gold. Where would it go, into the sea? And even if a single nation were to lose a good deal of its gold, that would be no tragedy if prices were to adjust as well. Suppose Britain lost half its gold. If at the same time all prices and incomes in Britain were exactly halved, then no one in the country would be any better or worse off. Even though people have only half as much gold, that smaller amount will buy the same quantity of goods and services. The *real* value of monetary gold (that is, the quantity of real commodities that the gold will buy) is unchanged. So, Hume argued, losing half or nine-tenths of a nation's gold is of no concern if the nation ends up with a balanced reduction of all prices and costs.

The second part of Hume's reasoning showed that there is an automatic mechanism that tends to keep international payments in balance under the gold standard. This explanation rested in part upon the quantity theory of prices outlined in Chapter 35, so we would do well to review the quantity theory here.

Gold and the Quantity Theory. Hume was, in fact, one of the earliest proponents of the quantity theory of prices. This doctrine holds that the overall price level in an economy is proportional to the supply of money. Under the gold standard, gold formed an important part of the money supply—either directly, in the form of gold coins, or indirectly when governments used gold as backing for paper money.

What would be the impact of a country's losing gold? First, the country's money supply would decline either because gold coins would be exported or because some of the gold backing for the currency would leave the country. Putting both these consequences together, we would find that a loss of gold leads to a reduction in the money supply. The next step, according to the quantity theory, is that prices and costs would change proportionally to the change in the money supply. If Britain loses 10 percent of its gold to pay for a trade deficit, the quantity theory predicts that Britain's prices, costs, and incomes would fall 10 percent. If gold discoveries in California increased gold supplies sharply, we would expect to see a proportional increase in the price level in the United States.

The Four-Pronged Mechanism. Now consider Hume's theory on international payments equilibrium. Suppose that America runs a large trade deficit and begins to lose gold. According to the quantity theory of prices, this loss of gold reduces America's money supply, driving down America's prices and costs.

As a result, (1) America decreases its imports of British and other foreign goods, which have become relatively expensive; (2) because America's domestically produced goods have become relatively inexpensive on world markets, America's exports increase. The opposite effect occurs in Britain and other foreign countries. When Britain's exports grow rapidly, it receives gold in return. Britain's money supply increases, driving up British prices and costs according to the quantity theory.

At this point, two more prongs of the Hume mechanism come into play: (3) British and other foreign exports have become more expensive, so the volume of goods exported to America declines; and (4) British citizens, faced with a higher domestic price level, now import more of America's low-priced goods.

The result of Hume's four-pronged gold-flow mechanism is to improve the balance of payments of the country losing gold and to worsen that of the country gaining the gold. In the end, an equilibrium of international trade and finance is reestablished at new relative prices, which keep trade and international lending in balance with no net gold flow. This equilibrium is a stable one and requires no tariffs or other government intervention.

Flexible Exchange Rates

Having seen how a gold standard works, we turn next to flexible exchange rates. A system of **flexible exchange rates** is one in which the foreign exchange rate is predominantly determined by the market forces of supply and demand. That is, in a flexible-exchange-rate system, the relative prices of currencies are determined by buying and selling among people, firms, and governments.

Under the gold standard, the dollar and the pound were tied in a $5-to-£1 relationship. But what would have happened in 1913 if the United States had decided not to define its dollar in terms of a fixed weight of gold? Would the dollar have sold for $4 per £1? Or $6 per £1? Since 1973, the world has learned that flexible exchange rates tend to fluctuate widely.

Within the class of flexible-exchange-rate systems, we can distinguish the two important subcases of a *free-floating* system and a *managed-floating* system. The difference between these two systems depends on the amount of government intervention. Government exchange-rate **intervention** occurs when the government buys or sells its own or foreign currencies to affect exchange rates. For example, the Japanese government on a given day might buy $1 billion worth of Japanese yen with U.S. dollars. This would cause a rise in value, or appreciation, of the yen. Governments generally tend to intervene heavily when they believe their country's foreign exchange rate is higher or lower than is desirable.

A **freely floating** exchange rate is one determined purely by supply and demand without any government intervention. In a **managed-floating** system, the government intervenes in exchange markets to affect the exchange rate.

Freely Floating Exchange Rates

The first case we examine is that of freely floating exchange rates. In a system of freely floating exchange rates, prices are determined by the forces of supply and demand, as was illustrated at the beginning of this chapter. Say that at an exchange rate of $1.50 per £1, Americans are importing many British goods, while the British are importing few American goods. This means that Americans will be demanding a large quantity of British pounds to buy British goods, but the British will be supplying few British pounds.

What will be the outcome? The excess demand for British pounds will bid up the price of pounds (or, equivalently, will bid down the price of the dollar).

How far will exchange rates move? Just far enough so that—at the new higher price of, say, $2 for the British pound—the foreign exchange market will be in equilibrium. The price of the pound must move up until the diminished quantity of British pounds demanded is equal to the increased supply of British pounds.

Two main steps are involved. (1) With the pound more expensive, it will cost more to import British goods, services, and investments, causing our demand for imports to fall off in the usual fashion. (2) With the dollar now cheaper, our goods will cost less to foreigners. They will want to purchase more of our export goods. (If we look at these two effects from the viewpoints of both countries, we have something much like the four-pronged mechanism of Hume.)

Managed Exchange Rates

In the freely floating exchange-rate system just described, the government is on the sidelines. It allows the foreign exchange market to determine the value of the dollar (just as it allows markets to determine the value of oats, GM stock, or copper).

Few countries, in reality, allow their currencies to float freely. Rather, they manage their exchange rates, intervening to prevent wide swings in exchange rates, or even to maintain a *parity* (an announced target exchange rate with other countries).

A particularly important example of a managed exchange-rate system, known as *pegged exchange rates,* prevailed during the period from World War II until 1971. Called the *Bretton Woods system,* it allowed countries to set fixed parities or pegged exchange rates with each other; the rates might be $2.40 per British pound, 4 German marks per $1, and so forth. Countries then took steps to defend the set of exchange rates. From time to time, when exchange rates deviated too far from the official rates, countries would adjust the official parities. The essence of the Bretton Woods system was that the exchange rates were fixed but adjustable—that is, fixed in the short run but adjustable in the long run.

Today, we see a variety of different exchange-rate systems coexisting. Western European countries have joined together in a system similar to the Bretton Woods system. But each of the three major currency areas—the U.S. dollar, the Japanese yen, and the European currencies—has floated more or less freely against the others since 1973. Many countries in Latin America peg their exchange rates to the U.S. dollar. In addition, almost all countries tend to intervene either (*a*) when markets become "disorderly" or (*b*) when exchange rates seem far out of line with the "fundamentals," that is, with exchange rates that are appropriate for existing price levels and trade flows. This system—with a mixture of different components—is called *managed floating.* We return to a full discussion of this system in the next section of this chapter.

B. Issues of International Economics

Now that we have analyzed the highlights of exchange rates and of the international monetary system, we will survey the history of international economic institutions along with current problems of the international economy.

Building International Institutions after World War II

After World War II, the United States emerged with its economy intact and was able to help rebuild the countries of allies and foes alike. The postwar international political system also responded to the needs of war-torn nations by constructing durable institutions within which the international economy could recover quickly. The four major economic institutions of the 1940s—the GATT (described in Chapter 37), the Bretton Woods exchange-rate system, the International Monetary Fund, and the World Bank—stand as monuments to wise and farsighted statecraft.

The Bretton Woods System

The economic and social turmoil of the 1930s deeply impressed economic thinkers of the 1940s. They were determined to avoid the economic chaos and competitive devaluations of the Great Depression.

In order to map out a new international economic order, the United States, Britain, and their major allies gathered in Bretton Woods, New Hampshire, in 1944. Under the intellectual leadership of J. M. Keynes and the American diplomat H. D. White, this landmark conference hammered out an agreement that led to the formation of the International Monetary Fund (IMF), the World Bank, and the Bretton Woods exchange-rate system. For the first time in history, nations agreed upon a system for regulating international financial transactions. Even though some of the rules have changed since 1944, the institutions established at Bretton Woods continue to play a vital role today.

The conference designed a framework for managing exchange rates that is known as the **Bretton Woods system.** Those who attended the Bretton Woods conference remembered well how the gold standard was too inflexible and served to deepen economic crises. To replace the gold standard, the Bretton Woods system established a parity for each currency in terms of both the U.S. dollar and gold. As the key or reserve currency, the parity of the dollar was pegged only in terms of gold, initially at $35 per ounce of gold. Other currencies were defined in terms of both gold and the dollar.

For example, the parity of the British pound was set at £12.5 per ounce of gold. Given the gold price of the dollar, this implied an official exchange rate between the dollar and the pound of $35/£12.5 = $2.80 per £1, which was thereby set as the official parity on the pound. Under the Bretton Woods system, therefore, because each currency's parity was established in terms of gold and the dollar, a set of exchange rates *among* currencies was fixed by international agreement.

However, when one currency got too far out of line with its appropriate or "fundamental" value, the parity could be adjusted. The German mark was adjusted upward, or revalued, on several occasions, while the British pound was devalued from \$2.80 per £1 to \$2.40 per £1 in 1967.

The ability to adjust exchange rates when fundamental disequilibrium arose was the central distinction between the Bretton Woods system and the gold standard. The Bretton Woods system was a *fixed but adjustable* exchange-rate system. Ideally, exchange-rate changes would be worked out among countries in a cooperative way. By creating a fixed but adjustable system, the designers of Bretton Woods hoped to have the best of two worlds. They could maintain the *stability* of the gold standard, a world in which exchange rates would be predictable from one month to the next, thereby encouraging trade and capital flows. At the same time, they would simulate the *adaptability* of flexible exchange rates, under which persistent relative price differences among countries could be adjusted to by exchange-rate changes rather than by the painful deflation and unemployment necessary under the gold standard.

The International Monetary Fund (IMF)

Another major contribution of the Bretton Woods conference was the establishment of the International Monetary Fund (or IMF), which still administers the international monetary system and operates as a central bank for central banks. Member nations subscribe by lending their currencies to the IMF; the IMF then relends these funds to help countries in balance-of-payments difficulties. In recent years, the IMF has played a key role in organizing a cooperative response to the international debt crisis and in helping socialist countries make the transition to the market.

How would an IMF mission operate? Suppose that Poland's program to introduce a market economy is in trouble because of a rapid inflation. It is having trouble paying interest and principal on its foreign loans. The IMF might send a team of specialists to pore over the country's books. The IMF team would come up with an austerity plan for Poland, generally involving reducing the budget deficit and tightening credit; these measures would slow GNP growth and reduce the trade deficit. When Poland and the IMF agree on the plan, the IMF would lend money to Poland, perhaps \$1 billion, to "bridge" the country over until its balance of payments improves. In addition, there would probably be a "debt rescheduling," wherein banks lend more funds and stretch out existing loans.

If the IMF program was successful, Poland's balance of payments would soon regain health, and the country would resume economic growth.

The World Bank

The Bretton Woods conference also established the World Bank. The Bank is capitalized by lending nations who subscribe in proportion to their economic importance in terms of GNP and other factors. The Bank makes low-interest loans to countries for projects that are economically sound but cannot get private-sector financing. As a result of such long-term loans, goods and services flow from the advanced nations to developing countries. In recent years, the World Bank has made new loans averaging \$25 billion per year.

While the loans are being spent, the advanced world is forgoing domestic spending. When the loans are being "serviced" or repaid, the advanced nations can enjoy somewhat higher imports of useful goods. Production in the borrowing lands will have risen by more than enough to pay interest on the loans; wages and living standards generally will be higher, not lower, because the foreign capital has raised GNP in the borrowing countries.

Demise of the Bretton Woods System

For the first three decades after World War II, the world was on a dollar standard. The U.S. dollar was the key currency; most international trade and finance were carried out in dollars and payments were most often made in dollars. Exchange-rate parities were set in dollar terms, and private and government reserves were kept in dollar balances.

The world economy thrived during this period. The industrial nations began to lower trade barriers and to make all their currencies freely convertible. The economies of Western Europe and East Asia recovered from war damage and grew at spectacular rates. But recovery contained the seeds of its own destruction. Dollars began to pile up abroad as Germany and Japan developed trade surpluses. Meanwhile, U.S. deficits were fueled by an overvalued currency, trade deficits, and growing overseas investment by American firms. Dollar holdings abroad grew from next to nothing in 1945 to $50 billion in the early 1970s.

By 1971, the amount of liquid dollar balances had become so large that governments had difficulty defending the official parities. People began to lose confidence in the "almighty dollar." And the lower barriers to capital flows meant that billions of dollars could cross the Atlantic in minutes. In August 1971, President Nixon formally severed the link between the dollar and gold, bringing the Bretton Woods era to an end. No longer would the United States automatically convert dollars into other currencies or into gold at $35 per ounce; no longer would the United States set an official parity of the dollar and then defend this exchange rate at all costs. As the United States abandoned the Bretton Woods system, the world moved into the modern era of managed flexible exchange rates.

Managed Floating Exchange Rates

When the old system broke down, there was no perfect new one to take its place. Leading IMF member countries tried unsuccessfully to agree on a new system to replace the Bretton Woods system. So without anyone's having planned it, the world has moved on to a managed floating-exchange-rate system. This system works as follows:

- A few countries allow their currencies to *float freely,* as has the United States for some periods in the last two decades. In this approach, a country allows markets to determine its currency's value and it rarely intervenes.
- Some major countries have *managed but flexible* exchange rates. Today, this group includes the United States and Japan. Under this system, a country will buy or sell its currency to reduce the day-to-day volatility of currency fluctuations. In addition, a country will sometimes engage in systematic intervention to move its currency toward what it believes to be a more appropriate level.
- Some nations pursue *flexible rates with target zones,* whereby they individually or collectively set broad zones within which currencies can fluctuate and they intervene to keep exchange rates within these zones.
- Many countries, particularly small ones, *peg* their currencies to a major currency or to a "basket" of currencies. Sometimes, the peg is allowed to glide smoothly upward or downward in a system known as a *gliding* or *crawling peg* (see question 7 at the end of this chapter).
- Finally, some countries join together in a *currency bloc* in order to stabilize exchange rates among themselves while allowing their currencies to move flexibly relative to the rest of the world. The most important of these blocs is the European Monetary System (discussed below).

Current International Economic Problems

Governments are increasingly concerned with the world economy, the prospects for international trade, and the economic linkages between them. Now that we have surveyed the determination of exchange rates, we will examine some critical issues of international economics.

The Volatile Dollar

During the years that followed the breakdown of the Bretton Woods system, industrial countries attempted to find an alternative that had the twin advantages of the earlier system—stability of exchange rates in the short run with adaptability of exchange rates over the long run. Figure 39-3 shows the average exchange value of the dollar against major currencies over this period. Note how stable the dollar's exchange rate was until the Bretton Woods system broke down in 1971; also examine the steady depreciation of the dollar from 1971 to 1980.

The decade of the 1980s witnessed a dramatic cycle of dollar rise and fall—appreciation and depreciation. The rise of the dollar began in 1980 after a tight monetary policy and loose fiscal policy in the U.S. drove interest rates up sharply. High interest rates, a conservative administration in the United States, and a cut in U.S. tax rates attracted mobile funds from other currencies to U.S. dollars. At the same time, economic difficulties in continen-

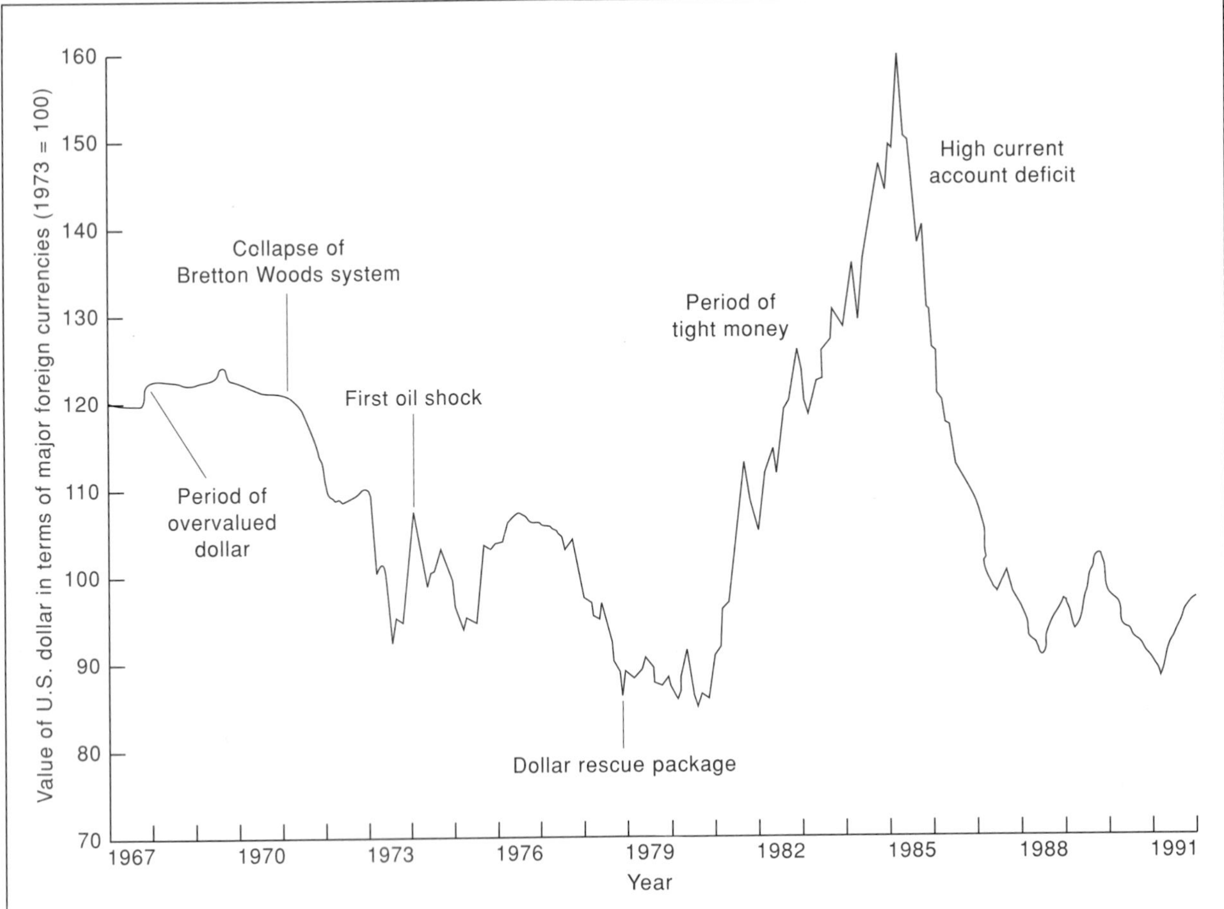

Figure 39-3. The foreign exchange value of the dollar

The dollar has shown extreme instability under flexible exchange rates. Before the collapse of the Bretton Woods system, the dollar's value was stable in exchange markets. After 1971, the dollar first drifted down, next rose sharply during the high-interest-rate era of the early 1980s, then collapsed as U.S. interest rates fell and the U.S. trade deficit mounted. (Source: Federal Reserve System.)

tal Europe, along with political unrest and a debt crisis in many Latin American countries, led foreigners to ask in effect, "Why risk your nest egg in socialist France or in strife-torn Brazil when you can obtain a high real return on your funds in the safe dollar?"

Figure 39-3 shows the result: from 1979 to early 1985, the exchange rate on the dollar rose 80 percent. Indeed, the dollar soared to levels far above those attained just before the Bretton Woods system collapsed because of an "overvalued dollar" in 1971. Many economists and policymakers became convinced that the dollar was overvalued in 1985, and a swift decline soon followed. Over the next 6 years, the dollar fell more than it had risen in the early 1980s.

Impacts of the Overvalued Dollar. Many economists believed that the dollar was "overvalued" in the early 1980s. An *overvalued currency* is one whose value is high relative to its long-run or sustainable level. What were the impacts of U.S. financial policies and the overvaluation of the dollar in the 1980s? The consequences were profound not only for the United States but for virtually the entire world economy.

The first results came as the high interest rates slowed economic growth in the United States and abroad. We learn in macroeconomics that high interest rates tend to reduce business and residential investment, thereby reducing aggregate spending, slowing economic activity, and raising unemployment. The United States experienced an economic slowdown beginning in 1980, with the trough of the recession coming in 1982.

In addition, the high U.S. interest rates pulled up the interest rates of other major countries. These high interest rates slowed investment in other industrial economies and triggered a sharp slowdown in overall economic activity in the industrial world. This slowdown began in 1981, and the European economies had not fully recovered from it by 1991. In addition, high interest rates increased debt-service burdens in poor and middle-income countries.

The next reaction came in exchange markets. As the dollar rose, American export prices increased and the prices of goods imported into the United States fell. As a result, America's exports declined while its imports mounted sharply. From 1980 to 1985, the prices of imported goods and services fell by 1 percent, while the prices of our exports in foreign currencies rose over 60 percent. In response, the volume of imports rose 42 percent while export volumes fell 5 percent.

The impact on the overall economy is measured by the changes in *real net exports,* which measure the trade balance in quantity terms; more precisely, real net exports are the quantity of exports minus the quantity of imports, where both are measured in constant dollars.

Figure 39-4 illustrates the dramatic effect of the rising exchange rate of the dollar on real net exports. From the peak in 1980 to the trough in 1986, real net exports declined by $216 billion, or 5.8 percent of 1986 GNP (all these figures are in 1982 prices).

What was the impact of the decline in real net exports upon the American economy? A drop in real net exports has a contractionary multiplier effect upon domestic output and employment. When foreigners spend less here and Americans spend more abroad, the demand for American goods and services declines, real GNP falls, and unemployment tends to rise. Economic studies indicate that the fall in real net exports was a major contributor to the deep recession in the early 1980s and tended to retard the growth of real GNP during much of the first half of the 1980s.

Deindustrialization of America. The overvalued dollar produced severe economic hardships in many U.S. sectors exposed to international trade. Industries like automobiles, steel, textiles, and agriculture found the demand for their products withering as their prices rose relative to the prices of foreign competitors. Unemployment in the manufacturing heartland increased sharply as factories were closed and the midwest became known as the "rust belt."

The political response to the soaring trade deficit took many forms. Economists tended to emphasize macroeconomic forces such as the overvalued dollar, tight monetary policy, and growing fiscal deficit. They called for reducing the government deficit to force down the dollar's exchange rate and reduce the trade deficit.

Many non-economists interpreted U.S. trade problems as indicative of "America in decline." They sometimes advocated economic protection against stronger trading partners like Japan, Korea, and Western Europe. Some argued for "industrial policies," fiscal aid to beleaguered industries to help stem the "deindustrialization of America."

The Dollar's Decline. In early 1985, the dollar peaked and began a sharp decline. The reversal was caused in part by governments that intervened by selling dollars and buying other currencies, in part by speculators who believed that the dollar was overvalued, and in part by lower relative dollar interest rates. As can be seen in Figure 39-3, the dollar declined steadily for the next 6 years, and by 1991 it had lost all the ground gained between 1980 and 1985.

The recovery in U.S. net exports after 1985 was slow but steady, and Figure 39-4 shows that the current and trade accounts remained in deficit into 1991. What was the reason for the slow improvement after the dollar's decline? Trade flows react to exchange-rate changes with a substantial delay because both prices and quantities change slowly in response to exchange-rate movements. Prices react slowly because importers into the United States tend to keep their dollar prices stable and squeeze their profit margins rather than lower their market shares. When importers ultimately raise

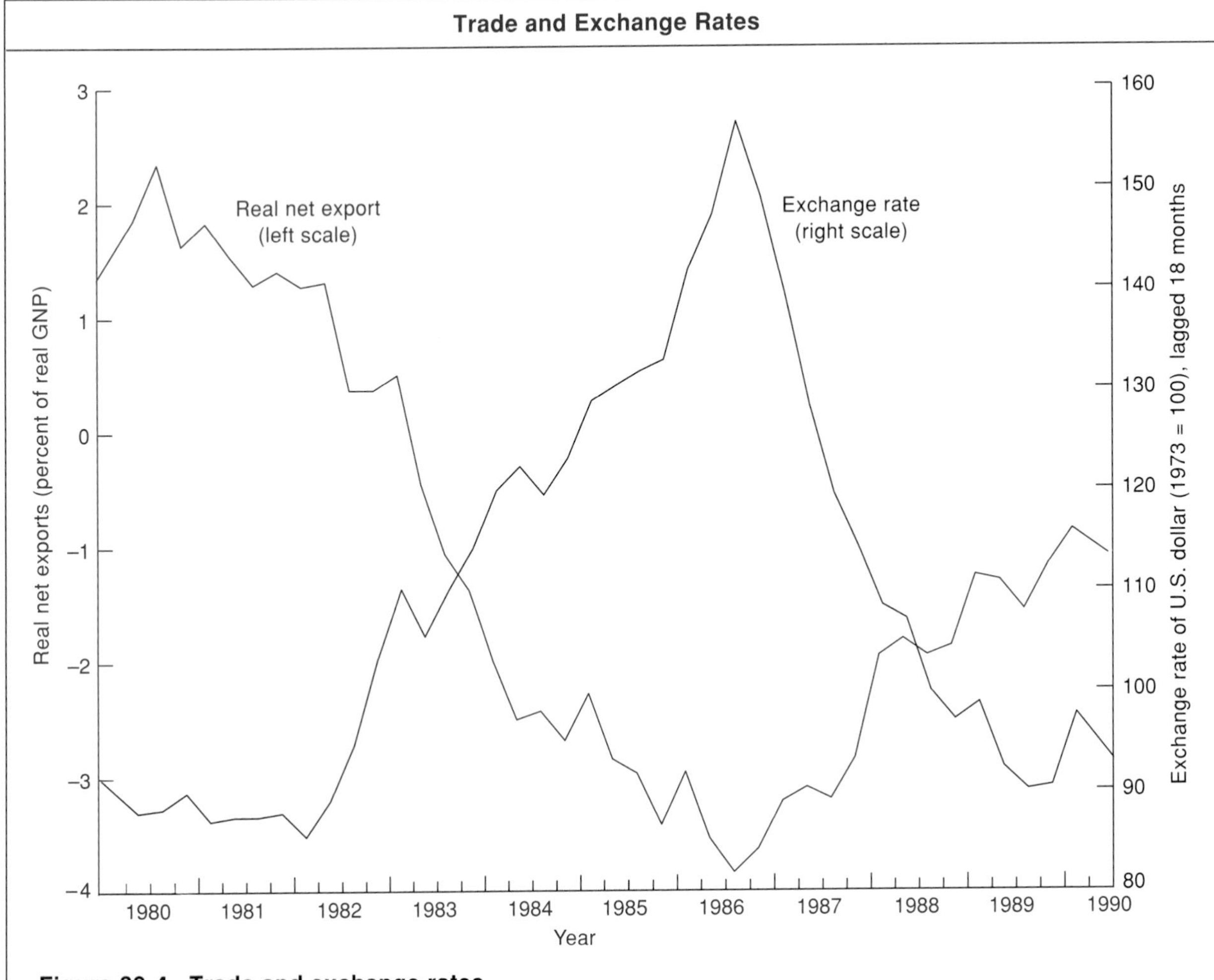

Figure 39-4. Trade and exchange rates

Real net exports react to exchange-rate changes, but with a time lag. The rising real exchange rate of the dollar during the early 1980s increased U.S. export prices and reduced prices of goods imported into the United States. As a result, real net exports (that is, exports minus imports, both measured in constant 1982 prices) fell sharply. When the dollar started to fall in 1985, real net exports began to react only after a considerable time lag. (Source: Real exchange rate is trade-weighted exchange rate corrected for differences in national price levels, from Federal Reserve Board; real net exports from U.S. Department of Commerce.)

their prices, people substitute domestic for imported goods only after they have evaluated and selected new products: brand loyalties become entrenched, so that Toyotas and Canons may retain a substantial market share many years after these products have migrated to the high end of the price range. All these forces imply that the full reaction to the exchange-rate depreciation of 1985–1991 may not be felt until well into the 1990s. As a result, the United States may continue to experience deficits in its trade and current accounts and in its real net exports for a substantial period of time.

Assessment of Flexible Exchange Rates

The year 1991 marks two decades of experience with flexible exchange rates. How well have they functioned? Figure 39-3 tells the story of how a key currency, the U.S. dollar, evolved over the 1970s and 1980s. Note how much greater were the fluctuations after the flexible-rate regime began in 1973.

Many economists and policymakers, having lived through the violent ups and downs of the last two decades, have concluded something like the following:

> We had high hopes that flexible exchange rates would allow our economies to adjust to changes in national economic conditions without unacceptable business cycles or currency fluctuations. But currencies left to free markets wander around like a bunch of drunken sailors. We must put some control over these wayward exchange rates by moving back toward the fixed or stable exchange rates of the Bretton Woods period.

The historical record reveals that flexible exchange rates have indeed performed less well than their advocates had hoped. Exchange rates have been extremely unstable, as the volatile dollar illustrates. Other countries, particularly Japan and those in Europe, also saw excessive fluctuations in their currencies.

Moreover, the sharp currency movements have had unwelcome macroeconomic effects. The dollar's rise caused a severe external deficit in the United States and turned the country into the world's largest debtor. The counterpart of the dollar's swings has left Japan and Germany with large trade surpluses. Thus, critics of flexible exchange rates argue that the exchange rate should not be left to the market but must be controlled by governments and central banks.

The EMS. Many countries have moved to curb exchange-market fluctuations. One early step was the creation in 1978 of a currency bloc known as the European Monetary System (or EMS). A group of West European countries, notably Germany, France, and Italy, designed this system along lines of the Bretton Woods regime; in the EMS, countries intervene to keep their relative exchange rates within narrow limits.

The EMS has some of the advantages of both worlds: The French and the Germans can conveniently transact with each other on quite predictable currency terms. At the same time, any fundamental change in world affairs, such as the major shift in American monetary policy in 1979 or the oil-price increases that have so often occurred, can be absorbed by allowing the EMS exchange rates to float flexibly upward or downward.

European countries agree that their experiment with a currency zone has been successful. Indeed, they are considering a plan to move beyond the EMS to a *common currency* under a blueprint known as the "Delors plan." Its objective is to replace the several central banks of Europe with a single European central bank (some call it the "Eurofed"). With a unitary monetary policy in place, a common currency could be issued. Many Europeans believe that a single currency, like the one enjoyed by the United States, will unify the continent politically and economically and sustain economic growth for many years to come.

Floating Rates and Discipline. We saw that fixed exchange rates, such as the gold standard, impose very tight discipline on a nation. If domestic prices began to rise and a balance-of-payments deficit occurred, gold would leave the country, leading to monetary contraction and recession or worse. A similar (albeit somewhat less tight) chain of events would occur under the Bretton Woods system.

With a floating-rate system, these tight constraints are removed. Countries are free to use macroeconomic policies to determine their own domestic price levels—they can be high-inflation countries or low-inflation countries without automatically triggering a balance-of-payments crisis. But removing the old constraints leads to new ones. Freedom to choose price levels does not mean that a nation can have any *real* wage rate it chooses.

Suppose the United States raises money wage rates 50 percent overnight. Our costs are now high. Our exports can no longer compete. The dollar floats down to correct the imbalance. Imports (raw materials, etc.) become more expensive, so U.S. prices rise. In the end, our prices are likely to rise about as much as money wage rates rose.

The moral here is that floating exchange rates eliminate the discipline of the gold or dollar standard on the *nominal* price and wage levels. But nothing can remove the irreducible constraint of an economy's real productivity level. Flexible exchange rates remove one set of constraints (the straightjacket of gold) and impose another (the harsh verdict of markets about a currency's true value).

Improving International Cooperation

During the turbulent 1980s, the United States came of age as a mature partner in world economic affairs. It saw its domestic monetary and fiscal policies spill over to affect exchange rates and trade flows; the country even found its unemployment rate buffeted by the ups and downs of foreign trade. The central lesson of the 1980s is clear: In a world where economies are increasingly linked by trade and capital flows, interdependence is unavoidable. No walls can prevent domestic actions from spilling over territorial boundaries. National strengths can be leveraged in a global marketplace, while national weaknesses fall prey to intense foreign competitors. Isolationism is today no more feasible in economic affairs than it is in political or military affairs.

All this means that exchange with other nations is an integral part of domestic economic welfare. This fact is captured in the old saying, "When America sneezes, Europe catches cold." An updated adage might read, "When the global economy is sick, the contagion spreads everywhere."

Since World War II, international economic cooperation has entered the agenda of domestic economic policy. Here are the major issues:

- *Trade agreements.* Nations can take measures to protect their industries through tariffs and quotas. These steps would reduce trade deficits and at the same time increase domestic output and employment. But this cure would be a "beggar-thy-neighbor" policy, in a sense exporting trade deficits and unemployment. Having learned the dangers of protectionism in the 1930s, nations have banded together in multinational trade treaties and agreements to desist from imposing trade restrictions.
- *International monetary arrangements.* Foreign exchange rates necessarily affect many nations. In the past, nations would sometimes manipulate their exchange rates to attain domestic political objectives—forcing a depreciation of their currencies to increase net exports, output, and employment. At other times, nations allowed their domestic inflation to spill over to other regions. In an attempt to curtail undesirable manipulation of exchange rates, nations now gather periodically to oversee exchange-rate policies and to ensure that no nation engages in "competitive devaluations" that export its unemployment. The process of "exchange-rate surveillance" is overseen by the IMF.
- *Macroeconomic coordination.* The most recent and controversial of cooperative steps include attempts to coordinate macroeconomic policy. Suppose the world economy is in recession. No single nation is powerful enough to bring the world economy back to its potential output. Moreover, if one small nation takes fiscal or monetary steps to increase its output, much of the stimulus spills over to other countries and, because open-economy multipliers are small, the home economy enjoys relatively less economic expansion. Even worse, if a small country expands on its own, not only will it find that much of the stimulus spills over its borders, but also it is likely to witness a turn in its trade account toward deficit.

  To break out of this bind, economists and policymakers have sometimes proposed "coordinated expansion," wherein all countries would take expansionary steps simultaneously. A coordinated fiscal or monetary expansion would find each country both causing and enjoying expansionary spillovers. Moreover, because foreign countries would be expanding, a nation could hope that its exports (driven up by expansion abroad) would rise as much as its imports (driven up by expansion at home). Such coordinated macroeconomic policies could also be used to contract global economic activity if that were called for. Today, the major market economies regularly meet to discuss their macroeconomic policies, particularly monetary policy, and from time to time policy measures are coordinated to improve overall macroeconomic performance.

America in Decline?

As the millenium approached, many observers worried that the United States was traveling rapidly down the road to economic and political decline. They pointed to a variety of symptoms: a declining national savings rate, a persistent federal budget deficit, slow productivity growth, and a large external deficit, which was turning the United States into the world's largest debtor nation. At the same time, the country appeared to lack the political will to take forceful steps to reverse these trends.

Against this backdrop, Yale historian Paul Kennedy published a massive study of economic change and political conflict, *The Rise and Fall of the Great Powers.*[2] Kennedy argued that, because of

[2] Paul Kennedy, *The Rise and Fall of the Great Powers: Economic Change and Military Conflict from 1500 to 2000* (Random House, New York, 1987). See especially the introduction, Chap. 1, and Chap. 8.

underlying long-term economic trends, the United States was likely to suffer a significant decline in political and military power in the decades to come.

After reviewing five centuries of economic, political, and military history, Professor Kennedy puts forth the following theses:

1. "The historical record suggests that there is a very clear connection in the long run between an individual Great Power's economic rise and fall and its growth and decline as an important military power (or world empire). . . . Both wealth and power are always relative. . . . " He buttressed his argument by a thorough historical study of Spain, France, the British Empire, the Soviet Union, and the United States.
2. "The relative strengths of the leading nations in world affairs never remain constant, principally because of the uneven rate of growth among different societies and of the technological and organizational breakthroughs which bring a greater advantage to one society than to another." Economic and technological developments from the development of steam power to the introduction of nuclear weapons illustrate the way technology changes the economic and political fortunes of nations differently and unpredictably.

Kennedy then applies these lessons of history to contemporary economic and political affairs. He notes that the U.S. share of world GNP and manufacturing has declined significantly since its zenith in 1945; that many critical American industries and skills have declined, to be replaced by those of foreign countries; that the political consensus has become less favorable to economic growth; and that high defense spending and research and development (R&D) has sapped the nation's civilian economy. At the same time, other regions—particularly Japan and the European Community—are growing rapidly, producing an increasing share of world GNP and manufacturing, and possessing the potential of becoming "Great Powers." From these and other facts, Kennedy concludes:

> The only answer to the question . . . of whether the United States can preserve its existing [military and political] position is "no"—for it simply has not been given to any one society to remain permanently ahead of all the others, because that would imply a freezing of the differentiated patterns of growth rates, technological advance, and military developments which has existed since time immemorial. . . . One is tempted to paraphrase Shaw's deadly serious quip and say, "Rome fell; Babylon fell; Scarsdale's turn will come."[3]

Kennedy's thesis provoked a storm of debate and criticism. Some argued that the lessons of Europe do not apply to a continental power like the U.S.; others believe that, as the exchange rate of the dollar falls and America gets its fiscal house in order, American industry will increase its share of world trade. Many point to U.S. victory in the Persian Gulf as proof that its economic problems are small and that its technological virtuosity is preeminent.

Perhaps the argument has greater weight for countries like the Soviet Union. Central planning, an overarching bureaucracy, lack of incentives, and militarization of science and technology proved a poor recipe for economic vigor. Although the Soviet Union was a military superpower, its economy fell further behind the market economies. The crumbling of the Soviet empire in the 1990s testifies to the growing importance of economic strength in national power today.

Epilogue: Affluence for What?

Whether America is on the path to decline or destined to be the economic superpower of the next century cannot now be foretold. The issues raised by Kennedy's bold hypothesis serve as a stern reminder of the continuing importance of productive efficiency and economic growth.

At a deeper level, we recognize in his words the age-old dilemma of choice, posed in a new form for wealthy societies: *affluence for what?* How shall we use the resources that have been made so productive by technological change? For guns or butter or machines? For guns to protect our oil lifeline abroad, ensuring energy supplies to the industrial world? Or for butter and other consumption goods, enjoying the fruits of our past investments with high consumption today and letting the future fend for itself? Or for machines and other forms of investment, in capital goods and education and research and environmental quality, all of which will ensure a higher standard of living for those who follow us?

[3] The quotes above are from Kennedy, ibid., pp. xxii, xv, and 533.

There are no right answers to these fundamental questions of economics. Each of us must reflect on our values and strive to work toward the greater good. We particularly like the observation of John F. Kennedy, who showed great wisdom in matters economic: "Now the trumpet summons us again—not as a call to bear arms [but in] a struggle against the common enemies of man: tyranny, poverty, disease, and war itself."

This plea might serve as a trumpet call for young economists as well. Even though market economies are many times wealthier than they were in the age of Adam Smith, the vitality of economics knows no diminishing returns. The catalogue of unsolved economic problems remains long. Yet we remain cautiously optimistic that the study of economics will enhance not only the gross national product but also those best things in life that are beyond the marketplace—freedom to criticize, freedom to change, and freedom to pursue one's own dreams.

SUMMARY

A. The Determination of Foreign Exchange Rates

1. International trade involves use of different national currencies, which are linked by relative prices called foreign exchange rates. When Americans import British goods, they ultimately need to pay in British pounds. In the foreign exchange market, British pounds might trade for $1.80 per £1 (or reciprocally, $1 would trade for £0.56).

2. In the foreign exchange market involving only two countries, the demand for British pounds comes from Americans who want to purchase goods, services, and investments from Britain; the supply of British pounds comes from Britons who want to import commodities or financial assets from America. The interaction of these supplies and demands determines the foreign exchange rate. More generally, foreign exchange rates are determined by the complex interplay of many countries buying and selling among themselves. When trade or capital flows change, supply and demand shift and the equilibrium exchange rate changes.

3. A fall in the market price of a currency is a depreciation; a rise in a currency's value is called an appreciation. In a system where governments announce official foreign exchange rates, a decrease in the official exchange rate is called a devaluation while an increase is a revaluation.

4. A well-functioning international economy requires a smoothly operating exchange-rate system, which denotes the rules and institutions that govern transactions among nations. Three important exchange-rate systems are: (*a*) the gold standard, in which countries define their currencies in terms of a given weight of gold and then buy and sell gold to balance their international payments; (*b*) a pure floating-exchange-rate system, in which a country's foreign exchange rate is entirely determined by market forces of supply and demand; and (*c*) a managed floating-exchange-rate system, in which government interventions and market forces interact to determine the level of exchange rates.

5. Classical economists like David Hume explained adjustments to trade imbalances by the gold-flow mechanism. Under this process, gold movements would change the money supply and the price level. For example, a trade deficit would lead to a gold outflow and a decline in domestic prices

that would (*a*) raise exports and (*b*) curb imports of the gold-losing country while (*c*) reducing exports and (*d*) raising imports of the gold-gaining country.

B. Issues of International Economics

6. After World War II, countries created a group of international economic institutions to organize international trade and finance. These included the International Monetary Fund (IMF), which oversees exchange-rate systems and helps countries with their balance of payments; the World Bank, which lends money to low-income countries; and the Bretton Woods exchange-rate system. Under the Bretton Woods system, countries "pegged" their currencies to the dollar and to gold, providing fixed but adjustable exchange rates. When official parities deviated too far from fundamentals, countries could adjust parities and achieve a new equilibrium without incurring the hardships of inflation or recession.
7. When the Bretton Woods system broke down in 1971, it was replaced by today's system of generally flexible exchange rates. Some large countries or regions allow their currencies to float independently; most small countries peg their currencies to the dollar or to other currencies; and most European countries adhere to the European Monetary System (EMS), which resembles closely the Bretton Woods system. Governments often intervene when their currencies get too far out of line with fundamentals or when exchange markets become disorderly.
8. The most dramatic development of the last two decades has been the rise and fall of the dollar. The dollar surged in 1980, and this appreciation led to a sharp fall in real net exports, exacerbating the 1980–1982 recession. The fall in the dollar after 1985 has gradually begun to cure the huge trade deficit of the United States.
9. Floating exchange rates appear to remove the automatic discipline of the earlier gold or dollar standards—allowing countries to pursue their own inflationary or non-inflationary policies. But in fact a new discipline emerges—that of markets which move exchange rates in response to divergent relative price levels or interest rates, or even to people's expectations about prices or interest rates.
10. Because of the increasing interdependence of national economies, countries often attempt to coordinate their economic policies. Important policy issues are:
    (a) National trade policies will affect the output and employment of other countries. A policy of protecting one's own industries by trade barriers is a "beggar-thy-neighbor" approach, in essence exporting unemployment and trade deficits.
    (b) Foreign exchange rates can affect relative prices and net exports. A rise in a nation's foreign exchange rate will depress that nation's net exports and output, while a fall in a nation's foreign exchange rate will increase net exports and output. Because of the significant impact of exchange rates on national economies, countries have entered into agreements on international monetary arrangements.

(c) In recent years, countries have often coordinated their macroeconomic policies, simultaneously trying to increase their national outputs or to lower their national inflation rates. By cooperating in fiscal or monetary policies, countries can take advantage of the expansionary or contractionary impacts that inevitably spill over the borders when output changes.

CONCEPTS FOR REVIEW

The international financial system
foreign exchange rate
supply of and demand for foreign currencies
currency: appreciation and depreciation; revaluation and devaluation
exchange-rate systems: gold standard, freely floating, managed floating
intervention
Hume's four-pronged gold-flow mechanism
fixed exchange rates; pegged parities

Current issues of international economics
World Bank and IMF
Bretton Woods system and its breakdown, EMS
volatility of flexible exchange rates
international economic cooperation
America in decline?

QUESTIONS FOR DISCUSSION

1. Define the following and explain the significance of each: foreign exchange rate, gold standard, Bretton Woods system, and freely floating exchange rate.
2. The following table shows some foreign exchange rates (in dollars per unit of foreign currency) as of mid-1991:

	Price	
Currency	Dollars per unit of foreign currency	Foreign currency per $1
Pound (Britain)	1.6325 ($/pound)	______
Franc (France)	0.1637 ($/franc)	______
Yen (Japan)	0.00726 ($/yen)	______
Won (South Korea)	0.00138 ($/won)	______
Mark (Germany)	0.5565 ($/DM)	______

Fill in the last column of the table with the reciprocal price of the dollar in terms of foreign currencies, being especially careful to write down the relevant units.

3. Figure 39-1 shows the demand and supply for British pounds in an example in which Britain and the United States trade only with each other. Describe the reciprocal supply and demand schedules for U.S. dollars. Explain why the supply of pounds is equivalent to the demand for dollars. Also explain the schedule that corresponds to the demand for pounds. Find the equilibrium price of dollars in this new diagram and relate it to the equilibrium in Figure 39-1.
4. James Tobin has written, "A great teacher of mine, Joseph Schumpeter, used to find puzzling irony in the fact that liberal devotees of the free market were unwilling to let the market determine the prices of foreign currencies. . . . " [*National Economic Policy* (Yale University Press, New Haven, Conn., 1966), p. 161]. For what reasons might economists allow the foreign exchange market to be an exception to a general inclination toward free markets?
5. Show an initial equilibrium in the foreign exchange market for Japanese yen (similar to that for pounds in Figure 39-1). Let the initial equilibrium be 150 yen to the dollar and consider the impact on the market equilibrium of the following:
   (a) The Japanese government decides to sell very large quantities of yen at 160 yen to the dollar.
   (b) Higher interest rates in New York lower the demand for yen.
   (c) The demand for Toyotas and Hondas by Americans increase sharply.

(d) Japan pays the United States in dollars for American forces in the Far East.

6. In the Louvre accord in 1987, major countries agreed to keep their currencies within "reference zones." Say that the United States and Germany agree to keep the German mark in the range of 1.60 to 1.80 marks to the dollar. Show with the help of a supply-and-demand diagram how the governments could implement this policy.
7. Figure 39-5 shows a proposal for a "gliding parity" or "crawling peg" for the exchange rate between the dollar and the German deutsche mark (DM). Such a system lets an exchange rate change a few percent per year. What are its pros and cons relative to fixed exchange rates or freely floating rates?

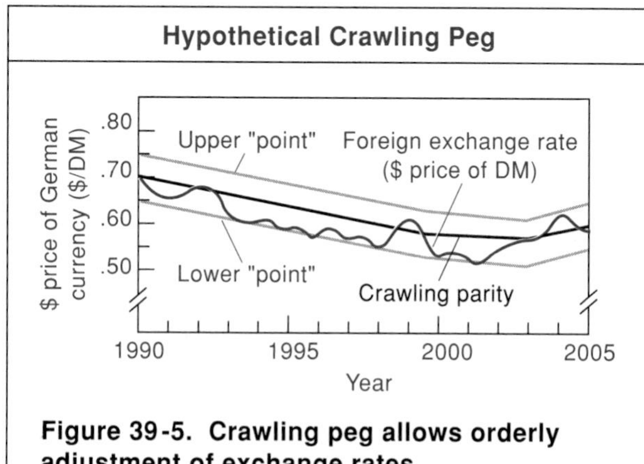

Figure 39-5. Crawling peg allows orderly adjustment of exchange rates

8. Suppose a country discovers oil, but it takes a decade to exploit the new find. What would happen to the country's trade balance after oil began to flow onto world markets? What might happen to the nation's freely floating currency once people realized that the trade balance would soon move into surplus? Why would the trade balance thus go into deficit in the period before the oil is actually recovered?
9. Consider the following three exchange-rate systems: classical gold standard, freely floating exchange rates, and Bretton Woods system. Compare and contrast the three systems with respect to the following characteristics:
   (a) Role of government vs. that of market in determining exchange rates
   (b) Degree of exchange-rate volatility
   (c) Method of adjustment of relative prices across countries
   (d) Need for international cooperation and consultation in determining exchange rates
   (e) Potential for establishment and maintenance of severe exchange-rate misalignment
10. The 1984 *Economic Report of the President* states:

    > In the long run, the exchange rate tends to follow the differential trend in the domestic and foreign price level. If one country's price level gets too far out of line with prices in other countries, there will eventually be a fall in demand for its goods, which will lead to a real depreciation of its currency.

    The first sentence espouses the "purchasing-power parity" or "PPP" theory of exchange rates. The PPP theory, which was proposed by David Ricardo in 1817 and by Sweden's Gustav Cassel around 1916, holds that floating exchange rates will move in proportion to relative prices in different countries; that is, if prices in the United States are rising 7 percent annually while those in Germany are rising 3 percent annually, the PPP theory holds that the U.S. dollar will tend to depreciate about 4 percent annually relative to the German mark. Explain the reasoning behind the PPP theory of exchange rates. In addition, using a supply-and-demand diagram like that of Figure 39-1, explain the sequence of events, described in the second sentence of the quotation, whereby a country whose price level is relatively high will find that its exchange rate depreciates.
11. Suppose America is running a trade deficit with output at the desired level, while Europe has a trade surplus with excessively high unemployment. What combination of coordinated exchange-rate changes and fiscal policies could move trade positions toward balance and output toward the desired levels?

GLOSSARY OF TERMS[1]

Ability-to-pay principle (of taxation). The principle that one's tax burden should depend upon the ability to pay as measured by income or wealth. This principle does not specify *how much* more those who are better off should pay.

Absolute advantage (in international trade). The ability of Country A to produce a commodity more efficiently (i.e., with greater output per unit of input) than Country B. Possession of such an absolute advantage does not necessarily mean that A can export this commodity to B successfully. Country B may still have the comparative advantage.

Actual, cyclical, and **structural budget.** The **actual budget** deficit or surplus is the amount recorded in a given year. This is composed of the **structural budget,** which calculates what government revenues, expenditures, and deficits would be if the economy were operating at potential output; and the **cyclical budget,** which measures the effect of the business cycle on the budget.

Adaptive expectations. See **expectations.**

Adjustable peg. An exchange-rate system in which countries maintain a fixed or "pegged" exchange rate with respect to other currencies. This exchange rate is subject to periodic adjustment, however, when it becomes too far out of line with fundamental forces. This system was used for major currencies during the Bretton Woods period from 1944 to 1971 and is called the **Bretton Woods system.**

Administered (or **inflexible**) **prices.** A term referring to prices which are set and kept constant for a period of time and over a series of transactions. (In contrast, refer to **price flexibility.**)

Aggregate demand. Total planned or desired spending in the economy during a given period. It is determined by the aggregate price level and influenced by domestic investment, net exports, government spending, the consumption function, and the money supply.

Aggregate demand (*AD*) curve. The curve showing the relationship between the quantity of goods and services that people are willing to buy and the aggregate price level, other things equal. As with any demand curve, important variables lie behind the aggregate demand curve, e.g., government spending, exports, and the money supply.

Aggregate supply. The total value of goods and services that firms would willingly produce in a given time period. Aggregate supply is a function of available inputs, technology, and the price level.

Aggregate supply (*AS*) curve. The curve showing the relationship between the output firms would willingly supply and the aggregate price level, other things equal. The *AS* curve tends to be vertical at potential output in the very long run but may be relatively flat in the short run.

Allocative efficiency. A situation in which no reorganization or trade could raise the utility or satisfaction of one individual without lowering the utility or satisfaction of another individual. Under certain limited conditions, perfect competition leads to allocative efficiency. Also called **Pareto efficiency.**

Antitrust legislation. Laws prohibiting monopolization, restraints of trade, and collusion among firms to raise prices or inhibit competition.

Appreciation (of a currency). See **depreciation** (of a currency).

Arbitrage. Speculation without risk. The act of buying a currency or a commodity in one market and simultaneously selling it for a profit in another market. Arbitrage is an important force in eliminating price discrepancies, thereby making markets function more efficiently.

Asset. A physical property or intangible right that has economic value. Important examples are plant, equipment, land, patents, copyrights, and financial instruments such as money or bonds.

Asset demand for money. See **demand for money.**

Automatic (or **built-in**) **stabilizers.** The property of a government tax and spending system that cush-

[1] Words in bold type within definitions appear as separate entries in the glossary. For a more detailed discussion of particular terms, the text will provide a useful starting point. More complete discussions are contained in Douglas Greenwald, ed., *Encyclopedia of Economics* (McGraw-Hill, New York, 1983); David W. Pearce, *The Dictionary of Modern Economics*, rev. ed. (MIT Press, Cambridge, Mass., 1983); *International Encyclopedia of the Social Sciences* (Collier and Macmillan, New York, 1968); and John Eatwell, Murray Milgate, and Peter Newman, *The New Palgrave: A Dictionary of Economics* (Macmillan, London, 1987), four volumes.

ions income changes in the private sector. Examples include unemployment compensation and progressive income taxes.

Average cost. Refer to **cost, average.**

Average cost curve, long-run (*LRAC*, or *LAC*) The graph of the minimum average cost of producing a commodity for each level of output, assuming that technology and input prices are given but that the producer is free to choose the optimal size of plants.

Average cost curve, short-run (*SRAC*, or *SAC*). The graph of the minimum average cost of producing a commodity, for each level of output, using the given state of technology, input prices, and existing plant.

Average product. Total product or output divided by the quantity of one of the inputs. Hence, the average product of labor is defined as total product divided by the amount of labor input, and similarly for other inputs.

Average propensity to consume. See **marginal propensity to consume.**

Average revenue. Total revenue divided by total number of units sold—i.e., revenue per unit. Average revenue is generally equal to price.

Average variable cost. Refer to **cost, average variable.**

Balance of international payments. A statement showing all a nation's transactions with the rest of the world for a given period. It includes purchases and sales of goods and services, gifts, government transactions, and capital movements.

Balance of trade. The part of a nation's balance of payments that deals with merchandise (or visible) imports or exports. When "invisibles," or services, are included, the total accounting for imports and exports of goods and services is called the **balance on current account.**

Balance on current account. See **balance of trade.**

Balance sheet. A statement of a firm's financial position as of a given date, listing **assets** in one column, **liabilities** plus **net worth** in the other. Each item is listed at its actual or estimated money value. Totals of the two columns must balance because net worth is defined as assets minus liabilities.

Balanced budget. See **budget, balanced.**

Bank, commercial. A financial intermediary whose prime distinguishing feature until recently was that it accepts checking deposits. Also it holds savings or time deposits and money market deposit accounts; sells traveler's checks and performs other financial services; and lends to individuals and firms. Since 1980, savings banks and other depository institutions have been allowed to accept checking accounts and are thus becoming more like commercial banks.

Bank money. Money created by banks, particularly the checking accounts (part of M_1) that are generated by a multiple expansion of bank reserves.

Bank reserves. Refer to **reserves, bank.**

Barriers to competition. Factors that reduce the amount of competition or the number of producers in an industry, allowing greater economic concentration to occur. Important examples are legal barriers, regulation, and product differentiation.

Barter. The direct exchange of one good for another without using anything as money or as a medium of exchange.

Benefit principle (of taxation). The principle that people should be taxed in proportion to the benefits they receive from government programs.

Bond. An interest-bearing certificate issued by a government or corporation, promising to repay a sum of money (the principal) plus interest at specified dates in the future.

Break-even point (in macroeconomics). For an individual, family, or community, that level of income at which 100 percent is spent on consumption (i.e., the point where there is neither saving nor dissaving). Positive saving begins at higher income levels.

Break-even price or **level,** or **point** (in microeconomics). For a business firm, that level of price at which the firm breaks even, covering all costs but earning zero profit.

Bretton Woods system. See **adjustable peg.**

Budget, balanced. A budget in which total expenditures just equal total receipts (excluding any receipts from borrowing).

Budget constraint. See **budget line.**

Budget deficit. For a government, the excess of total expenditures over total receipts, with borrowing not included among receipts. This difference (the deficit) is ordinarily financed by borrowing.

Budget, government. A statement showing, for the government in question, planned expenditures and revenues for some period (typically 1 year).

Budget line. A line indicating the combination of commodities that a consumer can buy with a given income at a given set of prices. If the graph shows food and clothing, then each point on the line represents a combination of food and clothing that can be bought for a certain income level and with a given set of prices for the two goods. Also sometimes called the **budget constraint.**

Budget surplus. Excess of government revenues over government spending; the opposite of **budget deficit.**

Built-in stabilizers. See **automatic stabilizers.**

Business cycles. Fluctuations in total national output, income, and employment, usually lasting for a period of 2 to 10 years, marked by widespread and simultaneous expansion or contraction in many sectors of the economy. In modern macroeconomics, business cycles are said to occur when actual GNP rises relative to potential GNP (expansion) or falls relative to potential GNP (contraction or recession).

C + I, C + I + G, or ***C + I + G + X* schedule.** A schedule showing the planned or desired levels of aggregate demand for each level of GNP, or the graph on which this schedule is depicted. The schedule includes consumption (*C*), investment (*I*), government spending on goods and services (*G*), and net exports (*X*).

Capital (capital goods, capital equipment). (1) In economic theory, one of the triad of productive inputs (land, labor, and capital). Capital consists of durable produced goods that are in turn used in production. The major components of capital are equipment, structures, and inventory. When signifying capital goods, reference is also made to real capital. (2) In accounting and finance, "capital" means the total amount of money subscribed by the shareholder-owners of a corporation, in return for which they receive shares of the company's stock.

Capital consumption allowance. See **depreciation** (of an asset).

Capital deepening. In economic-growth theory, an increase in the capital-labor ratio. (Contrast with **capital widening.**)

Capital gains. The rise in value of a capital asset, such as land or common stocks, the gain being the difference between the sales price and the purchase price of the asset.

Capital markets. Markets in which financial resources (money, bonds, stocks) are traded. These, along with **financial intermediaries,** are institutions through which savings in the economy are transferred to investors.

Capital-output ratio. In economic-growth theory, the ratio of the total capital stock to annual GNP.

Capital widening. A rate of growth in real capital stock just equal to the growth of the labor force (or of population), so that the ratio between total capital and total labor remains unchanged. (Contrast with **capital deepening.**)

Capitalism. An economic system in which most property (land and capital) is privately owned. In such an economy, private markets are the primary vehicles used to allocate resources and generate incomes.

Cartel. An organization of independent firms producing similar products that work together to raise prices and restrict output. Cartels are illegal under U.S. antitrust laws.

Central bank. A government-established agency (in the United States, the Federal Reserve System) responsible for controlling the nation's money supply and credit conditions and for supervising the financial system, especially commercial banks.

Change in demand vs. change in quantity demanded. A change in the quantity buyers want to purchase, prompted by any reason other than a change in price (e.g., increase in income, change in tastes, etc.), is a "change in demand." (In graphical terms, it is a shift of the demand curve.) If, in contrast, the decision to buy more or less is prompted by a change in the good's price, then it is a "change in quantity demanded." (In graphical terms, a change in quantity demanded is a movement along an unchanging demand curve.)

Change in supply vs. change in quantity supplied. This distinction is the same for supply as for demand, so see **change in demand vs. change in quantity demanded.**

Checking accounts (or **bank money**). A deposit in a commercial bank or other financial intermediary upon which checks can be written and which is therefore transactions money (or M_1). The major kinds of checking accounts are demand deposits (which can be withdrawn without notice and do not bear interest) and **NOW accounts** (which are indistinguishable from traditional demand deposits except that they earn interest). Checking accounts are the largest component of M_1.

Chicago School of Economics. A group of economists (among whom Henry Simons, F. A. von Hayek, and Milton Friedman have been the most prominent) who believe that competitive markets free of government intervention will lead to the most efficient operation of the economy.

Classical economics. The predominant school of economic thought prior to the appearance of Keynes' work; founded by Adam Smith in 1776. Other major figures who followed him include David Ricardo, Thomas Malthus, and John Stuart Mill. By and large, this school believed that economic laws (particularly individual self-interest and competition) determine prices and factor rewards and that the price system is the best possible device for resource allocation. Their macroeconomic theory rests on **Say's Law of markets.**

Classical theories (in macroeconomics). Theories emphasizing the self-correcting forces in the economy. In the classical approach, there is generally full employment and policies to stimulate aggregate demand have no impact upon output.

Clearing market. A market in which prices are sufficiently flexible to equilibrate supply and demand very quickly. In markets that clear, there is no rationing, unemployed resources, or excess demand or supply. In practice, this is thought to apply to many commodity and financial markets but not to labor or many product markets.

Closed economy. See **open economy.**

Coase theorem. A view (not actually a theorem) put forth by Ronald Coase that externalities or economic inefficiencies will under certain conditions be corrected by bargaining between the affected parties.

Collective bargaining. The process of negotiations between a group of workers (usually a union) and their employer. Such bargaining leads to an agreement about wages, fringe benefits, and working conditions.

Collusion. Agreement between different firms to cooperate by raising prices, dividing markets, or otherwise restraining competition.

Collusive oligopoly. A market structure in which a small number of firms (i.e., a few oligopolists) collude and jointly make their decisions. When they succeed in maximizing their joint profits, the price and quantity in the market closely approach those prevailing under monopoly.

Command economy. A mode of economic organization in which the key economic functions—*what, how,* and *for whom*—are principally determined by government directive. Sometimes called a "centrally planned economy."

Commodity money. Money with **intrinsic value;** also, the use of some commodity (cattle, beads, etc.) as money.

Common stock. The financial instrument representing ownership and, generally, voting rights in a corporation. A certain share of a company's stock gives the owner title to that fraction of the votes, net earnings, and assets of the corporation.

Communism. At the same time (1) an ideology, (2) a set of political parties, and (3) an economic system. A communist economic system is one in which private ownership of the means of production, particularly industrial capital, is prohibited (for such ownership of capital goods is believed to result in exploitation of workers). In addition, communism holds that income should be distributed equally, or, more ideally, according to "need." In today's communist countries, most capital and land are owned by the state. These countries are also characterized by extensive central planning, with the state setting many prices, output levels, and other important economic variables.

Comparative advantage (in international trade). The law of comparative advantage says that a nation should specialize in producing and exporting those commodities which it can produce at *relatively* lower costs, and that it should import those goods for which it is a *relatively* high-cost producer. Thus it is a comparative advantage, not an absolute advantage, that should dictate trade patterns.

Compensating differentials. Differences in wage rates among jobs that serve to offset or compensate for the nonmonetary differences of the jobs. For example, unpleasant jobs that require isolation for many months in Alaska pay wages much higher than those for similar jobs nearer to civilization.

Competition, imperfect. Refers to markets in which perfect competition does not hold because at least one seller (or buyer) is large enough to affect the market price and therefore faces a downward-sloping demand curve (or supply). Imperfect competition refers to any kind of imperfection—pure **monopoly, oligopoly,** or **monopolistic competition.**

Competition, perfect. Refers to markets in which no firm or consumer is large enough to affect the market price. This situation arises where (1) the number of sellers and buyers is very large and (2) the products offered by sellers are homogeneous (or indistinguishable). Under such conditions, each firm faces a horizontal (or perfectly elastic) demand curve.

Competitive equilibrium. The balancing of supply and demand in a market or economy characterized by **perfect competition.** Because perfectly competitive sellers and buyers individually have no power to influence the market, price will move to the point at which price equals both marginal cost and marginal utility.

Competitive market. See **competition, perfect.**

Complements. Two goods which "go together" in the eyes of consumers (e.g., left shoes and right shoes). Goods are **substitutes** when they compete with each other (as do gloves and mittens).

Compound interest. Interest computed on the sum of all past interest earned as well as on the principal. For example, suppose $100 (the principal) is deposited in an account earning 10 percent interest compounded annually. At the end of year 1, interest of $10 is earned. At the end of year 2, the interest payment is $11, $10 on the original principal and $1 on the interest—and so on in future years.

Concentration ratio. The percentage of an industry's total output accounted for by the largest firms. A typical measure is the **four-firm concentration ratio,** which is the fraction of output accounted for by the four largest firms.

Conglomerate. A large corporation producing and selling a variety of unrelated goods (e.g., some cigarette companies have expanded into such unrelated areas as liquor, car rental, and movie production).

Conglomerate merger. See **merger.**

Constant returns to scale. See **returns to scale.**

Consumer price index (CPI). A price index that measures the cost of a fixed basket of consumer goods in which the weight assigned to each commodity is the share of expenditures on that commodity by urban consumers in 1982–1984.

Consumer surplus. The difference between the amount that a consumer would be willing to pay for a commodity and the amount actually paid. This difference arises because the marginal utilities (in dollar terms) of all but the last unit exceed the price. Hence the monetary equivalent of the total utility of the commodity consumed may be well above the amount spent. Under rigorous assumptions, the money value of consumer surplus can be measured (using a demand-curve diagram) as the area under the demand curve but above the price line.

Consumption. In macroeconomics, the total spending, by individuals or a nation, on consumer goods during a given period. Strictly speaking, consumption should apply only to those goods totally used, enjoyed, or "eaten up" within that period. In practice, consumption expenditures include all consumer goods bought, many of which last well beyond the period in question—e.g., furniture, clothing, and automobiles.

Consumption function. A schedule relating total consumption to personal disposable income (*DI*). Total wealth and other variables are also frequently assumed to influence consumption.

Consumption-possibility line. Refer to **budget line.**

Cooperative equilibrium. In game theory, an outcome in which the parties act in unison to find strategies that will optimize their joint payoffs.

Corporate income tax. A tax levied on the annual net income of a corporation.

Corporation. The predominant form of business organization in modern capitalist economies. A corporation is a firm owned by individuals or other corporations. It has the same rights to buy, sell, and make contracts as a person would have. It is legally separate from those who own it and has "limited liability."

Correlation. The degree to which two variables are systematically associated with each other.

Cost, average. Total cost (refer to **cost, total**) divided by the number of units produced.

Cost, average fixed. Fixed cost divided by the number of units produced.

Cost, average variable. Total variable cost (refer to **cost, variable**) divided by the number of units produced.

Cost, fixed. The cost a firm would incur even if its output for the period in question were zero. Total fixed cost is made up of such individual contractual costs as interest payments, mortgage payments, and directors' fees.

Cost, marginal. The extra cost (or the increase in total cost) required to produce 1 extra unit of output (or the reduction in total cost from producing 1 unit less).

Cost, minimum. The lowest attainable cost per unit (whether average, variable, or marginal). Every point on an average cost curve is a minimum in the sense that it is the best the firm can do with respect to cost for the output which that point represents. Minimum average cost is the lowest point, or points, on that curve.

Cost-push inflation. Inflation originating on the supply side of markets from a sharp increase in costs. In the aggregate supply-and-demand framework, cost-push is illustrated as an upward shift of the *AS* curve. Also called **supply-shock** inflation.

Cost, total. The minimum attainable total cost, given a particular level of technology and set of input prices. Short-run total cost takes existing plant and other fixed costs as given. Long-run total cost is the cost that would be incurred if the firm had complete flexibility with respect to all inputs and decisions.

Cost, variable. A cost that varies with the level of output, such as raw materials, labor, and fuel costs. Variable costs equal total cost minus fixed cost.

Crawling (or **sliding**) **peg.** A technique for managing a nation's exchange rate that allows the exchange rate (or the bands around the rate) to "crawl" up or down by a small amount each day or week (say, 0.25 percent per week).

Credit. (1) In monetary theory, the use of someone else's funds in exchange for a promise to pay (usually with interest) at a later date. The major examples are short-term loans from a bank, credit extended by suppliers, or commercial paper. (2) In balance-of-payments accounting, an item such as exports that earns a country foreign currency.

Cross elasticity of demand. A measure of the influence of a change in one good's price on the demand for another good. More precisely, the cross elasticity of demand equals the percentage change in demand for good A when the price of good B changes by 1 percent, assuming other variables are held constant.

Crowding out. The proposition that government spending or government deficits reduce the amount of business investment.

Currency. Coins and paper money.

Currency appreciation (or **depreciation**). See **depreciation** (of a currency).

Current account. See **balance of trade.**

Cyclical budget. See **actual, cyclical,** and **structural budget.**

Cyclical unemployment. See **frictional unemployment.**

Deadweight loss. The loss in real income or consumer and producer surplus that arises because of monopoly, tariffs and quotas, taxes, or other distortions. For example, when a monopolist raises its price, the loss in consumer satisfaction is more than the gain in the monopolist's revenue—the difference being the deadweight loss to society due to monopoly.

Debit. (1) An accounting term signifying an increase in assets or decrease in liabilities. (2) In balance-of-payments accounting, a debit is an item such as imports that reduces a country's stock of foreign currencies.

Decreasing returns to scale. See **returns to scale.**

Deficit spending. Government expenditures on goods and services and transfer payments in excess of its receipts from taxation and other revenue sources. The difference must be financed by borrowing from the public.

Deflating (of economic data). The process of converting "nominal" or current-dollar variables into "real" terms. This is accomplished by dividing current-dollar variables by a price index.

Deflation. A fall in the general level of prices.

Demand curve (or **demand schedule**). A schedule or curve showing the quantity of a good that buyers would purchase at each price, other things equal. Normally a demand curve has price on the vertical or *Y* axis and quantity demanded on the horizontal or *X* axis. Also see **change in demand vs. change in quantity demanded.**

Demand for money. A summary term used by economists to explain why individuals and businesses hold money balances. The major motivations for holding money are (1) **transactions demand,** signifying that people need money to purchase things, and (2) **asset demand,** relating to the desire to hold a very liquid, risk-free asset.

Demand-pull inflation. Price inflation caused by an excess demand for goods in general, caused, for example, by a major increase in aggregate demand. Often contrasted with **cost-push inflation.**

Demography. The study of the behavior of a population.

Depreciation (of an asset). A decline in the value of an asset. In both business and national accounts, depreciation is the dollar estimate of the extent to which capital has been "used up" or worn out over the period in question. Also termed **capital consumption allowance** in national-income accounting.

Depreciation (of a currency). A nation's currency is said to depreciate when it declines relative to other currencies. For example, if the foreign exchange rate of the dollar falls from 6 to 4 French francs per U.S. dollar, the dollar's value has fallen, and the dollar has undergone a depreciation. The opposite of a depreciation is an **appreciation,** which occurs when the foreign exchange rate of a currency rises.

Depression. A prolonged period characterized by high unemployment, low output and investment, depressed business confidence, falling prices, and widespread business failures. A milder form of business downturn is a **recession,** which has many of the features of a depression to a lesser extent; the precise definition of a recession today is a period in which real GNP declines for at least two consecutive calendar quarters.

Derived demand. The demand for a factor of production that results (is "derived") from the demand for the final good to which it contributes. Thus the demand for tires is derived from the demand for automobile transportation.

Devaluation. A decrease in the official price of a nation's currency, as expressed in the currencies of other nations or in terms of gold. Thus when the official price of the dollar was lowered with respect to gold in 1971, the dollar was devalued. The opposite of devaluation is called **revaluation,** which occurs when a nation raises its official foreign exchange rate relative to gold or other currencies.

Developing countries. See **less developed country.**

Diminishing marginal utility, law of. The law which says that, as more and more of any one commodity is consumed, its marginal utility declines.

Diminishing returns, law of. A law stating that the additional output from successive increases of one input will eventually diminish when other inputs are held constant. Technically, the law is equivalent to saying that the marginal product of the varying input declines after a point.

Direct taxes. Those levied directly on individuals or firms, including taxes on income, labor earnings, and profits. Direct taxes contrast with **indirect taxes,** which are those levied on goods and services and thus only indirectly on people, and which include sales taxes and taxes on property, alcohol, imports, and gasoline.

Discount rate. (1) The interest rate charged by a Federal Reserve Bank (the central bank) on a loan that it makes to a commercial bank. (2) The rate used to calculate the present value of some asset.

Discounting (of future income). The process of converting future income into an equivalent present value. This process takes a future dollar amount and reduces it by a discount factor that reflects the appropriate interest rate. For example, if someone promises you \$121 in 2 years, and the appropriate interest rate or discount rate is 10 percent per year, then we can calculate the present value by discounting the \$121 by a discount factor of $(1.10)^2$. The rate at which future incomes are discounted is called the **discount rate.**

Discrimination. Differences in earnings that arise because of personal characteristics that are unrelated to job performance, especially those related to gender, race, or religion.

Disequilibrium. The state in which an economy is not in **equilibrium.** This may arise when shocks (to income or prices) have shifted demand or supply schedules but the market price (or quantity) has not yet adjusted fully. In macroeconomics, unemployment is often thought to stem from market disequilibria.

Disinflation. The process of reducing a high inflation rate. For example, the deep recession of 1980–1983 led to a sharp disinflation over that period.

Disposable income (*DI*). Roughly, take-home pay, or that part of the total national income that is available to households for consumption or saving. More precisely, it is equal to GNP less all taxes, business saving, and depreciation *plus* government and other transfer payments and government interest payments.

Dissaving. Negative saving; spending more on consumption goods during a period than the disposable income available for that period (the difference being financed by borrowing or drawing on past saving).

Distribution. In economics, the manner in which total output and income is distributed among individuals or factors (e.g., the distribution of income between labor and capital).

Division of labor. A method of organizing production whereby each worker specializes in part of the productive process. Specialization of labor yields higher total output because labor can become more skilled at a particular task and because specialized machinery can be introduced to perform more carefully defined subtasks.

Dominant equilibrium. See **dominant strategy.**

Dominant strategy. In game theory, a situation where one player has a best strategy no matter what strategy the other player follows. When all players have a dominant strategy, we say that the outcome is a **dominant equilibrium.**

Downward-sloping demand, law of. The rule that says that when the price of some commodity falls, consumers will purchase more of that good when other things are held equal.

Duopoly. A market structure in which there are only two sellers. (Compare with **oligopoly.**)

Durable goods. Equipment or machines that are normally expected to last longer than 3 years, e.g., machine tools, trucks, and automobiles.

Easy-money policy. The central-bank policy of increasing the money supply to reduce interest rates. The purpose of such a policy is to increase investment, thereby raising GNP. (Contrast with **tight-money policy.**)

Econometrics. The branch of economics that uses the methods of statistics to measure and estimate quantitative economic relationships.

Economic good. A good that is scarce relative to the total amount of it that is desired. It must therefore be rationed, usually by charging a positive price.

Economic growth. An increase in the total output of a nation over time. Economic growth is usually measured as the annual rate of increase in a nation's real GNP (or real potential GNP).

Economic regulation. See **regulation.**

Economic rent. See **rent, economic.**

Economic surplus. A term denoting the excess in total satisfaction or utility over the costs of production. Equals the sum of consumer surplus (the excess of consumer satisfaction over total value of purchases) and producer surplus (the excess of producer revenues over costs).

Economies of scale. Increases in productivity, or decreases in average cost of production, that arise from increasing all the factors of production in the same proportion.

Economies of scope. Economies of producing multiple goods or services. Thus economies of scope exist if it is cheaper to produce both good X and good Y together rather than separately.

Efficiency. Absence of waste, or the use of economic resources that produces the maximum level of satisfaction possible with the given inputs and technology. A shorthand expression for **allocative efficiency.**

Efficient-market theory. See **random-walk theory** (of stock market prices).

Elasticity. A term widely used in economics to denote the responsiveness of one variable to changes in another. Thus the elasticity of X with respect to Y means the percentage change in X for every 1 percent change in Y. For especially important examples, see **price elasticity of demand** and **price elasticity of supply.**

Employed. According to official U.S. definitions, persons are employed if they perform any paid work, or if they hold jobs but are absent because of illness, strike, or vacations. Also see **unemployment.**

Equilibrium. The state in which an economic entity is at rest or in which the forces operating on the entity are in balance so that there is no tendency for change.

Equilibrium (for a business firm). That position or level of output in which the firm is maximizing its profit, subject to any constraints it may face, and therefore has no incentive to change its output or price level. In the standard theory of the firm, this means that the firm has chosen an output at which marginal revenue is just equal to marginal cost.

Equilibrium (for the individual consumer). That position in which the consumer is maximizing utility, i.e., has chosen the bundle of goods which, given income and prices, best satisfies the consumer's wants.

Equilibrium, competitive. See **competitive equilibrium.**

Equilibrium, general. See **general equilibrium.**

Equilibrium, macroeconomic. A GNP level at which intended aggregate demand equals intended aggregate supply. At the equilibrium, desired consumption (*C*), government expenditures (*G*), investment (*I*), and net exports (*X*) just equal the quantity that businesses wish to sell at the going price level.

Exchange rate. See **foreign exchange rate.**

Exchange-rate system. The set of rules, arrangements, and institutions under which payments are made among nations. Historically, the most important exchange rate systems have been the gold exchange standard, the Bretton Woods system, and today's flexible-exchange-rate system.

Excise tax vs. sales tax. An excise tax is one levied on the purchase of a specific commodity or group of commodities (e.g., on alcohol or tobacco). A **sales tax** is one levied on all commodities with only a few specific exclusions (e.g., on all purchases except food).

Exclusion principle. A criterion by which public goods are distinguished from private goods. When a producer sells a commodity to person A and can easily exclude B, C, D, etc., from enjoying the benefits of the commodity, the exclusion principle holds and the good is a private good. If, as in public health or national defense, people cannot easily be excluded from enjoying the benefits of the good's production, then the good has public-good characteristics.

Expectations. Views or beliefs about uncertain variables (such as future interest rates, prices, or tax rates). Expectations are said to be **rational** if they are not systematically wrong (or "biased") and use all available information. Expectations are said to be **adaptive** if people form their expectations on the basis of past behavior.

Expenditure multiplier. See **multiplier.**

Exports. Goods or services that are produced in the home country and sold to another country. These include merchandise trade (like cars) and services (like transportation or interest on loans and investments). **Imports** are simply flows in the opposite direction—into the home country from another country.

External diseconomies. Situations in which production or consumption imposes uncompensated costs on other parties. Steel factories that emit smoke and sulfurous fumes harm local property and public health, yet the injured parties are not paid for the damages. The pollution is an external diseconomy.

External economies. Situations in which production or consumption yields positive benefits to others without those others paying. A firm that hires a security guard scares thieves from the neighborhood, thus providing external security services. Together with external diseconomies, these are often referred to as **externalities.**

External vs. induced variables. External variables are those determined by conditions outside the economy. They are contrasted with **induced variables,** which are determined by the internal workings of the economic system. Changes in the weather are external; changes in consumption are often induced by changes in income.

Externalities. Activities that affect others for better or worse, without those others paying or being compensated for the activity. Externalities exist when private costs or benefits do not equal social costs or benefits. The two major species are **external economies** and **external diseconomies.**

Factors of production. Productive inputs, such as labor, land, and capital; the resources needed to produce goods and services. Also called **inputs.**

Fallacy of composition. The fallacy of assuming that what holds for individuals also holds for the group or the entire system.

Federal Reserve System. The **central bank** of the United States.

Fiat money. Money, like today's paper currency, without **intrinsic value** but decreed (by fiat) to be legal tender by the government. Fiat money is accepted only as long as people have confidence that it will be accepted.

Final good. A good that is produced for final use and not for resale or further manufacture. (Compare with **intermediate goods.**)

Financial intermediary. An institution that receives funds from savers and lends them to borrowers. These include depository institutions (such as commercial or savings banks) and non-depository institutions (such as money market mutual funds, brokerage houses, insurance companies, or pension funds).

Firm (business firm). The basic, private producing unit in a capitalist or mixed economy. It hires labor and buys other inputs in order to make and sell commodities.

Fiscal-monetary mix. Refers to the combination of fiscal and monetary policies used to influence macroeconomic activity. A tight monetary–loose fiscal policy will tend to encourage consumption and retard investment, while an easy monetary–tight fiscal policy will have the opposite effect.

Fiscal policy. A government's program with respect to (1) the purchase of goods and services and spending on transfer payments, and (2) the amount and type of taxes.

Fixed cost. Refer to **cost, fixed.**

Fixed exchange rate. See **foreign exchange rate.**

Flexible exchange rates. A system of foreign exchange rates among countries wherein the exchange rates are predominantly determined by private market forces (i.e., by supply and demand) without government's setting and maintaining a particular pattern of exchange rates. Also sometimes called **floating exchange rates.** When the government refrains from any intervention in exchange markets, the system is called a pure floating exchange-rate system.

Floating exchange rates. See **flexible exchange rates.**

Flow vs. stock. A flow variable is one that has a time dimension or flows over time (like the flow through a stream). A stock variable is one that measures a quantity at a point of time (like the water in a lake). Income represents dollars per year and is thus a flow. Wealth as of December 1992 is a stock.

Foreign exchange. Currency or other financial instruments that allow one country to settle amounts owed to other countries.

Foreign exchange rate. The rate, or price, at which one country's currency is exchanged for the currency of another country. For example, if one British pound costs $1.40, then the exchange rate for the pound is $1.40. A country has a **fixed exchange rate** if it pegs its currency at a given exchange rate and stands ready to defend that rate. An exchange rate which is not fixed is said to float. See also **flexible exchange rates.**

Four-firm concentration ratio. See **concentration ratio.**

Fractional-reserve banking. A regulation in modern banking systems whereby financial institutions are legally required to keep a specified fraction of their deposits in the form of deposits with the central bank (or in vault cash). In the United States today, large banks must keep 12 percent of checking deposits in reserves.

Free goods. Those goods that are not **economic goods.** Like air or seawater, they exist in such large quantities that they need not be rationed out among those wishing to use them. Thus, their market price is zero.

Free trade. A policy whereby the government does not intervene in trading between nations—by tariffs, quotas, or other means.

Frictional unemployment. Temporary unemployment caused by changes in individual markets. It takes time, for example, for new workers to search among different job possibilities; even experienced workers often spend a minimum period of unemployed time moving from one job to another. Frictional is thus distinct from **cyclical unemployment,** which results from a low level of aggregate demand in the context of sticky wages and prices.

Full employment. A term that is used in many senses. Historically, it was taken to be that level of employment at which no (or minimal) involuntary unemployment exists. Today, economists rely upon the concept of the **natural rate of unemployment** to indicate the highest sustainable level of employment over the long run.

Galloping inflation. See **inflation.**

Game theory. An analysis of situations involving two or more decision makers with at least partly conflicting interests. It can be applied to the interaction of oligopolistic markets as well as to bargaining situations such as strikes or to conflicts such as games and war.

General equilibrium. An equilibrium state for the economy as a whole in which the markets for all goods and services are simultaneously in equilibrium. Since at these prices producers want to supply exactly the amount of goods that consumers want to buy, there are no pressures encouraging any agent in the economy to change behavior. By contrast, **partial-equilibrium analysis** concerns the equilibrium in a single market.

GNP. See **gross national product.**

GNP deflator. The "price" of GNP, that is, the price index that measures the average price of the components in GNP relative to a base year.

GNP gap. The difference or gap between potential GNP and actual GNP.

Gold standard. A system under which a nation (1) declares its currency unit to be equivalent to some fixed weight of gold, (2) holds gold reserves and will buy or sell gold freely at the price so proclaimed, and (3) puts no restriction on the export or import of gold.

Government debt. The total of government obligations in the form of bonds and shorter-term borrowings. Government debt held by the public excludes bonds held by quasi-governmental agencies such as the central bank.

Graduated income tax. See **income tax, personal.**

Gresham's Law. A law first attributed to Sir Thomas Gresham, adviser to Queen Elizabeth I of England, who stated in 1558 that "bad money drives out good"—i.e., that if the public is suspicious of one component of the money supply, it will hoard the "good money" and try to pass off the "bad money" to someone else.

Gross domestic product (GDP). The total output produced inside a country during a given year. Contrasts with **GNP,** which is the output produced by factors owned by the country.

Gross national product, nominal (or **nominal GNP**). The value, at current market prices, of all final goods and services produced during a year by a nation.

Gross national product, real (or **real GNP**). Nominal GNP corrected for inflation, i.e., real GNP = nominal GNP/GNP deflator.

Growth accounting. A technique for estimating the contribution of different factors to economic growth. Using marginal-productivity theory, growth accounting decomposes the growth of output into the growth in labor, land, capital, education, technical knowledge, and other miscellaneous sources.

Hedging. A technique for avoiding a risk by making a counteracting transaction. For example, if a farmer produces wheat that will be harvested in the fall, the risk of price fluctuations can be offset, or hedged, by selling in the spring or summer the quantity of wheat that will be produced.

High-powered money. Same as **monetary base.**

Horizontal equity vs. vertical equity. Horizontal equity refers to the fairness or equity in treatment of persons in similar situations; the principle of horizontal equity states that those who are essentially equal should receive equal treatment. **Vertical equity** refers to the equitable treatment of those who are in different circumstances; there are no universally accepted practical applications of vertical equity, although some hold that vertical equity requires progressive taxation.

Horizontal integration. Refer to **integration, vertical vs. horizontal.**

Horizontal merger. See **merger.**

Human capital. The stock of technical knowledge and skill embodied in a nation's work force, resulting from investments in formal education and on-the-job training.

Hyperinflation. See **inflation.**

Imperfect competition. Refer to **competition, imperfect.**

Imperfect competitor. Any firm that buys or sells a good in large enough quantities to be able to affect the price of that good.

Implicit-cost elements. Costs that do not show up as explicit money costs but nevertheless should be counted as such. For example, if you run your own business, then in reckoning your profit you should include as one of your implicit costs the wage or salary you could have earned if you had worked elsewhere. Sometimes called **opportunity cost** although "opportunity cost" has a broader meaning.

Imports. See **exports.**

Inappropriability. The inability of firms to capture the full monetary value of their actions; particularly applicable to inventive activity.

Incidence (or **tax incidence**). The ultimate economic burden of a tax (as opposed to the legal requirement for payment). Thus a sales tax may be paid by a retailer, but it is likely that the incidence falls upon the consumer. The exact incidence of a tax depends on the price elasticities of supply and demand.

Income. The flow of wages, interest payments, dividends, and other receipts accruing to an individual or nation during a period of time (usually a year).

Income effect (of a price change). Change in the quantity demanded of a commodity because the change in its price has the effect of changing a consumer's real income. Thus it supplements the **substitution effect** of a price change.

Income elasticity of demand. The demand for any given good is influenced not only by the good's price but by buyers' incomes. Income elasticity measures this responsiveness. Its precise definition is percentage change in quantity demanded divided by percentage change in income. (Compare with **price elasticity of demand.**)

Income statement. A company's statement, covering a specified time period (usually a year), showing sales or revenue earned during that period, all costs properly charged against the goods sold, and the profit (net income) remaining after deduction of such costs. Also called a **profit-and-loss statement.**

Income tax, negative. Refer to **negative income tax.**

Income tax, personal. Tax levied on the income received by individuals, either in the form of wages and salaries or income from property, such as rents, dividends, or interest. In the United States, personal income tax is **graduated,** meaning that people with higher incomes pay taxes at a higher average rate than people with lower incomes.

Income velocity of money. Refer to **velocity of money.**

Incomes policy. A government policy that attempts directly to restrict wage and price changes in an effort to slow inflation. Such policies range from voluntary wage-price guidelines to outright legal control over wages, salaries, and prices.

Increasing returns to scale. See **returns to scale.**

Independent goods. Goods whose demands are relatively separate from one another. More precisely, goods A and B are independent when a change in the price of good A has no effect on the quantity demanded of good B, other things equal.

Indexing (or **indexation**). A mechanism by which wages, prices, and contracts are partially or wholly adjusted to compensate for changes in the general price level.

Indifference curve. A curve drawn on a graph whose two axes measure amounts of different goods consumed. Each point on one curve (indicating different combinations of the two goods) yields exactly the same level of satisfaction for a given consumer. That is, the consumer is indifferent between any two points on an indifference curve.

Indifference map. A graph showing a family of indifference curves for a consumer. In general, curves that lie farther northeast from the graph's origin represent higher levels of satisfaction.

Indirect taxes. See **direct taxes.**

Induced variables. See **external vs. induced variables.**

Industry. A group of firms producing similar or identical products.

Inertial inflation. A process of steady inflation that occurs when inflation is expected to persist and the ongoing rate of inflation is built into contracts and people's expectations.

Infant industry. In foreign-trade theory, an industry that has not had sufficient time to develop the experience or expertise to exploit the economies of scale needed to compete successfully with more mature industries producing the same commodity in other countries. Infant industries are often thought to need tariffs or quotas to protect them while they develop.

Inferior good. A good whose consumption goes down as income rises.

Inflation (or **inflation rate**). The inflation rate is the percentage annual increase in a general price level. **Hyperinflation** is inflation at extremely high rates (say, 1000, 1 million, or even 1 billion percent a year). **Galloping inflation** is a rate of 50 or 100 or 200 percent annually. **Moderate inflation** is a price-level rise that does not distort relative prices or incomes severely.

Innovation. A term particularly associated with Joseph Schumpeter, who meant by it (1) the bringing to market of a new and significantly different product, (2) the introduction of a new production technique, or (3) the opening up of a new market. (Contrast with **invention.**)

Inputs. See **factors of production.**

Insurance. A system by which individuals can reduce their exposure to risk of large losses by spreading the risks among a large number of persons.

Integration, vertical vs. horizontal. The production process is one of stages—e.g., iron ore into steel ingots, steel ingots into rolled steel sheets, rolled steel sheets into an automobile body. **Vertical integration** is the combination in a single firm of two or more different stages of this process (e.g., iron ore with steel ingots). **Horizontal integration** is the combination in a single firm of different units that operate at the same stage of production.

Interest. The return paid to those who lend money.

Interest rate. The price paid for borrowing money for a period of time, usually expressed as a percentage of the principal per year. Thus, if the interest rate is 10 percent per year, then $100 would be paid for a loan of $1000 for 1 year.

Intermediate goods. Goods that have undergone some manufacturing or processing but have not yet reached the stage of becoming final products. For example, steel and cotton yarn are intermediate goods.

Intervention. An activity in which a government buys or sells its currency in the foreign exchange market in order to affect its currency's exchange rate.

Intrinsic value (of money). The commodity value of a piece of money (e.g., the market value of the weight of copper in a copper coin).

Invention. The creation of a new product or discovery of a new production technique. (Distinguish from **innovation**.)

Investment. (1) Economic activity that forgoes consumption today with an eye to increasing output in the future. It includes tangible capital (structures, equipment, and inventories) and intangible investments (education or "human capital," research and development, and health). Net investment is the value of total investment after an allowance has been made for depreciation. Gross investment is investment without allowance for depreciation. (2) In finance terms, investment has an altogether different meaning and denotes the purchase of a security, such as a stock or a bond.

Investment demand (or **investment demand curve**). The schedule showing the relationship between the level of investment and the cost of capital (or, more specifically, the real interest rate); also, the graph of that relationship.

Invisible hand. A concept introduced by Adam Smith in 1776 to describe the paradox of a laissez-faire market economy. The invisible-hand doctrine holds that, with each participant pursuing his or her own private interest, a market system nevertheless works to the benefit of all as though a benevolent invisible hand were directing the whole process.

Involuntary unemployment. See **unemployment.**

Iron law of wages. In the economic theories of Malthus and Marx, the theory that there is an inevitable tendency in capitalism for wages to be driven down to a subsistence level.

Keynesian economics. The body of thought developed by John Maynard Keynes holding that a capitalist system does not automatically tend toward a full-employment equilibrium. According to Keynes, the resulting underemployment equilibrium could be cured by fiscal or monetary policies to raise aggregate demand.

Labor force. In official U.S. statistics, that group of people 16 years of age and older who are either employed or unemployed.

Labor-force participation rate. Ratio of those in the labor force to the entire population 16 years of age or older.

Labor productivity. See **productivity.**

Labor supply. The number of workers (or, more generally, the number of labor-hours) available to an economy. The principal determinants of labor supply are population, real wages, and social traditions.

Labor theory of value. The view, often associated with Adam Smith and Karl Marx, that every commodity should be valued solely according to the quantity of labor required for its production.

Laissez-faire ("Leave us alone"). The view that government should interfere as little as possible in economic activity and leave decisions to the marketplace. As expressed by classical economists like Adam Smith, this view held that the role of government should be limited to (1) maintenance of law and order, (2) national defense, and (3) provision of certain public goods that private business would not undertake (e.g., public health and sanitation).

Land. In classical and neoclassical economics, one of the three basic factors of production (along with labor and capital). More generally, land is taken to include land used for agricultural or industrial purposes as well as natural resources taken from above or below the soil.

Least-cost rule (of production). The rule that the cost of producing a specific level of output is minimized when the ratio of the marginal revenue product of each input to the price of that input is the same for all inputs.

Legal tender. Money that by law must be accepted as payment for debts. All U.S. coins and currency are legal tender, but checks are not.

Less developed country (LDC). A country with a per capita income far below that of "developed" nations (the latter usually includes most nations of North America or Western Europe).

Liabilities. In accounting, debts or financial obligations owed to other firms or persons.

Libertarianism. An economic philosophy that emphasizes the importance of personal freedom in economic and political affairs; also sometimes called "liberalism." Libertarian writers, including Adam Smith in an earlier age and Milton Friedman and James Buchanan today, hold that people should be able to follow their own interests and desires and that government activities should be limited to guaranteeing contracts and to providing police and national defense, thereby allowing maximum personal freedom.

Limited liability. The restriction of an owner's loss in a business to the amount of capital that the owner has contributed to the company. Limited liability was an important factor in the rise of large corporations. By contrast, owners in partnerships and individual proprietorships generally have **unlimited liability** for the debts of those firms.

Long run. A term used to denote a period over which full adjustment to changes can take place. In microeconomics, it denotes the time over which firms can enter or leave an industry and the capital stock can be replaced. In macroeconomics, it is often used to mean the period over which all prices, wage contracts, tax rates, and expectations can fully adjust.

Long-run aggregate supply. The relationship between output and the price level after all price and wage adjustments have taken place, and the *AS* curve is therefore vertical.

Lorenz curve. A graph used to show the extent of inequality of income or wealth.

M_1, M_2. Refer to **money supply.**

Macroeconomics. Analysis dealing with the behavior of the economy as a whole with respect to output, income, the price level, foreign trade, unemployment, and other aggregate economic variables. (Contrast with **microeconomics.**)

Malthusian theory of population growth. The hypothesis, first expressed by Thomas Malthus, that the "natural" tendency of population is to grow more rapidly than the food supply. Per capita food production would thus decline over time, thereby putting a check on population. In general, a view that population tends to grow more rapidly as incomes or living standards of the population rise.

Managed float. The most prevalent exchange-rate system today. In this system, a country occasionally intervenes to stabilize its currency.

Marginal cost. Refer to **cost, marginal.**

Marginal principle. The fundamental notion that people will maximize their income or profits when the marginal costs and marginal benefits of their actions are equal.

Marginal product (*MP*). The extra output resulting from 1 extra unit of a specified input when all other inputs are held constant. Sometimes called marginal physical product.

Marginal product theory of distribution. A theory of the distribution of income proposed by John B. Clark, according to which each productive input is paid according to its **marginal product.**

Marginal propensity to consume (*MPC*). The extra amount that people consume when they receive an extra dollar of disposable income. To be distinguished from the **average propensity to consume,** which is the ratio of total consumption to total disposable income.

Marginal propensity to import (*MPm*). In macroeconomics, the increase in the dollar value of imports resulting from each dollar increase in the value of GNP.

Marginal propensity to save (*MPS*). That fraction of an additional dollar of disposable income that is saved. Note that, by definition, $MPC + MPS = 1$.

Marginal revenue (*MR*). The additional revenue a firm would earn if it sold 1 extra unit of output. In perfect competition, *MR* equals price. Under imperfect competition, *MR* is less than price because, in order to sell the extra unit, the price must be reduced on all prior units sold.

Marginal revenue product (*MRP*) (of an input). Marginal revenue multiplied by marginal product. It is the extra revenue that would be brought in if a firm were to buy 1 extra unit of an input, put it to work, and sell the extra product it produced.

Marginal tax rate. For an income tax, the percentage of the last dollar of income paid in taxes. If a tax system is progressive, the marginal tax rate is higher than the average tax rate.

Marginal utility (*MU*). The additional or extra satisfaction yielded from consuming 1 additional unit of a commodity, with amounts of all other goods consumed held constant.

Market. An arrangement whereby buyers and sellers interact to determine the prices and quantities of a commodity. Some markets (such as the stock market or a flea market) take place in physical locations; other markets are conducted over the telephone or are organized by computers.

Market economy. An economy in which the *what, how,* and *for whom* questions concerning resource allocation are primarily determined by supply and demand in markets. In this form of economic organization, firms, motivated by the desire to maximize profits, buy inputs and produce and sell outputs. Households, armed with their factor incomes, go to markets and determine the demand for commodities. The interaction of firms' supply and households' demand then determines the prices and quantities of goods.

Market equilibrium. Same as **competitive equilibrium.**

Market failure. An imperfection in a price system that prevents an efficient allocation of resources. Important examples are **externalities** and **imperfect competition.**

Market power. The degree of control that a firm or group of firms has over the price and production decisions in an industry. In a monopoly, the firm has a high degree of market power; firms in perfectly competitive industries have no market power. **Concentration ratios** are the most widely used measures of market power.

Market share. That fraction of an industry's output accounted for by an individual firm or group of firms.

Markup pricing. The pricing method used by many firms in situations of imperfect competition; under this method they estimate average cost and then add some fixed percentage to that cost in order to reach the price they charge.

Marxism. The set of social, political, and economic doctrines developed by Karl Marx in the nineteenth century. As an economic theory, Marxism predicted that capitalism would collapse as a result of its own internal contradictions, especially its tendency to exploit the working classes. The conviction that workers would inevitably be oppressed under capitalism was based on the **iron law of wages,** which holds that wages would decline to subsistence levels.

Mean. In statistics, the same thing as "average." Thus for the numbers 1, 3, 6, 10, 20, the mean is 8.

Median. In statistics, the figure exactly in the middle of a series of numbers ordered or ranked from lowest to highest (e.g., incomes or examination grades). Thus for the numbers 1, 3, 6, 10, 20, the median is 6.

Mercantilism. A political doctrine perhaps best known as the object of Adam Smith's attack in *The Wealth of Nations.* Mercantilists emphasized the importance of balance-of-payments surpluses as a device to accumulate gold. They therefore advocated tight government control of economic policies, believing that laissez-faire policies might lead to a loss of gold.

Merger. The acquisition of one corporation by another, which usually occurs when one firm buys the stock of another. Important examples are (1) **vertical mergers,** which occur when the two firms are at different stages of a production process (e.g., iron ore and steel), (2) **horizontal mergers,** which occur when the two firms produce in the same market (e.g., two automobile manufacturers), and (3) **conglomerate mergers,** which occur when the two firms operate in unrelated markets (e.g., shoelaces and oil refining).

Microeconomics. Analysis dealing with the behavior of individual elements in an economy—such as the determination of the price of a single product or the behavior of a single consumer or business firm. (Contrast with **macroeconomics.**)

Minimum cost. Refer to **cost, minimum.**

Mixed economy. The dominant form of economic organization in non-communist countries. Mixed economies rely primarily on the price system for their economic organization but use a variety of government interventions (such as taxes, spending, and regulation) to handle macroeconomic instability and market failures.

Model. A formal framework for representing the basic features of a complex system by a few central relationships. Models take the form of graphs, mathematical equations, and computer programs.

Moderate inflation. See **inflation.**

Momentary run. A period of time that is so short that production is fixed.

Monetarism. A school of thought

holding that changes in the money supply are the major cause of macroeconomic fluctuations. For the short run, this view holds that changes in the money supply are the primary determinant of changes in both real output and the price level. For the longer run, this holds that prices tend to move proportionally with the money supply. Monetarists often conclude that the best macroeconomic policy is one with a stable growth in the money supply.

Monetary base. The net monetary liabilities of the government that are held by the public. In the United States, the monetary base is equal to currency and bank reserves. Sometimes called **high-powered money.**

Monetary policy. The objectives of the central bank in exercising its control over money, interest rates, and credit conditions. The instruments of monetary policy are primarily open-market operations, reserve requirements, and the discount rate.

Money. The means of payment or medium of exchange. For the items constituting money, refer to **money supply.**

Money demand schedule. The relationship between holdings of money and interest rates. As interest rates rise, bonds and other securities become more attractive, lowering the quantity of money demanded. See also **demand for money.**

Money funds. Shorthand expression for very liquid short-term financial instruments whose interest rates are not regulated. The major examples are money market mutual funds and commercial bank money market deposit accounts.

Money market. A term denoting the set of institutions that handle the purchase or sale of short-term credit instruments like Treasury bills and commercial paper.

Money supply. The narrowly defined money supply (M_1) consists of coins, paper currency, plus all demand or checking deposits; this is narrow, or transactions, money. The broadly defined supply (M_2) includes all items in M_1 plus certain liquid assets or near-monies—savings deposits, money market funds, and the like.

Money-supply effect. The relationship whereby a price rise operating on a fixed nominal money supply produces tight money and lowers aggregate spending.

Money-supply multiplier. The ratio of the increase in the money supply (or in deposits) to the increase in bank reserves. Generally, the money-supply multiplier is equal to the inverse of the required reserve ratio. For example, if the required reserve ratio is 0.125, then the money-supply multiplier is 8.

Money, velocity of. See **velocity of money.**

Monopolistic competition. A market structure in which there are many sellers who are supplying goods that are close, but not perfect, substitutes. In such a market, each firm can exercise some effect on its product's price.

Monopoly. A market structure in which a commodity is supplied by a single firm. Also see **natural monopoly.**

Monopsony. The mirror image of monopoly: a market in which there is a single buyer; a "buyer's monopoly."

MPC. See **marginal propensity to consume.**

MPS. See **marginal propensity to save.**

Multiplier. A term in macroeconomics denoting the change in an induced variable (such as GNP or money supply) per unit of change in an external variable (such as government spending or bank reserves). The **expenditure multiplier** refers to the increase in GNP that would result from a $1 increase in expenditure (say on investment).

Multiplier model. In macroeconomics, a theory developed by J. M. Keynes that emphasizes the importance of changes in autonomous expenditures (especially investment, government spending, and net exports) in determining changes in output and employment. Also see **multiplier.**

Nash equilibrium. In game theory, a set of strategies for the players where no player can improve his or her payoff given the other player's strategy. That is, given player A's strategy, player B can do no better, and given B's strategy A can do no better. The Nash equilibrium is also sometimes called the **noncooperative equilibrium.**

National debt. Same as **government debt.**

National-income and -product accounting. A set of accounts that measures the spending, income, and output of the entire nation for a quarter or a year.

Natural monopoly. A firm or industry whose average cost per unit of production falls sharply over the entire range of its output, as for example in local electricity distribution. Thus a single firm, a monopoly, can supply the industry output more efficiently than can multiple firms.

Natural rate of unemployment. The unemployment rate at which upward and downward pressures on wage and price inflation are in balance, so that inflation neither rises nor falls. Equivalently, the unemployment rate at which the long-run **Phillips curve** is vertical.

"Near-money." Financial assets that are risk-free and so readily convertible into money that they are close to actually being money. Examples are money funds and Treasury bills.

Negative income tax. A plan for replacing current income-support programs (welfare, food stamps, etc.) with a unified program. Under such a plan, poor families would receive an income supplement and would have benefits reduced as their earnings increase.

Neoclassical growth model. A theory or model used to explain long-term trends in economic growth of industrial economies. This model emphasizes the importance of capital deepening (i.e., a growing capital-labor ratio) and technological change in explaining the growth of potential real GNP.

Net economic welfare (NEW). A measure of national output that corrects several limitations of the GNP measure.

Net exports. In the national product accounts, the value of exports of goods and services minus the value of imports of goods and services.

Net investment. Gross investment minus depreciation of capital goods.

Net national product (NNP). GNP less an allowance for depreciation of capital goods.

Net worth. In accounting, total assets minus total liabilities.

NNP. See **net national product.**

Nominal GNP. See **gross national product, nominal.**

Nominal (or **money**) **interest rate.** The **interest rate** paid on different assets. This represents a dollar return per year per dollar invested. Compare with the **real interest rate,** which represents the return per year in goods per unit of goods invested.

Noncooperative equilibrium. See **Nash equilibrium.**

Normative vs. positive economics. Normative economics considers "what ought to be"—value judgments, or goals, of public policy. **Positive economics,** by contrast, is the analysis of facts and behavior in an economy, or "the way things are."

NOW (negotiable order of withdrawal) account. An interest-bearing checking account. See also **checking accounts.**

Okun's Law. The empirical relationship, discovered by Arthur Okun, between cyclical movements in GNP and unemployment. The law states that when actual GNP declines 2 percent relative to potential GNP, the unemployment rate increases by about 1 percentage point. (Earlier estimates placed the ratio at 3 to 1.)

Oligopoly. A situation of imperfect competition in which an industry is dominated by a small number of suppliers.

Open economy. An economy that engages in international trade (i.e., imports and exports) of goods and capital with other countries. A **closed economy** is one that has no imports or exports.

Open-economy multiplier. In an open economy, income leaks into imports as well as into saving. Therefore, the open-economy multiplier for investment or government expenditure is given by

$$\text{Open-economy multiplier} = \frac{1}{MPS + MPm}$$

where MPS = marginal propensity to save and MPm = marginal propensity to import.

Open-market operations. The activity of a central bank in buying or selling government bonds to influence bank reserves, the money supply, and interest rates. If securities are bought, the money paid out by the central bank increases commercial-bank reserves, and the money supply increases. If securities are sold, the money supply contracts.

Opportunity cost. The value of the next best use (or opportunity) for an economic good, or the value of the sacrificed alternative. Thus, say that the best alternative use of the inputs employed to mine a ton of coal was to grow 10 bushels of wheat. The opportunity cost of a ton of coal is thus the 10 bushels of wheat that *could* have been produced but were not. Opportunity cost is particularly useful for valuing nonmarketed goods such as environmental health or safety.

Other things equal. A phrase that signifies that a factor under consideration is changed while all other factors are held equal or constant. For example, a downward-sloping demand curve shows that the quantity demanded will decline as the price rises, as long as other things (such as incomes) are held equal.

Output. See **total product.**

Paradox of value. The paradox that many necessities of life (e.g., water) have a low "market" value, while many luxuries (e.g., diamonds) with little "use" value have a high market price. It is explained by the fact that a price does not reflect the total utility of a commodity but its marginal utility.

Pareto efficiency (or **Pareto optimality**). See **allocative efficiency.**

Partial-equilibrium analysis. Analysis concentrating on the effect of changes in an individual market, holding other things equal (e.g., disregarding changes in income).

Partnership. An association of two or more persons to conduct a business which is not in corporate form and does not enjoy limited liability.

Patent. An exclusive right granted to an inventor to control the use of an invention for, in the United States, a period of 17 years. Patents create temporary monopolies as a way of rewarding inventive activity and are the principal tool for promoting invention among individuals or small firms.

Payoff table. In game theory, a table used to describe the strategies and payoffs of a game with two or more players. The profits or utilities of the different players are the **payoffs.**

Payoffs. See **payoff table.**

Perfect competition. Refer to **competition, perfect.**

Personal savings rate. The ratio of personal saving to personal disposable income, in percent.

Phillips curve. A graph first devised by A. W. Phillips, showing the tradeoff between unemployment and inflation. In modern mainstream macroeconomics, the downward-sloping "tradeoff" Phillips curve is generally held to be valid only in the short run; in the long run, the Phillips curve is usually thought to be vertical at the natural rate of unemployment.

Portfolio theory. An economic theory that describes how rational investors allocate their wealth among different financial assets—that is, how they put their wealth into a "portfolio."

Positive economics. Refer to **normative vs. positive economics.**

***Post hoc* fallacy.** From the Latin, *post hoc, ergo propter hoc,* which translates as "after this, therefore because of this." This fallacy arises when it is assumed that because event A precedes event B, it follows that A *causes* B.

Potential GNP. High-employment GNP; more precisely, the maximum level of GNP that can be sustained with a given state of technology and population size without accelerating inflation. Today, it is generally taken to be equivalent to the level of output corresponding to the natural rate of unemployment.

Potential output. Same as **potential GNP.**

Poverty. Today, the U.S. government defines the "poverty line" to be the minimum adequate standard of living.

PPF. See **production-possibility frontier.**

Present value (of an asset). Today's value for an asset that yields a stream of income over time. Valuation of such time streams of returns requires calculating the present worth of each component of the income, which is done by applying a discount rate (or interest rate) to future incomes.

Price-elastic demand (or elastic demand). The situation in which price elasticity of demand exceeds 1 in absolute value. This signifies that the percentage change in quantity demanded is greater than the percentage change in price. In addition, elastic demand implies that total revenue (price times quantity) rises when price falls because the increase in quantity demanded is so large. (Contrast with **price-inelastic demand.**)

Price elasticity of demand. A measure of the extent to which quantity demanded responds to a price change. The elasticity coefficient (price elasticity of demand = E_D) is percentage change in quantity demanded divided by percentage change in price. In figuring percentages, use the averages of old and new quantities in the numerator and of old and new prices in the denominator; disregard the minus sign. Refer also to **price-elastic demand, price-inelastic demand, unit-elastic demand.**

Price elasticity of supply. Conceptually similar to **price elasticity of demand,** except that it measures the supply responsiveness to a price change. More precisely, the price elasticity of supply measures the percentage change in quantity supplied divided by the percentage change in price. Supply elasticities are most useful in perfect competition.

Price flexibility. Price behavior in "auction" markets (e.g., for many raw commodities or the stock market), in which prices immediately respond to changes in demand or in supply. (In contrast, refer to **administered prices.**)

Price index. An index number that shows how the average price of a bundle of goods has changed over a period of time. In computing the average, the prices of the different goods are generally weighted by their economic importance (e.g., by each commodity's share of total consumer expenditures in the **consumer price index**).

Price-inelastic demand (or inelastic demand). The situation in which price elasticity of demand is below 1 in absolute value. In this case, when price declines, total revenue declines, and when price is increased, total revenue goes up. Perfectly inelastic demand means that there is no change at all in quantity demanded when price goes up or goes down. (Contrast with **price-elastic demand** and **unit-elastic demand.**)

Private good. See **public good.**

Producer price index. The **price index** of goods sold at the wholesale level (such as steel, wheat, oil).

Product, average. See **average product.**

Product differentiation. The existence of characteristics that make similar goods less-than-perfect substitutes. Thus locational differences make similar types of gasoline sold at separate points imperfect substitutes. Firms enjoying product differentiation face a downward-sloping demand curve instead of the horizontal demand curve of the perfect competitor.

Product, marginal. See **marginal product.**

Production function. A relation (or mathematical function) specifying the maximum output that can be produced with given inputs for a given level of technology. Applies to a firm or, as an aggregate production function, to the economy as a whole.

Production-possibility frontier (*PPF*). A graph showing the menu of goods that can be produced by an economy. In a frequently cited case, the choice is reduced to two goods, guns and butter. Points outside the *PPF* (to the northeast of it) are unattainable. Points inside it are inefficient since resources are not being fully employed, resources are not being used properly, or outdated production techniques are being utilized.

Productivity. A term referring to the ratio of output to inputs (total output divided by labor inputs is **labor productivity**). Productivity increases if the same quantity of inputs produces more output. Labor productivity increases because of improved technology, improvements in labor skills, or capital deepening.

Productivity growth. The rate of increase in **productivity** from one period to another. For example, if an index of labor productivity is 100 in 1990 and 101.7 in 1991, the rate of productivity growth is 1.7 percent per year for 1991 over 1990.

Productivity of capital, net. Refer to **rate of return.**

Profit. (1) In accounting terms, total revenue minus costs properly chargeable against the goods sold (refer to **income statement**). (2) In economic theory, the difference between sales revenue and the full opportunity cost of resources involved in producing the goods.

Profit-and-loss statement. Refer to **income statement.**

Progressive, proportional, and **regressive taxes.** A progressive tax weighs more heavily upon the rich; a regressive tax does the opposite. More precisely, a tax is progressive if the average tax rate (i.e., taxes divided by income) is higher for those with higher incomes; it is a regressive tax if the average tax rate declines with higher incomes; it is a proportional tax if the average tax rate is equal at all income levels.

Property rights. Property rights define the ability of individuals or firms to own, buy, sell, and use the capital goods and other property in a market economy.

Proportional tax. Refer to **progressive, proportional,** and **regressive taxes.**

Proprietorship, individual. A business firm owned and operated by one person.

Protectionism. Any policy adopted by a country to protect domestic industries against competition from imports (most commonly, a tariff or quota imposed on such imports).

Public choice (also **public-choice theory**). Branch of economics and political science dealing with the way that governments make choices and direct the economy. This theory differs from the theory of markets in emphasizing the influence of vote maximizing for politicians, which contrasts to profit maximizing by firms.

Public debt. See **government debt.**

Public good. A commodity whose benefits are indivisibly spread among the entire community, whether or not particular individuals desire to consume the public good. For example, a public-health measure that eradicates smallpox protects all, not just those paying for the vaccinations. To be contrasted with **private goods,** such as bread, which, if consumed by one person, cannot be consumed by another person.

Pure economic rent. See **rent, economic.**

Quantity demanded. See **change in demand vs. change in quantity demanded.**

Quantity equation of exchange. A tautology, $MV \equiv PQ$, where M is the money supply, V is the income velocity of money, and PQ (price times quantity) is the money value of total output (nominal GNP). The equation must always hold exactly since V is defined as PQ/M.

Quantity supplied. See **change in supply vs. change in quantity supplied.**

Quantity theory of prices. A theory of the determination of output and the overall price level holding that prices move proportionately with the money supply. A more cautious approach put forth by monetarists holds that the money supply is the most important determinant of changes in nominal GNP (see **monetarism**).

Quota. A form of import protectionism in which the total quantity of imports of a particular commodity (e.g., sugar or cars) during a given period is limited.

Random-walk theory (of stock market prices). Increasingly called the **efficient-market theory.** A view that holds that all currently available information is already incorporated into the price of common stocks (or other assets). Consequently, the stock market offers no bargains that can be found by looking at old or "stale" information or at easily available information (like recent price movements). Stock prices do change, however—on the basis of *new* information. If we assume that the chances of good news and of bad are 50:50, then stock prices will follow a "random walk," i.e., they are equally likely to move up or down.

Rate of inflation. See **inflation.**

Rate of return (or **return**) **on capital.** The yield on an investment or on a capital good. Thus, an investment costing $100 and yielding $12 annually has a rate of return of 12 percent per year.

Rational expectations. (1) For the narrow definition, see **expectations.** (2) More generally, part of a view of the economy held by proponents of **rational-expectations macroeconomics.**

Rational-expectations macroeconomics. A school, led by Robert Lucas and Thomas Sargent, holding that markets clear quickly and that expectations are rational. Under these and other conditions it can be shown that predictable macroeconomic policies have no effect on real output or unemployment. Sometimes called new classical macroeconomics.

Real GNP. GNP adjusted for price change. Real GNP equals nominal GNP divided by the GNP deflator. See **gross national product, real.**

Real interest rate. The interest rate measured in terms of goods rather than money. It is thus equal to the money (or nominal) interest rate less the rate of inflation.

Real wages. The purchasing power of a worker's wages in terms of goods and services. It is measured by the ratio of the money wage rate to the consumer price index.

Recession. A downturn in real GNP for two or more successive quarters. See also **depression.**

Regressive tax. Refer to **progressive, proportional,** and **regressive taxes.**

Regulation. Government laws or rules designed to control the behavior of firms. The major kinds are **economic regulation** (which affects the prices, entry, or service of a single industry, such as telephone service) and **social regulation** (which attempts to correct externalities that prevail across a number of industries, such as air or water pollution).

Rent, economic (or **pure economic rent**). This term was applied by nineteenth-century British economists to income earned from land. The total supply of land available is (with minor qualifications) fixed, and the return paid to the landowner is rent. The term is often extended to the return paid to any factor in fixed supply—i.e., to any input having a perfectly inelastic or vertical supply curve.

Required reserves. See **reserves, bank.**

Reserves, bank. That portion of deposits that a bank sets aside in the form of vault cash or non-interest-earning deposits with Federal Reserve Banks. In the United States, banks are required to hold 12 percent of checking deposits (or transactions accounts) in the form of reserves.

Reserves, international. Every nation holds at least some reserves, in such forms as gold, currencies of other nations, and special drawing rights. International reserves serve as "international money," to be used when a country encounters balance-of-payments difficulties. If a nation were prepared to allow its exchange rate to float freely, it would need no reserves.

Resource allocation. The manner in which an economy distributes its resources (its factors of production) among the potential uses so as to produce a particular set of final goods.

Returns to scale. The rate at which output increases when all inputs are increased proportionately. For example, if all the inputs double and output is exactly doubled, that process is said to exhibit **constant returns to scale.** If, however, output grows by less than 100 percent when all inputs are doubled, the process shows **decreasing returns to scale;** if output more than doubles, the process demonstrates **increasing returns to scale.**

Revaluation. An increase in the official foreign exchange rate of a currency. See also **devaluation.**

Revenue, average. Refer to **average revenue.**

Revenue, marginal. Refer to **marginal revenue.**

Revenue, total. Refer to **total revenue.**

Risk averse. A person is risk-averse when, faced with an uncertain situation, the displeasure from losing a given amount of income is greater than the pleasure from gaining the same amount of income.

Risk spreading. The process of taking large risks and spreading them around so that they are but small risks for a large number of people. The major form of risk spreading is **insurance,** which is a kind of gambling in reverse.

Sales tax. See **excise tax vs. sales tax.**

Saving. That part of income which is not consumed; in other words, the difference between disposable income and consumption.

Savings function. The schedule showing the amount of saving that households or a nation will undertake at each level of income.

Say's Law of markets. The theory that "supply creates its own demand." J. B. Say argued in 1803 that, because total purchasing power is exactly equal to total incomes and outputs, excess demand or supply is impossible. Keynes attacked Say's Law, pointing out that an extra dollar of income need not be entirely spent (i.e., the marginal propensity to consume is not necessarily unity).

Scarcity, law of. The principle that most things that people want are available only in limited supply (the exception being **free goods**). Thus goods are generally scarce and must somehow be rationed, whether by price or some other means.

Securities. A term used to designate a wide variety of financial assets, such as stocks, bonds, options, and notes; more precisely, the document used to establish ownership of these assets.

Short run. A period in which all factors cannot adjust fully. In microeconomics, the capital stock and other "fixed" inputs cannot be adjusted and entry is not free in the short run. In macroeconomics, prices, wage contracts, tax rates, and expectations may not fully adjust in the short run.

Short-run aggregate supply. The relationship between output and prices in the short run wherein changes in aggregate demand can affect output. Also represented by an upward-sloping or horizontal *AS* curve.

Shutdown price (or **point,** or **rule**). In the theory of the firm, the shutdown point comes at that point where the market price is just sufficient to cover average variable cost and no more. Hence, the firm's losses per period just equal its fixed costs; it might as well shut down.

Single-tax movement. A nineteenth-century movement, originated by Henry George, holding that continued poverty in the midst of steady economic progress was attributable to the scarcity of land and the large rents flowing to landowners. The "single tax" was to be a tax on economic rent earned from landownership.

Slope. In a graph, the change in the variable on the vertical axis per unit of change in the variable on the horizontal axis. Upward-sloping lines have positive slopes, downward-sloping curves (like demand curves) have negative slopes, and horizontal lines have slopes of zero.

Social overhead capital. The essential investments on which economic development depends, particularly for transportation, power, and communications. Sometimes called "infrastructure."

Social regulation. See **regulation.**

Socialism. A political theory that holds that all (or almost all) the means of production, other than labor, should be owned by the community. This allows the return on capital to be shared more equally than under capitalism.

Speculator. Someone engaged in speculation, i.e., who buys (or sells) a commodity or financial asset with the aim of profiting from later selling (or buying) the item at a higher (or lower) price.

Spillovers. Same as **externalities.**

Stagflation. A term, coined in the early 1970s, describing the coexistence of high unemployment, or *stag*nation, with persistent in*flation*. Its explanation lies primarily in the inertial nature of the inflationary process.

Stock, common. Refer to **common stock.**

Stock market. An organized marketplace in which common stocks are traded. In the United States, the largest stock market is the New York Stock Exchange, on which are traded the largest American companies.

Stock vs. flow. See **flow vs. stock.**

Strategic interaction. A situation in oligopolistic markets in which each firm's business strategies depend upon its rivals' plans. A formal analysis of strategic interaction is given in **game theory.**

Structural budget. See **actual, cyclical,** and **structural budget.**

Structural unemployment. Unemployment resulting because the regional or occupational pattern of job vacancies does not match the pattern of worker availability. There may be jobs available, but unemployed workers may not have the required skill; or the jobs may be in different regions from where the unemployed workers live.

Subsidy. A payment by a government to a firm or household that provides or consumes a commodity. For example, governments often subsidize food by paying for part of the food expenditures of low-income households.

Substitutes. Goods that compete with each other (as do gloves and mittens). By contrast, goods that go together in the eyes of consumers (such as left shoes and right shoes) are complements.

Substitution effect (of a price change). The tendency of consumers is to consume more of a good when its relative price falls (to "substitute" in favor of that good), and to consume less of the good when its relative price increases (to "substitute" away from that good). This substitution effect of a price change leads to a downward-sloping demand curve. (Compare with **income effect.**)

Supply curve (or **supply schedule**). A schedule showing the quantity of a good that suppliers in a given market desire to sell at each price, holding other things equal.

Supply shock. In macroeconomics, a sudden change in production costs or productivity that has a large and unexpected impact upon aggregate supply. As a result of a supply shock, real GNP and the price level change unexpectedly.

Supply-side economics. A view emphasizing policy measures to affect aggregate supply or potential output. This approach holds that high marginal tax rates on labor and capital incomes reduce work effort and saving.

Tariff. A levy or tax imposed upon each unit of a commodity imported into a country.

Tax incidence. See **incidence.**

Technological change. A change in the process of production or introduction of new products such that more or improved output can be obtained from the same bundle of inputs. It results in an outward shift in the production-possibility curve.

Technological progress. Same as **technological change.**

Terms of trade (in international trade). The "real" terms at which a nation sells its export products and buys its import products. It equals the ratio of an index of export prices to an index of import prices.

Tight-money policy. A central-bank policy of restraining or reducing the money supply and of raising interest rates. This policy has the effect of slowing the growth of real GNP, reducing the rate of inflation, or raising the nation's foreign exchange rate. (Contrast with **easy-money policy.**)

Time deposit. Funds, held in a bank, that have a minimum "time of withdrawal." Included in broad money (M_2) but not in M_1 because they are not accepted as a means of payment.

Token money. Money with little or no intrinsic value.

Total cost. Refer to **cost, total.**

Total factor productivity. An index of productivity that measures total output per unit of total input. The numerator of the index is total output (say GNP), while the denominator is a weighted average of inputs of capital, labor, and resources. The growth of total factor productivity is often taken as an index of the rate of technological progress.

Total product (or **output**). The total amount of a commodity produced, measured in physical units such as bushels of wheat, tons of steel, or number of haircuts.

Total revenue. Price times quantity, or total sales.

Trade balance. See **balance of trade.**

Trade barrier. Any of a number of protectionist devices by which nations discourage imports. Tariffs and quotas are the most visible barriers, but in recent years nontariff barriers (or NTBs), such as burdensome regulatory proceedings, have replaced more traditional measures.

Transactions demand for money. See **demand for money.**

Transfer payments, government. Payments made by a government to individuals, for which the individual performs no current service in return. Examples are social security payments and unemployment insurance.

Treasury bills (T-bills). Short-term bonds or securities issued by the federal government.

Underground economy. Unreported economic activity. The underground economy includes otherwise legal activities not reported to the taxing authorities (such as garage sales or services "bartered" among friends) and illegal activities (such as the drug trade, gambling, and prostitution).

Unemployment. (1) In economic terms, **involuntary unemployment** occurs if there are qualified workers who would be willing to work at prevailing wages but cannot find jobs. (2) In the official (U.S. Bureau of Labor Statistics) definition, a worker is unemployed if he or she (*a*) is not working and (*b*) either is waiting for recall from layoff or has actively looked for work in the last 4 weeks.

Unemployment, frictional. See **frictional unemployment.**

Unemployment rate. The percentage of the labor force that is unemployed.

Unemployment, structural. See **structural unemployment.**

Unit-elastic demand. The situation, between **price-elastic demand** and **price-inelastic demand,** in which price elasticity is just equal to 1 in absolute value. See also **price elasticity of demand.**

Unlimited liability. See **limited liability.**

Usury. The charging of an interest rate above a legal maximum on borrowed money.

Utility (also **total utility**) The total satisfaction derived from the consumption of goods or services. To be contrasted with **marginal utility,** which is the additional utility arising from consumption of an additional unit of the commodity.

Utility-possibility frontier. Analogous to the **production-possibility frontier;** a graph showing the utility or satisfaction of two consumers (or groups), one on each axis. It is downward-sloping to indicate that redistributing income from A to B will lower the utility of A and raise that of B. Points on the utility-possibility frontier display **allocative** (or **Pareto**) **efficiency.** For the allocation implied by these points, it is impossible to devise feasible outcomes that would make one party better off without making someone else worse off.

Value added. The difference between the value of goods produced and the cost of materials and supplies used in producing them. In a \$1 loaf of bread embodying \$0.60 worth of wheat and other materials, the value added is \$0.40. Value added consists of the wages, interest, and profit components added to the output by a firm or industry.

Value-added tax (or **VAT**). A tax levied upon a firm as a percentage of its value added.

Value, paradox of. See **paradox of value.**

Variable. A magnitude of interest that can be defined and measured. Important variables in economics include prices, quantities, interest rates, exchange rates, dollars of wealth, and so forth.

Variable cost. Refer to **cost, variable.**

Velocity of money. In serving its function as a medium of exchange, money moves from buyer to seller to new buyer and so on. Its "velocity" refers to the "speed" of this movement. The **income velocity of money** is defined as nominal GNP divided by the total money supply for the period in question, or $V \equiv P \times Q/M \equiv \text{GNP}/M$.

Vertical equity. See **horizontal equity vs. vertical equity.**

Vertical integration. Refer to **integration, vertical vs. horizontal.**

Vertical merger. See **merger.**

Voluntary unemployment. The unemployment that occurs when an individual perceives the value of wages to be less than the opportunity use of time, say in leisure.

Wealth. The net value of tangible and financial items owned by a nation or person at a point of time. It equals all assets less all liabilities.

Welfare economics. The normative analysis of economic systems, i.e., the study of what is "wrong" or "right" about the economy's functioning.

Welfare state. A practice whereby the government of a mixed economy uses its fiscal and regulatory policies to modify the market distribution of income and to provide service to the population.

What, how,* and *for whom. The three fundamental problems of economic organization. *What* is the problem of how much of each possible good and service will be produced with the society's limited stock of resources or inputs. *How* is the choice of the particular technique by which each good of the *what* shall be produced. *For whom* refers to the distribution of consumption goods among the members of that society.

Yield. Same as the **interest rate** or **rate of return** on an asset.

INDEX

Page references in **boldface** indicate Glossary terms.

Family Tree of Economics

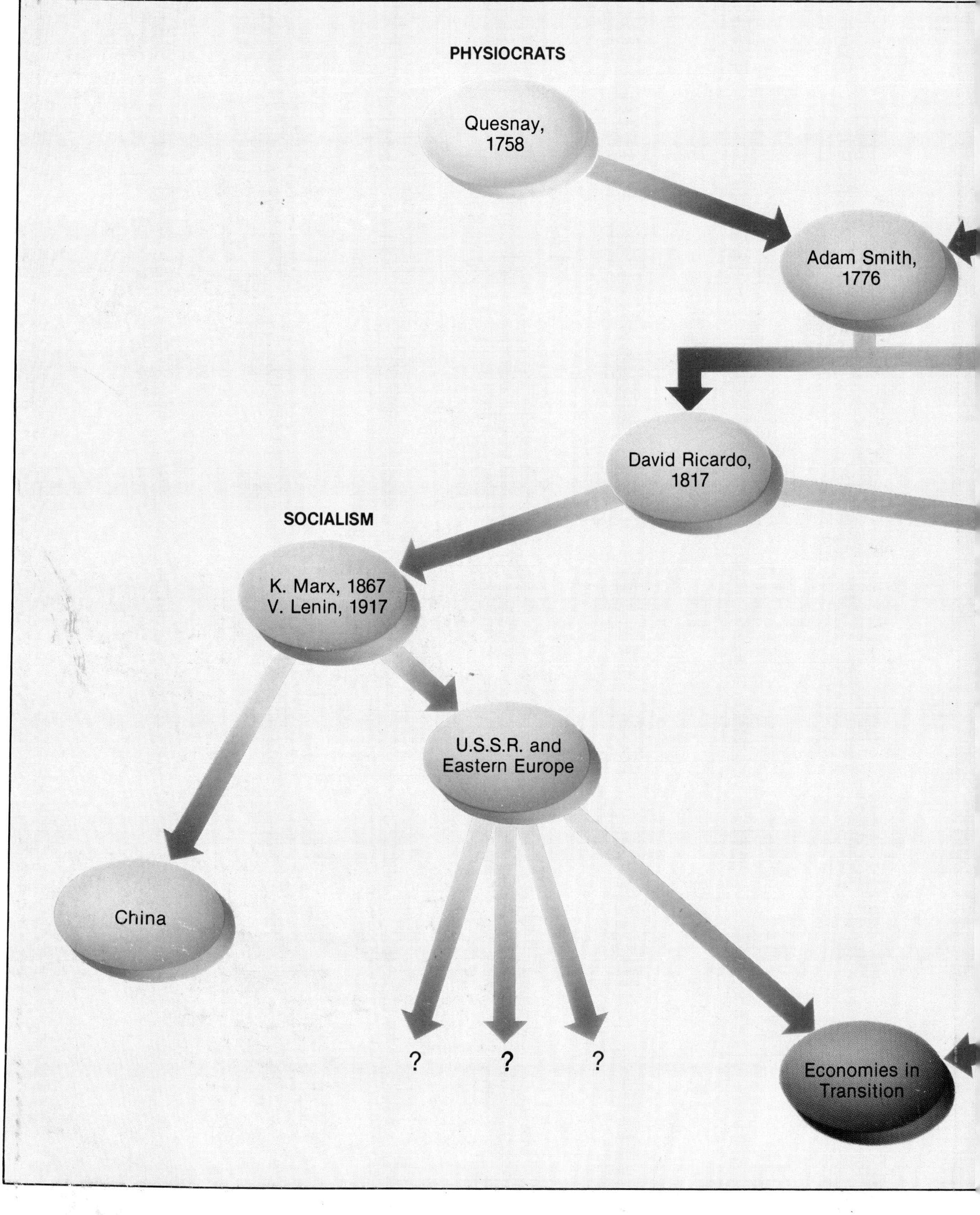